ENCYCLOPEDIA
OF CLINICAL
ASSESSMENT

Volume 1

Robert Henley Woody

General Editor

ENCYCLOPEDIA
OF CLINICAL
ASSESSMENT

Volume 1

Jossey-Bass Publishers

San Francisco • Washington • London • 1980

ENCYCLOPEDIA OF CLINICAL ASSESSMENT
Volume 1
by Robert Henley Woody, Editor

616.89
E 56

Library of Congress Cataloguing in Publication Data

Main entry under title:

Encyclopedia of clinical assessment.

Includes bibliographies and indexes.
1. Personality assessment. 2. Personality.
3. Mental illness—Diagnosis. I. Woody, Robert Henley.
BF698.4.E5   157'.7   80-10463
ISBN 0-87589-446-1 (set)
ISBN 0-87589-460-7 (v. 1)
ISBN 0-87589-461-5 (v. 2)

Manufactured in the United States of America

JACKET DESIGN BY WILLI BAUM

FIRST EDITION

Code 8007

The Jossey-Bass
Social and Behavioral Science Series

To my wife, Jane Divita Woody,
and to our children, Jennifer, Bobby, and Matthew;
and to the family members of the contributors.

Without doubt, support from loved ones
makes it all seem worthwhile.

Preface

In a way, the *Encyclopedia of Clinical Assessment* started in 1960 when I was in my first position as a psychologist serving two rural counties in northern Michigan. Since I was the first psychologist in the region, I was deluged with requests for diagnostic services. As might be expected, my patients reflected the full spectrum of problems and considerations, and I often thought that my professional training had not prepared me for the breadth of questions I was being asked to answer. I realized I needed a reference source that would allow me to better understand the particular dimensions reflected by a given patient and to be able to identify the options for action. But no such source was available.

Over the years, having found myself in various clinical contexts, I continued to recognize that the practitioner is constantly faced with tests of his or her knowledge—but no one person can possibly be a reservoir of all the information required. There is a need for reference materials, and yet the field of psychology and related disciplines involved with clinical assessment have not created such materials. When I took law courses, I was impressed with the plethora of legal reference materials available; the lawyer can go to legal tomes and often within minutes can find the primary knowledge for a given legal matter.

With this as a backdrop, I started working on an encyclopedia-like volume in 1969. My first attempt with co-editor Jane Divita Woody was *Clinical Assessment in*

Counseling and Psychotherapy (1973). Therein, we were able to bring together, along with some of our own ideas, chapters by such notable professionals as Frederick C. Thorne, John M. Hadley, Robert H. Geertsma, Milton F. Shore, John E. Houck, and James C. Hansen to create a textbook on the major categories of clinical assessment. But this work still did not fulfill the need for a basic reference source.

The present *Encyclopedia,* I believe, does fulfill that need. It attains the quality necessary to make it a worthwhile tool in the day-to-day functioning of the practitioner involved with clinical assessment.

In the introductory chapter, I develop a conceptual framework for clinical assessment and describe the organization and structure of the *Encyclopedia.* At this point, suffice it to note that the ninety-one chapters include dimensions that, when taken together, form a comprehensive coverage of the major topics of clinical assessment; and each of the 110 contributors is distinguished for his or her research on clinical assessment. Also, the chapters follow a similar format, thereby allowing the reader to make comparative analyses across chapters (or dimensions) and to move progressively from a general overview to greater in-depth understanding.

The *Encyclopedia* meets four objectives: (1) to make readers aware of the highly subjective nature of clinical assessment and to prepare them to maintain academically based objectivity; (2) to familiarize readers with the array of procedures available for clinical assessment, especially with the effects of the idiosyncratic characteristics of both the professional and the patient; (3) to realistically appraise the importance of clinical assessment for professional functioning and for societal development; and (4) to stimulate readers to make a commitment to continued professional growth through a melding of professional and personal self-concepts for responsible actions.

In approaching the task of developing the *Encyclopedia,* I was well aware from previous editorial duties that it would probably be difficult to get so many contributors to honor their commitments to produce a scholarly work within a designated time frame. Now that the work is completed, I want to congratulate the authors on the quality and comprehensiveness of their contributions.

Special appreciation is due to Marie Schonberner, my staff assistant, who became personally committed to the managerial aspects of this project. Her working relationship with the contributors was such that she was able to resolve many technicalities and salve numerous "personal preferences" that, if improperly attended, could have disrupted the development of the *Encyclopedia.* Without her help, this project could not have been produced so efficiently.

I would also like to express appreciation to Jane Divita Woody, my wife, for certain editorial assistance. Finally, there is no doubt that gratitude must go to my family and the families of the contributors for their acceptance of our professional roles.

Omaha, Nebraska   Robert Henley Woody
January 1980

Contents

Volume 1

Part One: Individual Development

Part Five: Personality Development

Volume 2

Part Seven: Sexuality

Part Eight: Learning and Education

Part Eleven: Planning and Prognostic Factors

Alphabetical
Listing of Chapters

The Editor

Robert Henley Woody is professor of psychology at the University of Nebraska at Omaha and is in private practice as a clinical and forensic psychologist with Woody Clinical Associates, Omaha. He earned a doctor of philosophy degree in counseling psychology in 1964 from Michigan State University, a doctor of science degree in health services research in 1975 from the University of Pittsburgh, and the postdoctoral certificate in group psychotherapy in 1969 from the Washington School of Psychiatry. During 1966-67, he was a postdoctoral fellow in clinical psychology at the University of London's Institute of Psychiatry. In addition, he has studied law at the Creighton University School of Law and the Ohio State University College of Law.

Prior to his present employment, he was assistant professor at the State University of New York at Buffalo, associate professor at the University of Maryland, dean for student development and director of counseling and mental health services at the Grand Valley State Colleges, and professor at Ohio University. Woody has been a visiting professor at Ohio State University and the University of Reading (England). Before his current professorship, he was dean for graduate studies and research at the University of Nebraska at Omaha.

Woody is a fellow of the American Psychological Association (divisions of Clinical Psychology, School Psychology, Counseling Psychology, and Psychological Hypnosis), the

American Association for Marriage and Family Therapy, the Society for Personality Assessment, and the American Society of Clinical Hypnosis. He received postdoctoral research fellowships from the U.S. Vocational Rehabilitation Services and the U.S. Office of Education. The American Board of Professional Psychology deemed Woody a diplomate in clinical psychology and the American Board of Psychological Hypnosis named him a diplomate in experimental psychological hypnosis.

Woody has authored or edited ten books and approximately two hundred articles for professional journals. His books include *Behavioral Problem Children in the Schools* (1969), *Clinical Assessment in Counseling and Psychotherapy* (with J. D. Woody, 1972), *Psychobehavioral Counseling and Therapy* (1971), and *Getting Custody* (1978).

Woody's present interests are forensic psychology, psychodiagnostics, and comparative theories of psychotherapy and behavior change. His recent research has focused on behavioral science criteria in child custody legal proceedings, psychological aspects of personal injury and wrongful death, and therapeutic strategies for holistic health.

Contributors

Thomas M. Achenbach, Ph.D., research psychologist, Laboratory of Developmental Psychology, National Institute of Mental Health

Robert S. Albert, Ph.D., professor of psychology, Pitzer College

Vernon L. Allen, Ph.D., professor of psychology, University of Wisconsin at Madison

Martin Amerikaner, Ph.D., assistant professor of education, Department of Counselor Education, University of Houston

Robert L. Anderson, Ph.D., professor of psychology, Eastern Michigan University

Stephen M. Auerbach, Ph.D., associate professor of psychology, Virginia Commonwealth University

Victoria Azara, Ph.D., psychologist, Churchill School, and adjunct assistant professor of educational psychology, New York University

Donald A. Bakal, Ph.D., associate professor of psychology and psychiatry, University of Calgary

Therese L. Baker, Ph.D., associate professor of sociology and division head of behavioral-social sciences, DePaul University

James R. Barclay, Ph.D., professor of educational psychology and counseling, University of Kentucky

David W. Barnett, Ph.D., assistant professor of school psychology, University of Cincinnati

Curtis L. Barrett, Ph.D., associate professor of psychology and director of adult psychology services, Department of Psychiatry and Behavioral Sciences, University of Louisville School of Medicine

Joseph F. Bertinetti, Ph.D., associate professor of counseling and guidance, University of Nebraska at Omaha

Ronald Blackburn, Ph.D., senior lecturer in clinical psychology, University of Aberdeen, Scotland

Brian F. Bolton, Ph.D., associate professor of rehabilitation, Arkansas Rehabilitation Research and Training Center, University of Arkansas at Fayetteville

Thomas G. Burish, Ph.D., assistant professor of psychology, Vanderbilt University

Roger V. Burton, Ph.D., professor of psychology and director of developmental psychology program, State University of New York at Buffalo

Alfred J. Butler, Ph.D., professor and chairperson of studies in behavioral disabilities, University of Wisconsin at Madison

William M. Casey, Ph.D., psychologist, Psychoendocrinology Program, Children's Hospital of Buffalo

Jay L. Chambers, Ph.D., professor of psychology and director of the Center for Psychological Services, College of William and Mary

William C. Coe, Ph.D., professor of psychology, California State University at Fresno

Robert W. Collins, Ph.D., associate professor of psychology, Grand Valley State Colleges

Ray A. Craddick, Ph.D., professor of psychology and director of clinical training, Georgia State University

James C. Crumbaugh, Ph.D., staff psychologist, Veterans Administration Hospital, Gulfport, Mississippi, and adjunct associate professor of psychology, University of Southern Mississippi

Richard H. Dana, Ph.D., professor of psychology, University of Arkansas at Fayetteville

Stephanie Z. Dudek, Ph.D., professor of psychology, University of Montreal

George Edmunds, Ph.D., lecturer in psychology, University of Glasgow, Scotland

R. William English, Ph.D., associate director of the Rehabilitation Research and Training Center in Mental Retardation, University of Oregon

Oliva M. Espin, Ph.D., assistant professor of counselor education, Boston University

Julian J. Fabry, Ph.D., staff psychologist, St. Joseph's Center for Mental Health, Omaha, Nebraska

Paul N. Foxman, Ph.D., staff psychologist, St. John's Mental Health Center, Santa Monica, California

Robert J. Gatchel, Ph.D., associate professor of psychology, University of Texas at Arlington

Robert H. Geertsma, Ph.D., professor and chairperson of medical education and communications and professor of psychiatry, University of Rochester School of Medicine and Dentistry

Judy Genshaft, Ph.D., assistant professor of exceptional children, Ohio State University

Robert W. Genthner, Ph.D., associate professor of psychology and director of clinical training, Eastern Kentucky University

Stephen H. Getsinger, Ph.D., chief of psychology service, Veterans Administration Medical Center, Fort Howard, Maryland

Vincent Glaudin, Ph.D., psychologist, Veterans Administration Hospital, Portland, Oregon, and associate professor of psychology, Portland State University

Charles J. Golden, Ph.D., assistant professor of medical psychology, Department of Psychiatry, University of Nebraska Medical Center

Marilyn E. Goodrich, D.S.Hyg., research intern, Educational Testing Service, Southern Regional Office, Atlanta, Georgia

Melvin A. Gravitz, Ph.D., independent practice of clinical psychology, Washington, D.C., and adjunct professor of clinical psychology, American University

Penelope J. Greene, M.A., teaching assistant, Department of Statistics, Harvard University

James C. Hansen, Ph.D., professor of counseling psychology, State University of New York at Buffalo

Martin Harrow, Ph.D., director of psychology, Michael Rees Medical Center, and associate professor of psychology, University of Chicago

Roger R. Harvey, Ph.D., associate professor of special education, University of Nebraska at Omaha

Edwin L. Herr, Ed.D., professor and head of counseling and educational psychology, Pennsylvania State University

Bonnie S. Himes, Ed.M., consultant, Niagara Falls Community Mental Health Center

Michael Hirt, Ph.D., professor of psychology, Kent State University

Aprile M. Holland, M.B.A., graduate teaching and research assistant, Department of Management, Georgia State University

Ann Howland, Ph.D., clinical psychologist, Athens Psychology Clinic, Athens, Ohio

George J. Huba, Ph.D., assistant research psychologist, Department of Psychology, University of California at Los Angeles

Max L. Hutt, Ph.D., consulting psychologist in private practice and professor of psychology (retired), University of Detroit

Louis H. Janda, Ph.D., assistant professor of psychology, Old Dominion University

Victor C. Joe, Ph.D., associate professor of psychology, Idaho State University

Marvin S. Kaplan, Ph.D., associate professor of graduate education, Kent State University

Martin Katahn, Ph.D., professor of psychology, Vanderbilt University

Jay Kuten, M.D., assistant professor of psychiatry, Boston University School of Medicine

Luciano L'Abate, Ph.D., professor of psychology, Georgia State University

Steen F. Larsen, Ph.D., associate professor of psychology, University of Aarhus, Denmark

Uriel Last, Ph.D., lecturer in psychology, Hebrew University, Jerusalem, Israel

Joseph C. LaVoie, Ph.D., professor of psychology, University of Nebraska at Omaha, and associate professor of medical psychology, Department of Psychiatry, University of Nebraska Medical Center

Billie S. Lazar, Ph.D., assistant professor of psychology, Department of Psychiatry, University of Illinois Medical Center

Eugene E. Levitt, Ph.D., director of psychology, Indiana University School of Medicine, and senior research associate, Indiana University Institute for Sex Research

Larry C. Loesch, Ph.D., associate professor of counselor education, University of Florida

Jan Loney, Ph.D., associate professor of psychiatry, University of Iowa

Gary Thomas Long, Ph.D., associate professor of psychology, University of North Carolina at Charlotte

Albert D. Loro, Jr., Ph.D., assistant professor of medical psychology, Department of Psychiatry, Duke University Medical Center

Lee J. Loshak, Ph.D., independent practice of clinical psychology, Brooklyn, New York, and clinical psychologist, Advanced Center for Psychotherapy, Forest Hills, New York

David J. McDowell, Ph.D. candidate, University of Maine, and clinical director, Milford Assistance Program, Inc., Milford, Massachusetts

Sam G. McFarland, Ph.D., associate professor of psychology, Western Kentucky University

Max G. Magnussen, Ph.D., associate director of the Pittsburgh Child Guidance Center and professor of clinical child psychiatry and psychology, University of Pittsburgh School of Medicine

Marlis E. Mann, Ed.D., associate professor of education, University of New Mexico

Robert P. Marinelli, Ed.D., associate professor of counseling and guidance and of rehabilitation counseling, West Virginia University

Joseph D. Matarazzo, Ph.D., professor and chairman of medical psychology, Department of Psychiatry, University of Oregon School of Medicine

Robert A. Mednick, Ph.D., postdoctoral fellow in psychoanalysis and psychotherapy, Postgraduate Center for Mental Health, New York, New York

Robert G. Meyer, Ph.D., professor of psychology, University of Louisville

John B. Miner, Ph.D., research professor of management and doctoral program coordinator, College of Business Administration, Georgia State University

Irvin Moelis, Ph.D., associate professor and chief of clinical child psychology, Department of Psychiatry, State University of New York Upstate Medical Center

Everett Moitoza, Ed.D., postdoctoral fellow in psychology, Brandeis University

Charles J. Morgan, Ph.D., professor of psychology and research associate, Institute for Environmental Studies, University of Washington

Donald L. Mosher, Ph.D., professor of psychology, University of Connecticut

Lloyd D. Noppe, Ph.D., lecturer in psychology, University of Wisconsin

John O'Connor, Ph.D., professor and chairperson of psychology, Western Kentucky University

Jacob L. Orlofsky, Ph.D., assistant professor of psychology, University of Missouri at St. Louis

Janet L. Ostrand, Ph.D., counseling psychologist, Student Counseling Services, University of Illinois at Chicago

Loren D. Pankratz, Ph.D., staff psychologist, Veterans Administration Hospital, Portland, Oregon, and assistant professor of medical psychology, Department of Psychiatry, University of Oregon Health Sciences Center

Timothy G. Plax, Ph.D., associate professor of speech communication, University of New Mexico

Selina Sue Prosen, Ph.D., assistant professor of education and counseling, Johns Hopkins University

Jaquelyn Liss Resnick, Ph.D., associate professor of counselor education and counseling psychologist, Psychological and Vocational Counseling Center, University of Florida

Malcolm H. Robertson, Ph.D., professor of psychology and director of clinical training, Western Michigan University

David C. Rowe, Ph.D., assistant professor of psychology, Oberlin College

Paul N. Russell, M.A., senior lecturer in psychology, University of Canterbury, Christchurch, New Zealand

Carolyn Saarni, Ph.D., associate professor of educational psychology, New York University

David A. Sabatino, Ph.D., professor and chairperson of special education, Southern Illinois University at Carbondale

Gary S. Sarver, Ph.D., assistant professor of psychology, Ohio University, and clinical psychologist, Athens Psychology Clinic, Athens, Ohio

Sylvan J. Schaffer, Columbia University Law School, and Ph.D. candidate in clinical psychology, American University

Paul G. Schauble, Ph.D., professor of psychology and counseling psychologist, Psychological and Vocational Counseling Center, University of Florida

Peter W. Sheehan, Ph.D., professor of psychology, University of Queensland, St. Lucia, Queensland, Australia

Alan G. Slemon, Ph.D., professor of education, University of Western Ontario

Thomas M. Stephens, Ed.D., professor of education and chairperson of exceptional children, Ohio State University

Fred D. Strider, Ph.D., associate professor of medical psychology, Department of Psychiatry, University of Nebraska Medical Center

Clifford H. Swensen, Ph.D., professor of psychological sciences, Purdue University

Kenneth R. Thomas, Ed.D., professor of studies in behavioral disabilities, University of Wisconsin at Madison

Jeffrey Urist, Ph.D., assistant professor of psychology, University of Michigan

Glen M. Vaught, Ph.D., professor of psychology, State University of New York at Oswego

Herman A. Walters, Ph.D., professor of clinical psychology, University of Montana

Peter H. Waxer, Ph.D., associate professor of psychology, York University, Downsview, Ontario, and chief psychologist, York-Finch General Hospital, Toronto

Michael S. Weissman, Ph.D., director of internship training and coordinator of psychological testing, Portsmouth Psychiatric Center, Portsmouth, Virginia

Norman E. Whitten, Sr., Ph.D., professor of anthropology, State University of New York at Oswego

Gregory H. Wilmoth, M.A., graduate student in psychology, University of Florida

Karl B. Zucker, Ph.D., professor of special education, Indiana State University

Robert Henley Woody

Introduction: A Conceptual Framework for Clinical Assessment

The *Encyclopedia of Clinical Assessment* is intended to be a compendium of behavioral science material for the practitioner. Thus, the goal is to marry art and science. Since the two sometimes make strange bedfellows, it seems best to preface the chapters with a conceptual framework for clinical assessment that will delineate the scope of objectives and clarify how the contents can be used in day-to-day practice. The final section sets forth the organization and structure of the *Encyclopedia*.

Clinical Assessment

Clinical assessment is a set of processes and procedures for human services professionals. It is inherent to all professional functions, be it the reaction in the initial contact with a prospective patient, the decision to accept or reject a patient, the services to be offered and the techniques to be used, the decision to terminate treatment, or the impression of the treatment's efficiency and relevance to treating other patients.

Clinical assessment is a professional service. Sundberg (1977, p. 30) emphasizes this point: "The human problems and decisions that psychological assessment addresses are ancient, but systematic study and development of exact measures for assessment date only from the late nineteenth century. Many of the aspects of professional assessment are similar to those of informal, everyday assessment, such as the processes of forming impressions of others. The major advantages of professional assessment are that trained people have special knowledge and skills and feel a distinct responsibility, with ethical concerns about the process."

Clinical assessment is much more than the use of psychological tests, as Maloney and Ward (1976, p. 38) clarify:

> Psychometric testing refers to the systematic study of individual differences among people along specified traits or dimensions. The essence of the psychometric test is that the description of people is done in objective, standardized, quantifiable ways. Psychological assessment, on the other hand, is more generally a process of solving problems. . . . (1) Psychometric testing is primarily measurement oriented, while psychological assessment is primarily problem oriented; (2) psychometric testing is primarily concerned with describing and studying groups of people, while psychological assessment focuses on a description and an analysis of a particular individual in a problem situation; (3) psychometric testing demands little if any clinical expertise other than that of a psychometrist, while the role of the clinician or expert is crucial and integral to the process of psychological assessment.

Within this statement are four critical points. First, clinical assessment is not restricted to objective, standardized, quantifiable procedures. For example, many of the data might come from interviews or observations. Second, clinical assessment is individually focused; more will be said about this shortly. Third, clinical assessment is problem oriented. Fourth, the diagnostician, that is, the assessor, has the responsibility of applying and maintaining astute clinical acumen.

As mentioned, clinical assessment focuses on the individual; that is, for the most part it is *idiographic,* as opposed to *nomothetic.* Idiographic assessment involves principles of individuality, whereas nomothetic evaluation is devoted to identifying universal laws. This does not mean, however, that the individual is viewed in isolation from universal laws or as being exempt from social influences.

At one point, clinical assessment was restricted primarily to a trait-and-factor determination for the individual. There were merely descriptions of the presence or absence of various factors thought to be critical to the assessment objectives and, perhaps, comparisons of the individual's characteristics with the seeming distribution of the factors among peers (for example, using percentiles). This isolated scope has broadened, and it is recognized that the individual is not compartmentalized and that he or she is in a state of constant growth and change as a result of being integrally involved with social systems. As Sundberg (1977) notes, the assessor adopts an ecological attitude toward causation, strives to identify the systems of importance to the person, and bases an analysis on the characteristics of the systems. These external social systems are then blended with the internal systems. Sundberg indicates that this means discerning "the perceived internal *self-system,* the person's consciousness of his or her own program, or perceptions of the self and one's possibilities," making "comparisons of the self-system with the environmental system," and delineating "the person's behavioral repertoire and the potential behavior that might result from learning and situational changes" (1977, p. 15). As might be expected, therapy would, therefore, be directed at altering the inputs to the individual from the many social systems in which he or she exists. Obviously these alterations need not be accomplished only through behavior modification (that is, conditioning) procedures per se, since it seems clear that essentially all forms of therapy rely on reinforcement processes and accept in fact that change can occur through eliminating inputs that promote "illness" and fostering inputs that will increase the likelihood of "healthy" percepts, feelings, and behavior (Woody, 1971). In sum, clinical assessment is individually oriented, but it always considers social existence; the objective is usually to help the person solve problems.

Clinical Judgment

Professional expertise in clinical judgment develops through formulating impressions, identifying "facts" that will be considered, and posing hypotheses. But these steps are only the beginning for the hypothesis-testing processes also include weighing clinical data and fitting outcomes into diagnostic models and classification systems. Although diagnosis and classification will be elaborated on later, it must be underscored here that each of these functions by the assessor involves clinical judgment. By its very nature, clinical judgment is subjective and represents using scientific knowledge and methods artistically.

Inspection of clinical assessment's evolution reveals that diagnosticians constantly make judgments. In tracing the history of psychological testing from approximately 1850 to the present, Kaplan, Hirt, and Kurtz (1967) cite the emergence of psychodynamic approaches that incontrovertibly depend on the professional's exercising judgment. Sundberg (1977) sets forth fifty key events in psychological assessment; from Galton's "Classification of Men According to their Natural Gifts" in 1869 to the behavioral assessment techniques using observations in 1976, it is obvious that the success or failure of assessment is connected to the quality of the professional's judgments during the assessment process. Bieri and others (1966) identify four historical phases for clinical judgment. The first phase involved an almost total reliance on introspective analysis, such as in the Freudian approach. A second stage occurred when there was increased concern for the adequacy of diagnostic procedures; in other words, it was a reliability-validity stage. Third, an extension of the reliability-validity phase led to an emphasis on clinical versus statistical prediction. The culminating fourth stage was the emergence of concern for developing theoretical models for the clinical judgment processes.

With this historical backdrop, any attempt to define clinical assessment should consider the views of Thorne (1961, p. 7):

Most parsimoniously, clinical judgment properly refers simply to the correctness of the *problem-solving thinking of a special class of per-*

sons, namely clinically trained persons with special levels of training, experience, and competence. Judgments concerning clinical matters can be made by anyone. Such *lay opinions* have only the weight of the level of intelligence, education, and experience of the person making them. It always remains to be demonstrated whether specialty training and experience make possible judgments of higher validity than lay opinions.

In so saying, Thorne introduces the notion that clinical assessment receives sanction from society. Thorne acknowledges that clinical judgments may be only slightly better, that is, more discerning, than common sense or pure chance solutions: "In cases where the differential is relatively small, then society itself must determine how much it can afford to pay for such a premium" (1961, p. 23).

Clinical judgment involves inferential accuracy, the assessor's "ability, given limited information about a target person (patient), to judge correctly other pertinent characteristics about that person and to identify behavioral exemplars as part of a pattern of behavioral consistencies" (Reed and Jackson, 1975, p. 475). Given the subjectivity inherent in making inferences, even by the most highly trained professional, it is not surprising that research does not yield consistent support for clinical judgments (Thorne, 1961). Clinical assessment is, however, a pragmatic creation of society. Thorne asserts that clinical judgment based on procedures that lack "complete scientific support and validation" must only profess "to be the best that can be offered at time and place" (1961, p. 21); he continues, "society must depend upon clinical decisions because of the practical and economic limitations of life situations" (p. 23).

Diagnosis

Clinical assessment usually accommodates a multifaceted diagnosis. One author offers three requirements for diagnosis: "the present functioning or characteristics should be evaluated and described; possible causative factors or etiology should be posited; and a prognosis should be made and a treatment approach recommended" (Woody, 1969, p. 77). Another recognizes six requirements: "observation, description, a delineation of causation or etiology, classification, prediction or prognosis, and control-modification or treatment plan" (Beller, 1962, p. 109). Yet, regardless of the number of requirements, diagnosis fulfills crucial functions. Shevrin and Shectman write that "a diagnostic point of view fosters a way of approaching clinical issues and conceptualizing them" (1973, p. 467). While diagnosis will lead to classification, it affords a broader clinical understanding of the case. As Arbuckle states: "Diagnosis may be considered as the analysis of one's difficulties and the causes that have produced them. More clinically, it may be thought of as the determination of the nature, origin, precipitation, and maintenance of ineffective abnormal modes of behavior. More simply, it may be considered as the development by the counselor of a deeper and more accurate understanding and appreciation of the client" (1965, p. 220).

Similarly, Shevrin and Shectman believe: "In the diagnosis of mental disorders the diagnostician, through the *medium of a personal relationship, elicits and observes* a range of *psychological functioning* which he considers *relevant on some theoretical grounds for* understanding the disorder so that he can make a *recommendation* which stands a good chance of being *acted on as a basis for dealing with the disorder*" (1973, p. 451). Beyond the misconception that classification is the sum and substance of diagnosis, Shectman states: "*Diagnosis can work when it is based not on labels but on establishing relation-*

ships which permit the observation of psychological functioning and in turn leads to an appreciation of a patient's internal experience and understanding of it and the drawing of proper conclusions" (1973, p. 524).

Clinical assessment emanates from human interaction. Logically, the diagnostic elements should be drawn from all segments of the interaction; they cannot be isolated to an interview or the administration of tests. In clinical assessment, diagnosis will and should always be present. Of course, carrying out the diagnostic function through the relationship between the diagnostician and patient is no simple accomplishment. Diagnostic efforts are always predicated on the qualities of the diagnostician and on his or her interactions with the patient.

It is important to examine how the specific factors considered in clinical assessment—namely, emotional and behavioral factors—influence or relate to the diagnostic processes. As reflected in the previously cited requirements for diagnosis (Woody, 1969; Beller, 1962), etiology or causation is critical to the diagnosis of emotional and behavioral problems. Woodruff, Goodwin, and Guze (1974) point to three types of causation: (1) *Necessary and sufficient* causes, which are uncommon, come from a specific infectious agent (for example, genes that produce disorders). (2) *Necessary but not sufficient* causes are conditions where a number of persons are exposed to the agent but only a few develop a problem (for example, the use of alcohol). (3) *Facilitating or predisposing that are neither necessary nor sufficient* causes represent a host of agents (biological, social, and psychological) that influence the likelihood of developing a problem. In clinical assessment of emotional and behavioral disorders, the majority of causations will be in the third category. Consequently, no clear-cut or discrete etiological agents will be discerned. Rather, clinical assessment will involve, first, a screening of the myriad of influences that could potentially have contributed to the current emotional or behavioral status of the patient and, second, a crude, at best, setting of priorities to establish which factors should receive therapeutic attention.

It would be convenient if emotional and behavioral problems could be separated by unique factors. The chapters in the *Encyclopedia* reveal that this is not possible. Frank examined research on the psychiatric diagnosis of various emotional disturbances and concluded that from the interviews, observations, and psychological tests relevant to the patient's symptoms "the data indicate that there does not seem to be any consistent relationship among the patterns of these various segments of personality" (1975, p. 63). He continues: "Psychiatric diagnoses, therefore, prove to be a purely descriptive system of classification, yielding no useful information regarding the life of the individual (beyond the observable in the present, that is, his symptoms), the prognosis for the person's rehabilitation, or what methods would best be cited to facilitate that rehabilitation. Moreover, though syndromes (that is, grouping of symptoms) *do* emerge from these data, few symptoms prove to be syndrome (that is, diagnosis) specific" (p. 64).

As might be assumed, diagnoses—especially with a nosology—are the products of professionalization. In other words, they are not absolute results from the patient's condition; they are created by professionals to facilitate delivery of services. Rosenhan clarifies the matter: "Unlike most medical diagnoses, which can be validated in numerous ways, psychiatric diagnoses are maintained by consensus alone" (1975, p. 464). He indicates that this is exemplified by the decision by the American Psychiatric Association to delete homosexuality from its list of mental disorders.

In this *Encyclopedia,* diagnosis is taken as a "fact of life" but not a practice deserving of unassailable "sanctity." It is a professional practice to facilitate services and—less honorably perhaps—professional identity.

Classification

A number of the chapters in the *Encyclopedia* reflect labels, and labels are based on *nosology,* the classification of diseases. For example, the chapters in Part Three, "Major Disorders," are intended to encompass the system set forth by the American Psychiatric Association's (1968) *Diagnostic and Statistical Manual of Mental Disorders* (second edition; commonly known as the DSM-II). Nosology is very much a part, rightly or wrongly, of contemporary clinical assessment, but it must be placed in a reasonable perspective.

The use of a classification system for emotional and behavioral problems is justified if it increases the efficacy of professional services on behalf of the patient. As Frank states: "Classification presumes ordering; an order presumes a reason for the ordering; a reason presumes some understanding" (1975, p. 73). There seems little room to quarrel with systems, methods, or procedures that allow professionals to better understand and, thus, better serve their patients. The question, however, remains: Does classification facilitate greater efficacy in clinical assessment? The answer, while qualified by numerous reservations, seems to be "yes." Even though he presents evidence that seriously questioned classification, Rosenhan (1975) acknowledges that individual differences will always make classification/categorization possible and that scientific understanding is predicated on use of classification. But he cautions that new classification systems for clinical assessment should demonstrate evidence of their utility before being allowed promulgation.

It seems prudent to assert that any classification system for emotional and behavioral problems should fulfill at least four evaluative criteria (Blashfield and Draguns, 1976). First, it must be possible to apply the system in a *reliable* fashion. That is, a given diagnostician must be able to replicate the judgment of another diagnostician. Further, multiple diagnosticians must be able to produce judgments that are in significant agreement with each other, which is easier said than done. For example, in a study that asked senior electroencephalographers to simply dichotomize electroencephalograms according to the classifications of "normal" or "abnormal," their percentage of agreement on the overall record classification was only 53.3 percent, even though they agreed on definitions for the categories beforehand (Woody, 1968). Second, the system should offer *coverage* relevant to a domain of patients. Regrettably, the greater the coverage, the lower the reliability. Third, a system must have *descriptive validity,* that is, relative homogeneity of categories within the classification system. Fourth, a system must have *predictive validity,* that is, a pragmatic utility for making treatment decisions. These four criteria create a tough challenge for clinical assessment, and Frank's analysis of research on psychiatric diagnosis supports that they are seldom fulfilled: "This study suggests that the system has only face validity, and yet I am sure clinicians will go right on using it, ignoring the research" (1975, p. 81). Although classification is fraught with limitations, it is still a function that society requires of the diagnostician.

The DSM-II is the foremost classification system for emotional and behavioral disorders, and it is frequently referred to in the *Encyclopedia.* Although a DSM-III is being prepared, it has not received empirical application to date, and thus *Encyclopedia* contributors have purposefully concentrated on its predecessor. Certain features of the DSM-III should be noted, however.

The disease-oriented model of the DSM-II will be expanded. Rather than encompassing the person's total environment in an ecological, nondisease model, the DSM-III promises to draw all sorts of social and psychological factors under the auspices of medicine and, consequently, of treatment by the disease approach. The DSM-III reportedly will eliminate a single classification statement and will utilize instead evaluative opinions according to a multiaxial diagnosis covering five areas: (1) formal psychiatric syndrome, (2) personality disorders (adults) and specific developmental disorders (children), (3) non-mental medical disorders, (4) severity of psychosocial stressors one year preceding disorder, and (5) highest level of adaptive behavior one year preceding disorder. Further details are provided by Schacht and Nathan (1977).

The DSM-III is not receiving unrestricted endorsement. For example, Schacht and Nathan point out that the DSM-III may be, in not-so-subtle fashion, more a promotion of psychiatry's control over other mental health disciplines than a functional contribution to the mental health needs of consumers. They comment: "The resulting document, then, may be likened to a symphony written by a committee—the notes are all there, but the way they are put together reflects the mediocrity inherent in such a process rather than integrated purpose and understanding" (1977, p. 1017). As might be expected, the American Psychological Association has embarked on a counterpart "Descriptive Behavioral Classification System." When the American Psychological Association's Task Force on Descriptive Behavioral Classification issued its progress report, it noted that "the proposed DSM-III fails to provide a satisfactory method of classification for the following reasons: (1) It is a disease-based model inappropriately used to describe problems of living; (2) it has consistently shown high levels of unreliability of the specific categories; (3) it is a mixed model, the groupings variously based on symptom clusters, antisocial behaviors, theoretical considerations, or developmental influences; (4) categories have been created or deleted based on committee vote rather than on hard data; (5) the labels have assumed strong judgmental qualities, frequently resulting in bias and social injustice; (6) it offers low capability for indication of treatment modality, prediction of outcome, or determination of required duration of interventions, characteristics both desirable clinically and of major importance to third party payors" (1977, p. 1). The message seems to be that the classification of emotional and behavioral disorders will receive a great deal of professional attention in the foreseeable future, but regrettably that attention may be motivated by professional self-interest (such as political and legal power to increase economic rewards to practitioners) rather than by the desire to develop a classification system that could be used for the benefit of patients.

Pragmatism

As a conceptual framework, this introduction has emphasized that clinical assessment is more than psychological testing—it is a complete set of processes and procedures, primarily devoted to idiographic problem solving and highly dependent on the subjective judgments and clinical acumen of professionals. As a main segment of clinical assessment, diagnosis extends throughout the relationship between the professional and the patient and is intended to improve understanding of the conditions that affect the patient and to facilitate therapeutic efficacy. The causes of emotional and behavioral problems are usually multifaceted and difficult to pinpoint. Thus, diagnoses are vulnerable to error, and diagnostic methods frequently lack reliability and validity (and other properties) that would assure that the benefits of using a certain classification system far outweigh possible liabilities for the patients. As previously suggested, specific processes in clinical assessment, for example, diagnostic classification, are not immune to being used as political issues for the economic benefits of a profession (and potentially at the expense, figuratively and literally, of the patient).

Clinical assessment, with all of its strengths and weaknesses, is a pragmatic undertaking. Even though clinical judgments and lay opinions may not differ that much and even though errors and practices of poor validity are a real possibility, patients continue to seek help from clinicians. Thus, the diagnostician is placed in a position where he or she must continue to make clinical judgments. Frank (1975, p. 73) captures the essence of pragmatism in the following statement:

> Part of the problem with an applied arm of science, be it medicine, clinical psychology, engineering, and so on, is that it tends to be an empirical endeavor. Confronted with the exigencies of daily problems, the applied scientist may have to try to resolve a situation without the (at least, adequate) help of research and theory. Most frequently, what has worked before is the first line of intervention; if that does not work, we will try something else, and if *that* does not work, perhaps we will stop and ask ourselves the important question: why? If the procedure works, we do not feel the need to confront the question of why it works: that is considered "academic." Sometimes one just does not have time to pose theoretical questions and/or test assumptions with adequate research; for example, there are patients who are in pain (physically or psychologically) *now,* and they need help, *now.* The reality of clinical work imposes a nonscientific approach. . . . [W]e say to our more research-oriented brethren: we will work as best as we can with what we have, you research the issue. [Yet] we frequently distrust the research: it deals with part processes, segments of the human, limited facets of the entire situation, that is, the totality of life in which this person is embedded; in short, "artificial." And so, without recourse to the very data that might modify our procedures for the better, we bungle on.

To bungle on is not acceptable, of course, to the applied behavioral science identity of clinical assessment practitioners. There must be continuing efforts to test, verify, and develop reliable and valid means for accomplishing clinical assessment. Research is essential —without it, clinical assessment will deteriorate. In the meantime, however, there is a societal mandate to practice, to apply clinical assessment skills, albeit that they may be as much art as science.

Organization and Structure

As the preceding comments reveal, clinical assessment has a number of inherent dimensions. The fundamental challenge in organizing this *Encyclopedia,* therefore, was to discern the dimensions that had to be covered so that the composite would provide a comprehensive scope. Theoretical and experimental dimensions necessary for a behavioral science foundation had to be accommodated, as did pragmatic considerations necessary for effective professional practice.

The literature of the past ten years was reviewed—particularly major assessment texts and professional journals relevant to clinical practice in general and clinical assessment in particular—to (1) create a tentative list of dimensions that should be covered, and (2) develop a roster of researchers who were studying these dimensions. The names of other researchers were included after perusing the membership lists of clinically relevant divisions of the American Psychological Association and of diplomates named by the American Board of Professional Psychology. Of particular interest were those people who were known for contributions to clinical assessment, for example, for published work that might not have been included in the ten-year journal review. These researchers, along with the topics that they had investigated, were matched with the dimensions to be covered. Although an effort was made to select contributors who had achieved eminence, consideration was also given to "new" investigators who were distinguished, for example, by the uniqueness of their research. Further, a select group of renowned clinical investigators were asked if they had any special interests that would complement the intended coverage of the *Encyclopedia*. After a tentative list of topics and potential contributors was compiled, personal invitations went out.

The result of this selection process is found in the ninety-one chapters. The authors represent a diversified and impressive array of contemporary investigators in the field of clinical assessment. There is a healthy blend of "senior" and "junior" contributors, and the topics provide the comprehensive scope needed for a reference of this nature.

The chapters are grouped in such a way that general and theoretical concerns are discussed before more specialized clinical concerns. The sequence is as follows: individual normal development to individual problems of adjustment and the broad area of personality to specialized areas, social functioning, and operational considerations.

One of the most distinctive features of the *Encyclopedia* is that each chapter follows a similar format, an inherent characteristic of encyclopedic resources. Thus, users may read as little or as much as they wish and still come away with increased understanding of the topic. Reading the first couple of sections results in generalized familiarity; further reading provides more refined understanding. Consequently, the sequence of contents, as structured by the outline followed by contributors, is progressive in depth and coverage.

This uniform approach to structuring chapters offers the advantage of allowing the reader to move back and forth between chapters, thereby promoting a comparative analysis of given clinical assessment dimensions. The following headings reflect the outline used in preparing each chapter.

The opening paragraphs provide a basic definition for the dimension under consideration. Each definition is designed to give an overview of the dimension's components and to increase conceptual understanding.

Background and Current Status. This section traces the evolution of the dimension, provides the historical and clinical antecedents, moves from the initiation phase to the present, and offers a here-and-now perspective.

Critical Discussion. For many of the dimensions, this will be the academic heart of the body of material in the chapter. Here the principle of progressive refinement is foremost. There are four subsections: *General Areas of Concern* presents what might be deemed the critical issues, follows up with an in-depth discussion on the same point, and considers any other points necessary to achieve a thorough analysis of the designated critical issues. *Comparative Philosophies and Theories* explores the philosophical and theoretical underpinnings for the delineated critical concerns and establishes the behavioral science "school(s)" most appropriate for the dimension. *Elaboration on Critical Points* moves further into refinement of the issues and, given the philosophical-theoretical framework, introduces new issues that fulfill the criteria of breadth and depth for the dimension. *Personal Views and Recommendations* allows the contributor to interpret the material from his or her vantage point as a specialist-investigator (whereas the preceding subsections were geared to be objective, this subsection is purposefully interpretive).

Application to Particular Variables. This section focuses on the numerous factors that affect the dimension, including, among other things, age, sex, education, socioeconomic factors, ethnic and racial factors, and dimension-specific disorders.

References. The sources referred to in each chapter were carefully selected to avoid burdening the reader with an undue number of citations. The references included are not exhaustive but are a primary resource for readers who wish to gain a more specialized understanding of the dimension.

As mentioned in the preface, this *Encyclopedia* is designed to make the reader aware of the subjective nature of clinical assessment and to promote optimum, academically based objectivity in clinical practice. In addition, the contents will help facilitate (1) an awareness of the methods that are suited and ill-suited for particular dimensions; (2) a realistic appraisal of the role clinical assessment can and should play in professional functioning and societal development; and (3) a commitment to continual professional growth on the part of the practitioner who turns to the *Encyclopedia* to help improve his or her case management.

References

American Psychiatric Association. *Diagnostic and Statistical Manual of Mental Disorders.* (2nd ed.) Washington, D.C.: American Psychiatric Association, 1968.

American Psychological Association's Task Force on Descriptive Behavioral Classification. "Progress Report." Washington, D.C.: American Psychological Association, July 1977 (mimeo).

Arbuckle, D. S. *Counseling: Philosophy, Theory, and Practice.* Boston: Allyn & Bacon, 1965.

Beller, E. K. *Clinical Process: The Assessment of Data in Childhood Personality Disorders.* New York: Free Press, 1962.

Bieri, J., and others. *Clinical and Social Judgment: The Discrimination of Behavioral Information.* New York: Wiley, 1966.

Blashfield, R. K., and Draguns, J. G. "Evaluative Criteria for Psychiatric Classification." *Journal of Abnormal Psychology,* 1976, *85,* 140-150.

Frank, G. *Psychiatric Diagnosis: A Review of Research.* New York: Pergamon, 1975.

Kaplan, M. L., Hirt, M. L., and Kurtz, R. M. "Psychological Testing: I. History and Current Trends." *Comprehensive Psychiatry,* 1967, *8,* 299-309.

Maloney, M. P., and Ward, M. P. *Psychological Assessment: A Conceptual Approach.* New York: Oxford University Press, 1976.

Reed, P. L., and Jackson, D. N. "Clinical Judgment of Psychopathology: A Model for Inferential Accuracy." *Journal of Abnormal Psychology,* 1975, *84,* 475-482.

Rosenhan, D. L. "The Contextual Nature of Psychiatric Diagnosis." *Journal of Abnormal Psychology,* 1975, *84,* 462-474.

Schacht, T., and Nathan, P. E. "But Is It Good for the Psychologists? Appraisal and Status of DSM-III." *American Psychologist,* 1977, *32,* 1017-1025.

Shectman, F. "On Being Misinformed by Misleading Arguments." *Bulletin of the Menninger Clinic,* 1973, *37,* 523-525.

Shevrin, H., and Shectman, F. "The Diagnostic Process in Psychiatric Evaluations." *Bulletin of the Menninger Clinic,* 1973, *37,* 451-494.

Sundberg, N. D. *Assessment of Persons.* Englewood Cliffs, N.J.: Prentice-Hall, 1977.

Thorne, F. C. *Clinical Judgment: A Study of Clinical Error.* Brandon, Vt.: Journal of Clinical Psychology, 1961.

Woodruff, R. A., Jr., Goodwin, D. W., and Guze, S. B. *Psychiatric Diagnosis.* New York: Oxford University Press, 1974.

Woody, R. H. "Inter-Judge Reliability in Clinical Electroencephalography." *Journal of Clinical Psychology,* 1968, *24,* 251-256.

Woody, R. H. *Behavioral Problem Children in the Schools: Recognition, Diagnosis, and Behavioral Modification.* New York: Appleton-Century-Crofts, 1969.

Woody, R. H. *Psychobehavioral Counseling and Therapy: Integrating Behavioral and Insight Techniques.* New York: Appleton-Century-Crofts, 1971.

ENCYCLOPEDIA
OF CLINICAL
ASSESSMENT

Volume 1

1

Max G. Magnussen

Child and Adolescent Development

The emphasis of this chapter is on the clinical assessment of children and youth. The developmental range covered extends from infancy through adolescence (0-18 years). Knowledge of developmental levels and processes is underscored as necessary to understand normal and deviant behavior.

Although there are many legitimate purposes for diagnosis (that is, discovering etiology, planning treatment, describing symptom clusters, and offering a prognosis), Cole and Magnussen (1966) focus on disposition and action as the ultimate critical goals for assessment. The value of any effort to establish a valid and accurate diagnosis depends, at least in part, on the utility of an assessment in suggesting differential action on the part of the child mental health personnel who are expected to use this information on behalf of the client. This is essentially an emphasis on assessment for treatment selection. Adoption of such a primary focus might well assist in the situations described by Hobbs (1975), who contends that many children are simply classified and labeled for a *no-service track*. If assessment were to be reserved for the major purpose of treatment selection, perhaps this labeling for no benefit to the client might be prevented.

1

Background and Current Status

Theories of human development have guided assessment and measurement activities. Freud formulated the initial systematic theory of personality and social development and provided a bridge between earlier theories based on instincts or other biological concepts. The psychoanalytic tradition stimulated assessment of personality and the psychosexual developmental stages. Piaget developed a systematic theory of cognitive development, concentrating on intellectual development and universal stages in cognitive development. Gestalt theorists and researchers have stressed that subjective meanings are influenced both by the context in which stimuli are perceived and by the previous experiences that the person has had with similar stimuli. As a consequence, assessment was often aimed in these directions. Behaviorists identified most closely with the experimental approach to the study of development and emphasized the physical environment (that is, the observable and measurable properties of stimuli) and its effects on the organism. Behavioral assessment and the study of situational specificity problems evolved from this theoretical foundation. Another major influence in child development has been the psychometric tradition, which stresses the measurement of characteristics and the development of norms. The orientation is heavily empirical and in marked contrast to the other approaches, which are heavily theoretical. This tradition has produced intelligence tests (permitting intellectual classification for educational placement), standardized personality tests and questionnaires, and age and sex norms for many developmental stages.

In 1952, with the development of the first edition of the American Psychiatric Association's *Diagnostic and Statistical Manual of Mental Disorders (DSM-I),* the psychiatric establishment attempted to provide a framework for the systematic classification of disorders. The focus was on the labeling of illness and pathology, and an attempt was made to classify individuals rather than discrete behaviors or traits.

Until recently the *DSM-II* (American Psychiatric Association, 1968) has been in use. This system paid a certain amount of attention to disorders of children and adolescents. The emphasis remained on labeling of deviance, but there was some recognition of developmental periods of children and youth.

Currently the third edition of the *Diagnostic and Statistical Manual of Mental Disorders (DSM-III)* is under active development. The draft version of this edition (American Psychiatric Association, 1977) indicates it is more comprehensive than the *DSM-II.* Moreover, in this edition diagnosis takes a multiaxial form; that is, each diagnosis contains information on at least five predetermined axes designed to be of value in categorizing, classifying, planning treatment, and predicting outcome. Axis II in the system devotes some attention to specific developmental disorders in children. The major problem with the system is the unproven assumption that psychiatric disorders are medical problems (see Salzinger, 1977; Schacht and Nathan, 1977; Shershow and Savodnik, 1977; Zubin, 1977-78). With more political finesse than scientific foundation, the preface of *DSM-III,* in effect, states that mental disorders are the result of organic failure in the human body. The problem with the medical model—and with political, social, and professional psychiatric influences on diagnosis—is that the service needs of clients, and perhaps the rights of patients to appropriate treatment, are largely ignored (that is, the model is predicated on values that are not always compatible with client needs and rights).

Critical Discussion

General Areas of Concern

An acknowledged crisis exists in child mental health. A majority of children in need of help are receiving inadequate (if any) professional services—services that are commonly late in coming and of unknown effectiveness. Surveys indicate that 30 percent of all children experience some form of school maladjustment (Glidewell and Swallow, 1969). Other studies (Langner and others, 1974) reveal that as many as half of all school children who are "markedly or severely impaired" due to emotional and behavioral difficulties are not even referred for professional treatment. There are barriers that now prevent this help from being given. Some of the barriers are external to the child mental health professions and services. Children and youth are underrepresented in the society in general. Although they comprise one quarter to one third of the nation's population, they do not receive a proportional amount of special resources. Furthermore, what constitutes children's rights continues to be a legal morass. Low national priorities for children and lack of sufficient funding are constant and common barriers to establishing and obtaining children's services. These roadblocks must be constantly attacked.

Other concerns include the questioning of the value of diagnosis for treatment selection, the importance of directly relating evaluation to decisions and dispositions to assist the person in societal interactions, and vigilance to the potentially damaging effects of labeling, particularly on children and youth. Deemphasizing preoccupation with individual pathology and focusing on competency (see Sundberg, Snowden, and Reynolds, 1978) in relationship to the person and the social situation and specific developmental level are advocated. Any clinical assessment theory or practice must consider the technical properties of measurement—the issues of validity, reliability, norms, standardization, and the utility of measurement. Magnussen (in press) enumerates the issues concerning psychometric properties in traditional tests for children and adolescents. Due to space limitations, and to a subsequent suggestion that assessment should be aimed at clinical decision making (Cole and Magnussen, 1966), only validity will be elaborated on here.

Validity pertains to the degree to which a test measures that which it was designed to measure. Validity in measurement terms concerns itself with the relationships of a test to other data about the individual. A systematic study of the relationships makes it possible to determine what the technique measures and to what degree it correlates with an independent criterion.

Why are some approaches valid and others not? One of the reasons must be that valid tests measure the abilities and characteristics actually needed in real-life functioning. This exceedingly important technical property of a test, validity, leads to differing viewpoints about the practical use of diagnosis. In keeping with any viewpoint, it is always essential to know the purpose for which the assessment has specified validity. In conventional classification, tests may possess content validity, criterion-related validity, or construct validity, or any combination of these (Anastasi, 1972). Content validity concerns the accuracy and completeness with which items sample the function that is being assessed. Criterion-related validity involves correlation of a score or item with an external criterion. Construct validity is a generalized, all-inclusive, kind of validity. Its use generally deals with research refutation or verification of theoretical constructs or experimental hypotheses concerning human behavior.

In applied clinical practice, validity coefficients of relatively low magnitude are often useful for making predictions for specified purposes or when large numbers of individuals are tested. In striving to make predictions for the individual case, however, one usually cannot obtain validity coefficients as high as those found in large normative samples.

Further practical issues in applied contexts have resulted in expanded definitions of validity. In the conventional orientation toward validity, the general goal of testing is interpreted as involving the prediction of human behavior. Typically, the purpose of a test is to forecast nontest behavior. Test validity considerations, such as construct and criterion validity, refer to some measurable aspect of the child, and the criterion for test validation is viewed as involving the behavior of the individual tested. Gough and Heilbrun (1965) state that the primary evaluation of an assessment technique identifies the criteria that are principally relevant to the test and determines how well the technique predicts what it seeks to predict, measures what it purports to measure, or defines what it is intended to define. An implicit rule is that assessment techniques predict, measure, or define some aspect of human behavior. In an alternative orientation to assessment, validity in terms of clinical decision making, the usefulness of information depends directly on how well that information aids in making dispositions for action. The validity of the procedure depends on an evaluation of the total effects of treatment on patients, a clinic, and, possibly, even a community.

Although this approach might logically evolve into a "diagnostic" procedure, its orientation toward clinical action (rather than patient behavior) differs from traditional diagnostic procedures (Cole and Magnussen, 1966). A treatment disposition might imply a diagnostic classification, but only indirectly (for instance, outpatient psychotherapy would be prescribed for a client with a neurotic condition rather than a serious psychotic condition). Primarily, dispositional assessment suggests that treatment procedures are evaluated *in addition to* the usual procedures of scientific validation. The question of the value of tests, when considered in their practical use, is *not* "Does the test correlate with a criterion?" Instead, the question becomes "Does the use of the test improve the success of the decision-making process?"—by making it more efficient, less costly, more accurate, more rational, or more clinically relevant. Levine (1968) raises these issues and concludes that much of the research on test validity is not relevant to the practical use of psychological tests. If one purpose of assessment is diagnostic classification, however, the typical procedure of validity has some degree of utility.

The matter of clinical versus statistical prediction remains active in the assessment field. Actuarial or statistical prediction refers to a method of statistically combining data to make a decision or prediction (Meehl, 1954). Recent studies (Nisbett and Borgida, 1975; Davis, 1976) find that clinicians predict less well than the actuarial models, in that they do not appropriately consider the base rates for the conditions they are predicting. As for clinical prediction, clinical judgment is still part of actuarial prediction (Sines, 1970). It is in this area of clinical decision making that clinical and actuarial methods are combined and hopefully provide suggestions of intervention strategies to assist clients.

Comparative Philosophies and Theories

While diagnosis is often looked upon as the end point in clinical assessment, it frequently falls short of truly differentiating those with a given label (such as schizophrenia or depression) from normals (Zubin, 1977-78). Minimal relationships have also been found between diagnostic labels and treatment selection. Perhaps due to a dissatisfaction with this finding, many clinicians are adopting the view that the classification or diagnosis of psychological disorders is useful only to the extent that one can determine the relationship between different disorders and specific treatment recommendations (Ross, 1974). Cole and Magnussen (1966) focus on disposition and action as the ultimate critical goals for assessment. They point out that a major assumption underlying any case is that the categorization of information about an individual enables the professional to utilize his or her skills and clinical facilities in an appropriate way leading to problem solution. It is their thesis that most diagnostic procedures are only loosely related, if at all, to disposition and treatment. They emphasize that the ultimate criterion for a meaningful clinical study of a patient rests with the ability to distinguish among a number of dispositions; therein one disposition will lead to action resulting in better handling of whatever problem exists, and not necessarily relate to the accuracy with which labels can be applied or agree with someone else (which is the basic approach for each *DSM*). They stress also that the usefulness of any information depends directly on how well that information helps in making treatment decisions.

If disposition can be shown to be a function of the information available about a case and the way that information is handled by the child mental health personnel, certain information would be necessary for a disposition. For example, the fact that a person is in distress, properly motivated, not dangerous to himself or others, and of average intelligence may be the minimal necessary and sufficient data used to determine selection for outpatient psychotherapy. Specific diagnostic labeling and further personality assessment may add little, if any, discriminative information to this particular disposition decision. In actual clinical practice, other purposes of diagnosis are legitimate and important. Nevertheless, clinicians should be explicit and open in the expression of their purposes for requiring certain clinical data. They should strive to relate the clinical information sought *directly* to the diagnostic purpose, whether for assessing etiology, prognosis, or treatment selection.

A further extension of this particular orientation deals with the amount and kind of clinical assessment data collected. In practice, the purposes for clinical evaluation are many, varied, and seldom made explicit. Data are frequently collected idiosyncratically, based on a clinician's "belief system." Once again, the requirement for the clinician is to make explicit and to directly relate the diagnostic data to the purpose of assessment. However, whether the purpose of diagnosis is selection of treatment or assignment of a diagnosis, the research literature suggests that relatively limited clinical information may be sufficient. In several studies (Sarbin, 1942; Kostlan, 1954; Sines, 1959; Weiss, 1963; Golden, 1964; Oskamp, 1965; Schwartz, 1967) that investigated accuracy of prediction as a function of varying amounts of information, the amount of data available to the judge was unrelated to the accuracy of his or her judgments. The use of multisource data (hospital intake information, biographical material, projective test data, interviews, and personality descriptions) yielded little increment in accuracy with increasing amounts of information.

This approach to clinical assessment was proposed in order to variously facilitate description and/or treatment. It seems logical, from a practical stance, that description in itself has little value or utility as separated from the treatment or disposition to be offered the client. Thus, the value of assessment is, ultimately, in its ability to positively affect the type and course of treatment to be provided. Cole and Magnussen (1966) suggest that diagnostic categories be developed which can be empirically related to treatment outcome. Such categories would assign patients to various forms of treatments (individual, family, or group) on the basis of variables shown to relate positively to outcome criteria.

With such a clinical decision-making approach, information necessary and sufficient to make a dispositional decision can be collected from many sources. Information that is derived from many different philosophical and theoretical assessment viewpoints might be incorporated into this decision making. As examples, decision-related data might be obtained from interviews, biographical information, naturalistic observations, social-contextual situations, inventories, rating scales, traditional objective and projective techniques, behavioral assessment, environmental assessment, medical diagnosis, competence assessment, developmental information, and particularly the child mental health resource environment.

In such a decision-making orientation, it cannot be assumed that treatment modalities are unitary phenomena. Each therapy relationship is unique and each patient-therapist combination might be a significant treatment variable. Although this is a thorny problem, one must assess the child mental health resources for both individual evaluation and program evaluation.

The importance of stressing competence, as opposed to deviance, especially as represented in the medical model approaches, requires more consideration. The negative effects and the potentially destructive impacts of labeling on children have been reported by Hobbs (1975). Concerns about negative labeling and test bias, particularly against minorities, have further stimulated reevaluation of the concept of intelligence. McClelland (1974) offers an alternative approach to the traditional notions of general intelligence and the technical characteristics of tests. He advocates criterion sampling; that is, having the test encompass the real-life samples that may be actually possessed by those with proficient behavior. McClelland elaborates on life-outcome criteria in terms of theory and practical application to challenge the ingrown world of traditional intelligence testing. He advocates the need to test for competence rather than for "intelligence."

Elaboration on Critical Points

Clinical assessment of children and youth involves the collection of data different from those required for the evaluation of adults. Data must be collected not only about the child's strengths and problems but about such areas as mastery of developmental tasks, functioning in the school and the community, and the parental management of and relationship with the child. Assessment must include the individual and the relevant person-situation interaction systems, such as the family, school, community, and child mental health resources. Assessment decisions may be influenced by factors related not directly to the client but to the clinician and the context in which the evaluation is conducted.

The basic common denominator in the evaluation of the individual and the program is the systematic and standardized collection of data from a variety of sources. In this form of data collection, freedom should be permitted to the clinicians and clients to engage in a variety of traditional and nontraditional assessment strategies and approaches. In fact, these approaches should be encouraged as long as the client's rights and benefits (in terms of positive payoff) are protected and assured.

Traditionally, the information collected through these methods of assessment is recorded in the form of narrative reports, the clinical chart, or the medical record. Another method of recording information obtained in the course of assessment is the standardized data collection instrument. The use of a standardized record-keeping system ensures that all data considered essential are collected, regardless of the discipline, theoretical preference, or experience of the clinicians involved with the client. Such a record-keeping system provides uniform, comparable, and retrievable data on all clients. The information can be directed to such uses as program evaluation, program planning, peer review, clinical administration, training, and clinical research. Standardized evaluation systems lend themselves to automation.

A standardized information system for child mental health services has been developed at the Pittsburgh Child Guidance Center (Magnussen and others, 1974; Snyderman and others, 1975). Having taken the position that the data should include the information necessary for making decisions about treatment, the investigators developed a model whereby such data would be identified. The position taken in developing the system has been that the information to be included is the minimal data necessary and sufficient to make decisions regarding the most appropriate form of disposition of treatment for the child and family. The interested reader is referred to a chapter (Snyderman, Magnussen, and Henderson, in press) that details the decision-making instrument and provides examples of clinical usage. Another chapter (Magnussen, in press) provides content on the historical antecedents to the system and basic clinical application of child assessment.

At the Pittsburgh Child Guidance Center, an entire program of clinical investigation is beginning to emerge based on the theoretical premise that informational categories need to be developed which can be empirically related to treatment planning (Cole and Magnussen, 1966). Currently in preparation for publication are findings on informational categories that differentiate selection of individual versus family therapy. Additional unpublished data point to directions in regard to psychiatric classification versus treatment selection. Another group of collaborators are collecting program information on the evaluation of child mental health services. The evaluation of treatment outcomes is complex and even more complicated with children due to the need to take into consideration expected developmental changes (Koocher and Broskowski, 1977; Waskow and Parloff, 1975). Additionally, investigators are conducting center-wide program evaluation studies on attrition and unilateral termination as it pertains to patient, clinician, contextual, treatment selection, and treatment outcome variables.

Rutter (1974) has been working in the area of competency evaluation with children. (For a review of the literature on competence in children at risk for severe psychiatric disorder, see Garmezy, 1974.) In Great Britain, Rutter reports, one in six children is raised in conditions of extreme social disadvantage characterized by poverty, poor housing, and family adversity. Of these, half are well adjusted, one in seven shows some outstanding ability, and one in eleven shows above-average attainment in mathematics. Rutter and his research group are searching for the positive influences and the sources of support and protection for children reared in deprivation. The goal is to find the sources of social competence and the nature of the protective influence. Studies so far have emphasized that the interaction of stress factors is especially important. Most studies show six factors to be strongly associated with childhood psychiatric disorder: (1) severe marital discord, (2) low social status, (3) overcrowding or large family size, (4) paternal criminality, (5) maternal psychiatric disorder, and (6) admission into the care of local authorities. When only one of these conditions is present, a child is no more likely to develop psychiatric problems than any other child. When two of the conditions occur, however, the child's psychiatric risk increases fourfold. The implication is that it may be of considerable value to eliminate some of the stresses even if others remain. It is also clear that genetic and environmental factors interact in ways that make it even more important, not less so, to do everything possible to improve environmental circumstances.

In looking for positive factors that protect children from the effects of chaotic homes, Rutter considered the school environment as possibly the most important. He and his colleagues are engaged in an intensive long-range study of twelve schools to try to find what schools can do to facilitate normal development in children from deprived homes. It is already clear that the answers do not lie in such factors as class size, staff/pupil ratio, or quality of buildings. Rather, the crucial differences are to be found in the atmosphere of the schools and their qualities as social institutions.

A complete understanding of child and adolescent development requires attention to and integration of several different lines of theory and research. In order to relate clinical assessment to developmental psychology, it is necessary to address the different developmental landmarks. The following descriptions of developmental stages are based on Brophy's (1977) discussion of cognitive and personality development from birth through adolescence. Development includes both growth, in terms of expanded mass, and differentiation toward higher levels or organization.

Infant Development (0-2). Piagetians view infants in their cognitive development as constantly in interaction with the environment, building schemas through accommodation and assimilation and guided by internal equilibration. This period is referred to as the sensorimotor phase.

Early language development tends to be theoretically explained through the conditioning processes. Language is acquired largely from exposure, and the contributions of instruction and reinforcement are differentially posited.

Social and personal development is most often addressed by psychoanalytic and social learning theorists. The learning theorists rely heavily on the concepts of modeling, reinforcement, and stimulation. Psychoanalytic theories provide concepts dealing with the interaction of genetics with socialization by mothers in terms of defined stages of psychosexual development.

The commonly considered developmental tasks of infancy include mastery of eye-hand coordination, sensory discrimination, and simple motor skills; in later infancy (age 1 to 2 years), developmental tasks include controlling body elimination, walking, talking, and commencing social play. Piaget provides theoretical guidelines on cognitive development. Learning to eat solid foods and the interaction with the caretaker are areas of focus for person-social development. Erikson theorizes that the development of "trust versus mistrust" centers around the early mother-child feeding interaction. Freud postulates that successful feeding experiences lead to positive outcomes, and problems in this area contribute to insecurity and mistrust. The development of moral judgment in infancy is theorized by Kohlberg to proceed from complete egocentrism toward higher levels of psychological refinement.

Early Childhood (2-6). Some of the common developmental tasks in early childhood include general body control, skill learning, use of imagery, learning about sex differences, learning through play, learning about right and wrong, manipulation, and exploration. Development continues from the global to the differentiated, and progress in different areas tends to proceed unevenly. The personality and social development theorists conceptualize this period in terms of "initiative versus guilt" (Erikson); "late anal," "phallic," and "oedipal" (Freud); and "early conventional morality" (Kohlberg). In cognitive theory, according to Piaget, this is the "preoperational stage"—characterized by skill development, egocentric cognitive and language development, and gradual assimilation of schemas to one another.

Middle Childhood (6-12). The major developmental tasks of middle childhood include: distinguishing fact from fantasy; elevated problem-solving capacity; mastering reading, writing, and arithmetic at school; relating to teachers and unfamiliar grownups; developing frustration tolerance and self-regulation of behavior and conscience; and meeting expectations of peers and reference groups. To Piaget, this is the "stage of concrete operations"; to Kohlberg it is the period of "advanced conventional morality"; to Erikson it is the phase of "industry versus inferiority"; to the Freudians it is the "latency" stage of psychosexual development.

Adolescence (12-19). The tasks to be mastered by the adolescent include adjusting to body changes, dealing with new emotions and feelings, obtaining gradual independence from peers and adults, questioning values, and mastering conceptual and theoretical factors in life and school.

Personal Views and Recommendations

In each clinical case, the evaluating clinician—taking into account the individual's competence, potentialities, and current environment—must translate into practical, useful terms the findings that facilitate the development and functioning of the child. In the past, much of the activity in this area of child assessment has been more in "the best interests" of the professionals, institutions, economics, and politics. Children and adolescents are minorities and lack power or political votes. Some children and youth have been further ignored due to racial, ethnic, sexual, and socioeconomic biases. One can easily perceive the interdisciplinary rivalry and power struggles. In the 1960s and early 1970s, with the social, political, and economic changes occurring, psychological testing came under serious attack. Legal suits alleged that minority group children were misplaced in special classes, based on tests biased against these groups. The controversial paper published by Jensen (1969) further stimulated immediate and intense responses from within and outside the professions. The entire controversy continues to broaden, as is pointed out in a review by Wade (1976). Block and Dworkin (1976) provide a thorough coverage on the raging struggle. Some of the outcomes of the consumer response include the well-known "Federal Fleece Awards," state and federal laws to limit and control use and kinds of assessment, increased professional liability, and elevated defensive practice of assessment.

In light of the many issues in clinical assessment and mental testing, I offer the following recommendations:

1. Cultural variables should be included only if they are relevant to the specific purpose of a particular assessment.
2. Tests should not be overvalued and used as sole sources of information for decision making; at the same time, they should not be totally undervalued and abandoned because of their obvious defects.
3. In deciding on any assessment technique, one must determine the utility of the assessment for the consumer of the assessment.
4. Decisions about any child's intellectual status require supplementary and confirmatory data from several significant sources.
5. Assessment should be focused on competence and the promotion of competence in a pluralistic and changing society.
6. Culture fairness requires assessment of the culturally relative environments, as well as the assessment of potential of the individual and the environment.
7. Assessment and treatment should be directly related, and emphasis should be on the appropriate placement to facilitate the individual's development, coping, and potentialities.
8. A clinical decision-making approach that considers all the relevant social systems and environments in the human development spectrum seems to be the direction of choice.

9. Ethical sensitivity to such issues as confidentiality, invasion of privacy (see Gross, 1962), openness of clinical records, right to the least restrictive treatment, the best interests of children, benefits outweighing risks, and the potentially negative effects of labeling must be emphasized.

A currently common source of concern is whether professional training appropriately prepares trainees for the real world as it pertains to assessment. Sundberg, Snowden, and Reynolds (1978) review the area and conclude that many university programs prepare students poorly for conducting evaluations in clinical settings. In addition, most university programs tend to ignore or minimize training in the assessment of children and youth, which requires special skills. Training programs have not generally provided adequate theory to guide the practice of assessment of children and adolescents. Rather, an emphasis has been on methodologies, traditional testing, behavioral assessment, or procedures ill suited to meet application realities. Professional competence to render quality service to children goes hand in hand with training to attain that competence and with certification to confirm that competence has been attained. At the professional level, the American Psychological Association has created a new Division of Children and Youth Services. This is an encouraging step forward. Problems remain in training and certification between and within professions, systems (mental health, education, and physical health), groups, and organizations.

Application to Particular Variables

Age. The clinical child diagnostician has available an array of assessment techniques that cover a broad developmental range. A sampling of the commonly used instruments that are frequently administered at each developmental level follows.

Infant tests usually cover the first eighteen months of life. The bulk of these examinations are controlled observations of sensorimotor development. Preschool tests typically cover the ages of 18 to 60 months. The child at these ages can sit, walk, communicate by language, manipulate objects, and interact in an interpersonal process. The procedures, therefore, are more varied and provide broad samplings of developmental behaviors. Examples of commonly used sets of methods at the infant and preschool level are the Gesell and Amatruda Developmental Schedules, which extend from the age of 4 weeks to 6 years. These schedules reflect the fine line between observations and standardized tests. The examinations are essentially an elaboration and refinement of the qualitative observation commonly conducted by pediatricians. Most of the items are made on the observation of the child's behavioral development in the motor, language, adaptive, and personal-social areas. The parent provides the examiner with supplemental information to compare with the norms in the four areas.

Uzgiris and Hunt (1975), inspired by Piaget's writings on infant intelligence, devised seven scales to survey an age range from 1 through 20 months. The scales assess visual pursuit and permanence of objects, development of means for obtaining desired environmental events, development of gestural imitation, development of vocal imitation, development of operational causality, construction of object relations in space, and development of schemes for relating to objects. This is an ordinal measurement device and the approach is being researched. It is a variation of traditional cognitive examination.

The Bayley Scales of Infant Development cover a range in age from 2 through 30 months and provide a tripartite basis for evaluation (mental [sensory], motor [coordination], and infant behavior [social]) of the child's developmental status. The Cattell Infant Intelligence Scale samples an age range from 3 to 30 months.

Beyond the developmental level of infancy and into preschool and school-age stages of growth, commonly utilized measures of intelligence include the Stanford-Binet Intelligence Scale (Form L-M, ages 2 years and over); the Wechsler Intelligence Scale for Children (WISC) (ages 5 to 15 years); and the Wechsler Intelligence Scale for Children— Revised (WISC-R) (ages 6 through 16 years).

Projective techniques that are commonly used to measure personality traits at different developmental levels include the Children's Apperception Test (CAT) (ages 3 to 10 years); the Rorschach, with norms (2 to 16 years) established by Ames and others (1952, 1959, 1974); the Rosenzweig Picture Frustration Study: Form for Children (ages 4 through 13 years); and the Thematic Apperception Test (TAT) (4 years and beyond).

Sex. When the variable of sex is deemed a critical factor in the assessment of a person, one must compare the person and the norms, in addition to the standardization concerning the procedure. The interpretation of the findings requires sensitivity to possible bias. If a procedure is sexually biased or reflects sexism, clinicians and consumers must aspire to correct this matter and not misuse, or perhaps use, any of the information gained from such a measurement.

Clinicians performing either diagnostic, treatment, or research functions with individuals have found that, among other attributes, the clinician's sex significantly affected client performance. Therefore, this variable must always be seriously considered—especially in contexts where sex differences exist between examiner and examinee.

Socioeconomic Status. For several decades the measurement of both intelligence and personality yielded findings that demonstrated differences between children from varying home backgrounds, socioeconomic levels, and urban versus rural settings. In general, it is not surprising that the differences found seem to have antecedent conditions in the living environments. One must carefully assess the normative and standardization information in interpreting any differences. Professional attention has become focused more sharply in this direction and toward attempts to develop alternative measurement devices.

Ethnic/Racial Factors. Ogbu (1978) rejects explanations that attribute academic retardation of minority children to heredity, home environment, or school surroundings. He asserts that caste-like status is a powerful, though subtle and hidden, determinant of behavior. This status works against minority families and the school experiences of their children. Because societal standards and values, including hypocrisy and prejudice, affect assessment strategies and philosophies, a culture-free test seems to be an impossibility. Therefore, the use of tests, particularly with ethnic and racial minorities, must be vigorously scrutinized. Samuda (1975) provides a comprehensive and well-balanced presentation of the issues, practices, theories, and research on assessment of minorities.

Physical Disorders. In order to consider the assessment findings in a proper perspective, the clinician must know the physical status of the child. Factors such as ill health, malnutrition, fatigue, use of certain medications, and allergies may have an influence on the examinee's assessment responses. Often the examiner must face special problems in evaluating children with different kinds of difficulties. Techniques and interpretation of findings must vary, as in any other type of clinical situation, in order to deal with evaluating the physically ill or physically handicapped child or adolescent.

Intellectual Factors. Since previous space in this chapter has been devoted to intellectual assessment, this section addresses the learning disabled. Much of the assessment literature about learning disability focuses on the functioning of the preschool or school-age child—specifically, on school-age programs and on early identification of and programming for the preschool child.

There is general agreement in the literature that the basic characteristics of the learning-disabled individual are different at the developmental stage of adolescence. The child who has manifested such characteristics as hyperactivity, variability of attention span, and difficulty in processing information within sensory modalities and across sensory modalities has usually, by adolescence, come to some terms with these specific areas of difficulty. By the time children reach adolescence, they have typically developed compensatory mechanisms for dealing with problems in processing information. They frequently have learned to cover up or conceal specific areas of difficulty and to avoid other problem areas. They have usually managed to master enough of the basics of perceptual-motor integration and are often able to perform creditably on most of the perceptual tests used with school-age children. The adolescent learning-disabled individual may be quite similar to the school-age learning-disabled child, however, in the area of academic lags.

It is certainly evident that unhelped learning-disabled children still have their learning problems when they reach high school. The ordinary problems of adjusting to adolescence are intensified by the additional problem of entering this developmental period with a history of failure, low self-esteem, negative attitudes about learning and the school, and some compensatory learning mechanisms which may not be efficient for negotiating learning tasks. In assessing learning difficulties at the high school level, one must look for: (1) discrepancies between expected achievement levels and actual achievement levels; (2) significant discrepancies between visual, motor, and auditory-verbal learning modes; and (3) negative attitudes toward the self, particularly toward the self as a learner.

One of the best all-around tests for assessing learning disability at the adolescent level is the WISC-R (or the WAIS, if the youth is above 16 years of age). A comprehensive developmental history is another source of clinical data. Projective tests might contribute by yielding information about how the adolescent perceives himself or herself in relationship to the world. Other tests often used as a source of perceptual-motor and projective data at the adolescent level are the Woodcock, the Durrell, the Key Math, and figure drawings. Such perceptual-motor tasks as the Bender-Gestalt, the Benton Visual Retention Test, and the Beery-Buktenica are often used as part of the test battery.

For the adolescent, assessment should be an ongoing process. Moreover, the clinician should have information, usually obtained through consultation with the classroom teacher, about special interests of the student and the student's attention span and ability to handle independent work in the classroom. Follow-up contacts with the school to determine the individual's response to interventions are important aspects of ongoing assessment with the adolescent.

Organic Dysfunctions. Imperfect as the current psychiatric diagnostic categories are, they are the nosological schemes with which the clinical child psychologist must cope. Inferences from intelligence tests or other clinical measurements are made through parallelisms between test responses and the symptom clusters of the traditional child psychiatric classifications. For example, in the category termed *brain damage* and *organicity,* one finds variable diffuseness of damage, different localization of structural insults, a variety of diseases, many disorders of different degrees of chronicity, and nonstatic status (that is, improvement and/or degeneration may occur)—especially with children. The wide variety of patterns in "brain-damaged" children challenges clinical psychologists to locate the differential effects on intellectual functioning. In clinical practice, where clinicians encounter many kinds of "organicity," it is impossible to find universal indices of scatter or deterioration. In some clinical instances, organically damaged children may demonstrate poorer functioning on memory items and the Performance Scale of the

there is some evidence that
~ered performance level
~ hemisphere dam-
performance
scales. A ⌐⌐⌐ ⌐rbal and
performance scales merits ⌐⌐⌐⌐ ⌐logical
assessment and clinical research in this area ⌐ ⌐d refinements in theory and practice.

With children, the conclusiveness of intratest variabu⌐ ⌐ini-
cians must depend a great deal on clinical experience. The human ⌐ ⌐-
chologist) and the psychometric instrument (the intelligence test) can ⌐ ⌐e
differential diagnostic process. Science and clinical art often combine in the a. ⌐g-
nostic application.

Functional Factors. Rabin and McKinney (1972) review empirical findings with intelligence tests and several nosological groupings of psychopathology. In the clinical assessment of children and youth, the clinician not only encounters the psychiatric classification difficulties presented by the *DSM-II* (and now *DSM-III*) but also the developmental process and the developmental level of the patient. In order for clinicians to make assessment predictions of reasonable accuracy, it is imperative to know the base rates of the functional disorder, the developmental level of patients assessed in the agency, and the base rates on these factors in the general population. These conditions are often unmet in the clinical assessment practice with children and youth.

Diagnoses of functional disorders or diseases, according to psychiatry, encounter many of the difficulties referred to in the classification of organicity. In particular is the nonstatic status, in the sense that improvement and/or deterioration may occur in children and youth as a function of the developmental process or developmental level of the individual.

Collective/Interactional Factors. The mind-boggling problems and issues in the clinical assessment of patients who suffer simultaneously from organic and functional disorders are easily recognized. The interaction effects between conditions that influence the individual's behavior are extremely difficult to determine and pinpoint. When the purpose of assessment is mainly to remediate and/or appropriately place the client, some of these issues concerning etiology and interaction between conditions are partially bypassed. At worst, the unknown in the individual's particular conditions are largely focused on the purpose of trying to appropriately facilitate development and reduce malfunctioning in the most practical and direct manner to benefit the client.

It is the interaction among examiner and examinee and context variables that provides the broad conceptual framework by which to understand the ingredients of the clinical assessment process. As one example, the examiner's professional status and interpersonal warmth may have a differential effect on examinees with different kinds of interpersonal difficulties. The effect may also be modified by the characteristics of the context in which the examination took place. Rosenthal (1969) has summarized a number of studies bearing on the effects of clinician expectancy in the use of clinical assessment techniques. The effects of an examiner's race have been reviewed by Sattler (1970). Masling (1960, 1966) has reviewed the literature on the examiner and situational variables that influenced the clinical findings. Verbal and nonverbal behavior of the examiner has been found to influence Rorschach productivity (Magnussen, 1960); the sequence of individual tests given in a battery also can exert a significant influence on the productivity of certain content in the Rorschach Test (Magnussen, 1967). The social-psychological aspects of the relationship among the examiner, the examinee, the assessment setting, and the clinical findings also have been reviewed (Magnussen, in press).

References

American Psychiatric Association. *Diagnostic and Statistical Manual of Mental Disorders.* (1st ed.) Washington, D.C.: American Psychiatric Association, 1952.

American Psychiatric Association. *Diagnostic and Statistical Manual of Mental Disorders.* (2nd ed.) Washington, D.C.: American Psychiatric Association, 1968.

American Psychiatric Association. *Diagnostic and Statistical Manual of Mental Disorders.* (3rd ed.) Washington, D.C.: American Psychiatric Association, 1977.

Ames, L. B., and others. *Child Rorschach Responses: Developmental Trends from Two to Ten Years.* New York: Hoeber Medical Division, Harper & Row, 1952.

Ames, L. B., and others. *Adolescent Rorschach Responses: Developmental Trends from Ten to Sixteen Years.* New York: Hoeber Medical Division, Harper & Row, 1959.

Ames, L. B., and others. *Child Rorschach Responses: Developmental Trends from Two to Ten Years.* New York: Brunner/Mazel, 1974.

Anastasi, A. "Psychological Testing of Children." In A. M. Freedman and H. I. Kaplan (Eds.), *The Child: His Psychological and Cultural Development.* Vol. I: *Normal Development and Psychological Assessment.* New York: Atheneum, 1972.

Block, N. J., and Dworkin, G. (Eds.). *The IQ Controversy.* New York: Pantheon, 1976.

Brophy, J. E. *Child Development and Socialization.* Chicago: Science Research Associates, 1977.

Cole, J. K., and Magnussen, M. G. "Where the Action Is." *Journal of Consulting Psychology,* 1966, *30,* 539-543.

Davis, D. A. "On Being Detectably Sane in Insane Places: Base Rates and Psychodiagnosis." *Journal of Abnormal Psychology,* 1976, *85,* 416-422.

Garmezy, N. "The Study of Competence in Children at Risk for Severe Psychopathology." In E. J. Anthony and C. Kupernik (Eds.), *The Child in His Family: Children at Psychiatric Risk.* Vol. 3. New York: Wiley, 1974.

Glidewell, J. C., and Swallow, S. C. *The Prevalence of Maladjustment in Elementary Schools.* Report prepared for the Joint Commission on Mental Health of Children. Chicago: University of Chicago Press, 1969.

Golden, M. "Some Effects of Combining Psychological Tests on Clinical Inferences." *Journal of Consulting Psychology,* 1964, *28,* 440-446.

Gough, H. G., and Heilbrun, A. B. *The Adjective Check List Manual.* Palo Alto, Calif.: Consulting Psychologists Press, 1965.

Gross, M. L. *The Brainwatchers.* New York: Random House, 1962.

Hobbs, N. *The Futures of Children: Categories, Labels, and Their Consequences.* San Francisco: Jossey-Bass, 1975.

Jensen, A. "How Much Can We Boost IQ and Scholastic Achievement?" *Harvard Educational Review,* 1969, *39* (1), 1-123.

Koocher, G. P., and Broskowski, A. "Issues in the Evaluation of Mental Health Services for Children." *Professional Psychology,* 1977, *8* (4), 583-592.

Kostlan, A. "A Method for the Empirical Study of Psychodiagnosis." *Journal of Consulting Psychology,* 1954, *18,* 83-88.

Langner, T. S., and others. "Treatment of Psychological Disorders Among Urban Children." *Journal of Consulting and Clinical Psychology,* 1974, *42,* 170-179.

Levine, D. "Why and When to Test: The Social Context of Psychological Testing." In

A. I. Rabin (Ed.), *Projective Techn* *duction.* New York: Spinger, 1968.

McClelland, D. C. "Testing for Compet̲e̲n̲c̲e̲ ̲R̲a̲t̲h̲e̲r̲ ̲T̲h̲a̲n̲ for 'Intelligence.'" In S. Chess and A. Thomas (Eds.), *Annual Progress in Child Psychiatry and Child Development.* New York: Brunner/Mazel, 1974.

Magnussen, M. G. "Verbal and Nonverbal Reinforcers in the Rorschach Situation." *Journal of Clinical Psychology,* 1960, *16* (2), 167-169.

Magnussen, M. G. "Effect of Test Order upon Children's Rorschach Animal Content." *Journal of Projective Techniques,* 1967, *31,* 41-43.

Magnussen, M. G. "Psychometric and Projective Techniques in the Examination of Children and Adolescents." In J. D. Noshpitz (Ed.), *Basic Handbook of Child Psychiatry.* New York: Basic Books, in press.

Magnussen, M. G., and others. *Clinical Data System: CDC Forms A, B, C, D, and E.* Pittsburgh: Pittsburgh Child Guidance Center, 1974.

Masling, J. "The Influence of Situational and Interpersonal Variables in Projective Testing." *Psychological Bulletin,* 1960, *57,* 65.

Masling, J. "Role-Related Behavior of the Subject and Psychologist and Its Effects upon Psychological Data." In D. Levine (Ed.), *Nebraska Symposium on Motivation.* Vol. 14. Lincoln: University of Nebraska Press, 1966.

Meehl, P. E. *Clinical vs. Statistical Prediction.* Minneapolis: University of Minnesota Press, 1954.

Nisbett, R. E., and Borgida, E. "Attribution and the Psychology of Prediction." *Journal of Personality and Social Psychology,* 1975, *32,* 932-943.

Ogbu, J. U. *Minority Education and Caste.* New York: Academic Press, 1978.

Oskamp, S. "Overconfidence in Case Study Judgments." *Journal of Consulting Psychology,* 1965, *29,* 261-265.

Rabin, A. I., and McKinney, J. P. "Intelligence Tests and Childhood Psychopathology." In B. B. Wolman (Ed.), *Manual of Child Psychopathology.* New York: McGraw-Hill, 1972.

Rogers, C. R. "The Necessary and Sufficient Conditions of Personality Change." *Journal of Consulting Psychology,* 1957, *21,* 25-103.

Rosenthal, R. "Unintended Effects of the Clinician in Clinical Interaction: A Taxonomy and a Review of Clinician Expectancy Effects." *Australian Journal of Psychology,* 1969, *21,* 1-20.

Ross, A. O. *Psychological Disorders of Children.* New York: McGraw-Hill, 1974.

Rutter, M. "Epidemiological Strategies and Psychiatric Concepts in Research on the Vulnerable Child." In E. J. Anthony and C. Kupernik (Eds.), *The Child in His Family: Children at Psychiatric Risk.* Vol. 3. New York: Wiley, 1974.

Salzinger, K. "But Is it Good for the Patient?" Paper presented at symposium on Psychological Taxonomy: An Alternative to DSM at 85th annual meeting of American Psychological Association, San Francisco, 1977.

Samuda, R. J. *Psychological Testing of American Minorities: Issues and Consequences.* New York: Dodd, Mead, 1975.

Sarbin, T. "Contribution of the Study of Actuarial and Independent Methods of Prediction." *American Journal of Sociology,* 1942, *48,* 593-602.

Sattler, J. M. "Racial 'Experimenter Effects' in Experimentation, Testing, Interviewing and Psychotherapy." *Psychological Bulletin,* 1970, *73,* 137-60.

Schacht, T., and Nathan, P. E. "But Is It Good for the Psychologists? Appraisal and Status of DSM-III." *American Psychologist,* 1977, *32,* 1017-1025.

Schwartz, M. L. "Validity and Reliability in Clinical Judgments of C-V-S Protocols as a Function of Amount of Information and Diagnostic Category." *Psychological Reports,* 1967, *20,* 767-774.

Shershow, J. C., and Savodnik, I. *The Neo-Kraepelinian Revival: A Critique. II: Conceptual Considerations.* Pittsburgh: Department of Psychiatry, University of Pittsburgh, 1977. (Mimeograph.)

Sines, J. O. "Actuarial vs. Clinical Prediction in Psychopathology." *British Journal of Psychiatry,* 1970, *116,* 129-144.

Sines, L. K. "The Relative Contribution of Four Kinds of Data to Accuracy in Personality Assessment." *Journal of Consulting Psychology,* 1959, *23,* 483-495.

Snyderman, B. B., Magnussen, M. G., and Henderson, P. B. "Standardized Data Collection." In J. D. Noshpitz (Ed.), *Basic Handbook of Child Psychiatry.* New York: Basic Books, in press.

Snyderman, B. B., and others. *Clinical Data System: CDC Forms A, B, C, D, and E.* Pittsburgh: Pittsburgh Child Guidance Center, 1975.

Sundberg, N. D., Snowden, L. R., and Reynolds, W. M. "Toward Assessment of Personal Competence and Incompetence in Life Situations." In M. R. Rosenzweig and L. W. Porter (Eds.), *Annual Review of Psychology.* Vol. 29. Palo Alto, Calif.: Annual Reviews, 1978.

Uzgiris, I. C., and Hunt, J. McV. *Assessment in Infancy: Ordinal Scales of Psychological Development.* Urbana: University of Illinois Press, 1975.

Wade, N. "IQ and Heredity: Suspicion of Fraud Beclouds Classic Equipment." *Science,* 1976, *194* (4268), 916-919.

Waskow, I. E., and Parloff, M. B. (Eds.). *Psychotherapy Change Measures.* Rockville, Md.: National Institute of Mental Health, 1975.

Weiss, J. H. "Effect of Professional Training and Amount of Accuracy of Information on Behavioral Prediction." *Journal of Consulting Psychology,* 1963, *27,* 257-262.

Zubin, J. "But Is It Good for Science?" *Clinical Psychologist,* Winter 1977-78, *31* (2), 1, 5-7.

2

Joseph C. LaVoie

Adult Development

Not many years ago, the topic of adulthood would have received scant attention from most individuals, with the exception of a few dedicated pioneers in the study of adulthood and aging. This situation has changed radically. With the advent of the 1970s, one can note a tremendous surge of interest in adulthood and aging, as evidenced by the appearance of numerous books—not only in the academic realm but also in the popular press. Three widely read nonacademic volumes are *Your Erroneous Zones* (Dyer, 1976), in which one is told how to overcome personal barriers through one's power; *Pulling Your Own Strings* (Dyer, 1978), which prescribes ways in which one can cope with pressures and manipulations and stop being a victim; and Sheehy's (1976) *Passages*, which maintains that each crisis of adulthood can be used to expand one's potential. Coping with crises so that one can live in accordance with one's desires is a recurrent theme in these books.

Why the sudden interest in the latter stages of the life span? Demographic information cited by Bischof (1976) suggests one reason. The population of the United States now contains more adults over the age of 21 years than in previous years, and life ex-

Note: I am greatly indebted to William R. Looft and Gerald R. Adams, who are responsible for my introduction to life-span psychology. I also want to recognize the assistance of William Easton in the preparation of this chapter.

pectancy has increased (males now live an average of 72 years, while females reach 77 years of age). This increase in numbers of older people has prompted an increased interest in adulthood and the aging process. This awakened interest, coupled with the advances in developmental methodology and the sophistication of statistical techniques, has challenged the view that the adult years follow a decrement or stagnation model and has focused professional attention on adulthood and aging as developmental periods.

A major problem facing the adulthood researcher is that of locating the period of adulthood in the life cycle. Bromley (1966) and Havighurst (1972) have used a chronological age breakdown, ranging from young adulthood (which begins around 18-21) to old age (which includes the years beyond 60 or 70). For Havighurst, the middle adult period includes the years between 30 and 60. Stegner (1978), however, claims that adulthood has a social meaning, since "one does not declare oneself to be an adult; one is perceived to be" (p. 277); and Kimmel (1974), contending that chronological age is not a meaningful indicator of adulthood, opts instead for a definition based on one's perceived age (How old do you feel?), which reflects social and biological age as well as chronological age. In this vein, Cameron (1969) asked a group of men and women, whose ages ranged from 14 to 90 years, the question "When is one old or middle-aged?" Their responses indicated that middle age comprises the years 40-55 and that old age begins at 65. The ten-year period between middle and old age was left undesignated. In general, investigators seem to use some type of age designation for the period of adulthood, and the most commonly accepted period is the years 30 through 60 or 70.

Background and Current Status

According to Groffman (1970), the roots of adult psychology can be traced to Aristotle and his thinking about the concept of development. But Adolph Quételet, the pioneer in life-span psychology, is credited with first using a scientific approach to the study of adult development. Quételet demonstrated that aging data best fit a developmental model rather than a mental stagnation model, and he used the cross-sectional method in data collection to measure age differences (Elias, Elias, and Elias, 1977). Other important contributions to the study of adulthood as a science were Galton's work on individual differences, correlational statistics, and the experimental psychology of adulthood; Hall's (1922) treatise on aging; and Wechsler's (1939) development of the Adult Intelligence Scale (WAIS). This individual test of mental ability, consisting of eleven subtests (six tests in the Verbal scale and five tests in the Performance scale), extended the psychometric assessment of intelligence from the upper age limits to which one was previously restricted with the Stanford-Binet. While the WAIS was available earlier, norms for persons older than 55 to 64 years were not available until 1955.

With Pressey's (Pressey, Janney, and Kuhlen, 1939) review of the experimental literature, the field of adult psychology came of age. In subsequent years, the appearance of government support for research on adulthood and aging, the continuation of data gathering on the adult populations in the longitudinal studies, the formation of a Division of Adulthood and Aging in the American Psychological Association, and the appearance of professional journals on adulthood and aging all contributed to the continued growth of adult psychology (Elias, Elias, and Elias, 1977). The establishment of gerontology centers and the formation of multidisciplinary programs, as well as the shift in developmental psychology programs in some psychology departments to a life-span approach, also contributed to the growth of this field. Accompanying this academic development was a major innovation in experimental design and research methodology—specifically, the methodological advancements offered by Schaie (1965, 1967) and Nesselroade (1970) and the contributions of Goulet and Baltes (1970). Their pioneer work enabled the researcher to separate age, time of measurement, and cohort effects and to assess age changes and age differences.

Recent developments in the psychology of adulthood are evident in the increased literature on the topic and in the concern with methodology (Schaie and Gribbon, 1975). Specific developments include the use of descriptive as well as experimental strategies to interpret age changes, increased contact with psychologists studying different segments of the life cycle, and the interest of gerontologists in life-span psychology. But the introduction of some sophisticated methodology has created a problem in the adult literature. It appears that the data on adulthood are based on cohort comparisons; therefore, the present findings may reflect generational differences rather than developmental processes (Schaie and Gribbon, 1975). This issue will be explored further in the discussion on methodology.

Critical Discussion

General Areas of Concern

The current focus in the psychology of adulthood seems to be on methodological issues—specifically, age change versus age differences and the effect of cohort; cognitive processes, particularly intelligence, learning capacity, and memory; perception and psychophysiology; personality, especially the disengagement controversy and the role of attachment across the life span; and changes in social roles.

Methodological Issues. Among the methodological issues isolated by Schaie and Gribbon (1975) is the matter of determining which model best fits the adult data. Previous findings in studies with young and old subjects have indicated age differences favoring younger subjects, thus supporting a decrement or stagnation model, which implies an ontogenetic decline (Schaie and Gribbon, 1975). Kuhlen (1963) and Schaie (1973) believe that these age differences can be interpreted as cohort effects resulting from differential experiences. Several alternative models of adult development have been suggested by Schaie and Gribbon (1975), but they conclude that a stability model seems to provide the best fit for intelligence data and many personality factors. Alternative models include (1) the decrement within compensation model, which assumes an age decline but compensation with a facilitating environment (Schaie and Gribbon, 1975); and (2) Wohlwill's (1973) concept of developmental function, which treats age as a dependent variable. Developmental function refers to the relationship between chronological age and the changes occurring in a response on some dimension of behavior across development.

Schaie and Gribbon (1975) have identified other problems facing the life-span researcher. These include the use of life-history analyses, reliability and generalization, and sampling problems resulting from attrition. The major problem, however, is the age change-age difference-sociocultural change issue. According to Schaie (Schaie, 1965; Schaie and Gribbon, 1975), longitudinal and cross-sectional designs evolve from the same developmental model, which extends development during childhood into the adult years in a linear fashion to some point of stability, after which biological deterioration, associated with aging, is assumed to occur. Therefore, these designs are confounded by age, time of measurement, and cohort effects. Since neither age changes from longitudinal research nor age differences from cross-sectional designs are free of these confoundings, Schaie has argued for the use of designs in which the three confounds are controlled. If one is interested in changes across age for successive cohorts, then the cohort-sequential design would be preferred; if one is concerned with age differences and time of measurement, the time-sequential design is preferred; but if one wishes to focus on generational effects or sociocultural change in adulthood without a concern for age differences, the cross-sequential design should be used. More complex analyses can be performed by combining two or more of the designs. Schaie (1977a) presents additional quasi-experimental designs that can be used to assess the effects of aging and other developmental changes during the adulthood.

Other advances in developmental methodology include the use of multivariate analyses to analyze age or time changes (Nesselroade, 1977) and the analyses of individual differences on multiple measures through the use of factor analytic models (Baltes and Nesselroade, 1973). Some of the more creative work involves the use of simulation models to assess the course of development and aging. The techniques to date have consisted of exposing animals to radiation, use of a multivariate approach to assess environmental change, acceleration of development through massed training or practice (that is, time compressed), and use of behavior modification techniques to accelerate development across the life span (Birren and Renner, 1977).

The problems associated with use of chronological age as an index of development have stimulated research on other indexes. One such measure that has demonstrated some utility is functional age, which considers performance at a specific age; that is, how a person actually functions. This measure assumes that the rate of aging differs for individuals across varying dimensions. As presently used, one's functional age can be estimated from ability tests, much like mental age (Schaie and Gribbon, 1975). A problem with the use of functional age is that it assumes a decrement model of aging. Studies using measures of functional age report a high correlation with chronological age; thus, it is difficult to determine any real advantages to using functional age. Troll (1975) has suggested that distance from death is a more useful index of development than distance from birth (chronological age). Other alternatives to chronological age include a self-perception approach such as that used by Kastenbaum and his associates (1972), who found that when people were asked how old they looked, their responses were similar to their actual age.

Psychometric Assessment of Cognition. The major issue emerging from the research on intelligence measures relates to the interpretation of age-related performance differences (Labouvie-Vief, 1977). The fluid versus crystallized intelligence model (Horn, 1970, 1976; Horn and Cattell, 1966, 1967) proposes that fluid intelligence (consisting of reasoning, figural relations, and memory tasks) is closely associated with biological aging because of its neurological basis. Crystallized intelligence (verbal aspects), although originating in fluid intelligence, is tied to experience and environmental effects. Therefore, fluid intelligence capacities ought to show a distinct decrement with aging, whereas crystallized intelligence should remain stable or possibly increase.

Both individual intelligence tests, primarily the Wechsler Adult Intelligence Scale (WAIS), and the Primary Mental Abilities (PMA) test provide the data base from which the arguments ensue regarding decrement in fluid or crystallized intelligence. To understand the issue, it becomes necessary to separate the cross-sectional data from those obtained through longitudinal studies. In his review of the cross-sectional findings, Botwinick (1977) notes that age differences are more evident in the performance subtests, which involve speed, than in the verbal subtests of the WAIS. Further, the performance decline seems to be more extensive after the age of 60. This age difference is present also in aged groups (individuals 60-89 years of age) that are matched on total score on the WAIS, as shown by Harwood and Naylor (1971). When speed is not a factor, such as in untimed tests, older adults show some improvement, but their gain is not as great as that displayed by younger adults (Botwinick, 1977). Other research utilizing a factor analysis of WAIS subtests shows that the performance element is related to the intelligence factor. However, education rather than age seems to be more highly correlated with intelligence in factor analytic studies. The apparent conclusion from the cross-sectional data is that age is not a major variable until the later years, when the decrement associated with performance emerges (Botwinick, 1977).

Caution must be exercised in the interpretation of these results because of certain methodological problems associated with the system of data collection. The problems, identified by a number of investigators (for example, Botwinick, 1977; Horn, 1976; Labouvie-Vief, 1977), relate to sampling and cohort confounding. Although random sampling is a necessary technique for research, such sampling in older populations increases the likelihood that persons selected will have lower levels of education than younger populations. Further, because of their education, these older people tend to score lower on the WAIS. Some data supporting this claim were reported by Green (1969), who found an age decline in a random sample of 25- to 64-year-olds that was not present in the sample matched for educational level. The education-matched sample showed stability on verbal measures into the 55-64 age range. Cohort problems arise because different age groupings (generations) are used who, because of the time of their birth, have different sociocultural experiences, which may influence the adequacy of their preparation for test taking.

Given the problems with cross-sectional studies and the nature of the findings (age differences), one can question whether the age decline also appears in longitudinal studies that show age changes. One such study (Kangas and Bradway, 1971) retested subjects from the Terman study, who were then in the 39-44 age range. Increases in IQ occurred for estimated Stanford-Binet scores as well as WAIS verbal and performance scores from an earlier measurement (when the subjects were 30 years of age); but the subjects were in the higher IQ ranges. In three other longitudinal studies reviewed by Botwinick (1977), similar results on verbal performance were found for high-IQ subjects and for military retirees. In the study using the Army General Classification Test with military retirees, Tuddenham, Blumenkrantz, and Wilkin (1968) noted a significant decline in the pattern analysis test (a performance score) over the thirteen-year period between the two testings. Longitudinal data from other studies indicate that the age trend for verbal and performance scores appears to continue into the 50s (Botwinick, 1977).

The data on individuals in old age (60 years and beyond) show that the aging trend noted earlier changes into a general decline in abilities. In a relevant study, Eisdorfer and Wilkie (1973) used WAIS scores on subjects 60-79 years of age over a ten-year period. Average decreases in scores for the 60- to 69-year-old group were less than for the 70- to 79-year-old group and were characteristic of the aging trend (a decrement in performance scores, with verbal scores remaining relatively stable) previously reported for adult subjects. However, the decrease for 70- to 79-year-olds was equally large for both verbal and performance scores. In his discussion of this data, Botwinick (1977) notes a selective dropout of subjects during the five-year extension of the study. This dropout factor had the effect of decreasing the age decline, which underscores the need for careful examination of longitudinal data. That is, the dropout pattern of subjects results in longitudinal data from individuals who perform at a higher level. Further, the retest interval influences the interpretation. When short retest intervals are used, the general age decline is replaced by an increase in some scores. Rhudick and Gordon (1973) found that 58- to 88-year-old subjects showed some increase in performance scores, whereas verbal scores decreased when a two-year retest interval was used. Long retest intervals, however, show the general age decline, but not in all studies. For example, Gilbert (1973) found that verbal performance did not change over a thirty-five- to forty-year period for a group of adults in the 60-74 age range.

It is evident that longitudinal studies do not necessarily resolve the interpretation problems associated with the effects of aging on intelligence. Sample attrition, subject bias at various ages with respect to testing, and the health and interest of the subjects contaminate the data. A further problem is that of a positive bias, resulting from the likelihood that younger cohorts (those less than 60) in the aged group may contain a greater number of less able subjects, who are more likely to die before 60; thus, older cohorts tend to be more able individuals. These effects may function to reduce actual age changes. Schaie (1965) and Baltes (1968) have suggested that a combination of cross-sectional and longitudinal analyses (that is, a cross-sequential analysis) can reduce the problem. This methodology was used in a longitudinal study by Schaie and colleagues (Schaie and Labouvie-Vief, 1974; Schaie, LaBouvie-Vief, and Buech, 1973; Schaie and Strother, 1968), who used the Primary Mental Abilities Test with subjects 21 to 70 years of age. Their design consisted of a fourteen-year longitudinal study, with three cross sections (of which two were seven years apart), and independent samples of same-age cohorts added at each testing.

The cross-sectional analyses across the fourteen years showed no decline in total score for those in the 21-50 age group, and the verbal portion of the test indicated general stability into the 60s. The performance measure tended to display the anticipated age effect. A decline in total PMA score was evident in the age group of 50-70 years, with the largest decrement appearing for the 70-80 age group. The longitudinal data generally followed the cross-sectional pattern. When Botwinick (1977) examined specific cohort groups in Schaie's study, he found that the cross-sectional and longitudinal data were similar for all age groups, except with the 53-67 age group, where the cross-sectional drop was greater than the longitudinal decrement. The independent cohorts showed a greater age decline than the longitudinal groups, perhaps due to selective dropout in the latter. Labouvie-Vief (1977) concludes from these data that intellectual development during adulthood shows stability and some increases, with decreases occurring in the 70s and 80s. Further, cohort, rather than age per se, seems to account for most of the variation in intellectual ontogeny, indicating the impact of changing environmental influences.

Some attention needs to be given to three other questions relating to intelligence. One question concerns the consistency of ability across age. Botwinick (1977) examined a number of studies relating to this question and concluded that individuals initially high in ability are likely to continue at this level whereas those of lower ability are likely to decline. Riegel and Riegel (1972) found this pattern for unfamiliar information, but the difference was less evident with familiar information. The other questions concern whether individuals with low initial ability tend to die sooner and whether a noticeable decrease in IQ precedes death (the notion of *terminal drop*). There is some evidence that low-scoring persons do experience death sooner, and verbal scores may be slightly more predictive of an earlier death. The data on *terminal drop* tend to be controversial. Some researchers (for example, Baltes and Schaie, 1974; Riegel, 1971; Riegel and Riegel, 1972) have reported that a noticeable decrement in performance occurs about five years before death.

A number of other factors influence the test performance of aged persons. Furry and Baltes (1973) found that test fatigue is a detrimental factor in performance with old people, and Botwinick (1977) suggests education and socioeconomic status as variables to be considered. Further, practice, but not incentives, has been shown to increase performance on a digit symbol test (Grant, Storandt, and Botwinick, 1978). Physiological measures have also been associated with WAIS performance measures. Wilkie and Eisdorfer (1971) noted higher scores for adults with lower blood pressure levels; greater intellectual decline than would be expected to occur with normal aging was present in those individuals with high blood pressure. Extent of brain damage appears to be associated with intellectual performance in institutionalized adults with neurophysiological disorders (Wang, 1973; Wang, Obrist, and Busse, 1970), and level of systemic disease is another related factor (Wilkie and Eisdorfer, 1971).

If the previously identified factors influence test performance, then intervention procedures with adults and aged persons could increase scores on psychometric measures. Several studies cited by Labouvie-Vief (1977) support this contention. Physical exercise programs have been found to increase adults' scores on performance measures, such as speed tests (Barry and others, 1966; Eisdorfer, 1969; Hoyer, Labouvie-Vief, and Baltes, 1973) and the Wechsler Memory Scale (Powell, 1974). Increased performance on figural relations tests (a measure of fluid intelligence) and generalization of training among 59- to 85-year-olds have been reported by Plemons, Willis, and Baltes (1978). Their four-week training session used a cognitive focus with such techniques as modeling, practice with feedback, and group discussion. Effects of training were present six months later on the near transfer tasks, and longer training periods showed greater long-term effects.

Piagetian Data on Cognition. According to Piaget (Inhelder and Piaget, 1958; Piaget, 1972; Piaget and Inhelder, 1969), the last stage of cognitive development (formal operations) appears about the age of 12, and the development of these thought structures continues through adulthood. Some investigators have recently proposed that cognitive growth occurs beyond formal operations. Arlin (1975) contends that divergent thinking and problem solving indicate advanced cognitive growth. Schaie (1977b) has proposed five adult cognitive stages which, he argues, evolve out of experience. The *acquisitive* stage is concerned with establishing independence and achieving competence, while more goal-directed formal operations occur during the *achieving* stage. Both stages evolve during young adulthood. The adulthood stages, extending from the 30s to the 60s, consist of the *responsible* stage (during which one integrates long-range goals in the solution of real-life problems) and, for some individuals, the *executive* stage. Development at this stage involves taking on the responsibility for social systems and developing cognitive strategies for integrating higher-order relationships. The final stage, *reintegrative*, involves simplification of cognitive demands to alleviate an overload, and problem solving is now directed toward immediate life concerns. This stage sequence is provocative, and Schaie (1977b) suggests that assessing competencies will require new measurement devices. Riegel's (1975b) contention that adult thinking is at a higher level (since adults must think and deal with contradictions) also implies the presence of a stage (or stages) beyond formal operations.

Although Piaget did not propose a regression in logical thought during adulthood, Hooper, Fitzgerald, and Papalia (1971) have proposed that such a decrement occurs because of the similarity between Piagetian operations and performance measures of fluid intelligence. Schaie's (1977b) reintegrative stage in adulthood also implies a restructuring. These issues stimulated a number of studies in which developmental trends in cognition were investigated during the adult years. Papalia (1972) used several conservation tasks with subjects ranging in age from 6 to over 65 years. Conservation performance in the adult sample decreased with age, with the largest decrement occurring in those subjects who were 65 and older. The order of decreasing scores for the aged population showed a reversal of the acquisition order for young children.

Papalia's findings were supported in a later study by Papalia, Salverson, and True (1973) with a group of 64- to 85-year-olds, who had some high school education, on tests of quantity conservation. Performance was at a lower level than younger age groups, and the decrement in performance was the inverse of usual acquisition. Graves (1972) reports that most adults (ages 20-40) in his study failed to conserve, but these subjects had low levels of education. In a study by Rubin and associates (1973), elderly persons (mean age 76 years) performed more poorly on conservation tasks than middle-aged people (mean age 44 years). However, Storck, Looft, and Hooper (1972) report that their 55- to 79-year-olds had weight conservation, and about 50 percent were conservers of volume. The apparent contradiction in findings has been clarified by Horn (1976), who maintains that educational level is the factor. Older subjects are likely to have less education, and these less educated subjects are found in the studies where decrements are reported.

Developmental trends in classification tend to mirror those reported for conservation. Denny and Lennon (1972) observed that 25-55-year-olds used different strategies than elderly persons (67-95 years old) in a classification problem. Middle-aged subjects grouped items by similarity, whereas elderly subjects used intricate classification designs similar to those of young children. Place of residence (nursing home versus neighborhood) was not a factor. In a later study with educational level as a variable, Denny and Cornelius (1975) reported that higher-educated elderly males performed better on class inclusion and multiple classification than less educated elderly males. No differences were found among elderly females, and the performance of 35-year-olds was significantly higher than that of the 75-year-old group. Design responses were not present in the 35- to 59-year-old subjects who were asked to group geometric stimuli into "same" categories by Denny (1974), but design and color groupings increased with age in the 60- to 95-year-old group. However, older persons (70-year-olds) in Kogan's (1974) study of categorization used a greater number of functional groupings, denoting what Kogan interpreted to be a more imaginative approach.

The possibility of modifying the effects of cognitive decline, noted in the psychometric area, has elicited interest in the Piagetian approach to cognition. Labouvie-Vief (1977), who presents the issue as that of inflexibility versus flexibility, concludes that cognitive processes are more plastic in old age than previously assumed, since intervention procedures seem to produce increments in performance. Tomlinson-Keasey (1972), using a problem-solving approach to training formal operational skills, observed significant increases in performance on appropriate tasks among the 12-, 20-, and 54-year-old females in her sample. However, persistence of the training was more evident in later posttests for the 20-year-olds, whereas the 54-year-olds showed a decrement. Use of a positive feedback procedure on surface conservation for nonconserving 65- to 75-year-old females increased conservation responses on this task and four of five other conservation measures in the Hornblum and Overton (1976) study, and this training effect was evident in six of eleven subjects after a six-week period.

In a number of studies a learning model has been used for constructing intervention strategies to remediate cognitive decrements. Sanders and associates (1975) found reinforcement training procedures effective in increasing concept identification among 63- to 85-year-old females in a four-day delayed posttest. Using an observational-learning paradigm with 65- to 91-year-olds, who previously classified on a primitive basis, Denny (1974) found that observation of a model classifying stimuli on the basis of similarity increased subsequent classification of familiar (but not unfamiliar) stimuli by these subjects. A cognitive modeling procedure, with fading of overt verbalization of task-relevant instructions by the model and subject, was used by Labouvie-Vief and Gonda (1976).

Their inductive-reasoning task used letter sets with females in the 63-95 age group. Training consisted of use of strategies, anxiety reduction, nonspecific training instruction, and a control group. Strategy and anxiety training were effective in the immediate posttest, whereas the anxiety reduction and nonspecific instruction groups showed the most positive effect in the two-week follow-up. Some generalization of training effects was present. More recent data by Sanders and Sanders (1978), in a follow-up study on the effects of training and reinforcement on conceptual performance, indicate that training effects were evident for a similar task administered twelve months later, but reinforcement was not a factor. Cognitive structures in older adults are amenable to change and intervention procedures based on a learning model. The interesting aspect is that most training studies have used training based on a learning model rather than a cognitive model.

   Learning. One of the problems in interpreting the learning literature is that most of the data are cross-sectional. Therefore, one is limited to discussing age differences rather than age changes or cohort differences, and there is also no systematic theory to account for age differences. A third characteristic of the research is that most of the studies are on verbal learning; thus, little information is available on other areas, such as discrimination and concept learning. The general lack of literature surveys is noteworthy, perhaps resulting from the belief that developmental deficits in learning are largely the product of performance differences rather than a decrease in ability to learn (Schaie and Gribbon, 1975). For example, increased anxiety in aged people is one factor influencing learning, and reinforcement for correct or incorrect responses decreases errors and trials to criterion (Leech and Witte, 1971). The two major variables producing age differences in verbal learning are pacing and the use of mediators; the latter has been identified as a problem with young children. Elderly people produce more errors when rate of stimulus presentation is increased in paired-associate learning, and they use verbal mediators less often.

   According to Arenberg and Robertson-Tchabo (1977), the most extensive data on age changes are found in the Baltimore study, in which paired-associate and serial-learning performance of 30- to 76-year-old males were investigated. Age differences in paired-associate learning were smaller for those males under 60 years of age, with the largest error rate occurring among the 69-76 age group, and pacing was a performance factor. A similar age pattern appeared for the serial-learning task. Considering these findings and the results from a number of other studies, it becomes apparent that presentation time and response time affect errors and trials to criterion among adult and aged subjects. However, other factors may mediate the pacing effect. Wilkie and Eisdorfer (1977) report that, when the presentation rate on a serial-learning task was increased, males (ages 60-79 years) with low verbal ability made more errors than males with high verbal ability or females of either verbal level.

   Although the decrement in verbal learning could be a retrieval problem, Witte and Freund (1976) found that learning rate among their 60- to 73-year-old females did not improve greatly when retrieval effects were minimized. The poor performance of the elderly apparently resulted from deficits in response and associative learning. On the basis of various studies, the most reasonable conclusion is that encoding and mediation deficits best explain the age differences. Inefficient encoding strategies—resulting from the failure of aged persons to use mediators and other encoding strategies, such as organization—are associated with poorer performance. Interestingly, older persons tend to use mediators when instructed to do so, and the use of efficient strategies seems to benefit the elderly more than younger persons. Information overload in the aging central nervous system is undoubtedly related to the problem. Older persons may comprehend and input too much information, thus increasing the complexity of the problem and the central processing requirements. Information overload may also produce greater interference, since problems with transfer and interference are more extensive among the elderly.

Discrimination, another form of learning, has received some attention in the adult and aging literature, and the general conclusion is that the performance of aged persons is very similar to that of young children. When a reversal-nonreversal shift paradigm (in which the subject has to change responses to a stimulus of a similar or different dimension) is used with older adults, reversal shifts are performed better than nonreversal shifts, suggesting a mediational deficiency and more reliance on selecting previously reinforced responses (Nehrke, 1973; Witte, 1971). Similarly, training that emphasizes the critical dimensions of stimuli improves discrimination in adults. The tendency of older adults to perceive too many relationships and increase the complexity of the problem is quite evident in their discrimination performance.

Memory. Currently, an information-processing model is the preferred mechanism for interpreting developmental changes in memory during the adulthood years. This type of model assumes a stage sequence, consisting of modality-specific sensory memory, primary or short-term memory, and secondary or long-term memory. Most of the data are cross-sectional, so the findings should be viewed as age differences rather than age changes. Within the sensory modality, perceptual processing seems to be an area influenced by the aging process. Information processing is slower in older adults, and reaction time to visual stimuli lengthens, as is evident in the research of Schonfield and Wenger (1975). They noted that older persons required more time to identify letters when an additional letter was added to a group of four. Auditory or echoic memory is not affected as greatly as visual or iconic memory. Studies on dichotic listening indicate that adults are more accurate in recall when information is presented to the right ear, perhaps resulting from the activity of the verbal center in the left hemisphere. This laterality difference occurs, however, only when ear order is unspecified, suggesting that older adults rely more on the right ear. Craik (1977) concludes that age decrements are present in dichotic listening, but the processes involved—storage, retrieval, or other—have not been identified.

The data on age differences in shifts necessitated by attention to input and recall are more definitive. Performance by older adults on tasks requiring division of attention shows a distinct decrement. The decrement in performance is more evident when a visual task is used, suggesting the involvement of information processing. This processing problem may arise in part because older adults focus on irrelevant stimuli. Kausler and Kleim (1978) observed that 61- to 88-year-old adults made more errors in a visual recognition task when four items were used than in a similar task with two items.

The reaction-time research of Anders, Fozard, and Lillyquist (1972) indicates that recognition of low-association visual stimuli is slower for 58- to 85-year-olds than the 33- to 43-year-olds. This age effect has been used as evidence for a deficit in retrieval from primary memory associated with aging. Older adults also experience more problems in verbal learning when the word pairs have low association value. However, Craik (1977) argues that few age differences occur in primary memory. For example, studies of free recall (a more acceptable measure of primary memory) indicate recency effects in subjects of varying ages. Memory span for digits, letters, and words shows some decrement across the adulthood years. Botwinick and Storandt (1974) found that memory span for letters decreased from 6.2 for 30-year-olds to 5.4 for 70-year-olds, but decline in this aspect of memory has been considered minimal by Craik (1977). It is also likely that some retrieval of one or more items from secondary memory may be involved in these paradigms. Other variations of the memory-span paradigm suggest that the performance

of older adults is lower when they are asked to recall reverse orders of words or to repro-
duce correct serial order of words from the end of a variable list. Both tasks probably
require some reorganization of information, and this process, like division of attention, is
sensitive to age effects. Rate of scanning in primary memory also seems to be influenced
by aging, but the effects are not clear. Anders, Fozard, and Lillyquist (1972) have reported slower scanning rates among older adults, although other data contest this effect.

Forgetting in primary memory does not seem to be a product of decay effects,
rate of presentation, or interference effects; and rate of forgetting is not affected greatly
by age differences. Wickelgren (1975) compared the performance of 19- to 24-year-olds
with that of 60- to 82-year-olds and found acquisition differences in a recognition
memory task, but forgetting rates across a 2.6-hour period were not different. Retention
is also influenced somewhat by modality of the information presentation in that auditory
information produces slightly improved recall. In general, primary memory retention in
older adults seems to be influenced more by the need for reorganization of information
than by interference (Craik, 1977).

The controversy over age differences in secondary memory revolves around the
acquisition versus retrieval issue, and there is evidence to support both explanations.
Acquisition deficits are present in older adults, especially in encoding of information,
which necessitates organization into meaningful units, and in the use of mediators. That
is, older people seem to use less effective strategies in organizing input for encoding and
in using various mediators (such as associations), which suggests a mental operations
deficit. However, Mistler-Lachman (1977) believes that environmental factors may influence encoding. She found that elderly people living in the community displayed greater
access to encoding dimensions than those living in a rest home.

Recall, which necessarily involves retrieval, is especially sensitive to aging effects.
Retrieval time for older adults increases with list length, although accuracy in recall in
five-item lists did not differ among age groups in the Anders and Fozard (1973) study.
Recall differences are most evident in longer lists, especially in the primary and middle
portion of the list (Craik, 1977). Since recognition does not involve recall, one would
expect fewer age differences, but the research in general shows that such effects are
present in both recognition and recall, regardless of the stimulus form (words or pictures).
Overall, the age decrement in recall is greatest when there is an absence of retrieval information, and the most noticeable decline in performance occurs after the age of 50 (Craik,
1977; Schonfield and Robertson, 1966).

Much of the speculation about forgetting in secondary memory has focused on
the effects of interference and the role of retrieval. Information overload and inability to
select out relevant cues may account for the interference effect, and thus decrease retrieval. Evidence for a retrieval deficit is evident in the work of Buschke (1974); he
showed that recall patterns of the same word list varied from trial to trial for adults (ages
34-50). Hultsch (1975) has pointed out that both cue- and trace-dependent forgetting
occur in adults over 50 years of age. That is, recall of categories (cue dependent forgetting) as well as actual words (trace dependent forgetting) decrease with age; the former,
involving higher-order memory units, showed greater decrement among the 65- to 83-
year-olds in Hultsch's study. Age differences have also been noted for nonverbal stimuli
(such as geometric designs), and older persons have been found to have deficits in recall-
ing and recognizing remote events from their past (such as school classmates), although
accuracy in this area continues at a quite high rate into the 70s (Craik, 1977).

The age decrement in secondary memory cannot be attributed solely to acquisition or retrieval deficits, according to Craik (1977). It is quite evident from the preceding

discussion that both explanations can be advanced, depending on the situation. Eysenck (1974) has asserted that the problem is with semantic forms of encoding. Older adults are less likely to use higher-order cognitive operations in processing information and do not reconstruct sufficiently to enhance retrieval cues.

Visual Perception. In the field of vision, the concern for the adult years has focused on changes in perceptual functioning—specifically, the structure of the eye—and visual information processing. The structural changes involve the eye lens, which loses transparency (that is, it becomes yellow, thus reducing the amount of light on the retina) and elasticity and increases in thickness, resulting in presbyopia (farsightedness). The decline in accommodation, which is most notable between 40 and 55 years, is evidence for loss in lens flexibility and visual acuity, and a decrease in depth perception occurs at about the same time (that is, after the age of 45). Pupil constriction and a decrease in adaptation to changing levels of illumination also occur with aging (Fozard and others, 1977). In one such study (cited by Elias, Elias, and Elias, 1977), a group of 16- to 19-year-olds dark-adapted five times more quickly than 80- to 89-year-olds, and about twice as fast as 40- to 49-year-olds, over a two-minute period.

Time required to identify a target also increases with age. Adults in the 50-55 age range require a stimulus presentation of about ten times the length needed by those in the 30-35 range, but older persons can extract information from a visual display for a longer time (Eriksen, Hamlin, and Breitmeyer, 1970). Older adults also require longer search times for a stimulus embedded in a complex display; their binocular rivalry decreases; they require more time to switch between views; and duration of aftereffect increases with stimulus time among 60- to 81-year-olds. Susceptibility to various geometrical illusions decreases from the early years to adulthood, but the Müller-Lyer illusion shows an increase from middle age to senescence (Fozard and others, 1977).

Auditory Perception. Decrease in auditory perception (presbycusis) follows the classic age trend. Some loss in hearing is usually present in males over 32 years of age and in females above 37 years. This decline in hearing is at the lower frequencies, but sex is a factor. Hearing loss for males is greater than for females at 2,000 Hz and above when age is controlled, although the loss at and below 1,000 Hz is slightly greater for females (Corso, 1977). However, exposure to deleterious noise levels may accelerate hearing loss. Pitch discrimination also declines in the 40s, with greater changes in the years beyond 55, especially at the higher frequencies. Similar to vision, the current research emphasis is on auditory processing and speech distortion.

Reaction time to auditory signals increases with age, possibly indicating a decrement in the auditory nervous system. Further, data on signal detection indicate that older adults can detect pure tones in the presence of noise as well as young adults can, but their decision criteria are more conservative. Thus, age differences in auditory perception are due to factors other than solely physiological deterioration. The onset of presbycusis produces a decline in the ability to understand speech and in auditory sensitivity (Corso, 1977). Understanding speech appears to remain quite stable from age 20 to 50, with a 25 percent loss occurring up to age 80, and this decrement is even higher under conditions of stress. According to Corso (1977), the decrement in speech perception is partially attributable to increases in auditory information-processing time, resulting from deterioration in both the peripheral and central auditory components.

Psychophysiology. Changes in EEG associated with age include an increase in slow waves, particularly a slowing of the alpha rhythm (Marsh and Thompson, 1977; Schaie and Gribbon, 1975). While slow-wave activity has been found to be highly correlated with IQ decline, controlling for health status, socioeconomic status, and education decrease this correlation (Schaie and Gribbon, 1975). During sleep, the effects of EEG seem to be more extensive than any other age-related factor. The percentage of sleep time in which rapid eye movement (REM) occurs decreases with age, but the most marked decline occurs around 80 (Marsh and Thompson, 1977; Schaie and Gribbon, 1975). Average evoked potentials following stimulation also show a decrease in amplitude up to 45 years and an increase in latency up to about 80 years for visual and somatosensory stimulation, while average evoked potential for auditory stimulation is the most stable, although individual differences need to be considered (Marsh and Thompson, 1977).

Age changes in arousal have been linked to behavioral decrements in older adults, and one of the positions taken is that both central and autonomic nervous systems need to be considered. Supporters of the underarousal explanation point to lower responsiveness to stimulation among older adults when GSR and heart rate are used as measures during conditioning and vigilance behavior (Marsh and Thompson, 1977). Alpha slowing has also been used as further support for underarousal. The overarousal position follows from the data related to sympathetic function, which shows that free fatty acid increases during tasks involving information processing. Lacey and Lacey (1970) have argued that the nature of the task and the experimental situation are critical factors in the autonomic pattern; thus, a unifying explanation seems difficult. Further, Schaie and Gribbon (1975) contend that behavioral manipulations of arousal in general have not shown age differences.

Reaction-time data show that age increases in simple reaction time are relatively small, while increases in choice reaction-time involving discrimination or disjunction tasks are quite evident in middle and old age (Elias, Elias, and Elias, 1977). Thus, as task difficulty increases, reaction time also increases more rapidly in older than in young adults, suggesting that information processing is affected. Although alpha rhythms are correlated with reaction time, and alpha decreases with age, this does not explain completely the increase in reaction time (Schaie and Gribbon, 1975). There is some evidence that longer reaction times are required by older adults (especially females) for nonverbal stimuli, which may suggest a problem with encoding strategies (Elias, Elias, and Elias, 1977).

Personality. Life-span psychology and its related methodology have enhanced the understanding of personality development during adulthood. This developmental view provides data relating to continuity and the presence of periods during which major personality changes may occur. Nevertheless, there are a number of problems with much of the data on adult personality. Some of the criticisms cited by Neugarten (1977) include extreme variation in samples, cohort confounding from cross-sectional studies, questionable validity and reliability of measures, generalizability to persons in different life periods, and failure to consider life events in the interpretation of age differences. The issue of continuity and discontinuity in adult personality is a major concern. Schaie and Parham (1976), in a cross-sequential study with 21- to 84-year-olds across a seven-year period, found evidence for stability on seventeen of nineteen factors of their Social Responsibility Scale, with major age changes restricted to excitability and humanitarian concern. Personality profiles for each of the eight cohorts in the study were constructed to examine change. Those changes which occurred in traits were attributable largely to cohort differences. The Berkeley longitudinal studies also support the contention that continuity in personality is present over time, especially for items relating to presentation of self and responses to socialization (Neugarten, 1977). Although factor analytic studies of the MMPI and 16 PF with adults in several age groups have shown some age differences, the results are mainly conflicting (Neugarten, 1977).

Age differences have been reported for a number of personality dimensions, but only those dimensions which seem to have rather broad implications for adulthood will be considered in this chapter. Egocentrism is present in adulthood; at least the communicative and spatial components have been isolated, although Looft (1972) maintains that egocentrism is not a salient dimension. Spatial egocentrism was noted by Looft and Charles (1971) in a group of 66- to 91-year-olds; however, these adults displayed great individual differences in their ability to decenter, and their egocentrism was not related to social interaction skills. Rubin (1973) found evidence of egocentrism only in his institutionalized 70- to 85-year-olds. Cognitive style (that is, reflection-impulsivity) has been studied in young adults (18- to 27-year-olds) and old adults (61- to 87-year-olds). Coyne, Whitbourne, and Glenwick (1978) found that older adults were more impulsive, as evidenced by their shorter response latencies and higher error scores, much like young children. But these investigators did not consider the alternative explanation that the adults may have been more anxious about their competency. The impulsiveness effect is contrary to the literature on cautiousness in adults and aged (for instance, Okun, Siegler, and George, 1978); that is, older adults are less likely to take risks.

Kohlberg's (1973) delineation of moral stages has elicited interest in the later development of moral judgment. Kohlberg contends that stage 5 (higher law and conscience orientation) and stage 6 (universal ethical principles) are not attained until adulthood, and this development is largely the result of experience, involving questioning, commitment, and role taking. The research on maturity of moral judgment tends to support Kohlberg's hypotheses, although an age decrement occurs. Bielby and Papalia (1975) report that the highest moral stage occurs in middle age (35- to 49-year-olds), with stage level declining in the aged group (65 years and older). Sex differences are usually present, as evidenced by males scoring somewhat higher than females, since the Kohlberg measure is based on justice and a struggle for power. Papalia and Bielby (1974) suggest that the variability in the moral reasoning of older adults may result from an identity crisis associated with aging. Their conclusion is based on data showing that moral development parallels ego development.

Research on locus of control and self-concept indicates that both personality dimensions are sensitive to age effects and consequences, such as institutionalization. Wolk (1976) found that internal control in noninstitutionalized older adults was associated with positive adjustment, satisfaction, and self-concept. A subsequent investigation by Reid, Haas, and Hawkings (1977) showed that expectancy of perceived control over desired outcomes was more highly correlated with self-concept for elderly males (65- to 83-year-olds) than females, but internal control for both sexes was correlated with positive adjustment. The age data on self-perception suggest that self-concept tends to increase with age into at least the 60s, although other sources report a mid-life depression (Troll, 1975), where adults worry about being old. Males apparently experience a greater change in self-concept during the 50s than females do. In a fourteen-year longitudinal study involving 21- to 84-year-olds, Schaie and Parham (1976) report a decline in social responsibility with age, although over the seven-year spans males scored higher than females on social responsibility, and older cohorts showed greater responsibility during the period of 1956-1963. In general, the peak of social responsibility appears to be attained during the years of 32-46.

One of the continuing controversies with respect to adult personality concerns the viability of disengagement as a characteristic of the aging adult. According to this notion, sometime after the 40s adults begin to withdraw from the social and physical world. By reducing involvement with society, it is assumed, one can transfer the conserved energy to ego enhancement. In essence, disengagement implies that the older adult severs attachments with people and objects. Psychological disengagement supposedly precedes social disengagement, which assumes that society withdraws from the aging adult. Since both assumptions have received much criticism, perhaps disengagement should be reconceptualized as selective withdrawal (Neugarten, 1977).

Dissatisfaction with the concept of disengagement and the need to view attachment as a life-span concept (Antonucci, 1976; Knudtson, 1976) have stimulated some provocative theorizing and research on adulthood attachments. Kalish and Knudtson (1976) have proposed that the notion of psychological and social disengagement ought to be shelved and replaced with the more useful construct of attachment. If attachment is more broadly perceived as involving groups and objects as well as a specific figure(s), then it seems logical that attachments continue throughout life. Further, some type of self-produced feedback from the attachment is probably necessary to provide one with a sense of control or power. Kalish and Knudtson (1976) note that, with increasing age, early objects of attachment disappear (for instance, parents die), children become more involved with their own families and activities, friends gradually die, familiar objects disappear, and beliefs and ideas may be out of synchrony with present ideologies. Thus, loss of attachment, coinciding with other transitions (such as the loss of spouse and sense of mastery), is experienced. This effect is counteracted somewhat as older adults establish new attachments with social service personnel, doctors, and institutional staff, although these new attachments are weaker and more easily broken. Further, children now become care givers where previously they were receivers of care. Central to these developmental changes in attachments is the notion of a confidante. Research among the aged shows that the only significant difference among the institutionalized and those living in a community was the presence of a confidante (Kalish and Knudtson, 1976). While confidante relationships are important, great individual differences in the number of confidantes and the frequency of contact can be found among adults. Stimulation overload may be a factor in accounting for these individual differences in attachment across the life span.

Several questions arise from this conceptualization of attachment. The substitution of attachment objects, the effect of age period, and factors such as proximity versus affect need to be considered. Most adults appear to maintain three or four best friends, regardless of place of residence; that is, friends lost in a move are replaced. Troll and Smith (1976) found that love of another person was more important for dyadic attachment and family integration than the physical distance separating the persons involved. Thus, maintenance of attachment bonds does not require frequent contact and proximity. The implications for adjustment and satisfaction in later years are quite evident, but the role of nonsocial objects is not clear. Attachment to nonsocial objects may result if adequate social attachments cannot be formed (Kalish and Knudtson, 1976).

Perhaps the most controversial issue in adult personality, and one of major concern, is that of personality and adaptation. These concepts have been treated as either integrated or independent. When independence is assumed, personality appears to be a reliable predictor of adaptation, although the particular traits may differ according to developmental period (Neugarten, 1977). However, the issue of whether the relationship remains stable across adulthood is a sticky one. The investigative focus on this problem has ranged from life periods to life events to a succession of events. Sheehy (1976), for example, focuses on crises during adulthood, especially the "mid-life crisis" and its traumatic impact on adjustment. Many of these life crises, according to Neugarten (1977), are anticipated and rehearsed, thus allaying their effect. It is only unexpected events that produce crises.

Further evidence negating the universality of a mid-life crisis can be found in the

Grant Study. Vaillant (1977, p. 41) argues that the "mid-life crisis" notion has been over-dramatized by the popular press. He further states, "The high drama in Gail Sheehy's best-selling *Passages* was rarely observed in the lives of the Grant Study men." According to Vaillant, these men responded to life events with growth-facilitating styles of adaptation, although some failures occurred. While one's identity, based on a commitment to a vocation and an ideology following a crisis, is usually attained in adolescence and young adulthood, the 40s are a time during which males reexamine their earlier identity. Through the ego mechanisms of defense, argues Vaillant, the Grant Study males were able to cope with conflict. That is, growth (development) emerged from conflict. Among the factors associated with the best-adjusted males (those who reached Erikson's stage of generativity) were a positive childhood experience, a career choice associated with father identification, a satisfying marriage, and the positive achievements of children.

Somewhat similar findings are reported by Sears (1977) in his follow-up of Terman's gifted men. The life-span satisfactions of these men were occupation and family life, resulting from work persistence into the later years and a stable marital relationship. Satisfaction in these areas could be predicted by positive affect and achievement in the 30s and resolution of childhood conflicts. Livson (1977) has identified two personality patterns that resulted in adaptation and adjustment in middle-aged females. The *independent* females were intellectual, achieving, introspective, and unconventional in early development, but at age 40 conflict, depression, and a regression to earlier identity stages seemed to be present; this crisis, however, was resolved by age 50. In contrast, the *traditional* women, seen as highly feminine, had a nonconflictful transition into middle age. Livson concludes that the major difference between the two groups was the fit between their life style and personality; that is, the *traditional* females' personality matched the more conventional female roles.

A few conclusions can be drawn regarding personality development during adulthood. First, there is evidence of stability in personality, although some age differences are evident in older adults, especially in those areas involving cognitive processes. Second, life-span changes in attachment more accurately characterize the aging adult's personal and social relationships. Third, positive adjustment and satisfaction in adulthood are the products of adapting to events and conflicts across the life span. When mid-life crises appear, these conflicts seem to emerge from an incongruity between one's life style and socially expected role; but such crises are not an inevitable consequence of adulthood.

Social Roles. The emergence of the women's movement, formation of female and male consciousness groups, a questioning of traditional sex roles, and changes in social institutions such as the family have challenged existing social-role prescriptions and proscriptions. One interesting offshoot of the apparent change in traditional roles is the increase in female crimes. Adler (1975) reports that female arrest rates are increasing several times faster than male rates, except for the crimes of murder and aggravated assault. This change has been attributed to social factors and the attainment of greater social and economic status for females. A brief discussion of other notable changes in traditional social roles follows.

Bem's (1974, 1977) research on psychological androgyny suggests that traditional concepts of masculinity and femininity limit one's behavior. According to Bem's investigations, the androgynous person (one who scores high on both masculinity and femininity) is less sex stereotyped and more nurturant, assertive, yielding, and self-reliant than someone who is highly masculine or feminine. It is implied, therefore, that the androgynous person is better able to cope and more psychologically healthy. Empirical support for this contention is mixed. Kelly and Worell (1977) note that higher self-esteem is not associated only with androgyny, since masculine-typed individuals seem to score as high on this trait. However, androgynous persons score higher than masculine or feminine individuals on social ascendancy and intellectuality on the Personality Research Form. In subsequent research by Jones, Chernovitz, and Hansson (1978), masculinity rather than androgyny was associated with flexibility and adjustment, as assessed by a number of measures (such as introversion-extraversion, locus of control, self-esteem, helplessness, and sexual maturity).

Another factor influencing social-role expectations is that of marital status. According to 1975 census data, 36.8 percent of the American males and 42.5 percent of the American females are single (divorced, separated, widowed, never married). An interesting trend among the never marrieds in this group is that an increasing number (54.1 percent of the 20- to 29-year-old females and 82.2 percent of the 20- to 29-year-old males) are choosing to remain single, according to 1975 data provided by Stein (1976). Part of the impetus for this divergence from marriage norms is the expanding opportunities for women, the concerns about obsolescence in traditional marriage, and the feeling that a single life style is more conducive to personal growth (Stein, 1976). The never-married group also includes middle-aged and older females and males. According to Stein (1976), one group of unmarried females consists of women with an undergraduate or graduate education, or a salary in excess of $20,000, who are highly achievement oriented and concerned with career expansion. Marriage may be more difficult for this group because there are fewer males whose salary, education, and interests are commensurate with theirs. However, older unmarried females seem to be better adjusted than their male counterparts. This difference may be a product of support systems in that males tend to establish less intimate relationships with other males than females do with other females. For the singles as a whole, a greater number of older singles comprise the separated, divorced, or widowed group. Among this group four of every five divorced persons remarry, and this reestablishment of marriage is more likely among males. Further, the number of possible marriage partners is more limited for women than for men, one reason being that women live longer than men.

Changing patterns in marriage have influenced social roles as well. One pattern seems to be the movement away from the traditional male dominance in the marriage. Although the female has had to make more extensive behavioral changes in the marital relationship than the male (Ahammer, 1973), the egalitarian marital relationship appears to be gaining in acceptance; this is exemplified by the *open marriage* (O'Neill and O'Neill, 1972), in which there is a commitment to self and the other's growth. Another pattern in the marital relationship is "swinging" (open sexual infidelity), which some investigators claim improves the marital relationship (Goldberg and Deutsch, 1977). Cohabitation, as an alternate to traditional marriage, has received more attention than other alternatives, although this relationship is found largely among young adults. There are many nuances in cohabitation. Macklin (1972) found that most cohabitants chose this relationship to fulfill intimacy needs arising out of loneliness, rather than to satisfy a need for sexual relations. Cohabitation is not replacing marriage, according to Hassett (1977); this life style merely serves as a mechanism to delay marriage for a time.

Social roles are also influenced by changes in the traditional family cycle. Two such changes are the increase in maternal employment and the greater numbers of single parents. Bronfenbrenner (1977), in chronicling the changes in American families, reports that over 50 percent of married women with school-age children are employed or seeking employment, and a majority of these mothers are working full time. Whereas younger mothers (those under 25) and those in families where the husband's income is below $5,000 have been more likely to work in the past, the most rapid increase in maternal employment is presently among mothers in middle- and high-income families. One obvious effect of this pattern is that fewer adults are present in the home to provide child care. This change and other assumed effects of maternal employment have been reviewed by Hoffman (1974); she contends that the available evidence does not support the notion that children in these families experience cognitive and emotional deprivation. Hoffman concludes from her review that the working mother provides a different role model, especially for girls. Girls with working mothers are more independent and have higher aspirations than girls with nonworking mothers. Further, working mothers who are able to resolve their dual role, find adequate child care, and are satisfied with their job seem to be as well adjusted and competent as nonworking mothers. Working mothers, at least those of lower socioeconomic status, do provide less adequate supervision for their children, but the data do not suggest that these children are more delinquent.

The increase in single parents is an outcome largely of separation and divorce, with unwed mothers comprising the second-largest category. The most rapid increase in single parenthood has occurred in families with children under 6 years of age, and about 95 percent of the single parents are women (Bronfenbrenner, 1977). Some insight into the effect of divorce on the parents and their children can be obtained from a series of studies, involving middle-class divorced parents and their preschool children matched with intact families, conducted by Hetherington, Cox, and Cox (1976, 1977). The divorced families experienced much distress, particularly during the first year, and at least one member of each family was under severe stress and experienced behavior problems. Divorce presented a number of specific problems for the parents: the tasks involved in maintaining a household as a single parent; disorganization in family routines, such as regular mealtimes and bedtimes for the children; role adjustment and interpersonal problems; and parent-child relations. Economic stress associated with two households was a major conflict among the couples.

Husbands and wives, in the Hetherington study, appeared to be differentially affected by the divorce. Wives showed a greater sense of helplessness, as indicated by higher external-control scores. They felt more anxious and less competent. This condition was especially evident in boys' mothers who were experiencing conflict in their parent-child relationship. Divorced mothers had significantly less social contact and felt isolated. Divorced fathers became more involved in their work and reported more conflicts with work, and their social life was more restricted, although sexual activity was more likely among divorced males. Both males and females experienced an extreme need for intimacy and a lack of satisfaction in their casual relationships. Anger and resentment were common feelings expressed by divorced couples, but this strong affect was tempered by ambivalence.

Some of the most evident effects of divorce recorded by Hetherington were observed in parent-child relations. A general lack of control occurred in divorced families: children less often had maturity demands made on them, communication problems arose, less affection was shown, and discipline was inconsistent. This patterning of inadequate parenting was more evident among mothers during the first year, but improvement was found in all areas during the second year following divorce. While the parenting problem was similar for divorced fathers, they tended to decline in affection and attachment to their children over the two-year period. Overall, the mothers' influence on the children increased while fathers became less influential.

Comparative Philosophies and Theories

Social/Psychological Theories. Bühler (1972), in her theory of human development, conceptualizes adulthood in terms of areas, tendencies, and experiences. Development is basically goal directed, thus implying the notion of intentionality of behavior.

Activities, personal relationships, and self-development and analysis are the three most significant areas of life, with degree of fulfillment contingent on satisfaction of needs, adaptation, and inner consistency. The adult years are perceived as a time of assessment of goals, with the acknowledgment of satisfaction or failure, whereas old age is the time when one acknowledges the degree of fulfillment of life goals.

Erikson's (1963) eight stages of development and Havighurst's (1953, 1972) developmental tasks are similar in that both theories consider development across the life span and assume that positive resolution results in happiness while negative resolution elicits despair. However, Erikson focuses on development, whereas Havighurst incorporates maturation, social influences, and personal values in his developmental tasks. A basic component of Erikson's theory is the epigenetic principle, which proposes that properties that were nonexistent at a previous period emerge as the result of development (Bischof, 1976). At each stage of development, Erikson has posed a polar conflict, the resolution of which determines development at the succeeding stages. Basic trust provides the primary block for future development, and, given positive resolutions during the life span, trust becomes faith at old age.

Acquisition of an identity must occur for a positive entry into adulthood. Although identity is not a stable state, one must nevertheless make a commitment to a vocation and adopt an ideology, thus enabling one to know "who I am" and "where I am going" and to "get one's head on straight." Successful resolution of the identity crisis enables one to resolve the stage of intimacy versus isolation during young adulthood, thus achieving affiliation and love. The problem facing the individual during middle adulthood is that of resolving the generativity versus stagnation crisis. According to Bischof (1976), Erikson believes that production and care emerge from generativity, which is a concern with accomplishments during one's adult life and caring for children. If one has been successful in coping with the conflicts faced during the life span, integrity can be achieved in old age, and one can feel a sense of personal satisfaction and fulfillment rather than despair over the failure to accomplish set goals. Wisdom is the basic virtue emerging at this time, when one is preparing for the eventuality of death. This synopsis seems to imply that conflict resolution is stable or permanent. Erikson, however, questions such an interpretation because it largely ignores the negative elements at each stage (Bischof, 1976). These elements, according to Erikson, are continually present and, therefore, influence the uncertainty of one's existence.

Havighurst (1972) proposes a series of developmental tasks that must be accomplished at each stage for successful development to occur. Unlike Erikson's stages, the developmental tasks of Havighurst, once mastered, are assumed to be stable throughout life. The developmental tasks facing the young adult revolve around marriage, family, and occupation, while the tasks facing the middle-aged person focus on achievement of responsibility, rearing adolescent children, personal and interpersonal adjustment, and physiological changes. During old age there is the need to resolve problems associated with physical well-being, retirement, death of a spouse, and changes in social role.

Both Erikson's and Havighurst's theories provide a framework for viewing human development. Although neither theory has generated much research, both Constantinople (1969) and LaVoie and Adams (in press) report moderate intercorrelations between Erikson's stages (from infancy—trust versus mistrust—through young adulthood—intimacy versus isolation).

Another stage conception of development, one that focuses mainly on adulthood and old age, has been proposed by Levinson (1977). While Levinson's initial theorizing was based on interview data from adult males, the continuing research includes females. Levinson views adult development as evolution of the life structure (the patterning of one's life at a given time). This life structure consists of a sociocultural world, participation in this world, and aspects of self (that which is experienced). Such components as occupation and family are central in one's life; other components, involving less investment of self, are peripheral. Within this general model, Levinson assumes that one's life structure evolves through a series of alternating stable and transitional stages. The developmental task at each stage involves decision making, constructing a life structure around the decisions, and attaining goals and values. Certain tasks are specific to each stage, much like the developmental tasks of Havighurst. During the transitional period, the major developmental task is termination of the existing structure and construction of a new structure. This stage necessitates self-examination, exploration of future direction, and movement toward decisions that facilitate new life structures at the next stage. Each period is defined by the primary developmental task necessary for restructuring the life structure—not by significant events, such as marriage or divorce, which can occur at any stage during adulthood. Four developmental stages in adulthood have been identified: early adulthood (17-45 years); middle adulthood (40-65 years); late adulthood (60-85 years); and late, late adulthood (over 80 years). Each transition for these stages terminates the preceding developmental stage and introduces the next stage.

The early adulthood stage initiates entry into adulthood by terminating the preadult stage and simultaneously facilitating the exploration of adulthood and its many choices and roles (involving occupation, relationships, and life style). A transition period, lasting from the late 20s to the early 30s, provides an opportunity to improve on this first adult life structure and to modify it where necessary. The manner in which this transition stage is resolved varies greatly. For some individuals, developmental crises occur during the 30s, as a result of an inability to construct a satisfactory life structure. Various marital, familial, and vocational problems may emerge at this period. Other individuals experience no serious problems and therefore change their structure in a constructive way. The termination of this transition stage ushers in the next stage, which is a crucial period in adult development.

The second adult life structure continues until 40 years of age and involves two major tasks: developing competence in one's vocation and progressing along a predetermined course (achieving success). Toward the end of this stage, one reaches a distincitve time that Levinson has labeled "BOOM" (Becoming One's Own Man). The task at hand is to become an accepted member of society, firmly entrenched in a meaningful occupation, and willing to accept responsibility and various pressures with the assumption of greater authority. Three variations in the development of one's life structure at this period have been identified by Levinson: (1) growth within a stable structure, where one enriches and refines self and achieves success and an inner identity; (2) failure within a stable structure, where one may achieve success but some event denotes failure; (3) a changing structure, where one finds the life structure unbearable because of a work, marital, or other problem and therefore one makes some drastic change, such as divorce or job termination.

The mid-life transition (the period from 40 to 45) is a major developmental period in Levinson's model because it introduces the stage of middle adulthood. This transitional period usually involves great turmoil and much introspection and self-examination. During this period the individual attempts to cope with illusions and the realization that things are not as one imagined. Much disappointment and bitterness may result as one examines past events and anticipates the future. Marital relationships are especially vulnerable because one must now confront the fantasized self in the relationship with the real self, and one must further determine how the quality of future heterosexual relationships can be improved. Similar self-examinations occur in one's occupational and social roles. In many respects this crisis period resembles the identity crisis during adolescence and young adulthood, described by Erikson. What emerges from this struggle varies with the individual. Some persons are left without an adequate structure. Others merely subsist, while still others find an enriched, creative, and fulfilled life. This transition period does not mark the end of growth. Development continues in the succeeding stages of late adulthood and beyond. The transition tasks differ, but the sequence continues.

Biological Theories of Aging. The impact of the social/psychological theories has been to characterize equilibrium and stability as desirable goals while viewing crises in a negative manner (Riegel, 1975a); therefore, achieving consonance, self-fulfillment, and self-actualization have become the concerns of adults today. That is, crises have obtained a negative stereotype, implying that one ought to experience only success. Riegel (1975a, p. 100) counterargues that stability and crises should be viewed "as mutually dependent though contradictory conditions that only in their dialectical conjunction make development possible at all." That is, development can only occur when disequilibrium is present.* The *genetic theory* assumes that one's life span is determined by genetic factors and that the long life of humans results from their cognitive capabilities. Related to this notion is Birren's (1960) *counterpart theory.* It proposes that the negative effects in old age were primarily important at an earlier period. For example, the absence of cell replacement in the central nervous system may be highly adaptive for survival through improving learning and retention but may result in a finite life span. Other theories note that, regardless of genetic programming, one's life span may be influenced by various environmental hazards, such as infectious diseases, accidents, or radiation.

Another group of theories are more physiological in their account of the aging process, and their concern is with the degeneration of life processes. As an example, the Gompertz (1825) model shows that the probability of death increases exponentially with advancing age. The most commonsense explanation, according to Kimmel, is the *wear-and-tear theory*, which suggests that the human body wears out like a machine because of the deterioration of the organs necessary for life. However, Kimmel argues that aging is more complicated than the gradual deterioration of an organ, since the interrelationship of many body systems is involved. A second theory, *homeostatic imbalance*, suggests that aging results from disequilibrium of vital physiological processes, such as pH levels. Several studies cited by Kimmel show a decreasing ability to maintain various body processes with increasing age and the accompanying effect of emotional stress. The *accumulation of metabolic waste* explanation proposes that aging occurs because human cells are adversely affected by the waste products of metabolism. The accumulation of waste products, however, may be more a symptom of aging than a cause. Aging has also been associated with the concept of *autoimmunity*, which relates aging to the production of antibodies that act against tissues. A final explanation is that of *cellular aging*, which implies that the ratio of cell death to cell production increases with age to the point where an insufficient number of body cells are present to continue life.

Elaboration on Critical Points

The central issue in adult psychology is the effect of aging on ability and performance. In order to accurately assess the effects of aging, cohort and time-of-measurement factors must be controlled. The most acceptable research alternative involves the use of chronological age to select the adult sample, and a quasi-experimental design for

*This discussion of biological theories is based on the explanations presented by Kimmel (1974).

the data collection. Age differences and changes have been most extensively charted in the area of cognitive processes. While some performance decrements associated with age were noted, this decline is more evident and extensive among adults over 50 years of age and when demands for higher-level cognitive operations, such as complex reasoning and maintaining invariance, are required. When confronted with problems in these areas, older adults do not use meaningful organization and transformations of information (that is, adequate encoding), resulting in what Eysenck (1974) has labeled a "processing deficit hypothesis." It is tempting to attribute this age-related decrement to neurological impairment associated with aging in the central nervous system, such as neuronal atrophy. Bondareff (1977) notes that neuronal loss is greater in the frontal cortex than in other parts of the brain; and there is some evidence that neuronal RNA metabolism declines with age, at least in animals. In general, however, neuronal loss is a questionable index of aging, since neurological decline can be modified. The intervention research shows that various training procedures can increase performance on both quantitative and qualitative measures of intelligence and that instructions on encoding, mediation, and retrieval improve learning and memory performance. In essence, the adult's cognitive system appears to be more flexible than assumed. Furthermore, an individual's general health, educational level, and willingness to take risks, in addition to test-taking variables and other environmental factors, must be considered when cognitive capacities during adulthood are assessed. At the present time, the data seem to support an information-processing-deficit explanation for age differences. That is, as individuals progress through middle age and into senescence, their information-processing system becomes overloaded more easily because these experienced adults have greater difficulty in discriminating the information irrelevant to a problem. When aided in this task, the adult shows improvement. By proposing an information-processing deficit, one is not denying neurological decline. Rather, the information-processing explanation provides a more precise explanation for the cognitive decline, including perception.

Personal Views and Recommendations

Two major aspects of adult development can be singled out for further consideration. These facets consist of the decrement in functioning associated with age (physical, cognitive, and affective) and the conflicts faced in adjusting to middle age. While some physiological decline is a natural concomitant of aging, its effect is not irreversible. That is, physical activity, health maintenance, continued education and training, ongoing social involvement, and opportunities to exercise personal control and to receive self-produced feedback are potentially powerful elixirs. There is a need for expanded research in all areas of adulthood, including the physiological changes (especially in the central nervous system) and their impact on cognition, personality, and social-role enactment. The concept of attachment and its utility as a developmental function needs further investigation and explication. Not to be overlooked is the need for further study on the effects of changing societal values on social role fulfillment in adulthood.

The perception of middle age as a crisis period needs to be rethought. Bardwick (1978) indicates that professionals generally overlook the constructive features of this developmental phase. She contends that healthy coping at this stage involves an acceptance of the reality that the tasks of young adulthood are ended and the realization that one is now free to create, to self-actualize, to become functionally autonomous, and to formalize new goals. That is, one now remobilizes and pursues new challenges, but with a different script and with the benefit of much experiential learning. Those who grow as a result of coping with adulthood will have a sense of future. Adulthood crises are not inevitable, and they are not necessarily negative. Through coping with crises and conflict, one achieves growth (that is, development in adulthood).

Application to Particular Variables

The importance of age is quite apparent, since the focus of this chapter was on age changes and differences across the stage of adulthood. For many developmental changes, the critical age seems to be around 50-60. That is, shifts, especially in cognitive functioning, are more evident at this time. Sex differences have not been dwelled on extensively in the adult psychology literature, although this is one area that may provide some additional insights, given the present knowledge about sex differences in earlier developmental stages. The major sex difference reported is the classic finding that females perform better on verbal measures in intelligence tests, while males score higher on performance measures. One rather important difference that has evolved from the research on adulthood is the influence of education, especially on cognitive measures. Older adults with more education perform at higher levels than their counterparts with lower levels of education. Socioeconomic status needs to be considered more than it has been (the population for most studies is middle class and Caucasian), since cognitive performance and general adjustment may be influenced by social-class factors.

References

Adler, F. "The Rise of the Female Crook." *Psychology Today*, 1975, *9*, 42-114.

Ahammer, I. M. "Social Learning Theory as a Framework for the Study of Adult Personality Development." In P. B. Baltes and K. W. Schaie (Eds.), *Life-Span Developmental Psychology: Personality and Socialization.* New York: Academic Press, 1973.

Anders, T. R., and Fozard, J. L. "Effects of Age upon Retrieval from Primary and Secondary Memory." *Developmental Psychology*, 1973, *9*, 411-415.

Anders, T. R., Fozard, J. L., and Lillyquist, T. D. "The Effects of Age upon Retrieval from Short-Term Memory." *Developmental Psychology*, 1972, *6*, 214-217.

Antonucci, T. "Attachment: A Life-Span Concept." *Human Development*, 1976, *19*, 135-142.

Arenberg, D., and Robertson-Tchabo, E. A. "Learning and Aging." In J. E. Birren and K. W. Schaie (Eds.), *Handbook of the Psychology of Aging.* New York: Van Nostrand Reinhold, 1977.

Arlin, P. K. "Cognitive Development in Adulthood. A Fifth Stage?" *Developmental Psychology*, 1975, *11*, 602-606.

Baltes, P. B. "Longitudinal and Cross-Sectional Sequences in the Study of Age and Generation Effects." *Human Development*, 1968, *11*, 145-171.

Baltes, P. B., and Nesselroade, J. R. "The Developmental Analysis of Individual Differences on Multiple Measures." In J. R. Nesselroade and H. W. Reese (Eds.), *Life-Span Developmental Psychology: Methodological Issues.* New York: Academic Press, 1973.

Baltes, P. B., and Schaie, K. W. "Aging and IQ: The Myth of the Twilight Years." *Psychology Today*, 1974, *7*, 35-40.

Bardwick, J. "Middle Age and a Sense of Future." *Merrill-Palmer Quarterly*, 1978, *24*, 129-138.

Barry, A. J., and others. "The Effects of Physical Conditioning on Older Individuals. II: Motor Performance and Cognitive Function." *Journal of Gerontology*, 1966, *21*, 182-191.

Bem, S. L. "The Measurement of Psychological Androgeny." *Journal of Consulting and Clinical Psychology,* 1974, *42,* 155-162.

Bem, S. L. "On the Utility of Alternate Procedures for Assessing Psychological Androgeny." *Journal of Consulting and Clinical Psychology,* 1977, *45,* 196-205.

Bielby, D., and Papalia, D. "Moral Development and Perceptual Role-Taking Egocentrism: Their Development and Interrelationship Across the Life Span." *International Journal of Aging and Human Development,* 1975, *6,* 293-308.

Birren, J. E. "Biological Theories of Aging." In N. W. Shock (Ed.), *Aging: Some Social and Biological Aspects.* Washington, D.C.: American Association for the Advancement of Science, 1960.

Birren, J. E., and Renner, V. J. "Research on the Psychology of Aging: Principles and Experimentation." In J. E. Birren and K. W. Schaie (Eds.), *Handbook of the Psychology of Aging.* New York: Van Nostrand Reinhold, 1977.

Bischof, L. J. *Adult Psychology.* (2nd ed.) New York: Harper & Row, 1976.

Bondareff, W. "The Neural Basis of Aging." In J. E. Birren and K. W. Schaie (Eds.), *Handbook of the Psychology of Aging.* New York: Van Nostrand Reinhold, 1977.

Botwinick, J. "Geropsychology." *Annual Review of Psychology,* 1970, *21,* 239-272.

Botwinick, J. "Intellectual Abilities." In J. E. Birren and K. W. Schaie (Eds.), *Handbook of the Psychology of Aging.* New York: Van Nostrand Reinhold, 1977.

Botwinick, J., and Storandt, M. *Memory Related Functions and Age.* Springfield, Ill.: Thomas, 1974.

Bromley, D. B. *The Psychology of Human Aging.* New York: Penguin Books, 1966.

Bronfenbrenner, U. "The Changing American Family." In E. M. Hetherington and R. D. Parke (Eds.), *Contemporary Readings in Child Psychology.* New York: McGraw-Hill, 1977.

Bühler, C. "The Course of Human Life as a Psychological Problem." In W. R. Looft (Ed.), *Developmental Psychology: A Book of Readings.* New York: Holt, Rinehart and Winston, 1972.

Buschke, H. "Two Stages of Learning by Children and Adults." *Bulletin of the Psychonomic Society,* 1974, *4,* 392-394.

Cameron, P. "Age Parameters of Young Adult, Middle-Aged, Old, and Aged." *Journal of Gerontology,* 1969, *24,* 201-202.

Constantinople, A. "An Eriksonian Measure of Personality Development in College Students." *Developmental Psychology,* 1969, *1,* 357-372.

Corso, J. F. "Auditory Perception and Communication." In J. E. Birren and K. W. Schaie (Eds.), *Handbook of the Psychology of Aging.* New York: Van Nostrand Reinhold, 1977.

Coyne, A. C., Whitbourne, S. K., and Glenwick, D. S. "Adult Age Differences in Reflection-Impulsivity." *Journal of Gerontology,* 1978, *33,* 402-407.

Craik, F. I. M. "Age Differences in Human Memory." In J. E. Birren and K. W. Schaie (Eds.), *Handbook of the Psychology of Aging.* New York: Van Nostrand Reinhold, 1977.

Denny, N. "Classification Abilities in the Elderly." *Journal of Gerontology,* 1974, *29,* 309-314.

Denny, N. W., and Cornelius, S. E. "Class Inclusion and Multiple Classification in Middle and Old Age." *Developmental Psychology,* 1975, *11,* 521-522.

Denny, N. W., and Lennon, M. L. "Classification: A Comparison of Middle and Old Age." *Developmental Psychology,* 1972, *7,* 210-213.

Dyer, W. W. *Your Erroneous Zones.* New York: Avon, 1976.

Dyer, W. W. *Pulling Your Own Strings.* New York: Crowell, 1978.

Eisdorfer, C. "Intellectual and Cognitive Changes in the Aged." In E. W. Busse and E. Pfeiffer (Eds.), *Behavior and Adaptation in Later Life.* Boston: Little, Brown, 1969.

Eisdorfer, C., and Wilkie, F. "Intellectual Changes with Advancing Age." In L. F. Jarvik, C. Eisdorfer, and J. E. Blum (Eds.), *Intellectual Functioning in Adults.* New York: Springer, 1973.

Elias, M. F., Elias, P. K., and Elias, J. W. *Basic Processes in Adult Developmental Psychology.* St. Louis: Mosby, 1977.

Eriksen, C. W., Hamlin, R. M., and Breitmeyer, R. G. "Temporal Factors in Visual Perception as Related to Aging." *Perception and Psychophysiology,* 1970, *7,* 354-356.

Erikson, E. H. *Childhood and Society.* (2nd ed.) New York: Norton, 1963.

Eysenck, M. W. "Age Differences in Incidental Learning." *Developmental Psychology,* 1974, *10,* 936-941.

Fozard, J. L., and others. "Visual Perception and Communication." In J. E. Birren and K. W. Schaie (Eds.), *Handbook of the Psychology of Aging.* New York: Van Nostrand Reinhold, 1977.

Furry, C. A., and Baltes, P. B. "The Effect of Age Differences in Ability-Extraneous Performance Variables on the Assessment of Intelligence in Children, Adults, and the Elderly." *Journal of Gerontology,* 1973, *28,* 73-80.

Gilbert, J. G. "Thirty-Five Year Follow-Up Study of Intellectual Functioning." *Journal of Gerontology,* 1973, *28,* 68-72.

Goldberg, S., and Deutsch, F. *Life-Span Individual and Family Development.* Belmont, Calif.: Wadsworth, 1977.

Gompertz, B. "On the Nature of the Function Expressive of Human Mortality and on a New Mode of Determining Life Contingencies." *Philosophical Transactions of the Royal Society* (London), 1825, *115,* 513-585.

Goulet, L. R., and Baltes, P. B. *Life-Span Developmental Psychology: Research and Theory.* New York: Academic Press, 1970.

Grant, E. A., Storandt, M., and Botwinick, J. "Incentive and Practice in the Psychomotor Performance of the Elderly." *Journal of Gerontology,* 1978, *33,* 413-415.

Graves, A. J. "Attainment of Conservation of Mass, Weight, and Volume in Minimally Educated Adults." *Developmental Psychology,* 1972, *7,* 223.

Green, R. F. "Age-Intelligence Relationship Between Ages Sixteen and Sixty-Four: A Rising Trend." *Developmental Psychology,* 1969, *1,* 618-627.

Groffman, K. J. "Life-Span Developmental Psychology in Europe: Past and Present." In L. R. Goulet and P. B. Baltes (Eds.), *Life-Span Developmental Psychology: Research and Theory.* New York: Academic Press, 1970.

Hall, G. S. *Senescence, the Last Half of Life.* New York: Appleton-Century-Crofts, 1922.

Harwood, E., and Naylor, G. F. K. "Changes in the Constitution of the WAIS Intelligence Pattern with Advancing Age." *Australian Journal of Psychology,* 1971, *23,* 297-303.

Hassett, J. "A New Look at Living Together." *Psychology Today,* 1977, *11,* 82-83.

Havighurst, R. J. *Human Development and Education.* New York: McKay, 1953.

Havighurst, R. J. *Developmental Tasks and Education.* (3rd ed.) New York: McKay, 1972.

Hetherington, E. M., Cox, M., and Cox, R. "Divorced Fathers." *Family Coordinator,* 1976, *25,* 417-428.

Hetherington, E. M., Cox, M., and Cox, R. "The Aftermath of Divorce." In J. H. Stevens, Jr., and M. Matthews (Eds.), *Mother-Child, Father-Child Relations.* Washington, D.C.: National Association for the Education of Young Children, 1977.

Hoffman, L. W. "Effects of Maternal Employment on the Child—A Review of the Research." *Developmental Psychology,* 1974, *10,* 204-228.

Hooper, F., Fitzgerald, J., and Papalia, D. "Piagetian Theory and the Aging Process: Extensions and Speculations." *Aging and Human Development,* 1971, *2,* 3-20.

Horn, J. L. "Organization of Data on Life-Span Development of Human Abilities." In L. R. Goulet and P. B. Baltes (Eds.), *Life-Span Developmental Psychology: Research and Theory.* New York: Academic Press, 1970.

Horn, J. L. "Human Abilities: A Review of Research and Theory in the Early 1970s." *Annual Review of Psychology,* 1976, *27,* 437-485.

Horn, J. L., and Cattell, R. B. "Refinement and Test of the Theory of Fluid and Crystallized Intelligence." *Journal of Educational Psychology,* 1966, *57,* 253-270.

Horn, J. L., and Cattell, R. B. "Age Differences in Fluid and Crystallized Intelligence." *Acta Psychologica,* 1967, *26,* 107-129.

Hornblum, J. N., and Overton, W. F. "Area and Volume Conservation Among the Elderly: Assessment and Training." *Developmental Psychology,* 1976, *12,* 68-74.

Hoyer, W. J., Labouvie-Vief, G., and Baltes, P. B. "Modification of Response Speed Deficits and Intellectual Performance in the Elderly." *Human Development,* 1973, *16,* 233-242.

Hultsch, D. F. "Adult Age Differences in Retrieval: Trace Dependent and Cue Dependent Forgetting." *Developmental Psychology,* 1975, *11,* 197-201.

Inhelder, B., and Piaget, J. *The Growth of Logical Thinking from Childhood to Adolescence.* New York: Basic Books, 1958.

Jones, W. H., Chernovitz, M. E. O'C., and Hansson, R. O. "The Enigma of Androgeny: Differential Implications for Males and Females." *Journal of Consulting and Clinical Psychology,* 1978, *46,* 298-313.

Kalish, R. A., and Knudtson, F. W. "Attachment Versus Disengagement: A Life-Span Conceptualization." *Human Development,* 1976, *19,* 171-181.

Kangas, J., and Bradway, K. "Intelligence at Middle Age: A Thirty-Eight Year Follow-Up." *Developmental Psychology,* 1971, *5,* 333-337.

Kastenbaum, R., and others. "The Ages of Me: Toward Personal and Interpersonal Definitions of Functional Aging." *Aging and Human Development,* 1972, *3,* 197-211.

Kausler, D. H., and Kleim, D. M. "Age Differences in Processing Relevant Versus Irrelevant Stimuli in Multiple Item Recognition Learning." *Journal of Gerontology,* 1978, *33,* 87-93.

Kelly, J. A., and Worell, J. "New Formulations of Sex Roles and Androgeny: A Critical Review." *Journal of Consulting and Clinical Psychology,* 1977, *45,* 1101-1115.

Kimmel, D. C. *Adulthood and Aging: An Interdisciplinary Developmental View.* New York: Wiley, 1974.

Knudtson, F. W. "Life-Span Attachment: Complexities, Questions, Considerations." *Human Development,* 1976, *19,* 182-196.

Kogan, N. "Categorizing and Conceptualizing Styles in Younger and Older Adults." *Human Development,* 1974, *17,* 218-230.

Kohlberg, L. "Continuities in Childhood and Adult Moral Development Revisited." In P. B. Baltes and K. W. Schaie (Eds.), *Life-Span Developmental Psychology: Personality and Socialization.* New York: Academic Press, 1973.

Kuhlen, R. G. "Age and Intelligence: The Significance of Cultural Change in Longitudinal vs. Cross-Sectional Findings." *Vita Humanae,* 1963, *6,* 113-124.

Labouvie-Vief, G. "Adult Cognitive Development: In Search of Alternative Interpretations." *Merrill-Palmer Quarterly,* 1977, *23,* 227-263.

Labouvie-Vief, G., and Gonda, J. N. "Cognitive Strategy Training and Intellectual Performance in the Elderly." *Journal of Gerontology,* 1976, *31,* 327-332.

Lacey, J. I., and Lacey, B. "Some Autonomic-Central Nervous System Interrelationships." In P. Black (Ed.), *Physiological Correlates of Emotion.* New York: Academic Press, 1970.

LaVoie, J. C., and Adams, G. R. "Erikson Developmental Stage Resolution and Attachment Behavior in Young Adulthood." *Adolescence,* 1979.

Leech, S., and Witte, K. L. "Paired-Associate Learning in Elderly Adults as Related to Pacing and Incentive Conditions." *Developmental Psychology,* 1971, *5,* 180.

Levinson, D. J. "The Mid-Life Transition: A Period in Adult Psychosocial Development." *Psychiatry,* 1977, *40,* 99-112.

Livson, F. B. "Patterns of Personality Development in Middle-Aged Women: A Longitudinal Study." *Aging and Human Behavior,* 1977, *7,* 107-115.

Looft, W. R. "Egocentrism and Social Interaction Across the Life Span." *Psychological Bulletin,* 1972, *78,* 73-92.

Looft, W. R., and Charles, D. C. "Egocentrism and Social Interaction in Young and Old Adults." *Aging and Human Development,* 1971, *2,* 21-28.

Macklin, E. "Heterosexual Cohabitation Among Unmarried College Students." *Family Coordinator,* 1972, *21,* 463-472.

Marsh, G. R., and Thompson, L. W. "Psychophysiology of Aging." In J. E. Birren and K. W. Schaie (Eds.), *Handbook of the Psychology of Aging.* New York: Van Nostrand Reinhold, 1977.

Mistler-Lachman, J. L. "Spontaneous Shift in Encoding Dimensions Among Elderly Subjects." *Journal of Gerontology,* 1977, *32,* 68-72.

Nehrke, M. F. "Age and Sex Differences in Discrimination Learning and Transfer of Training." *Journal of Gerontology,* 1973, *28,* 320-327.

Nesselroade, J. R. "Application of Multivariate Strategies to Problems of Measuring and Structuring Long-Term Change." In L. R. Goulet and P. B. Baltes (Eds.), *Life-Span Developmental Psychology: Research and Theory.* New York: Academic Press, 1970.

Nesselroade, J. R. "Issues in Studying Developmental Change in Adults from a Multivariate Perspective." In J. E. Birren and K. W. Schaie (Eds.), *Handbook of the Psychology of Aging.* New York: Van Nostrand Reinhold, 1977.

Neugarten, B. "Personality and Aging." In J. E. Birren and K. W. Schaie (Eds.), *Handbook of the Psychology of Aging.* New York: Van Nostrand Reinhold, 1977.

Okun, M. A., Siegler, I. C., and George, L. K. "Cautiousness and Verbal Learning in Adulthood." *Journal of Gerontology,* 1978, *33,* 94-97.

O'Neill, N., and O'Neill, G. *Open Marriage: A New Life Style for Couples.* New York: Evans, 1972.

Papalia, D. E. "The Status of Several Conservation Abilities Across the Life-Span." *Human Development,* 1972, *15,* 229-243.

Papalia, D. E., and Bielby, D. "Cognitive Functioning in Middle and Old Age Adults: A Review of Research Based on Piaget's Theory." *Human Development,* 1974, *17,* 424-443.

Papalia, D. E., Salverson, S., and True, M. "An Evaluation of Quantity Conservation Performance During Old Age." *Aging and Human Development,* 1973, *4,* 103-109.

Piaget, J. "Intellectual Evolution from Adolescence to Adulthood." *Human Development,* 1972, *15,* 1-12.

Piaget, J., and Inhelder, B. *The Psychology of the Child.* New York: Basic Books, 1969.

Plemons, J. K., Willis, S. L., and Baltes, P. B. "Modifiability of Fluid Intelligence in

Aging: A Short-Term Longitudinal Training Approach." *Journal of Gerontology,* 1978, *33,* 224-231.

Powell, R. R. "Psychological Effects of Exercise Therapy upon Institutionalized Geriatric Mental Patients." *Journal of Gerontology,* 1974, *29,* 157-161.

Pressey, S. L., Janney, J. E., and Kuhlen, J. E. *Life: A Psychological Survey.* New York: Harper & Row, 1939.

Reid, D. W., Haas, G., and Hawkings, D. "Locus of Desired Control and Positive Self-Concept of the Elderly." *Journal of Gerontology,* 1977, *32,* 441-450.

Rhudick, P. J., and Gordon, C. "The Age Center of New England Study." In L. F. Jarvik, C. Eisdorfer, and J. E. Blum (Eds.), *Intellectual Functioning in Adults.* New York: Springer, 1973.

Riegel, K. F. "The Prediction of Death and Longevity in Longitudinal Research." In E. Palmore and F. C. Jeffers (Eds.), *Prediction of Life Span.* Lexington, Mass.: Heath, 1971.

Riegel, K. F. "Adult Life Crises: A Dialectic Interpretation of Development." In N. Datan and L. H. Ginsberg (Eds.), *Life-Span Developmental Psychology: Normative Life Crises.* New York: Academic Press, 1975a.

Riegel, K. F. "From Traits and Equilibrium Towards Developmental Dialectics." In W. Arnold (Ed.), *Nebraska Symposium on Motivation.* Lincoln: University of Nebraska Press, 1975b.

Riegel, K. F., and Riegel, R. M. "Development, Drop, and Death." *Developmental Psychology,* 1972, *6,* 306-319.

Rubin, K. H. "Decentration Skills in Institutionalized and Noninstitutionalized Elders." In *Proceedings of the 81st Annual Convention.* Washington, D.C.: American Psychological Association, 1973.

Rubin, K. H., and others. "The Development of Spatial Egocentrism and Conservation Across the Life-Span." *Developmental Psychology,* 1973, *9,* 432.

Sanders, R. E., and Sanders, J. C. "Long Term Durability and Transfer of Enhanced Conceptual Performance in the Elderly." *Journal of Gerontology,* 1978, *33,* 408-412.

Sanders, J. C., and others. "Modification of Concept Identification Performance in Older Adults." *Developmental Psychology,* 1975, *11,* 824-830.

Schaie, K. W. "A General Model for the Study of Developmental Problems." *Psychological Bulletin,* 1965, *64,* 92-107.

Schaie, K. W. "Age Changes and Age Differences." *Gerontologist,* 1967, *7,* 128-132.

Schaie, K. W. "Methodological Problems in Descriptive Developmental Research on Adulthood and Aging." In J. R. Nesselroade and H. W. Reese (Eds.), *Life-Span Developmental Psychology: Methodological Issues.* New York: Academic Press, 1973.

Schaie, K. W. "Quasi-Experimental Research Designs in the Psychology of Aging." In J. E. Birren and K. W. Schaie (Eds.), *Handbook of the Psychology of Aging.* New York: Van Nostrand Reinhold, 1977a.

Schaie, K. W. "Toward a Stage of Adult Cognitive Development." *Aging and Human Development,* 1977b, *8,* 129-138.

Schaie, K. W., and Gribbon, K. "Adult Development and Aging." *Annual Review of Psychology,* 1975, *26,* 65-96.

Schaie, K. W., and Labouvie-Vief, G. "Generational Versus Ontogenetic Components of Change in Adult Cognitive Behavior: A Fourteen-Year Cross-Sequential Study." *Developmental Psychology,* 1974, *10,* 305-320.

Schaie, K. W., Labouvie-Vief, G., and Buech, B. U. "Generational and Cohort-Specific Differences in Adult Cognitive Functioning: A Fourteen-Year Study of Independent Samples." *Developmental Psychology,* 1973, *9,* 151-166.

Schaie, K. W., and Parham, I. A. "Stability of Adult Personality Traits: Facts or Fable?" *Journal of Personality and Social Psychology*, 1976, *34*, 146-158.

Schaie, K. W., and Strother, C. R. "A Cross-Sequential Study of Age Changes in Cognitive Behavior." *Psychological Bulletin*, 1968, *70*, 671-680.

Schonfield, D., and Robertson, B. A. "Memory Storage and Aging." *Canadian Journal of Psychology*, 1966, *20*, 228-263.

Schonfield, D., and Wenger, L. "Age Limitation of Perceptual Span." *Nature*, 1975, *253*, 377-378.

Sears, R. R. "Sources of Life Satisfaction of the Terman Gifted Men." *American Psychologist*, 1977, *32*, 119-128.

Sheehy, G. *Passages: Predictable Crises of Adult Life*. New York: Bantam Books, 1976.

Stegner, W. "The Writer and the Concept of Adulthood." In E. H. Erikson (Ed.), *Adulthood*. New York: Norton, 1978.

Stein, P. J. *Singles*. Englewood Cliffs, N.J.: Prentice-Hall, 1976.

Storck, P., Looft, W. R., and Hooper, F. H. "Interrelationships Among Piagetian Tasks and Traditional Measures of Cognitive Abilities in Mature and Aged Adults." *Journal of Gerontology*, 1972, *27*, 461-465.

Tomlinson-Keasey, C. "Formal Operations in Females from Eleven to Fifty-Four Years of Age." *Developmental Psychology*, 1972, *6*, 364.

Troll, L. E. *Early and Middle Adulthood*. Monterey, Calif.: Brooks/Cole, 1975.

Troll, L. E., and Smith, J. "Attachment Through the Life Span: Some Questions About Dyadic Bonds Among Adults." *Human Development*, 1976, *19*, 156-170.

Tuddenham, R. D., Blumenkrantz, J., and Wilkin, W. R. "Age Changes on AGCT: A Longitudinal Study of Average Adults." *Journal of Consulting and Clinical Psychology*, 1968, *32*, 659-663.

Vaillant, G. E. "The Climb to Maturity: How the Best and the Brightest Came of Age." *Psychology Today*, 1977, *11*, 34-110.

Wang, H. S. "Cerebral Correlates of Intellectual Functioning in Senescence." In L. F. Jarvik, C. Eisdorfer, and J. E. Blum (Eds.), *Intellectual Functioning in Adults*. New York: Springer, 1973.

Wang, H. S., Obrist, W. D., and Busse, E. W. "Neurophysiological Correlates of the Intellectual Function of Elderly Persons Living in the Community." *American Journal of Psychiatry*, 1970, *126*, 1205-1212.

Wechsler, D. *The Measurement of Adult Intelligence*. Baltimore: Williams and Wilkins, 1939.

Wickelgren, W. A. "Age and Storage Dynamics in Recognition Memory." *Developmental Psychology*, 1975, *11*, 165-169.

Wilkie, F. L., and Eisdorfer, C. "Intelligence and Blood Pressure in the Aged." *Science*, 1971, *172*, 959-962.

Wilkie, F. L., and Eisdorfer, C. "Sex, Verbal Ability, and Pacing Differences in Serial Learning." *Journal of Gerontology*, 1977, *32*, 63-67.

Witte, K. L. "Optimal Shift Behavior in Children and Young and Elderly Adults." *Psychonomic Science*, 1971, *25*, 329-330.

Witte, K. L., and Freund, J. S. "Paired-Associate Learning in Young and Old Adults as Related to Stimulus Concreteness and Presentation Method." *Journal of Gerontology*, 1976, *31*, 186-192.

Wohlwill, J. F. *The Study of Behavioral Development*. New York: Academic Press, 1973.

Wolk, S. "Situational Constraint as a Moderator of Locus of Control—Adjustment Relationship." *Journal of Consulting and Clinical Psychology*, 1976, *44*, 420-427.

3

James C. Hansen
Bonnie S. Himes

Normality

Nearly all investigators agree that there is no clear definition of normality or the various terms that may be used interchangeably. However, certain relevant dimensions of normality—namely, mental health, psychological maturity, adjustment, and a healthy personality—are crucial to an understanding of the concept.

According to Goldenson (1970), mental health is the ability to handle demands and situations without excessive stress and strain. A mentally healthy individual has a sense of well-being and functions effectively. Such a person works regularly, thinks clearly, manages emotions, enjoys life, and keeps on good terms with other people and self. For Szasz (1960) mental health is not the absence of mental illness; rather, it is the ability to make good choices in life. The adversary is not mental illness. The issue is problems in living, whether these be biological, economic, political, or sociopsychological: "Mental illness is a myth whose function it is to disguise and thus render more palatable the bitter pill of moral conflicts in human relations" (p. 118). For Laing (1969) a mentally healthy person is open, honest, and able to see things as they really are. This person does not engage in game playing or wear a mask.

Psychological maturity is seen in persons who are clearly aware of reality and do not run head on to violate it, though they do what they can to shape it to positive ends.

Because they are essentially at peace with themselves, they are also attentive to the needs of others. They enjoy productivity and work in accordance with their skills and tend to grow toward higher levels of competence (Cox, 1974).

Adjustment may be described as an individual's general adaptation to his or her environment and the demands of life—including the way that he or she relates to other people, handles responsibilities, deals with stress, and meets personal needs. It is not a static condition; since life is constantly changing, the ability to revise attitudes and behavior is an essential ingredient in adjustment. When adjustment breaks down and the individual cannot meet the demands of life without excessive strain or definite emotional symptoms, that individual probably needs psychological aid. The major aim of psychotherapy is to enable the distressed individual to achieve a more adequate adjustment; that is, a more effective and satisfying way of living (Goldenson, 1970).

In discussing the concept of a healthy personality, White (1973) stresses a feeling of competence with self, interpersonal situations, and skill accomplishment. White advocates individual differences and states that the goal of counselors is not to produce an ideal character type but to help people with problems in their own particular lives.

Background and Current Status

Normality implies a goal, a standard, something tangible, but its precise definition and measurement are elusive. The problem stems from the evolution of its usage, which borrows concepts from other fields. The notion that normality is quantifiable results from its use in mathematics and science. During the eighteenth century, the geometrical normal line was synonymous with "perpendicular" and usually referred to a line or plane that intersected another at right angles. By the mid nineteenth century, the term *normal* had come to mean conforming to or not deviating from the standard. For example, in 1840 the French referred to their regular system of primary schools as normal; in 1876 the *Encyclopaedia Britannica* defined *normal paraffins* as "those meeting the standard in which no carbon atom is combined with more than two other carbon atoms" (p. 557). Normal also connotes that which is positive or right; over the years the concept evolved to the point that the only requirement for normalcy is the lack of wrong. In 1866 the *Athenaeum* noted that "normality gives us only the negative notion of absence of defect" (p. 873).

The mental health field in the twentieth century has accepted these various connotations of normality. Normality is a positive goal that implies health and a certain degree of conformity. Attempts to define and quantify the concept have emphasized statistical terms (such as the normal probability curve), sociological terms (such as cultural relativity), and subjective terms (such as the individual's feelings of satisfaction in his or her relations to self and the external world).

Critical Discussion

General Areas of Concern

Psychological normality is difficult to define for a number of reasons. First, there is no sharp dividing line between normal and abnormal behavior but, rather, a continuous gradation from good to poor adjustment and from apparent absence of symptoms to extreme pathology. Second, an individual may shift to different positions along this continuum. Third, a definition of normality in terms of a statistical norm would overemphasize the average individual and tend to exclude deviations from the majority, such as geniuses, nonconformists, and even people who are completely free from conflicts. Fourth, a definition in terms of adaptation is bound to stress adjustment to a particular society at a particular time. Fifth, an individual's problems may be organic or functional rather than psychological.

Since no one definition of normality can cover the topic, several concepts need to be examined. A useful catalog of current concepts has been proposed by Offer and Sabshin (1974), who have categorized the following perspectives on normality. Normality as health assumes that behavior is within normal limits when no manifest psychopathology is present. In this context, health refers to a reasonable rather than an optimal state of functioning. Normality as utopia defines the ideal person or characteristics. Normality as average results from a mathematical principle of the bell-shaped curve; it involves a statistical measurement of individuals and conceives of the middle range as normal and both extremes as deviant. Normality as transactional systems stresses changes or processes rather than a cross-sectional definition. From an analysis of the various concepts, the clinician may derive a synthesis to assist in individual assessment.

Comparative Philosophies and Theories

Four concepts of normality (similar to those proposed by Offer and Sabshin) are presented here: normality as a biological and medical concept, normality as a cultural and social concept, normality as an ideal concept, and normality as a process.

Normality as a Biological and Medical Concept. A biological view of normal behavior refers to a certain point in time or the element of change over time. The biologist does not label any one act normal or abnormal but suggests that there is a broad, stable range of behaviors regarded as normal; such a view allows for individual diversities and for changes over time (Child, 1924). Biological normality is relative to evolutionary stages.

Herrick (1956) considers genetic influence the main determinant of behavioral patterns. Classical genetic theory suggests that normal people carry mostly normal genes. Consequently, abnormal people carry more abnormal genes, and abnormal behavior results from abnormal genes. This theory has led to efforts to understand the contribution of genetics to behavior. A more complex genetic theory is the balance theory, which suggests that there are many kinds of normal people, that such people are products of a great array of genotypes, and that the boundary between genetically normal and handicapped is not sharp. Geneticists agree that there is a close connection between heredity and behavior and that genetic factors affect the range of functions and behaviors in an individual.

In the medical field, physicians (including psychiatrists) have not attended to the normally functioning population. Their focus is on the exception to the rule; that is, the ill or abnormally functioning individual. When no manifest psychopathology is present, behavior is assumed to be normal. The absence of gross pathology or suffering is a description of the healthy condition and is considered synonymous with normality. Psychosomatic medicine presents a newer trend in psychiatry. In an attempt to bridge the gap between physical and mental conditions, Engel (1962) discusses disease and health as unsuccessful and successful adaptations to an environment.

Normality as a Cultural and Social Concept. Many anthropologists and sociologists avoid attempting a definition of normality because it reflects moral decisions. However, anthropologists concede that in every culture there is a wide range of individual types but that only a few are allowed to flourish. These are the dominant types that the majority of people adopt. A minority will be deviant or abnormal.

A more universal view of normality compares personality structures across cultures. Hsu (1961) suggests that there is a core difference between abnormal and normal behavior; namely, that evaluation of people's behavior can be made in terms of their ability to relate to other people. He emphasizes three factors: sociability, security, and status. In his view, only those individuals who cannot maintain any relationships anywhere should be considered abnormal. One should not equate abnormality with deviance from cultural values.

Wallace (1961) stresses the biocultural view, which considers the interaction between biological and cultural variables. One is always affected by biological makeup; however, mental health is "a state in which the person is performing to his own and others' satisfaction the roles appropriate to his situation in society" (p. 211).

Two views of normality that most anthropologists accept are cultural relativism (that is, what is considered abnormal in one culture is not necessarily indicative of abnormality in another culture) and functionalism (which evaluates the function of behavior in terms of the total personality, while recognizing that it is, in part, culturally determined).

Sociologists are likely to consider the question "What leads to deviance?" rather than "What is normality?" Cohen (1959), for example, excludes the psychiatric labels in his definition of deviant behavior. He suggests that deviance has to do with the relationships of action to societal expectations.

Merton (1949) approaches deviance and normality from a sociological point of view. He suggests that there is a break in the connection between culturally prescribed aspirations and socially structured ways to realize these aspirations. The concepts of deviancy and normality are linked together in that they serve to clarify each other. Without deviant behavior, it becomes difficult to interpret what is normal. It is important to examine the two terms together. It may be possible to view normal behavior within a deviant group. Such a member of this group has behavior that is suitable to the rest of the group.

Parsons (1958) views normality in terms of an individual's actions within a particular system. Health is defined as capacity. According to Parsons, each individual develops a capacity for effective performance, and this capacity varies qualitatively among individuals. In Parsons' (1959) ideas about the problem of normality and pathology, there is a need to evaluate the functioning of systems. When patterns are adapted and integrated, they are normal within the situations in which they are integrated. In this context, a system can be labeled successful; however, it becomes difficult to judge the value of that system and the likelihood of results beyond that particular system.

Normality as an Ideal Concept. The psychological view of normality can be approached statistically or clinically. Statistically, it is important to understand the concept of the average. Lambert Quételet's bell-shaped curve is based on his theory that nature strives to duplicate a particular model in every man and misses by varying degrees. His assumption is that the average man is nature's biological ideal. In a similar theory, Galton applied statistics to the measurement of mental ability. Investigation of the normal distribution of genius led him to believe that the frequency of genius could be predicted. In 1905 Alfred Binet employed the concept of mental age in the first standardized intelligence test. Binet's approach is the operational base for many psychological tests. A good psychological test, for example, can be defined as one that separates the average from both extremes in a meaningful way. Many tests, such as intelligence tests, use this norm or average to statistically represent the majority of the population. Most people fall within one standard deviation of the mean.

Other types of psychological tests involve clinical evaluations. Different interpretations are made of the varying clinical scores. In most cases tests like the Minnesota

Multiphasic Personality Inventory (MMPI) and the Thematic Apperception Test (TAT) define the average as clinically desirable. Each extreme on the normal curve indicates pathology. One has too much anxiety or too little. Use of the norm in this way suggests an idealization of the concept (Offer and Sabshin, 1974).

Several investigators have described normality in terms of ideal characteristics. Individuality of the person is stressed in the single case study. It appears impossible to use statistical criteria as the sole bases to judge a person's normality. Instead, the normal individual is seen as a nonexistent ideal. Clinicians are asked to compare the individual to an ideal.

Maslow and Mittelman (1951) enumerate three points that must be remembered in any study of the normal. First, the dynamics of mentally sick and mentally healthy individuals differ only quantitatively. Second, the use of the term *normal* in statistics connotes the average. Third, normality has a direct relationship to cultural adaptation. Social status, age, and sex must also always be kept in mind. Maslow and Mittelman list eleven manifestations of ideal psychological health:

1. Adequate feelings of security—feeling safe with others.
2. Adequate self-evaluation—including self-esteem and worthwhileness.
3. Adequate spontaneity and emotionality—ability to form and sustain emotional ties, give expression, and share and understand others' emotions.
4. Efficient contact with reality—absence of excessive fantasy, realistic outlook on life, and ability to change.
5. Adequate bodily desires and the ability to gratify them.
6. Adequate self-knowledge—adequate knowledge of motives, goals, and ambitions and realistic appraisal of abilities.
7. Integration and consistency of personality—full development of interests, flexibility of views, ability to concentrate, and no major conflicting trends in the personality.
8. Adequate life goals—achievable and worthwhile goals, coupled with persistence in accomplishing them.
9. Ability to learn from experience—receptiveness and lack of rigidity.
10. Ability to satisfy the requirements of the group—showing some likeness to the group, knowledgable of the group ways, and able to conform to the group.
11. Adequate emancipation from the group or culture—having some originality and independence, not requiring group approval, and appreciating cultural differences.

These criteria are somewhat difficult to assess and may be culturally bound and value-laden concepts. They seem to represent ideals with emphasis on creative aspects and the potentials of the individual.

Rogers (1963) believes that individuals are able to actualize themselves and can become fully functioning persons with the following characteristics:

1. They are open to experience and exhibit no defensiveness.
2. All experiences are available to awareness.
3. All symbolizations are as accurate as the experiential data permit.
4. Their self-structure is congruent with their experience.
5. Their self-structure is a fluid Gestalt, changing flexibly in the process of assimilation of new experience.
6. They experience themselves as the locus of evaluation.
7. They have no conditions of worth and experience unconditional self-regard.

8. They meet each situation with behavior that is a unique and creative adaptation to the newness of that moment.
9. They find their organismic valuing a trustworthy guide to the most satisfying behaviors because of effective reality testing.
10. They live with others in the maximum possible harmony.

Rogers' term *fully functioning person* is synonymous with optimal psychological adjustment and maturity. Such a person has nonspecific behaviors that enable him to adapt adequately to new situations. The normal individual, then, is in continual process of self-actualization.

Jahoda (1950) emphasizes six major criteria of mental health: (1) positive attitudes toward the self; (2) presence of growth, development, and self-actualization; (3) integration, including the balance of psychic forces, a unifying outlook on life, and resistance to stress; (4) autonomy and independence from social influences; (5) adequate perception of reality; and (6) environmental mastery. Jahoda (1958) rejects "absence of mental disease" as a criterion of mental health, since the notion of mental disease is subject to wide cultural variation and since a person's resources of strength and areas of vulnerability may vary independently of one another. That is, one should not decide arbitrarily that health and illness can usefully be represented as opposite ends of a single dimension.

Smith (1950) introduces the notion of optimum mental health, in contrast to the idea that every component in a mental health pattern should be maximized. Smith (1969) states that values are involved in defining mental illness or positive mental health. Behavioral scientists would do well to heed Smith's recommendation that clinicians make explicit their own value orientations. According to Smith, additional competing lists of mental health criteria contribute little to professional understanding. Instead, conceptual clarification may be more profitable. A major part of this becomes the acceptance and understanding of one's own values.

Smith prefers to use a "frame of reference" for the purpose of analyzing mental health. The three somewhat independent features of psychological well-being are adjustment, integration, and cognitive adequacy. Adjustment stems from the functional biological approach. The well-being of the individual in interaction with his or her environment depends on the satisfaction of needs. How the individual reduces tension, deals with frustration, and develops adjustive mechanisms all contribute to the achievement of homeostasis. The second criterion, integration, became a central concern with ego psychology and related emphasis on self-realization and self-consistency. The concept refers to the degree of coordination of needs, means, and goals and to one's resiliency under pressure. Smith's final criterion is adequacy of the individual's cognition of reality —both of self and of one's social environment, since distortions in the one are likely to imply complementary distortions in the other. Accuracy of perception is an essential accompaniment of maximal adjustment and integration.

Another description of normality as an ideal is available from analytical concepts. Freud's psychoanalytic theory has resulted in several notions regarding normality. First, there has been a general acceptance of psychopathology in everyday life. The range of behavior that Freud describes is broad and depends on inherent and developmental criteria. He views normality as "an ideal fiction" (Freud, 1937), an ideal at the end of the range. A healthy mature person would have adequate ego strength to cope with personal drives as well as social pressures. Ego strength and coping skills are developed through personal and social interaction during various developmental stages.

Jung ([1923] 1971) perceives the healthy individual striving for perfection, which cannot be reached. Instead, the individual tends toward completeness in terms of society. In Jungian psychology the collective norm is the sum total of all individual ways. It is this norm that each person tries to approximate but can never achieve. The mature person has found a satisfactory relationship to the norm and worked through to a concept of individuation.

In Adler's (1939) view, the normal person strives for more than self-centered goals. Adler suggests that the drives are shaped and channeled by social interest. The normal person sets his or her sights on social, cooperative goals; the neurotic focuses only on selfish, egocentric aims. Adler believes that normal persons can free themselves from conflicts of past events and create and change their own lives. In contrast, neurotic persons are unable to identify positive goals and expectations for themselves. Normality may encompass self-reliance, a power to effect changes in one's environment. The normal person (1) creates relationships in cooperation with others, (2) is able to solve personal problems, and (3) has a feeling of worth that is a function of social usefulness.

Rank (1925) defines normality as one of three categories into which people fall. The adjusted person accepts the popular will of the group. The neurotic individual has difficulties identifying with the group in a positive way; this person struggles with feelings of inferiority and guilt. The third type of individual most successfully accepts and affirms himself. This creative individual is in close harmony with personal abilities and ideals. According to Rank, it is the function of therapy to move the neurotic toward characteristics of the creative individual.

Hartmann (1960) employs ego psychology as a means of understanding normal behavior in children and adults. A person possesses various degrees of ego strength based on the complex interaction between biological and sociocultural aspects of human behavior. The ego strength determines the degree of stability and environmental adaptation. Health emerges with good adaptation to one's mental and physical environment.

Normality can be viewed as a personality that is well integrated. Of basic importance is the mastery of developmental stages. Erikson (1950) views the identity as a process evolving from the numerous disruptions and potential crises. A normal person is one who successfully overcomes the obstacles in each stage of development. A crucial factor is the early experience of the individual.

Normality as a Process. When normality is viewed as a process, the normal individual is seen as someone who effectively copes with life situations at each stage of development. One of the four functional perspectives on normality distinguished by Offer and Sabshin (1974) was normality as transactional systems. Normality as transactional systems suggests that normal behavior is the end result of interacting systems that change over time. Biologists adhere to this theory, as does Erikson (1950), with his description of progression through the stages of development. Each stage Erikson discusses builds on the preceding stages; what is learned in one stage contributes to the next.

Scientific theories needed to understand the "process" may not yet be fully developed. Offer and Sabshin classify conceptions of normality as processes tending toward adaptation. The process approach to normality may be best represented by various attempts to conceptualize and study effective coping behavior. Although this conceptualization is short of the full development of a systems theory of personality, many agree that active coping processes are part of an adequate formulation (Grinker, 1963; Smith, 1974). Successful prediction of health depends on the relationship between person and environment. It is important to determine the sources of stress on individuals in our society. With environments less stable than ever before, the individual is required to make extremely rapid changes. Mental health then depends on more flexibility of the individual.

Elaboration On Critical Points

Normal behavior involves appropriate organic conditions, self-esteem, social behavior, and work patterns, and it permits social and cultural variations. It is developmental in nature; that is, different behaviors are appropriate and necessary at different ages. Normal behavior is a process of continuous coping.

The organic condition of the person will affect behavior and therefore must be considered in clinical assessments.

Two aspects of normal behavior that are consistently noted involve appropriate and satisfactory relationships with other people and with oneself. Normal people are able to establish and maintain warm interpersonal relationships and are generally comfortable and satisfied with themselves. They may have some problems and/or desire changes, but their behavior does not cause others or themselves major difficulties.

Productive behavior is another aspect of normality that is frequently listed. Students should be productive in school and home, and adults should be able to maintain work. Excessive problems with work indicate some deviance from the norm. Work involves both production and adequate social behaviors.

Normal behavior meets the developmental tasks of the person's stage in life. The person's successful accomplishment of physical, social, and emotional tasks at one stage will affect his or her behavior at later stages.

Normal people recognize reality and can cope with the stress and strain of situations in their lives. They have developed appropriate problem-solving skills and defense reactions that help them to live more satisfactorily. This suggests that the normal person may experience problems but has abilities to meet them. Although there are ideal traits listed, they are, after all, ideals. The majority will not consistently achieve the ideal state. This idea gives some support to the concept of normal as average. The concept of average suggests that a person can have some problems and still behave in the range of normality.

Normality is not a static condition; rather, it is a process. Biological and sociocultural concepts accent the idea of relativity. A person's physical and emotional condition as well as the social situation will certainly fluctuate. Therefore, one's adjustment may vary.

There are social and cultural variations in normality. The family and cultural teachings will provide guidelines for acceptable behavior. Although there is room for cultural differences, individuals need to conform adequately to generally accepted behavior patterns.

Personal Views and Recommendations

Emphasis on normality may influence clinicians' viewpoints in diagnosing client behavior. More specific attention to the variability and many dimensions of normal behavior will give the clinician a broader perspective on the concept of psychopathology. It would emphasize developing a positive attitude about people, looking for the assets of the individual even when there are some problem behaviors. Rather than just labeling the person with a diagnostic category, the clinician can view the total behavior pattern. Clinicians can profit from knowledge regarding the biological bases of behavior and the sociological and anthropological influences on behavior patterns. A broader knowledge will improve the comparison of general concepts of normality with abnormal behavior.

Each clinician should develop a conceptual framework for normality which will assist in conceptualizing people. However, there are ethical considerations regarding the clinician's assessment. Specifically, the clinician's values may affect the diagnosis, and the clinician's value of normal mental health may affect the goals and process of therapy. Personal values may influence perceptions of behaviors of divergent racial or ethnic groups, different socioeconomic classes, or the opposite sex. Clinicians have worked from an implicit view of normality that is consistent with the central tendencies of Western culture. The literature suggests that diagnosis is an inappropriate alliance of morality, psychiatry, and politics in the labeling process (Scheff, 1975). Clinicians are accused of diagnosing according to their value assumptions, which get applied universally without an adequate transcultural definition of normal mood, thought, and behavior. The behavioral scientist's values also can significantly affect professional services. Maddi (1973) suggests that clients learn from the therapist a direction or orientation in which they can behave and therefore become more effective in behavior. Whether therapists recognize it or not, they give cues and reinforcements consistent with their own values. Often clients who are termed improved have shifted in their values toward those of the therapist.

Applications to Particular Variables

Age. Erikson (1950) and Havighurst (1951) describe the basic tasks that must be mastered at each stage of life if the individual is to achieve normal development and healthy adjustment. Failure to perform any of these tasks may hamper development in succeeding stages. The tasks are grouped around seven poles: (1) physical skills, (2) intellectual advancement, (3) emotional adjustment, (4) social relationships, (5) attitudes toward self, (6) attitudes toward reality, and (7) formation of values. To meet these requirements successfully, the individual must develop not only constantly increasing competence and understanding but also a sense of responsibility, a realistic outlook, and a capacity for self-direction.

In infancy and early childhood (age 0-6), the individual learns to take solid foods, walk, talk, and control elimination. There is development of trust in one's self and others, as well as respect for rules and authority. The individual explores the immediate environment and develops skills through play. Social skills involve learning to identify with one's own sex and relate to parents, siblings, other children, and adults. The child learns to control emotions and to distinguish right from wrong and acquires simple concepts of time, space, and safety.

In middle childhood (age 6-12), there is an expanding of knowledge and understanding of the physical and social world. Individuals adopt a masculine or feminine role and build attitudes of confidence and self-esteem. There is an increase in ability to take responsibility, academic skills, reasoning, and judgment. Individuals learn physical and social skills through hobbies, interests, and activities. They achieve increasing independence and self-reliance.

During adolescence (age 12-18), there is a gain in self-assurance and sense of identity. Individuals discover and accept personal limitations as well as strengths and must adjust to bodily changes. There is a developing sexual interest, and there are more mature relationships with peers. Adolescents increasingly achieve emotional independence from parents and establish personal, social, and ethical values. Adolescents explore their interests and abilities as preparation for an occupation, marriage, parenthood, and participation in the community. Erikson (1950) defines the adolescent's predicament as "finding an identity"; and, indeed, *identity crisis* has become a common diagnostic term when one is talking about disturbed adolescents or young adults. Having an identity connotes both an inner oneness with self and the assurance of possessing a recognizable posture in society. The opposite of having an identity is identity diffusion. The adolescent or young adult who has not "found the self" and is puzzled as to who he or she is and where he or she belongs is often said to suffer from identity diffusion.

In early adulthood (age 18-35), most individuals complete formal education and embark on an occupation. Individuals during this stage are finding and learning to live with a mate, establishing a home, and beginning to provide for the material and emotional needs of children. Young adults are in the process of developing a basic philosophy of life. They are searching for a congenial social group and participating in civic affairs. (Adjustment during this stage appears to be difficult. National statistics for age of first mental hospital admission show a rise from childhood to a peak in the stage of 25 to 34.)

During middle age (35-60), individuals are establishing a standard of living, building financial security for the remaining years, and taking greater social responsibility. They develop their free life, including adult leisure activities. Parents help teenage children become effective and stable adults. Individuals also adjust to the aging of their parents and accept their own physiological changes of middle age. For most individuals middle age brings anticipated changes in family, work, and health. Normal adjustment is easier when they expect life-cycle changes.

In later life, there is a process of adjusting to increasing physical limitations, reduced income, and the loss of friends or spouse. Individuals usually accept retirement as a way of life and find adequate living arrangements. They are affiliating with their own age group and maintaining active interests beyond themselves. They meet social and civic obligations within their ability and circumstances.

The well-adjusted aged continue the capacity to gain gratification and relieve their tensions. They appear to maintain their self-esteem, self-confidence, personal identity, purposefulness, and social role. They tend to keep busy at work or at play equivalents, which are within their physical capacities, commensurate with their intelligence and training, and from which they gain a sense of accomplishment.

Sex. Sex-related behaviors involve both biological characteristics and the effects of socialization. Research in development of the brain suggests some evidence of sex-linked differences. In the embryo, sex hormones are involved in the shaping of neural circuits in the hypothalamus, which is the part of the brain that directly influences the endocrine system (Bardwick, 1971). If development of the male is somewhat more complex, it may also be more hazardous. This leads to the view that sexual pathology among men is more common than among women. To the extent that there is central nervous system sex-typing, the predispositions to perceive and respond to stimuli will be influenced by the sex-type of the brain. The development of femininity and masculinity in the central nervous system can be seen as independent of the development of reproductive organs.

Normal adult behavior can occur only if the neural, hormonal, and experiential developments all have been within a normal range. The behavioral dispositions that may result from the sex-typing of the brain are the infant's personality qualities that will be socialized by being punished, rewarded, or ignored. It is unreasonable to ascribe human motivation solely to experiential factors and animal motivation solely to endocrine-constitutional factors. Both sets of factors contribute to the development of the personality in the human.

Most socialization for sex-role behavior tends to reinforce sex-stereotyped behaviors. Sex-role behaviors are first reinforced by the family and then in school (Vernoff, 1969). Normal behavior for males and females has to do with their self-concept, interpersonal relationships, and productivity (Mussen and Rutherford, 1963). Society generally views sex-stereotyped behavior as normal; therefore, individuals who deviate from the stereotype may experience more stress. When assessing an individual's behavior, the clinician must be aware of the biological component and the socialization of the person.

Education. Normal educational development involves age and grade attainment. Most children begin school at age 5 and are expected to advance one grade each year. Individuals who are retained (failed) have not met the prescribed educational tasks. Problems in educational development may occur because of intelligence, motivation, emotions, or special learning disabilities. Special assessment is required for each area. Problems in normal educational development often contribute to a lowering self-esteem and behavior problems in school. A lower self-esteem and poor social adjustment would be indications of difficulty with major variables of normal development.

Although intelligence is only one aspect of normal educational development, it is the primary subject of assessment when educational problems are observed. General intelligence has been widely studied, particularly in the last fifty years. It is defined in different ways, but nearly all definitions bring it into relation with adaptation. Intelligence has to do with learning, problem solving, judgment, and thinking. It can be called the cognitive side of one's capacity for adaptation, in rough contrast to the motivational aspects of the adjustment process (White, 1964). There is growing evidence that general intelligence is really a cluster of more or less independent abilities, but the concept of the IQ is so firmly entrenched that most studies of deviations in mental ability treat intelligence as though it were, in fact, general. There is also growing evidence that intelligence is not the utterly fixed, innate endowment it was once supposed to be; motivation and environment have some influence on it.

Vocation. Normal vocational behavior may be viewed in different stages throughout an individual's life. Super's (1957) concept of vocational development views the individual as moving through a series of life stages, each of which is characterized by a different vocational development task that elicits various vocational behaviors. The individual's final choice is reflective of the degree of thoroughness to which he has implemented his self-concept into the world of work. It appears, then, that vocational development is synonomous with the development of the self-concept and that vocational adjustment depends on the implementation of this self-concept in an occupation.

Super's concept of career development is built on the thesis that vocational life stages reflect the individual's life tasks and conflicts. He lists five vocational life stages: (1) Growth, (2) Exploration, (3) Establishment, (4) Maintenance, (5) Decline.

During the Growth stage, from the time of birth to the age of 14, the individual's self-concept develops through identification with significant others. During ages 4 through 10, a substage of Fantasy exists, during which needs are dominant and fantasy role playing is important. During the substage of Interest, from age 11 to 12, the individual's aspirations and activities are determined by the individual's likes and dislikes. Capacity, at ages 13 and 14, is the substage during which aptitudes and abilities are considered and job requirements, including necessary training, are examined.

During the Exploration stage, from age 15 through 24, the individual selects the occupation through which he or she can implement self-concept. The person may accomplish this implementation through self-examination, role tryouts, exploratory occupational activities in school, leisure activities, and part-time employment. Most of the choices made during this period are first explored and implemented in fantasy. During ages 15 through 17, the individual is in the Tentative substage, where consideration is given to personal needs, interests, capacities, values, and available opportunities. The Transition substage, from age 18 through 21, emphasizes reality decisions made as the individual enters the labor market or educational institution in an attempt to implement his or her self-concept. When an individual has located a seemingly appropriate field and has begun a job in an attempt at what may become his life work, he is 21 to 24 years of age and is in the substage called Realistic.

The Establishment stage begins about age 25 through 30 and may include a Trial substage. It also includes a substage of Stabilization, ages 31 through 44. If, in reality, the assumed field of work is commensurate with the individual's self-concept, then the substage of Trial is not a necessity. However, if the life work is not commensurate with the individual's self-concept, the individual becomes aware that he will make one or more changes before finding his life's work or will face a work that is merely a series of unrelated jobs. The Stabilization substage is characterized by a clearly established career pattern, which the individual seeks to stabilize.

The Maintenance stage, from age 44 to 64, finds the individual with a place in the world of work, which he or she attempts to hold or maintain.

Decline, the final stage, begins theoretically at age 65 and extends until death. There are two substages: Deceleration, ages 65 through 70; and Retirement, age 70 plus. The significant variable of this final stage is that work is terminated, regardless of the specific age.

Socioeconomic Status. Socioeconomic variables (wealth, income, occupation, status, community power, group identity, level of consumption, and family background) may have some impact on the assessment of normal behavior. There appears to be an inverse relationship between socioeconomic status and mental illness (Dohrenwend and Dohrenwend, 1974). However, the reasons for this are not evident. Is the higher mental illness in lower social class exclusively an economic reality, or is it the sum of varying social conditions or status relative to other groups?

The social stress-psychopathology relationship is one that is now receiving a great deal of attention, particularly with the new degree of ecological consciousness. Critical questions have been asked about mental health and the urban environment and the impact of rapid social change (Dunham, 1976; Kasl and Hamburg, 1975). A debate has been waged in the literature as to whether individual vulnerability, assumed to be endemic and almost genetic, produces a social class high in psychopathology or whether psychopathology is a response to high social stress in a particular social class. The debate has centered on, and is in fact clouded by, the inverse relationship between social-class status and frequency of mental illness. King (1978) states that the debate is a false one. First, a historical process of social selection is being compared with a phenomenal process of social stress. Implicit in the historical process is the operation of social stress as a cause. Second, social class is governed by society's values. A society designates poverty levels and classifies certain behaviors as abnormal. Values influence not only the numbers assigned to poverty level and the definition and treatment of psychopathology but also the relationship between poverty and psychopathology. The social process influencing poverty, the meanings culturally assigned to it, and the language expressing attitudes toward the poor adjoin to produce and accentuate psychopathology.

Although research suggests an inverse relationship between mental illness and social class, it seems inappropriate to make a decisive statement regarding mental health. The social and economic advantages may make it easier to develop behaviors that lead to better mental health. Many investigators, however, are encouraging professionals to avoid stereotypes and focus on the individual (King, 1978).

Ethnic/Racial Factors. Culture is the total way of life for a group of people, primarily the shared patterns of values, beliefs, and feelings that are characterized by a distinct code of conduct and definition of reality to satisfy biological and psychological needs. The primary concern with culture and normality/psychopathology is how behavior is structured, organized, and influenced by cultural rules or the extent that culture creates conditions of vulnerability, making the advent of mental illness more likely for individuals, groups, or the whole culture.

Ethnic personality results from growing up within a particular ethnic group. Ethnic identity involves internal and external role attribution. There may be some functional and dysfunctional aspects to ethnic identity. Ethnic identity helps with the subjective sense of social belonging, but excessive ethnic identity may reduce other identifications and thereby the scope of the personality (DeVos and Romanucci-Ross, 1975).

Although there may be some ethnic or racial norms for certain behaviors, the general dimensions of the concept are appropriate. A consistent research finding has been that race alone does not account for the prevalence of mental illness. In an examination of blacks, Puerto Ricans, Jews, and Italians, Rabkin (1976) found that both income and ethnicity were significant factors.

References

Adler, A. *Social Interest: Challenge to Mankind.* New York: Putnam, 1939.

Athenaeum. December 29, 1866, p. 873.

Bardwick, J. *Psychology of Women: A Study of Bio-Cultural Conflicts.* New York: Harper & Row, 1971.

Child, C. M. *Physiological Foundations of Behavior.* New York: Holt, Rinehart and Winston, 1924.

Cohen, A. K. "The Study of Social Disorganization and Deviant Behavior." In R. Merton, L. Bloom, and L. Cottrell, Jr. (Eds.), *Sociology Today.* New York: Basic Books, 1959.

Cox, R. D. "The Concept of Psychological Maturity." In S. Arieti (Ed.), *American Handbook of Psychiatry.* Vol. 1. New York: Basic Books, 1974.

DeVos, G., and Romanucci-Ross, L. (Eds.). *Ethnic Identity.* Palo Alto, Calif.: Mayfield, 1975.

Dohrenwend, B. P., and Dohrenwend, B. S. "Social and Cultural Influences on Psychopathology." *Annual Review of Psychology,* 1974, *25,* 417-452.

Dunham, H. "Society, Culture and Mental Disorder." *Archives of General Psychiatry,* 1976, *33,* 147-156.

Encyclopedia Britannica. Vol. 5. 1876, p. 557.

Engel, G. *Psychological Development in Health and Illness.* Philadelphia: Saunders, 1962.

Erikson, E. *Childhood and Society.* New York: Norton, 1950.

Freud, S. "Analysis Terminable and Interminable" [1937]. In J. Strachey (Trans.), *Collected Papers of Sigmund Freud.* Vol. 5. New York: Basic Books, 1959.

Goldenson, R. *The Encyclopedia of Human Behavior.* Vol. 2. New York: Doubleday, 1970.

Grinker, R. R. "A Dynamic Story of the 'Homoclite.' " In J. H. Masserman (Ed.), *Science and Psychoanalysis.* Vol. 6. New York: Grune & Stratton, 1963.

Hartmann, H. "Towards a Concept of Mental Health." *Britain's Journal of Medical Psychology,* 1960, *33,* 243-248.

Havighurst, R. *Developmental Tasks and Education.* New York: Holt, Rinehart and Winston, 1951.

Herrick, C. J. *The Evolution of Human Behavior.* Austin: University of Texas Press, 1956.

Hsu, F. (Ed.). *Psychological Anthropology: Approaches to Culture and Personality.* Homewood, Ill.: Dorsey Press, 1961.

Jahoda, M. "Towards a Social Psychology of Mental Health." In M. J. E. Senn (Ed.), *Symposium on the Healthy Personality.* New York: Josiah Macy Foundation, 1950.

Jahoda, M. *Current Concepts of Positive Mental Health.* New York: Basic Books, 1958.

Jung, C. G. "Psychological Types" [1923]. In G. Adler and others (Eds.), *The Collected Works of C. G. Jung.* Princeton, N.J.: Princeton University Press, 1971.

Kasl, S., and Hamburg, E. "Mental Health and the Urban Environment: Some Doubts and Second Thoughts." *Journal of Health and Social Behavior,* 1975, *16,* 268-282.

King, L. "Social and Cultural Influences on Psychopathology." *Annual Review of Psychology,* 1978, *29,* 405-433.

Laing, R. *The Divided Self.* New York: Pantheon Books, 1969.

Maddi, S. "Ethics and Psychotherapy." *Counseling Psychologist,* 1973, *4*(2), 78-96.

Maslow, A., and Mittelman, B. *Principles of Abnormal Psychology.* New York: Harper & Row, 1951.

Merton, R. *Social Theory and Social Structure.* New York: Free Press, 1949.

Mussen, P., and Rutherford, E. "Parent-Child Relations and Parental Personality in Relation to Young Children's Sex-Role Preferences." *Child Development,* 1963, *34*(3), 589-607.

Offer, D., and Sabshin, M. *Normality: Theoretical and Clinical Concepts of Mental Health.* New York: Basic Books, 1974.

Parsons, T. "Definitions of Health and Illness in the Light of American Values and Social Structure." In E. Gartley Jaco (Ed.), *Patients, Physicians and Illness.* New York: Free Press, 1958.

Parsons, T. "An Approach to Psychological Theory in Terms of the Theory of Action." In S. Koch (Ed.), *Psychology: A Study of Science.* Vol. 3. New York: McGraw-Hill, 1959.

Rabkin, J. G., and Struening, E. L. *Ethnicity, Social Class, and Mental Illness.* New York: Institute on Pluralism and Group Identity, 1976.

Rank, O. *The Artist and Other Contributions to the Psychoanalysis of Poetical Creation.* Leipzig: Internationaler Psychoanalytischer Verlag, 1925.

Rogers, C. "A Theory of Therapy, Personality, and Interpersonal Relationships as Developed in the Client-Centered Framework." In S. Koch (Ed.), *Psychology: A Study of Science.* New York: McGraw-Hill, 1963.

Scheff, T. *Labeling Madness.* Englewood Cliffs, N.J.: Prentice-Hall, 1975.

Smith, M. B. "Optima of Mental Health: A General Frame of Reference." *Psychiatry,* 1950, *13,* 503-510.

Smith, M. B. *Social Psychology and Human Values: Selected Essays.* Chicago: Aldine, 1969.

Smith, M. B. *Humanizing Social Psychology.* San Francisco: Jossey-Bass, 1974.

Super, D. E. *The Psychology of Careers.* New York: Harper & Row, 1957.

Szasz, T. "The Myth of Mental Illness." *American Psychologist,* 1960, *15*(2), 113-118.

Vernoff, J. "Social Comparison and the Development of Achievement Motivation." In C. Smith (Ed.), *Achievement Related Motives in Children.* New York: Russell Sage Foundation, 1969.

Wallace, A. F. C. "Mental Illness, Biology and Culture." In F. Hsu (Ed.), *Psychological Anthropology: Approaches to Culture and Personality.* Homewood, Ill.: Dorsey Press, 1961.

White, R. *The Abnormal Personality.* New York: Ronald Press, 1964.

White, R. "The Concept of Healthy Personality: What Do We Really Mean?" *Counseling Psychologist,* 1973, *4* (2), 1-17.

4

Luciano L'Abate
Marilyn E. Goodrich

Marital Adjustment

Marital adjustment (MA) is an umbrella term that covers positive and negative aspects defying diagnostic pigeonholing and systematic classification. Its assessment is by no means adequate due to a host of theoretical and practical problems to be reviewed. In this context, MA reflects how good and how functional the relationship between spouses is.

The division between researchers and clinicians has retarded systematic efforts at assessment. The former are interested mostly in normative aspects of MA, and the latter are mostly interested in application to deviant or negative instances of MA. Critical to an assessment of MA is the normal-abnormal distinction. Many assessment tools are based on evaluations of samples which are biased in unexpected directions. Are couples who ask for help "really" maladjusted? Is asking for help a criterion for maladjustment? Some clinicians would argue that asking for help is a sign of strength and that the most troublesome marriages do not come to the attention of clinicians. Criteria suffer by the use of referral as a measure of dysfunction.

This chapter concentrates on research since Burr's (1973) and Udry's excellent surveys (1974), with a few references to crucial studies since the beginning of this decade. Previous research has been reviewed by Barry (1970) and Hicks and Platt (1970). References to prior studies will be made if and when they are relevant to a historical understanding of recent studies. For reasons of imposed brevity, this review is highly selective and highly schematic. With notable exceptions, it must be kept in mind that normative aspects of MA have been in the hands of sociologists (Burr, 1973; Hicks and Platt, 1970; Udry, 1974), while MA of deviant couples has usually been the province of psychologists and mental health specialists. A few brave souls, such as Murstein (1976) and Centers (1975), have crossed the line. Since the work of Veroff and Feld (1970), it is clear that the marital relationship has come more and more under the scrutiny of psychologists (L'Abate, 1976).

Background and Current Status

Since the early attempts of Hamilton (1929), Bernard (1964), Burgess and Cottrell (1939), and Terman (1938) at an operational definition of marital success and failure, marriage has become more and more a subject of study for psychologists and mental health workers, to the point that a veritable technology to evaluate and improve marriage has developed (Guerney, 1977; L'Abate and L'Abate, 1977). Hand in hand with this technology, theory has developed to the point of increasing testability and practical applications (L'Abate, 1976; Lantz and Snyder, 1969; Murstein, 1974, 1976; Toman, 1976).

As the foregoing references (and they by no means include all of the literature to be cited) attest, the study of MA is progressing rapidly because of a variety of political, economic, and ideological developments, especially in the mental health field (Blood and Wolfe, 1960). Among these developments, acknowledgment should be given to (1) disenchantment with expensive, long-term individual psychotherapy; (2) realization that MA through the life cycle does not occur in a vacuum; and (3) a need for a more ecological, transactional view of behavior with a detailed appreciation for its most pervasive intimate human relationship: marriage.

Marital adjustment is an area in and of itself as defined by the term, but it also includes a variety of other dimensions that may range from a positive connotation (happiness, for example) to a negative one (conflict).

Marital Adjustment (MA). Bernard's (1964) review laid the foundations for evaluating the permanence of a marital relationship—that is, (1) how well it meets the needs and expectations of society; (2) its performance and endurance; (3) degree of unity, agreement, or consensus between mates; (4) degree to which it facilitates personality development; (5) degree of satisfaction or happiness. Problems in defining happiness were noted. Lantz and Snyder (1969) list six major factors to be considered in MA: (1) personality characteristics, (2) cultural backgrounds, (3) social participation, (4) economic status, (5) response patterns, and (6) sexual factors. Barry's (1970) review indicates that the husband is the major determinant of MA, against the popular belief that both partners are responsible.

Since the early measurement of MA by Locke (1951), his Marital Adjustment Inventory (MAI) is by now the most frequently used and validated of marital adjustment tests (Locke and Williamson, 1958; Kimmel and Van der Veen, 1974). Dhillon, Ganguli, and Basu (1975) also constructed a new measure of marital adjustment of promising reliability.

Udry (1974), in his comprehensive review of MA, recommends Orden and Bradburn's (1968) MA Balance Scale as a simpler and perhaps more accurate measure of MA than the Locke-Wallace scale. He also includes a revision of this scale with weighted scores. The reader is referred to this source as a basic reading in MA.

Spanier (1976) reviews most of the published measures of MA and related concepts, plus a Dyadic Adjustment Scale of considerable potential for clinical assessment. This is a highly recommended report for the interested researcher and clinician. Guerney (1977) and Murstein (1976) report a variety of tests and questionnaires to use in premarital and marital research. Cromwell, Olson, and Fournier (1976) review most of the available clinical instruments to assess MA and include a classification system for self-report methods, intrapersonal and interpersonal measures, and observational methods. This also is an important review for researchers or clinicians interested in evaluating interventional outcomes.

Communication and Conflict. Olson and Ryder (1970) contribute an inventory of marital conflicts based on experimental interaction. Raush and his associates (1974) investigated the interactions of newlywed couples through the use of role-playing improvisations designed to magnify differences. Interactions fell within six categories of initiation and response: thinking through, resolving, reconciling, appealing, rejecting, and coercing. With the help of quantitative informational analysis, they explored the effects of various factors on the foregoing modes of interaction: (1) orientation toward marriage; (2) sex differences; (3) issue-oriented versus relationship-oriented conflict; (4) stages of marriage; (5) nature of constructive and destructive conflict; and (6) reciprocity and the couple's concept of marriage as a unitary system. The see-saw of polarization (hawks and doves) and role reversal in marriage were also documented. Another innovative and crucial study is the work of Gottman, Markman, and Notarius (1977); they used a problem inventory and a coding of videotapes of marital interactions with distressed and nondistressed couples. They studied content, affect, and contextual differences, using a sequential analysis of metacommunication, expression of feelings, summarizing self versus other, feeling problems, nonverbal behavior during message delivery, and positive and negative reciprocity. Their results do not lend support to most behavioral or communicational models.

Another important contribution in this area is that of Thomas (1977), who provides a detailed code of verbal categories and a Verbal Problem Checklist, complete with a step-by-step approach for the amelioration of communication and decision making. Glick and Gross (1975) evaluate critically two major research strategies (questionnaires and simulation games) to assess marital communication and conflict. They suggest several methodological guidelines for future research.

Marital Happiness (MH). In Terman's (1938) view, the most predictive items of MH are (1) superior MH of parents, (2) childhood happiness, (3) lack of conflict with father and mother, (4) firm home discipline without undue harshness, (5) strong attachment to mother and father, (6) parental frankness about sex, (7) infrequent and mild childhood punishment, and (8) positive premarital attitude toward sex. It is difficult to separate what Hicks and Platt (1970) call instrumental affectiveness and temporal life-cycle variables from happiness and stability. They support Barry's (1970) findings concerning the crucial role of the husband. They also suggest that the concept of happiness and overreliance on "self-report measures" be discarded altogether, considering that many low-happiness marriages are stable. In their review, they note new instruments to assess this variable, instruments developed since Nye and MacDougall's (1959) early Marital Happiness Questionnaire. More recently, Howard and Dawes (1976) have argued that MH can be predicted on the basis of a simple linear model. They had twenty-seven married couples monitor their rates of sexual intercourse and arguments on a daily basis for thirty-five consecutive days, using a seven-point scale ranging from "very happy" to "perfectly happy," with a central midpoint. Rate of sexual intercourse minus the rate of arguments was highly predictive of self-ratings of MH. Azrin, Naster, and Jones (1973) developed a self-rating scale of MH on ten areas of marriage on a ten-point scale ranging from happy to unhappy. As Jacobson and Martin (1976) comment, they failed to show this scale's validity and reliability. This scale, however, has been found useful in assessment of marital change after enrichment by L'Abate (1977a).

Intimacy. The issue of intimacy in marriage is crucial, since this term can be as vague and ill defined as many of the terms used to describe or define marital interactions. Most marital conflicts are conceptualized according to a love-hate dichotomy (Bach and Wyden, 1969; Mace, 1976) that fails to deal with underlying feelings of hurt and fear of being hurt (L'Abate, 1977b). Using videotapes of three conflict-resolution models (anger à la Bach and Wyden, cool rational à la Ellis, and hurt à la L'Abate), Frey, Holley, and L'Abate (1979) were able to test the differential outcomes of these models with eleven couples as their own controls. Most couples liked the cool, calm, and collected model to solve problems, but sharing of hurt feelings was considered the most preferred model of conflict resolution to reach intimacy. (Conflict resolution and intimacy are not synonymous.)

Power and Decision Making. Safilios-Rothschild (1971), in her review, presents the multidimensionality of this concept and the need to evaluate individually its various aspects. Power, especially in marriage and the family, is a very slick and slippery concept to define. Rollins and Bahr (1976) differentiate it from control attempt, control, resources, and authority. They develop a theory specifying relationships among these five variables. The theory assumes that (1) power and control are social interaction constructs rather than attributes of individuals; (2) power and control are relevant constructs only when a conflict exists between the goals of marriage partners; and (3) authority, resources, and power do not exist independently of perceptions. Levin (1976) distinguishes between (1) rule-setting decisions that determine marital life style (orchestration) and (2) frequent administrative decisions necessary for ongoing routines (instrumentation). A self-report inventory, designed to describe decision-making processes, subjective perceptions of power, levels of marital satisfaction, and a comparative ratio of SES, substantiated resource theory (Blood and Wolfe, 1960). The spouse who had a greater ratio of resources had greater authority to orchestrate and to relegate instrumental decisions to the other spouse. The greatest degree of satisfaction was achieved when both types of decisions were made by both partners.

Marital Satisfaction (MS). Burr (1973) presents a variety of theoretical propositions about MS, relating it to (1) role discrepancies, (2) number of satisfactions and tensions (they are unrelated to each other), (3) compensations, (4) sentiments, (5) rewards and profits, (6) amount of interaction, (7) altruism and empathy, and (8) balance in the relationship. He differentiates MS from stability as dealing with two completely different variables, one subjective, the other objective.

This construct has been the subject of a great many studies concerned with its fluctuations along the life cycle. Miller (1976) used path analysis to test a theoretical model made up of seven antecedents of MS: (1) amount of anticipatory socialization, (2) ease of family role transitions, (3) length of marriage, (4) number of children, (5) amount of companionship, (6) family SES, and (7) child spacing. His subjects were 140 urban and suburban married individuals. Reported ease of most recent familial role transition and frequency of companionate activities had positive and direct effects on MS. Amount of companionship was inversely affected by number of children and positively influenced by social status. Developmental factors, such as length of marriage and stage of the family life cycle, were theoretically and empirically linked to MS through the number of children and frequency of companionate activities. Child spacing was affected by length of marriage and number of children but had no significant consequences for the model. Lee (1977) found a small positive association between age at marriage and MS as well as several indicators of spouse's marital role performance.

Self-Concept. Luckey (1964) found that satisfaction in marriage was related to the congruence of the husband's self-concept and that held of him by his wife. When husband and wife agreed that he was as he wanted to be (this tended to be like his father) and as she wanted him to be (this tended to be like her father), both were happier. Rathus and Siegel (1976) discuss the reliability and validity of a ten-item semantic differential self-concept scale. Unfortunately, this measure was validated on 165 males alone and not on couples. Kawash and Scherf (1975) administered the Marlowe-Crowne Social Desirability Scale, the Self-Esteem Inventory, and Rotter's Locus of Control Scale to 85 pairs of parents of university students. They found profound sex differences in homogeneity of self-perceptions, with females more homogeneous than males, and a significant correlation between social desirability and self-esteem scores. Askham (1976) emphasizes that intimate people seek to develop and maintain senses of personal identity and of stability, which may be in potential conflict with each other. This conflict can be resolved in a variety of ways, depending on the level of differentiation of the individual (L'Abate, 1976).

Stability. Marital stability may be defined generally as nondivorce. Lenthall (1977) distinguishes among three forms of stability: (1) normal marital satisfaction with its inevitable peaks and valleys; (2) enduring dissatisfaction; and (3) that combination of marital dissatisfaction and instability that leads to separation and divorce. This area involves a whole new line of research. Very little attention has been given to the low-happiness high-stability marriage. It is here that the "why" and "how" of MA become critical. Why do couples continue to live in a state of marital unhappiness? How do they go about living together interpersonally? It is also at this juncture that the simple correlational studies become almost useless. A more complex, dynamic approach is needed to explain the mix of two personalities in the intimacies of the marital relationship. What makes marriage stick? And what breaks it apart?

Levinger (1976) views marital cohesiveness as a special instance of group cohesiveness in general. The strength of the marital relationship is a direct function of the attractions within and barriers around the marriage, and an inverse function of such attractions to and barriers from other relationships. Pair cohesiveness describes the sum of the attractions and barriers inside a relationship minus the net attractions to and barriers around the most salient outside alternative. Attractions that help to cement a marriage derive from the partners' mutual need satisfaction—the needs for (1) physical subsistence and safety; (2) psychological security, love, and respect; and (3) self-actualization or fulfillment. Barriers against breakup can be coordinated to the partners' personal feelings of obligation—to each other, their children, and other members of their social network or to abstract moral values—and to normative pressures from external sources. Alternative attractions derive from competing sources of need satisfaction. A summary of the factors differentiating cohesion (stability) in marriage is as follows: (1) *Attractions:* material rewards (family income and home ownership); symbolic rewards (educational status, occupational status, social similarity); affectional rewards (companionship and esteem, sexual enjoyment); (2) *Barriers:* material costs (financial expenses); symbolic costs (obligation toward marital bond, religious constraints, pressures from primary groups, pressures from the community); affectional costs (feeling toward dependent children); (3) *Alternative Attractions:* material rewards (wife's independent social and economic status); symbolic rewards (independence and self-actualization); affectional rewards (preferred alternate sex partner, disjunctive kin affiliations). While Levinger admits that his conceptual framework is too simple to account for all the complexities, it does offer a way of translating the effects of external events, pressures, or shocks into psychological forces experienced in the marital dyad. The factors mentioned above should be seen as varying over time and social context.

Status. In the sociological literature, the term *status* has been related to various parameters of health and sickness (O'Gorman, 1977). Warheit and associates (1976), for instance, question the relationship between psychopathology and mental illness, especially in females. When demographic and marital-status factors are controlled (through multiple regressions), SES becomes the strongest predictor of mental illness in females. A great deal of stress in marriage seems related to status inequality between men and women (Glenn, Hoppe, and Weiner, 1974).

Critical Discussion

General Areas of Concern

The questionnaire remains the most frequent tool of assessment of MA and related terms, followed closely by ad hoc questionnaires and traditional tests, like the old standby Locke-Wallace MAI and a host of new-vintage tests that do not begin to possess the standards of validity and reliability achieved by the old standbys, due to the sheer frequency of studies using them and length of time since publication (Cromwell, Olson, and Fournier, 1976; Spanier, 1976).

The problem of definition looms large in the various meanings attributed to MA. It is not rare to find different terms, such as adjustment and happiness, measured by the same instrument. Most instruments are used as criteria and taken at their face value. The validity of most reliable instruments thus far used remains limited, if not questionable. By what criteria shall MA be evaluated? Stability? Permanence? Using either criterion, one would encompass some of the best as well as some of the worst marriages. What is the relationship of test instruments to theory? What theory shall one use to consider MA?

The most critical issues in this area are the following: (1) Theory is not adequately linked to test instruments or experimental tests. (2) Most normative research is done by sociologists, who seldom interview or question couples; hence, little is known about normative, interactive patterns in couples. (3) As a borderline area between mental health disciplines (psychiatry, clinical psychology, and social work) and sociology, marriage is interdisciplinary in nature; but research in the applied area, except for couples diagnosed on the basis of symptoms of one spouse, remains lagging. (4) Relationships among evaluation, intervention, and follow-up should be examined more fully (What can be learned about MA from intervention research?). (5) Textbook knowledge and primary data must be kept up to date. (6) Psychologists lack substantive knowledge about marriage (Where are the courses?). (7) We need to learn more about specificity of intervention; that is, which marriage dysfunction improves the most by which method at what cost? (8) The relationship between personality and marital adjustment is unknown (How is personality dysfunction related to marital dysfunction?).

Comparative Philosophies and Theories

Among the theoretical perspectives that can shed some light on MA, five may be identified: (1) classical psychoanalytic (Dicks, 1967); (2) psychoanalytic Adlerian; (3) behavioral and subgroups (reciprocity, social learning, reinforcement); (4) social exchange, equity, and balance theories; and (5) systems. The one with specific evidence to its credit is Adlerian theory (Toman, 1976). Weller, Nathan, and Hazi (1974), using the Nye and MacDougall (1959) scale, obtained reports of MH from 258 women in Israel. Birth order and report of marital bliss were significantly related, according to these rankings: (1) first-born husband, later-born wife; (2) later-born husband, first-born wife; (3) middle-born husband, middle-born wife; (4) only-child husband, first-born wife; (5) first-born husband, first-born wife; (6) later-born husband, later-born wife; and (7) only-child husband, only-child wife. Unfortunately, husbands were not used in these ratings.

Behavioral and exchange theories and their offshoots are clearly used in most interventional applications (Azrin, Naster, and Jones, 1973; Jacobson and Martin, 1976). L'Abate (1976) describes marriage according to an information systems viewpoint related to intrafamilial priorities. He and his coworkers (L'Abate, 1977a) have developed various instruments to test the theory, including a Marital Questionnaire designed to test specific postulates and derivations of the theory.

Elaboration on Critical Points

The major issue to consider in MA is the role of personality factors (Centers, 1975; Murstein, 1976). To what extent is MA a function of these and other situational factors? How can one separate demographic factors—that is, reference or ethnic group membership—from personality characteristics? A beginning stab in this direction has been made by L'Abate (1976), who postulates a dialectic continuum of personality differentiation according to degrees of likeness (symbiosis, sameness, similarity, differentness, oppositeness, and autism) that seem relevant to self-definition, mate selection, and MA. By definition, an individual in the middle of the continuum would not select someone toward the extreme ends. Marriages between differentiated individuals (in the middle of this continuum) have the greatest chance of turning out positively. Marriages between less differentiated individuals (sameness-oppositeness) are troublesome and may not last. Marriages between extremely undifferentiated individuals (symbiosis-autism) would probably be stable (misery loves company). Empirical testing of some propositions derived from this postulate is now in progress.

Personal Views and Recommendations

It is difficult to separate from any of the foregoing points what is objective and what are the investigators' personal views. As the most intense and prolonged intimate relationship, marriage remains the testing ground for personal confrontation (L'Abate and L'Abate, 1977). As a natural context for personality definition, it makes a great deal of research and study on personality in a *vacuum* irrelevant (Dunne and L'Abate, 1978). No wonder that the predictive validity of most personality tests and inventories is so limited. People have been asked to evaluate themselves in an artificial vacuum. Most of the test instruments (including the most popular ones like 16 PF and MMPI) do not begin to deal with relevant issues of self-definition in marriage. A man may define himself as a "good" husband. However, the best judge of this definition may be his wife. Similarly, he may be a better judge of his wife as a wife than she is of herself. Interviewing and evaluating individuals separately from their spouses is as artificial and irrelevant a practice as any propagated by traditional mental health ideology. The artificiality and irrelevance in clinical practice are perpetuated when individuals are seen alone, separately from their everyday relationships. It may not be unethical, but it is wasteful.

Another critical issue that makes for difficult progress in this area is the single-shot or at most double-barreled approach; that is, only one or two instruments are used, with little attention to issues of concurrent validity. This area is ripe for a multitrait, multimethod battery approach (L'Abate, 1977a), which would more realistically fit into the multidimensional nature of this variable.

There are three major classes of issues in the area of clinical assessment of MA and related terms: (1) Who should evaluate among professionals and by what criteria? (2) How should evaluation take place and for what purposes (that is, who should be the recipient of results: clients or professionals or both)? (3) What are the minimal standards for responsible assessment? To answer the last question, nine separate areas may be outlined: (1) responsibility, (2) competence, (3) moral and legal standards, (4) public statements, (5) confidentiality, (6) welfare of consumers, (7) professional relationships, (8) research activities, and (9) utilization of assessment techniques (an elaboration of these points is available from the authors).

By now, MA is a sufficiently substantive field to justify specialization at the graduate level. Unfortunately, most substantive training on the nature of marriage takes place in home economics and sociology, while most clinical applications take place in mental health settings. Consequently, scholars and researchers are left to learn about marriage indirectly, without the benefit of direct, clinical closeness and involvement. At the same time, clinicians who work with couples lack the substantive knowledge about marriage possessed by their more scholarly counterparts. A great many marriage counselors and therapists have become so as a result of trial and error and self-chosen training rather than by design and plan. Eventually, there may be a subspecialty of marital professionals who will be able to operate as researchers, scholars, and clinicians.

Application to Particular Variables

Age. The study of the relationship between age and adjustment has been approached from two perspectives: (1) life cycle and (2) age as a demographic variable. There is a change in the various measures of MS over the life cycle (Udry, 1974), with the least satisfaction during the childrearing years. Age at marriage is positively correlated with satisfaction and stability (DeLissovoy, 1973; Lee, 1977). Explanations for these findings have been sought within social and psychological contexts. Campbell (1977), in reporting the most comprehensive and latest study of marital satisfaction in the life cycle (with a review of previous studies), found that his indications of well-being could be considered measures of personality. Maas and Kuypers (1974), in a forty-year longitudinal study of married men and women, found a random pattern in the relationship between personality and life style. Continuities in personality (from early adulthood to old age) were evident—more so among the mothers than the fathers. Their data argue against the idea that old age in itself produces psychological decline. Lowenthal, Thurnher, and Chiriboga (1975), in examining adaptation during four critical stages of adulthood, found that differences between the sexes were far more significant than differences between the oldest and youngest of either sex viewed separately. Marital dissatisfaction was greatest among middle-aged women, but sex of the individual rather than his or her stage of life accounted for most of the variation within their sample.

DeLissovoy (1973) found that, for thirty-seven couples married in high school, variables associated with high risk of failure were premarital pregnancy, school dropout, low SES, husband and wife under 18 years of age, limited dating experience, and lack of adequate income. Kin network of economic and psychological support and church activities were identified as marriage-sustaining forces.

Sex. When sex is considered, it is evaluated directly in terms of sex differences in relation to MA and indirectly in terms of how the sexes differ in constructs (such as power, roles, or communication) correlated with MA. Udry (1974) concludes that wives more than husbands determine MA. He cites the findings of an eighteen-year longitudinal study of married couples, in which happy marriages were characterized by constancy in the husband's personality and great change in the wife's whereas unhappy marriages were noted for a great change in the husband and little change in the wife's personality. MH was thus related to the wife's ability to adapt and change to the marital relationship.

Marital status (married, single, divorced, widowed) itself (Campbell, 1977) and individual global happiness have been related in the sense that the married have been found to be happier than the unmarried. However, MH has been differentially related to sex. Married men had previously been found to be happier than married women in global happiness. Glenn (1975), however, from recent national survey data, found that husbands and wives had similar levels of reported MH but that there was a stronger relationship between MH and global happiness for the wives. In reconciling these findings with previous data showing an unusual prevalence of psychological stress among women, Glenn concludes that women exceed men in both the stress and the satisfaction they derive from marriage.

Social and psychological reasons for these sex differences have been explored. Balswick and Avertt (1977), noting that females are sex-role stereotyped as being more expressive than males, attempted to relate the differences to two variables: perceived parental expressiveness and interpersonal orientation. They found instead that females were more expressive of love, happiness, and sadness than males. The findings of Burke, Weir, and Harrison (1976) suggest that disclosure acts as an intervening variable between sex and MA. In their study of 189 husband-wife pairs, they found that wives disclosed significantly more often than husbands. Husbands and wives who were more likely to disclose to their spouse reported greater marital and life satisfaction.

Education. A consistent relationship has been shown between educational level and marital success; the higher the level of education, the lower the probability of divorce and the higher the probability of good marital adjustment (Udry, 1974). The relationship between education and MA, however, is far from clear, since educational attainment relates to a number of variables, which in themselves affect MA. Educational attainment is correlated with such variables as age at marriage and economic success, and it may possibly be related to personality and intellectual characteristics in that the ceasing or continuing of education may be a function of motivation and ability. Udry (1974) found that (1) the wife's educational level was not significantly related to marital stability but the husband's education was, when the wife's age at marriage was controlled; and (2) it was the husband's income rather than education that contributed to marital stability. Education did seem to make a difference, however, in whether unhappy marriage ended in divorce; less educated men and women tended to remain in unhappy marriages, while college-educated individuals tended to divorce if their marriages were unhappy. Similarity of educational level of both spouses is of modest importance in MS, but differences in education are associated with marital instability only when the wife is college educated and the husband is not. For women, educational level does seem to act as an intervening variable in transgenerational marital instability. Mueller and Pope (1977), from a national sample of women in the United States, obtained support for the conclusion that the repetitive effect of parent marital instability on the child's subsequent instability is greatest in early and limited-education marriages.

Socioeconomic Factors. The lower the social class, the less stable the marriage and generally the lower the MA (Udry, 1974). While the social and economic climate of lower-class life may not be conducive to marital happiness, paradoxically this very climate may make it more difficult than in the upper classes to dissolve marriages. Cross-class marriage in and of itself has not been found to be an important determiner of marital stress. The variable of primary importance in relation to MA is the husband's income. The lower the husband's income, the more unstable and maladjusted the marriage is likely to be. Accordingly, women whose marriages represent downward mobility are more likely to have unstable marriages than women whose marriages have resulted in upward mobility for them. Different social classes may represent quite different normative contexts, both in terms of resources and values, and these differences need to be considered in evaluating MA (Lorion, 1973).

Vocation. Until recent years, the focus in evaluating the relationship between vocation and MA would typically have been on the husband. Changing patterns of employment, however, with women representing approximately 52 percent of the work force in the United States, have made the working wife a norm rather than a rarity and have created new expectations, roles, and issues in the marital relationship. Rapoport and Rapoport (1977) give in-depth reports of five representative dual-career families; discuss the integration of personal, family, and work worlds; and describe five sets of dilemmas that affect MA: overload, norms, identity, social network, and role cycling. The authors also note that gratification came to these couples from mastery of these dilemmas, along with concomitant gains. Effects of employment status on MA is a complex issue, particularly in view of the changing norms in regard to who works in the marriage and in what capacity.

Ethnic-Racial Factors. Little is known about differences in marital adjustment among ethnic and racial groups. Interracial marriage has received attention, but it is difficult to assess outcome data because of the rarity of the event. According to Udry (1974), no major MA study has included interracial marriages. From what is known, he concludes that "No evidence indicates that interracial marriages are less stable than marriages in which both partners are of the same race" (p. 255).

Physical Disorders. The relationship between physical health and measures of MA has not been widely researched, but an association has been established. Pratt (1972) found that level of health and health-related behavior was higher in couples characterized by shared power, flexible division of tasks, and high level of companionship than in marriages characterized by unequal power, rigid sex-role differentiation, and low companionship level. When physical disability does occur, marriages can be greatly stressed, and whether marriages do adjust depends on many factors.

Intellectual Disorders. The effect of intellectual level on MA is a rarely researched area, and little is known. The assessment of MA in the intellectually handicapped presents unique difficulties in that they would be less likely to marry than others and the modality of assessment would more likely be based on researcher observation and anecdote than on instruments. Neutens' (1974) instrument for appraising maritally related attitudes of educable mentally handicapped teenage students may be of aid to other researchers interested in the MA of this population.

Psychiatric Disorders. The review of psychopathology in married couples by Crago (1972) offers a good introduction to this frequently researched area. She found that married couples as a group had a lower incidence of mental disorder, but when there was mental disorder within a marriage, both parties were likely to show disturbance. This finding may have been due to assortive mating or to marital interaction; her review of the literature offers evidence for both effects.

In relation to psychiatric patients with organic syndromes, the manic-depressive is perhaps the most likely to be in the marriage market after the disorder becomes manifest. Greene, Lee, and Lustig (1975) give a general overview of the treatment of marital disharmony where one spouse has a primary affective disorder. This article is helpful in that system theories of primary affective disorders are reviewed and suggestions for family therapists are presented. In relation to functional factors, Marshall and Neill (1977) found marked conflict and disruption in the marriages of twelve patients following intestinal bypass surgery for extreme obesity. Steinglass, Davis, and Berenson (1977) utilized clinical observation to develop an interactional model of alcoholism in families, based on general systems concepts. Feldman (1976) presents a theoretical exposition (covering systems, cognitive schema, and social initiation and reinforcement) of the relationship between depression and marital interaction. Bergner (1977) describes the marital system of the hysterical individual.

Collective/Interactional Factors. Terms used in describing pathological interaction run a broad gamut, but generally they fall into two categories: (1) *communication theories,* which focus on discrepancies between verbal statements and behavior; and (2) *role theories,* which suggest that marital conflicts arise when husband and wife come from families with different communication codes. Reciprocity of roles is necessary in maintaining equilibrium and stability, and breakdown of reciprocity leads to stress and concomitant symptomatology (Crago, 1972). Marital-role typologies include equalitarian, complementary, parallel, and symmetrical. Murphy and Mendelson (1973) provide evidence that faulty communication and marital maladjustment are related.

References

Askham, J. "Identity and Stability Within the Marriage Relationship." *Journal of Marriage and the Family,* 1976, *38,* 535-547.

Azrin, N. H., Naster, B. J., and Jones, R. "Reciprocity Counseling: A Rapid Learning-Based Procedure for Marital Counseling." *Behaviour Research and Therapy,* 1973, *11,* 365-382.

Bach, G., and Wyden, P. *The Intimate Enemy.* New York: Morrow, 1969.

Balswick, J., and Avertt, C. P. "Differences in Expressiveness: Gender, Interpersonal Orientation, and Perceived Parental Expressiveness as Contributing Factors." *Journal of Marriage and the Family,* 1977, *39,* 121-127.

Barry, W. A. "Marriage Research and Conflict: An Integrated Review." *Psychological Bulletin,* 1970, *73,* 41-54.

Bergner, R. M. "The Marital System of the Hysterical Individual." *Family Process,* 1977, *16,* 85-95.

Bernard, J. "The Adjustment of Married Mates." In H. T. Christensen (Ed.), *Handbook of Marriage and the Family.* Chicago: Rand McNally, 1964.

Blood, R. O., Jr., and Wolfe, D. M. *Husbands and Wives: The Dynamics of Married Living.* New York: Free Press, 1960.

Burgess, E. W., and Cottrell, L. S., Jr. *Predicting Success or Failure in Marriage.* Englewood Cliffs, N.J.: Prentice-Hall, 1939.

Burke, R. J., Weir, T., and Harrison, D. "Disclosure of Problems and Tensions Experienced by Marital Partners." *Psychological Reports,* 1976, *38,* 531-542.

Burr, W. R. *Theory Construction and the Sociology of the Family.* New York: Wiley, 1973.

Campbell, A. "Subjective Measures of Well-Being." In G. W. Albee and J. M. Joffe (Eds.), *Primary Prevention of Psychopathology.* Vol. 1: *The Issues.* Hanover, N.H.: University Press of New England, 1977.

Centers, R. *Sexual Attraction and Love: An Instrumental Theory.* Springfield, Ill.: Thomas, 1975.

Crago, M. A. "Psychopathology in Married Couples." *Psychological Bulletin,* 1972, *77,* 114-128.

Cromwell, R. E., Olson, D. H. L., and Fournier, D. G. "Tools and Techniques for Diagnosis and Evaluation in Marital and Family Therapy." *Family Process,* 1976, *15,* 1-49.

DeLissovoy, V. D. "High School Marriages: A Longitudinal Study." *Journal of Marriage and the Family,* 1973, *35,* 245-255.

Dhillon, P. K., Ganguli, H. C., and Basu, C. K. "Construction and Standardization of Two Scales of Marital Adjustment and Attitude Towards Family Planning." *Indian Journal of Psychology,* 1975, *50,* 25-32.

Dicks, H. V. *Marital Tensions.* New York: Basic Books, 1967.

Dunne, E. E., and L'Abate, L. "The Family Taboo in Psychology Textbooks." In *Teaching of Psychology,* 1978, *5,* 115-117.

Feldman, L. B. "Depression and Marital Interaction." *Family Process,* 1976, *15,* 389-395.

Frey, J., Holley, J., and L'Abate, L. "Intimacy Is Sharing Hurt Feelings: A Comparison of Three Conflict Resolution Models." *Journal of Marriage and Family Counseling,* 1979, *6,* 35-41.

Glenn, N. D. "The Contribution of Marriage to the Psychological Well-Being of Males and Females." *Journal of Marriage and the Family,* 1975, *37,* 594-600.

Glenn, N. D., Hoppe, S. K., and Weiner, D. "Social Class Heterogamy and Marital Success: A Study of the Empirical Adequacy of a Textbook Generalization." *Social Problems,* 1974, *22,* 539-550.

Glick, B. R., and Gross, S. J. "Marital Interaction and Marital Conflict: A Critical Evaluation of Current Research Strategies." *Journal of Marriage and the Family,* 1975, *37,* 505-512.

Gottman, J., Markman, H., and Notarius, C. "The Typography of Marital Conflict: A Sequential Analysis of Verbal and Nonverbal Behavior." *Journal of Marriage and the Family,* 1977, *39,* 461-477.

Greene, B. L., Lee, R. R., and Lustig, N. "Treatment of Marital Disharmony Where One Spouse has a Primary Affective Disorder (Manic Depressive Illness). I: General Overview—100 Couples." *Journal of Marriage and Family Counseling,* 1975, *1,* 39-50.

Guerney, B. G., Jr. *Relationship Enhancement: Skill-Training Programs for Therapy, Problem Prevention, and Enrichment.* San Francisco: Jossey-Bass, 1977.

Hamilton, G. V. *A Research in Marriage.* New York: A. and C. Bom, 1929.

Hicks, M. W., and Platt, M. "Marital Happiness and Stability: A Review of the Research in the Sixties." *Journal of Marriage and the Family,* 1970, *32,* 553-573.

Howard, J. W., and Dawes, R. M. "Linear Prediction of Marital Happiness." *Personality and Social Psychology Bulletin,* 1976, *2,* 478-480.

Jacobson, N. S., and Martin, B. "Behavioral Marriage Therapy: Current Status." *Psychological Bulletin,* 1976, *83,* 540-556.

Kawash, G. F., and Scherf, G. W. "Self-Esteem, Locus of Control, and Approval Motivation in Married Couples." *Journal of Clinical Psychology,* 1975, *31,* 715-720.

Kimmel, D., and Van der Veen, F. "Factors of Marital Adjustment in Locke's Marital Adjustment Test." *Journal of Marriage and the Family,* 1974, *36,* 57-63.

L'Abate, L. *Understanding and Helping the Individual in the Family.* New York: Grune and Stratton, 1976.

L'Abate, L. *Enrichment: Programmed Interventions with Couples, Families, and Groups.* Washington, D.C.: University Press of America, 1977a.

L'Abate, L. "Intimacy Is Sharing Hurt Feelings: A Reply to David Mace." *Journal of Marriage and Family Counseling*, 1977b, *3*, 13-16.

L'Abate, L., and L'Abate, B. L. *How to Avoid Divorce: Help for Troubled Marriages.* Atlanta, Ga.: John Knox Press, 1977.

Lantz, H. R., and Snyder, E. C. *Marriage: An Examination of the Man-Woman Relationship.* New York: Wiley, 1969.

Lee, G. R. "Age at Marriage and Marital Satisfaction: A Multivariate Analysis with Implications for Marital Stability." *Journal of Marriage and the Family*, 1977, *39*, 493-504.

Lenthall, G. "Marital Satisfaction and Marital Stability." *Journal of Marriage and Family Counseling*, 1977, *3*, 25-32.

Levin, E. L. "The Marital Power Structure." Unpublished doctoral dissertation, Georgia State University, 1976.

Levinger, G. "A Social Psychological Perspective on Marital Dissolution." *Journal of Social Issues*, 1976, *32*, 21-47.

Locke, H. J. *Predicting Adjustment in Marriage: A Comparison of a Divorced and a Happily Married Group.* New York: Holt, Rinehart and Winston, 1951.

Locke, H. J., and Wallace, K. "Short Marital-Adjustment and Prediction Tests: Their Reliability and Validity." *Marriage and Family Living*, 1959, *21*, 251-255.

Locke, H. J., and Williamson, R. C. "Marital Adjustment: A Factor Analysis Study." *American Sociological Review*, 1958, *23*, 562-569.

Lorion, R. P. "Socioeconomic Status and Traditional Treatment Approaches Reconsidered." *Psychological Bulletin*, 1973, *78*, 263-270.

Lowenthal, M. F., Thurnher, M., Chiriboga, D., and Associates. *Four Stages of Life: A Comparative Study of Women and Men Facing Transitions.* San Francisco: Jossey-Bass, 1975.

Luckey, E. H. "Marital Satisfaction and Personality Correlates of Spouse." *Journal of Marriage and the Family*, 1964, *26*, 217-220.

Maas, H. S., and Kuypers, J. A. *From Thirty to Seventy: A Forty-Year Longitudinal Study of Adult Life-Styles and Personality.* San Francisco: Jossey-Bass, 1974.

Mace, D. R. "Marital Intimacy and the Deadly Love-Anger Cycle." *Journal of Marriage and Family Counseling*, 1976, *2*, 131-137.

Marshall, J. R., and Neill, J. "The Removal of a Psychosomatic Symptom: Effects on the Marriage." *Family Process*, 1977, *16*, 273-280.

Miller, B. C. "A Multivariate Developmental Model of Marital Satisfaction." *Journal of Marriage and the Family*, 1976, *38*, 643-657.

Mueller, C. W., and Pope, H. "Marital Instability: A Study of Its Transmission Between Generations." *Journal of Marriage and the Family*, 1977, *39*, 83-93.

Murphy, D. C., and Mendelson, L. A. "Communication and Adjustment in Marriage: Investigating the Relationship." *Family Process*, 1973, *12*, 317-326.

Murstein, B. I. *Love, Sex, and Marriage Through the Ages.* New York: Springer, 1974.

Murstein, B. I. *Who Will Marry Whom?* New York: Springer, 1976.

Neutens, J. J. "An Evaluation Instrument for Appraising the Dating, Premarital, and Marital Related Attitudes of Educable Mentally Handicapped Teenage Students." *Dissertation Abstracts International*, 1974, *34*, 7470-7471.

Nye, I., and MacDougall, E. "The Dependent Variable in Marital Research." *Pacific Sociological Review*, 1959, *2*, 67-70.

O'Gorman, H. J. "Status Integration and Mental Illness." *Journal of Health and Social Behavior*, 1977, *18*, 91-92.

Olson, D. H., and Ryder, R. G. "Inventory of Marital Conflicts (IMC): An Experimental Interaction Procedure." *Journal of Marriage and the Family*, 1970, *32*, 676-680.

Orden, S. R., and Bradburn, N. M. "Dimensions of Marriage Happiness." *American Journal of Sociology,* 1968, *73,* 715-731.

Pratt, L. "Conjugal Organization and Health." *Journal of Marriage and the Family,* 1972, *34,* 85-95.

Rapoport, R., and Rapoport, R. *Dual Career Families Reexamined.* New York: Harper & Row, 1977.

Rathus, S. A., and Siegel, L. J. "Reliability and Validity of a Self-Concept Scale for Researchers in Family Relationships." *International Journal of Family Counseling,* 1976, *4,* 57-60.

Raush, H. L., and others. *Communication, Conflict, and Marriage: Explorations in the Theory and Study of Intimate Relationships.* San Francisco: Jossey-Bass, 1974.

Rollins, B. C., and Bahr, S. J. "A Theory of Power Relationships in Marriage." *Journal of Marriage and the Family,* 1976, *38,* 619-627.

Safilios-Rothschild, S. "The Study of Family Power Structure." In C. B. Broderick (Ed.), *A Decade of Family Research and Action.* Minneapolis: National Council on Family Relations, 1971.

Spanier, G. B. "Measuring Dyadic Adjustment: New Scales for Assessing the Quality of Marriage and Similar Dyads." *Journal of Marriage and the Family,* 1976, *38,* 15-28.

Steinglass, P., Davis, D. I., and Berenson, D. "Observation of Conjointly Hospitalized 'Alcoholic Couples' During Sobriety and Intoxication." *Family Process,* 1977, *16,* 1-16.

Terman, L. *Psychological Factors in Marital Happiness.* New York: McGraw-Hill, 1938.

Thomas, E. J. *Marital Communication and Decision Making.* New York: Free Press, 1977.

Toman, W. *Family Constellation.* New York: Springer, 1976.

Udry, J. R. *The Social Context of Marriage.* Philadelphia: Lippincott, 1974.

Veroff, J., and Feld, S. *Marriage and Work in America: A Study of Motives and Roles.* New York: Van Nostrand Reinhold, 1970.

Warheit, G. J., and others. "Sex, Marital Status and Mental Health: A Reappraisal." *Social Forces,* 1976, *55,* 459-570.

Weller, L., Nathan, O., and Hazi, O. "Birth Order and Marital Bliss in Israel." *Journal of Marriage and the Family,* 1974, *36,* 794-797.

5

Robert H. Geertsma

Family Functioning

The primary or nuclear family is usually defined as a unit of a social system consisting of two adults of different sexes who function as parents to one or more children. One-parent families, which are now common in our society, may be considered a truncated variant of the primary family. An extended family includes, in addition, other persons related by descent, marriage, or adoption. While primary and extended families have provided both a legal and a social model in our society, more recently various other groupings of adults and children are found living together and discharging family functions.

Family functioning involves the family as the unit of attention and analysis. It potentially encompasses all those activities and aspects of living together in which family members influence each other, whether by direct interaction and communication or otherwise by their behavior. In practice, some narrowing down of attention is necessary for certain clinical or investigational purposes. Typically, family functioning is taken to include the family's experiencing and adjusting to problems, and it also often includes characteristic patterns of interaction and the pursuit of economic, social, and childrearing activities.

Background and Current Status

Because it is a fundamental social and economic unit, the family has long been an object of demographic interest. Family functioning as a field of research and practice grew both from psychotherapeutic and social science roots. From the psychotherapeutic

movement, while intrapsychic processes were of prime interest, such maverick psychotherapists as H. S. Sullivan and P. Federn drew attention to the importance of the family
environment in treating schizophrenic patients. Other therapist-investigators, such as
Jackson and Weakland, assayed a form of family treatment in their investigations of
schizophrenia. Such therapists as John Bell began involving the whole family in the treatment of children and thus set the stage for the development of family therapy as a coherent new treatment approach. In the social sciences, Parsons and Bales provided a perspective on the family as a social system with patterned, recurrent transactions and
representing an aggregate that is more than the sum of its parts.

Although the family was studied as a social-cultural entity as early as the mid
1920s (Burgess, 1926) and was regarded in general terms as a primary vehicle for the
socialization of the child, it was the work of sociologists Parsons and Bales (1955) in the
mid 1950s that provided a conceptually workable view of the family as a social unit.
However, because of carryover of attention to intrapsychic events and individual psychopathology, subsequent workers in this area were slow to make use of their conceptualization. Interest in the family was then mounting among clinicians who viewed the family
as important in the genesis of emotional illness. Psychotherapists had long been interested
in social-cultural determinants of psychopathology (Fromm, 1941; Horney, 1939), and at
least one influential therapist viewed mental illness in terms of disturbed interpersonal
relationships (Sullivan, 1965). Erikson (1963), another therapist, convincingly described a
model of human development which assigned a major role to the social-cultural environment. These workers established the general expectation that the family is influential in
the development of emotional illness. The result was that specific family-related determinants of emotional illness were intensively sought. First, studies were pursued that
attempted to causally relate certain parental attitudes—such as maternal overprotection
(Levy, 1943), rejection, or inconsistency—to specific disorders in the child (such as
autism and sociopathy). The general belief that emotional illnesses are generated through
disturbed parent-child relationships had to be made specific by identification of the crucial pathological elements or events. Perhaps the high point of this now virtually abandoned search for the significant traits is presented in Fromm-Reichman's (1950) concept
of the schizophrenogenic mother.

The search for pathogenetic traits was paralleled by the work of a small number of
investigators who attempted to find disturbance within the total family group. Specifically, they sought to explain how schizophrenia occurs. It is interesting to note that the
search for the etiology of schizophrenia, rather than that of the more psychothera-
peutically treatable emotional illnesses, is associated with attention to the family unit.
Perhaps it was only when the conventional wisdom of prevailing psychotherapeutic practice was not applicable that a novel conceptualization could be pursued. In any case,
Ackerman (1958) and Lidz and his associates (1957) articulated the view that the study
of family processes might illuminate the etiology of schizophrenia. The pioneers in this
area (Bateson and others, 1956; Lidz and others, 1957; Wynne and others, 1958) studied
patterns of intrafamily interaction and communication. Seeking a key to the development
of schizophrenic psychopathology, these teams of investigators turned to the family as
providing a powerful, long-acting, and consistent set of influences on the ego development of the child. While definitive answers to the question of the etiology of schizophrenia did not emerge from these preliminary investigations, a number of intriguing and
important concepts were generated; for example, the concept of the double bind (Bateson and others, 1956), pseudomutuality and pseudohostility (Wynne and others, 1958),
family homeostasis (Jackson, 1957), and schismatic and skewed family structures (Lidz
and others, 1957). Scott and Ashworth (1969) suggested a mode of transmission termed

"shadow of an ancestor"; that is, schizophrenia may be generated in a child by a mother who has had prior experience with an insane ancestor; who herself has a fear of madness; and who centers all her attention on one child, caring for that child in a ritualistic manner devoid of satisfaction to herself. Vogel and Bell (1968) suggested that some parents resolve intrafamily tension by deflecting hostility toward a child who is selected to be a "scapegoat" for the entire family. The child is thus sacrificed to become emotionally ill in the service of preserving family homeostasis.

Clinical interest in the family grew apace in the 1960s and 1970s, spurred by the clinician's growing awareness of the problems and difficulties of family life in our society and by the growing confidence that family problems could be identified and treated. A number of approaches to family therapy were elaborated, with therapists drawing their conceptional and technical tools from the domain of individual therapy and from the discipline of family studies. Bowen (1966) and Minuchin (1974) were prime developers of treatment approaches to the family. Boszormenyi-Nagy and Spark (1973) and Stierlin (1974), emphasizing intrafamily relationships, proposed processes whereby emotional illness is produced in a child and suggested more or less specific corrective interventions.

While the clinical area burgeoned with family therapeutic ideas and approaches, researchers were intent on pursuing and elaborating their earlier work on intrafamily patterns of interaction and communication. Their investigations by and large were marked by conceptualization of the family as a unit, techniques of direct observation, and a movement toward increased methodological soundness.

Family therapy is not distinguished by careful, systematic initial assessment of family problems and resources. Assessment has tended to be handled within the clinical interaction, and evaluative techniques and tools have been neglected, both in their development and use. Cromwell, Olson, and Fournier (1976) note that the empirical development of such instruments is rare, information about those that are available is scattered, and practitioners prefer to use, if any, an instrument that is convenient, whether it is appropriate or not, or else follow fads. They also observe that researchers have not often been concerned about making their evaluative instruments available to practitioners.

Research workers in the area of family functioning appear to have exhausted the "trait" approach to family influence and are confronting a more complex approach, involving the family as a unit. They have followed various directions. One tack addresses discrepancies in role perceptions, expectations, and performances; another tack involves intrafamily communication patterns; a third emphasizes functioning to solve problems, make decisions, or play especially structured games. All these approaches aim at revealing and categorizing typical family behavior, with some investigators emphasizing content and others process.

The well-established findings that have emerged from experimental research work have not been overwhelming in number, but a few of the variables most closely related to the emotional health of families deserve mention. This treatment is representative and not meant to be complete. Communication "fragmentation" and "unclarity" have been repeatedly found to be high in severely disturbed families (Mishler and Waxler, 1968; Wynne and Singer, 1963). The "agreement/disagreement" ratio has been demonstrated to be higher in normal than disturbed families (Lennard and Bernstein, 1969; Mishler and Waxler, 1968; Riskin and Faunce, 1970). And "humor," "laughter," and "positive affect" were found to be greater in healthy families (Mishler and Waxler, 1968; Riskin and Faunce, 1970).

Findings such as the above may not, in contrast to the hypothetical constructions deriving from clinical work, present a systematic view of a functioning family. However, they do represent a careful sifting and testing of many interactional variables, using accepted methodological procedures, and in consequence they are scientifically credible and will serve as building blocks for future theories.

To sum up, the current status of research in family functioning suggests movement and progression, but not in a unified direction. Variety, lack of consistency, and pursuit of different ideas have predominated. Clinicians tend to put together broad views, while experimenters work to validate the significance of individual concepts and variables. A context of discovery prevails. The overall impression is one of an early developmental stage. Much sloppy work has been done, particularly that stemming from the clinical areas. Only in the determined efforts of the investigators with nonclinical aims do we begin now to see concern for methodological issues and an apparent agreement on approaching the family on a basis other than that of individual psychopathology. Concern for replication and validation, agreement on important variables, and integrative research and theorizing can only be looked forward to at this time. It is not surprising, then, that the assessment of family functioning is not currently highly developed. Its promise must await developments in both theory and methodology, which can be expected to flow from research on family functioning.

Critical Discussion

General Areas of Concern

The investigation of family functioning requires a set of variables and a data-gathering methodology. The handling of these basic components has drawn from the conceptually and methodologically rich areas of psychology, sociology, and psychiatry, with a resultant plethora of approaches, variables, and lexicons. Many promising variables have been suggested, and the number of methodologically sound investigations seems to be increasing. Clearly, the need is both for consolidation and finer focusing of variables and for closer attention to methodological issues. Unfortunately, investigators have a proclivity for restricting their attention to variables of their own first choosing and for repetitively pursuing the same methodological approaches.

The basic issue involved in consolidating approaches to family functioning hinges on the question of what is significant or likely to be significant and for what purposes. This is a difficult question to answer. A number of possible criteria of significance can be suggested: (1) outcome significance—the extent to which the concepts or variables are likely to be related to outcomes, such as the stability of the family, the emotional or physical health of family members, or their economic productivity; (2) treatment relevance—the extent to which the concepts or variables admit of therapeutic intervention; and (3) methodological soundness—the extent to which the approach follows methodologically sound lines, as with regard to systematic and objective observation, recording and coding, appropriate sample selection for generalization of findings, adequate controls, and attention to reliability and validity of measures. The first of these criteria, outcome significance, entails empirical questions; and, by and large, the significance of virtually all variables investigated or suggested has not been conclusively confirmed or disconfirmed. Thus, judgment must be deferred on the truly important variables—pending the results of appropriate studies.

Treatment relevance imposes a practical test that may not be important to the investigator and may not be demonstrated until relatively late in the investigational process. In addition, the term *treatment* is an abstraction which, as used here, must be qualified; that is, one must specify what type of treatment, in what circumstances, and by whom. The complexity generated by these qualifications makes the criterion of treatment relevance seem impractical if not impossible to apply.

The criterion of methodological soundness, then, should be considered carefully, since it seems to provide the most practical evaluative criterion. There is, however, the argument that this is a relatively new area and that it would be premature to impose rigid methodological criteria. Handel (1965) has suggested that it is even premature to attempt to differentiate normal and pathological families, inasmuch as an adequate typology of families has not yet been found. While this viewpoint seems reasonable in its recognition that scientific progress in an area includes, and perhaps requires, early work that is not heavily constrained by methodological considerations, at some point methodological soundness becomes critical. Therefore, those working in the area and those who read critically the reports of such work should be aware of relevant methodological issues.

Fontana (1966) has provided a methodological discussion of the search for the etiology of schizophrenia in the family. Retrospective accounts are considered untrustworthy, since they are open to error from (1) conceptual and language differences between investigators and respondents; (2) inaccuracy in recall of past events and feelings; (3) defensive forgetting, distortion, and justifying elaboration; and (4) social desirability and other response-set factors. Interaction studies are judged on the basis of (1) objective, systematic recording and coding of data; (2) validity and reliability of measures, with reliability pursued beyond interjudge agreement (which may reflect a shared bias); (3) attention to the possibility that current interaction patterns may be different from past patterns; (4) attention to the possibility that the task around which the observed interaction is organized may alter the interaction; and (5) attention to the possibility that the absence of some family member may alter the observed interaction. Given these qualifications, Fontana concludes that the interpretation of data acquired by direct recording and systematic coding provides a scientific approach to the etiology of emotional disorder.

Methodological reviews of empirical family studies have emphasized both the importance of methodological soundness and, until recently, a typical lack of it (Fontana, 1966; Jacob, 1975; Rabkin, 1965; Riskin and Faunce, 1972). Jacob (1975) lists six criteria of methodological soundness for family interaction studies: (1) experimental and control families should be comparable on demographic variables related to family interaction; (2) raters, coders, or judges should be "blind"; (3) agreement among independent judges as to the presence and frequency of the behaviors to be rated should be high; (4) data from male and female children should be analyzed separately; (5) experimental and control families should be observed in the same setting; and (6) potential effects of institutionalization and past or present treatment on observed differences should be minimized. Among the twenty-seven observational studies he reviewed that contained a disturbed nonschizophrenic group, he found that a great majority satisfied at least five of these criteria, whereas in the studies containing schizophrenic families, the majority failed to satisfy five of the criteria.

Comparative Philosophies and Theories

The philosophies and theories of family functioning can be approached from the point of view of classification schemes or the type of assessment approach taken. Since both substance and methodology are important, these two avenues will be discussed separately.

Family classification schemes have been pursued in various directions and are so numerous that they themselves justify classification or typing. Fisher (1977), who has reviewed and analyzed the family classification efforts of the past twenty years, identifies five types. For purposes of this discussion, a three-category typology is appropriate: (1) a typology based on individual diagnosis or problem; (2) a typology based on family pathology; and (3) a typology based on family interaction. Each of these types requires elaboration.

The diagnosis or presenting problem of an individual family member has been used to type families. This follows from and can be viewed as an attempt to apply the individual diagnostic approach to families. A standard diagnostic perspective or a more idiosyncratic system may be used, but in any case the family is not approached as a unit. In general terms, many investigators have termed families "schizophrenic" or "depressive" (or "normal") because of the psychiatric diagnosis on one member (or lack of such diagnosis for any family member). Serrano, McDonald, and Goolishian (1962), Goldstein, Judd, and Rodnick (1968), and Beavers, Lewis, and Gossett (1975) base their typologies on the role or behavior of the adolescent family member, who is presumed to be the focal point of family functioning.

In pathology-based approaches, families are typed according to the conflicts or disturbances present. Investigators taking this tack usually draw on their clinical or investigatorial experience with families, and their notions of what constitutes disturbance vary considerably. Duvall (1967) characterizes families as progressing through a series of stages, from childbearing through the death of one spouse, with each stage posing its own developmental task. Gruenbaum and Bryant (1966) suggest that family breakdown occurs when the task of a particular stage cannot be met. Ackerman (1958) describes seven types of disturbed families: (1) the externally isolated, (2) the externally integrated, (3) the internally unintegrated, (4) the unintended, (5) the immature, (6) the deviant, and (7) the disintegrated family. Vorland (1961) identifies the perfectionistic, the inadequate, the egocentric, and the unsocial family. Riskin and Faunce (1970), taking a global view of pathological family structures, present a scheme based on the severity and number of problems a family has. Their five types comprise (1) the multiproblem disagreeing family, (2) the multiproblem constricted family, (3) the family with an acting-out or under-achieving child, (4) the family with significant but undiagnosed problems, and (5) the well-functioning family. Minuchin (1974) classifies families on a dimension ranging from enmeshed to disengaged, with the concept of boundaries crucial. In enmeshed families the boundaries around family members become blurred and there is much intrafamilial contact. In disengaged families the boundaries are rigid and there is little intrafamilial contact. Richter (1974) has described family symptom neurosis and family character neurosis types, and Gehrke and Kirshenbaum (1967) identify repressive, delinquent, and suicidal family types. In the approaches exemplified by this group of investigators, the family is treated as a unit, but the conditions of observation leading to the classification systems tend not to be systematically or explicitly described.

The typologies based on family interactions generally derive from systematic observation of family behavior in some type of experimental or quasi-experimental setting. Conflict and difficulty are not pivotal. Understanding family dynamics is paramount. The work of Wynne and Singer, which was mentioned earlier, represents a relatively pure example of this type of approach. Reiss (1971), using a quasi-experimental setting, identifies environment-sensitive and consensus-sensitive family types. Farina and Dunham (1963) analyzed the verbal interactions of families containing schizophrenic sons. Classifying the families according to good or poor premorbid adjustment, they found fathers to be dominant in the good-premorbidity families, the mothers dominant in the poor-premorbidity families, and significantly greater conflict in the interpersonal communication of the poor-premorbidity families. Murrell and Stachowiak (1965) counted the number of times each family member spoke to each other member during work on four different group tasks. Families seeking help and families not seeking help were used. The investigators were interested in examining the stability of intrafamily patterns of interaction, the rigidity with which these patterns of communication were held in troubled and normal families, and the extent to which the authority structure is autocratic in troubled and normal families. They found interactional stability and differing patterns of authority. Haley (1962, 1967) approached the measurement of family interaction patterns using an instrument that automatically counts the number of times each family member's speech is followed by each other member's speech.

Family interaction types that are less pure, in the sense that a systematic observational base is not made explicit, are common. Ford and Rarrick (1974) type families according to their implicit involvement with the following family rules: (1) Children come first. (2) Two against the world (the spouses have united to feel safe in a world they both fear). (3) Share and share alike (the spouses each at times play the roles of child and parent). (4) Every man for himself (the marital relationship is primarily a means to gain some end and thus lacks an emotional nexus). (5) Until death do us part (the family is threatened by dissolution, but this is seen as justified only by death). The typology developed by Markowitz and Kadis (1964) is based on the central family member. Thus, they describe father-centered, mother-centered, child-centered, and family-centered families.

Approaches to assessment come mainly from assessment traditions involving the clinical interview, psychodiagnostic testing, and observational methods.

The interview has long been a mainstay for psychiatric diagnosis. It affords the interviewer much flexibility in exploring material that emerges from the interaction, but it entails the limitation that the subject is not required to respond to a standard stimulus situation (which would facilitate comparison of different subjects' responses). Since interview data are usually interpreted according to content, this approach depends on retrospection, the accuracy of which is questionable. In an effort to ensure that subjects provide comparable responses or information, investigators have introduced various types and degrees of structure into the interview format. Prescribed questions, lists of topics to be broached, and even representations of family members have been used. As long as the interviewer interacts on a contingent basis with subjects, the format can be considered to be that of an interview.

Watzlawick (1966) developed a standardized, semistructured interview in which families respond to situations designed to stimulate representative family interactions. For example, the family might be asked to plan an outing in which they all would participate.

Psychodiagnostic techniques generally present a standard problem or stimulus situation, the responses to which yield inferences about the family. Subjects may be tested individually or as a family unit. Insights into family functioning may be produced by these techniques, but reliability and validity of measures are typically not established.

Heller (1976) developed a paper-and-pencil test to measure family solidarity, which he terms *familism*. The test is administered to individual family members to assess their familistic attitudes. In a somewhat similar but less psychometrically rigorous vein, the Otto Family Strength Survey (Otto, 1963) is a paper-and-pencil test that makes an inventory of strengths in fifteen areas. A family or family member responds to each area by indicating none, little, some, or much. This instrument has the virtue of bringing to attention perceived strength rather than weakness and deviance, which are more commonly sought.

A number of methods used to assess individuals—for example, the Self-Disclosure

Questionnaire (Jourard, 1971), FIRO-B (Schutz, 1958), and the Interpersonal Check List (LaForge and Szurek, 1955)—can also be used to characterize families. Testing the individual members and then putting together the results may yield useful interpersonal patterns but does not deal with interactional patterns. The amount of work involved, the difficulty in interrelating the individual data, and the static rather than interactional focus have probably induced researchers and clinicians to seek other methods.

Family sculpture (Simon, 1972) has each family member in turn arranging the others to create a spatial tableau of the family. In the Conjoint Family Drawing technique (Bing, 1970) the family members draw a picture together to represent how they see themselves as a family. An elaboration of this technique involves supplying a range of media so that the family can produce a two- or three-dimensional family portrait (Rubin and Magnussen, 1974). In the Puppet Interview (Irwin and Mallory, 1975), each family member is asked to define the family problem, after which the family together makes up a story and then acts out the story using puppets. In the Family Thematic Apperception Test of Winter and Ferreira (1965), a family produces three stories based on nine TAT cards. The stories are then scored by a technique used to score TAT stories given by individuals. Kadushin and others (1969) have developed a Family Story Technique, in which a family produces a story for each of ten standard TAT cards and a picture of a family seated around a table set for a birthday party. The scoring is based on Horney's method of classifying interactions.

Observational approaches to the study of family interaction patterns have aimed at the understanding of both normal and abnormal personality development. While they pursue research rather than diagnostic questions, there is a strong presumption that such questions underlie and support diagnostic formulations. The approaches taken have drawn on small-group experimental methods, have often employed audio and video recording techniques, and have involved the generation of quantifiable data.

In observational approaches, some procedure is necessary to induce family members to interact, after which their interaction is observed or recorded, and then a scoring method applied. Early investigators often used Bales' Interpersonal Process Analysis scheme to score data. Wynne and his associates (1958) asked families to respond to Rorschach cards, producing agreed-upon responses. The verbal interactions of the family members were recorded and analyzed in terms of formal patterns of interaction and communication styles. Using this approach, they have identified disturbances in establishing, maintaining, and sharing foci of attention in families with a schizophrenic member. They classify communicational disturbance in terms of a continuum ranging from amorphous to fragmented.

Riskin and Faunce (1970) developed a set of scales which are applied to family interaction data from a semistructured interview. The scales involve clarity, topic, commitment, agreement, and intensity as rated from the family member's verbal interactions.

Mishler and Waxler (1967) used Strodtbeck s (1951) revealed-differences method to produce discussion among family members. The discussions were recorded and transcribed, and the transcripts coded according to several category systems to yield indexes for statistical analysis. Group, role, and situational effects were related to family types.

Ferreira (1963) and Ferreira and Winter (1965), using a modification of the revealed-differences technique, in which differences are not revealed, investigated decision making in families. Each of sixteen neutral items had three possible responses. After family members made their individual responses, they were asked to produce a group response. Four decision types were revealed: (1) unanimous (when family members all selected the same individual response), (2) majority (when the group response was that given by the majority of the individual responses), (3) dictatorial (when the group response was that given by a minority of the individual responses), and (4) chaotic (when the group response was different from all the individual responses). Normal families evidence more spontaneous agreement (agreement of the individual responses), greater parental than child influence on group responses, and fewer chaotic decisions.

Some investigators have employed game-like situations in order to reduce the response possibilities and make them more readily classifiable, although most of these have involved only parents. One that encompasses the entire family was developed by Haley (1962). The object of the game was to accumulate as much time as possible in "coalition," which was counted when any two family members simultaneously pressed certain buttons. Normal families achieved more coalition time than did families with a schizophrenic member, and their coalitions more often included the children.

Elaboration on Critical Points

An appreciation of any study of family functioning, as well as the comparison of studies, requires awareness of certain critical issues, the most general of which are briefly discussed below. Unfortunately, reports of studies do not always provide complete information on these issues.

Purposes. Investigators pursue different aims, often without making them explicit. The most common distinction here is between clinical and nonclinical purposes. Clinical interest involves the development of better therapeutic methods or the development of better methods of assessing the effectiveness of family therapy. Nonclinical purposes involve an understanding of family structure or functioning and may aim toward understanding the influence or operation of specific variables, such as mother dominance or shadow of the ancestor. From the point of view of the generation of knowledge, whether clinical or nonclinical purposes are paramount, the families studied must be considered as representative of some population of families.

The Family Unit Being Studied. It is important to know how the family unit being studied is defined—whether the parents and one (emotionally ill) child are being studied, or the parents and all their children (one of whom is emotionally ill). Also, the family's socioeconomic status, cultural-ethnic characteristics, and involvement in religious or in social, community, and academic pursuits may be important. All these parameters bear on the issue of generalizing findings to a population that is represented by the family studied. Studies using families in which a member is or has been psychiatrically ill are involved in the complex issues of psychiatric diagnosis and should make their diagnostic data and criteria known.

Setting. Where is the family studied and under what conditions? Most commonly a laboratory setting is used, although families at times have been observed in their homes. O'Rourke (1963) has studied the comparability of data derived from these two settings. This question bears on the issue of the representativeness and the stability of the behaviors observed ("Is the behavior observed in the laboratory similar to the behavior observed at home, or when no observer is present?"). The relationship between the investigators and the families studied can be considered an aspect of the setting; since it may color the observed behavior of the family, it is an extremely important factor. Not only how the investigators treat the subjects is of interest, but also how the subjects regard the investigators and their observational intrusion into the family space. In some studies (though it is not often reported) the subjects may be put through a standardized procedure by technicians and may never be seen by the investigators who designed the study and will interpret the results.

The Interactional Task. In general, investigators have used tasks that elicit commonly experienced family interactions (for instance, "Plan something together"); or they have constructed tasks to induce behaviors that are readily interpretable in terms of concepts or constructs in which they are interested (for example, in a game involving trains the bumping and obstruction of one spouse's train by the other's is interpreted as dominance); or they have used tasks that require responses for which an interpretative scheme has previously been worked out (for instance, Rorschach cards). The issue here is one of operationalizing the concepts that are of interest or, from the other side, specifying the concepts that are represented by the observed behaviors. It is important to note the rationale and cogency of conceptual leaps from abstract concepts like "dominance" or "homeostasis" to behaviors actually observed, and vice versa.

Methodological Soundness. This is really a set of complex issues and has been discussed above in as much detail as can be encompassed in this presentation. The difficulty in this area is that, although more methodological sophistication is desirable in family studies, investigational interest must not be deflected away from important variables and toward more easily measured but inane variables.

Personal Views and Recommendations

Family functioning is a flourishing field of research and practice. Its diversity of disciplines, purposes, methods, and concepts has produced a fertile mix; and continued growth can be expected. The question is what will be made of all this activity. So far, no approaches to treatment have been accepted as characteristic of family therapy (Group for the Advancement of Psychiatry, 1970), and researchers seem to be working at their own semi-independent notions of what is important. The evaluation of what should be done in the future (and what has been done in the past) depends on the evaluator's values. On the one hand is the prospect of evolution in this area through clinical-descriptive and clinical-theoretical contributions; on the other, the pursuit of research dealing with quantifiable data. Of course, some use of research methods and quantification can be expected of those basically working from a clinical perspective, and some impressionistic-theoretical contributions can be expected from those experimenters who are essentially quantitative in their approach. The future of a descriptive-theoretical movement is likely to depend on the "attractiveness" of the work of a few leaders—or possibly of a single dominating figure—who provide a useful approach to conceptualizing and managing clinical problems. It is very difficult, if not impossible, to predict or point out with confidence the directions that future work of this sort may take.

In experimental science the ideal progression in a field such as family functioning involves research validation of ideas deriving from the context of discovery, and then a knitting of these together to form more complex hypotheses and testable theories. The knowledge generated in this process is likely to have application to clinical or social problems, but the pursuit of such applications need not necessarily involve the experimenter. With this progression in mind, a number of recommendations can be made in the interest of expediting progress in this area.

It is important for scientific progress that research workers build on each other's findings—sharing the work and providing checks on the data and their interpretation. Such an approach should ultimately result in the construction of a more solidly established and larger corpus of knowledge. In order for this to happen, however, research workers will have to communicate and collaborate with each other more fully and more frequently. Also, important findings should be replicated; and investigators should include other workers' variables as markers in their own studies, so that results can be more easily interrelated.

It is perhaps only just that the "family" of research workers concerned with family interaction should be advised to attend to their own interaction. A number of means could be utilized to increase communication and collaboration—for instance, government-sponsored conferences, formation of a new professional society, publication of an experimental family work journal—but the basic requirement is that the investigators take a broad view of the development of their field and actively pursue interrelationships with one another.

Many matters should be conjointly considered by the research workers in this area. First of all, methodology deserves attention in order to avoid weaknesses in experimental design and execution. Agreement on such issues as appropriate controls, populations to be studied, and procedures for establishing reliability and validity of measures would promote a more uniform and higher quality of research. Sharing views on investigative approaches and strategies most likely to produce useful new data should also be helpful; and agreement on the cataloging of problems ranked according to priorities seems useful.

Substantively, the comparison, interrelating, and integrating of the variables, hypotheses, and theories being pursued by different investigators should be started and then maintained as the field progresses. Investigators who deal with observational data will doubtless persist in idiosyncratically labeling and categorizing what they see. The problem to be addressed involves translation and cross-indexing of variables—so that, no matter what different investigators call their variables, they and others will know whether the same or different variables (as defined on an operational level) are being used. At some time in the future, it can be hoped that a commonly used term will identify each observed entity.

Finally, cooperative studies can be recommended—projects of interinstitutional, or even national, scope. One type of study would involve teams of investigators, perhaps sponsored by a national agency, working on projects of larger scope than could be carried out by an individual or a single institution. Another type would involve individual researchers performing their own studies that were developed in conjunction with other researchers, so that common subjects, procedures, or variables are used, and study objectives are designed to provide interrelated, reinforcing findings. These types of studies, involving huge resources, are thinkable only for an area of major significance in our society; the family seems to have such significance. Fortunately, we do possess the behavioral science tools and competence to undertake the scientific study of the basic social institution in our society that the family represents.

Application to Particular Variables

Evidence for the effects of sex of child, age of child, and social class of family on family interaction appears to be accumulating. Sex of child has been found to significantly influence family interaction patterns in families with an emotionally disturbed member (Hetherington, Stouwie, and Ridberg, 1971) and in families with a schizophrenic member (Ferreira and Winter, 1965; Mishler and Waxler, 1968). Age of child (Ferreira and Winter, 1968; Murrell and Stachowiak, 1967) and social class of the family (Alkire, 1969; Becker and Iwakami 1969) have been found to be significantly related to family interaction. Further, the interaction of these variables may also be significant, as a study by Jacob (1974) indicates. He found an interaction between social class and parental influence (dominance). Thus, although in all families a 16-year-old son exerted greater influence than an 11-year-old son, in middle-class families the 16-year-old's gain in influence was associated with the mother's loss, whereas in lower-class families the son's gain was associated with the father's loss.

Demographic variables are usually not of primary interest to investigators, who prefer to pursue integrated, psychologically coherent views of family functioning. Nevertheless, attention to demographic variables is methodologically important. The comparability of experimental and control families should be arranged on demographic variables, at least on those that have been demonstrated to be significantly related to family interaction. The demographic characteristics of subject populations are especially important when the results of different studies are compared, since subject population differences on such variables may account for divergent results in studies using the same main variables or treatments.

References

Ackerman, M. W. *The Psychodynamics of Family Life.* New York: Basic Books, 1958.

Alkire, A. "Social Power and Communication Within the Families of Disturbed and Nondisturbed Preadolescents." *Journal of Personality and Social Psychology,* 1969, *13,* 335-349.

Bateson, G., and others. "Toward a Theory of Schizophrenia." *Behavioral Science,* 1956, *1,* 251-264.

Beavers, W. R., Lewis, J., and Gossett, J. T. "Family Systems and Individual Functioning: Mid-Range Families." Paper presented at American Psychiatric Association meeting, Anaheim, Calif., 1975.

Becker, J., and Iwakami, E. "Conflict and Dominance Within Families of Disturbed Children." *Journal of Abnormal Psychology,* 1969, *74,* 330-335.

Bing, E. "The Conjoint Family Drawing." *Family Process,* 1970, *9,* 173-194.

Boszormenyi-Nagy, I., and Spark, G. *Invisible Loyalties.* New York: Harper & Row, 1973.

Bowen, M. "The Use of Family Therapy in Clinical Practice." *Comprehensive Psychiatry,* 1966, *7,* 345-374.

Burgess, E. W. "The Family as a Unity of Interacting Personalities." *The Family,* 1926, *7,* 3-9.

Cromwell, R. E., Olson, D. H. L., and Fournier, D. G. "Tools and Techniques for Diagnosis and Evaluation in Marital and Family Therapy." *Family Process,* 1976, *15,* 1-49.

Duvall, E. R. *Family Development.* Philadelphia: Lippincott, 1967.

Erikson, E. H. *Childhood and Society.* New York: Norton, 1963.

Farina, A., and Dunham, R. M. "Measurement of Family Relationships and Their Effects." *Archives of General Psychiatry,* 1963, *9,* 64-73.

Ferreira, A. J. "Decision-Making in Normal and Pathological Families." *Archives of General Psychiatry,* 1963, *8,* 68-73.

Ferreira, A. J., and Winter, W. "Family Interaction and Decision Making." *Archives of General Psychiatry,* 1965, *13,* 214-223.

Ferreira, A. J., and Winter, W. "Decision Making in Normal and Abnormal Two-Child Families." *Family Process,* 1968, *7,* 17-36.

Fisher, L. "On the Classification of Families." *Archives of General Psychiatry,* 1977, *34,* 424-433.

Fontana, A. F. "Family Etiology of Schizophrenia: Is a Scientific Methodology Possible?" *Psychological Bulletin,* 1966, *66,* 214-227.

Ford, F. R., and Rarrick, J. "Family Rules: Family Life Styles." *American Journal of Psychiatry,* 1974, *44,* 61-69.

Fromm, E. F. *Escape from Freedom.* New York: Farrar, Straus & Giroux, 1941.

Fromm-Reichman, F. *Principles of Intensive Psychotherapy.* Chicago: University of Chicago Press, 1950.

Gehrke, S., and Kirshenbaum, M. "Survival Patterns in Family Conjoint Therapy." *Family Process,* 1967, *6,* 67-80.

Goldstein, M. J., Judd, L. L., and Rodnick, E. G. "A Method for Studying Social Influences and Coping Patterns Within Families of Disturbed Adolescents." *Journal of Nervous and Mental Disease,* 1968, *147,* 233-251.

Group for the Advancement of Psychiatry. *The Field of Family Therapy.* New York: Group for the Advancement of Psychiatry, 1970.

Gruenbaum, H. V., and Bryant, C. M. "The Theory and Practice of the Family Diagnostic: Theoretical Aspects and Resident Education." *Psychiatric Research Reports,* 1966, *20,* 150-162.

Haley, J. "Family Experiments: A New Type of Experimentation." *Family Process,* 1962, *1,* 265-293.

Haley, J. "Experiment with Abnormal Families: Testing Done in a Restricted Communication Setting." *Archives of General Psychiatry,* 1967, *17,* 53-63.

Handel, G. "Psychological Study of Whole Families." *Psychological Bulletin,* 1965, *63,* 19-41.

Heller, P. L. "Familism Scale: Revalidation and Revision." *Journal of Marriage and the Family,* 1976, *38,* 423-429.

Hetherington, E., Stouwie, R., and Ridberg, E. "Patterns of Family Interaction and Child Rearing Attitudes Related to Three Dimensions of Juvenile Delinquency." *Journal of Abnormal Psychology,* 1971, *78,* 160-176.

Horney, K. H. *New Ways in Psychoanalysis.* New York: Norton, 1939.

Irwin, E. C., and Mallory, E. S. "Family Puppet Interview." *Family Process,* 1975, *14,* 179-191.

Jackson, D. D. "The Question of Family Homeostasis." *Psychiatric Quarterly Supplement,* 1957, *31,* 79-90.

Jacob, T. "Patterns of Family Conflict and Dominance as a Function of Child Age and Social Class." *Developmental Psychology,* 1974, *10,* 1-12.

Jacob, T. "Family Interaction in Disturbed and Normal Families: A Methodological and Substantive Review." *Psychological Bulletin,* 1975, *82,* 33-65.

Jourard, S. M. *The Transparent Self.* New York: Van Nostrand, 1971.

Kadushin, P., and others. "The Family Story Technique and Intrafamily Analysis." *Journal of Projective Techniques and Personality Assessment,* 1969, *33,* 438-450.

LaForge, R., and Szurek, R. F. "The Interpersonal Dimension of Personality III: An Interpersonal Check List." *Journal of Personality,* 1955, *24,* 94-112.

Lennard, H. L., and Bernstein, A. *Patterns in Human Interaction: An Introduction to Clinical Sociology.* San Francisco: Jossey-Bass, 1969.

Levy, D. M. *Maternal Overprotection.* New York: Columbia University Press, 1943.

Lidz, T., and others. "The Intrafamilial Environment of the Schizophrenic Patient I: The Father." *Psychiatry,* 1957, *29,* 329-342.

Markowitz, M., and Kadis, A. L. "Parental Interaction as a Determinant in Social Growth of the Individual in the Family." *International Journal of Social Psychiatry, Special Edition,* 1964, *2,* 81-89.

Minuchin, S. *Families and Family Therapy.* Cambridge, Mass.: Harvard University Press, 1974.

Mishler, E. G., and Waxler, N. E. "Family Interaction Patterns and Schizophrenia: A Multi-Level Analysis." In J. Romano (Ed.), *The Origins of Schizophrenia.* Proceedings of the 1st Rochester International Conference on Schizophrenia. Amsterdam: Excerpta Medica Foundation, 1967.

Mishler, E. G., and Waxler, N. E. *Interaction in Families: An Experimental Study of Family Process and Schizophrenia.* New York: Wiley, 1968.

Murrell, S. A., and Stachowiak, J. G. "The Family Group: Development, Structure, and Therapy." *Journal of Marriage and Family Living,* 1965, *27,* 13-19.

Murrell, S. A., and Stachowiak, J. G. "Consistency, Rigidity, and Power in the Interaction Patterns of Clinic and Nonclinic Families." *Journal of Abnormal Psychology,* 1967, *72,* 265-272.

O'Rourke, J. F. "Field and Lab: The Decision Making Behavior of Family Groups in Two Experimental Situations." *Sociometry,* 1963, *26,* 422-435.

Otto, H. A. "Criteria for Assessing Family Strength." *Family Process,* 1963, *2,* 329-338.

Parsons, T., and Bales, R. F. *Family Socialization and Interaction Process.* New York: Free Press, 1955.

Rabkin, L. "The Patient's Family: Research Methods." *Family Process,* 1965, *4,* 105-132.

Reiss, D. "Intimacy and Problem Solving: An Automated Procedure for Testing a Theory of Consensual Experience in Families." *Archives of General Psychiatry,* 1971, *25,* 442-455.

Richter, H. E. *The Family as Patient.* New York: Farrar, Straus & Giroux, 1974.

Riskin, J., and Faunce, E. E. "Family Interaction Scales I: Theoretical Framework and Method." *Archives of General Psychiatry,* 1970, *22,* 504-512.

Riskin, J., and Faunce, E. E. "An Evaluative Review of Family Interaction Research." *Family Process,* 1972, *11,* 365-456.

Rubin, J., and Magnussen, M. G. "A Family Art Evaluation." *Family Process,* 1974, *13,* 185-200.

Schutz, W. C. FIRO: *A Three-Dimensional Theory of Interpersonal Behavior.* New York: Holt, Rinehart and Winston, 1958.

Scott, R. D., and Ashworth, P. L. "The Shadow of the Ancestor: A Historical Factor in the Transmission of Schizophrenia." *British Journal of Medical Psychology,* 1969, *42,* 13-32.

Serrano, A. C., McDonald, E. C., and Goolishian, H. A. "Adolescent Maladjustment and Family Dynamics." *American Journal of Psychiatry,* 1962, *118,* 897-910.

Simon, R. "Sculpting the Family." *Family Process,* 1972, *11,* 49-59.

Stierlin, H. *Separating Adolescents and Parents.* New York: Quadrangle, 1974.

Strodtbeck, F. L. "Husband-Wife Interaction over Revealed Differences." *American Sociological Review,* 1951, *16,* 468-473.

Sullivan, H. S. *Collected Works.* New York: Norton, 1965.

Vogel, E. F., and Bell, N. W. "The Emotionally Disturbed Child as the Family Scapegoat." In G. Handel (Ed.), *The Psychosocial Interior of the Family.* Chicago: Aldine, 1968.

Vorland, A. L., and Buell, B. "A Classification of Disordered Family Types." *Social Work,* 1961, *6,* 3-11.

Watzlawick, P. "A Structured Family Interview." *Family Process,* 1966, *5,* 155-172.

Winter, W. D., and Ferreira, A. J. "Story Sequence Analysis of Family TAT's." *Journal of Projective Techniques and Personality Assessment,* 1965, *29,* 392-397.

Wynne, L. C., and others. "Pseudo-Mutuality in the Family Relations of Schizophrenics." *Psychiatry,* 1958, *21,* 205-220.

Wynne, L. C., and Singer, M. T. "Thought Disorder and Family Relations of Schizophrenics: A Research Strategy." *Archives of General Psychiatry,* 1963, *9,* 191-198.

6

Marvin S. Kaplan

Parenting Assessment

The transformation of the familiar nouns *mother* and *father* into the verbal form *parenting* illustrates a critical shift in contemporary thinking. In contrast to the imagery evoked by the words *father, mother, or parent*—namely, one who begets, originates, and produces a product, generally identified as offspring, future generations, and the like—the term *parenting* implies an ongoing process involving extensive interactions among parent, child, and environment and requiring skillful handling of a wide range of task demands (such as nurturance and socialization). *Child care* in the past has typically referred to mothering, while the role of the father has been viewed as secondary and supportive (Rapoport, Rapoport, and Strelitz, 1977). Contemporary writers, in contrast, view parenting as a joint enterprise involving both the mother and the father. Consistent with this history, there is some research on mothering, very little research on fathering, and virtually no research on parenting (Rapoport, Rapoport, and Strelitz, 1977). In addition, current views increasingly emphasize that behavior is the outcome of the interaction of the person and the environment, but most research has focused on trait or dynamic factors within the person rather than on interactions.

A potentially useful approach to the assessment of parenting—incorporating both the idea of interaction and a focus on personal traits and dynamic factors within the individual—is the concept of competence, as proposed by Sundberg, Snowden, and Reynolds (1978). In accordance with this proposal, parenting can be described as a multifactored competence, including knowledge, skills, and attitudes. In order to assess such competence, one must assess the individual parents and their histories as persons who were "parented," parenting task demands, and the human and environmental resources and stresses of the particular setting.

Background and Current Status

Advice regarding childrearing can be found in the Old Testament (Gangel, 1977), in the works of philosophers such as John Locke and Jean-Jacques Rousseau, and in the writings of Puritan Americans. For example, Greven (1973, p. 4) notes that the Puritans were aware of the importance of parents as well as "the interrelationship between child-rearing methods, personality, and adult experience and belief." While there were differences among the Puritans, they shared a common concern for controlling and suppressing the autonomy of their children.

Although the scientific study of children can be said to have begun in 1877 with the publication of Charles Darwin's *Biographical Sketch of an Infant* (Denzin, 1977), the empirical studies of the mother-child relationship began in the 1930s. Brody (1956) reviewed the literature and noted: "Remarkably few investigators have been concerned with mothers themselves as persons who have particular tasks and particular conflicts" (p. 22). Brody also noted that most studies dealt with maternal attitudes rather than behaviors and that she found "no analysis of the functioning of mothers from a psychological point of view" (p. 28). She concluded that "the bulk of the literature is speculative, and specific data about what mothers do and feel [are] hardly available" (p. 28).

Apparently in these respects there have been only small changes in the past twenty years. Consequently, the studies that Brody summarized tended to deal with the question of the "maternal instinct" rather than the influence of social experience on the adequacy of maternal functioning. Levy (1943) concluded that maternal behavior is primarily constitutional and biological, while Deutsch (1945) stated that the capacity for satisfying motherhood is based on the mother's identification with her own mother. Levy also developed the concept of "maternal overprotection" (excessive contact, prevention of independent behavior) and concluded that this deficiency in maternal behavior is the result of harsh realities early in life, such as the death of parents, premature responsibilities, affect hunger, death, threatening illness of the child, and marital incompatibility. Studies of the effects of maternal deprivation, particularly of the institutionalized infant, were conducted by Spitz and Wolf (1946) and by Bowlby (1951). Bowlby (1973) concluded that failure of the infant or young child to obtain a warm, intimate, continuous relationship with his or her mother (or permanent mother substitute) is the probable cause of psychoneurosis and character disorders. Rutter (1974) reassessed the concept of maternal deprivation and concluded that it is essentially unproved, thus opening the door to experimentation in parenting.

In 1939 Symonds described twelve essentials of good parenting but, despite this, concluded that "It is difficult if not impossible to discriminate the kinds of persons who make good parents" (p. 110).

Brim (1959), consistent with current thinking, listed six factors as determinants of parenting behaviors: physical and intellectual factors, unconscious factors, cultural values, interpersonal and social contacts, structure of the family group, and ecological factors such as stress on the parents.

The evolution of the concept of parenting is associated with changes in belief about the nature of childhood, the breakdown of sex-stereotyped roles, and evidence indicating the importance of the father's role in child development. In addition, with the increasing movement of women into careers and out-of-the-home employment, the increased participation by fathers in child care has become essential.

Childhood was historically a "nightmare from which we have only recently awakened. The further back in history one goes, the lower the level of child care, and the more likely children are to be killed, abandoned, beaten, terrorized, and sexually abused" (DeMause, 1974, p. 1). Thus, it is only in the twentieth century that society has begun seriously to consider the needs of the child and the essential conditions for maximum growth and development. In the current period, there is concern for the empathic involvement of both parents in providing psychological conditions essential for development (DeMause, 1974).

The importance of fathering to the development of the child is a recent concern of social science. Biller (1971) reports that a review of research between 1929 and 1956 revealed only eleven publications on the father-child relationship but 160 studies concerned with the mother-child relationship. After reviewing the research on the father's role, Lynn (1974, p. 285) concludes that "children generally do not develop well in conflict-laden homes or in homes without a father, especially if the father's absence results from separation, desertion, or divorce." Walters and Stinnett (1977) believe that father absence is associated with lower masculine identification of male children. The younger the age of the child when the father leaves and the longer the absence, the greater the effect of paternal absence. Some recent studies have concluded that boys' masculinity is not significantly affected by fathers' absence (many factors influence masculinity); however, deficiencies are reported in social control and resistance to temptation (Santrock, 1975). Not only are boys negatively affected by father deprivation, but girls also manifest difficulties in personality development and feminine identification (Biller, 1971). An important goal of future research regarding the role of the father is the separation of the effect of marital discord from that of father absence on child development. Clearly, professionals are just beginning to obtain data on the contribution of the father to child development. (For additional reviews of the role of the father and father absence, see Biller and Meredith, 1975; Clarke-Stewart, 1977; DeFrain, 1974; Green, 1976; Herzog and Sudia, 1968; Lamb, 1976; Radin, 1976; and the National Council on Family Relations, 1976. Price, 1976, has developed a bibliography of literature related to the role of the father.)

Concern with parenting, as contrasted to mothering, has become of central importance in part because of the changes noted earlier. In addition, there is increasing concern for the psychological health of the interacting family unit. There is recognition that behavior must be viewed in its interactive context (Endler and Magnusson, 1976; Mischel, 1973; Mischel, 1975), rather than solely in terms of the characteristics within individuals. Parenting increasingly is viewed as part of a family system in which each part influences and is influenced by other parts of the system. Thus, parenting is viewed as a subsystem of the family unit, and the development of the child is dependent on the functioning of the family system (Minuchin, 1974).

Critical Discussion

General Areas of Concern

Parenting may be viewed as a multidimensional competence, presenting evaluation problems similar to those confronted in the assessment of the effective teacher and the effective psychotherapist. Psychotherapy, teaching, and parenting involve the relationship between a more and a less expert person, in which the more expert attempts to provide conditions that will maximize the growth of the less expert or competent. Psychotherapy, in contrast to parenting, is rich in theoretical formulations and research; but there are few widely accepted principles (concerning such issues as the goals of therapy and the importance of the characteristics of the therapist and the client) supported by empirical data. The conclusions generally supported by the literature regarding the effective therapeutic process (accurate empathy, nonpossessive warmth, and genuineness) may apply equally to effective parenting behavior (Truax and Mitchell, 1971). In the domain of teacher competence, despite much research, few clear conclusions have resulted. McNeil and Popham (1973, p. 220) note: "When one considers the idiosyncratic backgrounds of teachers and pupils, the great range of instructional objectives, and the immense variation in the environments where teaching occurs, it is unlikely that any process or personal attribute on the part of teachers will invariably produce pupil growth."

Similarly, as suggested by Paul (quoted by Bergin, 1971, p. 253), the question of effective parenting may become: "What treatment, by whom, is most effective for this individual with what specific problems and under which set of circumstances?" Paul's recommendation may be considered an ideal one for maximum effectiveness. A more humble goal regarding parenting may be to identify parents who are sufficiently deviant so that professionals may conclude that their behaviors, in most situations, would not facilitate child growth.

Parenting assessment thus presents a wide range of problems, including limited theory development, difficulty in defining effective childrearing process and child outcomes, lack of agreement in conceptualizing and measuring variables, in addition to difficulty in relating variables to one another. In short, it is an area that is in its infancy. Data are limited, and agreed-on conclusions are sparse because of the large number of variables and because studies have infrequently focused upon parents themselves. Potentially useful information may lie in the data on child development and pathology.

Much research on child development has made use of parent attitude data, which unfortunately has rarely shown a systematic relationship to child behavior (Hess, 1970). Symonds (1939) proposed that parental attitudes might be divided into the dimensions acceptance-rejection and dominance-submission, and these have essentially stood the test of time, although Schaefer (as reported in Martin, 1975) has demonstrated that eighteen maternal behaviors can be distinguished and arranged in a systematic circular order. Interestingly, children's reports of parent attitudes have been found to be more predictive of behavior or status than are measured parent attitudes (Goldin, 1969). Parent characteristics correlated with child behavior have been found in studies of delinquents and children described as disturbed, as well as in studies describing parents who physically abuse their children. In addition, data are reported regarding the characteristics of parents of competent children.

Perhaps the best-supported conclusion of the child development and child pathology literature is the social modeling concept—the belief that pathological parents produce pathological children while, conversely, psychologically healthy parents produce healthy children. In addition, extremes of permissiveness, control, or punitive rejection are associated with deviant child behavior, particularly aggression (Hetherington and Martin, 1972; Martin, 1975). Martin notes that, despite weaknesses in the research literature, "Parental warmth (and acceptance) continues to be a variable of exceptional importance. Nonacceptance is related to both withdrawn neurotic behavior and antisocial aggression across a wide age range" (p. 529). Similarly, Clarke-Stewart (1977) reports that competent children come from families in which parents are warm and attentive.

The data available from many studies of parents who have abused their children provide clues to the characteristics of deficient parents and parenting; these data also help to explain the etiology of this grossly deficient form of child care. Perhaps most widely accepted is the conclusion that abusing parents demand more from their infants and children than the children are capable of producing. In addition, such parents look to the child for reassurance, comfort, and a loving response but disregard the needs and limited abilities of the child (Steele and Pollock, 1974). Other studies essentially agree that such parents lack knowledge of specific age norms for children (Stainton, 1975) or have misinformation about children (Jayaratne, 1977). Certainly it can be questioned whether the problem is lack of cognitive knowledge of child development, lack of personal sensitivity, or conflicting parental needs. Most reports agree that such parents have themselves frequently been abused as children and have not experienced adequate parenting of their own (Gelles, 1972; Fontana and Schneider, 1978; Justice, 1976; Sameroff and Chandler, 1975; Stainton, 1975). As a result of such inadequate parenting, they in turn have unrealistic expectations of their children, which they enforce inconsistently (Sameroff and Chandler, 1975). Spinetta and Rigler (1972), in their review of the literature, report such parents to be immature, self-centered, and self-critical, while Justice (1976) describes abusive parents as narcissistic and seeking nurturing and comfort from the child. A useful conceptual framework on abuse is provided by Martin's (1976) analysis of the four typical approaches to the analysis of abuse: intrapsychic factors, social and cultural factors, psychopathology, and predisposing factors.

In contrast to the data on abusive parents, Clarke-Stewart (1973) found that the mothers of young children identified as competent were markedly sensitive and responsive to their children and effectively soothed and comforted them when they were distressed. These mothers mediated environmental stimuli, and their responses were consistent with the child's age and ability. The mother's intelligence test scores and knowledge of child development were highly correlated with positive attitudes toward the child and all variables defined as "optimal child care" (p. 54). In her extensive review of the research literature on child care, Clarke-Stewart (1977) concludes that the parents of socially competent children "model positive social behavior and reward both independent achievement and cooperation" (p. 61). In addition, such parents are responsive, but "discipline is consistent, . . . firm, . . . reasonable and rational; limits are clearly defined, are appropriate, and moderate in number; and enforcement is gentle" (p. 61).

Bronfenbrenner (1961, p. 100) notes that "Middle-class parents, as compared with lower-class parents, are more permissive of the child's spontaneous desires, express affection more freely, and prefer psychological techniques of discipline, such as reasoning or appeals to guilt, to more direct methods like physical punishment."

Factors associated with children's intellectual development are extensive verbal interaction, demand for high achievement, attentiveness, warmth, and high regard for both self and the child (Hess, 1969). Similarly, Baumrind (1972) reports that parents of children who were most self-reliant and self-controlled were content with themselves. While such parents were demanding, they were also warm, rational, and receptive to child communication. Baumrind refers to these parents as "high authoritative, a unique combination of high control and positive encouragement of the child's autonomous and independent strivings" (p. 202).

Walters and Stinnett (1977) reviewed over 200 studies of parent-child relationships. Although these studies largely confirm previously reported findings, Walters and Stinnett note, as does Clarke-Stewart (1977), that the direction of causation is not clear; that is, did the child's behavior lead to the parenting behavior or vice versa? Certainly a

neglected aspect of many parent-child studies is the extent to which the child's temperament and behavior have contributed to the parenting behavior and the resulting interaction. Walters and Stinnett conclude that parent-child relationships cannot be viewed
solely as products of parent's influence. In addition, they state that "Every generalization
concerning parent-child relationships must be qualified by a list of contingent conditions"
(p. 101).

Comparative Philosophies and Theories

Rapoport, Rapoport, and Strelitz (1977) report that there have been four approaches to parenting: biological, systems, cultural, and developmental. The biological
approach is represented by the work of ethologists and physical anthropologists, such as
Morris (1967), Ardrey (1974), Tiger and Fox (1972), and Bowlby (1951, 1973). These
authors, perhaps excluding Bowlby, are concerned with analogies between animal and
human behavior; and they view parenting as a part of mating and "nesting" behavior.
Systems theorists—including Minuchin (1974), Bateson (1972), and Haley (1976)—
emphasize the interactions within the family as the cause of child behavior. Leading early
theorists of this view include Parsons (1949), who proposed an often-cited model of
family functioning, and Bales (1950), who studied small task groups. Together, Parsons
and Bales (1955) developed the concept of the instrumental group leader (in families, the
father), who deals with external adaptation, and the expressive leader (the mother), who
focuses on the harmonization of roles, reduction of group tension, and increased commitment to the group. Thus, the role of the mother is defined as providing unconditional
love to the children, while the father's role is that of introducing societal rules and regulations into the family and rewarding children contingent upon performance. The cultural
emphasis, based on the ideas of Mead (1939a, 1939b), proposes that sex roles and parenting tasks change in accordance with the changing beliefs and values of the culture. Thus,
the current social norms are moving toward greater equality between the sexes in parenting responsibilities. The developmental position suggests that not only the child but also
the parents are affected by the stage of their respective life cycles. Thus, parents, too, go
through a series of life changes having specific tasks (marital pair without children, marital pair with young children, and the like), and these stages play a role in the definition of
key tasks to be performed.

Brown (1978) proposes that various developmental stages must be successfully
completed by the marital pair in order to create an environment for effective parenting.
These stage tasks include disconnection of the marital pair from families of origin, modification of career commitments and relationships with friends, and alteration of recreational activities. The relatively exclusive marital commitment facilitates effective parenting. Another task, Brown says, is the development of reciprocal nurturing between the
marital partners, which will later provide support for the child's development and will
invite nurturing attitudes from the child. Brown notes that environmental stresses interfere with nurturing, but that "maintaining integrative and positive nurturing attitudes in
the face of complex and conflictful feelings is a primary functional responsibility of
parenthood" (p. 25). The later development of childhood autonomy and individuation,
"while maintaining deep emotional connections" (pp. 26-27), can be effectively achieved
only if prior reciprocal nurturing has been accomplished. According to Brown, the failure
of the marital pair in establishing mutual nurturing is associated with marital dissatisfaction, disruptive cross-generational alliances, conflict, and less effective parenting.

Tallman (1971), after reviewing the task-group literature, proposes a modified
systems emphasis. He suggests that there are prerequisites for effective group (or family)

problem solving: *commitment* to the marital unit and to the child as a member; *resource control*, or the ability to control resources and thus to meet basic emotional needs as well as needs for food, clothing, and shelter; *consensus* between mates regarding goals, the means for goal attainment, and the allocation of tasks; and *boundary permeability*, or the ability of the family to keep control of their internal affairs but remain sufficiently open so that information and materials will enter the system.

Rapoport, Rapoport, and Strelitz (1977) conclude that the contemporary expectations in the social science literature require involvement and commitment to the parenting tasks, recognition that parenting involves the need to learn, ability to share problems and pleasures, and the need to adopt a teacher and learner attitude through life. White (1975) suggests that the caretakers of infants have three primary functions: *designer*, who plans the home environment to allow the infant both freedom and safety; *consultant*, who provides help consistent with the baby's purpose of the moment; and *authority*, who sets clearly enforced limits in language that the child can understand.

In the 1940s and 1950s, much of the research relevant to parenting was based on psychoanalytic theory (Brody, 1956) and was particularly concerned with such concepts as identification and resolution of the oedipal problem. Current research appears to be less obviously analytically based, and Bandura's theories of social learning (Bandura and Walters, 1963) have often served as an important conceptual framework. However, the analytic view of parenting is alive and well, as represented by Anthony and Benedak (1970).

Perhaps the most significant change in research in both child development and the study of parenting is the increased focus on naturalistic studies of parent-child interaction, as contrasted to the earlier use of attitude questionnaires and trait and dynamic theories of individual behavior. In this regard, Rowe, Murphy, and Cspkes (1975), surveying the literature on counselor effectiveness (results generally disappointing), recommend that "the focus of research should shift from the personality (characteristics) of the counselor to particular behaviors, skills and their relationships to counseling outcome" (p. 242). Similarly, in the area of instruction Hunt (1975) suggests the use of an interactional framework, asking "not which instruction program is better but rather for whom and for what purpose" (p. 218). Clearly, the determination of effective parenting must be situation, person, and skill specific.

Elaboration on Critical Points

As has been noted, many reviewers are critical of attitude data—particularly those derived from parental contact via either personal interview or questionnaire (Hess, 1970; Martin, 1975)—as a means of obtaining accurate and useful information for the evaluation of parenting. Currently favored are multiple sources of information and, especially, direct observation of interactions, naturalistic observation in the home, and structured and manipulated observations in the laboratory. After reviewing six sources of data regarding parenting behavior (parental interviews, conjoint family interviews, structured observations, unstructured observation, and diary and parental observations), Cox (1975) concludes that each has advantages and disadvantages and that employing only one is no longer satisfactory.

There are interesting data regarding the effect of observers and laboratory or clinic settings on family behavior. "As families are shifted from familiar to unfamiliar settings, from home to laboratory, or from unstructured to structured situations, there is a tendency for family members to register less negative emotion, exhibit more socially desirable responses, and ... assume socially prescribed role behavior" (Hetherington and

Martin, 1972, p. 33). Zegiob and Forehand (1975a) found that observed mothers (as contrasted with seemingly unobserved mothers) played more with their children and were more informal and more positive in verbal behavior. Observer effects on home observation are so consistent that they have come to be called the "girdle on/girdle off" phenomenon (Evans and Nelson, 1977). Such effects can be minimized if observers are similar to the parent in such characteristics as sex, race, and age, and "are inconspicuous, nonthreatening, friendly, and visit the family regularly" (Clarke-Stewart, 1977, p. 7). The evidence is clear that the behavior of parents is altered by observers, typically in the direction of increased social appropriateness. However, the effects on child behavior are less clear. Parents of deviant (clinic referrals) as well as nondeviant children were more successful in causing their children (4 to 8 years old) to behave in socially inappropriate ways and less successful in causing their children to behave in socially appropriate ways (Lobitz and Johnson, 1975). Thus, there is some evidence that parents will have difficulty hiding deviant child behavior from the observation of the clinician.

Despite limitations, interviews and questionnaires will undoubtedly remain important sources of data, especially when supplemented by other material. Interviewed parents are likely to be more accurate about recent events than earlier ones, although parents may not report accurately about interactions of which the culture does not approve (Yarrow, 1963). Yarrow also found that agreement, parent-parent and child-parent (regarding items on authority relations), ranged from 26 percent to 72 percent—making evident the need for multiple sources of information. Similarly, questionnaires often provide data of limited reliability and validity—as a result of such factors as socially appropriate responses, unclear meaning of items, and the demand for generalized conclusions from respondents; however, they have the advantage of providing a wide range of information and requiring limited expenditure of professional time. *Tests and Measurements in Child Development* (Johnson and Bommarito, 1971) provides the clinician with brief descriptions of devices ranging from structured interviews to tests and surveys and covering a wide range of parenting behaviors, attitudes, and environments.

White and his associates (1974), as part of the Harvard Preschool Project, have developed an adult assessment index (based in part on predictive evidence provided by Holmes and Rahe, 1967, and Holmes and Matsuda, 1974) designed to measure parenting stress. Abidin and Burke (1978) believe that such parental stress is especially critical in the first three years of life and are studying the predictive validity and reliability of this device.

Schneider, Hoffmeister, and Helfer (1976) have developed a questionnaire designed to "identify those parents who are more likely to have problems with parent-child relationships than is the general population" (p. 393). Fairly large-scale validation studies have been performed, providing evidence of successful differentiation among known samples of identified child abusers, those with high potential for abuse, model mothers, and mothers whose histories suggest little likelihood of their being abusive. Although the questionnaire was successful in identifying all known child abusers, its reliability is low. The best single predictive cluster in individual cases was that of "self-esteem," while the single best item distinguishing known abusers was "When I was a child my parents used severe physical punishment on me" (p. 405). The investigators report that 20 percent of their sample ($N = 500$) "have childrearing attitudes and experiences so similar to [those of] known abusers as to make them indistinguishable from nonabusers on any dimension except the absence of documented abuse" (p. 393). Schneider, Hoffmeister, and Helfer believe that a child with unique characteristics and a family crisis are necessary to precipitate an abusive act.

Wilson (1976) reports some success in the development of a "delivery room observation scale," which seeks to predict whether the mother-child interaction will facilitate child development. White (1975) remains skeptical of these devices, since "scales for assessing mother-infant interactions are almost as common as rejected research proposals" (p. 250).

Personal Views and Recommendations

The view of parenting as a subsystem within a developing family system offers a potentially productive way of understanding caretaker behavior in context. This model provides a framework for studying transactions within natural human environments, as contrasted to assessing the characteristics and processes within individuals.

Viewing parenting as a *competence* offers guidance regarding some of the components to be considered in the prediction (or concurrent assessment) of parenting. Integrating the findings of this review and the competence framework adapted from Sundberg, Snowden, and Reynolds (1978) suggests evaluation of the following five areas: *skills* in sharing pleasures and problems with others, in experiencing and conveying empathy, and in managing life change; *knowledge* of child development, at least to the extent that one's expectations of children are consistent with developmental levels; *attitudes* of reasonable contentment with self and others as well as willingness to make long-term commitments to others; *stress*, the ability to maintain day-to-day living and to cope with problems without significant impairment of relationships; *environmental resources*, having adequate and mutually supportive relationships with others as well as basic material resources; *parenting history*, the extent to which adequate parenting was experienced as a child.

Application to Particular Variables

Socioeconomic Status. Studies and reviews of the effects of socioeconomic status on childrearing behavior and attitudes (Clarke-Stewart, 1977; Deutsch, 1973; Hess, 1970; Pavenstedt, 1965; Walters and Stinnett, 1977) provide relatively consistent evidence of differences between middle- and lower-class parenting behavior. Middle-class parents are more permissive, express affection more freely, and tend to use rational forms of discipline rather than physical punishment and threats (Bronfenbrenner, 1961; Walters and Stinnett, 1977; Zegiob and Forehand, 1975b). Middle-class parents stress internal standards (Gecas and Nye, 1974), are higher on all measures of adult-initiated interaction related to the child's needs, are more positive and accepting of children, and are more likely to request, consult, and explain rather than coax and punish. Middle-class parents also provide fewer restrictions and verbally interact more frequently with their children. Parents of lower socioeconomic status have lower expectations for child attainment and stress obedience, cleanliness, and neatness (Clarke-Stewart, 1977; Gardner, 1978).

As a function of their caretaking environment, infants who suffered severe perinatal stress have been found to vary greatly in their IQ scores at 20 months: "The data have yet to produce a single predictive variable more potent than the familiar socioeconomic characteristics of the caretaking environment. . . . Socioeconomic status appears to have a much stronger influence on the course of development than perinatal history. . . . Supportive and normalizing environments appear able to eliminate the effects of early complications . . . while caretaking by deprived, stressed, or poorly educated parents tends to exacerbate difficulties" (Sameroff, 1975, pp. 274-275).

Somewhat in contrast to Sameroff's conclusions, Clarke-Stewart (1977) reports that during the first 6 months of infancy there are *no significant differences* in parenting behaviors related to socioeconomic status, although she reports such differences at ages beyond 6 months. White (1975, p. 244) reports that parenting requirements in the first 7 to 9 months of life are "so modest as to be available in even the poorest of homes. The picture changes when children begin to crawl about and to process language."

Socioeconomic status thus is a complex category. Clarke-Stewart (1977) notes that reported differences may be confounded by religious, racial, geographical, and ethnic differences, and behaviors may be a function of maternal resources, education, and perhaps biological differences. Sameroff (1975) suggests that socioeconomic differences may be confounded by the additional factors of family stability, intelligence, and parental education. Schaefer (1972) reports that lower levels of child learning and emotional problems are more related to family environment indices than to socioeconomic status. In short, the classification of families by socioeconomic level may cover more differences than are revealed, and there is clearly a need for consideration of the many variables hidden by this global term.

Marital Satisfaction. This variable is reviewed in Chapter Four of this volume. In addition, however, marital satisfaction has been found to be associated with child adjustment and competence (Clarke-Stewart, 1977; Stainton, 1975; Tan and Lawlis, 1976; Wente and Crockenberg, 1976).

Parental Pathology and Illness. The effect of these variables on parenting has been extensively reviewed by Grunebaum and associates (1975), McLean (1976), and Hirsch and Leff (1975), among others. In one significant study, Schacter and his associates (1977, p. 204) found that "women who have been hospitalized for mental illness do not respond as quickly or accurately to their infants' cues as do nonhospitalized women." Walters and Stinett (1977, p. 841) note that "Pathological symptoms of parents are present in the backgrounds of schizophrenic and emotionally disturbed children." However, these reviewers suggest that the direction of causation is not clear and in some cases may be from child to parent rather than from parent to child. Perhaps one reasonable conclusion is that the parent who has difficulty in maintaining his or her own day-to-day living "is not likely to [have] much resource left over to give to the child" (Clarizio and McCoy, 1976, p. 440).

Maternal Employment. A number of reviewers indicate that the critical factor in child care is not whether the mother is employed but whether she is satisfied with her role. Thus, employment as such is unrelated to childrearing patterns (Clarke-Stewart, 1977; Etaugh, 1974). Other authorities note the stresses created by the proliferation of maternal role demands, as well as the anxiety and guilt generated by employment (Johnson and Johnson, 1977) and the importance of adequate substitute child care (Harrell and Ridley, 1975). Etaugh (1974), in her review of the literature, found no evidence of difficulty in the adjustment of elementary school children and little effect on adolescents resulting from maternal employment. Interestingly, Etaugh reports that lower-class boys whose mothers are employed have less favorable views of their fathers. Etaugh, apparently not convinced that maternal employment is a crucial variable, concludes that "Child attachment to the mother is a function of the quality and intensity of mother-child interaction, rather than sheer availability" (p. 90).

Other Variables. Many other variables of importance to parenting have been studied. For example, Dresen (1976) has reviewed the problems of single parenting; Thompson (1968), Wilson and associates (1975), and Rapoport, Rapoport, and Strelitz (1977) have considered the problems and data regarding stepparenting; Bemis, Diers, and Sharpe (1976) deal with the teenage mother; Nydegger (1975) focuses on the effects of the age of fathers on childrearing; Stuart and Abt (1972) note the effect of separation and divorce; and Bronfenbrenner (1976) has considered the effects of social institutions on parenting and child development. Clearly, the number of variables affecting parenting is large.

References

Abidin, R., and Burke, W. T. "The Development of a Parenting Stress Index." Summary of paper presented at American Psychological Convention, Toronto, Canada, 1978.

Anthony, E. J., and Benedak, T. (Eds.). *Parenthood: Its Psychology and Pathology.* Boston: Little, Brown, 1970.

Appleton, T., Clifton, R., and Goldberg, S. "The Development of Behavior Competence in Infancy." In F. D. Horowitz and E. M. Hetherington (Eds.), *Review of Child Development Research.* Vol. 4. Chicago: University of Chicago Press, 1975.

Ardrey, R. *African Genesis: A Personal Investigation into the Animal Origins and Nature of Man.* New York: Dell, 1974.

Bales, R. F. *Interaction Process Analysis: A Method for the Study of Small Groups.* Reading, Mass.: Addison-Wesley, 1950.

Bandura, A., and Walters, R. H. *Social Learning and Personality Development.* New York: Holt, Rinehart and Winston, 1963.

Bateson, G. *Steps to an Ecology of Mind.* New York: Ballantine, 1972.

Baumrind, D. "Socialization and Instrumental Competence in Young Children." In W. Hartup (Ed.), *The Young Child.* Vol. 2. Washington, D.C.: National Association for Education of Young Children, 1972.

Bemis, J., Diers, E., and Sharpe, R. "The Teenage Single Mother." *Child Welfare,* 1976, *55,* 309-318.

Bergin, A. E. "The Evaluation of Therapeutic Outcomes." In A. E. Bergin and S. L. Garfield (Eds.), *Handbook of Psychotherapy and Behavior Change: An Empirical Analysis.* New York: Wiley, 1971.

Biller, H. B. *Father, Child, and Sex Role.* Lexington, Mass.: Heath, 1971.

Biller, H. B., and Meredith, D. *Father Power.* New York: Delacorte Press, 1975.

Bowlby, J. *Maternal Care and Mental Health.* Monograph Series 2. Geneva: World Health Organization, 1951.

Bowlby, J. *Separation.* New York: Basic Books, 1973.

Brim, O. G. *Education for Childrearing.* New York: Russell Sage Foundation, 1959.

Brody, S. *Patterns of Mothering.* New York: International Universities Press, 1956.

Bronfenbrenner, U. "Toward a Theoretical Model for Analysis of Parent-Child Relationships in a Social Context." In J. C. Glidwell (Ed.), *Parental Attitudes and Child Behavior.* Springfield, Ill.: Thomas, 1961.

Bronfenbrenner, U. "The Roots of Alienation." In N. Talbot (Ed.), *Raising Children in Modern America.* Boston: Little, Brown, 1976.

Brown, S. L. "Functions and Stresses of Parenting: Implications for Guidance." In L. E. Arnold (Ed.), *Helping Parents Help Their Children.* New York: Brunner/Mazel, 1978.

Clarizio, H., and McCoy, G. F. *Behavior Disorders in Children.* (2nd ed.) New York: Crowell, 1976.

Clarke-Stewart, K. A. "Interactions Between Mothers and Their Young Children: Characteristics and Consequences." *Monographs of the Society for Research in Child Development,* 1973, *38* (6-7, serial no. 153).

Clarke-Stewart, K. A. *Child Care in the Family.* New York: Academic Press, 1977.

Cox, A. "Annotations: The Assessment of Parental Behavior." *Child Psychology and*

Psychiatry, 1975, *16,* 255-256.

DeFrain, J. D. "A Father's Guide to Parent Guides: A Review and Assessment of the Paternal Role as Conceived in the Popular Literature." Paper presented at the annual meeting of the National Council on Family Relations, American Association of Marital and Family Counselors, St. Louis, Mo., 1974.

DeMause, L. (Ed.). *The History of Childhood.* New York: Psychohistory Press, 1974.

Denzin, N. K. *Childhood Socialization: Studies in the Development of Language, Social Behavior, and Identity.* San Francisco: Jossey-Bass, 1977.

Deutsch, C. P. "Social Class and Child Development." In B. M. Caldwell and H. N. Ricciuti (Eds.), *Review of Child Development Research.* Vol. 3. Chicago: University of Chicago Press, 1973.

Deutsch, H. *The Psychology of Women.* Vol. 2. New York: Grune & Stratton, 1945.

Dresen, S. "The Young Adult: Adjusting to Single Parenting." *American Journal of Nursing,* 1976, *76,* 1286-1289.

Endler, N. S., and Magnusson, P. "Toward an Interactional Psychology of Personality." *Psychological Bulletin,* 1976, *83,* 956-974.

Etaugh, C. "Effects of Maternal Employment on Children: A Review of Recent Research." *Merrill-Palmer Quarterly,* 1974, *20,* 71-98.

Evans, I. M., and Nelson, R. O. "Assessment of Child Behavior Problems." In A. R. Ciminero, K. Calhoun, and H. Adams (Eds.), *Handbook of Behavioral Assessment.* New York: Wiley-Interscience, 1977.

Fontana, V. J., and Schneider, C. "Help for Abusing Parents." In L. E. Arnold (Ed.), *Helping Parents Help Their Children.* New York: Brunner/Mazel, 1978.

Gangel, K. O. "Toward a Biblical Theology of Marriage and Family. Part One: Pentateuch and Historical Books." *Journal of Psychology and Theology,* 1977, *5,* 55-69.

Gardner, H. *Developmental Psychology.* Boston: Little, Brown, 1978.

Gecas, V., and Nye, F. I. "Sex and Class Differences in Parent-Child Interaction: A Test of Kohn's Hypothesis." *Journal of Marriage and the Family,* 1974, *36,* 742-749.

Gelles, R. J. *The Violent Home: A Study of Physical Aggression Between Husbands and Wives.* Beverly Hills, Calif.: Sage, 1972.

Goldin, P. C. "A Review of Children's Reports of Parent Behaviors." *Psychological Reports,* 1969, *71,* 222-236.

Green, M. *Fathering.* New York: McGraw-Hill, 1976.

Greven, P. J. *Child Rearing Concepts 1628-1861.* Itaska, Ill.: Peacock, 1973.

Grunebaum, H., and others. *Mentally Ill Mothers and Their Children.* Chicago: University of Chicago Press, 1975.

Haley, J. *Problem-Solving Therapy: New Strategies for Effective Family Therapy.* San Francisco: Jossey-Bass, 1976.

Harrell, J. E., and Ridley, C. A. "Substitute Child Care, Maternal Employment and the Quality of Mother Child Interaction." *Journal of Marriage and the Family,* 1975, *37,* 556-564.

Helfer, R. E., and Kempe, C. H. (Eds.). *Child Abuse and Neglect.* Cambridge, Mass.: Ballinger, 1976.

Herzog, E., and Sudia, C. "Fatherless Homes. A Review of Research." *Children,* 1968, *15,* 177-182.

Hess, R. D. "Parental Behavior and Children's School Achievement in Headstart." In E. H. Grotberg (Ed.), *Critical Issues in Research Related to Disadvantaged Children.* Princeton, N.J.: Educational Testing Service, 1969.

Hess, R. D. "Social Class and Ethnic Influences on Socialization." In P. H. Mussen (Ed.), *Carmichael's Handbook of Child Psychology.* New York: Wiley, 1970.

Hetherington, E. M., and Martin, B. "Family Interaction and Psychopathology in Children." In H. C. Quay and J. S. Werry (Eds.), *Psychopathological Disorders of Childhood.* New York: Wiley, 1972.

Hirsch, S. R., and Leff, J. P. *Abnormalities in Parents of Schizophrenics.* London: Oxford University Press, 1975.

Holmes, T. H., and Matsuda, M. "Life Change and Illness Susceptibility." In B. S. and B. P. Dohrenwend (Eds.), *Stressful Life Events.* New York: Wiley, 1974.

Holmes, T. H., and Rahe, R. H. "The Social Readjustment Rating Scale." *Journal of Psychosomatic Research,* 1967, *11,* 213-218.

Hunt, D. E. "Person-Environment Interaction: A Challenge Found Wanting Before It Was Tried." *Review of Educational Research,* 1975, *45,* 209-230.

Jayaratne, S. "Child Abusers as Parents and Children." *Social Work,* 1977, *22,* 5-9.

Johnson, C. L., and Johnson, F. A. "Attitudes Toward Parenting in Dual Career Families." *American Journal of Psychiatry,* 1977, *134,* 391-395.

Johnson, O. G., and Bommarito, J. W. *Tests and Measurements in Child Development: Handbook I.* San Francisco: Jossey-Bass, 1971.

Justice, B., and Justice, R. *The Abusing Family.* New York: Human Sciences Press, 1976.

Lamb, M. (Ed.). *The Role of the Father in Child Development.* New York: Wiley, 1976.

Levy, D. M. *Maternal Overprotection.* New York: Columbia University Press, 1943.

Lobitz, W. C., and Johnson, S. M. "Parental Manipulation of the Behavior of Normal and Deviant Children." *Child Development,* 1975, *45,* 719-726.

Lynn, D. B. *The Father: His Role in Child Development.* Monterey, Calif.: Brooks/Cole, 1974.

Lytton, H. "Observational Studies of Parent-Child Interaction: A Methodological Review." *Child Development,* 1971, *42,* 652-682.

McLean, P. D. "Parental Depression." In E. J. Mash, L. C. Handy, and L. A. Hammerlynet (Eds.), *Behavior Modification Approaches to Parenting.* New York: Brunner/Mazel, 1976.

McNeil, J. D., and Popham, J. W. "The Assessment of Teacher Competence." In R. M. W. Travers (Ed.), *Second Handbook on Teaching.* Chicago: Rand McNally, 1973.

Martin, B. "Parent-Child Relations." In F. D. Horowitz and E. M. Hetherington (Eds.), *Review of Child Development Research.* Vol. 4. Chicago: University of Chicago Press, 1975.

Martin, H. P. "The Environment of the Abused Child." In H. P. Martin (Ed.), *The Abused Child: A Multidisciplinary Approach.* Cambridge, Mass.: Ballinger, 1976.

Mead, M. *From the South Seas: Studies of Adolescence and Sex in Primitive Societies.* New York: Morrow, 1939a.

Mead, M. *Male and Female: A Study of the Sexes in a Changing World.* New York: Morrow, 1939b.

Minuchin, S. *Families and Family Therapy.* Cambridge, Mass.: Harvard University Press, 1974.

Mischel, W. "Toward a Cognitive Social Learning Reconceptualization of Personality." *Psychological Review,* 1973, *80,* 252-283.

Mischel, W. "On the Future of Personality Measurement." Paper presented at the symposium on The Future of Personality Assessment, American Psychological Association, Chicago, 1975.

Morris, D. *The Naked Ape: A Zoologist's Study of the Human Animal.* New York: McGraw-Hill, 1967.

National Council on Family Relations. "Fatherhood." *Family Coordinator,* 1976, *25* (special issue).

Nydegger, C. "Age and Paternal Behaviors." *Gerontologist,* 1975, *15,* 44-45.

Pavenstedt, E. A. "A Comparison of the Child Rearing Environment of Upper and Very Low Lower Class Families." *American Journal of Orthopsychiatry,* 1965, *35,* 89-98.

Parsons, T. "The Social Structure of the Family." In R. N. Anshew (Ed.), *The Family: Its Function and Destiny.* New York: Harper & Row, 1949.

Parsons, T., and Bales, R. F. *Family Socialization and Interaction Process.* New York: Free Press, 1955.

Price, B. A. "Bibliography of Literature Related to the Roles of Father." *Family Coordinator,* 1976, *25,* 489-513.

Radin, N. "The Role of the Father in Cognitive, Academic and Intellectual Development." In M. Lamb (Ed.), *The Role of the Father in Child Development.* New York: Wiley, 1976.

Rapoport, R., Rapoport, R. N., and Strelitz, Z. *Fathers, Mothers, and Society.* New York: Basic Books, 1977.

Rowe, W., Murphy, H. B., and Cspkes, R. A. "The Relationship of Counselor Characteristics for Counseling Effectiveness." *Review of Educational Research,* 1975, *45,* 231-246.

Rutter, M. *Maternal Deprivation Reassessed.* London: Penguin Books, 1974.

Sameroff, A. J. "Early Influences on Development: Fact or Fancy?" *Merrill-Palmer Quarterly,* 1975, *21,* 267-294.

Sameroff, A. J., and Chandler, M. J. "Reproductive Risk and the Continuum of Caretaking Casuality." In F. D. Horowitz and others (Eds.), *Review of Child Development Research.* Chicago: University of Chicago Press, 1975.

Santrock, J. W. "Father Absence, Perceived Maternal Behavior and Moral Development in Boys." *Child Development,* 1975, *46,* 753-757.

Schacter, J., and others. "Assessment of Mother-Infant Interaction: Schizophrenic and Non-schizophrenic Mothers." *Merrill-Palmer Quarterly,* 1977, *23,* 193-206.

Schaefer, E. S. "Parents as Educators, Longitudinal and Intervention Research." In W. Hartup (Ed.), *The Young Child.* Washington, D.C.: National Association for Education of Young Children, 1972.

Schneider, C., Hoffmeister, J. K., and Helfer, R. "A Predictive Questionnaire for Parental Problems in Mother-Child Interactions." In R. Helfer and C. H. Kempe (Eds.), *Child Abuse and Neglect.* Cambridge, Mass.: Ballinger, 1976.

Spinetta, J. J., and Rigler, D. "The Child Abusing Parent: A Psychological Review." *Psychological Bulletin,* 1972, *77,* 296-304.

Spitz, R. A., and Wolf, K. M. "Anaclitic Depression." In A. Freud, E. Kris, and H. Hartmann (Eds.), *The Psychoanalytic Study of the Child.* Vol. 2. New York: International Universities Press, 1946.

Stainton, M. C. "Non-accidental Trauma?" *Canadian Nurse,* 1975, *71,* 26-29.

Steele, B. F., and Pollock, C. B. "Psychiatric Study of Parents Who Abuse Infants and Small Children." In R. Helfer and C. H. Kempe (Eds.), *The Battered Child.* (2nd ed.) Chicago: University of Chicago Press, 1974.

Stuart, I. R., and Abt, L. E. *Children of Separation and Divorce.* New York: Grossman, 1972.

Sundberg, N. D., Snowden, L. R., and Reynolds, W. "Toward Assessment of Person Competence in Life Situations." *Annual Review of Psychology,* 1978, *29,* 179-344.

Symonds, P. M. *Psychology of Parent-Child Relations.* New York: Appleton-Century-Crofts, 1939.

Tallman, I. "Family Problem Solving." In J. Aldus (Ed.), *Family Problem Solving.* Hindsdale, Ill.: Dryden Press, 1971.

Tan, G., and Lawlis, G. F. "Correlational Study of Children's School Achievement and Parent Interactional Perceptions." *Psychological Reports,* 1976, *38,* 578-580.

Thompson, H. *The Successful Stepparent.* New York: Funk & Wagnalls, 1968.

Tiger, L., and Fox, R. *The Imperial Animal.* New York: Dell, 1972.

Truax, C. B., and Mitchell, K. M. "Research on Certain Therapist Interpersonal Skills in Relation to Process and Outcome." In A. E. Bergin and S. L. Garfield (Eds.), *Handbook of Psychotherapy and Behavior Change: An Empirical Analysis.* New York: Wiley, 1971.

Walters, J., and Stinnett, N. "Parent-Child Relationships: A Decade Review of Research." *Journal of Marriage and the Family,* 1977, *39,* 70-106.

Wente, A. S., and Crockenberg, S. B. "Transition to Fatherhood: Lamaze Preparation, Adjustment Difficulty and Husband-Wife Relationship." *Family Coordinator,* 1976, *25,* 351-357.

White, B. L. "Critical Influence in Origins of Competence." *Merrill-Palmer Quarterly,* 1975, *21,* 243-266.

White, B. L., and others. *Adult Assessment Scales.* Cambridge, Mass.: Harvard Preschool Project, Harvard University, 1974.

White, M. S. "Social Class, Child Rearing Practice and Child Behavior." *American Sociological Review,* 1957, *22,* 704-712.

Wilson, A. L. *Early Prediction of Parenting Potential.* University Microfilm, 76-12547. Ann Arbor, Mich.: Dissertation Abstracts International, 1976.

Wilson, K. L., and others. "Stepfathers and Stepchildren: An Exploratory Analysis from Two National Surveys." *Journal of Marriage and the Family,* 1975, *37,* 526-536.

Yarrow, M. R. "Problems of Methods in Parent-Child Research." *Child Development,* 1963, *34,* 215-226.

Zegiob, L. E., and Forehand, R. "An Examination of Observer Effects on Parent-Child Interaction." *Child Development,* 1975a, *46,* 509-512.

Zegiob, L. E., and Forehand, R. "Maternal Interactive Behaviors as a Function of Race, Socioeconomic Status and Sex of the Child." *Child Development,* 1975b, *46,* 564-568.

7

Edwin L. Herr

Career Development

The term *career development* (interchangeable with the earlier term *vocational development*) incorporates research and theory that describe the developmental processes and the conditions that influence the processes involved in choosing vocational goals and establishing a work identity. *Career maturity* (used interchangeably with *vocational maturity*) is typically conceived as a series of traits that interact to permit the individual to master developmental tasks associated with the exploration of self and career characteristics, the specification of vocational preferences, the establishment and advancement in a career pattern, and adjustments to a changing self in relation to career. The traits required of the career-mature individual vary with the life stage occupied. A person said to be career-mature at a particular point (for instance, at adolescence) would not necessarily be so at a later stage (such as middle age) unless appropriate developmental growth had occurred during the intervening period.

Career identity is a special case of self-identity. The term connotes the process by which individuals translate their self-concepts into occupational terms. That is, they convert their changing picture of themselves into decisions that give direction to the career pursued. Career identity can be positive or negative. Work can be central or peripheral in the choices that an individual makes. Regardless, the interaction of these factors produces career patterns (or job histories) that are continuous or discontinuous, linear or jagged, as they are observed within groups of persons across the life span.

103

Background and Current Status

The concept of life stages applied to vocational choice and adjustment is evident in the early work of Bühler (1933) and Super (1942). However, major stimulation to the notion of career development processes occurred in the 1950s as a result of the work of Ginzberg and his colleagues (1951), Havighurst (1953), and Super and his colleagues (Super, 1953, 1957; Super and Bachrach, 1957; Super and others, 1957). In the early 1950s, Super initiated the twenty-year Career Pattern Study, a longitudinal study of more than 100 men from the time they were in ninth grade until they were well into adulthood, and with it stimulated the process of conceptualizing, defining, and assessing vocational (later known as career) maturity. Since the first model of vocational maturity proposed by Super in 1954, other researchers, including Crites (1965), have refined and extended the concept.

Before 1950 the approach to vocational choice, placement, and adjustment was primarily that of improving methods of matching persons and jobs. The emphasis was on increasing psychometric sophistication in regard to identifying the traits required for success in different occupations and in effective measurement in persons of the presence of the traits by which occupations could be distinguished. If an individual's characteristics and the characteristics required in a particular job could be closely related, it was assumed, an effective match would ensue. Such a matching approach lay at the base of vocational guidance and counseling from the turn of the twentieth century until approximately 1950.

By 1950, however, some vocational psychologists were growing increasingly uncomfortable with a trait and factor approach to vocational guidance and vocational choice. They were beginning to ask developmentally and behaviorally focused questions: How do vocational goals develop, and what factors influence them? Can vocational goals be modified? Do vocational choices differ at different points in life? Do people differ in their decision-making skill? If so, why? On what bases do individual career patterns differ? Such questions broadened the perspectives of theorists and practitioners from predictions about immediate choice to intermediate and future choice as well. Simultaneously, the unit of study shifted from job or occupation to the broader notion of career—encompassing not only a concern about the content of work but also a broad spectrum of questions about the relationship between education and work, work and life style, work and leisure, work and personal goals.

As a dynamic and developmental view of occupational choice and career patterning began to emerge, redefinitions of the ways of helping persons choose also began. In a presidential address to the National Vocational Guidance Association, Hoppock (1950) concluded that the traditional views of vocational guidance were "beginning to crumble." In 1951 Super recommended revision of the official definition of vocational guidance adopted by the National Vocational Guidance Association in 1937. In place of that definition ("Vocational guidance is the process of assisting the individual to choose an occupation, prepare for it, enter upon and progress in it") Super (1951, p. 92) proposed that vocational guidance be considered "the process of helping a person to develop and accept an integrated and adequate picture of himself and of his role in the world of work, to test this concept against reality, and to convert it into a reality with satisfaction to himself and benefit to society." The 1951 definition of vocational guidance brought to the forefront a focus on self-understanding and self-acceptance as a base to evaluate occupational and educational alternatives available to the individual. The psychological nature of vocational choice was accepted as a given, although there was as yet little systematic theory to deal with such concepts.

Today, career development theory has become the conceptual glue providing both a rationale and a substance for current models of career education and of career guidance. In broad terms, career education is concerned about the existing relationship between education and work. It gives particular attention to the problems experienced by youth and adults in the transition from schooling to work or at points of occupational dislocation. Of specific concern to the federal government and to other social agencies have been alleged deficiencies in the ability of youth (1) to understand and act upon their aptitudes, values, and goals; (2) to make accurate self-appraisals; (3) to identify and differentiate between educational and occupational options available to them; (4) to make realistic career-related choices independent of others; and (5) to manifest attitudes and behavior conducive to job satisfaction and adjustment. Such individual deficiencies are alleged to be the result of inappropriate educational emphases, so that opportunities for occupational socialization are not adequately incorporated into schooling. It is contended that schools remain indifferent to facilitating the career development of students and to providing them with specific knowledge, attitudes, and skills comprising "employability." The assumption is that schooling in the United States has been oriented too much to college preparation or general education rather than to its utility in preparing persons with occupation-specific task skills and other behaviors required by the labor force.

Regardless of the debatable validity of some of the current criticisms of education in relation to work preparation, it has been necessary to identify the specific behaviors or organizing themes that might enhance relationships between education and work. Career development theory and research have provided major insight into the behavioral elements which are of consequence in the transition from school to work, reentry into the labor force, or occupational dislocation-relocation. Career development theory and research have also provided insight into how the behaviors are formed, how they differ across population and age groups, and when and how they might be modified.

Like career education, current models of career guidance have also benefited from the insights provided by career development theory in research. Career education has been defined by the United States Office of Education as "the totality of experiences through which one learns about and prepares to engage in work as part of her or his way of living" (Hoyt, 1975, p. 6). Career guidance is a major subsystem of the broad set of experiences described in the above definition of career education. As such, it attempts to help individuals personalize the many experiences constituting career education and develop systematic plans by which they can integrate work, family, leisure, and community roles. Career guidance can be considered a synthesizing process, in which individuals are helped to combine their self and career understanding in the decision making in which they engage. Thus, career guidance, as it is currently viewed, is not simply crisis centered and focused on immediate choice but addresses developmental questions relative to self and career identity. Beyond this, the intent is not only to remediate skill and information deficits which inhibit decision making but to systematically help persons learn to anticipate and plan from immediate choice options to intermediate and future choice directions. In other words, career guidance seeks to help persons attain career maturity. Career development theory and research have been instrumental in identifying the behaviors that comprise career maturity in different life stages.

Critical Discussion

General Areas of Concern

Five major areas of concern are pertinent to career development theory and research: (1) accommodation of multidisciplinary views of career development into a coherent frame of reference; (2) importance of creating a theory of career development interventions as well as a theory of career development behavior; (3) degree to which current models of career development are culture-bound or class-bound; (4) differences between the structural and the developmental aspects of career behavior; and (5) assessment of career development.

Because career development encompasses many types of behaviors and events across the life span, career development theory and research can be viewed through multidisciplinary lenses. However, the accommodation into a coherent theory of career development of insights emanating from psychology, economics, anthropology, and sociology, as well as subspecialties within each knowledge domain, is yet to be fully achieved. Similarly, not enough is known about career development interventions. A knowledge of the short-range effects of various career guidance techniques is available, but there are gaps in understanding of the comparative effects of many intervention processes in relation to specified criteria. Knowledge about the long-range effects of career development interventions is, at best, limited.

Regarding the third area of concern—the degree to which current models are culture-bound or class-bound—many of the original samples from which theory derived were middle-class white males in the United States; therefore, the same level of systematic inquiry has not been extended to women, to persons of diverse socioeconomic backgrounds, or to special populations such as minorities or the physically handicapped. Beyond these limitations within the United States, most American models of career development have not been tested in other nations.

The fourth area of concern is related to the structural versus the developmental aspects of career behavior. The first is a cross-sectional issue; the second is longitudinal. In the first instance, there is the question of what behaviors comprise career maturity at a particular life stage (such as adolescence). In the second case, the question is how such behaviors change over time and under what conditions. Considerable speculation about each of these areas is currently available in the different theoretical perspectives on career development. The empirical base necessary to examine these questions is substantially less complete.

The fifth area of concern has to do with the assessment of career development. Earlier models of career guidance were principally concerned with aptitude and interest assessment—predicting one's future performance from his or her actual or potential performance (aptitude) or the likely compatibility of an individual with persons occupying some educational or occupational role (interest). Each of these measurements provides information about the content of decisions to be made. Career development, however, goes beyond the issue of the content of decisions to one's readiness to make decisions. Therefore, assessment in career development must consider the individual's career maturity—his or her ability to choose, to plan, and to accept the consequences of choice and related issues. Research about this type of assessment is still in its infancy. There are career development assessment instruments with a considerable research base now commercially available, but these are generally useful primarily with adolescents, not college students or adults.

Comparative Philosophies and Theories

Trait and Factor. The clearest example of a descriptive approach to career behavior is the trait and factor approach. Based on theories of individual differences, this approach does not emphasize how such differences develop but rather how they relate to entry or success in different educational, occupational, or social alternatives. In this approach, one attempts to identify and measure the individual characteristics that are directly related to educational and occupational choice, to the learning of such choices, and to adjustment to or success in them. The individual behaviors usually considered of most importance in a trait and factor approach are aptitudes, interests, and values. The assumption on which a trait and factor approach rests is that an individual must have certain specific traits in order to perform effectively in a specific occupation or educational program. It is also assumed that these relationships between individual traits and educational or occupational factors can be determined through research and used to identify the odds of any individual's likely success in a particular type of alternative.

Economic or Decision Theory. Economic or decision theory assumes that career behavior unfolds in response to continuous decisions by which persons try to maximize their gain and minimize their loss. The gain or loss might be anything of value to a particular individual, such as income, prestige, social mobility, or spouse. Such approaches view choices as occurring under conditions of risk or uncertainty, which require individuals to reconcile several factors, such as the relative value of outcomes, the cost of attaining the outcomes, and the probability that each outcome may occur. Economic and decision theorists are concerned primarily with such matters as the way that individuals engage in risk-taking behavior, the reconciling of the costs and the likelihood of different alternatives occurring, the application of objective and subjective probabilities, and the clarity with which values are held and applied in decision making.

Sociological Approaches. According to sociological theorists, an individual's career development depends on such factors as family beliefs, sex, race, socioeconomic status, opportunities available or accessible, community attitudes about the value of different types of choices, and other factors beyond the control of the individual (but whose effects are likely to be internalized) that shape both motivations and information-seeking behavior. Put in another fashion, sociological approaches indicate that the place one occupies in the social stratum has a large effect on what opportunities one will know about, be encouraged to consider, or be able to act on. The assumption here is that the society is a large information percolation system which does not distribute information, encouragement, or resources equally and that these inequities shape career patterns differently.

Psychological Approaches. Psychological approaches tend to stress intrinsic individual motivation as the major factor in career development. These approaches concern themselves principally with inferred states or conditions that prompt persons to engage in career-related behavior. In some instances, psychological theorists explain career development in terms of Maslow's (1954) theory of prepotent needs; others believe that adult vocations are sought for their instinctual gratifications, as need for these is developed in early childhood; others connect the development of occupational interests with early childrearing practices. Whether the central focus is impulse gratification or need satisfaction, psychological theorists view career development as an unfolding process of individuals searching out and gravitating to environments consistent with their own self-classifications or which affirm their personal behavioral styles.

Developmental Emphases. Developmental approaches are most concerned with the career development tasks that people typically cope with at different life periods. Generally, developmental views of career development acknowledge that most persons have multipotentiality. A persistent theme in developmental perspectives on career development is that persons must master increasingly complex vocational development tasks at different life stages; if they do not do so, floundering, plateauing, or other forms of retarded career development will occur. Within this context, sociological factors, physical impairments, and related variables are incorporated to explain career behavior which is not smooth and linear across life stages. Central to several of the developmental perspectives on career development is the view that one chooses and behaves in accordance with the self-concept in relation to the demands or possibilities inherent in different choice opportunities. The self-concept is not static. It both shapes and is shaped by choices made. Therefore, career development at different life stages is at once a public translation of one's self-concept and a synthesis of what is desired and what is available.

Elaboration on Critical Points

Career development theory is an amalgam of views in which specific occupational choice and the patterning of occupational choices across the life span are each vital issues. Beyond these matters, however, the factors that account for continuity and discontinuity in the behaviors and the decisions comprising career development are important areas of inquiry. It is conventional wisdom that career development interacts with physical, intellectual, and emotional development and that a great number of stimuli influence it (for example, mass media, peers, and family). As in other types of growth and learning, persons vary in their readiness to engage in self-understanding, information about options available to them, and the responsibilities inherent in choice-making. Following are some of the most-used empirically based instruments for measuring the career maturity or the decision-making readiness of an individual:

The *Career Maturity Inventory* (CMI) (Crites, 1973) is composed of an attitude scale and a competence scale. The attitude scale assesses orientation to work, conceptions of the choice process, independence in decision making, preference for vocational choice factors, and involvement in the choice process. The competence test assesses self-appraisal, occupational information, goal selection, planning, and problem solving. The CMI is typically used from grade 6 through grade 12, although some researchers have used the instrument in the early years of college or postsecondary education.

The *Cognitive Vocational Maturity Test* (Westbrook and Parry-Hill, 1973) is composed of six subtests. The first five assess a subject's occupational knowledge (fields of work, work conditions, duties, and the education and attributes required for various occupations); the sixth (job selection) assesses the subject's ability to choose the most realistic occupation for a hypothetical student with specific ability, interests, and values. Normative data are available for grades 6 through 9.

The *Career Development Inventory, Form I* (Super and Forrest, 1972) is comprised of three scales designed to assess planning orientation (concern with choice, specificity of planning, and self-estimated knowledge of occupations), resources for exploration (knowledge and use of appropriate resources needed in planning), and information and decision making (actual occupational information and knowledge of vocational decision-making principles). Normative data are available for grades 8 through 12.

The *Career Skills Assessment Program* (College Entrance Examination Board, 1974) consists of six separate self-assessment areas: self-evaluation and development skills, career awareness skills, career decision-making skills, employment-seeking skills, work effectiveness skills, and personal economics skills. The skills in each assessment domain are grouped in four basic areas: (1) relating abilities, values, needs, and experience to career choices; (2) locating, evaluating, and interpreting information for career choices; (3) obtaining facts about career opportunities; and (4) learning educational requirements for various occupations. It is useful primarily for grades 9 to 12.

The *Assessment of Career Development* (American College Testing Program, 1974) consists of scales measuring occupational awareness (occupational knowledge and exploratory occupational experience), self-awareness (preferred job characteristics, career plans, and perceived needs for help), career planning and decision making (career-planning knowledge and career-planning involvement), and reactions to career guidance experiences. It is designed for use with students in grades 8 through 11.

The instruments described here are addressed specifically to aspects of the career development process. Each has a comprehensive research base and has demonstrated validity for career development assessment. Other experimental instruments are now being developed, but they have not yet achieved the level of empirical support that would justify their inclusion here.

As indicated previously, aptitude tests, as well as interest and value inventories, have relevance to career development. However, this is not their purported goal, nor do they address an individual's readiness for choice.

Personal Views and Recommendations

As suggested by the nature of the career development instruments currently available, there are gaps in measurement techniques just as there are gaps in career development theory and research. Career development does not begin with the seventh grade, nor does it stop at the end of the twelfth grade. But the available career development measures are largely confined to use with persons during these years. In many ways, this fact acknowledges that most of the research interest in career development has been directed, until recently, to the initial exploration period, which is seen as occurring primarily between the years of 14 and 25. While career development theory has addressed the life span, research studies have not been equally comprehensive. Although this situation is now changing, currently available career development assessment instruments have dealt primarily with those years in which research findings have been most fully available.

Current research efforts are being systematically directed to adults in mid-career crisis, middle-aged adults, pre-retirees, and other postsecondary school populations. There is little doubt that the near future will bring extensions to these populations of the career development assessment techniques now useful for adolescents. Except in some experimental procedures, this measurement goal has not yet been achieved.

Since the measurement of career development flows from the status of theory and research dealing with such phenomena, it is important to acknowledge the gaps that exist in the latter. Most of the accepted principles of career development theory have come from longitudinal studies of relatively small samples of middle-class white males. Beyond these studies, there are many cross-sectional studies dealing with various subpopulations. In large measure, these have not been assimilated into a comprehensive theory which combines longitudinal perspectives with those coming from various short-term, cross-sectional tests of hypotheses. Trends such as the growing similarity of male and female career patterns have had little acknowledgment in the theoretical or research literature.

There is as yet no comprehensive theoretical perspective on the career development of women, nor is there much systematic information on the career development of minority group members, whether classified racially, ethnically, or religiously. Relatively little attention has been given to the career development of the rural poor as compared with the urban poor. Systematic study of the effects of congenital versus later physical handicaps upon career development is yet to be undertaken. Virtually no attention has been given to the career development of homosexuals, the employment limitations they face, or the career guidance strategies appropriate to them (Herr, 1978).

With populations described as minority or poor, theory and research have not, for example, differentiated the effects of race from those of socioeconomic class in isolating different types of impaired or retarded career patterns. Relatively little is known about the effects of economic or cultural change upon career development in general or upon such specific factors as individual risk taking as a potent influence in shaping career behavior. Situational (sociological) variables have been hypothesized to be major influences on career development, but research testing the direct effects of such conditions upon personal choice making is spotty at best. It is clear that family history and socioeconomic status have an effect on an individual's self-concept and the career choices that he or she will make. The question is: How much of an effect, when, under what conditions, and for whom?

Application to Particular Variables

Age. Since individual career development evolves and changes throughout the life span, assessment techniques can be applied at any age. The behavior and development of elementary school children are more likely to be expressed in action rather than content; therefore, young children should be permitted to express their career development through action, role playing, dramatics, games, and ideas likely to be within their social radius. As career development assessment is applied to older populations, more emphasis can appropriately be placed on content and on paper-and-pencil or other more abstract measurement techniques. This does not preclude the use of direct-action exercises in which career development problem-solving exercises are the assessment content. It simply acknowledges the greater quantity of vocabulary and experiences that youth and adults bring to career development assessment as compared with children. It is also useful to note that many adults are as illiterate about themselves and their opportunities as children are. Thus, the career development concepts that need to be assessed in children, youth, or adults are not necessarily different; it is the language system and the assessment procedure that differ.

Sex. In general, the career development assessments identified above do not have different sex norms. The assumption is that the readiness for choice making, the ability to plan, and the possession of information are not sex related. The research evidence for this assertion is somewhat ambivalent. However, it does appear that females tend to get set in careers earlier than males. To the degree that this is so, career guidance efforts intended to facilitate the use of accurate information about the self and environmental opportunities, to keep career options open, and to assess readiness for and competency in career decision making need to occur at an earlier age for girls than for boys.

Among adults, many women and men have similar career patterns; where this is true, career assessment procedures can be similar. In the case of women reentering the labor market after many years of childrearing or other home- or family-oriented activities, it may be necessary to deal with basic feelings of anxiety or inability to cope with the pressures of a full-time job in the labor market before dealing with information or decision-making factors pertinent to specific choices.

Education. Problems of underemployment, unemployment, or indecisiveness about the type of commitment to work one wants to make occur among people of all educational backgrounds. Aside from the specific choice problem at issue, all of these persons need help in determining their readiness for choice, the information they need, the clarity of their self-understanding, and other factors assessed by career development measures.

Socioeconomic Status. Career development techniques previously discussed are appropriate across socioeconomic levels. However, persons at different socioeconomic levels will likely differ in the breadth of developmental experiences they have had, the career models to which they have been exposed, and the types of educational or occupational options they have been encouraged to consider and implement.

Vocation. Regardless of the type of vocational goal one wishes to explore or to which one aspires, the career development questions that need to be considered remain relatively constant.

Ethnic/Racial Factors. Career development assessment techniques have not been differentiated on ethnic or racial grounds. The assumption is that persons in such groups also need assistance in clarifying their self-characteristics and the options available to them. Beyond these needs, it is assumed that the counselor will be alert to and deal with developmental deficits that unrealistically limit the individual's aspirations, self-concepts, or information.

Disorders. Little research directly related to the career development of persons experiencing physical, intellectual, or psychiatric disorders has been undertaken. The assumption would be, as in any other measurement procedure, that career development assessment procedures would need to be tailored to take into account hearing or visual impairment or psychomotor difficulties. In the case of intellectual impairments, it may be necessary to deal with role playing, acting out, and other concrete forms of career development assessment rather than more abstract procedures. Frequently, such procedures can be carried on within the context of vocational evaluation or sheltered workshop techniques. Certain psychiatric disorders may preclude career development procedures. Assessment in career development is a reality-testing process; therefore, unless the individual's emotional stability is being managed, through chemical or other therapeutic interventions, so that adequate reality contact is present, career development assessment procedures should not be implemented.

References

American College Testing Program. *Assessment of Career Development: User's Guide and Report of Research.* Boston: Houghton Mifflin, 1974.

Bühler, C. *Der Menschliche Rebenslauf abs Psychologisches Problem.* Leipzig: Hirzel, 1933.

College Entrance Examination Board. *Career Skills Assessment Program: Sample Set.* New York: College Entrance Examination Board, 1974.

Crites, J. O. "Measurement of Maturity on Adolescence. I: Attitude Test of the Vocational Development Inventory." *Psychological Monographs,* 1965, *72,* 595.

Crites, J. O. *Administration and Use Manual for the Career Maturity Inventory.* Monterey, Calif.: CTB/McGraw-Hill, 1973.

Ginzberg, E., and others. *Occupational Choice.* New York: Columbia University Press, 1951.

Havighurst, R. J. *Human Development and Education.* New York: Longmans Green, 1953.

Herr, E. L. *Work-Focused Guidance for Youth in Transition: An R & D Approach for Vocational Education.* Occasional Paper 43. Columbus: Center for Vocational Education, Ohio State University, 1978.

Hoppock, R. "Presidential Address, 1950." *Occupations,* 1950, *28,* 497-499.

Hoyt, K. B. *An Introduction to Career Education: A Policy Paper of the U.S. Office of Education.* Washington, D.C.: U.S. Government Printing Office, 1975.

Maslow, A. H. *Motivation and Personality.* New York: Harper & Row, 1954.

Super, D. E. *Dynamics of Vocational Adjustment.* New York: Harper & Row, 1942.

Super, D. E. "Vocational Adjustment: Implementing a Self-Concept." *Occupations,* 1951, *30,* 88-92.

Super, D. E. "A Theory of Vocational Development." *American Psychologist,* 1953, *8,* 185-190.

Super, D. E. "Career Patterns as a Basis for Vocational Counseling." *Journal of Counseling Psychology,* 1954, *1,* 12-20.

Super, D. E. *The Psychology of Careers.* New York: Harper & Row, 1957.

Super, D. E., and Bachrach, P. B. *Scientific Careers and Vocational Development Theory.* New York: Bureau of Publications, Teachers College, Columbia University, 1957.

Super, D. E., and others. *Vocational Development: A Framework for Research.* New York: Bureau of Publications, Teachers College, Columbia University, 1957.

Super, D. E., and Forrest, D. J. *Career Development Inventory, Form 1: Preliminary Manual.* New York: Teachers College, Columbia University, 1972. (Mimeograph.)

Westbrook, B. W., and Parry-Hill, J. W., Jr. *The Construction and Validation of a Measure of Vocational Maturity.* Center Technical Paper 16. Raleigh: Center for Occupational Education, North Carolina State University, 1973.

8

Thomas M. Achenbach

Behavior Disorders of Children and Adolescents

As used here, the term *behavior disorders* designates behavior that is generally of concern to mental health professionals. It does not imply an exclusively behavioristic conception of etiology, assessment, or treatment, and it encompasses the terms *psychopathology, mental disorders,* and *emotional disturbance.* The relevant assessment data are necessarily behavioral, because psychological states are not directly observable. However, behavioral data include physiological responses and self-reports and may be used to infer psychological functioning. Although behavior disorders may be associated with mental retardation, learning disabilities, and organic dysfunctions, these topics will not be specifically discussed here, since they are presented elsewhere in this volume.

The developmental dimension provides the primary guide to assessment of behavior disorders from birth to maturity. Unlike adults, for whom subjective distress is usually the central focus of assessment, children must be assessed largely in terms of their deviance from the normal course of development. Even though all facets of development are intricately interwoven in the individual child, it is nevertheless helpful to view the adaptive challenges faced at successive ages from the separate perspectives of biological, emotional, cognitive, social, and educational development.

Marked changes in biological, cognitive, social, and educational status make it convenient to divide the topic into developmental periods during which different types of disorders become evident. Most disorders emerging during the *infant period,* from birth until about age 2, involve mismatches between children's biologically based needs in such areas as nurturance, digestion, sleep, toileting, motility, and responsiveness to various kinds of stimulation, on the one hand, and the constraints imposed by the external world, on the other. Many disorders originating in temperamental characteristics of the child and/or in parents' failure to read their child accurately may soon subside unless the resulting discomfort engenders a lasting pattern of maladaptive interactions among family members. In addition to disorders that arise out of mismatches between child and parent behavior, developmental delays in biologically based functions are often a cause for concern during this period. Delays in recognizing caretakers, manipulation of objects, motility, and vocalization may all signify biological deficits, emotional deprivation, or, in many cases, merely idiosyncratic lags that will be overcome later. However, rare but severe disorders of unknown origin that drastically affect personality development also become apparent during this period. The best known of these is early infantile autism, which may first be evident in unresponsiveness to social cues, overreaction to environmental changes, and a preoccupation with inanimate objects.

During the *preschool period*—from about the age of 2 to 5—the widening social world of the normal child, the growing importance of language, and increasing expectations for conformity to social decorum make developmental deviations in these areas the greatest cause for concern. Severe disorders such as autism may now become manifest in extreme avoidance of social interaction, ritualistic and bizarre behavior, reversal of personal pronouns, or a complete lack of normal speech. However, idiosyncrasies of biological maturation and social environment are still so great that behavioral norms remain very broad during this period.

During the *elementary school* period, from the age of about 6 to 11, our society begins to impose much more uniform expectations for progress in social, cognitive, emotional, and educational development. The primary vehicle for imposing these expectations is, of course, the school, and it is in response to school problems that a great upsurge in mental health referrals occurs during this period. Most of these referrals involve boys who are failing to progress academically and behaviorally according to the norms of the school culture. The most frequent problems include poor school performance, inability to concentrate, overactivity, and defiant behavior (Achenbach and Edelbrock, in press). The terms *hyperactivity* and *hyperkinesis* are currently enjoying great popularity as euphemisms for a wide variety of behavior that adults find obnoxious, although the validity of these labels is open to question.

During the *adolescent period*, from the age of about 12 to 20, new stresses can arise from the massive physiological changes of puberty; the advent of hypothetico-deductive thinking, which stimulates questioning of personal values and identities; and the lack of stable social roles available to young people in our society. During this period the adult forms of schizophrenia, antisocial behavior, and depression first become evident. The consequences of maladaptive behavior at this period are no longer confined so exclusively to the purview of the family, school, and mental health practitioners but begin to be manifest in such alternative forms as "dropping out," teenage pregnancy, unemployment, crime, and suicide. Although adolescence has traditionally been depicted as a time of *Sturm und Drang*, it is by no means certain that developmental stresses unique to this period are specifically responsible for either a significant increase in psychopathology or the forms that it assumes. Longitudinal research on general population samples has shown, for example, that the total incidence of disorders was not much greater at ages 14 and 15 than in the same samples at age 10 and that many of the disorders evident at ages 14 and 15 were continuations of adaptational problems evident earlier (Rutter and others, 1976). Rather than being specifically determined by stresses unique to adolescence, the disorders that begin to emerge in adult form during this period may result from biological, cognitive, and socioemotional characteristics that are simply not present earlier. However, research now under way on children believed to be at high risk for the adult disorders may reveal precursors that will enhance our understanding of the etiology, developmental course, and prevention of these disorders (Mednick and others, 1974).

Background and Current Status

Although adult disorders received considerable study during the nineteenth century and Emil Kraepelin's comprehensive taxonomy emerged in 1883, childhood disorders did not begin to attract attention until the turn of the twentieth century; systematic research has remained meager until very recently; and no comprehensive taxonomy is widely accepted as yet. Lightner Witmer, who started the first American psychological clinic at the University of Pennsylvania in 1896, is credited with originating the clinical assessment of childhood disorders in this country, as well as with coining the term *clinical psychologist.* However, Witmer's clinic was restricted primarily to helping children with educational problems. In 1909 the psychiatrist William Healy founded the Juvenile Psychopathic Institute (now the Institute for Juvenile Research) to perform clinical evaluations for the Chicago Juvenile Court, established in 1899 as the first juvenile court. But it was not until 1915, when surveys by the National Committee for Mental Hygiene revealed widespread emotional problems among school children, that children's mental health needs evoked much concern.

Originating mainly with demonstration clinics financed by the Commonwealth Fund and organized by the National Committee for Mental Hygiene in 1922, child guidance clinics became the primary vehicles for mental health services to children. Another outgrowth of this work was the American Orthopsychiatry Association, which was founded in 1924 as a professional organization of psychiatrists, psychologists, and social workers who worked clinically with troubled children. According to the prevailing clinical model, children were tested by psychologists and treated by psychiatrists, while their parents were interviewed by social workers. Assessment was viewed as a team enterprise in which the psychiatrist's clinical observations, the psychologist's tests—primarily intelligence tests at first but later joined by projectives—and the family history obtained by the social worker were synthesized into a case formulation by the psychiatrist. Despite subsequent changes in theories of psychopathology and its treatment, and a diversification of roles within each profession, this model still shapes professional functions in many clinical agencies.

Child guidance clinics have continued to serve as the primary vehicle for mental health services to children, but other vehicles have also evolved. These include clinical adjuncts that provide assessments and recommendations for children being processed by educational, legal, welfare, and placement agencies; residential and day facilities for severely disturbed children who cannot be adequately served on an outpatient basis; diversification of adult-oriented family service agencies and community mental health centers to include the assessment and treatment of children; and a growing army of private practitioners, at first mainly psychiatrists but now including psychologists, social workers, and educational specialists. Amid such diversity of practitioners, settings, and clienteles, there is no unanimity in conceptions of childhood behavior disorders or their assessment.

Critical Discussion

General Areas of Concern

Ideally, the purposes of clinical assessment are to determine the nature, etiology, and severity of a disorder and to guide optimal management, given the characteristics of the client and his or her life situation. Unfortunately, the lack of an accepted taxonomy, the paucity of well-validated assessment procedures, and professional ignorance about differential treatment effectiveness impede attainment of this ideal. As will become apparent from the discussion, problems of assessment are unlikely to be solved in isolation, because assessment constitutes but one aspect of an enterprise that is shaped by diverse theories of psychological functioning; instruments for evaluating it; the expectations children and their families bring to mental health services; the personal philosophies, qualifications, and vested interests of practitioners; the treatment options available; and assumptions about the prognosis for particular children. Despite being dependent on so many other considerations, the value of purely clinical assessment should be judged in terms of the course of action it can prescribe for the individual client. It is of questionable value if it cannot increase the accuracy of predictions or the quality of services rendered on behalf of clients. However, if we acknowledge that little is really known about the nature and treatment of children's behavior disorders, then assessment can also be viewed as a particularly central component of the research required to build a viable clinical science.

In practice, clinical applications of assessment have generally diverged from research applications. Observations in unstandardized clinical interviews, developmental histories as recalled by parents, and projective tests have provided the primary basis for clinical formulations of personality and family dynamics. While these may foster a sense of understanding the client's underlying personality and conflicts, research has shown that they are of limited reliability, even when studied under conditions more favorable than usually prevail in clinical settings (Chess, Thomas, and Birch, 1966; Suinn and Oskamp, 1969; Yarrow, Campbell, and Burton, 1970; Zubin, Eron, and Schumer, 1965). Although unreliable procedures are unlikely to produce valid results under any conditions, the question of validity is difficult to address at all, because the usual personality formulation rarely yields testable predictions, and outcome studies have not been designed to test the validity of treatment recommendations derived from clinical assessments.

A further problem is that assessment procedures and clinical models originating in the treatment of adult psychopathology have had undue influence on child assessment, where developmental factors may far outweigh personality dynamics in determining children's responses to assessment, as well as to treatment. Thus, a child's cognitive immaturity and inability to assume the role of patient may limit the value of personality formulations obtained in clinical assessment more severely than they might with mature and motivated adults. Whether personality formulations can actually enhance the effectiveness of predictions or treatment for adults has not in fact been demonstrated (Mischel,

1972), but, elusive as such evidence is for adults, it has not even been systematically sought for children.

Despite the lack of evidence for the efficacy of traditional personality assessment, a recent survey of 500 clinical psychologists (Wade and Baker, 1977) indicates that most of the respondents regarded such assessment as an important means of obtaining information about personality structure; the most favored tests by far were the Rorschach and the Thematic Apperception Test. (The proportion of respondents who assessed children was not reported, but, since many endorsed the Wechsler Intelligence Scale for Children, the findings are likely to reflect current assessment practices for children as well as adults.) Most of the respondents who used projective tests (81.5 percent), and even some of the respondents who used objective tests (38.9 percent), interpreted them in a personalized manner rather than using standardized scoring. Personal clinical experience was rated highest as the reason for using tests, with "answering assessment needs" and "graduate training experiences" following thereafter. "Statistical reliability and validity" ranked a poor fourth as a reason for using tests. The investigators conclude that clinicians in general did not view diagnosis, behavioral prediction, or assignment to treatment "as important benefits of test usage or as important reasons for recommending tests" (p. 879). Instead, "clinicians rated personal experience with tests as the most important factor in their decision to use tests" (p. 879). Yet, research shows that utilizing test data in a subjective, personalized fashion—as preferred by most of the respondents—is the least accurate approach to prediction, whether tests are scored objectively or not (Sawyer, 1966). Furthermore, unvalidated personal experience has been shown to produce highly biased illusions of correlation where no such correlation exists in psychodiagnostic data (Chapman and Chapman, 1971). How, then, can clinical assessment be expected to help disturbed children?

The contradictions between clinical assessment practices and research findings are symptomatic of the gulf that separates psychological research from applications. Nowhere is this gulf wider than in the area of childhood psychopathology. Despite a substantial body of research on child behavior and a substantial cadre of clinicians who assess children, there has been a minimum of programmatic research designed to resolve the problems of clinical assessment. Questionable as unvalidated assessment practices may be, the complaint of clinicians surveyed by Wade and Baker (1977)—namely, that they lack alternatives to traditional assessment—may be justified.

Comparative Philosophies and Theories

In comparing philosophies and theories of assessment, one must consider the developmental period and the general domain of disorders to which they pertain. During the infant period, for example, virtually all assessment techniques focus on behavioral milestones that can be reported by parents or tested by a trained examiner. The Gesell Scales of Infant Development have been prototypical of this approach (Gesell and Amatruda, 1947). Based on Gesell's theory of behavioral development as a maturational process like the unfolding of an embryo, the scales consist of items designed to measure the level of adaptive, motor, language, and personal-social behavior. Norms are provided for responses at four-week intervals up to the age of 1 year, three-month intervals to the age of 2, and six-month intervals to the age of 3. Gesell and his co-workers also argued for extending the normative developmental approach to assessment of older children, but his approach has remained the general model for assessment during only the first few years of life. Other infant scales now include the Bayley (1969) Scales of Infant Development, Uzgiris and Hunt's (1975) Piagetian scales, the Griffiths (1954) Scale, and Cattell's (1960) Mental

Test for Infants and Young Children, which is a downward extension of the Stanford-Binet. Although it was at first hoped that the developmental quotients (DQ) scored from infant tests would predict later IQ, longitudinal studies have demonstrated negligible correlations, except among very low-scoring children (Rubin and Balow, 1979). As a result, infant tests have come to be regarded largely as screening devices on which exceptionally low scores may indicate organic damage, disease, or severe environmental deprivation, whereas uneven performance may indicate specific handicaps, such as deafness, emotional disturbance, or autism.

Although no uniformly developmental approach is in general use beyond the infant period, developmental considerations have guided the selection and/or scoring of items for measures of specific functions, such as IQ and achievement tests, Koppitz's (1975) scoring of the Bender Gestalt Test for maturity of perceptual-motor functioning, the Illinois Test of Psycholinguistic Abilities for language development (Kirk, McCarthy, and Kirk, 1968), Harris's (1963) scoring of the Draw-a-Person Test, and the Vineland Social Maturity Scale (Doll, 1965). While these measures may all contribute to the assessment of behavior disorders in some cases, measures designed specifically to assess behavior disorders have not generally been constructed or calibrated on developmental principles. Among projective tests, responses to the Rorschach (Ames and others, 1972) and the Michigan Picture Test (Andrew and others, 1953) have been tabulated for various age groups, but deviations from these cannot necessarily be interpreted in developmental terms. The same is true for the adolescent norms provided for the Minnesota Multiphasic Personality Inventory (MMPI) and the norms provided for standardization samples on tests such as the Children's Manifest Anxiety Scale (Castaneda, McCandless, and Palermo, 1956) and on behavior checklists such as Quay and Peterson's (1975) Behavior Problem Checklist.

Besides the developmental approach to assessment—which is really practiced only with infants—the other main approaches can be roughly categorized as psychodynamic, family dynamic, and behavioral. The psychodynamic approach is designed to provide a case formulation in terms of the child's motives, conflicts, defenses, and ego identity, plus environmental pressures and psychodynamics of family members that may cast the child in a particular role. The more classically Freudian the approach, the greater the emphasis on phases of psychosexual development, drive regressions, fixations, and unconscious determinants. However, even without the orthodox Freudian emphasis, assessment directed toward a complex formulation of underlying personality is probably best labeled as psychodynamic, because it focuses on the configuration of motives and stresses within the individual personality, as opposed to overt behavior or the stresses within the family viewed as a system. The basis for psychodynamic assessment includes what the child says and does during unstructured playroom interviews, family history as reported by the parents, projective tests, and, in some cases, inferences drawn from performance measures, such as the Bender Gestalt, Draw-a-Person, and IQ tests.

The family dynamic approach, by contrast, elevates psychodynamic-like analyses to the level of the family. Here the focus is on the conflict of forces and roles within the family rather than within the individual. The child who is brought for assessment is regarded as merely the symptom of a disturbed family that has selected him or her to play the scapegoat or some other pivotal role in its shared stress. Because family dynamic assessment is typically practiced in settings where conjoint family therapy is the dominant treatment modality, the clinician often begins by meeting family members conjointly rather than making a separate assessment of the child, which might imply endorsement of the role to which the family has assigned the child. Although meeting separately with the child may sometimes be unavoidable, family dynamicists stress the importance of observing the family's interactions at every opportunity, including home visits where possible (Schomer, 1978).

The behavioral approach aims at identifying the specific deviant behaviors, the environmental conditions supporting them, and the possibilities for changing these conditions. Depending on the problems in question, this typically entails interviewing the parents to obtain the presenting complaint. It also entails interviews with the child, either alone or together with the parents; responses by the child to self-report measures, such as the Fear Survey Schedule (Wolpe, 1969); observations of the child under conditions where the deviant behavior can occur; and reports of behavioral observations by teachers and other relevant parties. Because behavioral assessment is intended to be an ongoing component of treatment, changes from base-rate levels of the deviant behavior are to be recorded during and after treatment.

Elaboration on Critical Points

The dramatic upsurge in behavior modification during the 1960s, and its apparent success in documenting its effectiveness where other approaches had not succeeded, opened a host of new vistas on behavior disorders. From reading the behavioral literature of the past decade, one might conclude that behavioral standards now prevail for the definition and documentation of disorders, their systematic amelioration, and the synthesis of assessment, treatment, and follow-up into a continuous process. Behavior modification has indeed had an influence through childrearing manuals and parent training groups, special education programs for retarded and extremely disturbed children, and the provision of new alternatives for clinical treatment of behavior disorders in children. Yet Wade and Baker's (1977) survey reveals little impact on clinical assessment practices. Why?

There seem to be three possible answers. First, because behaviorally oriented clinicians are more likely than traditional clinicians to do research, they are greatly overrepresented in the recent research literature. Second, the relatively high proportion of behavioral research involving analog situations, volunteer subjects having relatively minor and/or circumscribed complaints, and conditions that for other reasons are not representative of clinical practice has masked the failure of behavior modification to provide procedures readily assimilated by most clinical practitioners. Third, the enthusiasm of behavior modifiers for translating clinical problems into behavioral jargon has exaggerated the degree to which the problems are thereby solved. Recent attempts to diversify behavioral approaches, to integrate them with other approaches, and especially to take account of cognitive variables reflect recognition that the clinical problems cannot be so easily defined away.

Paralleling the course of behavior modification, chemotherapy—especially the use of stimulant drugs to treat hyperactivity—has also received wide publicity during the 1960s and 1970s. Like behavior modification, stimulants have been demonstrated to reduce certain problem behaviors in at least some children, although negative side effects occur and long-term follow-ups show that many treated children continue to do poorly in school (Douglas, 1975). Like behavior modification, stimulants have also sparked intense controversy, with opposing camps claiming either that they are being used to drug children into insensibility or that many children who need them are being unjustly deprived of their benefits.

A problem common to behavior modification, stimulant drugs, and almost every other treatment modality—old or new—is that each tends to be indiscriminately embraced by its proponents and rejected by its opponents, rather than being empirically compared with other approaches for well-defined classes of clients in order to determine which approach works best for whom. In order to build clinically applicable knowledge about type-of-client by type-of-treatment interactions, assessment procedures are needed to categorize children reliably and to quantify their disorders in such a way as to permit evaluation of differential treatment outcomes.

Personal Views and Recommendations

Despite a wealth of theories of psychopathology, no theory has provided generally accepted categories that discriminate among disturbed children with respect to etiology, course, or responsiveness to various interventions. Without an underpinning of conceptual categories, operational definitions cannot be effectively derived from existing theories, even if there were a theory sufficiently refined and accepted to warrant the effort. However, the less theoretical eclectic approach to taxonomy that has lent a semblance of structure to adult psychopathology since Kraepelin has also failed to produce accepted categories for child psychopathology.

Lacking a satisfactory taxonomy of childhood disorders, researchers have increasingly turned to multivariate techniques to identify syndromes of statistically associated behavior problems among children. Despite great diversity of subject samples, rating instruments, raters, and methods of analysis, there has been considerable convergence in the identification of certain syndromes. These syndromes can be divided into a small number of broad-band syndromes and a larger number of narrow-band syndromes, many of which can be subsumed by the broad-band syndromes (Achenbach and Edelbrock, 1978). Nearly all studies geared to the identification of broad-band syndromes have produced one that has been variously labeled as inhibited, shy-anxious, internalizing, and personality disorder, and a second syndrome that has been labeled as aggressive, acting out, externalizing, and conduct disorder. Table 1 shows the number of studies of parent, teacher, mental health worker, and case history ratings that have yielded these broad-band syndromes, which are designated in the table as Overcontrolled and Undercontrolled, respectively. Table 1 also lists two other broad-band syndromes and fourteen narrow-band syndromes that were each found in at least two studies of disturbed children. The labels are intended to reflect the common elements in syndromes that appear similar, whether or not these particular labels were used in the original studies. As can be seen from the table, a broad-band syndrome labeled Pathological Detachment was found in four studies, and one labeled Learning Problems was found in two studies. Narrow-band Aggressive, Delinquent, Hyperactive, and Schizoid syndromes were each found in from ten to fourteen studies, while Anxious, Depressed, Social Withdrawal, Somatic Complaints, Sexual Problems, Academic Disability, Immature, Obsessive-Compulsive, Uncommunicative, and Sleep Problems syndromes were each found in from three to six studies.

Although there can be little doubt about the existence of the two broad-band and four narrow-band syndromes found in from ten to sixteen studies, these may reflect only the behavior patterns that occur in both sexes over broad age ranges and in contexts accessible to diverse observers. The replicability of syndromes found in fewer studies may be underestimated, because many of the instruments employed were insufficiently differentiated and the samples too heterogeneous to reflect syndromes peculiar to one developmental period or sex. Furthermore, some syndromes, such as Sleep Problems and Somatic Complaints, are unlikely to be as evident to such diverse observers as other syndromes— for instance, the Hyperactive syndrome—are. Conservative as the picture emerging from Table 1 thus may be, it nevertheless demonstrates that considerable differentiation is possible among behavioral syndromes of childhood. Furthermore, the test-retest reliabilities

Table 1. Number of Studies in Which Syndromes Have Been Identified
Through Multivariate Analyses[a]

Syndrome	Case Histories	Mental Health Workers	Teachers	Parents	Total
		Source of Ratings			
Broad Band					
Overcontrolled	2	1	5	4	12
Undercontrolled	3	3	5	5	16
Pathological Detachment	3	–	1	–	4
Learning Problems	–	–	1	1	2
Narrow Band					
Academic Disability	–	1	–	3	4
Aggressive	3	4	1	6	14
Anxious	1	2	1	2	6
Delinquent	3	1	–	6	10
Depressed	2	1	–	3	6
Hyperactive	3	2	1	6	12
Immature	–	1	–	2	3
Obsessive-Compulsive	1	–	–	2	3
Schizoid	3	4	–	3	10
Sexual Problems	1	2	–	1	4
Sleep Problems	–	–	–	3	3
Social Withdrawal	1	1	1	3	6
Somatic Complaints	1	–	–	5	6
Uncommunicative	–	1	–	2	3

[a]See Achenbach and Edelbrock (1978) for details.

and long-term stabilities of syndrome ratings are quite adequate, although—as would be expected—interrater reliabilities are strongly affected by the similarity between the roles of the raters vis-à-vis the subjects and between the situations in which they see the subjects (Achenbach and Edelbrock, 1978).

The convergence of findings despite the diversity of methods indicates that the empirically derived syndromes offer at least a provisional means for describing, classifying, and communicating about children's behavior disorders. The information on which they are based is readily obtainable from informants who know the child well; these informants, particularly parents and teachers, should be utilized in the course of clinical evaluations anyway. However, a shortcoming of many of the studies summarized in Table 1 is that they have merely identified syndromes without providing means either for categorizing individual children in terms of the syndromes or for determining the correlates of particular syndromes. Insofar as correlates have been assessed, they have been mainly for the broad-band Overcontrolled versus Undercontrolled dichotomy. The correlates of this dichotomy indicate that undercontrolled children (and their families) are in more open conflict with other people, are less socially competent, are less appropriate candidates for traditional mental health services, and have poorer prognoses than overcontrolled children.

Several research programs are currently using cluster analysis to group children on the basis of profiles of scores they obtain across various syndromes (see Achenbach and Edelbrock, 1978). This procedure reveals similarities and differences in the overall patterning of behavior more precisely than does categorization according to single syndromes in a mutually exclusive fashion. To date, cluster-based taxonomies have been able to discriminate among children who differ significantly in demographic characteristics and in outcomes following typical child guidance clinic contacts. The findings indicate that the behavior patterns revealed through cluster analysis can be used to identify in advance children who do not benefit from mental health services as currently rendered and for whom new treatment modalities or better prescriptive selection of existing modalities must be developed.

While empirically based taxonomies are being further refined and more correlates are being established, a mutually beneficial convergence of the clinical and research applications of assessment can be facilitated if uniform assessment procedures are adopted. These procedures should be applicable to a variety of settings; they should facilitate communication about individual children; and they should be linked to expanding bodies of knowledge about the nature and course of behavior disorders, as well as their responsiveness to various interventions. At present, the best candidate assessment procedures of this sort appear to be the checklists from which the converging syndromes of behavior problems are derived. Among those sensitive primarily to broad-band syndromes, the most prominent are the Behavior Problem Checklist (Quay and Peterson, 1975), for use by a wide variety of raters; the Teacher Referral Form (Clarfield, 1974), for use by elementary school teachers; and the Kohn Symptom Checklist and Social Competence Scale (Kohn, 1977), for use by preschool teachers. Among those that reflect more differentiated syndromes are the School Behavior Checklist (Miller, 1972) and the Teacher Rating Scale (Conners, 1969), for elementary school teachers; the Child Behavior Checklist (Achenbach, 1979) and the Parents Questionnaire (Conners, 1973), for parent ratings; and the Devereux Child Behavior Rating Scale (Spivack and Spotts, 1966), for child care workers. In light of increasing recognition that positive adaptive competencies are likely to be as important as behavior problems, two of the instruments cited above have explicit social competence components (Achenbach, 1979; Kohn, 1977).

Because all the instruments are designed to be self-administered by people who interact with the child in everyday life, they do not require a sacrifice of time that would otherwise be used for clinical assessment. Even if none of the instruments is totally satisfactory for all purposes, assessment can be greatly enhanced if one or more of them are included with the clinician's or researcher's customary procedures—thereby facilitating a standardized description of clinically relevant behavior and providing a more systematic linkage between assessment of individual children and communicable knowledge about particular behavioral syndromes.

Application to Particular Variables

The clinical assessment of children must be thoroughly adapted to their developmental level. Children whose cognitive, social, physical, or educational development is well above or below the norm for their age cannot be expected to respond to assessment procedures in the same manner as children who are close to their age norm. Likewise, differences between children who deviate from a particular age norm and those who do not cannot necessarily be attributed to behavior disorders unless it is demonstrated that the differences are specifically correlated with the behavior disorders, rather than being a general function of the developmental level the deviant children have attained. For example, children diagnosed as psychotic often perform at lower cognitive levels than do normal children of the same age, and their cognitive retardation can affect their behavior. However, the retarded cognitive level and concomitant behavior should not be blamed on psychosis unless they constitute a regression from a previously attained premorbid level or unless there are other grounds for supposing that they are caused by the disorder. In short, developmental assessment should help to distinguish between (1) behavior that is deviant from norms for a child's age but not from his or her attained developmental level and (2) deviant behavior that is not attributable to merely the child's developmental level.

Keeping in mind the need to determine whether a child is developmentally deviant from the norms for his or her age, we can suggest some general guidelines for the ages at which various procedures are typically appropriate. Until about the age of 2 or 3, infant development tests of the Gesell and Bayley type provide the most central component of assessment. Unlike the IQ tests designed to tap cognitive functioning at later ages, infant development tests are generally designed to assess motor, social, and general adaptive functioning as well as early versions of mental functioning. Because infant tests are not very predictive of later functioning, they must be regarded as no more than indexes of current functioning in specific areas. When marked unevenness or deficits are found on infant tests, these may be indicative of organic abnormalities, adverse environmental conditions, or generalized slow development that may be overcome later.

IQ tests do not become stable indexes of the level and patterning of cognitive functioning until the end of the preschool period. However, numerous preschool screening instruments—including the Denver Developmental Screening Test (Frankenburg and Dodds, 1968), the Minnesota Child Development Inventory (Ireton and Thwing, 1974), and the Riley (1969) Preschool Developmental Screening Inventory—utilize parent reports and direct observation of performance on items like those of infant and IQ tests. This approach has also been extended upward to the age of 12 in Alpern and Boll's (1972) Developmental Profile.

The assessment of behavior disorders during the preschool period is handicapped by the broad range of difficult behavior that is nevertheless "within normal limits," the wide variation of biological maturation and social environments, and the lack of explicit behavioral norms like those that are later imposed by the school, peer, and adult cultures. Some of the same obstacles impede assessment during the infant period, but the range of behavior problems increases as children's motility, social contacts, and capacity for getting into trouble all increase, and as adults' progressively more stringent expectations for social decorum multiply the opportunities for conflict.

It is only toward the end of the preschool period that norms for behavior begin to become explicit and uniform enough to make the checklist approach a viable basis for assessment of specific behavioral syndromes, although some checklists are designed to reflect syndromes as early as the age of 3. Aside from checklists targeted on a single disorder—such as early infantile autism (Rimland, 1971)—the behavior checklist approach appears to be most valuable from the end of the preschool period until about the age of 16, after which behavioral norms once again become less distinct and teachers and parents are no longer in such favorable positions to report on behavior. Within the age range in which the checklist approach is most viable, the patterning and incidence of disorders vary in relation to sex and developmental level (see Achenbach, 1979); it is therefore important to orient assessment toward syndromes that have been derived in such a way as to reflect developmental and sex differences.

Assessment methods requiring self-reports by children are subject to the greatest developmental constraints. Children's responses to the ambiguous stimuli of projective tests are inevitably affected by their ability to understand the task and to verbalize their interpretations. Responses to projectives can certainly be obtained as early as the preschool period, but they are unlikely to reveal much about personality before the middle elementary school period, and the problem of gleaning information about the etiology, prognosis, or appropriate treatment for behavior disorders remains great at all ages.

Structured self-report measures are subject to response sets—such as "yea saying" and preference for the second of two proffered alternatives—that are especially strong in early childhood (Achenbach, 1978). For children whose educational development is in the normal range, simple written tests first become feasible around the age of 8 or 9. Of the few existing tests that are simple enough for use this early, however, the best known— the Children's Manifest Anxiety Scale (Castaneda, McCandless, and Palermo, 1956) and the General Anxiety Scale for Children (Sarason and others, 1960)—are vulnerable to yea-saying sets because all the pathological items are keyed in the positive direction. The MMPI is not appropriate with children until they have reached at least the cognitive and educational levels of the normal 12-year-old, although limitations on reading skills have sometimes been circumvented by tape-recorded administration (Baughman and Dahl-strom, 1968).

Like tests, assessment interviews must be geared to the developmental level of the child. A playroom setting is usual for children prior to adolescence, but this alone is not a sufficient concession to developmental differences. Unless the interviewer is thoroughly familiar with the range of playroom behavior typical of children of various backgrounds and developmental levels, it is too easy to mistake normal withdrawal, anxiety, or bois-terousness for pathological symptoms. The younger the child, the less he or she can assume the role of active informant in the interview setting. Yet, with standardized inter-view procedures that move gradually from an unstructured phase to systematic question-ing about fears, worries, unhappiness, and peer relationships, Rutter and Graham (1968) have obtained reasonably reliable and valid ratings of psychopathology with children as young as early elementary school age. At younger ages, the value of the playroom time available during most assessments is likely to be limited to providing general impressions of the child and noting behavioral clues to be followed up by obtaining information about behavior in other settings.

In addition to developmental level, the sex, socioeconomic status, and ethnicity of the child are important considerations in clinical assessment. As mentioned earlier, there are significant sex differences in the patterning and incidence of behavior problems, but most assessment instruments make little provision for sex differences, and only a few of the studies of empirically derived syndromes have been designed to reflect sex differences (see Achenbach and Edelbrock, 1978).

Because children's cognitive and educational attainments generally have moderate correlations with the socioeconomic status of their families, assessment procedures sensi-tive to developmental level will typically show that children from upper socioeconomic levels are more advanced than those from lower socioeconomic levels. A major exception is performance on infant tests, which does not generally correlate with socioeconomic level. As for behavioral problems, there appears to be no consistent correlation with socioeconomic level across age and sex, although certain types of delinquent behavior may be more frequent in lower-socioeconomic adolescent boys than in other groups (McDonald, 1969), and the incidence of early infantile autism has been found to be greatest in upper-socioeconomic families (see Achenbach, 1974, chap. 12).

Assessment procedures must, of course, be adapted to the linguistic and cultural backgrounds of individual children. However, the confounding of ethnicity with socio-economic status in this country makes it difficult to separate the effects of these two factors. To date, there is little firm evidence to support generalizations about the effect of ethnic differences on behavior disorders. Where attempts have been made to separate social-class effects from the effects of ethnic differences in the assessment of specific be-havioral problems, the social-class differences appear to dominate (Achenbach and Edel-brock, in press).

Two final but fundamental issues of particular relevance to the assessment of chil-dren concern the ethics of assessment and the proper training for assessment. Aside from broadly applicable standards of professional responsibility and the need to preserve confi-dentiality and to shun stigmatizing labels, the most urgent ethical question is whether unvalidated assessment and treatment practices should be perpetuated. If assessment can-not be demonstrated to contribute knowledge about children that in turn improves deci-sion making for their benefit, why assess? Unless mental health professionals accept responsibility for systematically evaluating the effects of what they do and for seeking new ways to help children who are not being helped by current services, the sale of these services cannot be justified.

As for training, the lack of clinical programs oriented toward children makes it necessary for many who wish to work with children to obtain their basic training in pro-grams dominated by adult models of psychopathology. Despite theoretical emphasis on the childhood origins of adult psychopathology, adult-oriented training tends to portray the child as a miniature adult, whose problems are construed as early versions of adult disorders and who enters the mental health system primarily as a patient seeking relief from stress. Because continuities between most child and adult disorders have not been verified, and because children do not typically assume the role of patient in relation to mental health services, training in developmental and educational processes, plus experi-ence with a wide variety of children of all ages outside formal clinical settings, would be preferable to the current tendency to make child training secondary to adult training. In addition to a firmer grounding in developmental psychology and greater independence from adult clinical models, training for assessment of children would benefit from an em-phasis on the systematic evaluation of procedures, with the goal of determining how the best possible dispositions can be made for each kind of problem in each kind of child and context.

References

Achenbach, T. M. *Developmental Psychopathology.* New York: Ronald Press, 1974.

Achenbach, T. M. *Research in Developmental Psychology: Concepts, Strategies, Methods.* New York: Free Press, 1978.

Achenbach, T. M. "The Child Behavior Profile: An Empirically Based System for Assess-ing Children's Behavioral Problems and Competencies." *International Journal of Men-tal Health,* 1979, *7,* 24-42.

Achenbach, T. M., and Edelbrock, C. S. "The Classification of Child Psychopathology: A Review and Analysis of Empirical Efforts." *Psychological Bulletin,* 1978, *85,* 1275-1301.

Achenbach, T. M., and Edelbrock, C. S. *Behavioral Problems and Competencies Reported by Parents of Normal and Disturbed Children Age 4 Through 16.* Monographs of the Society for Research in Child Development. Chicago: University of Chicago Press, in press.

Alpern, G. D., and Boll, T. J. *Developmental Profile.* Indianapolis: Psychological Develop-ment Publications, 1972.

Ames, L. B., and others. *Child Rorschach Responses.* New York: Brunner/Mazel, 1972.

Andrew, G., and others. *The Michigan Picture Test.* Chicago: Science Research Asso-ciates, 1953.

Baughman, E. E., and Dahlstrom, W. G. *Negro and White Children: A Psychological Study in the Rural South.* New York: Academic Press, 1968.

Bayley, N. *Bayley Scales of Infant Development: Birth to Two Years.* New York: Psychological Corporation, 1969.

Castaneda, A., McCandless, B. R., and Palermo, D. S. "The Children's Form of the Manifest Anxiety Scale." *Child Development,* 1956, *27,* 317-326.

Cattell, P. *The Measurement of Intelligence in Infants and Young Children.* New York: Psychological Corporation, 1960.

Chapman, L. J., and Chapman, J. P. "Associatively Based Illusory Correlation as a Source of Psychodiagnostic Folklore." In L. D. Goodstein and R. I. Lanyon (Eds.), *Readings in Personality Assessment.* New York: Wiley, 1971.

Chess, S., Thomas, A., and Birch, H. G. "Distortions in Developmental Reporting Made by Parents of Behaviorally Disturbed Children." *Journal of the American Academy of Child Psychiatry,* 1966, *5,* 226-234.

Clarfield, S. P. "The Development of a Teacher Referral Form for Identifying Early School Maladaptation." *American Journal of Community Psychology,* 1974, *2,* 199-210.

Conners, C. K. "A Teacher Rating Scale for Use in Drug Studies with Children." *American Journal of Psychiatry,* 1969, *126,* 884-888.

Conners, C. K. "Rating Scales for Use in Drug Studies with Children." In *Psychopharmacology Bulletin: Pharmacotherapy with Children.* DHEW Publication No. (HSM) 73-9002. Washington, D.C.: U.S. Department of Health, Education, and Welfare, 1973.

Doll, E. A. *Vineland Social Maturity Scale.* Circle Pines, Minn.: American Guidance Service, 1965.

Douglas, V. I. "Are Drugs Enough? To Treat or to Train the Hyperactive Child." *International Journal of Mental Health,* 1975, *4,* 199-212.

Frankenburg, W. K., and Dodds, J. B. *Denver Developmental Screening Test Manual.* Denver: University of Colorado Press, 1968.

Gesell, A., and Amatruda, C. S. *Developmental Diagnosis.* (2nd ed.) New York: Harper & Row, 1947.

Griffiths, R. *The Abilities of Babies: A Study in Mental Measurement.* New York: McGraw-Hill, 1954.

Harris, D. B. *Children's Drawings as Measures of Intellectual Maturity.* New York: Harcourt Brace Jovanovich, 1963.

Ireton, H., and Thwing, E. *Minnesota Child Development Inventory.* Minneapolis: Behavior Science Systems, 1974.

Kirk, S. A., McCarthy, J. J., and Kirk, W. D. *Illinois Test of Psycholinguistic Abilities.* Urbana: University of Illinois Press, 1968.

Kohn, M. *Social Competence, Symptoms, and Underachievement in Childhood: A Longitudinal Perspective.* New York: Wiley, 1977.

Koppitz, E. M. *The Bender Gestalt Test for Young Children.* Vol. 2. New York: Grune and Stratton, 1975.

McDonald, L. *Social Class and Delinquency.* London: Faber and Faber, 1969.

Mednick, S. A., and others (Eds.). *Genetics, Environment, and Psychopathology.* New York: American Elsevier, 1974.

Miller, L. C. "School Behavior Checklist: An Inventory of Deviant Behavior for Elementary School Children." *Journal of Consulting and Clinical Psychology,* 1972, *38,* 134-144.

Mischel, W. "Direct Versus Indirect Personality Assessment: Evidence and Implications." *Journal of Consulting and Clinical Psychology,* 1972, *38,* 312-324.

Quay, H. C., and Peterson, D. R. *Manual for the Behavior Problem Checklist.* Miami: University of Miami, 1975.

Riley, C. M. D. *Riley Preschool Developmental Screening Inventory.* Los Angeles: Western Psychological Services, 1969.

Rimland, B. "The Differentiation of Childhood Psychoses: An Analysis of Checklists for 2218 Psychotic Children." *Journal of Autism and Childhood Schizophrenia,* 1971, *1,* 161-174.

Rubin, R. A., and Balow, B. "Measures of Infant Development and Socioeconomic Status as Predictors of Later Intelligence and School Achievement." *Developmental Psychology,* 1979, *15,* 225-227.

Rutter, M., and Graham, P. "The Reliability and Validity of the Psychiatric Assessment of the Child. 1: Interview with the Child." *British Journal of Psychiatry,* 1968, *114,* 563-579.

Rutter, M., and others. "Adolescent Turmoil: Fact or Fiction?" *Journal of Child Psychology and Psychiatry,* 1976, *17,* 35-56.

Sarason, S. B., and others. *Anxiety in Elementary School Children: A Report of Research.* New York: Wiley, 1960.

Sawyer, J. "Measurement *and* Prediction, Clinical *and* Statistical." *Psychological Bulletin,* 1966, *66,* 178-200.

Schomer, J. "Family Therapy." In B. B. Wolman, J. Eagan, and A. O. Ross (Eds.), *Handbook of Treatment of Mental Disorders in Childhood and Adolescence.* Englewood Cliffs, N.J.: Prentice-Hall, 1978.

Spivack, G., and Spotts, J. *Devereux Child Behavior Rating Scale Manual.* Devon, Pa.: Devereux Foundation, 1966.

Suinn, R. M., and Oskamp, S. *The Predictive Validity of Projective Measures.* Springfield, Ill.: Thomas, 1969.

Uzgiris, I. C., and Hunt, J. McV. *Assessment in Infancy. Ordinal Scales of Psychological Development.* Urbana: University of Illinois Press, 1975.

Wade, T. C., and Baker, T. B. "Opinions and Use of Psychological Tests. A Survey of Clinical Psychologists." *American Psychologist,* 1977, *32,* 874-882.

Wolpe, J. *The Practice of Behavior Therapy.* Elmsford, New York: Pergamon Press, 1969.

Yarrow, M. R., Campbell, J. D., and Burton, R. V. "Recollections of Childhood: A Study of the Retrospective Method." *Monographs of the Society for Research in Child Development,* 1970, *35* (Serial No. 138).

Zubin, J., Eron, L., and Schumer, F. *An Experimental Approach to Projective Techniques.* New York: Wiley, 1965.

9

Malcolm H. Robertson

Neurotic Cues

The term *cue* denotes variations in kind and intensity of behavior. The term *neurotic* ascribes the variations of behavior to psychogenic dysfunctions of perception, thought, feeling, or action. The concept of neurotic cues may be viewed as bidimensional. The primary term, *neurotic*, can be conceptualized along a dimension identified as impairment of psychological functioning. The secondary term, *cue*, can be conceptualized along a dimension of incongruence of psychological functioning.

The concept of psychological impairment is an outcome dimension. It denotes a failure, as judged by personal and/or social norms, to adapt one's behavior to the changing conditions or exigencies of the psychosocial environment. In one sense, "The defining property of neurotic behavior is its rigidity, its inflexibility in the face of changed conditions" (Wachtel, 1973, p. 327). Both intrapersonal and interpersonal impairment are specified by psychological diagnosis. Diagnosis evaluates the degree of impairment (minimal, mild, moderate, or severe), the onset of impairment (acute or chronic), the psychological modality of impairment (sensory-somatic, perceptual-motor, cognitive-imaginative, affective-motivational, interpersonal actions), and the environmental modality (vocational, educational, recreational, sexual, marital, familial, and social adjustment).

The concept of incongruence is a process dimension identified and particularized through psychological or psychiatric assessment. Assessment is the discernment of cues of incongruence (that which is discrepant, inconsistent, conflicting, contradictory, or inappropriate in an individual's response to the psychosocial environment). A distinction may be made insofar as a phenotypic incongruence may correspond genotypically to a congruence of relatively stable dispositions of personality (Cohen, 1974).

Assessment specifies the intensity of the incongruence (slight, moderate, marked), the foci of incongruence (within or between psychological modalities), the frequency of incongruence (infrequent, frequent, very frequent), and the source of the incongruence (data from interviews, psychometric tests of intelligence and personality, projective techniques, and systematic observation of behavior in situ). Theoretically, as the incongruence of behavior increases in frequency, intensity, and number of foci and sources, the degree of impairment of psychological and environmental modalities also increases.

Finally, the two dimensions of impairment and incongruence may be combined into a single overall dimension, described by Carkhuff and Berenson (1967) as a deficient or defective integration, in which neurosis represents an integrative deficit or deficiency circumscribed by and limited to specific psychological modalities.

Background and Current Status

Near the end of the nineteenth century, Jean Charcot, Pierre Janet, Josef Breuer, and Sigmund Freud pioneered an investigation of the etiology of neurosis. Eventually, Charcot and Janet opted for a strictly biological basis of neurotic symptom formation, while Breuer and Freud tilted toward a psychological explanation. During the early 1900s, Freud constructed his theory of psychoneurosis (Millon, 1969; Ross and Abrams, 1965). The core idea was the struggle with and against sexual and aggressive instincts (id). During the first decade of life, instincts shift from one organ or zone of the body to another (psychosexual stages). At each psychosexual stage, instincts conflict with environmental obstacles and social taboos to create anxiety and frustration. The child's ego struggles to learn ways to satisfy the instincts without undue anxiety. Failure to do so at one or more of the psychosexual phases produces fixation—that is, character traits. After the first decade of life, stressful life situations cause regression to the point or points of fixation. Regression represents an exaggerated display of character traits (neurotic symptoms that symbolize the emergence of anxieties and defenses against anxieties associated with the critical psychosexual phases).

Differentiations of the term *neurosis* were made by Freud and some of his disciples (Ross and Abrams, 1965; Thompson, 1951). These included *psychoneurosis* (obsessions, phobias, hysterias), in which unconscious drives are expressed intrapsychically as compromise symptoms of wish versus fear; *actual neurosis* (neurasthenia, anxieties, hypochondriasis), in which unconscious instincts are blocked and expressed as states of heightened physiological tension; *organ neurosis* (conversions), in which the psychic conflict is transformed into physiological or physical disorders, later referred to as psychosomatic disorders and (after the 1952 publication of the *Diagnostic and Statistical Manual*) as psychophysiological disorders; *transference neurosis*, in which patients capable of a therapeutic relationship transfer their neurosis to this relationship, as distinguished from *narcissistic neurosis*, where the individual is incapable of a therapeutic relationship within which the neurosis can be expressed. Also identified were *war neuroses*, which Freud subsumed under his general theory of neurosis by adding the aggression instinct. Finally, Freud's concept of character structure, which was based on fixation at one or more psychosexual phases, was further developed by others (notably, Wilhelm Reich and Otto Fenichel). It characterized a condition in which neurotic symptomatology becomes integrated within the personality—a condition later referred to as character neurosis or disorder and (after publication of the *DSM*) as personality disorder.

The term *neurosis* has evolved along two parallel lines. The first consists of additions to, modifications of, and substitutions for Freud's theory between the early 1900s and the late 1950s. Carl Jung took three actions: (1) He accepted Freud's instinctual basis but included both positive and negative instincts. (2) He argued against the inevitability of conflict between instincts and reality. (3) He proposed that a continued denial or avoidance of positive instincts would transform normal expressions of thinking, feeling, and acting into abnormal ones (Millon, 1969). Another significant modification came from Otto Rank, who substituted birth trauma and its continuing effects as the core of neurosis (Kutash, 1965). The neurosis represents a failure to integrate the need for separation (becoming independent of others) with the need for security (becoming interdependent). Significant additions were made by Anna Freud, in her descriptive and conceptual analyses of defense mechanisms, and by Sandor Ferenczi, in his identification and delineation of stages of ego development (Thompson, 1951).

A substantial modification came from the socially oriented neo-Freudian group of Alfred Adler, Karen Horney, Harry Stack Sullivan, and Erich Fromm (Kutash, 1965; Thompson, 1951). For Adler the essence of neurosis is the relentless drive to achieve superiority and power in order to compensate for real and imagined weaknesses (Ford and Urban, 1963). Horney, Sullivan, and Fromm developed their theories independent of one another but had a common view of neurosis (Thompson, 1951). They contended that neurotic behavior results when an individual uses faulty methods to resolve severe interpersonal (as opposed to intrapersonal) anxiety. The various types of neurosis express different forms of coping maladaptively with interpersonal anxiety. The ego analysts (notably Heinz Hartmann, David Rapaport, and Erik Erikson) proposed that neurotic disorders reflect the failure of inborn positive ego capacities to unfold maturationally (Millon, 1969), due to deficiency of environmental stimulation (Hartmann and Rapaport) or to the cumulative effects of failure to complete normal developmental tasks (Erikson).

Significant substitutions for Freudian theory came primarily after 1940, with the self theorists (for example, Carl Rogers and Abraham Maslow) and the existentialists (Rollo May and V. E. Frankl). Rogers (1951, p. 508) defined neurosis as "a means of satisfying a psychic need which is not recognized in consciousness, by behavioral means which are considered consistent with the concept of the self and hence can be consciously accepted." Maslow (1962) focused on a hierarchical need structure, in which a disorder like neurosis results from the continued stress of satisfying lower-order needs of esteem, safety, and affection to the exclusion of fulfilling the self-actualization need. May, Angel, and Ellenberger (1958) held that neurosis develops when an individual cannot resolve his or her pervasive anxiety about self-identity. Frankl (1962) emphasized the neurotic individual's cumulative failure to resolve the normal experience of meaninglessness at each developmental stage, with the consequent loss of capacity to identify at each stage the new possibilities for discovering and living out the meaning of one's existence.

Between 1940 and the early 1950s, the behavioral position was articulated by Hans Eysenck, B. F. Skinner, and Joseph Wolpe. The formative influences were (1) the experimental neurosis research of Jules Masserman, Howard Liddell, and others, who drew upon the earlier conditioning studies of Pavlov; and (2) the translation of psychoanalytic principles and concepts into a learning theory framework by Neal Miller, John Dollard, and O. Hobart Mowrer (Kutash, 1965). Central to the behavioral position is the rejection of an "underlying" cause of neurosis and a definition of neurosis as no more or less than the presenting symptoms. The presenting symptoms represent strategies to avoid or escape from situationally centered anxieties. More narrowly, the cognitive/behavioral theorist Albert Ellis (1962) concludes that the crux of a neurosis is the pattern of irrational cognitions that produce maladaptive affects.

Within the same time frame, Fritz Perls' Gestalt theory (Fagan and Shepherd, 1970) presents a neurosis as a tiered concept of (1) disowning much of oneself by inauthentic actions; (2) intense anxiety about disowning and inauthenticity; (3) persistently felt deprivation of support from self and others; and (4) depression, despair, and self-rejection over one's self-imposed limitations and constricted style of life. It is debatable whether Eric Berne's transactional analysis theory is a modification of or a substitution for Freudian theory. If one views the parent, adult, child ego states as modifications of Freud's id, ego, and superego, then (in the author's judgment) a neurosis may be conceptualized as an integrative deficit in the ego-state functions.

In the evolution of theories of neurosis, the concept of anxiety has had a central role. Freud's writings on anxiety formed the base from which other theorists have examined the concept. In his early conception of neurosis, Freud concluded that repression causes anxiety. When threatened by sexual and aggressive impulses, the individual represses the impulse. The frustration that results from the repression is then physiologically converted into anxiety (Thompson, 1951). After 1920 Freud stressed the signaling function of anxiety. He reasoned that, like fear, anxiety is a signal to the ego of the arousal of id impulses and the need to activate defenses against the impulses. The special types of defenses elicited are the symptoms and character defenses of the ego (Thompson, 1951). He distinguished this type of anxiety (neurotic) from moral anxiety (threat from the superego) and from objective anxiety (threat from the environment). In addition to the signaling (learned) function of anxiety, Freud noted that anxiety can occur as a direct (innate) response to a traumatic situation (Izard, 1972). May (1977, p. 143) points out that Freud thought of the birth experience as the prototype of all anxiety: "Anxiety has its source, as far as a primal source is reactivated in later neurotic anxiety, in the fear of premature loss of or separation from the mother."

Rank based his theory of anxiety exclusively on the concept of birth (May, 1977). The primal anxiety of separation at birth is experienced throughout life in two forms: (1) developing autonomy by separating from significant others and (2) avoiding autonomy by remaining dependent on significant others. Neurotic symptoms represent efforts to cope with anxiety that is generated by the unresolved conflict between strong needs for autonomy and dependency. Neither Adler nor Jung formulated a systematic theory of anxiety.

Horney described two kinds of anxiety: basic anxiety and secondary anxiety (May, 1977). Basic anxiety arises out of the child's dependent relationship with hostile parents. The anxiety and accompanying helplessness lead to the formation of neurotic defenses or security measures. If the latter are threatened, secondary anxiety develops and necessitates additional defenses or security measures. Hostility is a critical component in both types of anxiety. Anxiety activates hostility, and hostile impulses in an anxious person generate additional anxiety; anxiety is then relieved by repression of hostility and the substitution (or exaggeration) of particular security measures. Like Horney, Sullivan underscored the role of helplessness in the child's susceptibility to anxiety. Anxiety follows from the fearful anticipation of the disapproval of significant persons on whom the child must depend (May, 1977). Preoccupation with reducing or avoiding anxiety causes constriction of self-awareness and restriction of emotional and social development.

Within self theory, Rogers views anxiety as an innate reaction that develops when a person becomes aware of responses that conflict with the self-image. If the person copes with the conflict-produced anxiety by denying in awareness the critical responses or by distorting them to fit the self-image, the foundation is established for the development of a neurotic disorder (Ford and Urban, 1963). Within existential theory, May (1977) concludes that neurotic anxiety always involves inner conflict. When persistent unresolved conflict results in repression of one horn of the dilemma or conflict, neurotic anxiety ensues. Neurotic anxiety generates feelings of helplessness, hopelessness, and inhibition of action. The outcome is an intensification of the original conflict or activation of a new conflict.

The early learning theorists (Miller, Dollard, and Mowrer) defined anxiety as a learned anticipatory response to an internal or external stimulus that signaled the presence of some type of threat. Neurotic symptoms are learned and strengthened because they reduce anxiety. However the symptoms are nonadaptive because they fail to resolve the threat and they prevent the development of adaptive responses. Later, Mowrer made a radical change in his formulation of anxiety (May, 1977). He argued that neurotic anxiety is the consequence of repression of the realistic superego responses of guilt and responsibility. For behavior therapists (notably, Wolpe and Eysenck), anxiety has a twofold role in the development of persistent nonadaptive conditioned responses, which are the neuroses (Ford and Urban, 1963). First, as both an innate and a learnable response, anxiety can be elicited by primarily neutral situational events, and thus become a nonadaptive response to the environment. Second, an individual may also learn nonadaptive responses to avoid or reduce anxiety as a response-produced stimulus (Ford and Urban, 1963).

In recent years, other formulations of anxiety have been set forth. On the basis of his factor analytic studies, Raymond Cattell concludes that anxiety is a function of the intensity of unfulfilled needs and the degree of uncertainty over their fulfillment. An individual is susceptible to neurotic anxiety and other symptoms to the degree that he or she lacks integrative actions, is unable to focus on external factors, and has incompatible needs (Epstein, 1972).

Cognitive theorists (such as Seymour Epstein, Irving Janis, and Richard Lazarus) view anxiety as a response that follows the perception and appraisal of threat. If the threat is unresolved, anxiety becomes diffuse and coping actions less effective. The defining quality of the anxiety experience is uncertainty about the nature of the perceived threat and how to cope with it (Epstein, 1972). George Mandler has posited a close relationship between helplessness and anxiety (Epstein, 1972). In stressful life situations, the person experiences normal arousal and distress. If unable to discover how to eliminate distress, the person feels helpless (and the cognitive component of helplessness is anxiety).

Charles Spielberger and other researchers distinguish between "state" and "trait" anxiety (May, 1977). State anxiety is a temporary emotional response associated with autonomic nervous system arousal. Trait anxiety is anxiety proneness, which originates in childhood experiences. Presumably, the higher the anxiety proneness, the greater the number of situations that elicit high state anxiety and the more likely it is that a person will develop neurotic responses to reduce or avoid anxiety.

To summarize, anxiety is a complex reaction that has perceptual, cognitive, physiological, and behavioral components, and possesses both stimulus and response properties. Interpersonal experiences, especially those of early life, critically influence the intensity of anxiety, the types of situations that elicit it, and the way in which the individual learns to cope with it. In addition, anxiety can precede or follow from a conflict of needs, feelings, motives, thoughts, or actions. Basic to the development of neurotic symptom formation is the interaction between persistent anxiety (expressed directly or implicitly in defenses) and unresolved conflict.

A further development of the term *neurotic* involved the progressive efforts to classify mental disorders. Prior to 1900 there were only sporadic attempts to do so. In 1915 Emil Kraepelin divided the neuroses into three groups: neurasthenias (states of fatigue, bodily symptoms, and poor attention), psychasthenias (phobias, obsessions, and compulsions), and hysterias (conversions and dissociations) (Millon, 1969).

Largely from inertia and force of habit, Kraepelin's classification was retained until 1952, when the first edition of the *Diagnostic and Statistical Manual of Mental Disorders (DSM-I)* was published. The second edition, *DSM-II* (American Psychiatric Association, 1968), was published with two objectives in mind: (1) to correct deficiencies in the classifications of *DSM-I*; (2) to make the *DSM* congruent with the classification of mental disorders in the eighth revision of the *International Classification of Diseases* (World Health Organization, 1968). For neurosis the modifications were as follows: the general category of psychoneurotic disorders was changed to neurosis; the word *neurosis* was substituted for the word *reaction* in the subcategories; the term *dissociative and conversion reactions* was changed to *hysterical neurosis, dissociative and conversion types*; and *psychoneurotic reaction, other,* was specified as *neurasthenia, depersonalization, hypchondriasis.*

Definitionally, neurosis is "a functional" concept denoting how a person thinks, feels, and acts (Saul, 1971). Specifically, it denotes a condition (as opposed to disease) of (1) impaired cognitive, affective, and behavioral functions, ranging from minimal to severe, with acute or chronic onset, and (2) psychogenic origin. Structurally, the term includes five critical components: (1) intense anxiety, free floating or circumscribed; (2) incomplete or poorly resolved conflict, covertly or overtly expressed; (3) defensive coping responses of varying degrees of self-awareness; (4) subjectively distressing signs of inefficiency and loss of psychological well-being; and (5) a heightened vulnerability to psychologically stressful life situations.

Dynamically, the term connotes an automatic process of protecting the self from intense anxiety aroused by a conflict between need satisfaction and self-esteem. The protective or defensive efforts crystallize into a particular pattern of symptoms, maintained primarily by partial or complete elimination of anxiety but also by the unsuccessful elimination of the conflict. Symptoms may be further strengthened by immediate or short-term gains, such as financial, attention-getting, or face-saving motives.

Etiologically, two types of developmentally sequential interactions are considered (Cohen, 1974). The first interaction is between organismically based characteristics (sex, size, attractiveness, intelligence, and psychophysiological reactivity) and socializing influences and pressures (from family, school, neighborhood, and peers). From this interaction, critical thought-feeling-action trait patterns evolve that constitute a predisposition to neurosis. The stage is then set for the second or developmentally later interaction between specific predispositions and precipitating events at different developmental levels (the stresses of normal developmental tasks as well as accidental stresses, such as the loss of significant others, failures, physical trauma, and illness).

Taxonomically, neurosis is a subset of mental disorders of adulthood. It is differentiated from (1) psychotic disorders by the absence of disorganization of personality and distortions or misinterpretations of reality; (2) personality disorders by the presence of marked subjective distress from which relief is desired; (3) psychophysiological disorders by the absence of primary dysfunctions of the autonomic nervous system; and (4) transient situational disturbances by the absence of overwhelming environmental stress and the presence of subclinical mental disorder. Types of neuroses are distinguished on the basis of predominant symptom formation: anxiety, conversion, dissociation, phobia, obsession-compulsion, depression, neurasthenia, depersonalization, or hypochondriasis (American Psychiatric Association, 1968).

Prognostically, the term suggests the following statements. Neuroses are considered amenable to treatment, with prognosis more favorable than for psychoses and personality disorders (Kutash, 1965) and less favorable than for the psychophysiological disorders and the transient situational disturbances. Because of secondary gains, symptoms may persist after environmental precipitants have been removed; in the absence of secondary gains, however, symptoms may improve spontaneously with changes in the life situation (Millon, 1969). Prognostic factors are many and varied (Kutash, 1965); they include severity of symptomatology, underlying conflicts, duration, manner of onset, rigidity of personality, age, intelligence, life situation, motivation for treatment, capacity for self-awareness, type of syndrome, tolerance for anxiety, variety and strength of defenses, and overall health. In general, the longer the duration and the more chronic the symptoms, the poorer the prognosis; similarly, the shorter the duration and the more acute the symptoms, the better the prognosis.

Diagnostically, the term is associated with both quantitative and qualitative assessment procedures, which include interviews, psychometric tests of intelligence and personality, projective techniques, and systematic observations of behavior in situ. Recent trends (Lanyon and Goodstein, 1971; Mash and Terdal, 1976; Mischel, 1968) favor (1) interviews based on structured and differentially weighted questions, which are derived from reliably obtained, consensually validated behavioral indexes, to yield both overall scores and component scores; (2) carefully constructed rating scales to assess specific behaviors in natural or controlled situations; and (3) self-report inventories or questionnaires that yield scores for clearly defined behavioral referents. Therapeutically, both individual and group treatment may be directed primarily toward the specific symptoms (as in the use of psychotropic drugs, behavior modification/therapy methods, hypnosis, and biofeedback) or primarily toward basic personality patterns (as in psychoanalytic methods) or equally to symptoms and personality patterns (as in client-centered, Gestalt, transactional analysis, rational-emotive, reality, and existential therapies).

Critical Discussion

General Areas of Concern

The objective of clinical assessment is to gather and evaluate information from which diagnostic decisions can be formulated about the degree and type of impairment of psychological and environmental modalities; these diagnostic decisions, together with an examination of the predisposing and precipitation factors, lead in turn to specific prognostic and therapeutic decisions. The accuracy of this process is still a debatable issue because of (1) the limited reliability, validity, and normative bases of the assessment procedures; and (2) the human errors and biases inherent in clinical judgments of data obtained from assessment procedures.

From assessment data the clinician discerns cues to differentiate neurotic symptoms from other types of symptoms and to reveal symptom configurations or syndromes and basic personality patterns. While clinicians differ in the importance attributed to different symptom cues and in the sensitivity imputed to various assessment methods, the referent point for cues is one or more of the specific psychological modalities (needs, images, sensations, motoric responses, affects, cognitions, motives, and actions).

Efforts continue to be made to develop syndrome classifications that not only discriminate commonalities among syndromes but also explicate etiological and therapeutic variables inherent in each syndrome. (Although *DSM-II* lacks these features, it is still the most frequently used classification of neurotic syndromes.) Similarly, efforts continue to be made to develop meaningful personality pattern classifications associated with particular neurotic symptom and syndrome cues.

Diagnosis of the type and severity of a neurosis begins with an assessment of neurotic cues associated with different levels of psychological functioning. Millon (1969) has proposed an assessment procedure in which four levels of abnormal functioning are examined. At the first level, deficient, excessive, or unusual characteristics of emotional expressiveness and social interaction are observed. At the second level, disturbances of consciousness, memory, feelings, and thought content (including pathological preoccupation) are noted from self-reports. At the third level, a determination is made of the impact of unconscious conflicts and defensive processes on emotional control and interpersonal coping strategies. At the fourth level, temperamental dispositions and biological defects or dysfunctions, as evidenced in physical examinations and laboratory tests, are evaluated. For the first three levels, neurotic cues can be identified by the use of the following assessment methods. First are tests of intellectual functioning, such as the verbal and performance sections of the Wechsler Adult Intelligence Scale (WAIS). Second are personality inventories, such as the Minnesota Multiphasic Personality Inventory (MMPI). Third are projective techniques, such as the Rorschach. Fourth is the diagnostic interview (structured or unstructured). Fifth are ratings of behavior on situational tasks or in natural settings. With the exception of behavioral ratings (which have had limited application to a neurotic population), a brief description of clinical usage of each method is given below.

On the WAIS, neurotic cues can be found in the character of the verbalizations (for instance, whether they are overdetailed or ambivalent); uneven quality of the answers (some easy items may be failed and more difficult ones passed); impaired attention and concentration on verbal tasks; psychomotor tension, which disrupts fine-motor manipulations; and extratest behavior (such as persistent self-criticism of responses). For an obsessive-compulsive syndrome, Ray Schafer (1948) identifies the most common cues as pedantic intellectualizing, rationalizing and doubting of answers, and an overall rigidity.

On the MMPI, neurotic cues can be identified from scale elevations, profile context of a particular scale elevation, and specific item content. For example, with primary elevation of the Hysteria scale (common in conversion syndrome), two types of items are frequently endorsed: complaints about specific body parts and denial of unacceptable personality traits (Pope and Scott, 1967). A primary elevation of the Psychasthenia scale may indicate compulsive actions, obsessional ideas, unreasonable fears, or anxious rumination (Marks and Seeman, 1963). Consequently, the profile context must be considered. For example, a secondary elevation on the Depression scale suggests an anxiety syndrome; similarly, a depressive syndrome is strongly indicated by a primary elevation on the Depression scale and a secondary elevation on the Psychasthenia scale. With a moderately elevated Schizophrenia scale, analysis of item content may yield cues suggestive of depersonalization or dissociation syndromes.

On the Rorschach, neurotic cues may be identified by the following: ideational productivity (for instance, moderate retardation of perceptual and associative responding); integrative quality of perception (for instance, a preponderance of vague and poorly conceived responses); emotional lability (for instance, denial or distortion of affective stimuli); content of responses (for instance, blocking or avoidance reactions). For a hysterical syndrome, Pope and Scott (1967) identify the principal cues as impulsiveness in thinking and acting, affective lability, excessive reliance on repression, and evidence of somatic concern.

Recently the diagnostic interview has had a more structured format and responses have been quantified. Structured interviews are of two types: qualitative or descriptive assessment of responses to a standard set of questions; and quantitative or differentially weighted assessment of responses to a standard set of questions. An example of the former is Arnold Lazarus' (1976) Multimodal Assessment, which provides a clinical appraisal of seven modalities: behavior, affect, sensation, imagery, cognition, interpersonal relationships, and physical condition and use of drugs. For a compulsive syndrome, examination of the first six modalities might yield the following cues: intrusive compulsions, anger, heightened awareness of autonomic functions, aggressive imagery, perfectionistic demands of self and others, and passive-aggressive relating. For a depressive syndrome, significant cues might be slowed psychomotor reactions, sadness, sensations of numbness, guilt-ridden imagery, self-castigating statements, and sharply curtailed social interaction.

Patients with neurotic symptom disorders, as differentiated from those with psychotic disorders, do not manifest gross perceptual misrecognitions, severe cognitive misinterpretations, and disorganized actions; secondarily, they do not display markedly dysphoric affect, bizarre motoric responses, terrifying images, hallucinatory sensations, grandiose motives, and needs often so pervasive as to preempt safety and health concerns. In addition, unlike the psychotic, the neurotic patient is aware of his impaired psychological functioning and wants to obtain relief from the impairment.

As differentiated from psychophysiological disorders, neurotic symptom disorders do not involve primary autonomic nervous system dysfunction or structural changes in the organs and viscera (Kolb/Noyes, 1968). In addition, unlike those with psychophysiological disorders, neurotic patients manifest intense affect of anxiety and depression, focal psychic conflicts, and defense mechanisms to avoid or escape from intense affect.

Neurotic symptom disorders are distinguished from the transient situational disturbances by the fact that environmental stress is of secondary importance to the development and maintenance of neurotic symptoms of distress and inefficiency; at the same time, a more encompassing impairment of environmental modalities (education, occupation, leisure, sex, marriage, parenthood, and social contact) usually accompanies neurotic disorders.

As distinguished from personality disorders, the onset of neurotic symptom disorders is more likely to be acute, with marked affective distress; symptoms are perceived as ego dystonic rather than ego syntonic; and conflicts are internally rather than externally focused.

Once the presence of symptomatic behavior has been identified and discriminated from symptoms of other disorders, the clinician then relies on syndrome cues (such as the type, confluency, consistency, and saliency of symptoms) to determine the closest fit between the symptomatic behavior and syndrome classification. Presented below are the characteristic symptom features of the nine neurotic syndromes listed in *DSM-II* (American Psychiatric Association, 1968).

Anxiety Syndrome. The predominant symptom pattern is one of acute affect (that is, nonspecific anxiety sometimes reaching panic proportions), often experienced in conjunction with unpleasant bodily sensations (American Psychiatric Association, 1968), motoric symptoms of restlessness and tremulousness, immobilized actions, and impaired perceptual attention and cognitive concentration. The major defense mechanism is diffuse displacement.

Hysterical Syndrome. There are two types: (1) In the *conversion type*, there is loss or limited use, without conscious intent, of sensory and motor functions incompatible with anatomical structure (Kolb/Noyes, 1968), combined with the absence of affective concern for the dysfunction. (2) In the *dissociative type* (or altered states of consciousness), there is selective loss of cognitive awareness (amnesia) of past experience and self-identity facts; perceptual misrecognition of significant others, sometimes combined with actions (fugue) that relocate the person in new surroundings and with a changed identity; somnambulism, in which complex activities are carried out in a sleeplike state for which there is amnesia; and multiple personality, characterized by two or more alternating autonomous sets of psychological modalities, especially cognitive and affective, for which there is unilateral or bilateral amnesia of one set for the other (Kutash, 1965). Though the conversion type is expressed somatically and the dissociation type behaviorally, they are considered similar in dynamics, and in both there are strong indications of secondary gain (Kutash, 1965). The primary defense mechanisms are repression, denial, and, in the dissociative type, perhaps reversal.

Phobic Syndrome. Phobias are characterized by persistent and intense affect of anxiety, sometimes bordering on panic, attached to some object or situation. They are accompanied by sensations of fainting, dyspnea, weakness, palpitations, and cold perspiration. The individual takes elaborate actions to circumvent the phobic object or situation, although he has perceptual recognition and cognitive awareness of the absence of real danger (American Psychiatric Association, 1968; Kolb/Noyes, 1968). The primary defense mechanism is circumscribed displacement.

Obsessive-Compulsive Syndrome. Obsessions and compulsions combine, with one or the other predominating. Specifically, the experience is one of persistently intrusive and unwanted images, cognitions, and motoric responses, accompanied by affective distress over the inability to stop the intrusions and a cognitive awareness of the irrationality or inexplicability of the intrusions (American Psychiatric Association, 1968; Kolb/Noyes, 1968). The primary defense mechanisms are isolation, undoing, displacement, and reaction formation (Millon, 1969).

Depressive Syndrome. There is strong and persistent affect of grief, guilt, and dejection, sometimes associated with an identified separation or loss and accompanied by moderately lethargic or agitated motoric responses, with actions tending toward isolation or withdrawal. The primary defense mechanisms are likely to be introjection and compensation.

Neurasthenic Syndrome. The presenting symptoms are sensations of chronic weakness, aches and pains, marked susceptibility to fatigue, often exhaustion, with affective distress about the symptoms but a lack of affective intensity on other matters (American Psychiatric Association, 1968; Kutash, 1965). Additional symptoms are distracting cognitions that impair concentration, a slowing of motoric responses, and actions characterized by a lack of productivity and interest in social relationships. The primary defense mechanisms are likely to be denial and displacement.

Depersonalization Syndrome. There is some similarity to the dissociative type of hysterical syndrome, as well as to elements sometimes present in depressive, hypochrondriacal, and obsessional syndromes. As a syndrome, it includes (1) an affective component of feelings of estrangement and unreality regarding one's body and identity; (2) a perceptual component in which objects, events, and people are perceived as strange, detached, unreal, and lacking in normal color and vividness; (3) a cognitive component of confusion, with a loss of conviction of self-identity and control over one's body; and (4) motoric responses that are often mechanical and stereotyped (Kolb/Noyes, 1968). Primary defense mechanisms are likely to be reversal and isolation.

Hypochondriacal Syndrome. In the hypochondriacal syndrome there is cognitive preoccupation with one's body, vague shifting sensations of bodily disturbances, affective distress (fear of disease) without loss of disturbance of psychological functions, sometimes following an accident or illness. There are also strong indications of secondary gain (American Psychiatric Association, 1968; Kutash, 1965). Denial and displacement are likely to be the primary defense mechanisms.

Personality Patterns. Personality pattern cues differ from syndrome cues insofar as the former subsume a wider range of behavior, with emphasis on inferred characteristics;

refer to more enduring or habitual responses; and connote a relational quality of pre-disposition to syndromes. Five commonly used or recently developed personality patterns are identified here.

1. *DSM-II* personality patterns or disorders (American Psychiatric Association, 1968): antisocial, asthenic, cyclothymic (affective), explosive, hysterical, inadequate, obsessive-compulsive, paranoid, passive-aggressive, schizoid. (See Chapter Eleven in this volume.)
2. Millon's (1969) personality patterns: aggressive; asocial, avoidant; conforming; cycloid; gregarious; narcissistic; negativistic; paranoid; schizoid; submissive.
3. Leary's (1957) interpersonal adjustment patterns: aggressive-sadistic, competitive-narcissistic, cooperative-overconventional, docile-dependent, managerial-autocratic, re-bellious-distrustful, responsible-hypernormal, self-effacing-masochistic.
4. Wolman's (1965) need satisfaction patterns: instrumental-hyperinstrumental, mutual-paramutual, vectorial-hypervectorial.
5. Wile's (1976) personality patterns or styles: oppositional-externalizing, personal excel-lence-performance, reductive-conventional, relationship-dependent, spiritualistic-cos-mic.

In Table 1, the nine neurotic syndromes are identified (by abbreviation) with their relation to the various personality patterns.

Table 1. Personality Patterns

Syndromes	APA (1968)	Millon (1969)	Leary (1957)	Wolman (1965)	Wile (1976)
Anx.	Pass.-aggress.	Conform., cycloid	Docile-depend.	Hyper-instru.	Relat.-depend.
Hyster., Conver.	Hyster.	Submiss., cycloid	Coop.-over-convent.	Para-mutual	Relat.-depend.
Hyster., Dissoc.	Hyster.	Avoidant	Coop.-over-convent.	Para-mutual	Relat.-depend.
Phob.	Hyster.	Submiss., cycloid	Docile-depend.	Hyper-vector.	Reduct.-convent.
Obsess.-Compul.	Obsess.-compul.	Conform., cycloid, paranoid	Self-effac.-masochist.	Hyper-vector.	Person. excell.
Depress.	Cyclothy.	Submiss., cycloid	Self-effac.-masochist.	Hyper-instru.	Relat.-depend.
Neuras.	Asthen.	Negativ., cycloid	Docile-depend.	Hyper-vector.	Opposit.-extern.
Despers.	Schizoid	Schizoid	Rebell.-distrust.	Para-mutual	Spirit.-cosmic
Hypochon.	Hyster.	Negativ., cycloid	Coop.-over-convent.	Hyper-vector.	Reduct.-convent.

Comparative Philosophies and Theories

Current theoretical positions are divided into four groups: cognitive/behavioral, phenomenological/humanistic, psychodynamic/intrapsychic, and trait/type.

The cognitive/behavioral position contends that the development, maintenance, and modification of behavior disorders are the same as for normal behavior; neurotic disorder is a label for behaviors that a person has acquired to cope with the stressful problems of daily living in an ever changing and complex environment (O'Leary and Wilson, 1975). Neurotic coping behaviors represent ways in which a person perceives, thinks, feels, and acts in specific situations. These behaviors are developed and maintained by (1) classically conditioned processes, in which responses become associated with external events; or (2) operantly conditioned processes of getting reinforcement, losing reinforcement, avoiding punishment, and getting punishment; or (3) cognitive, mediational process of vicarious learning, symbolic activities, and self-control mechanisms (Bandura, 1969). To a significant extent, maladaptive ways of thinking, feeling, and acting create environmental contingencies that help to strengthen and perpetuate the neurosis. To understand and predict neurotic behavior, one must examine antecedent stimulus variables; organismic variables (both psychological and physiological); the specific excesses and deficits of thinking, feeling, and acting; and the reciprocal impact of those excesses and deficits on the environment, which is primarily interpersonal (Goldfried and Pomeranz, 1968).

The phenomenological/humanistic position subsumes the self theorists, existential theorists, Gestalt theorists, many transactional analysis theorists, and a loosely knit group of theorists who advocate development of human potential. According to this position, neurosis develops when an individual's feelings, needs, motives, values, beliefs, and expectations run counter to socially approved or other-directed ones. The individual then experiences pervasive and protracted internal conflicts, which eventuate in self-estrangement or self-alienation. Unable or unwilling to relate meaningfully to self, the individual has limited awareness of his or her inner world, as well as that of significant others, with a resulting lack of personal and social identity (Millon, 1969). In contrast to patients with other disorders, neurotics are strongly inclined to subordinate their inner world to what they perceive or imagine to be the demands of expectations of the external world. In so doing, they fail to develop personal potentials to live productively and satisfyingly within and outside the self.

The psychodynamic/intrapsychic approach "hypothesizes motives, needs, conflicts, complexes, attitudes, and other underlying but not directly observable dispositions that produce varied manifestations similar to a physical disease" (Mischel, 1973, p. 336). The purpose of assessment and diagnosis is to infer the underlying dispositions in order to explain the array of symptomatic behaviors. The connection between the overt and the covert is often puzzling and elusive because of the defense mechanisms that intervene between the symptoms and their determinants. Neurotic disorders of adulthood are traceable to childhood anxieties and defenses against anxieties, with these anxieties and defenses experienced outside the center of conscious awareness (Millon, 1969). Defenses against anxiety undergo developmental progression compatible with maturation of sensory-motor, perceptual-cognitive, affective-motivational, and interpersonal processes. Anxieties of the early developmental stages are reactivated by stressful situations of adult life. A final proposition is that neurotic symptom formation is the outcome of escalating anxieties pressing against inadequate or weakened defenses, resulting in symptoms of internal and external impairment.

In the trait/type theory, neurosis is explained in terms of reliable and valid measures of traits derived from factor analysis. In the multifactorial theory (Cattell and Scheier, 1961), neurotic disorders differ from psychoses on a dimension of reality contact. Neurosis is thought to be a special type of personality pattern, in which the difference from normality is a function of differences in specific personality and situation factors. The differences are expressed in the formative years by the way in which external conflicts or barriers are overcome and, later developmentally, by the way in which internal conflicts or barriers are resolved. In contrast to normals, neurotics display poor problem-solving capacities, have an overreactive or underreactive temperament, grow up in a negatively toned family atmosphere, and show an energy deficiency (independent of conflict). Some personality factors raise the degree of neuroticism, while others lower it; and the interaction of the factors determines the type of neurosis. Eysenck and Rachman (1965) have presented a less elaborate factorial basis for describing neurosis by using only three factors; two factors, introversion-extraversion and neuroticism-emotionality, are related and are independent of the third factor, psychoticism. The neuroticism-emotionality factor has a stability-instability component and a temperament component. Types of neurotic disorders represent the varied composition of temperament, emotional instability, and introversion-extraversion.

Both psychodynamic/intrapsychic and trait/type positions accept the concepts of neurotic syndromes and stable personality patterns. This is consistent with their emphasis on the presence of maladaptive reactions and their willingness to conceptualize basic elements of behavior into higher-order concepts; however, they differ in the rational/subjective versus objective/empirical approach to assessment and diagnosis. In the phenomenological/humanistic position, syndromes and personality patterns are seldom utilized because this position conceptualizes disorders as problems of living productively and satisfyingly, rather than as illnesses, and emphasizes the absence of adaptive characteristics. The cognitive/behavioral position also eschews the use of syndromes and personality patterns, not only because of an emphasis on adaptive behavior that has not been learned but also because of a commitment to lower-order concepts of thought-feeling-action units of behavior. The trait/type and cognitive/behavioral positions share a commitment to empirically based principles of learning but differ in the former's acceptance of higher-order abstractions of behavioral phenomena. The psychodynamic/intrapsychic and phenomenological/humanistic positions, though differing in terms of an illness versus a problems-of-living model, have in common an emphasis on the interior life of the person. The cognitive/behavioral and phenomenological/humanistic positions differ in terms of empirical/objective versus intuitive/subjective methodology but show a mutual affinity in underscoring the responsibility of the individual for self-created and self-perpetuated problems.

Elaboration on Critical Points

As mentioned previously, five types of assessment methods provide data from which cues are discerned. Descriptively, cues vary according to degree of specificity, explicitness, verbal or nonverbal, frequency, saliency, consistency, and confluency. Cues also vary from lower-order concepts (such as sample) to higher-order concepts (such as sign or symbol) of neurotic symptom, syndrome, or personality pattern. The following is a brief example of sample, sign, and symbol for four different symptoms:

Sample: verbalized fear of disease; functional paralysis; suicidal thoughts; handwashing compulsion.

Sign: frequent anatomical percepts on the Rorschach; observation of histrionic or over-dramatized actions; sad, pessimistic themes on the TAT; persistently vacillatory responses in an interview.

Symbol: MMPI scale scores on Hs (hypochondriasis), Hy (hysteria), D (depression), Pt (psychasthenia).

Clinical judgment includes two types of reasoning (Shafer, 1948) from sample, sign, or symbol cues: (1) from interpretive reasoning to idiographic judgments about psychological modalities and the concomitant effects on environmental modalities; and (2) from diagnostic reasoning to nomothetic judgments about syndrome and personality pattern classifications. Clinical judgment has been dichotomized into (1) a subjective-experiential type, based on the clinician's experience with an assessment tool and with a particular clinical population; and (2) an objective-actuarial type, based on empirically determined relationships between assessment data and relevant criteria (for example, diagnostic, prognostic, and therapeutic variables). While research favors the objective type, its presently limited scope for individualized diagnostic, prognostic, and therapeutic decisions argues for its use as a complement to, rather than a substitute for, the subjective type (Millon, 1969).

Optimal reliability and validity of understanding and prediction for a neurotic patient depend on the degree to which assessment and diagnosis can be individualized. Walter Mischel (1968, p. 231) states: "The labeling of a person to conform to some classification may have powerful consequences, both applied privately by and publicly for the person." As Mischel implies, diagnosis is a type of evaluative personal and/or social judgment (Bandura, 1969; Mash and Terdal, 1976; Szasz, 1961), yet it is justifiable and useful: Research and clinical experience indicate that neurotics can be differentiated on the basis of symptomatic behavior as well as specific personality characteristics. Furthermore, some patients possess in common critical symptoms and personality characteristics that distinguish them from other groups of neurotic patients. Finally, past experience with these patient groups or syndromes can facilitate the individualizing of diagnostic, prognostic, and therapeutic decisions (Millon, 1969).

The specific strengths and weaknesses in this regard of the *DSM-II* classification have been noted by many investigators (for example, Millon, 1969). Its strengths are that neurotic symptoms can be discriminated from other symptoms in terms of severity; neurotic syndromes are differentiated by symptoms that cluster together; and neurotic syndromes are distinguishable from syndromes that emphasize the primary role of situational stresses, psychophysiological dysfunction, and pervasive and deeply ingrained habit patterns. Weaknesses are the relatively small weight given to prognostic and therapeutic variables compared to the weight given to symptomatology; the lack of differentiation among syndromes on etiological and developmental variables; the lack of clarity about significant commonalities among neurotic syndromes; and the use of ambiguous and inexact symptom criteria, resulting in low reliability for classifying a person in a particular syndrome.

While not yet a substitute for *DSM-II* in clinical usage, the recently developed *DSM-III* has overcome some limitations (Zubin, 1977-78). It synthesizes much of the progress in descriptive psychopathology, especially multivariate cluster and factor analytic studies, with greater reliability of behavior assessment and greater reliability of choice of diagnosis. The main limitations are the preference given to an illness model over other models and the fact that validity of the diagnostic groupings is still a moot issue due to limited knowledge of etiology.

The remaining critical points can be organized around three commonly employed models: illness, social learning, and actualization. Though semantic differences exist, the basic paradigm of personal distress/social inefficiency generated by defensive/protective reactions to conflict-centered fear/anxiety is central to all three models. The symptoms of the illness model are the behavioral deficits and excesses of the social learning model and the relating and communicating failures of the actualization model. While the issue of whether neurosis is qualitatively or quantitatively different from other disorders and from normality is unresolved, the three models accept the assumption of a severity continuum of mental disorders.

Neither the actualization nor the social learning model makes the sharp distinction between primary and secondary gain that the illness model does. For the former two, the concept of secondary gain means that the individual's symptoms do not provoke social condemnation and may even elicit social support and nurturance (Millon, 1969). Symptom substitution is a logical derivative of the illness model's assumption of symptoms linked to "underlying" causes, but it is incompatible with the social learning model's core meaning of neurosis as learned behavior deficits and excesses directly related to specific situations; it is also incompatible with the actualization model's core meaning of neurosis as a failure to communicate and relate authentically to oneself and others. Because unconscious determinants are of primary significance in the illness model and of secondary significance in the other two models, responsibility for one's problems and their alleviation is deemphasized in the former and emphasized in the latter two.

Within each model various therapeutic procedures have been developed to alleviate personal distress and overcome social ineffectiveness. In the illness and social learning models, the therapist is the change agent. In the former, the emphasis is on fostering insight into "underlying" causes, and symptom removal is a by-product; in the latter, the emphasis is on directly modifying the behavioral deficits and excesses, and insight is a by-product. In the actualization model, the client or patient is the change agent, and the therapist creates conditions conducive to accepting responsibility for self or discovering one's ability to communicate and relate differently and authentically to self and others.

While the three models recognize some form of the distinction between precipitating and predisposing factors, only the social learning model gives precipitating factors a major role. This model combines with social psychology and the professional specialty of community psychology to represent formative influences in research efforts to develop a taxonomy of situations or ecological events. The issue of predisposing factors is embedded in the basic questions about etiology, and the statement of Zubin (1977-78, p. 7) is timely: "One solution is to look for the common denominator running through all these models. . . . The thread . . . is the presence of a vulnerability . . . elicited by either exogenous or endogenous life events which produce sufficient stress to elicit an episode. . . . We need to find and differentiate markers of vulnerability from markers of the presence and absence of episodes. . . . The latter wax and wane with the episodes and disappear with the end of the episode, while the former persist in and out of episodes."

Personal Views and Recommendations

The *outcome* of psychological disorders may be designated as a loss of conscious control. In neurosis, one primarily loses control over one or more psychological modalities; the loss of control here is differentiated from that in psychoses on a severity dimension. In the psychophysiological disorders, the loss of control is in one or more components of the autonomic nervous system. In transient situational disturbances, the loss of control is primarily of one or more environmental modalities. In the personality disorders, the loss of control is manifested in the discordant or alienating quality of interpersonal habits.

The *process* of psychological disorders is determined by three classes of variables: precipitating, predisposing, and prevailing. With neurosis as a reference point, the class of precipitating variables includes (1) an external dimension of the quality and quantity of stress-producing situations; (2) an internal dimension of the perceptual, cognitive, and affective experience of the stress; and (3) a temporal dimension of past, present, or future. The class of predisposing variables includes the organismically and psychosocially determined vulnerabilities (the balance between the individual's strengths and weaknesses) to dysfunction of one or more psychological modalities. The class of prevailing variables refers to personality traits, some of which are common to all neurotic disorders, some common to one syndrome, and some characteristic of a particular individual.

A neurotic disorder is the culmination of the developmental and dynamic interaction of the three classes of variables. Factors such as onset and the environmental modalities affected are subsumed under the precipitation class; type and severity of disorder are subsumed under the predisposing class; and the accompanying personality features are subsumed under the prevailing class. Symptom substitution would express both predisposing and precipitating variables. Primary and secondary gain would be inferred from prevailing and precipitating variables. Environmental consequences of the disorder would be predictable from precipitating and predisposing variables. Therapeutic and other prognostic factors would be weighted differentially in all three classes of variables.

Clinical assessment is designed to provide data from which diagnostic conclusions may be drawn regarding the incongruities (that which is incompatible, inconsistent, conflicting, contradictory, or inappropriate) among and within the three classes of variables. Ideally, treatment is environmentally centered, in order to eliminate or modify the situational stresses and shore up environmental resources; and individually centered, in order to ameliorate and strengthen the specific perception-thought-feeling-action units of behavior in a sequential order from least to most dysfunctional. Practical criteria to evaluate treatment outcome might best be incorporated in quality-of-life indicators (such as working, leisure, eating, sleeping, social contact, earning, parenting, loving, liking for one's physical environment, and self-acceptance) (Blau, 1977).

Application to Particular Variables

Of the officially classified mental disorders, neurosis is the most prevalent; estimates range from a conservative 10 million to a more liberal 20-25 million (Kutash, 1965; Martin, 1971). Variability of estimates reflects different definitions among clinicians and researchers, varying cultural reactions to symptoms, and the discrepancy among epidemiological methods. An additional finding is that 30 to 60 percent of persons contacting general physicians and general hospitals and clinics can be classified as having a neurotic disorder (Kolb/Noyes, 1968; Kutash, 1965). Incidence is reported highest among divorced, then single, and next the married (Kolb/Noyes, 1968), and higher in congested urban areas than in rural areas (Millon, 1969). The different syndromes vary in reported incidence, with anxiety and depression the highest, the mixed (or "other") neuroses next, then conversions and obsessive-compulsive syndromes, with the lowest frequency for dissociative and phobic syndromes (Cattell and Scheier, 1961). Some factors contributing to a rise in incidence (or at least visibility) during the last two decades are the increase in insurance coverage for diagnosis and treatment and the burgeoning of comprehensive mental health complexes, especially crisis intervention centers.

Neurosis is classified primarily as a mental disorder of adulthood, due to the absence of easily recognized diagnostic signs in children and adolescents (Halpern, 1965). Because of the rigidity of the standard nomenclature and the greater fluidity of behavior in children and adolescents, many investigators (for instance, Eysenck and Rachman, 1965) prefer the traditional, more general classification of conduct and personality problems. Neurosis is most closely associated with the period between late adolescence and the late 30s, with some decline thereafter and a rise after age 60 (Cattell and Scheier, 1961; Kolb/Noyes, 1968). Masterson (1967) concludes that adolescent turmoil is a critical precipitant of neurosis between ages 11 and 14, though overestimated in depressive and anxiety reactions; that there is less continuity between early childhood and adolescence than for other disorders; and that impairment is usually of a mild degree, restricted to the psychological function affected by the type of symptom, and has a more favorable prognosis than the neurosis of adulthood. Cattell and Scheier (1961) have found that some neurotic factors increase with age (probably those associated with internalization of conflicts), others decrease with age (most likely those associated with external conflicts and barriers), and others stay the same (perhaps those associated with organismic/genetic influences).

The higher incidence in women (Cattell and Scheier, 1961; Fodor, 1974; Kolb/Noyes, 1968) is confounded by a number of factors, such as the greater readiness of women to admit to and seek help for emotional problems and the higher incidence of sex-role confusion during the last two decades (Gove and Tudor, 1973). With children, however, there is a significantly higher admission to clinics of boys than girls, age 5 to 9, with a sex-ratio reversal beginning in the later elementary years (Verville, 1967). Hysterical and phobic syndromes are reported to be more frequent in women than in men (Kolb/Noyes, 1968; Martin, 1971). From clinical experience, it seems that males show a higher incidence than females of obsessive-compulsive, anxiety, neurasthenia, and depersonalization syndromes, but there seems to be a lower incidence in males for depressive, hypochondriacal, hysterical, and phobic syndromes. One study (Coleman and Miller, 1975) found no difference in marital maladjustment scores of husbands and wives, but significantly more depressive reactions in the wives than in the husbands.

Neurosis has been cited as relatively more prevalent (and psychoses less prevalent) in the upper than in the lower socioeconomic groups (Hollingshead and Redlich, 1958). Other epidemiological studies (for instance, Dohrenwend and Dohrenwend, 1969) have noted a significant relationship between prevalence of symptoms and social class. Verville (1967) concludes that lower socioeconomic children show more problems than those of higher status and that the circular effects of inadequate education and lower socioeconomic status lead to problems in adjusting to middle-class norms. In addition, assessment analog studies have been carried out to demonstrate the effect of social-class bias on diagnosis (Di Nardo, 1975).

Symptoms such as anxiety, depersonalization, and depression are found cross-culturally and are traceable to stresses implicit in social and cultural backgrounds (Opler, 1965). Cultural variables can be expected to affect the form but not the frequency of mental disorders (Millon, 1969). According to Dohrenwend and Dohrenwend (1969, p. 169), "Symptom items themselves have different meanings and hence different implications for the persons in different subcultures." Cattell and Scheier (1961) report a higher incidence of anxiety and neurotic elements in some European and Asian countries than in the United States, and they attribute the variations to differences in affluence, education, and authoritarianism, with education and enlightened affluence leading to more effective prevention and treatment programs.

Although a higher frequency of psychopathology has been noted in blacks than in whites (Fischer, 1969; Genthner and Graham, 1976), some studies show that many of the reported racial differences in psychopathology disappear or are attentuated when age, sex, and social-class variables are held constant (Raskin, Crook, and Herman, 1975). Other studies (for example, Watkins, Cowan, and Davis, 1975) have found that diagnosis is a function of racial group rather than of purely social class and education; and Blake (1973) has noted that blacks are frequently overdiagnosed or underdiagnosed.

References

American Psychiatric Association. *Diagnostic and Statistical Manual of Mental Disorders.* (2nd ed.) Washington, D.C.: American Psychiatric Association, 1968.

Bandura, A. *Principles of Behavior Modification.* New York: Holt, Rinehart and Winston, 1969.

Blake, W. "The Influence of Race on Diagnosis." *Smith College Studies in Social Work,* 1973, *43,* 184-192.

Blau, T. H. "The Quality of Life Indicators." *Professional Psychology,* 1977, *8,* 464-473.

Carkhuff, R. R., and Berenson, B. G. *Beyond Counseling and Therapy.* New York: Holt, Rinehart and Winston, 1967.

Cattell, R. B., and Scheier, I. H. *The Meaning and Measurement of Neuroticism and Anxiety.* New York: Ronald Press, 1961.

Cohen, D. B. "On the Etiology of Neurosis." *Journal of Abnormal Psychology,* 1974, *83,* 473-479.

Coleman, R. E., and Miller, A. G. "The Relationship Between Depression and Marital Maladjustment in a Clinic Population: A Multitrait-Multimethod Study." *Journal of Consulting and Clinical Psychology,* 1975, *43,* 647-651.

Di Nardo, P. A. "Social Class and Diagnostic Suggestion as Variables in Clinical Judgement." *Journal of Consulting and Clinical Psychology,* 1975, *43,* 363-368.

Dohrenwend, B., and Dohrenwend, B. *Social Status and Psychological Disorder.* New York: Wiley, 1969.

Ellis, A. *Reason and Emotion in Psychotherapy.* New York: Lyle Stuart, 1962.

Epstein, S. "The Nature of Anxiety with Emphasis upon Its Relationship to Expectancy." In C. D. Spielberger (Ed.), *Anxiety: Current Trends in Theory and Research.* Vol. 2. New York: Academic Press, 1972.

Eysenck, H. J., and Rachman, S. *The Causes and Cures of Neurosis.* San Diego, Calif.: Robert Knapp, 1965.

Fagan, J., and Shepherd, I. L. (Eds.). *Gestalt Therapy Now.* Palo Alto, Calif.: Science and Behavior Books, 1970.

Fischer, J. "Negroes and Whites and Rates of Mental Illness: Reconsideration of a Myth." *Psychiatry,* 1969, *32,* 428-446.

Fodor, I. E. "Sex Role Conflict and Symptom Formation in Women: Can Behavior Therapy Help." *Psychotherapy,* 1974, *44,* 118-124.

Ford, D. H., and Urban, H. B. *Systems of Psychotherapy: A Comparative Study.* New York: Wiley, 1963.

Frankl, V. E. *Man's Search for Meaning.* Boston: Beacon Press, 1962.

Genthner, R. W., and Graham, J. R. "Effects of Short-Term Public Psychiatric Hospitalization for Both Black and White Patients." *Journal of Consulting and Clinical Psychology,* 1976, *44,* 118-124.

Goldfried, M., and Pomeranz, D. "Role of Assessment in Behavior Modification." *Psychological Reports,* 1968, *23,* 75-87.

Gove, W. R., and Tudor, J. F. "Adult Sex Roles and Mental Illness." *American Journal of Sociology,* 1973, *78,* 812-835.

Halpern, F. "Diagnostic Methods in Children's Disorders." In B. B. Wolman (Ed.), *Handbook of Clinical Psychology.* New York: McGraw-Hill, 1965.

Hollingshead, A. B., and Redlich, F. C. *Social Class and Mental Illness.* New York: Wiley, 1958.

Izard, C. E. *Patterns of Emotions: A New Analysis of Anxiety and Depression.* New York: Academic Press, 1972.

Kolb/Noyes, L. C. *Modern Clinical Psychiatry.* Philadelphia: Saunders, 1968.

Kutash, S. B. "Psychoneurosis." In B. B. Wolman (Ed.), *Handbook of Clinical Psychology.* New York: McGraw-Hill, 1965.

Lanyon, B. I., and Goodstein, L. D. *Personality Assessment.* New York: Wiley, 1971.

Lazarus, A. A. *Multimodal Behavior Therapy.* New York: Springer, 1976.

Leary, T. *Interpersonal Diagnosis of Personality.* New York: Ronald Press, 1957.

Marks, P. A., and Seeman, W. *Actuarial Description of Abnormal Personality.* Baltimore: Williams and Wilkins, 1963.

Martin, B. *Anxiety and Neurotic Disorders.* New York: Wiley, 1971.

Mash, E. J., and Terdal, L. G. *Behavior Therapy Assessment.* New York: Springer, 1976.

Maslow, A. *Toward a Psychology of Being.* New York: Van Nostrand, 1962.

Masterson, J. F. *The Psychiatric Dilemma of Adolescence.* Boston: Little, Brown, 1967.

May, R. *The Meaning of Anxiety.* New York: Norton, 1977.

May, R., Angel, E., and Ellenberger, H. F. (Eds.). *Existence: A New Dimension in Psychiatry and Psychology.* New York: Basic Books, 1958.

Millon, T. *Modern Psychopathology: A Biosocial Approach to Maladaptive Learning and Function.* Philadelphia: Saunders, 1969.

Mischel, W. *Personality and Assessment.* New York: Wiley, 1968.

Mischel, W. "On the Empirical Dilemmas of Psychodynamic Approaches: Issues and Alternatives." *Journal of Abnormal Psychology,* 1973, *82,* 335-344.

O'Leary, D. K., and Wilson, G. T. *Behavior Therapy: Application and Outcome.* Englewood Cliffs, N.J.: Prentice-Hall, 1975.

Opler, M. K. "Cultural Determinants of Mental Disorder." In B. B. Wolman (Ed.), *Handbook of Clinical Psychology.* New York: McGraw-Hill, 1965.

Pope, B., and Scott, W. *Psychological Diagnosis in Clinical Practice.* New York: Oxford University Press, 1967.

Raskin, A., Crook, T. H., and Herman, K. D. "Psychiatric History and Symptom Differences in Black and White Depressed Patients." *Journal of Consulting and Clinical Psychology,* 1975, *43,* 73-80.

Rogers, C. *Client-Centered Therapy.* Boston: Houghton Mifflin, 1951.

Ross, N., and Abrams, S. "Fundamentals of Psychoanalytic Theory." In B. B. Wolman (Ed.), *Handbook of Clinical Psychology.* New York: McGraw-Hill, 1965.

Saul, L. F. *Emotional Maturity: The Development and Dynamics of Personality and Its Disorders.* Philadelphia: Lippincott, 1971.

Schafer, R. *The Clinical Application of Psychological Tests.* New York: International Universities Press, 1948.

Szasz, T. *The Myth of Mental Illness.* New York: Harper & Row, 1961.

Thompson, C. *Psychoanalysis: Evolution and Development.* New York: Hermitage House, 1951.

Verville, E. V. *Behavior Problems of Children.* Philadelphia: Saunders, 1967.

Wachtel, P. L. "Psychodynamics, Behavior Therapy, and the Implacable Experimenter: An Inquiry into the Consistency of Behavior." *Journal of Abnormal Psychology,* 1973, *82,* 324-334.

Watkins, B., Cowan, M., and Davis, W. "Differential Diagnosis Imbalance as a Race-Related Phenomenon." *Journal of Clinical Psychology,* 1975, *31,* 267-268.

Wile, D. B. "Personality Styles and Therapy Styles." *Psychotherapy*, 1976, *13*, 303-307.

Wolman, B. B. (Ed.). *Handbook of Clinical Psychology*. New York: McGraw-Hill, 1965.

World Health Organization. *International Classification of Diseases*. (8th rev.) Public Health Service Publication No. 1693. Washington, D.C.: U.S. Government Printing Office, 1968.

Zubin, J. "But Is It Good for Science?" *Clinical Psychologist*, 1977-78, *31* (2), 1, 5-7.

10

Psychosomatic Disorders

Loren D. Pankratz
Vincent Glaudin

Most conceptualizations of psychosomatic disorders assume that emotional factors, such as stress or psychological conflicts, *cause* physical illness. The current diagnostic manual used in medical settings (*DSM-II*, American Psychiatric Association, 1968) promotes this view. It states clearly that psychophysiological disorders are "physical disorders of presumed psychogenic origin" and that physical symptoms are "caused by emotional factors." This formulation is based on questionable scientific evidence and tends to limit the scope of psychosomatic inquiry.

It is safer to say that many illnesses are *correlated* with social and psychological variables but are not necessarily caused by them. For example, Jenkins (1976a) has reviewed the extensive research on psychological and social risk factors for coronary disease. He points out that, with only a few exceptions, variables linking anxiety, life dissatisfactions, and personal problems to myocardial infarction are exclusively retrospective and should not be considered causal. The same may be said of other conditions presented as traditional psychosomatic illnesses. Kaplan (1975) flatly says that a definite causal relationship between psychological factors and true organic disease is merely an assumption. However, these appropriate notes of caution should not obscure the mass of research showing that life-style, personality variables, and life changes do correlate significantly with illness.

An assumption of correlation between somatic and psychological factors is not only sound scientifically; it is also clinically flexible and comprehensive. It heeds the assertion of Selby and Calhoun (1978) that the previous either-or thinking should give way to the notion of a continuum of contributing influences in psychosomatic disorders. It avoids the sterility of contemporary textbooks which merely review syndromes traditionally associated with stress or emotional problems. It permits inclusion of what Lachman (1972) calls "somatopsychic disorders," brings the emotional problems of chronic illness into perspective, and breaks down the barrier with rehabilitation medicine.

The diagnostic manual, *Psychological Factors Affecting Physical Disorder* (American Psychiatric Association, 1978), still eschewing the term *psychosomatic*, poses the addition of a category called "psychic factors in physical conditions." However, it seems more convenient to broaden the concept of psychosomatic disorder, as Wright (1977) suggests, than to create a series of new terms to describe the various ways in which organic disease interacts with personality variables. What is important is to avoid the assumption of a simple causal direction and/or to exclude a large group of patients who require assessment of emotional factors in their care.

Perhaps the broadest approach to psychosomatic disorders is in terms of "illness behavior" (Mechanic, 1962) and the "sick role" (Parsons, 1951). Sociologists have described how people perceive somatic events, selectively label symptoms, decide whether to seek treatment, decide on limiting responsibilities during illness, and cooperate with health care practitioners. In other words, there are normative aspects to illness behavior and the sick role. Therefore, the quality and degree of illness behavior must be assessed, at least informally, for every patient. Such an approach is likely to be more rewarding than focusing on a traditional group of syndromes. Moreover, assessment of illness behavior makes no assumptions about a primary psychological or organic etiology. It is likely that, in most cases, the clinician will encounter some *ongoing reciprocal interaction of somatic and psychological features.*

As the practice of medicine has increasingly become the treatment of chronic illness, excessive or inappropriate illness behavior may flourish, fed by specialization, repeated diagnostic studies, inadequately explained technical procedures, and dehumanizing institutions. The patient who presents a psychosomatic problem may well be one with organic pathology, emotional dependency, and social-psychological conditions that make the sick role attractive. In this respect, the emphasis in psychosomatic medicine has shifted from the etiology to the *course* of an illness.

Many patients with excessive illness behavior have become addicted to the medications prescribed to quiet their fears and pain. They become dependent on doctors, returning again and again with new symptoms as a way of interacting. Some patients "doctor-shop" or "hospital-shop," reluctant to admit that they are depressed, lonely, or worried about the future. Within this setting, the labeling of patients often inadvertently describes the interactional aspects of the patient-physician relationship. Slater (1965), for example, has pointed out that the diagnosis of hysteria is given frequently to patients whose illness behavior seems to demand more attention than the physician believes is deserved. Other common labels are hypochondriasis, functional disorder, organ neurosis, conversion reaction, psychogenic pain syndrome, psychophysiological reaction, depression, malingering, Munchausen Syndrome, and psychosomatic illness (see Table 1). These labels refer to various combinations of somatic symptoms, pain, depression, anxiety, and chemical dependency which constitute the varieties of *illness behavior syndromes* (Glaudin, Lipkin, and Loeb, 1978; Pilowsky, 1969). The illness behavior, rather than the primary psychological or organic origin of the disorder, should be the focus of assessment.

Table 1. Definition of Terms Related to Psychosomatic Disorders

Briquette's Syndrome	A specific disorder characterized by chronic, recurrent illness beginning before the age of 30, presenting with dramatic, vague, or complicated medical history (at least twenty-five medically unexplained symptoms over nine category groups).
Conversion Reaction	Traditionally considered to be a sudden manifestation of a sensory motor symptom as the result of the diversion of an intense emotional reaction.
Depression	Although there are specific types of depression, such as sadness, grief, and psychotic depression, the term *depression* is sometimes used to explain (or explain away) the symptoms generally associated with a clinical depression—sleeplessness, gastrointestinal problems, and lack of energy.
Factitious Illness	A self-induced injury or surreptitiously caused symptom generally thought of as implying more psychopathology than malingering, perhaps because the secondary gain is less obvious or absent.
Functional Disorder	A disorder with no demonstrated organic basis.
Functional Overlay	A physical symptom with an organic basis but probably intensified or maintained by emotional problems.
Hypochondriasis	A syndrome of obsessive (or excessive) preoccupation with health that is not resolved by negative findings or reassurance.
Hysteria	Used to denote symptoms that are overdramatized, frequently with a strange or naive detachment of responsibility.
Illness Behavior	Behaviors relating to the sick role but which have become inappropriate or excessive, blocking recovery and active life.
Malingering	Feigning a symptom or illness with conscious awareness, generally for the purpose of avoiding some responsibility or obtaining some benefit.
Munchausen Syndrome	Characterized by multiple hospitalizations at different places for complex or factitious illnesses. Sometimes called "hospital addiction."
Organ Neurosis	A functional disorder of a specific organ.
Psychogenic Pain Syndrome	Pain caused by emotional problems but expressed by complaining about some physical symptom.
Psychophysiological Reaction	An organic symptom or illness primarily caused by psychological distress.

Background and Current Status

All cultures of the world seem to have some belief system that other persons, places, things, or events may, if offended, do an individual physical harm by mystical means. This primitive belief is the root out of which our contemporary concepts of psychosomatic illness have grown (Herrick, 1976). The specifics of these belief systems, which vary from culture to culture, have been described by anthropologists, sociologists, and historians. For example, historians have provided good evidence that hysteria and hypochondriasis were well described by the Greeks in ancient times. Kaplan (1975) has provided an excellent brief review of the history of psychosomatic medicine and theory from early societies to the present.

The term *psychosomatic* was first used by J. C. A. Heinroth in 1818 to refer to mind and body in relation to his discussion of insomnia. But modern psychosomatic medicine probably can trace its roots back to Anton Mesmer (1734-1815) and his "animal magnetism"—although he treated his patients with such showmanship and dramatics that he was considered a scoundrel by those in the scientific world. Jean Charcot (1825-1893) explored the mechanisms of Mesmer's power, began to understand the role of hypnosis and suggestability, and presented his findings to medical societies. As a result, hypnosis was removed from the province of magic and became recognized as an acceptable method of treatment. Even today, in the literature on psychosomatic disorders, a large number of papers are based on hypnotic procedures. Freud was directly influenced by Charcot's ideas of suggestability and illness, although he gave up the specific use of hypnosis for free-association methods. From his earliest cases, Freud treated physical symptoms and analyzed the interaction of mind and body. He counteracted a strong trend of medicine at that time to focus narrowly on cellular pathology and disease entities. By treating the patient, not merely the disease, Freud set the tone for those who have followed in psychosomatic medicine.

In spite of its historical importance, psychoanalytic thought has waned in psychosomatic medicine in the last twenty years (Lipowski, 1977). The classical psychosomatic theories of the Chicago school (Alexander, 1950) have not received strong support by modern research (Sachar, 1972). Moreover, psychoanalysis has lost favor as a treatment modality for psychosomatic patients, who often lack motivation for self-examination, display limited ability to verbalize feelings, and present a risk of excessive dependency (Nemiah, 1975; Sifneos, 1973). Consequently, there have been suggestions that psychoanalysis is contraindicated for a great number of psychosomatic patients (Shands, 1975; Sifneos, 1973).

While Freud described the psychological mechanisms of psychosomatic disorders, others investigated the neurophysiological mechanisms for translating emotional reactions into physical symptoms. In this respect, two of the best-known neurophysiologists are Walter B. Cannon (1920) and Hans Selye (1946, 1950). Their work is remembered not only because of their significant discoveries but also because of their conceptual models, which have provided theories for continued research. As Lipowski (1977) has pointed out, we can never move beyond vague talk about a mysterious leap from mind to body unless we can identify the physiological mechanisms involved.

The most evident contemporary expression of psychophysiological inquiry in psychosomatic medicine is the exciting advancement in biofeedback (Birk, 1973; Pelletier, 1975; Schwartz, 1977). Recent innovations in instrumentation now make it possible for subjects to experience more closely than ever before the physical responses of the body and to train themselves to cope with stress-related symptoms. Meanwhile, our understanding of what life events contribute to stress has been enlarged by the research of Holmes and Rahe (1967). A third aspect of stress and psychophysiological inquiry has been made possible by the work of Friedman (1969) and his study of the Type A behavior pattern and its correlation with myocardial infarction.

The work with chronic pain has also stimulated some of the most innovative contemporary developments in psychosomatic medicine. These advancements have been shared with sociologists (Mechanic, 1959; Parsons, 1951), psychologists (Hilgard, 1969; Sternbach, 1974), and psychophysiologists (Beecher, 1966; Melzack and Wall, 1965). However, the most creative clinical conceptualization and application to the treatment of chronic pain has been provided by Wilbert Fordyce and his colleagues (Fordyce, 1976; Fordyce and others, 1968), who saw that some elements of the chronic pain syndrome could be described as learned illness behavior, subject to the same rules of learning as other operant behaviors. Once the concept of pain was broadened to include operant *behaviors* in addition to subjective *feelings*, assessment and treatment could proceed in terms of a learning model. Analyzed in this fashion, pain behaviors were often observed to be reinforced inadvertently by traditional medical treatments, such as pain-contingent responsiveness of doctors and nurses, pain medications on demand, reduction of social responsibility, and disability compensation benefits. To counteract this exacerbating medical and social environment, treatment programs have been established where these reinforcers are reversed and more positive or incompatible behaviors are learned (Bonica, 1975; Fordyce and others, 1968; Seres and others, 1977; Sternbach, 1974; Swanson and others, 1976). These programs have produced sufficiently successful results to attract the strong support of state industrial accident agencies and third-party payers.

There are only a few scattered reports of similar treatment units for general psychosomatic patients (Brautigan, 1974; Goldstein and Birnbom, 1976; Schernding, 1974). The list is slightly increased if one includes the more psychologically sophisticated rehabilitation programs for specific disorders, such as cardiac disease (Matheson, Sylvester and Rice, 1975) and pulmonary disease (Agle and others, 1973). Of those few psychosomatic inpatient units that treat a variety of adult disorders, the programs at Duke Medical Center (Reckless, 1971), at the University of Cincinnati Medical School, and at the Portland Veterans Administration Hospital seem to overlap significantly. The Cincinnati and Portland programs have a treatment strategy sufficiently similar to permit a joint report (Wooley and others, 1973). These programs combine the operant principles developed for chronic pain behavior with interpersonal skill training and family therapy. They assess and treat chronic illness behavior on the basis of a multidimensional model rather than being preoccupied with issues of primary etiology (Glaudin, Lipkin, and Loeb, 1978).

Holistic medicine is another promising contemporary trend in psychosomatic medicine. It has promise not merely because it attempts to be comprehensive and integrative (probably too comprehensive to define meaningfully at this time) but because it focuses on prevention. Holistic medicine attempts to confront the values and philosophies out of which life stresses arise (Pelletier, 1977). For example, many of the precursors of myocardial infarction and angina pectoris are now known, but the present system of health care is largely focused on the technology of after-the-fact repair and does little in helping patients come to grips with excessive competitiveness, aggression, impatience, and ceaseless striving for achievement. The holistic approach to illness addresses these issues and supports values that promote well being.

Although a revolution in the style of health care delivery is not imminent, a number of other changes may counteract the technological preoccupation, specialization, and dehumanization that aggravate psychosomatic illness. For example, there has been the recent elevation of *family practice* to a specialty status (Rakel, 1977). Moreover, strong voices from other medical specialties have influenced the style of medical practice. For example, Lipkin (1974) has suggested that the annual physical examination is a time to explore worries, review life-style issues, confront substance abuse, and explore frustrating relationships. Blackwell (1975) and Waldron (1977) have urged the physician to counsel the patient realistically rather than covering life problems with minor tranquilizers.

Health care delivery systems may help change our lives not because of a new bio-medical model of illness, as important as that would be (Engel, 1977), but because of the need to provide low-cost and affordable service to people (Garfield, 1970). The long lines of the "worried well" and "overutilizers" clog services for everyone. Cummings (1977) has reviewed some of the methods successfully used by one health maintenance organization, the Kaiser Foundation, for resolution of problems that present as medical needs but are also psychosocial in nature.

Critical Discussion

General Areas of Concern

Perhaps in no other area of psychological assessment is the presentation of findings as sensitive as in psychosomatic illness. The physician, the psychologist, and the patient are all likely to hear something quite different from the same report. It is easy to become drawn into philosophical discussions about the etiology of symptoms rather than focusing on helpful interventions and avoiding a destructive course of treatment, such as unwarranted surgery (Schlicke, 1977). Both Type I and Type II errors are possible: Type I errors representing an excessive search for organic factors when psychological courses of treatment are obvious; Type II errors constituting the attribution of every somatic symptom to psychological causes when in fact there are organic aspects of the syndrome which would respond to somatic therapy.

Type I Errors. Almost all standard textbooks of medicine acknowledge that a substantial portion of hospital beds are occupied by persons whose basic problems are social and psychological. Many of these patients have physical complaints that are part of a distinctive psychiatric syndrome (Wahl, 1975). A large percent of depressed patients, for example, have significant somatic complaints. However, the tragic aspect of this well-known generality is that behavioral disturbances are frequently uncharted on medical wards (Denney and others, 1966; Pankratz and Pankratz, 1973)—especially if the illness behavior is silence, withdrawal, passivity, and sadness, as opposed to loud, aggressive, or sexually repugnant behavior. It is so common to see an endless series of laboratory tests performed to chase an obvious symptom of depression that one of our consultants facetiously asks her residents to order "serum rhubarb levels." Obviously, if the aggressive physician looks long enough, some pathological result will be found (or caused!), reinforcing the further search for an organic disease process. A wiser clinician will seek a balance between labeling symptoms as "functional," on the one hand, and conducting an obsessive search for exotic diseases, on the other (Pankratz and Lipkin, 1978).

Type II Errors. History is replete with examples of illnesses once thought to be religious or psychological deviations which now respond promptly to a biological treatment. These include the early misunderstandings about vitamin deficiencies, the epilepsies, and syphilis. Also included here are disorders of movement, such as Huntington's disease, Sydenham's chorea, parkinsonism, and the more recent problems of tardive dyskinesia (a side effect of neuroleptic medications). Even today there is debate about the organic pathophysiology versus the psychological etiology of spasmodic torticollis, writer's cramp, Gilles de la Tourette syndrome, and disorders of sleep.

Follow-up studies on hysteria and conversion symptoms suggest that we should exercise continued caution in using psychodiagnostics and dismissing somatic treatment (Guze and Perley, 1963; Merskey and Buhrich, 1975; Slater and Glithero, 1965; Stefansson, Messina, and Meyerowitz, 1976). A large number of patients thought to have only functional symptoms have been shown subsequently to have organic disease, especially neurological complications. Indeed, even the documented Munchausen patient may present with serious medical problems, either as a primary disorder (Payne and Newlands, 1971) or secondarily as an iatrogenic problem (Allegra, Woodward, and Chandler, 1976). It seems that the clinician on the firing line is never safe!

Negative medical results never allow one to say with certainty that psychological intervention is sufficient and that no medical intervention will prove to be necessary. Laboratory tests do not exist for every possible human ill, and even results within normal limits on specific tests do not necessarily rule out all possible somatic treatments in the future. Furthermore, certain disorders with demonstrable anatomical or physiological changes—for example, degenerative arthritis—are not treatable by medication or surgery even if the problem is reliably identified. All these generalizations are so evident that they are truisms, yet they are common sources of blunders with psychosomatic patients. Moreover, they are rarely stated explicitly to the patient who *feels* and *believes* that he has an anatomical problem that the doctor should find and fix. The failure to be straightforward about a symptom that the patient "must learn to live with" is the focal point of many doctor-patient conflicts.

An Integrative Approach. To avoid both Type I and Type II errors, one must circumvent the pitfalls of etiology by reconceptualizing the assessment task. The first objective of psychological assessment should be description—especially of the problems that limit the patient. These should be the more public, observable problems that the patient can help to identify. Developmental predisposition and psychodynamics may add depth of understanding for the psychologist and the psychiatrist, but they are rarely useful for the patient or the referring physician. In a brilliant but little-known article, Saslow and Buchmueller (1949) suggest that the presence of a psychosomatic disorder in itself "predicts little about the severity of any associated behavior disorder, its frequency or duration; the difficulty, frequency, duration, or outcome of psychotherapy; the necessity to modify the behavior of significant persons in the patient's interactional system; or the personality assets of the patient upon which therapy can build" (p. 7).

Once the patient's behavioral deficits and assets have been clearly defined, it is helpful to describe the many *sources of pain* in the patient's life. Sources of pain include anatomical and physiological abnormalities but are not limited to these, since work pressures, family discord, financial worries, and even positive life changes also cause distress (Holmes and Rahe, 1967). The psychologist must also describe life style and habit patterns, such as eating, drinking, smoking, and sleeping, as possibly contributing to pain and symptom formation. The therapist can tell the patient quite truthfully that the identified social-psychological distress may or may not be significant in affecting the pain or other symptoms; perhaps it *aggravates* the symptom. At any rate, they can work together to see whether they can quiet some of the discomfort. In helping the psychosomatic patient cooperate with assessment and treatment, the experienced clinician is ever mindful of the threatening nature of this material, the importance of minimizing defensiveness, and the value of using the patient's own language to promote agreement and subsequent change (Watzlawick, Weakland, and Fisch, 1974).

Use of Tests. Formal testing is of special value in the psychological assessment of psychosomatic patients because the procedures are objective, highly standardized, and yield scores for precise communications. Additionally, test scores permit comparison of findings from one sample to another or as repeated measures over time. However, psychological testing has been criticized because its reliability is often questionable. It is probable that clinicians operate with a double standard; they recognize the poor reliability and the limitations of validity of many tests, but such awareness is apparently not crucial in their decision to use them (Wade and Baker, 1977). In this section, a number of tests pertinent to psychosomatic assessment will be mentioned, but the conscientious clinician will make important patient decisions based on these tests only after careful study in context.

Depression must be considered in the assessment of psychosomatic illness—either as a primary cause, a concomitant, or a secondary reaction to illness. Numerous *depression scales* are currently available. For severe conditions, there are the Hopelessness Scale (Beck and others, 1974) and the Will to Live Scale (Ellison, 1969). The most familiar depression scale (other than the MMPI) is probably the Beck Depression Inventory (Beck and others, 1961). This test has probably been the most consistently reliable self-rating measure of depression, although the clinician should be aware of the limitations of this scale for youths (Beck and Lester, 1973). Adjective checklists appear to be more appropriate for measuring the small changes of situational affect (Pankratz, Glaudin, and Goodmanson, 1972), so that one should consider using the Multiple Affect Adjective Check List (Zuckerman, Lubin, and Robins, 1965) or the Depression Adjective Check List (Lubin, 1965). An interesting variation of the affect checklist is the Paired Anxiety and Depression Scale, which requests the subject to make a forced choice between an adjective considered representative of anxiety and one representative of depression (Mould, 1975). There are several scales on which the patient is rated by an observer or interviewer. For this type, the Hamilton Scale for Depressive Illness is perhaps the most widely used (Hamilton, 1967).

The *Minnesota Multiphasic Personality Inventory* (MMPI) has been used to study organic and psychosomatic disabilities since its construction. For example, Wiener (1956) studied some 30,000 Minnesota disabled veterans, nearly all of whom had completed the MMPI. He found that patients with arthritis, flat feet, gunshot wounds, and ulcers were most likely to have elevations in hypochondriasis and depression relative to hysteria. High scores on the Hysteria Scale were common for the asthma, heart, and skin groups. Finally, there was a noticeable lack of emotional involvement in certain disabilities: the asthma group in terms of depression and the skin group in terms of hypochondriasis. Similar studies have been conducted for nearly every problem imaginable, with resulting special subscales (Dahlstrom and Welsh, 1960).

Special clinical subscales have limitations that should be clearly understood. Most subscales are devised from patients who show either "real" or "functional" problems. However, perhaps the largest groups of patients are those who display both organic and functional aspects of their illness. This problem has been illustrated with the low back pain patient. The low back pain scale of Hanvik (1951) was based on thirty organic and thirty functional patients. Freeman, Calsyn, and Louks (1976) note that most patients are not merely "real" or "functional" but present more complicated diagnostic problems because they demonstrate organic changes that are not sufficient to explain the full degree of reported pain. In comparing such "mixed" patients with more clearly organic patients and with more clearly functional patients they found that (1) both functional and organic patients were characterized by the classical Conversion "V" profile, and (2) mixed symptom patients differed significantly from the organic group but not from the functional group.

Friedman and Rosenman (1971, 1974) have described the behavior pattern of individuals who are heart attack prone. This personality profile, termed the *Type A constellation*, depicts the hard-driving individual who is hell-bent for success and heart attacks. This research is well known from popular writings and will not be further reviewed here because of the excellent summaries provided by Jenkins (1975, 1976b). Additionally, Jenkins (1976b) has identified the many different scales devised from the Type A behavior pattern and other scales devised to identify coronary-prone individuals.

Based on Rotter's Internal-External Locus of Control Scale, the *Health Locus of Control* test was specifically designed to identify expectancies of health-related behavior (Wallston and others, 1976). The early research on this instrument suggests that it is a valuable tool in identifying which subjects will expose themselves to more information about a given health condition (hypertension) and also which subjects will be likely to take steps to better their environment. This scale is worth watching for future developments.

The *Interpersonal Adjective Check List* is a nonthreatening and helpful instrument for understanding the interpersonal styles of patients. Originally designed in the Kaiser Hospital systems, it provides information about the personality styles of psychosomatic patients (Leary, 1957). It can also be completed by the patient to describe significant others or completed by others to describe the patient. This multidimensionality of the test makes it valuable for understanding the variety of social roles that a patient endorses.

Current clinical practice includes the use of a variety of *projective techniques* in assessing psychosomatic disorders (Lubin, Wallis, and Paine, 1971). Many clinicians seem to ignore standard scoring procedures for projectives and favor their own personalized standards (Wade and Baker, 1977), so that an already controversial problem is further complicated. The interested reader can consult a variety of texts and handbooks for further consideration of the topic. For example, Goldfried, Stricker, and Weiner (1971) provide a critical review of body-image boundary scoring and the relationship to physiological and other indexes.

Harrower, Thomas, and Altman (1975) conducted a unique study on the human figure drawings of former medical students who had subsequently developed emotional or somatic illness. Leaving aside the methodological and base-rate problems of the study, the results supported an interesting hypothesis. Subjects with somatic problems had greater portions of "outgoing attitudes," whereas subjects with emotional problems had a greater percentage of drawings in a "withdrawal pose." Even with drawings completed years previously, there were indications that in some the body would "take the rap," while in others the psyche would "take the rap."

Holmes and Rahe (1967) have devised a research instrument, variously known as the *Social Readjustment Rating Scale* or the *Schedule of Recent Experiences*, which has demonstrated the relationship between the amount of recent life changes and illness. The most recent summaries of this research can be found in Holmes and Masuda (1973) and Petrich and Holmes (1977). Anyone using this scale for research should consult the critical review, by Rabkin and Struening (1976), of methodology used with this scale.

Langner (1962) devised a twenty-two-item questionnaire, an *index of psychophysiological stress*, which has been used in a number of community surveys of psychiatric disorders. Recent factor analysis has shown this scale to be multidimensional; thus, one cannot be sure that it measures what it was intended to measure (Roberts, Forthofer, and Fabrega, 1976). However, Garrity, Marx, and Somes (1976) have conceptualized the scale as measuring psychophysiological strain, which includes psychological stress and physical malaise. They suggest that strain is the intervening variable between life experiences and illness episodes, problem days, and psychiatric impairment. They further suggest that strain is an efficient predictor of health breakdown and recommend this test as a prognostic instrument.

The *Sickness Impact Profile* (Gilson and others, 1975) is a survey which can be interviewer-administered or self-administered. It describes the level of functioning in those activities necessary for carrying on routine life activities. There are twelve categories, each representing a specific area of activity, such as mobility, alertness behavior, and home management. (A 1978 summary of the scale is available from the Department of Health Services, University of Washington, Seattle 98195.)

Brodman, Erdmann, and Wolff (1949) have presented a health questionnaire, the *Cornell Medical Index*, which the patient fills out to assist in the collection of medical and psychiatric data. It reviews the bodily systems to complement a standard medical history. The CMI's special value is demonstrating multiple-system complaint patterns frequently associated with illness behavior syndromes. It has been used to identify inductees who will later develop psychosomatic and psychiatric disabilities in military service (Brodman, and others, 1954). This predictive ability works on a rather straightforward theory: men with many medical complaints believe that they are sick and, if inducted, will serve like sick people. Men rejected for medical rather than psychiatric disorders, interestingly, generally do not think of themselves as sick except in the specific organ system of their structural disorder. The present authors believe that the Cornell Medical Index has much more promise than the few current studies on it would suggest.

The *Whiteley Index of Hypochondriasis*, introduced by Pilowsky (1967), is based on the samples of one hundred psychiatric patients diagnosed as manifesting hypochondriacal features and one hundred psychiatric patients showing few or none of these features. It has been used with cancer patients and shown to differentiate those who complain of much pain from those who do not complain of pain (Bond, 1971). This scale appears to measure a specific facet of anxiety about illness and is worthy of further consideration in a wide variety of contexts.

The *diary, personal log, self-charting,* and *symptom records* are all methods for getting the patient to observe and record his or her own behavior. Blachly (1967) used symptom charts to measure the influence of psychotropic drugs in an outpatient clinic population, but he also found that patients identified cyclic fluctuations of ailments, learned about the influence of interpersonal conflicts, and shaped their own behavior. In the Portland Illness Behavior Unit, patients are trained to monitor and graph pertinent somatic and emotional events, so that they can be described clearly at the daily "Symptom Group" (Glaudin, Lipkin, and Loeb, 1978). Behaviorally oriented therapists have used graphs and cumulative records for years, and it seemed only natural that data keeping would be turned over to the patients as more self-directed forms of behavior therapy became popular. Watson and Tharp (1972), for example, suggest that by tracking behavior the patient can become aware of what is being done *instead* of the desired behavior. But perhaps the most important part of self-collection of data is the participation of the patients, which binds them into the therapeutic alliance for both assessment and change.

Comparative Philosophies and Theories

Theoretical models and research paradigms have been constructed to explain why certain individuals develop psychosomatic disorders and why particular organ systems become symptomatic. One way to understand and compare models is to consider how much they focus on internal or external factors. Some of the biological, psychoanalytic, and personality studies have focused more on internal mechanisms. For example, there have been studies on the personality of patients who develop cancer, heart disease, and arthritis. Other studies—based on learning theory, social psychology, and stress—have focused more on external variables. Most theories do not emphasize both types of variables, although more interactional models and studies are needed. In treatment-oriented settings there has been less concern about etiology and more focus on the external factors in understanding the course and treatment of disorders.

Elaboration on Critical Points

The backdrop of all psychological assessment is the information gathered from the assessment interview. In the hands of a skilled examiner, the assessment interview is a rich and flexible technique that provides quality information for assessment. The careful interviewer attends to both the *content* (what the patient says about himself) and the *process* (the patient's manner, thinking, and affect as he interacts with the examiner). Enelow and Wexler (1965) have described the relationship of content and process in interviews of patients with medical complaints.

The interview can be called a *mental-status examination* if the data are presented systematically under headings such as appearance, intellectual functioning, affect, and orientation (Stevenson, 1969). Another model for reporting results in an objective system is the *problem-oriented record* (Weed, 1969). Although this system began with the purpose of improving medical charting, it also has some distinct advantages in psychiatric and rehabilitation programs (Grant and Maletzky, 1972; Pankratz and Poole, 1976).

In the assessment interview, the examiner communicates warmth and empathy in order to reduce defensiveness and enhance the quality of information volunteered. Yet he or she is firmly in control. Hypochondriacal recitals are terminated, and conversation is redirected to new content areas. The examiner maintains the flow of the interview by paraphrasing the content and the latent feeling in the patient's statements. For most patients it is effective to ask broad (open-ended) questions. Specific (closed-ended) questions may punctuate the examination, but any form of staccato questioning is avoided. Moreover, since patients frequently deny the relationship between emotional states and symptom exacerbation, leading questions—those requiring a patient to demonstrate insight into psychological conflicts—are avoided. Indeed, patients with functional symptoms seem excessively concerned with providing physical explanations of their problems (Brody, 1959; Cohen and others, 1953). In this situation the worst thing an examiner can do is attempt to persuade the patient to accept a psychological model for understanding his or her symptom. Moreover, the suggestion of psychotherapy is likely to be met with rejection (Guze and Perley, 1963). Instead, the assessment interview helps the patient tell his or her story of illness and treatment. Life-style and personal experiences are brought into the interview in a way that allows the patient to explain the problems of "living with illness." This *somatopsychic strategy* meets the patient's experiential reality and contributes to his or her sense of feeling understood. Any labeling must be done within the patient's own conceptualization of the problem, and the controversy over etiology must be avoided (Pankratz, 1979).

Personal Views and Recommendations

We have emphasized the following points in assessment of psychosomatic disorders: (1) More attention should be given to precipitating stress, the course of the illness, and contemporary factors maintaining symptoms rather than to predisposition and etiology. (2) A multidimensional model should be employed—in a way that permits specialists to describe the patient and contribute to a coordinated interventional plan rather than becoming trapped in a psychological versus somatic dichotomy. (3) A somatopsychic strategy should usually be employed in communicating with the patient, to reduce the threat of a psychological formulation. These are a few of the broad brush strokes to improve the picture of psychosomatic assessment.

The most realistic way to improve the psychological assessment and treatment of psychosomatic disorders is to provide these special services *within* existing health care programs, such as family practice, specialty medical clinics, and general hospital settings. In this way, competent psychological assessment will be provided where the patients present themselves initially—namely, to medical rather than to psychiatric or psychological settings. Resistance is reduced when the patients are treated in a medical setting that is based on a multidimensional model and that employs a somatopsychic strategy in communications. Therefore, the traditional family practice office, medical clinic, and general hospital must become places where psychological health care specialists, such as clinical psychologists, are part of the treatment team available to all patients. With this system, the highly specialized illness behavior unit in the medical center must represent a tertiary assessment and care resource for "treatment failures."

Ethical and political issues also will need to be confronted. For example, the common practice of maintaining psychosomatic patients on excessive amounts of Valium must change (Waldron, 1977). To avoid legitimizing illness behavior syndromes, physicians must provide the opportunity for psychosomatic assessment of patients *before* elective surgeries or other extensive exploratory procedures. At the same time, in order to avoid Type II errors, psychologists and psychiatrists must reflect on their own practices. In sum, each discipline attempting to serve the psychosomatic patient must curb the tendency toward narrowness and self-interest in order to provide each patient with a rational program of assessment and treatment.

Application to Particular Variables

Age. Physical illness has great potential for generating psychological problems. This seems especially true for children, because of the potential disruption of the developmental process. Psychological factors are also important across the entire disease process, all the way from the genesis of the disease to the recovery. However, so little is known of these processes in children that one must use extra caution when considering psychogenic causal factors, even in those disorders traditionally considered psychosomatic and even where there is clear evidence of psychological disturbance in the child or family. For example, Middleton (1972) has suggested that the basic responsivity of bronchial airways may play the major role in the development of childhood asthma. Furthermore, Block and his associates (Block, 1968; Block and others, 1964) showed that asthmatic children with fewer physical dispositions toward the problem had greater psychological problems. In addition, the mothers of these children with little physical predisposition more closely resembled mothers of psychologically disturbed children. There are, then, varying degrees of psychological contribution to a problem as well as a wide range of problems that may accompany a condition, complicating the recovery.

Wright and Fulwiler (1974) present an interesting variation on the problem of psychological stress secondary to illness. They followed burned children eighteen to sixty months after the burn episode. There seemed to be few significant differences between burned children and control children on measures of personality and adjustment. However, the mothers of burned children appeared significantly disturbed in comparison to

the mothers of the control children. The results are open to at least two different interpretations. The "burn" mothers may have been initially disturbed, and this disturbance
could have contributed to the child's accident. Or, more likely, the mothers may have had
difficulty adjusting to the accident, perhaps even feeling responsible for it in some way.

It is clear that advancing age brings more symptoms on a more frequent basis,
including those conditions generally considered psychosomatic (Schwab, Fennell, and
Warheit, 1974). For example, older patients report more indigestion, constipation, hypertension, weight difficulties, and colitis. However, the elderly probably have less discomfort than younger patients with similar disorders (Exton-Smith, 1961). Age itself may
not be the determining factor for increased symptoms. A more powerful determiner may
be the individual's location in the life cycle (Campbell, 1976). For example, being 40 may
have a dramatically different impact from being 40 *and* a grandmother. Thus, the perception of well-being and the presence of symptoms may be secondary to relationships in the
family and significant others.

Sex. Males are more likely to be troubled by asthma, stomach ulcer, and neuro-
dermatitis. Females are more likely to be troubled with colitis, headaches (including migraine), hypertension, rheumatoid arthritis, weight problems, and constipation. In the
epidemiological study of Schwab, Fennell, and Warheit (1974), females reported more
symptoms of a psychophysiological nature, and they were also more likely to report two
or more symptoms or conditions as occurring regularly. These differences are taken into
account by such tests as the MMPI, where females may have more complaints and still be
considered within "normal limits" on the Hysteria Scale. Females seem to report more
psychological stress, whereas males report more physiological symptoms (Roberts, Forthofer, and Fabrega, 1976). Sexual differences are undoubtedly influenced by childrearing
practices and socializing influences. For example, as a result of these influences, males
take more risks, seek medical care less readily, are less expressive about illness, and appear
more stoical than females (Mechanic, 1972). Generally, these factors are mentioned in
connection with the finding that pain thresholds tend to be lower in women.

Education. Education may be thought of as a socioeconomic variable that provides an individual with expanded role skills for coping. In terms of psychosomatic disorders, it is generally believed that the classical hysterical and functional patients are less
educated and more naive; but most of the studies on educational factors are confounded
by other socioeconomic factors. Moreover, illness has a powerful effect on people of all
educational levels. In 1969 those in poor health earned on the average about $7,000 a
year less than those in good health, regardless of educational level (Taubman and Wales,
1975).

Socioeconomic Factors. Illness has been related to social class in study after study
in this country and abroad. The socioeconomically disadvantaged have a dispropor-
tionately higher percent of physical illness, mental illness, psychosomatic illness, and mortality. Although McBroom (1970) has gathered one sample of evidence suggesting no relationship between illness and socioeconomic status, the overwhelming evidence suggests
that the poor are overrepresented in the ranks of the ill (Scott and Mackie, 1975).
Twaddle (1974) aptly points out that health and illness are themselves parameters of
social stratification; that is, health is taken into account when the worth of an individual
is assessed. Such evaluation, which may be an unconscious part of the health care system,
has a profound effect on the assessment process and the quality of care (Girard and Carlton, 1978). When the treating professional communicates a lack of respect for the
patient, the patient may be less likely to comply with prescribed treatment (Becker,
Drachman, and Kirscht, 1974; Becker and Maiman, 1975; Kirscht, Becker, and Eveland,

1976). Thus, the attitude of the examiner may influence the patient in a way that further prevents a resolution of the problem.

Vocation. The relationship between vocation and illness is clearly confounded by socioeconomic level, social mobility, status incongruity, physical activity level, age, and personality style. The vocation itself may interact with the personality of the worker. The Type A person works longer hours, feels time pressures, seeks responsibility, has a strong sense of duty, and wants to change jobs. These stress-related attitudes are perhaps more likely to be found in certain occupations, but one could conceive that they would be devastating in any occupation.

There is an extremely complex relationship among the variables of social class, vocation, and illness. An illness may cause loss of vocational opportunity and result in a lower social status. However, a particular symptom may arise because of a particular occupational/social setting. The injured Northwest logger provides an example of this complex problem. Back pains are an occupational hazard of the logger. Although a chronic low back pain might restrict the tennis of an accountant, a similar disability to a logger can mean the shattering of the "macho" self-concept as well as loss of job. The logger can no longer keep pace with friends in setting chokers, hauling elk out of the woods, or settling disputes. Usually the logger has little aptitude for a white-collar job, and the idea of it is unacceptable. Such conditions are a breeding ground for chronic pain complaints and illness behavior.

Racial/Ethnic Factors. Herrick (1976) has provided a review of the cross-cultural origins of psychosomatic and psychogenic illnesses according to anthropological and sociological findings. More current research on racial, ethnic, and cultural differences can be found in Zborowski (1952, 1969), Mechanic (1966), Twaddle (1969), and Sternbach (1974). These studies have generally focused on the expression of pain. However, it is also clear that different cultural groups vary in the extent to which they are willing to accept psychological interpretations of their complaints (Fink, Shapiro, and Goldensohn, 1969; Mechanic, 1963). Mechanic (1972) suggests that the ethnic differences noted in the literature may be the result of more objective symptoms, different interpretations of the same symptoms, the willingness to express concerns, or different vocabulary usage. In any event, the meaning and the role of illness are different among different cultures; for example, Cole and Lejeune (1972) point out that more achievement-oriented groups may use illness to justify failure to fulfill socially prescribed role obligations.

Physical Disorders. Strategies for the assessment of physical disorders have been discussed elsewhere in this chapter. There is, however, a little-known technique for the assessment of any sensory-loss symptom. Brady and Lind (1961) used a version of this technique in the assessment of a man with a two-year history of "hysterical blindness." They presented a task to him that could be solved more easily with a light cue. However, upon the introduction of the cue, the patient's performance actually *decreased* to less than what could be expected by chance alone. Theodor and Mandlecorn (1973) demonstrated a similar phenomenon with a young woman with tunnel vision. Subsequently, Pankratz, Fausti, and Peed (1975) proposed that the two-alternative forced-choice technique could be utilized as a general strategy for the assessment of any sensory loss. This strategy, subsequently called Symptom Validity Testing, is described further by Pankratz (1979), along with implications for treatment.

Neurological Disorders. Assessment of the psychosomatic features of neurological complaints is especially challenging and often requires special competence in neuropsychology. Problems labeled hysterical may later prove to mask a neurological condition. In contrast, symptoms that seem neurological—for example, complaints of cognitive inefficiency, poor memory, and defective concentration—may be related to depression. Fortunately, it is difficult to simulate organic brain damage (Benton and Spreen, 1961; Bruhn and Reed, 1975) or mental retardation (Spreen and Benton, 1963). Standard neuropsychological testing should be an adequate screen in most cases of simulation or malingering. However, some specific tests have been devised by André Ray in France (Lezak, 1976). These tests are based on the discrepancy between their difficult appearance and their relative ease in performance: The mentally retarded person will be able to complete the required tasks, whereas the malingerer will fail in an attempt to appear retarded.

Collective Psychosomatic Disorders. In an attempt to clarify the concept of hysterical psychosis, Hirsch and Hollender (1969) have described the anthropological aspects of that diagnosis. They identify several cultures in which unusual symptoms occur in a proscribed manner. Presumably these symptoms are learned or culturally transmitted. Schuler and Parenton (1943) have reviewed the history of epidemics of hysteria: dancing manias of the Middle Ages, strange behaviors of nuns, and witch hunts. Of more recent times the episodes of hysterical contagion have been primarily symptoms of physical illness. Gehlen (1977) has reviewed the theories of hysterical contagion and suggests that there are secondary gains in adopting the sick role during times of collective stress.

References

Agle, D. P., and others. "Multidiscipline Treatment of Chronic Pulmonary Insufficiency. 1: Psychologic Aspects of Rehabilitation." *Psychosomatic Medicine,* 1973, *35,* 41-49.

Alexander, F. *Psychosomatic Medicine: Its Principles and Applications.* New York: Norton, 1950.

Allegra, D., Woodward, J., and Chandler, J. "Munchausen as Physician and Patient." *Annals of Internal Medicine,* 1976, *85,* 262-263.

American Psychiatric Association. *Psychological Factors Affecting Physical Disorder.* Washington, D.C.: American Psychiatric Association, 1978.

Beck, A., and Lester, C. "Components of Depression in Attempted Suicides." *Journal of Psychology,* 1973, *85,* 257-260.

Beck, A., and others. "An Inventory for Measuring Depression." *Archives of General Psychiatry,* 1961, *4,* 53-63.

Beck, A., and others. "The Measurement of Pessimism: The Hopelessness Scale." *Journal of Consulting and Clinical Psychology,* 1974, *42,* 861-865.

Becker, M. H., Drachman, R. H., and Kirscht, J. P. "A New Approach to Explaining Sick-Role Behavior in Low-Income Populations." *American Journal of Public Health,* 1974, *64,* 205-216.

Becker, M. H., and Maiman, L. A. "Sociobehavioral Determinants of Compliance with Health and Medical Care Recommendations." *Medical Care,* 1975, *13,* 10-24.

Beecher, H. K. "Pain: One Mystery Solved." *Science,* 1966, *151,* 840-841.

Benton, A. L., and Spreen, O. "Visual Memory Test: The Simulation of Mental Incompetence." *Archives of General Psychiatry,* 1961, *4,* 79-83.

Birk, L. (Ed.). *Biofeedback: Behavioral Medicine.* New York: Grune and Stratton, 1973.

Blachly, P. H. "Self Rating Symptom Records: A Method of Educating Patients About Their Illness and Evaluating Treatment." *Diseases of the Nervous System,* 1967, *28,* 532-536.

Blackwell, B. "Minor Tranquilizers: Use, Misuse, or Overuse?" *Psychosomatics,* 1975, *16,* 28-31.

Block, J. "Further Consideration of Psychosomatic Predisposing Factors in Allergy." *Psychosomatic Medicine,* 1968, *30,* 202-208.

Block, J., and others. "Interaction Between Allergic Potential and Psychopathology in Childhood Asthma." *Psychosomatic Medicine,* 1964, *26,* 307-320.

Bond, M. R. "The Relation of Pain to the Eysenck Personality Inventory, Cornell Medical Index and Whiteley Index of Hypochondriasis." *British Journal of Psychiatry,* 1971, *119,* 671-678.

Bonica, J. J. "Organization and Function of a Pain Clinic." In A. Arias (Ed.), *Recent Progress in Anesthesiology and Resuscitation.* Amsterdam: Excerpta Medica Foundation, 1975.

Brady, J. P., and Lind, D. L. "Experimental Analysis of Hysterical Blindness." *Archives of General Psychiatry,* 1961, *4,* 331-339.

Brautigan, W. "Perspectives on the Psychotherapy of Psychosomatic Illnesses." *Journal Brasileiro de Psiquiatria,* 1974, *23,* 5-22.

Brodman, K., Erdmann, A. J., and Wolff, H. G. *Cornell Medical Index Health Questionnaire Manual.* New York: Cornell University Medical College, 1949.

Brodman, K., and others. "The Cornell Medical Index Health Questionnaire. VII: The Prediction of Psychosomatic and Psychiatric Disabilities in Army Training." *American Journal of Psychiatry,* 1954, *111,* 37-40.

Brody, S. "Value of Group Psychotherapy in Patients with Polysurgery Addiction." *Psychiatric Quarterly,* 1959, *33,* 260-283.

Bruhn, A. R., and Reed, M. R. "Simulation of Brain Damage on the Bender Gestalt Test by College Subjects." *Journal of Personality Assessment,* 1975, *39,* 244-255.

Campbell, A. "Subjective Measures of Well Being." *American Psychologist,* 1976, *31,* 117-124.

Cannon, W. B. *Bodily Changes in Pain, Hunger, Fear and Rage.* (2nd ed.) New York: Appleton-Century-Crofts, 1920.

Cohen, M. E., and others. "Excessive Surgery in Hysteria." *Journal of the American Medical Association,* 1953, *151,* 977-986.

Cole, S., and Lejeune, R. "Illness and the Legitimation of Failure." *American Sociological Review,* 1972, *37,* 347-356.

Cummings, N. A. "The Anatomy of Psychotherapy Under National Health Insurance." *American Psychologist,* 1977, *32,* 711-718.

Dahlstrom, W., and Welsh, G. *An MMPI Handbook.* Minneapolis: University of Minnesota Press, 1960.

Denney, D., and others. "Psychiatric Patients on Medical Wards." *Archives of General Psychiatry,* 1966, *14,* 530-535.

Ellison, D. L. "Alienation and the Will to Live." *Journal of Gerontology,* 1969, *24,* 361-367.

Enelow, A., and Wexler, M. "The Medical Interview." *Medical Times,* 1965, *93,* 1192-1200.

Engel, G. L. "The Need for a New Medical Model: A Challenge for Biomedicine." *Science,* 1977, *196,* 129-135.

Exton-Smith, A. N. "Terminal Illness in the Aged." *Lancet,* 1961, *2,* 305-308.

Fink, R., Shapiro, S., and Goldensohn, S. "The 'Filter-Down' Process to Psychotherapy in a Group Practice Medical Care Program." *American Journal of Public Health,* 1969, *59,* 245-260.

Fordyce, W. E. *Behavioral Methods for the Control of Chronic Pain and Illness.* St. Louis: Mosby, 1976.

Fordyce, W. E., and others. "Some Implications of Learning in Problems of Chronic Pain." *Journal of Chronic Diseases,* 1968, *21,* 179-190.

Fordyce, W. E., and others. "Operant Conditioning in the Treatment of Chronic Pain." *Archives of Physical Medicine and Rehabilitation,* 1973, *54,* 399-408.

Freeman, C., Calsyn, D., and Louks, J. "The Use of the Minnesota Multiphasic Personality Inventory with Low Back Pain." *Journal of Clinical Psychology,* 1976, *32,* 294-298.

Friedman, M. *Pathogenesis of Coronary Artery Disease.* New York: McGraw-Hill, 1969.

Friedman, M., and Rosenman, R. H. "Type A Behavior Pattern: Its Association with Coronary Heart Disease." *Annals of Clinical Research,* 1971, *3,* 300-312.

Friedman, M., and Rosenman, R. H. *Type A Behavior and Your Heart.* New York: Knopf, 1974.

Fuller, G. D. "Current Status of Biofeedback in Clinical Practice." *American Psychologist,* 1978, *33,* 39-48.

Garfield, S. "The Delivery of Medical Care." *Scientific American,* 1970, *222* (4), 15-23.

Garrity, T. F., Marx, M. B., and Somes, G. W. "Langner's 22-Item Measure of Psychophysiological Strain as an Intervening Variable Between Life Change and Health Outcome." *Journal of Psychosomatic Research,* 1976, *21,* 195-199.

Gehlen, F. L. "Toward a Revised Theory of Hysterical Contagion." *Journal of Health and Social Behavior,* 1977, *18,* 27-35.

Gilson, B. S., and others. "The Sickness Impact Profile: Development of an Outcome Measure of Health Care." *American Journal of Public Health,* 1975, *65,* 1304-1310.

Girard, D. E., and Carlton, B. E. "Alcoholism: Definition of the Problem and the Earlier Diagnosis." *Western Journal of Medicine,* 1978, *129,* 1-7.

Glaudin, V., Lipkin, J., and Loeb, B. "Evaluation of an Illness Behavior Program and Its Effect on Health Care Utilization." Unpublished research proposal, V.A. Hospital, Portland, Oregon, 1978.

Goldfried, M., Stricker, G., and Weiner, I. *Rorschach Handbook of Clinical and Research Applications.* Englewood Cliffs, N.J.: Prentice-Hall, 1971.

Goldstein, S. C., and Birnbom, F. "Hypochondriasis in the Elderly." *Journal of the American Geriatrics Society,* 1976, *24,* 150-154.

Grant, R. L., and Maletzky, B. M. "Application of the Weed System to Psychiatric Records." *Psychiatry in Medicine,* 1972, *3,* 119-129.

Guze, S. B., and Perley, J. J. "Observations on the Natural History of Hysteria." *American Journal of Psychiatry,* 1963, *119,* 960-965.

Hamilton, M. "Development of a Rating Scale for Primary Depressive Illness." *British Journal of Sociological and Clinical Psychology,* 1967, *6,* 278-296.

Hanvik, L. "MMPI Profiles in Patients with Low Back Pain." *Journal of Consulting Psychology,* 1951, *15,* 350-353.

Harrower, M., Thomas, C. B., and Altman, A. "Human Figure Drawings in a Prospective Study of Six Disorders: Hypertension, Coronary Heart Disease, Malignant Tumor, Suicide, Mental Illness, and Emotional Disturbance." *Journal of Nervous and Mental Disease,* 1975, *161,* 191-199.

Herrick, J. W. "Placebos, Psychosomatic and Psychogenic Illnesses and Psychotherapy: Their Theorized Cross-Cultural Development." *Psychological Record,* 1976, *26,* 327-342.

Hilgard, E. R. "Pain as a Puzzle for Psychology and Physiology." *American Psychologist,* 1969, *24,* 103-113.

Hirsch, S. J., and Hollender, M. H. "Hysterical Psychosis: Clarification of the Concept." *American Journal of Psychiatry,* 1969, *125,* 81-87.

Holmes, T., and Masuda, M. "Life Change and Illness Susceptibility." In J. P. Scott and E. C. Senay (Eds.), *Separation and Depression: Clinical and Research Aspects.* Washington, D.C.: American Association for the Advancement of Science, 1973.

Holmes, T., and Rahe, R. "The Social Readjustment Rating Scale." *Journal of Psychosomatic Research,* 1967, *11,* 213-218.

Jenkins, C. D. "The Coronary-Prone Personality." In W. D. Gentry and R. H. Williams (Eds.), *Psychological Aspects of Myocardial Infarction and Coronary Care.* St. Louis: Mosby, 1975.

Jenkins, C. D. "Recent Evidence Supporting Psychologic and Social Risk Factors for Coronary Disease." (First of two parts.) *New England Journal of Medicine,* 1976a, *294,* 987-994.

Jenkins, C. D. "Recent Evidence Supporting Psychologic and Social Risk Factors for Coronary Disease." (Second of two parts.) *New England Journal of Medicine,* 1976b, *294,* 1033-1038.

Kaplan, H. I. "Current Psychodynamic Concepts in Psychosomatic Medicine." In R. Pasnan (Ed.), *Consultation-Liaison Psychiatry.* New York: Grune and Stratton, 1975.

Kirscht, J. P., Becker, M. H., and Eveland, J. P. "Psychological and Social Factors as Predictors of Medical Behavior." *Medical Care,* 1976, *14,* 422-431.

Lachman, S. J. *Psychosomatic Disorders: A Behavioristic Interpretation.* New York: Wiley, 1972.

Langner, T. "A Twenty-Two Item Screening Score of Psychiatric Symptoms Indicating Impairment." *Journal of Health and Social Behavior,* 1962, *3,* 269.

Leary, T. *Interpersonal Diagnosis of Personality: A Functional Theory and Methodology for Personality Evaluation.* New York: Ronald Press, 1957.

Lezak, M. D. *Neuropsychological Assessment.* New York: Oxford University Press, 1976.

Lipkin, M. *The Care of Patients.* New York: Oxford University Press, 1974.

Lipowski, A. J. "Psychosomatic Medicine in the Seventies: An Overview." *American Journal of Psychiatry,* 1977, *134,* 57-62.

Lubin, B. "Adjective Check List for the Measurement of Depression." *Archives of General Psychiatry,* 1965, *12,* 57-62.

Lubin, B., Wallis, R. R., and Paine, C. "Patterns of Psychological Test Usage in the United States: 1955-1969." *Professional Psychology,* 1971, *2,* 70-74.

McBroom, W. H. "Illness, Illness Behavior and Socioeconomic Status." *Journal of Health and Social Behavior,* 1970, *11,* 319-326.

Matheson, L. N., Sylvester, R. H., and Rice, H. E. "The Interdisciplinary Team in Cardiac Rehabilitation." *Rehabilitation Literature,* 1975, *36,* 366-385.

Mechanic, D. "Illness and Social Disability—Some Problems in Analysis." *Pacific Sociological Review,* 1959, *2,* 37-41.

Mechanic, D. "The Concept of Illness Behavior." *Journal of Chronic Diseases,* 1962, *15,* 189-194.

Mechanic, D. "Some Implications of Illness Behavior for Medical Sampling." *New England Journal of Medicine,* 1963, *269,* 244-247.

Mechanic, D. "Response Factors in Illness: The Study of Illness Behavior." *Social Psychiatry,* 1966, *1,* 354-367.

Mechanic, D. "Social Psychologic Factors Affecting the Presentation of Bodily Complaints." *New England J rnal of Medicine,* 1972, *286,* 1132-1139.

Melzack, R., and Wall, P. D. "Pain Mechanisms: A New Theory." *Science,* 1965, *150,* 971-979.

Merskey, H., and Buhrich, N. A. "Hysteria and Organic Brain Disease." *British Journal of Medical Psychology,* 1975, *48,* 359-366.

Middleton, E. "Autonomic Imbalance in Asthma with Special Reference to Beta Adrenergic Blockage." *Advances in Internal Medicine,* 1972, *18,* 177-197.

Mould, D. E. "Differentiation Between Depression and Anxiety: A New Scale." *Journal of Consulting and Clinical Psychology,* 1975, *43,* 592.

Nemiah, J. "Denial Revisited: Reflections on Psychosomatic Theory." *Psychotherapy and Psychosomatics,* 1975, *26,* 140-147.

Pankratz, D., and Pankratz, L. "The Nursing Care Plan: Theory and Reality." *Supervisor Nurse,* 1973, *4* (4), 51-55.

Pankratz, L. "Symptom Validity Testing and Symptom Retraining: Procedures for Assessment and Treatment of Functional Sensory Deficits." *Journal of Consulting and Clinical Psychology,* 1979, *47,* 409-410.

Pankratz, L., Fausti, S. A., and Peed, S. "A Forced Choice Technique to Evaluate Deafness in the Hysterical or Malingering Patient." *Journal of Consulting and Clinical Psychology,* 1975, *43,* 421-422.

Pankratz, L., Glaudin, V., and Goodmanson, C. "Reliability of the Multiple Affect Adjective Check List." *Journal of Personality Assessment,* 1972, *36,* 371-373.

Pankratz, L., and Lipkin, J. "The Transient Patient in a Psychiatric Ward." *Journal of Operational Psychiatry,* 1978, *9* (1), 42-47.

Pankratz, L., and Poole, R. "The Use of Problem Oriented Records in Programs for the Functionally Handicapped." *Journal of Rehabilitation,* 1976, *42* (5), 12.

Parsons, T. *The Social System.* New York: Free Press, 1951.

Payne, J. E., and Newlands, J. S. "Munchausen Syndrome Masquerading as Pulmonary Embolism." *Medical Journal of Australia,* 1971, *1,* 661.

Pelletier, K. R. "Theory and Applications of Clinical Biofeedback." *Journal of Contemporary Psychotherapy,* 1975, *7,* 29-34.

Pelletier, K. R. *Mind as Healer, Mind as Slayer.* New York: Dell, 1977.

Petrich, J. P., and Holmes, T. "Life Change and Onset of Illness." *Medical Clinics of North America,* 1977, *61,* 825-838.

Pilowsky, I. "Dimensions of Hypochondriasis." *British Journal of Psychiatry,* 1967, *113,* 89-93.

Pilowsky, I. "Abnormal Illness Behavior." *British Journal of Medical Psychology,* 1969, *42,* 347-351.

Rabkin, J. G., and Struening, E. L. "Life Events, Stress and Illness." *Science,* 1976, *194,* 1013-1020.

Rakel, R. E. *Principles of Family Medicine.* Philadelphia: Saunders, 1977.

Reckless, J. B. "A Behavioral Treatment of Bronchial Asthma in Modified Group Therapy." *Psychosomatics,* 1971, *12,* 168-173.

Roberts, R., Forthofer, R., and Fabrega, H. "Further Evidence on Dimensionality of the Index of Psychophysiological Stress." *Social Science and Medicine,* 1976, *10,* 483-489.

Sachar, E. "Some Current Issues in Psychosomatic Research." *Psychiatric Annals,* 1972, *8* (2), 22-35.

Saslow, G., and Buchmueller, A. D. "Flexible Psychotherapy in Psychosomatic Disorders." *Human Organization,* 1949, *8,* 5-12.

Schernding, J. P. "From the Sanitorium to the Psychosomatic Clinic. III: Reflections on the Evolution of One Institution." *Revue de Médecine Psychosomatique et de Psychologie Médicale,* 1974, *16,* 373-386.

Schlicke, C. P. "Doctor, Is This Operation Necessary?" *American Journal of Surgery,* 1977, *134,* 3-12.

Schuler, E. A., and Parenton, V. J. "A Recent Epidemic of Hysteria in a Louisiana High School." *Journal of Social Psychology,* 1943, *17,* 221-235.

Schwab, J. J., Fennell, E. B., and Warheit, G. J. "The Epidemiology of Psychosomatic Disorders." *Psychosomatics,* 1974, *15,* 88-93.

Schwartz, G. "Psychosomatic Disorders in Biofeedback." In J. Maser and M. Seligman (Eds.), *Psychopathology: Experimental Models.* San Francisco: Freeman, 1977.

Scott, H. D., and Mackie, A. "Decisions to Hospitalize and Operate: a Socio-Economic Perspective in an Urban State." *Surgery,* 1975, *77,* 311-317.

Selby, J. W., and Calhoun, L. G. "Psychosomatic Phenomena: An Extension of Wright." *American Psychologist,* 1978, *33,* 396-398.

Selye, H. "The General Adaptation Syndrome and the Diseases of Adaptation." *Journal of Clinical Endocrinology and Metabolism,* 1946, *6,* 117-230.

Selye, H. *Physiology and Pathology of Exposure to Stress.* Montreal: Acta Press, 1950.

Seres, J. L., and others. "Evaluation and Management of Chronic Pain by Nonsurgical Means." In L. J. Fletcher (Ed.), *Pain Management: Symposium on the Neurosurgical Treatment of Pain.* Baltimore: Williams and Wilkins, 1977.

Shands, H. C. "How Are 'Psychosomatic' Patients Different from 'Psychoneurotic' Patients?" *Psychotherapy and Psychosomatics,* 1975, *26,* 270-285.

Sifneos, P. E. "Is Dynamic Psychotherapy Contraindicated for a Large Number of Patients with Psychosomatic Diseases?" *Psychotherapy and Psychosomatics,* 1973, *21,* 113-136.

Slater, E. "Diagnosis of 'Hysteria.' " *British Medical Journal,* 1965, *1,* 1395-1399.

Slater, E., and Glithero, E. "A Follow-Up of Patients Diagnosed as Suffering from 'Hysteria.' " *Journal of Psychosomatic Research,* 1965, *9,* 9-13.

Spreen, O., and Benton, A. L. "Simulation of Mental Deficiency on a Visual Memory Test." *American Journal of Mental Deficiency,* 1963, *67,* 909-913.

Stefansson, J. G., Messina, J. A., and Meyerowitz, S. "Hysterical Neurosis, Conversion Type: Clinical and Epidemiological Considerations." *Acta Psychiatrica Scandinavica,* 1976, *53,* 119-138.

Sternbach, R. A. *Pain Patients: Traits and Treatment.* New York: Academic Press, 1974.

Stevenson, I. *The Psychiatric Examination.* Boston: Little, Brown, 1969.

Swanson, D. W., and others. "Program for Managing Chronic Pain. I: Program Description and Characteristics of Patients." *Mayo Clinic Proceedings,* 1976, *51,* 401-408.

Taubman, P., and Wales, T. "Education as an Investment and a Screening Device." In F. Juster (Ed.), *Education, Income, and Human Behavior.* New York: McGraw-Hill, 1975.

Theodor, L. H., and Mandelcorn, M. S. "Hysterical Blindness: A Case Report and Study Using a Modern Psychophysical Technique." *Journal of Abnormal Psychology,* 1973, *83,* 552-553.

Twaddle, A. C. "Health Decisions and Sick Role Variations: An Exploration." *Journal of Health and Social Behavior,* 1969, *10,* 105-115.

Twaddle, A. C. "The Concept of Health Status." *Social Science and Medicine,* 1974, *8,* 29-38.

Wade, T. C., and Baker, T. B. "Opinions and Use of Psychological Tests: A Survey of Clinical Psychologists." *American Psychologist,* 1977, *32,* 874-882.

Wahl, C. "The Patient Whose Physical Symptoms Mask a Psychiatric Disorder." In R. Pasnan (Ed.), *Consultation-Liaison Psychiatry.* New York: Grune and Stratton, 1975.

Waldron, I. "Increased Prescribing of Valium, Librium and Other Drugs—An Example of the Influence of Economic and Social Factors on the Practice of Medicine." *International Journal of Health Services,* 1977, *7,* 37-62.

Wallston, B., and others. "Development and Validation of the Health Locus of Control (HLC) Scale." *Journal of Consulting and Clinical Psychology,* 1976, *44,* 580-585.

Watson, D., and Tharp, R. *Self-Directed Behavior: Self-Modification for Personal Adjustment.* Monterey, Calif.: Brooks/Cole, 1972.

Watzlawick, P., Weakland, J., and Fisch, R. *Change: Principles of Problem Formation and Problem Resolution.* New York: Norton, 1974.

Weed, L. L. *Medical Records, Medical Education and Patient Care.* Chicago: Press of Case Western Reserve University, 1969.

Wiener, D. "Personality Characteristics of Selected Disability Groups." In G. Welsh and W. Dahlstrom (Eds.), *Basic Readings on the MMPI in Psychology and Medicine.* Minneapolis: University of Minnesota Press, 1956.

Wooley, S. C., and others. *A New Behavioral Approach to Psychosomatic Medicine.* Williamsburg, Va.: Academy of Psychosomatic Medicine, 1973.

Wright, L. "Conceptualizing and Defining Psychosomatic Disorders." *American Psychologist,* 1977, *32,* 625-628.

Wright, L., and Fulwiler, R. "Emotional Sequelae of Burns: Effects on Children and Their Mothers." *Pediatric Research,* 1974, *8,* 931-934.

Zborowski, M. "Culture Components in Response to Pain." *Journal of Social Issues,* 1952, *8,* 16-32.

Zborowski, M. *People in Pain.* San Francisco: Jossey-Bass, 1969.

Zuckerman, M., Lubin, B., and Robins, S. "Validation of the Multiple Affect Adjective Check List in Clinical Situations." *Journal of Consulting Psychology,* 1965, *29,* 594.

11

Greek key border decoration

Curtis L. Barrett

Personality (Character) Disorders

Greek key border decoration

Personality or character disorders, unlike other mental disorders, are manifested in a social context. The label is not applied to describe individual distress, as in neurosis, or incapacity, as in psychosis or organic brain syndromes; instead, it reflects chronic maladjustment. Such maladjustment troubles society, in time, more than it troubles the individual. Seldom does this individual experience the crippling anxiety that is characteristic of the neuroses, the loss of functioning due to thought disorder characteristic of the schizophrenic process, the incapacity of organic brain syndromes, or the extremes of mood found in the affective disorders. Instead, one finds an apparently intact organism, with little severe symptomatology, that is unable to organize its behavior and complete tasks. In the words of *DSM II*: "This group of disorders is characterized by deeply ingrained maladaptive patterns of behavior that are perceptibly different in quality from psychotic and neurotic symptoms. Generally, these are lifelong patterns, often recognizable by the time of adolescence or earlier" (American Psychiatric Association, 1968, p. 41).

Background and Current Status

The term *character* or *personality disorder* developed from attempts to account for severe patterns of maladaptive behavior in the absence of the more classical symptoms of mental disorder (such as delusions, hallucinations, mania, melancholia). Because the behavior patterns were established early in life, it was reasonable to look for "constitutional factors" in the person. Meyer (1903), for example, attempted to describe the various types of "neurotic constitution." Some of his "types" might today fall into the category of personality disorder rather than neurosis. For example, he described the "hysterical constitution" as "consisting of crisis of an emotional character and an inter-paroxysmal condition of emotional weakness, nervousness, hyperesthesia and pains in the head or back, poor sleep, disagreeable dreams, globus, and vasomotor instability. The patients are mostly young girls or young women, unduly sensitive, depressed, easily alarmed; they feel nervous, lack emotional control" (p. 114). Meyer went on to point out that the more classical symptoms of hysteria—such as paralysis of a limb—may not occur.

Perhaps the first specific recognition of personality disorder was one that is considered in a separate chapter of this volume: antisocial personality. Stearns (1944) notes that as early as 1829 a patient who presented this disorder was observed in the Richmond lunatic asylum in Dublin. He appeared to be in control of his faculties but "exhibited a total want of moral feeling and principle." A physician commented: "He never was different than he now is; he has never evidenced the slightest mental incoherence on any one point, nor any kind of hallucination. The governors and medical gentlemen of the asylums have often had doubts about whether they were justified in keeping him as a lunatic. . . . He appears, however, so callous with regard to every moral principle and feeling . . . that any jury . . . would satisfy themselves by returning him as insane" (pp. 822-823).

The evolution of the present term *personality disorder* in clinical assessment can be traced through two distinct traditions. The first is psychoanalytic thought, wherein "character types" were defined in terms of theoretical tenets. Thus, one may find discussions of "anal character traits: the compulsive character" (Michaels, 1959). Persons having such character limits are described as orderly, frugal, and obstinate. The character *disorder* that such persons develop, according to this position, is "compulsive neurosis." Thus, the character "disorder" and character structure, short of the experience of neurotic anxiety, are blurred. The second tradition is the development of classificatory systems. The starting point is an arbitrary one, but it illustrates the importance of the "constitutional" thinking of Meyer, which was cited earlier. World War II presented the military with the problem of assessing persons who seemed to be unfit for military service. The 1938 version of the U.S. Navy *Diagnostic Nomenclature* included the following (cited by Stearns, 1944, p. 827):

- 1501   Constitutional psychopathic inferiority with psychosis
- 1502   Constitutional psychopathic state, criminalism
- 1503   Constitutional psychopathic state, emotional instability
- 1504   Constitutional psychopathic state, inadequate personality
- 1505   Constitutional psychopathic state, paranoid personality
- 1506   Constitutional psychopathic state, pathological liar
- 1507   Constitutional psychopathic state, sexual psychopathy

Using this nomenclature, one Navy neuropsychiatric service classified 80 (16 percent) of its first 500 admissions as "personality disorder."

None of the classificatory systems in use during World War II proved to be adequate to the task (Gardner, 1965). This and other factors led to the preparation of the *Diagnostic and Statistical Manual of Mental Disorders (DSM-I)* of the American Psychiatric Association in 1952. In *DSM-I* personality disorders were classified as disorders of psychogenic origin or without clearly defined tangible cause or structural assessment. They were grouped as follows:

- Personality pattern disturbance
    Inadequate personality
    Schizoid personality
    Cyclothymic personality
    Paranoid personality
- Personality trait disturbance
    Emotionally unstable personality
    Passive-aggressive personality
    Compulsive personality
    Personality trait disturbance, other
- Sociopathic personality disturbance
    Antisocial reaction
    Dyssocial reaction
    Sexual deviation
- Addiction
    Alcoholism
    Drug addiction
- Special Symptom Reactions
    Learning disturbance
    Speech disturbance
    Enuresis
    Somnambulism
    Other

The category "transient situational personality disorders" also was introduced as a "personality disorder." Covered were such diagnoses as "gross stress reaction" and "adjustment reaction of adolescence."

Clearly, *DSM-I* included a wide variety of symptomatic behavior under the term *personality disorder.* Implicit still was the idea of constitutional predisposition, either toward some maladjustive behavior over time or toward reaction to external stresses in maladaptive ways. However, it is quite difficult to determine a unifying characteristic for all the disorders that are listed together. For example, what do "learning disturbance" and "schizoid personality" have in common?

The 1968 revision of the *Diagnostic and Statistical Manual (DSM-II)* reflected considerable change in thinking about the personality disorder. Sexual deviations, drug addictions, and alcoholism were taken out of the category as were the "special symptom reactions." The distinction between personality pattern and personality trait was dropped. The emotionally unstable category became the "hysterical personality," and the "compulsive personality" became the "obsessive-compulsive personality." A new term, "explosive personality," appeared. Thus, in *DSM-II* one finds these personality disorders:

- Paranoid personality
- Cyclothymic personality (affective personality)

- Schizoid personality
- Explosive personality (epileptoid personality)
- Obsessive-compulsive personality (anankastic personality)
- Hysterical personality (histrionic personality)
- Asthenic personality
- Antisocial personality (see Chapter Twelve)
- Passive-aggressive personality
- Inadequate personality

It is this group that will be discussed at length with regard to clinical assessment.

The development of *DSM-II* has not resolved the assessment problems that the personality disorders present. In Europe the system devised by Schneider (1959) is used extensively, and it retains the "constitutional" emphasis noted above in other classificatory systems. Further, Schneider uses the term *abnormal personalities* to describe persons who deviate from the norm in certain ways even though they may not be in distress or cause society to suffer. For example, "hyperthymic psychopaths" deviate from the norm in that they are very cheerful and active; "attention-seeking psychopaths" are usually boastful, self-aggrandizing, and showy. The fact that the personalities and the abnormal personalities merge gradually into each other, in the system, indicates a continuous rather than a discontinuous conceptualization of this clinical phenomenon. No definite point of delineation exists.

A second contemporary issue with regard to the term *personality disorder* is also related to the continuity-discontinuity issue. That is, which of the personality disorders are entities unto themselves and which are related to major psychiatric illness? These questions will be considered later, when we deal more specifically with each of the personality disorders. However, to illustrate the issue, consider the similarity of behaviors associated with the cyclothymic personality and manic-depressive illness. Mood swings, over long periods of time, are characteristic of both. The difference is that the manic-depressive manifests extremes of mood swings and a loss of contact with the environment. Is there one disorder, varying in severity, or are these two disorders? How does one decide?

Attention to the personality disorders in any clinical assessment scheme is easily justified by their frequency of occurrence. Gardner (1965), for example, reports that, of 16,015 diagnoses made in psychiatric clinic and private office contacts over a three-year period (1960-1963), 5,689 (35.5 percent) were personality disorders (*DSM-I* classification system). This compares with 16 percent for neurotics and 26 percent for psychotics. But other evidence indicates that the assessment led to treatment for less than half of these persons. Thus, personality disorders continue to present not only the conceptual difficulties noted so far but also problems of disposition once assessment is completed.

Critical Discussion

To this point we have considered the personality or character disorders collectively and have made little comment on the subcategories. What has been said about the evolution of the general category applies as well to the subcategory. However, each subcategory needs to be considered individually.

Paranoid Personality

General Areas of Concern. According to *DSM-II,* the pattern of behavior observed in the paranoid personality is "characterized by hypersensitivity, rigidity, unwarranted suspicion, jealousy, envy, excessive self-importance, and a tendency to blame others and to ascribe evil motives to them. Interpersonal relations are often unsatisfactory for persons who exhibit such behaviors" (American Psychiatric Association, 1968, p. 42). It is necessary to avoid confusing paranoid personality with several other disorders: paranoia, involutional paranoia (involutional paraphrenia), paranoid states, and paranoid schizophrenia. *Paranoia,* a noun, refers to a "rare condition characterized by gradual development of an intricate, complex, and elaborate paranoid system based on and often proceeding logically from misinterpretation of an actual event" (p. 38). The essential characteristics are the delusional system and the absence of interference with the rest of the intellect and personality. *Paranoid,* as an adjective, signals the primacy of a delusional system and associated behavior in the disorder. Both paranoid states and paranoid schizophrenia involve loss of contact with reality, centered on the delusional system, and are classified as psychoses.

The fact that paranoid personality does not reflect a psychotic state in no way suggests, however, that persons presenting this disorder are easy to assess or to treat. The intimate, business, and social situations which they report are likely to be quite puzzling and often contain elements that make suspiciousness seem warranted. To secure external confirmation of the patient's data, the assessor/therapist must go beyond the one-to-one relationship and thereby may incur the patient's mistrust or may discover unexpected things. For example, what the patient presented as a close working relationship with an informant, who was sure to confirm the patient's complaint, may be found by the assessor to be quite the opposite. The informant, worn down by the patient, may simply have acquiesced. Such events feed the behavior pattern of the paranoid personality by confirming his or her worst fears.

The characteristic hypersensitivity of the patient with paranoid personality brings an overload of information to the therapy sessions. Correlations or "connections" that most professionals would attribute to chance carry great weight with the paranoid personality. For example, one person classified paranoid personality, whom I worked with in therapy for about two years, came to a session one day extremely upset. Earlier in the day the person had sold a piece of property for $16,000. Later the same day he became interested in another piece of property, asked the price, and was told that it was $16,500. This was presented as "clear" evidence that someone had the patient under surveillance: how else could the seller have "known"? Instances of this sort, day in and day out, keep such patients chronically off balance and deeply involved in a pseudocommunity: "an imaginary organization, composed of real and imagined persons, whom the patient represents as united for the purpose of carrying out some action upon him" (Cameron, 1963, p. 486). Their constant checking, asking for "confirmation" of their perceptions, and chronic reworking of past material destroys even their meager interpersonal support. Indeed, when the assessment includes interviews of significant others in the patient's life, a resigned, hopeless, exhausted quality in the persons interviewed is almost pathognomonic. They seem to have realized that the behavioral pattern resists all assaults of reason on it and that further therapeutic effort will only drain them more.

Comparative Philosophies and Theories. There is some evidence that paranoid personality is related to paranoid schizophrenia (Kay and Roth, 1967; Herbert and Jacobsen, 1967). Since paranoid schizophrenia is no better understood than paranoid personality, however, there seems little to be gained in exploring this possibility. To do so is to define one unknown in terms of another.

The dominant psychological formulations of the paranoid personality are the psychodynamic/psychoanalytic and the behavioral. The former stems from Freud's conceptualization of a process in which certain aspects of one's self come into consciousness, are unacceptably painful, and then become attributed to others. Of course, those attributes of others are delusional, and there is no confirmation of them from reality. The term *projection* was coined to explain this process, and it is still considered the major defense mechanism in paranoid personality. In the case of Schreber, a paranoid psychotic, Freud suggested that the defense is necessary because of underlying homoerotic impulses. The person defensively converts hate to love, can neither accept the loved persons nor hate them, and resolves the issue with the delusion "they hate me." Presumably a similar mechanism is at work in the development and maintenance of the paranoid personality. At any rate, by dealing with the hostile "pseudocommunity" (Cameron, 1963), such patients do not have to deal with their own hostile impulses.

Behavior theorists, such as Ullmann and Krasner (1969), see the paranoid individual as "one who thinks straight about a biased sample of information" (p. 438). The associated behavior patterns then develop according to general laws of learning, such as reinforcement and generalization, as do any other behavior patterns. However, a major factor in the process is the sort of stimulus value the suspicious, rigid, difficult person acquires. Generally, the person is a noxious social stimulus and others tend to avoid contact when possible. Isolation increases and reinforces the behavior patterns, and "reality testing" becomes less available.

Elaboration on Critical Points. Two points bear further emphasis here. First, the paranoid personality presents a significant assessment challenge. Accurate information is difficult to obtain, since the assessor/therapist easily can become part of a developing paranoid pseudocommunity. Thus, it is often necessary to utilize standard psychological assessment techniques, such as the Minnesota Multiphasic Personality Inventory (MMPI) or the Rorschach, to go beyond the intact, reasonable façade presented in early interviews. But such "testing" is done at the risk of rapidly losing the client due to lack of trust.

Second, the paranoid personality may be the early stage of a more serious disorder —for instance, a paranoid state—rather than stabilized at a less severe level. Cameron (1963) has noted a progression from "paranoid person" through "psychotic paranoid reaction." Cameron's first three stages—onset, early phases, and preliminary crystallizations—probably are indistinguishable from paranoid personality; the "final crystallization: the paranoid pseudocommunity" phase represents the first full departure from reality. It is no longer "as if" things are happening; the projected delusions have become real. "Paranoid action," such as flight or preemptory attack, is the last phase, although the patient may not enter it; if the phase is entered, however, the issue of dangerousness to self or others is raised. Therefore, the possibility of the patient's deterioration across time should be kept in mind as the assessment progresses.

Personal Views and Recommendations. There is little evidence, outside of case studies, that is relevant to the assessment and treatment of the paranoid personality. The critical feat to be accomplished is to gain the trust of a person who is chronically untrusting. Only with trust can the relationship be maintained and the assessment/treatment continued. This seems to be possible when the therapist assumes a classical Rogerian stance and attempts to understand the assumptive world in which the patient lives. This is a terribly wearing task. It takes considerable self-discipline not to label the "connections" that the patient makes as "preposterous" or "absurd"; but to confront in this way would only add one more person to the list of those who had done so.

While struggling to understand the patient's world, the therapist must make it clear that he or she accepts the patient but does not participate in the delusions. This can be done when the patient inevitably asks whether his or her "connection" is unreasonable. The therapist can respond that it is impossible to prove a negative. It cannot be

proven that a telephone is *not* tapped, that a car is *not* keeping a house under surveillance. What can be done is to understand how frightening it is for the patient to live in a
world where such things *could* happen. The therapist also can point out that immense
physical resources would be necessary to accomplish what is reported; for instance, that
the patient's "enemies" would have to influence everyone else in the patient's life—
plumber, drug store clerk, post office clerk—just to make life extraordinarily difficult for
the patient. From there it is a small step to comment on how important the patient must
be to anyone—for instance, the parents—who would spend so much to gain such influence. The need for such importance, it seems, is at the core of the problem anyway.
Finally, the therapist might take the initiative in pointing out "connections" that occur in
the patient's and the therapist's lives. The purpose is twofold: (1) to keep the relationship's potential conflicts current and (2) to model a response to life's inevitable frustrations.

Cyclothymic Personality (Affective Personality)

General Areas of Concern. The cyclothymic personality manifests variations of
mood in the absence of apparent exogenous explanatory factors. Whether the variations
of mood reflect fluctuations of the person's physiological state, idiosyncratic processing
of information from the environment, or interactions of these factors is unknown. As
described in *DSM-II*: "This behavior pattern is manifested by recurring and alternating
periods of elation and depression. Periods of elation may be marked by ambition,
warmth, enthusiasm, optimism, and high energy. Periods of depression may be marked by
worry, pessimism, low energy, and a sense of futility. These mood variations are not
readily attributable to external circumstances. If possible, the diagnosis should specify
whether the mood is characteristically depressed, hypomanic, or alternating" (American
Psychiatric Association, 1968, p. 42).

The cyclothymic personality is rather rare in that it constitutes less than 1 percent
of all personality disorders. Gardner (1965), for example, using *DSM-I* definitions,
found only thirteen persons who were so diagnosed out of a sample of 5,689 personality
disorders. Thus, the major interest in the disorder stems from its similarity to manic-
depressive illness. Indeed, some (for example, Winokur and Crowe, 1975) suggest that the
term *hypomanic* may be adequate to describe the disorder and to indicate its relationships to the more severe disorder.

Genetic studies (Kallmann, 1954) suggest that cyclothymic personality, if not
cyclothymic personality *disorder,* is found significantly more often in the background of
persons diagnosed as having manic-depressive illness. In the general population sample,
Kallmann found 0.7 percent to have cyclothymic personality. This, interestingly, compares with 0.8 percent of personality disorders found by Gardner (1965) to have cyclothymic personality *disorder.* Parents of manic-depressive patients were cyclothymic in
14.5 percent of Kallmann's cases; dizygotic co-twins were cyclothymic in 30.9 percent of
the cases. Unfortunately for assessment procedures, one cannot find evidence of the reverse: cyclothymic offspring of manic-depressives. However, it is reasonable to look for a
family history of manic-depressive illness as well as cyclothymic personality when considering the diagnosis of cyclothymic personality disorder.

Comparative Philosophies and Theories. Unfortunately, theories of personality
and theories of psychopathology often do not account for the same data in the same way,
which creates special implications for the objective assessment of the cyclothymic personality disorder. Personality theories consider mood swings and high or low rates of social
interaction reflective of personality traits, such as extraversion or introversion. The extra-

vert maintains high rates of social behavior and has a mood that is characteristically "high" while the introvert shows low rates of social interaction and is usually seen in a subdued mood. Theories of psychopathology, by contrast, categorize these behaviors and moods as less severe forms of a major category of psychopathology. Thus, cyclothymic personality is often thought of as subclinical manic-depressive illness and not a style of life.

Because the use of the term *cyclothymic personality disorder* is a clinical act that proceeds from no clear theoretical position, guidelines are needed to indicate what places the observed behavior outside normal limits. Three factors should be weighed heavily: severity of mood swings, absence of environmental precipitators, and positive family history of cyclothymic personality or manic-depressive illness. If all three factors are substantiated, a cyclothymic personality disorder may be diagnosed.

Elaboration on Critical Points. What justifies the term *disorder* in cyclothymic personality disorder? By *DSM-II* standards, applicable to all personality disorders, the behavior pattern must be *maladaptive.* This implies that such persons are prevented from effectively dealing with either their internal or their external environment. Yet the disorder is not diagnosed when a precipitating exogenous stress is present. It seems that the pattern of behavior may be *learned* and that it reflects a way to cope with interpersonal stresses.

Once more we consider the social stimulus value of the person who has initial temperament in the "cyclothymic" range. In the "manic" or "extraverted" phase, there probably is a great deal of social interaction, with attendant promises and commitments to others. Such commitments are reasonable given the high energy level of the person. Further, significant others, as they respond to what they see, expect the promises to be kept; as the mood swings downward slightly, however, the ability to meet the commitments decreases, and the significant others become disappointed and puzzled. As the mood swings upward, the person has a backlog of commitments to meet but also has the delusion of endless, abundant energy. In this state even more is taken on in the hope of social reinforcement, but with an inevitable result. If the environment (including the significant persons in the cyclothymic's life) is tolerant, there is no particular harm. In time a realistic level of expectation, based on the average energy available to the person, can be reached. But if the reinforcements are for *promise* of more and more performance, we see the makings of disorder. In time the person becomes a thorn in the side of others and enters the labeling process.

The puzzle of the lack of a "precipitating event"—for example, for depression—can be solved if the assessor focuses on the "manic" phase. What was promised? To whom? What compounding promises from past episodes were also unmet? What losses, with attendant grief responses, has the person suffered as a result of not doing what he or she led others to expect? Complete assessment of the cyclothymic personality disorder should include exploring these social learning aspects of the disorder.

Personal Views and Recommendations. As suggested, assessment should include examination of social learning factors in the development and maintenance of the patterns of behavior associated with all personality disorders. It is reasonable to assume that all persons assessed are coping with a unique internal environment that is biologically based. However, they also carry out social transactions with their environments, and these transactions have consequences. Among these consequences is the expectation that is set up by their environment. The feedback or reinforcement that they elicit in turn shapes them. Therefore, rational assessment strategy must result in an understanding of this process, of available models for such learning, and of inherited tendencies.

Schizoid Personality

General Areas of Concern. Individuals with schizoid personality disorder present a puzzling clinical picture. They appear to have normal ability to process information and to reason. However, in the face of events that would be disturbing to most people, they appear unmoved or even detached from the situation. Other aspects are summarized in *DSM-II*: "This behavior pattern manifests shyness, oversensitivity, seclusiveness, avoidance of close relationships, and often eccentricity. Autistic thinking without loss of capacity to recognize reality is common, as are daydreaming and the inability to express hostility and ordinary aggressive feelings" (American Psychiatric Association, 1968, p. 42).

In assessing persons in the category *schizoid personality,* one must ask "What constitutes *disorder*?" Noyes and Kolb (1963, pp. 648, 649), for example, say that the schizoid person is "the prototype of the ivory tower detached and abstract thinker. . . . The adult schizoid personality is typically aloof, unsociable, secretive, and uncomfortable in the close proximity of others, especially members of the opposite sex. He sometimes gives an impression of being self-sufficient but this impression arises from a defensive refusal to trust anyone, to confide in anyone." It appears, then, that any discomfort due to the disorder must be inferred by the observer. Otherwise, such persons go their own way and avoid social contact. What leads them to be diagnosed if they feel no discomfort? Probably nothing if they are adults and are socially successful. However, as children and adolescents such persons are forced into social situations, such as school. They appear to others to be "odd," "queer," or possibly even snobbish and therefore are likely to suffer at the hands of peers, who tease and harass them. Since they are constitutionally more sensitive to such wounds, there is strong negative reinforcement for social interaction.

Adults with the schizoid personality pattern are likely to be diagnosed when they do not meet social expectations, such as their holding a job. In this case they trouble others, usually relatives, who then try to influence the person to behave "normally." The lack of emotional response to such efforts often leads someone in the system to seek help.

Comparative Philosophies and Theories. Much of the interest in schizoid personality disorder stems from its assumed relationship to schizophrenia. Kretschmer (1936) believed that the two diagnoses reflect the same illness. Genetic studies are often cited to support this view. For example, Inouye (1961) studied monozygotic twins who were nonconcordant for schizophrenia; of twenty such pairs, he found that sixteen of the nonschizophrenic twins had schizoid personality.

Studies have also questioned whether persons with schizoid personality are at risk for development of schizophrenic disorder. One often cited, but now dated, study (Morris, Soroker, and Burruss, 1954) followed up shy, withdrawn children sixteen to twenty-seven years after they were diagnosed in a child guidance clinic. Of the fifty-four children, only two were maladjusted at follow-up, and one of these was schizophrenic. However, a burgeoning area of recent research, study of the "vulnerable child," suggests that there are identifiable personality antecedents of schizophrenia (Mednick and Schulsinger, 1970; Watt, 1974). For the time being, therefore, the assessor has no firm basis for deciding whether a diagnosis of schizoid personality includes a statement of risk for schizophrenia.

Psychodynamic formulations of schizoid disorder (see, for instance, Cameron, 1963) suggest that schizoid personality disorder originates in the earliest phases of life. Lack of basic trust produces anxiety and fears in the context of the primary human relationship, and these are never resolved. The person does not feel accepted and therefore will not risk the further hurt that could come from direct expression of anger or from competition.

Behavior theorists and behavior therapists (for instance, Ullmann and Krasner, 1969; Kanfer and Phillips, 1970) typically do not deal directly with the concept of schizoid personality disorder. However, it is interesting, from the point of view of assessment, to consider the psychodynamic and behavioral viewpoints together. The psychodynamic view is that this disorder originates in the period of life when the organism has no verbal language. That is, instead of pleasurable affect in an interpersonal situation, anxiety or fear is experienced. The association of people and fear presumably continues throughout life. But the diagnosis (*DSM-II*) also suggests that in conflictual interpersonal situations the schizoid is characterized by *non*response or "detachment." The assessment problem, therefore, is to determine whether the schizoid person responds affectively but inhibits motor response or whether the person experiences no discomfort at all. If an inappropriate affect is felt and leads to avoidance of people, then a desensitization program (or anxiolytic drug) is needed. If *lack* of response is the problem, then a procedure to increase the behavioral repertoire is the treatment of choice.

Elaboration on Critical Points. One difficulty with assessment of the schizoid personality is the definition of "disorder." As Mowrer (1948), among others, has pointed out, "disorder" cannot be defined as a deviation from some ideal model of the "normal" or "healthy" personality. Thus, "disorder" continues to be defined primarily by the complaints of a "client": either the person who manifests the personality pattern or a person who is troubled by someone who does. Assessment of the schizoid personality "disorder," one that is characterized by *lack* of overt response or expression of presumed affect (such as hostility), should address the question "Who is troubled?" Clinical experience suggests that the schizoid person—especially one who is occupationally successful—seldom enters the assessment/treatment system because of personal dissatisfaction with the current level of adjustment. Instead, such persons seek help because they want to change a life-style (for instance to marry) or because they fail to measure up to some significant person's expectations. The latter is illustrated by the 22-year-old son of a highly successful physician. The young man expressed no interest in the things that clearly motivated his father. He did not reject them as goals for others; he simply was content to live at a different socioeconomic and stress level. His father sought help for him, but assessment indicated that the young man had no desire to change. What was the locus of the disorder? Why was this person hospitalized? The answer lies in a community consensus that, given his intelligence and social opportunity, he *should have* wanted more involvement in his environment—even though the person himself did not think so.

Personal Views and Recommendations. More than any other of the personality disorders, the schizoid personality confronts the assessor with the question of how a person *should* be. Usually the assessor is presented with a person who is not impaired and not uncomfortable but who is clearly deviant in response pattern. It is hard not to agree with family members that the person is functioning far below potential and to project the feelings that the assessor would have if, for example, the same life-style were his or hers. But the application of the term *disorder* requires that someone be in distress and that the treatment be directed toward the person who is distressed. To do otherwise is to impose a style of life in which the person has no interest.

Explosive Personality (Epileptoid Personality)

This disorder will be considered only briefly, since—as Winokur and Crowe (1975, p. 1284) have said—"the birth of the term 'explosive personality' must surely have occurred in the presence of a group of experts sitting around a table and deciding the limits of acceptable behavior." According to *DSM-II,* "This pattern is characterized by gross outbursts of rage or of verbal or physical aggressiveness. These outbursts are strikingly different from the patient's usual behavior, and he may be regretful and repentant for them. These patients are usually considered excitable, aggressive, and overresponsive to environmental pressures. It is the intensity of the outbursts and the individual inability to control them that distinguishes this group" (American Psychiatric Association, 1968, p. 42).

It is possible, according to *DSM-II,* to include the "aggressive personality" in this group. However, this tends to muddy more water than it clarifies. In the case of the epileptoid personality, unlike the aggressive personality, a key to assessment is finding the person amnesic or puzzled about his violent actions. The effect of the puzzlement or amnesia has led Barrett and Meyer (1972) to argue that clinicians very seldom see persons with explosive personality disorders in their "psychopathological state." Such persons are more likely to be seen by the police, who for example, after answering a call about a domestic incident, may find a man and his family standing in awe of wrecked home furnishings. The person who committed the act is as puzzled about "what got into him" as are the rest of the family and the police, but unless property belonging to someone other than the person with the disorder has been damaged, there is likely to be no further action.

Obsessive-Compulsive Personality (Anankastic Personality)

General Areas of Concern. As *DSM-II* states, the obsessive-compulsive behavior pattern "is characterized by excessive concern with conformity and adherence to standards of conscience. Consequently, individuals in this group may be rigid, overinhibited, overconscientious, overdutiful, and unable to relax easily" (American Psychiatric Association, 1968, p. 43). This disorder is different from the neurosis of the same name in that the obsessive-compulsive neurosis is characterized by intrusion of unwanted thoughts, urges, or actions that the person is unable to stop and about which the person is anxious. In the personality disorder, the person typically does not experience significant distress. Indeed, Weintraub (1974, p. 86) notes that "epidemiological data have been difficult to obtain because most obsessive-compulsive characters do not seek treatment." What data there are indicate that the disorder constitutes about 2 percent (112/5,689) of diagnosed psychiatric disorders (Gardner, 1965).

The behaviors associated with obsessive-compulsive disorder (most notably, the repetitious acts, words, or thoughts) appear to serve humans in two fundamental ways. First, they permit guarding against fundamental, fatal error; second, they permit dealing with uncertainty. Both of these functions are illustrated well in the behavior of the competent airplane pilot. Flights begin well before the departure time with a ritualistic series of checks on the weather to be encountered. Closer to departure time there is a "preflight" ritual, in which the aircraft is inspected. Each inspection is conducted in precisely the same way. Just before takeoff, a checkoff list is completed, and it ends with the statement "Checkoff list complete." The recent crash of a chartered airliner bears grim testimony to what happens if one fails to use the checklist. An aileron lock was left installed, and the plane became uncontrollable immediately after it was airborne: all aboard were killed. The second function, reduction of uncertainty, is not quite so obvious. To continue the illustration, the probability that a flight will end safely is either 1 or 0; that is, it will or it will not. Most air disasters, however, stem from a very few causes, such as fuel mismanagement, midair collision, weather, or—rarely—catastrophic engine failure. None of these, obviously, can be avoided by a ritual; the probability remains 1 or 0 that they will occur. But the compulsive overt behavior (checking) and the obsessive thought (ruminating about the details of the airplane, oneself, and the flight) introduce a *sense* of being in control even when one is not. It is the positive emotional state (in control) that is sought, that reinforces, even though it is illusory. The anxiety associated with a real—if low-probability—danger is managed, and the person can go on.

If obsessive-compulsive character traits are "ego syntonic," fitting into the person's life-style, how does one assess the *disordered* state? Answering three questions will usually suffice in making the determination. Does the history of the person reveal a long-term pattern of obsessive-compulsive behavior? Does the history reveal a relatively high level of functioning even in the face of exaggerated obsessive-compulsive behavior? Is there evidence of significant lessening of function in the face of a significant new life stress? The first two establish the longevity of the behavioral pattern and its utility. The third establishes that disorder has occurred.

Salzman (1974, p. 226) provides a case illustration of the progression from behavioral characteristics to behavioral disorder in the case of an engineer:

> He would arrive at and depart from his plant according to his own schedule, and on many occasions he would work through the night. He was meticulously precise and had some hand-washing compulsions, as well as a total inability to settle for anything less than perfect performance on the job. While his lack of discipline tended to disrupt the laboratory routine, the management was extremely sympathetic and even increased his hourly pay. Periodically his preciseness and passion for order would resolve some hitherto unresolvable circuitry problem.
>
> Shortly after his marriage, his performance became more erratic and unreliable. . . . What had been considered merely odd and queer was now labeled as a character disorder that required therapy.

Weintraub (1974), proceeding from the "oral triad" (obstinacy, frugality, and orderliness), suggests that the obsessive-compulsive character may be a difficult person to live with or work with, because the need of such persons for control and for certainty extends well beyond themselves; their "rules" or required rituals also control the behavior of others without serving them. Thus, obsessive-compulsive persons are described as "loners," "inner directed," and "detached." They are controlling, and, when such control fails, they are likely to be combative. Perhaps the most noxious quality of such persons is their capacity to detach from the affective aspects of relationships and to focus on detail or procedure. Attempts to engage with the affective state intact face certain failure, since the definition of "correct" used by the obsessive-compulsive is usually idiosyncratic, not consensual. It is common to hear the obsessive-compulsive person, like the paranoid, describe the dissolution of relationships entirely in terms of the other person's weaknesses, errors, or incompetency.

Comparative Philosophies and Theories. The major formulations concerning obsessive-compulsives have come from the various psychoanalytic schools, and the major competing approach is grounded in learning theory. Both of these are well known and will be reported only sketchily here.

Psychoanalytic formulation of obsessive-compulsive neurosis, and by extension obsessive-compulsive character, emphasizes the "battle of the chamber pot" (Rado, 1974). The child's natural eliminative cycle is confronted by the mother's need to have the child establish voluntary control. Defiant defecation brings on punishment, or threats of it, and obedience to preserve the self. To this point reality has reigned; but if guilt becomes associated with defiance and punishment is perceived as "deserved," the situation changes. The child seeks to avoid rage by complying with vague, perfectionistic standards. It is a small step to conclude that directly expressed rage is inappropriate and to accept the meeting of standards as an end in itself. The resulting rigidity, from the point of view of assessment, may be regarded as pathognomic of the disorder.

Learning theory formulations of the obsessive-compulsive disorder, as one may expect, do not emphasize "character." Rather, they focus on the possible ongoing social reinforcement of the behaviors. Learning theorists believe that the disorder is caused by the reinforcement of superstitious behavior; that is, chance correlations between a behavior and a significant environmental event (positive *or* negative reinforcement). Mowrer (1960) has introduced the possibility that compulsions depend on temporal discrimination. The organism learns to differentiate "safe" from "dangerous" parts of the stimulus trace (situation). The organism does not act during the perceived "safe" period; when the "dangerous" time arrives, however, only the compulsive act (or obsessive thought process) can reduce the organism's distress.

Personal Views and Recommendations. The critical assessment task in the obsessive-compulsive character disorder is the determination that the person is no longer served by the thought process or the behavior. The use of obsessive-compulsive mechanisms is not only acceptable but, as noted, is systematically taught in many instances. One need not look far to find a "checklist" in use—for instance, in a service station or an airline cockpit. When the checklist, the controlling rule, becomes of more concern to the person than his or her own functioning, however, the diagnosis can be made. Experience indicates that the assessment will result when intimates or co-workers complain, and not because the person with the disorder is upset. What breaks down is the person's support system. It can no longer tolerate the elaborate, idiosyncratic "rules" that are imposed in order to control. Along with the obsessive-compulsive disorder, therefore, one may observe depression or possibly decompensation of the sort associated with loss of support.

Hysterical Personality (Histrionic Personality)

General Areas of Concern. Following *DSM-II*: "[Hysterical] behavior patterns are characterized by excitability, emotional instability, overreactivity, and self-dramatization. This self-dramatization is always attention seeking and often seductive, whether or not the patient is aware of its purpose. These personalities are also immature, self-centered, often vain, and usually dependent on others" (American Psychiatric Association, 1968, p. 43). Whether or not this disorder is found frequently in males (a point of enduring controversy), the diagnosis is used infrequently for men (Guze, Woodruff, and Clayton, 1972).

Hysterical personality disorder can be distinguished from hysterical neurosis on the basis of symptom severity. That is, hysterical neurosis in *DSM-II* includes a "dissociative type" and a "conversion type." The conversion type may involve dramatic physical symptoms (such as blindness or paralysis) and may mimic severe neuropathology. Equally dramatic are the markers of the dissociative type, in that they include multiple personality, fugue, and amnesia. Both neuroses have found their way to stage and screen as well as consulting room. But hysterical personality disorder has a much higher incidence. For example, Gardner (1965) reports that 1,038 of 16,015 patients (6.48 percent) referred to psychiatrists in a three-year period were diagnosed hysteric personality disorder. The dissociative type of hysteric neurosis occurred only twenty times (.12 percent); the conversion type occurred 239 times (1.49 percent).

Persons labeled "hysteric" are compelling social stimuli, since their symptoms, by definition, are exaggerated and attention seeking. Thus, the term is sometimes used in a pejorative way. That is, persons who, under stress, lose control are said to become "hysterical." In medical settings the label "hysteric" often serves to sum up a case and to justify dismissing it. But clinical practice shows that such disorders are difficult to treat and present diagnostic puzzles.

One diagnostic schema is Tupin's (1974) elaboration of Lazare (1971). Within hysterical personality disorder, a distinction is made between "healthy" (good or assertive) and "sick" (bad or dependent) characteristics. These distinctions further are referred to the patient's personality traits, life history, and psychodynamics (see Table 1). The healthy-sick distinction also reflects prognosis, since it is essentially a severity scale. That is, despite their having the same label, two persons might present different resources to the clinician.

Table 1. "Healthy" Versus "Sick" Characteristics of Hysterical Personality Disorder[a]

	Personality Traits
Healthy	Ambitious, competitive, buoyant, energetic, strict standards of behavior, aggressive, vain, histrionic, insensitive, overtalkative, coquettish, young appearing, emotionally expressive and labile, suspicious, impulsive, uneasy with women, competitive-destructive with men, successful, accomplished, caricature of femininity.
Sick	Low self-esteem, passive, dependent, helpless, withdrawn, pouty, obstinate, unpredictable, flighty, tentative, shy, sensitive, communicatively unclear, suggestible, compliant, frequent complaints of physical problems, feels overwhelmed, demanding, diminished guilt.

	Life History
Healthy	Frequently oldest, father's favorite, mother's assistant, responsible and engrossed in home, perceives mother as uninteresting, sexually frigid, nonworthy of emulation; the family may regard the patient as juvenile, inefficient, and cute. Ingratiating, emotional, often sexually inhibited, chooses older or unavailable men, may dominate in marriage; communicatively vague, strong emphasis on femininity, often successful in academics and vocations. Makes striking use of cosmetics, clothes to emphasize femininity and attractiveness, retains friendships, may belong to clubs or gangs in preadolescence, achievement and peer success in latency.
Sick	Often youngest child in family, described as cold, quarrelsome, ungiving, remote; mother perhaps absent, passive, or depressed, may have died early or have been ill; father may be seductive, dominant, or inaccessible; marital instability or great tolerance for abusive spouses, continued to true latency; preadolescence characterized by withdrawal, distorted peer relations with regression and demandingness, much fantasy, little achievement, poor peer relationships based on expectations of rescue and nurture, fears of rejection, childish, sexual promiscuity in exchange for nurturance and protection, academically and educationally erratic, poor tolerance of inner personal stress, and reacts with impulsivity, depression, psychosis, or conversion symptoms.

	Psychodynamics
Healthy	Oedipal conflicts predominate, obsessional defenses frequent, sexual issues are prominent, regression, manipulation, and control common, external reality, integrated ego and superego functions, has basic trust, can retain object relations, effective in insight-oriented psychotherapy.

Table 1 *(Continued)*

Sick	Oral conflicts prominent, condensation of genital and pregenital aims, poor integration of ego function, primitive sexually, confusion of internal and external reality, poor tolerance of tension, poor object relationships, periodic emotionality, may use alcohol or drugs, physical complaints and operations common, suicidal gestures, frigid, unaware of emotional problems within themselves, defensive failure leads to acting out, depression, distortions in internalized object relations.

[a]"Healthy" = good or assertive; "sick" = bad or dependent.

Source: Tupin (1974).

Tupin also notes the increasing recognition of the label *hysterical psychosis.* He concludes that this condition occurs almost exclusively in persons with hysterical personality disorder and lists the following other characteristics: "sudden dramatic onset related to a profoundly upsetting event or circumstance; manifestations include hallucinations, illusions, depersonalization, and unusual behavior; thought disorder, when occurring, is usually circumscribed and transient; affective volatility; rarely lasts longer than three weeks; minimal psychological deterioration or residue; object relatedness characterized by clinging dependence and control but healthier than [in] schizophrenics; the psychosis is frequently family (or culturally) syntonic" (Tupin, 1974, p. 76). No scientifically acceptable data have been found to indicate the incidence of this disorder; but it may be speculated that many of the "dramatic" responses of so-called acute psychotic episodes have been in persons who were "healthy" hysterical personality disorders.

Comparative Philosophies and Theories. There is a paucity of literature offering alternatives to the psychoanalytic view of the etiology of hysteric neurosis. It is therefore not surprising to find little systematic formulation of hysterical personality disorder that is not based on psychoanalytic theory. Behavioral approaches, like the psychoanalytic views, utilize similar mechanisms to account for a wide range of disorders. Emphasis is placed on reinforcement (for instance, for "show-off" behavior), the taking on of a social role, and phenomena such as modeling (Ullmann and Krasner, 1969). Barrett and Meyer (1972) offer this sort of behavioral formulation for a case of hysterical personality disorder. They conclude that the person's adult disorder resulted from the reinforcement (by parents and significant others) of childhood patterns of stealing, lying, and fabrication of wild stories. To maintain the same level of reinforcement and to make them age-appropriate, the individual had to resort to more extreme behaviors and stories. Eventually the social response was to bring the person's noxious behavior under control via incarceration and treatment.

Personal Views and Recommendations. The following case summary from clinical work with hysterical personality disorder suggests the quality of the disorder. Also, it proposes a similarity between the observations to be made in hysterical personality disorder and conversion hysteria.

Ms. J., a 30-year-old white female from a well-to-do rural family, was originally self-referred for treatment of an elevator phobia. She was severely incapacitated by her fear but responded well to behavioral treatment. During the course of the treatment, the hysterical personality disorder was observed. Her specific complaints centered on her marriage, headaches, and numerous interpersonal conflicts. She was overtly seductive in the therapy and attempted to sexualize the relationship. Her marital problems resulted in a divorce and significant adjustment problems as a single person. After some years she remarried, and there were problems from the beginning of the new marriage.

For present purposes we move to a time when she came in to ask for advice about how to handle her 4-year-old daughter's claim that she had been molested by her stepfather. Ms. J. was obviously upset but presented the information as strictly confidential. Arrangements were made to protect the child and to determine what had happened. The next day we were called by a social agency charged with controlling child abuse. Ms. J. had gone to that agency with her story. Indeed, it developed that she had consulted nearly a dozen persons and that her story had become more elaborate each time. At this point it was clear that Ms. J. and her children could be in serious danger. Her new husband, reportedly, had had a series of bizarre dreams and had some history of violence. Thus, there was risk that if he had sexually abused the child he could hurt or kill her to cover evidence. If he had not, he could see Ms. J.'s actions as a "last straw" assault on him and his professional reputation. That could lead to his doing violence to her. It was decided that Ms. J. should permit us to tell her husband that he had been reported and that, by law, the incident had to be a matter of public record. She and her children were to go out of town to a safe place until Mr. J.'s reaction and mental status could be determined.

The contrast between Ms. J.'s behavior before and after her advice hunting and report of her husband was astounding. Before, she was agitated, unable to sleep, physically distressed, disheveled, and distraught. After, she was impeccably dressed, calm, rational, and in control of herself. She acted as if nothing had happened. But in reality she was face to face with violence and the dissolution of her marriage. With the latter she faced return to the painful loneliness that she knew as a single person.

Ms. J.'s emotional state at the moment of greatest stress can be labeled "paradoxical calm." The paradox is that she showed a buildup to extreme agitation until she acted to place herself and her children in great danger; *then* she calmed. Further, while those around her were in a frenzy trying to work out the problem, she acted as if nothing had happened. It was as if she had escalated the problem to the point that someone *had* to take it over and that the takeover permitted Mrs. J. to assume the role of detached observer. There is a striking similarity between "paradoxical calm" as described here and *la belle indifférence* observed in conversion hysteria. Indeed, they appear to be functional equivalents.

This case also illustrates the function of the overt behavior of the person who presents with hysterical personality disorder. That is, when the situation is sufficiently extreme, someone else will claim ownership of the problem and see it to its solution. This takeover of the problem is won at the cost of self-esteem and the suffering of acute, self-induced distress. It also precludes the development of coping skills adequate for the subsequent stress. In time, of course, friends, relatives, and therapists catch on and cease to "take the bait." The resultant reality of loneliness and exposure of personal incompetence may precipitate a frankly psychotic disorder.

Asthenic Personality

General Areas of Concern. The following definition of asthenic personality is given in *DSM-II*: "This behavior pattern is characterized by easy fatigability, low energy level, lack of enthusiasm, marked incapacity for enjoyment, and oversensitivity to physical and emotional stress" (American Psychiatric Association, 1968, p. 43). The distinction between asthenic personality and neurasthenic neurosis is made on the basis of the person's *complaints* about chronic weakness. Complaint indicates that the disorder is "ego alien" or distressing, whereas in the personality disorder the characteristics are well integrated into the total personality ("ego syntonic"). Thus, the complaint associated with asthenic personality disorder is most likely to come not from the person but from the environment.

Comparative Philosophies and Theories. In Sullivan's (1956) view, behavioral deficits in the asthenic personality are caused by insecurity, which in turn results from unresolved anger. The person's "assumptive world," to use Frank's (1963) concept, is one in which punishment (disapproval, negative regard) is likely to follow most actions. The similarity of Sullivan's view to the behavioral view is striking. An organism subjected to an environment that offers little in the way of reward and a great deal of noncontingent punishment would be expected to show behavioral deficit. What remains to be understood is the apparent absence of "anxiety" or "expressed discomfort" as a result of the punishment. Most likely the behavioral formulation would postulate the existence of a reward system for assuming the "weak role."

Personal Views and Recommendations. The diagnostic category has little utility. Not only is the disorder rare, if it exists at all, but it also requires the clinician to make inferences that are difficult to make. That is, one must infer that the observed behavioral deficit and report of excessive fatigue exist in an organism that is within normal limits of biologically determined systemic activity and in an environment that provides average levels of reinforcement for activity. The gain apparent in applying the term as opposed to simply making these assessments seems to be minimal. Thus, it is recommended that the term be disregarded altogether.

Passive-Aggressive Personality

General Areas of Concern. In *DSM-II* passive-aggressive personality is described as "characterized by both passivity and aggressiveness. The aggressiveness may be expressed passively—for example, by obstructionism, pouting, procrastination, intentional inefficiency, or stubbornness. This behavior commonly reflects hostility which the individual feels he dare not express openly. Often the behavior is one expression of the patient's resentment at failing to find gratification in a relationship with an individual or institution upon which he is overdependent" (American Psychiatric Association, 1968, pp. 43-44).

Without question the passive-aggressive personality is one of the most complex and interesting of the personality disorders. The assessment requires an inference of hostility in the face of denial and a definition of aggression on the basis of *absence* of behavior rather than concrete action. Further, the term is applied routinely and indiscriminately in clinical settings to persons who are resistant, difficult, or unaccepting of the clinician's "wisdom." Precise use of the term in assessment is a challenge.

Weinstock (1965) reports that, of some 3,000 private practice cases studied, passive-aggressive personality was the most frequent diagnosis (16 percent). By comparison, the diagnosis of schizophrenia was made in 7 percent of these cases. The next most frequent personality disorder was compulsive personality (not a *DSM-II* term), which was applied in 14 percent of the cases. Gardner (1965) also found passive-aggressive personality to be the most frequently diagnosed personality disorder. In his study of 16,015 cases, the diagnosis was used in 1,569 cases (10 percent). Although Gardner used a separate category for the alcohol addictions (which accounted for an additional 7 percent of the total cases), it is common clinically to view the passive-aggressive personality as most susceptible to alcohol abuse.

The widespread use of the label *passive-aggressive personality* is even more remarkable since it was only coined officially in 1949 (Pasternack, 1974). This is taken to mean that the concept has good fit to clinical observation. In its short life, there has been some evolution. Instead of the single category, Cameron (1963), following *DSM-I* (American Psychiatric Association, 1952, p. 37), distinguishes three types: passive-dependent, passive-aggressive, and aggressive. In the passive-dependent type, the behavior is passive (dependent) and the *hostility* is inferred. In the aggressive type, the behavior is aggressive and appears to be hostile, but the *dependency* must be inferred; that is, the aggression is considered to be reactive and defensive, like adolescent rebellion, rather than being the integrated and goal-directed sort that forms the positive pole of aggressive behavior.

The present *DSM-II* definition of passive-aggressive personality translates almost directly to Cameron's second category. He uses the model of civil disobedience to illustrate the behavior. It is as if the person senses a set of rules on the part of an enemy—rules that the person can use to immobilize the enemy without incurring retaliation. An excellent description of the behavioral pattern can be found in *The Good Soldier Schweik* (Hašek, 1930). By following orders to the letter, Schweik reveals their absurdity and frustrates and infuriates his superiors.

The opportunity to assess passive-aggressive personality usually comes when the strategy is being most successful. That is, those subjected to it are so completely frustrated, so completely defeated, that they are on the brink of losing control and violating their own standards. This reveals the underlying hostility that the passive-aggressive person feels and exposes the essential aggressiveness of his action or inaction. The underlying fear of risking overt hostility may be expressed in panic or depression. It follows that one should investigate enigmatic anxiety states or depression to determine whether failure of a passive-aggressive life-style underlies it.

A particularly difficult form of the passive-aggressive personality is one in which the aggressive actions are expressed by others. Behind-the-scenes incitement, coupled with keeping a low profile in the presence of authority, makes the pattern difficult to detect. Usually the passive-aggressive individual provides an acceptable rationale for not being personally active ("I am handicapped and can't risk my job"). He also implies that he longs to be able to act directly ("If they did that to me, I'd . . ."). The collaboration of others in disguising the incitement adds to the difficulty of detecting it. When there is a threat of being exposed, the resultant anxiety is compounded. Not only is confrontation with authorities imminent but the person also risks exposure of cowardice to peers. Social rejection, humiliation, and abandonment strip the person of an elaborate social support system on which he has become dependent.

What is the prognosis of this disorder? No unequivocally acceptable research has been done on this topic. However, Small and his associates (1970) provide some estimates. Seventy-five of a sample of one hundred patients, who were diagnosed passive-aggressive personality, were followed up seven to fifteen years after hospitalization. Of the group, 15 percent were in psychiatric hospitals, some 30 percent had improved considerably, 29 percent were classified as severely disturbed. Prognosis was worst for patients who showed depression and alcoholism.

Comparative Philosophies and Theories. Systematic formulations of the etiology of passive-aggressive personality remain to be made. Clinical experience holds that "the origin of passive-aggressivity is rooted in childhood development. Raised most often by overly strict and harsh parents who stultify the child's basic trust, his dependency needs are never met. He harbors an intense resentment which he is frightened to express. . . .

Any protest is inhibited. At the same time, the parents reject the child's affections and are basically hostile toward him" (Pasternack, 1974, pp. 63, 68). Pasternack goes on to argue that what the child learns is that negative behavior at least earns attention. Taking the punishment is the price to be paid. It may be added that in time the person learns also to avoid or at least to defer the punishment also. This is accomplished through the deceptive behaviors described above.

Unfortunately, the present formulations lack grounding in any sort of empirical data. When one turns to the major alternative school of thought, behavior theory, the situation is no better. The familiar reinforcement, modeling, and anxiety reduction variables are paraded but still without empirical basis. The assessor is thus left to obtain an accurate history, infer hostility or dependence, and deduce the referred person's long-term behavioral pattern. Determining what caused the behavioral pattern to fail may then provide the best cue to the passive-aggressive personality disorder that is masked by an accurate depression or anxiety state.

Inadequate Personality

General Areas of Concern. According to *DSM-II,* the inadequate personality is "characterized by ineffectual responses to emotional, social, intellectual, and physical demands. While the [person] seems neither physically nor mentally deficient, he does manifest inadaptability, ineptness, poor judgment, social instability, and lack of physical and emotional stamina" (American Psychiatric Association, 1968, p. 44). The assessment of this personality disorder, then, requires two judgments. First, the person must be judged to be capable, by endowment, of normal functioning and free of environmental stress that would incapacitate a normally endowed person. Second, the person must be judged as ineffectual in accomplishing what he or she sets out to do.

How does one distinguish the inadequate personality from three other disorders that also involve apparent ineffectuality—namely, schizoid personality, asthenic personality, and passive-aggressive personality? Clearly, the schizoid personality brings to the social situation an air of detachment and distance, a lack of affective response (for instance, to failure), and an "odd" or "queer" quality. The asthenic personality is characterized by a rationale for task avoidance; there is a felt, vigorously reported lack of strength to become involved, but there is no concrete refusal. The passive-aggressive personality is similarly characterized by participation rather than refusal, but the participation also includes a strategy that will counter movement toward any authority's goal. By contrast, the inadequate personality endorses the goal, makes no complaint of disability, cannot be inferred to be acting on hostile feelings, but nevertheless fails or causes others to fail. In the vernacular, "He does not have an inferiority complex; he *is* inferior."

Personal Views and Recommendations. Gardner's (1965) data indicate that the incidence of inadequate personality is less than 1 percent of the patients seen in psychiatric practice. But if we consider the very real possibility that the major clinical feature—failure to perform—could have a different cause, the incidence may be even lower. For example, poor performance could be due to an anxiety overload that is experienced only under specific, performance-related circumstances. Outside the specific circumstances, the anxiety is not felt by the person and the clinician does not observe it, making it tempting to assign a label that reflects a genetic deficiency formulation, inadequate personality, and to miss the alternate diagnosis. Assessment that includes a "situational test," that is, replicating the actual situation in which inadequacy is reported, is recommended as a way to rule out performance anxiety in an apparent "inadequate personality."

References

Abse, D. W. "Hysterical Conversion and Dissociative Syndromes and the Hysterical Character." In S. Arieti (Ed.), *American Handbook of Psychiatry*. Vol. 3. (2nd ed.) New York: Basic Books, 1974.

American Psychiatric Association. *Diagnostic and Statistical Manual of Mental Disorders.* Washington, D.C.: American Psychiatric Association, 1952.

American Psychiatric Association. *Diagnostic and Statistical Manual of Mental Disorders.* (2nd ed.) Washington, D.C.: American Psychiatric Association, 1968.

Barrett, C. L., and Meyer, R. G. "Personality Disorders." In *Abnormal Psychology: Current Perspectives.* Del Mar, Calif.: CRM Books, 1972.

Cameron, N. *Personality Development and Psychopathology.* Boston: Houghton Mifflin, 1963.

Chrzanowski, G. "Neurasthenia and Hypochondriasis." In S. Arieti (Ed.), *American Handbook of Psychiatry*. Vol. 3. (2nd ed.) New York: Basic Books, 1974.

Frank, J. *Persuasion and Healing.* Baltimore: Johns Hopkins University Press, 1963.

Gardner, E. A. "The Role of the Classification System in Outpatient Psychiatry." In M. M. Katz, J. O. Cole, and W. E. Barton (Eds.), *Classification in Psychiatry and Psychopathology.* Washington, D.C.: U.S. Public Health Service, 1965.

Guze, S. B., Woodruff, R. A., and Clayton, P. J. "Sex, Age, and the Diagnosis of Hysteria." *American Journal of Psychiatry*, 1972, *129*, 747-748.

Hašek, J. *The Good Soldier Schweik.* New York: Doubleday, 1930.

Herbert, M. E., and Jacobson, S. "Late Paraphrenia." *British Journal of Psychiatry*, 1967, *113*, 461-469.

Inouye, E. "Similarity and Dissimilarity of Schizophrenia in Twins." In *Proceedings, Third World Congress of Psychiatry.* Toronto: University of Toronto and McGill Press, 1961.

Kallmann, F. "Genetic Principles in Manic-Depressive Psychosis." In J. Zubin and P. Hock (Eds.), *Depression: Proceedings of the American Psychopathological Association.* New York: Grune & Stratton, 1954.

Kanfer, F. H., and Phillips, J. S. *Learning Foundations of Behavior Therapy.* New York: Wiley, 1970.

Kay, D., and Roth, M. "Environmental and Hereditary Factors in the Schizophrenias of Old Age." *British Journal of Psychiatry*, 1967, *107*, 649-686.

Kretschmer, E. *Physique and Character.* London: Routledge & Kegan Paul, 1936.

Lazare, A. "The Hysterical Character in Psychoanalytic Theory—Evolution and Confusion." *Archives of General Psychiatry*, 1971, *25*, 131-137.

Mednick, S., and Schulsinger, F. "Factors Related to Breakdown in Children at High Risk for Schizophrenia." In M. Roff and D. Ricks (Eds.), *Life History Research in Psychopathology.* Minneapolis: University of Minnesota Press, 1970.

Meyer, A. "An Attempt at Analysis of the Neurotic Constitution." [1903]. In A. Lief (Ed.), *The Common-Sense Psychiatry of Dr. Adolf Meyer.* New York: McGraw-Hill, 1948.

Michaels, J. J. "Character Structure and Character Disorders." In S. Arieti (Ed.), *American Handbook of Psychiatry.* New York: Basic Books, 1959.

Morris, D., Soroker, E., and Burruss, G. "Follow-Up Studies of Shy, Withdrawn Children." *American Journal of Orthopsychiatry*, 1954, *24*, 743-754.

Mowrer, O. H. "What Is Normal Behavior?" In L. A. Pennington and J. A. Berg (Eds.), *An Introduction to Clinical Psychology.* New York: Ronald Press, 1948.

Mowrer, O. H. *Learning Theory and Behavior.* New York: Wiley, 1960.

Noyes, A. P., and Kolb, L. C. *Modern Clinical Psychiatry.* (2nd ed.) Philadelphia: Saunders, 1963.

Pasternack, S. "The Explosive, Anti-Social, and Passive-Aggressive Personalities." In J. R. Lion (Ed.), *Personality Disorders.* Baltimore: Williams and Wilkins, 1974.

Rado, S. "Obsessive Behavior." In S. Arieti (Ed.), *American Handbook of Psychiatry.* Vol. 3. (2nd ed.) New York: Basic Books, 1974.

Salzman, L. "Other Character-Personality Syndromes: Schizoid, Inadequate, Passive-Aggressive, Paranoid, Dependent." In S. Arieti (Ed.), *American Handbook of Psychiatry.* Vol. 3. (2nd ed.) New York: Basic Books, 1974.

Schneider, K. *Clinical Psychopathology.* New York: Grune & Stratton, 1959.

Small, I., and others. "Passive-Aggressive Personality Disorder." *American Journal of Psychiatry,* 1970, *126,* 973-983.

Stearns, A. W. "Unfit Personalities in the Military Services." In J. McV. Hunt (Ed.), *Personality and the Behavior Disorders.* New York: Ronald Press, 1944.

Sullivan, H. S. *Clinical Studies in Psychiatry.* New York: Norton, 1956.

Tupin, J. P. "Hysterical and Cyclothymic Personalities." In J. R. Lion (Ed.), *Personality Disorders.* Baltimore: Williams and Wilkins, 1974.

Ullmann, L. P., and Krasner, L. *A Psychological Approach to Abnormal Behavior.* Englewood Cliffs, N.J.: Prentice-Hall, 1969.

Watt, N. "Childhood and Adolescent Routes to Schizophrenia." In D. Ricks, A. Thomas, and M. Roff (Eds.), *Life History Research in Psychopathology.* Vol. 3. Minneapolis: University of Minnesota Press, 1974.

Weinstock, H. I. "The Role of Classification in Psychoanalytic Practice." In M. M. Katz, J. O. Cole, and W. E. Barton (Eds.), *Classification in Psychiatry and Psychopathology.* Washington, D.C.: U.S. Public Health Service, 1965.

Weintraub, W. "Obsessive and Paranoid Personalities." In J. R. Lion (Ed.), *Personality Disorders.* Baltimore: Williams and Wilkins, 1974.

Winokur, G., and Crowe, R. R. "Personality Disorders." In A. M. Freedman, H. I. Kaplan, and B. J. Sadock (Eds.), *Comprehensive Textbook of Psychiatry.* (2nd ed.) Baltimore: Williams and Wilkins, 1975.

12

The Antisocial Personality

Robert G. Meyer

The antisocial personality is typically a narcissistic, amoral, and impulsive individual who chronically manifests antisocial behavior. This individual also is typically unable to delay gratification, to deal effectively with authority, or to develop deep interpersonal relationships. The pattern is already apparent in adolescence or even early childhood, and the person shows the disorder across a wide performance spectrum, including school, vocational, and interpersonal behaviors. There is a heightened need for environmental stimulation and a lack of response to standard societal control procedures. The chronicity of the pattern is reflected in the individual's inability to profit from experience and is related to the inability to delay gratification.

The antisocial personality should be differentiated from the person whose antisocial behavior is the result of an impulse neurosis. In the impulse neurosis there is often a single focus for the acting-out behavior, as in kleptomania, and many of the factors noted above are not present. In addition, whereas the neurotic manifests intrapersonal anxiety over the violation of some introjected standard, the antisocial personality feels personal distress only when—as a result of his behavior—he is apprehended by the authorities.

Background and Current Status

The term *antisocial personality* reflects an evolution through a number of terms, the most widely known of which has undoubtedly been "psychopathic personality." In about 1800, Philippe Pinel coined the term *manie sans délire* to reflect the fact that these individuals manifest extremely deviant behavior but show no evidence of delusions, hallucinations, or other cognitive disorders (Cleckley, 1964). While Pinel was clearly including psychopathological categories other than the antisocial personality in his descriptions, James Prichard's label of "moral insanity," denoted in 1835, is a clear forerunner of the antisocial personality grouping. The general conceptualization grew in acceptance, and late in the nineteenth century the label *psychopathic inferiority*, introduced by Johann Koch (Cleckley, 1964), became the accepted term. Later variations included "psychopathic character," "psychopathic personality," and "psychopath." Expositions by a number of individuals, particularly by Cleckley (1964), brought the term into common usage.

Despite the foundation for the condition, the 1952 edition of the American Psychiatric Association's *Diagnostic and Statistical Manual of Mental Disorders (DSM-I)* muddied the issue by substituting the term *sociopathic personality* to cover the patterns that had traditionally been subsumed under the psychopath label. "Sociopathic" was used to emphasize the environmental factors allegedly generating the disorder and to de-emphasize the moralistic connotations that had become encrusted on the old terminology. Nevertheless, both concepts remained in lay and professional usages. The confusion was further heightened with the 1968 revision of the *Diagnostic and Statistical Manual (DSM-II)*, which included neither term; instead, the *DSM-II* substituted the label *antisocial personality*. Although this new term carries an inherent implication of specifically criminal behavior, many professionals agree that it is a clear improvement in that it implicitly refers to observable behavioral criteria; that is, to patterns of behavior that conflict chronically with agreed-upon societal norms.

The trend toward objective criteria for the application of the term continues in the latest revision of the *Diagnostic and Statistical Manual (DSM-III)*, and the term *antisocial personality* is also retained. Operational criteria for the term are delineated in *DSM-III* and refer to four areas: (1) evidence of the pattern in preadulthood, (2) problematic vocational or academic performance, (3) manifestations of more than one type of asocial or antisocial behavior, and (4) impaired interpersonal relationships.

In an excellent study, Gray and Hutchinson (1964) sampled a broad spectrum of Canadian psychiatrists and found that 83.7 percent considered the term *psychopathic personality* meaningful. Such a figure is remarkable, considering the notorious ability of mental health professionals to disagree on virtually everything. In another study, Spitzer and his associates (1967) checked for the diagnostic reliability of the standard diagnostic categories. Controlling for differential base rates and different ratios of deviance between the major diagnostic categories, they found the highest level of agreement ($r = .88$) in the respondents' ability to label persons in the category of antisocial personality. Interestingly, the lowest index of agreement ($r = .42$) was found with psychoneurotic reactions. Overall, the studies indicate that, from both the perspectives of reliability and meaningfulness, the category of antisocial personality is a useful one.

Critical Discussion

General Areas of Concern

As in any area of psychopathology, etiology and specificity of diagnosis are important. Many professionals feel that there is reasonable evidence to subdivide the antisocial personality into more discrete categories, which may reflect various etiologies. For example, researchers such as Lyken (1957) believe that the term *primary psychopath* should be reserved for those antisocial personalities that show very little anxiety or avoidance learning and that are particularly refractory to any standard social control. A special type of primary psychopath is the individual who shows a high level of aggression; numerous brain-wave disorders have been noted in the individuals (Hill, 1952). "Secondary psychopaths" are also generally considered antisocial personalities, but they show higher potential for avoidance learning and higher levels of anxiety than do primary psychopaths. Also, secondary psychopaths tend toward introversion, whereas the primary psychopath is extraverted.

Another concern is that the research data available on antisocial personalities are not based on adequate sampling techniques. Two populations are a favorite target of researchers: (1) persons (often college students) who score high on the Psychopathic Deviate (Pd (4)) scale of the Minnesota Multiphasic Personality Inventory (MMPI), and (2) incarcerated criminals. There are problems with both groups. Individuals high on the Pd scale (as psychology graduate students and medical students often are) may be creative, productive individuals who are contributing positively to society even though they do not accept some of the standard social mores. One can attempt a more refined approach by only using high scores on the Pd scale (4) when they are in conjunction with high scores on the Mania (Ma (9)) scale. This pattern often suggests to clinicians that they might be dealing with an antisocial personality. However, the word "might" should be emphasized, since any clinician knows that there are many exceptions to this axiom and makes no such designation without other context data. Researchers need to do likewise, or they must be willing to qualify their results in their discussions.

The use of an incarcerated criminal population is also a questionable practice. First, it assumes that the great majority of antisocial personalities are unsuccessful and are lodged in prisons. There are no data to back up this assumption, and logic would argue otherwise. A more critical error, however, lies in the assumption that the criminal population is largely composed of antisocial personalities. Anyone familiar with prisons is all too aware of the polyglot of individuals in residence. Neurotics and persons with marginal intellectual ability abound, and there are persons who often show no substantial prior pattern of antisocial behavior. Psychotics are not rare, nor are those individuals who are passive followers—willing to participate in any behavior in order to obtain even a glimmer of subgroup acceptance. All prisoners assert their innocence, and the research on jury selection and eyewitness reliability (for example, Gerbrasi, Zuckerman, and Reis, 1977) suggests that not all of them are simply playing a role. For studies to be definitive, more discriminating and exhaustive selection procedures are needed. It is a continual temptation to generalize to the antisocial personality from research on juvenile delinquent populations, but the leap in logic should be obvious.

A related problem is the treatment of antisocial personalities. They rarely present themselves in standard treatment placements, mainly because they seldom perceive themselves as having problems. When they do come into treatment, it is usually when they have been placed in a captive population, but then there are the confounding problems created by coercion and duress factors. Widom (1977) has used an ingenious technique to stimulate antisocial personalities in the community to come in for research purposes. This is at least a "foot in the door" for study or for treatment. Others have paid antisocial personalities to come into a treatment center to talk into a tape recorder, allegedly to provide history data on such a population. Several customers became so enamored of the process that they were willing to continue talking about themselves even after the pay stopped. Yochelson and Samenow (1976) report success with a confrontive type of therapy. They tell the client, usually an incarcerated criminal in their cases, that they know all about their lies and their anger. The effort is to "enhance their self-disgust" and, indirectly, to impress them enough to get them to stay in therapy. Such maneuvers could be construed as beating manipulators at their own game. Nevertheless, these approaches are refreshing attempts to deal with problems in the study and treatment of the antisocial personality.

Comparative Philosophies and Theories

As noted, there is general agreement on the reasonableness of the differentiation between the primary and the secondary psychopath. Since the secondary psychopath does show some "neurotic" characteristics, some theorists prefer to use the term *neurotic psychopath*. However, few are inclined to designate such individuals as primarily neurotic, and no such category in *DSM-II* or *DSM-III* would be an appropriate placement for these individuals. The terms are effective only if viewed as subcategorizations of the antisocial personality.

As in many other areas of psychopathology, there are various conceptualizations about the genesis of the disorder. Heredity, brain dysfunction, individual developmental experiences, and subcultural conformity are all promoted as generic to the antisocial personality, and are often seen as *the* factor by their proponents.

Cesare Lombroso's old theory that one can tell a criminal by certain physical features, such as a low forehead, has been discarded. However, more modern researchers, such as Mednick and Christiansen (1977), have shown that criminal behavior is affected by heredity—thus providing strong, though indirect, support for the belief that the antisocial personality also is affected by heredity. As yet, it is unclear how a hereditary component is mediated into behavior. Low general intellectual ability or specific deficits are possibilities. Brain dysfunction is a second potentially mediating factor between heredity and behavior, and differences in conditionability are a third. At present, however, data to indicate a clear hereditary component are only suggestive, and certainly there has been no clear link to mediating behaviors.

Phrenologists, who charted bumps on the skull to predict behavior, have been replaced by people like Wilder Penfield (Harmatz, 1978), who map the brain itself. However, the precise pinpointing allowed as an adjunct to occasions of required surgery is ethically unavailable to the typical researcher attempting to correlate antisocial behavior and brain dysfunction. Hence, because of ease and accessibility, the electroencephalogram (EEG) is often used. However, most EEG studies have had very mixed results. While this could reflect a lack of any association of brain dysfunction to antisocial behavior, it can just as well be explained by the crudity of the standard EEG as a measure. Improvements in technique (such as in the use of audio and visual evoked brain potentials as well as sophisticated scoring of more precise aspects of the EEG) are promising.

In spite of the problems in EEG measurement, an interesting phenomenon that has shown some replication is the abnormal temporal lobe slow-wave activity found in a greater proportion of antisocial personalities than in other subgroups of the criminal population. On the basis of this and similar research, Hare (1970) theorizes that the dysfunction is in the temporal lobes and limbic system, and these are considered to be central regulators for emotional and motivational behavior. The limbic system is particularly involved in the regulation of fear-motivated behaviors, and lesions in analogous areas in cats significantly lessen their ability to inhibit behaviors.

A related pattern of EEG abnormality, the positive-spike phenomenon, has been

shown to occur in a small subgroup of extremely impulsive and aggressive antisocial personalities in rates as high as 45 percent, while the incidence in the normal population is
only approximately 1 percent. The pattern is marked by positive polarity bursts of 6-8
cps and 14-15 cps activity in the temporal area of the brain.

At this point, it is reasonable to say that significant evidence of brain dysfunction
will be found in only a small proportion of antisocial personalities. Even when brain
dysfunction is detected, one is left with the vexing problem of establishing a causal sequence, an issue that has definite legal ramifications.

Other areas of particular research interest that might one day be linked with brain
dysfunction correlates are those of stimulation-seeking behavior and conditionability.
Quay (1965) theorizes that antisocial personalities almost constantly search for environmental stimulation and have only a minimal tolerance for sameness. This theory would fit
with the observations of lowered basal emotional responsibility in many of these individuals, and it could also be tied to Hare's theory of temporal lobe and limbic system
dysfunction. Quay also emphasizes cognitive aspects, using phrases such as "unable to
tolerate routine and boredom . . . impulsivity and lack of even minimal tolerance for
sameness which appear to be the primary and distinctive features" (p. 180).

Research into conditionability differences between antisocial personalities and
other groups has flourished recently. Over time, however, only one area has shown any
consistent replication: the electrodermal orienting and anticipatory responses, as measured by the galvanic skin response (GSR). From the perspective of the total organism,
theorists do not know what the standard GSR measurement is actually tapping. Consequently, GSR-related findings have not been of great theoretical usage. Alternative
measures of autonomic responsiveness (such as catecholamine output) could be more rewarding. Learning theory approaches to conditionability differences (see, for instance,
Lyken, 1957) also appear promising.

Factors in early childhood development, particularly the relationships with parents, have been studied as etiological factors. While one-to-one correlations between
parenting and antisocial patterns have not been found, two styles of parenting have often
been noted in the background of antisocial personalities. First is the cold and distant
parent, whose offspring are in similar fashion unable to empathize with others or to
understand the complexities of human relationships. The second parental style involves
parents who administer rewards and punishments with such inconsistency that it is impossible for the child to develop a clear role. More important, the child does not learn to
respond to anything more than rather concrete responses, a finding that fits well with
Lyken's (1957) research. In this second pattern, punishment is inconsistent, sporadic, and
ill timed; further, there is often a significant difference between the rules as verbalized
and as actually operationalized in the family. The parents (or surrogates)—and most often
the male—often provide a clear and direct model for such behaviors as aggression, alcoholism, sexual promiscuity, and interpersonal manipulation. Both styles produce individuals almost devoid of basic trust; this quality can, of course, serve as the foundation
for uncommitted interpersonal involvement.

This concept is not unlike the controversial ideas presented by Yochelson and
Samenow (1976). They believe that the antisocial personality is not a product of genetics
or of general environmental variables (such as poverty). Although they eschew comments
on etiology, they seem to be saying that early childhood influences are crucial in
forming entirely different "thinking patterns" in the antisocial individual. Their work has
significant methodological flaws, but their observations and theories warrant consideration.

Elaboration on Critical Points

While studies of the conditionability of physiological variables have not produced results of clarity and consistency, Lyken (1957) originated an interesting line of research, suggesting that a subgroup of antisocial personalities may be different in their conditioning to punishment stimuli. He divided criminal subjects into primary psychopaths, secondary psychopaths, and "normal" criminals and presented them with a "mental maze" consisting of a sequence of twenty choice points. At each point, the subject had a choice of four levers; one of the levers was the correct choice and was denoted as such by a green light. If the green light flashed, the subject moved on to the next array of four. But if the subject pulled a lever other than the correct one, he received a strong electric shock. Learning the sequence of correct levers was the overt task; avoidance of the punishment levers was the latent task. The three groups did not differ on the overt task. But the primary psychopaths were noticeably poorer at learning to avoid the punishing shock than either the neurotic psychopaths or the normal criminals were. Most important, Lyken's findings have been replicated by Schmauk (1970), though continued variations of the replication are in order, since this is a cornerstone study.

Schmauk's variation also produced another finding of interest: primary psychopaths *do* respond like normals when a tangible reinforcer, such as money, is used; but they do not learn the required response if the reinforcer is either electric shock or directions combined with social reprimand. Thus, if one presents punishment to primary psychopaths that is within their value system, they will learn the response. Ability to learn is not the issue; rather, it is a reduced tendency to respond—a finding that dovetails with Quay's (1965) theories.

From a societal perspective, there is a tremendous ethical problem in dealing with the antisocial personality. Even Pinel captured this issue in his concept "manie sans délire." Antisocial personalities show irrational behavior in that they are particularly refractory to experience, but they are not overtly "crazy" or bizarre in thought or action. The question is: Do we hold these individuals legally responsible for their behaviors, or are they "sick"? This becomes problematic when research reveals high correlations of a particular brain dysfunction pattern with a particular disorder, or if there is a high correlation between genetic deviation and a behavior pattern.

The problem is in defining causation. Let us consider the finding that a narrowly defined subset of extremely impulsive and aggressive antisocial personalities show the temporal lobe positive-spike phenomenon in rates as high as 45 percent while it is virtually absent in normals. Reason would suggest that these two different phenomena could be related causally. Yet they could be concomitant manifestations of a related disorder, or they could be caused by incremental cognitive states, or they could be unrelated.

In summary, the antisocial personality presents a murky conflux of four observations and issues: (1) an apparent rationality; (2) an apparent inability to process experience data effectively; (3) some evidence of behavior-determining variables, such as brain dysfunction; and (4) an absence of evidence of mediating variables. For good measure, consideration should be given to the free will/determinism issue and a varying level of political opinion in the populace relative to the "coddling of criminals." In actual practice, the legal system has usually acted under the assumption that the antisocial personality is responsible for all actions. An "irresistible impulse" defense has occasionally been employed successfully but is most often reserved for crimes of impulse or passion committed by otherwise respectable citizens. But the dilemma will persist, and more sophisticated techniques of assessment of brain disorder may isolate subsets of this diagnostic category with clear indicators of brain or genetic dysfunction.

Many practitioners have had little contact with the antisocial personality in their training or, for that matter, with many of the groups engaged in social deviations. Internships and residencies are loaded toward contact with psychotics, neurotics, and outpatient adjustment problems. Contrary to Cleckley's (1964) experience, the antisocial personality is uninterested in standard treatment modalities; hence, this type of person is not usually available for observation in the standard training program. Since most practitioners report that their work experience develops a broader scope than their training experience, they naturally manifest naiveté in first contact with the antisocial personality and the allied disorders. At least a short rotation through a prison or court clinic or even a juvenile detention center could be very helpful in rounding out the training experience.

Personal Views and Recommendations

While *antisocial personality* is clearly a meaningful and clinically useful term, certain subgroups within that designation may group together under various correlates, such as parental backgrounds or brain dysfunction patterns. Yet theorists in this area have been particularly vulnerable to assuming that any detected physiological differences are singularly and totally explanatory of the disorder. Any attempt to find a singular causal variable has inherent and substantial problems. First, mediating variables between the supposed cause and the manifested behavior have not been found, even when a correlation has been detected. Second, given the complexity of the syndrome, it seems highly improbable that any single variable can attain sufficient explanatory power. Such a quest is more often lodged in the researcher's very human need to reduce complexity rather than reflecting the probabilities of this research area.

There are potential linkups in the research findings. The finding of lowered GSR conditionability fits well with Quay's notion that the antisocial personality suffers from a deficiency in organismic arousal and thus manifests a chronically high level of stimulation seeking, and both can be peripherally related to the brain dysfunction literature. This developing concept is easily tied to the research trend initiated by Lyken (1957), and in any of these concepts heredity could play a role—but only as a predisposing factor, and probably not in all cases. Clear significance as a generic factor is possible in certain small subgroups within the overall diagnosis of antisocial personality. Parental inconsistency in affect and behavior, combined with modeling and peer culture influences, does appear to be of crucial importance. As Hare (1970, p. 109) notes, "One of the best predictors of adult psychopathy is having a father who was himself psychopathic, alcoholic, or antisocial."

Application to Particular Variables

DSM-III argues against applying the term *antisocial personality* to any individual prior to the age of 18. This is reasonable on several counts. First and foremost is the problem of getting rid of a label once it has been applied. Since adjustment is in a high state of flux at this age, such caution is important. Second, the individual may be what has been termed a subcultural socialized delinquent; that is, one whose behaviors are almost totally generated by the need for peer or gang acceptance. Such behavior may change radically if peer contacts change. It does seem reasonable to reserve the term for individuals who have shown a clear and chronic pattern of behavior. Yet for clinical purposes, it is worthwhile to note prepsychopathic or antisocial characteristics, which can be manifest rather early. Some professionals would argue that, even under a learning theory model, the pattern is almost irrevocably set early in childhood.

DSM-III states that the antisocial personality is significantly more common in males than in females and tends to occur later in females. Signs are often obvious in the male in early childhood, while in the female they more commonly appear first during puberty. There is every reason to believe that these differences reflect societal roles and expectations rather than any inherent propensities. In fact, concomitant with the rise of women's liberation has been a rise in occurrence of this disorder in females, just as there has been a lowering of the incidence of those disorders centering around passivity.

Considering that these individuals have definite problems adjusting to school, it is not surprising that they show educational achievement deficiencies in comparison to their estimated potential intellectual level. These deficiencies are often severe, and functional illiteracy may be a problem. Subtest variability on the WAIS may be marked, with higher scores obtained on subtests that are not so strongly school related.

Sporadically adequate individuals who are impulsive, antisocial, alcoholic, and/or unable to relate interpersonally would tend to sink to the bottom in any sociobehavioral network. Hence, it is not surprising that antisocial personalities tend toward the lower socioeconomic levels no matter what scale is employed. The ensuing progeny then have the double problem of trying to move out of a lower social class while lacking either an adequate head start or the appropriate behaviors and attitudes. Any racial differences as regards incidence can be explained more parsimoniously in terms of socioeconomic level and/or societal response and restriction.

Certain possible physiological peculiarities of the antisocial personality have already been noted. There has also been speculation that a chromosomal disorder, usually an extra Y chromosome, may be involved in antisocial behavior (Jacobs, Brunton, and Melville, 1965). This was first hypothesized as a causal factor in assaultists, and it was correlated with a specific physical appearance, termed Lincolnesque (it is thought that Lincoln was an XYY). However, follow-up data determined that few of these individuals are actually assaultive; and, conversely, few assaultists actually have the pattern.

There is evidence that aggressive antisocial personalities are more likely to be mesomorphic (the build of the powerful athlete) than would be expected statistically (Harmatz, 1978). This makes sense in that individuals who are slight in stature are less likely to be successful in using aggression to deal with the environment. Hence, such behaviors would tend to drop out of their repertoire, even if they had the initial push of heredity or modeling.

Cleckley (1964), a particularly influencial theorist, asserts that psychopaths are often intellectually superior, and this concept has influenced attitudes toward the antisocial personality. However, Cleckley is clearly in error here; such a characterization fits only the unique subsample that he was dealing with in his clinical practice. As a whole, antisocial personalities show lower than average scores on intelligence tests. This is logical considering their inability to adjust to school, and is especially so if genetic and/or brain dysfunction is involved.

It may be worthwhile to reiterate the interpersonal patterns characteristic of the antisocial personality. There are often signs and protestations toward a variety of interpersonal commitments, but carrying these to fruition is another matter. Like the passive-aggressive personality, the antisocial personality often uses aggression (or the threat thereof) for interpersonal manipulation and, unlike the passive-aggressive person, is likely to actuate the aggression. Behavior patterns are marked by impulsivity and sporadic adequacy. Such individuals are narcissistic and egocentric, show poor judgment, and do not seem to profit from interpersonal experiences. Social deviance in a variety of areas may be noted, but particularly in sexuality, aggression, honesty, and vocational and academic achievement.

References

Cleckley, H. *The Mask of Sanity.* (4th ed.) St. Louis: Mosby, 1964.

Gerbrasi, K., Zuckerman, M., and Reis, H. "Justice Needs a New Blindfold: A Review of Mock Jury Research." *Psychological Bulletin,* 1977, *84,* 323-345.

Gray, H., and Hutchinson, H. C. "The Psychopathic Personality: A Survey of Canadian Psychiatrists' Opinion." *Canadian Psychiatric Association Journal,* 1964, *9,* 450-461.

Hare, R. D. *Psychopathy: Theory and Research.* New York: Wiley, 1970.

Harmatz, M. *Abnormal Psychology.* Englewood Cliffs, N.J.: Prentice-Hall, 1978.

Hill, D. "EEG in Episodic Psychotic and Psychopathic Behavior: A Classification of Data." *EEG and Clinical Neurophysiology,* 1952, *4,* 419-442.

Jacobs, A., Brunton, M., and Melville, M. "Aggressive Behavior, Mental Subnormality, and the XYY Male." *Nature,* 1965, *208,* 1351-1352.

Lyken, D. T. "A Study of Anxiety in the Sociopathic Personality." *Journal of Abnormal and Social Psychology,* 1957, *55,* 6-10.

Mednick, S., and Christiansen, K. *Biological Basis of Criminal Behavior.* New York: Halstead, 1977.

Quay, H. C. "Psychopathic Personality as Pathological Stimulation Seeking." *American Journal of Psychiatry,* 1965, *122,* 180-183.

Schmauk, F. J. "Punishment, Arousal, and Avoidance Learning in Sociopaths." *Journal of Abnormal and Social Psychology,* 1970, *76,* 325-335.

Spitzer, R. L., and others. "Quantification of Agreement in Psychiatric Diagnosis: A New Approach." *Archives of General Psychiatry,* 1967, *17,* 83-87.

Widom, C. S. "A Method for Studying Noninstitutionalized Psychopaths." *Journal of Consulting and Clinical Psychology,* 1977, *45,* 674-683.

Yochelson, S., and Samenow, S. *The Criminal Mind.* New York: Aronson, 1976.

13

Fred D. Strider

Psychosis/
Schizophrenia: Cues

The primary dimension of the psychoses is the presence of severely disabling behavior, reflecting disorganized, impaired personality function. A current psychiatric dictionary (Hinzie and Campbell, 1970) suggests that generally the disorders labeled *psychoses* have in common one or more of five characteristics: (1) The psychoses are considered to be *severe* in their implications for the successful functioning of the individual, since they adversely affect all areas of the person's life. (2) The psychotic person is characterized by *withdrawal from reality*. Effective and rewarding relationships with other people are difficult to establish and maintain. The external objective world has little meaning and impor-

The author was supported in part by NIMH, Psychiatry Education Branch, Grant No. 14941-01. Portions of this chapter follow quite closely the formulations by Lehmann (1975), Millon (1969), and *DSM-III* (American Psychiatric Association, 1977a), which served as basic references for this chapter. The author wishes to express his gratitude to Merrill T. Eaton, Frank J. Menolascino, and William H. Reid for their helpful criticisms and suggestions.

tance or is perceived in a distorted, idiosyncratic manner. (3) The psychotic disorders also have in common a dimension of *emotional impairment* (affectivity). The person's emotional reactions are qualitatively and quantitatively different from the normal. (4) *Intellectual functioning* also is commonly impaired by psychotic processes. Language, thought processes, and judgment are disrupted. Hallucinations, delusions, and disturbed intellectual functions appear as reflections of disorganized thinking and feeling. (5) *Regression* also characterizes many psychotic processes. Not only is the psychotic individual's behavior maladaptive, but the individual may revert to behaviors characteristic of earlier developmental and adaptability levels and, eventually, may return to extremely primitive levels of intellectual and personality functioning.

Currently, the psychoses include the major affective disorders of involutional melancholia, manic-depressive illness, psychotic depressive reactions, the schizophrenias, the paranoid disorders, and the severely disrupted intellectual, emotional, and personality functioning accompanying organic brain syndromes and episodes of toxicity and intoxication.

Background and Current Status

Mental disorder was generally viewed by primitive man and early civilization as the effect of demoniac possession, usually as punishment for transgressions of religious teachings. Treatment in such civilizations involved exorcism and such painful and punitive techniques as starvation, flogging, and surgery. The demoniac explanation of mental illness persisted until the fifth century B.C., when Hippocrates proclaimed that the causes of disorders are within the patient and are not the result of actions by demons, gods, or spirits. Hippocrates' teachings advanced the practice of medicine by proposing biological causation and naturalistic treatment of diseases and by establishing the case history as a means of studying disease. He held that disorders are caused by imbalances of four basic body humors (blood, phlegm, yellow bile, and black bile), which can be readjusted by therapeutic practices such as diet, exercise, and bloodletting. The Greek physician Asclepiades, who lived a century before the birth of Christ, stressed the importance of naturalistic diagnosis, humane treatment, and environmental factors in disorders. He was the first to distinguish hallucinations from illusions and delusions and acute from chronic disease states. Also during this time, the Roman writer Celsus reorganized Hippocratic concepts into groups of disease states and proposed that mental disorders influence the entire functioning of the individual and are not the result of malfunction of a single organ alone. The Hippocratic theories of disease and treatment were abandoned after the fall of the Roman Empire; and during the Dark Ages the ideas of demonology, witchcraft, superstition, and demon possession were revived as explanations of disease and mental disorder.

In the Renaissance, the renewed interest in the classics was reflected in the revival of the Greek and Roman system of classification (based on the observations of Hippocrates), which divided mental disorders into five classes: (1) *phrenitis* (an acute disorder with fever), (2) *mania* (an acute disturbance without fever), (3) *melancholia* (a term used to designate any chronic disorder), (4) *hysteria* (a disorder of women characterized by agitation, pain and convulsions), and (5) *epilepsy* (a disorder characterized by recurrent convulsions). Two Renaissance physicians in Switzerland added to this classification system. Paracelsus added *vesania* (disorders caused by poisons), *lunacy* (a periodic disorder influenced by the phases of the moon), and *insanity* (diseases caused by heredity). Felix Platter (1536-1614) developed a four-category system, based entirely on the belief that careful and detailed observation of symptoms would reveal underlying disease entities. This system divided mental disorders into (1) disturbances of consciousness; (2) disturbances characterized by violence, despondency, delerium, or confusion; (3) mental exhaustion and mental deficiency; and (4) dementia.

The Dutch physician Johann Weyer (1515-1588), the first to use the term *psychosis* in its modern context, was the first physician to specialize in mental disorders and the first to successfully challenge the ideas of demonology. His advocacy of naturalistic explanations of mental illness and his insistence on humane medical treatment mark the beginning of the development of modern attitudes in the cause and treatment of mental disorders.

The success of humane methods of treating mental disorders was convincingly demonstrated by Philippe Pinel (1745-1826). His views that the mentally ill were uncooperative and unresponsive because they were deprived of liberty and fresh air led to the removal of chains and restraints, the provision of a pleasant environment, access to the outdoors, and a therapeutic atmosphere of kindness and sympathy. The role of hospital personnel was expanded from custodial functions. His methods were continued by his student Jean Esquirol (1772-1840), who published the first modern work on mental disorders in 1838.

The reforms of Pinel slowly pervaded Western approaches to the mentally ill. In America, Dorothea Lynde Dix in 1841 launched a reform movement against mistreatment of mental patients and crusaded for public responsibility for the mentally ill. The publication of Clifford Beer's book *A Mind That Found Itself* in 1908 brought to the attention of the public the mistreatment prevalent in the huge mental asylums throughout the country. Beer founded the Society for Mental Hygiene, which launched the mental health movement to foster the development and advancement of community and preventive psychiatry and to assist in removing the prejudice and disgrace that had been associated with mental disorders for centuries.

Progress in the natural and biological sciences strengthened the nosological approach in medicine. Wilhelm Griesinger's *Mental Pathology and Therapeutics*, when published in Europe in 1845, stressed the disease concept and inaugurated the search for brain pathology underlying mental illness. Benedict-Augustin Morel in 1856 proposed a disorder termed *dementia praecox* (precocious or rapid deterioration), which was diagnosed on the basis of age of onset and the course of the illness. Karl Ludwig Kahlbaum (1818-1899) extended this orientation in his classification system, based on the course and outcome of disorders. He contributed the terms *hebephrenia* and *catatonia*, still currently in use to describe variants of schizophrenia.

Emil Kraepelin (1856-1926) designed a nosological system that combined the somatic disease concepts of Griesinger with the longitudinal approaches of Kahlbaum. In 1899 he described two disorders that are still reflected in modern diagnostic manuals: *manic-depressive psychoses* and *dementia praecox*.

In the United States Adolf Meyer (1866-1950), although endorsing Kraepelin's system of diagnosis, believed that the mental disorders are not disease entities but psychobiological reactions to environmental stress. He considered schizophrenia to be the natural result of physical, social, and psychological factors in the life history of the individual. In his work one finds the beginnings of the psychobiological school of psychiatry and a combination of the physiological orientation of the nineteenth century and the psychodynamic orientation of the twentieth.

In 1911 Eugen Bleuler (1857-1939) introduced a new term, *schizophrenia*, to replace *dementia praecox*. The new term (meaning "split mindedness") was selected to reflect Bleuler's conviction that a splitting of the personality was the major feature of the disease. Bleuler's major contribution to the understanding of the psychotic disorders now termed schizophrenia was the replacement of Kraepelin's list of descriptive clinical characteristics with a hierarchy of symptoms which, to the present time, are considered to be central features of the disorder. Bleuler included as primary symptoms disturbances of *affect* and *association, ambivalence,* and *autism*; as secondary symptoms, delusions, hallucinations, negativism, and stupor.

Sigmund Freud, in the 1930s, believed that psychotic persons cannot form a transference relationship with the psychoanalyst and did not recommend the use of psychoanalysis with psychotic patients. In later years Carl Jung was to provide techniques for psychological understanding of psychotic symptoms. Other neo-Freudian analysts, Harry Stack Sullivan and Frieda Fromm-Reichman, adopted psychoanalytic techniques to treat psychotic individuals. In 1939 Gabriel Langfeldt proposed the useful concept of schizophreniform psychosis and distinguished between *reactive* and *process* schizophrenias. In the former, the schizophrenic symptoms are precipitated by stressful events in the life of an individual who was previously successful in meeting the challenges and responsibilities of living. The *process* schizophrenic symptoms appear without any identifiable sources of stress in the person's life and seem to be related to heredity and physiological or constitutional factors.

In 1942 Carl Schneider proposed that schizophrenia does not represent one single disorder but is the end product of the fragmentation of three basic processes, which are integrated in the normal individual: (1) an undisturbed feeling of identity, (2) continuity of psychic processes, and (3) contact with reality. Pathological impairment and breakdown of these processes results in three complexes of symptoms: (1) *thought withdrawal* (associated with symptoms such as thought stopping, thought hearing, and experiences of being controlled), (2) *derailment* (associated with symptoms such as despair, hallucinations, and lack of affect), and (3) *Faseln* (associated with delusions, looseness of association, and ego-alien impulses). In the analysis of these complexes, the underlying causes of schizophrenia may be revealed (Schneider, 1942).

To date, the newest revision of the *Diagnostic and Statistical Manual of Mental Disorders (DSM III)* (American Psychiatric Association, 1977a) has been prepared in draft form. This revision recommends that operational criteria be used as a basis for diagnostic determinations. Specific clinical phenomena that must be present are provided for each diagnostic entity. Disorders of psychotic proportions and characteristics are included in those sections dealing with organic mental disorders (which include disorders associated both with brain dysfunction and drug use), schizophrenic disorders, paranoid disorders, affective disorders, and listings for brief reactive psychosis and atypical psychosis.

The task force that prepared *DSM-III* has added new diagnostic categories, formulated operational criteria for each diagnosis, and adopted a "multiaxial" orientation to replace the "multicategory" approach of *DSM-II*. The multiaxial classification scheme is advocated because it allows for multiple categories to be coded on any one patient and introduces rules to follow in coding data on individual cases. This approach permits the diagnosis to include separate and independent characteristics for both clinical and research purposes.

In its "Guiding Principles," the task force acknowledges the concern among other professional groups that psychiatry has inappropriately assumed that the conditions described in its official nosology represent independent disease entities (the medical model). The decision was made to retain this medical model orientation to disorders as a "worthy hypothesis" that assumes the existence of organismic dysfunctions with relatively distinct clinical features, etiology, and course without assuming either single causative factors underlying each disorder or the primacy of biological, social, or environmental factors in all cases. The categorical approach, which describes the disorders as separate entities, connoting (if not denoting) entity status, was retained because it has practical advantages for communication, treatment, and research. In grouping the disorders into classes, the task force based its decisions on known necessary organic etiology, shared phenomenological characteristics, and commonly known or presumed necessary psychosocial etiological factors. These considerations represent the goals for nosological improvement targeted by the task force.

The *DSM-III* draft has recently been made available for additional field trials and to the public. Evaluative articles discussing issues in the theoretical and conceptual factors underlying *DSM-III* are now beginning to appear (see, for instance, Schacht and Nathan, 1977). It is premature to judge the effectiveness of *DSM-III* in actual practice before its implementation and without the advantage of empirical investigation. At the current state of knowledge, however, not all psychotic psychopathological conditions can be attributed to biological and physical impairments, although certain types (as for a most obvious example, the organic brain syndromes) can be so assigned. Even strong adherents of the medical model acknowledge that the manifestations of many of these disorders are, to a considerable extent, determined by the experiences of the individual and often by social, cultural, and environmental factors.

Critical Discussion

General Areas of Concern

The problems of specifying and delineating the kinds of behavior to be considered psychotic in nature and degree are long standing and complex. This section provides a synopsis of *DSM-III* formulations and a summary of the major clinical manifestations of the psychotic disorders.

Schizophrenia. According to *DSM-III*, the schizophrenic disorders are characterized by "a disorganization of a previous level of functioning which involves multiple aspects of psychological functioning" (American Psychiatric Association, 1977a, p. C:1) without organic brain disease. The schizophrenic illness always involves either delusions, hallucinations, or formal thought disorder. No single clinical behavioral manifestation is considered to be present in all forms of this disorder. Following is a list of psychological disturbances characteristic of the disorders considered to be schizophrenic in nature.

1. *Form of thought.* Disturbances in the form of thought have a variety of manifestations. Looseness of associations—in which the patient's verbal statements or ideas lack a coherent, logical, relevant relationship from one idea to the next—may occur. Poverty of ideas (vague or rambling speech) may be observed, or thinking may be illogical. Incoherence, use of neologisms (words of the patient's own making), perseveration (repetition of words or phrases), and blocking are other manifestations of thought disorder.
2. *Content of thought.* Content of thought may be impaired by characteristic delusions: that one is being persecuted; that unrelated events have special significance (ideas of reference); that one's thoughts are broadcast from one's head and that others can hear them; that others' thoughts are being inserted into one's mind or that one's thoughts are being removed; and that one's own feelings, impulses, and thoughts are not one's own.

3. *Perception.* Perception may be impaired by hallucinations, most commonly auditory in nature, in which voices heard from outside the head comment on the patient's ongoing behavior. Hallucinations of bodily sensations, particularly involving the genital areas of the body, are also common.

4. *Affect.* Emotional expressions are most commonly impaired by flattening of affect (in which the patient appears emotionally unresponsive, detached, alien, and remote) or by inappropriateness of affect (in which the individual's emotional expressions are incongruent with the content of speech or the nature of the social situation).

5. *Sense of self.* Frequently the schizophrenic individual experiences disturbances in, or loss of, the feeling of individuality, uniqueness, and self-direction.

6. *Volition.* Schizophrenic persons frequently have great difficulty in initiating and sustaining goal-directed activity as a result of inadequate interest, low drive levels, and ambivalence.

7. *Relationship to the external world.* Self-imposed isolation from the everyday world and sequestration are manifestations of schizophrenic processes. Schizophrenic patients frequently prefer to be isolated and left alone, being preoccupied with their own thoughts, beliefs, and fantasies, which may become extremely illogical and idiosyncratic. Sometimes the individual feels overwhelmed by the everyday world, which is perceived as threatening, frightening, or intractably complex.

8. *Motor behavior.* Motor behavior is disturbed during acute schizophrenic episodes and in severe and chronic conditions. Typical forms of disturbance include decrease in awareness of and reactivity to the environment and reduction of spontaneous movement and activity (catatonia). In catatonic rigidity, the individual adopts and maintains a rigid posture. In catatonic excitement, purposeless, excited, stereotyped behavior occurs without environmental influence. Other disturbances may include bizarre posturing, grimacing, and a peculiar condition (waxy flexibility) in which the patient's limbs may be placed in any position and remain there indefinitely.

Individuals who demonstrate operational criteria for a schizophrenic disorder may be further subcategorized into the following phenomenological subtypes of schizophrenia: *disorganized* (hebephrenic); *catatonic; paranoid; schizoaffective, depressed; schizoaffective, manic; undifferentiated;* and *residual.*

The essential feature of the *disorganized* subtype is incoherence and flat, incongruous, or silly affect. Unsystematized delusions or hallucinations are commonly associated features. Mannerisms, social withdrawal, and hypochondriachal complaints may also be present. Social impairment is usually extreme, and prognosis for improvement is poor. The disorder is characterized by poor premorbid adjustment, an early and insidious onset, deterioration, and a chronic progression of the disorder without significant improvement or remission.

In addition to the basic aspects of schizophrenia, the *catatonic* individual manifests psychomotor disturbance (stupor, rigidity, excitement, or posturing). The patient may demonstrate unpredictable alternating phases of stupor and excitement. Mannerisms, negativism, stereotyped behavior, and waxy flexibility are included in *DSM-III* as associated symptoms. Mutism is common. The catatonic schizophrenic disorder may be manifested in two different courses: (1) the patient may manifest the symptoms abruptly and subsequently experience remission and recurrences of the disorder; or (2) the patient may remain chronically disabled without remission.

The *paranoid* is characterized by the presence of, or preoccupation with, delusions of persecution or of grandeur or by hallucinations with such content. Delusions of jealousy may also be present. Frequently associated features include extreme (occasionally violent) anger, argumentativeness, fearfulness, delusions of reference, and preoccupation with difficulties about sexual identity, object choice, functioning, and autonomy. Formal thought disorder is often absent or may be mild in nature. The intellectual, emotional, and social functioning of the individual may remain unaffected, except perhaps in those areas associated with the delusional beliefs. If the delusions are acted on, emotional responsiveness may also remain unimpaired. More commonly, however, the individual's social behavior is affected by attitudes related to the paranoid delusions. Interpersonal interactions have a stilted, formal, or extremely intense quality.

The *schizoaffective, depressed* individual displays a mixture of depressive and schizophrenic symptoms. The *schizoaffective, manic* has both manic and schizophrenic symptoms. The *undifferentiated* individual manifests psychotic symptoms of delusions, hallucinations, formal thought disorder, or bizarre behaviors, but either does not demonstrate the symptoms of the other subtypes or demonstrates the symptoms of more than one subtype.

The *residual* subtype is used to characterize an individual who has experienced a schizophrenic episode and in recovery does not demonstrate prominent psychotic symptoms but remains impaired by limitations related to the disorder. During the schizophrenic episode, delusions or hallucinations may be present, but they are usually devoid of the emotional qualities typically associated with them. In remission, the individual may be eccentric, withdrawn, and/or emotionally unresponsive or may show some mild forms of schizophrenia.

DSM-III further specifies that these disorders be characterized in terms of the course of the illness to date in the person's life. The *acute* designation is used to indicate a sudden onset of the disorder (the appearance of schizophrenic symptoms within three months from the first signs of increasing psychopathology), a short course of the disorder (less than three months), and full recovery from previous episodes of the disorder. The *subacute* designation is recommended when the course of the disorder is closer to acute than chronic. A designation of *subchronic* is recommended for instances in which symptoms persist for longer than three months. The *chronic* designation reflects instances in which significant signs of the disorder are present, more or less continuously, for at least two years of the patient's life. The designation *in remission* is used when the individual's behavior met the full criteria for a schizophrenic disorder in the past but now shows no signs of the disorder.

Paranoid Disorders. The paranoid disorders include *paranoia, shared paranoid disorder,* and *paranoid state* and are characterized by persistent persecutory delusions or delusions of jealousy in the absence of symptoms suggestive of schizophrenia, organic brain dysfunction, manic disorder, or depressive disorder. In many ways, these disorders share similar features with the disorders of paranoid schizophrenia and the paranoid form of personality disorder. Persecutory delusions may be either simple or elaborate. Commonly, the delusions have a single theme or a series of associated themes. Examples include the conviction that one is the object of conspiracy, spying, or malicious gossip or that one is being followed, drugged, or poisoned. The delusion may have slight basis in fact but has been extrapolated far out of proportion. Persecutory themes are seldom present in delusions of jealousy. Rather, on the basis of little or no evidence, the individual concludes that his or her mate is unfaithful. The associated features of the paranoid disorders develop from the individual's actions related to the delusional beliefs. Expressions, occasionally violent, of anger and resentment and ideas or delusions of reference are common. Self-imposed isolation, seclusiveness, eccentric behavior, and suspiciousness are also prevalent. Injustice collecting and related letter writing and litigiousness are common characteristics.

The disorder designated *paranoia* is characterized by the insidious development of a chronic, unshakable paranoid delusional system and changes in interpersonal relationships, emotional reactions, and behavior consistent with that system. The patient's thinking ordinarily remains clear, orderly, and intact. The *shared paranoid disorder (folie à deux)* is developed on the basis of a close relationship (ordinarily familial) with another psychotically paranoid person. The paranoid delusion comes to be partly or completely shared by the two individuals. If the person can be separated from the originally paranoid individual, the delusional beliefs ordinarily diminish or disappear. The *paranoid state* is a residual category used to describe acute paranoid reactions that are most commonly associated with changes in work or living situations and that do not manifest the criteria for either *paranoia* or *shared paranoid disorder*. The *paranoid state*, as defined herein, represents a paranoid disorder appearing at a time of considerable psychological stress associated with changes in life situations. Paranoid disorders that do not fall into the above categories are designated as *unspecified paranoid disorders*.

Affective Disorders. The affective disorders are characterized by a primary disturbance of mood—prolonged emotions that permeate the entire functioning of the individual and usually involve either elation or depression. These disorders are grouped into several categories, including: (1) *episodic affective disorders*, sustained disturbances that appear from time to time and are clearly distinguishable from previous levels of functioning; and (2) *intermittent affective disorders*, chronic disorders, usually without clearly definable onsets, which may or may not reach psychotic proportions and in which there are recurrent periods of depressed mood and associated depressive symptoms (ranging from a few hours to several days) between periods of normal emotional functioning (ranging from days to weeks).

The *intermittent affective disorder* diagnosis replaces previous diagnostic classifications of *depressive, hypomanic,* or *cyclothymic personality.* The *episodic affective disorders* include *depressive disorder, manic disorder,* and *bipolar affective disorder.* These disorders tend to be recurring ones, although the individual usually returns to previous levels of psychological functioning and does not show deterioration or impairment of abilities and psychological functions between episodes. (*Involutional melancholia*, which was previously a separate diagnostic classification, is now included in the *DSM-III* classification *depressive disorder.*)

The *depressive disorder* is characterized by a prominent, persistent period of depressive mood or by a pervasive loss of interest in pleasure or in the capacity to experience pleasure. Other symptoms of depression—such as sleep disturbance, appetite disturbance, changes in body weight, psychomotor agitation or retardation, diminished ability to think or concentrate, decreased energy, feelings of self-reproach or guilt, feelings of anxiety, and thoughts of death or suicide—may also be present. In addition, the individual may display a sad or forlorn appearance, tearfulness, irritability, fearfulness or brooding, concern with physical health, or symptoms of panic attacks or phobias. Paranoid symptoms ranging from suspiciousness to delusional ideas may also appear. In psychotic depressive episodes, paranoid and/or depressive delusions may be present. Such patients may believe that they are being persecuted for sinfulness or that they are destitute and impoverished. They may have nihilistic delusions of world or personal destruction or hypochondriacal delusions of severe illness. Transient hallucinations have been known to occur in psychotically depressed individuals. The episode of depressive disorder is considered to be psychotic in severity when delusions or hallucinations are part of the patient's symptoms.

The *manic disorder* is characterized by a distinct period of time when the individual's demonstrated mood is either elevated, expansive, or irritable and when other symptoms of the manic syndrome (such as hyperactivity, excessive involvement in activities without consideration of possible or probable painful consequences, pressure of speech, flight of ideas, inflated self-esteem, decreased need for sleep and rest, and distractability) are present. Manic individuals may be either expansive and euphoric or irritable and angry. The classic symptoms include elation, hyperactivity, exuberant and unflagging sociability, expansiveness, grandiosity, lack of judgment, and disorganized, flamboyant, bizarre behavior. Speech is loud, rapid, and difficult to interpret. Ideas vary abruptly from topic to topic based on distracting stimuli and associations—the classic manic symptom termed "flight of ideas." Inflated self-esteem may range from uncritical self-confidence to delusions of grandeur. Manic individuals have been known to go without sleep for extended periods in heightened states of arousal. In some individuals, manic states are intermingled with depressive symptoms. Hallucinations related to the patient's mood may also occur. Impairment may range from mild to severe and may be considered to have reached psychotic levels with the appearance of delusions or hallucinations; at this level the individual requires protection from the consequences of his or her actions and, in some instances, to prevent death from physical exhaustion.

Both manic and depressive disorders may appear as single or recurrent episodes of impairment or as alternating episodes of mania and depression. These *bipolar affective disorders* are characterized by one or more manic and one or more depressive episodes or by one episode of illness that combines both features.

Brief Reactive Psychosis and Atypical Psychosis. The term *brief reactive psychosis* is used to designate psychotic reactions that follow severe environmental stress and typically last from several hours to several weeks. The psychotic behaviors are variable, but most show some relationship to the precipitating events. The category *atypical psychosis* is used to designate psychotic reactions that do not meet the criteria for organic delusional syndromes or the schizophrenic, paranoid, affective, or brief reactive psychotic disorders.

Psychoses Associated with Organic Brain Syndromes. Psychotic behavior may be manifested as a consequence of or in conjunction with impairment of brain function. Six organic brain syndromes are included in the *DSM-III* category of organic mental disorders and represent groupings of symptoms that reflect localization, rate of onset, progression, and duration of underlying brain pathology. *DSM-III* does not divide the organic mental disorders into psychotic and nonpsychotic and acute and chronic (irreversible) forms. Disorders relatively similar to the concept of organic psychotic disorders in the new classification are *delirium, dementia, amnestic syndrome, hallucinosis,* and the *organic delusional syndrome.*

Delirium is characterized by the rapid appearance of disorganization of higher mental functions related to a widespread disturbance of brain metabolism. The essential abnormality in psychological functioning is impairment of information processing. The delirious individual has difficulty maintaining, focusing, and shifting attention. Thinking processes may be accelerated and disorganized or slowed and impoverished. Abstract concept formation and reasoning are severely impaired, as is perceptual discrimination. The individual may have difficulty in distinguishing between dreams, perceptions, illusions, and hallucinations and may develop delusions based on these inaccurate perceptions. Memory is usually impaired during the delirious period as a result of defective information processing. Cognitive disturbances fluctuate unpredictably, and the individual may show periods of unimpaired intellectual activity—commonly termed "lucid intervals." Psychomotor behavior may also be impaired, with hyperactivity, hypoactivity, or alterations between the two. Sleep disturbances, nightmares, vivid dreams, and an inability to differentiate between dream states and reality are common, as are unpredictable emotional reactions. Severely impaired individuals may require close management to ensure that basic physical needs are met and to protect the individual from harmful actions directed against self or others. The duration of delirium is usually brief, depending on the influence of the causal agent affecting brain metabolism. When such influence continues, the individual may develop dementia.

Dementia is characterized by decrement in intellectual functioning and is reserved for those instances in which impairment occurs after full maturation of the brain. Common characteristics of dementia include impairments in memory, problem solving, judgment, and the ability to learn new skills. Forgetfulness or difficulty in dealing with novel situations, particularly under the pressure of time, are common initial symptoms. The individual may attempt to avoid such tasks and reacts with anxiety, anger, and irritability when such avoidance is not possible. Personality changes—usually accentuations or modifications of premorbid personality characteristics—are common. Emotional lability, impulsiveness, and loss of emotional and impulse control may result in socially maladaptive behavior. The impairment of intellectual, occupational, and social skills is invariably perceived by the individual. Anxiety, depression, and the intensified use of defense strategies to manage such feelings result in emotional and behavioral changes. In instances where dementia is progressive, the individual may become apathetic (although episodes of irritability and anger may appear at times). Disinhibition of emotions and impulses may result in boorish and inappropriate social conduct, unusual sexual behavior, legal difficulties, and deterioration in personal habits, appearance, and hygiene. Dementia increases the vulnerability of the individual to all stressors. Life changes become especially difficult to cope with successfully. The disorder may appear suddenly or may have a gradual onset, depending on the underlying brain pathology. The course of the syndrome is highly variable and may be progressive, static, or, in a few instances, reversible.

The *amnestic syndrome* appears to result from impairment of the ability to consolidate recent information into permanent memory stores, so that the individual is unable to remember events for longer than several minutes after their occurrence. Although the individual may be able to demonstrate intact immediate memory skills, loss of memories of the recent past is common. The amnestic syndrome may appear in otherwise intellectually normal individuals but may be accompanied by other disturbances in time orientation, perception, and concept formation. The individual may also lose initiative, be emotionally bland, and attempt to fill in the memory gaps with confabulations. The syndrome may have a sudden onset or be gradual in development and, depending on the underlying brain pathology, may or may not be partially or fully reversible. Impairment may vary from slight to total incapacitation. Causal factors include encephalitis, bilateral temporal ischemia, head injury, carbon monoxide poisoning, and brain hypoxia.

Hallucinosis is characterized by recurring or persistent hallucinations, which occur during a state of full wakefulness, while the person is alert and oriented to time, place, and person. The individual may or may not be aware that the hallucinations are not real. Specific organic etiological factors are most likely to produce hallucinations in a specific sensory modality and to involve distortion of environmental stimuli. The most common causal factors in hallucinosis are alcoholism, hallucinogens, sensory deprivation, deafness, blindness, brain tumors, epilepsy, and toxic and infectious disorders.

The *organic delusional syndrome* is reserved for those disorders in which delusions are the predominating symptoms of underlying brain pathology, including head injury, brain tumors, and drug misuse. These delusions may vary from simple, poorly formed paranoid delusions to highly organized delusional states similar to the paranoid schizo-phrenic syndrome. Mild intellectual impairment and thought disorders may be associated symptoms. Eccentricities of grooming and appearance, ritualistic and stereotyped be-havior, abnormal motor activity, and depressive mood are associated factors. Impairment and course of the disorder vary, depending on the underlying etiological factors.

Comparative Philosophies and Theories

Currently, theoretical explanations of the psychotic disorders fall into six general (and not always considered mutually exclusive) categories: (1) physical and biological; (2) psychodynamic, intrapsychic, and social-interactional; (3) phenomenological and existen-tial; (4) behavioral; (5) sociological; and (6) descriptive-classification models (Lehmann, 1975; Millon, 1969).

The physical and biological models assume that anatomical, biological, neurologi-cal, physiological, and/or biochemical factors are the primary determinants of psychotic disorders. Research using these models has sought to investigate and compare natural bio-logical variability in humans and to correlate such variability with the variants of behavior deemed psychotic. In studies of heredity, body structure, physical maturation, and neuro-anatomical and biochemical variability and abnormality, researchers have sought to iden-tify common patterns of biological defect and disorder in psychotic reactions. An impres-sive amount of recent data has accumulated over the years linking hereditary factors to schizophrenia and manic-depressive disorders. Kallmann (1953), for example, has sug-gested that genetic factors may predispose individuals to schizophrenia and manic-depres-sive disorders. Other research has sought to relate psychotic disorders to diseases of the individual (especially important in the organic brain syndromes), nutritional deficiencies, drugs, and complications of pregnancy and birth.

Kretschmer (1925) and Sheldon (1954) attempted to relate psychopathological conditions to morphological or physical variations in human body structure. The ecto-morphic or asthenic body type has been correlated with schizophrenia and schizoid dis-orders; the endomorphic or pyknic body type, with manic-depressive disorders; and the mesomorphic body type, with antisocial and paranoid disorders. These research efforts have been the object of severe criticism. At the present time, constitutional factors are not easily divorced from psychogenic and environmental influences, and it seems appro-priate to conclude that both may operate to produce psychopathological conditions (but in an interactive and complicated way that has yet to be explicated).

Attempts to relate psychotic conditions to neurological impairments are, of course, most clearly developed in the organic brain syndrome. Postulates that relate schizophrenic conditions to neurological defects are at this time equivocal. The best-known work in this area stems from the work of Rosenthal (1968). He concluded that there are two distinct types of schizophrenic syndromes: *process schizophrenia*, caused by a neurological defect; and *reactive schizophrenia*, resulting from environmental and experiential factors. Rosenthal's work has led to a substantial amount of research effort and has made an important contribution both to the understanding of the schizophrenic syndrome and to clinical practice. At this time, however, specific neurological defects underlying the process schizophrenia syndromes have yet to be delineated and estab-lished.

Over the last two decades, pharmacological and biochemical investigators have yielded an impressive data base of findings related to schizophrenia. Even with the accu-mulation of such a large data base, the exact relationship between certain pharma-cological agents and the symptoms of schizophrenia is still clouded. Two general or global hypotheses have been forwarded: (1) that schizophrenia results from a dysfunction in one or more of the cerebral dopaminergic systems and (2) that the symptoms of schizophrenia arise from an abnormal, endogenous-produced accumulation of a psychotogen, such as a methylated amine—particularly the methylated indoleamines and the methoxylated phenylethylamines.

Similarly, a biological basis has not been firmly established for the affective disorders, and the mechanisms by which efficacious drugs reduce or eliminate the symptoms of the affective disorder have not been clearly delineated. Two primary hypotheses have been evoked to explain affective disorders. The first hypothesis suggests that affective disorders arise from functional changes in the nonadrenergic system. The second hypothesis relates the primary deficit to a deficit in the central serotonergic system. One variation in these hypotheses, which may eventually be more applicable although more complex, is the relative or balance hypothesis; this hypothesis postulates a disturbance in the relative relationship between two or more of these neurotransmitter systems.

The biogenic amine hypotheses (whether directed at affective disorders or at schizophrenia) are not yet to be considered as theories. These hypotheses have been, are, and will be useful in the future if the biological understanding of the disorders is to become a reality.

One problem with the hypotheses thus forwarded is that they may be too simplistic, since they are predicated only on aberrant neurotransmitter systems, on abnormal metabolites, or on reduced or increased levels of one or more neurotransmitters (small molecules that convey information between neurons). For the most part, these hypotheses do not take into account substances referred to as neuromodulators (substances that increase or decrease neuronal activity). Although the concept of neuromodulators is not new, it is gaining in importance as an explanation for deficits in the hypotheses presently forwarded. One such group of substances, the *endorphins* (endogenous morphine-like compounds), may be neuroregulators in the brain with regard to opnoid tolerance and dependence, analgesia, and various abnormal behavioral states such as the schizophrenic. Although it is too early to characterize the recently discovered enkephalins as neurotransmitters or neuromodulators, these pentapeptides may similarly be of importance in neuroregulation of pain, analgesia, and certain types of mental illness.

The integration of the prevailing hypotheses and present concepts may permit, in the not too distant future, an encompassing biochemical theory or theories for specific mental illnesses (Copenhaver, 1978).

Psychodynamic, intrapsychic, and social-interactional models feature motivational factors in the individual and factors influencing the nature and quality of interpersonal relationships. In these models, which are variations of the medical disease model, psychological conflict and trauma are viewed as the underlying basic "disease"; this "disease," in turn, gives rise to individual and defensive reactions (unconscious defense mechanisms) that ameliorate the experience of anxiety. These mechanisms, however, involve denial and distortion of awareness, and/or reality, and, although successful in decreasing the experience of anxiety, may lead to maladaptive behavior.

Psychodynamic theories have been most successful in promoting understanding and treatment of neurotic disorders; they have not contributed substantially to an understanding of psychotic reactions. In the classical Freudian view, schizophrenia represents a primary disturbance of the individual's ability to form object relations. This disturbance precludes psychotherapy because the patient is unable to form a transference relationship with the analyst. The psychotic behavior (viewed as representing the effects of defense mechanisms erected to control high levels of anxiety related to traumatic experiences in early childhood) is regarded as the result of essentially the same process seen in neurotic behavior.

Klein (1950), a psychoanalyst, has proposed that certain of the psychotic disorders represent final stages of regression; that is, a return to positions common to those developmental stages that determine the individual's basic perception of the world. In this way, in addition to the primary impairment in object relations, the theory seeks to show that the underlying orientations of individuals to self and others produce the differing symptoms of schizophrenia, depression, and paranoia. At the same time, theoretical explanations emphasizing or elaborating on the neo-Freudian view—which posits disturbances in interpersonal relationships, family communications, and family relationships —are most widely used in psychodynamic explanations and treatment of psychotic disorders. London (1973) has identified two psychoanalytic orientations to schizophrenia: the unity theory, in which the disorder is related to unconscious conflict occurring in early life; and the specific theory, in which schizophrenia is seen as a deficiency state.

Phenomenological-existential approaches to psychotic disorders deemphasize aspects of theory and technique and focus on an understanding of the psychotic patient's phenomenological experiences, which are accepted and explored by the therapist on their own merits. Following the philosophical theories of the existential philosophers, Binswanger (1963), May (May, Angel, and Ellenberger, 1958; May and Von Kaam, 1963), Boss (1963), Frankel (1966), and Minkowsky (1953) base their views of the psychotic disorders on the assumption that one must accept and confront the inevitable dilemma and vicissitudes of life in order to discover authentic meaning in one's existence. Through the relationship with the patient, the therapist seeks to develop an interpersonal experience (being together) that will lead to mutual understanding and acceptance of phenomenological experience; this understanding, in turn, will lead to a discovery of meaning and purpose in life, so that the need for psychotic modes of adaptation is transcended.

Behavioral theorists (Eysenck, 1959, 1960; Jenkins, 1950; Skinner, 1953; Wolpe, 1958; Yates, 1970) view psychotic behaviors as learned, maladaptive behavior patterns of long standing that arise as a function of patterns of reinforcement in early life. In this approach, the psychotic patient's behavior is closely studied and analyzed. Maladaptive response patterns are then disintegrated through nonreinforcement, and adaptive and socially desired behaviors are reinforced through operant and classical conditioning. This approach has been extremely successful. Currently such programs are viewed critically, however, since they may involve what some professionals regard as infringement of civil rights of patients and exercise undue influence in the selection of behaviors targeted for modification.

Sociological interpretations of psychotic reactions relate to findings that the way in which psychopathology is manifested in behavior is determined by cultural and social influences. To explain the sociological finding that schizophrenic patients tend to be found more frequently in ghetto and socioeconomically deprived areas of society (Farris and Dunham, 1939), the *drift hypothesis* holds that these areas attract schizophrenics and other deviant and disadvantaged individuals, whereas the *breeder hypothesis* alleges that such disadvantaged environments contribute to the development of schizophrenic reactions (Lehmann, 1975).

R. D. Laing (1967) has combined both phenomenological and sociological considerations into a view that schizophrenic behavior is an understandable and liberating reaction to the contradictions and untenable demands of a destructive, "sick" society. Other sociological theorists have advocated the position that psychotic behaviors are nurtured and developed in a social context (Ullmann and Krasner, 1975) and that the psychotic disorders represent labels for stigmatizing and controlling persons whose deviant behavior is intolerable to society and to "the establishment" (Lement, 1951; Spiker and Denzin, 1968).

Approaches that seek to understand and conceptualize psychotic disorders through the classification and statistical processing of clinical observation have been termed descriptive-classification models (Lehmann, 1975). These approaches fall into three categories: the simple, clinical description of syndromes; the combining of nosological classifications on the basis of clinical findings; and the use of statistical methods of factor and cluster analysis of clinical data for development of systems of classification.

Elaboration on Critical Points

Clearly, advances have been made in the clinical diagnosis and treatment of the psychotic disorders. There is, however, little agreement on the "existence" of such clinical entities, their nature (assuming that they do represent or approach natural and not artificial scientific classifications), and even the degree to which modern methods of diagnosis and treatment represent humane innovations or are practices designed to regulate witchcraft in modern disguise, as some members of the antipsychiatry movement suggest.

The assessment of persons for purposes of diagnosis and treatment currently focuses on a diagnostic interview; diagnostic examinations (usually including a physical and neurological examination; appraisal of the individual's functioning in his or her social milieu, through social work procedures; and psychological tests); and, where indicated, specialized diagnostic studies (such as additional psychiatric interviews and specialized medical and laboratory tests). The results of all these procedures are considered and integrated into a diagnosis made according to the current diagnostic nosology. These results also form a basis for selecting treatment methods, with alternative diagnoses to be considered or ruled out, and a prognosis of the probable future course of the disorder.

The diagnostic interview is a procedure for collecting data and observations of the patient. The interviewer obtains information about the present symptoms (the chief complaint); history of past illnesses, as well as the present illness; and the patient's educational, social, family, marital, and vocational history (Eaton, Peterson, and Davis, 1976). This information provides a basis for determining, in a psychodynamic formulation, the specific psychological, environmental, familial, and social factors that are relevant to the present disorder and to treatment and prognostic predictions. Observations of the patient during this period provide the data for a statement of the patient's current functioning, termed the "mental status."

In the mental-status examination, the current psychological characteristics of the patient are most clearly documented for selection and diagnosis of current symptom characteristics. Currently a mental-status examination includes the following appraisals: a general description of the appearance, behavior, psychomotor activity, and attitude toward the examination; manner and type of speech; state of consciousness; affective or emotional state; level of activity; stream of thought; content of thought; orientation as to time, place, and person; memory; information and intelligence-level estimation; concentration; abstract thinking; judgment; insight; dreams, fantasies, and value systems; other tests as appropriate; and appraisal of the reliability of the patient as an accurate reporter of his or her situation (Freedman, Kaplan, and Sadock, 1975). These data provide the basis for selecting diagnosis to be considered descriptive of the patient's current functioning and disorder. Physical examinations and laboratory tests are used to identify relevant physical and biological factors either causing or contributing to the patient's disorder.

Social work procedures provide supplementary information regarding etiological factors and identify assets and liabilities in the present social environment.

The diagnostic interview has long been the subject of much criticism as a reliable and valid diagnostic procedure. A recent advance in diagnostic procedures in the determination of psychosis is reported by the World Health Organization (1973). The report describes the determination of criteria and procedures for increasing the reliability of diagnostic determinations of schizophrenia in various societies included. Dissatisfaction with the interview as an unreliable technique, especially for use in research studies, has given rise to a variety of rating scales for use in making clinical judgments and systematizing observations of patients. Among those widely in use are Hamilton Depression Scale (Hamilton, 1960, 1969), Hamilton Anxiety Scale (Hamilton, 1959), State-Trait Anxiety Inventory—a self-evaluation questionnaire (Spielberger, Gorsuch, and Lushene, 1970; Spielberger, Lushene, and McAdoo, 1977), Brief Psychiatric Rating Scale (Overall and Gorham, 1962), Katz Adjustment Scale (Katz and Lyerly, 1963), Wittenborn Psychiatric Rating Scale (Wittenborn, 1950, 1972), Inpatient Multidimensional Psychiatric Scale (Lorr and Klett, 1966), Discharge Readiness Inventory (Hogarty and Ulrich, 1971a, 1971b, 1972), and Nurses Observation Scale for Inpatient Evaluation (Honigfeld and Klett, 1965; Honigfeld, Gillis, and Klett, 1966).

The use of standardized psychological tests of intelligence and personality functioning is a customary practice in diagnostic procedures in identifying psychotic individuals. Although psychological tests are seldom used as a sole basis for diagnostic determination, they are frequently used in the selection of an appropriate diagnosis. Test results may assist also in planning treatment programs, better understanding the patient's personality, planning programs of education and rehabilitation, and assessing improvement or deterioration in functioning or adjustment. The most widely used tests for psychosis are intelligence tests and personality tests.

Nearly all the psychotic disorders involve either temporary or permanent impairment of intellectual functioning. The most widely used method in the clinical assessment of adult intellectual functioning is the Wechsler Adult Intelligence Scale (WAIS). The Wechsler procedures provide evaluation of the patient's (1) fund of general information and factual knowledge, (2) judgment in conventional social situations, (3) arithmetic skills, (4) abstract verbal generalization skills, (5) immediate rote memory, (6) vocabulary skills, (7) psychomotor speed skills, (8) discriminatory perceptual acuity, (9) analysis and synthesis of abstract relationships, (10) social perceptiveness, and (11) spatial relationships. The WAIS has been used in the diagnosis of organic brain dysfunction and in assessing the effects of known or suspected organic brain impairment. Neuropsychological assessments use the Wechsler scales in conjunction with more specific tests of psychomotor speed and coordination, sensory and tactile performance, abstract concept formation and reasoning, and perception (Golden, 1978). In persons with organic brain syndromes, the diagnosis of psychosis is ordinarily assessed on the basis of the presence of additional symptoms characteristic of a psychotic disorder.

In contemporary clinical practice, the most frequently used personality tests are the Minnesota Multiphasic Personality Inventory (MMPI), the Rorschach, the Thematic Apperception Test (TAT), and the Sentence Completion Test. The Bender Gestalt Test has been used as a test of both organic brain dysfunction and personality functioning. Other personality tests, such as the California Personality Inventory (CPI) and the 16 Personality Factors Test (16 PF), are used in some instances, but their use is not yet widespread.

The Minnesota Multiphasic Personality Inventory, the most widely used personality inventory in clinical assessment, was originally developed by Hathaway and McKinley (1967) to identify mentally disturbed individuals and to distinguish different forms of psychopathology. This test is used both as a screening device and as part of a larger battery of psychological tests to describe the personality characteristics of the patient, to distinguish normal from disturbed individuals, and to classify patient populations (Cronbach, 1970). In recent years the MMPI has also been used in actuarial fashion for predicting patient diagnoses, personality characteristics, and response to treatment methods (Gilberstadt and Duker, 1965).

The Rorschach, the most frequently used instrument in psychological assessment in the 1940s, continues to be a popular method of personality appraisal (Exner, 1974). Principally used in differential diagnosis, determination of psychodynamics, and identification of psychopathology and intrapsychic conflict, the Rorschach has been found especially useful in detecting schizophrenia and other psychotic processes when such are difficult to detect in structured or diagnostic interviews. Specifically, it can detect poor contact with reality, overgeneralization, unconventionality of thinking, idiosyncrasy of thought, peculiarities of language and thinking, and suicide potential (Carr, 1975).

The Thematic Apperception Test (TAT), developed by Henry Murray in 1943, has also been used extensively in clinical practice and in research studies of personality. As originally developed, the test was used as a projective technique whereby, through inspection of the hero's role in the stories elicited by the cards, the examiner could identify the feelings and needs of the individual, forces in the environment, and outcomes between the interaction of the two. Other interpretive approaches to the cards have been developed over the years. In most contemporary clinical situations, the TAT is used as a means of identifying psychodynamics as these are reflected in the individual's perception of and interaction with other significant figures in his or her environment (Carr, 1975).

The Sentence Completion Test is composed of a number of incomplete sentences which the patient completes in his or her own words. The test is used most frequently for eliciting relatively conscious attitudes and orientations toward significant figures and interpersonal events. It is useful in the evaluation of psychotic persons to identify areas of impairment and relative intactness.

Personal Views and Recommendations

The conceptualization, diagnosis, and treatment of the psychotic disorders, like the manifestations of such states, has throughout history reflected the social, cultural, moral, and ethical values of the society toward deviancy. In the past twenty years in America, sweeping social change has led to a significant reexamination and change in attitudes toward moral and ethical values. Traditional views of all mental disorders, especially the psychoses, have been subject to considerable scrutiny. The traditional model, the medical disease model, has received criticism on theoretical, moral, and ethical grounds. The severity of impairment involved in all the psychotic disorders almost invariably has involved some form of custody or confinement, not only to protect the person from the consequences of unrealistic action but also to protect others from unrealistic and unwarranted acts directed against them. In recent years this approach has been reconsidered along a variety of dimensions. The traditional attitude, which provided for diminished responsibility of the psychotic persons for the consequences of actions, has been questioned.

New state laws, enacted in response to nationwide civil rights movements, have resulted from reexamination of traditional practices of commitment. Consumer advocacy movements have affected the mental health fields through legislation that (1) establishes patients' "right to treatment" and (2) provides guidelines for evaluating treatment programs to ensure that that right is not violated (Mental Health Law Project, 1973; Miller, 1976). Concerns with issues of privacy have resulted in new conventions and regulations regarding the confidentiality of patient records. The courts have addressed issues involving informed consent in granting permission for treatment procedures. Current legal rulings require that the patient or a responsible person in guardianship status have full understanding of the options available, the reasons for, the nature of, and the probability of benefit and risk in order to provide consent for treatment procedures.

Moral and ethical issues related to the process and provision of psychotherapy are a current focus of concern as well. Physical procedures such as psychosurgery, electroconvulsive therapy, and the use of psychotropic medications have been subjected to renewed investigation and regulation.

The American Psychological Association (1977b) has recently developed new standards for the provision of psychological services and new ethical standards for psychological research (American Psychological Association, 1973). Concerns about the practices of research investigators and violation of the civil rights of such subjects have also resulted in federal legislation regarding research with human subjects.

All these developments, when viewed in their historical context, represent a continuous effort to better understand a group of persons whose deviant behavior is enigmatic and frightening and considered dangerous and destructive. They also represent attempts to provide strategies of treatment that maximize the human rights and dignity of such persons, who have been subjected to abuse and mistreatment throughout the history of man.

Application to Particular Variables

Schizophrenic disorders rarely have an onset in childhood, although some subclinical features may be seen in retrospect in the childhood of adult patients. In general, schizophrenic disorders of the process category have an onset in adolescence, whereas the onset of the affective disorders is evenly distributed throughout adult life. Manic and bipolar forms of the disorder tend to begin in early adulthood—slightly later, on the average, than schizophrenia. Age also appears to determine the manifestations of the symptoms of the affective disorders. In children affective disorders may appear as increases in separation anxiety, school refusal, or school phobia. In adolescent boys affective disorders may be manifested in negativistic and antisocial behavior. Affective disorder symptoms may appear in early adolescence as sulkiness, unwillingness to cooperate in family activities and endeavors, and withdrawal into solitude. Depression becomes more prominent—and more severe—as a presenting symptom in middle and late adulthood, and the risk of suicide in individuals with affective disorders increases with age. In elderly adults affective disorder manifestations may appear in dementia-like symptoms, apathy, loss of initiative and interest in usual pursuits, and disturbances in concentration. Paranoid disorders tend to have ages of onset later than those observed in schizophrenia. Some forms of paranoid disorder (formerly termed involutional reactions) tend to be associated with the menopause in women and the climacteric in men. The organic brain syndromes encompass a wide variety of etiologies and brain dysfunctions and appear at all age levels.

Academic difficulties are commonly observed in schizophrenic individuals, both in the premorbid personality type and in the psychotic episode following onset of the disorder. Academic and intellectual skills are variously impaired during periods of remission, depending on the subtype of schizophrenia involved and the degree of residual impairment of intellectual and motivational functioning of the individual. Academic and educational impairment is common in schizophrenias of the process variety but is much less common, except during periods of active psychosis, in the schizophrenias of the reactive type. Impairment in reactive schizophrenia is often due more to disorders of concentration and adaptation than to intellectual deficit as such. Almost all the organic brain disorders involve impairment of intellectual functioning, at least during acute episodes of psychotic illness. Many of these disorders result in chronic impairments which differentially affect intellectual and academic abilities.

Schizophrenia is by no means restricted to any socioeconomic level, although research indicates that it is most frequently found in lower socioeconomic groups. Whether this phenomenon represents the downward "drifting" of severely impaired individuals or whether schizophrenia is developed as a consequence of the stress and deprivation inherent in conditions of poverty remains an open question. Patients suffering from affective disorders are severely impaired in social and vocational functioning during acute episodes of illness, but they may be able to function successfully in vocational settings at other times. Occupational functioning as such is rarely impaired in paranoid disorders, although impairment of social functioning associated with the disorder may, and frequently does, create significant problems for the individual in vocational settings. The organic brain syndromes often impair vocational functioning.

Most epidemiological studies indicate that, in all societies studied, schizophrenia occurs in approximately 1 percent of the population. To the extent that schizophrenia is associated with poor and disadvantaged status, the incidence may be higher among such groups in a given society. The affective disorders do not appear to be associated with a particular ethnic or racial status. Some forms of the paranoid disorders are associated with immigrant status, but this disorder is found in all ethnic and racial groups, as are the organic brain syndromes.

References

American Psychological Association. *Ethical Principles in the Conduct of Research with Human Participants.* Washington, D.C.: American Psychiatric Association, 1973.

American Psychological Association. *Ethical Standards for Psychological Research.* Washington, D.C.: American Psychiatric Association, 1976.

American Psychiatric Association. *Diagnostic and Statistical Manual of Mental Disorders.* (3rd ed.) Washington, D.C.: American Psychiatric Association, 1977a.

American Psychological Association. *Standards for Providers of Psychological Services.* Washington, D.C.: American Psychiatric Association, 1977b.

Anastasi, A. *Psychological Testing.* (4th ed.) New York: Macmillan, 1976.

Binswanger, L. *Being-in-the-World.* (J. Needleman, trans.) New York: Basic Books, 1963.

Boss, M. *Psychoanalysis and Daseinsanalysis.* New York: Basic Books, 1963.

Brown, W. R., and McGuire, J. "Current Psychological Assessment Practices." *Professional Psychology,* 1976, 7 (4), 475-494.

Carr, A. C. "Psychological Testing of Intelligence and Personality." In A. M. Freedman, H. I. Kaplan, and B. J. Sadock (Eds.), *Comprehensive Textbook of Psychiatry.* (2nd ed.) Baltimore: Williams and Wilkins, 1975.

Cleveland, S. E. "Reflections on the Rise and Fall of Psychodiagnostics." *Professional Psychology,* 1976, 7 (3), 309-318.

Cohen, R. A. "Manic-Depressive Illness." In A. M. Freedman, H. I. Kaplan, and B. J.

Sadock (Eds.), *Comprehensive Textbook of Psychiatry*. (2nd ed.) Baltimore: Williams and Wilkins, 1975.

Copenhaver, J. H. Personal communication, June 1978.

Cronbach, L. J. *Essentials of Psychological Testing*. (3rd ed.) New York: Harper & Row, 1970.

Eaton, M. T. Personal communication, June 1978.

Eaton, M. T., Peterson, M., and Davis, J. A. *Psychiatry*. (3rd ed.) Flushing, N.Y.: Medical Examination Publishing Company, 1976.

Exner, J. E., Jr. *The Rorschach: A Comprehensive System*. New York: Wiley, 1974.

Eysenck, H. J. "Learning Theory and Behavioral Therapy." *Journal of Mental Science,* 1959, *105,* 61-67.

Eysenck, H. J. *Behavior Therapy and the Neuroses*. Elmsford, N.Y.: Pergamon Press, 1960.

Farris, R. E. L., and Dunham, H. W. *Mental Disorders in Urban Areas*. Chicago: University of Chicago Press, 1939.

Frankel, V. "Logotherapy and Existential Analysis: A Review." *American Journal of Psychotherapy,* 1966, *20,* 252-260.

Freedman, A. M., Kaplan, H. I., and Sadock, B. J. *Modern Synopsis of Comprehensive Textbook of Psychiatry*. Baltimore: Williams and Wilkins, 1975.

Gilberstadt, H., and Duker, J. *Handbook of Clinical and Actuarial MMPI Interpretation*. Philadelphia: Saunders, 1965.

Golden, C. J. *Diagnosis and Rehabilitation in Clinical Neuropsychology*. Springfield, Ill.: Thomas, 1978.

Hamilton, M. "The Assessment of Anxiety States by Rating." *British Journal of Medical Psychology,* 1959, *32,* 50-55.

Hamilton, M. "A Rating Scale for Depression." *Journal of Neurology, Neurosurgery and Psychiatry,* 1960, *23,* 56-62.

Hamilton, M. "Standardized Assessment and Recording of Depressive Symptoms." *Psychiatria, Neurologia, Neurochirurgia,* 1969, *72,* 201-205.

Hathaway, S. R., and McKinley, J. C. *Minnesota Multiphasic Personality Inventory: Manual for Administration and Scoring*. New York: Psychological Corporation, 1967.

Hinzie, L. E., and Campbell, R. J. *Psychiatric Dictionary*. (4th ed.) New York: Oxford University Press, 1970.

Hogarty, G. E., and Ulrich, R. *The Discharge Readiness Inventory (DRI)*. Baltimore: Friends Medical Science Research Center, 1971a.

Hogarty, G. E., and Ulrich, R. *The User's Manual for the Discharge Readiness Inventory*. Baltimore: National Educational Consultants, 1971b.

Hogarty, G. E., and Ulrich, R. "The Discharge Readiness Inventory." *Archives of General Psychiatry,* 1972, *26,* 419-426.

Honigfeld, G., Gillis, R., and Klett, C. J. "Nosie-30: A Treatment Sensitive Ward Scale." *Psychological Reports,* 1966, *19,* 180-182.

Honigfeld, G., and Klett, C. J. "The Nurses' Observation Scale for Inpatient Evaluation: A New Scale for Measuring in Chronic Schizophrenia." *Journal of Clinical Psychology,* 1965, *21,* 65-71.

Huston, P. E. "Psychotic Depressive Reaction." In A. M. Freedman, H. I. Kaplan, and B. J. Sadock (Eds.), *Comprehensive Textbook of Psychiatry*. (2nd ed.) Baltimore: Williams and Wilkins, 1975.

Jenkins, R. L. "Nature of the Schizophrenic Process: A Working Hypothesis for Therapy." *Archives of Neurological Psychiatry,* 1950, *64,* 243-262.

Kallmann, F. J. *Heredity in Health and Mental Disorders*. New York: Norton, 1953.

Kaplan, H. I., and Sadock, B. J. "Psychiatric Report." In A. M. Freedman, H. I. Kaplan, and B. J. Sadock (Eds.), *Comprehensive Textbook of Psychiatry.* (2nd ed.) Baltimore: Williams and Wilkins, 1975.

Katz, M. M., and Lyerly, S. B. "Methods for Measuring Adjustment and Social Behavior in the Community: I. Rationale, Description, Discriminative Validity, and Scale Development." *Psychological Reports,* 1963, *13* (21), 503-535.

Klein, M. *Contributions to Psychoanalysis, 1921-1945.* London: Hogarth Press, 1950.

Kraepelin, E. *Psychiatrie.* (8th ed.) Vol. 4. Leipzig: Barth, 1909-1915.

Kretschmer, E. *Physique and Character.* New York: Harcourt Brace Jovanovich, 1925.

Laing, R. D. *The Politics of Experience.* New York: Ballantine, 1967.

Langfeldt, G. *The Schizophreniform States.* Copenhagen: Munksgaard, 1939.

Lehmann, H. E. "Schizophrenia: Introduction and History." In A. M. Freedman, H. I. Kaplan, and B. J. Sadock (Eds.), *Comprehensive Textbook of Psychiatry.* (2nd ed.) Baltimore: Williams and Wilkins, 1975.

Lement, E. M. *Social Pathology.* New York: McGraw-Hill, 1951.

Lewandowski, D. G., and Saccuzo, D. P. "The Decline of Psychological Testing." *Professional Psychology,* 1976, *7,* 177-184.

Lieberman, R. P. "Behavior Modification of Schizophrenia: A Review." *Schizophrenia Bulletin,* 1972, *6,* 37-48.

London, N. J. "An Essay on Psychoanalytic Theory: Two Theories of Schizophrenia. Part I: Review and Critical Assessment of the Development of the Two Theories." *International Journal of Psycho-Analysis,* 1973, *54,* 169-178.

Lorr, M., and Klett, C. J. *Inpatient Multidimensional Psychiatric Scale: Manual.* (Rev. ed.) Palo Alto, Calif.: Consulting Psychologists Press, 1966.

May, R., Angel, A., and Ellenberger, H. (Eds.). *Existence. A New Dimension in Psychiatry and Psychology.* New York: Basic Books, 1958.

May, R., and Von Kaam, A. "Existential Theory and Therapy." In J. Masserman (Ed.), *Current Psychiatric Therapies.* Vol. 3. New York: Grune and Stratton, 1963.

Mental Health Law Project. *Basic Rights of the Mentally Handicapped: Right to Treatment; Right to Compensation for Institution-Maintaining Labor; Right to Education.* Washington, D.C.: Mental Health Law Project, 1973.

Miller, K. S. *Managing Madness: The Case Against Civil Commitment.* New York: Free Press, 1976.

Millon, T. *Modern Psychopathology.* Philadelphia: Saunders, 1969.

Minkowski, E. *La Schizophrénie.* (2nd ed.) Paris: Desclée De Brouwer, 1953.

Mora, G. "Historical and Theoretical Trends in Psychiatry." In A. M. Freedman, H. I. Kaplan, and B. J. Sadock (Eds.), *Comprehensive Textbook of Psychiatry.* (2nd ed.) Baltimore: Williams and Wilkins, 1975.

Overall, J. E., and Gorham, D. R. "The Brief Psychiatric Rating Scale." *Psychological Reports,* 1962, *10,* 799-812.

Polatin, P. "Psychotic Disorders: Paranoid States." In A. M. Freedman, H. I. Kaplan, and B. J. Sadock (Eds.), *Comprehensive Textbook of Psychiatry.* (2nd ed.) Baltimore: Williams and Wilkins, 1975.

Rosenthal, D. "An Historical and Methodological Review of Genetic Studies in Schizophrenia." In J. Romano (Ed.), *Origins of Schizophrenia.* Amsterdam: Excerpta Medica Foundation, 1968.

Sadock, B. J. "Organic Brain Syndromes: Introduction." In A. M. Freedman, H. I. Kaplan, and B. J. Sadock (Eds.), *Comprehensive Textbook of Psychiatry.* (2nd ed.) Baltimore: Williams and Wilkins, 1975.

Schacht, T., and Nathan, P. E. "But Is It Good for the Psychologists? Appraisal and Status of DSM-III." *American Psychologist*, 1977, *32*, 1017-1025.

Schneider, C. *Die Schizophrenen Symptomverbande*. Berlin: Springer, 1942.

Sheldon, W. H., and others. *The Varieties of Human Physique: An Introduction to Constitutional Psychology*. New York: Harper & Row, 1940.

Sheldon, W. H., and others. *Atlas of Men: A Guide for Somatotyping the Male at All Ages*. New York: Harper & Row, 1954.

Sheldon, W. H., and Stevens, S. S. *The Varieties of Temperament: A Psychology of Constitutional Differences*. New York: Harper & Row, 1942.

Skinner, B. F. *Science and Human Behavior*. New York: Macmillan, 1953.

Spielberger, C. D., Gorsuch, R. L., and Lushene, R. E. *Manual for the State-Trait Anxiety Inventory (Self-Evaluation Questionnaire)*. Palo Alto, Calif.: Consulting Psychologists Press, 1970.

Spielberger, C. D., Lushene, R. E., and McAdoo, W. G. "Theory and Measurement of Anxiety States." In R. Cattell and R. Dreyer (Eds.), *Handbook of Modern Personality Theory*. New York: Appleton-Century-Crofts, 1977.

Spiker, S. P., and Denzin, N. K. *The Mental Patient: Studies in the Sociology of Deviance*. New York: McGraw-Hill, 1968.

Stone, A. A., and Stromberg, C. D. *Mental Health and Law: A System in Transition*. Rockville, Md.: Center for Studies of Crime and Delinquency, National Institute of Mental Health, 1975.

Szasz, T. S. *The Myth of Mental Illness*. New York: Harper & Row, 1960.

Szasz, T. S. *Psychiatric Slavery*. New York: Free Press, 1977.

Ullmann, L. P., and Krasner, L. *A Psychological Approach to Abnormal Behavior*. (2nd ed.) Englewood Cliffs, N.J.: Prentice-Hall, 1975.

Wittenborn, J. R. "A New Procedure for Evaluating Mental Hospital Patients." *Journal of Consulting Psychology*, 1950, *14*, 500-501.

Wittenborn, J. R. "Reliability, Validity, and Objectivity of Symptom Rating Scales." *Journal of Nervous and Mental Disease*, 1972, *154*, 79-87.

Wolpe, J. *Psychotherapy by Reciprocal Inhibition*. Stanford, Calif.: Stanford University Press, 1958.

World Health Organization. *Report of the International Pilot Study of Schizophrenia*. Vol. 1. Geneva: World Health Organization, 1973.

Yates, A. J. *Behavior Therapy*. New York: Wiley, 1970.

Zilboorg, G., and Henry, G. W. *A History of Medical Psychology*. New York: Norton, 1941.

Zubin, J. "But Is It Good for Science?" *Clinical Psychologist*, 1977-78, *31*, 1, 5-7.

Zubin, J., and Spring, B. "Vulnerability—A New View of Schizophrenia." *Journal of Abnormal Psychology*, 1977, *86*, 103-126.

14

Charles J. Golden

Organic Brain Syndromes

Organic brain syndromes represent mental conditions resulting from an impairment of brain tissue function caused by such maladies as cerebrovascular disorders, head trauma, tumors, degenerative diseases of the brain, and disorders of the brain due to alcohol and other substances. The basic symptoms for the disorder include impairment of orientation, memory, verbal or nonverbal intellectual functions, judgment, perceptual and motor functions, and emotional feeling or expression. The syndrome may occur with all or only one of these symptoms and may occur with or without an accompanying psychosis. The disorder may be classified as acute (reversible) or chronic (irreversible). The type of syndrome manifested depends on the cause of the dysfunction, the location of the dysfunction in the brain, the extent of the dysfunction, the age of onset, time since onset, and the premorbid status of the patient.

Background and Current Status

The relationship between brain function and behavior was recognized as early as 3500 B.C. in the Edwin Smith Papyrus, with some evidence suggesting that this relationship had been observed since the Upper Paleolithic period (Chapman and Wolff, 1959). By 500 B.C., Pythagoras had identified the brain as the site of human reasoning. While ancient theorists could agree that human thought and intellectual abilities are to be found in the brain, there was considerable disagreement over which brain structures are responsible for intellect. The predominant view before the Rennaissance localized thought in the ventricles, the fluid-filled cavities that cushion the brain from trauma (Chapman and Wolff, 1959). Later theorists identified the center of mental processes in such areas as the pineal gland, a structure located in the center of the brain; and Lancisi theorized that the corpus callosum, a band of fibers connecting the left and right hemisphere, is responsible for mental functions (Luria, 1966). It was not until the nineteenth century that modern concepts about brain function began to develop.

Early in the nineteenth century, the German physician Franz Joseph Gall (1758-1828) postulated that the brain consists of a number of discrete organs, each of which is responsible for a single psychological skill, such as "wit" or "reading" (Krech, 1962). Gall postulated that the size of a given organ (area) of the brain determines the individual's ability in the psychological skill controlled by that organ. Thus, if the "wit" organ is large, the individual has a high capacity for being witty. Gall was the first major investigator to suggest that specific psychological functions are localized in specific organs or areas of the brain. This theory is known as the localizationist position.

The localization theory was given credibility in 1861 by the French surgeon Paul Broca, who—on the basis of autopsies completed on two patients who had lost the ability to use expressive speech—reported that he had found the brain area where motor speech is localized. Hailed by many as a major advance, Broca's work led to countless investigations attempting to localize specific psychological functions. These led to numerous published articles announcing various discoveries: the localization of receptive speech (by Carl Wernicke in 1874), motor and sensory areas (by Gustav Fritsch and E. Hitzig in 1870), and word blindness, or inability to read (by G. Kliessmaul in 1877). By the late nineteenth and early twentieth centuries, localizationist books included maps detailing the function of each area of the brain.

Despite the popularity of localizationist theories in the nineteenth century, many scientists rejected such theories. As early as 1840, Pierre Flourens mounted a series of attacks against localizationist theories, advocating instead an equipotentialist theory. According to this theory, intellectual and psychological skills are a product of the brain as a whole, rather than specific, localized areas. In the early twentieth century, many neurologists (for instance, Goldstein, 1927; Head, 1926; and Lashley, 1929) adopted an equipotential viewpoint. While these theorists accepted the idea that basic motor and sensory functions are localized, they believed that all higher intellectual functions are products of the brain as a whole. Any injury to the brain, no matter where it is located, will impair these higher intellectual skills. This was in contrast to the localization-based belief that only injuries to a specific area can impair a given intellectual skill.

Presently, both the localization and the equipotential positions have their adherents, and increasing numbers of practitioners advocate a combined position. Both theories have had a substantial impact on the assessment of organic brain syndromes in clinical neuropsychology. Individuals advocating an equipotential viewpoint have concentrated on finding a test or tests that can measure the underlying higher intellectual skills impaired in all forms of brain injury. Psychologists assuming a localization position have concentrated on finding batteries of tests that measure each of the psychological skills mediated by the brain, thus allowing one to assess not only the psychological status of the patient but, by inference, the physiological status of specific areas of the brain (Golden, 1978).

Within the last two decades, neuropsychology has become an increasingly specialized field, practiced by individuals with training beyond that usually given to a clinical psychologist. This training has included courses in neurology as well as intensive training in psychological assessment (Golden, 1976). In addition, the relationship of neuropsychology to other neurosciences has been constantly evolving. Where once psychology was involved only in discriminating brain-injured patients from those who were not brain injured, the psychologist is becoming more involved in questions of localizing disorders, assessing treatment programs, determining patient prognosis, and planning rehabilitation programs (Smith, 1975).

Critical Discussion

General Areas of Concern

Purpose of the Examination. Psychologists differ considerably on the role of the psychologist and the psychological examination in cases of suspected organic brain dysfunction (Luria and Majovski, 1977). Traditionally, the psychologist has had the role of identifying the presence or absence of such a syndrome. Many psychologists now question this traditional approach. In the first place, they contend that the approach is not useful for understanding or treating the patient, since the psychological diagnosis of organic brain syndrome simply becomes a part of the patient's chart and has little influence on treatment procedures or outcome. Second, they contend that not all organic brain syndromes are equivalent and that a detailed, extensive psychological examination is required if one is to understand the organic brain syndrome (Reitan, 1966).

A final objection to the traditional model is related to improvements in neurology and neuroradiology. Previously, the only instruments available to physicians to establish the presence of an organic brain syndrome involved great pain to the patient and a significant risk of death. While this could be justified as a necessary risk for a patient with a suspected brain tumor, it could not be justified in the case of an individual suspected of having a diffuse, untreatable atrophy of the brain. Thus, an important diagnostic role fell to the psychological tests, which were neither painful nor dangerous. New X-ray techniques, however, can visualize brain atrophy without pain or significant threat to the patient's life (New and Scott, 1974). Thus, many discriminations once asked of the psychologist have become the province of the neuroradiologist. This, many have argued, suggests that the psychologist should perform a different role in neurodiagnostics (Golden, 1976).

One alternate role involves a detailed analysis of the organic brain syndrome as it is expressed in the individual patient. This includes the evaluation of such skills as general intelligence, perceptual-motor functioning, language, flexibility, speed of response, attention, and concentration (Benton, 1975). Smith (1975) has identified four roles for the neuropsychological examination: an aid in diagnosis, especially in more difficult cases; a baseline against which future progress may be measured; an aid in making prognostic statements; and an aid in planning rehabilitation programs. The last three roles are becoming increasingly important in many settings—along with the more traditional diagnostic role, which still remains.

Individual Versus Standardized Testing. Proponents of the individualized approach advocate choosing tests for a patient on the basis of the referral question, initial historical information, and initial and subsequent clinical impressions. The psychologists using this approach argue that an individualized examination allows the clinician to concentrate the testing efforts in those areas of greatest deficit for the patient (Lezak, 1976).

Theoretically, this approach allows the clinician to arrive at a detailed evaluation of the patient in the smallest amount of time for both the psychologist and the patient. Opponents of this approach point out that the accuracy of the procedure is highly dependent on the skill of the individual clinician. If the correct tests are given on the basis of the clinician's judgment, then a highly effective examination may result. However, if the tests selected fail to measure the patient's deficits appropriately, then the examination will be inadequate at best and misleading at worst (Golden, 1978). In addition, opponents contend, this approach does not allow for the collection of systematic data across patients and disorders; as a result, the conclusions that can be reached from series of patients, or at least the scientific validation of those conclusions, are limited (Reitan, 1966).

Because of these limitations, many clinicians have chosen to use a standard test or test battery selected to represent all the major dimensions deemed relevant in the evaluation of the suspected organic brain syndrome patient. Since all patients receive the same evaluation, all are evaluated on these dimensions. This helps avoid errors in test selection by inexperienced clinicians. The approach also allows for the systematic collection of data on all subjects, yielding research in test performance patterns characteristic of various neurological disorders seen by the clinician. The research allows for test interpretation based more on objective results than on clinical experience and intuition (Reitan, 1966). The standardized approach also has limitations. First, the more comprehensive the examination, the longer it will take. Some of the more comprehensive test batteries may take one day or more to complete (Smith, 1975). If the examination is made shorter, it must often delete examination of some skills, thus introducing the possibility of diagnostic errors. Finally, a standardized test battery may fail to address areas that are significant for a given patient but not for patients in general (Lezak, 1976).

Quantitative Versus Qualitative Procedures. The quantitative approach attempts to reduce all test performance to a set of numbers that can be used in comparisons with performance by normal and impaired normative groups (Anastasi, 1976). On the basis of such comparisons, a diagnostic decision may be made. Proponents of the quantitative approach emphasize its reliance on objective indices that are reproducible across investigators and clinicians and its emphasis on research results gathered under controlled conditions (Reitan, 1966).

The qualitative approach emphasizes the way in which a person attempts to complete a test rather than the individual's score (Luria, 1966, 1973). This allows the clinician to understand the underlying processes that cause a patient's performance (Lezak, 1976). Once these underlying processes are understood, the clinician is able to identify the source of the brain dysfunction and its importance to the individual's recovery and rehabilitation treatment (Luria and Majovski, 1977). Proponents of the qualitative approach may change test procedures in an attempt to get a clearer picture of a client's performance, violating the standardized testing approach necessary for quantitative data (Lezak, 1976).

Single Tests Versus Test Batteries. Traditionally, many psychologists have used only a single test in the evaluation of organic brain syndrome. These tests are most commonly measures of abstract attitude or the related measures of complex constructional abilities (Goldstein and Scheerer, 1941). These tests were assumed to be highly sensitive to all forms of brain dysfunction, so that they could usefully discriminate between brain-injured and other patients (Shipley, 1940, 1946). It has come to be recognized, however, that a single-test approach is generally not effective (Koppitz, 1975). An individual test may be less than 80 percent accurate even when one is comparing organic and normal patients; it is even less accurate when one is comparing organic and other pathological populations (Golden, 1978). Thus, many clinicians have chosen a multitest approach, with decisions based on the patient's overall performance (McFie, 1975). Ideally, the tests in a test battery represent different abilities which are affected in brain damage. For example, one would not give two tests that request drawings from a patient.

The use of test batteries also allows for more complex interpretive approaches (Reitan, 1966). A test that represents right hemisphere performance may be compared with a test that represents left hemisphere performance. Verbal tests and tests of right-side motor and sensory functions are considered representative of left hemisphere performance; nonverbal tests and left-side motor and sensory tests are considered representative of right hemisphere performance (Small, 1973). If an individual's performance on a nonverbal test, for example, is markedly poorer than his performance on a verbal test, that might suggest an injury in the right hemisphere.

With test batteries, a pattern analysis of test results may also be employed. For example, the score on a set of three tests might not differentiate between schizophrenic and organic patients, but the overall configuration of the tests might be diagnostically useful. Pattern analysis may represent one of the most powerful tools available to the clinical neuropsychologist in more difficult, subtle cases of organic brain syndrome (Reitan, 1966).

Personality Assessment. As noted previously, an organic brain syndrome may occur with or without psychosis. Evaluation of the psychosis typically follows general clinical assessment strategies, although certain precautions must be taken. For example, in cases where visual impairment is present, tests like the Rorschach might give inappropriate results due to the perceptual effects of the brain injury rather than any accompanying psychosis. Similar problems might occur if the client has severe spatial rotation problems. On the MMPI some forms of brain dysfunction may cause inappropriately high Hypochondriasis, Depression, Hysteria, and Schizophrenia scores because the symptoms of the neurological disorder are identical to those used to detect the personality disorder. A related issue is the effects of severe personality pathology on test performance. The problems involved and ways of handling them will be discussed later.

Comparative Philosophies and Theories

Two major theories—equipotential and localization—have dominated the field. Both theories have had a profound impact on the development of clinical assessment tools, as well as on determining the role of the clinical psychologist in the treatment of the organic brain syndrome patient.

Equipotential Theory. Equipotential theory, as described earlier, involves the assumption that all areas of the brain make an equal contribution to overall intellectual function (Krech, 1962). Thus, the area of brain injury is unimportant; only the amount of brain injury relates to behavioral deficit (Lashley, 1929). Equipotential theories assume that all forms of brain injury are essentially alike, differing only in degree. Many equipotential theorists place a strong emphasis on deficits in abstract or symbolic ability, which are presumed to accompany all forms of organic brain syndrome. The patient is thought to operate on only a concrete level, so that he or she is unable to respond to abstract or symbolic statements (Goldstein, 1927).

The equipotential view has heavily influenced the development of psychological tests. Numerous researchers have attempted to find tests that measure the basic deficit common to all brain-injured patients in order to find the ideal test or tests (see Yates, 1954). Such research has not been as successful as one might expect from equipotential theories. While tests have been found on which brain-injured persons reliably do more poorly than persons who are not brain injured, the tests have not been discriminating enough for day-to-day clinical work (Golden, 1978).

Localization Theory. Localization theory assumes that each area within the brain is responsible for specific psychological skills (Luria, 1966). Thus, *where* an individual is injured becomes the primary concern of the organic brain assessment. Extent of injury is important only insofar as a larger injury will involve more areas of the brain and thus disrupt many skills. However, similarly sized lesions in different parts of the brain will produce significantly discrepant effects (Krech, 1962). In evaluating an individual patient, a psychologist working from this theory must recognize that few injuries are truly limited to a specific area. Tumors, for example, may cause increased intracranial pressure, thus impairing areas of the brain far removed from the tumor itself (Smith, 1975). Head traumas will disrupt functions in the hemisphere that is hit as well as in the opposite hemisphere, which is thrust against the skull (Bannister, 1973). Stroke victims often have impaired cerebral circulation in general (Chusid, 1970). In almost any injury there is likely to be impairment in many skills in areas removed from the injury, especially during the acute phases of the disorder. As the patient recovers, these deficits will become less prominent (Golden, 1978).

Localization theories differ in the kinds of psychological skills that are thought to be localized (Luria, 1966). Some theorists would localize, in specific centers of the brain, such complex skills as reading and writing (Nielsen, 1946). Other theorists emphasize the localization of skills such as auditory analysis (Luria, 1973). Some argue for the localization of personality traits, such as patience (Kleist, 1933).

Elaboration on Critical Points

Psychological research has not wholly supported either the localization or the equipotential theory. The equipotential theory cannot account for the specific, limited deficits that occur in some patients without any general impairment in abstract abilities or other similar skills (Nielsen, 1946). Localization theories are hard pressed to explain why a specific deficit, such as dysgraphia (inability to write), may occur with deficits almost anywhere in the left hemisphere and with many injuries in the right hemisphere (Luria, 1966).

Unable to accept either theory, many have looked toward an alternative. The creation of one such model has been credited to J. Huhlings Jackson, an English neurologist whose primary works were published in the last half of the nineteenth century (Luria, 1973). Jackson observed that most psychological functions are not unitary abilities but are made up of more basic skills. Thus, one cannot talk about localizing "writing" but must talk about the localization of such abilities as seeing what is to be written, visually encoding what is seen, analyzing the codes into letters, analyzing the kinesthetic and motor movements necessary to do the writing, commanding the beginning of the writing sequence, and monitoring the writing until the task is finished, with appropriate feedback and corrections to the motor movements as necessary (see Hebb, 1942; Ingham, 1948; Levin, 1953). According to Jackson, although very basic skills can be localized, all observable behavior is a complex interaction of numerous basic skills, so that the brain as a whole is involved in most actual behavior. Thus, the theory combines both localization and equipotential viewpoints to form a theory that can account for the experimental evidence generated to support both views (Golden, 1978; Luria, 1966, 1973).

Jackson's views can be seen in their most developed form in the theories of the Russian neuropsychologist A. R. Luria. In Luria's view (1973), all behavior is based on functional systems, which are the patterns of interaction among the localized areas of the brain that are necessary to produce a given behavior. Any injury that interrupts any part of a functional system will disrupt all behaviors based on that functional system. The more complex the behavior, the more complex the functional systems on which it is based. Consequently, highly complex intellectual skills, such as the ability to abstract, are most sensitive to brain injury because a great many functional systems must be involved to produce the behavior.

Personal Views and Recommendations

At present neuropsychology reflects the confusion of a field that has undergone a rapidly accelerating growth within the past two decades. There seems to be a steady tendency toward the acceptance of a theory of brain function that lies between the localization theory and the equipotential theory, along the lines suggested by Jackson and Luria. In addition, neuropsychological evaluations are moving away from using a single test to decide on the presence or absence of organicity to a test battery approach which recognizes the diversity of the effects of brain injury. However, because of the length of standard test batteries that are able to fully evaluate the patient's skills, some people have advocated the individualized approach, in which the tests are selected for each patient individually. While this approach is useful in the hands of an experienced clinician, it may not reveal anything but the obvious in the hands of the novice not highly trained in neuropsychology. Unfortunately, a lack of intense training in clinical neuropsychology is a common state among most clinical psychologists, many of whom are called on to do these evaluations. As a compromise with practical reality and the need of the patient, there will be an increasing emphasis on the development of comprehensive test batteries that are tailored specifically for the neuropsychological patient and can be completed in one to three hours. Some attempts have been made in this direction already, although no such test battery has become generally accepted.

A final trend in the field is a union of quantitative and qualitative methods in neuropsychology. Tests can be developed that are standardized but still allow for qualitative assessment of the patient, especially those qualitative dimensions important to neuropsychology. At present, this joint type of analysis is used informally by many clinicians. In the future, it should become a more formal part of the neuropsychological assessment.

With the emergence of neuropsychology as a subspecialty of clinical psychology, the question of proper training and certification to do neuropsychological evaluation has arisen. Under the current licensing and training models, it is assumed that all psychologists are qualified to interpret neuropsychological examinations. However, it has become apparent that practice in neuropsychology takes an extensive amount of specialized training, not only in clinical assessment but also in the related fields of neurology, neurophysiology, and psychiatry. Only if an individual has an adequate background in these areas, along with a minimum of one year's experience in neuropsychological assessment under a clinical neuropsychologist, can we be sure that he or she is able to function at the levels of performance being established in the field. Thus, requirements along these lines should be made the minimum requirements for using the title of neuropsychologist in the future.

Such requirements call for new directions in the training of clinical psychologists. First, training programs should recognize the experiences that competence in the assessment of organic brain dysfunction requires. There is a need for more programs to recognize neuropsychology as a formal subspecialty and to provide course and practicum work adequate for a subspecialty, including the collateral training that is necessary. At present, only about one out of every five or six schools offers training that will give the student a sufficient background in clinical neuropsychology. In addition, internship opportunities in neuropsychology, as well as postdoctoral training, should be expanded and provide the opportunity for adequate training of the Ph.D. in clinical neuropsychology.

Application to Particular Variables

Age. Tests that are sensitive to brain injury also tend to be highly sensitive to the effects of aging (Reitan, 1955; Teuber and Rudel, 1962). Some have theorized that age effects are caused by changes in the brain which accompany aging, thus providing a theoretical basis for the observed sensitivity of neuropsychological tests (Golden and Schlutter, 1978). This sensitivity makes it important for the neuropsychologist to consider age effects in analyzing test performance. However, it is also important to look closely at the results for patterns of test performance suggesting brain injury that may be masked by age-corrected scores. The patterns seen with various conditions are not altered by age (Golden, 1978; Reitan, 1955).

Neuropsychological test performance of children is highly dependent on age. In addition, injuries to children have significantly different effects depending on age. Boll (1974) has observed that, in general, the earlier the injury, the more severe the neuropsychological effects. With older children, an injury's effects become more like an adult's injury (Reed and Reitan, 1969). Although focal injuries, confined to one hemisphere, may show less effects when they occur early because of the ability of the young brain to reorganize itself (Annett, 1973; Geschwind, 1972; Milner, 1974), such injuries occur rarely in most children (DeRenzi and Piercy, 1969). In more generalized injuries, there is no largely intact brain tissue to support a reorganization of higher brain functions (Golden, 1978).

Another significant problem in children is separating problems caused by delayed development and mental retardation from those caused by actual brain injury. In many cases the distinction cannot be made, and in actual practice the distinction is often not important in terms of treating the child. In cases where the distinction is important (for instance, when a psychologist sees a 6-year-old child with problems resulting from a recent, localized injury), the differentiation between delayed development, mental retardation, and brain injury is much clearer (Golden, 1978).

Education. The role of educational levels in test results has been controversial (Benton, Levin, and Van Allen, 1974; Finlayson, Johnson, and Reitan, 1977; Prigatano and Parsons, 1976; Vega and Parsons, 1967). Upon inspection, it is clear that many tests require a minimum level of education. For example, one cannot usefully administer a test involving reading ability to a person who has never learned to read. In addition, Finlayson, Johnson, and Reitan (1977) report significant educational effects on the Seashore Rhythm Test, a measure of one's ability to compare two nonverbal rhythmic patterns, while Benton, Levin, and Van Allen (1974) report educational effects on a test of geographical orientation, a measure of spatial skill. The educational effects being observed may be related to general IQ, since individuals who go on to each succeeding level of education tend to have a higher average IQ. This relationship, as well as the effects of educational level on commonly used tests, needs to be the subject of more extensive research.

Physical Disorders. Peripheral disorders that impair motor movement, especially the movement of the hands and the mouth, can in many instances seriously affect the accuracy and validity of many neuropsychological tests. In such patients it is often necessary to substitute tests requiring little motor coordination for many of the tests used in neuropsychology. One excellent example of such a test is the Raven's Matrices (Raven, 1960), which allows a spatial skills assessment to be made in a manner that minimizes motor involvement. Multiple-choice verbal tests are useful for patients with impaired peripheral or central speech functions (Golden, 1978; Lezak, 1976).

Intelligence. The review by Matthews (1974) clearly suggests that individuals with lower intelligence perform less adequately on neuropsychological tests than individuals with normal intelligence do. Interpretation of the results must be adjusted on the basis of the patient's expected level of performance.

Functional Factors. A major problem in the assessment of organic brain dysfunction has been separating deficits caused by brain injury from deficits caused by functional disorders. In many cases the level of performance exhibited by individuals with chronic functional disorders is indistinguishable from the performance of the organic patient (Watson and others, 1968; see also the review by Heaton, 1976). Thus, alternative diagnostic processes often must be used in making this discrimination.

One important difference between brain-injured and schizophrenic patients is the consistency of their performance. Organic patients are highly consistent in the areas where they have a deficit. Functional patients, in contrast, may show highly variable performance from test to test or on the same test across several testing sessions (Pincus and Tucker, 1974). Sometimes this inconsistency can be observed within a test battery; at other times a full retesting of a patient may be necessary before a firm diagnostic conclusion can be reached (Golden, 1978). Another important strategy is examining the test results for patterns of performance consistent with brain injury (Reitan, 1966). While the schizophrenic may show impaired performance, rarely will that performance suggest a specific organic disorder as it should in the case of the true organic brain syndrome patient. A final strategy attempts to minimize the performance deficit in functional patients by scheduling shorter testing sessions to maximize performance motivation and minimize fatigue (Golden, 1977). In addition, changes in the patient's medication may also improve performance significantly (Heaton, 1976).

References

Anastasi, A. *Psychological Testing.* (4th ed.) New York: Macmillan, 1976.

Annett, M. "Laterality of Childhood Hemiplegia and the Growth of Speech and Intelligence." *Cortex,* 1973, *9,* 4-33.

Bannister, R. *Brain's Clinical Neurology.* London: Oxford University Press, 1973.

Benton, A. L. "Psychological Tests for Brain Damage." In A. M. Freedman, H. I. Kaplan, and B. J. Sadock (Eds.), *Comprehensive Textbook of Psychiatry.* (2nd ed.) Baltimore: Williams and Wilkins, 1975.

Benton, A. L., Levin, H. S., and Van Allen, M. W. "Geographic Orientation in Patients with Unilateral Brain Disease." *Neuropsychologia,* 1974, *12,* 183-188.

Boll, T. J. "Behavioral Correlates of Cerebral Damage in Children Aged 9 Through 14." In R. M. Reitan and L. A. Davison (Eds.), *Clinical Neuropsychology: Current Status and Applications.* Washington, D.C.: Winston and Sons, 1974.

Chapman, L. F., and Wolff, H. "The Cerebral Hemispheres and Highest Integrative Functions of Man." *Archives of Neurology,* 1959, *1,* 357-424.

Chusid, J. *Correlative Neuroanatomy and Functional Neurology.* (14th ed.) Los Altos, Calif.: Lange, 1970.

DeRenzi, E., and Piercy, M. "The Fourteenth International Symposium of Neuropsychology." *Neuropsychologia,* 1969, *7,* 583-585.

Finlayson, M. A. J., Johnson, K. A., and Reitan, R. M. "Relationship of Education to Neuropsychological Measures in Brain Damaged and Non-Brain Damaged Adults." *Journal of Consulting and Clinical Psychology*, 1977, *45*, 536-542.

Geschwind, N. "Language in the Brain." *Scientific American*, 1972, *226*, 76-86.

Golden, C. J. "The Role of the Psychologist in the Training of the Neurologically Impaired." *Professional Psychology*, 1976, *7*, 579-584.

Golden, C. J. "The Validity of the Halstead-Reitan Neuropsychological Battery in a Mixed Psychiatric and Neurological Population." *Journal of Consulting and Clinical Psychology*, 1977, *45*, 1043-1051.

Golden, C. J. *Diagnosis and Rehabilitation in Clinical Neuropsychology.* Springfield, Ill.: Thomas, 1978.

Golden, C. J., and Schlutter, L. C. "The Interaction of Age and Diagnosis in Neuropsychological Test Results." *International Journal of Neuroscience*, 1978, in press.

Goldstein, K. "Die Lokalisation in der Grosshirnrinde" (Localization in the Cortex). In A. Bethe (Ed.), *Handbuch der Normalen und Pathologischen Physiologie (Handbook of Normal and Pathological Physiology).* Berlin: Springer, 1927.

Goldstein, K. *The Organism.* New York: American, 1939.

Goldstein, K., and Scheerer, M. "Abstract and Concrete Behavior: An Experimental Study with Special Tests." *Psychological Monographs*, 1941, *53* (Whole Number 239).

Head, H. *Aphasia and Kindred Disorders of Speech.* Cambridge: Cambridge University Press, 1926.

Heaton, R. K. "The Validity of Neuropsychological Evaluations in Psychiatric Settings." *Clinical Psychologist*, 1976, *6*, 10-11.

Hebb, D. O. "The Effect of Early and Late Brain Injury upon Test Scores and the Nature of Normal Adult Intelligence." *Proceedings of the American Philosophical Society*, 1942, *85*, 275-292.

Ingham, S. "Cerebral Localization of Psychological Processes Occurring During a Two Minute Period." *Journal of Nervous and Mental Disease*, 1948, *107*, 399-391.

Kleist, K. *Gehirnpathologie (Pathology of the Brain).* Leipzig: Barth, 1933.

Koppitz, E. M. *The Bender Gestalt Test for Young Children.* Vol. 2. New York: Grune and Stratton, 1975.

Krech, D. "Cortical Localization of Function." In L. Postman (Ed.), *Psychology in the Making.* New York: Knopf, 1962.

Lashley, K. S. *Brain Mechanisms and Intelligence.* Chicago: University of Chicago Press, 1929.

Levin, M. "Reflex Action in the Highest Cerebral Centers: A Tribute to Huhlings Jackson." *Journal of Nervous and Mental Disease*, 1953, *118*, 481-493.

Lezak, M. D. *Neuropsychological Assessment.* New York: Oxford University Press, 1976.

Luria, A. R. *Higher Cortical Functions in Man.* New York: Basic Books, 1966.

Luria, A. R. *The Working Brain.* New York: Basic Books, 1973.

Luria, A. R., and Majovski, L. V. "Basic Approaches used in American and Soviet Clinical Psychology." *American Psychologist*, 1977, *32*, 959-968.

Matthews, C. G. "Applications of Neuropsychological Test Methods to Mentally Retarded Subjects." In R. M. Reitan and L. A. Davison (Eds.), *Clinical Neuropsychology: Current Status and Applications.* Washington, D.C.: Winston, 1974.

McFie, J. *Assessment of Organic Intellectual Impairment.* New York: Academic Press, 1975.

Milner, B. "Sparing of Language Function After Early Unilateral Brain Damage." *Neurosciences Research Program Bulletin*, 1974, *12*, 213-217.

New, P. J., and Scott, W. R. *Computed Tomography of the Brain and Orbit.* Baltimore: Williams and Wilkins, 1974.

Nielsen, J. M. *Agnosia, Apraxia, Aphasia.* New York: Hoeber, 1946.

Pincus, J. H., and Tucker, G. J. *Behavioral Neurology.* New York: Oxford University Press, 1974.

Prigatano, G. P., and Parsons, O. A. "Relationship of Age and Education to Halstead Test Performance in Different Patient Populations." *Journal of Consulting and Clinical Psychology,* 1976, *44,* 527-533.

Raven, J. C. *Guide to the Standard Progressive Matrices.* London: Lewis, 1960.

Reed, J. C., and Reitan, R. M. "Verbal and Performance Differences Among Brain Injured Children with Lateralized Motor Deficits." *Perceptual and Motor Skills,* 1969, *29,* 747-752.

Reitan, R. M. "The Distribution According to Age of a Psychologic Measure Dependent upon Organic Brain Function." *Journal of Gerontology,* 1955, *10,* 338-340.

Reitan, R. M. "A Research Program on the Psychological Effect of Brain Lesions in Human Beings." In N. R. Ellis (Ed.), *International Review of Research in Mental Retardation.* New York: Academic Press, 1966.

Shipley, W. C. "A Self-Administering Scale for Measuring Intellectual Impairment and Deterioration." *Journal of Psychology,* 1940, *9,* 371-377.

Shipley, W. C. *Institute of Living Scale.* Los Angeles: Western, 1946.

Small, L. *Neuropsychodiagnostics in Psychotherapy.* New York: Brunner/Mazel, 1973.

Smith, A. "Neuropsychological Testing in Neurological Disorders." *Advances in Neurology,* 1975, *7,* 49-110.

Teuber, H. L., and Rudel, R. G. "Behavior After Cerebral Lesions in Children and Adults." *Developmental Medicine and Child Neurology,* 1962, *4,* 3-20.

Vega, A., and Parsons, O. A. "Cross Validation of the Halstead-Reitan Tests for Brain Damage." *Journal of Consulting Psychology,* 1967, *31,* 619-625.

Watson, C. G., and others. "Differentiation of Organics from Schizophrenics at Two Chronicity Levels by Use of the Reitan-Halstead Organic Test Battery." *Journal of Consulting and Clinical Psychology,* 1968, *32,* 679-685.

Yates, A. J. "The Validity of Some Psychological Tests of Brain Damage." *Psychological Bulletin,* 1954, *51,* 359-379.

15

Joseph F. Bertinetti

Substance Abuse

Substance abuse is the "unapproved use of a group of drugs that have the properties of altering mood and behavior" (Glasscote and others, 1972). Substances that have the potential to be abused include licit drugs (amphetamines; barbiturates; synthetic sedatives; and synthetic narcotics, such as methadone and opium derivatives other than heroin), illicit drugs (marijuana, heroin, and d-lysergic acid diethylamide), alcohol, gasoline, tobacco, caffeine, and model glue. Althouth food is abused by many, it will not be treated herein as a substance commonly abused. Conservative estimates list alcohol abusers at some 9 million (Albano, 1974) and opiate abusers at 485,000 (Glasscote and others, 1972). Abusers of licit drugs are extremely difficult to document because of the reporting system used. Pepper (1970) cites examples of the dilemma when 4 billion doses, or half of the stimulant drugs produced in this country yearly, end up in illegal distribution systems.

Background and Current Status*

Substance abuse has existed as long as mankind. In ancient religion and medicine, substances found in nature were used to produce psychological experiences. People were adept at extracting, grinding, and distilling essential oils and potions for either medicinal

*Many of the historical comments in this section are based on the analysis and views of Fuqua (1978).

or religious purposes. Some of these substances and their preparation have been handed down to contemporaries, who still employ them to produce altered states of consciousness. According to White and Albano (1974), all the modern industrialized states have some difficulty with substance abuse. The more open and less controlled an economy, the more options become available for the individual to produce a unique life style. By extension, the more freedom the individual has, the more he or she will abuse drugs. White and Albano believe that the most obvious substance abuse problems are found in countries where social mobility is strained or the society is under great tension; such countries include the United States, Great Britain, Japan, and Israel.

Of the many different substances that are potentially abusive, the drugs derived from opium have been used and abused for centuries. According to archeologists, the earliest users of the opium poppy were simple neolithic farmers in the mountainous areas of the eastern shore of the Mediterranean Sea. Clay tablets of the Sumerians, over 6,000 years old, referred to opium as the "plant of joy." Medical use of opium was referenced in the Ebers Papyrus, an Egyptian medical treatise around the sixteenth century B.C., as well as by the famous Greek physician Galen. Galen prescribed opium as a cure for epilepsy, venomous bites, melancholy, and essentially all maladies. In addition to its medicinal qualities, opium was used in the making of candies and cakes in ancient Greece.

Historical accounts of the "magical" qualities of opium continue with the Arabs. The ancient Arab physician al-Biruni wrote of opiate addiction. During the zenith of the Arab empire, alcohol usage was forbidden by the holy writings in the Koran, but opium and hashish were not forbidden and, in fact, became the principal means of euphoria. As the Arab empire spread to India and China, so did the spread and cultivation of the poppy to produce opium.

Early in the nineteenth century, a discovery by the German chemist Friedrich Wilhelm Sertürner led to the development of morphine. Morphine was found to be ten times stronger than opium, and it became widely used in medicine as a pain killer of known strength and reliability. Another significant date in the history of drug use and abuse occurred forty-nine years after Sertürner's contribution. Alexander Wood perfected an efficient drug delivery system—the hypodermic needle. Prior to Wood's contribution, morphine had to be taken orally, which meant that the rate of absorption of the drug into one's bloodstream was different for every person. Consequently, the pain-killing potential of the drug became limited.

During the American Civil War, morphine became the most-used pain killer in both armies. In addition to its pain-killing properties, it also proved useful in combating diarrhea and dysentery. Because it was used so extensively, addiction often resulted. For several decades following the Civil War, morphine addiction was so common in veterans of both sides that the term "soldier's disease" developed to describe its effects. In the years following the Civil War, the patent medicine industry flourished; and patent medicines increased the number of people addicted to substances, especially opium and morphine, since all such remedies contained a good percentage of both.

Near the close of the nineteenth century, a semisynthetic opiate was to have a pronounced effect on substance abuse. The Bayer Company became interested in marketing this new wonder drug as a cough suppressant. As part of the Bayer Company's marketing techniques, the name chosen for the drug was heroin. Physicians found the properties of this semisynthetic opiate helpful in providing some relief for those suffering from morphine addiction.

The earliest use of the barbiturates can be traced to 1903, when the first barbiturate, Verinol, was produced. Physicians welcomed this substance to provide patients relief for anxiety and insomnia, both of which were being treated with various opiates and alcohol. Opiates and alcohol, however, both produced many undesirable psychological, physiological, and social side effects. Today most instances of abuse for the barbiturate class of substances are found among 30- to 55-year-olds from middle-class family backgrounds in the United States, accounting for from 400,000 to 490,000 individuals who take depressants and tranquilizers for nonmedical purposes (Domestic Council Drug Abuse Task Force, 1975).

The next group of substances commonly abused are the stimulants or amphetamines. All amphetamines are synthetic. The earliest discovery of compounds having chemical properties similar to amphetamines can be traced to the last decade of the nineteenth century. However, the substance did not receive wide use until the 1930s when it was introduced as a Benzedrine bronchial inhaler. It soon became known for its usefulness in promoting wakefulness and mental alertness and in controlling the appetite. During World War II, soldiers readily downed tablets and capsules to achieve a quick pick-me-up. In postwar Japan the abuse of amphetamines was especially pronounced; as many as 15 million Japanese were classified as abusers of the substance. Amphetamines, like other substances, are abused when they are used solely for their "rush" and euphoric effect, or to exceed one's physical and mental limits, rather than for a specific medicinal purpose.

Related to the amphetamines is a natural substance called cocaine, one of the most potent stimulants known. Cocaine in its raw form is an extract from the coca bush leaf. Its widespread use by the Indians of South America was noted by Spanish explorers in the early 1500s. Notable people (among them Sigmund Freud, John Philip Sousa, and Arthur Conan Doyle's Sherlock Holmes) soon hailed cocaine as a cure for everything from headaches to depression. Cocaine was acclaimed the drug of the century. Coca-Cola, thought by many to be the "national drink," employed a cocaine-based formula in its drink until 1903. Cocaine enjoyed a monopoly until the early 30s, when amphetamines became available. Amphetamines toppled cocaine from its place because they were cheaper, lasted longer, and could be swallowed or injected rather than snuffed or snorted. Until the early 1960s cocaine virtually disappeared except for use as an anesthetic for certain ophthalmologic surgeries. In the 1960s it was reintroduced as a fad drug.

Marijuana and related substances have been known for thousands of years, since the ancient Greeks and Chinese. Marijuana was originally prescribed as a medicine. The Spaniards brought the plant to Central America in the mid-sixteenth century, and the British introduced it to America in the early 1600s. Its principal use at that time was not for smoking the plant but as a source of hemp, an important commodity in the economy of the American colonies. Its popularity was so intense that at one time only cotton and tobacco outranked hemp as the principal cash crops. Both marijuana and hashish, a marijuana derivative, contain tetrahydrocannabinols (THC). The concentration of THC affects the mind-altering properties of these substances; the higher the concentration, the greater will be the results of smoking the substances. Marijuana has seen a new rise in popularity in the last two decades. Many users of this substance have advocated its decriminalization, and strong lobby groups are attempting to eradicate its presence on the controlled-substance list. One state, New Mexico, has decriminalized its use for certain individuals undergoing chemotherapy for cancer; in this instance, the drug has offset some of the undesirable side effects of chemotherapy.

Lysergic acid diethylamide (LSD) introduces the area of the hallucinogens. Contained in this family are synthetic and semisynthetic compounds. LSD, first discovered in 1938, has properties that give new "insights" to its users. Users experience mind-altering situations, colors become alive, sound is seen. Perception of one's self becomes extremely keen. Other hallucinogens are peyote; mescaline, a substance extracted from peyote and used principally (and legally) by native Americans in religious rituals; Phenaclidine (PCP), also known as "angel dust," which is being abused by many adolescents today; and Psilocybin and its derivative, Psilocin, obtained from certain species of mushrooms.

Another group of substances, the inhalants, are volatile chemicals that produce intoxication when they are inhaled. The categories or groups include anesthetics (such as ether, chloroform, and nitrous oxide), aerosol propellants, and volatile solvents (such as glue, nail polish, paint remover, and gasoline). In every case of use other than for the intended purpose of the manufacturer, a definition of abuse seems appropriate. Adolescents and preadolescents are the main abusers of substances in this category.

Tobacco, another commonly abused substance, acts as a mild stimulant when smoked. Nicotine derived from tobacco increases the heart rate and increases blood pressure through greater cardiac activity and by peripheral constriction of the blood vessels (Carney, 1974).

Caffeine, the psychoactive agent in coffee, also has its roots in history. The Arabs used coffee as early as 900 A.D. (Ray, 1978). In addition to acting as a stimulant of the central nervous system and as a diurectic, caffeine has been found to produce anxiety, neurosis, nervousness, irritability, insomnia, and gastrointestinal disturbances (Greden, 1974).

Alcohol, perhaps the largest single substance available today, has been used and abused for centuries. Mead, an alcoholic beverage made from honey, was known in the Paleolithic Age, about 8000 B.C. Beer and berry wine were used about 6400 B.C. Grape wine dates from 400 B.C. Distilled products first became available in Arabia about 800 A.D. (Ray, 1978).

Substance abuse today continues as it has for centuries. In the United States, the extent of use of various substances is indicated by data from the National Institute of Drug Abuse (NIDA) and the National Prescription Audit of NIDA. These agencies have furnished the following data concerning the users of various substances and the number of prescriptions and refills for the period May 1976 to April 1977: (1) narcotics, 522,000 users, 2,345,000 prescriptions and refills; (2) analgesics, 34,000,000 prescriptions and refills; (3) barbiturates and related sedatives, 1,060,000 users, 19,416,000 prescriptions/refills; (4) minor tranquilizers, 1,360,000 users, 98,495,000 prescription/refills; (5) alcohol, 92,300,000 users; (6) major tranquilizers, 11,936,000 prescriptions; (7) inhalants, 375,000 users; (8) amphetamines and related stimulants, 1,780,000 users, 5,500,000 prescriptions/refills; (9) cocaine, 1,640,000 users; (10) nicotine, 64,570,000 users; (11) cannabis, 16,210,000 users; and (12) hallucinogens, 7,140,000 users. In addition, the use of coffee and its main derivative, caffeine, has been estimated at 16 pounds per person per year.

Critical Discussion

General Areas of Concern

To effectively assess substance abuse, one must employ both subjective and objective techniques. The subjective process of evaluation is satisfied primarily through observation and interviewing; the objective, principally by the use of standardized inventories, such as the Minnesota Multiphasic Personality Inventory (MMPI) and other personality tests, and also by the use of laboratory tests to ascertain content of substance.

Subjective evaluations, made by observation, can determine whether certain psychomotor functions are impaired; whether general appearance is neglected; and whether anxiety or lethargy, depending on the type of substance used, is apparent.

Objective assessment is more difficult to acquire. In the assessment of alcohol abuse, most investigators (for example, Armstrong, 1958; Rosen, 1960; Syme, 1957) agree that no unique premorbid alcohol abusive personality has been discovered; however, some empirical evidence suggests that a cluster of personality traits may appear after abuse has been established. Some of these traits are low stress tolerance (Lisansky, 1960); dependency (Blane, 1968; Witkin, Karp, and Goodenough, 1959); negative self-image, feelings of isolation, insecurity, and depression (Irwin, 1968; Weingold and others, 1968; Wood and Duffy, 1966). Jones (1968), Robins (1966), Hilgard and Newman (1963), and Sampson (1965), report on longitudinal studies of persons who abuse alcohol.

In studies of substance abuse other than alcohol, Hill, Haertgen, and Glaser (1960) and Gilbert and Lombardi (1967) present data derived from the MMPI. Their findings indicate that scale 4, Psychopathic Deviate Scale, is predominant in the profile. According to Martin and Inglis (1965), drug abusers are less tolerant of pain than nondrug abusers are. Halstead and Neal (1968), using the Eysenck Personality Inventory, found abusers ranking themselves as neurotic introverts. Wishnie (1977) considers substance abuse a manifestation of impulsive behavior.

Other studies mention antecedents for drug abuse behavior. Hamburg, Kraemer, and Jahnke (1975) studied junior and senior high school students and found that drug abuse for this group was progressive; they began with coffee or tea and progressed to wine and beer, hard liquor, tobacco, marijuana or hashish, hallucinogens, stimulants or depressants, and, finally to narcotics. In another study (Smith and Fogg, 1975), student drug users were compared to nonusers on twenty-three variables over a five-year period. The investigators found marijuana users and hard drug users to be more rebellious, less ambitious, less self-reliant, less accepted, and unsocial. In a similar study Jessor (1975) concluded that marijuana abuse among junior high students is associated with prior deviant attitudes and behavior.

In a study of male chronic LSD abusers, Welpton (1968) found that these abusers had major difficulties with sexual identification, dependency needs, and control of aggression. Sutker's (1971) research indicates that a psychopathic personality predates the onset of heroin abuse. Chein and his associates (1964) concluded that heroin abuse among adolescents is an extension of or a development out of personality disturbance and maladjustment.

Cohen, White, and Schooler (1971) used the Leary Interpersonal Check List to compare personality characteristics of hallucinogen abusers with the characteristics of a nonuser control group. The abusers proved to be more dependent, passively hostile individuals with identity problems. Another study, by Hartung, Baxter, and McKenna (1970), using the Holtzman Inkblot Technique, compared hallucinogen users with nonusers; the results indicated no significant differences with respect to body image or degree of defensiveness.

Smart and Jones (1970) compared MMPI profiles of hallucinogen users with those of nonusers and found a higher incidence of psychopathology among the user group. Naditch (1974) concluded that use of hallucinogens covaries positively with regression and negatively with adjustment.

Finally, Himmelsbach (1974) found that opiate abusers tend to be emotionally unstable people, persons who display inadequate and immature personalities, persons with character disorders, persons with psychoneuroses, or hedonists.

How does one intelligently assess the abuser from the nonabuser on the basis of all these findings? The answer: Not well enough, since the characteristics noted for substance abusers are also found in nonabusers.

Other comparisons of abusers have attempted to delineate certain social conditions (such as deprived living conditions, inadequate income, or minority group membership) that may be related to substance abuse. Perhaps there is some validity in research findings that support these contentions. However, they still do not explain why others who experience similar conditions do not resort to substance abuse.

If the research were consistent across substance types rather than abuser types, perhaps some patterns would emerge. Most research in this area, however, is beset by a number of conceptual and methodological problems (Gorsuch and Butler, 1976). Conceptually, researchers espouse specific theories and then carry out their research in ways that uphold the theory. As Platt (1975) points out, most researchers use a narrow group of personality dimensions, primarily those provided for by the MMPI. Furthermore, most studies on substance abuse focus on use or nonuse of a given drug while concurrent use of other drugs is ignored (Braucht and others, 1973). Khavari, Mabry, and Humes (1977) found that most studies of hallucinogen abuse deal with subjects from specific populations—students, societal dropouts, and patients in emergency treatment facilities—and do not account for personality variables of users who are not in these categories.

The personality correlates of substance use and abuse have been determined by the use of univariate variance-component models of analysis. Brill, Crumpton, and Grayson (1971); Simon and associates (1974); and Crain, Ertel, and Gorman (1975) have compared users with nonusers across personality traits. Khavari, Mabry, and Humes criticize this procedure on both conceptual and methodological grounds. Bock (1975), however, advocates the use of multivariate statistical procedures.

Comparative Philosophies and Theories

Many hypotheses have been offered to explain why an individual abuses substances. Dole and Nyswander (1967) believe that heroin use results in metabolic alteration, which "impels" the individual to continue use and abuse of the drug. Just as Fenichel (1945) classified substance abuse and addiction as impulse neuroses, Ray (1978) believes that drug-taking behavior is a form of neurotic behavior. Berger and Porterfield (1969) claim that individuals use and abuse substances for three basic reasons: as escape mechanisms, to achieve acceptance in a subculture, and to express hosility toward respectable society and the establishment. Savitt (1963) states that the abuser is usually unable to experience love and gratification through the usual channel of incorporation and introjection. The *Diagnostic and Statistical Manual of Mental Disorders (DSM-II)* (American Psychiatric Association, 1968) treats substance dependence as a personality disorder characterized by deeply ingrained, maladaptive patterns, often recognizable by the time of adolescence or earlier.

Ewing (1967) indicates that the nonnarcotic abuser is a passive-aggressive personality, passive-dependent type, who manipulates others and has a history of a weak or absent father and an indulgent but rejecting mother.

Wikler (1970) expresses the importance of primary reinforcement in conditioning leading to substance abuse; thus, alcohol, depressants, and tranquilizers tend to be used to release inhibitions; narcotics are used to reduce aggression, hunger, pain, fatigue, sexual desire, and fantasy; amphetamines are used to reduce hunger, fatigue, and depression; and hallucinogens are used to intensify fantasy.

Blachly (1970) considers substance abuse a seductive behavior whereby the victim actively participates in his or her own victimization. Maurer (1970) studied students and substance abuse and found that abusers generally feel that society has not provided them with the emotional competence necessary to cope with the world without chemicals. Naditch (1975) identified three dimensions of motives for LSD use: use for pleasure, use with therapeutic intent, and reluctant use as response to peer pressure.

Fracchia and his associates (1975), using the Edwards Personal Preference Schedule, derived four factors that distinguish heroin abusers; they tend to be nonconformists, unable to form close friendships, and exhibitionists and have no need for order and endurance. Kurtines, Hogan, and Weiss (1975), using the California Psychological Inventory, compared heroin addicts with psychiatric patients, incarcerated delinquents, undergraduate marijuana users, and police officers. Results indicated heroin users to be normal in terms of social poise and self-esteem; however, they were significantly more hostile, rebellious, and irresponsible than any of the comparison groups.

Hypotheses concerning the etiology of alcohol abuse are also abundant in the literature. Williams (1947) advocates a genotrophic theory, postulating that an inherited metabolic defect causes the need for certain dietary substances in excess amounts to those provided in the ordinary diet. Investigators such as Popham (1953) and Lester (1960) reject this theory; others—for instance, Mardones (1951), Randolph (1956), and Karolus (1961)—have attempted to extend it. However, there is no empirical evidence to support such a theory.

Endocrine theories—such as expressed by Gross (1945), Lovell and Tintera (1951), and Smith (1949)—attempt to explain alcohol abuse as an endocrine dysfunction. Goodwin and associates (1973) suggest that alcoholism in humans is partly based on the individual's heredity. Other studies—such as Goodwin and Guze (1974), Cruz-Coke (1964), Camps and Dodd (1967), Rodgers (1966), McClearn and Rodgers (1959), and Schukit, Goodwin, and Winokur (1972)—advocate the genetic model of alcohol abuse. The number of compounding variables in most of these studies, however, mitigates the validity of their results.

Elaboration on Critical Points

The task of developing an instrument to objectively assess one's propensity to abuse substances is a complex one. Measurement or assessment of substance abusers is usually made on populations of abusers, although several longitudinal studies have attempted to predict proneness with nonabusive samples. The inevitable problem of interpretation arises: Did the traits found in these studies precede the abusive behavior, which can then be viewed as causal, or are these traits a consequence of the abuse, which by observation already exists?

Many theorists have unsuccessfully attempted to construct instruments with predictive validity. Scientifically, such an instrument would have to be administered to every person at a certain age. Longitudinal data would then have to be maintained by someone at considerable expense. A number of independent variables—such as socioeconomic class; geographical location; political and legal climate of one's community, state, and nation; the national economy; and the availability of substances—might also have to be taken into consideration. These variables are obviously uncontrollable. Available techniques and instrumentation do not, of course, provide for this myriad of variables.

Personal Views and Recommendations

Substance abuse is not a twentieth-century phenomenon. It has been a problem in many societies over many centuries. Although no specific clinical measures exist presently to adequately measure the abuser, both prior to and after first usage of a substance, research should not be abandoned. In particular, careful studies of genetic and biological makeup may provide clues that will enable researchers to formulate measurable constructs to identify the abuser.

It is probably unrealistic to believe that we can eliminate the substance abuse problem by eradicating the substances altogether. American history provides a glaring example of such an attempt, when alcohol was prohibited in the 1920s. Prohibition through legislation proved to be unworkable. People of that era, like their predecessors, felt that substances are a necessity of life and thus demanded their availability. Other attempts to eradicate or otherwise control and rectify abuse problems by treating those who become substance abusers have likewise not been as successful as might have been expected. For example, a 99 percent recidivism rate is expected for opiate abusers who receive treatment.

From a developmental perspective, most people live in a drug culture. People are exposed to an acceptance of drugs from birth on. The mass media, as constant propagandists, remind people constantly to use medications and potentially abusive products. It is no wonder that substances are welcomed—to such an extent that many people insist on having a prescription from the physician for whatever is troubling them. Physicians comply because they feel it is medically correct and therapeutic, and it assures their political and economic control of the health industry. The extreme use of mood-altering prescriptive drugs is evidenced by the fact that in 1970 more than two hundred million prescriptions were filled for tranquilizing drugs. This alone might support the premise that contemporary American life is a drug culture.

Even after many centuries it appears that substance abuse continues to be a fact of life. Many techniques have been applied to eradicate various substances—without success. Many approaches have been formulated to predict propensity to abuse substances—again without success. Perhaps one method, education—not in the sense of telling people what the substances are but in educating them to respect substances and to use them in a judicious manner—has not been as effectively used as it might.

Application to Particular Variables

Analogous to venereal disease, there are no class boundaries, geographies, or sex roles that immunize against substance abuse. Research has, however, attempted to differentiate among certain groups. Carney (1971) found that, in general, females participate less often in all risky behaviors, including smoking tobacco. However, once a female does become a habitual smoker of tobacco, it is more difficult for her to stop than for a male (Schauble, Woody, and Resnikoff, 1967). Also, a female's use of other drugs is more likely and the intensity of her general problems becomes greater than for the average male smoker. The street addict, or abuser of many substances, has been identified as primarily a young Negro, Puerto Rican, or Chicano heroin abuser (Bates, 1966; Chambers, Moffett, and Jones, 1968; Robins and Murphy, 1967).

Abusers tend to come from fatherless, broken homes. Fewer than a third have completed high school. Most have poor work histories prior to and following initial substance use. Chambers, Hinesley, and Moldestad (1970) and Chambers and Inciardi (1971) found that the Negro female abuser came from a deprived, deviant ghetto background, as did her male counterpart. Similar generalizations have been made about Puerto Rican males and females. That is, they tend to come from deprived, deviant environments and readily engage in criminal activities. Female Puerto Rican substance abusers usually sell illegal substances more than their Caucasian or black counterparts to help support their abuse pattern (Ball and Pabon, 1965; DeFleur, Ball, and Snarr, 1969; Preble, 1966; Preble and Casey, 1969). According to Chambers, Cuskey, and Moffett (1970), 10 percent of the abusers in the United States are Chicano, although Chicanos account for only 2 percent of the population.

Many of the aforementioned studies might lead one to theorize that only members of minority groups are substance abusers. The various abuse patterns of nonminority groups have not been reported as accurately as they might have been. Perhaps many social and cultural advantages, such as better living conditions and more social opportunities, are afforded nonminority members. Substance abuse, however, still occurs in the form of alcohol abuse and other licit substance abuse rather than just in the form of illicit substance abuse. Those from nonminority groups who do abuse substances usually see their actions as resulting from their being medical patients; they do not consider themselves addicts or psychiatrically involved persons (Stephens and Levine, 1971). Other studies of Caucasian, middle-aged morphine abusers include those of Ball (1965) and O'Donnell (1969).

Black (1975) used the MMPI to assess Vietnam veterans who abused heroin. His findings showed neither greater nor less psychopathology and sociopathology than for reported samples of civilian substance abusers. In another study Kojak and Canby (1975) found U.S. Army heroin abusers in Thailand to have gross difficulties in living and working, lower intelligence levels, and poor social skills. Nail, Gunderson, and Arthur (1974) compared drug abuse patterns and social backgrounds of black and Caucasian U.S. Navy enlisted men. Their findings suggest that different cultural patterns may underlie drug abuse behaviors of the two groups. Weppner and his associates (1976) compared patients in a county hospital emergency room receiving assistance for drug overdose with patients already in a treatment facility for drug abuse. Findings indicated that the emergency room group of abusers were primarily female, older, and abusers of prescription drugs.

References

Albano, R. F. "Alcohol and Social Abuse." In W. White, Jr., and R. F. Albano (Eds.), *North American Symposium on Drugs and Drug Abuse.* Philadelphia: North American Publishing Company, 1974.

American Psychiatric Association. *Diagnostic and Statistical Manual of Mental Disorders.* (2nd ed.) Washington, D.C.: American Psychiatric Association, 1968.

Armstrong, J. D. "The Search for the Alcoholic Personality." *Annals of the American Academy of Political and Social Science,* 1958, *315,* 40-47.

Ball, J. C. "Two Patterns of Narcotic Drug Addiction in the United States." *Journal of Criminal Law, Criminology and Police Science,* 1965, *56,* 203-211.

Ball, J. C., and Pabon, D. O. "Locating and Interviewing Narcotic Addicts in Puerto Rico." *Sociology and Social Research,* 1965, *49* (4), 401-411.

Bates, W. M. "Narcotics, Negroes, and the South." *Social Forces,* 1966, *45,* 61-67.

Berger, F. M., and Porterfield, J. "Drug Abuse and Society." In R. Whittenborn (Ed.), *Drugs and Youth: Proceedings of the RAPCUS Symposium on Drug Abuse.* Springfield, Ill.: Thomas, 1969.

Blachly, P. H. "The Seductive Threshold as a Concept for Prophylaxis of Drug Abuse." In P. H. Blachly (Ed.), *Drug Abuse: Data and Debate.* Springfield, Ill.: Thomas, 1970.

Black, F. W. "Personality Characteristics of Viet Nam Veterans Identified as Heroin Abusers." *American Journal of Psychiatry,* 1975, *132,* 748-749.

Blane, H. T. *The Personality of the Alcoholic: Guises of Dependency.* New York: Harper & Row, 1968.

Bock, R. D. *Multivariate Statistical Methods in Behavioral Research.* New York: McGraw-Hill, 1975.

Braucht, G. N., and others. "Deviant Drug Use in Adolescents: A Review of Psychosocial Correlates." *Psychological Bulletin,* 1973, *79,* 92-106.

Brill, N. Q., Crumpton, E., and Grayson, H. M. "Personality Factors in Marijuana Use." *Archives of General Psychiatry,* 1971, *24,* 163-165.

Camps, F. E., and Dodd, B. E. "Increase in the Incidence of Nonsecretors of ABH Blood Group Substance Among Alcoholic Patients." *British Journal of Medicine,* 1967, *1,* 30-31.

Carney, R. E. *Risk-Taking Behavior.* Springfield, Ill.: Thomas, 1971.

Carney, R. E. "The Abuser of Tobacco." In J. G. Cull and R. E. Hardy (Eds.), *Types of Drug Abusers and Their Abuses.* Springfield, Ill.: Thomas, 1974.

Chambers, C. D., Cuskey, W. R., and Moffett, A. D. "Demographic Factors in Opiate Addiction Among Mexican-Americans." *Public Health Reports,* 1970, *85,* 523-531.

Chambers, C. D., Hinesley, R. K., and Moldestad, M. "Narcotic Addiction in Females: A Race Comparison." *International Journal of the Addictions,* 1970, *5,* 257-278.

Chambers, C. D., and Inciardi, J. A. "Criminal Careers of Female Narcotic Addicts." Paper presented at Institut International de Sociologie, 1971.

Chambers, C. D., Moffett, A. D., and Jones, J. P. "Demographic Factors Associated with Negro Opiate Addiction." *International Journal of the Addictions,* 1968, *3,* 329-343.

Chein, L., and others. *The Road to H.* New York: Basic Books, 1964.

Cohen, C., White, E., and Schooler, J. "Interpersonal Patterns of Personality for Drug-Abusing Patients." *Archives of General Psychiatry,* 1971, *24,* 353-358.

Crain, W. C., Ertel, D., and Gorman, B. S. "Personality Correlates of Drug Preferences Among College Undergraduates." *International Journal of the Addictions,* 1975, *10,* 849, 856.

Cruz-Coke, R. "Colour Blindness and Cirrhosis of the Liver." *Lancet,* 1964, *2,* 1064-1065.

DeFleur, L. B., Ball, J. C., and Snarr, R. W. "The Long-Term Social Correlates of Opiate Addiction." *Social Problems,* 1969, *17,* 225-234.

Dole, V., and Nyswander, M. "Heroin Addiction: A Metabolic Disease." *Archives of Internal Medicine,* 1967, *120,* 19-24.

Domestic Council Drug Abuse Task Force. *White Paper on Drug Abuse.* Washington, D.C.: U.S. Government Printing Office, 1975.

Ewing, J. A. "Addiction to Non-narcotic Addictive Agents." In A. M. Freedman and H. I. Kaplan (Eds.), *Comprehensive Textbook of Psychiatry.* Baltimore: Williams and Wilkins, 1967.

Fenichel, O. *The Psychoanalytic Theory of Neurosis.* New York: Norton, 1945.

Fracchia, J., and others. "Manifest Psychological Needs of Heroin Addicts." *Comprehensive Psychiatry,* 1975, *16,* 133-136.

Fuqua, P. *Drug Abuse: Investigation and Control.* New York: McGraw-Hill, 1978.

Gilbert, J. G., and Lombardi, D. M. "Personality Characteristics of Young Male Narcotic Addicts." *Journal of Consulting Psychology,* 1967, *31,* 536-538.

Glasscote, R. M., and others. *The Treatment of Drug Abuse: Programs, Problems, Prospects.* Washington, D.C.: American Psychiatric Association and National Association for Mental Health, 1972.

Goodwin, D. W., and Guze, S. B. "Heredity and Alcoholism." In B. Kissin and H. Beileiter (Eds.), *The Biology of Alcoholism.* Vol. 3. New York: Plenum, 1974.

Goodwin, D. W., and others. "Alcohol Problems in Adoptees Raised Apart from Alcoholic Biological Parents." *Archives of General Psychiatry*, 1973, *28*, 238-243.

Gorsuch, R. L., and Butler, M. C. "Initial Drug Abuse: A Review of Predisposing Social Psychological Factors." *Psychological Bulletin*, 1976, *83*, 120-137.

Greden, J. F. "Anxiety or Caffeinism: A Diagnostic Dilemma." *American Journal of Psychiatry*, 1974, *131*, 1082-1089.

Gross, M. "The Relationship of the Pituitary Gland to Some Symptoms of Alcoholic Intoxication and Chronic Alcoholism." *Quarterly Journal of Studies on Alcoholism*, 1945, *6*, 25-35.

Halstead, H., and Neal, C. D. "Intelligence and Personality in Drug Addicts: A Pilot Study." *British Journal of Addiction*, 1968, *63*, 237-240.

Hamburg, B. H., Kraemer, H. C., and Jahnke, W. "A Hierarchy of Drug Use in Adolescence: Behavioral and Attitudinal Correlates of Substantial Drug Use." *American Journal of Psychiatry*, 1975, *132*, 1155-1163.

Hartung, J., Baxter, J., and McKenna, S. "Body Image and Defensiveness in an LSD-Taking Subculture." *Journal of Projective Techniques and Personality Assessment*, 1970, *34*, 316-332.

Hilgard, J. R., and Newman, M. F. "Parental Loss by Death in Childhood as an Etiological Factor Among Schizophrenic Alcoholic Patients Compared with a Non-patient Community Sample." *Journal of Nervous and Mental Disease*, 1963, *137*, 14-28.

Hill, H. E., Haertgen, C. A., and Glaser, R. "Personality Characteristics of Narcotic Addicts as Indicated by the MMPI." *Journal of General Psychology*, 1960, *62*, 127-139.

Himmelsbach, C. K. "Opiate Addiction." In J. C. Cull and R. E. Hardy (Eds.), *Types of Drug Abusers and Their Abuses*. Springfield, Ill.: Thomas, 1974.

Irwin, T. "Attacking Alcohol as a Disease." *Today's Health*, 1968, *46*, 21-23, 72-74.

Jessor, R. "Predicting Time of Onset of Marihuana Use: A Developmental Study of High School Youth." In D. J. Lettieri (Ed.), *Predicting Adolescent Drug Abuse: A Review of Issues, Methods and Correlates*. Washington, D.C.: U.S. Government Printing Office, 1975.

Jones, M. C. "Personality Correlates and Antecedents of Drinking Patterns in Adult Males." *Journal of Consulting and Clinical Psychology*, 1968, *32*, 2-12.

Karolus, H. E. "Alcoholism and Food Allergy." *Illustrated Medical Journal*, 1961, *119*, 151-152.

Khavari, K. A., Mabry, E., and Humes, M. "Personality Correlates of Hallucinogen Use." *Journal of Abnormal Psychology*, 1977, *86*, 172-178.

Kojak, G., and Canby, J. P. "Personality and Behavior Patterns of Heroin Dependent American Servicemen in Thailand." *American Journal of Psychiatry*, 1975, *132*, 246-250.

Kurtines, W., Hogan, R., and Weiss, D. "Personality Dynamics of Heroin Use." *Journal of Abnormal Psychology*, 1975, *84*, 87-89.

Lester, D. "A Biological Approach to the Etiology of Alcoholism." *Quarterly Journal of Studies on Alcohol*, 1960, *21*, 701-703.

Lisansky, E. S. "The Etiology of Alcoholism: The Role of Psychological Predisposition." *Quarterly Journal of Studies on Alcohol*, 1960, *21*, 314-343.

Lovell, H. W., and Tintera, J. W. "Hypoadvenocorticism in Alcoholism and Drug Addiction." *Geriatrics*, 1951, *6*, 1-11.

Mardones, J. "On the Relationship Between Deficiency of B Vitamins and Alcohol Intake in Rats." *Quarterly Journal of Studies on Alcohol*, 1951, *12*, 563-575.

McClearn, G. E., and Rodgers, D. A. "Differences in Alcohol Preference Among Inbred Strains of Mice." *Quarterly Journal of Studies on Alcoholism*, 1959, *20*, 691-695.

Martin, J. E., and Inglis, J. "Pain Tolerance and Addiction." *British Journal of Social and Clinical Psychology*, 1965, *4*, 224-229.

Maurer, J. I. "Students and Drugs—Trip or Treat." In P. H. Blachly (Ed.), *Drug Abuse: Data and Debate.* Springfield, Ill.: Thomas, 1970.

Naditch, M. P. "Acute Adverse Reactions to Psychoactive Drugs, Drug Usage, and Psychopathology." *Journal of Abnormal Psychology*, 1974, *83*, 394-403.

Naditch, M. P. "Relation of Motives for Drug Use and Psychopathology in the Development of Acute Adverse Reactions to Psychoactive Drugs." *Journal of Abnormal Psychology*, 1975, *84*, 374-385.

Nail, R. L., Gunderson, E., and Arthur, R. J. "Black-White Differences in Social Background and Military Drug Abuse Patterns." *American Journal of Psychiatry*, 1974, *131*, 1097-1102.

O'Donnell, J. A. *Narcotic Addicts in Kentucky.* Washington, D.C.: U.S. Government Printing Office, 1969.

Pepper, C. *Congressional Record—House.* Vol. 116, Part 25, Sept. 24, 1970. Washington, D.C.: U.S. Government Printing Office, 1970.

Platt, J. J. " 'Addiction Proneness' and Personality in Heroin Addicts." *Journal of Abnormal Psychology*, 1975, *84*, 303-306.

Popham, R. E. "A Critique of the Genotrophic Theory of the Etiology of Alcoholism." *Quarterly Journal of Studies on Alcohol*, 1953, *14*, 228-237.

Preble, E. "Social and Cultural Factors Related to Narcotics Use Among Puerto Ricans in New York City." *International Journal of the Addictions*, 1966, *1*, 30-41.

Preble, E., and Casey, J. "Taking Care of Business—The Heroin User's Life on the Street." *International Journal of the Addictions*, 1969, *4*, 1-24.

Randolph, T. G. "The Descriptive Features of Food Addiction: Addictive Eating and Drinking." *Quarterly Journal of Studies on Alcohol*, 1956, *17*, 198-224.

Ray, O. *Drugs, Society and Human Behavior.* St. Louis: Mosby, 1978.

Robins, L. N. *Deviant Children Grow Up: A Sociological and Psychological Study of Sociopathic Personality.* Baltimore: Williams and Wilkins, 1966.

Robins, L., and Murphy, G. "Drug Use in a Normal Population of Young Negro Men." *American Journal of Public Health*, 1967, *57*, 1580-1596.

Rodgers, D. A. "Factors Underlying Differences in Alcohol Preference Among Inbred Strains of Mice." *Psychosomatic Medicine*, 1966, *28*, 498-513.

Rosen, A. C. "A Comparative Study of Alcoholic and Psychiatric Patients with the MMPI." *Quarterly Journal of Studies on Alcohol*, 1960, *21*, 253-266.

Sampson, E. E. "The Study of Ordinal Position: Antecedents and Outcomes." In B. A. Maher (Ed.), *Progress in Experimental Personality Research.* Vol. 2. New York: Academic Press, 1965.

Savitt, R. A. "Psychoanalytic Studies on Addiction: Ego Structure in Narcotic Addiction." *Psychoanalytic Quarterly*, 1963, *32*, 43-57.

Schauble, P. G., Woody, R. H., and Resnikoff, A. "Educational Therapy and Withdrawal from Smoking." *Journal of Clinical Psychology*, 1967, *23*, 518-519.

Schukit, M. A., Goodwin, D. A., and Winokur, G. "A Study of Alcoholism in Half Siblings." *American Journal of Psychiatry*, 1972, *128*, 1132-1136.

Simon, W. E., and others. "A Comparison of Marijuana Users and Nonusers on a Number of Personality Variables." *Journal of Consulting and Clinical Psychology*, 1974, *42*, 917-918.

Smart, R., and Jones, D. "Illicit LSD Users: Their Personality Characteristics and Psychopathology." *Journal of Abnormal Psychology*, 1970, *75*, 286-292.

Smith, G. M., and Fogg, C. P. "Teenage Drug Use: A Search for Causes and Conse-quences." In D. J. Lettieri (Ed.), *Predicting Adolescent Drug Abuse: A Review of Issues, Methods and Correlates.* Washington, D.C.: U.S. Government Printing Office, 1975.

Smith, J. J. "A Medical Approach to Problem Drinking." *Quarterly Journal of Studies on Alcohol,* 1949, *10,* 251-257.

Stephens, R., and Levine, S. "The Street Addict Role: Implications for Treatment." *Psychiatry,* 1971, *4,* 351-357.

Sutker, P. B. "Personality Differences and Sociopathy in Heroin Addicts and Non-addict Prisoners." *Journal of Abnormal Psychology,* 1971, *78,* 247-251.

Sviland, M. A. P. "The Heroin Addict on Methadone Maintenance: His Attitudes, Re-sistance to Psychotherapy and Identity Problems." In *Proceedings of the 80th Annual Convention of the American Psychological Association.* Washington, D.C.: American Psychological Association, 1972.

Syme, L. "Personality Characteristics and the Alcoholic." *Quarterly Journal of Studies on Alcohol,* 1957, *18,* 288-302.

Weingold, H., and others. "Depression as a Symptom of Alcoholism: Search for a Phe-nomenon." *Journal of Abnormal Psychology,* 1968, *73,* 195-197.

Welpton, D. R. "Psychodynamics of Chronic Lysergic Acid Diethylamide Use." *Journal of Nervous and Mental Disease,* 1968, *147,* 377-385.

Weppner, R. S., and others. "Effects of Criminal Justice and Medical Definitions of a Social Problem upon the Delivery of Treatment: The Case of Drug Abuse." *Journal of Health and Social Behavior,* 1976, *17,* 170-177.

White, W., Jr., and Albano, R. F. (Eds.). *North American Symposium on Drugs and Drug Abuse.* Philadelphia: North American Publishing Company, 1974.

Wikler, A. "Some Implications of Conditioning Theory for Problems of Drug Abuse." In P. H. Blachly (Ed.), *Drug Abuse: Data and Debate.* Springfield, Ill.: Thomas, 1970.

Williams, R. J. "The Etiology of Alcoholism: A Working Hypothesis Involving the Inter-play of Heredity and Environmental Factors." *Quarterly Journal of Studies on Alco-hol,* 1947, *7,* 567-587.

Wishnie, H. *The Impulsive Personality.* New York: Plenum, 1977.

Witkin, H. A., Karp, S. A., and Goodenough, D. R. "Dependence in Alcoholics." *Quar-terly Journal of Studies on Alcohol,* 1959, *20,* 493-504.

Wood, H. P., and Duffy, E. L. "Psychological Factors in Alcoholic Women." *American Journal of Psychiatry,* 1966, *123,* 341-345.

16

Thomas G. Burish

Type A/B Behavior Patterns

Friedman (1969, p. 84) describes the coronary-prone behavior pattern as "a characteristic action-emotion complex which is exhibited by those individuals who are engaged in a relatively *chronic struggle* to obtain an *unlimited* number of *poorly defined* things from their environment in the *shortest period of time* and, if necessary, against the opposing efforts of other things or persons in this same environment." People who manifest this behavior pattern are referred to as Type A individuals, whereas people who exhibit the opposite pattern of behavior (that is, people who live a relatively unhurried, relaxed, satisfied, serene style of life) are referred to as Type B individuals. The primary dimension along which Type A and Type B individuals vary is their "coronary proneness": Type A individuals are more likely to develop angina pectoris (a disorder involving a distinct type of chest pain), myocardial infarction (a disorder involving necrosis of heart tissue, commonly called heart attack), and other coronary heart diseases (CHD) than are Type B individuals. In addition, Type A individuals show relatively extreme degrees of impatience; mental and physical alertness; deep commitment to their occupation or profession; tenseness of facial musculature; rapid and animated speech, with frequent bursts of increased volume; hurried eating habits; feelings of being under almost continuous time pressure; and a vague guilt or uneasiness about relaxing or slowing down (Jenkins, 1975; Suinn, 1977). Research aimed at extracting the major dimensions of Type A behavior from among all these characteristics (see, for example, Zyzanski and Jenkins, 1970) has generally resulted in the specification of three major factors: (1) competitive, hard-driving striving for achievement; (2) an exaggerated sense of time urgency; and (3) an over-involvement in one's job and professional responsibilities, often to the relative neglect of other aspects of one's life.

Background and Current Status

The observation that people who develop cardiovascular disease exhibit a charac-teristic pattern of behavior dates back many years. For example, in 1897 Sir William Osler wrote: "In the worry and strain of modern life arterial degeneration is not only very common, but develops often at a relatively young age. For this I believe that the high pressure at which men live and the habit of working the machine to its maximum capac-ity are responsible rather than excesses in eating or drinking" (pp. 153-154). Later, the Menningers (1936) hypothesized that strong (and usually repressed) aggressive tendencies also contribute to CHD. Dunbar (1943) described coronary disease patients as hard-driving, goal-oriented individuals who devote most of their life to their work. In Kemple's (1945) view, coronary-prone individuals manifest "a persistent pattern of aggressiveness and drive to dominate. . . . They are usually very ambitious and strive compulsively to achieve goals incorporating power and prestige" (p. 87).

In spite of these consistent clinical descriptions, the idea of a "coronary-prone behavior pattern" was never widely accepted in professional circles until several years later, when cardiologists Meyer Friedman and Ray Rosenman began publishing an impres-sive series of experimental demonstrations of the existence of a coronary-prone behavior pattern, which they referred to as the Type A pattern. Their work on coronary-prone behavior was spurred by the observation that many of the traditional "risk factors" for coronary disease did not adequately predict differences in incidence of the disease among various groups of people (Friedman and Rosenman, 1957). However, these scientists did notice that such risk factors as serum cholesterol level and blood coagulation time were related to job pressures and demands, with increases in these factors occurring during times of increased occupational stress and decreasing during times of decreased occupa-tional demand and pressure (Friedman, Rosenman, and Carroll, 1958). These findings led to the formulation "of a specific overt behavior pattern (pattern A) that we believed either was associated with or actually induced abnormal changes in serum cholesterol level and blood clotting time" (Friedman and Rosenman, 1959, p. 1286). In their initial empirical test of the relationship between Type A behavior and CHD, Friedman and Rosenman (1959) first asked men in various businesses and corporations to identify ac-quaintances who fit the Type A or Type B behavior descriptions; then they personally interviewed these men to assess the "degree of development of his particular behavior pattern" (p. 1287). Further study of these individuals indicated that coronary artery disease was seven times more prevalent in Type A individuals than in Type B individuals and that this finding could not be explained by differences in exercise, cigarette smoking, or drinking and eating habits. For the first time, the existence of a coronary-prone be-havior pattern was thus empirically demonstrated.

The contemporary view of Type A and Type B behavior patterns is strongly grounded on the early work of Friedman and Rosenman. However, the Type A and Type B behaviors originally described by Friedman and Rosenman are currently viewed as extreme end points of a behavioral continuum along which all people vary. As Jenkins (1975) has noted, no one Type A individual exhibits all the behaviors characteristic of this pattern, and the ones that he does display will not all be exhibited to the same degree. The same is true of Type B individuals. The crucial distinction between Type A and Type B individuals is thus one of degree: Type A individuals exhibit more behaviors characteristic of this pattern more often and to a greater extent than do Type B individuals.

Type A behavior is currently considered neither an invariable personality trait nor a universal response to certain situations. Instead, it is considered a function of both the individual *and* the environment. Thus, Type A individuals are more likely to exhibit this behavior pattern in challenging, competitive environments; and, correspondingly, challenging, competitive environments are more likely to produce (or attract) Type A individuals.

In contrast to the definition of the Type A/B dimension, which has changed little over recent years, current techniques for assessing these patterns vary considerably from the original peer-nomination method used by Friedman and Rosenman. In general, current assessment strategies are more objective than the peer-nomination procedure, and greater efforts have been made to establish their validity. These current strategies, which include a structured interview, a battery of performance tests, and a paper-and-pencil questionnaire, will be discussed in detail in a later section of the chapter. However, it should be noted at this point that the current procedure for validating *any* Type A/B assessment instrument is to establish its predictive validity in designating the occurrence of CHD and not its construct validity in actually measuring Type A and Type B behaviors. That is, a particular tool is currently considered a valid index of Type A and B behaviors to the extent that Type A ("coronary-prone") individuals develop CHD and Type B ("noncoronary-prone") individuals do not. Whether the tool actually assesses "competitiveness" or "time urgency" or any other supposedly relevant behavior appears to be of less importance.

Critical Discussion

General Areas of Concern

Theoretically, practically, and even historically, the central issue in the assessment of Type A behavior has been its association with the development of CHD. Over twenty retrospective and prospective studies have investigated this relationship, and most of these report very positive findings. In general, these studies indicate not only that Type A behavior is significantly related to CHD but also that it may be one of the most predictive risk factors for coronary disease so far discovered (Rosenman and others, 1966). The most impressive research in this area is based on the prospective "Western Collaborative Group Study," in which approximately 3,000 initially healthy men were followed for over eight years. Each of these men was categorized as Type A or B on the basis of a structured interview, and his cardiovascular status, blood lipids, coagulation time, and smoking, drinking, and eating habits were monitored regularly. Results published after two and a half years (Rosenman and others, 1966), four and a half years (Rosenman and others, 1970), and eight and a half years (Rosenman and others, 1975), consistently indicated that Type A behavior was related to CHD. Specifically, among the 257 men who had developed clinical CHD within the span of eight and a half years, there were over twice as many Type A as Type B individuals. Moreover, even after twelve other coronary risks were statistically controlled (such as serum cholesterol, blood pressure, and cigarette usage), the relationship between Type A behavior and CHD remained statistically significant. This finding suggests that the relationship was not an artifact of the association of Type A behavior with one or more other risk factors.

In addition to documenting the relationship of Type A behavior to both the incidence and the prevalence of CHD, some investigations have also shown that this behavior pattern is related to the degree of atherosclerosis, as determined by coronary angiography (see Jenkins, 1976), and to the occurrence of reinfarction in people who already have coronary disease (Jenkins and others, 1971). There is also some indication that the more intense the Type A behavior pattern, the more strongly it is related to coronary disease (Friedman, 1969), although this trend has not held up in all studies (see, for example, Keith, Lown, and Stare, 1965). Finally, attempts have been made to assess whether the relationship between Type A behavior and CHD applies equally to both myocardial infarction and angina pectoris. The results of these studies have been mixed, with some (for example, Rosenman and others, 1975) reporting a significant relationship between Type A behavior and both myocardial infarction and angina pectoris and others (for example, Keith, Lown, and Stare, 1965) reporting a relationship for only one or the other of these disorders. A recent item analysis of one of the questionnaires used to assess Type A/B behaviors (the Jenkins Activity Survey for Health Prediction) has suggested that there may in fact be two or three different patterns of Type A behavior and that each of these patterns may be primarily related to the development of a single type of coronary disease (Jenkins, Zyzanski, and Rosenman, 1978). These findings are important because they provide both a possible explanation for some of the inconsistencies in previous research and the means by which to increase the specificity of predicting CHD in the future. Overall then, it appears, then, that Type A behavior is related to the incidence, prevalence, recurrence, and perhaps severity of CHD. Moreover, there is some evidence that different facets or patterns of Type A behavior may be especially predictive of specific types of coronary pathology.

Closely related to research on the relationship between Type A behavior and CHD has been the search for a convenient and accurate method of assessing Type A/B behaviors. Two of the early instruments developed for this purpose eventually proved to be unreliable and hence have largely been abandoned. The first, the peer-nomination method, simply consists of describing the Type A and B behavior patterns to a group of individuals and then having these people classify their friends or fellow workers along the A/B continuum. Unfortunately, the consistency between raters in classifying their peers is less than desirable (Caffrey, 1968) and, of course, varies uncontrollably from study to study. A second early technique involved the polygraphic measurement of chest respiration, body movements, and hand clenching while subjects listened to a tape recording designed to elicit Type A behavior (Friedman and Rosenman, 1960). This technique was eventually judged to be insensitive and unreliable, sometimes even classifying more coronary patients as Type B than Type A (Keith, Lown, and Stare, 1965; Rosenman and others, 1966).

The first widely accepted and well-validated procedure for measuring Type A/B behaviors was the standard structured interview, originally designed by Rosenman and Friedman (Rosenman and others, 1964). This technique, which is currently one of the two most popular A/B assessment procedures, takes from twenty to thirty minutes to administer and consists of twenty-seven questions covering four topic areas: (1) ambition and drive, (2) competitiveness, (3) emotional expression, and (4) impatience and time urgency (Jenkins, Rosenman, and Friedman, 1968). However, the classification of a person as Type A or B depends more on the person's expressive gestures and motor behaviors than on the content of his or her answers. The ultimate behavioral classification thus results from an intuitive summing by the interviewer of the nature and intensity of the person's responses as well as his or her behaviors during the interview. A person may receive a classification of "fully developed" or "incompletely developed" Type A or Type B, with a rare fifth classification of "intermediate" given to people whose behavior does not clearly fall into an A/B category.

Although the interview technique is generally regarded as the most accurate method of assessing Type A/B behavior (Dembroski and others, in press), it suffers from several weaknesses. First, the interview procedure is relatively long and is generally impractical for assessing large groups of individuals. Second, since no objective criteria for administering or interpreting the interview have been published, it is impossible to assess whether one is consistently and accurately classifying people as Type A or B. Also, the fact that no objective administration and scoring guidelines exist essentially means that the only way to become an interviewer is to train under Friedman, Rosenman, or one of their trainees. In addition to being inconvenient, such training is very time consuming, taking up to one month (Jenkins, Rosenman, and Friedman, 1967).

Because of these problems, several other techniques for assessing the A/B behavior dimension have been developed. These include a battery of performance tests (Bortner and Rosenman, 1967); a 14-item semantic differential type of rating scale (Bortner, 1969); and several techniques of voice analysis (see, for example, Scherwitz, Berton, and Leventhal, 1977; Schucker and Jacobs, 1977), in which such characteristics as speed of ·speaking and emphasis in answering are measured or rated. Of these three techniques, analysis of voice characteristics seems to be the most promising for the following reasons: (1) it provides an objective, nontechnical, and reliable method of assessment; (2) initial evaluations of its ability to predict the prevalence of CHD are very positive; and (3) it provides a potentially accurate and reliable method of objectively scoring the structured interview and for discriminating which verbal behaviors emitted during the interview are most important for identifying Type A and B behaviors.

Clearly the most popular and best-researched alternative to the structured interview, however, is the Jenkins Activity Survey for Health Prediction (JAS). The JAS is a self-administered, computer-scored, 54-item questionnaire, which has both student (see Glass, 1977) and adult forms and takes only a few minutes to complete. Since the first draft of the JAS appeared in 1964, it has gone through numerous revisions and has been compared to the structured interview in both retrospective and prospective studies of CHD. While the overall agreement between the two techniques is statistically significant, ranging from 65 to 73 percent (Dembroski and others, in press), it is far from perfect, suggesting that the two techniques may be measuring different aspects of Type A and B behaviors. This notion is supported by research indicating that the JAS and the structured interview generally measure the same content but that the interviewer, in making a final classification, tends to downplay the content but weigh heavily the interviewee's speech characteristics. (Scherwitz, Berton, and Leventhal, 1977). Thus, classification by the JAS may not closely agree with that by the interview because, whereas the former focuses exclusively on *what* the person says, the latter focuses primarily on *how* the person says it. This difference in emphasis does not by itself argue that one technique is necessarily more valid than the other; however, preliminary research has in fact suggested that the interview method may be a better predictor of CHD (see Dembroski and others, in press).

The development of relatively reliable and valid assessment techniques, such as the structured interview and the JAS, has allowed researchers to begin to investigate other issues evolving from the relationship of Type A behavior to CHD. One such issue involves the question of how Type A behavior develops. To date, four studies of a developmental nature have been carried out. The first (Matthews and Glass; reported in Glass, 1977) indicated that Type A behavior can be identified in children as young as 9 years old; however, the second (Matthews and Krantz, 1976), an investigation of Type A and B behavior patterns in monozygotic and dizygotic twins, found no genetic basis for this behavior, and the third (Matthews, Richin, and Glass; reported in Glass, 1977) found no systematic basis for its development in the way that Type A and B mothers interact with their sons. The final study (Bortner, Rosenman, and Friedman, 1970) did find a weak tendency for Type A and B fathers to have Type A and B sons, respectively, but could not uncover the mechanism by which such paternal influence might operate. Overall, then, there are virtually no data that suggest how Type A and B behavior patterns develop. Because of this lack of data, and because the same conditions that produce Type A behavior in early life may increase the risk of coronary disease in later life, this area needs and merits further research.

Another area which has gained increased attention concerns the development of strategies for modifying or controlling Type A behavior. Again, there has been a dearth of relevant research. To date, only two experimental investigations relate directly to this issue, and neither provides convincing evidence that Type A behavior can be significantly changed. Suinn and Bloom (1978) found that a six-session "Cardiac Stress Management Program" did not produce a significant overall decrease in Type A scores as measured by the JAS, although it did significantly reduce the "Speed and Impatience" and the "Hard-Driving" subscales of this measure. The treatment also resulted in a significant decrease in self-reported anxiety and in a nonsignificant decrease in systolic and diastolic blood pressure, although in the latter case the results did not reach statistical significance. Roskies and his associates (1978) assigned healthy Type A individuals to either a dynamically or a behaviorally oriented therapy program aimed at reducing their Type A behaviors. After fifteen weekly sessions, subjects in both treatment groups showed significant reductions in serum cholesterol and systolic blood pressure and a general increase in reported life satisfaction. Unfortunately, however, the investigators did not include a no-treatment control group, nor did they remeasure Type A behavior after their treatment program was completed; hence, it is impossible to tell whether the reported changes were in any way related to the treatments or to a change in behavior patterns. Clearly, much more work needs to be done to determine whether Type A behavior can be modified and, more important, whether the modification of Type A behavior will lead to a decrease in the incidence of CHD.

Comparative Philosophies and Theories

Perhaps the most important theoretical issue at present concerns the processes by which Type A behavior produces an increased risk of CHD. Present-day theorizing on this issue takes place at two levels. First, several researchers have investigated the pathophysical correlates of Type A behavior, speculating that perhaps Type A individuals are more likely than Type B individuals to suffer CHD because they have higher serum lipid levels, faster blood coagulation times, and the like. Other researchers have gone one step further, speculating about why Type A individuals in turn display these pathophysical reactions. Theorizing at this level generally focuses on the social-personality attributes of Type A individuals, especially on the manner in which they experience and cope with stress.

Consonant with the first level of theorizing, research has indeed confirmed that Type A individuals are more likely to exhibit physiological and endocrine states that can increase the risk of CHD. For example, in comparison with Type B individuals, Type A individuals have significantly greater beta-lipoprotein concentrations (Rosenman and Friedman, 1963), faster blood-clotting times (Friedman and Rosenman, 1959), greater heart rate variability (Dembroski, McDougall, and Shields, 1977), and higher serum cholesterol and serum lipid levels (Rosenman and Friedman, 1961, 1963). During waking hours Type A individuals also secrete more epinephrine and more norepinephrine, and this increased catecholamine secretion may in turn be responsible for the increased serum lipids and blood-clotting time (Friedman and others, 1960). Finally, and perhaps most important, results of the Western Collaborative Group Study (Friedman and others, 1968) indicate that, no matter what the cause of death, autopsy findings reveal significantly more atherosclerosis and coronary occlusion in Type A than in Type B individuals.

The findings reviewed above support the theory that the crucial link between Type A behavior and CHD may be the development of damaging physioendocrinological conditions. However, we still do not know why Type A individuals develop these pathophysical reactions to a greater extent than do Type B individuals. According to several researchers, the answer to this question may lie in the nature of Type A behavior itself. Specifically, they hypothesize (1) that stress can lead to physiological states that increase the risk of CHD and (2) that Type A behaviors tend to increase and perpetuate high levels of stress. It follows from these two premises that Type A individuals would be more likely than Type B individuals to develop CHD. As previously discussed, the conclusion of this theory is well supported; we will now look briefly at the two premises.

The first premise, that stress can lead to damaging physioendocrinological consequences and eventually to coronary disease, is supported by research in a variety of areas. For example, several studies have shown that serum cholesterol level rises as a result of stress (Friedman, Rosenman, and Carroll, 1958; Rahe and others, 1971). Other research documents a positive relationship between stress and increased secretion of certain adrenal medulla hormones—most notably, adrenaline and noradrenaline (Mason, 1972; Selye, 1956). These hormones, in turn, may directly contribute to myocardial infarction by elevating blood pressure and increasing the aggregation of blood platelets, and these changes may, in turn, lead to thrombosis (Glass, 1977). Finally, a growing body of research has directly related the clinical presence of CHD to stress arising from such situations as the death of a close relative (Parkes, Benjamin, and Fitzgerald, 1969), excessive work and responsibility (House, 1975), and a variety of general life dissatisfactions (Glass, 1977; Jenkins, 1976). All in all, these findings clearly indicate that stress can enhance the risk of CHD.

That Type A individuals live under increased stress *because* of their Type A behaviors is the second basic premise. The rationale for this premise has been clearly stated by Suinn (1977, pp. 56-57): "If one examines the characteristics of the Type A individual, it becomes clear that this individual lives in an environment of many stresses. These stresses may derive from deadlines, or the competitiveness, or the drive towards success, or the overcommitment to work responsibilities. Stress may also develop secondarily as a result of the impatience experienced by the Type A individual when achievement is being blocked. . . . What I am saying is that the Type A individuals tend to put themselves in situations which involve stress, for example, because of their drive, competitiveness, achievement orientation, or self-imposition of deadlines." Suinn also points out that the Type A individual deals with this increased stress by increasing his or her Type A behavior; that is, the more deadlines the Type A person sets and the more responsibilities taken on, the more impatient, hard-driving, and competitive this individual becomes. Thus, a self-perpetuating, stress-inducing cycle is established. Recent research appears to support Suinn's theory. For example, Dembroski and MacDougall (1978) found that Type A individuals have a strong preference for working alone under pressure, a characteristic that may "impose stress beyond what the situation requires by needlessly increasing one's job load or responsibility" (p. 32). Similarly, Carver, Coleman, and Glass (1976) found that Type A individuals not only exerted greater effort on a treadmill exercise test than did Type B individuals but also tended to deny or suppress their feelings of fatigue. This characteristic of ignoring fatigue or pain may exacerbate the intensity of the stress. Thus, for example, Type A individuals are more likely to ignore early signs of heart problems and delay seeking treatment, and as a result "an ongoing infarction might become more severe, or prodromal fatigue might result in full-fledged heart attack" (p. 465). Clearly, Type A behavior can readily and perhaps dangerously increase stress and the risk of CHD.

A more specific and at this point speculative theory about the relationship between Type A behavior and stress has been put forward by Glass (1977). Glass hypothesizes that Type A behavior is actually a coping strategy used by some individuals to maintain control over their environment. Thus, Type A individuals work longer, faster, and more aggressively. In addition, when faced with an *uncontrollable* situation, Type A individuals are more likely, after an initial flurry of activity aimed at gaining control, to give up trying and instead to assume a posture of helplessness. Glass summarizes his theory and relates it to CHD as follows: "In other words, Pattern A subjects experience the alternation of active coping and giving up more frequently and intensely than Pattern B subjects. . . . To the extent that coronary disease is influenced by a cycle of hyper-reactivity and hypo-reactivity, the greater likelihood of the disease in As might be explained in terms of the cumulative effects of the excessive rise and fall of catecholamines released by the repetitive interplay of Pattern A and uncontrollable stress" (p. 172). Although Glass cites a number of published and unpublished studies that seem to support his theory, he admits that it is probably oversimplified and will require some modification. Nevertheless, it provides one of the first and most detailed attempts to link Type A behavior with stress and CHD.

Elaboration on Critical Points

Three critical points emerge from the empirical and theoretical work thus far carried out on Types A and B behavior. First, although there is an unmistakable relationship between Type A behavior and coronary disease, so much so that Type A behavior can rightfully be declared a risk factor for the development of this disease, the data accumulated so far do not demonstrate a causal relationship between Type A behavior and subsequent coronary pathology. It is possible, for example, that some third and as yet unidentified factor is responsible for both the behavior and the disease. In other words, although Type A behavior may be a useful *predictor* of CHD, at this point we cannot say conclusively that it directly causes CHD.

Second, although statistically significant, the relationship between Type A behavior and CHD is not exceptionally strong. Many people who develop CHD are not Type A individuals, and many Type A individuals continue on for years without developing CHD. As a clinical tool, the presence of Type A behavior can best be used as a guide to appraising in advance those individuals in a large group of people who are most likely to develop CHD. (Of course, other risk factors should also be considered in such an appraisal.) The prediction of CHD in an individual or a small group of individuals on the basis of behavior patterns cannot yet be recommended.

Finally, the relationship of stress to both Type A behavior and CHD seems to be an important one. Although it has repeatedly been stated that Type A behavior is not the same as stress (see, for example, Jenkins, 1975), nevertheless it appears that Type A individuals generally lead more stressful lives, perhaps because of their Type A behavior. Both Type A behavior and the stress it produces may eventually be linked to the development of coronary pathology. Moreover, reduction of the high levels of stress experienced by Type A individuals may be necessary before effective therapeutic modification of the behavior pattern can be made (Suinn, 1977).

Personal Views and Recommendations

Since cardiovascular disease is the major source of death in the United States, it is clearly of substantial importance to continue research on the nature of Type A behavior and its relationship to CHD. Three specific recommendations can be made in this regard. First, while the global concept of Type A behavior is clearly a meaningful one, it seems worthwhile to pursue the possibility that there are actually several different patterns or at least components of Type A behavior. The work by Jenkins and his colleagues on the major factors of the JAS and the differential relationship of various JAS items to various types of coronary pathology provides an important starting point for such research.

Second, additional research is needed on the nature and development of Type B behavior. Unfortunately, most investigators have focused rather exclusively on Type A behavior and have either ignored Type B behavior or have simply referred to it as the "absence of Type A." Nonetheless, it is equally important, both practically and theoretically, to know why Type B individuals do not develop CHD as to know why Type A individuals do; in fact, in terms of developing programs aimed at preventing CHD, it may even be more important. With a minimum of additional planning, many researchers can and should study the nature of Type B behavior at the same time they are studying Type A.

Finally, our understanding of the environmental and genetic determinants of Type A behavior, as well as the causal relationship between this behavior pattern and CHD, might be substantially increased if an animal model for studying Type A behavior could be produced. This point has been made previously by Jenkins (1976), but it has apparently received little attention.

Application to Particular Variables

Regrettably, the vast majority of research performed with Type A and B populations has been largely limited to white, middle-class, middle-aged males. Overall, there is thus little information available on the differential incidence or nature of Type A behavior among other populations. Obviously, this is an area that needs further research.

Age. Although research has indicated that coronary disease in general is more common in older (over 50) than younger age groups, few data have been collected on the differential incidence of Type A/B behaviors as a function of age. The research which has been conducted suggests that the association between Type A behavior and CHD is stronger in younger, as opposed to older, age groups (see, for example, Shekelle, Schoenberger, and Stamler, 1976). This relationship is not surprising and simply suggests that older individuals are likely to succumb eventually to some type of cardiovascular problem independent of their behavior type. Thus, it is in the prediction of early CHD that Type A behavior can and apparently does make its most significant contribution.

Sex. The overwhelming majority of research on Type A/B behaviors has been carried out with males. In general, the limited research on females suggests that the incidence of Type A behavior is lower, and the relationship to CHD is weaker among women than among men. However, the incidence of Type A behavior among females appears to be increasing and its relationship to CHD appears to be growing stronger as the employment and vocational equality of women also rises (Rosenman and Friedman, 1961; Waldron and others, 1977).

Education. There appears to be a weak positive relationship between education and Type A behavior, such that high school and college graduates are more likely to display Type A behavior than are individuals who have not earned a high school diploma (Keith, Lown, and Stare, 1965; Rosenman and others, 1975).

Socioeconomic Status. As determined by income, there is no evidence of a relationship between Type A behavior and socioeconomic status (Rosenman and others, 1975).

Vocation. Individuals in the professional and managerial occupations tend to display more Type A behavior than individuals in other occupations. However, this relationship is not a strong one, and there are Type A and B individuals at all occupational levels (Glass, 1977; Jenkins, 1975).

Ethnic/Racial Factors. Insufficient data exist to draw conclusions about, or even point to trends in, the relationship between race and behavior pattern. However, the possibility that such trends exist is suggested in a study of Waldron and associates (1977), which found that the particular manner in which Type A behavior is displayed by blacks may be different from the way it is displayed by whites. Specifically, whereas "job involvement" and "hard driving and competitive" summarized much of the Type A behavior in whites, "striving to advance" and "hard working" were better descriptors for blacks.

Disorders. With the exception of two studies and, of course, research on cardiovascular problems, no experimental investigations have been carried out on the relationship of Type A and B behavior patterns to various physical, intellectual, or psychiatric disorders, considered either individually or in an interactive fashion. The first study, reported by Friedman and Rosenman (1960), found that neurotic subjects, like normal control subjects, manifested significantly less Type A behavior than did subjects with CHD. Unfortunately, however, in this early study the investigators employed an unreliable method of assessing Type A behavior, the polygraphic method (see earlier discussion on assessment techniques); thus, their finding of a relative lack of Type A behavior in neurotic individuals must be regarded with caution. The second study, reported by Glass (1977), found that hospitalized alcoholics scored as high on the JAS as did hospitalized coronary patients and that both of these groups scored higher than normal control subjects. These findings led Glass to speculate that a large proportion of alcoholics may be Type A individuals and also that "alcoholism and clinical CHD may be alternative outcomes of Pattern A behavior" (p. 139). To date, no further research has been carried out either to replicate Glass's finding of a relationship between alcoholism and Type A behavior or to support his hypothesis that alcoholism may in some cases result from Pattern A behavior.

References

Bortner, R. W. "A Short Rating Scale as a Potential Measure of Pattern A Behavior." *Journal of Chronic Diseases,* 1969, *22,* 87-91.

Bortner, R. W., and Rosenman, R. H. "The Measurement of Pattern A Behavior." *Journal of Chronic Diseases,* 1967, *20,* 525-533.

Bortner, R. W., Rosenman, R. H., and Friedman, M. "Familial Similarity in Pattern A Behavior." *Journal of Chronic Diseases,* 1970, *23,* 39-43.

Caffrey, B. "Reliability and Validity of Personality and Behavioral Measures in a Study of Coronary Heart Disease." *Journal of Chronic Diseases,* 1968, *21,* 191-204.

Carver, C. S., Coleman, A. E., and Glass, D. C. "The Coronary-Prone Behavior Pattern and the Suppression of Fatigue on a Treadmill Test." *Journal of Personality and Social Psychology,* 1976, *33,* 460-466.

Dembroski, T. M., and MacDougall, J. M. "Stress Effects on Affiliation Preferences Among Subjects Possessing the Type A Coronary-Prone Behavior Pattern." *Journal of Personality and Social Psychology,* 1978, *36,* 23-33.

Dembroski, T. M., MacDougal, J. M., and Shields, J. L. "Physiologic Reactions to Social Challenge in Persons Evidencing the Type A Coronary-Prone Behavior Pattern." *Journal of Human Stress,* 1977, *3,* 2-9.

Dembroski, T. M., and others. "Assessment of Coronary-Prone Behavior." In T. M. Dembroski (Ed.), *Coronary-Prone Behavior.* New York: Springer, in press.

Dunbar, H. F. *Psychosomatic Diagnosis.* New York: Hoeber, 1943.

Friedman, M. *Pathogenesis of Coronary Artery Disease.* New York: McGraw-Hill, 1969.

Friedman, M., and Rosenman, R. H. "Comparison of Fat Intake of American Men and Women." *Circulation,* 1957, *16,* 339-347.

Friedman, M., and Rosenman, R. H. "Association of Specific Overt Behavior Pattern with Blood and Cardiovascular Findings." *Journal of the American Medical Association,* 1959, *169,* 1286-1296.

Friedman, M., and Rosenman, R. H. "Overt Behavior Pattern in Coronary Disease." *Journal of the American Medical Association,* 1960, *173,* 1320-1325.

Friedman, M., Rosenman, R. H., and Carroll, V. "Changes in the Serum Cholesterol and Blood Clotting Time in Men Subjected to Cyclic Variation of Occupational Stress." *Circulation,* 1958, *17,* 852-861.

Friedman, M., and others. "Excretion of Catecholamines, 17-Ketosteroids, 17-Hydroxy-corticoids and 5-Hydroxyindole in Men Exhibiting a Particular Behavior Pattern (A) Associated with High Incidence of Clinical Coronary Artery Disease." *Journal of Clinical Investigation,* 1960, *39,* 758-764.

Friedman, M., and others. "The Relationship of Behavior Pattern A to the State of the Coronary Vasculature: A Study of Fifty-One Autopsy Subjects." *American Journal of Medicine,* 1968, *44,* 525-535.

Glass, D. C. *Behavior Patterns, Stress, and Coronary Disease.* New York: Wiley, 1977.

House, J. S. "Occupational Stress as a Precursor to Coronary Disease." In W. D. Gentry and R. B. Williams (Eds.), *Psychological Aspects of Myocardial Infarction and Coronary Care.* St. Louis: Mosby, 1975.

Jenkins, C. D. "The Coronary-Prone Personality." In W. D. Gentry and R. B. Williams (Eds.), *Psychological Aspects of Myocardial Infarction and Coronary Care.* St. Louis: Mosby, 1975.

Jenkins, C. D. "Recent Evidence Supporting Psychologic and Social Risk Factors for Coronary Disease." *New England Journal of Medicine,* 1976, *294,* 987-994, 1033-1038.

Jenkins, C. D., and others. "Association of Coronary-Prone Behavior Scores with Recurrence of Coronary Heart Disease." *Journal of Chronic Diseases,* 1971, *24,* 601-611.

Jenkins, C. D., Rosenman, R. H., and Friedman, M. "Development of an Objective Psychological Test for the Determination of the Coronary-Prone Behavior Pattern in Employed Men." *Journal of Chronic Diseases,* 1967, *20,* 371-379.

Jenkins, C. D., Rosenman, R. H., and Friedman, M. "Replicability of Rating the Coronary-Prone Behavior Pattern." *British Journal of Preventive and Social Medicine*, 1968, *22*, 16-22.

Jenkins, C. D., Zyzanski, S. J., and Rosenman, R. H. "Coronary-Prone Behavior: One Pattern or Several?" *Psychosomatic Medicine*, 1978, *40*, 25-43.

Keith, R. A., Lown, B., and Stare, F. J. "Coronary Heart Disease and Behavior Patterns: An Examination of Method." *Psychosomatic Medicine*, 1965, *27*, 424-434.

Kemple, C. "Rorschach Method and Psychosomatic Diagnosis: Personality Traits of Patients with Rheumatic Disease, Hypertensive Cardiovascular Disease, Coronary Occlusion, and Fracture." *Psychosomatic Medicine*, 1945, *7*, 85-89.

Mason, J. W. "Organization of Psychoendocrine Mechanisms: A Review and Reconsideration of Research." In N. S. Greenfield and R. A. Sternbach (Eds.), *Handbook of Psychophysiology*. New York: Holt, Rinehart and Winston, 1972.

Matthews, K. A., and Krantz, D. S. "Resemblance of Twins and Their Parents in Pattern A Behavior." *Psychosomatic Medicine*, 1976, *38*, 140-144.

Menninger, K. A., and Menninger, W. C. "Psychoanalytic Observations in Cardiac Disorders." *American Heart Journal*, 1936, *11*, 10-21.

Osler, W. *Lectures on Angina Pectoris and Allied States*. New York: Appleton-Century-Crofts, 1897.

Parkes, C. M., Benjamin, B., and Fitzgerald, R. G. "Broken Heart: A Statistical Study of Increased Mortality Among Widowers." *British Medical Journal*, 1969, *1*, 740-743.

Rahe, R. H., and others. "Psychologic Correlates of Serum Cholesterol in Man: A Longitudinal Study." *Psychosomatic Medicine*, 1971, *33*, 399-410.

Rosenman, R. H., and Friedman, M. "Association of Specific Behavior Pattern in Women with Blood and Cardiovascular Findings." *Circulation*, 1961, *24*, 1173-1184.

Rosenman, R. H., and Friedman, M. "Behavior Patterns, Blood Lipids, and Coronary Heart Disease." *Journal of the American Medical Association*, 1963, *184*, 934-938.

Rosenman, R. H., and others. "A Predictive Study of Coronary Heart Disease: The Western Collaborative Group Study." *Journal of the American Medical Association*, 1964, *189*, 103-110.

Rosenman, R. H., and others. "Coronary Heart Disease in the Western Collaborative Group Study: A Follow-Up of Two Years." *Journal of the American Medical Association*, 1966, *195*, 86-92.

Rosenman, R. H., and others. "Coronary Heart Disease in the Western Collaborative Group Study: A Follow-Up Experience of 4½ Years." *Journal of Chronic Diseases*, 1970, *23*, 173-190.

Rosenman, R. H., and others. "Coronary Heart Disease in the Western Collaborative Group Study: Final Follow-Up Experience of 8½ Years." *Journal of the American Medical Association*, 1975, *233*, 872-877.

Roskies, E., and others. "Changing the Coronary-Prone (Type A) Behavior Pattern in a Non-Clinical Population." *Journal of Behavioral Medicine*, 1978, *1*, 201-216.

Scherwitz, L., Berton, K., and Leventhal, H. "Type A Assessment and Interaction in the Behavior Pattern Interview." *Psychosomatic Medicine*, 1977, *39*, 229-240.

Schucker, B., and Jacobs, D. R. "Assessment of Behavioral Risk for Coronary Disease by Voice Characteristics." *Psychosomatic Medicine*, 1977, *39*, 219-228.

Selye, H. *The Stress of Life*. New York: McGraw-Hill, 1956.

Shekelle, R. B., Schoenberger, J. A., and Stamler, J. "Correlates of the JAS Type A Behavior Pattern Score." *Journal of Chronic Diseases*, 1976, *29*, 381-394.

Suinn, R. M. "Type A Behavior Pattern." In R. B. Williams and W. D. Gentry (Eds.), *Behavioral Approaches to Medical Treatment*. Cambridge, Mass.: Ballinger, 1977.

Suinn, R. M., and Bloom, L. J. "Anxiety Management Training for Type A Persons." *Journal of Behavioral Medicine,* 1978, *1,* 25-35.

Waldron, I., and others. "The Coronary-Prone Behavior Pattern in Employed Men and Women." *Journal of Human Stress,* 1977, *3,* 2-18.

Zyzanski, S., and Jenkins, C. D. "Basic Dimensions Within the Coronary-Prone Behavior Pattern." *Journal of Chronic Diseases,* 1970, *22,* 781-795.

17

Robert J. Gatchel

Learned Helplessness (Physiological Concomitants)

A number of reports in the literature through the years suggest that the lack of control over aversive events can produce dramatic negative consequence. Bettelheim (1943), for example, described the *Muselmäner* (walking corpses) in Nazi concentration camps who, apparently because of their extreme sense of hopelessness, developed symptoms of apathy and withdrawal that many times resulted in death due to no known organic cause. Richter (1957) and Seligman (1975) have also documented instances of "sudden death" in animals, apparently resulting from a perceived uncontrollability over a stressful environment.

Investigators (for instance, Averill, 1973; Janis, 1958; Lazarus, 1966; Lefcourt, 1973) have pointed out that feelings of helplessness and lack of control appear to interfere significantly with one's ability to respond adaptively to a stressful situation. This phenomenon has come to be known as *learned helplessness*. The concept of learned helplessness initially evolved from a series of experiments conducted by Seligman and colleagues on traumatic avoidance learning in dogs (Overmier and Seligman, 1967; Seligman and Maier, 1967). Seligman (1975) has proposed that learned helplessness develops when an organism learns that responding and reinforcement (escape) are independent. This learning undermines the motivation for initiating instrumental responses.

Seligman (1975) has further proposed that the learned helplessness concept may serve as a model for reactive depression in man, so that the experimental procedure for producing learned helplessness may yield symptoms associated with naturally occurring reactive depression. Some researchers claim that the psychological state of depression is associated with a decrease in electrodermal activity (Greenfield and others, 1963; McCarron, 1973) and an increased heart rate (Kelly and Walter, 1968; McCarron, 1973). As noted by McCarron (1973), this finding of diminished electrodermal responding to stimulus input supplements the common clinical observations of dulled affect, psychomotor retardation, and general feelings of sadness and hopelessness in depressed subjects. Some investigators, however, have reported opposite electrodermal results (Lewinsohn, Lobitz, and Wilson, 1973; Zuckerman, Persky, and Curtis, 1968). A systematic review of the different types of depressed patients and methodologies employed in these studies will need to be conducted before any physiological response pattern associated with depression can be delineated on the basis of these investigations. Gatchel and colleagues (Gatchel, McKinney, and Koebernick, 1977; Gatchel and Proctor, 1976) have attempted to assess the physiological changes instigated by a learned helplessness task and to evaluate whether the physiological response patterns are similar to those reported in certain studies of depression. This research will be reviewed in detail later in this chapter.

Background and Current Status

As mentioned, the concept of learned helplessness was initially developed from a series of studies on traumatic avoidance learning in dogs (Overmier and Seligman, 1967; Seligman and Maier, 1967). Seligman (1975) has proposed a conditional probability theory to account for the learned helplessness effect. It is beyond the scope of this present chapter to evaluate the alternative theoretical learning accounts of this effect. However, certain researchers have recently questioned the learning principles on which Seligman assumes the learned helplessness phenomenon to be based. For example, Levis (1976) suggests that an extension of an Amsel frustration-type model may be a more heuristic alternative to the conditional probability model proposed by Seligman to account for learned helplessness. Regardless of the exact learning factors that underlie the effect, there can be little doubt from the research conducted to date that the lack of control has a dramatic impact upon cognitive, emotional, and motivational responding in subjects exposed to aversive situations (see Seligman, 1975). This has been demonstrated in a wide variety of studies employing both infrahuman and human subjects.

During the past few years, there has been a great amount of research on the effects of learned helplessness on human subjects in both laboratory and "real-life" situations. Laboratory studies, such as those by Gatchel and Proctor (1976) and Hiroto and Seligman (1975), have demonstrated the generality of the learned helplessness effect, with the resultant impairment process produced in both cognitive and instrumental tasks. These investigations utilized an experimental paradigm in which subjects were pretreated with a series of inescapable aversive tones and the degree of resultant impairment measured on a subsequent solvable anagram solution task. During the pretreatment phase with inescapable tones, subjects assumed they could escape the tones by pressing a button in a certain sequence. However, unknown to them, the button pressing was independent of tone termination so that subjects were unable to terminate the tones. These subjects were compared to (1) a group of subjects pretreated with escapable aversive tones (they could terminate the tone by pressing the button four times) and (2) a control group that passively listened to the tones without attempting to escape them. This control group was included to assess the effects of simple noise presentation without the added factor of attempting to control it. It is the perception of possible control, and then the subsequent frustration and inability to control a stimulus, which is assumed important in the learned helplessness phenomenon. Results demonstrated that the group pretreated with the inescapable noise evidenced greatly impaired performance during anagram solution test trials relative to control and escapable pretreatment groups. These data demonstrate that instrumental inescapability can generate cognitive interference. As indicated by Hiroto and Seligman (1975), this finding of cross-modal helplessness is of considerable theoretical interest; that is, it indicates a general "organismic" impairment which transfers to cognitive tasks.

In "real-life" situations some recent studies suggest the importance of the perception of control over a stressful situation in reducing the aversive emotional impact of that situation. For example, in hospital patients (Langer, Janis, and Wolfer, 1975), nursing home residents (Langer and Rodin, 1976; Schulz, 1976), and individuals exposed to crowded situations (Langer and Saegert, 1977), the introduction of some perception of control over their stressful life situations produces a reduction in the aversive emotional impact of these situations.

Critical Discussion

General Areas of Concern

As indicated earlier, Seligman (1975) has suggested that the learned helplessness concept may serve as a model for reactive depression in man. If this model is correct, then the experimental procedure for producing learned helplessness should yield symptoms associated with this clinical disorder. Studies by Gatchel and colleagues (Gatchel, McKinney, and Koebernick, 1977; Gatchel and Proctor, 1976) examined the relationship between learned helplessness and reactive depression in terms of physiological responding. In brief, the findings indicated that learned helplessness is associated with *less* phasic electrodermal responding to aversive events, while depression is associated with *greater* responding to the uncontrollable aversive stimuli.

Gatchel and Proctor (1976) utilized an experimental paradigm, described earlier in this chapter, for producing cross-modal learned helplessness in human subjects. Throughout the experiment, heart rate and electrodermal responses were monitored, and differences between groups and changes over tasks were analyzed. The results demonstrated specific physiological concomitants of the learned helplessness effect. Compared to escapable and control group subjects, the inescapable group subjects demonstrated lower tonic and phasic electrodermal responding. This response pattern was interpreted as a concomitant of decreased task involvement and motivation in learned helplessness subjects that was prompted by their learning that responding and reinforcement (escape) were independent. These subjects also demonstrated a greater frequency of spontaneous electrodermal activity relative to the escapable and control group subjects.

The above physiological concomitants of the learned helplessness effect consisted of deactivation responses (lower tonic and phasic electrodermal responses) as well as activation responses (greater spontaneous electrodermal activity). These findings of "fractionation" of electrodermal responses were interpreted in terms of an explanation suggested by Kilpatrick (1971) and Schwartz (1974). These investigators suggest that tonic electrodermal levels may be most responsive to cognitive and vigilance tasks, or what Schwartz refers to as "cortical arousability." In contrast, spontaneous electrodermal activity may be most expressive of emotional or limbic system stress, referred to by Schwartz as "subcortical reactivity." Although Schwartz has indicated that this is an oversimplified explanation, it was viewed as consistent with the data from the Gatchel and Proctor study. Escapable group subjects, who would be expected to have a greater degree of vigilance and task involvement during the experimental pretreatment task than inescapable group subjects because of the probability of escaping, had higher tonic electrodermal levels. Concurrently, these subjects had a lower frequency of spontaneous electrodermal fluctuations relative to inescapable group subjects. This would be expected due to the greater emotional stress in the inescapable group subjects, prompted by their inability to escape the aversive noise.

     In a follow-up to the above study, Gatchel, McKinney, and Koebernick (1977) directly assessed whether the physiological concomitants of learned helplessness are similar to the physiological response patterns found in naturally occurring depression. The same experimental paradigm employed in the Gatchel and Proctor (1976) study was utilized in this present experiment. The only additional feature of the investigation was that half of the subjects in each of the three groups (inescapable, escapable, and control) were depressed, as measured on the Beck Depression Inventory (Beck, 1967); the other half were nondepressed. Results of this study indicated that the depressed subjects in the control group, who passively listened to the aversive tones without attempting to escape them, demonstrated more impaired performance at subsequently solving anagrams than the nondepressed subjects in the control group. Inescapable noise produced impairments in nondepressed subjects similar to those demonstrated by the depressed subjects in the control group. Thus, the results demonstrate a similarity of impairment on a cognitive anagram task in laboratory-induced learned helplessness and naturally occurring depression. Similar results have also been reported by Miller and Seligman (1975).

     This study indicates, then, that learned helplessness is associated with *less* phasic electrodermal responding to the aversive tones, as was similarly found in the Gatchel and Proctor (1976) study, while depression is associated with *greater* responding to the uncontrollable aversive stimuli. Thus, there may be different underlying deficits in laboratory-induced learned helplessness and naturally occurring depression.

Comparative Philosophies and Theories

     The electrodermal response data support the view that learned helplessness develops when an organism learns that responding and reinforcement (escape) are independent. This learning undermines the motivation for initiating instrumental responses. The lower tonic and phasic electrodermal responses, which can be viewed as indicants of reduced autonomic arousal, can be viewed as concomitants of decreased task involvement and motivation in the learned helplessness subjects. Indeed, typical findings have shown a relationship between autonomic arousal and motivational level. For example, Malmo (1965) found that conditions of low and high incentive could be differentiated on the basis of a measure of sweat gland activity. The reduction in responding in the learned helplessness subjects was even greater than that evidenced by control group subjects, who were instructed to sit and passively listen to the tones. Since all groups received identical patterns of tones, differences in rate of habituation to the tones could not account for these results. Rather, the learning over pretreatment trials by the inescapable learned helplessness group subjects that responding and escape are independent, and the resultant decrease in task involvement and motivation, seems to be the most parsimonious explanation of these data.

Results of the Gatchel, McKinney, and Koebernick (1977) study indicate that there is not a direct parallel between learned helplessness and naturally occurring depression with respect to electrodermal responding. The greater electrodermal responding to uncontrollable aversive stimuli found in depressed subjects, relative to the nondepressed subjects, parallels independent findings reported by Lewinsohn, Lobitz, and Wilson (1973) and Zuckerman, Persky, and Curtis (1968). Lewinsohn, Lobitz, and Wilson (1973) indicate that these data may suggest that depressed individuals are more sensitive to aversive stimuli than nondepressed persons are. These investigators also suggest that the emotional disruption experienced by depressed individuals may prompt them to avoid and withdraw from unpleasant social situations.

In contrast to the Lewinsohn and Zuckerman studies, some investigators (for example, McCarron, 1973) claim that clinical depression is associated with decreased electrodermal responding. The possible reasons for these conflicting results, such as different methodologies and types of depressed subjects employed in the various studies, will need to be explored before any physiological pattern associated with depression can be unequivocally delineated.

Elaboration on Critical Points

The previously cited studies indicate that there is not a direct parallel between learned helplessness and naturally occurring depression with respect to physiological responding. Laboratory-induced learned helplessness was found to be associated with *less* electrodermal responding, while depression was found to be associated with *greater* responding to uncontrollable aversive events. This difference suggests that there may be different underlying mechanisms involved in these two phenomena.

The decreased electrodermal responding suggests the presence of a motivational deficit and decreased task involvement in the learned helplessness effect. In depression, with its accompanying greater electrodermal activity, the deficits may result from greater involvement of cognitive interference effects. However, this is merely speculative. Additional research is needed to examine the relative importance of cognitive and/or motivational deficits in learned helplessness and depression. Moreover, as noted by Gatchel, McKinney, and Koebernick (1977), one must also consider the possibility that learned helplessness, with its accompanying motivational deficit, is an early symptom of depression and that cognitive interference problems become more important factors later in the developmental course of this disorder. Future studies should examine this possibility.

Personal Views and Recommendations

Additional research is needed to investigate other symptoms (such as depressed mood and psychomotor retardation) generated by the learned helplessness procedure and to determine the effect of these symptoms on physiological responding. Do the individuals who demonstrate the greatest amount of altered physiological responding also display the greatest deficits in these other concurrent behaviors? Also, the assessment of a host of other physiological responses, besides just heart rate and electrodermal activity, would provide a more comprehensive determination of the physiological mechanisms involved in learned helplessness.

This additional research will further evaluate the relationship between learned helplessness and reactive depression in terms of physiological responding. If the concept of learned helplessness is a valid model for reactive depression, then certain intervention strategies can be developed to modify the cognitive distortion. For example, the response-reinforcement contingencies in the individual's environment might be restructured; or "cognitive restructuring" therapeutic techniques, which are beginning to show promise in the area of behavior therapy (Davison and Neale, 1974), might be effectively employed.

Because the standard learned helplessness induction procedure exposes subjects to uncontrollable stress, investigators must obtain proper informed consent of all experimental subjects and treat them in accordance with the ethical standards of the American Psychological Association, as stated in *Ethical Principles in the Conduct of Research with Human Participants* (1973). Moreover, careful and complete debriefing of subjects is essential to ensure that there are no negative aftereffects following the completion of the experiment. This is especially critical if subjects have been prescreened for experimental participation because of elevated levels of anxiety, depression, or other psychological problems.

Any investigator recording physiological responses in a study will require appropriate training in the proper use of physiological monitoring equipment, such as a polygraph. Some training in the area of psychophysiology is also essential, since it will provide the investigator with an understanding of the wide variety of factors—electrical, environmental, physiological, and psychological—that can significantly affect the accurate measurement of physiological responses. Unfortunately, many investigators who employ physiological recording techniques in their research do not have appropriate training in this area. They are, therefore, not aware of the important factors that need to be taken into consideration in psychophysiological investigations.

Finally, and most important, since physiological response monitoring usually involves possible electrical hazards to subjects, because of the direct attachment of electrodes to their bodies, electrical safety precautions need to be given top priority in any study. Biomedical research safety standards have been developed to ensure such electrical safety in studies employing human subjects (see Roveti, 1973).

Application to Particular Variables

Age. The physiological studies conducted to date on learned helplessness have employed college students. Since the age of the subject has been found to affect the magnitude of physiological responding, one cannot automatically assume that the same physiological effects of learned helplessness found with college students will necessarily be observed in other age groups. Although this age factor should not significantly affect the basic physiological responding-learned helplessness effect found in the earlier reviewed studies, additional physiological studies employing different age groups need to be conducted.

Educational/Intellectual Level. The educational/intellectual level of subjects might have an effect on results if a cognitive task (such as an anagram solution task), which has been a commonly used test of learned helplessness in past research in this area, is employed in a study. Education/intelligence level would be expected to significantly affect performance on such tasks, which, in turn, might affect physiological responding.

Race. The studies assessing physiological concomitants of learned helplessness employed Caucasian subjects. Since there are documented racial effects on physiological response levels, especially electrodermal responses (for instance, blacks and other dark-skin races have higher tonic skin resistance levels than Caucasians), one might well expect the basic physiological responding-learned helplessness relationship to be affected by the race of the subjects.

Physical Disorders. Physical disorders might be important if the individual is on some type of medication for the disorder. In such an instance, it will be important to determine whether such medication has a significant effect on the physiological responses being measured in a particular study.

Psychiatric Disorders. If an organic disorder has a significant negative impact on cognitive functioning, then an investigator would not want to employ cognitive tasks in the learned helplessness procedure. Rather, motor tasks would have to be employed. Organic brain damage can also affect physiological responding in some instances. An investigator will have to be aware of this possibility. Moreover, if these individuals are on a drug regimen, it will be important to determine whether the various drugs have a significant effect on physiological responding. There are also differences in physiological responding between normal subjects and psychiatric patients with various forms of functional psychopathology, such as anxiety neurosis, depression, and schizophrenia. For example, Gatchel, McKinney, and Koebernick (1977) found differences in electrodermal responding between depressed and nondepressed subjects. This functional psychopathology factor will therefore have to be controlled for.

Variables of No Apparent Importance. The learned helplessness studies conducted by Gatchel and colleagues found no sex difference effects. Factors such as socioeconomic level, vocational level, and ethnicity of subjects should also not affect the basic learned helplessness findings.

References

Averill, J. R. "Personal Control over Aversive Stimuli and Its Relationship to Stress." *Psychological Bulletin,* 1973, *80,* 286-303.

Beck, A. T. *Depression: Clinical, Experimental, and Theoretical Aspects.* New York: Hoeber, 1967.

Bettelheim, B. "Individual and Mass Behavior in Extreme Situations." *Journal of Abnormal and Social Psychology,* 1943, *38,* 417-452.

Davison, G. C., and Neale, J. M. *Abnormal Psychology: An Experimental Clinical Approach.* New York: Wiley, 1974.

Gatchel, R. J., McKinney, M. E., and Koebernick, L. F. "Learned Helplessness, Depression, and Physiological Responding." *Psychophysiology,* 1977, *14,* 25-31.

Gatchel, R. J., and Proctor, J. D. "Physiological Correlates of Learned Helplessness in Man." *Journal of Abnormal Psychology,* 1976, *85,* 27-34.

Greenfield, N., and others. "The Relationship Between Physiology and Psychological Responsivity: Depression and Galvanic Skin Response." *Journal of Nervous and Mental Disease,* 1963, *136,* 535-539.

Hiroto, D. S., and Seligman, M. E. P. "Generality of Learned Helplessness in Man." *Journal of Personality and Social Psychology,* 1975, *31,* 311-327.

Janis, I. L. *Psychological Stress.* New York: Wiley, 1958.

Kelly, D., and Walter, C. "The Relationship Between Clinical Diagnosis and Anxiety Assessed by Forearm Blood Flow and Other Measurements." *British Journal of Psychiatry,* 1968, *114,* 611-626.

Kilpatrick, D. G. "Differential Responsiveness to Two Electrodermal Indices to Psychological Stress and Performance of a Complex Cognitive Task." *Psychophysiology,* 1971, *9,* 218-226.

Langer, E. J., Janis, I. L., and Wolfer, E. J. "Reduction of Psychological Stress in Surgical Patients." *Journal of Experimental Social Psychology,* 1975, *11,* 155-165.

Langer, E. J., and Rodin, J. "The Effects of Choice and Enhanced Personal Responsibility for the Aged: A Field Experiment in an Institutional Setting." *Journal of Personality and Social Psychology,* 1976, *34,* 191-198.

Langer, E. J., and Saegert, S. "Crowding and Cognitive Control." *Journal of Personality and Social Psychology,* 1977, *35,* 175-182.

Lazarus, R. S. *Psychological Stress and the Coping Process.* New York: McGraw-Hill, 1966.

Lefcourt, H. M. "The Function of the Illusions of Control and Freedom." *American Psychologist,* 1973, *28,* 417-425.

Levis, D. J. "Learned Helplessness: A Reply and Alternative S-R Interpretation." *Journal of Experimental Psychology: General,* 1976, *105,* 47-65.

Lewinsohn, P. M., Lobitz, W. C., and Wilson, S. " 'Sensitivity' of Depressed Individuals to Aversive Stimuli." *Journal of Abnormal Psychology,* 1973, *81,* 259-263.

McCarron, L. T. "Psychophysiological Discrimination of Reactive Depression." *Psychophysiology,* 1973, *10,* 223-230.

Malmo, R. B. "Finger Sweat Prints in the Differentiation of Low and High Incentive." *Psychophysiology,* 1965, *1,* 231-240.

Miller, W. R., and Seligman, M. E. P. "Depression and Learned Helplessness in Man." *Journal of Abnormal Psychology,* 1975, *84,* 228-238.

Overmier, J. B., and Seligman, M. E. P. "Effects of Inescapable Shock upon Subsequent Escape and Avoidance Responding." *Journal of Comparative and Physiological Psychology,* 1967, *63,* 28-33.

Richter, C. P. "On the Phenomenon of Sudden Death in Animals and Man." *Psychosomatic Medicine,* 1957, *19,* 191-198.

Roveti, D. *Electrical Safety Test Procedures for the Hospital.* Annapolis, Md.: Instrutek, 1973.

Schulz, R. "Effects of Control and Predictability on the Physical and Psychological Well-Being of the Institutionalized Aged." *Journal of Personality and Social Psychology,* 1976, *33,* 563-573.

Schwartz, G. E. "Meditation as an Altered State of Consciousness: Current Findings on Stress Reactivity, Attentional Flexibility, and Creativity." Paper presented at 82nd Annual Convention of American Psychological Association, New Orleans, Sept. 1974.

Seligman, M. E. P. *Helplessness.* San Francisco: Freeman, 1975.

Seligman, M. E. P., and Maier, S. F. "Failure to Escape Traumatic Shock." *Journal of Experimental Psychology,* 1967, *74,* 1-9.

Zuckerman, M., Persky, H., and Curtis, G. C. "Relationships Among Anxiety, Depression, Hostility, and Autonomic Variables." *Journal of Nervous and Mental Disease,* 1968, *146,* 481-487.

18

Jan Loney

Childhood Hyperactivity

Perhaps the most frequently cited primary symptoms of the hyperkinetic syndrome are *hyperactivity* (overactivity, fidgetiness), *inattention* (distractibility, forgetfulness), *impulsivity* (recklessness, inability to delay gratification), and *excitability* (irritability, low frustration tolerance). The prototypical hyperactive child emerges from the descriptive literature as a youngster notably long on motility and short on restraint. Numerous experts (for example, Cantwell, 1975; Minde, 1977; O'Malley and Eisenberg, 1973; Rie, 1975; Ross and Ross, 1976; Routh, in press; Sandoval, Lambert, and Yandell, 1976; Schain, 1975; Stewart and others, 1966; Wender, 1971; Werry, 1968a) have painted the diagnostic picture of a child in perpetual motion; a child who flits around and blurts out but who doesn't finish assignments or chores; a child with a short and highly flammable fuse; a child of the present, who neither benefits from the past nor plans for the future.

Many experts also list one or more secondary symptoms—symptoms that are less salient or integral features of the hyperkinetic syndrome or that have developed from a negative interaction between the child's primary symptoms and aspects of his or her social environment. Lists enumerating these secondary or resultant symptoms often include low self-esteem, academic skill deficits, and delinquent acts; however, some authors consider learning impediments and/or aggressive behaviors (fighting, stealing, defiance) to be primary symptoms (Morrison and Stewart, 1971; Safer and Allen, 1976; Wender, 1971).

Background and Current Status

Systematic descriptions of children who would now be recognized as having the hyperkinetic syndrome or minimal brain dysfunction date back over 50 to 100 years (Ebaugh, 1923; Hoffmann, 1845; Still, 1902). Throughout the 1930s and 1940s, various investigators proposed etiological theories involving organic brain damage (Bradley, 1937; Kahn and Cohen, 1934; Orton, 1937; Strauss and Lehtinen, 1947). A major impetus to further interest and research was provided by Laufer's description of the hyperkinetic impulse disorder (Laufer and others, 1957). An influential paper by Clements and Peters (1962) offered the concept of minimal brain dysfunction as an antidote to psychogenic theories regarding the etiology of children's behavior problems. Soon thereafter, another important paper, by Stewart and associates (1966), presented data on thirty-two boys and five girls between 5 and 11 years of age who displayed overactivity and a short attention span at psychiatric referral. Comparison of these data with data from a group of normal first graders enabled these researchers to present one of the first empirical descriptions of the hyperactive child syndrome.

Much of the early writing and research on childhood hyperactivity proceeded from the assumption or tried to establish the fact that innate or acquired organic pathology is responsible for the hyperkinetic child's atypical behavior. However, although it was always obvious that brain trauma and neurological disease can produce hyperactive behavior patterns, it became equally clear that many hyperactive children do not manifest unequivocal organic pathology. The search abated for connections between hyperkinetic symptoms and organic indicators (perinatal adversities, developmental lags, neurological signs, electroencephalographic abnormalities, perceptual-motor disturbances, and the like). The term *minimal brain dysfunction* (MBD) came into use to indicate the presence of one or more of a set of symptoms considered to reflect the operation of subtle cerebral abnormalities or lesions.

Meanwhile, investigators tried to demonstrate that the set of symptoms thought to comprise the MBD syndrome are interrelated (Routh and Roberts, 1972; Werry, 1968b). Most of these studies involved the factor analysis of an assortment of scores, ratings, and descriptors which were presumed to covary in the MBD syndrome. However, instead of identifying a single MBD factor consisting of most of the hypothetical MBD measures, these analyses typically produced a large number of *source factors*. That is, the dimensions that were identified corresponded to the sources of the data (one factor consisting only of teacher ratings, another consisting only of psychometric scores, still another consisting only of EEG measures). Naturally, results such as these discouraged those who viewed the MBD syndrome as a set of interrelated symptoms and suggested that the MBD population is a heterogeneous one.

Partly as a result of the apparent dead ends to which the pursuit of the MBD concept was leading, an increasing number of investigators deemphasized etiological considerations and chose to study childhood hyperactivity. For some this represented the choice of a behavioral model; hyperactivity was viewed as a behavioral-psychological dimension or trait rather than as a syndrome or as one symptom of a medical disorder.

For others the model was still essentially a medical one, and the use of the terms *hyperkinetic* or *hyperactive child syndrome* signified mainly that an invariable organic etiology was not presumed. Most of those who studied children with the hyperkinetic syndrome used exclusionary criteria to eliminate psychotic, retarded, and epileptic children from their samples and thus to reduce the heterogeneity of their study groups.

A natural by-product of the shift in terminology was an accelerated concern with the definition of *hyperactivity*. A variety of distinctions were drawn and debated: (1) between the frequency or duration of movement and the intensity of movement (Pope, 1970); (2) between purposeless, disorganized, frenetic activity and activity that is goal directed; (3) between activity that is qualitatively and quantitatively age-appropriate and activity that is not. As both debate about terminology and research on diagnosis continued, the belief gradually strengthened that the essential difficulty of these children is with attention rather than activity. Research by Dykman and colleagues (1971) and by Douglas (1972) did much to emphasize and clarify the central role of inattention. The stage was set for still another shift in terminology, which the American Psychiatric Association formally noted by changing the "hyperkinetic reaction of childhood" of its 1968 *Diagnostic and Statistical Manual of Mental Disorders (DSM-II)* to the "attention deficit disorder" of its forthcoming revision (*DSM-III*).

As the terminology was changing over time, there were marked increases in the amount of both professional and public attention being paid to childhood hyperactivity. Books, articles, research investigations, and congressional hearings all attested to continuing controversies about whether the hyperkinetic/minimal brain dysfunction (HK/MBD) syndrome exists and what, if anything, should be done to treat it. Between the 1950s and 1970s, hundreds of studies were published, most of them investigating either the general effectiveness or the specific effects of drug treatment. Increasing numbers of children were diagnosed and treated with central nervous system (CNS) stimulants.

While there is evidence to suggest that the number of drug-treated children may now have reached an asymptote (Safer, Krager, and Earhart, 1978), a great many children are receiving stimulant medication. Several authors have analyzed the recent HK/MBD "epidemic" (Conrad, 1976; Freeman, 1976). There is little doubt that the existence of the CNS stimulant drugs, primarily Ritalin and Dexedrine, contributed to the rising proportion of children considered hyperkinetic. Here was a simple, effective, and relatively inexpensive treatment. A prescription for medication, combined with the diagnosis of minimal brain dysfunction, tended to relieve parents' worries about their possible role in the development and maintenance of their child's difficulties and to defuse parents' anger about their child's "bad" or "stupid" behavior. To provide a medical syndrome was to provide an explanation that was external to both parents and child. Therefore, no one was to blame (Whalen and Henker, 1976). To furnish, in addition, a medical treatment was to ameliorate home and school problems, sometimes with dramatic completeness and speed. Many physicians—faced with the fact that an individual child's response to medication was impossible to predict, convinced that the side effects of medication posed only minor and transitory risks, and impressed with the effects of stimulants on the problems of their patients—opted for trials of medication with children whose brain dysfunction was extremely minimal. Both clinicians and researchers, faced with the fact that very few children were uniformly hyperactive in all situations and at all times, drifted away from definitions that required cross-situational and cross-temporal symptomatology. Thus, more and more children were diagnosed and treated. In addition, changing societal factors may have contributed to genuine increases in hyperactive behavior (Block, 1977) and thus to increases in medical diagnoses and treatment.

The hyperkinetic syndrome, by one or another of a variety of names, is estimated to affect from 5 to 20 percent of American school children and to account for about 50 percent of referrals to outpatient clinics and similar settings. Because many definitions of the syndrome have been offered, ranging from highly clinical and subjective to entirely objective and operational, much of the variation in prevalence figures can be attributed to differences in terminology and perspective. When the medical approach is used, the important variables will be (1) the symptom behaviors considered relevant to diagnosis, (2) the sources of information used, and (3) the distinction made between normal and abnormal behaviors. When parents and teachers are asked to describe children by checking lists of descriptors, as many as half of all elementary school boys may be called restless and inattentive (Lapouse and Monk, 1958; Werry and Quay, 1971). When scores on rating scales are used to estimate prevalence, the number of children considered hyperactive will be a direct function of the cutoff point chosen; in a normal distribution of scores, a cutoff point two standard deviations above the mean will identify 2 to 3 percent of the sample as hyperactive (Sprague, 1977).

Some people believe that the hyperkinetic child is a by-product of our noisy and frenetic society or a figment of our overactive imaginations. Others are made restless and irritable by the fact that definitions of hyperkinesis vary more across situations and across time than does the hyperkinetic child. Experts do seem to agree on terminology (Schrager and others, 1966) more than they do in practice (Kenny and others, 1971). Clearly, however, the presence of childhood hyperactivity is accepted in the literature concerning behavior disorders, and an orderly and unified approach to its assessment and diagnosis must precede a more settled state of knowledge about prevalence, etiology, treatment, and course.

Critical Discussion

General Areas of Concern

A major issue in the assessment of the hyperkinetic syndrome is the identification and evaluation of methods of measurement. Numerous assessment methods have been employed or proposed.

Clinical decisions have long relied heavily on the psychiatric interview, during which a parent (usually the mother) is asked about the child's development and current problems. Although most such interviews are tailored to suit the style and theories of the individual clinician and the needs and circumstances of the particular parent, any number of semistructured formats for the parent interview have been developed. These formats can consist of specific questions for the interviewer to ask the parent or of lists of specific topical areas to be covered, with questions of the interviewer's choice. Rutter has done some of the best research work comparing different interview strategies and, along with many clinicians, considers the parent interview a primary source of descriptive diagnostic information (Rutter and Brown, 1966). While the parents' perceptions of their children are both subjective and unsystematic, their sheer exposure to the child's behavior over numerous situations and years of time makes them potential experts on some matters. Clinical or semistructured interviews with the child, in which he or she is asked questions about current problems and observed in the interview situation, are generally acknowledged to be much less fruitful for and relevant to diagnosis. However, there is reason to be dubious about the validity of the more retrospective and historical material derived from the parent interview (Yarrow, Campbell, and Burton, 1970), and it is a clinical truism that some parents, for a variety of reasons, are simply not good informants.

Research studies of the HK/MBD syndrome often involve the administration of lengthy batteries of psychological and educational tests. Several traditional tests—most notably, the Wechsler Intelligence Scale for Children (WISC), the Wide Range Achievement Test (WRAT), the Goodenough-Harris Draw-A-Person Test (DAP), and the Bender Gestalt Visual Motor Test—are included more or less routinely. Less frequently, projective tests or children's personality inventories are used. While differences between HK/MBD children and control or comparison groups are reported, these differences usually are not large, consistent, or specific enough to serve diagnostic purposes. Typically, there is substantial overlap between HK/MBD groups and normal (undiagnosed) groups, and there is even more overlap between HK/MBD groups and groups containing referred children with other diagnoses. Among the most promising of the familiar tests is the WISC. Dykman and his colleagues (Ackerman, Dykman, and Peters, 1977; Stevens and others, 1967) have repeatedly found differences between HK/MBD youngsters and controls on the WISC *ACID factor* (a combination of the child's scores on the Arithmetic, Coding, Information, and Digit Span subtests). This factor has regularly appeared in factor analyses of the WISC among various populations, and poor performance is thought to result from inattention, distractibility, and memory deficits or from the child's use of global as opposed to analytic problem-solving strategies. Several less traditional psychological tests have been used in research studies of childhood hyperactivity because, like the WISC ACID factor, they appear to measure functions that are central to or diagnostic of the HK/MBD syndrome. For example, both Kagan's Matching Familiar Figures (MFF) and the Porteus Maze Test are considered to yield measures of impulsivity, and both have discriminated between HK/MBD and other groups with encouraging regularity.

Other measures have come from laboratory studies of vigilance, attention, and related phenomena. Probably the most useful of these laboratory measures is the Continuous Performance Test (CPT). In its typical form, sequences of stimuli (such as letters) are presented, and the child indicates whenever a particular stimulus (such as a specific letter or letter combination) appears. In a series of careful studies of hyperactive children, Douglas and her collaborators have employed laboratory measures, such as delayed-reaction-time tasks and the CPT, as dependent variables (Sykes, Douglas, and Morgenstern, 1973; Sykes and others, 1971), and Kupietz has investigated the potentiality of an auditory vigilance task as an assessment device (Kupietz, 1976; Kupietz, Camp, and Weissman, 1976).

The search for organic indicators of the HK/MBD syndrome has ranged throughout the neurological examination and the electroencephalogram with equivocal success. Satterfield and Braley (1977) have carried out studies pointing to the possible diagnostic utility of EEG evoked potentials.

The use of rating scales and questionnaires is widespread, particularly in studies of treatment efficacy. Parent scales—most notably, the Werry-Weiss-Peters (Werry, 1968a)—are used to sample parents' perceptions of the child's behavior in various home situations (for instance, at the dinner table or watching TV). The validity of parent rating scales is reduced to the extent that parents lack appropriate norms for their child's behavior. Validity is also influenced by subjective parental factors. Parents may emphasize or minimize the child's need for help, or they may focus on their own emotional reactions to the child's behavior rather than on the behavior's actual frequency or duration. Lobitz and Johnson (1975) found that children identified as deviant or nondeviant by parental report do not differ in observed behavior, and Barkley and Ullman (1975) found low- or zero-order correlations between parental ratings and objective measures of activity and distractibility. While the clinical problem presented by a nondeviant child with over-anxious or hostile parents is as real as that presented by a deviant child and his or her parents, the validity of parental rating in establishing the diagnosis of childhood hyperkinesis is in doubt. Rapoport and Benoit (1975), however, have shown some correlation between mothers' diaries and clinic observations.

In studies where parent and teacher rating scales are used simultaneously, teachers' ratings have proved more sensitive to the effects of drug treatment (Sleator and von Neumann, 1974; Sprague and Sleator, 1973). In addition to purely methodological problems, discrepancies in ratings made by parents and teachers may reflect valid cross-situational variation in the child's behavior. Furthermore, both parents and teachers vary widely in their ability to manage or tolerate behavior that is truly deviant in kind or intensity, and these variations are reflected in their ratings of children.

To make or supplement diagnosis and to document the efficacy of both drug and behavior treatments, rating scales filled out by the child's teacher are most frequently used. Teachers are college educated, and they have the rest of the classroom and their past experience to rely on when judging a child's behavior. Several studies attest to teachers' ability to identify children who will behave deviantly during classroom observation (Bolstad and Johnson, 1977). A teachers' rating scale developed by Conners (1969) and refined to improve its discriminability is the most commonly encountered. It exists in two forms: (1) a 39-item form with five factorially derived scales (aggressive conduct disorder, inattention, withdrawal, hyperactivity, and sociability); and (2) a 10-item form, either administered separately or embedded in a longer version. Norms and validation data for the Conners scale are presented by Werry (Werry and Hawthorne, 1976; Werry, Sprague, and Cohen, 1975), and a significant correlation between the Conners scale and observations of children's behavior in the classroom is demonstrated in a study by Christensen (1975). Sprague (1977) suggests the use of a cutoff score of 15 (two standard deviations above the mean) on the Conners scale to identify probably hyperkinetic children, and numerous investigators have followed that advice in screening referrals. Despite the weaknesses inherent in teacher ratings, such a cutoff score provides one of the few explicit and replicable methods for selecting samples of hyperkinetic children.

Blunden, Spring, and Greenberg (1974) developed a parallel teachers' rating scale and classroom observation system for studies of hyperactivity. Of several factors in the rating scale, only one (impulsivity) correlated significantly with the comparable classroom observation category.

In large-scale intervention studies, home and/or school observation systems are employed in verifying diagnosis and assessing treatment efficacy. Home observations are often avoided as cumbersome, artificial, and intrusive, but classroom observations made by trained personnel have proved useful in various contexts. The classroom observation method originated with child behavior modification studies; specific problem behaviors in the classroom (such as talking out or standing up in class) were chosen and counted as attempts to reduce their frequency were made. One of the earliest uses of classroom observation in drug treatment studies was reported by Sprague, Barnes, and Werry (1970). They observed more off-task behavior and fewer positive student-teacher interactions in methylphenidate-treated than in placebo groups. This form of explicit monitoring has also found a use in diagnosis. A recent revision of the Illinois-Stony Brook observation system by Abikoff, Gittelman-Klein, and Klein (1977) shows a promising level of discrimination between hyperkinetic youngsters and normals. Another promising system is being developed by Williams and his colleagues, utilizing videotapes which are scored subsequently in the laboratory (Williams, Vincent, and Elrod, 1977). Classroom observation methods have the obvious advantage of increased objectivity and the obvious disadvantage of increased expenditures of time and money.

Many of those who have used observation methods have also taken the opportunity to observe normal children or children with other behavior problems in the classroom or to record data on teacher behavior or student-teacher interactions (Forness and Esveldt, 1975; Weissenburger and Loney, 1977; Williams, Vincent, and Elrod, 1977). These expansions of attention from the referred child to include other persons in the environment provide (in the case of classmates) a frame of reference within which to judge the degree to which the child's behavior is really deviant and (in the case of teachers) an idea of the antecedents and consequences of the child's on- and off-task behaviors. Both types of information can be useful in establishing diagnosis and planning treatment, and both constitute an invitation to study dyadic and higher-order interactions.

Another setting for observation is the clinic: the waiting room, the clinician's office, the examining room, or the playroom. The waiting room is often crowded and inaccessible and, perhaps for that reason, little studied. The office and the examining room have acquired poor reputations because behavior in the one-to-one setting with a cordially authoritative person in white garb does not seem to call forth the child's worst, although it may demonstrate the degree of control of which the child is capable. Playroom studies have proved practical and typically involve dividing the floor of the room into segments, supplying several identical sets of play materials, and recording segment changes, duration of toy contact, and frequency of several locomotion behaviors during both structured and unstructured periods. These studies have been useful primarily in showing that HK/MBD children are not overactive in free or unstructured play situations (Pope, 1970; Roberts and Ray, 1978; Routh and Schroeder, 1976; Schleifer and others, 1975) but that their behavioral difference from other children reveals itself under conditions of constraint, restriction, and external pacing—where tasks are to be performed, sustained attention paid, and motion inhibited. External distractions are of questionable relevance (Worland, North-Jones, and Stern, 1973; Zentall and Zentall, 1976). Several mechanical devices for recording activity—such as accelerometers, actometers, and pedometers—have been tested in the playroom (Bell, 1968a; Schulman and Reisman, 1959). The unobtrusive simplicity of such measures commends them as supplementary sources of data, despite some vexing questions about their reliability (Barkley and Ullman, 1975; Johnson, 1971).

The most common conclusion about hyperactivity is that diagnostic information should be sought from various perspectives and sources and through a variety of methods. One is encouraged simultaneously (1) to hope that the results of numerous procedures from various sources will converge on a single diagnostic conclusion and (2) to anticipate that some clear etiology or treatment direction will emerge if enough diagnostic clues are unearthed. To some extent, this diagnostic advice derives from the inconsistency and variability of the hyperkinetic child's behavior. To some extent, it is due to continuing ambiguities surrounding the diagnosis as such. To some extent, it reflects the fact that hyperactivity can have many different causes (Fish, 1971). Finally, to some extent, it reflects on the unreliability of our measurements, tests, and scales.

We need a set of systematic and objective diagnostic procedures that will furnish verifiable measures of the behaviors distinguishing the hyperkinetic child from his or her peers. At present, the most promising types of measures appear to be ratings made by the child's teacher, combined with observations in a structured playroom setting and, whenever possible, observations in the classroom. While classroom observation is expensive and logistically complex (Forness, 1975), it is of undeniable value. Harris, Vincent, and Williams (1977) suggest that stable classroom data can be collected within a relatively short observational period. Each of these types of measures should contribute both to the diagnostic decision and to the monitoring of effects during intervention and follow-up.

In cases where the problem behavior occurs mainly in the home, one will have to rely heavily on the parent interview for diagnosis and on parental records of objectively counted target behaviors for monitoring purposes. Standardized observations of parent-child interactions in the clinic playroom might also be adopted for these cases (Touwen and Kalverboer, 1973), and several intriguing studies have explored behavior in such dyadic situations (Barkley and Cunningham, 1979; Campbell and others, 1977; Routh, in press).

The requisite studies attempting to establish the reliability and validity of various diagnostic methods continue to appear. The interrater reliability of most observational systems ranges from acceptable to excellent. Agreements between teachers on rating scales are more difficult to document because any two teachers will typically see a given child at different times and in different situations. Temporal stability or test-retest reliability has received little attention (Harris, Vincent, and Williams, 1977).

Reports of correlations between various methods of assessing hyperactive problem behaviors are scattered throughout the literature. Statistically significant correlations have been found between teacher ratings and playroom behavior (Rapoport and others, 1971) and between teacher ratings and classroom behavior, but the magnitude and consistency of correlations between methods have seldom been impressive. More ambitious studies reporting correlations among two or more methods of measuring two or more problem behaviors have also been published. A comparison of several measures of distractibility and of activity in two observation contexts (play and task) was made by Barkley and Ullman (1975). Another study of relationships across measures in the classroom setting, using Campbell and Fiske's (1958) multitrait-multimethod analytic model, has been reported by Vincent, Williams, and Elrod (1977). In both of these studies, the size of the intercorrelations and the numbers of children studied have been small, and the magnitude of the correlations has been affected to an unknown degree by such factors as the restricted range of scores within clinic populations. It is easy to join with those who suggest that larger-scale multitrait-multimethod studies would have great utility for evaluating methods of measurement (Sandoval, 1977). The extent to which the generally low across-measure correlations should be attributed to situational variability or to imprecise measures is at present unknown.

Comparative Philosophies and Theories

The world's psychological, psychiatric, and educational literature is crowded with competing theories about childhood hyperactivity. When it comes to etiology, the theories range from those that postulate a genetically transmitted disorder of monoamine metabolism (Wender, 1976) to those that consider the disorder mythological (Coleman, 1978; Schmitt, 1975). Between the metabolic and the mythological, there are theories both psychological and social. Lead, fluorescent lighting, and food additives have all been implicated. There are multifactorial (Kenny and Clemmens, 1975) and "hydraulic parfait" (Arnold, 1976) models. When it comes to course and outcome, some view HK/MBD as a mere maturational lag, and others conclude that it presages adult psychosis and criminality. And controversies about treatment have been continual (Grinspoon and Singer, 1973; Sroufe and Stewart, 1973). One hopes that some of the facts necessary to choose among these theories will come from ongoing research.

Elaboration on Critical Points

In 1935 Childers wrote a strikingly modern paper on "hyper-activity" in children —describing overtalkativeness, boastfulness, attention seeking, and "divertability of attention" and presenting empirical data on hyperactive and nonhyperactive patients across numerous potential etiological variables. Childers also reported a follow-up study of groups in which hyperactivity had led to delinquency. He found what later researchers (Ackerman, Dykman, and Peters, 1977; Minde and others, 1971; Minde, Weiss, and Mendelson, 1972; Weiss and others, 1971) confirmed as well—namely, that locomotor hyperactivity gradually disappears but that sullenness and other manifestations of a lack of inhibition persist. Like many subsequent investigators, Childers concluded that childhood hyperactivity results from a number of factors.

This multiple etiology and the associated heterogeneity of hyperkinetic/MBD children have led to more than four decades of searching for homogeneous subgroups within the HK/MBD population. The impetus for much of this searching is an underlying assumption that a homogeneous subgroup will have a single etiology and will respond to a uniform treatment. Such an assumption is easily derived from the theory that the HK/MBD syndrome is a medical disorder, and several authors have presented methods for partitioning the large and diverse group of HK/MBD children into smaller, less diverse groups (Chess, 1960; Marwit and Stenner, 1972; Ney, 1974). Most of the proposed subgrouping methods are based on differences in presumed etiology, with the major distinctions being between constitutional and acquired behavior patterns or between physical and psychological causes for hyperactive behavior. As yet, however, there has been little empirical verification of these distinctions, and the ratio of questions to answers remains high.

Although the common view of childhood hyperactivity portrays a youngster in perpetual motion ("organically driven"), more and more attention is being given to the numerous children whose hyperactivity varies from situation to situation or from time to time. It is now widely acknowledged that many children display genuine problem behavior in only some situations, but few of the resulting questions have been asked or answered. Likewise, studies have only begun to identify the parameters of situations and the characteristics of children that make for variation in activity level (Ellis and others, 1974; Shaffer, McNamara, and Pincus, 1974). For whatever reasons, such children may be more responsive to situational variation than normal children are. If so, they would—as one kind of hyperactive child—be even more different than are normals from those hyperactive children who are constantly hyperactive in virtually all situations. One would certainly expect a child with situational hyperactivity to respond differently to behavioral treatment (that is, to changes in a situation) than a child with constant hyperactivity. There has been speculation that constant and unremitting hyperactivity is more often associated with organic etiology, and there are some data connecting organicity with better response to stimulant drug treatment (Conrad and Insel, 1967). But, beyond the intriguing work of Campbell and others (Campbell, Endman, and Bernfeld, 1977; Campbell and others, 1977; Schleifer and others, 1975), relatively little is known about differences between these and other potential subgroups.

In an influential paper, Fish (1971) has distinguished between hyperactivity as a syndrome (a collection of interrelated symptoms with a common etiology) and hyperactivity as a symptom. A particular symptom and a behavioral trait may be synonymous. In psychiatric diagnosis, however, a symptom is usually considered to be a sign of a medical disorder. In psychological assessment, a trait is more apt to be considered merely as highly similar behaviors that covary. It is beginning to seem that hyperactivity may not be a syndrome, a symptom, *or* a trait—that in some important respects hyperactivity is a *state*. An essential characteristic of a state is that it shows cross-situational and cross-temporal variation. Since the behavior of hyperactive children shows just such variation, the effective identification and separation of state (situation or setting) variation, child (symptom, trait, or syndrome) variation, instrument (method or measurement) variation, and informant (perspective) variation would be a worthwhile achievement.

Many experts (for example, Cantwell, 1975; Wender, 1971) distinguish between core or primary symptoms and resultant or secondary symptoms. They believe that the interaction between hyperactivity-inattention and environmental stresses produces such secondary symptoms as delinquent behavior and low self-esteem. According to this view, children with antisocial *and* hyperactive behavior have a more severe or advanced form of the HK/MBD syndrome (Stewart and others, 1966). Hyperactive and aggressive behaviors are essentially inseparable or unseparated components of childhood conduct disorder (Kupietz, 1976; Quay, 1979; Quay and Quay, 1965). Recent work by Loney, Langhorne, and Paternite (1978) suggests that hyperactivity and aggression are independent dimensions of HK/MBD symptomatology and that aggression accounts for more of the variation in HK/MBD boys than hyperactivity does. There is evidence to suggest that the hyperactive children who are referred are those who are more aggressive (Campbell, 1974; Firestone and Douglas, 1975; Shaffer, McNamara, and Pincus, 1974). The confusing heterogeneity of views about the necessity for or possibility of separating hyperactivity and aggression contributes to controversy about various other questions. Fish (1971), for example, believes that amphetamines act therapeutically on negative and aggressive children, whether they are hyperactive or not. Loney and associates (in press) present data indicating that methylphenidate acts on hyperactive children, whether they are aggressive or not.

As has been demonstrated repeatedly, both drug treatment and behavior modification can exert beneficial effects that do not seem to depend on whether the symptomatology or problem behavior is primarily physical or psychological in its origins. Specifically, any tendency to consider response to drug treatment as diagnostic proof of MBD has been discredited (Rapoport and others, 1978). Behavioral assessment provides a detailed description of explicit problem behaviors, and behavioral intervention aims to supply positive or negative consequences that will alter the probability of the recurrence of the behaviors; the causes for the problem behaviors and the manner in which they were learned do not often receive central attention. In contrast, medical diagnosis aims to identify a syndrome and its associated etiology, which in turn will suggest a particular treatment. However, it is doubtful that present medical treatments for hyperactivity offer that much specificity; they relieve symptoms but usually do not cure the patient. Thus, except when hyperactivity is associated with fairly explicit and remedial causes, knowledge about etiology in a particular case will be speculative and not necessarily germane to treatment choice (Werry, 1974). Drug treatment is a poor choice for children from chaotic families, for example, not so much because of psychological etiology as because of the likelihood that the treatment will not be properly carried out. Chaotic families are also unlikely to succeed with a behavioral treatment program. In both cases pessimism about treatment is occasioned by the fear that treatment will fail.

Few behavioral disorders have been the focus of as much ethical concern as has hyperkinesis. Almost everyone who has discussed the topic has criticized the unreliabilities inherent in the diagnosis. Loney and Ordoña (1975) provide an example of two psychiatrists whose rates of diagnosing hyperkinesis differed significantly in two randomly assigned sets of patients from the same clinic case load. Given the undeniable subjectivity of most definitions of the HK/MBD syndrome, it is clear that one person's "exuberance and spunk" can be another person's "overactivity and noncompliance." Several authors have attacked the concepts themselves, arguing that the hyperkinetic/MBD syndrome is imaginary. This position usually amounts to saying that so-called childhood hyperactivity exists only in the eye (and on the nerves) of the beholder.

A great deal of skepticism and dismay has been expressed about drug treatment. Some critics merely decry the ingestion of chemical agents. Others point out that there are still insufficient data on the long-term value of drug treatment and on the short- and long-term effects on growth and heart functioning. Special concern has been expressed about the possible role played by prescribed medication in later drug abuse. The few empirical studies bearing on the question suggest that hyperactive children are not placed at risk for later drug abuse by treatment with stimulant drugs (Beck and others, 1975). Similarly, there has been considerable concern about the negative effects and self-fulfilling prophecies that may emanate from the diagnosis itself. Studies of labeling and attribution are beginning to be advocated and reported (Whelen and Henker, 1976). When the child is professionally diagnosed or considered referable, the severity of parental discipline (Stevens-Long, 1973) and of child-reported teacher disapproval (Loney, Whaley-Klahn, and Weissenburger, 1976) may be reduced—perhaps because the child's behavior is not thought to be under voluntary control. The subtleties of the psychological impact of diagnosis and treatment obviously need further evaluation.

A large factor in the continuation of such controversies is, of course, that they are derived from differences in the values and principles held by the participants and as such are not really subject to significant modification from external data or counterarguments. But another problem is the absence of relevant data from one crucially important person: the child. The hyperactive child has not often been asked, directly or indirectly, whether his or her behavior or other peoples' reactions to it are a source of personal unhappiness. Many observers have noted that the nub of so-called hyperactive behavior is its annoyance value to parents, teachers, and/or peers; some are beginning to study the entire social/ psychological matrix in which the child operates. For example, Kupietz (1976) suggests that children be tested under conditions chosen to maximize their motivation. Another beginning could be made by developing separate measures of child behavior and parents' reactions to that behavior.

The topic of childhood hyperactivity, particularly at its intersections with minimal brain dysfunction and learning disabilities, stirs the concerns of parents, pediatricians, psychologists, psychiatrists, social workers, and various education professionals. Intradisciplinary controversies about etiology, assessment, and treatment choice can only produce interdisciplinary confusion. This is clearly a situation where sophisticated across-disciplinary collaboration is required, and training efforts can profitably be directed to enhancing knowledge and communication. The contributions of parents, teachers, and health professionals must be coordinated across the early and middle childhood years (Berlin, 1974; Feighner and Feighner, 1974), and the necessary commitment to continuity of care must be built into preparation for professional role functions.

The drug treatment of hyperactive children makes special demands on professional monitoring and follow-up procedures (Solomons, 1973). Studies by Sprague, Sleator, and their associates (Sleator and von Neumann, 1974; Sprague and Sleator, 1973) provide ideas about using periodic placebo trials in clinical practice. Studies by the same investigators (Sprague and Sleator, 1975, 1977) of dose-response relationships suggest that many of the clinical dosages that produce control of hyperactivity are too high for optimal learning. The necessity for using multiple measures of treatment response is well conveyed by these studies. The substantial literature on behavior modification also offers numerous good examples of methods for decision making and treatment monitoring in the individual case (Sulzbacher, 1975). Given the present state of knowledge, it would probably be helpful if students in various health and educational disciplines were exposed to the variety of theories and encouraged to adopt a questioning and flexible outlook as the search for answers proceeds. Continuing and concerned evaluation of the overall progress of each individual child is a vastly more important goal for training than is either a broad concern with etiological theories that have little pragmatic value, or a narrow reliance on a single method of intervention that will not be completely effective for all hyperactive children.

Personal Views and Recommendations

There is reason to wonder whether the diagnostic dilemmas of childhood hyperactivity will eventually yield more completely and understandably to medical or to psychological models. In research to date, groups that are homogeneous in symptomatology have tended to be heterogeneous in etiology and outcome, whereas groups that are similar in course or treatment response have appeared to be dissimilar in etiology. Some believe that the notion of a hyperkinetic *syndrome* has little to support it (Ross and Ross, 1976); but perhaps smaller subgroups, defined in ways that are not presently accepted or contemplated, might prove to be homogeneous in etiology and course (Ackerman, Dykman, and Peters, 1977). Without making an irrevocable choice, one might wish that psychological models would also be pursued. Such a model might empirically isolate measures of symptom factors, identify measures of antecedent variables, and derive measures of outcome dimensions. The use of multiple regression procedures would then enable investigators to identify the variables associated with different symptoms and outcomes and to estimate the amount of variation accounted for by each variable. It is worth noting that modern multivariate statistical procedures will accommodate the noncontinuous, nonlinear, and nominal data which might be involved (Harris, 1975).

These essentially correlational approaches would not allow causal inferences; therefore, they could not conclusively demonstrate etiology or treatment efficacy. They might, however, allow one to make individual predictions about treatment response and adolescent outcome—predictions derived from data on the individual child and associated with a specific level of confidence. Fairly sizable multiple correlations would be required for this kind of prediction, and they would have to have survived cross-validation studies. However, since predictions about individual children are presently made from clinical experience and from research on heterogeneous groups, the multiple regression approach seems to have considerable potential.

Regardless of the ultimate utility of multivariate approaches for individual prediction, answers to many of the important questions about treatment choice and potential outcomes could be suggested by multivariate studies which identified the relative contribution of environmental and symptom variables. Such an approach was taken by Paternite and Loney (in press) in a study indicating that much of the predictable variation in adolescent outcome is accounted for by aggressive symptomatology at referral. Similar findings have been reported in the comprehensive follow-up study being conducted by Weiss and her colleagues (Minde and others, 1971; Minde, Weiss, and Mendelson, 1972; Weiss and others, 1971). These results suggest that hyperactivity and aggression should be assessed separately at referral (Loney, Langhorne, and Paternite, 1978) and that long-term prognostic statements should be derived from a consideration of aggressive (as opposed to hyperactive) symptomatology. It begins to appear that hyperactivity and inattention are of little importance in the eventual outcome of the hyperactive child; this might explain why drug treatment with CNS stimulants does not predict long-term outcome, although it does reduce hyperactive symptoms.

Application to Particular Variables

It is widely recognized that most activity measures decline across the childhood years. Routh, Schroeder, and O'Tuama (1974) showed developmental changes in open-field activity scores in the playroom and on the Werry-Weiss-Peters rating scale for parents. Similar developmental changes have been seen in teacher ratings (Spring and others, 1977). The belief that clinical overactivity disappears as the child becomes older has been amended as the result of follow-up studies (Minde and others, 1971; Minde, Weiss, and Mendelson, 1972; Weiss and others, 1971). It appears that older hyperactive children *are* less likely to engage in the peripatetic and noisy behavior of their younger years, but differences from peers in both activity and attention tend to remain into adolescence. Differences between erstwhile HK/MBD individuals and normal controls appear to be even less striking by adulthood (Hechtman and others, 1976). These age-related changes in the nature and intensity of hyperactive behaviors tend *not* to be directly reflected in definitions of the HK/MBD syndrome. Thus, one can expect most definitions to produce more identified hyperkinetic children at younger than at older ages.

Many more boys than girls are diagnosed as hyperkinetic; sometimes the discrepancy is as large as 10 to 1. Some regard this sex ratio as evidence for a genetic etiology; others use the discrepancy to argue just as forcefully for a psychological role theory (Levine, Kozak, and Shaiova, 1977). Probably because of their relative rarity, very few studies of hyperactive girls are reported (Prinz and Loney, 1974); and almost all studies of hyperactive children include both boys and girls, without separate analyses for sex.

In addition to the poor peer relationships and classroom management problems occasioned by the child's hyperactivity and inattentiveness, he or she is also likely to have difficulties in learning and retaining academic material. Consequently, a substantial literature on learning disability overlaps with the literature on HK/MBD. Samples of hyperkinetic elementary school children contain many children who have repeated one or more grades and/or who read, spell, or calculate far worse than their peers (Ackerman, Dykman, and Peters, 1977; Minde and others, 1971; Minde, Weiss, and Mendelson, 1972). Conversely, samples of learning-disabled elementary school children contain many children who are hyperactive.

Hyperactivity occurs and responds to treatment across a wide socioeconomic range (Alley, Solomons, and Opitz, 1971; Hoffman and others, 1974). Paternite, Loney, and Langhorne (1976) suggest that primary HK/MBD symptomatology (hyperactivity and inattention) is not related to socioeconomic status (SES) but that secondary symptomatology (aggressive interpersonal behavior and self-esteem deficits) is more severe among lower-SES children. Paternite and his colleagues conclude that SES-related differences in parenting styles (for instance, parental laxity and hostility) account for more variation in secondary symptomatology than does SES as such. To date, the connections between parenting styles and hyperactive symptomatology have been little studied. Cunningham and Barkley (1979) have done observational studies documenting that the parents of hyperactives use stronger disciplinary methods than the parents of normals. Bell (1968b) has pointed out the difficulty of determining the direction of causality in parent-child interactions, and Chess (1969) has noted the reverberating effects of a temperamentally difficult child within the family circle. Stevens-Long (1973) has shown that parents tend to choose more severe discipline for more active children shown in films. Wender (1976) has noted that a child can, independently, have bad parents and MBD. He notes, however, that the "badness" of both child and parent in their respective family roles can have a common genetic basis.

Adult follow-up studies that might document different vocational choices or avocational preferences among hyperactive individuals have not yet been completed. Borland and Heckman (1976) found that formerly hyperactive young adults were employed at lower SES levels than either their brothers or their fathers, but the influence of the hyperactive young men's poorer academic records on their wages is not completely accounted for. The employers of hyperactive young adults apparently do not see them as much different from normal controls (Hechtman and others, 1976).

Virtually no separate analyses have been reported for racial and ethnic subgroups within the numerous studies of various aspects of hyperactivity. Spring and associates (1977) report differences in teacher ratings of the behavior of black, white, and oriental children. Other studies of teacher rating scales have noted both regional differences (Werry and Hawthorne, 1976) and cross-cultural similarities (Minde and Cohen, 1978; Sprague, Cohen, and Eichlseder, 1977).

There appear to be no laboratory findings associated with hyperactivity. Waldrop, Pedersen, and Bell (1968) report that minor physical anomalies of the type found in Down's Syndrome are more frequent among hyperactive boys, and several intriguing investigations of physical anomalies in hyperactive and comparison groups have been reported (Rapoport and Quinn, 1976; Firestone, Lewy, and Douglas, 1976).

Palkes and Stewart (1972) found differences in intelligence test scores between hyperactive and normal children. They concluded that hyperactive children have less intellectual endowment, independent of their problems with attention and related functions, and that their reduced academic functioning results from their lower intellectual ability. In a cross-sectional study, Loney (1974) found reduced intellectual functioning in older (fifth-grade) hyperactive boys but not in younger (second-grade) ones. Loney concluded that the intellectual deficits are essentially motivational ones that develop across time and do not reflect innate differences in capability. The accumulated research suggests that, for whatever reason, hyperactive groups do worse on intelligence tests, especially on subtests that require sustained attention.

Although many hyperactive youngsters show indicators of organic pathology (soft neurological signs, a history of adverse circumstances surrounding birth, poor performance on perceptual tests, and the like), many more do not. Similarly, some children with organic pathology are hyperactive, and some are not. Thus, no organic sign can presently be considered pathognomonic (Dubey, 1976; Werry, 1972). At the same time, organic etiological theories are being tested by several groups of investigators (Satterfield and Braley, 1977; Wender, 1976), and subgroups of children may well be identified in whom organic features are major determinants.

Many writers have postulated the existence of a subgroup of children whose hyperactive behavior is a product of psychological stress and/or family disharmony. Few studies of this type of child have been reported. In adolescent follow-up studies, however, several psychological consequences of childhood hyperactivity have been noted. Low self-esteem and delinquent behavior are frequently cited examples (Mendelson, Johnson, and Stewart, 1971). There is some question whether these psychological symptoms are the consequences of early hyperactivity or of early aggression. Adolescent symptoms such as low self-esteem and delinquent behavior appear to be associated with the existence of childhood aggression and with the presence of adverse economic circumstances and family disharmony (Loney and others, 1976).

The study of social and interactional aspects of childhood hyperactivity is in its infancy. The most common method of investigation has been observational studies of interactions in mother and child dyads (Routh, in press). Ingenious studies of interactions between hyperactive children and their peers have also begun to appear (Whalen and others, 1979). A recent paper by Block (1977) invites researchers to explore the etiology of hyperactivity from a broader cultural perspective.

References

Abikoff, H., Gittelman-Klein, R., and Klein, D. F. "Validation of a Classroom Observation Code for Hyperactive Children." *Journal of Consulting and Clinical Psychology*, 1977, *45*, 772-783.

Ackerman, P. T., Dykman, R. A., and Peters, J. E. "Teenage Status of Hyperactive and Nonhyperactive Learning Disabled Boys." *American Journal of Orthopsychiatry*, 1977, *47*, 577-596.

Alley, G. R., Solomons, G., and Opitz, E. "Minimal Cerebral Dysfunction as It Relates to Social Class." *Journal of Learning Disabilities*, 1971, *4*, 16-20.

Arnold, L. E. "Minimal Brain Dysfunction: A Hydraulic Parfait Model." *Diseases of the Nervous System*, 1976, *37*, 171-173.

Barkley, R. A. "Predicting the Response of Hyperkinetic Children to Stimulant Drugs: A Review." *Journal of Abnormal Child Psychology*, 1976, *4*, 327-348.

Barkley, R. A., and Cunningham, C. E. "The Effects of Ritalin on the Mother-Child Interactions of Hyperactive Children." *Archives of General Psychiatry*, 1979, *36*, 201-208.

Barkley, R. A., and Ullman, D. G. "A Comparison of Objective Measures of Activity and Distractibility in Hyperactive and Nonhyperactive Children." *Journal of Abnormal Child Psychology*, 1975, *3*, 231-244.

Beck, L., and others. "Childhood Chemotherapy and Later Drug Abuse and Growth Curve." *American Journal of Psychiatry*, 1975, *132*, 436-438.

Bell, R. Q. "Adaptation of Small Wristwatches for Mechanical Recording of Activities in Infants and Children." *Journal of Experimental Child Psychology*, 1968a, *6*, 302-305.

Bell, R. Q. "A Reinterpretation of the Direction of Effects in Studies of Socialization." *Psychological Review*, 1968b, *75*, 81-95.

Berlin, I. "Minimal Brain Dysfunction: Management of Family Distress." *Journal of the American Medical Association*, 1974, *229*, 1454-1456.

Block, G. "Hyperactivity: A Cultural Perspective." *Journal of Learning Disabilities*, 1977, *10*, 48-52.

Blunden, D., Spring, C., and Greenberg, L. M. "Validation of the Classroom Behavior Inventory." *Journal of Consulting and Clinical Psychology*, 1974, *42*, 84-88.

Bolstad, O. D., and Johnson, S. M. "The Relationship Between Teachers' Assessment of Students and the Students' Actual Behavior in the Classroom." *Child Development*, 1977, *48*, 570-578.

Borland, B. L., and Heckman, H. K. "Hyperactive Boys and Their Brothers: A Follow-Up Study." *Archives of General Psychiatry*, 1976, *33*, 669-675.

Bradley, C. "The Behavior of Children Receiving Benzedrine." *American Journal of Psychiatry*, 1937, *94*, 577.

Campbell, D. T., and Fiske, D. W. "Convergent and Discriminant Validation by the Multitrait-Multimethod Matrix." *Psychological Bulletin*, 1959, *56*, 81-105.

Campbell, S. B. "Cognitive Styles and Behavior Problems of Clinic Boys: A Comparison of Epileptic, Hyperactive, Learning-Disabled, and Normal Groups." *Journal of Abnormal Child Psychology*, 1974, *2*, 307-312.

Campbell, S. B., Endman, M. W., and Bernfeld, G. "A Three-Year Follow-Up of Hyperactive Preschoolers into Elementary School." *Journal of Child Psychology and Psychiatry*, 1977, *18*, 239-249.

Campbell, S. B., and others. "A Two-Year Follow-Up of Hyperactive Preschoolers." *American Journal of Orthopsychiatry*, 1977, *47*, 149-162.

Cantwell, D. P. *The Hyperactive Child.* Jamaica, N.Y.: Spectrum, 1975.

Chess, S. "Diagnosis and Treatment of the Hyperactive Child." *New York State Journal of Medicine,* 1960, *60,* 2379-2385.

Chess, S. "Genesis of Behaviour Disorders." In J. G. Howells (Ed.), *Modern Perspectives in International Child Psychiatry.* New York: Brunner/Mazel, 1969.

Childers, A. T. "Hyper-activity in Children Having Behavior Disorders." *American Journal of Orthopsychiatry,* 1935, *5,* 227-243.

Christensen, D. E. "Effects of Combining Methylphenidate and a Classroom Token System in Modifying Hyperactive Behavior." *American Journal of Mental Deficiency,* 1975, *80,* 266-276.

Clements, S. D., and Peters, J. E. "Minimal Brain Dysfunctions in the School-Age Child." *Archives of General Psychiatry,* 1962, *6,* 17-29.

Coleman, L. "Problem Kids and Preventive Medicine: The Making of an Odd Couple." *American Journal of Orthopsychiatry,* 1978, *48,* 56-70.

Conners, C. K. "A Teacher Rating Scale for Use in Drug Studies with Children." *American Journal of Psychiatry,* 1969, *126,* 152-156.

Conrad, P. *Identifying Hyperactive Children.* Lexington, Mass.: Heath, 1976.

Conrad, W. G., and Insel, J. "Anticipating the Response to Amphetamine Therapy in the Treatment of Hyperkinetic Children." *Pediatrics,* 1967, *40,* 96.

Cunningham, C. E., and Barkley, R. A. "The Interactions of Normal and Hyperactive Children with Their Mothers in Free Play and Structured Tasks." *Child Development,* 1979, *50,* 217-224.

Douglas, V. I. "Stop, Look and Listen: The Problem of Sustained Attention and Impulse Control in Hyperactive and Normal Children." *Canadian Journal of Behavioural Science,* 1972, *4,* 259-282.

Dubey, D. R. "Organic Factors in Hyperkinesis: A Critical Evaluation." *American Journal of Orthopsychiatry,* 1976, *46,* 353-366.

Dykman, R. A., and Ackerman, P. T. "Hyperactive Boys as Adolescents." Paper presented in symposium on hyperactive children, at meeting of American Psychological Association, Chicago, 1975.

Dykman, R. A., and others. "Specific Learning Disabilities: An Attentional Deficit Syndrome." In H. R. Myklebust (Ed.), *Progress in Learning Disabilities.* Vol. 2. New York: Grune and Stratton, 1971.

Ebaugh, F. G. "Neuropsychiatric Sequelae of Acute Epidemic Encephalitis in Children." *American Journal of Diseases of Children,* 1923, *25,* 89-97.

Ellis, M. J., and others. "Methylphenidate and the Activity of Hyperactives in the Informal Setting." *Child Development,* 1974, *45,* 217-220.

Feighner, A. C., and Feighner, J. P. "Multimodality Treatment of the Hyperkinetic Child." *American Journal of Psychiatry,* 1974, *131,* 459-463.

Firestone, P., and Douglas, V. "The Effects of Reward and Punishment on Reaction Times and Autonomic Activity in Hyperactive and Normal Children." *Journal of Abnormal Child Psychology,* 1975, *3,* 201-216.

Firestone, P., Lewy, F., and Douglas, V. I. "Hyperactivity and Physical Anomalies." *Canadian Psychiatric Association Journal,* 1976, *21,* 23-26.

Fish, B. "The 'One Child, One Drug' Myth of Stimulants in Hyperkinesis." *Archives of General Psychiatry,* 1971, *25,* 193-203.

Forness, S. R. "Looking: Use of Classroom Observation in Early Identification." In R. Rutherford and J. Buckhalt (Eds.), *Distinguished Lectures in Special Education.* Los Angeles: University of Southern California Press, 1975.

Forness, S. R., and Esveldt, K. C. "Classroom Observation of Children with Learning and Behavior Problems." *Journal of Learning Disabilities,* 1975, *8,* 49-52.

Freeman, R. D. "Minimal Brain Dysfunction, Hyperactivity, and Learning Disorders: Epidemic or Episode?" *School Review,* 1976, *85,* 5-30.

Grinspoon, L., and Singer, S. B. "Amphetamines in the Treatment of Hyperkinetic Children." *Harvard Educational Review,* 1973, *43,* 515-555.

Harris, G., Vincent, J., and Williams, B. "Temporal Stability of Behavior Profiles and Behaviors for Hyperactive and Control Children." Paper presented at meeting of American Psychological Association, San Francisco, Aug. 1977.

Harris, R. J. *A Primer of Multivariate Statistics.* New York: Academic Press, 1975.

Hechtman, L., and others. "Hyperactives as Young Adults: A Preliminary Report." *Canadian Medical Association Journal,* 1976, *115,* 625-630.

Hoffman, S. P., and others. "Response to Methylphenidate in Low Socioeconomic Hyperactive Children." *Archives of General Psychiatry,* 1974, *30,* 354-359.

Hoffmann, H. *Der Struwwelpeter: Oder Lustige Geschichten und Drollige Bilder.* Leipzig: Insel-Verlag, 1845.

Johnson, C. F. "Hyperactivity and the Machine: The Actometer." *Child Development,* 1971, *42,* 2105-2110.

Kahn, E., and Cohen, L. H. "Organic Drivenness: A Brain Stem Syndrome and an Experience." *New England Journal of Medicine,* 1934, *210,* 748-756.

Kenny, T. J., and Clemmens, R. L. "Hyperactivity: A Multi-Factorial Model." Paper presented at annual meeting of American Psychological Association, Washington, D.C., 1975.

Kenny, T. J., and others. "Characteristics of Children Referred Because of Hyperactivity." *Journal of Pediatrics,* 1971, *79,* 618-622.

Kupietz, S. S. "Attentiveness in Behaviorally Deviant and Nondeviant Children. I: Auditory Vigilance Performance." *Perceptual and Motor Skills,* 1976, *43,* 1095-1101.

Kupietz, S. S., Camp, J. A., and Weissman, A. D. "Reaction Time Performance of Behaviorally Deviant Children: Effects of Prior Preparatory Interval and Reinforcement." *Journal of Child Psychology and Psychiatry,* 1976, *17,* 123-131.

Lapouse, R., and Monk, M. A. "An Epidemiologic Study of Behavior Characteristics in Children." *American Journal of Public Health,* 1958, *48,* 1134-1144.

Laufer, M. W., and others. "Hyperkinetic Impulse Disorder in Children's Behavior Problems." *Psychosomatic Medicine,* 1957, *19,* 38-49.

Levine, E. M., Kozak, C., and Shaiova, C. H. "Hyperactivity Among White Middle-Class Children." *Child Psychiatry and Human Development,* 1977, *7,* 156-168.

Lobitz, G., and Johnson, S. "Normal Versus Deviant Children: Multimethod Comparison." *Journal of Abnormal Child Psychology,* 1975, *3,* 353-374.

Loney, J. "The Intellectual Functioning of Hyperactive Elementary School Boys: A Cross-Sectional Investigation." *American Journal of Orthopsychiatry,* 1974, *44,* 754-762.

Loney, J., Langhorne, J. E., Jr., and Paternite, C. E. "An Empirical Basis for Subgrouping the Hyperkinetic/MBD Syndrome." *Journal of Abnormal Psychology,* 1978, *87,* 431-441.

Loney, J., and Ordoña, T. T. "Using Cerebral Stimulants to Treat MBD." *American Journal of Orthopsychiatry,* 1975, *45,* 564-572.

Loney, J., and others. "The Iowa HABIT: Hyperkinetic/Aggressive Boys in Treatment." Paper presented at meeting of Society for Life History Research in Psychopathology, Ft. Worth, 1976.

Loney, J., Whaley-Klahn, M. A., and Weissenburger, F. E. "Responses of Hyperactive Boys to a Behaviorally-Focused School Attitude Questionnaire." *Child Psychiatry and Human Development*, 1976, 6, 123-133.

Loney, J., and others. "Hyperkinetic/Aggressive Boys in Treatment: Predictors of Clinical Response to Methylphenidate." *American Journal of Psychiatry*, 1978, 135, 1487-1491.

Marwit, S. J., and Stenner, A. J. "Hyperkinesis: Delineation of Two Patterns." *Exceptional Children*, 1972, 38, 401-406.

Mendelson, W., Johnson, N., and Stewart, M. A. "Hyperactive Children as Teen-Agers: A Follow-Up Study." *Journal of Nervous and Mental Disease*, 1971, 153, 273-279.

Minde, K. "Hyperactivity: Where Do We Stand?" In M. E. Blaw, I. Rapin, and M. Kinsbourne (Eds.), *Topics in Neurology*. Jamaica, N.Y.: Spectrum, 1977.

Minde, K., and Cohen, N. J. "Hyperactive Children in Canada and Uganda: A Comparative Evaluation." *Journal of the American Academy of Child Psychiatry*, 1978, 17, 476-487.

Minde, K., Weiss, G., and Mendelson, W. "A Five Year Follow-Up Study of 91 Hyperactive School Children." *Journal of the American Academy of Child Psychiatry*, 1972, 11, 595-610.

Minde, K., and others. "The Hyperactive Child in Elementary School: A 5-Year Controlled Follow-Up." *Exceptional Children*, 1971, 38, 215-221.

Morrison, J., and Stewart, M. A. "A Family Study of the Hyperactive Child Syndrome." *Biological Psychiatry*, 1971, 3, 189-195.

Ney, G. N. "Four Types of Hyperkinesis." *Canadian Psychiatric Association Journal*, 1974, 19, 543-550.

O'Malley, J. E., and Eisenberg, L. "The Hyperkinetic Syndrome." *Seminars in Psychiatry*, 1973, 5, 95-103.

Orton, S. *Reading, Writing, and Speech Problems in Children*. New York: Norton, 1937.

Palkes, H., and Stewart, M. "Intellectual Ability and Performance of Hyperactive Children." *American Journal of Orthopsychiatry*, 1972, 42, 35-39.

Paternite, C. E., and Loney, J. "Childhood Hyperkinesis: Relationships Between Symptomatology and Home Environment." In C. Whalen and B. Henker (Eds.), *Hyperactive Children: The Social Ecology of Identification and Treatment*. New York: Academic Press, in press.

Paternite, C. E., Loney, J., and Langhorne, J. E., Jr. "Relationships Between Symptomatology and SES-Related Factors in Hyperkinetic/MBD Boys." *American Journal of Orthopsychiatry*, 1976, 46, 291-301.

Pope, L. "Motor Activity in Brain-Injured Children." *American Journal of Orthopsychiatry*, 1970, 40, 783-794.

Prinz, R., and Loney, J. "Teacher-Rated Hyperactive Elementary School Girls: An Exploratory Developmental Study." *Child Psychiatry and Human Development*, 1974, 4, 246-257.

Quay, H. C. "Classification." In H. C. Quay and J. Werry (Eds.), *Psychopathological Disorders of Childhood*. (2nd Ed.) New York: Wiley, 1979.

Quay, H. C., and Quay, L. C. "Behavior Problems in Early Adolescence." *Child Development*, 1965, 36, 215-220.

Rapoport, J. L., and Benoit, M. "The Relation of Direct Home Observations to the Clinic Evaluation of Hyperactive School-Age Boys." *Journal of Child Psychology and Psychiatry*, 1975, 16, 141-147.

Rapoport, J. L., and others. "Playroom Observations of Hyperactive Children on Medication." *Journal of the American Academy of Child Psychiatry*, 1971, 10, 524-534.

Rapoport, J. L., and others. "Dextroamphetamine: Cognitive and Behavioral Effects in Normal Prepubertal Boys." *Science,* 1978, *199,* 560-563.

Rapoport, J. L., and Quinn, P. O. "Minor Physical Anomalies (Stigmata) and Early Developmental Deviation: A Major Biologic Subgroup of 'Hyperactive Children.' " *Mental Health in Children,* 1976, *3,* 271-290.

Rie, H. E. "Hyperactivity in Children." *American Journal of Diseases of Children,* 1975, *129,* 783-789.

Roberts, M. A., and Ray, R. S. "A Behavioral Assessment of Situational Differences in the Activity Level of Hyperactive and Normal Boys." Unpublished paper, 1978.

Ross, D. M., and Ross, S. A. *Hyperactivity: Research, Theory, and Action.* New York: Wiley, 1976.

Routh, D. K. "The Nature, Causes, and Management of Hyperactivity." In P. Magrab (Ed.), *Psychological Management of Pediatric Problems.* Baltimore: University Park Press, in press.

Routh, D. K., and Roberts, R. D. "Minimal Brain Dysfunction in Children: Failure to Find Evidence for a Behavioral Syndrome." *Psychological Reports,* 1972, *31,* 307-314.

Routh, D. K., and Schroeder, C. S. "Standardized Playroom Measures as Indices of Hyperactivity." *Journal of Abnormal Child Psychology,* 1976, *4,* 199-207.

Routh, D. K., Schroeder, C. S., and O'Tuama, L. A. "Development of Activity Level in Children." *Developmental Psychology,* 1974, *10,* 163-168.

Rutter, M. L., and Brown, G. W. "The Reliability and Validity of Measures of Family Life and Relationships in Families Containing a Psychiatric Patient." *Social Psychiatry,* 1966, *1,* 38-53.

Safer, D., and Allen, R. *Hyperactive Children: Diagnosis and Management.* Baltimore: University Park Press, 1976.

Safer, D., Krager, J., and Earhart, J. Baltimore County Department of Health, personal communication, 1978.

Sandoval, J. "The Measurement of the Hyperactive Syndrome in Children." *Review of Educational Research,* 1977, *47,* 293-318.

Sandoval, J., Lambert, N. M., and Yandell, W. "Current Medical Practice and Hyperactive Children." *American Journal of Orthopsychiatry,* 1976, *46,* 323-334.

Satterfield, J. H., and Braley, B. W. "Evoked Potentials and Brain Maturation in Hyperactive and Normal Children." *Electroencephalography,* 1977, *43,* 43-51.

Schain, R. J. "Minimal Brain Dysfunction." *Current Problems in Pediatrics,* 1975, *5,* 1-30.

Schleifer, M., and others. "Hyperactivity in Preschoolers and the Effect of Methylphenidate." *American Journal of Orthopsychiatry,* 1975, *45,* 38-50.

Schmitt, B. D. "The Minimal Brain Dysfunction Myth." *American Journal of Diseases of Children,* 1975, *129,* 1313-1324.

Schrager, J., and others. "The Hyperkinetic Syndrome: Some Consensually Validated Behavioral Correlates." *Exceptional Children,* 1966, *32,* 635-637.

Schulman, J. L., and Reisman, J. M. "An Objective Measure of Hyperactivity." *American Journal of Mental Deficiency,* 1959, *64,* 455-456.

Shaffer, D., McNamara, N., and Pincus, J. H. "Controlled Observations on Patterns of Activity, Attention, and Impulsivity in Brain-Damaged and Psychiatrically Disturbed Boys." *Psychological Medicine,* 1974, *4,* 4-18.

Sleator, E. K., and von Neumann, A. "Methylphenidate in the Treatment of Hyperkinetic Children." *Clinical Pediatrics,* 1974, *13,* 19-24.

Solomons, G. "Drug Therapy: Initiation and Follow-Up." *Annals of New York Academy of Science,* 1973, *205,* 335-344.

Sprague, R. L. "Psychopharmacotherapy in Children." In M. F. McMillan and S. Henae (Eds.), *Child Psychiatry: Treatment and Research.* New York: Brunner/Mazel, 1977.

Sprague, R. L., Barnes, K. R., and Werry, J. S. "Methylphenidate and Thioridazine: Learning, Reaction Time, Activity, and Classroom Behavior in Disturbed Children." *American Journal of Orthopsychiatry,* 1970, *40,* 615-628.

Sprague, R. L., Cohen, M. N., and Eichlseder, W. "Are There Hyperactive Children in Europe and the South Pacific?" Paper presented in symposium on the hyperactive child, at meeting of American Psychological Association, San Francisco, 1977.

Sprague, R. L., and Sleator, E. K. "Effects of Psychopharmacologic Agents on Learning Disorders." *Pediatric Clinics of North America,* 1973, *20,* 719-735.

Sprague, E. L., and Sleator, E. K. "What Is the Proper Dose of Stimulant Drugs in Children?" *International Journal of Mental Health,* 1975, *4,* 75-104.

Sprague, R. L., and Sleator, E. K. "Methylphenidate in Hyperkinetic Children: Differences in Dose Effects on Learning and Social Behavior." *Science,* 1977, *198,* 1274-1276.

Spring, C., and others. "Validity and Norms of a Hyperactivity Rating Scale." *Journal of Special Education,* 1977, *11,* 313-321.

Sroufe, L. A., and Stewart, M. A. "Treating Problem Children with Stimulant Drugs." *New England Journal of Medicine,* 1973, *289,* 407-413.

Stevens, D. A., and others. "Presumed Minimal Brain Dysfunction in Children." *Archives of General Psychiatry,* 1967, *16,* 281-285.

Stevens-Long, J. "The Effect of Behavioral Context on Some Aspects of Adult Disciplinary Practice and Affect." *Child Development,* 1973, *44,* 476-484.

Stewart, M. A., and others. "The Hyperactive Child Syndrome." *American Journal of Orthopsychiatry,* 1966, *36,* 861-867.

Still, G. F. "The Coulstonian Lectures on Some Abnormal Physical Conditions in Children." *Lancet,* 1902, *1,* 1108-1012, 1077-1082, 1163-1168.

Strauss, A. A., and Lehtinen, L. *Psychopathology and Education of the Brain Injured Child.* New York: Grune and Stratton, 1947.

Sulzbacher, S. I. "The Learning-Disabled or Hyperactive Child." *Journal of the American Medical Association,* 1975, *234,* 938-941.

Sykes, D. H., Douglas, V. I., and Morgenstern, G. "Sustained Attention in Hyperactive Children." *Journal of Child Psychology and Psychiatry,* 1973, *14,* 213-220.

Sykes, D. H., and others. "Attention in Hyperactive Children and the Effect of Methylphenidate (Ritalin)." *Journal of Child Psychology and Psychiatry,* 1971, *12,* 129-139.

Touwen, B. C., and Kalverboer, A. F. "Neurologic and Behavioral Assessment of Children with Minimal Brain Dysfunction." *Seminars in Psychiatry,* 1973, *5,* 79-94.

Vincent, J. P., Williams, B. J., and Elrod, J. T. "Ratings and Observations of Hyperactivity Multitrait-Multimethod Analyses." Paper presented at meeting of American Psychological Association. San Francisco, 1977.

Waldrop, M., Pedersen, F. A., and Bell, R. Q. "Minor Physical Anomalies and Behavior in Preschool Children." *Child Development,* 1968, *39,* 391-400.

Weiss, G., and others. "Studies on the Hyperactive Child. 8: Five-Year Follow-Up." *Archives of General Psychiatry,* 1971, *24,* 409-414.

Weiss, G., and others. "Effect of Long-Term Treatment of Hyperactive Children with Methylphenidate." *Canadian Medical Association Journal,* 1975, *112,* 159-165.

Weissenburger, F. E., and Loney, J. "Hyperkinesis in the Classroom: If Cerebral Stimulants are the Last Resort, What Would Be a First Resort?" *Journal of Learning Disabilities,* 1977, *10,* 339-348.

Wender, P. H. *Minimal Brain Dysfunction in Children*. New York: Wiley-Interscience, 1971.

Wender, P. H. "Minimal Brain Dysfunction: An Overview." Paper read at meeting of American College of Neuropharmacology, 1976.

Werry, J. S. "Developmental Hyperactivity." *Pediatric Clinics of North America*, 1968a, *15*, 581-598.

Werry, J. S. "Studies on the Hyperactive Child. 4: An Empirical Analysis of the Minimal Brain Dysfunction Syndrome." *Archives of General Psychiatry*, 1968b, *19*, 9-16.

Werry, J. S. "Organic Factors in Childhood Psychopathology." In H. C. Quay and J. S. Werry (Eds.), *Psychopathological Disorders of Childhood*. New York: Wiley, 1972.

Werry, J. S. "Minimal Brain Dysfunction (Neurological Impairment) in Children." *New Zealand Medical Journal*, 1974, *80*, 94-100.

Werry, J. S., and Hawthorne, D. "Conners' Teacher Questionnaire—Norms and Validity." *Australian and New Zealand Journal of Psychiatry*, 1976, *10*, 257-262.

Werry, J. S., and Quay, H. C. "The Prevalence of Behavior Symptoms in Younger Elementary School Children." *American Journal of Orthopsychiatry*, 1971, *41*, 136-143.

Werry, J. S., Sprague, R. L., and Cohen, M. N. "Conners' Teacher Rating Scale for Use in Drug Studies with Children—An Empirical Study." *Journal of Abnormal Child Psychology*, 1975, *3*, 217-229.

Whalen, C. K., and Henker, B. "Psychostimulants and Children: A Review and Analysis." *Psychological Bulletin*, 1976, *83*, 1113-1130.

Whalen, C. K., and others. "Peer Interaction in a Structured Communication Task: Comparisons of Normal and Hyperactive Boys and of Methylphenidate (Ritalin) and Placebo Effects." *Child Development*, 1979, *50*, 388-401.

Williams, B. J., Vincent, J. P., and Elrod, J. T. "The Behavioral Components of Hyperactivity." Paper presented at annual meeting of American Psychological Association, San Francisco, 1977.

Worland, J., North-Jones, M., and Stern, J. A. "Performance and Activity of Hyperactive and Normal Boys as a Function of Distraction and Reward." *Journal of Abnormal Child Psychology*, 1973, *1*, 363-377.

Yarrow, M. R., Campbell, J. D., and Burton, R. V. "Recollections of Childhood: A Study of the Retrospective Method." *Monographs of the Society for Research in Child Development*, 1970, *35*, Serial 138.

Zentall, S. S., and Zentall, T. R. "Activity and Task Performance of Hyperactive Children as a Function of Environmental Stimulation." *Journal of Consulting and Clinical Psychology*, 1976, *44*, 693-697.

19

Robert W. Collins

Enuresis
and Encopresis

Enuresis and encopresis are technical terms referring to functional difficulties in bladder and bowel control, respectively. Eliminative control ordinarily is accomplished in the sequence bowel-asleep, bowel-awake, bladder-awake, bladder-asleep (Stein and Susser, 1967). Encopresis and diurnal (daytime) enuresis can be recognized when a child is between 2 and 3 years of age. The last stage of bladder control in sleep appears to be particularly difficult to achieve for a significant minority of children from 4 to 5 years of age and beyond. In fact, bedwetting (nocturnal enuresis) may be regarded as the most chronic and prevalent of all childhood disorders.

Organic causes and complications of bladder and bowel incontinence are almost always sought but rarely found. While maturational and hereditary mechanisms are undoubtedly implicated, they clearly interact with personal-societal concerns and toilet-training procedures. The effectiveness of the various surgical, biochemical, and behavioral conditioning interventions attests to the highly interactive nature of enuresis or encopresis. The visibility of enuretic and encopretic symptoms lends an objectivity to clinical assessment procedures which is not generally found for other functional disorders. This realization, the robustness of modern medical and behavioral sciences, and the centuries-old concerns surrounding soiling promise increased freedom from the problem of urinary and fecal incontinence.

Background and Current Status

Enuresis is a New Latin derivation from the Greek word *enourein,* meaning "to urinate in." Its incidence in children has been a cause of concern for centuries. Encopresis is a modern term, invented in the mid 1920s (Halpern, 1977). The general paucity of information on encopresis, until very recently, contrasts greatly with the much more copious information on enuresis. An almost phobic aversion to feces has apparently characterized most cultures to this time. For example, fecal incontinence is the primary reason for removing the elderly from home care and placing them in extended-care facilities (Atthowe, 1972).

Nocturnal enuresis was recognized as worthy of attention as long ago as 1550 B.C., when it was described in the pediatric section of an ancient Greek volume (Glicklich, 1951). Thomas Phaer, the father of English pediatrics, headed a paragraph in his 1544 *Boke of Children* with the title "Of Pyssying in the Bedde" (Glicklich, 1951). Psychoanalytic speculation has suggested that enuresis is a form of aggression against the parents or a depression expressed in weeping through the bladder (Blackwell and Currah, 1973; Lovibond, 1964). In the modern era it rated an international conference in England (Kolvin, MacKeith, and Meadow, 1973).

Encopresis should be viewed in the context of centuries-old concerns with promoting bowel movements, on the one hand, and inhibiting them to prevent soiling, on the other (Beekman, 1977). Both processes have been viewed as essential to good physical health. In Freud's view, even personality development is affected by the various outcomes or processes associated with achieving bowel control (Erikson, 1963; Fine, 1973, 1975); and psychoanalytic observers specifically attribute to the "anal stage" of personality development such traits as stubbornness, orderliness, pedantry, rebelliousness, a drive for autonomy, and a fondness for molding and manipulating.

The worldwide incidence of nocturnal enuresis for children aged 4 years and older ranges from 10 to 33 percent (Cooper, 1973; de Jonge, 1973; Kaffman and Elizur, 1977; Lovibond, 1964; Oppel, Harper, and Rider, 1968). The chronicity of bedwetting is reflected in the statistics from some twelve surveys, which indicate that the actual probability of a child's becoming dry in any twelve-month period for any age beyond 4 years is not more than 1 in 4 (Lovibond and Coote, 1970) and could be as low as one in seven (de Jonge, 1973). Even if the child does attain continence, the probability that he or she will relapse can be as high as 1 in 4 (Oppel, Harper, and Rider, 1968). Children who have relapsed are termed secondary or acquired enuretics. Functional urinary incontinence since birth is known as primary or persistent enuresis.

The incidence of diurnal enuresis is much lower than that for nocturnal enuresis, from 2 to 5 percent (de Jonge, 1973). The presence of enuresis in rhe daytime is highly predictive of nocturnal enuresis. The reverse, diurnal enuresis given nocturnal enuresis, is somewhat less likely (de Jonge, 1973; Stein and Susser, 1967). However, some diurnal symptoms often remain for nocturnal enuretics in the form of frequency, urgency, and small bladder capacities (Lovibond and Coote, 1970; Zaleski, Gerrard, and Shokeir, 1973). Parental and societal sensitivity to daytime urinary incontinence appears to be much greater than that to bedwetting, which can be somewhat more successfully hidden and tolerated.

The incidence of encopresis in the Western world is about 1.5 percent, with boys manifesting the disorder much more often than girls (Bellman, 1966; Halpern, 1977). One should rule out the organic syndrome known as Hirschsprung's disease (involving an absence of nerve fibers in the rectum or large intestine) before diagnosing encopresis (Halpern, 1977; Wright, 1973); only about 5 percent of cases of fecal incontinence, however, are attributable to Hirschsprung's disease (Wright, 1973). There is little agreement on the nomenclature for the various forms of encopresis. Basically, there are the retentive and nonretentive forms. Retentive encopresis is most common (Bellman, 1966; Wright, 1975). It is characterized by frequent spotting throughout the day because of forced leakage around a large bolus or a fecalith. The nonretentive form is often associated with mental retardation or a lack of toilet training. As with enuresis, a further distinction can be made between primary and secondary encopresis, depending on whether or not the condition has been present from birth.

Critical Discussion

General Areas of Concern

A lack of bladder and bowel control is a natural condition of infancy. The usual question, then, of why a given child is incontinent is not nearly so interesting as the question of why or how a child manages eventually to achieve bladder and bowel control. The recast question helps to avoid blaming maturation, heredity, stress, incompetent or malevolent parents, and/or a deeply disturbed child. Instead, these same factors can be viewed from the perspective of how they can be fostered, altered, or overcome to promote bladder and bowel continence. Both modern biomedical and behavioral scientific research give good cause to believe that progress is being made in dealing with this newer question. For example, the old question implied that incontinence must be explained in terms of some underlying emotional disorder. The evidence that has emerged from research on bedwetting strongly suggests that the opposite position is largely true. That is, the unfortunate persistence of incontinence in and of itself leads to personal and societal reactions, which are the bases for the accompanying emotional problems of a significant minority of enuretic and encopretic children (Lovibond, 1964; Shaffer, 1973; Yates, 1970).

There are several ways in which physiological factors appear to be associated with incontinence. A contribution of heredity has often been suggested by the well-recognized familial incidence of enuresis. This observation has been strengthened by studies with identical twins (Bakwin, 1973). Maturational readiness for the development of bladder and bowel control is also important. The usual caution by child care experts, especially those of a psychoanalytic persuasion, is not to begin toilet training too early. However, toilet training *after* some given age may also be especially difficult to accomplish. One recent study, for example, supports the advantages of early toilet training initiated in the 15- to 19-month-old range (Kaffman and Elizur, 1977). A higher rate of nocturnal enuresis was found for children over 4 years old when their toilet training had been delayed to after 20 months of age.

Control of the retention or expulsion of waste products has to be tailored to complex societal demands about the appropriate time and place for elimination. This task, especially for a young child, is exceedingly complex. He or she must develop control over both the external and the internal milieu. Bedwetting is complicated even further because of its association with sleep, where the appropriate awareness and control is more difficult to accomplish. Here control may depend on awakening to toilet, accommodating more urine through the night, or even lessening the production of urine in sleep. One may very well wonder how young children can possibly learn the complex toileting cues and skills required for continence. The development of potent behavior conditioning regimens for toilet training has answered some questions about what should be learned (Azrin and Foxx, 1974; Collins, 1973; Halpern, 1977; Mowrer and Mowrer, 1938; Wright, 1973, 1975); and the contention that these behavior therapy approaches may have undesirable psychological or physiological consequences has not been supported (Collins, 1973, 1976; Geppert, 1953; Yates, 1970).

Comparative Philosophies and Theories

The biomedical and behavioral perspectives have merged as the predominant means for dealing with enuresis and encopresis. With respect to enuresis, biomedical researchers stress such factors as an unstable bladder, a lack of coordination between the sphincter and detrusor (bladder) muscle, and structural anomalies of the urinary tract. Their preferred modes of treatment are medication and surgery. Some degree of success has been achieved in treating enuresis with the tricyclic antidepressants (Blackwell and Currah, 1973), or by surgical transection of the bladder (Hindmarsh, Essenhigh, and Yeates, 1977), or by surgically invasive procedures to distend the bladder (Ramsden and others, 1976). However, some enuretics do not display any of the symptoms identified by the biomedical researchers as important. Even if such factors do exist, they might still be responsive to behavioral treatment procedures. For example, bladder-retraining programs do appear to be effective for the so-called unstable bladder (Allen, 1977; Svigos and Matthews, 1977).

Much of what has been observed for bladder function and enuresis could be applied to the relationship between colonic function and encopresis. One important difference between bladder and bowel dysfunction is that the problem for the bowel is more likely to be that of retention (and concomitant leakage) rather than sporadic or uncontrolled expulsion (Bellman, 1966; Wright, 1975). Biomedical interventions have typically taken the form of medications and surgery. The use of behavioral procedures appears to be as applicable for encopresis as for enuresis (Butler, 1977; Engel, Nikoomanesh, and Schuster, 1974; Epstein and McCoy, 1977; Halpern, 1977; Kohlenberg, 1973; Wright, 1973, 1975).

The behavioral research viewpoint on incontinence is represented by Mowrer and Mowrer (1938) in their early conceptualization of nocturnal enuresis as a *habit deficiency*. That is, incontinence is the result of a failure to utilize the stimuli and responses necessary for accomplishing bowel or bladder control. The Mowrers developed a device that is commonly known today as a bedwetting alarm. It is widely available through the major mail-order houses and medical supply outlets (Collins, 1976). The Mowrers theorized that the bedwetting alarm mediates a classical conditioning process, whereby the pressure cues arising from the bladder, which are still present at the sounding of the alarm, take over in eliciting the awakening and/or sphincter contraction necessary for continence.

A reanalysis of the basis for the effectiveness of the bedwetting alarm has been offered from an operant conditioning viewpoint (Azrin, Sneed, and Foxx, 1974). This view emphasizes all the reinforcing *consequences* that typically follow when one responds to the alarm by awakening and toileting (among them, smaller wet spots and dry nights). Azrin and his colleagues have developed a more elaborate conditioning program to specifically reinforce additional behaviors that should serve to mediate continence through the night.

Azrin and Foxx (1971) had earlier employed operant conditioning techniques for the daytime toilet training of the institutionalized retarded. A popular book for the layman detailing their daytime toileting procedures for normal children, entitled *Toilet Training in Less Than a Day,* was published in 1974. Wright (1973, 1975) has independently developed similar procedures especially for treating encopresis. Operant conditioning or biofeedback techniques have also been successfully focused on developing the internal biological responses, such as the anal sphincter response, relevant to bowel control (Engel, Nikoomanesh, and Schuster, 1974; Kohlenberg, 1973).

Elaboration on Critical Points

The biomedical and behavioral theoretical viewpoints are not incompatible or mutually exclusive. The behavioral view simply assumes that, whatever the cause for lacks in awareness and responding appropriate to achieving or maintaining continence, the appropriate learning can take place for an essentially intact system and organism. For the vast majority of cases of urinary incontinence, with the possible exception of the very elderly (Collins and Plaska, 1975), this assumption has been extraordinarily productive (Azrin and Foxx, 1971; Doleys, 1977; Stewart, 1975). The behavioral treatments appear to be both more effective and longer lasting than surgical techniques and medications when applied to the usual childhood cases of urinary incontinence. Combined biomedical and behavioral treatment interventions for urinary incontinence have been extraordinarily rare, though this need not be the case (Collins, 1976). One reason for this state of affairs may be that the behavioral conditioning procedures are effective and basically benign.

The combined biomedical-behavioral approach has emerged as more fruitful for the treatment of encopresis. Halpern (1977) and Wright (1973, 1975) have successfully employed a mixture of both conditioning and medications. Engel, Nikoomanesh, and Schuster (1974) have successfully combined surgical and operant conditioning procedures for the treatment of encopresis.

Personal Views and Recommendations

Encopresis and diurnal enuresis are so manifest and disturbing that they require almost immediate attention. Nocturnal enuresis can be more successfully hidden but is nevertheless so annoying and destructive of family relationships that it should also be treated as soon as possible. Before treatment for enuresis or encopresis is initiated, a physical examination, an intake interview, and a behavioral baseline are necessary.

Many physicians prefer to avoid intensive examinations. The findings are usually negative; even if they are positive, a behavioral intervention still may be indicated during or following medical correction. Successful treatments of related conditions—such as diabetes, urinary tract infections, or constipation—often do not remove the enuretic or encopretic symptoms.

In the intake interview for enuresis, one should obtain information about past and present attempts at treatment; any history of prior continence; presence of diurnal incontinence; and indications of current urgency or excessive frequency of urination, both as to time and place. Because of the importance of parental supervision during treatment, one must also determine the parents' willingness and ability to carry out the treatment. For example, single parents or employed parents often present special problems which may have to be specifically overcome in order for adequate treatment to take place. Some assessment of the parent-parent and parent-child relationships is also germane to successful treatment. Factors concerning the child must also be examined but typically do not play a large role. To assist in evaluating a child, a parent should complete a behavior symptom checklist (Collins, 1973). Care must be taken not to "pathologize," since many apparent signs of subject resistance are merely secondary to the enuresis and readily disappear with firm, supportive intervention. Most children are intellectually capable and willing enough to follow treatment instructions.

A behavioral baseline for enuresis should include time and place of accidents, spontaneous arousals in the night to toilet, size of wet spots in the morning, and bladder capacities before bedtime and upon arising in the morning. One all-day recording of toileting frequencies and bladder capacities is also recommended once a week. Continued monitoring of these same variables, whatever the form of treatment, is highly desirable.

The intake interview for encopresis is concerned with many of the same factors noted previously for enuresis, except as they involve bowel movements. However, the emotional and interactional conflicts are often more intense and complicated because of the generally greater aversion to fecal incontinence. The subject's reactions to the bathroom and sitting on the toilet should be determined, since they will often have to be specifically dealt with in treatment. Psychoanalytic concerns may have more credibility for this problem area, but again "pathologizing" should be avoided. Because psychological and physiological complications can result if this condition is left untreated, intervention for fecal incontinence is recommended as soon as the child can comprehend and participate in the treatment procedures. Most children can be successfully treated by 3 years of age.

The baseline for encopresis requires hourly checks for soiling. The amount, color, and viscosity of the stools should be estimated. The application of any routine aids to promote defecation should be noted.

Medical interventions for what appear to be primarily behavioral problems are mainly unwarranted. One exception would be for encopresis, where suppositories are a part of the usual behavioral intervention treatment program (Halpern, 1977; Wright, 1973, 1975). Another exception would be for bedwetting where special circumstances—for instance, family vacations—might suggest employing a temporary measure, such as the use of a tricyclic antidepressant. Finally, for adult primary enuretics who have failed to respond to any treatment, a bladder transection to reduce neural innervation of the detrusor might be considered (Essenhigh and Yeates, 1973; Parsons, O'Boyle, and Gibbon, 1977).

Once initiated, a behavior modification program requires strict adherence and plenty of support (Collins, 1973). Successful treatment followed by a relapse does not constitute a failure of the original treatment, since anything that is learned is subject to being "forgotten." Typically, relearning proceeds without incident from another course of conditioning. The failure of a conditioning regimen does not appear to have serious consequences and is apparently benign (Collins, 1973). However, successful treatment results in overall better psychological benefits (Doleys, 1977). More heroic medical examination or treatment procedures might well be reserved for use after conditioning interventions have been shown to be unsuccessful for individual cases.

Traditional psychotherapeutic procedures are not generally indicated for the treatment of encopresis and enuresis. However, the professional person must remain alert to the employment of the appropriate psychotherapy procedures to deal with the reactive features of incontinence or its treatment. In a relatively small proportion of cases, it may be necessary to intervene with behavior therapy or psychotherapy on a preliminary basis to allow subsequent meaningful behavioral and/or medical interventions.

The social and personal costs of allowing enuresis and encopresis to continue unabated are well documented and are to be avoided. Even physical costs become more likely, since there is an increased possibility of bladder infection, bladder trabeculation, and other organic complications if specific treatment is not undertaken (Collins, 1976; Wright, 1973). All these considerations are perhaps most obvious for encopresis and diurnal enuresis and less so for nocturnal enuresis, which can often be successfully hidden. Statements by professionals that a child will simply outgrow his or her incontinence must be regarded as approaching the unethical at this time. This judgment is strengthened by the existence of presently available, relatively inexpensive, and effective treatments for enuresis and encopresis.

Application to Particular Variables

Age. The clinician must be wary of self-reports from children about the severity or incidence of the usual enuretic or encopretic symptoms, since children tend to deny or underestimate their problem. Parental observations appear to be generally adequate and tend to correspond well with subsequent detailed baseline observations. Geriatric subjects who have reverted to incontinence may react negatively or in a confused way about their enuretic and encopretic episodes; here too, the reports of outside observers and baseline observation are necessary.

Sex. Eliminative disorders in general appear to occur more often for boys than for girls. For enuresis this predominance has been reported to be as high as 2 to 1 and for encopresis as high as 3.4 to 1 (Bellman, 1966; de Jonge, 1973; Essen and Peckham, 1976). Sex appears to be unrelated to behavioral treatment outcomes for enuresis or encopresis.

Socioeconomic Status. Enuresis generally is more common among children of unskilled and semiskilled workers than among children with fathers in professional and managerial occupations (Essen and Peckham, 1976). Related statistics for encopretic children do not exist.

Education. Enuretic children have been shown to obtain lower scores on reading, mathematics, and general-ability tests than nonenuretics (Essen and Peckham, 1976). These differences persisted even after allowance for sex, social class, crowding, and the number of older and younger children in the household. Similar data on encopretic children are lacking.

Physical Factors. Low-birth-weight children have been shown to be more likely to be diurnally and nocturnally enuretic than full-birth-weight children (Oppel, Harper, and Rider, 1968). Surprisingly, height has emerged as a statistically significant factor. Enuretic children are shorter than nonenuretics (Essen and Peckham, 1976). This factor persisted even after social class, sex, crowding, and the number of older or younger children in the household had been controlled for. The height difference proved to be very small— only 1.1 cm, on the average, at 11 years of age.

Intellectual Factors. One of the more common indicators of mental retardation is the age at which the various levels of toilet training continence is established. The incidence of enuresis and encopresis is much higher at any given age for the retarded than for intellectually normal children. These differences are probably even greater for institutionalized children. The incidence of nocturnal enuresis among the institutionalized severely retarded runs as high as 70 percent (Azrin, Sneed, and Foxx, 1973). Azrin and Foxx (1974) have noted that effective toilet training requires a minimal intellectual competence (which they term "instructional readiness"). They provide a simple test for parents to conduct to see whether their child is ready for training. If the child can carry out eight of the ten instructions they give, then the child is considered ready and should be treated.

References

Allen, T. "The Non-neurogenic Neurogenic Bladder." *Journal of Urology,* 1977, *117,* 232-238.

Atthowe, J. M. "Controlling Nocturnal Enuresis in Severely Disabled and Chronic Patients." *Behavior Therapy,* 1972, *3,* 232-239.

Azrin, N. H., and Foxx, R. M. "A Rapid Method of Toilet Training the Institutionalized Retarded." *Journal of Applied Behavior Analysis,* 1971, *4,* 89-99.

Azrin, N. H., and Foxx, R. M. *Toilet Training in Less Than a Day.* New York: Simon and Schuster, 1974.

Azrin, N. H., Sneed, T. J., and Foxx, R. M. "Dry Bed: A Rapid Method of Eliminating Bedwetting (Enuresis) of the Retarded." *Behaviour Research and Therapy,* 1973, *11,* 427-434.

Azrin, N. H., Sneed, T. J., and Foxx, R. M. "Dry-Bed Training: Rapid Elimination of Childhood Enuresis." *Behaviour Research and Therapy,* 1974, *12,* 147-156.

Bakwin, H. "The Genetics of Enuresis." In I. Kolvin, R. C. MacKeith, and S. R. Meadow (Eds.), *Bladder Control and Enuresis.* Philadelphia: Lippincott, 1973.

Beekman, D. *The Mechanical Baby.* Westport, Conn.: Lawrence Hill, 1977.

Bellman, M. "Studies in Encopresis." *Acta Paediatrica Scandinavica,* Supplement, 1966, *170,* 1-151.

Blackwell, B., and Currah, J. "The Psychopharmacology of Nocturnal Enuresis." In I. Kolvin, R. C. MacKeith, and S. R. Meadow (Eds.), *Bladder Control and Enuresis.* Philadelphia: Lippincott, 1973.

Butler, J. F. "Treatment of Encopresis by Overcorrection." *Psychological Reports,* 1977, *40,* 639-646.

Collins, R. W. "Importance of the Bladder-Cue Buzzer Contingency in the Conditioning Treatment for Enuresis." *Journal of Abnormal Psychology,* 1973, *82,* 299-308.

Collins, R. W. "Applying the Mowrer Conditioning Device to Nocturnal Enuresis." *Journal of Pediatric Psychology,* 1976, *4,* 27-30.

Collins, R. W., and Plaska, T. "Mowrer's Conditioning Treatment for Enuresis Applied to Geriatric Residents of a Nursing Home." *Behavior Therapy,* 1975, *6,* 632-638.

Cooper, C. E. "Cross-Cultural Aspects of Bedwetting." In I. Kolvin, R. C. MacKeith, and S. R. Meadow (Eds.), *Bladder Control and Enuresis.* Philadelphia: Lippincott, 1973.

de Jonge, G. A. "Epidemiology of Enuresis: A Survey of the Literature." In I. Kolvin, R. C. MacKeith, and S. R. Meadow (Eds.), *Bladder Control and Enuresis.* Philadelphia: Lippincott, 1973.

Doleys, D. M. "Behavioral Treatments for Nocturnal Enuresis in Children: A Review of the Recent Literature." *Psychological Bulletin,* 1977, *84,* 30-54.

Engel, B. T., Nikoomanesh, P., and Schuster, M. M. "Operant Conditioning of Recto-sphincteric Responses in the Treatment of Fecal Incontinence." *New England Journal of Medicine,* 1974, *290,* 646-649.

Epstein, L. H., and McCoy, J. F. "Bladder and Bowel Control in Hirschsprung's Disease." *Journal of Behavior Therapy and Experimental Psychiatry,* 1977, *8,* 97-99.

Erikson, E. *Childhood and Society.* New York: Norton, 1963.

Essen, J., and Peckham, C. "Nocturnal Enuresis in Childhood." *Developmental Medicine and Child Neurology,* 1976, *18,* 577-589.

Essenhigh, D. M., and Yeates, W. K. "Transection of the Bladder with Particular Reference to Enuresis." *British Journal of Urology,* 1973, *45,* 299-305.

Fine, R. *The Development of Freud's Thought.* New York: Aronson, 1973.

Fine, R. *Psychoanalytic Psychology.* New York: Aronson, 1975.

Geppert, T. V. "Management of Nocturnal Enuresis by Conditioned Response." *Journal of the American Medical Association,* 1953, *152,* 381-383.

Glicklich, L. B. "An Historical Account of Enuresis." *Pediatrics,* 1951, *8,* 859-876.

Halpern, I. "The Treatment of Encopretic Children." *Journal of the American Academy of Child Psychiatry,* 1977, *16,* 478-499.

Hindmarsh, J. R., Essenhigh, D. M., and Yeates, W. K. "Bladder Transection for Adult Enuresis." *British Journal of Urology,* 1977, *49,* 515-521.

Kaffman, M., and Elizur, E. "Infants Who Become Enuretics: A Longitudinal Study of 161 Kibbutz Children." *Monographs of the Society for Research in Child Development,* 1977, *42* (2), Serial No. 170.

Kohlenberg, R. J. "Operant Conditioning of Human Anal Sphincter Pressure." *Journal of Applied Behavior Analysis,* 1973, *6,* 201-208.

Kolvin, I., MacKeith, R. C., and Meadow, S. R. (Eds.). *Bladder Control and Enuresis.* Philadelphia: Lippincott, 1973.

Lovibond, S. H. *Conditioning and Enuresis.* London: Pergamon Press, 1964.

Lovibond, S. H., and Coote, M. A. "Enuresis." In C. G. Costello (Ed.), *Symptoms of Psychopathology: A Handbook.* New York: Wiley, 1970.

Mowrer, O. H., and Mowrer, W. M. "Enuresis: A Method for Its Study and Treatment." *American Journal of Orthopsychiatry,* 1938, *8,* 436-459.

Oppel, W. C., Harper, P. A., and Rider, R. V. "The Age of Attaining Bladder Control." *Pediatrics,* 1968, *42,* 614-626.

Parsons, K. F., O'Boyle, P. J., and Gibbon, N. O. K. "A Further Assessment of Bladder Transection in the Management of Adult Enuresis and Allied Conditions." *British Journal of Urology,* 1977, *49,* 509-514.

Ramsden, P. D., and others. "Distension Therapy for the Unstable Bladder: Later Results Including an Assessment of Repeat Distensions." *British Journal of Urology,* 1976, *48,* 623-629.

Shaffer, D. "The Association Between Enuresis and Emotional Disorder: A Review of the Literature." In I. Kolvin, R. C. MacKeith, and S. R. Meadow (Eds.), *Bladder Control and Enuresis.* Philadelphia: Lippincott, 1973.

Stein, Z., and Susser, M. "Social Factors in the Development of Sphincter Control." *Developmental Medicine and Child Neurology,* 1967, *9,* 692-706.

Stewart, M. A. "Treatment of Bedwetting." *Journal of the American Medical Association,* 1975, *232,* 281-283.

Svigos, J. M., and Matthews, C. D. "Assessment and Treatment of Female Urinary Incontinence by Cystometrogram and Bladder Retraining Programs." *Obstetrics and Gynecology,* 1977, *50,* 9-12.

Wright, L. "Handling the Encopretic Child." *Professional Psychology,* 1973, *4,* 137-144.

Wright, L. "Outcome of a Standardized Program for Treating Psychogenic Encopresis." *Professional Psychology,* 1975, *6,* 453-456.

Yates, A. J. *Behavior Therapy.* New York: Wiley, 1970.

Zaleski, A., Gerrard, J. W., and Shokeir, M. H. K. "Nocturnal Enuresis: The Importance of a Small Bladder Capacity." In I. Kolvin, R. C. MacKeith, and S. R. Meadow (Eds.), *Bladder Control and Enuresis.* Philadelphia: Lippincott, 1973.

20

Gary S. Sarver
Ann Howland

Epilepsy

Epilepsy refers to a paroxysmal (convulsive) discharge of neurons in the central nervous system. Usually, one or more neurons begin uncontrolled firing, which spreads to and recruits other nearby neurons and leads to the various seizure symptoms, the nature of which depends on the extent of the recruitment and the site of the initial discharge. These uncontrollable discharges may occur subclinically with obvious sensory, motor, autonomic, or psychic symptoms. Occasionally, clinical seizures may present with complex disorders of personality or mentation, which can be easily confused with psychopathologies resulting from nonneurological causes.

When the paroxysmal discharges, or seizures, occur in an enduring and predictable pattern, the term *epilepsy* refers to a disease process. However, seizure activity can also be a symptom of neurological dysfunction resulting from an acquired lesion, a metabolic disorder, or a systemic disorder. Therefore, it is necessary to distinguish between two types of seizures: those that have an enduring and predictable presentation of idiosyncratic symptoms and those that are symptomatic of an acquired neurological dysfunction. The term *epilepsy* refers to both types: a disease with fairly proscribed treatment approaches (anticonvulsant medication and surgical techniques) and a set of symptoms of

295

some other underlying neurological dysfunction which requires immediate medical diagnosis and varied treatment approaches.

Classification of epilepsies varies as a function of divergent criteria used for nosological purposes. Criterion groups include epilepsies variously classified according to the original neuronal site of the paroxysmal discharge, or the presenting symptoms, or the etiology of the disease process, as well as other miscellaneous considerations.

Further, the diagnosis of epilepsy is complicated by the similarity in its symptom presentation to that of traditional psychopathologies as well as to other syncopal (transient loss of consciousness) episodes. Epilepsy may often be confused with hysteria; transient ischemic attacks (for example, basilar artery insufficiency); changes in blood pressure secondary to cardiovascular disease (for example, pulmonary embolism or orthostatic hypotension); changes in blood chemistry (for example, hypoglycemia); and other miscellaneous diseases, such as narcolepsy (irresistible attacks of sleep) or cataplexy (leg weakness and subsequent falling to the ground, often precipitated by a strong emotion).

Background and Current Status

Epilepsy was initially attributed to demonic possession because of the dramatic presentation of the convulsive disorder. Unfortunately, the transient and cyclical nature of the disorder lent itself quite readily to such a paradigm, and treatment was aimed at driving away the offending spirit. Hippocrates first argued (about 400 B.C.) that seizure activity reflects disordered brain functioning, and subsequent investigators proposed a separation between seizures of known cause and those of unknown cause. However, following this early Greek enlightenment, no substantial progress was made until the 1800s, and the idea of demonic possession was episodically reconsidered.

As the functioning of the central nervous system unfolded, the available knowledge about epilepsy expanded. Basically, knowledge of the central nervous system began with the peripheral nerves, moved to the spinal cord, and then to the cerebral hemispheres; the etiological theories of epilepsy followed this same route. Initially, epileptic seizures were believed to originate in the peripheral nerves, where the symptoms appeared. Then the spinal cord and the cerebral hemispheres, respectively, were believed to be the site of epileptic seizures. Finally, in the period 1870-1873, the cortex was recognized as a significant source of seizure activity. At this time, John Hughlings Jackson attributed epilepsy to a sudden and excessive discharge of gray matter within the brain (Taylor, 1931). He approached seizures from the perspective of whether consciousness was lost or retained. Later, in the early 1900s, Gowers (1901) distinguished between epilepsies with a known organic cause and those with no known organic cause.

The modern era of epilepsy research began with the advent of the electroencephalogram in the 1930s. The EEG permitted actual confirmation of neurological concomitants during the seizure discharge and aided in understanding interictal (between-seizure) patterns and their relationship to varied seizure disorders.

Critical Discussion

General Areas of Concern

General concerns about epilepsy include (1) the nature of the disease process, (2) the etiology of the nondisease symptomatic process, (3) the differentiation of epilepsy from other syncopal attacks, and (4) the differentiation of epilepsy and its sequelae from other psychiatric disorders.

The paroxysmal discharge of neurons may be either focal or general in nature. If it is focal, a specific group of neurons is involved, and the observed behaviors reflect the disordered functioning of that particular area. Focal seizures occurring in areas of the brain which have known and easily observable symptoms (such as sensory or motor disturbances) are more easily diagnosed than those that occur in areas of the brain where the particular function is unknown or subtle (such as the frontal lobe). Focal seizures can present with either simple or complex symptoms. If the simple focal seizure remains focal, there is usually no loss of consciousness. Simple focal seizures can be classified as motor seizures or sensory seizures (Heilman, Watson, and Greer, 1977).

Simple motor seizures present with clonic "jerky" motor movements in localized groups of muscles—for instance, in the arm, the leg, or the head. The most common anatomical sites for the initiation of the seizure activity are the corner of the mouth, the great toe, and the thumb—probably because a proportionately greater cortical area is devoted to these motoric movements as compared to others. If the seizure recruits, or spreads along the precentral motor gyrus, it is termed Jacksonian Epilepsy. Following this seizure, there may be a weakness of the involved muscles, referred to as Todd's Paralysis. During the seizure the EEG will usually demonstrate a synchronous spike and/or wave, with possible phase reversals over the area of the cortex corresponding to the locus of the discharge. Involvement of the accessory motor cortex usually leads to deviation of the head and eyes to the side that is contralateral to the locus of the seizure activity. The contralateral arm may also be raised at the shoulder, and at the beginning of the seizure the patient often walks in a circle. Generally, as the locus of the seizure moves anteriorly in the frontal cortex, the nature of the muscle and motoric movements changes from simple to complex motor unit involvement. If the simple motor seizure involves the dominant hemisphere, there may be disorders of language functioning—such as difficulties in initiating speech or difficulties in decoding and/or encoding language (aphasic difficulties).

Simple sensory seizures involve paroxysmal discharges from the area around the postcentral gyrus, and usually present with disorders of the somesthetic senses of touch, temperature, pain, and pressure, although more complex disorders are possible. Sensory Jacksonian seizures are similar to the motor counterpart, except that the locus of the motor seizure tends to be cortical, while that of the sensory seizure tends to be subcortical (Lende and Popp, 1976). Other simple sensory seizures can involve visceral or autonomic functions, but these are usually quite rare.

Complex focal epilepsies are usually a variant of temporal lobe epilepsy. There is usually some impairment of consciousness, and memory loss or fugue state for the ictal (seizure) period is not uncommon. Temporal lobe seizures are the most likely to be confused with psychiatric disturbances, because they produce complex disorders of memory, vision, audition, touch, taste, and smell, and hallucinations are not uncommon. The involvement of the olfactory and gustatory senses sometimes produces a lip-smacking and chewing movement known as an uncinate fit. There may be episodes of *déjà vu* or *jamais vu*, as well as complex psychomotor automatisms wherein the individual, during the seizure, produces a series of behaviors that may appear either normal or grossly abnormal to others, but the individual will have no memory for such behaviors.

If the recruitment of nearby neurons continues during a focal seizure, it may develop into a generalized seizure. In generalized seizures there is usually no apparent primary focus, although there may be demonstrable neurological symptoms; there is also usually a loss of consciousness, with concomitant diffuse motoric involvement.

Heilman, Watson, and Greer (1977) have classified generalized seizures as either primary or secondary. Primary generalized seizures have no demonstrable etiology and no apparent neurological deficits; and the first seizure occurs during childhood, with an EEG that demonstrates a bilateral, synchronous, and paroxysmal discharge. These are usually thought to be genetic in origin and are consistent with the idea of epilepsy as a disease. Primary generalized seizures are classified as petit mal and grand mal.

Petit mal presents with brief interruptions of consciousness—referred to as the "absence," from the French *absence d'esprit.* Technically, the first seizure must occur in childhood, with a demonstrated EEG characterized by a three-per-second spike and wave pattern synchronous between the hemispheres. The child does not usually fall but stares off into space and cannot be redirected by others. Rhythmic eyeblinks may accompany these episodes. In more complex presentation there may be associated changes in muscle tone, mild clonic movements, automatisms, or loss of bladder control. The frequency of these attacks can vary from 1 to 200 per day.

There are two distinct phases to the grand mal seizure, the tonic phase and the clonic phase. The tonic phase usually, but not always, begins with the aura. The nature of the aura varies with the focal site of the paroxysmal discharge. Thus, the patient's aura may involve disturbances in sensations of taste, sight, smell, or sound, as well as disorders of memory, personality, or cognition. Indeed, days or hours prior to the seizure, the patient may present with personality changes, especially increased tension and irritability. There may also be local myoclonic contractions. The degree and pervasiveness of the muscular contractions sometimes cause the air to be forced from the lungs so quickly as to produce an audible yelp from the patient. These contractions produce a rigidity, which is usually maintained for about thirty seconds. However, in some enduring cases with prolonged respiratory arrest, the patient may become cynotic, with consequent neurological sequelae. The clonic phase follows the tonic phase and is characterized by robust rhythmic convulsant movements of the entire body, usually resulting in an arched back. There may be concomitant loss of bladder and, rarely, bowel control, as well as nonreactive pupils and a pathognomonic Babinski reflex. Following this massive motoric seizure, the patient may gradually arouse or may drop off to sleep. If the patient does not regain consciousness during the interictal period, he or she is said to be in "status epilepticus." When the patient does regain consciousness, he or she may complain of headache, fatigue, and clouded memory. The frequency of grand mal seizures varies from as few as one or two in a lifetime to several serial seizures occurring many times a day.

Secondary generalized seizures are usually the consequence of acquired diffuse neurological disease and are usually accompanied by demonstrable neurological signs and symptoms. The types of seizures seen in this category are similar to those seen in the primary generalized seizure category, although there may be greater variation in symptoms, depending on the site, extent, and nature of the lesions.

From the psychodiagnostic vantage point, epilepsy, especially complex variations of temporal lobe epilepsy, can present as psychopathologies. Indeed, it has been estimated that 30 percent of first mental hospital admissions involve neurological problems, with a substantial portion of these attributable to variations of epilepsy (Geschwind, 1974).

The essential diagnostic problem with epilepsy is to differentiate it from other syncopal attacks and from psychological problems, as well as to determine its etiology. Syncope, a transient loss of consciousness, can closely resemble an epileptic seizure. Causes of syncope may range from hysteria to a transient ischemic attack (TIA), wherein there is a basic attenuation of regional blood flow due to any of a variety of cardiovascular or blood chemistry problems. Prodromal symptoms include nausea, cold sweats, dizziness, and weakness. The onset is usually gradual, and the patient, after becoming prone, will usually recover in a few minutes. Incontinence, convulsive motoric movements (for example, tonic "yelp"), postictal fatigue, and neurological signs are rare with both hysterical fits and TIAs. Additionally, hysterical seizures usually require an audience, and the secondary gain is often apparent. Seizures occurring during sleep are rarely hysterical in origin. With TIAs, there are often other confirming neurological indications.

Other causes of impaired consciousness and/or muscle tone that mimics, but is not, epileptic in nature include drop attacks, cataplexy, and narcolepsy. With drop attacks, the patient experiences a sudden weakness of the legs and will fall to the ground without losing consciousness. This is usually due to basilar artery insufficiency, although there may be other neurological causes for these episodes. In cataplexy there is a sudden loss of muscle tone, usually precipitated by strong emotion. (In epileptics with limbic system involvement, however, a strong emotion can similarly precipitate an epileptic seizure.) Narcolepsy refers to attacks of irresistible sleepiness in an otherwise well-rested individual. These attacks usually occur when the patient is not physically active. This disease is more common in males, usually begins in late adolescence or early adulthood, and has no known etiology.

As previously mentioned, cognitive and psychological problems may accompany several seizure disorders. Basically, the nature of the symptoms will vary according to the site (whether frontal, temporal, parietal, or occipital lobe), as well as the nature and extent of the lesion. With more sophisticated psychological symptomatology, it becomes difficult to determine whether the emotional problems are a consequence of the social implications of having the disease or result from the very same lesion. However, knowledge concerning dysfunctional patterns for each lobe can aid in making a diagnosis.

With the exception of the precentral gyrus, which is a relatively common lesion site, epileptic loci in the frontal lobe are rarer than in other areas of the brain. With frontal lobe lesions, accompanying cognitive and emotional symptoms include decreased judgment, decreased social tact, loss of personal hygiene, manic irritability, decreased initiative, and heightened sexual interests (Benson and Blumer, 1975; Davison and Bagley, 1969; Rodin, Katz, and Lennox, 1976; Small, Small, and Hayden, 1966). Thus, these patients may present with either depressive or sociopathic symptomatology. Most often, however, frontal lobe pathologies result from progressive destructive lesions and not from epileptic disorders. Frontal lobe automatisms are possible, but they are difficult to differentiate clinically from temporal lobe automatisms (Geir and others, 1977). During the seizure the typical clinical manifestations of frontal lobe dysfunction may include disruption of ongoing activity, memory disturbances, verbalizations, deviations of head and eyes, falls, tonic-clonic movements, and simple motor automatisms—in that order (Geier and others, 1977).

The proposed "epileptic personality" is most often associated with temporal lobe epilepsy. Aside from the seizure activity previously discussed, there are reliable interictal personality attributes commonly found with temporal lobe epileptics. These include an obsessive concern with detail; a sober affect, with little or no sense of humor; increased religiosity; increased aggressiveness; and, sometimes, paranoid ideation (Bear, 1977a). Right temporal lobe epileptics tend to be more overtly emotional, while left temporal lobe epileptics are more often verbal (that is, philosophical or religious) (Bear, 1977b; McIntire, Pritchard, and Lombroso, 1976).

Whereas an estimated 10 to 25 percent of all outpatient epileptics have personality disorders, 50 percent of temporal lobe epileptics with limbic system involvement have interictal personality disorders (Benson and Blumer, 1975). Because medial temporal lobe structures are involved in emotion and sexuality, it is not uncommon to see decreased sexual interests, increased religiosity, and increased aggressive and violent behaviors. This alternation between violent behaviors and religiosity sometimes produces wide patterns of behavior manifested by aggressive acting-out episodes followed by deep guilt and remorse.

The emotional factors can also influence the control and management of seizures. In complex temporal lobe psychomotor seizures, strong emotions precipitated the ictus but could not be recalled postictally (Feldman and Paul, 1976). Typically, temporal lobe seizures may begin subcortically and then spread to the ipsilateral cortex and then to the contralateral cortex. If the spread of the subcortical focus does not reach the ipsilateral cortex, then the patient is likely to report the aura without the behavior change (Lieb and others, 1976). In addition, Remillard and his associates (1977) studied a group of patients with a unilateral temporal lobe focus and found that 73 percent also had a contralateral lower cranial nerve VII weakness (Remillard and others, 1977).

In addition to the personality disturbances that can be caused by the lesion, there may be personality changes secondary to having the epilepsy. Phobias, however, are rarely seen as sequelae (Benson and Blumer, 1975).

There may also be disorders associated with disruption of the language pathways. Auditory information usually reaches the dominant (usually the left) hemisphere, where it is received on the superior temporal gyrus in an area known as Heschl's Gyrus. From here, the information proceeds posteriorly to the area around the parietal-temporal junction known as Wernicke's area, where verbal information is decoded for understanding and encoded for expression. From Wernicke's area, the information proceeds anteriorly to Broca's area, where it is encoded for the proper motoric movements of speech. Disruption along this pathway can lead to various aphasias, depending on the site and extent of the lesion.

Knowledge concerning the etiology of symptomatic seizures is much more complete than the theories concerning the etiology of nonacquired seizures. However, transient symptomatic seizures may eventually evolve into a cyclical epileptic disorder. Common known causes of seizures include the following:

1. *Neoplasms.* Neoplasms may be primary intracranial tumors, or they may be secondary, having metasticized from other parts of the body. Depending on the rate of growth and the location of the tumor, there may be signs of increased intracranial pressure (for instance, papilladema), with headache, nausea, and vomiting. There may also be neurological symptoms present to aid in the localization of the tumor.
2. *Multifocal diseases.* Multifocal diseases, which are usually degenerative, primarily attack the myelin sheath surrounding the nerve fibers. Multiple sclerosis and tuberous sclerosis are examples of such a disease process. Aside from neurological findings, these disease processes are typically recurrent and episodic, with symptoms and lesions appearing over time and in various parts of the central nervous system.
3. *Metabolic and nutritional disorders.* Metabolic and nutritional disorders may produce seizures as a result of compromised cellular functioning and consequent damage to cells. Such is often the case in dehydration with high fevers (for instance, hypernatremia) and can be seen with disorders of protein, carbohydrate, and lipid storage, as well as with endocrine dysfunction. Electrolytic imbalances may lead to decreased convulsive threshold.
4. *Circulatory disorders.* Seizures occurring with circulatory disorders usually result from compromised circulation, which can lead to chronic anoxia and subsequent infarction of brain tissue. Seizures may also result from sudden stroke due to embolic phenomena.

5. *Infectious diseases.* Individuals with infections often have a regional spread of the disease to the subdural or epidural space, with the subsequent establishment of meningitis, encephalitis, and epidural and/or subdural abscesses. Indeed, temporal lobe epilepsy often can result from the regional spread of otitis media (middle ear infections), leading to an abscess and establishment of an irritative focus.

6. *Trauma.* Physical insult to the brain tissue itself or compromised cerebral functioning as a consequence of physical trauma elsewhere in the body can lead to damage or the establishment of an irritative lesion.

7. *Toxic disturbances.* The ingestion of toxic substances—such as lead, glue fumes, mercury, carbon monoxide, alcohol, and drugs (including antipsychotics)—and kidney disorders can lead to neurological damage.

Primary generalized seizures are thought to be either genetic in origin or acquired prenatally or during the birth process. As will be seen later, the age of onset for the first seizure may provide a clue to the etiology.

Comparative Philosophies and Theories

Many studies lend credence to the hypothesis that at least some forms of epilepsy, especially when first observed in childhood, have a genetic component. Wolf and his associates (1977) found that 42 percent of a group of children who were seen after they had had their first febrile (resulting from high fever) convulsions had a positive family history of febrile convulsions and 16 percent had a positive family history of nonfebrile seizures. Interestingly, when the child had the febrile seizure, 30 percent of the parents were unaware that the child had even had a fever; and 81 percent of the children had had the fever for less than 24 hours at the time of the seizure.

Annegers, Huhmar, and Krokfors (1976) found that mothers who had epilepsy were more likely to produce children who had epilepsy (febrile or nonfebrile). There was no increase in the probability of the child's having epilepsy, however, if the father was epileptic. Jensen (1976) found that, with temporal lobe epileptics who required surgical relief for their symptoms, the family history revealed 30 percent of the family members with epilepsy, 49 percent with neurological diseases, and 46 percent with psychiatric problems.

Epilepsy can also be caused by events surrounding the birth process and subsequent postnatal development. Boros and Nystrom (1977) examined the etiology of seizures during the first three months of life: 45 percent of the seizures were due to perinatal asphyxia, 13 percent to postnatal shock, and 10 percent to hypoglycemia; in 21 percent the etiology was unknown. Four years later, a follow-up study revealed that, regardless of the etiology, 37 percent of the children had abnormal development, 42 percent had a neurological deficit, and 32 percent had chronic seizure problems. Jensen (1976) examined etiologies in temporal lobe epilepsy and found a history of birth trauma in 38 percent, postnatal head trauma in 35 percent, cerebral infection in 24 percent, febrile conditions in 9 percent, and unknown causes in 16 percent.

The incidence of seizures in children under 16 years of age is approximately 14.7 per thousand (Hagberg and Hansson, 1976). Harder (1977) found that the probability of a child's having a seizure before the age of 5 years is about 3 percent, with the greatest risk period being between 6 and 27 months. The implications of having just one seizure can be seen in a study done by Harrison and Taylor (1976). They followed such children for more than twenty-five years and found that 66 percent had problems. Of these, 10 percent died, 11 percent were institutionalized, 7 percent were able to make home visits, and 25 percent had chronic epilepsy.

Generally, epileptic patients with focal seizures tend to be small at birth and are commonly delivered in the breech position to older mothers with a history of high blood pressure during pregnancy (Tervila, Huhmar, and Krokfors, 1975). The presence of atypical neurological signs at birth may be associated with later development of seizures. Indeed, the probability of a child's having a febrile seizure by age 7 years is greater in children who have had neurological or developmental abnormalities at birth (Nelson and Ellenberg, 1976). Bachman, Hodges, and Freeman (1976), using computerized axial tomography, found that 30 percent of children with focal motor seizure or slow-wave and spiking EEG records had demonstrable structural brain abnormalities. The most common structural change was atrophy, either focal or generalized. Gestaut (1976) found similar results with an examination of adult patients with chronic lesions.

Earle, Baldwin, and Penfield (1953) shed some light on the high incidence of temporal lobe epilepsy. They demonstrated that during the birth process the pressure applied to the head can cause a transient herniation of the medial temporal area against the tentorium. The posterior cerebral artery and the choroidal arteries, comparatively large in the newborn, would then be subject to ischemia and subsequently produce the commonly found medial temporal sclerosis. This finding is further supported by the observation that medial temporal lobe structures, especially the hippocampus and the amygdala, have relatively low seizure thresholds compared to other parts of the brain (Kaada, 1953). Clinically, this lower threshold can permit the appearance of seizures without easily demonstrable neurological signs or symptoms.

In adults the base rates of various etiologies are quite different. Earnest and Yarnell (1976) found that, of adults admitted to the hospital for seizures, 41 percent had a history of alcohol abuse and that, of these, 60 percent were having seizures secondary to the withdrawal. Of the remaining alcohol-related etiologies, 20 percent had a history of trauma, 5 percent had vascular problems, 2 percent had syncope, 2 percent had neoplasms, and 2 percent were idiopathic. In a nonalcoholic population, the incidences were 16 percent for trauma, 12 percent for vascular problems, 5 percent for syncope, 5 percent for tumor, 4 percent for infection, 4 percent for toxic-metabolic states, and 5 percent for other reasons. In adults over 69 years of age, studies indicate that cardiovascular disorders account for 30 percent of seizures; trauma accounts for 8 percent; toxic-metabolic problems are responsible for 10 percent; tumor accounts for 2 percent; and 50 percent are due to unknown causes (Earnest and Yarnell, 1976).

Treatment of seizure disorders falls under two basic categories: chemotherapy and surgery. While there have been attempts at using biofeedback, the results are not yet convincing.

The pharmacological agents most frequently used include diphenylhydantoin (Dilantin), phenobarbital (Luminal), and primadone (Mysoline), among others. From a psychiatric point of view, it should be noted that antipsychotics (Phenothiazines) lower the threshold for seizures, while minor tranquilizers (Librium, Valium, Serax) raise the threshold for seizures.

One anticonvulsant should be sufficient to control seizures when appropriate blood levels have been achieved. Shorvon and Reynolds (1977) found that introducing a second anticonvulsant improved only 36 percent of their patients, and that even this improvement was attributed to a greater probability of achieving optimum blood levels of at least one anticonvulsant. Lennox-Buchthal (1975) found that a maintenance dose of phenobarbital for children was effective in preventing a recurrence of seizure activity. However, pediatricians may not be aware that patients with febrile seizures need maintenance on phenobarbital; 15 percent of pediatricians prescribe it for a moderate period of time, while 54 percent prescribe it only during the time of the febrile illness (Lennox-Buchthal, 1975).

Driessen and Hoppener (1977) found that 28 percent of epileptic patients either failed to take their anticonvulsants or took then irregularly. Failure to take such drugs may be one of the most common causes of seizure activity.

Elaboration on Critical Points

The diagnosis of epilepsy requires a reasonable grasp of clinical neurology, clinical psychology, and medical psychology. Even with knowledge of these areas, diagnosis remains difficult.

While the EEG can be helpful in making a diagnosis, the false negative rate has been estimated to be as high as 25 percent (Boshes and Gibbs, 1972), even in patients who are known to have epilepsy. Further, there is a developmental change in EEG rhythms such that normal rhythms for children can be pathognomonic when seen in adults; and the change occurs gradually, so that the gradations are difficult to interpret with confident accuracy. Generally, it is not until age 14 to 16 years that normal adult EEG rhythms can be seen with regularity.

Various stimuli are employed during the EEG recording in an attempt to produce abnormal rhythms. Photic or auditory stimuli are presented at such a frequency as to stress the system, so that paroxysmal discharges—if they can be produced at all—will show up on the EEG. EEGs often are recorded during sleep, since paroxysmal discharges are more likely to occur during sleep than at other times.

Children more often present with primary generalized seizures, because their immature brain is more likely to be susceptible to a general recruitment and paroxysmal discharge. When focal epilepsies occur in children, they are usually associated with either the temporal or the occipital lobe. However, this midtemporal locus may be an expression of the tentorial herniation mentioned previously, but not demonstrated clinically until much later in development.

Differentiating psychopathologies from seizure activity is likely to remain the most difficult task, since the psychomotor automatisms may look like pathological behaviors to the nontrained observer. In addition, the lesion that causes the clinical manifestation of the seizure activity also has an effect on the personality. Finally, psychopathology can result from the way in which other people behave toward the epileptic individual.

Personal Views and Recommendations

The concepts of symptomatic and functional epilepsy appear useful from a diagnostic, treatment, and research standpoint. It is safe to assume that, even in seizure activity of unknown etiology, there is a structural change in the brain.

Perhaps the most vexing problem involves psychosurgery to remove the lesion. Here the evidence is mixed, with both negative and positive results. Here, too, philosophical questions—most notably, whether professionals know enough about the brain to start removing portions of it—come to the fore. Perhaps recent developments, such as computerized axial tomography, will permit the further development of epilepsy research, so that the next five years will produce new knowledge that will aid in the diagnosis and treatment of this disorder.

Finally, effective societal education appears in order to deal with and eradicate undeserved stereotypes, which are an unnecessary hindrance to most epileptic patients.

Application to Particular Variables

There is no need to recapitulate the previous information concerning age. However, some additional information is in order. First, it is not unusual for children to "outgrow" epilepsy by the time they reach puberty. The reasons for this remain basically unknown. Second, with increased age the nature of the seizure may change from relatively generalized seizures at birth to more well-defined focal seizures in the adult.

Focal seizures in children tend most often to be in the occipital area and the mid-temporal area, while focal seizures in adults tend to be in the anterior temporal lobes. Seizures secondary to trauma tend to be more focal in the "compartmentalized adult brain" and more generalized in the immature child's brain.

Perhaps of most importance is the finding that the age at which the individual first experiences seizure activity can be related to the etiology. According to Penfield and Jasper (1954), when the first seizure is seen from age 0 to 2 years, the probable causes, in descending order, are birth injury, degenerative disease, and congenital abnormalities; from age 2 to 10 years, the most frequent causes are birth injury, febrile conditions, trauma, and idiopathic causes; from age 10 to 20 years, the most frequent causes are idiopathic, trauma, and birth injury; from age 20 to 35 years, the most common causes are trauma and neoplasms; from age 35 to 55, the most frequent causes are neoplasms, trauma, and vascular diseases; and from 55 to 70 years, the most frequent causes are vascular problems and neoplasms. Previous research, however, indicates that alcohol is the most common cause of seizures in adults.

Regarding gender, all seizure types are more frequently found in males, with the exception of petit mal epilepsy and its three-per-second spike and wave, found more often in females (Boshes and Gibbs, 1972). Insofar as alcoholism and drug abuse, endocrine dysfunction, and metabolic problems are related to sex differences, consequent seizure activity will demonstrate a sex difference.

Seizures do not necessarily indicate educational problems. Whether seizures will lead to educational difficulties depends on the nature, extent, and site of the lesion, as well as the age at which it was acquired. Generally, the younger the individual at the time of the seizure and related lesion, the better the recovery. However, there is an exception in that individuals having seizures characterized by hypsarhythmia (West's Syndrome) are most likely to suffer from mental retardation. Generally, the higher the IQ, the better the prognosis in individuals afflicted with a seizure disorder.

Stores and Hart (1976) studied children who had epilepsy but were able to attend the public schools. They found that children with generalized seizures did not have particular reading problems, whereas children who had focal epilepsy had significant reading problems—especially if the focal epilepsy occurred in the left temporal lobe in males. They also found that Dilantin depressed reading ability more than other anticonvulsants. Another factor that influences educational ability is the secondary effect of having an illness, coupled with the parents' response to it. Sometimes parents unintentionally produce some degree of psychopathology when they become overprotective or feel considerable guilt over their child's disorder.

Although the rate of mental retardation in epileptics is three to four times higher than in the general population, it is associated with the degree of brain damage involved, and not with having epilepsy per se.

Socioeconomic-class differences in maternal psychopathology, maternal nutrition during pregnancy, medical care, and the like, can contribute to the development of seizure activity.

Seizures in relatively intact individuals can be well controlled with medication and present no particular vocational problems. Perhaps the greatest handicap is resistive public stereotypes. To the degree that the seizure activity represents neurological dysfunction that interferes with daily living, there can be vocational problems. The potential for employment in these cases is best determined by a thorough medical and neuropsychological examination with an assessment of cognitive and behavioral strengths and weaknesses.

At the present time there are no known differences due to ethnic background which cannot be more parsimoniously explained by other parameters of socioeconomic differences.

Intellectual impairment need not be a concomitant of epilepsy. However, the degree of cognitive impairment will vary with the anatomical site of the pathological process. In general, focal epilepsies, especially in the left temporal lobe, are associated with reading problems. These reading problems may be somewhat compounded by the specific attenuation of reading caused by Dilantin. Also, hypsarhythmia in the first year of life is associated with later mental retardation.

The nature of the lesion is less critical, generally, than the locus of the lesion. Large lesions in "silent" areas of the brain may be less disruptive than small lesions in more critical areas. In addition, the age at which the lesion is acquired has important implications for outcome; generally, the older the child, the more enduring will be the effects.

As discussed previously, psychiatric concerns are important in differential diagnosis. Various psychopathologies can be related to the behavioral effects of the lesion itself, either as part of an aura or as part of the seizure. In addition, psychopathologies may result from the disruptive social and interpersonal effects of having the seizure disorder.

References

Annegers, J. F., Huhmar, E. D., and Krokfors, E. "Seizure Disorders in Offspring of Parents with a History of Seizures—A Maternal-Paternal Difference?" *Epilepsia*, 1976, *17*, 1-9.

Bachman, D. S., Hodges, F. J., and Freeman, J. M. "Computerized Axial Tomography in Chronic Seizure Disorders of Children." *Pediatrics*, 1976, *58*, 828-832.

Bear, D. M. "Quantitative Analysis of Interictal Behavior in Temporal Lobe Epilepsy." *Archives of Neurology*, 1977a, *34*, 454-467.

Bear, D. M. "The Significance of Behavioral Change in Temporal Lobe Epilepsy." *McLean Hospital Journal*, 1977b, *85*, 9-21.

Benson, D. F., and Blumer, D. (Eds.). *Psychiatric Aspects of Neurological Disease.* New York: Grune and Stratton, 1975.

Boros, S. J., and Nystrom, J. "Neonatal Seizures: Quality of Survival." *Minnesota Medicine*, 1977, *60*, 99-102.

Boshes, L. D., and Gibbs, F. A. *Epilepsy Handbook.* Springfield, Ill.: Thomas, 1972.

Davison, K., and Bagley, C. "Schizophrenia-Like Psychoses Associated with Organic Disorders of the Central Nervous System—Review of the Literature." *British Journal of Psychiatry*, 1969, *116*, 113-184.

Driessen, O., and Hoppener, R. "Transient Anterior Horn Cell Dysfunction in Diphenyl-hydantion Therapy." *European Neurology*, 1977, *15*, 131-134.

Earle, K. M., Baldwin, M., and Penfield, W. "Incisural Sclerosis and Temporal Lobe Seizures Produced by Hippocampal Herniation at Birth." *Archives of Neurology and Psychiatry,* 1953, *69,* 27.

Earnest, M. P., and Yarnell, P. R. "Seizure Admissions to a City Hospital: The Role of Alcohol." *Epilepsia,* 1976, *17,* 387-393.

Feldman, R. G., and Paul, N. L. "Identity of Emotional Triggers in Epilepsy." *Journal of Nervous and Mental Disease,* 1976, *162,* 345-353.

Geier, S., and others. "Automatisms During Frontal Lobe Epileptic Seizures." *Brain,* 1976, *99,* 447-458.

Geier, S., and others. "The Seizures of Frontal Lobe Epilepsy: A Study of Clinical Manifestations." *Neurology,* 1977, *27,* 951-958.

Geschwind, N. *Selected Papers On Language and the Brain.* Boston: Reidel, 1974.

Gestaut, H. "Conclusions: Computerized Transverse Axial Tomography in Epilepsy." *Epilepsia,* 1976, *17,* 337-342.

Glaser, G. H. "The Problem of Psychosis in Psychomotor Temporal Lobe Epileptics." *Epilepsia,* 1964, *5,* 271-278.

Gowers, W. R. *Epilepsy and Other Chronic Convulsive Diseases: Their Causes, Symptoms and Treatment.* (2nd ed.) London: Church, 1901.

Hagberg, G., and Hansson, O. "Childhood Seizures." *Lancet,* 1976, no. 2, 208.

Harder, P. "Primary Immunization and Febrile Convulsions in Oxford 1972-5." *British Medical Journal,* 1977, *2,* 490-493.

Harrison, R. M., and Taylor, D. C. "Childhood Seizures: A 25-Year Follow-Up: Social and Medical Prognosis." *Lancet,* 1976, no. 1, 948-951.

Heilman, K. M., Watson, R. T., and Greer, M. *Handbook for Differential Diagnosis of Neurologic Signs and Symptoms.* New York: Appleton-Century-Crofts, 1977.

Jensen, I. "Temporal Lobe Epilepsy: Etiological Factors and Surgical Results." *Acta Neurologica Scandinavica,* 1976, *53,* 103-118.

Kaada, B. R. "Somatomotor, Autonomic and Electrocorticographic Responses to Electrical Stimulation of Rhineuciphobia and Other Forebrain Structures in Primates, Cats and Dogs." *Acta Physiologica Scandinavica,* Supplement 83, 1953, *24,* 1-2.

Lende, R. A., and Popp, A. J. "Sensory Jacksonian Seizures." *Journal of Neurosurgery,* 1976, *44,* 706-711.

Lennox-Buchthal, M. A. "Comments on Prophylactic Treatment for Febrile Convulsions." *Acta Neurologica Scandinavica,* 1975, Supplement 60, 77-78.

Lieb, J. P., and others. "A Comparison of EEG Seizure Patterns Recorded with Surface and Depth Electrodes in Patients with Temporal Lobe Epilepsy." *Epilepsia,* 1976, *17,* 137-160.

McIntire, M., Pritchard, P. B., and Lombroso, C. T. "Left and Right Temporal Lobe Epileptics: A Controlled Investigation of Some Psychological Differences." *Epilepsia,* 1976, *17,* 377-386.

Nelson, K. B., and Ellenberg, J. H. "Predictors of Epilepsy in Children Who Have Experienced Febrile Seizures." *New England Journal of Medicine,* 1976, *295,* 1029-1033.

Penfield, W., and Jasper, H. *Epilepsy and the Functional Anatomy of the Human Brain.* Boston: Little, Brown, 1954.

Remillard, G. M., and others. "Facial Assymetry in Patients with Temporal Lobe Epilepsy, A Clinical Sign Useful in the Lateralization of Temporal Epileptogenic Foci." *Neurology,* 1977, *27,* 109-114.

Rodin, E. A., Katz, M., and Lennox, D. "Difference Between Patients with Temporal Lobe Seizures and Those with Other Forms of Epileptic Attacks." *Epilepsia,* 1976, *17,* 313-320.

Shorvon, S. D., and Reynolds, E. H. "Unnecessary Polypharmacy for Epilepsy." *British Medical Journal,* 1977, *8,* 1635-1637.

Small, J. G., Small, I. F., and Hayden, M. P. "Further Psychiatric Investigations of Patients with Temporal and Nontemporal Epilepsy." *American Journal of Psychiatry,* 1966, *123,* 303-310.

Stores, G., and Hart, J. "Reading Skills of Children with Generalized or Focal Epilepsy Attending Ordinary School." *Developmental Medical Child Neurology,* 1976, *18,* 705-716.

Taylor, J. (Ed.). *Selected Writings of John Hughlings Jackson.* Vol. 1: *On Epilepsy and Eleptiform Convulsions.* London: Hodder and Stoughton, 1931.

Tervila, L., Huhmar, E. O., and Krokfors, E. "Cerebral Birth Injury as a Cause of Epilepsy." *Annual Chronicles of Gynecology,* 1975, *64,* 118-122.

Wolf, S. M., and others. "The Value of Phenobarbital in the Child Who Has Had a Single Febrile Seizure: A Controlled Prospective Study." *Pediatrics,* 1977, *59,* 378-385.

21

Donald A. Bakal

Headache

Headache is a disorder that is psychobiological in origin. A schematic of the *psycho-biological* model of headache is presented in Figure 1. This model views illness as resulting from complex interactions of environmental, psychological, physiological, genetic, and biochemical variables. A key assumption of the model is that headache is the result of a predisposition for the disorder, which becomes manifest in the presence of stress-related

Figure 1. Diathesis-Stress Model of Headache

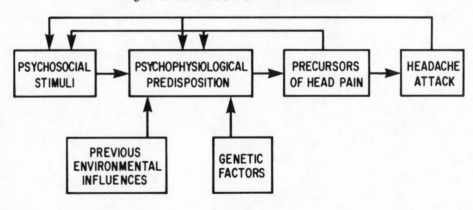

events. Furthermore, with repeated attacks the psychobiological predisposition may come to operate independently from psychosocial stressors, creating a condition that is puzzling to both the practitioner and the patient.

Background and Current Status

The classic research of Harold Wolff (Dalessio, 1972), which began in the 1930s, marked the beginning of modern psychophysiological headache research. Prior to Wolff's observations, headache appeared in medical texts under the general heading of "diseases of the central nervous system." Wolff provided empirical and clinical support for the psychophysiological nature of headache from several perspectives. First, he demonstrated that headache can originate from pathophysiological reactions of vascular and musculoskeletal mechanisms in the absence of central nervous system disease. Second, he provided family history data to support the hypothesis of an inherited predisposition for some forms of headache. Third, he presented clinical observations indicating that pathological emotions and personality traits are often central to chronic headache patients.

Wolff strongly believed in the existence of two distinct classes of psychobiological headache, migraine and muscle contraction, each with a separate etiology and symptomatology. Later an Ad Hoc Committee on Classification of Headache (1962) was to formalize the distinction between migraine and muscle contraction headache. The committee defined migraine headache as "recurrent attacks of headache, widely varied in intensity, frequency, and duration. The attacks are commonly unilateral in onset; are usually associated with anorexia and sometimes with nausea and vomiting; in some [instances] are preceded by, or associated with, conspicuous sensory, motor, and mood disturbances; and are often familial" (p. 127). A further distinction was made between the classic migraine and the common migraine, with the intent of separating those individuals exhibiting the sensory and motor preheadache symptoms from those individuals not exhibiting these symptoms. However, the distinction generally is not observed in the literature, and both forms are simply referred to as migraine. The muscle contraction headache refers to a class of headache previously called tension or nervous headache. Phenomenologically, a headache of this type is characterized by sensations of tightness and persistent band-like pain located bilaterally in the occipital and/or forehead regions.

Graham and Wolff (1938) established that migraine headache is associated with cranial vasodilatation. They administered ergotamine tartrate, a vasoconstrictive substance, to subjects during the headache phase of the migraine attack and simultaneously recorded extracranial vasomotor activity from the superficial temporal and occipital arteries. The vasoconstrictive effect of the drug was evident in large decreases in the magnitude of the pulse amplitudes. In addition, subjects showed a concomitant decline in the subjective intensity of headache. Later, Wolff adopted a similar procedure to demonstrate that vasoconstriction precedes the headache attack in migraineurs and accounts for some preheadache sensory disturbances (Dalessio, 1972). Visual disturbances during the preheadache phase were believed to result from vasoconstriction of the vessels serving the eye. Five migrainous subjects who were experiencing visual disturbances were required to inhale carbon dioxide. Carbon dioxide produces an immediate vasodilatory effect on cerebral vessels. Following the inhalation, the visual disturbances disappeared and the headache state did not follow.

Wolff also established that sustained contraction of the head and neck muscles can lead to pain (Dalessio, 1972). Since the resulting pain is of an aching rather than a throbbing quality, Wolff believed that muscle activity has little significance for understanding the etiology of migraine headache. In one study, Tunis and Wolff (1954) reported increases in neck and forehead electromyographic potentials in a group of migrainous headache sufferers who were experiencing an attack of head pain that was described as "something less than migraine." These data were interpreted as confirmation of the clinical observation that migraine patients suffer from periodic tension headaches:

> There is another type of head pain which occurs in migraine patients. It may be present concomitantly or in the interval between migraine headache attacks. Such headache is nonpulsatile, of low or moderate intensity, and may last for days, weeks, or years. The individual feels as if he has a hat on when he has none; that his neck is in a cast; that his shoulders are sore; that if he could be rubbed he would feel more comfortable. Action potentials recorded from the head and neck muscle during such a headache indicate vigorous contraction [Ostfeld and Wolff, 1958, p. 1503].

Interestingly, Tunis and Wolff also observed that cranial vasoconstriction occurred during the muscle contraction headache. In this instance, the vasoconstriction was assumed to be an outcome of the increased muscle activity.

The role of family history in migraine was first demonstrated by Allan (1928). He found a family history of migraine in one or both parents in 349 of 382 migrainous patients. Goodell, Lewinton, and Wolff (1954) found a similar family history in 84 percent of their migraine patients; 44.2 percent had one parent with migraine, and 69.2 percent had both parents afflicted. In a more recent study, Waters (1971) found little support for the hypothesis that family history is a good predictor of migraine. He concluded that far too much emphasis has been placed on the hereditary basis of migraine. The possibility that muscle contraction headache might have a constitutional basis has not been examined.

Personality variables, like family history, were considered by Wolff to be paramount in understanding the predisposition for migraine. Wolff was influenced by the theoretical ideas of Dunbar (1935) and Alexander (1950). Dunbar suggested that various personality characteristics are associated with specific physiological disorders, while Alexander believed that specific emotional states are capable of provoking specific physiological disorders. Consistent with their descriptions of the emotions and personality traits found in cardiovascular disorders, Wolff (1937) described the migrainous personality as ambitious, perfectionistic, orderly, inflexible, and excessively reserved. Attacks in individuals with these personality attributes, he contended, are triggered by emotional states involving frustration, fear of failure, self-doubt, criticism, and resentment.

One might have expected Wolff's research to stimulate a wave of interest in the psychophysiological mechanisms controlling headache, but in actuality it failed to do so. Psychologists generally remained unaware of his observations (Bakal, 1975). Medical researchers, however, began to extend Wolff's hypothesis concerning the vasoconstriction-vasodilatation sequence of migraine. One of the first studies was performed by Elkind, Friedman, and Grossman (1964). They used a tissue clearance technique which involves the measurement of the rate at which an injected isotope is removed from tissue, with the rate being proportional to blood flow through that tissue. They found that blood flow decreases during the prodromal phase of migraine and increases during the headache phase. Interestingly, they derived their procedure from an earlier finding that an increase in the muscle blood flow also occurs in the presence of muscle contraction headaches (Onel, Friedman, and Grossman, 1961). Other investigators who observed an increase in blood flow during the headache phase of migraine failed to include subjects with muscle contraction headaches as part of their design.

After confirmation of the vascular changes associated with migraine, medical researchers began to search for vasoactive substances that might mediate these changes. Conceptually, this had the effect of shifting attention away from psychobiological mechanisms, and migraine began to be viewed as a disease of regulation. Serotonin, or 5-hydroxy-tryptamine, received the most attention, although histamine, renin, kinins, tyramine, adrenaline, and prostaglandins were also considered as possible precursors of migraine. Serotonin is a potent vasoconstrictor of scalp arteries, and it was assumed that the depletion of plasma serotonin results in the extracranial vasodilatation characteristic of the migraine headache. Several studies had demonstrated decreases in serotonin levels during headache attacks (see review by Sjaastad, 1975). However, not all migraine patients showed the expected fall in serotonin levels during an attack. Some patients showed no change in the serotonin levels while other patients actually showed increases in serotonin levels. Furthermore, the observed changes in serotonin levels (or any other substance) could have been a consequence rather than a cause of the headaches. No efforts were made to integrate the physiological and biochemical research with formulations concerning the role of stress, emotion, and personality in migraine. That is, medical researchers did not consider how the hypothesized physiochemical mechanisms underlying migraine might interact with emotional and personality variables.

Interest by psychologists in the psychophysiology of headache began with the appearance of clinical biofeedback research. Two publications in particular sparked this interest: the first, by Sargent, Green, and Walters (1972); the second, by Budzynski and his associates (1973). Sargent, Green, and Walters reported considerable success in reducing migraine attacks by having subjects raise their finger temperature with the aid of autogenic training. Autogenic training involves the simultaneous regulation of mental and somatic functions by meditating on passive activities. Sargent and his associates hypothesized that the voluntary increase of finger temperature is correlated with an increase in blood flow to the peripheral regions and with a decrease of blood flow to the cranial regions. Although no physiological data were presented in support of this hypothesis, the study initiated interest in the possibility of self-control of the vascular mechanisms underlying migraine. Similarly, Budzynski and his associates found that training in frontalis electromyogram biofeedback was capable of reducing headache activity in people suffering from muscle contraction headaches. They also reported a concomitant decline in frontalis electromyogram activity that was maintained at a three-month follow-up.

Medical scientists are continuing their search for biochemical precursors of the pathophysiological vascular reactions of migraine headache. Personality and emotional aspects of migraine are now receiving less theoretical attention and are viewed as having secondary significance in the etiology of the disorder. This is the case even though emotional factors are still cited as the major trigger of migraine. The following commentary on the "psychosomatic" status of migraine illustrates the uncertainty associated with the significance of psychosocial variables:

> Emotional disturbance is the commonest single trigger mechanism, and is the most important cause of frequent and severe attacks. There is, however, nothing specific about the emotional stimulus, nor is there a consistent personality type in migraine subjects. Certainly personality reactions and patterns of behavior recur in migraine subjects: a tendency to anxiety reactions, sensitivity to stress, and difficulty in handling aggressive and hostile drives. In this respect, migraine is similar to many other "psychosomatic diseases" without demonstrable pathology but characterized by disorders of homeostasis. In some patients extrinsic physical and biochemical precipitants are prominent and the "psychosomatic ele-

ment" is slight. In most migraine patients, however, psychologic factors are important but are secondary rather than precipitating etiologic agents [Pearce, 1977, p. 125].

Much of the confusion regarding the precise role of emotional variables is traceable to the fact that many patients do not believe that their attacks are precipitated by emotional episodes. Dalsgaard-Nielsen (1965), for example, observed that although 68 percent of a patient group recognized that psychosocial stressors could precipitate an attack, 32 percent denied this possibility. Moreover, all the patients believed that many of the attacks occurred spontaneously, with no apparent cause. Because of the apparent absence of psychosocial influences in many occurrences of migraine, clinicians have suspected that physical factors, especially certain foodstuffs, may be the primary triggers of migraine attacks. There is little evidence to support this hypothesis. Wine and chocolate are often implicated, and both are known to contain tyramine (which is a vasodilator substance). In one of the few studies available, Moffett, Swash, and Scott (1974) identified twenty-five migrainous individuals, all of whom initially stated that their headaches could be precipitated by the consumption of chocolate. Subjects were told that they would be required to eat two different kinds of chocolate, but in actuality one of the samples consisted of a placebo made from a noncocoa substance. Only a small percentage of the subjects reported experiencing headache following ingestion of the chocolate, and this percentage was not different from that reported for the placebo condition. This study suggests that foodstuffs are not likely to account for a significant proportion of headache attacks.

Critical Discussion

General Areas of Concern

The belief that muscle contraction and migraine headaches are distinct syndromes with separate etiologies (and therefore requiring separate treatment) represents the one aspect of headache assessment that is seldom questioned. Migraine is defined as headache that is: (1) unilateral in onset, (2) preceded by sensory aura, (3) accompanied by nausea and vomiting, and (4) associated with a throbbing kind of pain. Muscle contraction headache is defined as frontal and/or occipital pain in the absence of the above migraine characteristics. The descriptions of these syndromes are based on clinical consensus rather than empirical findings. In one empirical study, Ziegler, Hassanein, and Hassanein (1972) attempted to isolate symptom clusters specific to muscle contraction and migraine headache. They administered a 27-item symptom questionnaire to a large sample of headache sufferers and, after factor analyzing the responses, discovered that no single factor emerged which represented the two traditional categories.

In contrast to these traditional categories, a unitary model of headache predicts that muscle contraction and migraine headache symptoms are common to all headache sufferers. Indirect support for such a model can be found in population surveys of headache incidence. Although migraine is assumed to account for only a small percentage of clinical headaches, migrainous symptoms are quite familiar to headache sufferers in the general population. Waters (1974) surveyed 2,000 adults in Wales and found that the majority of respondents reporting headaches were familiar with one or more migrainous symptoms. Of the respondents reporting headache during the preceding year, 62 percent of the males and 73 percent of the females reported experiencing at least one of the following three migrainous symptoms: (1) unilateral distribution of the headache, (2) a warning that the headache was coming, and (3) nausea or vomiting accompanying the headache. The presence of one of the symptoms was not necessarily predictive of the presence of the other two symptoms. However, the likelihood of one or more of these symptoms being reported increased with headaches that were rated as severe. This investigator has collected patient self-observation data which indicate that severe headache sufferers, regardless of diagnosis, are equally familiar with head pain locations thought to be specific to each class of headache patients (Bakal and Kaganov, 1977). The subjects were provided with a headache frequency record and required to monitor their headache activity for a two-week period. The reported locations of head pain obtained from a group of migraine sufferers, a group of muscle contraction headache sufferers, and a group diagnosed as manifesting both muscle contraction and migraine symptoms were compared. The diagnoses were made by neurologists in accordance with the guidelines of the Ad Hoc Committee on Classification of Headache (1962). There were no significant differences between the groups in terms of their reported locations of head pain. Additional self-report data indicated that the only difference between migraine and muscle contraction patients was that more migraine than muscle contraction headache subjects reported the presence of nausea and vomiting. In addition, all the subjects indicated that their headache condition had worsened over the years.

Have physiological characteristics unique to muscle contraction and migraine been identified? Not really, since, beginning with Wolff, most investigators have failed to compare the two classes of headache patients on similar measures. Typically, researchers have compared either migraine or muscle contraction patients with headache-free controls, but seldom have they simultaneously compared migraine and muscle contraction patients with one another. Therefore, such studies do not prove that the demonstrated vascular or muscular changes are, in fact, specific to the headache group under consideration. In the few studies that have included both migraine and muscle contraction patients, the differences found have been quantitative rather than qualitative. For example, two independent studies (Bakal and Kaganov, 1977; Pozniak-Patewicz, 1976) observed greater head and neck electromyographic activity in migraine than in muscle contraction patients, both during headache and headache-free periods. A similar lack of comparison data between migraine and muscle contraction headache sufferers characterizes the early biochemical research. Although the more recent literature indicates a trend to include both categories of patients, no effort is being made to equate the groups in terms of severity of headache. Admittedly, migraine by definition is a more severe disorder than muscle contraction headache, but it does not seem reasonable to compare data obtained from patients experiencing severe migraine attacks with data obtained from patients experiencing mild and nonspecific muscle contraction headaches. Efforts to minimize gross disparities in severity would allow greater confidence to be placed in data revealing group differences (should they still occur).

Viewing chronic headache in terms of severity does not mean that the critical psychophysiological processes mediating the headaches are identical across all sufferers. It does imply, however, that similar psychophysiological processes initiate the headache disorder, with the processes becoming more involved as the disorder increases in severity. Heightened muscle activity, for example, may be the major cause of less severe headaches, but with repeated attacks vascular systems may also become involved, along with autonomic disturbances that mediate nausea and vomiting. A similar sequence may underlie the predisposition for headache; that is, the predisposition initially may be the continuous presence of heightened neck and head muscle activity but in time may come to involve vascular and autonomic components. Within the diathesis-stress framework, it is also likely that, with increasing severity, structural changes occur in the central nervous system. For example, Sicuteri (1976) has hypothesized that chronic migraine is associated with structural changes in the central nervous system mechanisms controlling monamine turnover. The outcome of these changes might be a patient who experiences attacks in the absence of any specific stimulus.

Comparative Philosophies and Theories

Medically oriented theorists might reject a unitary explanation of the psychobiological processes underlying muscle contraction and migraine headache. The presence of muscle contraction symptoms in migraineurs has long been recognized but is interpreted as evidence that migraineurs are susceptible to more than one *kind* of headache. The possibility that severe muscle contraction headache sufferers may experience migrainous symptoms is not considered. The following statement on diagnosis, taken from Lance (1973, p. 94), reflects the medical position toward symptom overlap in migraine patients: "In view of the wide variation in clinical symptoms, it is remarkable that there is usually little difficulty in the diagnosis of migraine, the reason being the repetitive paroxysmal nature of the disorder. Difficulty arises when the frequency of attacks is such that migraine recurs almost daily or where migraine is superimposed upon daily tension headache. In both instances it may be difficult to sort out the vascular component from the background of nervous tension or depression."

The key to understanding the medical distinction between muscle contraction and migraine headaches is found in the description of migraine as a *paroxysmal* disorder. Migraine, unlike muscle contraction headache, is believed to occur suddenly and without provocation. At first glance, this characteristic of migraine seems at odds with the widely held notion that migraine is frequently triggered by emotional variables. There is some confusion in medicine regarding the precise role that psychological variables play in headache. Some physicians, for example, use the term *psychogenic headache* to describe headaches that are heavily influenced by psychological variables. What is a psychogenic headache? There is no adequate definition for their term, but when a large number of physicians were asked the question, the most frequent responses included reference to tension or muscle contraction headache. Not a single respondent considered migraine as a possible candidate (Packard, 1976). Because of its presumed paroxysmal nature, medical scientists consider migraine a disease that is more similar in nature to epilepsy than to muscle contraction headache. In fact, migraine has been called "autonomic epilepsy," the suggestion being that the headache constitutes only one aspect of the disease syndrome (Lennox, 1960). From this perspective, it becomes apparent why medical scientists are reluctant to attribute more than secondary significance to psychological variables in understanding the etiology of chronic headache.

Elaboration on Critical Points

By shifting attention to the psychobiological mechanisms controlling headache, we can develop a more integrated approach to the study of this disorder. New psychophysiological constructs may also emerge. Psychosomatic researchers, in general, have looked for psychological antecedents of disease rather than psychobiological components of disease. Numerous efforts have been made to establish the significance of pathological emotions and personality traits across a diversity of disorders, including headache, hypertension, heart disease, asthma, and epilepsy. These efforts have not yielded strong empirical relationships between psychological antecedents and specific disorders. Instead, the empirical relationships have been low in magnitude and nonspecific in nature (Luborsky,

Docherty, and Penick, 1973). Emotions and personality traits involving resentment, frustration, depression, anxiety, and helplessness are the most frequently reported antecedents, regardless of the disorder. More critical is the fact that, in many instances of disease, psychological antecedents are not identifiable. The commonly adopted solution to this conceptual dilemma is to assume (as many researchers have done with migraine) that only in some instances of a specific disorder are psychological variables critical.

Difficulties associated with the psychophysiological understanding of headache are identical to the difficulties associated with psychophysiological formulations of any disorder. Although the diathesis-stress model depicts the various levels of constructs involved in a disorder, there remains an absence of constructs to account for the *interaction* of these constructs (for example, psychological stress and dilatation of the arteries). Also absent are constructs to explain the self-sustaining nature of the disorder. These conceptual problems will receive more attention in the near future, for there is a growing interest in developing models that integrate the social, psychological, and physiochemical components of health and illness into a holistic framework (Bakal, 1979; Engel, 1977; Schwartz, in press; Schwartz and Weiss, 1977). This new approach has been called "behavioral medicine," and the hope is that behavioral medicine will come to mean something more than the implied dualism associated with the older term "psychosomatic medicine."

With respect to headache, cautious optimism for the holistic approach already exists, mainly because of the successful application of behavioral treatment strategies. A number of studies have reported success in reducing the frequency and severity of chronic headache attacks with biofeedback, relaxation training, and cognitive-coping training (Bakal and Kaganov, 1977; Mitchell and White, 1977; Stoyva, 1977). The successes are occurring in spite of the fact that the exact psychophysiological processes being altered in behavioral treatment programs have as yet to be identified. Here is where it is necessary to exercise caution. Clinicians often prescribe frontalis electromyographic training for muscle contraction headache and temperature training for migraine, even though these physiological measures have not been differentially implicated in the two categories of headache patients (Bakal, 1975). Not all studies have found a strict correlation between changes in the physiological parameter and headache activity. Epstein and Abel (1977), for example, observed decreases in tension headaches following frontalis electromyographic activity. Legewie (1977) has provided three alternatives for conceptualizing the processes operative during biofeedback training. First, there is the possibility of direct symptom control, in which the function trained is an immediate correlate of the clinical symptom. Second is the possibility of indirect symptom control, in which the function trained is a correlate of a higher-level system that controls the system. Third, there is the possibility of therapeutic gains that are completely independent of biofeedback training, changes which are most often discussed within the context of the placebo effect. We favor the second possibility in that patient acceptance of a treatment model is likely accompanied by real change in the psychobiological processes that are maintaining the problem.

Personal Views and Recommendations

It seems that similar psychobiological processes are operative in chronic headaches that are variously diagnosed as muscle contraction or migraine. One physiological parameter that is hypothesized to underlie the predisposition for headache is tonic muscle activity in the neck and head regions. This somatic activity may or may not be recognized by the headache sufferer. With the most severe headaches, the predisposition likely includes a vascular component, which could possibly be reflected in increased peripheral resistance resulting from increased sympathetic tone. Medical theorists might argue that this position cannot account for instances of migraine that are truly paroxysmal (for instance, those that occur once every six months and without apparent cause). This may be true, but the vast majority of headache sufferers seen in clinics (and probably most headache sufferers in the general population) do not exhibit this pattern. Their headaches are much more frequent and are varied in symptomatology. It appears, then, that severe headaches reflect the outcome of the patient's inability to cope with less intense headaches, accompanied by an increasing involvement of physiological systems that mediate both the predisposition for headache and the actual headache attack.

This conceptualization of headache suggests the presence of a critical psychobiological predisposition that must be altered in order to bring the disorder under control. Behavioral treatment may be capable of achieving this objective. However, a cautionary note is in order, since the successes reported to date have been short term in nature and without supporting documentation of any significant long-term changes in the psychophysiological status of the patient. It is possible to illustrate the dangers of short-term assessment with a patient who at three-months follow-up reported remarkable improvement in her condition, but who at six-months follow-up reported that her headache activity had returned to the pretreatment level. At this point, it cannot be said whether the long-term practice of behavioral treatment strategies will lead to permanent changes in the mechanisms mediating the attacks. In general terms, the behavioral literature has brought about recognition that the patient must assume an active role in his or her treatment. Ultimately, the philosophy of patient responsibility may be the greatest contribution of the psychophysiological perspective, for its adoption by the public at large is necessary before the incidence of this debilitating disorder will be significantly reduced.

Application to Particular Variables

Headaches begin to appear in children at approximately 7 years of age (Bille, Ludvigsson, and Sanner, 1977). A surprising number of young adolescents are familiar with headache. Deubner (1977) observed that 75 percent of a sample of 10- to 12-year-olds reported having experienced headache. Sixty-three percent of the subgroup were also familiar with at least one of the traditional migraine symptoms. Interestingly, the parents of the children believed that the headaches had increased in severity with increasing age. One area of assessment that requires attention is the age at which children begin to comprehend the meaning of stress.

Severe headache is more frequent in females than in males, with the difference being more pronounced in data derived from clinical populations. In a general population survey (Deubner, 1977), 22.1 percent of the female adolescents and 15.5 percent of the males reported severe headache symptoms (presence of two or more migrainous symptoms). Waters and O'Connor (1975) found prevalence rates in adults (21 years and over) to be 23.2 percent for the females and 14.9 percent for the males.

There is no known relationship between the incidence of headache and education. At one time it was believed that migraine is a disorder of the intelligent, but Waters (1971) found no support for this hypothesis. Waters observed, however, that patients of higher intelligence were somewhat more likely to seek assistance for headache.

Although the majority of headaches are psychophysiological in nature, headache may also be the result of organic disease, and this possibility demands that the patient be under continual supervision of medical specialists. Furthermore, the headache mechanism often is intricately related to more pervasive psychological problems. A recommended procedure for assessing and treating headache patients is to follow the cognitive-behavioral framework that has been developed for chronic pain patients (Turk and Genest, in press). Patients are encouraged to conceptualize pain in a manner that incorporates the idea that they can do something to alter the experience. Assessment and treatment focus on life-style change; relaxation and biofeedback methods; attention-focusing strategies; and direct alterations of self-statements concerning pain and change.

References

Ad Hoc Committee on Classification of Headache. "Classification of Headache." *Journal of the American Medical Association,* 1962, *179,* 717-718.

Alexander, F. *Psychosomatic Medicine: Its Principles and Applications.* New York: Norton, 1950.

Allan, W. "The Inheritance of Migraine." *Archives of Internal Medicine,* 1928, *42,* 590-599.

Bakal, D. A. "Headache: A Biopsychological Perspective." *Psychological Bulletin,* 1975, *82,* 369-382.

Bakal, D. A. *Psychology and Medicine: Psychobiological Dimensions of Health and Illness.* New York: Springer, 1979.

Bakal, D. A., and Kaganov, J. "Muscle Contraction and Migraine Headache: Psychophysiologic Comparison." *Headache,* 1977, *17,* 208-214.

Bille, B., Ludvigsson, J., and Sanner, G. "Prophylaxis of Migraine in Children." *Headache,* 1977, *17,* 61-63.

Budzynski, T. H., and others. "EMG Biofeedback and Tension Headache: A Controlled Outcome Study." *Psychosomatic Medicine,* 1973, *35,* 484-496.

Dalessio, D. J. "Headache." In C. G. Costello (Ed.), *Symptoms of Psychopathology.* New York: Wiley, 1970.

Dalessio, D. J. *Wolff's Headache and Other Head Pain.* New York: Oxford University Press, 1972.

Dalsgaard-Nielsen, T. "Migraine and Heredity." *Acta Neurologica Scandinavica,* 1965, *41,* 287-300.

Deubner, D. C. "An Epidemiologic Study of Migraine and Headache in 10-20 Year Olds." *Headache,* 1977, *17,* 173-180.

Dunbar, H. F. *Emotions and Bodily Changes.* New York: Columbia University Press, 1935.

Elkind, A. H., Friedman, A. P., and Grossman, J. "Cutaneous Blood Flow in Vascular Headaches of the Migraine Type." *Neurology,* 1964, *14,* 24-30.

Engel, G. L. "The Need for a New Medical Model: A Challenge for Biomedicine." *Science,* 1977, *196,* 129-136.

Epstein, L. H., and Abel, G. G. "An Analysis of Biofeedback Training for Tension Headache Patients." *Behavior Therapy,* 1977, *8,* 37-47.

Goodell, H., Lewinton, R., and Wolff, H. G. "Familial Occurrence of Migraine Headache." *Archives of Neurology and Psychiatry,* 1954, *72,* 325-334.

Graham, J. R., and Wolff, H. G. "Mechanism of Migraine Headache and Action of Ergotamine Tartrate." *Archives of Neurology and Psychiatry,* 1938, *39,* 737-763.

Lance, J. W. *Mechanism and Management of Headache.* London: Butterworth, 1973.

Legewie, H. "Clinical Implications of Biofeedback." In J. Beatty and H. Legewie (Eds.), *Biofeedback and Behavior.* New York: Plenum, 1977.

Lennox, W. G. *Epilepsy and Related Disorders.* Vol. 1. Boston: Little, Brown, 1960.

Luborsky, L., Docherty, J. P., and Penick, S. "Onset Conditions for Psychosomatic Symptoms: A Comparative Review of Immediate Observation with Retrospective Research." *Psychosomatic Medicine,* 1973, *35,* 187-204.

Mitchell, K. R., and White, R. G. "Behavioral Self-Management: An Application to the Problem of Migraine Headaches." *Behavior Therapy,* 1977, *8,* 213-221.

Moffett, A. M., Swash, M., and Scott, D. F. "Effect of Chocolate in Migraine: A Double-Blind Study." *Journal of Neurology, Neurosurgery, and Psychiatry,* 1974, *37,* 445-448.

Onel, Y., Friedman, A. P., and Grossman, J. "Muscle Blood Flow Studies in Muscle-Contraction Headaches." *Neurology,* 1961, *11,* 935-939.

Ostfeld, A. M., and Wolff, H. G. "Identification, Mechanisms, and Management of the Migraine Syndrome." *Medical Clinics of North America,* 1958, *42,* 1497-1509.

Packard, R. C. "What Is Psychogenic Headache?" *Headache,* 1976, *16,* 20-23.

Pearce, J. P. "Migraine: A Psychosomatic Disorder." *Headache,* 1977, *17,* 125-128.

Pozniak-Patewicz, E. " 'Cephalic' Spasm of Head and Neck Muscles." *Headache,* 1976, *16,* 261-266.

Sargent, J. D., Green, E. E., and Walters, E. D. "The Use of Autogenic Training in a Pilot Study of Migraine and Tension Headaches." *Headache,* 1972, *12,* 120-124.

Schwartz, G. E. "Psychobiological Foundations of Psychotherapy and Behavior Change." In S. L. Garfield and A. E. Bergin (Eds.), *Handbook of Psychotherapy and Behavior Change.* New York: Wiley, in press.

Schwartz, G. E., and Weiss, S. M. "What Is Behavioral Medicine?" *Psychosomatic Medicine,* 1977, *39,* 377-381.

Sicuteri, F. "Migraine: A Central Biochemical Dysnociception." *Headache,* 1976, *16,* 145-159.

Sjaastad, O. "The Significance of Blood Serotonin Levels in Migraine." *Acta Neurologica Scandinavica,* 1975, *51,* 200-210.

Stoyva, J. "Why Should Muscular Relaxation Be Clinically Useful? Some Data and 2½ Models." In J. Beatty and H. Legewie (Eds.), *Biofeedback and Behavior.* New York: Plenum, 1977.

Tunis, M. M., and Wolff, H. G. "Studies on Headache: Cranial Artery Vasoconstriction and Muscle Contraction Headache." *Archives of Neurology and Psychiatry,* 1954, *71,* 425-434.

Turk, D. C., and Genest, M. "Regulation of Pain: The Application of Cognitive and Behavioral Techniques for Prevention and Remediation." In C. P. Kendall and S. D. Hollan (Eds.), *Cognitive-Behavioral Interventions: Theory, Research, and Procedures.* New York: Academic Press, in press.

Waters, W. E. "Migraine: Intelligence, Social Class, and Family Prevalence." *British Medical Journal,* 1971, *2,* 77-81.

Waters, W. E. "The Pontypridd Headache Survey." *Headache,* 1974, *14,* 81-90.

Waters, W. E., and O'Connor, P. J. "Prevalence of Migraine." *Journal of Neurology, Neurosurgery, and Psychiatry,* 1975, *38,* 613-616.

Wolff, H. G. "Personality Features and Reactions of Subjects with Migraine." *Archives of Neurology and Psychiatry,* 1937, *37,* 895-921.

Ziegler, D. K., Hassanein, R., and Hassanein, K. "Headache Syndromes Suggested by Factor Analysis of Symptom Variables in a Headache Prone Population." *Journal of Chronic Diseases,* 1972, *25,* 353-363.

22

Martin Katahn

Obesity

Obesity refers to an excessive accumulation of adipose tissue. It should be differentiated from the term *overweight*, which refers to some deviation from standards based on desirable weight charts (Metropolitan Life Insurance Company, 1969) derived for actuarial purposes to predict longevity. One can be overweight without necessarily being obese. Persons with large muscle mass (football players), for example, may be overweight but not obese. For psychiatric or psychological purposes, obesity is commonly diagnosed as a "psychophysiologic gastrointestinal reaction—obesity" (American Psychiatric Association, 1968, 006-580); in some cases, as a result of "personality trait disturbance—compulsive eating" (American Psychiatric Association, 1968, 000-x5y); and occasionally as a response to stress falling within the "transient situational personality disorders" (American Psychiatric Association, 1968, 000-180 and following categories).

Background and Current Status

The words of Hippocrates are usually cited as proof that obesity was present and recognized as a health hazard in ancient times: "Sudden death is more common in those who are naturally fat than in lean persons" (*Aphorisms,* II, 44). This is as true today as it was in ancient times. In connection with other illness, however, he appeared to contradict himself: "In all maladies those who are fat about the belly do best; it is bad to be thin and wasted there" (II, 35). Perhaps he was observing here that the mortality rate is indeed higher for underweight persons suffering from tuberculosis, influenza, and pneumonia.

The word *obesity* first appeared in English usage in the early seventeenth century. As a synonym for *corpulence,* a term in prior Middle English usage, it referred both to excessive bulk of body and to the condition of being fleshy or fat; and it has traditionally been viewed as caused by overeating. Thus, a "reducing diet" has been the traditional remedy. The use of controversial dietary regimens in medical treatment (such as high-protein, low-carbohydrate combinations) dates back at least to 1863, when a physician prescribed such an unbalanced diet for an obese gentleman named William Banting. It was so successful that Mr. Banting published it. Present-day fad diet recommendations are frequently variations on this early theme. As discussed below, it is only in the recent past that the contribution of underactivity, rather than feeding abnormality, has received the attention it apparently deserves (Mayer, 1968).

Over the years, evidence has been gathered that links obesity to coronary disease, hypertension, diabetes, kidney and gall bladder dysfunction, arthritis, other orthopedic dysfunctions, varicose veins, serious accidents, obstetrical and gynecological problems, and a host of other medical problems. But the extent of the relationship, or the point at which the degree of obesity becomes an increased risk factor, remains debatable (Keys, 1975).

No single standard exists on which to base a judgment of obesity. Desirable weights in height/weight charts are frequently presumed to reflect an acceptable ratio of fat to lean body mass, even though the tables were not derived for that purpose. The charts are convenient to use, however, and clinicians and researchers often set 10, 15, or 20 percent over desirable weight to indicate the presence of obesity, in spite of the possibility of error. In a general adult population, it might be expected that persons 20 percent over desirable weight would possess a large percent of body fat, as determined by more direct means. In a recent study, however, only about one out of five overweight males (25 percent over average weight for age and height) was considered to be obese by skinfold measurement of body fat (Seltzer and others, 1970). In borderline cases, therefore, occupation and activity levels, which might indicate relatively large muscle mass, should be considered before a judgment of obesity is made.

Since other difficulties exist in the use of height/weight tables—for instance, difficulties in establishing body frame size and in making comparisons across populations different from those that were used in the standardization study—more direct means of estimating body fat are receiving increased attention. These include underwater weighing, estimation of body fat from body potassium, inert gas uptake, and others more fully described and discussed by Grande (1975) and Garrow (1975). Of all the more direct assessment techniques, skin caliper measurement of surface body fat is quite convenient and likely to have the greatest utility for research and clinical purposes. Standards for obesity and nomograms for estimating body fat from skinfold measurement have been published (Seltzer and Mayer, 1965; Sloan and Weir, 1970). Another potentially useful technique, anthropometric measurement (body circumference at various sites), is presented by Katch and McArdle (1977), with instruction in its use and charts for calculation of percent of body fat.

Some investigators set the criterion for obesity as a function of skin caliper measurement at one or more sites, such as 23 mm at the triceps for males and 30 mm for females. Others set a percentage fat criterion, with 14-16 percent body fat in males and 18-20 percent body fat in females considered acceptable, and with 25 percent and 30 percent body fat for males and females, respectively, as the criteria for obesity. Measurement is made at several skinfold sites, and an equation derived to predict body fat from hydrostatic weighing is used as embodied in the nomograms mentioned above. Trained athletes will have considerably less than average body fat, with long-distance runners and heavily muscled weight lifters or football players as low as 4.5 percent to 7 percent. (Some body fat is essential for the support and cushioning of internal organs; 4.5 percent to 5 percent is about as low as a person can get.) Since both marathon runners and football players may have minimal body fat, it is obvious that body build and overall size may not be good indicators of adiposity.

Critical Discussion

General Areas of Concern

Obesity is considered "the greatest single preventable cause of death in the United States" (Stunkard, 1973) because of its contribution as an increased risk factor in diabetes, coronary disease, hypertension, and other illnesses. The obese condition also may contribute to various personality disorders and emotional problems, especially in children and adolescents and in adults with childhood-onset obesity. Such persons may suffer from a negative physical self-concept, social anxieties, and distortions in the perception of their own body characteristics that resist change both during and following weight loss. In spite of the belief that obesity is both preventable and curable, its prevalence is increasing in technological societies, where food is abundant and the need for physical exertion is diminishing. Various estimates designate anywhere from 50 to 80 million individuals as obese in the United States.

Although obesity is caused by a regulatory defect in energy intake or energy expenditure, professionals do not adequately understand or cannot control either the biological or the psychological factors contributing to the condition; consequently, they have not been particularly successful in preventing or remedying obesity. Of all persons entering treatment for obesity, 25 percent may lose as much as 20 pounds and 5 percent as much as 40 pounds, but the odds are high that the weight will be regained within two years. Various estimates place the recidivism rate as high as 95 percent. Recent optimism over the effectiveness of behavioral treatments (Stunkard, 1972) may be misplaced, since results relating to *long-term* effectiveness are presently inconclusive. Behavioral treatments designed to modify maladaptive eating patterns appear to achieve modest results (an average of 8-13 pound weight loss) that would be of reasonable benefit for persons slightly to moderately obese. Fewer than half of the participants in a recently reported intensive program appeared capable of maintaining or continuing their losses, and only 10 percent lost to within 20 pounds of desirable weights during a 12- to 18-month follow-up. There was wide variation among individuals, with both large gains and losses relative to starting weights (Jeffrey, Wing, and Stunkard, 1978). Anorexic drug and diet therapies have proven so ineffective that it is naive to continue to expect success with these approaches. However, as various neurohormonal bases for the condition are discovered and subject to easy and reliable diagnosis, chemical remedies may be found.

Since obesity can result from defects in the regulation of food intake, energy expenditure, or metabolic processes, singly or in combination, it is obvious that treatment requires a thorough assessment of all possible contributing factors. A recent thorough physical examination of all participants in a weight reduction program is needed, either to rule out or to understand the existence of known metabolic factors and thus to be aware of the contribution of existing disease to the problem. Persons requiring insulin, medication for hypertension that reduces heart rate during physical activity, or other hormone therapies may find it extremely difficult to lose weight except on a drastically reduced caloric intake, which of itself presents other health hazards. Diets at 1,200 calories or below, even when designed by nutritionists, are likely to be deficient in the B vitamins, calcium, and iron. Long-term adherence to low caloric intakes without adequate nutritional supplementation can result in feelings of fatigue, irritability, insomnia, and depression. While such feelings can also result from the withdrawal from preferred foods and the giving up of eating as a response to emotional states, the contribution of nutritional deficiencies should not be overlooked.

Even when no known defects are discovered in basal metabolism, metabolic changes (which are very difficult to measure except under well-controlled laboratory conditions) will occur in just about all persons who undertake caloric restriction. In an effort to conserve energy and preserve weight at some established "set point" (see discussion below), basal metabolism may drop anywhere from 10 to 45 percent (Apfelbaum, 1975). In addition, the energy expended during digestion and in physical activities is reduced (referred to as a reduction in thermogensis). Thus, for example, many persons who have been consuming 2,000 calories to maintain established, stabilized body weights may lose little or no weight when they reduce their intake by 500 calories and continue with their customary levels of activity.

Childhood-onset obesity is likely to be associated with hyperphasia or hypercellularity (an increased number of fat cells) as well as hypertrophy (an increased cell size), while adult-onset obesity is associated only with hypertrophy. Many authorities feel that hyperphasia may make it more difficult for individuals who have been overweight since childhood or adolescence to lose to and maintain a lower weight. Long-standing family influences may also result in patterns of eating and activity that are hard to change.

Both genetic and environmental influences may contribute to the following relationship between obese parents and obese children: if neither parent is obese, the probability that an offspring will become obese is about 10 percent; if one parent is obese, it becomes approximately 40 percent; and if both parents are obese, it approaches 80 percent. The contribution of the environment is illustrated in an indirect way with family pets: when dog owners have normal physique, the incidence of obesity in their pets is 25 percent; when owners are obese, the incidence rises to 45 percent (Mason, 1970). As Dwyer and Mayer (1975, p. 108) state: "The more fat there is, the earlier in life it accumulated, the longer it has remained; the more difficult it is to treat and the less likelihood of success." An understanding of these contributing genetic and historical factors on the part of both therapist and client may help in their joint commitment to a weight-loss regimen, since individuals with extreme difficulties are wont to ask "Why can't I lose weight as fast as so and so?—I eat even less than she does!"

Metabolic and historical factors aside, it is still the present imbalance between energy intake and overall energy expenditure that leads to obesity and the maintenance of excess weight. At some point, no matter what the contributing physiological factors may be, a reduced energy intake and an increased energy expenditure via physical activity will result in weight loss. Thus, it is essential to get adequate baselines of existing caloric intake and activity levels in order to assess where the problem lies and to develop a workable intervention program. With respect to eating, it is customary to record all eating episodes, duration and place of eating, social aspects, activities associated with eating, perceived degree of hunger, mood, and food type and quantity by volume and calories (Jordan and Levitz, 1975). Various environmental and self-control strategies or more intensive therapy directed at interpersonal or emotional correlates can then be instigated, as appropriate to the individual case. Excellent guides to the behavioral approach to the modification of maladaptive eating patterns are available (Mahoney and Mahoney, 1976; Stuart, 1978).

Perhaps the limited success so far reported with the behavioral approach is due to the relatively great emphasis on eating patterns, with much less emphasis on the modification of activity patterns. As Mayer's (1968) summary of the literature indicates, many obese individuals *eat less* than their thin counterparts. The energy imbalance is in their relative inactivity. With records kept on daily activities, similar to the records on eating behavior, the therapist can employ various environmental restructuring procedures and incentives to increase energy expenditure. The key to ultimate success in weight maintenance after weight loss may lie not in diet but in one's developing a more active life style.

Comparative Philosophies and Theories

"Set-point" theory suggests that an established weight is set as a function of genetic factors or early feeding experiences. It may, for any given individual, be below, at, or above the average weight for any given reference population. The body attempts to regulate its metabolic processes in such a way as to preserve its set-point weight. Thus, overeating in the lean and undereating in the obese will not necessarily lead to changes in weight directly predictable from variability in calorie intake. If individuals are below set-point weights, it is easy for them to gain until the set point is reached, after which time an increased caloric intake is less likely to increase weight any further. An abundance of evidence exists to support this notion (Bray, 1975). The issue is whether a new set point can be established after weight loss and, if so, what factors could contribute to such a change.

The behavioral approach emphasizes the contributing factors in the antecedents and consequences of eating, including internal cues that may trigger eating behavior. Levitz (1975) and Rodin (1975) examined the evidence that the eating behavior of the obese is relatively unrelated to internal cues but is primarily under the control of external stimulation, as proposed by Schacter (1968). Although the results are often conflicting, there is some evidence that the externality hypothesis may hold for the moderately obese under certain limited conditions, such as high cue salience or prominence, while excessive corpulence may more often be correlated with glandular, metabolic, or emotional disorders.

Although reports on behavioral therapies are most popular in the present literature, these reports pay relatively less attention to the emotional and interpersonal difficulties that increase with degree of obesity than they do to other aspects of the antecedents and consequences of eating. Similarly ignored are the family conflicts that arise frequently whenever one member undertakes as drastic a change in life style as is entailed in a long-term weight management effort. These other psychological issues, as well as nonbehavioral approaches to obesity, have been extensively studied by Bruch (1957; 1973), Mayer (1968), and Stunkard (1958, 1976). Recent evidence (Rand and Stunkard, 1977) suggests considerably greater impact on weight loss and its emotional correlates as a result of psychoanalytic treatment than was reported by Stunkard in his earlier articles.

Allon (1975) analyzes the stigma attached to obesity in our culture, in which the condition of fatness is variously viewed as a sin, a disease, a crime, or as ugliness. The National Association to Aid Fat Americans (NAAFA) has been formed to combat the social discrimination which fat people must face in their daily lives and to strengthen their sense of pride and self-esteem. Grosswirth (1971) and Louderback (1970) have researched the dynamics of the stigma in American society and provide encouragement to the obese. Their work, contrary to its original purpose ("Whatever you weigh is right"), may help reduce the tension, shame, and guilt associated with being fat and actually make it more possible for overweight persons to lose weight whenever they decide to undertake a weight management effort.

Commercial programs to help overweight persons lose weight abound; and, because of the dismal lack of long-term success, the obese shop from program to program for the ultimate solution. Weight Watchers stresses sound nutrition and planned menus of approximately 1,200 calories per day (based on their own products) and has recently developed behavioral modules and added an emphasis on increasing physical activity. TOPS (Take Off Pounds Sensibly) is a nonprofit self-help organization with less structure than Weight Watchers and somewhat more emphasis on negative reinforcement, such as group disapproval to combat improper eating behavior. Overeaters Anonymous is a group based on principles similar to those of Alcoholics Anonymous. YMCAs also offer weight reduction programs, with instruction on diet and physical fitness. However, since the YMCA programs emphasize physical activity in a setting where fat persons must mingle with athletes and persons of normal weight becoming fit, overweight people tend to drop out unless special groups are set up for them with the help of a weight management specialist.

Elaboration on Critical Points

The reduction in metabolism during dietary restriction and the lack of thermic effect after eating (a rise in metabolism after eating, present in persons of normal weight but frequently absent in the obese) can be partially combated if exercise of moderate to vigorous intensity is added to the weight reduction program (Miller, 1975; Whipp and others, 1975). Weight maintenance after modest weight losses in a behavioral program can be facilitated by self-monitoring and minimal contact (scheduled weigh-ins) over an extended period of time (Hall, Bass, and Monroe, in press). From other behavioral studies, it appears that oral-sensory effects of ingested food are more important determinants of intake, satiety, and hunger than the actual caloric value of food consumed (Wooley and Wooley, 1975). What individuals "think" they have eaten determines consequent hunger ratings, and such thoughts are influenced by quantity, sweetness, and texture. Following a preload, subjects adjust subsequent eating according to the volume rather than the caloric value of the initial intake. That oral factors, rather than the nutrition received, govern feelings of satiety is demonstrated in experiments using intravenous feeding (Jordan, 1975).

Many additional hypotheses have been offered to account for obesity and its resistance to change, but, as summarized by Hagan (1976), research evidence is controversial with respect to the following questions: (1) Do the obese experience psychogenic hunger? (2) Are they more field dependent than persons of average weight? (3) Do they risk other psychological disturbances as a result of dieting? (4) Do they have a greater responsivity to the palatability of food? (5) Are they less responsive to internal sensations relating to hunger and satiation? (6) Do they defend their established weight, via a changing taste sensitivity that varies according to whether a person is at set-point weight or below?

With respect to some combination of foods that might facilitate weight loss, all sorts of faulty rationales exist to support contentions that a high-protein, low-carbohydrate diet or a low-protein, high-carbohydrate diet or a low-carbohydrate, high-fat diet or some other unbalanced type of diet is most effective. Drastically unbalanced diets do tend to demand a slightly higher energy cost in their utilization, compared with a well-balanced diet of equal calories, but the difference is small. It is the overall caloric intake that counts; and, if one is to lose weight efficiently, energy expenditure needs to be greater than energy intake. Unless long-term factors leading to overeating and under-activity are remedied, either during the period of weight loss or immediately after, weight will in almost all cases be regained when dieters "go off" their diets.

Personal Views and Recommendations

A comprehensive approach to the assessment and treatment of obesity will involve attention to the possible contribution of faulty eating and activity patterns, and to the role of known genetic, metabolic, environmental, interpersonal, and emotional factors. Individuals can be trained to keep adequate records of all aspects of their eating and activity patterns, probably within 10 percent of their actual caloric intakes and expenditures. On the basis of such records, each individual can be guided to an appropriate regimen. Even when actual weight loss does not coincide with a theoretical prediction based on estimates that assume normal resting and activity metabolism, remedies are available. If adequate records are kept, one can simply assume metabolic conservation (or some other physical disorder discussed below) when weight loss does not occur on an intake of 1,000 calories a day in a woman or 1,200-1,500 calories in a man. In certain rare instances, persons have had to cut calories to as low as 800 per day and institute fifteen-minute walks after meals to achieve an average weight reduction of slightly less than 1 pound per week. Drastic measures of this sort seem to be necessary more frequently for women 40 to 90 pounds over desirable weights than for men. Caloric restriction to 1,000 calories or below and walking after meals may also be necessary to facilitate weight loss for individuals on medications that slow metabolic processes and for diabetics whose insulin facilitates conversion of carbohydrates to fat.

Because most obese individuals are relatively inactive, they are in very poor physical condition with respect to muscular and cardiovascular endurance. Because they cannot expend great amounts of energy for an extended period of time, weight loss at the beginning of a weight management program depends primarily on caloric restriction. It seems, however, that commitment to a walking program and flexibility exercises is still an important feature, even at the start of a weight management effort. If the effort is to be ultimately successful, the activity component must increase. Further, to reach and maintain ideal weight, *one must become addicted to an active life style.* Physically well-conditioned persons have no difficulty expending energy at 7 to 10 or even 12 times their resting metabolic rates in physical activities (such as jogging, bicycling, swimming, or tennis). Their heart rates are no higher in these activities than those of obese persons expending energy at only 3 to 4 times their resting metabolic rates, such as during walking at approximately 5 to 7 km per hour (3 to 4 miles per hour). When formerly obese persons become capable of, and do perform, moderate to vigorous activity for an hour to an hour and a half a day, approximately five days a week, they seem to have little difficulty keeping weight off, in spite of caloric intakes that may actually exceed the amounts they consumed prior to weight reduction. In cases where no cardiovascular disease exists, the limiting factors in exercise are muscular weakness and the likelihood of bone or joint injuries. Care must be used in encouraging vigorous body movement until strength and flexibility have increased and considerable weight has been lost.

Unfortunately, most physical fitness leaders do not know how to relate to overweight people to help them deal with the problems they will face (pain, self-consciousness, and management of time) when they make an effort to increase their activity to a level where positive physical and emotional benefits are experienced. Similarly, most health professionals who deal with obesity do not have the facilities, time, or inclination to act as models for the obese people with whom they work. Useful collaborations between community health and athletic facilities are possible. Clinicians may find it helpful to make contact with their local YMCAs, where adequate assessment of physical fitness (including assessment of body fat) can be done and fitness programs especially for overweight persons can be organized.

Obese individuals also need to be helped to make additional changes to combat loneliness, social embarrassment, interpersonal relationships that encourage obesity, and the emotional correlates of overeating and underactivity. For many persons, a group therapeutic atmosphere seems to be more effective than individual treatment. In other cases, combined individual and group therapy may be useful when individuals fail to make progress in a group setting.

When obesity reaches morbid dimensions (100 percent over desirable weight, with a potential threat to life), radical treatments—such as extended complete fasts; protein-sparing fasts using low-calorie protein liquid or powders; or the intestinal bypass operation, in which a portion of the small intestine is removed—may have to be employed. Persons on fasts and protein replacements need careful medical and nutritional supervision because of the potential for severe physiological reactions, including cardiac malfunctions that in rare cases may cause death. However, in view of the extreme difficulty faced by the clinician attempting to help the morbidly obese achieve a significant weight loss, the field could profit from further research on the utility of combining protein-sparing fasts with behavior modification. The bypass operation has a fairly high mortality rate (variously reported to be from 4 percent to 10 percent) as well as a host of uncomfortable side effects (for instance, a prolonged period of diarrhea). A large percentage of persons undergoing that operation require reconnection, with subsequent weight gain. It is a treatment not to be recommended except when there is an imminent threat to life.

Anorexic drugs and hypnotherapy have short-term effects, and chorionic gonadotrophin is apparently useless except as a motivating factor that seems to help individuals adhere to a low-calorie diet (usually 500-600 calories per day) for a short period of time. These approaches have little to recommend them.

There are a number of ethical considerations relating to the obese condition and its management. There is discrimination against the obese in both the vocational and the educational arenas. Fat adolescents are less likely to be accepted by a preferred elite university, and both employment and opportunities for job advancement are less available to the obese. Advertisers, clothing manufacturers and retailers, and most of the specialists who treat the condition make obesity appear immoral and ugly. In view of the environmental and metabolic causes of obesity, this situation is more unethical or immoral than the condition itself, which is neither of these things. In this regard, the efforts of NAAFA are important.

It is certainly unethical for those who treat obesity or write books on diet to promise miraculous, lasting results with little effort on the part of the client. Self-help manuals should not make claims to the public that are unsupported by research. Researchers testing various treatments or theoretical issues in time-limited programs involving random assignment of participants to treatment or control groups should make their objectives clear to prospective subjects, since most studies of this sort are not designed to help all participants reach and maintain ideal weight. A majority of persons exposed to time-limited, fragmentary behavioral approaches may fail in achieving their weight objectives and become inoculated against possibly helpful behavioral strategies when they are incorporated into more comprehensive, long-term treatment efforts. Researchers with children and adolescents should be particularly concerned over whether their design will contribute to an ultimate failure experience for many of their participants at critical periods in their lives, and thus contribute to the growth and maintenance of a negative self-concept.

In addition to these many ethical considerations, there are a number of implications for the training and certification of professional weight management specialists. Because of the complexity of the obese condition, most workers in the field do not understand all its metabolic, nutritional, psychological, interpersonal, emotional, and physical fitness aspects and therefore cannot offer comprehensive evaluation and treatment. Thus, collaborative efforts among specialists in medicine, nutrition, psychology, exercise physiology, and physical fitness are most likely to be in the clients' best interests. Interdisciplinary continuing education is in order, and those responsible for the primary training of people who expect to work with obesity need to assure that basic knowledge of contributing factors and treatment approaches is in the curriculum.

Specialists desiring to broaden their own understanding of the assessment and treatment of obesity in its many aspects will find the following sources most useful. The self-help manuals by Stuart (1978) and Mahoney and Mahoney (1976) provide an excellent overview of the behavioral approach to assessing and modifying faulty eating patterns. Much of the basic research using behavioral strategies is reprinted in Foreyt (1977). A complete picture of theory and research relating to physiological, epidemiological, medical, and other psychological aspects of obesity can be found in three excellent collections of papers: Bray (1975); Silverstone (1975); and Williams, Martin, and Foreyt (1976). Guthrie's (1975) fine standard reference text on nutrition contains a special chapter on weight control. Stunkard's (1978) book is especially recommended for its comprehensive treatment of set-point theory, metabolic complexities, and virtually all other major issues touched upon in this chapter. Katch and McArdle (1977) have designed a useful text particularly for the professional preparation of persons from any of the health-related disciplines who wish to deal with obesity. It covers basic information, assessment, and treatment procedures in the areas of nutrition, weight control, and exercise.

Application to Particular Variables

The incidence of obesity increases in both men and women until around age 60, at which point it appears to decline (possibly as a result of longevity). Metabolic processes slow down, and activity levels fall slowly in the 30s and more quickly in the 40s. Many older inactive individuals may have a relatively large proportion of adipose tissue and still fall within the desirable weight range according to the published tables.

Obesity is more prevalent among lower-class women than among women in the upper classes, and it is probably more prevalent among middle- and upper-class men than among lower-class men, but the relationship is not as strong.

Dietary control and behaviorally oriented weight management programs are less successful with minority group members than they are with the white middle class. It is unclear whether the relative lack of effect is due to educational or to cultural differences that influence both food preferences and receptivity to therapeutic strategies.

Individuals who are involved in heavy work and who exercise frequently will have less adipose tissue than those in sedentary occupations. They may still be "overweight," relative to height/weight charts, however, as a result of increased muscle mass. When individuals change from active to sedentary vocations (the football player who retires to sell insurance), muscle mass decreases and fat mass tends to increase.

A number of physical disorders may relate to obesity. In humans, as in other animals, it is quite certain that abnormalities of the hypothalamus will result in abnormalities in feeding behavior and activity. It is also quite certain that many other central nervous system and neurohormonal factors, of which there is sparse knowledge, are involved. A depressed level of energy needs may be related to a depressed level of thyroxin, secreted by a thyroid gland, which controls basal metabolism. High insulin levels may increase the rate at which adipose tissue is formed. An imbalance among endocrine secretions may produce an abnormal distribution of body fat in various parts of the body. Some persons who have difficulty losing weight may be resistant to fat-mobilizing substances (such as epinephrine). Various properties of fat cells—for instance, their sensitivity to insulin—appear to change as their size increases with obesity. Furthermore, individuals differ genetically in the level of enzymes available that affect both fat storage and fat mobilization. A high level of enzymes that facilitate lipogenesis (fat formation) and a low level of lipase (the fat-splitting enzyme that breaks down fats for use as energy) will predispose a person to obesity. The level of these enzymes may vary fivefold across individuals. Furthermore, once fat has been deposited in adipose tissue, the cells will more readily store fat after its removal than before.

Among psychiatric disorders, any organic condition that affects feeding and activity levels is likely to affect weight. As a special group, the mentally retarded of all ages are more susceptible to obesity and inactivity than persons of normal intelligence, and constitute a population that deserves more attention.

References

Allon, N. "The Stigma of Overweight in Everyday Life." In G. A. Bray (Ed.), *Obesity in Perspective*. Report No. NIH75-708. Washington, D.C.: U.S. Department of Health, Education and Welfare, 1975.

American Psychiatric Association. *Diagnostic and Statistical Manual of Mental Disorders*. Washington, D.C.: American Psychiatric Association, 1968.

Apfelbaum, M. "Influence of Level of Energy Intake on Energy Expenditure in Man: Effects of Spontaneous Intake, Experimental Starvation, and Experimental Overeating." In G. A. Bray (Ed.), *Obesity in Perspective*. Report No. NIH75-708. Washington, D.C.: U.S. Department of Health, Education and Welfare, 1975.

Bray, G. A. (Ed.). *Obesity in Perspective*. Report No. NIH75-708. Washington, D.C.: U.S. Department of Health, Education and Welfare, 1975.

Bruch, H. *The Importance of Overweight*. New York: Norton, 1957.

Bruch, H. *Eating Disorders: Obesity, Anorexia Nervosa, and the Person Within*. New York: Basic Books, 1973.

Dwyer, J., and Mayer, J. "The Dismal Condition: Problems Faced by Obese Adolescent Girls in American Society." In G. A. Bray (Ed.), *Obesity in Perspective*. Report No. NIH75-708. Washington, D.C.: U.S. Department of Health, Education and Welfare, 1975.

Foreyt, J. P. (Ed.). *Behavioral Treatments of Obesity*. Elmsford, N.Y.: Pergamon Press, 1977.

Garrow, J. S. "The Regulation of Body Weight." In T. Silverstone (Ed.), *Obesity: Its Pathogenesis and Management*. Lancaster, England: Medical and Technical Publishing Co., 1975.

Grande, F. "Assessment of Body Fat in Man." In G. A. Bray (Ed.), *Obesity in Perspective*. Report No. NIH75-708. Washington, D.C.: U.S. Department of Health, Education and Welfare, 1975.

Grosswirth, M. *Fat Pride: A Survival Handbook.* New York: Jarrow Press, 1971.

Guthrie, H. A. *Introductory Nutrition.* Saint Louis: Mosby, 1975.

Hagan, R. L. "Theories of Obesity: Is There Any Hope for Order?" In B. J. Williams, S. M. Martin, and J. P. Foreyt (Eds.), *Obesity: Behavioral Approaches to Dietary Management.* New York: Brunner/Mazel, 1976.

Hall, S. M., Bass, A., and Monroe, J. "Continued Contact and Monitoring as Follow-Up Strategies: A Long-Term Study of Obesity Treatment." *Addictive Behavior,* in press.

Jeffrey, R. W., Wing, R. R., and Stunkard, A. J. "Behavioral Treatment of Obesity: The State of the Art 1976." *Behavior Therapy,* 1978, *9,* 189-199.

Jordan, H. A. "Physiological Control of Food Intake in Man." In G. A. Bray (Ed.), *Obesity in Perspective.* Report No. NIH75-708. Washington, D.C.: U.S. Department of Health, Education and Welfare, 1975.

Jordan, H. A., and Levitz, L. S. "A Behavioral Approach to the Problems of Obesity." In T. Silverstone (Ed.), *Obesity: Pathogenesis and Management.* Lancaster, England: Medical and Technical Publishing Co., 1975.

Katch, F. I., and McArdle, W. D. *Nutrition, Weight Control and Exercise.* Boston: Houghton Mifflin, 1977.

Keys, A. "Overweight and the Risk of Heart Attack and Sudden Death." In G. A. Bray (Ed.), *Obesity in Perspective.* Report No. NIH75-708. Washington, D.C.: U.S. Department of Health, Education and Welfare, 1975.

Levitz, L. S. "The Susceptibility of Human Feeding Behavior to External Controls." In G. A. Bray (Ed.), *Obesity in Perspective.* Report No. NIH75-708. Washington, D.C.: U.S. Department of Health, Education and Welfare, 1975.

Louderback, L. *Fat Power: Whatever You Weigh Is Right.* New York: Hawthorne Books, 1970.

Mahoney, M. J., and Mahoney, K. *Permanent Weight Control: A Total Solution to the Dieter's Dilemma.* New York: Norton, 1976.

Mason, E. "Obesity in Pet Dogs." *Veterinarian Record,* 1970, *86,* 612-616.

Mayer, J. *Overweight: Causes, Costs, and Control.* Englewood Cliffs, N.J.: Prentice-Hall, 1968.

Metropolitan Life Insurance Company. "New Weight Standards for Men and Women." *Statistical Bulletin,* Nov.-Dec. 1969, *40,* 3.

Miller, D. S. "Overfeeding in Man." In G. A. Bray (Ed.), *Obesity in Perspective.* Report No. NIH75-708. Washington, D.C.: U.S. Department of Health, Education and Welfare, 1975.

Rand, C. S., and Stunkard, A. J. "Psychoanalysis and Obesity." *Journal of the American Academy of Psychoanalysis,* 1977, *5* (4), 459-497.

Rodin, J. "Responsiveness of the Obese to External Stimuli." In G. A. Bray (Ed.), *Obesity in Perspective.* Report No. NIH75-708. Washington, D.C.: U.S. Department of Health, Education and Welfare, 1975.

Schacter, S. "Obesity and Eating." *Science,* 1968, *161,* 751-756.

Seltzer, C. C., and Mayer, J. "A Simple Criterion of Obesity." *Postgraduate Medicine,* 1965, *38,* 101-107.

Seltzer, C. C., and others. "Reliability of Relative Body Weight as a Criterion of Obesity." *American Journal of Epidemiology,* 1970, *92,* 339-350.

Silverstone, J. T. *Obesity: Pathogenesis and Management.* Lancaster, England: Medical and Technical Publishing Co., 1975.

Sloan, A. W., and Weir, J. B. "Nomograms for Prediction of Body Density and Total Body Fat." *Journal of Applied Psychology,* 1970, *28,* 221-222.

Stuart, R. B. *Act Thin, Stay Thin.* New York: Norton, 1978.

Stunkard, A. J. "Physical Activity, Emotions, and Human Obesity." *Psychosomatic Medicine,* 1958, *20,* 366-372.

Stunkard, A. J. "New Therapies for the Eating Disorders: Behavior Modification of Obesity and Anorexia Nervosa." *Archives of General Psychiatry,* 1972, *26,* 391-398.

Stunkard, A. J. "Obesity." In Arieti (Ed.), *American Handbook of Psychiatry.* New York: Basic Books, 1973.

Stunkard, A. J. *The Pain of Obesity.* Palo Alto, Calif.: Bull Press, 1976.

Stunkard, A. J. (Ed.). *Obesity: Basic Mechanisms of Treatment.* Philadelphia, Pa.: W. B. Saunders, 1978.

Whipp, B. J., and others. "Exercise and Energetics and Respiratory Control Following Acute and Chronic Elevation of Caloric Intake." In G. A. Bray (Ed.), *Obesity in Perspective.* Report No. NIH75-708. Washington, D.C.: U.S. Department of Health, Education and Welfare, 1975.

Williams, B. J., Martin, S. M., and Foreyt, J. P. (Eds.). *Obesity: Behavioral Approaches to Dietary Management.* New York: Brunner/Mazel, 1976.

Wooley, O. W., and Wooley, S. C. "Short-Term Control of Food Intake." In G. A. Bray (Ed.), *Obesity in Perspective.* Report No. NIH75-708. Washington, D.C.: U.S. Department of Health, Education and Welfare, 1975.

23

Clifford H. Swensen

Ego Development

The two main definitions of the term *ego* both contain the concept of organization. That is, the ego is regarded either as the aspect of the personality that organizes and integrates the personality as a whole or as the organization of the personality. In other words, organization of the personality structure is seen as either the essence of the ego or the product of the ego. The ego organizes or is the typical organization from which the person's perceiving, thinking, and behaving flow. The underlying processes are the processes of perception, thinking, and problem solving; and the behavior manifested is a function of these processes. The term *development* implies that the ego is not static but, rather, a dynamic and changing process and that this course of change follows some typical sequence.

Background and Current Status

Ego development has a much shorter history than the term *ego*. The concepts of the self, the me, the I, or the ego can be traced back to antiquity. Certain characteristics of the person seem to demand some such concept. People have a concept of themselves as a unity with a continuous history. People who knew me as a 5-year-old boy might have a quite different perception of me from those who knew me as a 50-year-old college professor, and people who know me as a professor certainly have a different conception of me from those who know me as a father or a grocery store customer. But I experience myself as one. The 5-year-old boy, the 50-year-old college professor, and the father are all the same "me." This experience of unity and continuity implies the experience of some unifying "me," within which all those different ages and roles are contained.

The concept of "ego" was more specifically and explicitly developed by Freud in his elaboration of the structure of the personality (Munroe, 1955), in the first third of the twentieth century. In Freud's conception, the personality structure is composed of three parts: the id, the ego, and the superego. The id contains the basic drives, the superego contains the values and the conscience, and the ego integrates the demands of the id and the constraints of the superego with the demands of the real world outside. In Freud's view, the ego serves those three "harsh masters" in much the same way, perhaps, as a waiter in a restaurant must try to satisfy the demands of his customers, the headwaiter, and the cook.

Within the psychoanalytic school, a series of revisions of the original Freudian theory led to the conceptualization of the ego as having power and functions of its own, apart from the demands of the id and the strictures of the superego. This line of evolution led to Erikson's (1950) description of a lifelong process of development.

The concept of "development" was not a new idea within Freudian psychology. Freud (1933) originally conceptualized the ego as developing out of the clash between the demands of the id, on the one hand, and harsh requirements of the outside world, on the other hand. The ego developed to enable the person to satisfy the demands of the id within the strictures laid down by the outside world. However, the Freudian stages of personality development ended with the achievement of adulthood. Erikson extended these stages to cover the life span.

Erikson (1950) postulated that each stage of life poses a crisis that must be resolved by the person before he can move on to the resolution of the following stages. The resolution of the crises of these stages—or the failure to resolve a crisis, so that one becomes fixated at a stage—determines a person's fundamental orientation toward life. These stages, and the consequent result of the resolution or failure to resolve the crisis at that stage, are the following: (1) infancy: trust versus mistrust; (2) early childhood: autonomy versus shame, doubt; (3) preschool years: initiative versus guilt; (4) school age: industry versus inferiority; (5) adolescence: identity versus identity confusion; (6) young adulthood: intimacy versus isolation; (7) middle age: generativity versus stagnation; and (8) old age: integrity versus despair.

Erikson was working essentially within the psychoanalytic framework. At that same time, in the World War II and postwar era, Ausubel (1950) developed a concept of ego development that sought to integrate the findings of general psychology, outside of the psychoanalytic stream, within one theory. Ausubel postulated that there are two critical stages of ego development: early childhood and preadolescence. In early childhood the interactions of the child and the parents must be such that the child is able to "satellize"; that is, become a satellite to his parents. In the preadolescent stage the child must be able to reverse the process—become independent and "desatellize" from the parents. Ausubel did not postulate normal adult stages of development, although he did hypothesize a variety of consequences in adulthood as a result of various kinds of resolution to the satellization and desatellization process.

During the 1950s and 1960s a series of developments in several different areas of research appeared to converge toward a cognitive paradigm for the human personality—a paradigm that would include not only psychoanalytic and psychiatric concepts but concepts from other areas of psychology as well (Swensen, 1977). These concepts and research results have, to a large extent, been integrated into Loevinger's (1966, 1976) and Loevinger, Wessler, and Redmore's (1970) scheme of ego development.

Piaget's (1926, 1928, 1932) concepts of the intellectual development of children began to enter the mainstream of developmental psychology. These concepts stimulated Kohlberg's (1969) research into moral development. Concomitantly, Sullivan's (1953) concept of the self was elaborated into a theory of development of the self system by Sullivan, Grant, and Grant (1957), whose stages have been used as a basis of research on the treatment of delinquent juveniles (Jesness, 1971; Palmer, 1971). The character typology developed by Sullivan, Grant, and Grant fit very closely the results of an independent sociological study of character development (Peck and Havighurst, 1960). Within social psychology, research on cognitive complexity (Bieri, 1966; Harvey, 1963, 1966) produced a four-stage theory of cognitive development, progressing from simple to complex, from subservience to authority to independence. All these developments, within diverse areas of psychology, pointed toward a process of development in the perceptual and thinking processes of humans, which were manifested in human behavior.

Loevinger (1976) integrated these strands into a conception of ego development that has seven basic stages and two half-stages or levels. These stages and levels are the following: (1) presocial, symbiotic stage; (2) impulsive stage; (3) self-protective stage; (4) conformist stage; (5) self-aware level, transition from conformist to conscientious stage; (6) conscientious stage; (7) individualistic level, transition from conscientious to autonomous stage; (8) autonomous stage; and (9) integrated stage. Loevinger (1970) also created a sentence completion test for measuring ego development.

Critical Discussion

General Areas of Concern

The essential underlying idea in the concept of ego development is that the organization of the personality (that is, the ego) goes through a process of change over the life of the person. This process of change follows a certain sequence. Basically, the sequence begins with a simple and undifferentiated ego that becomes increasingly more complex and differentiated. With this increase in complexity and differentiation, other changes also take place. In the earliest stage there is no cognitive differentiation between the person and the environment. As development proceeds, there is increasingly extensive differentiation among persons, situations, objects, feelings, thoughts, and actions. Initially, there is no integration among the various needs, responsibilities, and relationships; ultimately, there is a harmonious integration of the various internal and external forces in the person's life. Initially, the person is totally self-centered; ultimately, he is able to understand, appreciate, and share the feelings, thoughts, needs, and experiences of other people. Initially, the person is unable to relate to other people, except for the satisfaction of the most basic personal needs; ultimately, he is able to relate intimately and harmoniously with other people. Finally, the person is at first totally at the mercy of the intermediate environment; ultimately, he can exercise some control over the environment, either through changing the environment or through choosing an environment.

Since this process of change follows a certain sequence (from the simple to the increasingly complex), it must be the same for all people; that is, all people must go through intermediate stages of complexity. A person develops from simplicity to increasingly more complex stages in the same invariant fashion that one grows from being two feet tall to being five feet tall—by being, in sequence, three feet tall, then four feet tall, and finally reaching five feet.

How this process of development takes place is not entirely clear. However, all theorists more or less agree that it emerges out of the interaction between the natural process of growth in the individual, on the one hand, and the forces in the environment, on the other hand. The major forces in the environment, of course, are primarily other people (in the early stages of development, the parents). Some theorists stress one aspect more than the other. Erikson (1968) suggests that the growth is based on an "epigenetic principle." That is, any organism develops in accordance with some basic ground plan. As the person at a specific stage in the ground plan of development interacts with the forces in the society and culture, the succeeding stage emerges. In Loevinger's (1976) view, the drives within the individual change (for instance, during adolescence) and thereby disrupt an earlier equilibrium; consequently, a new, more complex, equilibrium must be established that integrates this change.

It seems likely that the changes in development during childhood are, to some extent, a function of biological changes. As children develop motor coordination, they become capable of moving over wider areas of the physical environment and of manipulating various tools and objects. Thus, they are exposed to new experiences, which must be assimilated and integrated into their ego structure. Because of this increased development of skill, their parents come to expect certain new behavior from them. They are now expected to feed and dress themselves with less and less help from the parents. In short, the biological change brings about changes in the experiences of the child and the expectations other people have for the child; and this disturbs the ego equilibrium of the infant, who is totally cared for by the parents. When adolescence arrives (and with it sexual maturity), the individual is faced with integrating a whole new set of changes. The biological drives have changed; the body size, strength, and configuration have changed; and the expectations other people have for the adolescent have changed. Biological changes probably become somewhat less important during the long adult years of life; social changes, however, may be quite dramatic. With marriage a new set of social relationships develops. With the arrival of children, another set of social relationships develops, and these relationships change as one's children grow and leave home. Even if a person does not marry, he must adjust to the fact that most other people do marry, and being a single person at age 25 is not the same as being a single person at age 45. With the coming of retirement and old age, the loss of roles and declining powers and health induce a new set of changes. Particularly with the onset of old age and chronic illness and the marked change in physical capacity, biological factors may once again come to play a significant part in inducing ego development.

Comparative Philosophies and Theories

In general, self theory or ego theory has proved useful as a part of a global personality theory or as a theory on the functioning of a specific aspect of personality; it has not had much relevance to the areas of psychology concerned with the functioning of subsystems within the person. Studies of perception, sensation, cognition, learning, and social interaction have all, more or less, proceeded without reference to the ego (and to some extent without too much reference to each other). Behavior theory has provided a basis for integrating such research, and attempts have been made to apply behavior theory to more holistic concerns; but no real integration has taken place. Modern psychology has been, to a large extent, divided into the "three cultures" of behaviorism, psychoanalysis, and humanism. McKeachie (1976) suggests that the developments within cognitive psychology may provide a basis for the integration of these three diverse cultures. The processes of perceiving and thinking that organize the personality as a whole are the domain of ego development. The chief significance of the concept of ego development is that it may well provide a basis for a paradigm that will integrate all of psychology.

As Segal and Lachman (1972) point out, the difficulties with the behavioristic S-R paradigm have led experimental psychologists into areas that were formally rejected as mentalistic; that is, into research into cognitive processes. Similarly, researchers in the behavioristic wing of clinical psychology have begun to study cognitive processes (Meichenbaum, 1977). In these two areas there are examples of movement toward a convergence. This convergence is reflected in Loevinger's (1976) integration of several strands of development in social psychology, sociology, developmental psychology, and clinical psychology. The developments in experimental psychology and behavior therapy suggest that the behavioristic strand may also be integrated into one overarching paradigm.

Elaboration on Critical Points

The concept of ego development that will be elaborated here is that of Loevinger (1976). Her scheme is utilized for two main reasons. First, she attempts to integrate a wider variety of other approaches to ego and ego development with psychology in general and to a greater degree than do those presenting other schemes; in the process, she not only includes much of what the other approaches include but provides the data from other developmental research. Second, she has developed a sophisticated measuring device for assessing ego development (Loevinger, Wessler, and Redmore, 1970).

The Loevinger stages will be presented in sequence. The symbol in parentheses after the name of the stage is Loevinger's symbol for each stage. She avoids numbering her stages because numbering leads to difficulties when new stages are identified or new conceptualizations developed. The Loevinger stages are as follows:

- *Presocial Stage (I-1).* At birth the baby does not differentiate self from the environment. A child who fails to differentiate self from the environment is autistic.
- *Symbiotic Stage (I-1).* After the baby has differentiated self from the environment and from other people, these other people are seen only as supplying the baby's needs. The relationship with other people is a symbiotic relationship. The baby develops out of this stage with the development of language.
- *Impulsive Stage (I-2).* The child expresses his separate identity through the expression of impulses. Parents curb these impulses—at first by physical restraint and later by reward and punishment. The child views others primarily as persons who either provide him with or deprive him of what he wants. He is not concerned with moral values but with whether actions lead to punishment or reward. Since impulses often lead to disapproval and punishment, the child is concerned with his impulses, especially aggressive and sexual impulses. He lives primarily in the present and has little concern with or awareness of the past or the future.
- *Self-Protective Stage (I-Delta).* The child begins to anticipate short-term rewards and punishments. There is no moral concern with right or wrong but, rather, a concern with not getting caught at doing things that will bring punishment. The child blames trouble or punishment on the environment, other people, or personal characteristics for which he cannot be held personally responsible. Relationships are seen as competitive, or as "zero-sum" games in which there are winners and losers. The primary concern of the person at this stage is to gain personal advantage and to avoid being taken advantage of by other people. The good life is a life of fun, material plenty, and little work or responsibility.
- *Conformist State (I-3).* The person perceives that certain rules govern situations and

relationships with other people. At this stage he obeys the rules because they are the rules. He recognizes that other people have needs and desires, but these needs and desires are seen in stereotyped ways. Primary identification is with the person's own group. Other ethnic, religious, or racial groups are seen in stereotyped ways. The person is particularly concerned with prestige, status, and what other people think. There is an awareness of values, but the punishment for failing to meet certain values is the disapproval of other people. Behavior is seen in terms of its external manifestations, rather than in terms of any internal motivation or in terms of psychological factors. The person has a conception of motivation, but it is in rather shallow concepts such as "love" or "hate" or "ambition." The psychological explanation of the conformist person is at the level of the cliché.

- *Self-Aware Level (I-3/4).* The self-aware level is the modal level in current American society. It is called a "level," rather than a stage, because it is perceived as a transition step between two main stages. The person at this level has begun to perceive that the rules learned at the conformist stage do not always make sense when applied to specific situations and that rules sometimes conflict with one another. Further, the person perceives that groups other than his own have rules that work just as well as his own group's rules. However, persons at this level, if they belong to an established social group, are often cautious about expressing personal opinions that are at variance with the accepted opinions and values of their group.

- *Conscientious Stage (I-4).* The person begins to be concerned with personal values. He is often acutely self-critical, because he has become aware of internal feelings, needs, and motivations. He is also aware of the feelings, needs, and motivations of other people. Both self and others are seen in more complex, more highly differentiated ways than is true at the less complex stages. The person has transcended primary concern with external rewards and punishments, whether material or social, and has become more concerned with internal evaluation. At this stage the person has developed a broader time perspective, being able to see the contribution of the past to the present and to anticipate the contribution of the present to the future.

- *Individualistic Level (I-4/5).* This transitional level is characterized by an increased concern for emotional dependence and an increased sense of individuality. The person has become aware that an individual may be financially and physically independent of others but still may remain emotionally dependent on them. The person who develops beyond the conscientious stage becomes more tolerant of self and other people. The moralism of earlier stages begins to be replaced with an awareness of inner conflict. At this level the person typically perceives behavior in terms of psychological causality.

- *Autonomous Stage (I-5).* The person perceives the individuality of other people and accepts other people for what they are. The person is aware of inner conflicts and is able to cope with them. He does not necessarily have more inner conflicts than people at less complex stages but is more consciously aware of the conflicts that exist. There is a realization that some conflict is inherent in the human condition, so that conflict is accepted as a part of life. The person values personal autonomy and respects the autonomy of other people. At this stage the parent is willing to let his children make their own mistakes. Personal relationships are especially cherished by people at this stage, and self-fulfillment is a primary goal.

- *Integrated Stage (I-6).* The person has transcended the conflicts of the preceding stage and not only accepts the individuality of other people but values it. This stage may correspond to Maslow's (1970) concept of the self-actualizing person.

In considering a scheme with such breadth, one may pursue evaluation at both the theoretical and the technical levels. Here consideration will be given to the theoretical problems with the model. In a later section discussion will focus on the sentence completion test and its applicability to various populations.

When one presents Loevinger's conceptualizations to an audience, one of the first questions asked is: "Isn't this scheme just a case of value judgment? Aren't the more complex levels just an example of a particular society's, or even a particular individual's, system of values?" To the question about society Loevinger (1976) replies that all societies are built on conformity; they presumably pressure people to function at the conformist stage and punish people who do not function at this stage. To the criticism that the system of stages may reflect the originator's own values Loevinger replies that her conceptualization is in substantial agreement with the general trend of the schemes of other theorists. Moreover, since the scheme is essentially based on an ascending order of cognitive differentiation and integration, its expression in particular ways of perceiving, thinking, and behaving does not necessarily imply any particular content. For example, although hippies would not typically be considered as conforming to the rules of the larger American culture, one study found that hippies are predominantly at the conformist level of development (Haan, Stroud, and Holstein, 1973). Another study (Candee, 1974) found that people who subscribe to the New Left ideology scored at six different levels of ego development, from the self-protective stage through the autonomous stage. At the simpler stages the subjects were concerned with the effects of politics on themselves, while at the more complex stages they viewed politics in terms of human development and justice.

More serious questions have been raised by Hauser (1976). In a conclusion to an extensive review of the research on ego development, he points out that many questions have been raised but not answered by Loevinger's theory. One question concerns the invariant order of stages. No data have been produced to support the contention that each person must progress through each stage, in order, in the course of development. Other questions have to do with how the process of ego development functions and how ego development relates to other systems. The process by which change takes place from one stage to another has not been elaborated on. Nor has the process by which ego, or the organization, integrates the various processes of the personality structure been described. Similarly, the relationship of ego development to physical development, intellectual development, and psychosexual development has not been specified.

Personal Views and Recommendations

Besides providing a possible basis for integrating all of psychology, ego development also has significance of a more mundane nature. Specifically, if there is a process of development in the way people typically perceive, think about, and solve problems presented to them by the world around them, this information should be of considerable significance to those who are concerned with predicting, controlling, and changing behavior. That is, it should have significance for clinical, counseling, school, and forensic psychology. As mentioned, the basic ideas have already been applied to developing treatment procedures for juvenile delinquents (Jesness, 1971; Palmer, 1971). The concept also has been integrated into a paradigm for studying interpersonal relationships (Swensen, 1977); therefore, it should be applicable to the marriage relationship and the psychotherapeutic interaction. One study has found that the level of ego development is related to adjustment to retirement (Kohlhepp, 1976). Any concept that is concerned with the organization of the totality of human personality should have applicability to any situation within which human beings are found.

Application to Particular Variables

A concept as global as the concept of ego development has application to all groups. The only limitation to its use is the measuring device by which ego development is assessed. Ego development is assessed either from responses in interviews (see, for example, Ausubel, 1950) or from responses to a sentence completion test (Loevinger, Wessler, and Redmore, 1970). Both require an ability to understand and respond to language, and the acquisition of language marks the transition from the presocial stage to the impulsive stage. Therefore, the fact that a subject cannot respond appropriately to an interview or to the sentence completion test would appear to be evidence that this subject is at the presocial stage (unless, of course, the person's inability to speak or write stems from physical disabilities). The appropriate language for the subject should be used, however, and the lack of language acquisition should clearly not be the result of some sensory deficit.

The assessment of ego development seems to have limited use in the usual clinical setting because particular clinical facilities (or other assessment centers) draw their clientele from people who range over a rather narrow band of ego development. Assessment of the clients in a university psychological services center revealed that more than 75 percent were from the self-aware level. The remainder were from the conformist stage and the conscientious stage. Assessment of the inmates in a juvenile detention center revealed that over half of them were at the self-protective stage and most of the remainder were at the impulsive stage. A current study of alcoholics receiving treatment in a psychiatric hospital has found over two thirds of them at the conformist stage. A series of studies of married couples in the immediate preretirement and postretirement ages has found all of them at or above the conformist stage and about two thirds of them at the self-aware level.

What, then, is the value of the concept and the measurement of level of ego development? Its value appears to lie largely in its ability to explain phenomena; its measurement, therefore, would be most useful in research that is directed toward understanding a particular kind of behavior.

A study cited earlier (Candee, 1974) found that ego development is related not to the content of political belief but to the way in which people think about political belief. Some people saw political ideology in terms of how it applied personally to themselves. Others, at the more complex levels of ego development, saw political ideology in terms of how it applied to the more abstract principles of justice and the promotion of human development. Obviously, politics and political action have a different meaning and will result in a different behavior by these two groups of people. A study of juvenile delinquents (Gumper, 1976) found that most of the delinquents were at the impulsive and self-protective stages; four subjects, however, were at the conscientious stage. These delinquents at the more complex stage were qualitatively different from their colleagues. They were leaders, and their delinquent acts were in part a personal statement on their view of their society. The simpler delinquents got into trouble mostly because they were unable to anticipate the reaction of other people to their behavior.

Three studies suggest that ego development level is significantly related to the way in which men and women view sex roles and to the way in which they relate to each other (Black, 1973; Erickson, 1977; Kohlhepp, 1976). There appear to be two specific "break" points in level of ego development which affect how people relate to other people. At the conformist stage the person develops a rather stereotyped view of the social group and its rules—a view that lends itself easily to, among other things, sex-role stereotyping. At the conscientious stage the person transcends sex-role and other kinds of stereotyping and begins to relate to other people as individuals (Black, 1973). Erickson (1977) found that people at the conscientious stage and more complex stages are clearly different from people at simpler stages in their perceptions and beliefs concerning the role of women in society, clearly favoring equality of choice for women. In a study of married couples, Kohlhepp (1976) found that over time the amount of marriage interaction and expression of love between husband and wife declines for couples at the conformist stage; but for the couples at the conscientious stage and more complex stages, the amount of marriage interaction and expression of love increases. The implication of this research is that, for marriage to escape the ruts of habit and ritual, the husband and wife must transcend the socially prescribed husband-wife roles. However, to be able to do this, they must develop beyond the conformist stage of ego functioning.

The concept of ego development, then, appears to have substantial potential implications for understanding human behavior and for planning treatment procedures for working with people who exhibit problem behavior. For general clinical application, a substantial amount of research still must be conducted. The measurement of ego development in a clinical setting, however, could be of value in obtaining data that would be useful in this research enterprise.

References

Ausubel, D. P. *Ego Psychology and Mental Disorder.* New York: Grune & Stratton, 1950.

Bieri, J. "Cognitive Complexity and Personality Development." In O. J. Harvey (Ed.), *Experience: Structure and Adaptability.* New York: Springer, 1966.

Black, J. H. "Conceptions of Sex Role." *American Psychologist,* 1973, *28,* 512-526.

Candee, D. "Ego Developmental Aspects of New Left Ideology." *Journal of Personality and Social Psychology,* 1974, *30,* 620-630.

Erickson, V. L. "Beyond Cinderella: Ego Maturity and Attitudes Toward the Rights and Roles of Women." *Counseling Psychologist,* 1977, *7,* 83-88.

Erikson, E. H. *Childhood and Society.* New York: Norton, 1950.

Erikson, E. H. *Identity: Youth and Crisis.* New York: Norton, 1968.

Freud, S. *New Introductory Lectures on Psycho-Analysis.* New York: Norton, 1933.

Gumper, L. L. "Interpersonal Maturity Level, Ego Development, and Friendships of Juvenile Offenders." Unpublished master's thesis, Purdue University, 1976.

Haan, N., Stroud, J., and Holstein, C. "Moral and Ego Stages in Relationship to Ego Processes: A Study of 'Hippies.' " *Journal of Personality,* 1973, *41,* 596-612.

Harvey, O. J. (Ed.). *Motivation and Social Interaction: Cognitive Determinants.* New York: Ronald Press, 1963.

Harvey, O. J. (Ed.). *Experience: Structure and Adaptability.* New York: Springer, 1966.

Hauser, S. T. "Loevinger's Model and Measure of Ego Development: A Critical Review." *Psychological Bulletin,* 1976, *83,* 928-955.

Jesness, C. F. "The Preston Typology Study: An Experiment with Differential Treatment in an Institution." *Journal of Research in Crime and Delinquency,* 1971, *8,* 38-52.

Kohlberg, L. "Stage and Sequence: The Cognitive-Developmental Approach to Socialization." In D. A. Goslin (Ed.), *Handbook of Socialization Theory and Research.* Chicago: Rand McNally, 1969.

Kohlhepp, K. A. "The Effects of Ego Development and Pre- and Post-Retirement Status on Marriage Relationships." Unpublished master's thesis, Purdue University, 1976.

Loevinger, J. "The Meaning and Measurement of Ego Development." *American Psychologist*, 1966, *21*, 195-206.

Loevinger, J. *Ego Development: Conceptions and Theories.* San Francisco: Jossey-Bass, 1976.

Loevinger, J., Wessler, R., and Redmore, C. *Measuring Ego Development.* (2 vols.) San Francisco: Jossey-Bass, 1970.

McKeachie, W. J. "Psychology in America's Bicentennial Year." *American Psychologist*, 1976, *31*, 819-833.

Maslow, A. H. *Motivation and Personality.* (2nd ed.) New York: Harper & Row, 1970.

Meichenbaum, D. *Cognitive-Behavior Modification.* New York: Plenum, 1977.

Munroe, R. *Schools of Psychoanalytic Thought.* New York: Dryden Press, 1955.

Palmer, T. B. "California's Community Treatment Program for Delinquent Adolescents." *Journal of Research in Crime and Delinquency*, 1971, *8*, 74-92.

Peck, R. F., and Havighurst, R. J. *The Psychology of Character Development.* New York: Wiley, 1960.

Piaget, J. *The Language and Thought of the Child.* New York: Harcourt Brace Jovanovich, 1926.

Piaget, J. *Judgment and Reasoning in the Child.* New York: Harcourt Brace Jovanovich, 1928.

Piaget, J. *The Moral Development of the Child.* New York: Free Press, 1932.

Segal, E. M., and Lachman, R. "Complex Behavior of Higher Mental Process: Is There a Paradigm Shift?" *American Psychologist*, 1972, *27*, 46-55.

Sullivan, C., Grant, M. Q., and Grant, J. D. "The Development of Interpersonal Maturity: Applications to Delinquency." *Psychiatry*, 1957, *20*, 373-385.

Sullivan, H. S. *The Interpersonal Theory of Psychiatry.* New York: Norton, 1953.

Swensen, C. H. "Ego Development and the Interpersonal Relationship." In D. Nevill (Ed.), *Humanistic Psychology: New Frontiers.* New York: Gardner Press, 1977.

24

Uriel Last

Ego Strength

Ego strength refers to the degree of adequacy or efficiency with which individuals display various ego functions in their transactions with themselves and with the environment. It also refers to the degree of competence with which individuals regulate impulses and cope with environmental impositions. In this sense, a strong ego is one that has "developed substantial competence in dealing with impulse and environment" (White, 1963, pp. 138-139). As a prognostic term, ego strength refers to the potential ability of a person to benefit from psychodynamically oriented psychotherapy. The relevant capabilities are defined in the form of a list of ego functions whose degree of efficiency must be assessed on an implicit or explicit quantitative scale.

Background and Current Status

In any consideration of ego strength, the term *ego* indicates the meaning elaborated in Freud's "structural theory" (Freud, 1923). Within this framework, Freud defined the ego as "a coherent organization of mental processes" (p. 17). The defensive processes or functions of the ego were at first the most closely studied functions (Freud, 1926). Only later, in *New Introductory Lectures,* did Freud (1933) elaborate on various ego functions crucial for adaptation other than defensive ones. Freud's final statement regarding ego functions is contained in *An Outline of Psychoanalysis* (1940).

341

Freud did not provide a systematic approach for assessing ego functions or a sound method for appraising ego strength. This situation improved somewhat as a result of the 1938 International Psychoanalytic Convention in Paris, which was devoted to discussing the issue of ego strength and ego weakness. Although no theoretical definition emerged there, two significant theoretical contributions were a product of that symposium. Nunberg (1938) attempted to classify the determinants of ego strength and ego weakness according to their locus of origin. In his view, some determinants—such as oversensitivity to displeasure, proneness to experience anxiety or guilt, and the presence of symptoms— seem to originate within the ego system. Others—for instance, instinct strength and narcissism—emanate from the id system. Nunberg concluded that optimal, rather than maximal or minimal, functioning of each determinant is implied for indicating ego strength. Fenichel (1938) attempted to answer the question "When is an ego strong?" by examining the degree of adequacy with which certain ego capabilities are displayed. He considered (1) the ability to tolerate tension and excitation; (2) the ability to make valid judgments and to carry out intentions in the face of obstacles; (3) the ability to control and channel instinctual impulses; (4) the ability to modulate the more archaic dynamisms of the superego; and (5) the ability to reconcile and harmonize conflicting elements within the ego. This "abilities" conception brought to light the need to consider the possibility that "strength" may be manifested in some of the abilities or functions and not in others, as well as the recognition that a multifaceted approach to assessment of ego strength is a prerequisite to any global appraisal of the construct.

In the early 1950s a whole array of systematic assessment procedures for ego strength emerged and started to proliferate. Pascal and Sutell (1951) proposed an ego strength index based on Bender Gestalt performances. Their scoring system is based on the assumption that accuracy in reproducing test items represents the individual's capacity to respond adequately to environmental stimuli. They label this capacity of adaptive coping with environmental demands as ego strength. Klopfer and his associates (1951, 1954) developed a Rorschach-derived measure of ego strength—the Rorschach Prognostic Rating Scale (RPRS). It constitutes an attempt to use Rorschach responses to predict patients' responses to psychotherapy, assuming that ego strength encompasses all those capabilities necessary to benefit from psychotherapy. At about the same time, Barron (1953) suggested an ego strength scale (Es scale) constructed of Minnesota Multiphasic Personality Inventory (MMPI) items. The scale seemed to reflect the constructive forces that enable a person to cope with an emotional crisis, profit from psychological support and insights, and avoid maladaptive patterns of emotional reactions.

Cattell (1957), through factor analysis of psychometric data from behavior ratings and questionnaire responses, extracted a source trait that he called ego strength (source trait C), which seems to be a major personality dimension. This source trait is one of the variables that can be measured by means of the Sixteen Personality Factor (16 PF) Questionnaire (Cattell, Eber, and Tatsuoku, 1970) and other related questionnaires designed for specific populations. According to Cattell and his associates, the ego-weak person is easily annoyed by things and people; is dissatisfied with the world situation, his family, the restrictions of life, and his own health; and feels unable to cope with life in general. He shows generalized neurotic responses in the form of phobias, psychosomatic disturbances, sleep disturbances, and hysterical obsessional behavior. Ego strength is conceived of by Cattell as the absence of neurotic symptomatology and the presence of emotional stability and capacity to cope with emotional difficulties, while giving expression to drives in a well-balanced way.

A different approach to the assessment of ego strength (which relies on clinical ratings based on interview and observation data, rather than on psychodiagnostic or psychometric data) is exemplified by Karush and associates (1964), in their proposed profile of adaptive balance for ego strength assessment. They assume that ego strength can be evaluated by the person's ability to balance various adaptive efforts. They list nine behavioral and experiential areas, each of which can be rated for each person on a nine bipolar scale. The resultant adaptive balance curve, indicating the degree and composition of ego strength, can then be used for various purposes, such as to predict therapeutic outcome.

Bellak's (1967) Global Ego Strength Scale involves the rating of psychological and behavioral characteristics relevant to each stated ego function. These are rated on a six-point amount scale as well as on a six-point appropriateness scale. This attempt grew out of an earlier idea proposed by Bellak to construct an ego strength scale based on a person's life history and symptoms—a scale that would resemble intelligence scales (for instance, as developed by Wechsler). Bellak's continuous efforts to construct measures of ego functions that could indicate ego strength culminated in a report on a systematic study of ego functions in schizophrenics, neurotics, and normals (Bellak, Hurvich, and Gediman, 1973). Bellak and his associates point out that, as with intelligence, the total adaptive ability, ego strength, often tends to be thought of as a unitary phenomenon, whereas clinicians have been struck by the variant afflictions of different ego functions. In the light of analogy with intelligence scales, Bellak, Hurvich, and Geidman found it useful to define twelve ego functions, which may overlap or correlate with each other in varying ways. For each assessed person, a profile of the degree of adequacy of twelve ego functions may be obtained. The range of well or ill functioning may be stated, and a characteristic level of functioning may be determined.

Bellak's twelve ego functions may be assessed from three different sources: clinical interview; laboratory experimental procedures; and psychodiagnostic procedures, including the Bender Gestalt Test, human figure drawings, the Wechsler Adult Intelligence Scale, the Rorschach, and the Thematic Apperception Test. However, it is emphasized that the clinical interview must be tailored to elicit information on each of the twelve ego functions. Their interview plan is structured to contain sets of specific questions, each pertinent to a corresponding ego function. For each assessed subject, a profile is then obtained, which indicates the level of adequacy for all twelve rated ego functions.

Bellak's list of twelve ego functions is a recent attempt to formulate a comprehensive repertoire of ego functions, following former attempts such as those of Hartmann (1939); Beres (1956); Arlow and Brenner (1964); and Grinker, Werble, and Drye (1968). Bellak and his associates enumerate the following ego functions: (1) reality testing; (2) judgment; (3) sense of reality of the world and of the self; (4) regulation and control of drives, affects, and impulses; (5) object relations; (6) thought processes; (7) adaptive regression in the service of the ego; (8) defensive functioning; (9) stimulus barrier; (10) autonomous functioning; (11) synthetic-integrative functioning; and (12) mastery-competence.

The contemporary status of the ego strength concept must be appraised in the light of three considerations: (1) developments in conceptualization of ego and ego functions, (2) validity and utility of operational approaches to the measurement and assessment of ego strength, and (3) degree of proliferation in professional use and application.

As to the first consideration, it seems that the time is ripe for a formulation of an ego model different from the ego model which has dominated the scene since Freud's formulations; namely, the "bundle of functions" model exemplified by Bellak, Hurvich, and Gediman (1973). Haan (1977), for instance, has attempted to formulate an ego model that takes into account the multifaceted nature of its functions and explicates a proposed basic structure underlying the various enumerated ego functions. Her taxonomy of ego processes, while not pretending to encompass the entire range of human ego capabilities, refers to ten generic processes, each having three possible modes of operation: coping, defending, or fragmenting. The ten generic ego processes are divided into four sectors: (1) cognitive functions, subsuming discrimination, detachment, and means-ends symbolization; (2) reflexive-intraceptive functions, subsuming delayed response, sensitivity, and time reversion; (3) attention-focusing functions, subsuming selective awareness; and (4) affect- and impulse-regulating functions, subsuming diversion, transformation, and restraint. This taxonomy refers to most of the commonly mentioned ego functions, but it has the additional merit of being comprehensively organized. The specific characteristic of Haan's work is her effort to state, in parallel to defense operations of the ego, those functions that represent the rational, logical, productive, loving, and playful aspects of ego actions characteristic of healthy optimal personality functioning. Haan supplements her conceptual ego model with pertinent rating procedures (which have already served as assessment devices in a number of investigations).

The second consideration in appraising the contemporary status of ego strength deals with the validity and utility of the available procedures for operationalization and assessment of ego strength. Various measures of ego strength have failed to correlate with each other, thus raising serious questions about their validity. Furthermore, the validity and utility of the two most applied measures of ego strength, Barron's Es scale and the RPRS, have been questioned. Barron's Es scale was found to be related more to well-being or absence of psychopathology than to any criterion with a direct conceptual relationship with ego strength. Klopfer's RPRS, while doing better than Barron's Es for prediction of therapeutic outcome, could be eventually replaced by discrete Rorschach variables or simple combinations of such variables. This state of affairs might, of course, hinder further application of these assessment procedures.

The use of the concept of ego strength is at least implicit in many considerations conducted in any psychodynamically oriented clinical team. Its use is widespread when both diagnosis and prognosis are discussed; but it is usually applied in a very vague and globalistic manner, which does not allow one to gain the full heuristic significance this term could provide for the psychodynamically oriented practitioner and scholar. Without further specification and qualification, its application may be limited. Alone, it is not sophisticated or useful enough for practical clinical objectives.

Critical Discussion

General Areas of Concern

The concept of ego strength implies consideration of the two components of the label. The first component, ego, has, in the framework of psychoanalysis and ego psychology, a structural-functional meaning. The second component, strength, is saturated with economic-quantitative significance. The full meaning and possible utilities of the ego strength concept can be outlined, therefore, only (1) after a detailed analysis and explication of what constitutes an "ego" and ego functions; (2) after quantitative operations are proposed to assess at least certain aspects of these functions; and (3) after the assessment procedures are put to an empirical test for their validation.

As mentioned, ego strength serves to appraise the degree to which a person is equipped to benefit from psychotherapy. Within the framework of psychoanalysis, it is assumed that, in order to gain from therapy, one must display certain capabilities—for instance, the capacity to endure frustration and emotional tension and the capacity to reconcile contradictions. But the range of application of the concept must not be restricted to the area of psychotherapeutic outcome. It can also be a valuable concept in the assessment of an individual's ability to adapt successfully and to withstand stressful events.

Unfortunately, however, research findings usually point out serious problems in the validation of ego strength measures. First of all, as mentioned earlier, it has proved to be particularly difficult to demonstrate a positive relationship between different measures of ego strength. Werts (1960) and Herron, Guido, and Kantor (1965) tried to intercorrelate various ego strength measures; they obtained matrices of correlation coefficients which did not deviate in their composition from chance expectations.

Since its publication, Barron's Es scale has been applied to a variety of diagnostic and prognostic criteria and incorporated into the scoring profiles provided by many scoring services of MMPI answering sheets. In a recent review of the status of Barron's Es scale, Dahlstrom, Welsh, and Dahlstrom (1975) conclude that, as a predictor of response to psychoanalytically oriented psychotherapy, the scale has received little cross-validation beyond Barron's (1953) original results. Factor analysis (Stein and Chu, 1967) and review of relevant research data (Frank, 1967) revealed that Barron's Es scale appears to be measuring mainly "well-being" (Stein and Chu) or absence of psychopathology (Frank). Stein and Chu conclude that "Barron's scale is related to the construct ego strength conceptually and empirically only in part. . . . Three clusters—(a) emotional well-being, (b) cognitive well-being, (c) physical well-being—show empirical validity only in a gross sense; that is, when extreme groups such as psychiatric and normal groups are compared. These same dimensions, however, lack validity for finer discriminations, such as between abnormal groups. Similar findings from other studies add a consistency to this conclusion" (p. 160). Frank's conclusion is similar: "Research does demonstrate that the Es scores of individuals displaying discernible patterns of psychopathology sui generis are statistically distinguishable from and consistently lower than those of control, overtly nonpathological groups" (p. 184). According to Frank, however, Es scores do not differentiate in most instances between psychotics and neurotics (that is, between more and less sick groups). Further, he indicates that hospitalization or psychotherapy has not resulted in a significant rise in Es scores over time. Dahlstrom, Welsh, and Dahlstrom (1975) question the mere psychological sense and rationale of the scale and its use. They claim that, since Es scores are inversely related to the degree of manifest psychopathology, it follows that patients who are most in need of help (very low scores on Es) are said to benefit from it least and those in need of help least (very high scores on Es) are supposed to benefit most.

Es scores seem to be practically useless as an outcome of treatment criterion and as predictors of outcome. Despite all these well-established conclusions, the Es scale is still the most widely used measure of ego strength—apparently due simply to the ease of its administration and scoring.

The status of Klopfer's RPRS as a measure of ego strength is, at least, equivocal. Scoring and weighting a variety of Rorschach variables as required by the procedure are quite complex, technically difficult, high in skill requirements, and time consuming. While such practical considerations should in no way enter into the appraisal of the validity of the procedure, they restrict its use in practice. Garwood (1977), in a recent survey of 13 RPRS studies (published between 1953 and 1974), states that, indeed, the RPRS predicts therapeutic outcome for a wide variety of patient populations and therapeutic techniques, including behavior modification, and should be regarded, therefore, as a valuable prognostic instrument. Correlations between RPRS scores and therapeutic outcomes range from r = .38 to r = .80. However, other research findings cast some doubts on the usefulness of the RPRS. There is evidence that some discrete Rorschach variables may predict therapeutic outcome as well as or even better than the full scale (Endicott and Endicott, 1964; Kirkner, Wisham, and Giedet, 1953; Seidel, 1960; Sheehan and others, 1954). This state of affairs motivated Last and Weiss (1976) to propose a different Rorschach-derived ego strength measure, composed of four discrete variables which are summed additively to an ego strength measure. These variables are (1) sharply perceived human movement responses ($M+$), (2) sharply perceived animal movement responses ($FM+$), (3) sharply perceived space responses ($S+$), and (4) color-determined responses with a good form component ($FC+$ or $CF+$).

Comparative Philosophies and Theories

Comparative approaches relevant to the issue of ego strength may be considered from two points of view, one of content and one of form. From the first point of view, one must refer to theoretical conceptualizations that have affinity with our focal concept. These conceptualizations are derived either from popular notions, such as "strength of character" and "will power," or from theory or research undertakings, such as White's (1963) competence notion and Haan's (1977) coping mode of ego functioning. All these conceptions deal with positive, healthy, constructive, rational, and playful aspects of personality functioning, rather than with mere psychopathological aspects or their absence.

From a formal point of view, it is obvious that ego strength is a multifaceted or multidimensional concept and is similar in this respect to intelligence. Both ego strength and intelligence encompass whole arrays of interrelated abilities or functions, and both allow hypotheses and construct models referring to their nature, basic composition, and structure. Many of the methodological and conceptual considerations pertaining to intelligence may likewise be relevant when one is trying to deal systematically with ego strength.

Elaboration on Critical Points

What is clearly implied by theoreticians, clinicians, and researchers is the need for a useful ego model. Such a comprehensive model could provide new impetus toward developing better assessment procedures of ego strength which would have utility both in clinical and research practice.

The crucial problem in the past seems to have been that of enumerating an exhaustive list of discrete ego functions, which could then be assessed to compose a global score of their efficiency or adequacy. The outcome of every such attempt seemed to be a quite haphazard collection of functions, without any reference to their interrelatedness or to their underlying structure.

Another principal issue regards the organization and hierarchical structure of ego functions. According to theory, the ego, in addition to its specific functions, exerts a regulating and organizing process, which acts on all other ego functions in order to harmonize their simultaneous operation (in the light of adaptive goals). Assessment procedures, however, have not taken this important consideration into account. The synthetic function is treated as just one additional function among others, so that its significant uniqueness (which implies a certain hierarchy of ego functions and, hence, a specifiable organization) is disregarded.

Personal Views and Recommendations

The potential usefulness of the ego strength concept and its practical application are clearly limited by the disadvantages displayed by all available assessment procedures.

This inefficiency may be, in part, attributed to an inclination toward utilizing, through modification or specialized scoring systems, well-established psychodiagnostic instruments, without referring seriously to what is implied by theoretical considerations. One course to improve the state of affairs would require, therefore, a better convergence between theoretical notions and the way in which available procedures are applied. Another course of improvement is a concurrent development of theoretical models of ego functioning and concomitant assessment procedures. What is needed is a comprehensive ego functions taxonomy that will resemble Guilford's (1967) systematic attempt to encompass the cognitive domain (intelligence) by means of a multifaceted model, rather than Wechsler's (1958) approach (which assembles a bunch of vaguely defined abilities to operationally define intelligence). Haan's (1977) ego model comes closer to the ideal than any former attempt, and it may eventually serve as a point of departure for further developments.

Application to Particular Variables

The concept of ego strength may be applicable to personality assessment for a wide range of populations varying in age, sex, education, socioeconomic background, vocational background, and ethnic and racial background. Whenever an ego, functioning even to a minimal degree, may be attributed to the person under consideration, the term *ego strength* may be relevant. The application of the term to persons afflicted by a variety of psychopathological conditions is of special pertinence. Applying the term *ego strength* enables the clinician to assess globally a patient's state of mental health and well-being and to differentiate relatively intact capacities from functions affected by the psychopathological condition. This differential appraisal of ego functions may enable the clinician to suggest a rational and sound therapeutic or rehabilitative program. Despite the wide-ranging theoretical applicability of the term, however, the actual appraising of ego strength may be limited by the nature of the assessment devices and their own applicability to the various aforementioned populations. Thus, the use of Barron's Es scale may be limited in its application to the same extent as the MMPI, and the application of the RPRS must be restricted to those populations to which the Rorschach can be administered and scored. One could of course use assessment methods such as clinical interview and careful observation, methods which are applicable to practically anyone.

The main purpose that the term *ego strength* may serve is the appraisal of a person's suitability for various assigned treatments. It is assumed that vulnerability or susceptibility of patients to certain types of psychotherapy is determined by those personality characteristics comprising ego strength. The issue of pretreatment definition of therapeutic goals and rational planning and assignment of patients to appropriate therapeutic techniques and therapists should be stressed during training and certification procedures. Inappropriate assignment to a therapeutic procedure and the subsequent misfortunes may, of course, have ethical as well as legal implications. In this regard, appropriate assessment of ego strength may be a useful safeguard.

References

Arlow, J. A., and Brenner, C. *Psychoanalytic Concepts and the Structural Theory.* New York: International Universities Press, 1964.

Barron, F. "An Ego Strength Scale Which Predicts Response to Psychotherapy." *Journal of Consulting Psychology,* 1953, *17,* 327-333.

Bellak, L. *The Broad Scope of Psychoanalysis.* New York: Grune & Stratton, 1967.

Bellak, L., Hurvich, M., and Gediman, H. K. *Ego Functions in Schizophrenics, Neurotics, and Normals.* New York: Wiley, 1973.

Beres, D. "Ego Deviation and the Concept of Schizophrenia." *Psychoanalytic Study of the Child,* 1956, *11,* 164-235.

Cattell, R. B. *Personality and Motivation.* New York: World, 1957.

Cattell, R. B., Eber, H. W., and Tatsuoku, M. M. *Handbook for the Sixteen Personality Factor Questionnaire.* Champaign, Ill.: Institute for Personality and Ability Testing, 1970.

Dahlstrom, W. G., Welsh, G. S., and Dahlstrom, L. E. *An MMPI Handbook.* Vol. 2. Minneapolis: University of Minnesota Press, 1975.

Endicott, N. A., and Endicott, J. "Prediction of Improvement in Treated and Untreated Patients Using the Rorschach Prognostic Rating Scale." *Journal of Consulting Psychology,* 1964, *28,* 342-348.

Fenichel, O. "Ego Strength and Ego Weakness" [1938]. In D. Rapaport and H. Fenichel (Eds.), *The Collected Papers of Otto Fenichel.* New York: Norton, 1954.

Frank, G. H. "A Review of Research with Measures of Ego Strength Derived from the MMPI and the Rorschach." *Journal of General Psychology,* 1967, *77,* 163-206.

Freud, S. *The Ego and the Id* [1923]. In *Standard Edition of the Complete Psychological Works of Sigmund Freud.* Vol. 19. London: Hogarth Press, 1961.

Freud, S. *Inhibitions, Symptoms and Anxiety* [1926]. In *Standard Edition.* Vol. 20. London: Hogarth Press, 1959.

Freud, S. *New Introductory Lectures on Psychoanalysis* [1933]. In *Standard Edition.* Vol. 22. London: Hogarth Press, 1964.

Freud, S. *An Outline of Psychoanalysis* [1940]. In *Standard Edition.* Vol. 23. London: Hogarth Press, 1964.

Garwood, J. "A Guide to Research on the Rorschach Prognostic Rating Scale." *Journal of Personality Assessment,* 1977, *41,* 117-119.

Grinker, R. R., Werble, B., and Drye, R. C. *The Borderline Syndrome.* New York: Basic Books, 1968.

Guilford, J. P. *The Nature of Human Intelligence.* New York: McGraw-Hill, 1967.

Haan, N. *Coping and Defending.* New York: Academic Press, 1977.

Hartmann, H. *Ego Psychology and the Problem of Adaptation* [1939]. New York: International Universities Press, 1958.

Herron, W. G., Guido, S. M., and Kantor, R. E. "Relationship Among Ego Strength Measures." *Journal of Clinical Psychology,* 1965, *21,* 403-404.

Karush, A., and others. "The Evaluation of Ego Strength. I: A Profile of Adaptive Balance." *Journal of Nervous and Mental Disease,* 1964, *139,* 236-253.

Kirkner, F. J., Wisham, W. W., and Giedet, F. H. "A Report on the Validity of the Rorschach Prognostic Rating Scale." *Journal of Projective Techniques,* 1953, *17,* 465-470.

Klopfer, B., and others. "Introduction: The Development of a Prognostic Rating Scale." *Journal of Projective Techniques,* 1951, *15,* 421.

Klopfer, B., and others. *Developments in the Rorschach Technique.* Vol. 1. New York: Harcourt Brace Jovanovich, 1954.

Last, U., and Weiss, A. A. "Evaluation of Ego Strength Based on Certain Rorschach Variables." *Journal of Personality Assessment,* 1976, *40,* 57-66.

Nunberg, H. "Ego Strength and Ego Weakness" [1938]. In *The Practice and Theory of Psychoanalysis.* Vol. 1. New York: International Universities Press, 1960.

Pascal, G. R., and Sutell, B. J. *The Bender Gestalt Test.* New York: Grune & Stratton, 1951.

Seidel, C. "The Relationship Between Klopfer's Rorschach Prognostic Rating Scale and Phillips' Case History Rating Scale." *Journal of Consulting Psychology*, 1960, *24*, 46-49.

Sheehan, J., and others. "A Validity Study of the Rorschach Prognostic Rating Scale." *Journal of Projective Techniques*, 1954, *18*, 233-239.

Stein, K. B., and Chu, C. L. "Dimensionaliy of Barron's Ego Strength Scale." *Journal of Consulting Psychology*, 1967, *31*, 153-161.

Wechsler, D. *The Measurement and Appraisal of Adult Intelligence.* Baltimore: Williams and Wilkins, 1958.

Werts, C. E. "Multi-Dimensional Analysis of Psychological Constructs." Unpublished doctoral dissertation, University of Minnesota, Minneapolis, 1960.

White, R. W. "Ego and Reality in Psychoanalytic Theory." *Psychological Issues,* 1963, *3* (3, entire issue).

25

Stephen H. Getsinger

Ego Delay

Ego delay is the process by which the psychic apparatus interposes a temporal duration in psychophysiological functioning between stimulation of the organism by internal or external forces and motor responses initiated for the purpose of adaptation and drive reduction. From a strictly physiological viewpoint, growing levels of tissue need (drive) create increasing levels of neural excitation and tension for the organism. From a topographical viewpoint, this process remains beyond awareness (unconscious) until the tension reaches a critical threshold. At this point, a conscious image is formed by the ego of an object satisfying the particular issue need.

From a structural viewpoint, the id is the unconscious reservoir of drive seeking immediate gratification of need and operating via the primary process and pleasure principle. In contradistinction to the id, the ego (as the repository of consciousness) contains the psychic representation of the satisfying object. By its various executive functions, the ego mobilizes the organism to achieve gratification and discharge of energy via secondary process and the reality principle. Ego delay is, thus, the temporal duration during which the executive dimension of the psyche mobilizes its resources and functions in order to

Note: Opinions expressed in this chapter are those of the author and not necessarily those of the Veterans Administration.

act on reality in such a way that drive and tension can be safely reduced and psychophysiological equilibrium restored.

Background and Current Status

The ego delay concept is most directly attributed to Freud (1933), but philosophical roots for the concept can be found in Descartes, who developed a dualistic notion of the mind's relationship to the body, with a strong emphasis on cognition as the cornerstone of human existence; Kant, who specified a priori functions of the mind independent of the external world; Spinoza, who developed a strictly deterministic view of the psyche; and Newton, who expanded determinism to include the entire universe in terms of the principle of the conservation of energy. Even more importantly, nineteenth-century scientific discoveries and notions preceded and stimulated Freud's thinking. These include Charles Bell's distinction between motor and sensory neurons; Johannes Müller's development of a model of specific energies of sensory neurons and the concepts of reaction and conduction times; Gustav Fechner's construction of a bridge between physical and mental activity through the employment of Weber's Law; Hermann von Helmholtz's theories of the speed of neural activity and his conception of the human organism as an energy system; and Julius Robert Mayer's application of the conservation of energy principle to biology.

The construct of ego delay can be traced through each of Freud's unfolding models of the psyche. The construct reached its most articulate form, however, in his structural model (Freud, 1911, 1915a, 1915b, 1933). It is here that he postulated the constructs of the id, the ego, and the superego as the psychic determinants of organismic functioning. The construct of the ego became Freud's answer to the following questions: What keeps the unconscious from becoming conscious and serves as the organ of attention, memory, judgment, and defense? What forms the image of conscious thought as it moderates between instinctual demand and environmental reality? What delays the discharge of instinctual drive and creates the concepts of past, present, and future? It is the ego—the executor of the psyche. Freud moved in his theoretical development from a topographical model, through genetic and dynamic models, to a structural approach, where the ego became a prime focus in theory building and therapy.

Post-Freudians, with the exception of Jung, have been ego psychologists. Refinements in psychoanalysis came in their articulation of the structural model of the ego, including means and dynamics by which it implements the imperative of delay in psychic functioning. Fenichel (1945) defined the neurotic as a person suffering from an undersupply or an oversupply of impulse control. The neurotic is unable to tolerate rising psychic tensions and escapes these through denial, narcotization, dependence, and depression. Acting out in neurosis is a failure in the ego delay mechanism when past and present are inaccurately differentiated. From this temporal confusion, an impulse neurosis may develop characterized by restlessness and hyperactivity. Hartmann (1939, 1939-1959) saw ego delay as a process freeing energy from primitive drives and channeling it into various psychic activities. The ego adapts to reality to the extent that it effects creative detours between stimulation and response. Ego strength includes the capacity for planning, thereby necessitating a delay process. Memory is another ego-delaying mechanism leading to potential adaptation.

Anna Freud (1966) suggested that anxiety may serve as a trigger for the ego-delaying mechanisms; she theorized that the various defenses protect the ego from effects of impulsivity and hyperactivity. Erikson (1968) traced the delay function through its social transformations and linked the genetic model of Freud to particular developmental crises. In Erikson's view, regression is the result of the loss of the ego's capacity to maintain an adaptive temporal perspective and expectation. French (1970) focused on this expectative function of the ego as essentially a creative act of delay, in which the organism maintains hope. For him, mental health is related to the amount of psychic tension the organism can tolerate without disintegration. Parsons (1964) theorized that ego delay is important as a social reality and is linked to systemic concerns of pattern maintenance, adaptation, tension reduction, regulation, integration, and goal attainment. The most comprehensive review of the ego delay construct—from both qualitative and quantitative vantage points— was done by David Rapaport (1945-46; see also J. Rapaport, 1967); he was also the first psychologist to explore the construct psychometrically.

Development of the delay construct was not confined to psychoanalytic writers and theorists. Wundt (1874) linked physiological and psychological functioning and includes impulses with feelings and ideas as the three elements of consciousness. Pavlov (1928) differentiated both external and internal inhibition in terms of the conditioned reflex. He studied external inhibition, but he did not theorize about the real nature of internal inhibition. McDougall (1923) included the concepts of energy discharge and transformation in his model of social psychology. Although Tolman (1932) did not speak of the ego directly, he differentiated reflexive from docile (learned) behavior and talked about goal directedness, purposiveness, expectations, and memory—concepts presupposing a temporal duration between stimulation and response. Goldstein (1940) described abstract behavior as delayed and concrete behavior as impulsive and disorganized. Köhler (1947) conceived of the psyche as an energy system, compared brain mechanisms to electric circuits, and postulated structures through which delay is created and terminated by processes of equilibrium and closure. His work formed the basis for Lewin's (1951) energy model, with its concepts of tension, disequilibrium, need, and force. Hull (1952) included concepts of drive, intensity, inhibitory potential, negative drive, and conditioned inhibition in his brand of organismic behaviorism. Piaget (1969) described less mature behavior as impulsive, immediate, and lacking the capacity of reversibility—all indicating a lack of delay capacity between stimulation and response. Eysenck (1965) developed a personality typology based on psychophysiological studies in which the capacity to delay motoric discharge is basic to the model. His "extravert" craves stimulation and excitement, takes high risks, and is generally impulsive. His "introvert" is reserved, controlled, and retiring (taking many looks before leaping).

Critical Discussion

General Areas of Concern

As a dynamic construct, the ego delay process can be conceptualized as operating along a continuum typified by polar points labeled action versus thought. Although there are no pure types, it is useful thinking dialectically to contrast two ideal (stereotypic) types characterized by the relative activation or inactivation of the delay mechanism by drawing on the findings and concepts of many authors, especially Eysenck (1965).

The prototype of low ego delay (LED) is characterized by little tendency toward inhibition between stimulation and response. To the extent that intelligence includes the capacity for reflection, analysis, and planned action, this type will obtain lower aptitude and intelligence test scores (especially where the ability to manipulate abstract symbols is concerned). In tasks emphasizing high levels of motor skills (especially precision motor control), the LED type will perform poorly. EEG readings may appear unreliable, indicating (at times) pathologically low or high levels of cortical arousal.

Behaviorally, the LED type is impulsive, hyperactive, reckless, and aggressive. Because of erratic psychophysiological rhythms, the biological clock is frequently accelerated. Internal time goes much faster than objective time, and there is a tendency toward boredom. Time seems to pass very slowly; once it has passed, however, it seems (subjectively) shorter than it was in reality. The past and present appear to merge with the future into timelessness and to remain undifferentiated in any clear way. Since the internal clock moves swiftly, the future is far distant, and the LED type appears unwilling to postpone the gratification of needs to the future.

Since creative expectation and planning are benchmarks of educational processes, the LED type may do poorly in school or on the job (unless it is one in which energy output in short durations is more important than accuracy over the long run). Perceptually, there may be a strong tendency toward closure, where relevant perceptual stimuli are often unattended to because they do not appear important at first look. A strong probability exists for the discharge of drive through physical means. Much time is spent in pursuing sexual and aggressive drives. Rather than changing the self, the LED type will leap to change the environment. These attempts may be quite successful, because of the strong energy thrust behind them; but they may sometimes be ineffective, because of a lack of selective attention or the capacity to focus and achieve a high level of ego organization. As tension mounts and boredom increases, the LED type may be chronically understimulated and may spend a good deal of time livening up the environment by seeking new thrills.

Although primarily directed toward the environment (extraversive), the LED type frequently conditions poorly and may appear unable to learn from experience. Due to a chronic state of understimulation, stimulating drugs may intensity perceptions, thereby allowing the processing of more relevant information and, thus, lengthening ego delay. Depressants lower ego delay even further and may lead to the acting out of impulses. A low level of cortical excitation is complemented by a high level of cortical inhibition and low levels of persistence and endurance. Although the LED types are more tolerant of pain, they are especially intolerant of sensory deprivation. The LED type is particularly susceptible to mania and sociopathy and may commit highly aggressive and violent acts.

At the other end of the continuum is the high ego delay type (HED). This type is characterized by a highly introversive tendency relevant to the handling of impulses. Oriented toward the cognitive (as contrasted with the affective) realm, the HED type is highly controlled and prefers to avoid intense levels of stimulation. Since this type is more sensitive to environmental press, persons in this category condition more swiftly and appear less subject to extinction. Capable of a lengthened attention span (closely binding psychic energy), the HED type is less susceptible to boredom and generates reactive inhibition slowly and dissipates it more quickly. The HED type shows more infrequent oscillations in autonomic nervous system activity. The use of stimulating drugs with this type lowers ego delay. The HED type exhibits a chronically high level of cortical activity with low levels of cortical inhibition.

Since the HED type is capable of sustained attention to the point of vigilance, the persons aligned with HED process more information and seem to tolerate sensory deprivation well, although their pain tolerance is low. Psychopathological reactions seen in this type include obsessions, phobias, ruminative anxiety, and depression. Since the biological clock moves slower than the objective clock, the HED type experiences time as passing quickly but, from a subjective viewpoint, perceives time durations as longer than they really were (since more information than the LED type was processed by this type during the period).

As far as intelligence includes the ability to manipulate higher-level abstractions cortically, the HED type is more intelligent than the LED type. This characteristic is also revealed in a greater tendency to anticipate and plan for future events and an extended future perspective. However, this type shows a tendency to have experiences when the past, present, and future are meaningfully integrated. The HED type is more apt to perceive the self as the locus of control, probably because of the greater resources available to this type for modifying both the self and the environment. Occupationally, the HED type functions most effectively in situations where sustained effort is more important than exuberance and where effective planning is a necessity.

Researchers have reported the following specific findings concerning the ego delay mechanism:

1. The ego delay mechanism appears to have a psychophysiological basis (Cahoon, 1969; Hoagland, 1933; Kappers, 1930; Mawson, 1977).

2. This psychophysiological basis constitutes a biological clock, which orders physiological behavior and psychological processes (National Institute for Mental Health, 1970; Thor, 1962).

3. The ego delay mechanism is particularly important in cognitive functioning (for example, in attention, concentration, abstract reasoning, and planning). (See Davids, 1969; Geiwitz, 1965; Getsinger, 1977, in press a and b; Levine and others, 1959; Spivack, Levine, and Sprigle, 1959; Spreen, 1963.)

4. The ego delay construct relates in anticipated directions to other more general personality constructs: introversion/extraversion (Buchwald and Blatt, 1974; Spreen, 1963; Veach and Touhey, 1971); religious belief/disbelief (Brown, 1965); locus of control (Friel, 1969; Shybut, 1970); retentive personality traits (Campos, 1966); vocational development (Getsinger, 1977; Holtzman, Swartz, and Thorpe, 1971); sensation seeking (Zuckerman, 1971; Zuckerman and others, 1972); psychopathology (Barabasz, 1970; Barndt and Johnson, 1955; Cappella, Gentile, and Juliano, 1977; Davids, 1969; Densen, 1977; Douglas, 1972; Getsinger, 1975, 1976; Goldstone and Goldfarb, 1962; Johnson and Petzel, 1971; Robinson, 1971; Ross, 1976; Rychlak, 1972; Stern, 1977).

Comparative Philosophies and Theories

Concern with the actual assessment of the ego delay concept is long standing. As reported in Judges 7, Gideon (in anticipating a battle between his Israelites and the Midianites) led his troops down to the river to drink. Those soldiers who scooped water into their hands and remained in a vigilant status (HED) were selected to do battle, while those who lay down to drink directly from the water (LED) were not selected to do battle. Following this line of assessment, various unobtrusive measures can give an indication of ego delay processes. Bellak, Hurvich, and Gediman (1973) suggest that assessment of the following behaviors via interview or observation can provide an index of ego delay: (1) drive for physical activity, (2) levels of emotionality and excitability, (3) extent of mood shifts, (4) level of rebelliousness, (5) level of impatience, (6) tolerance of frustration, (7) tolerance for anxiety, (8) level of aggressiveness, (9) accident proneness, and (10) tolerance for homicidal and suicidal impulses.

Similar information can be deduced from content analyses of stories produced in the administration of the Thematic Apperception Test (TAT) (Allison, Blatt, and Zimet, 1968). Since examinees are instructed to respond to the TAT cards by producing stories with past, present, and future orientations, another indication of ego delay is obtained through analyses of productions in terms of temporal orientation (Fisher and Fisher, 1953; Lipgar, 1969). Persons who produce stories with extended future orientations (HED) can be differentiated from persons whose stories reveal that they live in an eternal present characterized by swift rise and discharge of drive energies (LED).

Another projective technique used in the assessment of ego delay is the Rorschach. Beck (1947, 1952) suggests that one indicator of ego strength obtainable from Rorschach productions is the *F+* response. Persons who produce responses with clearly differentiated form have the capacity to (1) center attention, (2) produce clear percepts, (3) form clearly demarcated mental images, (4) link forms from the past with present stimuli, and (5) select clearly from relevant memory images. A further measure of ego delay capacity available from Rorschach data is the *Erlebnistypus* score, formed by the ratio of human movement to color responses. Individuals showing a high ratio of *M* to *C* are conceptualized as having an introversive as contrasted with extraversive tendency. This delay of closure (Schachtel, 1966) is indicative of the HED type. Research evidence on this score tends to support these theoretical formulations, especially the LED type's tendency to have a different temporal orientation from that of the HED type (Barocas, 1971; Buchwald and Blatt, 1974).

Standardized objective test procedures of a self-report nature provide a plethora of techniques for the assessment of the ego delay construct. The Minnesota Multiphasic Personality Inventory (MMPI) has several scales which when viewed in profile purport to differentiate impulsive (LED) from normal individuals. Elevations on scales 4 (Psychopathic Deviate) and 9 (Hypomania) when in conjunction above *T* scores of 70 indicate a behavioral picture of emotional instability, impulsivity, low social conformity, and hyperactivity. These are all characteristics of the LED type. See Gilberstadt and Duker (1965) for a full description of this profile. Elevations on these scales within normal limits (*T* scores of 50 to 70) still suggest a healthy tendency toward motoric discharge and less inhibition of need. Persons demonstrating this profile are characterized as adventurous, verbal, active, frank, and energetic (Dahlstrom, Welsh, and Dahlstrom, 1960).

Eysenck's Personality Inventory measures extraversive/introversive tendency via self-report and thereby taps the ego delay concept. Individuals scoring high in extraversive tendency endorse items suggesting impulsivity (for example, craving for excitement, taking dares, shouting at people, short attention spans, and high social needs); these are signs of an LED type (Edmunds, 1977; Howarth, 1976). Research suggests that this extraversive or LED tendency may relate to hasty decision making, sensation seeking, low frustration tolerance, and impulsive buying (Plomin, 1976).

Jackson's (1976) Personality Inventory contains a risk-taking scale that taps the ego delay domain with similar items, and Rosenzweig's Picture Frustration Test (Rosenzweig and Rosenzweig, 1976) provides another projective device for measuring the lower frustration component of LED. Holland's Vocational Preference Inventory allows for the assessment of self-control tendency via preference for risky or dangerous occupations when contrasted with relatively safe ones (Holland, 1965, 1966). Using a similar theoretical rationale, Kunce (1967) developed a measure of accident proneness (LED), using scores obtained from the Strong Vocational Interest Blank. Subjects scoring much higher on the Aviator than the Banker scale were found to have a higher than average accident rate. Scales measuring sensation seeking (Zuckerman, 1971; Zuckerman and others, 1972) and risky decision making (Plax and Rosenfeld, 1976) also tap the ego delay domain.

An intriguing approach to the delay construct is through the techniques of time estimation. Two frequently used techniques (production and verbal estimation) have been found to be negatively correlated (McConchie and Rutschmann, 1971). When the method of production is used, subjects are asked to produce a specified interval of time (such as a thirty-second interval) by starting and stopping a clock. Persons who reliably "jump the gun," stopping the clock short of the interval, produce intervals of time less than the standard and are conceptualized as LED; conversely, subjects who produce intervals longer than the standard are conceptualized as HED. When the method of verbal estimation is used, subjects simply tell the examiner how much time they believe has elapsed in a specified standard interval. Subjects who underestimate in this condition are conceptualized as having slower internal clocks and HED; conversely, subjects who overestimate are conceptualized as having faster internal clocks and LED.

Elaboration on Critical Points

Since most of the techniques just described are well reviewed in the references provided, this elaboration will be restricted to the temporal estimation techniques, which are not well reviewed elsewhere. Research results with temporal measures of ego delay have produced some construct validity for these techniques. For example, Spivack, Levine, and Sprigle (1959) used the method of production and found IQ scores positively correlated with temporal scores (HED). Spreen (1963) found production delay scores positively correlated with IQ and verbal delay scores positively correlated with introversion scores. Baer, Wukasch, and Goldstone (1963) found production delay scores positively correlated with higher levels of aspiration. Brown (1965) found evidence linking time estimates and religious belief. Geiwitz (1965) linked time estimates with a tendency toward extended future perspective. Rychlak (1972) found that anxiety tends to bind persons to the immediate present, shortening future perspective and possibly thereby lowering ego delay capacity. However, Holtzman, Swartz, and Thorpe (1971) found inaccuracy in time estimation negatively correlated with anxiety—perhaps because anxiety makes one more aware of time's passage. Additionally, they found ego delay negatively correlated with human and popular responses to Holtzman Inkblots; in this context, this finding may mean that HED types form more abstract and uncommon responses to objective stimuli.

Getsinger (1976) used the production method for assessment of ego delay and found that sociopaths obtained significantly lower ego delay scores than more self-actualizing subjects did. Among patients referred for vocational rehabilitation procedures, those with higher ego delay tendencies evidenced higher tested vocational aptitudes and were more successful occupationally than LED types (Getsinger, 1977). In further research, LED subjects were found to experience little differentiation among the time zones, a rejection of the present, and an overidentification with the past (Getsinger, 1973, 1975). Unpublished research shows ego delay negatively correlated with chronicity and strong dominance of the past time mode, and positively correlated with future dominance and long-term adjustment following psychiatric hospitalization (Getsinger and Leon, 1979). These findings tend to support the construct validity of temporal estimates as measuring some aspect of the ego delay process.

Freud insisted that the core structure of psychic processes is rooted in physiological mechanisms. Thus, one would expect measures of ego delay capacity to be related to psychophysiological measures. Hoagland (1933) found that the subjective sense of the speed of time varies directly with body temperature, and he concluded that this is evidence for a biological clock. Although this construct has been criticized by some (Ornstein, 1969), the evidence linking temporal phenomena to psychophysiological processes appears strong (Cahoon, 1969; National Institute for Mental Health, 1970; Thor, 1962).

Personal Views and Recommendations

Ego delay as a metapsychological construct should be assessed via a multitechnical approach. From the point of view of the diagnostician, available physiological measures, a careful clinical interview, selected projective test data, self-report inventories, cognitive measures, and time estimates should be considered. Where the paths of evidence tend to converge, therein lies the highest probability for accurate diagnostic judgment. For example, a recent examinee produced a history replete with frequent moves around the country, abuse of drugs, and brushes with the law (because of fighting in bars). Psychophysiological measures were abnormal, with a disturbed sleep rhythm pattern. MMPI findings revealed a classic 4-9 profile (elevated Psychopathic Deviate and Hypomania scales). TAT stories were brief and oriented primarily toward the present. Content analyses revealed poor control of sexual and aggressive drives. The patient's behavior during the interview was restless and revealed a short attention span. When he was asked to produce a thirty-second interval, on four consecutive trials his longest interval was only six seconds. There was little doubt that this patient's behavior was more like the LED than the HED type. Extreme care, however, should be given in making clinical judgments based on only one measure or on one assessment technique. It should be remembered that ego delay is a metatheoretical construct and is useful descriptively—but does not "exist" in reality apart from its behavioral ad psychophysiological bases.

Application to Particular Variables

This section will be restricted to the assessment of ego delay via the techniques of time estimation. Research in the area of age and ego delay indicates that children and aged persons show a tendency toward LED (Bain, 1971; Bell, 1972; Crawford and Thor, 1967; Davids, 1969; Lynch, 1968). The technique should not be used with persons who are too young to comprehend the instructions. Evidence on sexual differences indicates that there may be important differences between males and females in time-related tasks. Males and females appear to differ in their attitudes toward time and their ability to estimate time under differing conditions (Bell, 1972; Getsinger, 1973, 1974). This could affect the performance of males and females in situations in which time must be estimated, such as speeded testing. However, the effects of gender on ego delay are unclear at this time. Findings linking ego delay to obtained educational level are speculative, but unpublished research indicates a positive correlation between ego delay and the level of education subjects obtained (Hart, Getsinger, and Norman, 1978).

Research on socioeconomic levels indicates that social class may be a factor in delay, with persons from lower socioeconomic levels showing a tendency toward the LED pattern (Leshan, 1952). Other findings indicate that this tendency may be influenced by racial and/or political considerations (Lessing, 1971). In the area of vocational choice and development, Getsinger (1977) found ego delay scores positively correlated with vocational aptitude test scores and employment status following vocational rehabilitation procedures. Holland (1966) developed the hypothesis that vocational preference relates to personality factors such as ego delay, but there is minimal research supporting the notion that vocational or career choice is linked to the delay mechanism (Holtzman, Swartz, and Thorpe, 1971). As to racial considerations in ego delay assessment, there is minimal research in this area, with no clear findings. Similarly, no known studies have explored the relationship of ego delay to physical disability. However, research does link intellectual deficits with LED patterns (Getsinger, 1977; Levine and others, 1959; Spreen, 1963).

Studies of psychiatric patients indicate that organic disabilities modify temporal behaviors in expected directions. Specifically, schizophrenics (Densen, 1977; Dilling and Rabin, 1967; Johnson and Petzel, 1971), sociopaths and delinquents (Barabasz, 1970; Barndt and Johnson, 1955; Getsinger, 1976; Hare, 1970; Mawson, 1977; Mawson and Mawson, 1977), and children with learning disabilities (Cappella, Gentile, and Juliano, 1977; Douglas, 1972; Ross, 1976) all evidence LED patterns, perhaps because of organic deficits and abnormalities. Functional disorders have been hypothesized to relate to ego delay but have been infrequently researched. Although Stern (1977) indicates that narcissism may alter temporal behavior, this has not been researched. Hart, Getsinger, and Norman (1978) show ego delay scores positively correlated with the MMPI Hysteria scale scores among patients committed for psychiatric hospitalization, but this finding has not been interpreted. Campos (1966) found a positive correlation between ego delay and an anality scale (which makes sense from a psychoanalytic perspective). Davids (1969) found that emotionally disturbed children showed the LED pattern more than normals did. Getsinger and Leon (1979) found ego delay positively correlated with long-term adjustment following psychiatric hospitalization (which is consistent with the theoretical model described herein).

References

Allison, J., Blatt, S. J., and Zimet, C. N. *The Interpretation of Psychological Tests.* New York: Harper & Row, 1968.

Baer, P. E., Wukasch, D. C., and Goldstone, S. "Time Judgment and Level of Aspiration." *Perceptual and Motor Skills,* 1963, *16,* 648.

Bain, D. A. "Time Conception, Self-Concept and Responsibility in Seven and Ten Year Old Children of White Middle-Class Community." *Dissertation Abstracts,* 1971, *31,* 5835.

Barabasz, A. F. "Time Estimation and Temporal Orientation in Delinquents and Nondelinquents: A Re-examination." *Journal of General Psychology,* 1970, *82,* 265-267.

Barndt, R. J., and Johnson, D. M. "Time Orientation in Delinquents." *Journal of Abnormal and Social Psychology,* 1955, *51,* 343-345.

Barocas, H. A. "Temporal Orientation, Human Movement Responses and Time Estimation." *Journal of Personality Assessment,* 1971, *35,* 315-319.

Beck, S. J. *Rorschach's Test.* Vol. II: *A Variety of Personality Pictures.* New York: Grune & Stratton, 1947.

Beck, S. J. *Rorschach's Test.* Vol. III: *Advances in Interpretation.* New York: Grune & Stratton, 1952.

Bell, C. R. "Accurate Performance of a Time-Estimation Task in Relation to Sex, Age, and Personality Variables." *Perceptual and Motor Skills,* 1972, *35,* 175-178.

Bellak, L., Hurvich, M., and Gediman, H. K. *Ego Functions in Schizophrenics, Neurotics, and Normals.* New York: Wiley, 1973.

Brown, L. B. "Religious Belief and Judgment of Brief Duration." *Perceptual and Motor Skills,* 1965, *20,* 33-34.

Buchwald, C., and Blatt, S. J. "Personality and the Experience of Time." *Journal of Consulting and Clinical Psychology,* 1974, *42,* 639-644.

Cahoon, R. L. "Physiological Arousal and Time Estimation." *Perceptual and Motor Skills,* 1969, *28,* 259-268.

Campos, L. P. "Relationship Between Time Estimation and Retentive Personality Traits." *Perceptual and Motor Skills,* 1966, *23,* 59-62.

Cappella, B., Gentile, J. R., and Juliano, D. B. "Time Estimation by Hyperactive and Normal Children." *Perceptual and Motor Skills,* 1977, *44,* 789-790.

Crawford, M. J., and Thor, D. H. "Time Perception in Children in the Absence of External Synchronizers." *Acta Psychologica,* 1967, *26,* 182-188.

Dahlstrom, W. G., Welsh, G. S., and Dahlstrom, L. E. *An MMPI Handbook.* Vol. I: *Clinical Interpretation.* Minneapolis: University of Minnesota Press, 1960.

Davids, A. "Ego Functions in Disturbed and Normal Children: Aspiration, Inhibition, Time Estimation, and Delayed Gratification." *Journal of Consulting and Clinical Psychology,* 1969, *33,* 61-70.

Densen, M. "Time Perception and Schizophrenia." *Perceptual and Motor Skills,* 1977, *44,* 436-438.

Dilling, C. A., and Rabin, A. I. "Temporal Experience in Depressive States and Schizophrenia." *Journal of Consulting Psychology,* 1967, *31,* 604-608.

Douglas, V. I. "Stop, Look, and Listen: The Problem of Sustained Attention and Impulse Control in Hyperactive and Normal Children." *Canadian Journal of Behavior Science,* 1972, *4,* 259-281.

Edmunds, G. "Extraversion, Neuroticism and Different Aspects of Self-Reported Aggression." *Journal of Personality Assessment,* 1977, *41,* 66-70.

Erikson, E. *Identity, Youth and Crisis.* New York: Norton, 1968.

Eysenck, H. J. *Fact and Fiction in Psychology.* New York: Penguin Books, 1965.

Fenichel, O. *The Psychoanalytic Theory of Neurosis.* New York: Norton, 1945.

Fisher, S., and Fisher, R. L. "The Unconscious Conception of Parental Figures as a Factor Influencing Perception of Time." *Journal of Personality,* 1953, *21,* 496-505.

French, T. M. *Psychoanalytic Interpretations.* New York: Quadrangle Books, 1970.

Friel, C. M. "Cognitive Style and Temporal Behavior." *Dissertation Abstracts,* 1969, *29,* 4365.

Freud, A. *The Ego and the Mechanisms of Defense.* New York: International Universities Press, 1966.

Freud, S. "Formulations Regarding the Two Principles in Mental Functioning" [1911]. In *Collected Papers.* Vol. 4. New York: Basic Books, 1959.

Freud, S. "Repression" [1915a]. In *Collected Papers.* Vol. 4. New York: Basic Books, 1959.

Freud, S. "The Unconscious" [1915b]. In *Collected Papers.* Vol. 4. New York: Basic Books, 1959.

Freud, S. *The Complete Introductory Lectures on Psychoanalysis* [1933]. New York: Norton, 1966.

Geiwitz, P. J. "Relationship Between Future Time Perspective and Time Estimation." *Perceptual and Motor Skills,* 1965, *20,* 843-844.

Getsinger, S. H. "Ego Strength and Temporal Behavior." Unpublished doctoral dissertation, University of Missouri-Columbia, 1973.

Getsinger, S. H. "Temporal Estimation, Sex and Ego Strength." *Perceptual and Motor Skills,* 1974, *38,* 322.

Getsinger, S. H. "Temporal Relatedness: Personality and Behavioral Correlates." *Journal of Personality Assessment,* 1975, *39,* 405-408.

Getsinger, S. H. "Sociopathy, Self-Actualization and Time." *Journal of Personality Assessment,* 1976, *40,* 398-402.

Getsinger, S. H. "Ego-Delay and Vocational Behavior." *Journal of Personality Assessment,* 1977, *41,* 91-95.

Getsinger, S. H. "Dreaming, Religion and Health." *Journal of Religion and Health,* in press,a.

Getsinger, S. H. "Psychotherapy and the Fourth Dimension." In *Psychotherapy: Theory, Research and Practice,* in press,b.

Getsinger, S. H., and Leon, R. "Ego-Delay, Temporal Perspective and Post-Hospital Adjustment of Neuropsychiatric Patients." Unpublished manuscript, 1979.

Gilberstadt, H., and Duker, J. *A Handbook for Clinical and Actuarial MMPI Interpretation.* Philadelphia: Saunders, 1965.

Goldstein, K. *Human Nature in the Light of Psychopathology*. Cambridge, Mass.: Harvard University Press, 1940.

Goldstone, S., and Goldfarb, J. L. "Time Estimation and Psychopathology." *Perceptual and Motor Skills*, 1962, *15*, 28.

Hare, R. D. *Psychopathy: Theory and Research*. New York: Wiley, 1970.

Hart, R. R., Getsinger, S. H., and Norman, W. B. "Taped Hypnotic Time Distortion and Modification of Ego-Delay." Unpublished manuscript, 1978.

Hartmann, H. *Ego Psychology and the Problem of Adaptation* [1939]. New York: International Universities Press, 1958.

Hartmann, H. *Essays on Ego Psychology* [1939-1959]. New York: International Universities Press, 1964.

Hoagland, H. "The Physiological Control of Judgments of Duration: Evidence for a Chemical Clock." *Journal of General Psychology*, 1933, *9*, 267-287.

Holland, J. L. *Manual for the Vocational Preference Inventory*. Palo Alto, Calif.: Consulting Psychologists Press, 1965.

Holland, J. L. *The Psychology of Vocational Choice*. Waltham, Mass.: Ginn, 1966.

Holtzman, W. H., Swartz, J. D., and Thorpe, J. S. "Artists, Architects, and Engineers— Three Contrasting Modes of Visual Experience and Their Psychological Correlates." *Journal of Personality*, 1971, *39*, 432-449.

Howarth, E. "A Psychometric Investigation of Eysenck's Personality Inventory." *Journal of Personality Assessment*, 1976, *40*, 173-185.

Hull, C. L. *A Behavior System*. New Haven, Conn.: Yale University Press, 1952.

Jackson, D. N. *Manual for the Jackson Personality Inventory*. Goshen, N.Y.: Research Psychologists Press, 1976.

Johnson, J. E., and Petzel, T. P. "Temporal Orientation and Time Estimation of Chronic Schizophrenics." *Journal of Clinical Psychology*, 1971, *27*, 194-196.

Kappers, C. V. *The Evolution of the Nervous System in Convertebratae, Vertebratae and Man*. Utrecht: Bohn, 1930.

Köhler, W. *Gestalt Psychology*. New York: Liveright, 1947.

Kunce, J. T. "Vocational Interests and Accident Proneness." *Journal of Applied Psychology*, 1967, *51*, 223-225.

Leshan, L. "Time Orientation and Social Class." *Journal of Abnormal and Social Psychology*, 1952, *47*, 589-592.

Lessing, E. E. "Comparative Extension of Personal and Social Political Future Time Perspective." *Perceptual and Motor Skills*, 1971, *33*, 415-422.

Levine, M., and others. "Intelligence, and Measures of Inhibition and Time Sense." *Journal of Clinical Psychology*, 1959, *15*, 224-226.

Lewin, K. *Field Theory in Social Sciences*. New York: Harper & Row, 1951.

Lipgar, R. M. "Treatment of Time in the T.A.T." *Journal of Projective Techniques and Personality Assessment*, 1969, *33*, 219-229.

Lynch, D. J. "Future Time Perspective and Impulsivity in Old Age." *Dissertation Abstracts*, 1968, *28*, 4296-4297.

McConchie, R. D., and Rutschmann, J. "Human Time Estimation: On Differences Between Methods." *Perceptual and Motor Skills*, 1971, *32*, 319-336.

McDougall, W. *Outline of Psychology*. New York: Scribner's, 1923.

Mawson, A. R. "Hypertension, Blood Pressure Variability, and Juvenile Delinquency." *Southern Medical Journal*, 1977, *70*, 160-164.

Mawson, A. R., and Mawson, C. D. "Psychopathy and Arousal: A New Interpretation of the Psychophysiological Literature." *Biological Psychiatry*, 1977, *12*, 49-74.

National Institute for Mental Health. *Biological Rhythms in Psychiatry and Medicine.* Chevy Chase, Md.: National Clearinghouse for Mental Health Information, National Institute for Mental Health, 1970.

Ornstein, R. E. *On the Experience of Time.* New York: Penguin Books, 1969.

Parsons, T. *Social Structure and Personality.* New York: Free Press, 1964.

Pavlov, I. P. *Lectures on Conditioned Reflexes.* New York: International Universities Press, 1928.

Piaget, J. *The Child's Conception of Time.* New York: Ballantine, 1969.

Plax, T. G., and Rosenfeld, L. B. "Correlates of Risky-Decision Making." *Journal of Personality Assessment,* 1976, *40,* 413-418.

Plomin, R. "Extraversion: Sociability and Impulsivity." *Journal of Personality Assessment,* 1976, *40,* 24-30.

Rapaport, D. *Diagnostic Psychological Testing.* (2 vols.) Chicago: Year Book Medical Publishers, 1945-46.

Rapaport, J. (Ed.). *The Collected Papers of David Rapaport.* New York: Basic Books, 1967.

Robinson, C. L. "Future Time Perspective in Non-Incarcerated Juvenile Delinquents." *Dissertation Abstracts International,* 1971, *32,* 1225-1226.

Rosenzweig, S., and Rosenzweig, L. "Guide to Research on the Rosenzweig Picture Frustration (P-F) Study, 1934-1974." *Journal of Personality Assessment,* 1976, *40,* 599-606.

Ross, A. O. *Psychological Aspects of Learning Disabilities and Reading Disorders.* New York: McGraw-Hill, 1976.

Rychlak, J. F. "Manifest Anxiety as Reflecting Commitment to the Psychological Present at the Expense of Cognitive Futurity." *Journal of Consulting and Clinical Psychology,* 1972, *38,* 70-79.

Schachtel, E. G. *Experiential Foundations of Rorschach's Test.* New York: Basic Books, 1966.

Shybut, J. "Internal vs. External Control, Time Perspective and Delay of Gratification of High and Low Ego Strength Groups." *Journal of Clinical Psychology,* 1970, *26,* 430-431.

Spivack, G., Levine, M., and Sprigle, H. "Intelligence Test Performance and the Delay Function of the Ego." *Journal of Consulting Psychology,* 1959, *23,* 230-235.

Spreen, O. "The Position of Time Estimation in a Factor Analysis and Its Relation to Some Personality Variables." *Psychological Record,* 1963, *13,* 455-464.

Stern, M. E. "Narcissism and the Defiance of Time." In M. C. Nelson (Ed.), *The Narcissistic Condition.* New York: Human Sciences Press, 1977.

Thor, D. "Diurnal Variability in Time Estimation." *Perceptual and Motor Skills,* 1962, *15,* 451-454.

Tolman, E. C. *Purposive Behavior in Animals and Men.* New York: Appleton-Century-Crofts, 1932.

Veach, T. L., and Touhey, J. C. "Personality Correlates of Accurate Time Perception." *Perceptual and Motor Skills,* 1971, *33,* 765-766.

Wundt, W. *Principles of Physiological Psychology.* London: Macmillan, 1874.

Zuckerman, M. "Dimensions of Sensation-Seeking." *Journal of Consulting and Clinical Psychology,* 1971, *36,* 45-52.

Zuckerman, M., and others. "What Is the Sensation Seeker? Personality Trait and Experience Correlates of the Sensation-Seeking Scales." *Journal of Consulting and Clinical Psychology,* 1972, *39,* 308-321.

26

Roger V. Burton
William M. Casey

Moral Development

Moral concerns are distinguished from other concerns in that their resolution is considered essential to the maintenance of human relationships. Moral development, then, refers to those categories of human development that have a sense of compellingness or "oughtness" attached to them. The psychological study of this broad domain has focused on three principal aspects or dimensions: cognitions, emotions, and behaviors.

Moral reasoning refers to the cognitive processes involved in making decisions about abstract moral conflicts or dilemmas (see Chapter Twenty-Seven in this volume) and will be referred to here primarily in the context of its relationship to affect and behavior.

The second dimension of moral development, affect, refers to the emotions that one experiences before, during, or after moral thoughts or actions. Within this dimension, a distinction has been drawn between guilt (an unpleasant feeling experienced due to commission of a wrong or omission of a right) and shame (apprehension associated with possible discovery of one's misdeed by another).

Finally, and perhaps of greatest importance, moral behavior refers to overt moral conduct. This generally takes the form of altruism (voluntary commission of a prosocial act) or resistance to temptation (inhibition of deviant acts).

Though the term *moral development* may connote the concept of a unitary system, the dimensions listed above are both theoretically and empirically distinguishable. The relatively low degree of consistency within modes and the complex interactions across the modes indicate that the specific determinants of responses in each mode may be quite different.

Background and Current Status

As most students learn in introductory courses in philosophy, there are three basic positions taken in essays addressed to the development of a proper moral code in children: (1) the Rousseauian doctrine that human beings are innately good (if they are given room to grow and flourish, without being corrupted by modern civilization, they will eventually develop into morally mature adults); (2) the Christian-Freudian position that human beings, because of original sin, are innately corrupt (the task of life is to bring evil and destructive urges under rational control); and (3) the middle position of Locke and the empiricists that human beings are neither good nor evil but rather are born as "blank slates" (whatever they come to be is a direct result of what the world has made of them). Even in its origins, then, "morality" has been conceptualized in quite distinct ways.

The philosophical models described above produced comparably different orientations to the psychological study of moral development. They became represented in the three principal works on moral development in the present century. These writings parallel both the philosophical models and the three primary dimensions of morality discussed earlier.

Rousseau's notion that humans possess a positive potential for development is represented by another Genevan: Piaget's (1932) classic monograph on moral judgment in children. Although half of the work is addressed to the correspondence between compliance and conceptions of rules in marble games, the study is mainly known for what it found in the purely cognitive moral judgment area. Using material from clinical interviews, Piaget demonstrated that children pass through two broad stages in the development of their moral reasoning. The first stage is described as a "morality of constraint," in which the young child believes that rules are sacred and unchangeable, that the morality of an act is judged by its consequences, and that punishment automatically follows when one has deviated. In the second stage, the stage of "autonomous morality," the child recognizes that rules are arbitrary social agreements, that the morality of an act is more appropriately judged by intentions than by consequences, and that punishment may be independent of the morality of the behavior.

The belief that a human is innately corrupt became clearly represented in the writing of Freud (1923), who asserted that the conscience, or superego, is responsible for affective responses associated with moral conflicts. Though Freud described conscience as essentially unidimensional, evolving as a result of the identification process, he focused on feelings of guilt following deviations, rather than on other aspects of morality. Freud saw the development of the superego as the internalization of parental standards, since the parents administer punishments for deviations, and thus as essential for the survival of society. At the same time, he observed that an overly severe superego is responsible for many forms of psychopathology.

The concept that we enter this world as a "blank slate" has its psychological counterpart, or descendant, in learning theory, with its focus on the role of experience in the development of moral conduct. The classic study of resistance to temptation was conducted by Hartshorne and May (1928). Using deceptive behavior as an operational definition of dishonesty, these investigators devised thirty-three tests to measure cheating, lying, and stealing in children. Their data led them to conclude that honest behavior tends to be a function of specific situational constraints (the "doctrine of specificity") rather than being a transsituational personality trait. Furthermore, few systematic relationships could be found between honest conduct and verbal allegiance to honesty.

With moral development conceptualized and examined in this threefold manner, there followed over the succeeding half-century a series of attempts to both pursue and merge these disparate points of view. Representative of these attempts was the study by Sears, Maccoby, and Levin (1957), who proposed a learning theory reinterpretation of the psychoanalytic concept of identification. They emphasized, as had Freud, the importance of the early dependency relationship between the child and parent in the development of conscience. Examining a variety of dimensions of parent-child relationships, they found parental warmth and reinforcement of role modeling to be key factors in the internalization of parental standards. However, a serious problem existed concerning the lack of independence of the data sources, since information concerning both childrearing practices and child behavior came from interviews with the parents (Yarrow, Campbell, and Burton, 1968). In a later replication, Sears, Rau, and Alpert (1965) added behavioral measures and failed to support the concept of a unitary conscience, in which resistance to temptation and posttransgression guilt would be strongly related.

In the 1960s investigators continued to explore more directly the antecedents and the interrelationships of moral behaviors, thoughts, and actions. They examined both the experimental conditioning of anxiety and the facilitating role of cognitive mediators in this process and demonstrated that temporal and intensity parameters of punishment affect both posttransgression anxiety and resistance to temptation (Aronfreed, 1968; Parke, 1969; Solomon, Turner, and Lessac, 1968). High-intensity punishment administered prior to completing a proscribed act seemed to be most effective in promoting self-control. However, there was also some evidence that, when combined with a clear rationale, delayed punishment of low intensity may be most effective.

The work of Hoffman (1970) also demonstrates the direction that moral development research took in the 1960s. Hoffman has focused on parental discipline techniques as antecedents of children's morality. He has suggested that childrearing techniques may be separated into three categories: power assertion, love withdrawal, and induction. Hoffman and his colleagues have argued that power-assertive techniques, in which the parent capitalizes on his or her physical power or control over material resources, plays a consistently negative role in moral development. Love withdrawal, which produces anxiety around parental disapproval, has some positive effects, though primarily in encouraging an externalized morality, based on salient external supports. Hoffman maintains that inductive techniques, in which the parent provides reasons for requiring particular behaviors, is most conducive to an internalized morality.

Hoffman's (1976) efforts also illustrate a further step in the evolution of moral development research; namely, an increasing attention to altruism. Though Murphy (1937), decades ago, extensively investigated the roots of positive social responses in children, relatively little systematic investigation of prosocial behavior was conducted until the 1960s. Perhaps partially because of the powerful influence of Freud's view of humans as essentially egoistic, researchers had primarily addressed themselves to questions concerning inhibition of deviant behavior, rather than promotion of positive behavior. In the 1960s a large body of research began to grow, exploring the roots of altruism from both behavioral (Bryan and London, 1970) and cognitive-developmental (Lickona, 1974) perspectives.

A further illustration of another direction that contemporary research and theorizing has followed is found in the writing of Mischel and Mischel (1976) and Burton (1963, 1977). Mischel has formulated a cognitive social learning approach to morality that considers both competence and performance variables. While cognitions and beliefs are important "construction competencies," they interact with more direct determinants of performance, such as expected consequences and self-regulatory abilities. Burton, in a similar fashion, has suggested possible modes of interface between behavioral and cognitive-developmental approaches to research in morality. He and his collaborators have engaged in a program of research based on a social learning model that predicts that moral conduct is determined by transfer both from direct behavioral training in specific moral situations and from the conceptual moral labels learned during training (Burton, 1963). Instead of assessing situational variables for individual tests of moral conduct, these studies directly explore the antecedents of individual differences in the tendency to be consistent or inconsistent in moral conduct; that is, what leads to more or less of a trait of honesty. These studies indicate that the use of broadly applicable terms during training in moral conduct will increase children's consistency of moral behavior across situations (Burton, 1976b; Casey, 1978; Casey and Burton, 1978).

The extension of Piaget's work by Kohlberg (1964) and his colleagues in the last two decades (described in detail in Chapter Twenty-Seven of this volume) also should be mentioned. While research in the 1950s had concentrated on moral conduct and emotion, Kohlberg, with his emphasis on the development of moral reasoning styles, has significantly redirected the orientation of a whole field of psychological research.

The present status of the psychological study of moral development can be summarized in the following statements:

First, there is currently a growing concern about moral development among researchers and educators. This concern is evidenced by the recent publication of numerous books and journals that encompass a wide range of moral development issues (see DePalma and Foley, 1975; Graham, 1972; Lickona, 1976b; Mussen and Eisenberg-Berg, 1977; Wright, 1971; and the journals *Moral Education Forum* and *Journal of Moral Education*).

Second, the two facets of moral development currently receiving the greatest attention are prosocial behavior and moral reasoning. The reasons for this are not clear, though one underlying cause may be societal concern over indoctrination of arbitrarily proscribed sets of standards. Prosocial values seem to be more consensually accepted, while moral reasoning research and education strive to focus on the structure rather than the content of thought. In the educational domain, Kohlberg's theory of moral reasoning and the values clarification approach (Simon, Howe, and Kirschenbaum, 1972) are becoming increasingly popular. The Kohlberg orientation has a greater appeal to some educators because of its developmental foundation; the values clarification approach attempts to be more content free.

Third, while efforts in the past have been directed toward demonstrating the validity of theoretical viewpoints that have focused on particular dimensions of moral development, there has developed a movement toward integration of various perspectives and recognition of the complex interplay between the dimensions. For example, questions concerning the role of cognitive mediators in moral conduct, the relationship between empathy and altruism, and the dyadic interaction between child conduct and parental beliefs and behavior are being seriously addressed. In other words, the concept of a unitary "conscience" that is a direct consequence of a specific socialization procedure and that underlies a unidimensional morality is giving way to more complex questions, and ultimately to more complex explanations.

Critical Discussion

General Areas of Concern

In the area of moral development, the following issues may be of greatest importance to clinicians today: First, how can moral development be measured? That is, what are the measurement techniques available for assessing a person's morality and the antecedents of it? Second, what are the relationships between different aspects of moral development? That is, in making an assessment of one domain, how confident can one be that one has also obtained a measure of another domain? Third, what are appropriate goals for moral education programs? To the extent that goals are agreed on, how can they best be obtained? Fourth, what are the ethical issues that must be resolved in both research and therapeutic practice dealing with the moral domain?

Assessment Techniques. The following assessment techniques have been used in examining moral development: (1) Parent and child interviews of either a clinical or a highly structured nature have been extensively used in the past. In such an interview, the parents provide information concerning past and present socialization practices that they utilize, in addition to information concerning their child's behavior. The child may be asked about his or her behavior and/or moral knowledge or beliefs. The major difficulty, of course, with such interviews concerns the veridicality of the information obtained. Particularly if such reports touch on highly sensitive areas (and this is often true with moral issues), socially undesirable responses may be omitted. Furthermore, there is ample evidence (Yarrow, Campbell, and Burton, 1970) that retrospective accounts of childhood frequently demonstrate low validity. (2) Projective techniques have often been utilized by clinicians and researchers in order to assess thoughts and feelings, particularly guilt. Again, empirical evidence for the validity of such techniques is sparse. As Burton (1971) has pointed out, the use of fantasy confession in doll play to assess a child's conscience is based on the untested assumptions that fantasy confession is related to overt confession, that overt confession is a sign of guilt, and that guilt and resistance to temptation are related aspects of conscience. The evidence provides no support for this set of assumptions. (3) The prevailing method of assessing moral judgment stage in the United States is currently Kohlberg's structured moral judgment interview. Since this has been under constant revision and has not been published in a standardized format, it is unavailable and not useful to most clinicians. The Defining Issues Test, an objective instrument that measures moral reasoning comprehension rather than production, has recently become available (Rest and others, 1974). Because of the absence of validity studies to date, it has been used primarily for research rather than as a clinical instrument. The major weakness of the moral judgment scales for clinical use is the absence of any evidence that changes in moral orientation are accompanied by changes in moral actions. (4) In studies of value preference, the most popular and easily usable measure has been the Rokeach Value Survey, in which "instrumental" and "terminal" values are rank-ordered. Rokeach (1973) presents voluminous data concerning the reliability and validity of this scale. However, the validational measures of "behavior" tend to be very broad indices of value choices that are public (such as past participation in a civil rights group) and not situationally specific private moral conflicts (such as cheating on an examination or on income tax). Furthermore, when persons are questioned about their beliefs after moral actions have already been taken, a cognitive dissonance interpretation of the apparent consistency seems to fit the data very well (Burton, 1976b). (5) The most direct method of measuring moral development is to assess conduct. Traditional "resistance to temptation" measures have included both experimental situations, in which cheating, lying, and stealing may be covertly detected, and naturalistic observations of deviant or prosocial behavior, such as donations or sharing. Each of these techniques has its own problems. Situationally contrived tests may be artificial and not representative of real-life situations. Naturalistic observation can be obtrusive and extremely time consuming. Nevertheless, appropriately used behavior assessment has the distinct advantage of circumventing subjective inference and social desirability difficulties. (6) Finally, particularly in the study of antisocial forms of morality, school and court records, teacher ratings, and sociometric questionnaires may be utilized. The validity of such reports depends on the skill of the creator of the scale and the manner in which the data are obtained. To summarize this statement concerning measurement of moral development, few validated standardized tests exist. Consequently, researchers and clinicians are most often left to their own devices to create measures that they believe will best represent the facet of morality in which they are interested.

   Consistency of Dimensions. The concept of a "unidimensional conscience" receives little support from empirical research. The issue of consistency may be considered from both within and between dimensions. Burton's (1963) reanalysis of the Hartshorne and May (1928) data demonstrated that, though one may speak of a moderate trait of honesty, correlations between different measures of honesty vary greatly as a function of the physical or perceived similarity of temptation situations. In regard to affective responses, the use of projective stories and interviews following temptation situations may or may not produce consistency across alternative measures of guilt and anxiety reactions to temptations. A recent review of factors involved in the correspondence between words and deeds (Casey, 1977) indicates that the linkage between what one says and what one does is complex but at the same time can be studied directly rather than either assumed (thus ignoring much empirical evidence) or rejected (thus denying what is experienced by everyone many times daily). The magnitude of the relations appears to depend on how broadly based the categories are. Broad, general categories appear to be subject to response sets reflecting the respondent's implicit theory about appropriate reactions following a moral dilemma (Grinder and McMichael, 1963). The more refined and specific the response categories become, the less consistency is manifested across the response categories. An extensive study of the generality of moral judgment was carried out by Johnson (1962), who studied five dimensions posited by Piaget as involved in moral development: (1) immanent justice, (2) intentionality, (3) retribution as a basis for punishment, (4) efficacy of severe punishment, and (5) collective guilt versus individual responsibility. There was substantial agreement across items within each area. However, when the different dimensions were intercorrelated, the magnitudes of the correlations, though all positive, were greatly decreased and comparable to the intercorrelations produced by the honesty tests of Hartshorne and May (1928). In spite of the expectations that common intellectual underpinnings would produce consistency across the alternative measures, the evidence for unidimensionality is about the same as for behavioral tests. In his extension of Piaget's work on moral judgment, Kohlberg (1976) found that almost all individuals manifest more than 50 percent of responses at a single stage, with the remaining responses at adjacent stages. However, Rest (1976) has pointed out that rarely does a subject respond 100 percent at a single stage and that such factors as different test stimuli, manner of presentation of stories, and amount of irrelevant information may all contribute to within-subject inconsistency in moral reasoning. In one study (Rest and others, 1974)

Rest's Defining Issues Test correlated at the .68 level with Kohlberg's measure of moral stage for a group of subjects. Clearly, there is a need for both short-term test-retest reliability information on moral judgment measures and for longitudinal data that separate developmental changes from regression-toward-the-mean effects (Holstein, 1976).

Another type of question concerns the relationships between different dimensions of moral development. From a learning theory perspective, there is no necessary relationship between them (Burton, 1971; Burton, Maccoby, and Allinsmith, 1961). For example, guilt and resistance to temptation may be produced by distinct independent mechanisms. In general, projective measures of guilt have demonstrated little correspondence with measures of overt conduct. Likewise, confession of guilt fails to relate strongly to incidence of cheating, perhaps because most cheaters never confess their misdeed. The relationship of moral reasoning to moral conduct and guilt is also an ambiguous one (Burton, 1976a). Wright (1971) has pointed out that whether an individual resists temptation, feels guilt, or helps others is partly determined by how he or she cognitively construes the situation. However, he also adds that moral situations that we talk about are usually very different from those in which we face an actual moral challenge, when the pressures at work may be quite different.

Empirical studies of the relationship between moral judgment and guilt or conduct present a confusing picture. Haan, Smith, and Block (1968) found behavioral differences in social activism to be related to moral judgment maturity on Kohlberg's scale. Ruma and Mosher (1967) discovered that measured guilt related significantly to the first three Kohlberg stages. Kohlberg (1969) has reported a tendency for adults with a principled moral orientation to be less willing to shock a victim in a Milgram obedience experiment. However, attempts to replicate this finding have been unsuccessful (Podd, 1972). Kohlberg (1976) has argued that the relationship of the development of judgment to action is something to be studied and theoretically conceptualized but that this issue does not relate to the "validity" of moral judgment measures. Lickona (1976a) has also noted that interdimension consistency may exist from a subject's point of view, even though there appears to be an inconsistency to the observer. Nevertheless, if moral judgment is not related in some significant fashion to overt moral behavior, it may be of theoretical significance to the academician but is of little value to the clinician. Finally, the correlations between overt behavior and ratings by teachers or peers likewise are relatively low. Research findings suggest that subject variables like social class, grades, IQ, and general impulsivity tend to influence observers' ratings of moral behavior.

The low generality within modes and the complex interactions that exist across the dimensions of morality indicate that high correlations and consistent relationships are unlikely to occur. In making an assessment of a child or a group of children, clinicians would be unwarranted in assuming that a measurement of one dimension provides an approximate measure of another dimension.

Goals for Moral Education Programs. A National Conference for Planning for Moral/Citizenship Education met in Philadelphia in 1976 and established as a priority substantive issue a clear definition of "moral/citizenship." However, the operational definitions that emerged ranged from curbing impulses to making rational moral decisions. In a similar vein, Sanders and Wallace (1975), in a survey of teacher and parent opinions concerning moral education, found a wide range of opinion concerning values (if any) that should be learned. But despite this disagreement on one level, there is some consensus in our society on such values as honest behavior (Rokeach, 1973), mature decision making, personal responsibility for one's actions, and concern for others.

On the basis of the available evidence, some cautious statements can be made about how such goals can most effectively be achieved. Lickona (1976a) has summarized some of these methods in his discussion of what optimizes moral development. Punishment, particularly in combination with verbal mediators, seems to be effective in producing initial inhibitory skills necessary for self-restraint. Punishment used for moral training works best in a context of love. However, though a "morality of constraint" is necessary to some extent, especially if ethical conduct is placed in a developmental perspective (Burton, Maccoby, and Allinsmith, 1961), a further goal of moral education is to stimulate an appreciation of rules and principles at a higher level of abstraction. The goal of moral socialization is to produce an individual who abides by a code of prescribed conduct, not proscriptions. To achieve this goal, inductive techniques are probably more effective. A reasoning approach should be appropriate to a child's current cognitive level and should attempt to create a mild state of disequilibrium in the child. Lickona directly suggests that if such "cognitive conflict" is conducive to moral development, particularly moral reasoning development, then educators ought to deal head on with opposing viewpoints that provoke controversy. Discussion of "real-life" moral dilemmas might be conducive not only to stimulation of abstract moral reasoning but also to clarification of personal values and ultimately to more rational behavioral decisions. Finally, moral development of every sort is directly susceptible to the effects of modeling. This has been illustrated most clearly in research on prosocial behavior and succinctly captured by the title of Bryan's (1975) chapter on altruism in children: "You Will Be Well Advised to Watch What We Do Instead of What We Say."

Ethical Issues. Serious and complex ethical issues arise in the domain of moral development. Clinicians and educators constantly face the risk of committing injustices to individuals by labeling, making unwarranted influences about character, assuming origins of deviant behavior, and indoctrinating an arbitrary or subjective set of values. At the same time, they cannot ignore a real responsibility for providing their professional expertise in stimulating desirable moral development in the family, schools, and greater society.

Researchers have become increasingly attentive to the ethical responsibility they have for the protection of subjects, whether they are adults or children. The Watergate era has made the whole society aware of the possible abuses that can occur when the rights of individuals are disregarded. There exists a current trend to disparage psychological investigations of moral behavior through techniques that employ deception, one-way observation, and measurement of overt behavior. Perhaps an even greater ethical disaster would develop, however, if researchers simply reverted to the use of only questionnaires and the study of only socially desirable behaviors. If progress is to be made in our scientific understanding of moral development, it must be founded on a strong empirical data base that provides objective information about all the aspects of morality in which we are interested. It would be ethically irresponsible for clinicians, educators, or researchers to provide recommendations that go beyond such a data base.

Comparative Philosophies and Theories

Though Freudian theory has had a major historical impact on moral development theory and research, the two dominant theoretical approaches today are social learning theory and cognitive-developmental theory. The social learning approach, embodied in the work of Aronfreed, Burton, Hoffman, and Mischel, focuses on socialization antecedents of conduct and affect, the use of conditioning and modeling principles to explain development, theoretical independence of various dimensions of morality, and the modifiability of behavior. Cognitive-developmental approaches, like those of Piaget and Kohlberg, focus on structural aspects of reasoning processes, holistic change, and antecedents and correlates of moral judgment development. Each approach implicitly suggests appropriate goals and measures for progress in moral development, as described in previous sections.

Elaboration on Critical Points

Of theoretical interest to researchers and of practical concern to parents is the question "Can reliable moral conduct be learned solely through positive reinforcement?" Skinner avers that reliance on positive reinforcement alone will shape desirable moral conduct better than any combination of schedules involving punishment. Furthermore, clinical studies show that punitive training for conscience development can have deleterious effects that should be avoided. Minimizing and, when possible, eliminating punishment, therefore, seems humane and also often functionally desirable. Nevertheless, consideration of theory and all available evidence indicates that some affective arousal, even if very low in magnitude, is necessary for cognitive structure to exert directive power over overt behavior. Once a response to avoid fear arousal has been learned well, performance can occur very reliably even though only a trace of the original affect is now involved (Solomon and Wynne, 1954). This "anxiety conservation" seems especially likely when one considers the human capacity to employ verbal mediators to direct behavior. The calm, unemotional conduct of the older child or the adult, then, is often founded on avoidance of punishment earlier in the socialization history. It seems realistic, therefore, to view punishment as a necessary and inevitable aspect of limit setting in the socialization of children.

Personal Views and Recommendations

It is recommended that the assumption of correspondence between modification of value statements and modification of conduct, particularly in a clinical or institutional setting, be seen as unjustified. A current tendency to rely on moral judgment or value preference for the clinical appraisal of morality ignores the substantial empirical evidence regarding the discrepancy between words and deeds and can lead to egregious errors with individual patients. If a clinician is concerned, therefore, with the behavioral dimension of a client's moral structure, examinations of verbalizations cannot at the present time provide an adequate assessment. If modification of conduct is a therapeutic goal, changes in values or moral judgment should not be considered as indicative of progress in therapy. In addition to clarifying moral values through discussion, the clinician needs to provide the patient with situations for acting on moral decisions.

Application to Particular Variables

Age. No reliable age differences have been found for specific experimental tests of resistance to temptation. However, if the behavioral measure is consistency of conduct, older children tend to be more morally consistent than younger children. Unfortunately, longitudinal evidence is unavailable on changes in conduct on specific measures or in generality of moral conduct. With story-completion measures of guilt, age is correlated with a decreasing emphasis on external punishment and an increasing acceptance of personal responsibility for one's moral actions. In marked contrast to the moral conduct tests, the moral judgment measures of Piaget and Kohlberg are highly correlated with age because that was a requirement in the development of these measures.

Sex. There are no overall consistent sex differences in moral conduct. Other factors that interact with sex, such as motivational aspects of temptation situations and sex of the adult administering the test, seem to account for differences when they appear. Girls display greater guilt on some self-report and story-completion measures, but this appears to reflect sex-role expectations that girls are to be more compliant and obedient to the moral code. There is no systematic empirical support for the Freudian notion of a stronger male conscience.

Education. Intelligence and academic ability correlate moderately with honesty on experimental tasks. However, this is most evident in academic types of tests, where previous differences in incentive to deviate may produce different histories. More intelligent children may be more sensitive to the potential risks involved in deviating, rather than being more "moral" in a pure sense. There is little evidence for an association between intelligence and guilt. There is a strong correlation between intelligence and Kohlberg's stages of moral reasoning, although Kohlberg believes that certain stages of cognitive development are necessary, but not sufficient, conditions for development of the parallel moral reasoning stages.

Socioeconomic Status. Norms and group codes are major determinants of moral behavior. However, caution must be exercised in assuming what the prevailing norms of a particular social or economic class may be. For example, while middle-class parents may extol the value of honesty, they may also create strong pressures to succeed or to excel. While group norms can be assumed to exert a strong influence on morality, specifications of the exact nature of a norm may be extremely difficult. Also, values placed on some behaviors vary widely as a function of subcultural group norms. Moral judgment interviews appear biased in favor of those groups with the most education and the greatest verbal skills.

Physical Disorders. Some attempts have been made in the past to relate physique to personality characteristics of deviant groups, such as delinquents (Glueck and Glueck, 1950). Interestingly, the evidence for such a relationship suggests that characteristics seen as desirable in middle-class youngsters—intelligence, athletic build, leadership—tend to be associated with delinquency. To the extent that such a relationship exists, perhaps these characteristics enable a child in a high-risk delinquency subculture to begin a pattern of deviance more successfully than children without these generally desirable qualities. However, the data really are not yet robust enough to do more than speculate on an interpretation.

Intellectual Factors. As stated above, many moral development measures correlate positively with intelligence and education, though this relationship is probably mediated by third variables, such as sensitivity to risk and motivation to deviate. To the extent that intellectual disorders would interfere with all kinds of learning, they would also interfere with moral learning. The presence or absence of behavioral inhibitions and guilt in mentally deficient individuals has not generally been regarded as appropriate to the domain of moral development. Most moral measurement techniques assume an average level of physical and intellectual competence. Nevertheless, the evidence that is available suggests that the moral development (both behavioral and reasoning) of retarded children is comparable to that of normals (Stephens, Miller, and McLaughlin, 1969).

Organic Dysfunctions. Eysenck (1976) has argued that "conscience" is essentially the conditioning of anxiety. Both social and biological factors may be responsible for the failure of appropriate conditioning. Eysenck suggests that individuals vary in their "conditionability" because of genetic predispositions that produce different levels of cortical arousal. Low cortical arousal leads to poor conditioning potential and impulsive, sensation-seeking behavior. If these genotypic factors interact with certain environmental influences, the phenotype produced is the psychopath; that is, the antisocial person who apparently experiences no remorse. Eysenck remains cautious about the validity of this approach to psychopathic behavior, and it has not yet received adequate research scrutiny. It does, however, generate a number of testable hypotheses concerning organic bases of deviant behavior.

Functional Disorders. Though Freud would have listed many of the neuroses as consequences of overdeveloped superegos, most functional psychiatric disorders do not lend themselves to analysis through contemporary theories and research in moral development. A few of the behavior disorders of childhood and adolescence listed in the *Diagnostic and Statistical Manual of Mental Disorders* may be conceptualized in terms of inadequate moral development. For example, unsocialized aggressive reactions or group delinquent reactions may be viewed as a result of lack of proper socialization. Whether interpretations of current research in moral development can be extended to larger social problems remains to be seen. Assessment and diagnosis of these disorders, however, has not typically been conducted with measurement techniques used to examine moral development.

References

Aronfreed, J. *Conduct and Conscience: The Socialization of Internalized Control over Behavior.* New York: Academic Press, 1968.

Bryan, J. H. "You Will Be Well Advised to Watch What We Do Instead of What We Say." In D. J. DePalma and J. M. Foley (Eds.), *Moral Development: Current Theory and Research.* Hillsdale, N.J.: Erlbaum, 1975.

Bryan, J. H., and London, P. "Altruistic Behavior by Children." *Psychological Bulletin,* 1970, *73,* 200-211.

Burton, R. V. "Generality of Honesty Reconsidered." *Psychological Review,* 1963, *70,* 481-499.

Burton, R. V. "Correspondence Between Behavioral and Doll-Play Measures of Conscience." *Developmental Psychology,* 1971, *5,* 320-332.

Burton, R. V. "Interface Between the Behavioral and Cognitive-Developmental Approaches to Research in Morality." In B. Presseisen (Ed.), *Topics in Cognitive Development.* Vol. 2: *Language and Operational Thought.* New York: Plenum, 1977.

Burton, R. V. "Honesty and Dishonesty." In T. Lickona (Ed.), *Moral Development and Behavior: Theory, Research, and Social Issues.* New York: Holt, Rinehart and Winston, 1976a.

Burton, R. V. "Assessment of Moral Training Programs: Where Are We Going?" Paper presented at 84th annual convention of American Psychological Association, Washington, D.C., 1976b.

Burton, R. V., Maccoby, E. E., and Allinsmith, W. "Antecedents of Resistance to Temptation in Four-Year-Old Children." *Child Development,* 1961, *32,* 689-710.

Casey, W. M. "Words and Deeds: A Variety of Perspectives." Unpublished manuscript, State University of New York at Buffalo, 1977.

Casey, W. M. "Teaching Children to Be Honest Through Verbal Self-Instructions." Paper presented at annual meeting of Eastern Psychological Association, Washington, D.C., 1978.

Casey, W. M., and Burton, R. V. "Verbal Control of Moral Behavior." Paper presented at 5th biennial Southeastern Conference on Human Development, Atlanta, 1978.

DePalma, D. J., and Foley, J. M. (Eds.). *Moral Development: Current Theory and Research.* Hillsdale, N.J.: Erlbaum, 1975.

Eysenck, H. "The Biology of Morality." In T. Lickona (Ed.), *Moral Development and Behavior: Theory, Research, and Social Issues.* New York: Holt, Rinehart and Winston, 1976.

Freud, S. *The Ego and the Id.* London: Hogarth Press, 1923.

Glueck, S., and Glueck, E. *Unravelling Juvenile Delinquency.* New York: Commonwealth Fund, 1950.

Graham, D. *Moral Learning and Development: Theory and Research.* New York: Wiley, 1972.

Grinder, R. E., and McMichael, R. E. "Cultural Influence on Conscience Development: Resistance to Temptation and Guilt Among Samoans and American Caucasians." *Journal of Abnormal and Social Psychology,* 1963, *66,* 503-507.

Haan, N., Smith, M. B., and Block, J. "Moral Reasoning of Young Adults: Political-Social Behavior, Family Background, and Personality Correlates." *Journal of Personality and Social Psychology,* 1968, *10,* 183-201.

Hartshorne, H., and May, M. A. *Studies in the Nature of Character.* Vol. 1: *Studies in Deceit.* New York: Macmillan, 1928.

Hoffman, M. L. "Moral Development." In P. H. Mussen (Ed.), *Carmichael's Manual of Child Psychology.* Vol. 2. New York: Wiley, 1970.

Hoffman, M. L. "Empathy, Role-Taking, Guilt, and Development of Altruistic Motives." In T. Lickona (Ed.), *Moral Development and Behavior: Theory, Research, and Social Issues.* New York: Holt, Rinehart and Winston, 1976.

Holstein, C. B. "Irreversible, Stepwise Sequence in the Development of Moral Judgment: A Longitudinal Study of Males and Females." *Child Development,* 1976, *47,* 51-61, 1962.

Johnson, R. C. "A Study of Children's Moral Judgments." *Child Development,* 1962, *33,* 327-354.

Kohlberg, L. "Development of Moral Character and Moral Ideology." In M. L. Hoffman and L. W. Hoffman (Eds.), *Review of Child Development Research.* Vol. 1. New York: Russell Sage Foundation, 1964.

Kohlberg, L. "Stage and Sequence: The Cognitive-Developmental Approach to Socialization." In D. A. Goslin (Ed.), *Handbook of Socialization Theory and Research.* Chicago: Rand McNally, 1969.

Kohlberg, L. "Moral Stages and Moralization: The Cognitive-Developmental Approach." In T. Lickona (Ed.), *Moral Development and Behavior: Theory, Research, and Social Issues.* New York: Holt, Rinehart and Winston, 1976.

Lickona, T. "A Cognitive-Developmental Approach to Altruism." Paper presented at 82nd annual meeting of American Psychological Association, New Orleans, 1974.

Lickona, T. "Critical Issues in the Study of Moral Development and Behavior." In T. Lickona (Ed.), *Moral Development and Behavior: Theory, Research, and Social Issues.* New York: Holt, Rinehart, and Winston, 1976a.

Lickona, T. (Ed.). *Moral Development and Behavior: Theory, Research, and Social Issues.* New York: Holt, Rinehart and Winston, 1976b.

Macauley, J., and Berkowitz, L. (Eds.). *Altruism and Helping Behavior.* New York: Academic Press, 1970.

Mischel, W., and Mischel, H. N. "A Cognitive Social Learning Approach to Morality and Self-Regulation." In T. Lickona (Ed.), *Moral Development and Behavior: Theory, Research, and Social Issues.* New York: Holt, Rinehart and Winston, 1976.

Murphy, L. B. *Social Behavior and Child Personality.* New York: Columbia University Press, 1937.

Mussen, P., and Eisenberg-Berg, N. *Roots of Caring, Sharing, and Helping.* San Francisco: Freeman, 1977.

Parke, R. D. "Effectiveness of Punishment as an Interaction of Intensity, Timing, Agent Nurturance, and Cognitive Structuring." *Child Development,* 1969, *40,* 213-235.

Piaget, J. *The Moral Judgment of the Child.* New York: Harcourt Brace Jovanovich, 1932.

Podd, M. "Ego Identity Status and Morality: The Relationship Between Two Developmental Constructs." *Developmental Psychology,* 1972, *6,* 497-507.

Rest, J. "New Approaches in the Assessment of Moral Judgment." In T. Lickona (Ed.), *Moral Development and Behavior: Theory, Research, and Social Issues.* New York: Holt, Rinehart and Winston, 1976.

Rest, J., and others. "Judging the Important Issues in Moral Dilemmas." *Developmental Psychology,* 1974, *10,* 491-501.

Rokeach, M. *The Nature of Human Values.* New York: Free Press, 1973.

Ruma, E. H., and Mosher, P. L. "The Relationship Between Moral Judgment and Guilt in Delinquent Boys." *Journal of Abnormal Psychology,* 1967, *72,* 122-127.

Sanders, N. M., and Wallace, J. D. *Teacher and Parent Opinion Concerning Moral/Ethical Education in the Public Schools: A Report of an Institute for Survey Research Study.* Philadelphia: Research for Better Schools, 1975.

Sears, R. R., Maccoby, E. E., and Levin, H. *Patterns of Child Rearing.* New York: Harper & Row, 1957.

Sears, R. R., Rau, L., and Alpert, R. *Identification and Child Rearing.* Stanford, Calif.: Stanford University Press, 1965.

Simon, S., Howe, L. W., and Kirschenbaum, H. *Values Clarification: A Handbook of Practical Strategies for Teachers and Students.* New York: Hart, 1972.

Solomon, R. L., Turner, L. H., and Lessac, M. S. "Some Effects of Delay of Punishment on Resistance to Temptation in Dogs." *Journal of Personality and Social Psychology,* 1968, *8,* 233-238.

Solomon, R. L., and Wynne, L. C. "Traumatic Avoidance Learning: The Principles of Anxiety Conservation and Partial Irreversibility." *Psychological Review,* 1954, *61,* 353-385.

Stephens, W. B., Miller, C. K., and McLaughlin, J. A. "The Development of Moral Conduct in Retardates and Normals." Paper presented at biennial meeting of Society for Research in Child Development, Santa Monica, Calif., 1969.

Wright, D. *The Psychology of Moral Behavior.* New York: Penguin Books, 1971.

Yarrow, M. R., Campbell, J. D., and Burton, R. V. *Child Rearing: An Inquiry into Research and Methods.* San Francisco: Jossey-Bass, 1968.

Yarrow, M. R., Campbell, J. D., and Burton, R. V. "Recollections of Childhood: A Study of the Retrospective Method." *Monographs of the Society for Research in Child Development,* 1970, *35* (5), Serial No. 138.

27

Gregory H. Wilmoth
Sam G. McFarland
John O'Connor

Moral Reasoning

"Moral reasoning" and its synonym "moral judgment" refer to the cognitions and reasoning processes whereby individuals determine which of their moral standards, if any, should govern their behavior in a specific situation. Moral reasoning refers to cognitions that precede and govern behavior, rather than to reasons that follow behavior as justifications and/or rationalizations. It is distinguished from moral knowledge (awareness of socially sanctioned moral rules), from moral feelings (shame, guilt), and from moral behaviors (resistance to temptation, honesty, helping behaviors), although these constructs are generally assumed to be related to moral reasoning.

Like reasoning in general, moral reasoning frequently becomes more complex, abstract, differentiated, integrated, and comprehensive with age and experience. Theories and research have generally assumed that moral reasoning undergoes a series of systematic, qualitative changes, which can be represented in developmental-stage schemes. While the terms *moral development* and *moral maturity* may include the dimensions of moral knowledge, feelings, and behavior, they most commonly refer in contemporary usage to the dimension of moral reasoning.

Theorists generally assume that an individual's moral thought is a structured whole; however, various components are distinguishable. The component of role-taking ability appears particularly relevant to clinical and counseling psychology. Role-taking ability refers here to the cognitive capacity to step outside one's own perspective and to view events from the perspective of another person, the larger society, a neutral third party, or the entire human family. Like the larger unity of moral reasoning, role-taking ability is assumed to pass through developmental stages. It is also assumed to be necessary but not sufficient for mature moral thought in general.

Background and Current Status

Loevinger (1976) has traced the philosophical ideas from which contemporary psychologists have constructed theories of moral development. Kohlberg (1970, 1976), the most influential contemporary theorist, has identified his primary philosophical influences as Plato, John Dewey, and John Rawls. Specifically, Kohlberg summarizes eight elements of the Platonic view to which he adheres: (1) virtue is ultimately one, not many, and it is always the same ideal form regardless of time or culture; (2) this ideal form is called justice; (3) virtue is knowledge of the good, and he who knows the good chooses the good; (4) knowledge of virtue is philosophical knowledge or intuition of the ideal form of the good, not correct opinion or acceptance of conventional beliefs; (5) the good can be taught; (6) the teaching of the good is more a calling out than an instruction because the good is known all along, at least at a low level; (7) the same good is known differently at different levels, and direct instruction is ineffective across levels; and (8) one teaches virtue by asking questions and leading individuals upward, not by giving answers or instilling knowledge that was not in the mind before. Kohlberg objects, however, to Plato's notion of justice. Whereas Plato believes that a just society is one in which each individual occupies his proper place in the social hierarchy, Kohlberg defines justice as equality.

From Dewey, Kohlberg adopted the following notions: (1) critical, analytic, and reflective thought are necessary for moral growth; (2) to comprehend the meaning of personal conduct, one must be fully aware of one's social existence; and (3) social justice is the heart and center of morality. This tradition of moral thought centered in social justice was further developed by Rawls (1971).

The shift from viewing moral reasoning and moral development as philosophical issues to viewing them as psychological and scientific constructs is seen in the writings of Baldwin (1902), McDougall (1908), Mead (1934), and Piaget (1932). Many of the philosophical ideas noted above reappear in these theories in increasingly scientific form. Seven components of these theories mark the evolution to current theories of moral reasoning: (1) the assumption that justice is the center of mature moral thought; (2) the conception of changes in moral reasoning as developmental, emphasizing the processes of arriving at moral judgments and minimizing the importance of moral content that is learned; (3) the thesis that development consists of qualitative changes, identified as stages, rather than quantitative increases; (4) an emphasis on role playing as a necessary stimulus to moral development; (5) the construction, by Piaget, of clinical assessment methods to measure moral judgment; (6) the construction of an empirically derived theory of the development of moral reasoning in children; and (7) the extension of this theory to encompass lifelong moral development.

The bulk of recent interest has centered on the stage theories of Piaget (1932) and Kohlberg (1969). Both theorists propose that moral reasoning passes through a series of mental structures (referred to as stages), with each stage representing a qualitatively different organization and pattern of moral thought from the preceding one. Both theorists assume that (1) the development of moral reasoning consists of changes in the structure of one's reasoning about moral choices rather than of changes in specific moral contents (for example, specific actions that are condemned or approved); (2) the stages form an invariant sequence, in which no stages are "skipped," up to that point at which the individual reaches the highest stage or fixates at some stage below the highest; and (3) the sequence of stages is universal, so that individuals in all cultures begin at the same stage and pass through the stages in the same order, although one's culture might accelerate or retard the speed of moral development.

Piaget proposes that children, following a period of amorality in early childhood, display two successive stages of moral thought. The earlier stage is variously labeled heteronomous morality, moral realism, objective morality, or a morality of constraint. Four principles define this stage: (1) rules are viewed as absolute, sacred, and immutable; (2) judgments of rightness are based on the duty of obedience to adult authority; (3) judgments of wrongness are based on the magnitude of the consequences of an act, while intentions and motivations are discounted; and (4) posttransgression justice is served by expiatory punishment. The transition to the stage of autonomous morality, also called a morality of cooperation, is based on a shift in the reasons for respect for the rules of the social order. The shift is from respect based on the prestige and power of the authority to respect based on the function of the rules to ensure fairness, cooperation, and reciprocity. There are four consequences: (1) rules are now viewed as changeable when circumstances dictate or when all concerned parties agree; (2) rightness is grounded in reciprocity with others and in honoring one's own commitments; (3) judgments of wrongness now consider intentions, motives, and mitigating circumstances; and (4) punishment which makes restitution to the victim best serves posttransgression justice. Piaget claims that children in an environment of mutual respect and equality in social interaction will develop into autonomous morality by early adolescence.

Kohlberg's theory, empirically derived from longitudinal, cross-sectional, and cross-cultural samples, encompasses lifelong development. For Kohlberg moral development constitutes a progressive movement toward basing moral judgments on increasingly comprehensive conceptions of justice. Kohlberg (1968, 1976) defines three levels of moral reasoning, each level consisting of two stages possessing the same structuring principle:

> *Preconventional Level.* Rules and social expectations are not yet internalized; externally mediated consequences of one's actions determine judgments of action's goodness or badness.
>> *Stage 1.* Orientation toward punishment and unquestioning deference to superior power. The physical consequences of action, regardless of their human meaning or value, determine its goodness or badness [1968, p. 26].
>> *Stage 2.* Right action consists of that which instrumentally satisfies one's own needs. . . . Elements of fairness, of reciprocity, and equal sharing are present, but they are always interpreted in a physical, pragmatic way . . . [rather than as] loyalty, gratitude, or justice [1968, p. 26].
> *Conventional Level.* The self is identified with or has internalized the rules and expectations of others [1976, p. 33].
>> *Stage 3.* Good behavior is that which pleases . . . others and is ap-

proved by them. [There is much] conformity to stereotypical
images of what is majority or "natural" behavior. Behavior is often
judged by intention [1968, p. 26].

Stage 4. Right behavior consists of doing one's duty [obeying fixed
rules], showing respect for authority, and maintaining the given
social order [1968, p. 26].

Postconventional Level. [The person] has differentiated his self from the
rules and expectations of others and defines his values in terms of self-
chosen principles [1976, p. 33].

Stage 5. Right action . . . [is] defined in terms of standards which
have been critically examined and agreed upon by the whole society. [There is a clear] awareness of the relativism of personal
values and opinions and a corresponding emphasis upon procedural
rules for reaching consensus. [There is also an] emphasis upon the
"legal point of view," but with . . . the possibility of changing law
in terms of rational considerations of social utility. . . . Outside the
legal realm, free agreement and contracts are the binding elements
of obligation [1968, p. 26].

Stage 6. [The individual is oriented] toward the decisions of conscience and toward self-chosen ethical principles. . . . These principles are abstract and ethical (the Golden Rule . . .); they are not
concrete moral rules like the Ten Commandments. Instead, they
are universal principles of justice, of the reciprocity and equality of
human rights, and of respect for the dignity of . . . individual persons [1968, p. 26].

According to Kohlberg, preconventional thought characterizes "most children
under 9, some adolescents, and many adolescent and adult criminal offenders" (Kohlberg,
1976, p. 33). Conventional thought is common to most adolescents and adults in most
societies. Only a minority of adults develop postconventional moral thought, and rarely
before age 20.

Kohlberg's theory has had dynamic influence since it was first published in 1963.
It has engendered debate from philosophy, social learning theory, and psychodynamic
theory, and it has inspired massive and diverse research. Applied research and pragmatic
usage of Kohlberg's theory have centered on the areas of moral education and the treatment of delinquency and antisocial behavior. Two periodicals, the *Journal of Moral Education* and *Moral Education Forum,* are exclusively devoted to moral education issues and
research. Many school systems have instituted moral education programs based in large
part on Kohlberg's model. Commercial instructional media are available. Since a number
of studies have found that delinquents and adult criminals often exhibit lower moral-stage
reasoning than their age peers, several attempts to reduce antisocial behavior by improving moral reasoning have been reported. Few other clinical applications of Kohlberg's
model have been reported to date.

Selman (1976; Selman and Damon, 1975) has recently proposed a stage theory of
role-taking ability which appears to embody the stage assumptions identified by Piaget
and Kohlberg. Selman's scheme is described here, since it is the only moral reasoning
scheme that has generated research on clinical applications. The stages are:

Stage 0: Egocentric Role Taking (about ages 4 to 6). The child
recognizes that others have desires and make judgments, but these are
assumed to be identical to the child's own. Therefore, the child does not
recognize that his desires may conflict with another's desires.

Stage 1: Social-Informational Role Taking (about ages 6 to 8). The child now realizes that the feelings and judgments of others may differ from his own, since others are in different situations or have different information. The child can now distinguish between intentional and unintentional actions. Still, the child assumes that his own perspectives are "right" or "true" and cannot place himself in the perspective of others.

Stage 2: Self-Reflective Role Taking (about ages 8 to 10). The child is able to reflect on his own behavior and motives from the perspective of another. Since the child recognizes that others can do the same, the child can anticipate others' reactions to his motives as well as to his behaviors. Friendship is a matter of giving and receiving specific favors.

Stage 3: Mutual Role Taking (about ages 10 to 12). The child realizes that both self and another in a social exchange can consider each other's point of view mutually and simultaneously. Thus, friendship is no longer seen as just immediate acts of "back scratching" but as longer-term mutuality. Additionally, the child sees for the first time that both parties can place themselves in the perspective of a third party who comprehends both sets of motives and the relationship between the parties.

Stage 4: Social and Conventional System Role Taking (about ages 12 to 15+). The adolescent can now take the perspective of the general social system, the "generalized other," as well as the perspective of a third party.

Selman suggests that an understanding of a child's role-taking stage allows the educator and the clinician to "understand how the child looks at the world, and to avoid expectations of conceptual and emotional abilities that the child has not yet developed" (Selman, 1976, p. 300). In addition, clinicians can recognize that a child's lack of role-taking ability may cause maladaptive social behavior and affective reactions to social situations. In Selman's judgment, therapists frequently focus too exclusively on the affective domain and fail to see that a child's reactions (hostility, withdrawal, and the like) may be caused by a cognitive inability to take the role of other persons. Therapeutic intervention that is aimed at gains in role-taking ability can be a key element in improving a child's social functioning. No stage-developmental theory has been developed to date which extends role-taking stages into adulthood.

Critical Discussion

General Areas of Concern

Three concerns regarding moral reasoning appear particularly significant for the practitioner: (1) How can moral reasoning be measured? (2) How can the development of moral reasoning be facilitated? (3) How can the construct of moral reasoning be used to produce therapeutic gains?

How can moral reasoning be measured? Piaget's method of assessment is rather straightforward. Children are presented two stories and are asked to judge between the central actors on a dimension relative to Piaget's stage theory. For example, a child may be asked to judge whether a child who broke many cups accidentally in one story or a child who broke one cup while violating a parent's rules in another story "did worse," a dilemma that allows a child to choose either in terms of the magnitude of the consequences or the wrongdoer's intentions. Probes may be used following the child's answers to explore further intricacies in moral reasoning.

Kohlberg has used morally ambiguous stories with a series of open-ended, probing questions following each story. In the most famous example, a man faces the dilemma of stealing a drug that might save his wife's life. The respondent is asked to elaborate on the wrongness or rightness of the act, the role of the husband's love and responsibilities in the decision, the importance of the law and of the druggist's rights, and the proper response of a criminal judge to the theft. Questions are structured to elicit the respondent's reasoning behind his choices.

A respondent's stage score may be determined by various procedures, all of which require extensive training. For instance, stage scores might be assigned to each sentence, or to each story, or to predefined "aspects" or "issues," or to a global subjective evaluation of the overall moral reasoning of the respondent. A moral maturity score is sometimes calculated as a weighted average of the amount of the respondent's usage of each stage.

Kohlberg's scoring procedures have been revised almost yearly since 1958, so extreme caution must be used in comparing scores between studies. Reliability estimates vary markedly from story to story, rater to rater, and test to retest. Kurtines and Grief (1974) reviewed the psychometric properties of Kohlberg's instrument and found no estimates of temporal stability. Since that time, Kohlberg (1976) has reported an 88 percent test-retest stage classification agreement, while Rest (1977) reports one study that found a reliability estimate of $\gamma = .44$. The assessment of moral reasoning is dramatically affected by the story content, response characteristics of the situation, and characteristics of the examiner. For example, individuals are theoretically unable to understand moral reasoning two or more stages above their own, but no known study reports the functioning stage of examiners. If the researchers who use the instruments are representative of the samples collected, most of them should be unable to comprehend principled reasoning. In summary, scoring procedures are in such disarray that their use in a clinical setting is questionable.

Rest (1975, 1976) has recently developed an objective test of moral judgment called the Defining Issues Test (DIT). For each of six morally ambiguous stories, subjects are asked to rate the importance of each of twelve issues in deciding what should be done. The twelve issues are written to exemplify concerns that are characteristic of the different stages. The indices of moral reasoning available from these ratings include (1) the proportion of moral reasoning at the principled stages, (2) the rejection of lower-stage reasoning, and (3) the stage that a respondent uses most frequently. Rest (1976) reports a $\gamma = .68$ correlation between the subjects' proportion of principled reasoning and their scores on Kohlberg's stories. The ease of use and the good psychometric properties of the DIT are encouraging, though Rest (1976) does not consider the DIT and Kohlberg's stories as equivalent measures. The DIT is available only for research purposes and with Rest's approval.

How can the development of moral reasoning be facilitated? A number of factors commonly believed to affect moral development do not correlate with the developmental stages. For instance, the amount and kind of punishment; the presence or absence of religious training; parental strictness versus permissiveness; and, except in extreme cases, the degree of parental affection are all unrelated to the child's level of moral judgment. Different levels of these variables may, however, affect moral feelings and moral behaviors.

Moral reasoning theorists also reject the notion that the highest stages can be directly "taught," as though they consisted of memorizing and practicing moral principles. Kohlberg (1970), for example, has specifically deemphasized this "bag of virtues" approach. On theoretical grounds, this approach cannot produce high stages of moral reasoning because the attainment of each stage is based on an understanding of the preceding stage and its limitations for resolving moral problems. Research on Kohlberg's theory indicates that children cannot understand moral reasoning that is more than one stage above their own. When children (or college students) are given an example of moral reasoning that is two or more stages above their own and are asked to restate the reasoning in their own words, they generally reveal that they have misunderstood or misinterpreted the reasoning.

Three factors appear to be particularly important in the development of moral reasoning. The first of these factors is the development of concrete and formal operational thought. Research on Piaget's theory is generally consistent with his argument "that the child's level of moral development is anchored to his general level of cognitive functioning" (Lickona, 1976, p. 229), although some research is unsupportive. Keasey (1975) has shown that concrete operational thought appears to precede the development of Kohlberg's stage 2 and that formal operational thought precedes the development of the postconventional, principled stages.

Second, role-taking opportunities, particularly those made available by equalitarian peer interaction, apparently are important for moral development. Studies on both the Piaget and the Kohlberg theories generally support this view, although the findings are not unanimous. Kohlberg (1976) has recently illustrated the importance of role taking by citing examples of two extreme groups. American orphanage children, whose peer interactions were described as "fragmentary" and "deprived," had the lowest levels of moral thought of any sample Kohlberg and his associates had observed; in contrast, Israeli kibbutz children, who engaged in intense peer interaction, showed the most rapid moral development of any group. However, the role-taking experience required to develop postconventional morality may not be satisfied by peer interaction. Stage 6 morality, based on the abstract principles of justice and equality, theoretically requires the ability to place oneself in the role of any human group or individual, including those outside one's personal experience. Therefore, imaginative role taking appears necessary for the development of Kohlberg's highest stages.

Third, dialogue concerning moral issues is the central feature of the application of Kohlberg's theory to education. Dialogue has several functions, such as (1) attuning the individual to moral considerations, (2) encouraging the person to develop general rules for moral behavior from the specifics of one's own experience, (3) facilitating the discovery of the weaknesses of moral thought, (4) exposing the individual to more advanced reasoning that does not have these weaknesses, and (5) providing the opportunity for imaginative role taking with unencountered groups and individuals. The importance of moral dialogue in moral development is strongly supported by research. Parents who encourage moral dialogue are more likely to witness moral-stage advances in their children.

Several other factors, less central theoretically, have also been suggested. Piaget emphasizes the importance of independence from adult constraint for the development of autonomous morality, but the research to date offers very limited and circumscribed support. In fact, some research supports the opposite view—namely, that authoritative adult didactic training can increase autonomous moral reasoning. Kohlberg reports, however, that in junior high schools where students were permitted an active role in the formulation of rules governing student behavior, students increased their understanding and use of such moral principles as justice, rights, procedural fairness, equality, and reciprocity. Moral change can also be influenced by modeling, as many studies have shown, but Piagetian and social learning theorists still debate both the processes by which modeling has its influence and the nature of the change.

How can the construct of moral reasoning be used to produce therapeutic gains?

Surprisingly, the therapeutic relevance of moral reasoning has received almost no research and little speculation. Selman's (1976) work stands alone in pointing to therapeutic implications and in outlining a therapeutic program. Even here, the outline is skimpy, and the supporting research is limited to the few case studies that Selman has reported.

In Selman's view, a child's social fear, withdrawal, and anger, as well as his need for attention and his low self-esteem, are all frequently rooted in deficits in role-taking skills. For example, an 8-year-old is more likely to start a fight (or withdraw in fear) if he fails to differentiate purposive and unintentional actions. When the teacher does not attend to every request, the child is more likely to believe that the teacher hates him if he is unable to take the teacher's role and see the competing demands for the teacher's attention. In a vicious cycle, the child's feelings of being hated may lead to even more attention seeking and to ever increasing feelings of rejection. These cognitive deficits may isolate the child from peers, produce a chain of emotional traumas, and interfere with moral reasoning.

While many therapists focus almost exclusively on the emotional consequences, Selman suggests that a therapy aimed at improving the child's role-taking skills may strike closer to the problem's center. The process is simply one of providing careful and repeated explanation to the child of the reasons behind others' behaviors and of making the social need for rules and social structures as clear as possible to the child. This process may most effectively take place in a setting of legitimate social interactions, such as a school or a summer camp. If Selman's case studies are representative, gains in role-taking stages often result in improved social relations, moral development, and ego development as well.

Other clinical implications of moral reasoning are speculative, but they may be far reaching. Marriage and family problems might, at times, be rooted in moral reasoning differences between the members. Intergenerational conflicts in the family may reflect disagreements resting on different underlying stages of moral reasoning. Marriage partners whose moral reasoning is separated by more than one stage might well find difficulty in maintaining the mutual respect necessary for enduring love. For example, a person whose morality is centered around the abstract principles of justice and equality (Kohlberg's stage 6) will no doubt view a partner's law-and-order morality (stage 4) as retarded. The law-and-order partner might, as research has shown, misinterpret the partner's failure to worship the conventional laws as preconventional lawlessness.

Comparative Philosophies and Theories

At least seven alternate models of moral reasoning have appeared in recent years. In general, these models are not stage-developmental in nature and do not embody the stage assumptions of the theories previously described. None of the authors of these theories appear to have discussed their clinical use.

Bronfenbrenner (1962) constructed a moral reasoning typology based on his comparative study of Russian and American character socialization. The five types are (1) self-oriented, where the individual is motivated by impulses of self-gratification; (2) authority oriented, in which the adult and authority values are rigidly accepted; (3) peer oriented, in which one is motivated by conformity to nonauthority reference groups; (4) collective oriented, in which commitment to group goals takes precedence over individual values; and (5) objectively oriented, in which the individual makes judgments on the basis of moral principles rather than on the basis of orientations toward social agents. This initially nonstructural model has recently been integrated with Kohlberg's approach (Garbarino and Bronfenbrenner, 1976). It varies from the Kohlberg model in two respects:

first, while the levels are viewed as universal in their developmental sequence, the stages within a level are not necessarily sequential, invariant, or universal; second, the dominant integrating value pattern of the society is seen as determining the moral type of its members. Individuals will develop a morality of principles only in a "pluralistic" society, one that allows the free expression of competing ideologies.

Hoffman (1970) has identified three orientations of conscience: (1) external, oriented toward the avoidance of detection and punishment; (2) conventional, oriented toward a strict adherence to the rules and norms of a society; and (3) humanistic, oriented toward human needs and feelings, which are considered as important extenuating conditions for applying moral rules. These orientations are developmental and structural only in the sense that specific patterns of parenting are associated with their use by children.

McCord and Clemes (1964) have distinguished four moral reasoning orientations based on the two dichotomous dimensions of deontology versus ontology and extrinsic versus intrinsic standards. The "normatist" (deontological and extrinsic) believes that moral standards reside in extrinsic social norms, order, and authority; an action is moral if it is consistent with society's norms and laws. An "integratist" (ontological, extrinsic) also perceives moral standards as externally derived but focuses on the consequences of an action in judging its moral worth. A "phenomenalist" (deontological, intrinsic) views moral standards as intrinsically individual and relative and judges moral actions according to the intention of the performer to cooperate, conform, and agree, rather than by their consequences. The "hedonist" (ontological, intrinsic) also believes in individual moral standards but evaluates the moralness of an action by the degree to which it achieves its intrinsic, hedonistic goal.

Schlenker and Forsyth (1977) derived four ethical postures, somewhat similar to those of McCord and Clemes, from subjects' responses to the ethicality of controversial research practices. "Teleologists" judge moral actions by weighing their good (pleasure, happiness, social welfare) versus bad (pain, suffering) consequences. "Deontologists" judge actions against an a priori, universal, and immutable moral standard, which generally states that persons must always be treated as ultimate ends and never as means to some other end. "Pragmatic skeptics" and "idealistic skeptics" both deny the existence of universal moral principles and emphasize cultural, situational, and individual relativity. Pragmatic skeptics calculate the morality of an act as the teleologists do—that is, by weighing its consequences; the pragmatic skeptics, however, consider only good versus bad consequences of personal hedonistic concern. Idealistic skeptics endorse a universal rule of protecting people's welfare, but they assume that this rule is relative to their personal and cultural standards.

Perry (1970) presents one of the most complex and detailed models of ethical development. Moral reasoning progresses through nine positions in a sequential, but not invariant, movement (since regression to earlier positions is an empirical feature of the theory). The complexity of this scheme prevents its description here.

Hogan (1973, 1974, 1975) has proposed a character structure ontogenesis model of moral development in which mature moral judgment is seen as the combined product of five factors: (1) moral knowledge, defined as the awareness and comprehension of the moral rules of a society; (2) socialization, the degree to which one has internalized these rules as personally obligatory; (3) empathy, the capacity and disposition to regulate one's actions with awareness of the expectations of others; (4) autonomy, the ability to make moral judgments without being influenced by peer pressure or the dictates of authority; and (5) ethical attitude, the perception of moral rules as either instrumentally valuable for regulating social conduct or valuable for personal integrity. Moral maturity is measured by the frequency with which one uses any of four predefined moral concerns: (1) concern for the sanctity of the individual, (2) judgments based on the spirit (function) rather than the letter of the law, (3) concern for the welfare of society as a whole, and (4) capacity to see both sides of an issue. Hogan and Dickstein's (1972) measure of mature moral reasoning is empirically related to Kohlberg's levels of moral reasoning in a strongly positive way (Wilmoth and McFarland, 1977).

Haan (1978) has proposed a stage-developmental scheme of five "levels of interpersonal morality." Advances from stage to stage do not occur on the basis of increasingly abstract logic and rationally derived truths, as they do for the other stage theorists, but rest on the "evolution of differentiated, sensitive, intersubjective understanding" (pp. 287, 289). The levels, which appear to parallel Selman's stages in many ways, cannot be easily capsuled. As with Selman's stages, the child develops an increasingly sophisticated understanding of self and others in moral exchanges. At level 1 the child has no view of self as separate from others and thus has no understanding of moral exchange. At level 2 the child realizes his separateness from others but believes that others feel and behave exactly as he does; the child assumes that they, like himself, will respond in a tit-for-tat, eye-for-an-eye manner. At level 3 the child sees the self as a good member of a good human community but is naive about his own goodness and the goodness of others. The child does not see himself objectively enough to recognize that he can and does sin against the common good. At level 4 the child sees himself and others with enough depth to recognize that bad faith and others' peculiar individualities may contribute to social inequality; hence, the child becomes legalistic and rule oriented in moral exchanges and unforgiving of violations. At level 5 the child sees himself with enough objectivity to recognize that he, as well as others, may contribute to moral imbalances. As the child develops detachment and humor about himself, he becomes more forgiving and more willing to accept flexible loyalty rather than rule observance. The individual sees that good moral exchanges require taking chances on good faith and cannot be based on legalistic prescriptions.

Elaboration on Critical Points

Two critical issues require comment: (1) How well does the available evidence substantiate the stage-developmental models of moral reasoning? (2) Do differences in moral reasoning produce important differences in behavior?

The evidence bearing on the validity of the models is at times strongly supportive, occasionally contradictory, and often points to needed theoretical refinements. Many age-stratified samples have verified the two-stage progressions identified by Piaget, but the separate aspects of Piaget's stages (the nature of rules, the "badness" of acts, the uses of punishment) have distinctive rather than unitary age onset and termination profiles, indicating developmental independence instead of integrated stage progression. Counter to the stage-theory assumption of the impossibility of regressions, social learning theorists have shown that heteronomous reasoning can be increased by modeling in children who have already attained substantial autonomous reasoning. Advocates of Piaget's theory question the stability of these regressions, however, since these children eventually return to autonomous reasoning. Social learning theorists still debate the mechanisms responsible for moral development, emphasizing the role of modeling and reinforcements instead of the child's deductive abilities.

Research on Kohlberg's theory supports the hypothesized stage progression more strongly for the lower stages than for the higher ones, where several alternate paths of development have been suggested. The theoretical requirement of moral reasoning consistency across situations is well documented, but inconsistencies in individuals' moral reasoning are also common. In addition to apparently random intrasubject inconsistencies, subjects frequently reason lower on sexual dilemmas than on other stories. Kohlberg's theory is strongly supported by the fact that individuals (1) can comprehend clearly their own stage and all stages below their own, (2) have some difficulty with the stage just above their own, and (3) show little understanding of still higher stages. Also, subjects who are exposed to samples of moral reasoning from several stages are most influenced by the reasoning from one stage above their own.

Rest (1977) has argued that the simple stage models proposed by Piaget and Kohlberg must be replaced by a more complex model that allows for more stage overlap; the use of different stages for different moral issues; and the continued development of the type of thinking represented by each stage, even after the next stage has been acquired. Rest questions the assumption that all moral reasoning fits within a single structural whole for most people.

The claim that the stages are universal to all cultures, made by both Piaget and Kohlberg, has received the strongest criticism. For example, Simpson (1974) presents philosophical, logical, anecdotal, and nonexperimental evidence to support her contention that Kohlberg's theory suffers from a scientific and Western cultural bias. This issue is unresolved.

The importance of moral reasoning for moral behavior is most frequently discussed in connection with Kohlberg's theory. At least two factors militate against strong and simple relations. Since stages are defined by their structure and not by their content, individuals at the same stage do not always agree on the morality of specific actions. Second, social pressure, ego needs, and many other factors might cause one to behave in a manner that is inconsistent with one's moral judgments. Kohlberg recognizes that higher-stage reasoning does not guarantee more moral behavior, but he says that such reasoning does make moral behavior possible. While someone with stage 6 moral reasoning may backslide, no one without stage 6 reasoning will consistently act with stage 6 principles.

The empirical relations between moral reasoning and behavior, therefore, vary from study to study. Kohlberg (1969) found that stage 6 subjects, unlike all others, generally refused to administer shocks in the Milgram (1963) obedience experiment, but one attempt to replicate this finding failed (Podd, 1972). Some studies have found positive relations between Kohlberg's stages and helping behavior, but others have not. The stages are negatively related to racial prejudice and to cheating, although the latter relationship is found for men only. Preconventional and postconventional students participated in campus civil disobedience more frequently than did conventional subjects.

Personal Views and Recommendations

Given the assessment difficulties and the paucity of research on clinical uses of moral reasoning, there seems to be no basis for recommending moral reasoning as a diagnostic dimension to clinical practitioners. The moral reasoning tests can be abused by those who would score them without sufficient training, since the scoring systems are subtle and complex. Anyone who wishes to investigate the clinical relevance of Kohlberg's stages should attain training, such as in one of Kohlberg's summer workshops. No one should presume to self-teach the scoring of responses to the Kohlberg stories. Since moral reasoning is not, at present, a dimension of proven value in clinical practice, no special issues are raised for general training and certification. Moral-stage scores can be abused, however, if they are used to determine clinical treatment, since their value for clinical prescriptions is untested. Careful research on the relevance of moral reasoning might point the way to valuable clinical applications in the future.

Application to Particular Variables

Since the moral reasoning instruments have generally not been used for diagnostic purposes in therapeutic settings, no published guidelines on using them in these settings with particular populations are available. For those who choose to use them despite the warnings, the following additional warnings are warranted:

1. Since age is highly correlated with moral reasoning, judgments about a child's moral advancement or retardedness should recognize what is normal for age peers.

2. Many but not all studies show that females score lower than males on Kohlberg's stages. One plausible explanation is that the moral dilemmas are biased to reflect traditionally masculine concerns, although women may possess a different conception of morality than men (Gilligan, 1977).

3. Since respondents' verbal fluency tends to bias judges' ratings in a positive direction, well-educated, verbally fluent clients might be scored as more advanced in moral reasoning than they actually are. The scores of uneducated clients might reflect the opposite bias.

4. Middle- and upper-class respondents tend to score higher on both Piaget's and Kohlberg's stages. Both rater bias and middle-class biases in the dilemmas may contribute to these differences.

5. Vocation does not appear to be a major source of scaling bias, except as vocational differences reflect sex, educational, and socioeconomic differences.

6. The lower stage scores typically obtained by nonwhite, non-American samples may reflect a cultural bias in the dilemmas; the confounding with socioeconomic level, education, and verbal dialect; and/or the biases of the scorers, as shown by the lack of lower stage scores for blacks when these factors are controlled (Harris, 1970).

7. Descriptive norms and suggested assessment procedures exist for deaf children (Nass, 1964) and for mentally retarded persons aged 6 to 20 (Mahaney and Stephens, 1974).

8. Collective/interactional disorders may be frequently rooted in immature moral reasoning. Selman's and Kohlberg's models may prove fruitful for both analysis and treatment. Psychopathic delinquents have significantly lower role-taking skills and lower scores on Kohlberg's stages than do nondelinquents of the same age and socioeconomic level. Neurotic and subcultural delinquents, however, have moral reasoning equivalent to their age and socioeconomic peers (Jurkovic and Prentice, 1977). Sociopathic children also reveal lower levels of moral reasoning (Campagna and Harter, 1975). Hawk and Peterson (1974) found that delinquents and counselors who both scored high on the Psychopathic Deviant (Pd) scale of the Minnesota Multiphasic Personality Inventory were clearly differentiated on preconventional (delinquents) versus postconventional (counselors) moral reasoning. Maladaptive aggression decreases with maturity on Kohlberg's stages (Anchor and Cross, 1974). Manipulation, defined as using another person as a means to one's own ends, is frequently associated with adult stage 2 reasoning. College females operating with preconventional moral reasoning tended to form mutually manipulative relations with men to gain emotional affection and warmth through an exchange for sexual encounters (D'Augelli and Cross, 1975).

Rehabilitation programs based on Kohlberg's moral development model have been designed for delinquents and adult prisoners. Kohlberg, Scharf, and Hickey (1972) report on an intervention program in which a model cottage of twenty-two inmates and staff established a participatory, "just" community by writing a constitution, establishing a disciplinary procedure, and creating a self-governing structure. Moral discussion sessions focused on interpersonal dilemmas and on dilemmas between group norms and personal behavior. The inmates increased their identification with the group and its governance structure, and they engaged in the active maintenance and orderly functioning of the group as a social institution. Overall, these programs have met with mixed success. As part of a vocational training program, Candee (1977) has combined Kohlberg's model and Selman's model in an attempt to develop the role-taking skills and moral reasoning of interns —and thereby to improve medical care. Apart from these programs and that of Selman, described previously, no other uses of moral reasoning for collective/interactional disorders have been reported.

References

Anchor, K., and Cross, H. "Maladaptive Aggression, Moral Perspective, and the Socialization Process." *Journal of Personality and Social Psychology*, 1974, *30*, 163-168.

Baldwin, J. M. *Social and Ethical Interpretations in Mental Development.* New York: Macmillan, 1902.

Bronfenbrenner, U. "The Role of Age, Sex, Class and Culture in Studies of Moral Development." *Religious Education*, 1962, *57*, 3-17.

Campagna, A., and Harter, S. "Moral Judgment in Sociopathic and Normal Children." *Journal of Personality and Social Psychology*, 1975, *31*, 199-205.

Candee, D. "Role-Taking, Role Conception, and Moral Reasoning as Factors in Good Physician Performance: A Pilot Study." *Moral Education Forum*, 1977, *2* (2), 14-15.

D'Augelli, J., and Cross, H. "Relationship of Sex Guilt and Moral Reasoning to Premarital Sex in College Women and in Couples." *Journal of Consulting and Clinical Psychology*, 1975, *43*, 40-47.

Garbarino, J., and Bronfenbrenner, U. "The Socialization of Moral Judgment and Behavior in Cross-Cultural Perspective." In T. Lickona (Ed.), *Moral Development and Behavior: Theory, Research, and Social Issues.* New York: Holt, Rinehart and Winston, 1976.

Gilligan, C. "In a Different Voice: Women's Conception of the Self and of Morality." *Harvard Education Review*, 1977, *47*, 481-517.

Haan, N. "Two Moralities in Action Contexts: Relationships to Thought, Ego Regulation, and Development." *Journal of Personality and Social Psychology*, 1978, *36*, 286-305.

Harris, H. "Development of Moral Attitudes in White and Negro Boys." *Developmental Psychology*, 1970, *2*, 376-383.

Hawk, S., and Peterson, R. "Do MMPI Psychopathic Deviancy Scores Reflect Psychopathic Deviancy or Just Deviancy?" *Journal of Personality Assessment*, 1974, *38*, 362-369.

Hoffman, M. "Conscience, Personality, and Socialization Techniques." *Human Development*, 1970, *13*, 90-126.

Hogan, R. "Moral Conduct and Moral Character: A Psychological Perspective." *Psychological Bulletin*, 1973, *79*, 217-232.

Hogan, R. "Dialectical Aspects of Moral Development." *Human Development*, 1974, *17*, 107-117.

Hogan, R. "Moral Development and the Structure of Personality." In D. DePalma and J.

Foley (Eds.), *Moral Development: Current Theories and Research.* Hillsdale, N.J.: Erlbaum, 1975.

Hogan, R., and Dickstein, E. "A Measure of Moral Values." *Journal of Consulting and
Clinical Psychology,* 1972, *39,* 210-214.

Jurkovic, G., and Prentice, N. "Relation of Moral and Cognitive Development to Dimensions of Juvenile Delinquency." *Journal of Abnormal Psychology,* 1977, *86,* 414-420.

Keasey, C. "Implications of Cognitive Development for Moral Reasoning." In D. DePalma
and J. Foley (Eds.), *Moral Development: Current Theories and Research.* Hillsdale,
N.J.: Erlbaum, 1975.

Kohlberg, L. "The Child as a Moral Philosopher." *Psychology Today,* Sept. 1968, pp.
25-30.

Kohlberg, L. "Stage and Sequence: The Cognitive-Developmental Approach to Socialization." In D. A. Goslin (Ed.), *Handbook of Socialization Theory and Research.* Chicago: Rand McNally, 1969.

Kohlberg, L. "Education for Justice: A Modern Statement of the Platonic View." In N.
Sizer and T. Sizer (Eds.), *Moral Education: Five Lectures.* Cambridge, Mass.: Harvard
University Press, 1970.

Kohlberg, L. "Continuities in Childhood and Adult Moral Development Revisited." In P.
Baltes and K. Schaie (Eds.), *Life-Span Developmental Psychology: Personality and
Socialization.* New York: Academic Press, 1973.

Kohlberg, L. "Moral Stages and Moralization: The Cognitive-Developmental Approach."
In T. Lickona (Ed.), *Moral Development and Behavior: Theory, Research, and Social
Issues.* New York: Holt, Rinehart and Winston, 1976.

Kohlberg, L., Scharf, P., and Hickey, J. "The Justice Structure of the Prison: A Theory
and an Intervention." *Prison Journal,* 1972, *51,* 3-14.

Kurtines, W., and Grief, E. "The Development of Moral Thought: Review and Evaluation
of Kohlberg's Approach." *Psychological Bulletin,* 1974, *81,* 453-470.

Lickona, T. "Research on Piaget's Theory of Moral Development." In T. Lickona (Ed.),
Moral Development and Behavior: Theory, Research, and Social Issues. New York:
Holt, Rinehart and Winston, 1976.

Loevinger, J. *Ego Development: Conceptions and Theories.* San Francisco: Jossey-Bass,
1976.

McCord, J., and Clemes, S. "Conscience Orientation and Dimensions of Personality." *Behavioral Science,* 1964, *9,* 19-29.

McDougall, W. *An Introduction to Social Psychology.* London: Methuen, 1908.

Mahaney, E., and Stephens, B. "Two Year Gains in Moral Judgment by Retarded and
Nonretarded Persons." *American Journal of Mental Deficiency,* 1974, *79,* 134-141.

Mead, G. H. *Mind, Self and Society.* Chicago: University of Chicago Press, 1934.

Milgram, S. "Behavioral Study of Obedience." *Journal of Abnormal and Social Psychology,* 1963, *67,* 371-378.

Nass, M. "Development of Conscience: A Comparison of the Moral Judgments of Deaf
and Hearing Children." *Child Development,* 1964, *35,* 1073-1080.

Perry, W. G. *Forms of Intellectual and Ethical Development in the College Years: A
Scheme.* New York: Holt, Rinehart and Winston, 1970.

Piaget, J. *The Moral Judgment of the Child.* New York: Free Press, 1932.

Podd, M. "Ego Identity Status and Morality: The Relationship Between Two Developmental Constructs." *Developmental Psychology,* 1972, *6,* 497-507.

Rawls, J. *A Theory of Justice.* Cambridge, Mass.: Harvard University Press, 1971.

Rest, J. "Recent Research on an Objective Test of Moral Judgment: How the Important

Issues of a Moral Dilemma Are Defined." In D. DePalma and J. Foley (Eds.), *Moral Development: Current Theories and Research.* Hillsdale, N.J.: Erlbaum, 1975.

Rest, J. "New Approaches in the Assessment of Moral Judgment." In T. Lickona (Ed.), *Moral Development and Behavior: Theory, Research, and Social Issues.* New York: Holt, Rinehart and Winston, 1976.

Rest, J. "The Stage Concept in Moral Judgment Research." Unpublished manuscript, 1977.

Schlenker, B., and Forsyth, D. "On the Ethics of Psychological Research." *Journal of Experimental Social Psychology,* 1977, *13,* 369-396.

Selman, R. "Social-Cognitive Understanding: A Guide to Educational and Clinical Practice." In T. Lickona (Ed.), *Moral Development and Behavior: Theory, Research, and Social Issues.* New York: Holt, Rinehart and Winston, 1976.

Selman, R., and Damon, W. "The Necessity (but Insufficiency) of Social Perspective Taking for Conceptions of Justice at Three Early Levels." In D. DePalma and J. Foley (Eds.), *Moral Development: Current Theory and Research.* Hillsdale, N.J.: Erlbaum, 1975.

Simpson, E. "Moral Development Research: A Case Study of Scientific Cultural Bias." *Human Development,* 1974, *17,* 81-1-6.

Wilmoth, G., and McFarland, S. "A Comparison of Four Measures of Moral Reasoning." *Journal of Personality Assessment,* 1977, *41,* 396-401.

28

Jay L. Chambers

Personal Needs
Systems

Needs (or motives) are considered to be the movers or initiators of action. From the motivational viewpoint, all actions are attempts to satisfy a need or a combination of needs. Some needs (for instance, security or achievement needs) are named for external goals, conditions, or incentives which, when attained, will satisfy the need. Other needs (for instance, the aggression, sex, or play needs) are named for the behavior used to satisfy the need. Both internal and external conditions arouse, evoke, or affect needs.

The term *need* implies a deficit; that is, there is something lacking that the person desires to obtain. Certain needs, however, are based on the giving of one's self to others; thus, the metaphorical connotation of a need as a deficit is misleading. What all needs or motives have in common is the aim to increase satisfaction and avoid dissatisfaction. Just as a few kinds of sensations can combine to create many distinctive food tastes, so cognitive, emotional, and sensory factors can combine to make many kinds of discriminable satisfactions. Types of satisfactions appear to be additive in evolutionary development. Higher forms tend to inherit, accumulate, and add to the satisfaction capabilities exhibited by lower forms. Behaviors and satisfactions cannot be reduced to equivalencies, since the same identifiable satisfaction (such as sexual satisfaction) can be attained by a wide variety of behaviors and the same behavior can satisfy different needs. Thus, satisfactions function as convergent centers for associations between stimuli and responses.

Personal needs refer to needs of humans as individuals, as contrasted to the drives of animals or the needs of groups or organizations. A need system is concerned with more than linear causal relationships between isolated needs and behavioral variables; instead, it is concerned with sets of needs that are interrelated, by an organizing principle, to form a whole. The organizing principle of the motivation system is the aim to maximize satisfaction and minimize dissatisfaction for *all* needs. In order to meet this aim, the need elements are related to each other in ways that provide internal checks and balances, so that any one need or group of needs will not monopolize the time and energy available to the system. Need systems are considered to be subsystems of the total personality. The need system, for example, is interactive with the endocrine system on the physical side and a belief system on the psychological side. Although a personal need system is individualized, some general structural characteristics of human motivation systems are assumed to be common to most people.

Background and Current Status

The historical antecedents of present motivational concepts are imbedded in philosophical and religious issues (Edwards, 1972). Some of these issues are presently of little concern, and some are now viewed from a different perspective. Hedonism can be viewed as a motivation-oriented philosophy concerned with maximizing satisfaction of needs, not all of which are necessarily pleasurable or sensual. The Platonic and Aristotelian idea of an inner struggle between reason and emotion can be interpreted in terms of motivational conflict. For Plato the primary motive is to maximize virtue. St. Augustine developed this motivational theory into a conflict between the desire for virtue and the desire for pleasure. His resolution of this conflict was to love God and do as one pleases. St. Paul's statement regarding sinning ("That which I would do, I do not, and that which I would not do, I do") has been considered a forerunner of self-conscious awareness of inner motivational conflicts. In medieval times motivational factors were implied in arguments regarding the operation of the will. Moral philosophers, religious leaders, and theologians have been concerned with motivation in terms of good and bad desires and passions.

In literature many of the great artists, from Chaucer to Henry James, have been highly sensitive to and skilled in depicting the subjective passions and desires of their characters. Motivation portrayed in literature is, of course, highly intuitive and reveals the writer's own implicit theories regarding relationships between motives and character or personality.

Freud (1910) developed motivation concepts as one of the dominant factors in his personality theory. He took particular pains to explain abnormal behavior in motivational terms, thus rejecting views that abnormal behavior is necessarily the result of organic deficit or a manifestation of demonic possession. Motivational explanations of behavior attained much wider acceptance after Freud demonstrated that needs often function at unconscious levels. Several philosophers and writers (for example, Schopenhauer, Gustav Fechner, Eduard von Hartmann, Nietzsche, and Goethe) were aware of and had written about unconscious mental processes before Freud (Edwards, 1972). It was Freud, however, who forced the concept of the unconscious into the consciousness of psychiatrists

and psychologists and later into the public mind. His success in establishing this important psychological concept was due in part to his linking of unconscious mental processes
to behavior via motivation. Freud's analysis of motivation was very reductive; that is, he
telescoped most motivation into the categories of sex and aggression, or life (Eros) and
death (Thanatos). Psychoanalysts and personality theorists later broadened the motivation spectrum to include needs for superiority, social affiliation, self-actualization,
homeostasis, positive self-regard, self-consistency, and others.

At approximately the same time that Freud was developing many of his important
theoretical concepts, McDougall (1923) developed a theory of "hormic psychology,"
which emphasized psychophysical dispositions and sentiments. These were transitional
concepts between the accepted idea of instinct and the developing concepts of needs or
motives. McDougall's theory has had some continuing influence among behaviorists and
learning theorists, whereas Freud's influence has been most strongly felt among clinicians.

Murray (1953), with a background in medicine and psychoanalysis, was the first
theorist to apply a systems approach to motivation. The efforts of Murray and his co-
workers from areas such as psychology, sociology, and anthropology resulted in the Murray need system, one of the most comprehensive motivation classification systems developed to date. Murray described interactions and relationships between needs, using terms
such as *prepotency, fusion, subsidiation,* and *conflict.* Perhaps because he did not emphasize a general organizing principle, which would integrate the parts into a systematic
whole, the Murray needs have been used more as a motivation taxonomy than as a dynamic system.

Maslow (1970) produced a shorter and more general list of needs than the Murray
classification. He also developed a stronger systems organization for his theory than did
Murray. Maslow's needs are ordered hierarchically by the organizing principles of necessity for survival and the desire for self-actualization.

Angyal (1965) applied a systems approach to his holistic personality theory. Although he did not develop a list of motives or specify any particular set of specific needs,
he wrote about motivation from a formalized systems perspective, and he created concepts of autonomy and homonomy as general organizing principles in his dualistic theory
of motivation.

Psychologists, such as Maslow and Angyal, who have introduced systems thinking
into psychological theories were probably influenced, either directly or indirectly, by
Bertalanffy. Bertalanffy, a biologist, began to develop and expound a systems approach in
the 1930s as an alternative to mechanistic and vitalistic views of life. In applying systems
thinking to psychology and the social sciences, Bertalanffy theorized that man, because
of his ability to create and live in a world of symbols, occupies a special place in the
world. With symbols to represent future events, a person can act with true intention and
purpose (motivation concepts) and is not bound by causal deterministic principles, as
lower-level organisms are. Bertalanffy (1968) called his approach *general system theory,*
although in his later writings he viewed systems thinking as more of a philosophical perspective than a theoretical model (Bertalanffy, 1975).

The systems perspective has had and continues to have some influence in psychology, particularly in clinical assessment. Many researchers use the term *system* to describe
complex, multivariate phenomena even though they do not state what principles are implied by the term. Clinicians also look for interactions among personality variables and
attempt to organize the variables into a comprehensive whole. The systems perspective
has an affinity with holistic philosophy and is closely related to Lewin's (1936) field
theory and to Gestalt psychology, particularly as formulated by Köhler (1947).

Motivation continues to be an important construct in contemporary personality theory. Neo-behaviorists and humanists use motivation concepts to help account for responses and actions. Theorists with a cognitive orientation have traditionally been less interested in motivation. However, a synthesis between cognitive constructs (such as belief and expectation) and motivational concepts seems to be emerging (Weiner, 1974). There is some evidence of an increasing interest in a systems approach to clinical problems. Bertalanffy was elected an honorary fellow of the American Psychiatric Association in 1967. Miller (1978), as director of the Mental Health Research Institute at Ann Arbor, Michigan, conducted an active program of research in general systems theory. One of the fruits of this program is an excellent set of statements and principles to guide systems research in the clinical area and in the broader area of living systems. Family systems therapy, a recent formalized approach, considers the family as a social system that establishes a mental health environment for its members (Dodson, 1977). Psychologists have found systems theory helpful in studying social interactions in the area of community psychology (Rappaport, 1977).

Thus, from several areas there is a convergence of interests in motivation and systems theory. These interests, combined with new concepts and techniques, should encourage the development of personal need systems assessment.

Critical Discussion

General Areas of Concern

There are two major concerns regarding motivation assessment. The first concern is the well-recognized problem of developing better techniques for assessing and measuring motivation. This problem results from the fact that motives are constructs and, as such, are identified and measured indirectly, by inference, rather than by direct observation. Despite this difficulty, motivation has persisted as a theoretical construct because relationships between situational conditions and behavior are too complex to be useful or understandable without some reduction via unifying constructs.

Clinicians currently use standardized tests and interview material to assess motivation. Examples of standardized tests are the Edwards Personal Preference Schedule, the Stern Activities Index, and the Personality Research Form. Projective tests (such as the Thematic Apperception Test) can also be placed in this category, since the materials, administration, and scoring procedures have standardized versions.

Objective motivation tests are often used with an assumption that they measure the "strength" of needs. This is generally an untenable assumption, since the strength of a need is not constant and varies markedly from situation to situation. In clinical assessment, measures that relate to success and failure in satisfying motives may be more useful than measures that indirectly attempt to measure the potential strength of motives.

The information usually obtained about needs by objective tests is based on (1) self-ratings of behavior assumed to express the various needs measured, (2) values and attitudes regarding the needs, or (3) beliefs about the needs. Self-reports of behavior may be distorted by social desirability factors, degree of self-awareness, willingness to reveal information, and other factors. In addition, the same type of behavior may be quite differently motivated in different people (for example, one person may work hard to satisfy an achievement need, whereas another works equally hard to avoid blame or failure). Attitudes and beliefs may modify and control need expressions, but they are not, in any traditional sense, the same as needs, nor are they direct measures of the strength of needs.

Another motivation assessment problem has to do with the reliability of measurements between instruments. When the same population has been tested with different instruments designed to measure Murray needs, correlations between measures of needs labeled the same by the different tests have been disappointingly low (Fiske, 1973; Megargee and Parker, 1968). Examination of the items measuring the needs reveals some possible causes for these disturbing results. Inventory items often combine several discriminable needs in one statement. The combinations vary from one test to another. It is not surprising that the results differ, since the items are often asking quite different and quite complex questions. A fictitious example, not too unrepresentative of some actual items, illustrates the point. Suppose that subjects are asked to indicate how strongly they agree with the following statement: "I work hard to obtain recognition and power." The assumption might be made that this is a simple n achievement item. It can, however, be considered a complex statement that refers to needs for achievement, exhibition, and dominance. Subject responses will differ according to the varying emphasis placed on these three need elements. A sequential factor—the assumption that hard work will be followed by recognition and power—further complicates the statement. The statement also implies some hierarchical values, in that hard work is considered a means to the more important ends of acquiring power and recognition. Better agreement among the different test measures could be attained if simple need elements were used and if sequential and attitudinal factors were analyzed and controlled.

The operation of needs at different levels of consciousness creates assessment difficulties, some of which may be related to intratest reliability. If a need functions differently at different consciousness levels, the measures that tap different levels may not agree, even if they are valid for the particular stratum they measure. Many contradictions and inconsistencies in the behavior of individuals may be caused in part by shifts in motivation from one level of consciousness to another. The explanatory and predictive value of motivation assessment instruments would be considerably enhanced if reasonable estimates of the consciousness level measured could be provided. Motivation data thus classified would be very useful for developing more comprehensive theoretical models of motivation.

In practice, clinicians are more likely to use interview material than standardized test results to assess motivation. The success of this approach depends on the judgment and skill of individual clinicians, since there is little agreement among clinicians regarding such techniques. Free association and dream analysis are used by psychoanalytically oriented clinicians. Each therapist has his or her own techniques for eliciting client information, but the data thus obtained are usually not subjected, in any formal way, to motivational analysis. Improvement in objective motivation assessment may result in improved theoretical models, which, in turn, may lead to the development of more widely accepted interview techniques for need assessment.

The second major concern regarding motivation assessment has to do with the need to approach this assessment from a systems perspective. The main argument for adopting a systems approach to motivation is that motives operate in a systematic way. From a systems viewpoint, significant needs do not function as isolated forces but as elements in a system of interrelated elements. It is necessary to understand the structure and internal organization of a need system to understand how individual need elements function as mediators between situational and behavioral variables. This concern will be examined primarily for its research implications, since assessment techniques are often first developed to meet research interests and needs.

A systems-oriented researcher starts with a set of elements that are logically independent but interrelated by common aims or functions. With the set of elements selected and defined, the researcher proceeds to study the structure of relationships between the elements and to note the types of structural changes which the system can generate. Structural changes in the system are simultaneous and interactive, rather than linear and mechanistic; therefore, temporal and causal factors are important considerations in an analysis of structural change.

Although experimentation with an isolated variable is inconsistent with a systems approach, focus on a single variable is not. When the focus is on a single variable, the other elements in a system should not be controlled but should be monitored for structural changes. The elements in a system cannot be controlled without destroying the integrity of a system. "Controlling" the other elements in a nonstatistical or absolute way is analogous to studying the effects of physical exercise on heartbeat while trying to hold breathing constant.

Some specific examples may illustrate how systems thinking may be applied to research and assessment problems. Assume that an experiment has proved that chemical x destroys insect y. If the investigation goes no further and x is used as a pesticide to kill y, there could be some unfortunate reverberating consequences throughout the ecological system of which y and human beings are elements. A systems-oriented researcher would study the effects of x on the entire environmental system of y before recommending action.

Turning to the clinical area, a therapist and client may agree that the client is too passive and needs to be more aggressive. If the aggressive element in a client's motivational system has been strongly associated with an unrealistic fear of blame and punishment, then encouraging aggressiveness may escalate a conflict in the client. As the pressure to be aggressive increases, so does the associated fear of blame. The exacerbated conflict may produce rash, impulsive, desperate reactions, the consequences of which may further undermine the client's self-confidence. A systems-oriented therapist, after gaining an understanding of the client's motivation system, would work toward helping the client differentiate the aggression and blame avoidance needs. When the client can differentiate between situations where it is appropriate to be aggressive and situations where the consequences of blame and punishment make it appropriate to inhibit aggression, normal aggressiveness will be asserted.

Comparative Philosophies and Theories

Perhaps the strongest opponent of a systems approach is the philosophical position that, because of its inferential nature, motivation cannot be adequately and reliably assessed and is not, therefore, useful in a theoretical model. This represents the pure behaviorist stand. There are neo-behavioristic learning theorists who include motivation as an intervening variable, but they tend to limit their motivational interests to physiological needs that can be easily manipulated for experimental purposes. Although some behavioral therapists select and use, for shaping purposes, situational factors that have strong incentive or motivating power, their focus of interest is on modifying observable behavior and manipulating controllable motivating stimuli.

Disregarding the basic assumption of systems theory—that a system is composed of more than one element—several personality theorists have attempted to reduce motives to one broadly inclusive category. Reinforcement (learning theory), libido (psychoanalysis), and self-acceptance (client-centered therapy) are examples of attempts to reduce motivation to a single important or all-inclusive category. There is no question about the usefulness and necessity of reduction as an aid to scientific understanding. In some instances, however, simplification can become simplistic and can create the illusion of understanding at the expense of overlooking or ignoring critical distinctions.

Trait theory (Allport, 1961) and typology provide other alternatives to motivation analysis. Trait theory focuses attention on aspects of a person's behavior that are consistently expressed despite varying situational factors. Trait assessment is often useful for predictive purposes, based on the observation that past experience is the best guide to the future. Correct prediction based on past performance does not, however, necessarily promote better understanding of behavior. When successful, trait assessment can lead to prescriptions for shaping or modifying a trait—for instance, when a person is correctly assessed as having a strong trait of emotional reactivity and is persuaded to avoid stress or to take tranquilizers. On the whole, however, the clustering of behaviors into traits does not provide much of a handle for helping people understand or change cognitive, emotive, or motivational functions that may be strongly involved in their general welfare.

Another major competitor of a need system approach is cognitive theory. Cognitive theory, particularly as developed by Kelly (1963), explains behavior as the natural consequence of the way a person construes the world. From a purely cognitive point of view, motivation can be incorporated, absorbed, and disappear without loss or trace. For example, a person's need for dominance can be restated as his or her own construction of the belief that directing and controlling others is desirable and/or necessary. Ellis (1962) has developed a psychotherapy approach (rational emotive therapy or RET) that is strongly cognitive in orientation. Ellis feels that beliefs are important determiners of personality, but he also states that beliefs should be in accord with reality and that unrealistic beliefs are the cause of neurosis. The assumption of reality as an orienting point for cognitive structure differs in philosophy from the view that reduction of cognitive dissonance or the resolution of internal contradictions in the belief system is the primary cognitive goal.

Elaboration on Critical Points

Three previously mentioned motivation assessment problems will be briefly reviewed and elaborated in this section. These problems are the definition of need elements, multivariate simultaneous measurement of elements, and hierarchical and sequential relationships between need elements.

A useful model cannot be constructed for a system without the proper elements. The solar system may serve as a familiar model for elaboration of this point. If observations were available for only one planet in a solar system, a systems model could not be constructed. If observations were available for two or three planets, covariation of the locations of these elements could show some systematic relationships, but considerable variance still would be unaccounted for. If a series of simultaneous orbital locations of the sun, all the planets, and their satellites were available, then a model could be constructed that would be isomorphic with the movements in the solar system. In this model gravity would serve as the organizing principle, and the sun would be the dominant element in a hierarchical structure. The solar system offers an oversimple analogy for a personal need system, but it illustrates the importance of defining the significant elements in a system. In motivation assessment there is as yet little agreement about need elements.

With regard to the second problem, multivariate simultaneous measures provide necessary data for determining the basic structure of a system. A system state is defined as the interrelationship of the elements at a given point in time. Because of structural changes in a dynamic system, the observation of a single state can provide only a limited knowledge of the basic structure. If a series of structural states are observed, however, the basic structure of a system can be more reliably determined. Also, it may be possible to observe restructuring processes from a series of states. The familiar example provided by pictures obtained by a weather satellite may illustrate this point. The weather system usually changes relative to geographical locations, but a series of satellite pictures with other additional data can show that certain elements, such as cloud formations and pressure cells, maintain consistent relationships. A series of such pictures can also be used to make a time-lapse "movie" to study both constancy and change in the weather system structure.

Most psychological tests that assess motivation do not take into account the temporal factor; that is, they are designed to measure traits rather than a system structure. For example, a motivation test may indicate that a subject has a strong tendency to assert both aggression and nurturance. What is not determined is whether the subject attempts to assert both needs simultaneously or whether one need is inhibited while the other is expressed. The latter structure would produce quite different behavior with quite different consequences than the former.

Chambers and Surma (1977) has used the Picture Identification Test to obtain simultaneous measures of a number of need elements. For this test, subjects are asked to rate how strongly they feel each of twenty-two needs is revealed by the expression in a facial photograph. Since a photograph represents a person at a particular moment, the responses of a subject are focused on a stimulus representing a particular point in time. A series of such photograph ratings will produce several motivational states, from which a personal need structure can be derived.

The expression "hierarchical relationships between needs" refers to the order of priority assigned to needs for seeking satisfaction. It is assumed that hierarchical relationships are determined partly by personal and partly by situational factors. Attention here will be limited to personal factors.

Two basic personal factors are involved in the urgency or power attributed to a need. One may be labeled the ontological factor; the other, the value or attitudinal factor. The ontological factor has to do with beliefs held by a person about reality. If a person believes that human nature is basically combative and that life is hard and cruel, then he is likely to give priority to needs such as aggression and defendance. These beliefs may dictate priority regardless of the individual's values or attitudes about "the way things are." It is also true, however, that values or attitudes contribute to the priorities placed on needs. For example, a person may place priority on benevolent activities because of strong feelings that it is good to be nurturant despite ontological beliefs that life and people are not generally kind and benevolent.

Priorities are also created by strong beliefs about the proper or necessary sequencing of motivation. For example, if a person believes that the only way to satisfy a need for dominance is to acquire power through hard work, he will first give priority to achievement as a means to the more valued end of power and status.

Some of these considerations have been dealt with theoretically by Murray and Maslow. Some Thematic Apperception Test scoring techniques provide means for assessing subsidiation and sequential themes. Most of the more objectively scored instruments, however, have not attempted this type of assessment refinement.

Personal Views and Recommendations

The following proposals have, to a large extent, been implied by the foregoing analyses. The order in which the recommendations are presented indicates priorities based in part on a necessary and logical sequence and, to some extent, on personal interests and values.

The first priority is to establish a realistic and acceptable set of need elements. A suggested approach to this problem is to define need elements in terms of discriminable satisfactions. Each type of satisfaction is a nexus for situational, personal, and behavioral variables. The types of satisfactions that can be identified and differentiated by most people would define the basic need elements.

Assessment instruments should be designed that provide multivariate simultaneous measures of need elements. Such measures can be analyzed to reveal the state of a need system at a particular point in time. From a series of motivational states, the basic structure of a system can be identified. Adaptive or creative restructuring processes may also be perceived from a series of states that cover a period of change. Instruments should not attempt to directly measure the strength of need elements in a subject but should aim at measuring more constant personal factors that moderate or control needs. Factors relating to success and failure in satisfying needs are of particular importance.

Measures should be designed that explicitly identify the hierarchical structure of the personal need system. Multidimensional scaling and hierarchical clustering techniques can provide information regarding subsystem structure and hierarchical structure. Subjects' beliefs about necessary sequences of need expression or means-ends relationships between needs should also be studied systematically.

Assessment techniques should be designed that measure need functions at different levels of consciousness. Projective techniques reach unconscious levels more effectively than self-rating inventories. Strong emotional reactions or moods are often triggered by unconsciously held beliefs. Emotions are reactions to success (positive emotions) or failure (negative emotions) in satisfying needs. Techniques enabling clients to bring into consciousness the beliefs that trigger strong emotions might be effective for assessing need functions at unconscious levels.

Relationships should be investigated between need system structures and nosological classifications or other broad adjustment and personality categories. Developmental studies of an individual's need system structuring at different ages would be useful for both theoretical and practical assessment purposes. Interactions between need systems and other subsystems of the total personality should be studied.

The instruments designed should provide interpretations that the client can understand and find useful. Such knowledge can be used by clients to develop their own personality theory. Implicit personality theories play an important role in shaping behavior and personality. If made explicit, neurotic elements in an implicit theory may be modified toward more realistic views. Motivation test results designed for client understanding can promote collaborative therapeutic efforts between clients and clinicians.

Personal need system assessment has not developed to the extent that special ethical considerations are indicated. The usual ethical clinical concerns are, of course, necessary, with perhaps some extra caution in interpretation, since motives are indirectly assessed and function to a large extent at unconscious levels. Neither the clinician nor the client can afford to feel very confident about a particular motivation interpretation until considerable supporting evidence has been developed. It is also important to remember that, from a systems perspective, the same behavior can have many different causal or interactive motivational relationships. There is seldom, if ever, a single, simple motivational explanation for any human action.

Application to Particular Variables

Most need assessment instruments have been designed for and used with young adults, primarily college students. Some projective techniques that assess motivation have been adapted to wider age ranges; for example, the Children's Apperception Test is an adaptation of the Thematic Apperception Test.

Relationships between traditional motivation measures and demographic factors have not been extensively explored. Personal need systems data for such variables as age, socioeconomic level, and education are even less available.

Although sex differences usually require separate norms for most traditional motivation measures, the available data for personal need systems measures show little differences in the need structures of males and females. Present evidence, based largely on Picture Identification Test results, indicates that there is a general normal need system structure and that people with emotional and mental disorders tend to deviate from this norm. Deviations are greatest among psychotics, who tend to have poorly structured need systems. In general, nosological groups show less conceptual-perceptual differentiation between needs than do normals (Chambers and Surma, 1977).

References

Angyal, A. *Neurosis and Treatment.* New York: Viking Press, 1965.

Allport, G. *Pattern and Growth in Personality.* New York: Holt, Rinehart and Wilson, 1961.

Bertalanffy, L. von. *General System Theory.* New York: Braziller, 1968.

Bertalanffy, L. von. *Perspectives on General System Theory.* New York: Braziller, 1975.

Buros, O. K. *The Mental Measurements Yearbook.* Highland Park, N.J.: Gryphon Press, 1972.

Chambers, J. L., and Surma, M. E. "Need Associations and Psychopathology." *Journal of Personality Assessment,* 1977, *41* (4), 358-367.

Cofer, C. N. *Motivation and Emotion.* Glenview, Ill.: Scott, Foresman, 1972.

Dodson, L. S. *Family Counseling: A Systems Approach.* Muncie, Ind.: Accelerated Development, 1977.

Edwards, P. (Ed.). *Encyclopedia of Philosophy.* Vols. 5 and 8. New York: Macmillan, 1972.

Ellis, A. *Reason and Emotion in Psychotherapy.* New York: Lyle Stuart, 1962.

Fiske, D. W. "Can a Personality Construct Be Validated Empirically?" *Psychological Bulletin,* 1973, *80,* 69-72.

Freud, S. *General Introduction to Psychoanalysis* [1910]. (J. Riviere, Trans.) New York: Doubleday, 1943.

Gray, W. *General Systems Theory and Psychiatry.* Boston: Little, Brown, 1969.

Kelly, G. *A Theory of Personality.* New York: Norton, 1963.

Köhler, W. *Gestalt Psychology.* New York: Liveright, 1947.

Landfield, A. W., and Cole, J. K. (Eds.). *1976 Nebraska Symposium on Motivation.* Vol. 24. Lincoln: University of Nebraska Press, 1977.

Lewin, K. *Principles of Topological Psychology.* New York: McGraw-Hill, 1936.

McDougall, W. *Outline of Psychology.* New York: Scribner's, 1923.

Maslow, A. *Motivation and Personality.* (2nd ed.) New York: Harper & Row, 1970.

Megargee, E. I., and Parker, G. V. "An Exploration of the Equivalence of Murray Needs as Assessed by the Adjective Checklist, the TAT, and Edwards Personal Preference Schedule." *Journal of Clinical Psychology,* 1968, *24* (1), 47-51.

Miller, J. G. *Living Systems.* New York: McGraw-Hill, 1978.

Murray, H. A. *Explorations in Personality.* New York: Oxford University Press, 1953.

Rappaport, J. *Community Psychology: Values, Research, and Action.* New York: Holt, Rinehart and Wilson, 1977.

Tomkins, S. *The Thematic Apperception Test.* New York: Grune & Stratton, 1950.

Weiner, B. (Ed.). *Cognitive Views of Human Motivation.* New York: Academic Press, 1974.

29

David C. Rowe

Temperament

The term *temperament* refers to variation in the intensity or style of behavior. A number of temperamental traits appear to indicate the intensity of the expression of emotional states; for example, the expression of anxiety, as in the temperament of Neuroticism (Eysenck, 1967), and the expression of anger, as in Emotionality (Buss and Plomin, 1975). Another behavioral style refers to the ability to control or inhibit behavior. This dimension is reflected in temperamental traits such as Restraint (Guilford, Zimmerman, and Guilford, 1976). There are also large individual differences in motoric energy levels, and these are tapped by temperamental traits referring to activity levels of various kinds. Degree of preference for contact with others, or Sociability, also is considered a temperament (Buss and Plomin, 1975). In general, temperaments are thought of as broad aspects of personality that persist across a variety of situations and are also relatively stable qualities of behavior. The concept of temperament also carries the implication of a hereditary influence, though modern psychologists would not accept this as an a priori assumption. Genetic influence on temperamental traits must be first verified through behavioral genetic research.

Background and Current Status

The study of temperament can be traced back to the origins of scientific thought. In 460-377 B.C., as part of his theory of medicine, Hippocrates proposed that humors circulating in the body give rise to temperamental traits. For example, the sadness of the melancholic was thought to be caused by an excess of "black bile." Five centuries later this theory was systematized and extended by Galen, who theorized that blends of the four fundamental types of humors—melancholic (sad), choleric (quick to action), sanguine (warmhearted), and phlegmatic (calm)—could produce mixed temperaments. Hippocrates and Galen intended their theories primarily as explanations of disease, but they were also used to account for the behavior of normal individuals. The ancient four-temperament theory has not been used as the explicit basis for any twentieth-century theory, though Eysenck (1967) indicates that his model of temperament corresponds roughly to the Galenian. Furthermore, the connection of temperament and mental illness remains a focus of active research.

Another source of twentieth-century theory is Jung's (1921) theory of psychological types—namely, the extraverted and introverted personality types, which arise from the way that libido (instinctual energy) is displaced, either toward the external world or internally. The extravert's traits include interest in events, sociability, impulsiveness, and enthusiasm; the introvert's traits are mainly the opposite of these four characteristics. These ideas about the organization of personality appealed to quantitatively oriented psychologists because they suggested what traits might covary and what relationships might exist between personality and psychopathological conditions; for instance, Jung's prediction that hysterics are extraverted. Guilford's (1959) and Eysenck's (1967) theories of temperament both originated in attempts to confirm Jung's ideas empirically by means of factor analysis.

Guilford was one of the first researchers to attempt to delineate the structure of temperament. In the 1930s Guilford's early studies were aimed at clarifying the nature of extraversion and introversion and involved identifying traits through factor analyses of questionnaire items, no small undertaking at the time. Although some of the traits could be placed on an extraversion-introversion continuum, Guilford concluded that a multidimensional representation of personality was more correct. A series of studies led to the discovery of additional traits (Guilford and Guilford, 1934, 1936, 1939a, 1939b). In 1949 this work culminated in the publication of the Guilford-Zimmerman Temperament Survey (GZTS), which had scales for the ten major traits uncovered by Guilford's research program. Though these traits were selected so as to be independent, they are correlated to some extent. Guilford (1975) has developed a hierarchical model of personality which regards the ten GZTS traits as forming four second-order traits: Social Activity, Emotional Stability, Paranoid Disposition, and Extraversion-Introversion. It should be noted that this last second-order trait is *not* identical to Eysenck's E-I.

Eysenck's ambitious theory of temperament is both descriptive and experimental. The descriptive work concerns factor analytic identification of major temperamental traits. In an early study Eysenck (1947) factor-analyzed the symptoms of inpatient neurotics and found two factors: Neuroticism (N) and Extraversion-Introversion (E-I). In 1956 Eysenck's questionnaire for N and E-I was developed from a combined factor analysis of items from one of Guilford's questionnaires and items from an inventory of neurotic symptoms. Given the later disagreements between Eysenck and Guilford (Eysenck, 1977; Guilford, 1977), it is noteworthy that Eysenck initially used Guilford's items in the construction of his personality measure. A modest negative correlation was found between the measures of N and E-I, which was not predicted from Eysenck's theoretical view that they are independent personality dimensions. For this reason, the questionnaire was later revised and published as the Eysenck Personality Questionnaire, reducing somewhat the correlation between N and E-I. In his experimental work, Eysenck developed behavioral test measures of the temperament dimensions that borrowed creatively from laboratory tests of learning and perception. For a variety of measures—including tests of conditioning, figural aftereffects, sedation thresholds, and perceptual constancy—Eysenck predicted differential performance depending on temperamental type. By and large, these predictions were supported within Eysenck's laboratory, though there was sometimes difficulty in replicating them elsewhere (Berlyne, 1968). Because the performance of psychotics on these laboratory tests did not seem to depend on either dimension, Eysenck (1952) added Psychoticism as a third dimension of temperament. Recently he has published a questionnaire measure of Psychoticism and reported findings on its positive relationship with psychosis and criminal behavior (Eysenck and Eysenck, 1976).

Many of Eysenck's predictions are loosely derived from physiological models of each of the temperaments. Physiological models of N and E-I were first proposed in the 1950s and later revised in the *Biological Basis of Personality* (Eysenck, 1967). A physiological model of Psychoticism, which is probably the most speculative of the three models, was proposed by Eysenck and Eysenck (1976). Greatly simplified, the models can be summarized as follows: Psychoticism is related to an excess of male hormones, Neuroticism to the degree of reactivity of the autonomic nervous system, and Extraversion to the balance of mutual arousal and inhibition linking the cortex with the reticular formation. Unquestionably, the model of E-I has generated the most research, possibly because it connects, through the concepts of Pavlov and Hull, hypothetical neurological states with the ability to learn through classical and instrumental conditioning. Contrary to what one might expect on commonsense grounds, introverts are predicted to be more rapid learners than extraverts because the former are assumed to possess excitable nervous systems which more easily consolidate new stimulus-response connections.

Several twentieth-century theorists have tried to relate temperament to body type. The most influential of these theories was developed by Sheldon and Stevens (1942). The three basic body types of Sheldon's constitutional psychology are mesomorphy (muscular), endomorphy (fat), and ectomorphy (thin, light boned). Corresponding to each body type is a "dynamic aspect" consisting of presumably correlated traits. For example, mesomorphy was hypothesized to be associated with the somatotonic temperament, which includes need for exercise (not unexpectedly), aggressiveness, and claustrophobia. Although Sheldon's studies supported these relationships, they were methodologically flawed because Sheldon made the ratings of both somatotype and temperament. Subsequent studies using better methods generally reported only modest relationships between body type and temperament.

Two theories grew out of modern research on temperament. Thomas and his colleagues (1963) were impressed with the degree of individual differences in personality evident in infancy. In 1956 they started the New York Longitudinal Study (NYLS) of personality development, following children from 3 months of age to adolescence. A theory of temperament was developed inductively from parental reports of child behavior and direct observation of selected infants. The NYLS group has also explored the relationship of temperament to psychiatric disorders (Thomas and Chess, 1977; Thomas, Chess, and Birch, 1968). Buss and Plomin (1975) borrowed from Diamond (1957) the idea that temperaments are general dispositions shared by man and phylogenetically related animal species. In addition, they argued that a temperamental trait should be longitudinally stable, present in adults, and, most important, inherited. According to their theory and research, four temperaments—emotionality, activity, sociability, and impulsivity—at least provisionally meet these criteria.

Critical Discussion

General Areas of Concern

For the clinician confronting the large array of personality assessment options, some justification for using a temperament description of personality structure may be necessary. While most assessment devices, such as the Minnesota Multiphasic Personality Inventory (MMPI), yield a multidimensional picture of personality, they do not reveal important facts about the etiology of behavior disorder, whereas many temperament theories are primarily attempts to explain the etiology of psychiatric illness and adjustment problems. Eysenck (1957, 1961), Buss and Plomin (1975), and Thomas and Chess (1977) claim that temperaments, in part, determine psychiatric disorders. Given today's lack of consensus about the etiology of psychiatric disorders, the temperament theories are subject to opposition from other viewpoints. Nevertheless, if the temperament explanations are correct, or at least somewhere close to the truth, they offer the clinician an assessment system that should provide a real understanding of disorders, in addition to simple description. Moreover, temperaments may be important for less severe life problems. Temperaments can set the tone for social interactions, dampen or magnify the impact of the environment, and create problems when the mix of environment and temperament is incompatible. It should be emphasized that temperament explanations do not ignore the environment. Most temperament theories maintain that environmental stresses contribute to psychiatric problems. However, temperament theories are an antidote to those theories that rely on purely environmental factors by their attention to the role of a person's characteristics in the etiology of disturbance.

Studies of twins have shown a genetic component to variation in temperament (Buss and Plomin, 1975; Eysenck, 1967; Eysenck and Eysenck, 1976; Thomas and Chess, 1977). Although these studies implicate *both* environmental and genetic factors in the etiology of temperament, it is clear that genetic influence separates temperamental traits from other traits ascribed to purely environmental factors.

Temperament may lead to maladjustment or psychiatric illnesses through several paths. One way is through the inheritance of an extreme temperament. Almost any temperament, taken at the extreme, might create adjustment problems. For instance, inheritance of low Sociability might result in debilitating shyness, or inheritance of high Sociability might interfere with the independent pursuit of goals. Another way for temperament to produce psychiatric or adjustment problems involves interactions between temperament and environment. This analysis preserves the distinction between an underlying trait and symptoms that appear only when environmental stresses are introduced. It is important to consider whether the environmental stress is independent of the temperament or represents a reaction, albeit inappropriate, to the temperament. In the former case, temperament and environment can be considered as two separate causes acting jointly to produce maladjustment. In the latter, the environment might, in effect, be created by reactions to the temperament. For example, if a high-activity child should disrupt a classroom, his or her behavior may provoke very negative responses from the teacher. Thus, the child's behavior has provoked the teacher's reactions, but they, in turn, may be what is psychologically harmful to the child. As this example was intended to suggest, the relationship between temperament and pathology may be very complex, involving "vicious circles" and multiple causes, rather than any simple, unidirectional pattern of causation.

Comparative Philosophies and Theories

The temperament system proposed by the New York Longitudinal Study (NYLS) provides a framework for clinical intervention in infancy and early childhood (3-8 years). One of the first discoveries of the NYLS was that nine temperaments adequately describe the behavior in this age range: (1) Approach/Withdrawal, (2) Activity, (3) Adaptability, (4) Rhythmicity, (5) Intensity of Reaction, (6) Mood, (7) Threshold of Responsiveness, (8) Distractibility, and (9) Attention Span (Thomas and others, 1963). Thomas, Chess, and Birch (1968) investigated the relationship between the temperaments and psychiatric disturbance. About one third of the children who participated in the longitudinal study were diagnosed as having some type of psychiatric disturbance. The prevalence of certain temperaments and temperament syndromes was greater in this group than in the non-diagnosed comparison group. The Difficult and Slow-to-Warm-Up temperament syndromes were associated with disorder, while the Easy syndrome appeared to confer some immunity. The Difficult syndrome includes high Intensity of emotional reactions, lack of Rhythmicity of bodily functions, and poor Adaptability to new people and situations; the Easy syndrome is the opposite of these characteristics. The Slow-to-Warm-Up temperament is similar to the Difficult, except that better adaptation is made to new situations. Several other temperaments, including high Distractibility and either high or low Activity, were related to disturbance, though the statistical data are not strong (Thomas, Chess, and Birch, 1968). In a related line of research, Graham, Rutter, and George (1973) found that temperament is predictive of psychiatric disturbance in the children of a mentally ill parent.

One of the major contributions of the NYLS study is the idea of parent guidance therapy. A review of case histories revealed that most of the children with disorders were under stress because of incompatibility between their temperament and the environment. For example, a demand that a Slow-to-Warm-Up (STWU) child rapidly adjust to new situations led to the development of symptoms (see Thomas, Chess, and Birch, 1968, for other examples). The purpose of parent guidance is to improve the temperament-environment "goodness of fit" by advising parents on ways of bringing their attitudes and behaviors into harmony with their children's temperamental capabilities. To continue the previous illustration, parents were asked to expose STWU children to new people and situations slowly. Note that the attempt is made to change the handling of the child, not his or her temperament. How effective is this approach? In the NYLS sample, about 64 percent of the clinically diagnosed children responded favorably (though no untreated control group is available). These data suggest that the NYLS system of temperament can be applied in counseling parents and teachers about childhood behavior problems. A number of assessment devices are available for the NYLS temperaments, and they are reviewed by Thomas and Chess (1977).

Eysenck also conceptualizes psychiatric disturbance as arising from temperamental disposition (Eysenck, 1957; Eysenck and Eysenck, 1976). Empirical research has found that the following three temperaments characterize different diagnostic categories: (1) high Psychoticism (paranoid ideation, insensitivity to others), psychosis; (2) high Extraversion (a mixture of Impulsivity and Sociability), psychopathy; and (3) high Neuroticism (anxiety), neurosis. The situation is actually somewhat more complex, because each diagnosis is associated with a profile of scores on the PEN traits. For instance, hysteria is attributed to a combination of high N and medium E.

Eysenck believes that neurosis and psychopathy are *learned*. The temperaments set up conditions that make acquisition of the symptoms more likely. Neurosis is attributed to the acquisition of conditioned fears and anxieties from simultaneous dispositions toward strong anxiety responses (high Neuroticism) and rapid learning (Introversion). Psychopathy may result from the inability of the extraverted individual to learn proper modes of conduct through conditioning. Other predictions are made from these temperaments. Extraverts, because they are assumed to accumulate "reactive inhibition" (mental fatigue) quickly, are supposed to be susceptible to frequent rest pauses on tasks that require sustained attention. In agreement with this hypothesis, extraverts do not perform as well as introverts on monotonous industrial tasks and school work (Eysenck and Eysenck, 1968). The poorer vigilance performance of extraverts has also been confirmed in laboratory tests (Eysenck, 1967; Harkins and Geen, 1975).

Eysenck's theory has been successfully applied to educational counseling, industrial psychology, and psychiatric diagnosis (see Eysenck and Eysenck, 1968). However, if one were to follow Eysenck's recommendations, his personality dimensions would replace psychiatric nosologies. Moreover, he suggests that classification in the PEN system allows for rational choice of behavior therapy (see Eysenck and Rachman, 1965). Use of Eysenck's theory in this way would probably require a strong faith in it. Some chinks in the empirical armor, however, indicate that this theory should be used only where there is empirical support for an application. Berlyne (1968) and Brody (1972) both reviewed the literature on the *central* assumption equating extraversion-introversion with conditionability and found it to be equivocal. Thus, the generalization that introverts condition easily is not justified (see also Eysenck, 1965). There are also some weaknesses in Eysenck's dimensional system. Criminals, who should be placed with psychopaths (see Eysenck, 1964), do *not* typically score high on Extraversion (see Cochrane, 1974). Despite these provisos, Eysenck's theory is certainly worth investigation by clinicians, especially those who share his behavior therapy bent.

Applications of the Guilford theory are summarized in the *Guilford-Zimmerman Temperament Survey* (GZTS) *Handbook* (Guilford, Zimmerman, and Guilford, 1976). In the past twenty-five years, the GZTS has been correlated with just about every conceivable personality trait, performance skill, and occupational category. This material is ably presented in the *Handbook*. Clinicians may find the chapters on the clinical interpretation and use of the GZTS in counseling to be especially helpful. The major uses are the identification of adjustment problems and vocational guidance. Furthermore, Jacobs (1976) has found ways to apply the GZTS in implementing behavior therapy. GZTS profiles have been found for managerial personnel, nurses, religious occupations, and teachers, to mention a few. Not all groups are equally well identified; for example, teachers and secretaries had rather undistinguished profiles, while several traits distinguished managers from the general population. This information, combined with that on interest and values, should provide a good basis for vocational counseling. Two scales, Restraint (low impulsivity) and Thoughtfulness, are associated with academic achievement and may help pinpoint underachievers. A small amount of work has been done with abnormal populations. Not surprisingly, abnormal groups are low on emotional stability, and schizophrenics are also low on sociability. Expectations for GZTS relationships depend primarily on common-sense interpretations of the traits' meanings and do not imply causal mechanisms or genetic factors. From the vantage of pure assessment, this may not present a problem— witness the success of the empirically derived MMPI—but for those hoping to find a theory of behavior, Guilford's temperaments may be disappointing.

Elaboration on Critical Points

The various theories differ chiefly in the number and content of their temperaments. To some extent, these differences are semantic. Thomas and Chess's Intensity, Guilford's Emotional Stability, Buss and Plomin's Emotionality, and Eysenck's Neuroticism all refer to the strength of emotional responses. Nevertheless, subtle differences between the temperaments can be recognized in a close reading of item content. For example, Buss and Plomin's Emotionality does not include items referring to guilt and worry, a major component of Eysenck's Neuroticism scale. The use of just a few traits, as in Eysenck's theory, results in a broad description of personality but may sacrifice the finer discrimination of several homogeneous traits. Eysenck, in his typically uncompromising way, claims that the use of broad, second-order traits captures *all* the interesting information about personality. However, this extreme position does not seem justified, because information is always lost when relatively independent traits are combined.

In this regard, the current controversy over the structure of Extraversion is relevant. Guilford (1975, 1977) has challenged the unity of Eysenck's Extraversion; he finds its two component traits—Sociability and Impulsivity—to be independent, a position shared by Buss and Plomin (1975). Eysenck (1977) has answered Guilford's criticisms with a defense of a unitary E-I. To some, these arguments, based as they are on interpretations of complex factor analytic solutions, may seem to have little substance. However, if Sociability and Impulsivity should have different external correlates, this would be strong evidence for the use of separate measures of each. Eysenck reports that the Sociability items on the E-I scale fail to predict criminal behavior, while the Impulsivity items do so (Eysenck and Eysenck, 1976). Thus, it would seem wise to use separate measures of S and I or, if one is using Eysenck's Extraversion, at least to examine the correlates of the S and I items separately. Extraversion scores appear to be more strongly related to Sociability than to Impulsivity (see Plomin, 1976), a fact that should be borne in mind in the interpretation of results.

Personal Views and Recommendations

Temperaments are important because of their repeatedly established relationships to psychological disturbance. The preliminary New York Longitudinal Study results show that a temperament-based intervention can be successful. The work of Thomas, Chess, and Birch (1968) contains a rich lode of advice to clinicians on the use of temperament concepts in therapy. Eysenck's theory is most accessible to learning theory-oriented clinicians, who can take advantage of its implications for behavioral treatments. However, the MMPI provides a better measure than the Eysenck Personality Questionnaire for the assessment of standard diagnostic categories. The Guilford-Zimmerman Temperament Survey is competitive with Cattell's Sixteen Personality Factor Questionnaire (16 PF) (Cattell, 1957) and the California Psychological Inventory (CPI) (Gough, 1969). The GZTS may provide a better analysis of personality structure than the 16 PF because of the instability of the latter's factor structure and its grouping of seemingly disparate behaviors into traits. From a technical viewpoint, the GZTS and the California Psychological Inventory can be rated about equally. It is recommended that the clinician compare them for particular applications. The CPI, unlike the GZTS, is a criterion-based instrument and is probably stronger for identifying particular groups, such as delinquents. However, the GZTS gives a less redundant sample of personality traits and contains a number of traits that do not overlap with the CPI. As a measure of a broad range of personality traits, each with important correlates, the GZTS is probably superior. Buss and Plomin's temperament theory lacks the normative data necessary for most practical applications and should be used primarily for research.

Application to Particular Variables

Temperamental characteristics are available for assessment at all ages. Measures can be found for infants (Carey, 1970), for children (Buss and Plomin, 1975; Rowe and

Plomin, 1977; Eysenck and Eysenck, 1976; Thomas and Chess, 1977), and for adolescents and adults (Eysenck and Eysenck, 1975; Guilford, Zimmerman, and Guilford, 1976). Longitudinal data indicate that temperamental traits are moderately stable from childhood into adolescence and early adulthood (see review by Buss and Plomin, 1975). Temperament does appear to change over the adult years, with decreases in Extraversion and Psychoticism (Eysenck and Eysenck, 1976) and increases in Restraint (Guilford, Zimmerman, and Guilford, 1976). Users of temperament inventories should check age norms to determine whether corrections are necessary when comparing groups with markedly different mean ages.

Other demographic characteristics are important to consider in the assessment of temperament. Since the primary measure is the questionnaire, literacy is clearly a requirement, though the reading level demanded by most inventories is not high. Some temperamental traits in children have been quantified through direct observation or instrumentation; for example, the use of the actometer for the assessment of activity level (Loo and Wenar, 1971; see brief review of these methods in Buss and Plomin, 1975). Sex differences are found for some temperamental traits. Guilford, Zimmerman, and Guilford provide separate norms by sex for Activity, Ascendance, and Masculinity. Buss and Plomin (1975) and Eysenck and Eysenck (1976) also report some sex differences. It is worth emphasizing that these sex differences are usually small. High social class is typically associated with temperamental traits indicative of better social adjustment—for instance, Emotional Stability (Guilford, Zimmerman, and Guilford, 1976). Some racial differences have been reported for temperament (Eysenck and Eysenck, 1976; Guilford, Zimmerman, and Guilford, 1976). It is uncertain whether they represent true differences or reflect subcultural variation in the interpretation of questionnaire items.

Temperament measures can be used for a variety of industrial and clinical applications. Tests such as the Eysenck Personality Questionnaire and the Guilford-Zimmerman Temperament Survey have been used for personnel selection and vocational counseling. The actual value of a temperament inventory for personnel selection hinges on many factors, including base rates and selection ratios; Wiggins (1973) provides a thorough discussion of the problems and advantages associated with selection by personality tests. Temperament can also be used in psychiatric diagnosis. Eysenck's personality test can identify different psychiatric diagnoses through score profiles on the PEN traits (Eysenck and Eysenck, 1976). Buss and Plomin theorize that childhood hyperactivity is the result of a combination of activity and impulsivity. Whether or not this hypothesis is correct, the symptoms of hyperactivity do appear to correspond to an extreme of these temperaments. Ross and Ross (1976) evaluate some of the instruments designed specifically for diagnosis of hyperactivity. In addition, temperaments have been used in the measurement of therapy outcomes. Changes in temperament appear to be associated with recovery (Coppen and Metcalfe, 1965; Ingaham, 1966). Because behavior problems are alleviated when parents change their rearing practices to make them more congruent with their child's temperament, knowledge of temperament seems useful for pediatricians, psychologists, social workers, and other professionals who counsel parents.

References

Berlyne, D. E. "Behavior Theory as Personality Theory." In E. F. Borgatta and W. W. Lambert (Eds.), *Handbook of Personality Theory and Research*. Chicago: Rand McNally, 1968.

Brody, N. *Personality: Research and Theory*. New York: Academic Press, 1972.

Buss, A. H., and Plomin, R. *A Temperament Theory of Personality Development*. New York: Wiley, 1975.

Carey, W. B. "A Simplified Method for Measuring Infant Temperament." *Journal of Pediatrics,* 1970, *77,* 188-194.

Cattell, R. B. *Personality and Motivation: Structure and Measurement.* New York: World, 1957.

Cochrane, R. "Crime and Personality: Theory and Evidence." *Bulletin of the British Psychological Society,* 1974, *27,* 19-22.

Coppen, A., and Metcalfe, M. "Effect of a Depressive Illness on MMPI Scores." *British Journal of Psychiatry,* 1965, *111,* 236-239.

Diamond, S. *Personality and Temperament.* New York: Harper & Row, 1957.

Eysenck, H. J. *Dimensions of Personality.* London: Routledge & Kegan Paul, 1947.

Eysenck, H. J. *The Scientific Study of Personality.* London: Routledge & Kegan Paul, 1952.

Eysenck, H. J. *The Dynamics of Anxiety and Hysteria: An Experimental Application of Modern Learning Theory to Psychiatry.* London: Routledge & Kegan Paul, 1957.

Eysenck, H. J. "Classification and the Problem of Diagnosis." In H. J. Eysenck (Ed.), *Handbook of Abnormal Psychology: An Experimental Approach.* New York: Basic Books, 1961.

Eysenck, H. J. *Crime and Personality.* Boston: Houghton Mifflin, 1964.

Eysenck, H. J. "Extraversion and the Acquisition of Eyeblink and GSR Conditioned Responses." *Psychological Bulletin,* 1965, *63,* 258-270.

Eysenck, H. J. *The Biological Basis of Personality.* Springfield, Ill.: Thomas, 1967.

Eysenck, H. J. "Personality and Factor Analysis: A Reply to Guilford." *Psychological Bulletin,* 1977, *84,* 405-411.

Eysenck, H. J., and Eysenck, S. B. *Manual for the Eysenck Personality Inventory.* San Diego: Educational and Industrial Testing Service, 1968.

Eysenck, H. J., and Eysenck, S. B. *Psychoticism as a Dimension of Personality.* London: Hodder and Stoughton, 1976.

Eysenck, H. J., and Rachman, S. *The Causes and Cures of Neurosis: An Introduction to Modern Behavior Therapy Based on Learning Theory and the Principles of Conditioning.* San Diego: Knapp, 1965.

Eysenck, S. B., and Eysenck, H. J. *Manual for the Eysenck Personality Questionnaire.* San Diego: Educational and Industrial Testing Service, 1975.

Gough, H. *Manual for the California Psychological Inventory.* (Rev. ed.) Palo Alto, Calif.: Consulting Psychologists Press, 1969.

Graham, P., Rutter, M., and George, S. "Temperamental Characteristics as Predictors of Behavior Disorders in Children." *American Journal of Orthopsychiatry,* 1973, *43,* 328-339.

Guilford, J. P. *Personality.* New York: McGraw-Hill, 1959.

Guilford, J. P. "Factors and Factors of Personality." *Psychological Bulletin,* 1975, *82,* 802-814.

Guilford, J. P. "Will the Real Factor Extroversion-Introversion Please Stand Up? A Reply to Eysenck." *Psychological Bulletin,* 1977, *84,* 412-416.

Guilford, J. P., and Guilford, R. B. "Factors in a Typical Test of Introversion-Extroversion." *Journal of Abnormal and Social Psychology,* 1934, *28,* 377-399.

Guilford, J. P., and Guilford, R. B. "Personality Factors S, E, and M and Their Measurement." *Journal of Personality,* 1936, *2,* 109-127.

Guilford, J. P., and Guilford, R. B. "Personality Factors D, R, T, and A." *Journal of Abnormal and Social Psychology,* 1939a, *34,* 21-36.

Guilford, J. P., and Guilford, R. B. "Personality Factors N and GD." *Journal of Abnormal and Social Psychology,* 1939b, *34,* 239-248.

Guilford, J. S., Zimmerman, W. S., and Guilford, J. P. *The Guilford-Zimmerman Temperament Survey Handbook.* San Diego: Educational and Industrial Testing Service, 1976.

Harkins, S., and Geen, R. G. "Discriminability and Criterion Differences Between Extroverts and Introverts During Vigilance." *Journal of Research in Personality,* 1975, *9,* 335-340.

Ingaham, J. G. "Changes in MPI Scores in Neurotic Patients: A Three-Year Follow-Up." *British Journal of Psychiatry,* 1966, *112,* 931-939.

Jacobs, A. "Uses of the GZTS in the Contemporary Counseling Center." In J. S. Guilford, W. S. Zimmerman, and J. P. Guilford, *The Guilford-Zimmerman Temperament Survey Handbook.* San Diego: Educational and Industrial Testing Service, 1976.

Jung, C. G. *Psychological Types* [1921]. In H. Read, M. Fordham, and G. Adler (Eds.), *Collected Works.* Vol. 6. New York: Pantheon Books, 1953.

Loo, G., and Wenar, C. "Activity Level and Motor Inhibition: Their Relationship to Intelligence Test Performance in Normal Children." *Child Development,* 1971, *42,* 967-971.

Plomin, R. "Extraversion: Sociability and Impulsivity?" *Journal of Personality Assessment,* 1976, *40,* 24-30.

Ross, D. M., and Ross, S. A. *Hyperactivity: Research, Theory, and Action.* New York: Wiley, 1976.

Rowe, D. C., and Plomin, R. "Temperament in Early Childhood." *Journal of Personality Assessment,* 1977, *41,* 150-156.

Sheldon, W. H., and Stevens, S. S. *The Varieties of Temperament: A Psychology of Constitutional Differences.* New York: Harper & Row, 1942.

Thomas, A., and Chess, S. *Temperament and Development.* New York: Brunner/Mazel, 1977.

Thomas, A., Chess, S., and Birch, H. G. *Temperament and Behavior Disorders in Children.* New York: New York University Press, 1968.

Thomas, A., and others. *Behavioral Individuality in Early Childhood.* New York: New York University Press, 1963.

Wiggins, J. W. *Personality and Prediction: Principles of Personality Assessment.* Reading, Mass.: Addison-Wesley, 1973.

30

Robert W. Genthner

Personal Responsibility

Personal responsibility can be conceptualized as a continuum of victimization. Individuals at the lowest levels of this continuum are not willing to accept the consequences of personal actions. When they focus on personal problems, they mask personal role and responsibility by searching for the faults of others. Individuals at the highest levels accept total responsibility for personal problems. They do not see themselves as victims and are willing to act responsibly to solve personal problems. If they need help in resolving personal problems, they choose an ally rather than someone on whom they can depend totally. The ally is always a resource person, not someone who takes responsibility away from the person.

The following is a brief description of a scale representing five anchor points on this continuum of victimization:

- *Level 1.* The individual takes no responsibility for his life and almost never accepts the consequences of personal actions.
- *Level 2.* The individual has depersonalized his approach to life problems. He sees specific external forces (sex, job, mate, and so forth) as the cause of his problems. Because

he is pursuing a solution to personal problems by anger or depersonalized exploration, he does have some sense of personal responsibility.
- *Level 3.* The individual reveals a partial commitment to personal responsibility. That is, he verbalizes some responsibility for values, feelings, thoughts, and behaviors but blames others as often as he accepts responsibility for the personal problems.
- *Level 4.* The individual voices total responsibility for his life but is not committed to an effective action program to solve personal problems.
- *Level 5.* The individual takes total responsibility for his life. He is capable of making accurate discriminations between personal (internal) contributions and external contributions, yet he never *dwells* on how others have contributed to his problems. There is an indication of responsible, personal action directed toward resolving his problems decisively. The individual fully accepts the consequences of personal behavior.

Background and Current Status

The notion of humans as personally responsible is founded in existential philosophy. For example, in *The Sickness unto Death,* Kierkegaard ([1849] 1941, p. 25) writes of personal responsibility for despair: "Every actual instant of despair is to be referred back to possibility, every instant the man in despair is contracting it, it is constantly in the present tense, nothing comes to pass here as a consequence of a bygone actuality superseded: at every actual instant of despair the despairer bears as his responsibility all the foregoing experience in possibility as a present." Heidegger (1962) discusses the experience of anxiety as a function of a person's authenticity or inauthenticity. The authentic person is totally responsible for being in the world (that is, concerned with present possibilities rather than denying them). The inauthentic individual denies his possibilities and denies personal responsibility for the present and the past. Sartre (1943), a student of Heidegger's, credits the individual with full and sole responsibility. For Sartre, choice always exists because suicide is always possible for each living person. A person is never trapped by circumstances, because he always has the choice of life or death. It is from these philosophical bases that the existential and phenomenological psychologists (for instance, Binswanger, 1963; Boss, 1963; Frankl, 1963; Laing, 1959; Maslow, 1968; Rogers, 1961) developed their theories and treatment systems.

With its foundation in existential philosophy, the evolution of the concept of personal responsibility and its relationship to present-day clinical assessment can best be understood relative to psychotherapy systems. As early as Freud, patients' increased personal responsibility has been a goal of psychotherapy. While the philosophical assumptions of psychoanalysis are deterministic, Freud ([1927] 1949, p. 53) wrote that the purpose of psychotherapy is to give "the patient's ego freedom to choose one way or the other"; and with this choice comes responsibility for the consequences. Psychoanalysis does not, however, fully embrace the notion that humans are personally responsible for their lives and life circumstances. Freud saw people as victims of their inner drives and as needing a strong culture to keep them in check.

Carl Rogers, in the early 1950s, revolutionized psychotherapy, in both technique and theory, with his introduction of personal responsibility as a measurable goal of psychotherapy. While the European existentialists were developing the theoretical notion of individual responsibility in psychotherapy, Rogers was the first to operationalize the concept in a process scale that allows for measurement. Contrary to psychoanalysis, Rogers fully embraced the notion that humans are personally responsible; he postulated that they are free and not determined. Instead of external control and societal regulation, Rogers saw the need for people to express their inner potentials unhampered by the "shoulds" and constraints of society. In describing healthy functioning, Rogers (1961, p. 71) says that man becomes more psychologically healthy as he "moves away from a state where his thinking, feeling, and behavior are governed by the judgments and expectations of others, and towards a state in which he relies upon his own experiences for his values and standards." Rogers states specifically that, as a person begins to actualize, he becomes more "responsible" for personal problems: "The person lives his problems subjectively, feeling responsible for the contributions he has made in the development of his problems" (p. 157).

More current psychotherapy systems have also explicated their goal of greater client responsibility. Ellis's (1963) rational-emotive therapy views the person as directly responsible for his life. Ellis maintains that it is what people say to themselves about an event, and not the event itself, that causes them to feel certain ways. Thus, Ellis asserts that people are personally responsible for their feelings and are not made to feel certain ways by other people or events. Rational-emotive therapy helps people to change their self-communications in order to change their feeling responses. It teaches people to be responsible for what they are feeling, instead of being victims of external events. A rational-emotive therapist would estimate the degree to which persons take responsibility for their life by their self talk. For example, people who tell themselves that they "should have done something" (in the past) or "should do something" (in the future) would be viewed as not living rationally and thus not taking responsibility for their behavior. Similarly, a person who says "They made me angry" would not be functioning responsibly, since rational-emotive therapy maintains that people make themselves angry by what they say intrapersonally.

More recently, Perls has emphasized the need for greater personal responsibility as a core element to healthy functioning. He equates the lack of personal responsibility with poor psychological adjustment: "We are infantile because we are afraid to take responsibility in the now. To take our place in history, to be mature means giving up the concept that we have parents, that we have to be submissive or defiant, or the other variations on the child's role that we play" (Perls, 1970, p. 17). Perls describes pathology as projecting one's feelings onto others and, therefore, throwing the responsibility for one's own responses and actions onto others. In order to own these feelings, to identify them as part of oneself, one must be "willing to take full responsibility—responsibility for yourself, for your actions, feelings, thoughts" (Perls, 1970, p. 29).

In one of his final works, Perls (1973) maintains that neurosis is the denial of personal responsibility through the use of either confluence, introjection, retroflection, or the previously mentioned projection: "What the patient does through these mechanisms is, in essence, to shirk responsibility for his behavior. . . . To reintegrate the neurotic we have to make use of whatever share of responsibility he is willing to take" (p. 79).

The notion of personal responsibility within more behavioristic orientations developed along different lines. Initially, personal responsibility was a strictly humanistic term. The early behaviorists believed that the external environment causes behavior and that the individual is not responsible in any way. One of the first breaks from this position was made by Homme (1965), a student of Skinner. Homme argued that the so-called "private events" of the mind are in fact conditionable, and he outlined techniques for "covert control" of specific thoughts. After Homme, the notion of covert conditioning was developed and expanded by Cautela (1966, 1967), who offered the self-control technique of covert sensitization, whereby imagery and aversive techniques are used to provide the client with a means of self-control. This issue of self-control later influenced the development of a theory of reciprocal determinism, emphasizing the complex causal interaction between the organism and its environment (Bandura, 1969, 1971; Thoresen and Mahoney, 1974).

Mahoney (1972, 1974; Mahoney and Thoreson, 1974) and Meichenbaum (1974) are cognitively oriented behaviorists whose work is consistent with issues of personal responsibility. Meichenbaum uses behavioral techniques to help people become aware of and in control of their thinking. Like Ellis, he believes that thoughts create emotions and that changing inner dialogue will change emotions and overt behavior. Mahoney offers four general categories of research on self-control techniques: stimulus control, self-monitoring, self-reward, and self-punishment. In each of these techniques, the emphasis is on putting the client-patient in charge of his life.

While there is an abundance of theoretical speculation concerning the term *personal responsibility,* the empirical literature is only at a beginning stage of development. Kirtner and Cartwright (1958) used a typology system of five discrete categories, indicating various degrees of *personal responsibility,* to rate psychotherapy recipients. They found that subjects rated most personally responsible were more likely to have a successful therapy experience. Kirtner and Cartwright's research efforts grew out of Roger's theory of client-centered therapy and are consistent with the Rogerian notion that healthy functioning is related to seeing oneself as the source of one's circumstances.

A concept from personality theory that has received much attention and is parallel to personal responsibility is the theoretical construct of locus of control (Rotter, 1966). From his work within social learning theory, Rotter developed an internal-external locus of control (I-E) scale for measuring the degree to which individuals attribute their receiving reinforcements to their own behavior. Internalized persons see the self as in control of their receiving reinforcements and would theoretically be considered high in personal responsibility. Externalized persons see the control of reinforcements as external to the self and thus see the self as less responsible for personal life. The I-E scale is a 23-item forced-choice paper-and-pencil test. There have been several reviews of the extensive literature (Joe, 1971; Lefcourt, 1966, 1972; Minton, 1967; Phares, 1976), as well as an overview of the development, theory, and research of the concept of locus of control and its place in personality theory (Phares, 1976).

Adapting the theoretical notions of internal versus external locus of control to Kirtner and Cartwright's typology system, Pierce, Schauble, and Farkas (1970) developed a five-point continuous rating scale for measuring client internalization. They found that, with a brief, straightforward intervention, they could positively change clients on the I-E dimensions. In another study, Schauble and Pierce (1974) found that internalization ratings were related positively to rated change in Minnesota Multiphasic Personality Inventory (MMPI) protocols.

A rating system for assessing personal responsibility was refined and developed by Genthner and Jones (1976). In a preliminary study, they were able to establish construct validity, reliability, and rater trainability for a five-point rating system developed to assess personal responsibility (Genthner, 1974). They found that personal responsibility ratings of taped interviews were significantly correlated with fifteen scales of the California Personality Inventory, including an average score which was a measure of overall adjustment. This study also found that, after a brief training period, graduate student raters could achieve high levels of conceptual agreement in their ratings of personal responsibility. In other studies (Genthner, 1976; Neuber and Genthner, 1977; Palmer and Genthner, 1977), reliability and construct validity were further established for the personal responsibility rating system. Personal responsibility ratings were correlated positively with an experienced psychologist's ratings of psychological effectiveness (Genthner, 1976) and were correlated negatively with scores on the Taylor Manifest Anxiety Scale (Palmer and Genthner, 1977). Personal responsibility ratings appear also to be significantly related to

Erikson's (1959) notion of identity achievement (Neuber and Genthner, 1977). Beyond the construct validity studies mentioned above, personal responsibility ratings were also found to discriminate human relations training outcome. Trainees who were rated high in personal responsibility gained more from training than trainees rated low in personal responsibility on indices designed to measure ability to communicate effectively (Genthner and Falkenberg, 1977).

In addition to the empirical work with the Genthner (1974) personal responsibility rating system, there has been some initial attempt to adapt the system to the treatment of families. Genthner and Veltkamp (1977) theorize that intervention strategies with families should take into account the level of responsibility of the family. A family functioning at the lowest levels of responsibility, where the members feel hopeless and resigned to the failure of the family, would probably not benefit from family therapy, at least not initially. Families functioning at middle levels of responsibility would probably benefit from a family systems type of intervention, and families functioning near the highest levels of responsibility would probably need only a problem-solving type of intervention.

Personal responsibility has also been assessed by means of Shostrom's (1972) Personal Orientation Inventory (POI). The POI is a measure of self-actualization and was developed from humanistic notions of psychological health and growth. The dimension of the POI that is equivalent to personal responsibility is Inner Directedness. Shostrom's definitions of inner-directed and other-directed people are highly consistent with the notions of personal responsibility.

> *The Inner-Directed Person.* The inner-directed person appears to have incorporated a psychic "gyroscope" which is started by parental influences and later on is further influenced by other authority figures. The inner-directed man goes through life apparently independent, but still obeying this internal piloting. The source of inner direction seems to be implanted early in life and the direction for the individual is inner in the sense that he is guided by internal motivation rather than external influences. This source of direction becomes generalized as an inner core of principles and character traits.
>
> *The Other-Directed Person.* The other-directed person appears to have been motivated to develop a radar system to receive signals from a far wider circle than just his parents. The boundary between the familial authority and other external authorities breaks down. The primary control feeling tends to be fear or anxiety of the fluctuating voices of school authorities or the peer group. There is a danger that the other-directed person may become oversensitive to "others' " opinions in matters of external conformity. Approval by others becomes for him the highest goal. Thus, all power is invested in the actual or imaginary approving group. Manipulation in the form of pleasing others and insuring constant acceptance becomes his primary method of relating. Thus, it can be seen that the original feeling of fear can be transformed into an obsessive, insatiable need for affection [Shostrom, 1972, p. 17].

Shostrom has extensively validated his POI scale, and since its development the scale has been used in numerous studies. The POI manual/bibliography (Shostrom, 1972) provides an appropriate introduction to this instrument.

One obvious problem with a review of the research on the construct of personal responsibility is that there are variations in the definition of the concept from study to study. Differing definitions, the general lack of empirical validity, and reliance on face validity for some scales designed to measure the concept make a statement based on the general findings tenuous at best.

Critical Discussion

General Areas of Concern

Personal responsibility is not synonymous with social responsibility. When a personally responsible person assumes social responsibility (by obeying social mores or societal laws), he does so not out of fear or reprisal or negative sanction but, rather, because doing so is consistent with who he is at that given moment. Thus, being personally responsible means being "responsible for," not "responsible to." Personal responsibility originates from within. The personally responsible individual is responsible for his choices and is responsible to an inner authority rather than an external authority.

Another form of responsibility dealt with extensively in the psychological literature is the concept of attribution of responsibility. Based on Heider's (1958) model of the psychology of interpersonal relations, attribution theory concerns the way in which a person interprets causality in his world. Attribution theorists are interested in evaluating the focus and amount of blame that an individual attributes to others. In contrast, personal responsibility investigators are interested in blame only to the degree that it masks the individual's perspective of personal responsibility in a given situation. While there is an overlap, the core focus is different for the two approaches.

To clarify the issue of blame and personal responsibility, it should be understood that personal responsibility is not blame or fault. To blame oneself for one's life consequences is as irresponsible as to blame others. Personal responsibility postulates, "I am the source of meaning in my life." It is a shift in focus from "who is at fault" to "how can I understand myself and my personal constructs from this experience so that I can act fully on my life." It is a shift from a past focus to a focus on the present. The past is useful only in its present meaning.

The difference between attribution of responsibility and personal responsibility may become clear with an example of attribution of inadequacy from Valins and Nisbett (1971). They tell of the rejecting attitude of established combat units toward new recruits. The new recruit erroneously attributes this rejection to his own inadequacy and decides "They hate me," rather than "This is the way they treat all new recruits." The latter attribution is the accurate one from Valins and Nisbett's perspective. A personally responsible perspective would be less interested (but not uninterested) in the "accurate" attribution; instead, it would note that the new recruit is willing to define himself by the acceptance or rejection of his seasoned colleagues and is unwilling to take responsible action to change an uncomfortable situation.

Another concern has to do with personal responsibility relative to the acculturation process. Most people learn their values and points of view from parents, teachers, peers, and other socializing agents. This process of acculturation is often subtle and powerful and so complete that people believe that their points of view and value systems are facts and, therefore, unchallengeable. When a person loses the sense that his values create the meaning in a given situation, he develops a "should" perspective—for example, "I should be popular and well liked." When such an individual is disliked, he blames the world for not treating him better, or he blames himself for not getting more approval. He fails to see that his discomfort is generated out of his value system, not out of an observable fact (for instance, that he was not invited to a party). A more general value that is learned through culture is that one should be happy, calm, and serene and that it is wrong to feel hurt, upset, or angry. A personally responsible individual, however, allows for discomfort and recognizes the source of the discomfort as his own desires. For example, if he wants a promotion and does not get it, he does not feel that he is a victim of those making the decision but recognizes that he did not do whatever was necessary to get the promotion. He still may feel bad about not getting the promotion, but he owns the bad feelings. He then is free to evaluate whether he is willing to do what is necessary to get what he wants in this situation (that is, a promotion)."

Because one learns how to behave from others, he often feels less than responsible for personal behavior. Self comments might include "I did it because that's the way you're supposed to do it" or "I did it to please." The person constructs many reasons why he behaves in a certain way. It is these whys that interfere with personal responsibility. They explain behavior away from the behaver; they determine behavior separate from the doer. Behavior that is personally responsible is experienced as being the behaver. That is, "I am what I am doing from moment to moment" or "I do not behave because of my point of view or because someone has taught me to behave this way but, rather, because I have chosen to behave this way in the moment." Thus, with personal responsibility there can be no excuse for behavior. As Horosz (1975) explains, there can be no system of totality that is ultimately responsible; there is only the individual human orderer. What a person learns from his socializing agents is best understood as a guide, not a determinant of behavior.

Comparative Philosophies and Theories

While the concept of personal responsibility is most identified with existentialism as a philosophical system, some attempts have been made to reconcile it with more behavioristic perspectives. The existentialists believe that individuals are personally responsible because they have freedom to choose and with this freedom comes the responsibility for the consequences of their choices. The behaviorists, in contrast, believe that behavior is determined. In Skinner's (1971) view, since a person's behavior is a function of his environmental contingencies, he cannot be held responsible for either positive or negative accomplishments. More recent behaviorists (for instance, Bandura, 1971; London, 1969; Mahoney, 1974) have taken issue with this strict environmental determinism. Craighead, Kazdin, and Mahoney (1976) offer a convincing argument that reconciles personal responsibility and behaviorism. They posit that "the act of holding people responsible or making them accountable for their behavior is in itself a very important environmental event" (p. 174). Their concept of "reciprocal determinism" views behavior and environment as reciprocally determined. That is, environments can cause behavior and behavior can cause environments. Therefore, a person "can take an active role in self-determination" (p. 176). They are careful not to suggest that free will is in force in this self-determination. The self-determining behaviors are, from their point of view, caused by previous environments and behaviors.

A comparison of personal responsibility from a social learning perspective (Rotter's, 1966, internal-external locus of control) and personal responsibility from an existential perspective (Genthner's, 1974, personal responsibility rating system) reveals some major differences between these two basically similar approaches. Empirically, two studies (Genthner and Jones, 1976; Palmer and Genthner, 1977) have found no relationship between personal responsibility ratings and internal-external locus of control scale (I-E) scores. The difference between the personal responsibility rating system and the locus of control construct is apparent in the items of the I-E scale used to assess locus of control. One item on the I-E scale is "Most people don't realize the extent to which their lives are controlled by accidental happenings." This statement might be endorsed by one person rated low in personal responsibility and rejected by another. The individual who rejects the statement might do so not because he believes that he is responsible for his life but because he believes "If it weren't for my enemies (mate, boss, or whomever), I would be free to live my life."

A second difference between I-E and PR is apparent in the definition of the person rated high in personal responsibility versus the person who scores in the internal direction on the I-E scale. An internalized person is defined as someone who *believes* that he has control over his reinforcements. A person rated high in PR must have an effective *behavioral* program to receive a high PR rating. Therefore, personal responsibility has an action component that is excluded from or only implied in locus of control theory.

A third possible difference between PR and I-E is that I-E may not be a linear measure of adjustment. Phares (1976) speculates that I-E may, in fact, be a curvilinear measure of adjustment. People at the extremes—that is, extreme internalizers as well as extreme externalizers—may both be representative of poor adjustment. In contrast, PR appears to be a linear measure of adjustment.

Elaboration on Critical Points

The issue of personal responsibility relative to freedom and determinism might be best understood from Kuhn's (1970) treatise on the revolution of science. Kuhn maintains that science does not grow in linear fashion but, rather, grows through paradigmatic shifts. That is, perspectives are enhanced or changed not because of advances in technology or information but because of a shift in point of view. For a long time, Uranus was regarded as a star. When the point of view shifted and the possibility of its being a planet was considered, it and twenty other planets were discovered over the next ten years. Kuhn further maintains that shifts in point of view do not uncover reality but, in fact, create a reality that did not exist prior to the paradigm. This reasoning is consistent with Horosz's (1975) statement that freedom and determinism are paradigms used to order experience and thus do as much to determine experience as they do to explain it.

If personal responsibility is to become an effective life perspective, a paradigmatic shift must take place—a shift away from the point of view that "I am determined and thus things happen to me out of my control" to the point of view that "I can influence my life condition and its meaning." Thus, personal responsibility requires that the person is neither free nor determined but rather that he construe his life from either an influence or a no-influence perspective. If people construe themselves as externally determined, then they will in fact be determined; their paradigms will ensure this. Similarly, if they construe themselves as free, they will in fact be free.

Personal Views and Recommendations

There are two points of view that deserve emphasis. The first is that the assessment of personal responsibility offers clinical data that are directly related and relevant to treatment. The second is that personal responsibility is a conceptualization that offers assessment along a continuum of normalcy rather than pathology. With this point of view, it is possible to avoid the stigmatization that often comes with traditional diagnostic systems. For example, persons labeled schizophrenic or neurotic become the disease. They are schizophrenics or some other disease or disorder. The labeling process offers no alternative and views the person labeled as determined by the disorder. In contrast, personal responsibility is a perspective that people in treatment can learn. They can learn the entire continuum and therefore are given the possibility of alternative ways of behaving and of viewing themselves.

Personal responsibility is a complex construct. It is a compromise between a pure art-philosophy point of view and a more scientific point of view. Because it has not been reduced to its component parts, it has preserved its utility to the practitioner. Because it has, in some forms, demonstrated empirical respectability (in that it is a concept that can be reliably measured), it has attained some scientific rigor.

In addition to the previous points, two major ethical considerations deserve emphasis. The first is that the potential for causing pain to another person through labeling is always an issue in clinical assessment. There is a danger implicit in all evaluation procedures that the evaluator can describe the person being evaluated as "wrong" or deny his dignity in some manner through the use of the evaluation tool. This is especially important with personal responsibility evaluations because of the potential for denying one's own responsibility by demanding that others be more responsible. When working with personal responsibility, a therapist might erroneously believe that "Nothing I do or say can hurt the other person because he is fully responsible for all that happens to him."

The second major ethical concern is a continuation of the issue of denying another person's experience. In postulating a set of alternative attitudes to pathology, one can use personal responsibility to say, "You should be more responsible, and the way you feel is not valid." Thus, personal responsibility is used not to facilitate growth but to deny the person evaluated his experience of being a victim. From clinical experience, it has been observed that people who are functioning at low levels of personal responsibility experience themselves as victims and thus are victims. The job is not to deny their experience but to empathize with it, give it space to exist, and offer alternative perspectives that might free them from this victim perspective. People need to feel safe before they can experiment with the possibility of being responsible for their lives.

Application to Particular Variables

Personal responsibility appears to be a concept that has developmental implications (Genthner and Hartley, 1976). That is, because children are dependent on adults for their survival needs, it is difficult for them to experience themselves as autonomous and responsible. Thus, as children grow and mature into adults, they more fully realize their autonomy and physically and psychologically give up dependence on their parents and surrogate parents. Within these limits, relative personal responsibility can be obtained for all ages. There appears to be no restriction of personal responsibility on the basis of sex, educational level, socioeconomic status, vocation, or ethnic/racial factors.

Personal responsibility assessments of the physically handicapped—people who have lost a limb, have been paralyzed, or have a terminal disease—will give insight into the person's level of adjustment to this life incident. How responsible a person can be for his life after a critical incident will determine the quality of life he has after the adjustment period. When psychosis is viewed from a personal responsibility perspective, a new dimension is added to the disorder. If, instead of viewing a psychotic as a victim of a disease, the clinician teaches the person to own his hallucinations and delusions, the possibility of a transformation is greater.

References

Bandura, A. *Principles of Behavior Modification.* New York: Holt, Rinehart and Winston, 1969.

Bandura, A. "Vicarious and Self-Reinforcement Process." In R. Glaser (Ed.), *The Nature of Reinforcement.* New York: Academic Press, 1971.

Binswanger, L. *Being-in-the-World: Selected Papers of Ludwig Binswanger.* (Edited and with critical introduction by J. Needleman.) New York: Basic Books, 1963.

Boss, M. *Psychoanalysis and Daseinanalysis.* New York: Basic Books, 1963.

Cautela, J. R. "Treatment of Compulsive Behavior by Covert Sensitization." *Psychological Record,* 1966, *16,* 33-41.

Cautela, J. R. "Covert Sensitization." *Psychological Reports,* 1967, *20,* 459-468.

Craighead, W. E., Kazdin, A. E., and Mahoney, M. J. *Behavior Modification Principles: Issues and Applications.* Boston: Houghton Mifflin, 1976.

Ellis, A. *Reason and Emotion in Psychotherapy.* New York: Lyle Stewart, 1963.

Erikson, E. H. "Ego Development and Historical Change." *Psychological Issues,* 1959, *1,* Monograph 1.

Frankl, V. *Man's Search for Meaning: An Introduction to Logotherapy.* New York: Washington Square Press, 1963.

Freud, S. *The Ego and the Id* [1927]. (J. Riviere, Trans.) London: Hogarth Press, 1949.

Genthner, R. W. *A Manual for Rating Personal Responsibility.* Richmond: Eastern Kentucky University, 1974.

Genthner, R. W. "An Empirical Investigation of the Personal Responsibility Rating System." *Journal of Psychology,* 1976, *92,* 53-56.

Genthner, R. W., and Falkenberg, V. A. "Changes in Personal Responsibility as Function of Interpersonal Skills Training." *Small Group Behavior,* 1977, *8,* 533-539.

Genthner, R. W., and Hartley, B. "Some Developmental Aspects of Personal Responsibility." Unpublished manuscript, Eastern Kentucky University, 1976.

Genthner, R. W., and Jones, D. E. "Personal Responsibility: Validity, Reliability, and Rater Trainability." *Journal of Personality Assessment,* 1976, *40,* 269-275.

Genthner, R. W., and Veltkamp, L. "A System for Assessing Family Function-Dysfunction." *International Journal of Family Counseling,* 1977, *5,* 79-85.

Heidegger, M. *Being and Time.* New York: Harper & Row, 1962.

Heider, F. *The Psychology of Interpersonal Relations.* New York: Wiley, 1958.

Homme, L. E. "Perspectives in Psychology. XXIV: Control of Coverants, the Operants of the Mind." *Psychological Record,* 1965, *15,* 501-511.

Horosz, W. *The Crises of Responsibility.* Norman: University of Oklahoma Press, 1975.

Joe, V. C. "Review of the Internal-External Control Construct as a Personality Variable." *Psychological Reports,* 1971, *28,* 619-640.

Kierkegaard, S. *The Sickness unto Death* [1849]. Princeton, N.J.: Princeton University Press, 1941.

Kirtner, W. L., and Cartwright, D. S. "Success and Failure in Client Centered Therapy as a Function of Initial Responsibility in Therapy Behavior." *Journal of Consulting Psychology,* 1958, *22,* 329-335.

Kuhn, T. S. *The Structure of Scientific Revolutions.* (2nd ed.) Chicago: University of Chicago Press, 1970.

Laing, R. D. *The Divided Self: An Existential Study of Sanity and Madness.* London: Tavistock, 1959.

Lefcourt, H. M. "Internal Versus External Control of Reinforcement: A Review." *Psychological Bulletin,* 1966, *65,* 206-220.

Lefcourt, H. M. "Recent Developments in the Study of Locus of Control." In B. A. Maher (Ed.), *Progress in Experimental Personality Research.* Vol. 6. New York: Academic Press, 1972.

London, P. *Behavior Control.* New York: Harper & Row, 1969.

Mahoney, M. J. "Research Issues in Self-Management." *Behavior Therapy,* 1972, *3,* 45-63.

Mahoney, M. J. *Cognition and Behavior Modification.* Cambridge, Mass.: Ballinger, 1974.

Mahoney, M. J., and Thoresen, C. E. (Eds.). *Self-Control: Power to the Person.* Monterey, Calif.: Brooks/Cole, 1974.

Maslow, A. F. *Toward a Psychology of Being.* (2nd ed.) New York: Van Nostrand, 1968.

Meichenbaum, D. *Cognitive Behavior Modification.* Morristown, N.J.: General Learning Press, 1974.

Minton, H. L. "Power as a Personality Construct." In B. A. Maher (Ed.), *Progress in Experimental Personality Research.* Vol. 4. New York: Academic Press, 1967.

Neuber, K. A., and Genthner, R. W. "The Relationship Between Ego Identity, Personal Responsibility and Facilitative Communication." *Journal of Psychology,* 1977, *95,* 45-49.

Palmer, C., and Genthner, R. W. "Attribution of Responsibility as a Function of a Failure Experience." Unpublished manuscript, Eastern Kentucky University, 1977.

Perls, F. "Four Lectures." In J. Fagan and I. L. Shepherd (Eds.), *Gestalt Therapy Now.* New York: Harper & Row, 1970.

Perls, F. *The Gestalt Approach and Eyewitness to Therapy.* Palo Alto, Calif.: Science and Behavior Books, 1973.

Pierce, R. M., Schauble, P. G., and Farkas, A. "Teaching Internalization Behavior to Clients." *Psychotherapy: Theory, Research, and Practice,* 1970, *7,* 217-220.

Phares, J. E. *Locus of Control in Personality.* Morristown, N.J.: General Learning Press, 1976.

Rogers, C. R. *On Becoming a Person: A Therapist's View of Psychotherapy.* Boston: Houghton Mifflin, 1961.

Rotter, J. B. "Generalized Expectancies for Internal Versus External Control of Reinforcement." *Psychological Monographs,* 1966, *80* (whole no. 609).

Sartre, J. P. *Being and Nothingness* [1943]. New York: Washington Square Press, 1956.

Schauble, P. G., and Pierce, R. M. "Client in Therapy Behavior: A Therapist's Guide to Progress." *Psychotherapy: Theory, Research, and Practice,* 1974, *11,* 229-234.

Shostrom, E. L. *Personal Orientation Inventory Manual.* San Diego: Educational and Industrial Testing Service, 1972.

Skinner, B. F. *Beyond Freedom and Dignity.* New York: Knopf, 1971.

Thoresen, C. E., and Mahoney, M. J. *Behavioral Self-Control.* New York: Holt, Rinehart and Winston, 1974.

Valins, S., and Nisbett, R. E. "Attribution Process in the Development and Treatment of Emotional Disorder." In E. E. Jones and others (Eds.), *Attribution: Perceiving the Causes of Behavior.* Morristown, N.J.: General Learning Press, 1971.

31

Michael S. Weissman

Decisiveness

Decisiveness is defined here as the ability of the individual to engage in the decision-making process. This global theoretical construct is further considered to encompass a number of specific components, including Need for Information, Confidence in Decisions, Risk Taking (the willingness of the individual to choose "risky" alternatives, alternatives with a relatively low probability of achieving the desired outcome), Tendency to Defer Decisions, Self-Appraisal of Decisiveness, and Peer Rating of Decisiveness (Weissman, 1974, 1976). These components are not intended to be exhaustive or entirely mutually exclusive or independent; rather, they are considered to be one step in the development of a clinically and theoretically useful construct.

As a general theoretical construct, decisiveness is considered an important attribute that reflects certain styles or patterns of reaching decisions. By implication, then, decisiveness is a construct that purports to reflect the manner in which the individual interacts with the environment when choices are available. In addition, decisiveness connotes an attitude about oneself and hence affects one's sense of competence, self-esteem, and ability to "cope" or deal with problem situations.

Background and Current Status

The ability to make decisions is a vital human characteristic, as has been emphasized by philosophers and religious leaders for centuries. In more recent times, the so-called "existentialists," coming from both religious and secular traditions, have noted the crucial importance of a person's capacity to choose values, roles, and meaning in life, as evidenced in a theme repeated throughout the work of Sartre, "I am my choices," and in Paul Tillich's statement, "Man becomes truly human only at the moment of decision." William James (1893), in the early days of modern psychology, stated that "there is no more miserable human being than one in whom nothing is habitual but indecision." However, decisiveness has remained essentially untouched by scientific psychology until recent years.

A considerable body of literature exists on decision making, but by far the major portion of this literature is devoted either to understanding the various factors that affect the decision-making process or to developing models (usually mathematical) that shed light on the decision-making process. Thus, there are many comprehensive studies on the effect of such variables as personality traits, skill versus chance conditions, amount of payoff, values, or prior training on decision making. This type of research treats the decision-making process as a *dependent* variable rather than an independent variable—that is, a characteristic of individuals in and of itself. Similarly, complicated mathematical analogs of the decision-making process explore optimal decision-making strategies, expected gains set against objective costs, and input-output equations. Here, too, the focus is on the decision-making process, not on decisiveness as a characteristic of individuals, especially as this characteristic relates to other aspects of the individual's personality and overall functioning. In fact, a review of the literature readily reveals that decisiveness as a "personality variable" (analogous to obsessiveness, ego strength, self-esteem, and so on) has been essentially ignored. Certainly, there are theoretical and clinical perspectives (for instance, competence theory, which will be discussed later) that are closely related to decisiveness. Also, Janis and Mann (1977) discuss decision making in their recent comprehensive treatment; but here, too, the major emphasis is not on decisiveness as a personality attribute or characteristic of individuals with specific clinical implications. Thus, unlike the large body of previous research, the present discussion is an attempt to examine the actual assessment of decisiveness as a personality trait (including construct validity) and the relationship between decisiveness and the individual's ability to cope with life and its stresses.

By definition, the present discussion assumes that decisiveness has great relevance in the attempt to understand contemporary man. This viewpoint is supported by Toffler (1970), who points out the adverse consequences of a society that places an ever increasing demand on the individual to make more decisions than he or she can handle. In addition to the obvious qualitative importance of being able to investigate one's general ability to make decisions, the quantitative importance of being able to accurately assess a person's ability to negotiate particular kinds of decision-making situations is clear. How quickly can one act in a given situation? How much information is necessary before a particular person will act, as opposed to another person, who may be "less decisive"? What is the best way to select from a number of individuals the one who will cope best with situations that require choosing among "risky" alternatives? Our increasingly complex society can clearly benefit from having the tools available to answer such questions.

Critical Discussion

General Areas of Concern

Given the lack of previous research on decisiveness as a personality construct, it is necessary to (1) define specific parameters constituting decisiveness, (2) evaluate the interrelationship of these parameters, (3) develop specific procedures for measurement,

and (4) assess the relationship of the various parameters of decisiveness to other important variables of interest. Although the major focus of the present discussion will be on
the assessment of decisiveness itself, including the construct validity of the term, some
preliminary results describing the relationship of decisiveness to a number of measures of
psychological adjustment will be offered later.

As alluded to previously, decisiveness is herein viewed from the perspective of six
specific parameters: (1) Need for Information, (2) Confidence in Decisions, (3) Risk Taking, (4) Tendency to Defer Decisions, (5) Self-Appraisal of Decisiveness, and (6) Peer
Rating of Decisiveness. The first four parameters can be considered as (1) "situation specific," in that their assessment depends on the specific decision-making situation confronting the individual; and (2) "objective," in that their assessment requires a behavioral
evaluation of an individual's performance in the decision-making situation. The last two
parameters are more impressionistic, or perhaps even subjective, in that they involve a
general assessment of one's own or another's ability to make decisions, without relying on
behavioral, quantitative assessment. In terms of construct validity, there is obvious interest in the extent to which the various parameters correlate with each other, the extent to
which they overlap, and the extent to which they are in fact independent or "orthog-
onal" constructs, and hence cannot be subsumed under the same general construct of
"decisiveness."

The six major parameters of decisiveness were isolated on the basis of an extensive
review of the literature on decision making, as well as on the basis of an interest in developing impressionistic measures of decisiveness which might be suitable for direct clinical
application. Need for Information, as an indicator of the individual's readiness to make a
decision, has obvious face validity as a construct and is directly based on the Expanded
Judgment Task (Audley, 1964; Brody, 1963; Irwin and Smith, 1957; Irwin, Smith, and
Mayfield, 1956; Singer and Roby, 1967). Assessment involves requiring a subject to make
a decision in a situation where the subject chooses how much information is needed before reaching the decision (Brody, 1963). Confidence in Decisions also possesses obvious
face validity as a component of decisiveness, and assessment involves asking the subject to
supply a self-confidence rating on each decision reached in the Expanded Judgment Task
(using a ten-point Likert-type scale). Risk Taking as a construct has been the focus of
much research. In the present discussion, it is seen as reflecting an individual's implicit
attitude concerning his competence as a decision maker. This position is supported by
Jellison and Riskind (1970), who conclude that there is a close relationship between risk
taking and perceived ability. In an assessment of this dimension, Kogan and Wallach
(1964) used the Choice Dilemma Questionnaire, in which twelve hypothetical situations
are described and the subject is directed to indicate the minimum level of certainty before
he would choose a risky but desirable alternative. The fourth parameter of decisiveness,
Tendency to Defer Decisions, a construct under development by Ivan Steiner at the University of Massachusetts (unpublished at the time of the present research), relates to one's
willingness to engage in the decision-making process. Assessment involves presenting ten
hypothetical situations and asking the subject to indicate on a seven-point scale how he
feels about making the decision, as opposed to deferring it to someone else mentioned in
the situation.

The final two parameters, Self-Appraisal of Decisiveness and Peer Rating of Decisiveness, are constructs developed by Weissman (1974, 1976) and are intended to assess
decisiveness from an impressionistic point of view, being based on self-perceived ability to
engage in different types of decisions (Self-Appraisal of Decisiveness) or on one's view of
another's ability to make decisions (Peer Rating of Decisiveness). Both the Peer Rating
and the Self-Appraisal instruments use parallel seven-item questionnaires asking either the

subject or a "peer" who knows the subject to rate on a seven-point scale the subject's ease in making decisions, degree of anxiety in decision making, the amount of time required to reach decisions, whether big or small decisions are more difficult, and how the subject compares to his or her friends in decision-making ability.*

Space limitations prevent a comprehensive, detailed description of the specific test items comprising each decisiveness measure, the complete experimental procedure, and the entire series of statistical analyses employed to assess construct validity and the relationship of decisiveness to a variety of psychological adjustment measures. The reader is referred to the previous papers for this material (Weissman, 1974, 1976). However, a general summary of the results of these studies is offered below, with the major emphasis on the construct validity of decisiveness as a trait.

The abovementioned assessment procedures were administered to a group of 228 (120 females, 108 males) volunteer college students. With one exception, all of the decisiveness measures were shown to be internally reliable through the use of inter-item and item-total Pearson product-moment correlation coefficients, with all coefficients being significant at the p = .001 level. Split-half reliability measures and a comprehensive series of factor analyses supported the internal reliability of five of the six decisiveness measures. The one exception involved ambiguous results for the Tendency to Defer Decisions instrument, which showed poor internal reliability, suggesting that this instrument actually contains a number of relatively independent factors. In addition, the Self-Appraisal of Decisiveness instrument and the Peer Rating of Decisiveness instrument yielded lower inter-item and item-total correlations for two of the seven questions, namely, the items that asked whether "big" or "small" decisions are more difficult to make. Thus, it appears that five of the six major parameters of decisiveness emerge intact as internally reliable constructs, while there does not appear to be the same internal reliability for the Tendency to Defer Decisions instrument.

In contrast to the good internal reliability of each decisiveness instrument, the correlations between the decisiveness measures were relatively low. This finding seems to support the view that decisiveness is not a global characteristic of individuals but, rather, a multidimensional construct. However, the particular pattern of relationships between the decisiveness measures suggests some correlation among certain measures. Specifically, the four "behavioral" or "task-oriented" measures of decisiveness identified previously tend to correlate better with each other than with the two impressionistic (self and peer) measures. Similarly, these two impressionistic measures correlate fairly well with each other. This observed correlation among the behavioral measures, on the one hand, and between the impressionistic measures, on the other hand, speaks for the convergent validity of the decisiveness measures within the two observational modes, but not across modes.

As mentioned, Weissman's (1974, 1976) previous research involved examining the relationship between decisiveness and a variety of indicators of psychological adjustment. Since the major focus of the present discussion is on the assessment of decisiveness (and not specifically on the relationship of decisiveness to other psychological concerns), these latter data will only be summarized briefly. In essence, it was found that the two impressionistic measures of decisiveness (Self-Appraisal of Decisiveness and Peer Rating of Decisiveness) related to more adjustment measures than did the four behavioral measures. More specifically, it was found that persons who see themselves as decisive also see them-

---

*These two questionnaires each use seven questions to tap five general aspects of decisiveness.

selves as more satisfied, less depressed, less alienated, and more pleased with themselves, and generally rate their overall functioning as higher. Interestingly, persons who are rated as decisive by their peers are also generally seen as better adjusted in other areas. The behavioral measures of decisiveness were observed to relate more strongly to those adjustment measures that were also not self-ratings (measures such as grade point average, scholastic aptitude test scores, and some of the peer ratings of performance).

Two general conclusions emerged from this analysis of the relationship of the decisiveness measures to a number of adjustment measures. First, virtually all the significant results were in a positive direction. That is, "decisive" individuals appear better adjusted and perform better in a variety of situations. Second, the relationship between decisiveness and adjustment is much less general than expected; particular dimensions of decisiveness relate only to particular dimensions of adjustment. In the Weissman studies the obvious question of contamination of these data due to methods variance was assessed, and it was shown that indeed a significant component of the correlation between decisiveness and adjustment could be contributed to response bias, but there appeared to be at least a significant component of "true" correlation between the adjustment measures and the decisiveness measures. These conclusions were based on several multitrait, multimethod analyses.

Comparative Philosophies and Theories

A number of theoretical perspectives relate to the position that decisiveness is an important personality trait that is related to other aspects of psychological adjustment. For example, White's (1963, 1971) competence theory emphasizes that much of an individual's behavior is motivated by a need to experience the consequences of one's actions. White argues that, to the degree that the individual is successful in attempts to affect the world, he or she develops a feeling of efficacy, and cumulative experiences of efficacy result in a sense of competence. White then goes on to relate this sense of competence to one's overall self-esteem. This theme is consistent with the work of Seligman (1973), who defines depression as "a belief in one's own helplessness" and who states: "A cure for depression occurs when the individual comes to believe that he is not helpless and that an individual's susceptibility to depression depends on the success or failure of his previous experience with controlling the environment" (p. 43). Both of these perspectives, therefore, emphasize the importance of being able to take action; by inference, one can see that decisiveness emerges as a common denominator to both of these perspectives. Similarly, Rotter's (1964) locus of control construct (and much of the literature based on this construct) indicates that individuals who experience themselves as having some control over their lives demonstrate better psychological adjustment in a variety of areas (Epstein and Komorita, 1970; Fitch, 1970; Joe, 1971; Seligman, 1973). As discussed earlier, decisiveness is viewed as closely related to Rotter's concept of the individual whose locus of control is "internal."

Elaboration on Critical Points

The above discussion and the results of research clearly must be seen as a first step toward the development of a theoretically useful and valid notion of decisiveness. While decisiveness was found to be a multidimensional rather than a monolithic trait, the various dimensions clearly showed some interrelationship. This observation, coupled with the fact that the relationship between the decisiveness measures and the adjustment measures was not a general one but, rather, a function of the particular dimensions under consideration, indicates a need to develop specific measures of different aspects of decisiveness in order to evaluate an individual's likelihood of coping with a particular situation.

Personal Views and Recommendations

Although the results of relevant investigations should be viewed as tentative, the importance of decisiveness as a personality trait that relates to other aspects of psychological adjustment is clear, and further research to document this relationship and to refine assessment techniques is indicated.

Application to Particular Variables

The Weissman research, which involved college students, does not indicate that the assessment of decisiveness has any particular limitations with regard to age, sex, education, socioeconomic status, ethnic or racial groups, or particular diagnostic categories. Rather, it is felt that the above-discussed procedures are applicable to all segments of the population, although some of the techniques may need to be modified for the assessment of children and perhaps for those with severe intellectual deficits.

References

Audley, R. J. "Decision-Making." *British Medical Journal,* 1964, *20* (1), 20-27.

Brody, N. "Need Achievement, Test Anxiety, and Subjective Probability of Success in Risk-Taking Behavior." *Journal of Abnormal and Social Psychology,* 1963, *66* (5), 413-418.

Epstein, R., and Komorita, S. S. "Self-Esteem, Success-Failure, and Locus of Control in Negro Children." *Developmental Psychology,* 1970, *4,* 2-8.

Fitch, G. "Effects of Self-Esteem, Perceived Performance, and Choice on Causal Attributions." *Journal of Personality and Social Psychology,* 1970, *16* (2), 311-315.

Irwin, F. W., and Smith, W. A. S. "Value, Cost, and Information as Determiners of Decision." *Journal of Experimental Psychology,* 1957, *54,* 229-232.

Irwin, F. W., Smith, W. A. S., and Mayfield, J. F. "Tests of Two Theories of Decision in an Expanded Judgment Situation." *Journal of Experimental Psychology,* 1956, *51,* 216-218.

James, W. *Psychology.* New York: Holt, Rinehart and Winston, 1893.

Janis, I. L., and Mann, L. *Decision Making: A Psychological Analysis of Conflict, Choice, and Commitment.* New York: Free Press, 1977.

Jellison, J. M., and Riskind, J. "A Social Comparison of Abilities Interpretation of Risk-Taking Behavior." *Journal of Personality and Social Psychology,* 1970, *15* (4), 375-390.

Joe, V. C. "Review of the Internal-External Control Construct as a Personality Variable." *Psychological Reports,* 1971, *28,* 619-640.

Kogan, N., and Wallach, M. A. *Risk-Taking: A Study in Cognition and Personality.* New York: Holt, Rinehart and Winston, 1964.

Rotter, J. B. *Clinical Psychology.* Englewood Cliffs, N.J.: Prentice-Hall, 1964.

Seligman, M. E. P. "Fall into Helplessness." *Psychology Today,* 1973, *7* (1), 43-48.

Singer, E., and Roby, T. B. "Dimensions of Decision-Making Behavior." *Perceptual and Motor Skills,* 1967, *24* (2), 571-595.

Toffler, A. *Future Shock.* New York: Random House, 1970.

Weissman, M. S. "Decisiveness: Its Nature and Its Relationship to Psychological Adjustment." Unpublished doctoral dissertation, University of Massachusetts, Amherst, 1974.

Weissman, M. S. "Decisiveness and Psychological Adjustment." *Journal of Personality Assessment,* 1976, *40* (4), 403-412.

White, R. W. "Ego and Reality in Psychoanalytic Theory—A Proposal Regarding Independent Ego Energies." *Psychological Issues,* 1963, *3* (3), monograph 11.

White, R. W. "The Urge Towards Competence." *American Journal of Occupational Therapy,* 1971, *25* (6), 271-274.

32

Timothy G. Plax
Marlis E. Mann

Risk Taking

Investigators (see Kusyszyn, 1973) have proposed a wide range of identifiers in their attempts to define the risk-taking construct. The most commonly used labels have been risk taking, risk aversion, risk avoidance, risky-shift phenomenon, risky and conservative decision making, chance taking, cautiousness, risk preference, chance activity preference, risk propensity, venture response, risk orientation, impulsivity, gambling, chance orientation, risk sensitivity, probability preference, decision behavior, extreme behavior, risky values, coping, risk assumption, and adaptation capability. Regardless of which identifier is used, the risk-taking construct has been most frequently conceptualized as an individual's orientation toward taking chances in a decision-making situation. Operationally, an individual is typically given an instrument assessing his or her willingness to take risks on tasks either in an imaginary or a real-life decision-making situation.

Risk-taking tests normally are hypothetically based. Both individual and situational characteristics that can potentially influence decision behavior are generally included when risk taking is assessed and definitions are advanced. For example, if a person possesses a particular personality trait that is supposed to predispose risk, then the focus is on an individual risk-relevant characteristic. However, if a person is placed in an environment that is inherently risk arousing or that affects the individual's risk behavior, then an investigator is dealing with a pertinent situational determinant. Risk also appears in a manipulated form. For example, an individual may be placed in an experimenter-constructed risky situation. In addition, interactions between the individual and situational components are often of experimental concern.

Background and Current Status

Research in risk taking originated with the elaboration and explication of formal decision-making models. Early investigators examined the choices among gambles differing in probability of winning and losing on a risk-taking task. For example, in three gambling experiments Edwards (1953, 1954a, 1954b) discovered a preference among subjects for outcomes with specific probabilities. Specifically, when offered alternative bets having the same expected value, his subjects chose low probabilities of losing large amounts of money over high probabilities of losing small amounts. This type of gambling study has often been replicated and is commonly referred to as the Edwards Type Experiment.

From decision-making models, risk-taking research moved to the assessment of individual differences with regard to probability preference. This line of risk-taking investigation focused on the need to achieve and the fear of failing as determinants of risk behavior. Early research attempted to discriminate among individuals with regard to predicting at least one personality or motivational variable associated with risky decision making. For example, Atkinson (1957) demonstrated that the tendency to overestimate chances to win is especially likely to be associated with a high need for achievement. Other research, however, has assumed that an individual's risk orientation influences all perceptions and behavior. Morris (1957), for instance, in an examination of personality characteristics of gamblers, suggested that specific traits may be central to gambler-nongambler differences. Studies such as Morris' support risk taking as a predispositional and not simply a situational construct. However, the earlier and more traditional lines of decision theory research continue.

In comparison to many other areas of the behavioral sciences, the risk-taking construct has remained relatively limited, both qualitatively and quantitatively. Its overall relevance and growth have been restricted to a great extent by Stoner's (1961) isolation of the risky-shift phenomenon and the plethora of subsequent studies concerned with this effect. Essentially, Stoner found that group decisions following discussion to consensus were riskier than the decisions advocated by the same group members as individuals. This finding has emerged as the most commonly used definition of the phenomenon.

Although the risky-shift effect was in direct contrast to the long research tradition comparing the productivity of individuals in isolation and in groups, it influenced a division of subsequent risk-taking theory construction and research into individual versus group concerns. Ironically, two decades after the discovery of the phenomenon, serious doubt has been cast on its very existence (Plax and Rosenfeld, 1976a). For an excellent review and critical analysis of over a decade of risky-shift research, see Cartwright, 1971.

Critical Discussion

General Areas of Concern

An examination of contemporary individual risk-taking literature reveals five quantitatively defined research concerns: (1) applied, or essentially nontheoretically based, risk-taking research; (2) research focusing on problems in the assessment of risk; (3) research dealing with correlates of risk taking; (4) research handling risk taking situationally (either as an independent or a dependent variable); and (5) theory-based risk-taking research.

By far the most prolific area, applied risk-taking research covers a diverse range of interests. Several interesting examples can easily be cited. Singh (1968), investigating the relationship between anxiety and risk taking among successful and unsuccessful farmers, found positive correlations for both groups. Brown (1970) compared the risky decision-making propensity of business and public school administrators. Those in business were found to be greater risk takers than those in the public schools. Kennedy, Phanjoo, and Shekim (1971) found no support for the hypothesis that attempted suicides are excessive risk takers who overindulge in gambling and have traffic accidents. Chaubey (1972) found no consistent effect of family type (Indian villagers) and size on risk-taking behavior. Hayes (1973), investigating risk taking in retarded children, indicates that in certain risk situations (switch games) retarded children take at least as many risks as nonretarded children do. Tamerin and associates (1975) investigated the awareness of risk-taking implications of excessive drinking and attitudes toward drinking in hospitalized alcoholics. Results indicated that, despite an understanding of the consequences, the subjects anticipated difficulty in quitting drinking. These studies are representative and should illustrate the wide diversity in applied risk-taking research.

Research focusing on problems in the assessment of risk has included both the classic and still accurate review by Slovic (1964) and several more contemporary studies. Slovic (1971), for example, constructed and administered two structurally similar risk-taking tasks in order to evaluate intertask consistency. Results suggest that high correlations are unlikely between measures of risk in structurally different settings or between riskiness and other behaviors. Similar results are reported by Horne (1972). Stroebe and Fraser (1971), using choice dilemma items (*the most commonly used risk measure reported in the literature*) to examine the relationship between an individual's willingness to take risks and his or her confidence in making decisions, demonstrated that individuals indicate more confidence in extreme rather than moderate decisions. Lafferty and Higbee (1974), examining the realism/risk-taking relationship, report that individuals tend to be less risky when decisions are made for real consequences (payoffs), as opposed to hypothetical consequences. They conclude, as Slovic (1971) did, that one should exercise caution when equating real risk behavior with hypothetical risk. Pretesting has also been examined and concluded to be a threat to the validity of risk-taking research (Gaskell, Thomas, and Farr, 1973).

In research concerned with correlates of risk taking, Scodel, Ratoosh, and Minas (1959) describe low risk takers, as contrasted with high risk takers, as other directed, socially assimilated, and middle-class oriented. According to Cameron and Myers (1966), subjects high in exhibition, aggression, or dominance prefer risks with high payoffs and a low probability of success, and individuals high in autonomy and endurance tend to desire low-payoff risks and a high probability of success. Sherman (1968) found support for a relationship between an individual's risk-taking attitude and strategic choices during game playing. He concludes that a player's choices, in a variety of game situations, seemed to be influenced by an individual's overall personality. Sheridan and Shack (1970) report that volunteers for experimental research (risk takers) were significantly more accepting of themselves and significantly less dependent on their environment for their motivation than nonvolunteers. Volunteers also tended to be more self-actualized. Plax and Rosenfeld (1976b), in developing a risk-taking personality profile, were able to identify individuals who were willing to take risks when making decisions. Taken together, the variables contributing to this pattern of willingness to take risks characterize a dynamic task-oriented individual. The above studies, consistent with numerous contemporary findings, provide strong support for a predispositional interpretation of riskiness.

Reports by investigators addressing risk taking from a situational perspective have appeared less frequently in the literature than those concerned with either personality or application. However, enough situational research has been published to warrant a separate divisional concern. The projects that have been reported are interesting. Lieblich (1968), investigating the effects of stress on risk-taking behavior, reports an increase in risk under varying stress conditions. Zimmerman and Krauss (1971) investigated the influence of severity and agency of censure (self, family, peer group, and society) on risk taking. In the high censure condition, societal censure reduced the amount of risk taking assessed most effectively; however, with low censure self-censure proved most effective. In a survey-type experiment, Higbee and Lafferty (1972) asked whether people are more risky in situations which they judge as unimportant than in those which they assess as important. Results supported a significant negative relationship between willingness to take risks and importance of topic for males but not for females. Moore and colleagues (1973), examining the effects of taking risks on learning a new concept, report that a willingness to take risks interfered with concept acquisition in two good-negative and good-positive instance conditions. Experimental conditions were manipulated with positive and negative attributes regarding the concept. However, risk did improve acquisition in good-positive instance conditions and when two poor-negative and poor-positive instance conditions were manipulated. Walsh and Stillman (1974) investigated the disclosure or deception procedures by subjects who had been debriefed but asked not to disclose information regarding a risk-taking experiment. Subjects who agreed to maintain confidentiality about the experiment disclosed less than a control group that had not been asked to remain silent. These situationally based studies illustrate a contemporary concern with risk as both an antecedent and a consequent condition.

Examples of the more theoretically based risk-taking research are reviewed in the section elaborating on critical points.

Comparative Philosophies and Theories

Investigators of risk taking have launched their theoretically based research predominantly from two perspectives: formal decision-making theory and motivational or expectancy theory.

The original risk-taking research grew out of a concern with the subjectively expected utility component of formal decision-making theory. As an alternative to formal decision theory, risk-taking assessments were typically made in terms of the probability of perceived decision choices (Edwards, 1953, 1954a, 1954b, 1954c, 1961). Most of the research applying decision theory to the study of risk has been both generalized and inconsistent. Slovic (1964) reviews the early research in this area, concentrating on assessment, and Rapoport and Wallsten (1972) offer a detailed discussion of risk in formal decision theory.

Motivational theory is predominantly the outgrowth of Atkinson's concern with the determinants of risk-taking behavior (Atkinson, 1957; Atkinson and Feather, 1966; Atkinson and Litwin, 1960; Atkinson and others, 1960). The focus of his theory is on need for achievement and fear of failure as correlates of risk behavior. According to Atkinson, individuals possessing high levels of achievement motivation will exhibit moderate risk behavior, whereas persons with a high motive to minimize failure will tend to avoid taking risks. These approach-avoidance tendencies are reported to be greatest when the subjective probability of success is $p = .50$. Research has been reasonably consistent in the testing of Atkinson's propositions as they were originally stated.

Less heuristic theoretical formulations have also been proposed. For a comparison of theories see Alker (1969).

Elaboration on Critical Points

Tests of the Atkinson theory have been numerous. Weinstein (1969), for example, in determining relationships among several measures of the need for achievement and risk preference, found support for the Atkinson model, but only for preferences in vocational choice. Hamilton (1974) tested Atkinson's propositions directly. The predicted relationships occurred, but with a subjective probability of success of slightly less than $p = .40$, not the $p = .50$ originally suggested by Atkinson. Investigating the determinants of risk taking in power situations in which power could be exercised, McClelland and Teague (1975) asked subjects either to make choices of different risks among various positions on the public issues or to pick an opponent for an arm-wrestling match. In both of the subjects' choice situations, Atkinson's model for predicting risk-taking behavior failed to predict choices. Roberts (1974) investigated the risk-taking choices of achieve-success and avoid-failure individuals performing a shuffleboard task. Levels of achievement and success and of avoidance and failure were measured with tests of insight and anxiety. Achieve-success oriented subjects preferred intermediate-risk choices, whereas avoid-failure persons preferred extreme-risk choices. Examining the effects of need for achievement on the willingness to take risks of males and females playing shuffleboard, Roberts (1975) found support for Atkinson's original predictions. As suggested by these and earlier studies, Atkinson's motivational theory has in most cases been supported in the literature.

Examples of risk-taking research following from formal decision-making theory are even more numerous than for motivational theory. In 1967 Coombs proposed the portfolio theory; that is, a risky decision-making model which applies to multiple play of single gambles and to mixtures of gambles. The theory suggests that when gambling there is a preferred degree of risk taking at each level of expected value and that an individual will attempt to maximize an expected value in making a choice between available games which deviate in their level of risk the same amount from their respective risk levels. Results of subsequent empirically based research support the theory (Coombs and Huang, 1970; Hall and Weir, 1974).

Investigating whether risk taking is a function of incentive condition, range of payoffs, and an alternative to gambling, Petersen, Kanarick, and Hergenhahn (1968) found no support for their hypothesis that incentive would have a greater effect on gambling behavior when tested as affecting subjects' individuality rather than as a between-subjects variable. Payne and Braunstein (1971) explored the risk-taking preferences among differing gambles with an equal underlying probability distribution. Subjects' preferences for betting were shown to be associated with displayed probabilities. In a risky situation in which subjects could acquire as much information as they desired before making probability guesses, Radzicki (1975) tested the success of probabilistic diagnosing. Individuals were asked to judge which of a certain number of known populations a sample belonged to. Responses and acquired information increased, and probability guess correctness decreased, parallel to a rise in the number of alternative states of nature. As the above studies illustrate, decision theorists interested in risk have been as diverse as they have been numerically productive.

Personal Views and Recommendations

An analysis of the theoretical and experimental risk-taking literature reveals several serious shortcomings, important ethical considerations, and implications for training and certification. Perhaps the most obvious shortcoming is the large body of inconsistent findings in contemporary risk-taking investigations. This is not a new condition. Slovic (1964) addresses the same issue in an earlier paper. Although empirically representative concerns exist in the literature, no substantial theoretical framework can be constructed from any of them. Interested investigators can isolate empirical evidence that can be used to argue in support of hypotheses predicting in any direction. A primary contributor to this state of affairs is the lack of a clear understanding of risk taking (see Tomkins, 1971). However, the number of conceptual definitions advanced is inexhaustible. Conceptions of risk taking range from specific definitions such as "the relative magnitude of approach and avoidance tendencies" (Schroeder and Schroeder, 1970, p. 459) to broader discussions of the "tendency to prefer long shots with higher payoffs over sure things with lower payoffs" (Jones and Gerard, 1967, pp. 628-639). This ambiguity also prevails in the operational area (Knowles and others, 1973). For example, Slovic (1964) insightfully divides types of risk-taking assessment into three categories, which have been used in a variety of experimental and clinical contexts. One group he refers to as the response set and judgmental measures. These range from gambling tendency instruments to personality tests. A second group Slovic labels simply as risk-taking questionnaires. These include inventories assessing risk taking from an awareness of an individual's life experiences. The third category Slovic calls probability and variance preference measures. These devices essentially allow for the assessment of preferences among gambles differing in probability of winning and losing. These three operational divisions remain the same in the more current literature on risk taking. Although attempts to clarify both conceptual and operational definitions have been made, no agreement has as yet been reached (Touhey and Mason, 1972). Researchers need expend more effort toward rigorously defining the risk-taking variable.

A second major problem area is the shortsightedness of available risk-taking theories (Milburn and Billings, 1976). Although Atkinson's motivational theory is normally supported by the literature, it is presently two decades old and needs redefinition. Few attempts have been made to extend the theory or to integrate any other social theory or theories into his original expectancy framework (Touhey and Villemez, 1975). The result of this approach to theory construction would be a more fully developed basis from which to reason and test risk-taking predictions. An additional contributor to the presently weak theoretical condition is the overemphasis on research formulating and testing probability and utility models of risk taking (Scodel, Ratoosh, and Minas, 1959). There appear to be a number of inherent weaknesses in these models. The most obvious problem is a lack of fit between a particular theory and the chosen risk-taking operation. The most severe weakness is that they stand as an alternative to sound formal decision-making theory (Rapoport and Wallsten, 1972). However, from the increasing number of published reports advancing risk-taking models, it appears that the study of risk taking is moving progressively backward, making no real theoretical progress. Developing already existing models should take precedence over advancing new ones.

An overemphasis on application also contributes to the weak theoretical condition and inconsistency of findings. Even a cursory literature review reveals a predominance of applied projects. This condition has facilitated a severe fragmentation of the field. It appears as if just about every conceivable real-life setting and/or unique population has been plugged into a risk-taking paradigm. The examples range from farmers in India to mentally retarded second graders in upstate New York. This concern with application may well be the consequence of isolating the risky-shift phenomenon (see Plax and Rosenfeld, 1976a). The effect drastically split research energies leveled at this individual and group risk taking into separate studies. Since the division, researchers have for the most part moved away from basic individual risk-taking investigation. Basic research (see Kerlinger, 1977) is needed before the empirical fragmentation can be stopped.

Another noticeable shortcoming is the lack of agreement on how risk-taking behavior should be assessed. As previously mentioned, Slovic (1964) addressed the assessment issue in early risk-taking research, and measurement continues to be a concern (see McCauley, Kogan, and Teger, 1971; Ermalinski, 1972). Contributing further to the measurement problem are numerous methodological weaknesses. Examples range from context effects (Ortendahl, 1975) to completely faulty paradigms (Steiner, Jarvis, and Parrish, 1970). Adding even further to the problems inherent in the risk-taking literature is a lack of long-term programmatic investigations or attempts to meaningfully interpret published findings other than from an experimental perspective. Until efforts are made to correct these problem areas, risk taking will remain a theoretically underdeveloped area of investigation.

While risk taking remains a relatively underdeveloped area, enough potentially misunderstood information has been reported to create an ethical concern. From an empirical perspective, a fundamental consideration involves concluding too narrowly from the risk-taking literature. This practice would be greatly misleading and should be avoided. No data currently exist to warrant any completely *right* or *wrong* statements concerning risk-taking behavior. In fact, there is reason to question any use of what emerges from the literature other than to generate more experimental research. However, any interpretation of findings should include a complete explanation of the weaknesses inherent in a large portion of the published risk-taking research.

Although there is presently no empirically proven risk-taking assessment procedure that a clinician can use in therapy, it appears important for therapists to create a positive attitude in their clients toward taking risks. This position is justified on the grounds that risk is an integral part of our lives. Of course, encouraging extremely high or low levels of risk behavior could be dangerous. However, if a client is first counseled about the dangers of overindulgent risk taking, moderate levels of riskiness could be suggested. Naturally, in formulating their risk recommendations, counselors and therapists should be sensitive to the temperaments of individuals and groups. In these clinical contexts situational ethics constitute the rule rather than the exception. However, caution is advised, and clinicians are referred to Slovic's (1964) risk-taking article for a complete set of definitions and a thorough list of possible procedures that can be used in a variety of therapeutic contexts.

If practitioners are to become sensitive to the shortsightedness of inaccurately applying or misinterpreting the risk-taking literature, specific educational requirements need to be established. Initially, students must conceptually understand risk-taking behavior as a complex activity. Next, risk-relevant theoretical and methodological courses should be required in all clinically oriented plans of study. In order to make this design operational, departmental and academic program certification might be at least partially contingent on the completeness of risk-taking course offerings. This criterion might well apply to both experimental and clinical programs. In addition, advanced experimental/ clinical study should include, at the very least, training in the psychometric and sociometric aspects of risk assessment and an intern experience with a public facility in which risk-taking training is an important organizational component. The establishment of these requirements could stimulate the necessary sophistication and incentive to develop the risk-taking area more substantially.

Application to Particular Variables

Correlations between age and risk taking have been investigated on a number of occasions. Specifically, risk taking has been hypothesized to be related to age categories (Chaubey, 1974; Okun and Siegler, 1976; Vroom and Pahl, 1971; Walesa, 1975), birth order (Weller, Eytan, and Sollel, 1976), age and degree of disclosure (Routledge, Repetto-Wright, and Howarth, 1974), age and avoidance behavior (Botwinick, 1969; Okun and di Vesta, 1976), children in each developmental phase (Bradfer-Blomart, 1965-66; Walesa, 1972), motivational conditions and the intellectual performance of the elderly (Birkhill and Schaie, 1975), and the impulsiveness of children (Kopfstein, 1973).

Sex difference investigations have been concerned with the willingness to take driving risks (Carlson and Cooper, 1974), situations in which the types of available risks are appropriate to a certain age group (Tongberg, 1971), classroom-related risk taking (Bradley, Snyder, and Kathan, 1972; Stukalin, 1973; Thomas and Garvin, 1973), the modeling of a chance type of risk task (Montgomery and Landers, 1974), the influence of peer pressure on risky drug use (Schuman and Polkowski, 1975), stereotyped decisions under conditions of risk (Goldsmith, 1972), real payoff gambling (Heilizer and Cutter, 1971), risk-mindedness (Walesa, 1975), risk willingness in threatening and nonthreatening situations (Moon, 1974), the preferred level of risk taking on a shuffleboard task (Pankove and Kogan, 1968), and risk preferences in perceived important and unimportant situations (Higbee and Lafferty, 1972).

Several contemporary risk-taking projects, most accurately classified as educational, have been concerned with risk taking and divergent thinking (Jose, 1970; Rudder, 1972), risky decision making and the training of counselors (Moran, 1971), risk in educator receptivity to initiating sex education programs (Giacquinta, 1975), riskiness and reading test scores (Crealock, 1973), risk-taking behaviors of sixth, seventh, and eighth grade students and open-space or traditional school settings (Anifant, 1972), and risk-taking tendencies and performance on multiple-choice tests (Quereshi, 1974).

A few recent studies have examined the relationship between risk taking and socioeconomic variables. Representative are studies focusing on cultural poverty and the willingness to take risks in the future (Maida, 1970); rapid economic development and risk taking (Chaubey and Sinha, 1974); family income, rural home environment, and individual risk-taking attitudes (Cecil, 1972); social position and risky decision making (Fleming, 1973); and socioeconomic status and risk taking defined as willingness to be innovative (Gartrell, Wilkening, and Presser, 1973).

Researchers have also shown an interest in the importance of risk in vocational behavior. Investigations in the vocational area have been concerned with risk taking in choice of profession (Davidshofer, 1976); attitudes toward taking chances in a chosen occupational field (Roberts and Wicke, 1972); the risk attitudes of business and agricultural entrepreneurs (Singh and Singh, 1972); the relationship between risk taking and anxiety (Singh, 1970); differences between the risk attitudes of educators and business managers (Miskel, 1974); the values of narcotics users (Miller, Sensenig, and Reed, 1972); the belief differences among managers from varying international regions (Cummings, Harnett, and Stevens, 1971); and perceived environmental control and risky decision making (Higbee, 1972).

Six contemporary studies are concerned with either ethnic or racial risk taking. These reports examined the risk taking of individuals in Africa and Europe (Poortinga and Spies, 1972), the effect of religious preference on riskiness (Chandler and Rabow, 1969), the gambling of Indians and Canadians (Carment, 1974), the risk preferences of Canadian and United States college students (Touhey, 1971); black and white undergraduate student risk propensity and racial identification (Kapel and Wexler, 1972), and varieties of risk behavior among black and white prison inmates (Edelman, 1971).

Published risk-taking research concerned with physical disorders is quite limited. Two recent studies examined sensory and motor control and risk behavior (Beshai, 1971) and risk-taking changes among patients in a physical development clinic (West, Fretz, and MacDonald, 1970). Research on intellectual disorders has included examinations of risk taking among mentally retarded persons (Hayes, 1973; McManis and Bell, 1968; Murphy, 1975; Zisfein and Rosen, 1974) and the influence of intelligence on riskiness in psychiatric and surgical patients (Steiner, 1972). Investigations of risk taking and psychiatric disorders include two recent studies on organic disorders—one concerned with conceptual shifting in chronic alcoholics (Tarter and Parsons, 1971); the other, an ethological model of schizophrenia (Singh and Gang, 1974)—and numerous studies of functional disorders: risk taking linked to schizophrenia (Spencer, 1975), drug use (Rouse and Ewing, 1973; Salzman and others, 1972), suicide attempts (Kennedy, Phanjoo, and Shekim, 1971; Adams, Giffen, and Garfield, 1973; Jacobson, 1973; Kochansky, 1973), drinking behavior (Beauchamp, 1975; Cutter, Green, and Harford, 1973; Tamerin and others, 1975), runaway behavior (Kessler and Wieland, 1970), sociopathy (Gluck, 1972), future criminal actions in a prison population (Gilbert, 1973; Roe, Howell, and Payne, 1974), youth offenses (Krauss, Coddington, and Smeltzer, 1971; Moser and Moser, 1973), compulsive gambling and marital disharmony (Pokorny, 1972), and convict psychopathy (Abudabbeh, 1974; Krauss, Robinson, and Cauthen, 1972).

Finally, risk-taking investigators have focused on collective/interactional activities. Material in this area might also be obtained from an examination of the risky-shift literature (for example, Plax and Rosenfeld, 1976a); however, a number of studies have been reported that most appropriately fall into this collective-interactional risk-taking category. These studies have associated risk-taking with counselor willingness to accept case-in-service clients (Moran, Winters, and Newman, 1972), disrupted cooperative behavior patterns (Marwell, Schmitt, and Shotola, 1971), therapist-patient interactions (Berger, 1972), sensitivity training (Allan and Allan, 1971), remedial achievement programs (Klein, Quarter, and Laxer, 1969), and generalized interpersonal behavior (Weinstein and Martin, 1969).

References

Abudabbeh, N. N. "An Investigation of the Relationships Between Psychopathy and Intelligence, Risk-Taking and Stimulation Seeking." *Dissertation Abstracts International,* 1974, *35,* 3,501.

Adams, R. L., Giffen, M. B., and Garfield, R. "Risk-Taking Among Suicide Attempters." *Journal of Abnormal Psychology,* 1973, *82,* 262-267.

Alker, H. A. "Rationality and Achievement: A Comparison of the Atkinson-McClelland and Kogan-Wallach Formulations." *Journal of Personality,* 1969, *37,* 207-224.

Allan, T. K., and Allan, K. H. "Sensitivity Training for Community Leaders." *Proceedings of the Annual Convention of the American Psychological Association,* 1971, *6,* 577-578.

Anifant, D. C. "Risk-Taking Behavior in Children Experiencing Open Space and Traditional School Environment." *Dissertation Abstracts International,* 1972, *33,* 2,491.

Atkinson, J. W. "Motivational Determinants of Risk Taking Behavior." *Psychological Review,* 1957, *64,* 359-372.

Atkinson, J. W., and Feather, N. T. (Eds.). *A Theory of Achievement Motivation.* New York: Wiley, 1966.

Atkinson, J. W., and Litwin, G. H. "Achievement Motive and Test Anxiety Conceived as Motive to Approach Success and Motive to Avoid Failure." *Journal of Abnormal and Social Psychology,* 1960, *60,* 52-63.

Atkinson, J. W., and others. "The Achievement Motive, Goal Setting, and Probability Preferences." *Journal of Abnormal and Social Psychology,* 1960, *60,* 27-36.

Beauchamp, D. E. "A Note on the Notion of Social Drinking." *Drug Forum,* 1975, *4,* 289-293.

Berger, M. M. "The Relationship of Increasing Options to Choice: The Human Prerogative." *American Journal of Psychoanalysis,* 1972, *32,* 203-205.

Beshai, J. A. "Behavioral Correlates of the EEG in Delinquents." *Journal of Psychology,* 1971, *79,* 141-146.

Birkhill, W. R., and Schaie, K. W. "The Effect of Differential Reinforcement of Cautiousness in Intellectual Performance Among the Elderly." *Journal of Gerontology,* 1975, *30,* 578-583.

Botwinick, J. "Disinclination to Venture Response Versus Cautiousness in Responding: Age Differences." *Journal of Genetic Psychology,* 1969, *115,* 55-62.

Bradfer-Blomart, J. *Le Comportement Imprudent Chez l'Enfant.* [Imprudent Behavior in Children.] *Psychologica Belgica,* 1965-66, *6,* 45-53.

Bradley, L., Snyder, C. R., and Katahn, M. "The Effects of Subject Race and Sex and Experimenter Race upon Classroom-Related Risk-Taking Behavior." *Psychonomic Science,* 1972, *28,* 362-364.

Brown, J. S. "Risk Propensity in Decision Making: A Comparison of Business and Public School Administrators." *Administrative Science Quarterly,* 1970, *15,* 473-481.

Cameron, B., and Myers, J. L. "Some Personality Correlates of Risk-Taking." *Journal of General Psychology,* 1966, *64,* 51-60.

Carlson, K., and Cooper, R. "A Preliminary Investigation of Risk Behavior in the Real World." *Personality and Social Psychology Bulletin,* 1974, *1,* 7-9.

Carment, D. W. "Risk-Taking Under Conditions of Chance and Skill in India and Canada." *Journal of Cross-Cultural Psychology,* 1974, *5,* 23-35.

Cartwright, D. "Risk-Taking by Individuals and Groups: An Assessment of Research Employing Choice Dilemmas." *Journal of Personality and Social Psychology,* 1971, *20,* 361-378.

Cecil, E. A. "Factors Affecting Individual Risk-Taking Attitudes." *Journal of Psychology,* 1972, *82,* 223-225.

Chandler, S., and Rabow, J. "Ethnicity and Acquaintance as Variables in Risk-Taking." *Journal of Social Psychology,* 1969, *77,* 221-229.

Chaubey, N. P. "Indian Family Structure and Risk-Taking Behaviour." *Indian Journal of Psychology,* 1972, *47,* 213-221.

Chaubey, N. P. "Effect of Age on Expectancy of Success and on Risk-Taking Behavior." *Journal of Personality and Social Psychology,* 1974, *29,* 774-778.

Chaubey, N. P., and Sinha, D. "Risk-Taking and Economic Development." *International Review of Applied Psychology,* 1974, *23,* 55-61.

Coombs, C. H. "Portfolio Theory: A Theory of Risky Decision-Making." *Psychonomic Bulletin,* 1967, *2,* 19.

Coombs, C. H., and Huang, L. "Tests of a Portfolio Theory of Risk Preference." *Journal of Experimental Psychology,* 1970, *85,* 23-29.

Crealock, C. M. "Risk-Taking and Reading Test Performance." *Dissertation Abstracts International,* 1973, *35,* 253.

Cummings, L. L., Harnett, D. L., and Stevens, Q. J. "Risk, Fate, Conciliation and Trust: An International Study of Attitudinal Differences Among Executives." *Academy of Management Journal,* 1971, *14,* 285-304.

Cutter, H. S., Green, L. R., and Harford, T. C. "Levels of Risk Taken by Extroverted and Introverted Alcoholics as a Function of Drinking Whiskey." *British Journal of Social and Clinical Psychology,* 1973, *12,* 83-89.

Davidshofer, C. O. "Risk-Taking and Vocational Choice: A Reevaluation." *Journal of Counseling Psychology,* 1976, *23,* 151-154.

Edelman, M. W. "Varieties of Risk-Taking Behavior Among Prison Inmates." *Dissertation Abstracts International,* 1971, *32,* 7,570.

Edwards, W. "Probability Preferences in Gambling." *American Journal of Psychology,* 1953, *66,* 349-364.

Edwards, W. "Probability Preferences Among Bets with Differing Expected Values." *American Journal of Psychology,* 1954a, *67,* 56-67.

Edwards, W. "The Reliability of Probability Preferences." *American Journal of Psychology,* 1954b, *67,* 68-95.

Edwards, W. "Variance Preferences in Gambling." *American Journal of Psychology,* 1954c, *67,* 441-452.

Edwards, W. "Behavioral Decision Theory." In P. H. Mussen and M. R. Rosenzweig (Eds.), *Annual Review of Psychology.* Palo Alto, Calif.: Annual Reviews, 1961.

Ermalinski, R. "Questionnaire Responses Regarding Risk-Taking Behavior with Death at Stake." *Psychological Reports,* 1972, *31,* 435-438.

Fleming, J. J. "Social Position and Decision-Making Involving Risk." *Human Relations,* 1973, *26,* 67-76.

Gartrell, J. W., Wilkening, E. A., and Presser, H. A. "Curvilinear and Linear Models Relating Status and Innovative Behavior: A Reassessment." *Rural Sociology,* 1973, *38,* 391-411.

Gaskell, G. D., Thomas, E. A., and Farr, R. M. "Effect of Pretesting on Measures of Individual Risk Preferences." *Journal of Personality and Social Psychology,* 1973, *25,* 192-198.

Giacquinta, J. B. "Status, Risk, and Receptivity to Innovations in Complex Organizations: A Study of the Responses of Four Groups of Educators to the Proposed Introduction of Sex Education in Elementary School." *Sociology of Education,* 1975, *48,* 38-58.

Gilbert, W. W. "Ethical Risk as a Behavioral Predictor in a Prison Population." *Dissertation Abstracts International,* 1973, *34,* 2,351-2,352.

Gluck, S. D. "Egocentricity, Delay of Gratification and Risk-Taking in Sociopaths." *Dissertation Abstracts International,* 1972, *33,* 2,808-2,809.

Goldsmith, R. W. "Proneness to Behavioral Stereotypy in a Decision-Making Context." *Psychological Research Bulletin,* 1972, *12,* 49.

Hall, R., and Weir, R. "Laterality Effects in Risk Preference: A Test of the Portfolio Theory." *Acta Psychologica,* 1974, *38,* 351-355.

Hamilton, J. O. "Motivation and Risk-Taking Behavior: A Test of Atkinson's Theory." *Journal of Personality and Social Psychology,* 1974, *29,* 856-864.

Hayes, C. S. "Risk-Taking by Retarded and Nonretarded Children." *Psychological Reports,* 1973, *32,* 738.

Heilizer, F., and Cutter, H. S. "Generality and Correlates of Risk-Taking." *Journal of General Psychology,* 1971, *85,* 259-283.

Higbee, K. L. "Perceived Control and Military Riskiness." *Perceptual and Motor Skills,* 1972, *34,* 95-100.

Higbee, K. L., and Lafferty, T. "Relationships Among Risk Preferences, Importance and Control." *Journal of Psychology,* 1972, *81,* 249-251.

Horne, W. C. "Risk-Taking and Ethical Risk-Taking: No Relationship." *Psychological Reports,* 1972, *30,* 492.

Jacobson, H. M. "An Investigation of the Relationship Between Risk-Taking Characteristics, Belief in Internal-External Control, Emotional Reactivity, and the Lethality of the Suicide Plan in Women Who Have Attempted Suicide." *Dissertation Abstracts International,* 1973, *34,* 2738-2739.

Jones, E. E., and Gerard, H. B. *Foundations of Social Psychology.* New York: Wiley, 1967.

Jose, T. A. "Convergent-Divergent Thinking Abilities and Risk-Taking in Children." *Phillipine Journal of Psychology,* 1970, *3,* 22-35.

Kapel, D. E., and Wexler, N. "Conceptual Structures of High Risk Black and Regular Freshmen Toward College Related Stimuli." *Journal of Negro Education,* 1972, *41,* 16-25.

Kennedy, P. F., Phanjoo, A. L., and Shekim, W. O. "Risk-Taking in the Lives of Parasuicides (Attempted Suicides)." *British Journal of Psychiatry,* 1971, *119,* 281-286.

Kerlinger, F. N. "The Influence of Research on Education Practice." *Educational Researcher,* 1977, *6,* 5-12.

Kessler, C. C., and Wieland, J. "Experimental Study of Risk-Taking Behavior in Runaway Girls." *Psychological Reports,* 1970, *26,* 810.

Klein, J. P., Quarter, J. J., and Laxer, R. M. "Behavioral Counseling of Underachievers." *American Educational Research Journal,* 1969, *6,* 415-424.

Knowles, E. S., and others. "Risk-Taking as a Personality Trait." *Social Behavior and Personality,* 1973, *1,* 123-136.

Kochansky, G. E. "Risk-Taking and Hedonic Mood Stimulation in Suicide Attempters." *Journal of Abnormal Psychology,* 1973, *81,* 80-86.

Kopfstein, D. "Risk-Taking Behavior and Cognitive Style." *Child Development,* 1973, *44,* 190-192.

Krauss, H. H., Coddington, R. D., and Smeltzer, D. J. "Ethical Risk Sensitivity of Adolescents in Legal Difficulty: First Contact and Repeat Contact Groups." *Journal of Social Psychology,* 1971, *83,* 213-217.

Krauss, H. H., Robinson, I. E., and Cauthen, N. R. "Variables Which Influence Ethical Risk-Taking Among Convicts." *Proceedings of the Annual Convention of the American Psychological Association,* 1972, *7,* 225-226.

Kusyszyn, I. "Gambling, Risk-Taking and Personality: A Bibliography." *International Journal of the Addictions,* 1973, *8,* 173-190.

Lafferty, T., and Higbee, K. L. "Realism and Risk-Taking." *Psychological Reports,* 1974, *34,* 827-829.

Lieblich, A. "Effects of Stress on Risk-Taking." *Psychonomic Science,* 1968, *10,* 303-304.

McCauley, C., Kogan, N., and Teger, A. I. "Order Effects in Answering Risk Dilemmas for Self and Others." *Journal of Personality and Social Psychology,* 1971, *20,* 423-424.

McClelland, D. C., and Teague, G. "Predicting Risk Preferences Among Power Related Tasks." *Journal of Personality*, 1975, *43*, 266-286.

McManis, D. L., and Bell, D. R. "Risk-Taking by Reward-Seeking, Punishment-Avoiding, or Mixed-Orientation Retardates." *American Journal of Mental Deficiency*, 1968, *73*, 267-272.

Maida, P. R. "The Relationship of Risk-Taking and Future Orientations of Persons in a Rural Pennsylvania Low-Income Area." *Dissertation Abstracts International*, 1970, *31*, 837.

Marwell, G., Schmitt, D. R., and Shotola, R. "Cooperation and Interpersonal Risk." *Journal of Personality and Social Psychology*, 1971, *18*, 9-32.

Milburn, T. W., and Billings, R. S. "Decision-Making Perspectives from Psychology: Dealing with Risk and Uncertainty." *American Behavioral Scientist*, 1976, *20*, 111-126.

Miller, J. S., Sensenig, J., and Reed, T. E. "Risky and Cautious Values Among Narcotic Addicts." *International Journal of the Addictions*, 1972, *7*, 1-7.

Miskel, D. "Intrinsic, Extrinsic, and Risk Propensity Factors in the Work Attitudes of Teachers, Educational Administrators, and Business Managers." *Journal of Applied Psychology*, 1974, *59*, 339-343.

Montgomery, G. T., and Landers, W. F. "Transmission of Risk-Taking Through Modeling at Two Age Levels." *Psychological Reports*, 1974, *34*, 1187-1196.

Moon, C. E. "Variation in Children's Risk-Taking Behavior as a Function of External Evaluation, Self-Concept, Locus of Control, Sex, and Anxiety." *Dissertation Abstracts International*, 1974, *34*, 5725.

Moore, J. W., and others. "The Effect of Risk on Concept Acquisition." *Journal of Experimental Education*, 1973, *42*, 51-58.

Moran, M. F. "The Effects of Differential Training on the Risk Variable in the Counselor Decision-Making Process." *Rehabilitation Research and Practice Review*, 1971, *2*, 9-15.

Moran, M. F., Winters, M., and Newman, J. "A Scale for Measuring the Risk-Taking Variable in Rehabilitation Counselor Decision-Making." *Rehabilitation Counseling Bulletin*, 1972, *15*, 211-219.

Morris, R. P. "An Exploratory Study of Some Personality Characteristics of Gamblers." *Journal of Clinical Psychology*, 1957, *13*, 191-193.

Moser, A. J., and Moser, K. A. "Locus of Control as a Determinant of Environmental Manipulation in the Youthful Offender." *Corrective and Social Psychiatry and Journal of Applied Behavior Therapy*, 1973, *19*, 35-39.

Murphy, S. "Expanding Horizons for MRs." *Innovations*, 1975, *2*, 21-26.

Okun, M. A., and di Vesta, F. J. "Cautiousness in Adulthood as a Function of Age and Instructions." *Journal of Gerontology*, 1976, *31*, 571-576.

Okun, M. A., and Siegler, I. C. "Relation Between Preference for Intermediate Risk and Adult Age in Men: A Cross-Cultural Validation." *Developmental Psychology*, 1976, *12*, 565-566.

Ortendahl, M. "Context Effects on Delay Processes." *Göteborg Psychological Reports*, 1975, *5*, 1-8.

Pankove, E., and Kogan, N. "Creative Ability and Risk-Taking in Elementary School Children." *Journal of Personality*, 1968, *36*, 420-439.

Payne, J. W., and Braunstein, M. L. "Preferences Among Gambles with Equal Underlying Distributions." *Journal of Experimental Psychology*, 1971, *87*, 13-18.

Petersen, R. C., Kanarick, A. F., and Hergenhahn, B. R. "Effects of Incentive as a Within- and Between-Subjects Variable in Risk-Taking." *Psychonomic Science*, 1968, *12*, 279-280.

Plax, T. G., and Rosenfeld, L. B. "Dogmatism and Decisions Involving Risk." *Southern Speech Communication Journal,* 1976a, *41,* 266-277.

Plax, T. G., and Rosenfeld, L. B. "Correlates of Risky Decision-Making." *Journal of Personality Assessment,* 1976b, *40,* 413-418.

Pokorny, M. R. "Compulsive Gambling and the Family." *British Journal of Medical Psychology,* 1972, *45,* 355-364.

Poortinga, Y. H., and Spies, E. "An Attempt to Compare Risk-Taking in Two Culturally Different Groups." *Psychologica Africana,* 1972, *14,* 186-199.

Quereshi, M. Y. "Performance on Multiple-Choice Tests and Penalty for Guessing." *Journal of Experimental Education,* 1974, *42,* 74-77.

Radzicki, J. "The Effect of Some Situational Factors on Probabilistic Diagnosing." *Polish Psychological Bulletin,* 1975, *6,* 147-156.

Rapoport, A., and Wallsten, T. S. "Individual Decision Behavior." In P. H. Mussen and M. R. Rosenzweig (Eds.), *Annual Review of Psychology.* Palo Alto, Calif.: Annual Reviews, 1972.

Roberts, G. C. "Effect of Achievement Motivation and Social Environment on Risk-Taking." *Research Quarterly,* 1974, *45,* 42-55.

Roberts, G. C. "Sex and Achievement Motivation Effects on Risk-Taking." *Research Quarterly,* 1975, *46,* 58-70.

Roberts, J. M., and Wicke, J. O. "Flying and Expressive Self-Testing: An Exploratory Consideration." *Journal of Safety Research,* 1972, *4,* 60-68.

Roe, A. V., Howell, R. J., and Payne, I. R. "Comparison of Prison Inmates with and Without Juvenile Records." *Psychological Reports,* 1974, *34,* 1,315-1,319.

Rouse, B. A., and Ewing, J. A. "Marijuana and Other Drug Use by Women College Students: Associated Risk-Taking and Coping Activities." *American Journal of Psychiatry,* 1973, *130,* 486-491.

Routledge, D. A., Repetto-Wright, R., and Howarth, C. I. "A Comparison of Interviews and Observation to Obtain Measures of Children's Exposure to Risk as Pedestrians." *Ergonomics,* 1974, *17,* 623-638.

Rudder, C. S. "A Study of the Relationship Between Semantic Divergent Thinking and Types of Risk-Taking Behavior in Fifth Grade Children." *Dissertation Abstracts International,* 1972, *33,* 1528.

Salzman, C., and others. "The Psychology of Hallucinogenic Drug Discontinuers." *American Journal of Psychiatry,* 1972, *129,* 755-761.

Schroeder, C. A., and Schroeder, S. R. "Decision Conflict in Children in a Risk Situation." *Psychological Record,* 1970, *20,* 457-463.

Schuman, S. H., and Polkowski, J. "Drug and Risk Perceptions of Ninth-Grade Students: Sex Differences and Similarities." *Community Mental Health Journal,* 1975, *2,* 184-194.

Scodel, A., Ratoosh, P., and Minas, S. "Some Personality Correlates of Decision-Making Under Conditions of Risk." *Behavioral Science,* 1959, *4,* 19-28.

Sheridan, K., and Shack, J. R. "Personality Correlates of the Undergraduate Volunteer Subject." *Journal of Psychology,* 1970, *76,* 23-26.

Sherman, R. "Personality and Strategic Choice." *Journal of Psychology,* 1968, *70,* 191-197.

Singh, M. M., and Gang, R. G. "An Ethological Model of Schizophrenia: A Preliminary Investigation." *Diseases of the Nervous System,* 1974, *35,* 157-165.

Singh, N. P. "A Study of the Relationship Between Anxiety and Risk-Taking Amongst Successful and Unsuccessful Agricultural Entrepreneurs of Delhi." *Manas: A Journal of Scientific Psychology,* 1968, *15,* 111-119.

Singh, N. P. "Risk-Taking and Anxiety Among Successful and Unsuccessful, Traditional and Progressive Agricultural Entrepreneurs of Delhi." *British Journal of Social and Clinical Psychology*, 1970, *9*, 301-308.

Singh, N. P., and Singh, K. "Risk-Taking Among Agricultural and Business Entrepreneurs of Delhi." *Psychologia: An International Journal of Psychology in the Orient*, 1972, *15*, 175-180.

Slovic, P. "Assessment of Risk-Taking Behavior." *Psychological Bulletin*, 1964, *61*, 220-233.

Slovic, P. *Information Processing, Situation Specificity, and the Generality of Risk-Taking Behavior*. Eugene: Oregon Research Institute, 1971.

Spencer, J. "The Mental Health of Jehovah's Witnesses." *British Journal of Psychiatry*, 1975, *126*, 556-559.

Steiner, J. "A Questionnaire Study of Risk-Taking in Psychiatric Patients." *British Journal of Medical Psychology*, 1972, *45*, 365-374.

Steiner, J., Jarvis, M., and Parrish, J. "Risk-Taking and Arousal Regulation." *British Journal of Medical Psychology*, 1970, *43*, 333-348.

Stoner, J. A. "A Comparison of Individual and Group Decisions Including Risk." Unpublished master's thesis, School of Industrial Management, Massachusetts Institute of Technology, 1961.

Stroebe, W., and Fraser, C. "The Relationship Between Riskiness and Confidence in Choice Dilemma Situations." *European Journal of Social Psychology*, 1971, *1*, 519-526.

Stukalin, J. J. "A Study of Disadvantaged Eleven-Year-Olds' Risk-Assumption as Related to Locus of Control, Flexible Thinking, and Demographic Factors." *Dissertation Abstracts International*, 1973, *34*, 1762-1763.

Tamerin, J. S., and others. "The Awareness of Risk and Personal Relevance in Alcoholics." *Diseases of the Nervous System*, 1975, *36*, 67-70.

Tarter, R. E., and Parsons, O. A. "Conceptual Shifting in Chronic Alcoholics." *Journal of Abnormal Psychology*, 1971, *77*, 71-75.

Thomas, G. P., and Garvin, A. D. "Sex Differences in Risk-Taking on Essay Tests." *Journal of Student Personnel Association for Teacher Education*, 1973, *12*, 32-36.

Tomkins, S. S. "A Theory of Risk-Taking Behavior." In R. E. Carney (Ed.), *Risk-Taking Behavior: Concepts, Methods, and Applications to Smoking and Drug Abuse*. Springfield, Ill.: Thomas, 1971.

Tongberg, S. A. "Risk-Taking Judgments in Adulthood." *Dissertation Abstracts International*, 1971, *32*, 1261.

Touhey, J. C. "Risk-Taking Preferences of College Students in Canada and the United States." *Psychological Reports*, 1971, *29*, 512.

Touhey, J. C., and Mason, E. P. "Relationship of Flexibility and Category Width to Risk-Taking Strategy." *Journal of Experimental Research in Personality*, 1972, *6*, 259-263.

Touhey, J. C., and Villemez, W. J. "Need Achievement and Risk-Taking Preference: A Clarification." *Journal of Personality and Social Psychology*, 1975, *32*, 713-719.

Vroom, V. H., and Pahl, B. "Relationship Between Age and Risk-Taking Among Managers." *Journal of Applied Psychology*, 1971, *55*, 399-405.

Walesa, C. "The Development of Decision Processes: Experimental Tests of Children at School Age." *Roczniki Filozoficzne: Annales de Philosophie (Polish Annals of Philosophy)*, 1972, *20*, 101-142.

Walesa, C. "Children's Approaches to Change- and Skill-Dependent Risk." *Polish Psychological Bulletin*, 1975, *6*, 131-138.

Walsh, W. B., and Stillman, S. M. "Disclosure of Deception by Debriefed Subjects." *Journal of Counseling Psychology,* 1974, *21,* 315-319.

Weinstein, E., and Martin, J. "Generality of Willingness to Take Risks." *Psychological Reports,* 1969, *24,* 499-501.

Weinstein, M. S. "Achievement Motivation and Risk Preference." *Journal of Personality and Social Psychology,* 1969, *13,* 153-172.

Weller, L., Eytan, R., and Sollel, M. "Birth Order and Risk-Taking Among Kibbutz and City Youth." *British Journal of Social and Clinical Psychology,* 1976, *15,* 103-104.

West, J. D., Fretz, B. R., and MacDonald, M. J. "Modifying Risk-Taking Behavior." *Child Development,* 1970, *41,* 1083-1088.

Zimmerman, J., and Krauss, H. H. "Source and Magnitude of Censure in Predictions of Unethical Behavior." *Psychological Reports,* 1971, *28,* 727-732.

Zisfein, L., and Rosen, M. "Self-Concept and Mental Retardation: Theory, Measurement and Clinical Utility." *Mental Retardation,* 1974, *12,* 15-19.

33

Jaquelyn Liss Resnick
Martin Amerikaner

Self-Disclosure

Self-disclosure, defined as the art of revealing personal information about oneself to another (Jourard, 1971), has generated much discussion and research among behavioral scientists in the past twenty years. Humanistically oriented personality theorists have discussed the importance of self-disclosure to healthy personal functioning; social psychologists have studied the factors influencing the several parameters of disclosing behavior; and clinicians have examined the implications of client and therapist self-disclosure within the process of therapy.

As interest in the field has grown, alternative labels have been used by investigators to reflect their unique interests and perspectives. Altman and Taylor (1973) use the term *social penetration* to describe the "multilevel behavioral process" of exchanging personal information at several levels of intimacy. Suchman (1965) takes a phenomenological orientation, using the terms *revealingness* and especially *authentic revealingness* to capture the experiential components of self-disclosure. Other terms central to the discussion of self-disclosure include *reciprocity, dialogue,* and *authentic* or *real self*. Reciprocal disclosure, sometimes called the "dyadic effect" (Jourard, 1971), refers to the tendency for individuals to match the level of disclosure of conversational partners (Cozby, 1973). Dialogue is described by Jourard (1978) as an active, ongoing process whereby two people reveal themselves to each other and listen to the disclosures of the other in order to "understand and make oneself understood" (p. 47). This dialogue process is contrasted to interaction where the goal of one or both is to negate, change, or in some other way manipulate the perspective of the other. Persons engaged in dialogue are revealing and discovering their authentic, "real" selves, whereas interaction not involving dialogue is designed to reveal only the "public" selves of the participants. (See Jourard, 1974, for a fuller discussion of authentic and public selves.)

In developing a more complete understanding of self-disclosure, both content and process dimensions have been researched using a variety of methods. Studies have focused on the topic areas people choose to reveal (and to not reveal), the partners chosen for different degrees of disclosure, and the social factors which influence the pace, intimacy, and other components of the disclosure process. Methodologists have studied the utility of several assessment techniques, including self-report questionnaires and scales designed to rate disclosure in conversational behavior.

As several investigators have noted, self-disclosure is not a unitary or single-dimensional construct (Chelune, 1978; Cozby, 1973). Five parameters have been identified as central to self-disclosure: (1) amount or breadth of disclosed personal information; (2) degree of intimacy of disclosed material; (3) a time dimension related to rate and duration of disclosure; (4) the affective or emotional "charge" accompanying verbal disclosure; and (5) the overall flexibility or inflexibility of a person's disclosing behavior in varying social contexts (Chelune, 1975a).

Background and Current Status

In discussion of his early research on self-disclosure, Jourard (1971) cites the writings of Edmund Husserl, Martin Heidegger, Jean-Paul Sartre, and Maurice Merleau-Ponty as providing a philosophical basis for his work. Especially important is Buber's (1937) description of "I-Thou" relationships, to which Jourard (1971, 1974) refers in describing the relevance of self-disclosure and dialogue to authentic, healthy personal functioning.

Psychological theorists also have contributed to the historical context of interest in self-disclosure. The relationship between self-expression and personal growth has been discussed by Rogers and his associates (Rogers and Dymond, 1954). Rogers (1961) considers self-disclosure both a characteristic of self-acceptance and the means to achieve this end. Sullivan (1954) notes the therapeutic value of client self-disclosure, in contrast to abstract interactions, which lack personal disclosure. Other theorists (Bateson and others, 1956; Laing, 1959; Mowrer, 1961; Reusch, 1957) have related blocked, distorted, and inauthentic communication to individual and interpersonal dysfunctions.

The psychoanalytic conception of the therapeutic relationship was challenged by Jourard (1960) in his inclusion of therapist self-disclosure as appropriate and of therapeutic value in the therapy hour. Jourard (1960, 1974) expanded Rogers' (1961) conditions necessary for a therapeutic environment to include authentic dialogue between therapist and client. In this model, therapist disclosure serves both to assist the development of a trusting relationship and to allow the therapist to act as a facilitative "larger consciousness" and role model.

Social psychologists have examined the role of self-disclosure in interpersonal relationships within the context of social exchange and social penetration (Cozby, 1973). Altman and Taylor (1973) propose a model of social penetration, which integrates reward-cost concepts of exchange theory with situational determinants and personality characteristics that influence disclosure. Reciprocity of disclosure has been viewed as a result of social exchange process, where self-disclosure serves as a social reward (Worthy,

Gary, and Kahn, 1969). Jourard (1959, 1964) has also described the reciprocity effect in terms of modeling, with the initial discloser, by his or her own example, "inviting" the recipient to disclose. Many studies have sought to explore the factors that determine whether the invitation to disclose will be accepted.

Research on self-disclosure has focused on two general methodological approaches. The first has investigated the personality and social factors that influence the level of disclosure by subjects. In their early questionnaire studies, Jourard and his associates (Jourard, 1959; Jourard and Landsman, 1960; Jourard and Lasakow, 1958) examined the relationship of demographic and cultural parameters to self-disclosure. These studies used self-report and paper-and-pencil instruments and were correlational in nature. While the self-report approach was being developed and more sophisticated instruments were being constructed, another methodology was developed to investigate the ongoing self-disclosure process itself (Epting, Suchman, and Barker, 1977). Within therapeutic settings, studies examined both the influence of therapist behavior on client revealingness and the relationship of this self-exploration to client movement and growth in therapy (Truax and Carkhuff, 1965, 1967). In laboratory studies, investigators experimentally examined the parameters that influenced subjects' disclosures during ongoing interactions (Jourard, 1971).

Current studies in the self-disclosure field can be seen as more carefully designed developments of earlier work. These are based on a more sophisticated theoretical understanding of the elements of self-disclosing behavior (such as nonverbal and paralinguistic behaviors) and the variables that influence individual self-disclosure. Chelune's (1976a, 1976b) effort to assess the multiple dimensions of communication demonstrates an awareness of the complex nature of the disclosure process, as well as the difficulty involved in quantifying that process. Another recent development is the attempt to move beyond brief interactions of strangers in a laboratory setting to the study of disclosure patterns and reciprocity over time as it occurs in long-term relationships such as friendships (Derlega, Wilson, and Chaiken, 1976). The relationship of self-disclosure to healthy personality functioning is still of theoretical and clinical importance, although empirical investigation has yet to demonstrate the hypothesized (Jourard, 1974) curvilinear relationship between disclosure and healthy functioning.

Critical Discussion

General Areas of Concern

Three major areas must be considered in the assessment of self-disclosure: (1) the multidimensional nature of the construct; (2) the varying perspectives from which self-disclosure can be measured; (3) the factors known to affect self-disclosure behaviors, including the social context in which it occurs.

Dimensions of Self-Disclosure. Five parameters have been identified as central to the construct of self-disclosure: (1) *amount*, (2) *intimacy*, (3) *duration*, (4) *affect*, and (5) *flexibility*.

Early self-disclosure research was content oriented, dealing with the amount of information disclosed to specified others. Assessment involved use of the Jourard Self-Disclosure Questionnaire (JSDQ) and the self-report rating scale developed by Jourard and Lasakow (1958) or modifications derived from it (Jourard, 1964, 1968, 1971). The original instrument (JSDQ-60) consists of six ten-statement categories of aspects of self. Degrees of past self-disclosure on the sixty items are reported with regard to four target persons: mother, father, same-sex friend, and opposite-sex friend or spouse. Scores can be obtained for overall disclosure, for each target person, and for each topic category.

The general psychometric quality of the JSDQ-60 is considered quite good (Chelune, 1978); the reliability and construct validity are sound, but the predictive validity is questionable. However, with appropriate instruction set (willingness to disclose to a specified target), the predictive ability improves (Jourard and Resnick, 1970). Besides altered instruction set, modification of the instrument has included varying the number of items, the rating scale, and the target persons.

Objective measures of amount include content analysis of actual interviews and of written transcripts of taped interviews. The number of words spoken; the number of items or topics covered; and the number of sentences, thought units, and statements about self have all been tabulated as basic units of analysis in the measure of amount of self-disclosure (Chelune, 1978).

Several instruments have been developed for assessing the degree of intimacy of self-disclosures. Taylor and Altman (1966) scaled 671 statements concerned with aspects of self for intimacy, with the intent that the items could be used in the development of self-disclosure measures. One such scale is the Intimacy Rating Scale (Strassberg and Anchor, 1975), which rates intimacy on the basis of content alone. Jourard and Resnick's (1970) procedure for obtaining self-report data on disclosure in actual interviews combines intimacy and amount into a single composite score. Topics selected from Taylor and Altman's (1966) pool of low, medium, and high intimacy values were rated on a three-point scale for amount of disclosure. A weighted score was obtained by multiplying the amount by the intimacy value of the topic (1, 2, or 3).

The third dimension of self-disclosure, duration, refers to the time spent disclosing. It has been assumed that speech duration is related to self-disclosure output or willingness to disclose (Doster and Strickland, 1971). Questions have been raised as to whether duration of speech is necessarily related to the quantity or quality of self-disclosure (Block and Goodstein, 1971). However, Goodstein and associates (1976) found that, especially from the recipient's point of view, the amount of self-disclosure is equated with the amount of participation in a group. Although duration has not been found to be related to the number of references to self, the relationship between duration and ratings of depth of disclosure has been consistently reported, indicating that the longer one speaks about oneself, the more intimate the disclosures become or are perceived to become (compare Chelune, 1978, p. 305).

Since the concise, explicit speaker is penalized by measures of duration, rate of disclosure has been used to reflect disclosure per unit of time, independent of individual speech rhythms (Chelune, 1975b, 1976a). Comparisons of measures of rate and duration of disclosure are needed to shed further light on this parameter.

"Reaction time" and "silence quotient" have been used as temporal factors (Doster, 1972, 1975; Doster and Strickland, 1971), with lengthy reaction times and high silence quotients considered to reflect cautiousness in preparing verbal disclosures. However, within the counseling context silences were found to enhance the counselor's perceptions of counselee self-disclosure (Fischer and Apostal, 1975).

A departure from the preceding research methodologies is found in studies using a process conception of self-disclosure, where variables contributing to a person's style of communication and paralinguistic characteristics of verbal productions are treated as additional sources of data (Epting, Suchman, and Barker, 1977). The implication is that an "appropriate affective charge," which plays an important role in communication, can be attached to the revelation of intimate information (Chelune, 1975a).

Bayne (1974) has raised the issue of whether instruments such as the JSDQ assess the authentic disclosure of self to others, since they do not allow assessment of whether an item reported as disclosed is real or false. Barker (1971-72) has labeled this dimension of self-disclosure "revealingness" or "authentic revealingness," defined as being open and true in a relationship to another, so that he may know one's real self, as opposed to being false or phony so as to obscure knowledge about oneself.

Rating scales developed to assess this affective dimension of self-disclosure derive in part from the Process Scale (Walker, Rablen, and Rogers, 1960), which measures the degree of self-exploration, rigidity of concepts, and degree of immediate experiencing. Self-disclosure as an ongoing process has also been measured by the Experiencing Scale (Gendlin and Tomlinson, 1967) and the Depth of Intrapersonal-Exploration Scale (Truax, 1962). A frequently used scale in clinical settings is the Helpee Self-Exploration Scale (Carkhuff, 1969). It is a five-point scale, with self-exploration defined at level 3 as the voluntary introduction by the helpee of personally relevant material, although the style may be mechanical and unemotional. Above level 3, the helpee introduces personally relevant material with increasing emotional proximity; below level 3 there is no voluntary introduction of such material. Helper Self-Disclosure has also been operationalized on a five-point rating scale (Carkhuff, 1969).

The Revealingness Scale (Suchman, 1965), developed specifically for use in laboratory and field studies of personal communication, is designed to produce finer differentiation at the less revealing end of process dimensions than those scales designed primarily for psychotherapeutic interactions. In samples of spoken behavior, language style, voice quality, and content are simultaneously evaluated on a seven-point rating scale. Brooks (1974) has refined the REV to include an additional rating category for affective involvement in external content. Also, verbal segments are rated for their modal (rather than highest) level of response.

Other measures of affect can be used with written samples of disclosure. The Self-Disclosure Sentence Blank (Greene, 1964) contains twenty incomplete sentences. The instructions call for completion of the items in an open and straightforward manner. Ratings of self-disclosure, based on samples in the scoring manual, are made on a five-step scale. The Personal Approach Rating Scale (Carpenter, 1966) assesses the dimension reflecting a personal versus an impersonal view of others. Subjects are asked to write ten or twenty sentences to describe a specific target person. The sentences are scored as personal, impersonal, or unscorable. A Personal Approach Score (PAS) is obtained as a ratio of personal statements to the sum of personal and impersonal statements multiplied by a constant. Doster's (1971) Disclosure Rating Scale also rates disclosures along a superficial-personal continuum.

Self-descriptive essays scored for depth of self-disclosure and authenticity have been used by Burhenne and Mirels (1970) and by Pedersen and Breglio (1968). Janofsky (1971) measured self-disclosure by counting the number of "I" statements followed by affect words. Responses to TAT cards as a source of data for ratings of openness have been used by Hamshire and Farina (1967), who developed a five-point rating scale and a scoring manual based on story characteristics. Chelune (1975b) has developed a content analysis system that independently assesses the judged degree of congruence between content and affective manner of presentation.

The fifth dimension of self-disclosure, flexibility, refers to the ability to modulate self-disclosure levels according to the interpersonal and situational demands of various social situations (Chelune, 1976a). Whereas Jourard (1964) believes that there is an optimal level of disclosure correlated with mental health, Chelune (1975a) suggests that individual flexibility in disclosure across situations—rather than some overall, consistently optimal degree of "willingness to disclose"—might be the important dimension in healthy functioning. The assessment of disclosure flexibility necessitates repeated measures of each subject across time and situations; a single "level of disclosure" score is insufficient. Beginning work in the development of methods for assessing disclosure flexibility has been done by Chelune (1975b, 1976b).

Measurement Perspective. Self-disclosure can be measured from the perspective of the sender, the recipient, or an objective or neutral observer (Goodstein and Reinecker, 1974). The sender typically uses self-report inventories or rating scales. The recipient often uses rating scales; projective techniques can also be employed, and peer nominations are possible in a group situation. The neutral observer may use a variety of rating scales or may use objective measures, such as number of words or time spent talking. Researchers must take into consideration that these three different perspectives may yield different assessments of self-disclosure. A study by Goodstein and associates (1976) indicates that judgments based on the recipient's and the sender's perspective may involve the use of different criteria, yielding discordant results. Eland, Epting, and Bonarius (in press) found that ratings of disclosure by the sender and the recipient sometimes differed from those made by a neutral judge.

Factors Affecting Self-Disclosure. Self-disclosure is a function of social-situational factors and the personality of the discloser. One important social-situational factor is the target person (the recipient of the disclosure). The relationship between the discloser and the target person, the discloser's liking for the target, and the sex and race of the target will all affect a particular disclosure. The verbal and nonverbal behavior of the target also is a powerful determinant of self-disclosure. Jourard (1959) has described the dyadic effect, an input-output correlation of revealingness operating on the principle that "disclosure begets disclosure." The dyadic effect has been demonstrated in questionnaire (Jourard and Lasakow, 1958; Jourard and Landsman, 1960; Jourard and Richman, 1963) and in interview research (Jourard, 1968; Jourard and Jaffee, 1970; Jourard and Resnick, 1970; Matarazzo, Wiens, and Saslow, 1965). Heller, Davis, and Myers (1966) found that greater interviewer activity produced higher proportions of subject verbalization and that interviewer silence was verbally inhibiting, producing the least interviewee talk time. Similar trends have been found in small groups (Chittick and Himelstein, 1967; Himelstein and Kimbrough, 1963). In a clinical setting, verbal and nonverbal counselor behavior (in the form of the "core conditions" of empathy, positive regard, and genuineness) have a demonstrated relationship to helpee self-exploration (Carkhuff, 1969; Truax and Carkhuff, 1965, 1967).

The content or topic of self-disclosure is also a relevant variable. Some aspects of self are more public and, therefore, more readily disclosed than private aspects, which may be disclosed only under certain circumstances (Jourard, 1964). Another variable that affects self-disclosure has been termed "setting condition" (Chelune, 1978). Setting conditions can refer to the experimental laboratory or to natural settings, such as a blind date.

Numerous studies have examined the relationship between self-disclosure and demographic and personality factors. Sex differences; differences among racial, national, religious, and socioeconomic groups; and birth order and age differences in self-disclosure have all been reported (Chelune, 1978; Cozby, 1973; Jourard, 1971). A wide variety of personality measures have been correlated with self-disclosure. Although the correlations are generally low and appear equivocal, Cozby (1973) notes that a consistently positive relationship has been found between self-disclosure and measures of social extraversion. Altman and Taylor (1973) suggest that self-disclosure be examined within the context of specific relationships and settings and indicate that the search for relationships between "trait disclosure" and other personality measures is unrealistic.

Comparative Philosophies and Theories

The concept of self-disclosure is grounded in humanistic-existential-phenomeno-logical theory (Jourard, 1971). Personality theorists have related self-disclosure to healthy personality (Jourard, 1971). Clinicians have developed theoretical models specifying conditions that facilitate helpee self-exploration (Carkhuff, 1969; Carkhuff and Berenson, 1967; Rogers, 1961; Truax and Carkhuff, 1967). Social psychologists have sought to explain self-disclosing behavior in theories of social exchange, social penetration, and social modeling (Altman and Taylor, 1973; Cozby, 1973; Doster and Brooks, 1974; Jourard, 1964).

Elaboration on Critical Points

Self-disclosure is a multidimensional concept, with at least five dimensions identified as factors. However, the assessment of self-disclosure has usually been unidimensional. Occasionally, two or three dimensions are considered together (Doster and Brooks, 1974), and sometimes two dimensions are confounded in a single measure (Suchman, 1965). The only known instrument for assessing all five dimensions independently is the Self-Disclosure Coding System (Chelune, 1975b), a complex system consisting of eleven coding categories and a detailed scoring manual. However, the relationships among the dimensions of self-disclosure remain to be established.

The level of analysis in assessment must be spelled out, since contradictory results can occur. Goodstein and associates (1976) found that neutral observers rating the same individual's disclosure by content rather than process analysis judged the most revealing statements to come from persons both self-ranked and group-ranked as low disclosers. Measurement perspective and the sociosituational context in which measurement occurs are other factors that must be taken into account before results of studies can be interpreted in a meaningful way (Eland, Epting, and Bonarius, in press).

Personal Views and Recommendations

To illuminate the concepts of flexibility and appropriateness of disclosure, the self-disclosure process needs to be assessed in ongoing relationships, especially in natural settings, with repeated measurements over time. Process variables such as changes in direction or topic (see Grater and Claxton, 1976) provide fruitful avenues of research.

Authenticity of disclosure is another dimension that needs more attention in assessment procedures. Along these lines, Gitter and Black (1976) have operationalized the term *gilding,* which they define as communicative behavior intended to falsify what the speaker believes to be true. Risk taking and trust in a relationship are other factors that must be integrated into professional understanding of self-disclosure. Areas of current psychological concern that need clarification with regard to their impact on self-disclosure include power, sex-role expectation (Derlega and Chaiken, 1976), and sex-role identification.

Experimentation in self-disclosure often involves encouraging naive subjects to disclose themselves to other naive subjects or to clinically untrained experimenter cohorts. Since self-disclosure may uncover or expose the subject to personal conflicts or confusion, provisions should be made for debriefing and the availability of appropriate referral to professionals, if necessary. As in all psychological research and assessment, the confidential nature of all disclosed material must be assured to all subjects and, of course, respected by the researcher.

Application to Particular Variables

Numerous demographic characteristics of the discloser (such as age, sex, education, ethnicity, race, religion, and socioeconomic status, as well as vocational affiliation and role) are known to have significant relationships to self-disclosure (Jourard, 1971). Furthermore, these same factors, as characteristics of the recipient, affect self-disclosure. For example, racial differences occur in self-disclosure, depending on the racial identity of the speaker and of the target person as well (Singleton, 1976).

The assessment instruments reviewed previously have been used with diverse populations of young adults and adults. To extend the age range, other measures have been developed for particular use with children and adolescents (Chelune, 1978; Rivenbark, 1971; Skypeck, 1967; Vondracek and Vondracek, 1971).

There is some evidence for Jourard's (1964, 1971) theory that authentic self-disclosure is related to the healthy personality, while neurosis is related to inability to know one's real self and make it known to others. Psychological adjustment, self-concept, and self-actualization have been significantly correlated with amount of self-disclosure (Jourard, 1971; Lombardo and Fantasia, 1976; Shapiro and Swensen, 1977). High disclosers have been found not only to reveal more but to be more sincere than their low-disclosing counterparts, who reveal less and are more likely to falsify the image that they present, using gilding to mask what they do not wish to reveal (Gitter and Black, 1976). Shimkunas (1972) found that disturbed individuals tend to disclose little about themselves and that schizophrenics actively avoid intense personal interactions by verbalizing peculiar beliefs and autistic concepts.

References

Altman, I., and Taylor, D. A. *Social Penetration: The Development of Interpersonal Relationships.* New York: Holt, Rinehart and Winston, 1973.

Barker, E. N. "Humanistic Psychology and Scientific Method." *Interpersonal Development,* 1971-72, *2*, 137-172.

Bateson, G., and others. "Towards a Theory of Schizophrenia." *Behavioral Science,* 1956, *1*, 251-264.

Bayne, R. "Does the JSDQ Measure Authenticity?" *Journal of Humanistic Psychology,* 1974, *14*, 79-86.

Block, E. L., and Goodstein, L. D. "Comment on 'Influence of an Interviewer's Disclosure on the Self-Disclosing Behavior of Interviewees.' " *Journal of Counseling Psychology,* 1971, *18*, 595-597.

Brooks, L. "Interactive Effects of Sex and Status on Self-Disclosure." *Journal of Counseling Psychology,* 1974, *21*, 469-474.

Buber, M. *I and Thou.* New York: Scribner's, 1937.

Burhenne, D., and Mirels, H. "Self-Disclosure in Self-Descriptive Essays." *Journal of Consulting and Clinical Psychology,* 1970, *35*, 409-413.

Carkhuff, R. R. *Helping and Human Relations.* Vol. 2. New York: Holt, Rinehart and Winston, 1969.

Carkhuff, R. R., and Berenson, B. G. *Beyond Counseling and Therapy.* New York: Holt, Rinehart and Winston, 1967.

Carpenter, J. C. "The Construct Personal-Impersonal." Unpublished master's thesis, Ohio State University, 1966.

Chelune, G. J. "Self-Disclosure: An Elaboration of Its Basic Dimensions." *Psychological Reports,* 1975a, *36,* 79-85.

Chelune, G. J. "Studies in the Behavioral and Self-Report Assessment of Self-Disclosure." Unpublished doctoral dissertation, University of Nevada at Reno, 1975b.

Chelune, G. J. "A Multidimensional Look at Sex and Target Differences in Disclosure." *Psychological Reports,* 1976a, *39,* 259-263.

Chelune, G. J. "The Self-Disclosure Situations Survey: A New Approach to Measuring Self-Disclosure." *JSAS Catalog of Selected Documents in Psychology,* 1976b, *6,* 111-112.

Chelune, G. J. "Nature and Assessment of Self-Disclosing Behavior." In P. McReynolds (Ed.), *Advances in Psychological Assessment IV.* San Francisco: Jossey-Bass, 1978.

Chittick, E. V., and Himelstein, P. "The Manipulation of Self-Disclosure." *Journal of Psychology,* 1967, *65,* 117-121.

Cozby, P. "Self-Disclosure: A Literature Review." *Psychological Bulletin,* 1973, *79,* 73-91.

Derlega, V. J., and Chaiken, A. L. "Norms Affecting Self-Disclosure in Men and Women." *Journal of Clinical and Consulting Psychology,* 1976, *44,* 376-380.

Derlega, V. J., Wilson, M., and Chaiken, A. L. "Friendship and Disclosure Reciprocity." *Journal of Personality and Social Psychology,* 1976, *34,* 578-582.

Doster, J. A. "The Disclosure Rating Scale." Unpublished rating manual, University of Missouri, 1971.

Doster, J. A. "Effects of Instructions, Modeling, and Role Rehearsal on Interview Verbal Behavior." *Journal of Consulting and Clinical Psychology,* 1972, *39,* 202-209.

Doster, J. A. "Individual Differences Affecting Interviewee Expectancies and Perceptions of Self-Disclosure." *Journal of Counseling Psychology,* 1975, *22,* 192-198.

Doster, J. A., and Brooks, S. J. "Interviewer Disclosure Modeling, Information Revealed, and Interviewee Verbal Behavior." *Journal of Consulting and Clinical Psychology,* 1974, *42,* 420-426.

Doster, J. A., and Strickland, B. R. "Disclosing of Verbal Material as a Function of Information Requested, Information About the Interviewer, and Interviewee Differences." *Journal of Consulting and Clinical Psychology,* 1971, *37,* 187-194.

Eland, F. A., Epting, F. R., and Bonarius, H. "Self-Disclosure and the Reptest Interaction Technique (RIT)." In P. Stringer and D. Bannister (Eds.), *Construct Theory and Social Psychology.* New York: Academic Press, in press.

Epting, F., Suchman, D. I., and Barker, E. N. "Some Aspects of Revealingness and Disclosure." In D. D. Nevill (Ed.), *Humanistic Psychology: New Frontiers.* New York: Gardner Press, 1977.

Fischer, M., and Apostal, R. "Selected Vocal Cues and Counselor's Perceptions of Genuineness, Self-Disclosure, and Anxiety." *Journal of Counseling Psychology,* 1975, *22,* 92-96.

Gendlin, E. T., and Tomlinson, T. M. "A Scale for the Rating of Experiencing." In C. R. Rogers and others (Eds.), *The Therapeutic Relationship and Its Impact: A Study of Psychotherapy with Schizophrenics.* Madison: University of Wisconsin Press, 1967.

Gitter, A. G., and Black, H. "Is Self-Disclosure Self-Revealing?" *Journal of Counseling Psychology,* 1976, *23,* 327-332.

Goodstein, L. D., and others. "Measurement of Self Disclosure in Encounter Groups: A Methodological Study." *Journal of Counseling Psychology,* 1976, *23,* 142-146.

Goodstein, L. D., and Reinecker, V. M. "Factors Affecting Self-Disclosure: A Review of the Literature." In B. A. Maher (Ed.), *Progress in Experimental Personality Research*. Vol. 7. New York: Academic Press, 1974.

Grater, H., and Claxton, D. "Counselor Empathy Level and Client Topic Changes." *Journal of Counseling Psychology*, 1976, *23*, 407-408.

Greene, R. "Sentence Completion Test for Measuring Self-Disclosure." Unpublished master's thesis, Ohio State University, 1964.

Halverson, C., and Shore, R. "Self-Disclosure and Interpersonal Functioning." *Journal of Consulting and Clinical Psychology*, 1969, *33*, 213-217.

Hamshire, H. H., and Farina, A. "Openness as a Dimension of Projective Test Responses." *Journal of Consulting Psychology*, 1967, *31*, 525-528.

Haymes, M. "Self-Disclosure and the Acquaintance Process." Unpublished manuscript, Cornell University, 1969.

Heller, K., Davis, J. D., and Myers, R. A. "The Effects of Interviewer Style in a Standardized Interview." *Journal of Consulting Psychology*, 1966, *30*, 501-508.

Himelstein, P., and Kimbrough, W. "A Study of Self-Disclosure in the Classroom." *Journal of Psychology*, 1963, *55*, 437-440.

Janofsky, A. I. "Affective Self-Disclosure in Telephone Versus Face-to-Face Interviews." *Journal of Humanistic Psychology*, 1971, *11*, 93-103.

Jourard, S. M. "Self-Disclosure and Other Cathexis." *Journal of Abnormal and Social Psychology*, 1959, *59*, 428-431.

Jourard, S. M. "Some Implications of Self-Disclosure Research for Counseling and Psychotherapy." Paper presented at conference on personality theory and counseling, University of Florida, Gainesville, 1960.

Jourard, S. M. *The Transparent Self*. New York: Van Nostrand, 1964.

Jourard, S. M. *Disclosing Man to Himself*. New York: Van Nostrand, 1968.

Jourard, S. M. *Self-Disclosure: An Experimental Analysis of the Transparent Self*. New York: Wiley-Interscience, 1971.

Jourard, S. M. *Healthy Personality: An Approach from the Viewpoint of Humanistic Psychology*. New York: Macmillan, 1974.

Jourard, S. M. "Education as Dialogue." *Journal of Humanistic Psychology*, 1978, *18*, 47-52.

Jourard, S. M., and Jaffe, P. E. "Influence of an Interviewer's Behavior on the Self-Disclosing Behavior of Interviewees." *Journal of Counseling Psychology*, 1970, *17*, 253-257.

Jourard, S. M., and Landsma, M. J. "Cognition, Cathexis, and the 'Dyadic Effect' in Men's Self-Disclosure Behavior." *Merrill-Palmer Quarterly of Behavior and Development*, 1960, *6*, 178-186.

Jourard, S. M., and Lasakow, P. "Some Factors in Self-Disclosure." *Journal of Abnormal and Social Psychology*, 1958, *56*, 91-98.

Jourard, S. M., and Resnick, J. L. "Some Effects of Self-Disclosure Among College Women." *Journal of Humanistic Psychology*, 1970, *10*, 84-93.

Jourard, S. M., and Richman, P. "Factors in the Self-Disclosure Inputs of College Students." *Merrill-Palmer Quarterly of Behavior and Development*, 1963, *9*, 141-148.

Laing, R. D. *The Divided Self*. London: Tavistock, 1959.

Lombardo, J. P., and Fantasia, S. C. "The Relationship of Self-Disclosure to Personality, Adjustment, and Self-Actualization." *Journal of Clinical Psychology*, 1976, *32*, 765-769.

Matarazzo, J. D., Wiens, A. M., and Saslow, G. "Studies of Interview Speech Behavior."

In L. Krasner and L. P. Ullmann (Eds.), *Research in Behavior Modification: New Developments and Their Clinical Implications.* New York: Holt, Rinehart and Winston, 1965.

Mowrer, O. H. *The Crisis in Psychiatry and Religion.* New York: Van Nostrand, 1961.

Pedersen, D. M., and Breglio, V. J. "Personality Correlates of Actual Self-Disclosure." *Psychological Reports,* 1968, *22,* 495-501.

Reusch, J. *Disturbed Communication.* New York: Norton, 1957.

Rivenbark, W. H. "Self-Disclosure Patterns Among Adolescents." *Psychological Reports,* 1971, *28,* 35-42.

Rogers, C. *On Becoming a Person.* Boston: Houghton Mifflin, 1961.

Rogers, C., and Dymond, R. *Psychotherapy and Personality Change.* Chicago: University of Chicago Press, 1954.

Shapiro, A., and Swensen, C. H. "Self-Disclosure as a Function of Self-Concept and Sex." *Journal of Personality Assessment,* 1977, *41,* 144-149.

Shimkunas, A. M. "Demand for Intimate Self-Disclosure and Pathological Verbalizations in Schizophrenia." *Journal of Abnormal Psychology,* 1972, *80,* 197-205.

Singleton, D. E. "Racial Self-Designation, Self-Disclosure and Counselor Preference." Unpublished doctoral dissertation, George Washington University, 1976.

Skypeck, G. "Self-Disclosure in Children Ages Six Through Twelve." Unpublished master's thesis, University of Florida, 1967.

Strassberg, D. S., and Anchor, K. N. "Rating Intimacy of Self-Disclosure." *Psychological Reports,* 1975, *37,* 562.

Suchman, D. I. "A Scale for the Measurement of Revealingness in Spoken Behavior." Unpublished master's thesis, Ohio State University, 1965.

Sullivan, H. S. *The Psychiatric Interview.* New York: Norton, 1954.

Taylor, D. A., and Altman, I. "Intimacy-Scaled Stimuli for Use in Studies of Interpersonal Relations." *Psychological Reports,* 1966, *19,* 729-730.

Truax, C. B. "A Tentative Scale for the Measurement of Depth of Intrapersonal Exploration (DX)." Discussion Paper No. 29. Madison: Wisconsin Psychiatric Institute, 1962.

Truax, C. B., and Carkhuff, R. R. "Client and Therapist Transparency in the Psychotherapeutic Encounter." *Journal of Counseling Psychology,* 1965, *12,* 3-9.

Truax, C. B., and Carkhuff, R. R. *Toward Effective Counseling and Psychotherapy: Training and Practice.* Chicago: Aldine, 1967.

Vondracek, S., and Vondracek, F. W. "The Manipulation and Measurement of Self-Disclosure in Preadolescents." *Merrill Palmer Quarterly,* 1971, *17,* 51-58.

Walker, A. M., Rablen, R. A., and Rogers, C. R. "Development of a Scale to Measure Process Change in Psychotherapy." *Journal of Clinical Psychology,* 1960, *16,* 79-85.

Worthy, M., Gary, A. L., and Kahn, G. M. "Self-Disclosure as an Exchange Process." *Journal of Personality and Social Psychology,* 1969, *13,* 59-63.

34

Paul N. Foxman

Tolerance for Ambiguity: Implications for Mental Health

Tolerance for ambiguity refers to the degree to which a person can cope effectively with unstructured or open-ended situations. In this sense, tolerance for ambiguity represents the extent of a person's willingness and/or ability to accept experiences at variance with conventional reality, as well as the degree to which free play of thought processes is allowed under such circumstances. There appear to be stable individual differences in levels of tolerance for ambiguity as a general cognitive and perceptual orientation to the

world. These differences have been found to reflect differences in other personality variables. This chapter reviews the concept of tolerance for ambiguity in terms of its implications for mental health, including applications to self-actualization, creativity, the psychology of consciousness, psychotherapy, and Rorschach testing in clinical settings.

Tolerance for ambiguity appears to be a stable response style, with individual differences in the degree to which it is exhibited. High tolerance for ambiguity has been
linked to a number of adaptive personality traits and is considered a reflection of high
levels of psychological health.

A number of perceptual measures have been used to assess degree of tolerance for
ambiguity, but the Rorschach appears to be high in both construct validity and interjudge
reliability for this purpose (Foxman, 1976; Klein, Gardner, and Schlesinger, 1962; Klein
and Schlesinger, 1951).

Background and Current Status

The concept of tolerance for ambiguity is rooted historically in a series of attempts to establish a set of perceptual behaviors that could define personality organization. The theoretical framework for this effort was psychoanalytic, with special reference to
the ideas of the "ego psychology" theorists (Gardner, 1964; Gardner and others, 1959;
Hartmann, 1939; Klein, 1949, 1954, 1958; Rapaport, 1958). In that framework, tolerance
for ambiguity was conceptualized as a conflict-free ego function that operates, along with
other mechanisms, to regulate adaptation to internal and external stimuli. The term *cognitive controls* was used to refer to these regulatory mechanisms, with the idea that each is a
distinct response orientation aroused by specific stimulus conditions. Tolerance for ambiguity was proposed as the response orientation aroused by unstructured or open-ended stimulus conditions.

Developmentally, cognitive controls were thought to mature over time from innate
structures that "accommodate" to external stimulation during formative years. This idea
overlapped with work on cognitive development by Piaget (1952), particularly in the importance attributed to external stimulation in the maturation of cognitive and perceptual
functioning. In further developing this idea, cognitive control theorists also drew on the
well-known Hebb studies of stimulation deprivation (Heron, Bexton, and Hebb, 1953;
Heron, Doane, and Scott, 1956), which indicated that cognitive functioning is impaired by
inadequate external stimulation. Theoretically, then, cognitive controls, such as tolerance
for ambiguity, were considered to be relatively stable personality traits, with individual
differences to be explained in terms of differences in the amount and quality of external
stimulation during childhood.

With cognitive control theory as a foundation, research on tolerance for ambiguity
began with the assessment of individual differences in performance on a number of perceptual measures. The measures included the Apparent Movement Test, the Aniseikonic Lenses
Test, and the Rorschach, all of which involve a conflict between what is experienced subjectively and what is known conceptually to be true. Collectively, these measures were conceived of as assessing individual differences in capacity for dealing effectively with unstable
and ambiguous situations. In that research the term *tolerance for ambiguity* came to be
associated primarily with the Rorschach, and a rating system was developed which enabled
Rorschach protocols to be scored on this single dimension. High tolerance for ambiguity was
assumed to be adaptive.

Another step in the evolution of research on tolerance for ambiguity was taken by a
number of studies linking high tolerance for ambiguity with other ostensibly adaptive
personality traits, such as tolerance for ethnic differences (Block and Block, 1951), toler-

ance for interpersonal conflict (Martin, 1954), and disposition to inhibit premature closure and dichotomous thinking (Frenkel-Brunswik, 1949-50). On the basis of these correlations, high tolerance for ambiguity was considered to be not only adaptive in itself but also to reflect high levels of psychological health. It was even implied that the degree of tolerance for ambiguity could be used as a valid index of psychological health or, in the theoretical framework of that period, of "adaptive equilibrium" (Klein, Gardner, and Schlesinger, 1962).

Tolerance for ambiguity overlaps conceptually with a current theory of self-actualization and thus appears to be relevant to clinical assessment and intervention. The widely cited works of Maslow (1962), Jourard (1968), and others in this vein emphasize the capacity for suspending conventional modes of thinking and perceiving and accepting alternative models of reality as necessary conditions for personal growth. Similarly, high tolerance for ambiguity, as assessed by performance on the Rorschach, would be reflected in freedom to depart from conventional meanings and in capacity for considering alternatives to stereotyped percepts.

A number of prevailing theories of creativity appear to coincide with the concept of tolerance for ambiguity. For example, Schachtel (1961) has identified creativity in terms of "allocentric perception," or the free play of attention, thought, feeling, and perception in stimulus encounters. Similarly, Bush (1969) believes that scientific creativity requires a capacity for considering multiple interpretations, unusual relationships, and new possibilities. These perceptual and cognitive styles strongly resemble the response styles that would be exhibited in the Rorschach protocols of individuals rated high in tolerance for ambiguity.

The concept of tolerance for ambiguity also appears to be relevant to the psychology of consciousness, as articulated by Ornstein (1972); he and others have asserted that each hemisphere of the brain mediates a separate mode of cognitive functioning. One is the rational and analytic mode, mediated apparently by the left brain hemisphere. The other is the intuitive and relational mode, which includes fantasy and imagination, mediated apparently by the right brain hemisphere. (This model applies to the 95 percent of the population which is right-handed; the reverse applies to left-handed individuals.) The right brain mode appears to be dominant during altered states of consciousness, such as in hypnosis and meditation, and regulates the free play of fantasy and unstructured associative elaboration of thought which are characteristic of high tolerance for ambiguity. This coincidence suggests that the degree of tolerance for ambiguity may be related to the extent to which people can experience right brain modes of cognitive functioning.

Critical Discussion

General Areas of Concern

The use of performance on the Rorschach as a measure of tolerance for ambiguity raises a number of reliability and validity questions. For example, the criteria for judging tolerance for ambiguity emphasize a subject's level of comfort with the task and attitude toward responses more than the standard signs by which Rorschach protocols are usually scored. The rating of Rorschach protocols for degree of tolerance for ambiguity, therefore, relies heavily on clinical judgment. As a result, there is always a question of interjudge reliability, or the degree to which one judge would tend to agree with another. In one study where an analysis of interjudge reliability is reported, a high correlation was found between ratings of tolerance for ambiguity made independently by two judges (Foxman, 1976). Few other studies, however, have dealt with this particular reliability issue or with the question of test-retest reliability. Thus, the reliability of the rating system for judging tolerance for ambiguity from Rorschach protocols should be considered questionable.

As a measure of tolerance for ambiguity, however, the Rorschach can be said to have high face validity (conceptual similarity between what the test measures and the personality construct to be assessed). The Rorschach asks subjects to depart from the obvious qualities of the stimuli and to respond instead of what the designs "might or could be" or what they "remind one of." The task is unstructured, and no rules of interpretation or other instructions are offered. Furthermore, it is usually apparent from the preliminary instructions that there are no right or wrong answers (although some subjects may attempt to respond "correctly"). The Rorschach is thus an ambiguous, open-ended task that calls for precisely those perceptual and cognitive processes defined in the concept of tolerance for ambiguity.

The Rorschach can also be said to have high construct validity as a measure of tolerance for ambiguity, in that performance on this test correlates highly with performance on other measures of similar perceptual and cognitive behavior. It was found in one study, for example, that performance on the Apparent Movement Test correlated highly with high and low tolerance for ambiguity classifications of subjects who performed on the Rorschach (Klein, Gardner, and Schlesinger, 1962). The Apparent Movement Test generates an ambiguous state in a stimulus presentation which creates the illusion of movement. The accepted range of movement is the criterion measure on this test, and wide ranges of accepted movement require high tolerance for the conflict between known versus apparent stimulus movement. The Apparent Movement Test, in other words, appears to measure tolerance for a perceptual conflict similar to that assessed by the Rorschach.

With respect to the validity question, Klein and Schlesinger (1951) found that performance on the Apparent Movement Test could be predicted accurately from tolerance for ambiguity scores on the Rorschach. Since the two tests appear to measure the same domain of behavior, it could be said that the Rorschach has high predictive validity as a measure of tolerance for ambiguity. Overall, then, as a measure of tolerance for ambiguity, the Rorschach seems to have secure validity but equivocal reliability.

Standard Rapaport procedure (Rapaport, Gill, and Schafer, 1945) usually is followed when the Rorschach is used to measure tolerance for ambiguity; therefore, a basic knowledge of Rorschach testing is required. However, Rorschach performance can be rated for degree of tolerance for ambiguity by certain criteria developed specifically for this purpose. In general, what distinguishes between high and low tolerance for ambiguity in Rorschach performance is the degree to which a person can respond comfortably to the task as an opportunity for fantasy and projection without excessive concern with the "reasonableness" of responses. Individual differences along this dimension are revealed in a number of ways and are summarized as follows:

High tolerance for ambiguity:
1. A generally dilated record.
2. An attitude of great "distance" from the blot, of freedom to fantasy and to project.
3. Tending to have more than one response per area, not confined to the conspicuous.
4. Ideas take precedence over form—form not necessarily compelling; hence, $F-$s may be given.
5. Content not stereotyped.
6. Free use of determinants other than form.
7. Fabulations and even confabulations, or $D \rightarrow W$s.
8. Attitude of comfort with task: free of critical comments and expressions of dissatisfaction.

Low tolerance for ambiguity:

1. A generally constricted record, sometimes including rejections.
2. An attitude of consistent "closeness" to the blot, accepting it insistently as part of conventional reality, not feeling free to fantasy or to project.
3. Tending to have only one response per area, typically to the most conspicuous and usual area; many populars.
4. A high *F+%* record.
5. Restricted content, tending to be stereotyped.
6. A form-primary record; use of other determinants infrequent.
7. May have space responses or sharply formed *Dr*s.
8. Attitude of discomfort with task: complaints about vagueness of instructions, questions about how to respond, other indications of anxiety or impatience (hurrying the task, pushing cards away after responses, and so on).

These criteria may conflict in some instances with traditional diagnostic theory in Rorschach testing. For example, it is usually considered maladaptive or pathological for subjects to produce responses with poor form level, confabulations, or $D \rightarrow W$ locations. Such responses, however, may be consistent with overall comfort with the task, with freedom to "play" with alternative meanings, and thus with high tolerance for ambiguity. When used as a measure of tolerance for ambiguity, therefore, Rorschach data must be analyzed independently of the usual diagnostic norms. Furthermore, since the criteria involve the subtleties of nonverbal behavior and verbalizations other than responses per se, clinical experience is essential in rating Rorschach protocols for degree of tolerance for ambiguity.

One troubling issue in the assessment of tolerance for ambiguity is raised by the fact that in previous research the ratings of Rorschach protocols were made relative to sample groups only. Thus, there is no fixed standard of high and low tolerance for ambiguity, so that the results from any one study are not generalizable to another. Apparently, the nature of the rating criteria makes it difficult to objectify the scale. This limitation, combined with other reliability questions, has probably discouraged the use of the Rorschach in research on tolerance for ambiguity.

In spite of these issues, the use of the Rorschach to assess tolerance for ambiguity is relatively simple and cost-effective in terms of time. Once a verbatim Rorschach protocol is obtained by standard administration, the rating of degree of tolerance for ambiguity can be accomplished in a matter of minutes (a four-point scale is typically used). The Rorschach data do not require elaborate scoring or interpretation other than the single rating of tolerance for ambiguity.

Furthermore, the administration of the Rorschach can be modified in the interest of time by limiting arbitrarily the number of responses allowed for each card without sacrificing the behavioral sample to be rated (Foxman, 1976). Conceivably, the test could be modified even further by omitting the inquiry, since it would not necessarily be required for ratings of tolerance for ambiguity. However, no studies have used the Rorschach in this way, and the resulting behavioral sample to be rated might be too compressed to serve as a basis for making reliable judgments.

Comparative Philosophies and Theories

The concept of tolerance for ambiguity can be compared with such processes as self-actualization, creativity, meditation, and psychotherapy, as well as a theory of consciousness and the psychoanalytic view of cognitive development. These parallels have been discussed in previous sections. Chapter Thirty-Five reviews tolerance for ambiguity in relation to ethnocentrism and other personality variables.

Elaboration on Critical Points

The important issues involved in the assessment of tolerance for ambiguity concern the reliability and validity of using Rorschach performance as a behavioral sample. These issues were discussed in detail in the preceding section.

Personal Views and Recommendations

It would be unfortunate if the concept of tolerance for ambiguity were to wither because of the assessment limitations associated with it. The concept is worth preserving and developing because it appears to have even wider applicability now than when it was first introduced. In overlapping with the concept of self-actualization, for example, tolerance for ambiguity could be used as a behavioral index of attained level of self-actualization. This was done, in fact, in a recent study; Foxman (1976) found that level of self-actualization, when assessed independently, correlated significantly with degree of tolerance for ambiguity. On this basis, the assessment of tolerance for ambiguity in clinical settings may help discriminate between people in levels of readiness to change. Similarly, assessment of tolerance for ambiguity could be used in clinical settings as a pretest and a posttest of treatment effectiveness for evaluation purposes.

Tolerance for ambiguity appears to have clinical applicability to a number of psychotherapeutic techniques (such as meditation, hypnosis, relaxation training, and yoga) which appear to overlap with this cognitive dimension. Such techniques involve alterations in consciousness and are growing in popularity as adjuncts to traditional verbal interventions. In many forms of meditation and relaxation training, for example, one must be capable of tolerating decreased control over the direction of mental content as well as the unpredictability of what may thus come into consciousness. The cognitive set involved in these and related techniques overlaps with tolerance for ambiguity, which refers precisely to the degree to which individuals can suspend habitual thought processes and cope with less structured states. A rating of a person's level of tolerance for ambiguity, therefore, may serve as a baseline for what to expect as shifts to less familiar and less structured modes of consciousness are experienced. Clinically, assessment of tolerance for ambiguity might also be used to screen out those individuals who may not be ready to handle techniques involving this type of consciousness change.

With respect to other possible applications, tolerance for ambiguity overlaps with a number of theories of creativity, such as those articulated by Schachtel (1961) and Bush (1969). As noted, these theories identify free play of thought processes and capacity for considering multiple interpretations and alternative relationships as essential to creativity. Since these processes appear to be the same as those involved in high tolerance for ambiguity, assessment of tolerance for ambiguity may be useful in vocational settings where prediction of creative potential is important. In other vocational settings assessment of tolerance for ambiguity may also be useful in screening for jobs that involve ambiguous or unstructured conditions.

Application to Particular Variables

Research on tolerance for ambiguity suggests that this dimension is independent of sex differences, intellectual level within the normal range, education, and vocational background (Gardner and others, 1959; Foxman, 1976). There is some evidence that low tolerance for ambiguity is associated with ethnocentrism, or low tolerance for ethnic differences (Block and Block, 1951). Previous research has not considered directly the relationship between tolerance for ambiguity and psychiatric status.

In view of the developmental aspect of cognitive control theory, it would be appropriate and meaningful to study tolerance for ambiguity with children. Previous research in this area is limited, and the Rorschach criteria for assessing degree of tolerance for ambiguity have not yet been adapted for children.

References

Block, J., and Block, J. "An Investigation of the Relationship Between Intolerance of Ambiguity and Ethnocentrism." *Journal of Personality,* 1951, *19,* 303-311.

Bush, M. "Psychoanalysis and Scientific Creativity, with Special Reference to Regression in the Service of the Ego." *Journal of the American Psychoanalytic Association,* 1969, *17* (1), 136-190.

Foxman, P. "Tolerance for Ambiguity and Self-Actualization." *Journal of Personality Assessment,* 1976, *40* (1), 67-72.

Frenkel-Brunswik, E. "Intolerance of Ambiguity as an Emotional and Perceptual Personality Variable." *Journal of Personality,* 1949-50, *18,* 108-143.

Gardner, R. "The Development of Cognitive Structures." In C. Sheerer (Ed.), *Cognition: Theory, Research, Promise.* New York: Harper & Row, 1964.

Gardner, R., and others. "Cognitive Control: A Study of Individual Consistencies in Cognitive Behavior." *Psychological Issues,* 1959, *1* (entire issue, 4).

Hartmann, H. *Ego Psychology and the Problem of Adaptation* [1939]. New York: International Universities Press, 1958.

Heron, W., Bexton, W., and Hebb, D. "Cognitive Effects of a Decreased Variation in the Sensory Environment." *American Psychologist,* 1953, *8,* 366.

Heron, W., Doane, B., and Scott, T. "Visual Disturbances After Prolonged Perceptual Isolation." *Canadian Journal of Psychology,* 1956, *10,* 13-18.

Jourard, S. M. *Disclosing Man to Himself.* New York: Van Nostrand, 1968.

Klein, G. "Adaptive Properties of Sensory Functioning: Some Postulates and Hypotheses." *Bulletin of the Menninger Clinic,* 1949, *13,* 16-23.

Klein, G. "Need and Regulation." In M. R. Jones (Ed.), *Nebraska Symposium on Motivation.* Lincoln: University of Nebraska Press, 1954.

Klein, G. "Cognitive Control and Motivation." In G. Lindzey (Ed.), *Assessment of Motives.* New York: Holt, Rinehart and Winston, 1958.

Klein, G., Gardner, R., and Schlesinger, H. "Tolerance for Unrealistic Experiences: A Study of the Generality of a Cognitive Control." *Brisith Journal of Psychology,* 1962, *53,* 41-55.

Klein, G., and Schlesinger, H. "Perceptual Attitudes Toward Instability. 1: Prediction of Apparent Movement Experiences from Rorschach Responses." *Journal of Personality,* 1951, *19,* 289-302.

Martin, B. "Intolerance of Ambiguity in Interpersonal and Perceptual Behavior." *Journal of Personality,* 1954, *22,* 499-503.

Maslow, A. *Toward a Psychology of Being.* New York: Van Nostrand, 1962.

Ornstein, R. *The Psychology of Consciousness.* San Francisco: Freeman, 1972.

Piaget, J. *Origins of Intelligence in Children.* New York: International Universities Press, 1952.

Rapaport, D. "The Theory of Ego Autonomy: A Generalization." *Bulletin of the Menninger Clinic,* 1958, *22,* 12-35.

Rapaport, D., Gill, M., and Schafer, R. *Diagnostic Psychological Testing.* Vol. 1. Chicago: Year Book Medical Publishers, 1945.

Schachtel, E. *Metamorphosis.* New York: Basic Books, 1961.

Schafer, R. *Psychoanalytic Interpretation in Rorschach Testing: Theory and Application.* New York: Grune & Stratton, 1954.

35

Selina Sue Prosen

Ambiguity Tolerance

Ambiguity tolerance refers to an internal process that influences the way in which a person structures information about ambiguous situations where he is confronted by an array of unfamiliar, complex, or incongruent cues. Since people exhibit wide variations in their reactions to ambiguous situations, it is possible to differentiate levels of ambiguity tolerance. Differences in levels of ambiguity tolerance are thought to predispose an individual to variations in cognitive operations as well as changes in emotional states.

A person with a low level of ambiguity tolerance may experience psychological stress or threat when confronted with an ambiguous situation. As a result, such a person tends to react to a situation prematurely, reaching conclusions that often are based on inadequate or distorted stimulus sampling. By contrast, the person who is tolerant of ambiguity is comfortable with situations that lack cues for immediate response. Such a person neither distorts nor denies complexity or incongruity. In fact, it is possible for a highly tolerant person to experience ambiguity as desirable and challenging. The individual who is tolerant of cognitive ambiguity is also believed to be accepting of emotional ambivalence.

The ability to tolerate cognitive and emotional ambiguity has been examined as a potentially coherent personality characteristic, which supposedly predisposes an individual to respond in a predictable manner to a particular stimulus condition. This supposition has provided the impetus for research from many disciplines. Some of the research has incorporated concepts of perception, cognition, and motivation in efforts designed to uncover a unity of response patterns among individuals with regard to their ability to tolerate ambiguity.

Background and Current Status

The treatment of ambiguity as a cognitive and emotional personality variable was introduced by Frenkel-Brunswik (1948) as an outgrowth of her work on studies associated with ethnocentrism. Her observations of persons who exhibited "intolerance of ambiguity" led her to describe them as "disinclined to think in terms of probability" (p. 268). Instead, such individuals tended to favor stereotypes and showed a marked discomfort with ambiguity. Frenkel-Brunswik (1949) postulated a close connection between tolerance of ambiguity and the psychoanalytic concept of coping with ambivalence; that is, an individual who is able to accept his or her feelings of ambivalence is also more likely to be able to tolerate ambiguity. She concluded that "denial of emotional ambivalence and intolerance of cognitive ambiguity may be different aspects of a fairly coherent characteristic" (p. 140). The individual who is intolerant of ambiguity tends to seek black-white answers. This tendency sometimes leads the intolerant person to reduce the amount of information used from the environment. The avoidance of thinking in terms of probability and the preference for concreteness predominate in the cognitive style of such an individual.

In their classic study *The Authoritarian Personality,* Adorno and his co-workers (1950) related intolerance of ambiguity to a constellation of personality traits, including ethnocentrism, rigidity, superstition, and submission to authority. Most of the original data related to ambiguity tolerance as a cognitive and emotional variable were gathered through interviewing and projective testing. However, Frenkel-Brunswik (1949) also reported on a series of perceptual experiments designed to test differences in reactions to perceptual ambiguity on the part of subjects high and low on ethnocentrism.

Pursuing Frenkel-Brunswik's ideas, Block and Block (1951) used an autokinetic situation as a measure of ambiguity tolerance and found a significant relationship between low tolerance and high scores on the Berkeley Ethnocentrism Scale. O'Connor (1952) also found a positive relationship between high ethnocentrism and intolerance for ambiguity; however, she used a paper-and-pencil attitude measure (Walk's A Scale) rather than a perceptual task to test for ambiguity tolerance.

Davids (1955) reported somewhat different results. Using a selected set of Rorschach cards to measure visual ambiguity and a test of auditory ambiguity, he found no significant relationship between tests of ambiguity tolerance and authoritarianism. He concluded that high authoritarianism and ambiguity intolerance may be two different constructs. Other studies, however, by Millon (1957) and Bhushan (1971), have supported the positive relationship of these two constructs.

According to these early studies, then, a person with low ambiguity tolerance would (1) solve problems with less than adequate information, (2) fail to see fluctuations in ambiguous drawings, (3) quickly stabilize judgments of autokinetic movement, and (4) believe that society is inherently structured along ethnocentric dimensions (Brown, 1953).

Frenkel-Brunswik's (1948, 1949) work has influenced the subsequent efforts of other researchers in three ways. First, a number of studies have examined the relationship between ambiguity tolerance and authoritarianism and its correlates with ethnocentrism, dogmatism, and rigidity. Second, her idea that a person's perceptual reactions to ambiguity may be indicative of his emotional responses has influenced a number of researchers to employ visual or auditory tasks as measures of ambiguity. Third, her influence can be seen in work by Smock (1955), who hypothesized that experimentally induced psychological stress would result in increased intolerance for ambiguity. By employing a series of ambiguous cards (similar to those used by Frenkel-Brunswik), Smock found support for the idea that "stress results in an inability in some individuals to withhold response . . . until adequate cues are present for an appropriate response" (p. 182). In a later study Smock (1957) concluded that the effect of anxiety arousal on a perceptual task could be either a tendency toward impulsivity or an excessive cautiousness of response, thus suggesting that both response styles may be indicators of difficulty with ambiguity.

Concerns regarding the accuracy of measures of ambiguity tolerance were raised by Kenny and Ginsberg (1958). In addressing the issue of construct validity, they proposed, first, to test the relationship between a number of measures that had been used up to that time; and, second, to test the relationship of these measures to authoritarianism. The outstanding finding of their study was the lack of evidence of a positive relationship between perceptual and attitudinal measures of ambiguity tolerance. They concluded that, given the measures available, there was little support for either a general construct of tolerance of ambiguity or the assumption that tolerance of ambiguity is a correlate of authoritarianism.

In the development of an attitudinal scale to measure its dimensions, Budner (1962) defined tolerance of ambiguity as "the tendency to perceive ambiguous situations as desirable" and intolerance of ambiguity as "the tendency to perceive (interpret) ambiguous situations as sources of threat" (p. 29). Further, Budner indicated that ambiguous situations have cues that are unfamiliar, complex, or incongruent and that a person with a low ambiguity tolerance might respond to such cues by submission, wherein the individual decides that the situation cannot be altered, or by denial, wherein the individual performs some act to alter objective reality. Budner also clearly distinguished between rigidity (a response tendency irrespective of phenomena) and tolerance of ambiguity (a tendency to evaluate phenomena in a particular way). Because of this evaluative function, Budner posited that "a measure of attitudes and values probably taps the construct more directly than a measure requiring inferences about observed behavior" (p. 32).

Apparently a number of researchers have agreed with him. In the years since its publication, Budner's Tolerance-Intolerance of Ambiguity Scale has been used in more studies of ambiguity tolerance than any other similar measure. Examples of its use may be found in McDaniel (1967), Crandall (1968), Gruberg (1969), Harlow (1973), Shavit (1975), and Chasnoff (1976).

Subsequent to Budner's attitudinal measure, three similar instruments have been developed. The first, by Rydell and Rosen (1966), is a sixteen-item true-false scale which has been used in studies by Pawlicki and Almquist (1973) and Kreitler, Maguen, and Kreitler (1975). Attempting to improve on the low reliability of the sixteen-item Rydell and Rosen scale, MacDonald (1970) added four items to form the AT-20, which related positively to performance in an ambiguous task, the F scale of authoritarianism, dogmatism, rigidity, and church attendance. The AT-20 scale has been used in studies by Chabassol and Thomas (1975) and MacDonald, Walls, and LeBlanc (1973). The most recent paper-and-pencil measure of ambiguity tolerance, the MAT-50, was developed by Norton (1975). He reported both high internal and test-retest reliabilities and gave evidence for adequate construct validity. However, the instrument awaits use by others.

Since 1962, in addition to the development of four paper-and-pencil attitudinal measures, several researchers have continued to pursue the use of perceptual stimuli to assess ambiguity tolerance. Representing this approach are Bochner (1965); Davids (1968); Derogatis, Gorham, and Moseley (1968); and Rogers, Pasewark, and Fitzgerald (1975).

A growing number of recent studies have focused on the relevance of ambiguity tolerance to therapist effectiveness. Repeated findings attest to ambiguity tolerance as one of the few dimensions of therapist personality which is related to overall effectiveness.

Several researchers have studied the relationship of ambiguity tolerance to "locus of control" (MacDonald, Walls, and LeBlanc, 1973; Pawlicki and Almquist, 1973; Shavit, 1975). There continues to be interest in the relationship of ambiguity tolerance to dogmatism (Bates, 1969; Norton, 1975; Chabassol and Thomas, 1975).

Quantitatively, the interest in ambiguity tolerance continues and, in fact, seems to have increased. Qualitative assessments of its viability are more difficult to make, but there has been clear interest in improving measurement of the construct as well as recognition of the gaps in validation.

Critical Discussion

General Areas of Concern

Wide differences exist in the extent to which individuals are psychologically threatened by ambiguous perceptions. At one extreme is the individual who experiences ambiguity as a desirable goal and deliberately seeks it out; at the other extreme is the person who, when threatened by ambiguity, constructs delusions to allay anxiety. Thus, the potential outcomes in behavior may range from artistic creativity and scientific problem solving to denial, withdrawal, and hallucinations. Most people, of course, function between these extremes.

Descriptions of other personality functions of a person who is intolerant of ambiguity may include high degrees of authoritarianism, ethnocentrism, submission to authority, and expectations of an external locus of control of reinforcement. The person will probably also be characterized by a rigid and dogmatic cognitive style that tends to be "field dependent" and concrete.

To date, most research has attempted either to define ambiguity tolerance or to determine its relationship to other personality constructs or cognitive styles. The issue of whether or not it can be modified—and, if so, under what conditions—has yet to be addressed. With a working definition and some beginning tools of assessment, the next logical step is the development and testing of strategies of modification.

Attempts at definitions of this concept have followed two methodological routes. Beginning with O'Connor's (1952) use of Walk's A Scale, several paper-and-pencil attitudinal measures have been developed by Budner (1962), Rydell and Rosen (1966), MacDonald (1970), and Norton (1975). Budner's scale has been employed in a greater number of studies than any other instrument. The second methodological route, beginning with Frenkel-Brunswik's (1949) perceptual experiments, has used a variety of visual and or auditory stimuli to assess ambiguity tolerance. This approach can be seen in Block and Block (1951), Smock (1955, 1957), and Davids (1955, 1968). One effort by Kenny and Ginsberg (1958) to correlate the two types of measures (attitudinal and perceptual) resulted in failure. It should be noted, however, that they used an attitudinal measure (Walk's A Scale) that was criticized by Erlich (1965) for its lack of internal consistency.

There has been no attempt to replicate the Kenny and Ginsberg effort with any of the more recent and reliable attitudinal measures.

The continuing concern with appropriate definition of ambiguity tolerance was recently addressed by Kreitler, Maguen, and Kreitler (1975). Using ten different attitudinal and perceptual measures, they concluded that there may be three distinct or essentially uncorrelated dimensions of ambiguity tolerance, each of which lends itself to a distinctive type of measurement. These dimensions may be described as (1) an inability to accept multiple interpretations of a given situation, (2) an inability to accept situations that are difficult to categorize, and (3) an inability to respond to contradictions or polarities.

Continued efforts to refine operational definitions of ambiguity tolerance should be encouraged. However, because of the variety of instrumentation (both attitudinal and perceptual) used to assess ambiguity tolerance, it is difficult to draw comparisons across studies. The lack of experimentation designed to either increase or decrease ambiguity tolerance needs to be remedied. Until such time, the question of whether or not modification is feasible or desirable remains to be answered.

Comparative Philosophies and Theories

Frenkel-Brunswik (1949) hypothesized that an individual's ability to accept the coexistence of love and hate toward the same object is related to his ability to accept the coexistence of positive and negative features in any object, group, or event. She further speculated that an early precipitator of the tendency to avoid ambiguity of any sort is the child's attempt to master aggressive impulses toward the parent. Tendencies toward premature closure of stimulus sampling, jumping to generalizations, and carrying over inappropriate response sets can be as evident in cognitive and perceptual reactions as they are in the social and emotional spheres. She concluded that if intolerance of ambiguity "should turn out to be a formal characteristic of the organism independent of content, experiments on perceptual ambiguity could be used as diagnostic tools" (p. 126).

A somewhat related speculation about the consistency of motivational processes and perception can be seen in Bruner's (1957) description of "perceptual defense." People exhibit differences in the range of alternatives for which they are "perceptually set." When those who are tuned for a narrow range of alternatives are confronted with the unexpected, they find cognitive identification and categorizing impeded. This kind of cognitive processing may be described as "rigid," "stuck," and ultimately intolerant of ambiguity. Bruner attributed this circumstance to an interference in perceiving (not to a failure to perceive).

Smock (1955) suggested that ambiguity creates stress because it disrupts the organism's striving for a "stable" or "familiar" environment. To reduce the anxiety, the "individual under stress may make some response before adequate 'information' is available for the most appropriate response" (p. 183). Intolerance of ambiguity, then, is a learned response to anxiety.

An extension of this formulation to the cognitive processes of schizophrenics was attempted by Draguns (1963). He postulated that idiosyncratic utilization of limited perceptual or cognitive data is what leads to the distorted conceptual system of the schizophrenic. Caution, suspicion, or avoidance in the face of ambiguity becomes the characteristic cognitive response mode. In an assessment of responses to ambiguity, Heilbrun (1972) found differences among late adolescent paranoid males in that some responded to ambiguity by the "premature assignment of meaning" (p. 293), whereas others responded by excessive delay. In either instance, the anxiety created by ambiguity was evident, even though the manifestation of the maladaptiveness of the response was, as Draguns had hypothesized, highly idiosyncratic.

The most recent theoretical explication of ambiguity tolerance has been advanced by Kreitler, Maguen, and Kreitler (1975) under the rubric of "cognitive orientation theory." In their schema, cognitive processes for orienting behavior operate on "molar" and "submolar" levels. Ambiguity tolerance is classified as a molar process, since it is elicited when a particular bit of cognitive input cannot be adequately processed on a reflex (submolar) level. In this regard, tolerance of ambiguity is more akin to a predisposition to action than to action per se. They conclude that "The concept of 'intolerance of ambiguity' could prove to be of great importance if properly used for the analysis of perception, social interaction, and pathological reaction" (p. 238).

Elaboration on Critical Points

Ambiguity tolerance has been used to describe an internal process that may result in a characteristic style of emotional and cognitive responding. It originally evolved from a psychoanalytic framework in which it was thought to be associated with responses to ambivalence. Two distinct approaches of measurement have characterized most of the research. In one, attitudinal paper-and-pencil surveys have been used; in the other, variations of visual and auditory perceptual tasks have been used. An early effort to intercorrelate these two methodologies met with little success (Kenny and Ginsberg, 1958). Nevertheless, interest in both types of instrumentation has continued.

Both perceptual and attitudinal measures of ambiguity tolerance have been employed with varying degrees of success to correlate it with other personality dimensions (such as authoritarianism, ethnocentrism, dogmatism, and locus of control).

To date, relatively little effort has been devoted to assessing differences in ambiguity tolerance as a function of age, sex, race, or socioeconomic status. There has, however, been continuing interest in the significance of high ambiguity tolerance as a variable contributing to therapist effectiveness.

On the periphery of the research are a few efforts to apply the concept to some aspects of psychiatric diagnosis. However, the early idea of Frenkel-Brunswik (1949-50) that perceptual tasks of ambiguity might prove useful as diagnostic tools for unifying emotional, social, and cognitive personality evaluations has yet to be adequately validated. In fact, the issue of whether ambiguity response sets generalize remains a question for investigation.

Personal Views and Recommendations

Given the heuristic appeal of the concept of ambiguity tolerance, the following areas might be the most useful for further pursuit. Comparative data about differences in ambiguity tolerance as a function of age, sexual, and racial differences are needed. With the very limited data now available, it appears that females may be less tolerant of ambiguity than males, while racial and ethnic minorities may be more tolerant than the wider population. If this is so, it raises questions that could be explored about the effects of socialization on this characteristic.

There is also a need to carefully and systematically evaluate the attitudinal scales being used in a number of studies to measure ambiguity tolerance. There is no discussion of any of these instruments to be found in appropriate references (such as the *Mental Measurements Yearbooks*); given the volume of research being conducted with these instruments, this type of scrutiny would be desirable.

With the more refined instruments now available, an effort also should be made to duplicate the early and singular effort by Kenny and Ginsberg (1958) to intercorrelate perceptual and attitudinal measures of ambiguity tolerance.

Finally, there is a dearth of experimental evidence on whether ambiguity tolerance is a characteristic that can be modified and, if so, what types of interventions might be appropriate for this task. Until this question is addressed in some systematic manner, behavioral scientists will be able to do little more than describe the state of the organism with regard to ambiguity tolerance.

Application to Particular Variables

Ambiguity tolerance has been studied in children (Smock, 1955, 1957), adolescents (Chabassol and Thomas, 1975; Shavit, 1975), college students (Zacker, 1973), and adults (Rogers, Pasewark, and Fitzgerald, 1975). In each of these studies, it was possible to identify subjects who differed in their levels of tolerance of ambiguity. In one study of ambiguity tolerance as a direct function of age, Hampton (1967) found that tolerance of ambiguity increased from preadolescence through young adulthood. Differences between age groups were also examined by Rogers, Pasewark, and Fitzgerald (1975), who found that 18- to 22-year-old females were not significantly different from 80-year-old females in their judgments of the magnitude of an ambiguous perceptual stimulus (perceived movement in a light source). However, having once made such a judgment, the older (60-80) subjects were less flexible than younger subjects in changing this judgment. Thus, while neither tolerance nor intolerance seems to be definitively indicative of a particular age, the lack of comparative data for adults between 22 and 60 years of age or for young children versus adolescents or adults on this dimension opens many questions to research.

Researchers have on the whole focused more on differences among males (Davids, 1968) or females (Pawlicki and Almquist, 1973) than on differences between males and females. A single exception is a study by Hampton (1967). He reported that Latin-American females have a developmental pattern of tolerance for ambiguity which is more similar to that of blacks than it is to Latin-American males. The most definitive examination of ethnic and racial variations in ambiguity tolerance was also reported in this same study. A comparison of blacks, Latin-Americans, and Anglos revealed that blacks and Latin-Americans, in general, had higher levels of ambiguity tolerance than Anglos, but they did not differ significantly from each other. This sparse exploration of sex and ethnic-racial factors clearly suggests a need for further testing of these differences.

Any suggestion of the use of ambiguity tolerance as a clinical tool for the differential diagnosis of specific physical or psychological disorders must be approached with extreme caution because only minimal investigation has been directed at assessing dysfunction. One preliminary study of a physiological correlate of ambiguity tolerance was reported by MacDonald, Walls, and LeBlanc (1973). They surveyed 400 female undergraduates on use of drugs and found a slight positive relationship between the use of marijuana and a high tolerance for ambiguity. However, there was no relationship for those subjects who identified themselves as the heaviest users of drugs. The relationship between drug and possibly alcohol use and ambiguity tolerance should be further investigated.

Examples of the use of ambiguity tolerance to assess functional disorders reflect several different areas of interest. Draguns (1963) compared chronic schizophrenics to normal subjects and found that the schizophrenics gave earlier recognition responses to an ambiguous perceptual task and a higher rate of responses to an ambiguous cognitive task. McReynolds, Collins, and Acker (1964) found support for the notion that delusional schizophrenics seek closure more than nondelusional schizophrenics do. Hilf, Wittner, and Kopell (1969) demonstrated that paranoids have difficulty utilizing corrective feedback in an ambiguous perceptual situation. Heilbrun (1972) examined variations in the responses of paranoid adolescent males to ambiguity; later (Heilbrun, 1975) he postulated an information-processing model to explain delusion formation as a function of the attempt to reduce anxiety created by ambiguity. In light of the current status of the concept of ambiguity tolerance, its use in clinical assessment of dysfunction should be approached with the same restraint that one would maintain with any idea that is in an exploratory stage.

The relationship of ambiguity tolerance to educational underachievement was assessed by Davids (1968) in a comparison of ten gifted adolescent males (mean IQ = 130) and twenty underachieving males (mean IQ = 128) enrolled in a remedial reading program. By using a perceptual measure of cognitive flexibility, Davids found that the underachievers were more impulsive in their approach to cognitive tasks and showed greater rigidity and less tolerance of ambiguity in their cognitive functioning. These findings led Davids to suggest that analysis of cognitive style at an early age might be helpful not only to identify potentially creative students but also to intervene in modifying impulsivity among underachievers.

In a related study, Cropley and Sikand (1973) found that "creative thinkers" differed significantly from both normal controls and schizophrenics in their ability to tolerate high levels of ambiguity and in their capacity to take high cognitive risks. Further examinations of the interrelationships of ambiguity tolerance, cognitive style, and educational achievement are worthy of pursuit.

The relevance of ambiguity tolerance to vocational performance has had some recent attention. In a population of fifty-four engineers, Harlow (1973) found that, for those who reported a high level of job satisfaction, ambiguity tolerance was positively related to a desire for upward mobility. By contrast, O'Reilly, Bretton, and Roberts (1974), using a sample of 250 military personnel, failed to find any relation between ambiguity tolerance and preference for promotion. They suggest that the construct is either situation dependent or in need of better measurement.

The one vocational group for whom ambiguity tolerance has been demonstrated to be a significant variable is the counselor-therapist group. Several studies have found a significant relationship between therapist effectiveness and high levels of ambiguity tolerance. Examples of these findings are reported in Chasnoff (1976); Foote, Davis, and Marks (1975); Tucker and Snyder (1974); Gruberg (1969); McDaniel (1967); and Brams (1961). These research efforts suggest that levels of therapist ambiguity tolerance may be related to level of verbal activity, need for structuring in the interview, preference for cognitive versus affective responses to the client, and choice of basic counseling orientation. Although these ideas are still in the exploratory stages, they merit further investigation, so that the therapist can be helped to make an assessment of how, and to what extent, his or her operations in regard to ambiguity impede or facilitate various therapeutic interventions.

References

Adorno, T. W., and others. *The Authoritarian Personality.* New York: Harper & Row, 1950.

Bates, S. D. "A Study of Tolerance-Intolerance of Ambiguity and Its Relationship to Dogmatism." Unpublished doctoral dissertation, University of South Dakota, 1969.

Bhushan, L. I. "A Study of Leadership Preference in Relation to Authoritarianism and Intolerance of Ambiguity." *Journal of the Indian Academy of Applied Psychology,* 1971, *8,* 34-38.

Block, J., and Block, J. "An Investigation of the Relationship Between Intolerance of Ambiguity and Ethnocentrism." *Journal of Personality,* 1951, *19,* 303-311.

Bochner, S. "Defining Intolerance of Ambiguity." *Psychological Record,* 1965, *15,* 393-400.

Brams, J. M. "Counselor Characteristics and Effective Communication in Counseling." *Journal of Counseling Psychology,* 1961, *8,* 25-30.

Brown, R. W. "A Determinant of the Relationship Between Rigidity and Authoritarianism." *Journal of Abnormal and Social Psychology,* 1953, *48,* 469-476.

Bruner, J. S. "On Perceptual Readiness." *Psychological Review,* 1957, *64,* 123-152.

Budner, S. "Intolerance of Ambiguity as a Personality Variable." *Journal of Personality,* 1962, *30,* 29-50.

Chabassol, D., and Thomas, D. "Needs for Structure, Tolerance of Ambiguity and Dogmatism in Adolescents." *Psychological Reports,* 1975, *37,* 507-510.

Chasnoff, S. F. "The Effects of Modeling and Ambiguity Tolerance on Interview Behavior." *Counselor Education and Supervision,* 1976, *16,* 46-51.

Crandall, J. E. "Effects of Need for Approval and Intolerance of Ambiguity upon Stimulus Preference." *Journal of Personality,* 1968, *36,* 67-83.

Cropley, A. J., and Sikand, J. S. "Creativity and Schizophrenia." *Journal of Consulting and Clinical Psychology,* 1973, *40,* 462-468.

Davids, A. "Some Personality Correlates of Intolerance of Ambiguity." *Journal of Abnormal and Social Psychology,* 1955, *51,* 415-420.

Davids, A. "Cognitive Styles in Potential Scientists and in Underachieving High School Students." *Journal of Special Education,* 1968, *2,* 197-201.

Derogatis, L. R., Gorham, D. R., and Moseley, E. C. "Structured vs. Interpretive Ambiguity: A Cross-Cultural Study with the Holtzman Inkblots." *Journal of Projective Techniques and Personality Assessment,* 1968, *32,* 66-73.

Draguns, J. R. "Responses to Cognitive and Perceptual Ambiguity in Chronic and Acute Schizophrenics." *Journal of Abnormal and Social Psychology,* 1963, *66,* 24-30.

Ehrlich, D. "Intolerance of Ambiguity, Walk's A Scale: Historical Comment." *Psychological Reports,* 1965, *17,* 591-594.

Foote, M., Davis, W., and Marks, S. E. "Tolerance of Ambiguity: A Variable in Client and Counsellor Pairing." *Canadian Counsellor,* 1975, *9,* 63-68.

Frenkel-Brunswik, E. "Tolerance Toward Ambiguity as a Personality Variable." *American Psychologist,* 1948, *3,* 268.

Frenkel-Brunswik, E. "Intolerance of Ambiguity as an Emotional and Perceptual Personality Variable." *Journal of Personality,* 1949, *18,* 108-143.

Gruberg, R. R. "A Significant Counselor Personality Characteristic: Tolerance of Ambiguity." *Counselor Education and Supervision,* 1969, *8,* 119-124.

Hampton, J. D. "Ambiguity Tolerance as a Function of Age, Sex, and Ethnicity." *Dissertation Abstracts,* 1967, *27* (12-A), 4128.

Harlow, D. N. "Professional Employees' Preference for Upward Mobility." *Journal of Applied Psychology,* 1973, *57,* 137-141.

Heilbrun, A. "Tolerance for Ambiguity in Late Adolescent Males: Implications for a Development Model of Paranoid Behavior." *Developmental Psychology,* 1972, *7,* 288-294.

Heilbrun, A. "A Proposed Basis for Delusion Formation Within an Information-Processing

Model of Paranoid Development." *British Journal of Social and Clinical Psychology*, 1975, *14*, 63-71.

Hilf, F., Wittner, W., and Kopell, B. "Feedback Utilization of Paranoid Patients." *Journal of Nervous and Mental Disease*, 1969, *149*, 491-494.

Kenny, D., and Ginsberg, R. "The Specificity of Intolerance of Ambiguity Measures." *Journal of Abnormal and Social Psychology*, 1958, *56*, 300-304.

Kreitler, S., Maguen, T., and Kreitler, H. "The Three Faces of Intolerance of Ambiguity." *Archiv für Psychologie*, 1975, *127*, 238-250.

McDaniel, S. W. "Counselor Selection: An Evaluation of Instruments." *Counselor Education and Supervision*, 1967, *6*, 142-144.

MacDonald, A. "Revised Scale for Ambiguity Tolerance: Reliability and Validity." *Psychological Reports*, 1970, *26*, 791-798.

MacDonald, A. P., Walls, R. T., and LeBlanc, R. "College Female Drug Users." *Adolescence*, 1973, *8*, 189-196.

McReynolds, P., Collins, B., and Acker, M. "Delusional Thinking and Cognitive Organization in Schizophrenia." *Journal of Abnormal and Social Psychology*, 1964, *69*, 210-212.

Millon, T. "Authoritarianism, Intolerance of Ambiguity and Rigidity Under Ego and Task-Involving Conditions." *Journal of Abnormal and Social Psychology*, 1957, *55*, 29-33.

Norton, R. "Measurement of Ambiguity Tolerance." *Journal of Personality Assessment*, 1975, *39*, 607-619.

O'Connor, P. "Ethnocentrism, 'Intolerance of Ambiguity,' and Abstract Reasoning Ability." *Journal of Abnormal and Social Psychology*, 1952, *47*, 562-530.

O'Reilly, C. A., Bretton, G. E., and Roberts, K. H. "Professional Employees' Preference for Upward Mobility: An Extension." *Journal of Vocational Behavior*, 1974, *5*, 139-145.

Pawlicki, R. E., and Almquist, C. "Authoritarianism, Locus of Control, and Tolerance of Ambiguity as Reflected in Membership and Nonmembership in a Women's Liberation Group." *Psychological Reports*, 1973, *32*, 1331-1337.

Rogers, M. L., Pasewark, R. A., and Fitzgerald, B. J. "Autokinetic Effect and Aging." *Perceptual and Motor Skills*, 1975, *40*, 514.

Rydell, S., and Rosen, E. "Measurement and Some Correlates of Need-Cognition." *Psychological Reports*, 1966, *19*, 139-165.

Shavit, H. "Personality Adjustments as a Function of Interaction Between Locus of Evaluation and Tolerance of Ambiguity." *Psychological Reports*, 1975, *37*, 1204-1206.

Smock, C. "The Influence of Psychological Stress on the 'Intolerance of Ambiguity.'" *Journal of Abnormal and Social Psychology*, 1955, *50*, 177-182.

Smock, C. "The Relationship Between 'Intolerance of Ambiguity' Generalization and Speed of Perceptual Closure." *Child Development*, 1957, *28*, 27-36.

Tucker, R. C., and Snyder, W. U. "Ambiguity Tolerance of Therapists and Process Changes of Their Clients." *Journal of Counseling Psychology*, 1974, *21*, 577-578.

Zacker, J. "Authoritarian Avoidance of Ambiguity." *Psychological Reports*, 1973, *33*, 901-902.

36

Charles J. Morgan
Penelope J. Greene

Altruism

The central issue in a discussion of altruism concerns the relative merits of the interests of self and other in determining personal actions. In contrast with *egoism,* when the individual acts directly in his or her own interests, an individual whose actions appear to be directed toward the benefit of others is said to act *altruistically,* especially if there is some personal sacrifice involved. A recurring problem is whether "true" altruism is indeed possible. If individuals whose acts are apparently directed toward the benefit of others are expecting some delayed personal benefit, then the behavior would be disguised egoism rather than altruism.

Background and Current Status

The term *altruism* was coined by the positivist philosopher Auguste Comte from the Italian *altrui,* meaning "of or to others," and was introduced into English by his translators and commentators. Comte attempted to form a positivist religion with sociologists (another word coined by Comte) as its priests. His slogan was "live for others," and universal altruism was to solve all social ills.

While the term *altruism* did not exist before Comte, discussion of egoism and the interests of others is quite old. The modern intellectual heritage begins approximately in the mid seventeenth century with Thomas Hobbes, who defended both psychological and ethical egoism. He argued that our actions not only are but should be determined by our interests. But the question of whether some actions have no selfish component continued. Finally, in the early eighteenth century, Joseph Butler provided a decisive refutation of psychological egoism, which can best be summarized by the statement that self-interest in unrestrained form might become so prevalent as to contradict its own end, the private good. David Hume argued that not all action springs from our individual interests. We praise bravery and virtue in an enemy, even though they are directed against us: "The social virtues . . . have a natural beauty and amiableness, which at first, antecedent to all precept or education, recommends them to the esteem of uninstructed mankind, and engages their affection" (quoted in Milo, 1973, p. 39). Hume suggested that this natural affection springs from the utility of the social virtues in maintaining an orderly society, which is not, after all, indifferent to us. Similarly, Immanuel Kant argued that we have a moral duty to help others, whether we love them or not.

It was against this background of metaphysical argument and the social reforms of the American and French Revolutions that Comte proposed altruism as a guiding principle and as a panacea for all social ills. The idea was widely accepted, but after the 1930s social science interest in altruism dwindled, maintained largely by the work of Sorokin (1950).

The 1960s saw a revival of interest in altruism. Gouldner (1960) suggested that all societies share a "norm of reciprocity" which forbids harming and requires individuals to help those who have helped them. Leeds (1963; see also Gouldner, 1973) suggested that there exists a norm of giving or beneficence which requires helping those who really need help, regardless of whether they are potentially able to repay. Berkowitz and Daniels (1963) proposed a norm of social responsibility, requiring that help be extended to dependent others. And then, in 1964, Kitty Genovese was stalked, raped, and knifed to death in New York. Thirty-eight people saw or heard the attack, but no one called the police for half an hour. The incident shocked and outraged those who heard about it. This incident sparked what is now one of the more active areas of social psychological investigation: the experimental study of the factors that determine whether one person will help another (see, for instance, Latané and Darley, 1970). A second research tradition focuses on specifying the internal mechanisms involved in a decision to help (see Aronfreed, 1970). Finally, there is the question of socialization: How does an individual learn to behave in (apparently) altruistic ways (see Ruston, 1976)?

The importance of this research lies in its implications for a conceptualization of a normal, healthy human being and for the light it sheds on the relationship of one person to surrounding others. While it is of great theoretical significance, the concept of altruism has not been well articulated for clinical applications (current textbooks do not index the term), and the few available attempts to use direct assessment techniques in clinical applications have shown that general mental health and altruism are not correlated (Plumez, 1975; Sawyer, 1966).

It has been shown that empathy is a powerful mediator of altruistic behavior (Krebs, 1975), and Rogers (1951) has argued persuasively for the importance of an empathic attitude on the part of the therapist. It may be that patients who sense empathy on the part of the therapist are especially ready to believe that the therapist will act in the patient's best interest.

Critical Discussion

General Areas of Concern

There are four basic questions: (1) What motivates acts of apparent altruism? (2) Under what conditions would we expect one person to help another? (3) How did apparent altruism evolve? and (4) Is true altruism possible? Answers to these questions tend to diverge, and the divergences stem from disagreements at the fundamental level of *why* a person acts. The "why" can be analyzed in terms of the reinforcement history, the immediate cost-benefit ratio, the expectations of others, the socialization process, and/or innate behavioral tendencies. Since many of the concerns are philosophical and/or theoretical in nature, they are elaborated in the next section.

Comparative Philosophies and Theories

As for *motivation,* the "problem" with apparently altruistic behavior, as noted by Krebs (1970), is that it seems contradictory to predictions from Freudian theory, learning theory, and evolution theory. How is it that a person will act against his or her own self-interests; how can this behavior be maintained, since by definition it is not reinforced; and how could it have evolved, since altruists would tend to leave fewer descendants than selfish individuals?

The philosophical debate stems from the issue of intent and morality. In his discussion of the evolution of a moral sense, Darwin (1871, p. 482) stated, "I am aware that some persons maintain that actions performed impulsively . . . do not come under the dominion of the moral sense, and cannot be called moral. They confine this term to actions done deliberately, after a victory of opposing desires." Such a distinction, in Darwin's view, is irrelevant or impossible, especially since it is impossible to distinguish between motives.

Following this tradition, apparent altruism can be organized into three motivational categories: (1) no conscious intent, (2) conscious intent to help, and (3) disguised selfishness. An example of the first category would be the perspective of Latané and Darley (1970), where *any* helping behavior qualifies as altruism; all that is required is that the behavior effectively help another. Aronfreed (1970) falls into the second category by considering only those acts that are motivated by empathic or vicarious experience from the effects on others. The third category has been utilized by Trivers (1971) in his discussion of reciprocal altruism: As a species with repeated interactions and memories, a person may help others who can later reciprocate.

Regarding the second concern, *conditions,* the psychological theories reflect the underlying philosophical debate. Explanations of human altruism often take the form of arguing that the altruistic act has some hidden payoff, that it is "really" selfish. Variations of this argument are used by reinforcement theorists and normative theorists. Reinforcement theorists (for example, Krebs, 1970) argue that apparently altruistic behavior, like any other behavior, is maintained by reinforcement; but the reinforcers are simply not apparent, since they are internal feelings such as satisfaction and well-being. Normative theorists, such as Aronfreed (1970), hold that violating the norms of prosocial behavior, which the individual has internalized under threat of sanctions from others, exposes the person to feelings of guilt and, possibly, further sanctions.

There is experimental support for both of these approaches. Weiss, Buchanan, and Alstatt (1971) demonstrated that acting altruistically in the absence of external rewards or punishments is itself reinforcing; thus, behaving altruistically may be internally reinforcing, as predicted by the reinforcement theorists. Horowitz (1971), however, found that members of a social service group were more, rather than less, likely to help if they believed that another person was observing their actions, thereby supporting the normative position. There is nothing necessarily contradictory here. Clearly, people do learn, think in symbolic terms, and anticipate the reactions of others. It should be noted, however, that attempts to alter altruistic behavior by direct reinforcement have been unimpressive (Ruston, 1976).

The presence of others is a significant variable in predicting or explaining altruism. In the seminal series of experiments stimulated by the Genovese murder, Latané and Darley (1970) investigated whether and how the presence of others influences one's willingness to help. They repeatedly found that in the presence of others an individual was *less* likely to help than if he or she were the only one present. In some cases this inhibition was so strong that groups of three were less likely to offer help than were lone individuals. Latané and Darley propose two possible underlying mechanisms. First is the "diffusion of responsibility" mechanism; that is, a lone witness bears the entire responsibility for assisting, while this responsibility is diffused among several when there is more than one witness present. Second is the "social influence" hypothesis; that is, the inaction of others misleads each individual into interpreting the situation as one that does not require attention. Other investigators (for instance, Piliavin, Rodin, and Piliavin, 1969), however, demonstrated that the presence of others does *not* inhibit action. Thus, this research area was left without any theoretical coherence. The theoretical model of Morgan (1978) unified these discrepant results. The diffusion effect is coupled with varying individual propensities (or thresholds) to intervene. That is, as group size increases, not only does the diffusion effect lessen each member's perceived responsibility but, at the same time, the group becomes increasingly likely to contain at least one member with a particularly high propensity to help. This diffusion/threshold effect is mediated by the relative costs and benefits of intervening: in general, the greater the cost of acting, the more pronounced the diffusion effect.

Evolution, the third theoretical problem, is central to the very understanding of human altruism. In their explanations of human altruism, normative and learning theorists rely on internal cognitive mechanisms (not necessarily conscious) that can be programmed by experience, so that the individual feels bad (is punished) when he fails to act altruistically in an appropriate situation and feels good (is rewarded) when he does act altruistically in an appropriate situation. But the ease with which the members of a species can learn something is itself an outcome of natural selection (Wilson, 1975). If altruists, in fact, fare worse reproductively than nonaltruists do, they will ultimately leave fewer genes behind; consequently, the ability to *learn* to behave altruistically (that is, the internal cognitive mechanisms that can be programmed to make altruism rewarding) would disappear from the population.

In his presidential address to the American Psychological Association, Campbell (1975, p. 1115) argues that extremes of human sociality—such as celibate priests, Kamikaze pilots, and self-sacrificial honesty and generosity—"cannot have been achieved on a genetic basis." There are, in fact, two models for the evolution of altruism that are capable of accounting for these behaviors.

The first model is that of kin selection (Hamilton, 1964; Maynard Smith, 1964), which follows from the observation that relatives share genes. This is simply a more general statement of the evolutionary principle behind parental care. Parents are selected to make appropriate sacrifices for their offspring, since these offspring are their genetic representatives in the next generation. Parents who neglect their needy young tend not to pass on their genes. Similarly, other relatives share some proportion of an individual's genes, inherited from common ancestors. Thus, if the altruistic act directed toward one of these relatives benefits more than it costs the altruist (in proportion to their degree of relatedness), then the genes of the altruist show a net gain. The second model specifies the conditions under which altruism might be expected among nonrelatives (conditions such as individual recognition, repeated interactions, and memory), provided there is a sufficiently high probability of reciprocity to self or to relatives (Trivers, 1971).

The biosocial argument on human altruism, then, holds that tendencies toward altruistic behavior have been shaped by natural selection and are part of the human heritage. Campbell (1975) expresses a more common conceptualization when he argues that "social evolution has had to counter individual selfish tendencies which biological evolution has continued to select as a result of genetic competition among the cooperators" (p. 1115).

True altruism, the fourth concern, focuses on whether an act deemed truly altruistic depends on the definition of self-interest. If self-interest is viewed narrowly as hedonism, then true altruism is a frequent occurrence. But if self-interest is viewed in an evolutionary perspective, with inclusive fitness and the spread of genes as the measure of benefit, then true altruism would never be selected. It might occasionally occur, but only as a mistake or as a relatively short-lived genotype or phenotype. Acts of apparent altruism can, from an evolutionary framework, be grouped into three categories: nepotism, reciprocity, and "foolishness."

Elaboration on Critical Points

The divergences in the three views (behaviorist, normative, and sociobiological) are at the level of the basic conceptualization of human nature. Learning theorists see humans as *tabulae rasae* (blank tablets), to be freely written on and molded by experience and reinforcement. Freudians and normative theorists view humans as innately selfish, with altruistic behavior the result of socialization and the internalization of norms. Finally, sociobiologists also see selfishness as part of human nature, but they regard the prosocial virtues as part of the same innate nature.

Additionally, the three types of theorists differ in their view of the individual's relationship to society and surrounding others. Learning theorists tend to deal with isolated individuals. Normative theorists are aware of the importance of others but tend to lump them into a collective "society" (which they endow with an existence in its own right). Sociobiologists see the individual as enmeshed in a network of other individuals, each pursuing personal goals (and each with some innate prosocial tendencies); human social systems, then, represent the accumulation of individual strategies. Note that this is not necessarily a reductionist view; emergent charactersitics of social aggregates (such as mobs) can result from selection at the individual level for differential responses given solitary or social conditions (Greene and Barash, 1976).

The philosophical debate concerning intentionality has generated some semantic misunderstandings. When biologists discuss personality traits such as altruism, they are not concerned with the existence or nature of internal motivation or cognition. Rather, they define the terms explicitly by the *consequences* (for instance, benefiting another individual at some apparent personal cost) of the act (note the similarity to behaviorism).

Personal Views and Recommendations

The individual is linked to the group around him because copies of the individual's genes are carried by relatives in the group and because the others in the group may reciprocate altruistic acts at a later time, "repaying" the individual's initial costs. Neitszche distinguished between the "little wisdom" of consciousness and the "big wisdom" of the organism as a whole. It appears that the human feeling of responsibility evolved in the first place through the operations of both kin selection and reciprocal altruism, because the interests of the individual are, as Roberts (1965) suggests, mixed up with the interests of others. The experience of a feeling of responsibility is the mechanism whereby the human organism, in its "big wisdom," judges where its interests lie. An individual's interests, defined in terms of inclusive fitness, may even be maximized by an act of apparent self-sacrifice.

The norms of reciprocity and beneficence provide a *precise* description of the behavior that would maintain a network of reciprocal altruists. One major problem with reciprocal altruism is that cheaters—those who accept altruism from others but do not themselves act altruistically—have an advantage over the altruists. Altruists are at an advantage only when they direct their altruism toward each other, so that they are ultimately repaid, with interest. Unless the altruists can spot the cheaters, the tendency to cheat will spread through the population, eventually replacing the tendency to act altruistically. Individuals who do not act according to the norms of reciprocity and beneficence are the cheaters who accept help from others but do not return it, and they will be spotted as violators of the norms. An altruist can then withhold altruistic acts from them, for to help them is ultimately, as well as immediately, costly.

This analysis suggests that the norms of reciprocity and beneficence have a double function. First, by their moral nature they help the individual resist the temptation to engage in actions that are beneficial in the short term but costly in the long run. They help motivate the individual to act altruistically, which is to his long-run advantage, even though it is costly in the short term. Second, they provide a means of spotting the cheaters who take advantage of the altruism of others but are not themselves altruistic.

Norms do not exist in the interests of the social system, nor are they opposed to the interests of the individual actors. They are accounting criteria, the offspring of cost-benefit analysis, and they exist in the long-run interests of the individual actors. This view of norms accords well with how they are actually used in social interaction. There is clearly a moral element in norms, and they are clearly intended as guides to personal behavior. At the same time, there is a recognition that one may act counter to the norms. One should help one's fellows, but perhaps one will not.

Besides serving as guides for personal behavior, norms serve as accounting criteria by which the behavior of others is judged; thus, norms promote individual adjustments in interactions with others. Sometimes one learns by direct experience that another person has cheated. This is rather painful, and most people try not to let the same person cheat them twice. That person was judged against moral, normative criteria and found wanting; interactions with him or her were therefore adjusted accordingly. Note also that the norms do not *require* that help be given under conditions of high personal cost, although this is commonly felt to be noble and worthy behavior.

Application to Particular Variables

Ruston (1976) has reviewed the literature on age and altruism. The available literature is, of course, contradictory. Some studies find that sharing increases with age; others find that competitiveness, not cooperation, increases with age; and still others find no differences with age. The studies of Staub are probably the most revealing. Staub (1970) investigated the maturational aspects of the intervention response. Children in kindergarten, first, second, fourth, and sixth grades heard a distressed child in the next room. The subject children were alone or with another child of the same age and sex. For the *alone* subjects, age was positively associated with likelihood of helping, up to the fourth grade; but between the fourth and the sixth grade, the tendency to give help declined (that is, sixth graders were less likely to help than fourth graders). There was an interesting parallel in the results for pairs of children. In kindergarten and in the first and second grades, pairs of children were more likely to help than were lone children of the same age, but they were less likely to help than lone fourth and sixth graders. Pondering these results, Staub (1971) speculated that there were conflicting behavioral expectations (in this case, remaining in the classroom versus leaving to assist a crying child in an adjacent room), and the children were worried that in going into the next room they would violate one of these rules. By manipulating the rules under which the children were operating (that is, allowing children to leave the room if a pencil sharpener was needed), he showed that this was indeed true; under this condition, many children left the room with pencil in hand to assist the crying child. The interesting point was the demonstration that altruistic behavior does not develop in a simple linear fashion and that it takes place after an unconscious balancing of the costs and benefits likely to follow.

Most studies that have included a sex variable have failed to find a male-female difference. Among those that did find sex differentials, there is a slight preponderance of studies showing females to be more helpful. There is some possibility that the differences are situation specific, but no coherent theory of male-female differences in altruistic situations has been offered.

A typical reaction following the Genovese murder was to assert that the nonaction of the witnesses was peculiar to New York (or at least to large cities) and that it would not happen in small towns. Again, it appears not to be that simple. Merrens (1973) found that people living in midwestern cities and towns were more helpful than New Yorkers on several simple requests for help (for instance, giving local directions), and Korte and Kerr (1975) found that help was more likely in nonurban than in urban areas. But Schneider and Mockus (1974) failed to find a rural-urban difference, and Weiner (1976) found that subjects raised in rural areas were less helpful than those raised in urban areas.

References

Aronfreed, J. "The Socialization of Altruistic and Sympathetic Behavior: Some Theoretical and Experimental Analysis." In J. Macauley and L. Berkowitz (Eds.), *Altruism and Helping Behavior.* New York: Academic Press, 1970.

Berkowitz, L., and Daniels, L. R. "Responsibility and Dependency." *Journal of Abnormal and Social Psychology,* 1963, *66,* 429-436.

Campbell, D. T. "On the Conflicts Between Biological and Social Evolution and Between Psychology and Moral Tradition." *American Psychologist,* 1975, *30,* 1103-1126.

Darwin, C. *The Descent of Man.* New York: Modern Library, 1871.

Gouldner, A. W. "The Norm of Reciprocity." *American Sociological Review,* 1960, *25,* 161-178.

Gouldner, A. W. "The Importance of Something for Nothing." In A. W. Gouldner (Ed.), *For Sociology: Renewal and Critique.* New York: Basic Books, 1973.

Greene, P. J., and Barash, D. P. "On the Genetic Basis of Behavior, Especially Altruism." *American Psychologist,* 1976, *31,* 359-361.

Hamilton, W. D. "The Genetical Theory of Social Behavior." *Journal of Theoretical Biology,* 1964, *7,* 1-52.

Horowitz, I. A. "The Effect of Group Norms on Bystander Intervention." *Journal of Social Psychology,* 1971, *83,* 265-273.

Korte, C., and Kerr, N. "Response to Altruistic Opportunities in Urban and Nonurban Settings." *Journal of Social Psychology,* 1975, *95,* 183-184.

Krebs, D. L. "Altruism—An Examination of the Concept and a Review of the Literature." *Psychological Bulletin,* 1970, *73,* 258-302.

Krebs, D. L. "Empathy and Altruism." *Journal of Personality and Social Psychology,* 1975, *32,* 1134-1146.

Latané, R., and Darley, J. M. *The Unresponsive Bystander: Why Doesn't He Help?* New York: Appleton-Century-Crofts, 1970.

Leeds, R. "Altruism and the Norm of Giving." *Merrill Palmer Quarterly,* 1963, *9,* 229-240.

Maynard Smith, J. "Group Selection and Kin Selection." *Nature,* 1964, *201,* 1145-1147.

Merrens, M. R. "Non-Emergency Helping Behavior in Various Sized Communities." *Journal of Social Psychology,* 1973, *90,* 327-328.

Milo, R. *Egoism and Altruism.* Belmont, Calif.: Wadsworth, 1973.

Morgan, C. J. "Bystander Intervention: Experimental Test of a Formal Model." *Journal of Personality and Social Psychology,* 1978, *36,* 43-55.

Piliavin, I. M., Rodin, J., and Piliavin, J. A. "Good Samaritanism: An Underground Phenomenon?" *Journal of Personality and Social Psychology,* 1969, *13,* 289-299.

Plumez, H. H. "The Relationship Between Altruism and Mental Health." *Dissertation Abstracts International,* 1975, *36* (6-B), 3,011-3,012.

Roberts, M. *Responsibility and Practical Freedom.* Cambridge, England: Cambridge University Press, 1965.

Rogers, C. *Client-Centered Therapy.* Boston: Houghton Mifflin, 1951.

Ruston, J. P. "Socialization and the Altruistic Behavior of Children." *Psychological Bulletin,* 1976, *83,* 898-913.

Sawyer, J. "The Altruism Scale: A Measure of Co-operative, Individualistic and Competitive Interpersonal Orientation." *American Journal of Sociology,* 1966, *71,* 407-416.

Schneider, F. W., and Mockus, Z. "Failure to Find a Rural-Urban Difference in Incidence of Altruistic Behavior." *Psychological Reports,* 1974, *35,* 294.

Sorokin, P. *Altruistic Love: A Study of American "Good Neighbors" and Christian Saints.* Boston: Beacon Press, 1950.

Staub, E. "A Child in Distress: The Influence of Age and Number of Witnesses on Children's Attempts to Help." *Journal of Personality and Social Psychology,* 1970, *14,* 130-140.

Staub, E. "Helping a Person in Distress: The Influence of Implicit and Explicit 'Rules' of Conduct on Children and Adults." *Journal of Personality and Social Psychology,* 1971, *17,* 137-144.

Trivers, R. L. "The Evolution of Reciprocal Altruism." *Quarterly Review of Biology,* 1971, *46,* 35-57.

Weiner, F. H. "Altruism, Ambience, and Action: The Effects of Rural and Urban Rearing on Helping Behavior." *Journal of Personality and Social Psychology,* 1976, *34,* 112-124.

Weiss, R. F., Buchanan, W., and Alstatt, L. "Altruism Is Rewarding." *Science,* 1971, *171,* 1262-1263.

Wilson, E. O. *Sociobiology: The New Synthesis.* Cambridge, Mass.: Harvard University Press, 1975.

37

Janet L. Ostrand

Dominance

Indicative of the concept of dominance are such words and phrases as confident, self-reliant, outgoing, strong, persuasive, resourceful, verbally fluent, and having leadership potential and initiative. Contraindicative are such words and phrases as meek, apathetic, shy, retiring, suggestible, slow in thought and action, and avoiding situations of tension and decision. When disassociated from terms like *aggression* and *authoritarianism*, which are unrelated concepts, dominance seems to denote a healthy ego state. Assertiveness, a concept related to dominance, became an increasingly popular topic during the 1970s. The social ethic of the decade promoted self-respect, openness, and an active orientation to life, which also are elements of dominance.

Psychologists aligned with an intrapsychic school of thought define dominance as a *feeling* (of self-esteem or self confidence), whereas behavioral psychologists define the concept as a *behavior* (control or directiveness). Maslow (1939) pointed out the necessity of separating dominance feelings, or ego level, from dominance behavior and indicated that one dynamic cannot be predicted from the other.

Background and Current Status

The term *dominance* initially appeared in 1865, within the study of biology in work done by Gregor Mendel on the various phenomena of inheritance and was discussed in terms of dominant and recessive genes. The concept of psychological dominance appears in the physiological, clinical, social, and experimental specialties of psychology. The development of the concept is rooted in Kempf's (1920) work on the nature and bodily mechanisms of emotion. Among the functions of the cerebrospinal system, Kempf contended that the autonomic functions are dominant. Adler (1929), a neoanalyst, discussed dominance as the will to power, resulting from the individual's attempts to compensate for feelings of inferiority. Maslow (1936, 1940), in his studies with primates, stressed dominance as a central dimension for comparative analysis. Other experimental investigations at an infrahuman level have indicated that experienced animals establish dominance quickly, often in the absence of fighting, and that, once it is established, dominance is highly stable (Maroney, Warren, and Sinha, 1959; Miller and Murphy, 1956). Other observations suggest that social learning plays a critical part in the dominance relations among primates (Imanishi, 1960). Bales (1956) and Berkowitz (1956) have studied the effect of dominance behavior in human communication networks.

Theory and research indicate that dominance is an inherent drive (Adler, 1929; Maslow, 1936), existing within the general population (Maslow, 1939; Veroff and Veroff, 1971) as a major form of human motivation (Stagner, 1961). Furthermore, results of correlational and factor analytic studies support the view that dominance is psychologically healthy (Bergin and Soloman, 1963; Cattell and Eber, 1962; Maslow, 1939) and is a characteristic important to leadership (Edwards, 1959; Gough, 1965, 1969). There are indications that dominance might also promote physical health. Among studies conducted with infrahuman primates, leaders had the lowest heart rate, a fact that reflects absence of emotional tension (Cherkovich and Tatogan, 1973).

Approaches conducive to the assessment of dominance include formal testing, observation, interviews.

The quality measured by tests is best ascertained by the given scale's stated definition of dominance, including characteristics it ascribes to high and low scorers, along with intercorrelational studies between the instrument's Dominance scale scores and other personality variables. Self-report inventories that include Dominance scales are the Adjective Check List (ACL), the Bernreuter Personality Inventory, the California Psychological Inventory (CPI), the Edwards Personal Preference Schedule (EPPS), the Guilford-Zimmerman Temperament Survey, and the Sixteen Personality Factor Questionnaire (16 PF). Among the projective techniques, the Thematic Apperception Test (TAT) includes a scoring procedure to estimate a subject's perceived need and press for dominance.

Another viable approach to the assessment of dominance is the observation of persons as they participate in an activity with others (for instance, in a dyad or a small group). Since dominance is a social interaction variable, observation is an important methodology. Within a dyad or a small group, phenomena to be observed include which person arises as the natural leader (since leadership is important to dominance) and which person appears to be called on to settle arguments. Groups whose total composition averages high on dominance are likely to show more effective role interaction and democratic procedures. Members are likely to feel free to participate, to raise group problems, and to criticize group defects.

Another assessment technique available to a psychologist is the interview. The psychologist wants to listen to clients' reports about their relationships with people and their self-perceived inferiorities, as well as to observe clients' relationships with the interviewer during the course of the discussion.

Critical Discussion

General Areas of Concern

Points of contention and apparent confusion among theory and research concern such questions as the following: (1) What is the relationship between dominance and the concepts of ascendance, authoritarianism, and aggression? (2) Are dominance features healthy or neurotic tendencies? (3) Is dominance mainly dependent on physiological processes or psychological functions? (4) Is there a dominance drive independent of specific social situations? The relationship of ascendance, authoritarianism, and aggression will be reviewed in this section; the remaining issues will be discussed as they evolve in the review of theory.

Ascendance may be defined as the tendency to dominate others; an ascendant person, for example, might tend to monopolize conversations, interrupt others, and resist any efforts to change his opinion (Berkowitz, 1964).

Authoritarianism is similar in some ways to ascendance. However, high authoritarians may be either dominant or submissive, depending on the position in which they find themselves. When these people are in authority (or power) positions, they tend to use their authority to control others; when they are in the subordinate positions, they accept this status and submit to the person or persons in superior positions (Berkowitz, 1964). People who manifest high authoritarianism epitomize closed-mindedness; they view the world in the absolutes of either-or, right-wrong, black-white, without integrating the varied aspects of a situation. Adorno and his co-workers (1950) conceptualize such a belief system as the "authoritarian personality" and developed the Fascism (F) scale to measure that dimension. Allport (1944) defines a similar entity as "power people" and sees them as reacting to self-perceived threats and deprivations arising from their own conflicts and insecurity. Reactive egos tend to perceive their neighbors and associates as threats rather than collaborators.

Some theorists (for instance, Dollard and others, 1939) believe that aggression is a secondary phenomenon arising from frustration. Typically, aggressive people are extrapunative (Rozenzweig, 1944) or manifest outward aggression, but they also may display intrapunitive or self-punishment features. The emergent dynamic is of a person who alternately lashes out at people and then withdraws and sulks.

The terms *authoritarianism, aggression,* and *power people* depict a person who feels insecure and who is not relating well to others. In contrast, Gough (1964) lists the characteristics of dominance as leadership ability, persistence, and social initiative. Similarly, Edwards (1959) describes dominance as the ability to argue from one's point of view, to lead, to be selected as head of committees, and to settle arguments between others. Both descriptions reveal a person who interacts well with others. In fact, in Gough's California Psychological Inventory (CPI) the Dominance scale is part of a six-scale cluster assessing a person's level of poise, ascendance, and self-assurance. The remaining five scales are Capacity for Status, Sociability, Social Presence, Self-Acceptance, and Well-Being. Authoritarians tend to be self-doubting and to have problems in social relationships.

An apparent difficulty among assessment techniques is that some instruments define dominance in factors more closely resembling aggression and authoritarianism than self-acceptance and self-confidence. For example, Cattell and Eber (1962, p. 14) describe high scorers on the Dominance scale of the Sixteen Personality Factors Questionnaire (16 PF) as "tending to be austere, a law unto themselves, hostile or extrapunitive, authoritarian."

Comparative Philosophies and Theories

Much of the confusion about dominance as a healthy versus neurotic character-istic is inherent in personality theory itself. Maslow (1939) concluded that dominance feelings are virtually identical with self-esteem; a similar conclusion was reached in a study conducted by Bergin and Soloman (1963). Furthermore, Bernreuter (1933) found dominance, as measured by the Bernreuter Personality Inventory, to be negatively related to introversion and instability. Adler (1929), however, did not distinguish between domi-nance behavior and dominance feeling; he conceptualized dominance as a neurotic need for power. Much of Adler's theory rests on a need within people to compensate for per-ceived inferiority. He conceptualized this need as the will to power or to strive from below to above. In his earlier work Adler posited compensation for a defective organ system as the basis of the will to power, but in his later volumes he spoke of a real or an imagined inferiority. Adler believed that the will to power is a fundamental drive and that it can be thwarted by some perceived inferiority. This thwarting mechanism focuses the attention of the individual on the defect, and a life plan is laid down to compensate for the deficiency. The nature of the will to power seems to be largely a matter of available psychophysiological energy, like Freud's libido. The difference is largely in the aims or objects to which it becomes selectively attached (Stagner, 1961). Adler's discussion of the will to power (or dominance) is couched almost entirely in negative terms as a reaction against inferiority or inadequacy.

Stagner (1961) has done considerable work integrating material from Adler with that of other researchers. Experimental and observational data gathered by Stagner sup-port the notion of a positive dominance drive, an innate tendency to achieve a status superior to that of others in the same species. Murchison (1935) and Schjelderup-Ebbe (1935) studied the fighting behavior of chickens, which continues until a stable domi-nance status or "pecking order" is evolved. This need to establish dominance seems inde-pendent of food, sex, and other drives. However, it can be intensified by injections of male sex hormones; that is, roosters so treated will actually achieve higher dominance status. Maslow (1936) showed that monkeys and anthropoid apes manifest a dominance drive that, in his view, is not a derivative of hunger, sex, or other bodily needs. In an attempt to extrapolate his work to humans. Maslow (1939, 1942) conducted studies that pointed to the social nature of dominance striving and indicated that it is a normal and major form of human motivation. While human material is inevitably more complex than that obtained from animal observation, he believed that the same generalizations could be applied in both investigations.

Elaboration on Critical Points

Three main points emerge: (1) that dominance is within a Gestalt of personality variables, (2) that dominance feeling must be separated from dominance behavior, and (3) that socialization and acculturation have important effects on dominance. From research and theory, dominance feeling—or ego level, as Maslow (1939) prefers to call it—has emerged not as an entity in and of itself, but existing within a cluster or syndrome. Domi-nance feeling relates positively to such variables as self-confidence, self-esteem, leadership, sociability, and friendliness, but negatively to shyness, timidity, self-consciousness, and embarrassment. Such a syndrome is apparent in the research of Bernreuter (1933) and Maslow (1939). Dominance feeling, or ego level, is an awareness within the self and a generalized approach to life, much of it internalized in the early life of an individual. Dominance behavior tends to be more situation specific than dominance feeling and, as such, is under greater social control. The inhibitory control by cultural pressures is far greater and more effective for dominance behavior than for dominance feeling; this partially explains the uncertain correlation between the two dynamics (Maslow, 1939).

Personal Views and Recommendations

There are indications of an inherent dominance drive, which is dependent on persons' feelings about themselves as well as on the influences of socialization. To a large extent, personality is a social product, but in a different sense than social mores or folkways, which tend to be specific and to hold for definite situations and circumstances and can vary over time in any one culture. In contrast, personality is the internalization of social experience during the early life of an individual and tends to remain a relatively stable portion of the person's approach to life (Maslow, 1939). The internalized social experiences appear related to issues of self-worth. People who are self-accepting tend to be more accepting of others, even of those who may hold opposing viewpoints. Individuals who feel insecure are likely to be rigid persons who score high on measures of authoritarianism or on Dominance scales that measure factors more closely resembling authoritarianism than ego level.

Extensive correlational studies between dominance and authoritarianism and between dominance and self-acceptance or self-confidence could allow researchers to determine which personality dynamics are being measured by Dominance scales. The definitions alone and even the manuals and handbooks do not provide sufficient data, because they include different concepts under the single heading "Dominance." Using the California Psychological Inventory (CPI), Ostrand (1976) found a correlation of $r = .66$ ($p < .01$) between the Dominance and Self-Acceptance scales of the CPI, whereas the correlation between the CPI Dominance scale and the Adorno (and others) Fascism (F) scale was $r = .02$ and not significantly different from zero. Similarly, using the Adjective Check List (ACL), Gough (1965) found an intercorrelation of $r = .05$ between the Dominance and Aggression scales of that instrument, whereas the correlation between the Dominance and Self-Confidence scales was $r = .65$.

Research suggests, then, that dominance can be viewed as a healthy trait, indicating feelings of security and confidence within the self. Persons who are self-accepting and self-confident will tend to approach their goals in ways that neither demean nor demoralize others but frequently enhance them—which tends to be unlike the behavior of authoritarian and aggressive personalities. To form an analogy, the differences between dominance and authoritarianism appear to be like the differences between assertiveness and aggression.

There remains, however, a paucity of information about dominance in relationship to practitioners. Among the research that has been conducted, Bergin and Soloman (1963), using the Edwards Personal Preference Scale (EPPS), found a significant posttest increase in EPPS Dominance with eighteen postinternship students in clinical and counseling psychology. Similarly, Passons and Dey (1972), using Gough's Adjective Check List (ACL), found a posttest increase in the practicum trainees' Self-Confidence, a variable positively correlated with dominance. Ostrand, Moses, and Delaney (1976) found a significant increase in Dominance scale scores on the California Psychological Inventory (CPI) for students who had conducted a one-semester supervised counseling practicum in educational psychology. In another study using counselor trainees in clinical and counseling psychology and psychiatric social work, CPI Dominance scores were significantly higher for students in a counseling practicum than for students not in a practicum (Ostrand, 1976).

Questions about dominance in reference to counselor training are (1) whether counselor education programs need to enhance a feeling of dominance in their students and (2) whether such a goal is possible. There are indications that dominance feeling is internalized in the early life of an individual but that it is reinforced by experience throughout life. Furthermore, it is generally believed that the counseling practicum is an emotionally heightened experience for counselor trainees because it is a new experience and an ego-involving experience concerning the question "Am I a good counselor?" If the practicum is a highly emotional experience, then counselor trainees should be likely candidates for psychological change. Gough and Heilbrun (1965) call this high emotional level an "available anxiety" and hypothesize that such anxiety may facilitate change. If dominance feeling can be enhanced during the time of the counselor program, and research indicates that it can (Bergin and Soloman, 1963; Ostrand, 1976), how will this feeling or self-percept affect counselor behavior? It might be predicted that a person who is experiencing enhanced feelings of self-worth and self-confidence would be a more effective counselor. However, the relationship between counselor dominance feeling and counselor effectiveness is uncertain; more research is needed in the area.

Investigation into the concept of dominance involves problems and responsibilities common to most psychological research. Researchers can assure themselves of professional conduct by becoming familiar with the American Psychological Association's "Ethical Standards for Psychologists." Especially relevant are Principle 1, which discusses the psychologist's responsibility as a scientist, and Principle 2, which delineates research precautions. To summarize, psychologists investigate in those areas where they believe society will benefit; and they assume obligations for the welfare of all their research subjects and resist exposing them to undue stress. The principles may seem especially relevant when one is dealing with persons who have physical, intellectual, and psychiatric disorders, but they are equally important to all populations. For example, students might erroneously believe that a course grade depends on their scores on a Dominance scale and become highly distressed at that prospect. All subjects, therefore, should be informed about the study as fully as possible prior to testing and thoroughly debriefed on termination of the study.

Application to Particular Variables

Among adolescents and adults, there is a possibility that dominance alters somewhat with age, showing signs of reduction in adults from middle to old age (Cattell, Eber, and Tatsuoka, 1970). Research conducted by Gough (1969), however, indicates that high school students and young delinquents have the lowest CPI Dominance scores among people in any age or occupational group. An explanation might be that adolescents in general have had less time to test reality and that the experience of young delinquents, though also limited, has largely been unsuccessful. The elderly have had many more experiences but might have less stamina to deal with life; this condition is manifested in decreased dominance. The results of research on age are inconclusive. A curvilinear dominance pattern is hypothesized, with scores peaking at middle adulthood (a time of life when experience and energy are substantial).

Dominance patterns are not significantly different for males and females. Studies using identical research instruments and similar observation techniques report dissimilar results. It might be assumed that acculturation effects would make females less dominant than males, but the results of observations, interviews, and tests are inconsistent with that assumption.

Generally, dominance behavior is related negatively to school achievement (up to graduate university work), because docility seems to enhance examination performance (Cattell, Eber, and Tatsuoka, 1970). The pattern may discontinue at the graduate school level because persons in training to become professionals must display an ability to work with people; at this level, that ability can be as important as test performance.

Data are unavailable on the relevance of socioeconomic factors, but a trend toward reduced dominance would be predicted for persons living in poverty (this condition being a debilitating experience). For people born into poverty, there is truly little hope of rising above it, and the condition fosters dependency on others for mere survival.

Among vocational categories, higher Dominance scores are obtained by athletes, sales managers, personnel directors, and public administrators, whereas lower scores are obtained by farmers, cooks, janitors, musicians, and printers. In general, dominance is higher among persons who prefer to work with people and lower for those who prefer to work with objects and ideas, although results are inconclusive, especially among research scientists (Cattell, Eber, and Tatsuoka, 1970; Gough, 1969).

Physically ill people can experience many frustrations in their attempts to deal with their body and environment. Thus, they can become intolerant, selfish, and controlling (Barker and others, 1953). Such a behavior syndrome is sometimes referred to in the professional literature as dominance, but it is more closely related to the dynamics herein aligned with aggression. Ill people can be manipulative and almost completely usurp the lives of those most devoted to them, but this combination of great power and extreme weakness places such persons in a difficult conflict. They are grateful to their benefactors, but they are also resentful of their subordinate relationship to them (Barker and others, 1953). This pattern is unlike dominance, which denotes an acceptance of the self and others.

Among the psychiatric classifications, organic reaction types are characterized by changes in the intellectual sphere (dementia); by affective disorders that take the form of emotional instability (so that, for instance, the person will laugh or weep without sufficient cause and often in an explosive way); and by character change in the form of conduct foreign to the person's natural disposition (Henderson and Batchelor, 1962). Such intellectual, emotional, or characterological conditions are not conducive to dominance.

Persons with chronic functional pathology tend to live less intensely than others; they are conspicuous for their apathy, indifference, and lack of initiative (low dominance). The apathy often represents a defense against aggressive and sadistic impulses (Fenichel, 1945). Other low-dominance people are fixated at the stage of primary narcissism and wish to regain feelings of omnipotence and, hence, self-esteem from sources outside themselves. Among such people there are many subtypes, including aggressive personalities and those who seek nurturance through submissiveness. Many simultaneously try both methods. In brief, dominance tends to denote a healthy ego state; therefore, it is negatively correlated with functional psychiatric conditions.

Dominance is strongly related to feelings of self-worth or self-esteem. Persons who are indigent, unhealthy, or poorly educated may be seen as suffering from a privation; therefore, lower dominance levels might be hypothesized for them. However, the results of interviews, observations, and tests often are inconsistent with such a hypothesis. A reason may be that people at all levels can experience feelings of confidence or insecurity, regardless of personal or social status. Some distinguished research scientists have felt ineffectual because they have failed to win a Nobel Prize (or maybe two prizes), whereas some people with subnormal intelligence trained for objectively routine jobs have felt good about themselves.

The question is, of course, why are some persons self-accepting and others not?

Self-esteem appears to be a phenomenon internalized in an individual's early years and, likely, reinforced by experience throughout life (Katz and Kahn, 1966). The difference between persons who are self-confident and dominant and those who are self-doubtful and passive or aggressive appears to be related to another variable, the ability to cope. The coping mechanism is dependent on a feeling of inner strength, a feeling within people that they will get by, they will endure, no matter what circumstances arise. Accordingly, dominance, self-esteem, self-confidence, and the ability to cope are interrelated dynamics that appear to have an inconsistent correspondence with tangible privations.

References

Adler, A. *Problems of Neurosis.* London: Routledge & Kegan Paul, 1929.

Adorno, T. W., and others. *The Authoritarian Personality.* New York: Norton, 1950.

Allport, G. W. "The Psychology of Participation" [1944]. In R. W. Marks (Ed.), *Great Ideas in Psychology.* New York: Bantam Books, 1966.

Bales, R. F. *Factor Analysis of the Domain of Values in the Value Profile Test.* Cambridge, Mass.: Laboratory of Social Relations, Harvard University, 1956.

Barker, R. G., and others. *Adjustment to Physical Handicap and Illness: A Survey of the Social Psychology of Physique and Disability.* New York: Social Science Research Council, 1953.

Bergin, A. E., and Soloman, S. "Personality and Performance Correlates of Empathic Understanding in Psychotherapy." *American Psychologist,* 1963, *18,* 393-397.

Berkowitz, L. "Personality and Group Position." *Sociometry,* 1956, *19,* 210-222.

Berkowitz, L. *Advances in Experimental Psychology.* New York: Academic Press, 1964.

Bernreuter, R. G. "The Theory and Construction of the Personality Inventory." *Journal of Social Psychology,* 1933, *4,* 383-405.

Cattell, R. B., and Eber, H. W. *Sixteen Personality Factor Questionnaire: Manual for Forms A and B.* Champaign, Ill.: Institute for Personality and Ability Testing, 1962.

Cattell, R. B., Eber, H. W., and Tatsuoka, M. M. *Handbook for the Sixteen Personality Factor Questionnaire.* Champaign, Ill.: Institute for Personality and Ability Testing, 1970.

Cherkovich, G. M., and Tatogan, S. K. "Heart Rate (Radiotelemetrical Registration) in Macaques and Baboons According to Dominance-Submissive Rank in a Group." *Folia Primatologica,* 1973, *20,* 265-273.

Dollard, J., and others. *Frustration and Aggression.* New Haven, Conn.: Yale University Press, 1939.

Edwards, A. L. *Edwards Personal Preference Schedule Manual.* New York: Psychological Corporation, 1959.

Fenichel, O. *The Psychoanalytic Theory of Neurosis.* New York: Norton, 1945.

Gough, H. G. *California Psychological Inventory Manual.* Palo Alto, Calif.: Consulting Psychologists Press, 1964.

Gough, H. G. *California Psychological Inventory Manual.* Palo Alto, Calif.: Consulting Psychologists Press, 1969.

Gough, H. G., and Heilbrun, A. G., Jr. *Adjective Check List Manual.* Palo Alto, Calif.: Consulting Psychologists Press, 1965.

Guilford, J. P., and Zimmerman, W. S. *The Guilford-Zimmerman Temperament Survey Manual.* Beverly Hills, Calif.: Sheridan Supply Co., 1949.

Henderson, D., and Batchelor, I. *Textbook of Psychiatry.* London: Oxford University Press, 1962.

Imanishi, K. "Social Organization of Subhuman Primates in Their Natural Habitat." *Current Anthropology*, 1960, *1*, 393-407.

Katz, D., and Kahn, R. L. *The Social Psychology of Organizations.* New York: Wiley, 1966.

Kempf, E. J. *Psychopathology*. St. Louis: Mosby, 1920.

London, P. *Modes and Morals of Psychotherapy*. New York: Holt, Rinehart and Winston, 1964.

Maroney, R. J., Warren, J. M., and Sinha, M. M. "Stability of Social Dominance Hierarchies in Monkeys." *Journal of Social Psychology*, 1959, *50*, 285-293.

Maslow, A. H. "Role of Dominance in Social and Sexual Behavior of Infra-human Primates." *Journal of Genetic Psychology*, 1936, *48*, 310-338.

Maslow, A. H. "Dominance, Personality, and Social Behavior in Women." *Journal of Social Psychology*, 1939, *10*, 3-39.

Maslow, A. H. "Dominance-Quality and Social Behavior in Infra-human Primates." *Journal of Social Psychology*, 1940, *11*, 313-324.

Maslow, A. H. "Self-Esteem (Dominance-Feeling) and Sexuality in Women." *Journal of Social Psychology*, 1942, *16*, 259-294.

Miller, R. E., and Murphy, J. V. "Social Interaction of Rhesus Monkeys. I: Food-Getting Dominance as a Dependent Variable." *Journal of Social Psychology*, 1956, *44*, 249-255.

Murchison, C. "Experimental Measurement of Social Hierarchy in Gallus Domesticus." *Journal of General Psychology*, 1935, *12*, 3-39.

Murray, H. A. *Thematic Apperception Test Manual.* Cambridge, Mass.: Harvard University Press, 1943.

Ostrand, J. L. "Effects of Supervised Counseling on Dominance." *Counselor Education and Supervision*, 1976, *16*, 117-124.

Ostrand, J. L., Moses, H. A., and Delaney, D. J. "A Study of Selected Personality Variables During Practicum." *Illinois Guidance and Personnel Association Quarterly*, 1976, *4*, 111-114.

Passons, W. R., and Dey, G. R. "Counselor Candidate Personal Change and the Communication of Facilitative Dimensions." *Counselor Education and Supervision*, 1972, *12*, 57-62.

Rozenzweig, S. "An Outline of Frustration Theory." In J. McV. Hunt (Ed.), *Personality and Behavior Disorders.* New York: Ronald Press, 1944.

Schjelderup-Ebbe, T. "Social Behavior of Birds." In C. Murchison (Ed.), *Handbook of Social Psychology*. Worcester, Mass.: Clark University Press, 1935.

Stagner, R. *Psychology of Personality*. New York: McGraw-Hill, 1961.

Veroff, J., and Veroff, J. B. "Theoretical Notes on Power Motivation." *Merrill Palmer Quarterly*, 1971, *17*, 59-69.

38

Disturbed Thinking

Albert D. Loro, Jr.

Since thinking is an introspective experience, it has no observable external referent. Clinicians typically use deviant behavior (such as bizarre language or unusual problem-solving approaches) as the clinical evidence for the presence of disturbed thinking. Disturbed thinking, then, is a clinical sign of an internal process that is inferred on the basis of unusual behavior. Implicit in this clinical inference is the operating assumption that a person's behavior reflects, to some extent, internal mediating events (Chapman and Chapman, 1973).

During a routine clinical assessment, the presence of disturbed thinking is determined by a critical examination of thought content (what a person says, does, or thinks) and thought process (how a person speaks, performs, or thinks). While both types of data are important to collect and evaluate, most clinicians and theorists emphasize the formal, process, or structural aspects of disturbed thinking.

It is important to make a distinction between disturbed thinking and schizophrenic thinking. Disturbed thinking could be displayed by any person with psychological problems, such as a manic, a hysteric, or an obsessive-compulsive. Schizophrenic thinking is a specific class of disturbed thinking and appears to be characteristic of, and generally peculiar to, most types of schizophrenia.

Background and Current Status

Emil Kraepelin (1856-1926) made the first major contributions to the literature on disturbed thinking. He noted that a deterioration in the capacity to think is a primary characteristic of dementia praecox, a clinical syndrome of progressive mental deterioration that is inevitable and begins in adolescence. Later, Eugen Bleuler (1857-1939) reclassified and reformulated several of Kraepelin's clinical entities of dementia praecox under the diagnostic category of schizophrenia. Bleuler coined the diagnostic label of schizophrenia and inferred that the splitting of associative threads in the minds of severely disturbed patients is responsible for the fundamental symptoms of schizophrenia, such as autism and ambivalence (Bleuler, 1911).

From 1910 until 1950, the study of disturbed thinking was gradually upgraded and empirically refined with the development and use of psychological testing. Using objective and projective testing instruments, psychologists were able to begin specifying tasks and questions that were useful in assessing disturbed thinking (Rapaport, 1951; Rapaport, Gill, and Schafer, 1946). In the late and middle 1950s, the clinical treatment of schizophrenia markedly improved with the advent of antipsychotic drugs and the major tranquilizers. These medications clearly reduced the symptoms of schizophrenia, including the frequency of severely disturbed thinking.

Because of therapeutic advances and the continued widespread use of psychotropic drugs, it is currently difficult to select suitable patients for research on disturbed thinking (Chapman and Chapman, 1973). In spite of this research complication, disturbed thinking holds a prominent position as a significant presenting symptom in modern clinical assessment. Specifically, disturbed thinking is widely accepted as the primary clinical sign of schizophrenia, and the topics of disturbed and schizophrenic thinking continue to generate massive amounts of clinical and empirical research (see, for example, Chapman and Chapman, 1973; Weiner, 1966).

Critical Discussion

General Areas of Concern

Given the importance of disturbed thinking in clinical assessment, it is necessary to consider the following questions: (1) How might one conceptualize disturbed thinking? (2) How might one distinguish among the various types of disturbed and schizophrenic thinking? (3) What are the implications of disturbed thinking for differential diagnosis?

Disturbed thinking is best conceptualized along a continuum ranging from slightly disturbed thinking to schizophrenic or severely disturbed thinking (Harrow and Quinlan, 1977). Using this approach, the practicing clinician places the various types of disturbed thinking (for example, loose associations and peculiar language) in a proper clinical perspective. At the same time, the clinician may draw on prior diagnostic experience, psychometric data, and empirical evidence to systematically evaluate and position disturbed thinking along this continuum.

Most importantly, a continuum of disturbed thinking is necessary for accurate differential diagnosis. The utility of this approach is best illustrated with several research findings. For example, acutely schizophrenic patients tend to manifest idiosyncratic (unconventional and bizarre) thinking rather than personally overinvolved thinking (Adler and Harrow, 1974). Similarly, circumstantial or tangential thinking is more indicative of schizophrenia than are the less explicit forms of thought disturbance, such as peculiar language or nonfocused thinking (Weiner, 1966). Further, some types of disturbed thinking generally believed unique to schizophrenia, such as consistent logical errors (Arieti, 1974) and stereotypy or perseveration (Kraepelin, 1919), occur in nonschizophrenic populations. That is, normal college students sometimes reason illogically, and brain-damaged patients frequently perseverate (Chapman and Chapman, 1973). At the same time, disturbed thinking, while important, is not the only critical factor in diagnosing schizo-phrenia. Other areas of disturbance—including perception and attention, motor behavior, social skills, and contact with reality—must be thoroughly evaluated (Davison and Neale, 1974). In addition, disturbed thinking is not the essential psychodiagnostic factor in dis-tinguishing schizophrenia from depressive and manic-depressive psychoses. Specifically, symptoms commonly associated solely with schizophrenia, such as severely disturbed thinking, are found with surprising frequency in both depressive and manic patients (McCabe, 1976; Skodol, Buckley, and Salamon, 1976). Skodol, Buckley, and Salamon (1976) found certain central factors (such as longitudinal course, family genetics, and drug responsiveness) more useful than the presence of disturbed thinking for making a differential diagnosis among schizophrenic, depressive, and manic-depressive disorders. Finally, experienced clinicians may be unreliable in their attempts to identify and eval-uate disturbed thinking by means of typical and traditional clinical methods, such as proverb interpretations (Andreasen, 1977; Andreasen, Tsuang, and Canter, 1974). In short, if one considers disturbed thinking alone, he will find it extremely difficult to make an accurate differential diagnosis, because disturbed thinking is not unique to schizophrenia, although the severe types of thought disturbance—including neologisms, word salad, and clang associations—are frequently indicative of schizophrenia (Davison and Neale, 1974). With these diagnostic issues in mind, the following rule applies in clini-cal assessment: *The greater the extent to which disturbed thinking violates realistic con-siderations and conventional rules of language, the more frequently it is displayed, the longer it persists, and the more inconsistent it is with available evidence, the more likely the thinking is indicative of schizophrenia* (Weiner, 1966).

Comparative Philosophies and Theories

Several elegant philosophies and numerous documented theories have been formu-lated about the nature and etiology of disturbed thinking. Since these complicated philos-ophies and elaborate theories cannot be adequately described and discussed in a few sen-tences, primary source material describing some of the major theories of disturbed thinking should be consulted (Arieti, 1974; Cameron, 1938, 1939; Chapman, Chapman, and Miller, 1964; Shakow, 1962, 1963; Wynne and Singer, 1963). In addition, critical reviews examining these and other theoretical formulations of disturbed thinking are highly recommended (Buss, 1966; Buss and Lang, 1965; Chapman and Chapman, 1973; Lang and Buss, 1965; Maher, 1966; Payne and Hewlett, 1960).

Elaboration on Critical Points

One of the most difficult clinical assessment tasks involves making an accurate differential diagnosis. Identifying disturbed thinking during a routine clinical assessment, while clinically important and diagnostically significant, can pose perplexing problems. These difficulties may stem from the complex nature of thought processes, the different theories and terms describing disturbed thinking, or the high value traditionally placed on disturbed thinking as a diagnostic sign. The complexity of disturbed thinking is best appreciated when one places thought processes on a continuum. This continuum extends from fallacious, erroneous, illogical thinking (usually exhibited by nonpsychiatric pa-tients) to mildly disturbed thinking (typically displayed by neurotics or individuals experiencing situational stress) to severely disturbed thinking (usually characteristic of schizophrenics). With the aid of clinical training, psychometric data, mental-status infor-mation, and empirical research, a clinician gains some sense of the diagnostic significance of thought disturbance. In contrast, intensive study of and exposure to the numerous theories and explanations about disturbed thinking tend to produce questions and confusion rather than concise answers (Loro, 1976). Some of these questions are a result of conflicting findings in the various studies of disturbed thinking. Chapman and Chapman (1973) contend that a significant portion of the research about disordered thinking possesses major methodological flaws, such as a lack of adequate control groups, biased sampling of subjects, and poorly constructed assessment instruments. These research deficiencies may partially explain the contradictory findings reported in professional publications. Other questions and areas of confusion may be a result of the complexity of disturbed thinking. Thinking is a complex internal process that is impossible to investigate directly. Clinicians must, therefore, evaluate the products (verbalizations) or results (responses to questions) of thinking rather than the actual thinking process. Because of this limitation, studies of disturbed thinking demand a high degree of clinical acumen, experimental rigor, and theoretical expertise. Unfortunately, only a few behavioral scientists meet these professional requirements and add some clarity to this confusing body of research. Typically, investigators of disturbed thinking are strong in clinical acumen and weak in experimental rigor and theoretical knowledge. At the same time, professional inertia results in clinicians' proliferating and elaborating traditional conceptualizations of disturbed thinking in spite of evidence to the contrary. For example, some practicing clinicians emphasize the presence of concretistic or personally overinvolved thinking as a critical factor in diagnosing schizophrenia (Chapman and Chapman, 1973)—even though numerous studies (Adler and Harrow, 1974; Davison and Neale, 1974; Maher, 1966) point out the need for alternative, multidimensional factors in diagnosing schizophrenia. Specifically, several relevant areas of functioning—including disturbances in mood, behavior, attention, and perception—must be considered along with an assessment of thought disturbance. For example, family communication patterns (Wynne and Singer, 1963), social-marital history (Phillips, 1953), and drug responsiveness (Skodol, Buckley, and Salamon, 1976) may all be important for diagnosing schizophrenia. Besides this systematic and comprehensive diagnostic approach, the clinician must be aware of the critical diagnostic significance of certain disorders of perception and attention (hallucinations) or cognition (delusions). These disorders are usually sufficient signs for diagnosing schizophrenia without the presence of severe thought disturbance (Davison and Neale, 1974).

Finally, there are no reliable and standardized methods or instruments for gathering data about disturbed thinking. As mentioned, traditional methods have been questioned and criticized. Andreasen (1977) found experienced mental health professionals unreliable in their efforts to evaluate the diagnostic meaning of patient proverb interpretations. And even though experienced clinicians may be able to determine the schizophrenicity of verbal responses (Hunt and Arnhoff, 1956; Hunt and Jones, 1958), they may not be able to consistently differentiate severely disturbed thought processes from unusual types of literary passages (Andreasen, Tsuang, and Canter, 1974). In short, in spite of the importance of disturbed thinking in clinical assessment, the evaluation of disturbed thinking lacks an adequate assessment technology.

Personal Views and Recommendations

Sophisticated clinical assessment requires the systematic collection and meticulous evaluation of all relevant data. When viewed in this context, the presence of disturbed thinking provides one important piece of a complicated psychodiagnostic puzzle. In past years, the value of disturbed thinking in the clinical assessment of schizophrenia was emphasized (Rapaport, 1951; Rapaport, Gill, and Schafer, 1946; Weiner, 1966). At the present time, the importance of disturbed thinking in clinical assessment appears over-emphasized and its usefulness as a critical diagnostic sign seems strained (Andreasen, Tsuang, and Canter, 1974; Harrow and Quinlan, 1977). A more reasonable clinical approach may involve viewing disturbed thinking as a necessary, but not sufficient, clinical sign of schizophrenia. Therefore, when a patient manifests severely disturbed thinking, the clinician will make a tentative diagnosis of schizophrenia and seek other pertinent corroborating evidence (Skodol, Buckley, and Salamon, 1976), prior to a final diagnosis. Overall, this assessment strategy is preferable to diagnosing schizophrenia purely on the basis of disturbed or severely disturbed thinking.

In addition to this general diagnostic recommendation, three specific recommendations pertain to disturbed thinking and its importance in training, certification, and continuing education. First, clinicians need to familiarize themselves with the basic types of disturbed thinking (Loro, 1976; Weiner, 1966). With this knowledge, the practicing clinician can make important clinical judgments about the form and severity of disturbed thinking (Adler and Harrow, 1974). Second, accurate clinical assessment requires evaluating the diagnostic significance of disturbed thinking vis-à-vis other symptoms (Andreasen, Tsuang, and Canter, 1974). This allows an examination of the degree of disturbed thinking in the context of other relevant diagnostic information (Harrow and Quinlan, 1977; Skodol, Buckley, and Salamon, 1976). Finally, in order to formulate appropriate psychotherapeutic and psychiatric treatment plans (Adler and Harrow, 1974; Maher, 1966; McCabe, 1976), the practicing clinician needs information about the prognostic importance of the various types and degrees of disturbed thinking.

Application to Particular Variables

The psychodiagnostic and prognostic significance of disturbed thinking during a clinical assessment seems dependent on one demographic variable and related to three dimensions of psychopathology. After the presence of severely disturbed thinking is detected, the developmental level of a patient needs to be considered. Specifically, normal or delayed adolescent turmoil may produce some relatively bizarre forms of thinking. These thought disturbances, however, are a result of the typical developmental crises of adolescence rather than a schizophrenic reaction (Weiner, 1966). Therefore, the presence of severely disturbed thinking in an adolescent may not be a clinical sign of schizophrenia.

In addition, when one is assessing the prognostic significance of severely disturbed thinking in adult schizophrenia, the type of onset, kind of premorbid adjustment (social and sexual adjustment prior to development of symptoms), and presence of paranoid ideation are important. Specifically, patients who experience an acute, rapid onset of schizophrenia tend to display relatively clear and blatant symptomatology, such as the presence of bizarre thinking. Usually, acute schizophrenia occurs in response to an emotionally painful experience. In contrast, chronic schizophrenic patients display a gradual, insidious onset of symptoms, which do not seem related to a particular incident or painful experience. Generally, patients diagnosed as acute schizophrenics have a better prognosis than patients diagnosed as chronic schizophrenics (Davison and Neale, 1974). Patients with a good premorbid adjustment tend to experience a more rapid onset of severe symptoms (blatant, idiosyncratic thought disturbance) than do patients with a poor premorbid adjustment (Phillips, 1953). Further, patients with a good premorbid adjustment tend to be equally divided between those who manifest paranoid symptoms (delusions) and those who do not; but almost all patients with a poor premorbid adjustment do not display paranoid symptoms (Goldstein, Held, and Cromwell, 1968; Neale, Kopfstein, and Levine, 1972). In short, an adult schizophrenic who manifests severely disturbed thinking or paranoid delusions, experiences acute problems, and had a good premorbid adjustment has an excellent treatment prognosis.

References

Adler, D., and Harrow, M. "Idiosyncratic Thinking and Personally Overinvolved Thinking in Schizophrenic Patients During Partial Recovery." *Comprehensive Psychiatry*, 1974, *15*, 57-67.

Andreasen, N. J. C. "Reliability and Validity of Proverb Interpretation to Assess Mental Status." *Comprehensive Psychiatry*, 1977, *18*, 465-472.

Andreasen, N. J. C., Tsuang, M. T., and Canter, A. "The Significance of Thought Disorder in Diagnostic Evaluations." *Comprehensive Psychiatry*, 1974, *15*, 27-34.

Arieti, S. *Interpretation of Schizophrenia.* (2nd ed.) New York: Basic Books, 1974.

Bleuler, E. *Dementia Praecox or the Group of Schizophrenias* [1911]. (J. Zinkin, Trans.) New York: International Universities Press, 1950.

Buss, A. H. *Psychopathology.* New York: Wiley, 1966.

Buss, A. H., and Lang, P. J. "Psychological Deficit in Schizophrenia. 1: Affect, Reinforcement and Concept Attainment." *Journal of Abnormal Psychology*, 1965, *70*, 2-24.

Cameron, N. "Reasoning, Regression, and Communication in Schizophrenics." *Psychology Monographs*, 1938, *50*, 1-34.

Cameron, N. "Deterioration and Regression in Schizophrenic Thinking." *Journal of Abnormal and Social Psychology*, 1939, *34*, 265-270.

Chapman, L. J., and Chapman, J. P. *Disordered Thought in Schizophrenia.* Englewood Cliffs, N.J.: Prentice-Hall, 1973.

Chapman, L. J., Chapman, J. P., and Miller, G. A. "A Theory of Verbal Behavior in Schizophrenia." In B. A. Maher (Ed.), *Progress in Experimental Personality Research.* Vol. 1. New York: Academic Press, 1964.

Davison, G. C., and Neale, J. M. *Abnormal Psychology: An Experimental Clinical Approach.* New York: Wiley, 1974.

Goldstein, M. J., Held, J. M., and Cromwell, R. L. "Premorbid Adjustment and Paranoid-Nonparanoid Status in Schizophrenia." *Psychological Bulletin*, 1968, *70*, 382-386.

Harrow, M., and Quinlan, D. "Is Disordered Thinking Unique to Schizophrenia?" *Archives of General Psychiatry*, 1977, *34*, 15-21.

Hunt, W. A., and Arnhoff, F. "The Repeat Reliability of Clinical Judgment of Test Responses." *Journal of Clinical Psychology*, 1956, *12*, 289-290.

Hunt, W. A., and Jones, N. F. "Clinical Judgment of Some Aspects of Schizophrenic Thinking." *Journal of Clinical Psychology*, 1958, *14*, 235-239.

Kraepelin, E. *Dementia Praecox and Paraphrenia* [1919]. (R. M. Barclay, Trans.) New York: Krieger, 1971.

Lang, P. J., and Buss, A. H. "Psychological Deficit in Schizophrenia. 2: Interference and Activation." *Journal of Abnormal Psychology*, 1965, *70*, 77-106.

Loro, B. "The Confusing Area of Disturbed Thinking." *Journal of Personality Assessment*, 1976, *40*, 475-482.

McCabe, M. S. "Symptom Differences in Reactive Psychoses and Schizophrenia with Poor Prognosis." *Comprehensive Psychiatry*, 1976, *17*, 301-307.

Maher, B. A. *Principles of Psychopathology.* New York: McGraw-Hill, 1966.

Neale, J. M., Kopfstein, J. H., and Levine, A. "Premorbid Adjustment and Paranoid

Status in Schizophrenia: Varying Assessment Techniques and the Influence of Chronicity." Paper presented at 80th annual convention of American Psychological Association, Honolulu, 1972.

Payne, R. W., and Hewlett, J. H. "Thought Disorder in Psychotic Patients." In H. J. Eysenck (Ed.), *Experiments in Personality*. Vol. 2. London: Routledge & Kegan Paul,
1960.

Phillips, L. "Case History Data and Prognosis in Schizophrenia." *Journal of Nervous and
Mental Disease*, 1953, *117*, 515-525.

Rapaport, D. *The Organization and Pathology of Thought*. New York: Columbia University Press, 1951.

Rapaport, D., Gill, M., and Schafer, R. *Diagnostic Psychological Testing*. Vol. 2. Chicago:
Year Book Medical Publishers, 1946.

Shakow, D. "Segmental Set: A Theory of the Formal Psychological Deficit in Schizophrenia." *Archives of General Psychiatry*, 1962, *6*, 17-33.

Shakow, D. "Psychological Deficit in Schizophrenia." *Behavior Science*, 1963, *8*,
275-305.

Skodol, A., Buckley, P., and Salamon, I. "The Ubiquitous Symptoms of Schizophrenia."
Comprehensive Psychiatry, 1976, *17*, 511-516.

Weiner, I. *Psychodiagnosis in Schizophrenia*. New York: Wiley, 1966.

Wynne, L. C., and Singer, M. T. "Thought Disorder and Family Relations in Schizophrenia. 2: A Classification of Forms of Thinking." *Archives of General Psychiatry*,
1963, *9*, 199-206.

39

Billie S. Lazar
Martin Harrow

Primitive Drive-Dominated Thinking

Primary process thinking, a concept that originated in psychoanalytic thinking and has been extended to nonanalytic approaches, is defined as a mode of thinking that disregards time and logical and realistic considerations and is dominated by instinctual drives (Holt, 1956). This has been contrasted with secondary process thinking, which is defined as a mode of thinking that is orderly, logical, and realistic. The mode of thinking is inferred from a

Preparation of this chapter was supported in part by Grant No. MH-26341 from the National Institute of Mental Health.

497

person's verbalizations or visual-motor productions, and primary process thinking may be identified either by illogical and unrealistic organization or by drive-dominated thinking. Drive-dominated thinking is a form of primary process thinking with libidinal or aggressive content. The two types of drive-dominated thinking are primitive drive-dominated thinking (direct, intense, raw, blatant, and inappropriate for social conversation) and socialized drive-dominated thinking (still a form of primary process thinking, but less direct, blatant, and raw and more appropriate for social conversation than primitive drive-dominated thinking).

Primitive drive-dominated thinking is hypothesized to become manifest when primitive drive material intrudes into awareness; that is, when id impulses seek expression or discharge or in response to environmental stimuli. One can use the term *primitive drive-dominated thinking* to describe behavioral manifestations or as a hypothetical construct to explain a range of behaviors.

The notion of drive-dominated thinking is based on the assumption that all thought and perception are to some extent organized by drives, as well as by the requirements of the external reality and of the logical structure of ideas. To distinguish primary process thinking from secondary process thinking (that is, orderly, logical, realistic thinking), Holt (1970a, 1956, 1966, 1977; Holt and Havel, 1960) notes that one must consider the extent to which drive is involved. In Holt's view, the more primary the thinking, the more it is organized and compelled by drives.

Primitive drive-dominated thinking has been measured by Holt's (1956, 1966, 1970a, 1970b, 1977; Holt and Havel, 1960) system for scoring Rorschach responses for primary process manifestations. The scoring system has two general categories of primary process manifestations: (1) content manifestations of libidinal and aggressive drive representations, which presumably reflect drive-dominated thinking; and (2) "formal" manifestations of thought, which reflect nondrive aspects of primary process thinking and which may be used to assess deviations from the logical, orderly, and realistic thinking that characterizes secondary process thought. Examples (from Holt, 1970b) of "formal" manifestations of primary process thinking which contain no libidinal or aggressive drive content include "The North Pole, because it is at the top," an example of autistic logic; "A butterfly," an example of a verbal condensation of bat and butterfly; and, "People flying through the air," an example of a contradiction of reality.

Each of the two kinds of drive-dominated thinking, libidinal and aggressive, may be manifested on a continuum from socially appropriate phenomena at the secondary process pole (socialized drive) to socially inappropriate phenomena at the primary process pole (primitive drive). The designation of libidinal and aggressive content as either primitive drive or socialized drive was made by Holt (1956) and is based on what he thought should be included on theoretical grounds and the results of several groups of Rorschach records (1977). In the following examples (from Holt, 1970b) the italicized term inside the parentheses is a manifestation of primitive drive-dominated thinking, and the other term is an example of socialized drive. Libidinal drive includes oral (*nursing,* eating), oral-aggressive (*cannibalism,* biting), anal (*excretory organs,* dirt), sexual (*genitalia,* marriage), exhibitionistic-voyeuristic (*nudity,* underwear), homosexuality (*overt homosexual act,* transvestism), and miscellaneous libidinal drive (*contraception,* embryo). Aggressive drive includes subject aggression (*murder,* fighting), object aggression (*being tortured,* illness), and results of aggression (*mutilated,* injured). Primitive subject aggression has been called sadistic aggression, and primitive object aggression has been called masochistic aggression.

Holt also assesses the controls and defenses which, according to psychoanalytic theory, are used to reduce the blatancy and increase the social appropriateness of the drive-dominated material, and the effectiveness with which these controls and defenses are employed. Note, however, that the concept of drive-dominated thinking can stand independently of the other components of Holt's system.

Background and Current Status

In his work on the theory of sexuality, Freud ([1905] 1953) defined an instinct or drive as a psychic representation of an inner somatic source of stimulation. He distinguished "drives," which are derived from erogenous zones (oral, anal, genital, and phallic), and "partial drives" (exhibitionistic, voyeuristic, sadistic, masochistic, homosexual, and narcissistic). In his paper on the two principles of mental functioning, Freud ([1911] 1958) discussed a pleasure principle, where the person gains gratification immediately and by any means, and a reality principle, where action is constrained by thought, tension is supported by delay, and gratification is obtained through realistic means. In 1915 Freud described an instinct as "a concept on the frontier between the mental and the somatic" (1957, p. 112); that is, a mental representation of internal stimuli and a measure of the demand made on the mind's energy. He continued to include sado-masochism under the sexual instincts. By 1920 (1955) and 1923 (1961a), Freud distinguished sexual instincts, whose energy is used by the ego to help the id master its tensions, from death instincts, which are expressed by destructive tendencies. In 1930 (1961b) he viewed the aggressive instincts as independent from, but secondary to, the libidinal instincts; finally, in 1933 (1964) he hypothesized two distinct classes of instincts, libidinal and aggressive.

Hartmann (1939) postulated two kinds of energy available for the ego's use: (1) The primary autonomous ego apparatuses (such as perception and memory) have neutral energy available for the ego's use. (2) Instinctual drive energy also may be neutralized; that is, freed drive may be made available for the ego's use (secondary autonomy of ego functions). Neutralization is a process by which libidinal or aggressive energies are changed to a noninstinctual form (Hartmann, 1964). Presumably, as energy becomes more neutralized, thinking changes from primary process to secondary process.

Various attempts have been made to operationalize drive-dominated thinking. The most prominent is Holt's system (1970b), described elsewhere in this chapter. Shaw (1948) and Pascal and others (1950) asked subjects whether they could see sexual content on the Rorschach ("testing the limits" for sex). Haley, Draguns, and Phillips (1967) and Lerner (1975) reviewed scales that assess aggression on the Rorschach. Elizur's (1949) Rorschach Content Test, the first to measure aggression systematically, differentiates more intense hostility from milder hostility. Other scales include DeVos's (1954) scale, which has scores for global hostility, oral aggression, and intentions; the Palo Alto Destructive Content Scale (Finney, 1955; Storment and Finney, 1953), which was validated against behavioral criteria; and Murstein's (1956) scale, which assesses the intensity of hostility and the place on the phylogenetic scale of the agent of hostility. Rychlack and O'Leary (1965) developed an "unhealthy content scale," which consists mainly of aggressive and exhibitionistic-voyeuristic content; since 15 to 20 percent of their samples of normal children and adolescents saw such content on the Rorschach, Rychlack and O'Leary conclude that it cannot be regarded as unhealthy.

Pine (1960) and Eagle (1964) modified Holt's (1956) measures so that they could be applied to the Thematic Apperception Test (TAT). Similarly, Harrow and associates (Harrow and Quinlan, 1973; Harrow and others, 1976; Quinlan, Harrow, and Carlson, 1973) combined Holt's categories to score for aggressive, oral, sexual (excluding homosexual), and miscellaneous (for example, anal or homosexual) drives.

Critical Discussion

General Areas of Concern

The concept of primitive drive-dominated thinking has at least five questions associated with it: (1) Is primitive drive-dominated thinking a situational variable or an enduring and stable one? (2) Do the standard measures that purport to assess this construct—measures such as the Holt (1970b) system—really measure it adequately? (3) Does primitive drive-dominated thinking differentiate among nosological groups? (4) How can one reconcile the issue of ego autonomy (Gill and Brenman, 1959; Holt, 1965a, 1967b; Miller, 1962; Rapaport, [1951] 1967a, [1953] 1967b, [1957] 1967c)—the independence of ego functions from drives—with the influence of primitive drives on perceptual organization and behavior? (5) Is the concept of primitive drive-dominated thinking viable, in view of theoretical formulations that the concept of drive energy may be unnecessary and that some motives may be completely autonomous from drives (Gill, 1959; Holt, 1965a, 1965b, 1967a, 1967b, 1976; Schafer, 1972, 1973a, 1973b; White, 1960, 1963)?

Situational or Stable Variable. One factor that relates to the stability of primitive drive-dominated thinking is the relative contribution of psychological variables and environmental variables. Primitive drive-dominated thinking has been operationalized according to what is raw and shocking and inappropriate for social discussion (Holt, 1970b). The subject's inability to *recognize* and edit possibly inappropriate expressions of drive content seems to play an important role in the overt appearance of the drive content and in some severe types of psychopathology (such as schizophrenic disorders), although the mechanisms by which the recognition and editing processes occur are poorly understood at present (Harrow, Oberlander, and Prosen, 1978; Harrow and Prosen, 1977, 1978). As social mores change, measures of primitive drive-dominated thinking may change accordingly; comparative studies then would be difficult to evaluate. If measures remain the same, apparent changes in drive-dominated thinking may be the result either of changes in social values or of actual differences among individuals. From previous research, questions around this issue have been raised to help explain the absence of a relationship between creativity and primitive drive-dominated thinking (Lazar, 1975, 1977). Similar reasoning would apply to cross-cultural studies.

Holt (1970b) notes that some studies (Gray, 1969; Phillip, 1959) have found much consistency in the production of primary process thinking over time. Heath (1965) reports that primitive material becomes less consistent over time. Other studies suggest that drive-dominated thinking can be changed by manipulating the individual or the environment. Researchers have been able to increase drive-dominated thinking by manipulating their subjects' state of consciousness through hypnosis (Fromm, Oberlander, and Gruenewald, 1970; Levin and Harrison, 1976; West, Baugh, and Baugh, 1963), by reading aggressive passages (Silverman, 1967; Silverman and Goldweber, 1966), inducing artificial hostility (Abrams, 1962, cited in Haley, Draguns, and Phillips, 1967), instruction (Eagle, 1964), and placing subjects in perceptual isolation (Goldberger, 1961), although perceptual isolation does not always result in an increase in drive-dominated thinking (Holt, 1965a; Miller, 1962).

Measures. One may question whether the libidinal and aggressive content scores defined by Holt (1970b) adequately operationalize the concept of primitive drive-dominated thinking. Holt's system was developed according to theoretical principles and some empirical Rorschach records and seems to have construct validity. However, after ten revisions (Holt, 1970b) the system still may not be complete and is subject to further change. Since primitive drive-dominated thinking is a construct and not a "thing," additional theoretical work and empirical studies using the Holt system can lend additional support, but not verification, to the question of whether the Holt system adequately measures primitive drive-dominated thinking.

Primitive drive-dominated thinking has been quantified according to Holt's (1970b) primitive (level 1) versus socialized (level 2) drive and his Defense Demand score, a six-point scale that reflects closeness to the primary process pole of thinking and the blatancy and social appropriateness of material. In addition, Goldberger's (1961) measure of adaptive regression, the product of Defense Demand and of a control score called Defense Effectiveness, takes into account both drive and the way it is handled. This latter measure is reminiscent of Anna Freud's ([1936] 1946) suggestion that, rather than "id impulse," one should speak of "id impulses modified by ego defensive means." Fishman (1973) notes that the adaptive regression score creates a mathematical artifact which is similar to the Defense Effectiveness rather than to the Defense Demand score; he concludes that the relevant factor is the capacity to deal adaptively with the primary process material, rather than the intensity of the primary process thinking. Similarly, Holt (1956, 1966, 1977; Holt and Havel, 1960) notes that drive may be used for fun or creative purposes through ego-controlled relaxation of defenses or because of ego weakness, which results in an involuntary breakthrough of this material. Thus, one view is that what is salient for understanding personality is the way in which drive is handled, rather than the level of drive as such. Other studies (discussed in the final section of this chapter) have found relationships between drive and other variables (such as sex and psychopathology).

Differentiating Groups. Many formulations have been made about the ability of measures to differentiate primitive drive-dominated thinking among nosological groups. The evidence available in this area is discussed in the final section of this chapter. While these formulations have much appeal, the evidence to support them is scanty, and results of research have varied considerably. Further empirical investigation is required to replicate previous studies in this area and to refine methodology. Similarly, results of research have varied in assessing whether primitive drive-dominated thinking differentiates creative from noncreative people. The question of whether this variable is useful for explaining personality is an open one.

Ego Autonomy. The issue of ego autonomy concerns the way in which ego functions exert control over drives and external stimuli. Ego autonomy involves controlled, active ego functioning in an organized way in which behavior is based on a decision that takes into account and evaluates drives, motives, and values as well as realistic considerations: the impairment of ego autonomy involves passive, uncontrolled ego functioning in an unorganized way in which behavior occurs without such a decision. Autonomy of the ego, as conceptualized by Hartmann ([1939] 1958) refers to the independence of ego functions from libidinal and aggressive drive energies. Rapaport ([1951] 1967a, [1953] 1967b, [1957] 1967c) characterizes ego autonomy as the ability to delay or modify a response so that behavior is not determined completely by drives or by external stimuli. To illustrate, consider a person with a strong wish to smoke who is unable to obtain a seat in the "smoking section" of an airplane. Autonomous ego functioning might include (1) a decision to delay smoking until the end of the flight with the pleasant anticipation of a cigarette, or (2) the negotiation of exchanging seats with a passenger in the "smoking section," while the impairment of ego autonomy might be reflected by the uncontrollable urge which leads a person to light a cigarette immediately without regard for airplane regulations or by experiencing an overwhelming discomfort about which he feels he can do nothing. Rapaport theorizes that the ability to respond to the drives "guarantees" relative autonomy from external stimuli in that behavior is not determined completely by the environment; conversely, he suggests that the ability to respond to external stimuli "guarantees" relative ego autonomy from the drives in that behavior is not determined completely by the drives. That is, Rapaport postulates that ego autonomy from id drives and ego autonomy from environmental stimulation have a reciprocal relationship. This hypothesis seems to assume that *either* drives *or* external stimuli determine behavior and does not seem to take into account synthesizing and reality-testing ego functions. Gill and Brenman (1959) note that autonomy does not mean absence of information, as Rapaport assumed; they view autonomy as the ability to deal with drive or external stimuli. Gill and Brenman conclude that autonomy from the drives and autonomy from environmental stimulation are related positively, rather than negatively, as Rapaport suggested. Miller (1962, p. 15) further characterizes ego autonomy as "a capacity for self-government in relation to demanding and nondemanding aspects of id and environment." He points out that behavior dominated by drives cannot be regarded as autonomous, and he agrees with Gill and Brenman that ego autonomy from the id and ego and autonomy from the environment have a corresponding relationship.

Using Holt's (1970b) system to operationalize drive and ego control (autonomy or activity), Lazar (1975) attempted to test the opposing views of Rapaport ([1957] 1967b) versus Miller (1962) and Gill and Brenman (1959). Results were inconclusive and pointed to the many problems in methodology, including operationalizing these concepts and over-simplifying a very complex problem.

Holt (1965b) notes that he cannot explain the mechanism by which an autonomous, active person is able to delay impulse, resist outer influences, and choose according to his or her values. Holt (1965a, p. 157) also suggests that rather than study the autonomy of the ego from the drives or the environment, a more useful study would be "to describe the relative roles of drive, external stimuli and press, and various inner structures in determining behavior, and the complex interactions between them." Holt's empirical system may be useful for examining the manner in which, and the conditions under which, primitive drive emerges and influences perceptual organization, and the ways in which ego structures control and modify drive influences.

Drive Energy and Motivation. Hyman (1975) has reviewed and evaluated various criticisms made against libido theory: (1) that it is both mechanistic and vitalistic; (2) that it anthropomorphizes and results in conceptual and language confusion; (3) that it is dualistic, mentalistic, and scientifically isolated; and (4) that psychoanalytic theory still is a young and immature body of thought. Hyman points out that arguments against libido theory pick on its weaknesses, which can be changed without changing the thrust of the theory itself. Other problems associated with the notion of drive energy are that (1) the concept can be measured only by the data it is supposed to explain; (2) it is incompatible with biological findings and with the notion that organisms are open rather than closed systems; and (3) it is not based on clinical observation (Holt, 1965b, 1967a, 1972; Schafer, 1973a). Taking a rather strong stance, Schafer (1972) has proposed a complete reformulation of psychoanalytic thinking and terminology, dispensing with the notion of instinctual drive whose psychic energy is discharged. More recently Holt (1977, p. 376), distinguishing the concept of primary process from that of energy, has stated that "much of what [Freud] wrote about the primary process was based upon clinical observation and profound insights that will have lasting value, whatever the fate of his metapsychological elaborations may be." In the same vein, Gill (1959) observes that the concept of primitive drive, rather than that of libido theory, is what psychoanalysts tend to defend.

Although Gill (1959) notes that primitive drive and nondrive factors play a role in determining behavior, motivation for him still seems to involve drives or drive derivatives. Hendrick's (1942) instinct to mastery and Mittleman's (1954) motility urge are in the direction of autonomous and noninstinctual ego motives. Similarly, White (1960) views Erickson's (1950) stages of development from the perspective that adaptive ability is an end in itself. He (1963) postulates that ego energies are independent of libidinal and aggressive instincts and conceives of an active ego serving the purpose of competence. He suggests that, although Freud initially defined the main function of the ego as mediating between the drives and the environment, the central concern should have been the process by which the ego relates with reality. Holt (1976) notes that, although sex and aggression are important, motives such as fear, anxiety, and curiosity also are important and cannot be reduced to sex or aggression. He has further demonstrated that the concept of drive can be replaced by the concept of wish for a more useful theory of motivation.

Elaboration on Critical Points

Several issues associated with the concept of primitive drive-dominated thinking have been discussed. On the one hand, some studies have found consistency in the production of primary process thinking over time, which suggests that it is a stable variable; on the other hand, drive-dominated thinking has been increased by manipulating the individual or the environment, which lends weight to the view that it is a situational variable. Some writers believe that the capacity to deal adaptively with drive, rather than the intensity of drive, is the salient variable for understanding personality, although this view is open to question. Results of studies vary in supporting the notion that primitive drive-dominated thinking differentiates among various groups, so that no conclusion can be drawn here. The issue of the autonomy of ego functions from libidinal and aggressive drive energies and from environmental stimuli still has not been resolved. Holt (1965a) suggests that a more useful study would be to consider the roles of drive, external stimuli, and internal structure in determining behavior. The notions of primary process and primitive drive-dominated thinking can stand independently of libido theory, which has several difficulties associated with it. Theories of motivation have ranged from involving only drives or drive derivatives to completely excluding them. Holt (1976), who notes the importance both of drive and nondrive variables, suggests that the concept of wish could replace the concept of drive for a more useful theory of motivation.

Personal Views and Recommendations

A drive theory of motivation is too simplistic and does not fit clinical observations. As Holt (1976) has noted, clinical observations of libidinal and aggressive manifestations are too important to be ignored, although other motivations (such as mastery, curiosity, and fear) also should not be forgotten. Appropriately, the metapsychological theory is being modified, and primitive drive-dominated thinking still has a place, but not the central place it previously occupied.

The energy model does not seem to be essential to the concept of primitive drive-dominated thinking, as Gill (1959) has pointed out, and has many problems associated with it. However, a conceptual dilemma arises. That is, the concept of primitive drive-dominated thinking may be meaningful when it is defined in terms of social appropriateness and the way in which drive is handled. Empirically, this concept has been found to relate to other variables; that is, it does appear to be valid. But does drive-dominated thinking have theoretical value in addition to construct validity and empirical validity? Some studies, using Holt's measures, have reported findings that are consistent with theoretical expectations (for example, Dudek, 1968; Rychlack and O'Leary, 1965; Zimet and Fine, 1965); but the results of other studies, such as the present authors' investigations of primitive drive-dominated thinking in schizophrenia and in creativity (Harrow and others, 1976; Lazar, 1975, 1977), were not consistent with theory. At this time, additional empirical studies and conceptual analysis of the concept of primitive drive-dominated thinking are needed.

Application to Particular Variables

Age. The Holt system for scoring the Rorschach was constructed from records taken from adults (Holt and Havel, 1960). Much of the research on primitive drive-dominated thinking has been with adults and college students, although some studies have been with children (Lucas, 1961; Rogolsky, 1968; Rychlack and O'Leary, 1965) and adolescents (Getzels and Jackson, 1962; Silverman, Lapkin, and Rosenbaum, 1962). No studies were found that applied the concept to geriatric subjects.

In a study of psychiatric patients aged 15 to 63, Pascal and others (1950) found a low negative relationship between age and number of genital symbols seen on the Rorschach; since they also found a negative relationship between total number of responses and age, total number of responses may be an intervening variable.

Sex. Males tend to manifest more hostility on the Rorschach than females (DeVos, 1954; Muramatsu, 1962; Rychlack and O'Leary, 1965). The study of psychiatric patients by Harrow and others (1976) revealed that males manifest more socialized drive on the Rorschach than females and show a tendency toward more primitive drive-dominated thinking and primitive sexual drive. Pascal and others (1950), however, found no difference between males and females in total number of sexual responses seen on the Rorschach; they found that males gave more vagina responses than penis responses and that females gave the same number of vagina responses as penis responses. In a sample of college students (Pine, 1960), females had more primary process on the Rorschach (and, by implication, more drive-dominated thinking) than males, although males manifested more variation in the poor control of this material.

Education. Hartmann ([1939] 1958) discussed the relationship between mental development and instinctual drive; he suggested that the taboo about instinctual drive hampers intellectual development. Fromm (1960) showed that the discharge of drive (for example, masturbation during the examination) may lead to failure on some Stanford-Binet items, and Rychlack and O'Leary (1965) found that people who express more "unhealthy content" (aggressive and exhibitionistic-voyeuristic content) have lower intelligence quotients. Pascal and associates (1950), however, found a low positive correlation between education and number of genital symbols seen on the Rorschach; educational level ranged from grades 4 through 16. In other studies, primitive oral drive and intelligence were found to be positively correlated (Holt, 1966), and subjects who passed the Hanfmann-Kasanin Concept Formation test in less than thirty minutes gave more oral responses on the Rorschach than those who took over thirty minutes; aggressive responses did not differentiate the two groups (Von Holt and others, 1960). Pine (1959) found almost no primitive drive on a science test, and a small, nonsignificant positive correlation between primitive drive and literary quality on the TAT; he did find that overall drive was positively related to literary quality. Among subjects of above average intelligence, highly creative (and relatively less intelligent) adolescents expressed more aggression and violence than less creative (and more intelligent) adolescents (Getzels and Jackson, 1962). In several studies primitive drive-dominated thinking (Lazar, 1975, 1977) and primary process thinking (Pine, 1962; Rogolsky, 1968) generally were not related to creativity, although Pine's results varied according to his sample. Gray (1969) also suggests that the positive relationship found between creativity and primary process is the result of a common variable, productivity.

Socioeconomic Status. Holt's system was constructed on well-educated adults with high socioeconomic status (SES) (Holt and Havel, 1960). The working hypothesis by Harrow and others (1976) is that primitive drive-dominated thinking is related to several factors—among them, the lack, or the loss, of social skills which were learned over the course of development in our society; the authors assume that the upper-middle-class patient population had good "training" in controlling socially inappropriate drive material. Rychlack and O'Leary (1965) found that more unhealthy content comes from lower-SES children than higher-SES children, which they relate to the fact that low-SES people are open, honest, sincere, and straightforward.

Vocation. Among male unemployed actors, primitive oral drive correlated with enjoying sensuous experience, achievement drive, and intellect, and primitive anal drive correlated with poor functioning (Holt, 1966). Actors exceeded stage directors in the production of primary process material (Ribeiro da Silva, 1962). Fromm (1969) scored primitive drive-dominated thinking in two paintings by the Dutch painter Hieronymus Bosch and then speculated on his personality dynamics. Dudek (1968) found that good artists manifest more controlled primitive drive-dominated thinking than bad artists. She (1970) also found that writers have more oral aggression than painters; the writers tended to be more concerned with sex and aggression, and the painters with identity. Lazar (1975, 1977) found that art students use more socialized drive on the Rorschach than business students, but these two groups do not differ in primitive drive-dominated thinking.

Among psychotherapists, control of primary process is necessary for conjunctive empathy (Bachrach, 1968). Peace Corps trainees who completed their assignment in Africa during a border war manifested more active object aggression on the Rorschach than those who did not (Sullivan and Bernstein, 1963).

Ethnic-Racial Factors. DeVos (1954) found no difference in total hostile responses of three groups of Japanese Americans (Issei, Kibei, and Nisei), although the groups differed in kinds of hostility; sado-masochism was more prevalent in the Japanese than in a sample of Americans. Muramatsu (1962) used the DeVos (1954) hostility scores in a stratified and representative sample of Japanese.

Nonpsychotic Anglo-Saxon, Mexican, and Negro psychiatric patients did not differ in "open" or actual hostility on the Rorschach. The Anglo-Saxons and Mexicans, however, exceeded the Negroes in potential hostility, while the Negroes showed more "victim hostility," suggesting a sense of being surrounded by impending violence (Johnson and Sikes, 1965).

Physical Disorders. Banks (1962) found a relationship between primary process thinking and recovery from tuberculosis. In normals, Oberlander (1967) found a positive relationship between primitive drive-dominated thinking and autonomic arousal, measured by pupil dilation.

Organic Dysfunction. An increase in primary process thinking was related to taking lysergic acid diethylamide (LSD) (Phillip, 1959). Tucker, Quinlan, and Harrow (1972), using samples of drug-taking (mostly LSD) and nondrug-taking psychiatric patients, found that drug-taking patients showed more primitive drive-dominated thinking; the two groups did not differ as much in other signs of "formal" thought disorder. These investigators conclude that drug taking does not cause an increase in primitive drive-dominated thinking but that use of drugs is a result, in part, of "drive-dominated" aspects of premorbid personality.

Functional Disorders. Results differentiating diagnostic categories have varied. In one study, number of sexual responses on the Rorschach did not differentiate normals, neurotics, and psychotics, although more paranoids gave anal responses than normals and other psychotics (Pascal and others, 1950). Haley, Draguns, and Phillips (1967) note that the Palo Alto scale of aggression (Finney, 1955; Storment and Finney, 1953) distinguished normals, neurotics, and schizophrenics, while the Elizur (1949) scale did not.

Moylan, Shaw, and Appleman (1960) scored the Rorschach protocols of paranoid schizophrenics and passive-dependent and passive-aggressive personalities for aggressive, passive, and neutral responses. In support of their hypotheses, passive-aggressive patients gave more aggressive responses than passive-dependent or paranoid patients, and passive-dependent patients gave a greater percentage of passive responses. Due to procedural and scoring difficulties, they suggest that results be interpreted cautiously.

Beres (1956) and Bellak (1966) believe that schizophrenics have difficulty in regulating and controlling instinctual drives. Research suggests that schizophrenics give poorly controlled oral-aggressive responses (Lavoie, 1964). Adolescent schizophrenics and adolescent neurotics and personality disorders do not differ in primitive drive on the Rorschach, although the neurotics and personality disorders have somewhat more controlled primitive drive (Silverman, Lapkin, and Rosenbaum, 1962).

In this same area, Harrow and others (1976) found that primitive drive-dominated thinking only weakly differentiated young acute schizophrenic patients from young nonschizophrenic psychiatric patients, although other aspects of bizarre and primary process thinking differentiated these groups at higher levels of significance. This study also found that process schizophrenics and reactive schizophrenics did not differ in primitive drive-dominated thinking. In Zimet and Fine's (1965) sample, however, process schizophrenics used more primary process thinking than reactive schizophrenics. In an exploratory study, bizarre and idiosyncratic responses on a proverbs test were not a function of intrusion of primitive drive material (Harrow and Prosen, 1978). The research team interpreted these results as suggesting that drive-dominated thinking is not the major cause of bizarre schizophrenic language. Saretsky (1966) found that schizophrenics treated with chlorpromazine improved in coping ability of primitive primary process (he implied drive-dominated thinking), although the amount and extent of primitiveness were not reduced.

Harrow and others (1976) found that patients with sociopathic tendencies revealed more signs of primitive drive-dominated thinking than those who did not have these tendencies.

References

Abrams, S. "A Refutation of Erikson's Sensitization-Defense Hypothesis." *Journal of Projective Techniques,* 1962, *26,* 259-265.

Bachrach, H. "Adaptive Regression, Empathy, and Psychotherapy: A Theory and Research Study." *Psychotherapy,* 1968, *5,* 203-209.

Banks, H. C. "The Relationship of the Flexibility of Ego Defenses to the Rate of Recovery in Tuberculosis Patients." Unpublished doctoral dissertation, New York University, 1962.

Bellak, L. "The Schizophrenic Syndrome: A Further Elaboration of the Unified Theory of Schizophrenia." In L. Bellak (Ed.), *Schizophrenia: A Review of the Syndrome.* New York: Grune & Stratton, 1966.

Beres, D. "Ego Deviation and the Concept of Schizophrenia." *Psychoanalytic Study of the Child,* 1956, *11,* 142-177.

DeVos, G. "A Comparison of the Personality Differences in Two Generations of Japanese-Americans by Means of the Rorschach Test." *Nagoya Journal of Medical Science,* 1954, *17,* 153-265.

Dudek, S. Z. "Regression and Creativity." *Journal of Nervous and Mental Disease,* 1968, *147,* 535-546.

Dudek, S. Z. "The Artist as a Person." *Journal of Nervous and Mental Disease,* 1970, *150,* 232-241.

Eagle, C. J. "An Investigation of Individual Consistencies in the Manifestations of Primary Process." Unpublished doctoral dissertation, New York University, 1964.

Elizur, A. "Content Analysis of the Rorschach with Regard to Anxiety and Hostility." *Rorschach Research Exchange and Journal of Projective Techniques,* 1949, *13,* 247-287.

Erikson, E. H. *Childhood and Society.* New York: Norton, 1950.

Finney, B. C. "Rorschach Test Correlates of Assaultive Behavior." *Journal of Projective Techniques,* 1955, *19,* 6-16.

Fishman, D. B. "Holt's Rorschach Measure of Adaptive Regression, Mathematical Artifact, and Prediction of Psychotherapy Outcome." *Journal of Personality Assessment,* 1973, *37,* 328-333.

Freud, A. *The Ego and the Mechanisms of Defence* [1936]. New York: International Universities Press, 1946.

Freud, S. *Three Essays on the Theory of Sexuality* [1905]. In *Standard Edition of the Complete Psychological Works of Sigmund Freud.* Vol. 7. London: Hogarth Press, 1953.

Freud, S. "Formulations Regarding Two Principles in Mental Functioning" [1911]. In *Standard Edition of the Complete Psychological Works of Sigmund Freud.* Vol. 12. London: Hogarth Press, 1958.

Freud, S. "Instincts and Their Vicissitudes" [1915]. In *Standard Edition of the Complete Psychological Works of Sigmund Freud.* Vol. 14. London: Hogarth Press, 1957.

Freud, S. *Beyond the Pleasure Principle* [1920]. In *Standard Edition of the Complete Psychological Works of Sigmund Freud.* Vol. 18. London: Hogarth Press, 1955.

Freud, S. *The Ego and the Id* [1923]. In *Standard Edition of the Complete Psychological Works of Sigmund Freud.* Vol. 19. London: Hogarth Press, 1961a.

Freud, S. *Civilization and Its Discontents* [1930]. In *Standard Edition of the Complete Psychological Works of Sigmund Freud.* Vol. 21. London: Hogarth Press, 1961b.

Freud, S. *New Introductory Lectures on Psychoanalysis* [1933]. In *Standard Edition of the Complete Psychological Works of Sigmund Freud.* Vol. 22. London: Hogarth Press, 1964.

Fromm, E. "Projective Aspects of Intelligence Tests." In A. I. Rabin and M. R. Haworth (Eds.), *Projective Techniques with Children.* New York: Grune & Stratton, 1960.

Fromm, E. "The Manifest and the Latent Content of Two Paintings by Hieronymus Bosch: A Contribution to the Study of Creativity." *American Imago,* 1969, *26,* 145-166.

Fromm, E., Oberlander, M. I., and Gruenewald, D. "Perceptual and Cognitive Processes in Different States of Consciousness: The Waking State and Hypnosis." *Journal of Projective Techniques and Personality Assessment,* 1970, *34,* 375-387.

Getzels, J. W., and Jackson, P. W. *Creativity and Intelligence.* New York: Wiley, 1962.

Gill, M. M. "The Present State of Psychoanalytic Theory." *Journal of Abnormal and Social Psychology,* 1959, *58,* 1-8.

Gill, M. M., and Brenman, M. *Hypnosis and Related States.* New York: International Universities Press, 1959.

Goldberger, L. "Reactions to Perceptual Isolation and Rorschach Manifestations of Primary Process." *Journal of Projective Techniques,* 1961, *25,* 287-302.

Gray, J. J. "The Effect of Productivity on Primary Process and Creativity." *Journal of Projective Techniques and Personality Assessment,* 1969, *33,* 213-218.

Haley, M., Draguns, J. G., and Phillips, L. "Studies of Rorschach Content: A Review of Research Literature. Part II: Nontraditional Uses of Content Indicators." *Journal of Projective Techniques and Personality Assessment,* 1967, *31,* 3-38.

Harrow, M., Oberlander, J., and Prosen, M. "How Does Bizarre Schizophrenic Language

Originate?" Paper presented at 131st annual meeting of American Psychiatric Association, Atlanta, May 8-12, 1978.

Harrow, M., and Prosen, M. "Schizophrenic Associations and Intermingling." In *Scientific Proceedings of the 130th Annual Meeting of the American Psychiatric Association.* Washington, D.C.: American Psychiatric Association, 1977.

Harrow, M., and Prosen, M. "Intermingling and Disordered Logic as Influences on Schizophrenic 'Thought Disorders.' " *Archives of General Psychiatry,* 1978, *35,* 1213-1218.

Harrow, M., and Quinlan, D. "Primary Process Thinking and Schizophrenia." Paper presented at 126th Annual Meeting of the American Psychiatric Association, Honolulu, May 7-11, 1973.

Harrow, M., and others. "Primitive Drive-Dominated Thinking: Relationship to Acute Schizophrenia and Sociopathy." *Journal of Personality Assessment,* 1976, *40,* 31-41.

Hartmann, H. *Ego Psychology and the Problem of Adaptation* [1939]. New York: International Universities Press, 1958.

Hartmann, H. *Essays on Ego Psychology: Selected Problems in Psychoanalytic Theory.* New York: International Universities Press, 1964.

Heath, D. H. *Explorations of Maturity.* New York: Appleton-Century-Crofts, 1965.

Hendrick, I. "Instinct and the Ego During Infancy." *Psychoanalytic Quarterly,* 1942, *11,* 33-58.

Holt, R. R. "Gauging Primary and Secondary Processes in Rorschach Responses." *Journal of Projective Techniques,* 1956, *20,* 14-25.

Holt, R. R. "Ego Autonomy Re-evaluated." *International Journal of Psychoanalysis,* 1965a, *46,* 151-167.

Holt, R. R. "A Review of Some of Freud's Biological Assumptions and Their Influence on His Theories." In N. S. Greenfield and W. C. Lewis (Eds.), *Psychoanalysis and Current Biological Thought.* Madison: University of Wisconsin Press, 1965b.

Holt, R. R. "Measuring Libidinal and Aggressive Motives and Their Controls by Means of the Rorschach Test." In D. Levine (Ed.), *Nebraska Symposium on Motivation.* Lincoln: University of Nebraska Press, 1966.

Holt, R. R. "Beyond Vitalism and Mechanism: Freud's Concept of Psychic Energy." In J. H. Masserman (Ed.), *Science and Psychoanalysis.* Vol. 11. New York: Grune & Stratton, 1967a.

Holt, R. R. "On Freedom, Autonomy, and the Redirection of Psychoanalytic Theory: A Rejoinder." *International Journal of Psychiatry,* 1967b, *3,* 524-536.

Holt, R. R. "Implication of Some Contemporary Personality Theories for Rorschach Rationale." In B. Klopfer and others (Eds.), *Developments in the Rorschach Technique.* Vol. 1. New York: Harcourt Brace Jovanovich, 1970a.

Holt, R. R. *Manual for the Scoring of Primary Process Manifestations in Rorschach Responses.* (10th ed.) New York: Research Center for Mental Health, New York University, 1970b.

Holt, R. R. "Freud's Mechanistic and Humanistic Images of Man." In R. R. Holt and E. Peterfreund (Eds.), *Psychoanalysis and Contemporary Science.* New York: Macmillan, 1972.

Holt, R. R. "Drive or Wish? A Reconsideration of the Psychoanalytic Theory of Motivation." *Psychological Issues,* 1976, *9* (whole No. 36).

Holt, R. R. "A Method for Assessing Primary Process Manifestations and Their Control in Rorschach Responses." In M. A. Rickers-Ovsiankina (Ed.), *Rorschach Psychology.* (2nd ed.) New York: Krieger, 1977.

Holt, R. R., and Havel, J. "A Method for Assessing Primary and Secondary Process in the

Rorschach." In M. A. Rickers-Ovsiankina (Ed.), *Rorschach Psychology*. New York: Wiley, 1960.

Hull, C. L. *Principles of Behavior*. New York: Appleton-Century-Crofts, 1943.

Hyman, M. "In Defense of Libido Theory." *Annual Review of Psychoanalysis*, 1975, *3*, 21-36.

Johnson, D. L., and Sikes, M. P. "Rorschach and TAT Responses of Negro, Mexican-American, and Anglo Psychiatric Patients." *Journal of Projective Techniques and Personality Assessment*, 1965, *29*, 183-188.

Lavoie, G. "Les Processus Primaires et Secondaires chez les Mères d'Enfants Schizophrènes." Unpublished doctoral dissertation, University of Montreal, 1964.

Lazar, B. S. "Creativity, Primary Process Manifestations, and Ego Activity and Passivity." Unpublished doctoral dissertation, University of Chicago, 1975.

Lazar, B. S. "Creativity and Regression on the Rorschach." Paper presented at meeting of American Psychological Association, San Francisco, August 1977.

Lerner, P. M. "Assessing Hostility by Means of the Rorschach: A Review." In P. M. Lerner (Ed.), *Handbook of Rorschach Scales*. New York: International Universities Press, 1975.

Levin, L. A., and Harrison, R. H. "Hypnosis and Regression in the Service of the Ego." *International Journal of Clinical and Experimental Hypnosis*, 1976, *24*, 400-418.

Lucas, W. B. "The Effects of Frustration and the Rorschach Responses of Nine-Year-Old Children." *Journal of Projective Techniques*, 1961, *25*, 199-204.

Miller, S. C. "Ego Autonomy in Sensory Deprivation, Isolation, and Stress." *International Journal of Psychoanalysis*, 1962, *43*, 1-20.

Mittleman, B. "Motility in Infants, Children, and Adults: Patterning and Psychodynamics." *Psychoanalytic Study of the Child*, 1954, *9*, 142-177.

Moylan, J. J., Shaw, J., and Appleman, W. "Passive and Aggressive Responses to the Rorschach by Passive-Aggressive Personalities and Paranoid Schizophrenics." *Journal of Projective Techniques*, 1960, *24*, 17-20.

Muramatsu, T. (Ed.). *Nihonjin: Bunka to Pasonarity no Jissho-Taki Kenkyu (The Japanese: Study in Culture and Personality)*. Nagoya: Reimei Shobo, 1962.

Murstein, B. I. "The Projection of Hostility on the Rorschach and as a Result of Ego Threat." *Journal of Projective Techniques*, 1956, *20*, 418-428.

Oberlander, M. I. "Pupillary Reaction Correlates of Adaptive Regression." Unpublished doctoral dissertation, University of Chicago, 1967.

Pascal, G. R., and others. "A Study of Genital Symbols on the Rorschach Test: Presentation of Method and Results." *Journal of Abnormal and Social Psychology*, 1950, *45*, 286-295.

Phillip, A. E. "The Effect of Lysergic Acid Diethylamide (LSD-25) on Primary Process Thought Manifestations." Unpublished doctoral dissertation, New York University, 1959.

Pine, F. "Thematic Drive Content and Creativity." *Journal of Personality*, 1959, *27*, 136-151.

Pine, F. "A Manual for Rating Drive Content in the Thematic Apperception Test." *Journal of Projective Techniques*, 1960, *24*, 32-45.

Pine, F. "Creativity and Primary Process: Sample Variations." *Journal of Nervous and Mental Disease*, 1962, *134*, 506-511.

Quinlan, D., Harrow, M., and Carlson, K. *Manual for Assessment of Deviant Responses on the Rorschach*. (ASIS/NAPS #02211.) New York: Microfiche Publications, 1973.

Rapaport, D. "The Autonomy of the Ego" [1951]. In M. M. Gill (Ed.), *The Collected Papers of David Rapaport.* New York: Basic Books, 1967a.

Rapaport, D. "Some Metapsychological Considerations Concerning Activity and Passivity" [1953]. In M. M. Gill (Ed.), *The Collected Papers of David Rapaport.* New York: Basic Books, 1967b.

Rapaport, D. "The Theory of Ego Autonomy: A Generalization" [1957]. In M. M. Gill (Ed.), *The Collected Papers of David Rapaport.* New York: Basic Books, 1967c.

Ribeiro da Silva, A. "Atrizes, Atôres, e Diretores do Brasil Através do Teste de Rorschach." *Arquivos Brasileiros de Psicotécnia,* 1962, *14,* 5-30.

Rogolsky, M. M. "Artistic Creativity and Adaptive Regression in Third Grade Children." *Journal of Projective Techniques and Personality Assessment,* 1968, *32,* 53-62.

Rychlak, J. F., and O'Leary, L. R. "Unhealthy Content in Rorschach Responses of Children and Adolescents." *Journal of Projective Techniques and Personality Assessment,* 1965, *29,* 354-367.

Saretsky, T. "Effects of Chlorpromazine on Primary Process Thought Manifestations." *Journal of Abnormal Psychology,* 1966, *71,* 247-252.

Schafer, R. "Internalization: Process or Fantasy?" *Psychoanalytic Study of the Child,* 1972, *27,* 411-436.

Schafer, R. "Action: Its Place in Psychoanalytic Interpretation and Theory." *Annual of Psychoanalysis,* 1973a, *1,* 159-196.

Schafer, R. "Concepts of Self and Identity and the Experience of Separation-Individuation in Adolescence." *Psychiatric Quarterly,* 1973b, *42,* 42-59.

Shaw, B. " 'Sex Populars' in the Rorschach Test." *Journal of Abnormal and Social Psychology,* 1948, *43,* 466-470.

Silverman, L. H. "A Study of the Effects of Subliminally Presented Aggressive Stimuli on the Production of Pathologic Thinking in a Nonpsychiatric Population." *Journal of Nervous and Mental Disease,* 1965, *141,* 443-455.

Silverman, L. H. "An Experimental Approach to the Study of Dynamic Propositions in Psychoanalysis: The Relationship Between the Aggressive Drive and Ego Regressions." *Journal of American Psychoanalytic Association,* 1967, *15,* 376-403.

Silverman, L. H., and Goldweber, A. M. "A Further Study of the Effects of Subliminal Aggressive Stimulation on Thinking." *Journal of Nervous and Mental Disease,* 1966, *143,* 463-472.

Silverman, L. H., Lapkin, B., and Rosenbaum, I. S. "Manifestations of Primary Process Thinking in Schizophrenics." *Journal of Projective Techniques,* 1962, *26,* 117-127.

Storment, C. T., and Finney, B. C. "Projection and Behavior: A Rorschach Study of Assaultive Mental Hospital Patients." *Journal of Projective Techniques,* 1953, *17,* 349-360.

Sullivan, J. S., and Bernstein, I. "Personality Measures of Peace Corps Volunteers to Somalia." Unpublished manuscript, New York University, 1963.

Tucker, G. J., Quinlan, D., and Harrow, M. "Chronic Hallucinogenic Drug Use and Thought Disturbance." *Archives of General Psychiatry,* 1972, *27,* 443-447.

Von Holt, H. W., and others. "Orality, Image Fusions, and Concept-Formation." *Journal of Projective Techniques,* 1960, *24,* 194-198.

West, J. V., Baugh, V. S., and Baugh, A. P. "Rorschach and Draw-a-Person Responses of Hypnotized and Non-hypnotized Subjects." *Psychiatric Quarterly,* 1963, *37,* 123-127.

White, R. W. "Competence and the Psychosexual Stages of Development." In Marshall R.

Jones (Ed.), *Nebraska Symposium on Motivation.* Lincoln: University of Nebraska Press, 1960.

White, R. W. "Ego and Reality in Psychoanalytic Theory." *Psychological Issues,* 1963, *3,* Monograph 11.

Zimet, C. N., and Fine, H. J. "Primary and Secondary Process Thinking in Two Types of Schizophrenia." *Journal of Projective Techniques and Personality Assessment,* 1965, *29,* 93-99.

40

Michael Hirt
Judy Genshaft

Information-
Processing Deficit

Information processing is most frequently conceptualized within a cybernetics model; that is, the organism is perceived as a computer. Within such a framework, information processing involves an attentional or input stage, during which stimuli or information from the environment enters the system and is used in forming a memory code. Subsequently, the organism has to store, categorize, and organize this information in a manner that will facilitate its retrieval. Finally, the organism has to examine the categories it has developed, make various decisions concerning the relevance and suitability of available information, and select the appropriate response.

There are many reasons why this process may not function optimally and why incorrect or otherwise inappropriate responses may result. For example, incomplete, incorrect, or irrelevant units of information may enter the system because of faulty initial screening of available stimuli. Correct information may become "lost" in the system because of memory deficits created by lags in information-processing time or because of interference effects by excessive and/or inappropriately selected units of information or distracting associations elicited by internal (or external) stimuli. Finally, incorrect responses may be selected because higher-order processing or integration is hampered by central nervous system impairment or cognitive deficits often found in thinking disorders.

Background and Current Status

An early conceptualization of the relevance of information processing to clinical behavior was Bleuler's (1911) distinction between those schizophrenics who process too little information from the environment and those who process too much information. In the area of minimal brain damage, there has also been considerable theorizing about a possible attentional deficit. Laufer and Denhoff (1957) postulated a lack of cortical control over subcortical areas as a consequence of either a failure of inhibitory control or filtering mechanisms in the cortex.

In the area of psychodiagnostic assessment, particularly within an ego psychology framework, increasing attention has been focused on cognitive or perceptual organization. Thus, instead of emphasizing interpersonal or intrapersonal dynamics in assessment, the hierarchical organization and integration of psychological processes are examined.

The role of information processing evolved very differently in assessment and psychopathology. Both were greatly influenced, however, by the "New Look" in perception, which emerged in the late 1940s (Klein, 1951). This approach emphasized relationships between dynamic aspects of personality and observable behavioral concomitants. Thus, relationships between styles of defense and styles of perception were sought, in order to identify the broader range of perceptual and character patterns referred to as cognitive styles.

In assessment, interest developed in the role of stylistic variables as modifiers and determinants in the processing and organizing of environmental data. Test responses were used to make inferences about people's ability to integrate thought and affect, delay and control expression, and relate the stylistic variables to current environmental demands. The emphasis was on behavioral manifestations of defense mechanisms and their effectiveness in maintaining adaptive functioning.

In psychopathology, cognitive variables, particularly the information processing of schizophrenic patients, were beginning to be examined. Focusing on attentional deficits, most cognitive theories evolved within Broadbent's (1958) filtering model. According to this model, cognitive impairment occurs because limited information is available for processing. Specifically, a breakdown in the initial or attentional filtering of environmental information results in the "overloading" of the individual's capacity to process information. This overloading with both relevant and distracting stimuli causes a failure in the process of selecting and, therefore, in responding to relevant stimuli.

Current usage of psychological tests is most meaningful from the premise that test data reflect broad organizing forces. Critical variables (such as perceptual styles, the use of memory, and the nature of thought associations) operate within a framework that is organized and patterned. Concurrent with this orientation, such functions as intelligence (which previously had been considered a relatively independent and discrete trait) are now evaluated within a framework of integrated and interrelated personality functioning. Intelligence is viewed as an area of application of basic personality resources, in which certain functions (such as perception and memory and organization) are brought to bear in problem-solving situations.

As indices of psychological deficit in clinical groups, models of information processing differ on the basis of where in this process they postulate the locus of the deficit to occur. Attentional theories emphasize the faulty input of information. These theories have evolved from observations of performance on two general types of tasks: (1) those in which extraneous cues are to be ignored and (2) those in which a large number of cues must be sampled. From both types of tasks, it appears that attention can be divided into an initial stage, in which stimuli are simply registered by the senses, and a second stage, in which information is temporarily stored in the form of a "picture" or image of the stimuli. Information is processed only from this storage stage or icon (Neisser, 1967). Because the icon decomposes very rapidly, selection of the necessary and appropriate information must be accomplished promptly. Even if this step is accomplished adequately, subsequent information processing may suffer because the organism is capable of processing only a limited amount of information per unit of time (Broadbent, 1958). This limitation, coupled with the rapid decay of information stored in the icon, also serves to severely limit the amount of information actually processed and available for processing. A filtering mechanism is often hypothesized to select the information that gets screened or selected for passage to a decision-making channel, which also has access to long-term storage of information.

In addition to schizophrenic patients, individuals with minimal brain damage have been described as deficient in sustained attentiveness. Their performance on simple and complex tasks (for example, reaction time, vigilance, and scanning rates) indicates that they are cortically underaroused, respond more impulsively than controls, and experience greater difficulty with various complex attainment tasks.

Critical Discussion

General Areas of Concern

It is difficult to evaluate the status of information-processing deficit unless one has a good working definition of attention. Unfortunately, no widely accepted definition is available (Neale and Cromwell, 1970). Partly to resolve this dilemma, six broad subdivisions of attention have been suggested: (1) concentration on a given task and attempted exclusion of potentially interfering stimuli; (2) vigilance, which suggests a state of readiness in the hope of detecting a prespecified event whenever it occurs; (3) selective attention, in which stimuli from only one source are registered and responded to; (4) scanning behavior, which involves searching among a set of stimuli for a predetermined subset or single stimulus; (5) activation, which is similar to vigilance but is a more general state of arousal and preparedness for any forthcoming event; and (6) set, a preparation to respond cognitively or motorically in a certain way.

One useful method for dealing with the various phenomena included in "attention" is to emphasize intensiveness and selectiveness (Berlyne, 1970). Intensiveness describes fluctuations in the general state of the individual and his total processing capacity over time. Selectiveness refers to the distribution of the individual's processing capacity among the stimuli within his perceptual field. While the intensive and selective aspects of attention are not independent, they are influenced by such situational variables as the rate of incoming stimulation and the response requirements of the task.

Dykman and Ackerman (1976) have schematically presented the interrelationship between behavior and aspects of information processing (see Figure 1). They point out the circular nature of behavior, insofar as a given behavior may be a consequence of deficiencies in one or more of these basic processes and may also be a precipitant by interfer-

Figure 1. Schematic Representation of Interrelationship Between Behavior and
Aspects of Information Processing

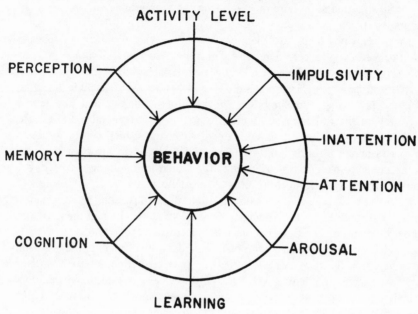

ing with other processes. Nevertheless, it is possible to describe an information-processing model that relies primarily on arousal, attention, memory, and central processing.

Arousal has a major role in sensitizing the individual to respond. While this is a relatively discriminant process (in the sense of maximal sensitization taking place in those parts of the central nervous system most involved with and necessary for responding to a given set of stimuli), arousal is also a global phenomenon (because even the simplest responses involve so much of the nervous system). Arousal thus activates the organism's filtering systems and attention. Indeed, the activation of attention implies that a certain amount of filtering or selectivity has already occurred and that attention is focused and directed. Furthermore, competing stimuli may elicit various degrees of intensity of arousal; the stimulus eliciting the most intense arousal generally is attended to, whereas other stimuli, whose arousal potential is less intense, are excluded.

Arousal may activate the organism to attend to either internal or external events. When it is attending to external events, there is usually a reduction in those functions associated with attention to internal events, such as long-term memory and central processing (although these two modes of attending are not mutually exclusive).

After attending to stimuli, particularly from external events, the organism must store the information in short-term memory. This is memory for recent events and tends to decay within minutes unless events are rehearsed. Short-term memory is limited in the amount of information it can retain. This limit is highly variable; once it is reached, however, information has to be either eliminated or consolidated before new information can be stored. This process of elimination or storage requires central processing strategies and is not carried out by short-term memory itself.

While short-term memory holds recently acquired information, long-term memory holds old information, acquired over a span of time ranging from the immediate past to a lifetime ago. In spite of this vast range of information, long-term memory is not infinite, and there is a constant exchange, with information from short-term memory being transferred to and replacing material held in long-term memory. The efficiency and permanency of information stored are most influenced by the primacy of material, which leads to the most efficient information storage, and by the extent to which materials are mentally rehearsed, which helps give them greater permanency. Primacy and rehearsal are, in turn, influenced by such considerations as the organism's state of arousal, the saliency of stimuli, and intervening events which may be distracting.

Central processing is most usefully conceptualized to include those aspects of information processing that emphasize the selection, gathering, and storage of information, as well as the utilization of such information. In a general sense, the element of intention is the most important component in distinguishing central processing from other phases in the information-processing sequence. Central processing deals with the encoding and selective retrieval of information stored in long-term memory. It assists in the transfer of material from short-term to long-term memory, and it involves (1) search behavior of memory banks, (2) the organization of memory, and (3) a constant interplay between the organism and its immediate environment in deciding on the most appropriate response. For purposes of clarification, the concept of "ego" (that is, an executor of behavior, which mediates between the organism and its environment) may be compared to central processing. To be maximally effective, some mediation requires (1) the reception of information (environmental demands), (2) the assessment and interpretation of such information, (3) numerous judgments and comparisons about alternate responses and their possible consequences, and (4) ultimate decisions about the most appropriate response and its implementation. Thus, central processing is a continuous process that undergoes change even while producing change in the cognitive structure and organization of the organism.

Comparative Philosophies and Theories

Given the disparity and ambiguity of defining "attention," it is not surprising that perhaps the most precise statement which can be made about attentional deficits and which is consistent with the various attentional theories is that there is an input dysfunction. This is a concept of perceptual nature and is seen as an artifact of the state of the organism in an arousal model. It is assumed that the organism has a malfunction in its ability to direct or orient receptors in an efficient manner. This deficiency is considered a function of the organism's state of physiological arousal. Only slightly different is the position that emphasizes a filtering model. This position is also concerned with the initial processing of stimulation but assumes that all information is available to the organism for initial processing. Both positions consider attention to be the preprocessing of information prior to any encoding or central processing. They differ, however, in stressing either the role of arousal or such cognitive variables as overinclusive thinking and distraction. All these theories consider the cognitive deficit to be a consequence of some malfunctioning prior to the point at which information enters central processing.

Those theories that emphasize the role of central processing are founded, to various degrees, on Broadbent's (1958) filtering model of cognitive processing. Broadbent compares the nervous system to a single communication channel. This channel is limited in the amount of sensory information it is capable of processing. Furthermore, sensory information does not enter this channel directly. Information for processing is selected from short-term memory, which is a general repository of sensory perceptions. Since information held in short-term memory is forgotten rapidly, and since the organism is limited in how much information it can process per unit of time, it is clear that cognitive deficits may occur due to processing variables.

Elaboration on Critical Points

Without attempting to identify the locus of the cognitive deficit, whether it is attentional or of a processing nature, the filtering model may be applied in various contexts. Within this framework, psychodiagnostic assessment focuses on the individual's cognitive and/or perceptual organization. Thus, attention is given to the informal aspects of perceptual or memory processes, rather than the contents involved. These cognitive styles are relatively consistent and truly dominate the manner in which a person views the environment. In spite of the individual forms that cognitive styles may assume, people may be categorized along some dimensions representing those styles. In other words, the manner in which a particular person receives, organizes, stores, and utilizes perceptions of the world permits classification along certain dimensions (such as leveling-sharpening and field dependence-independence).

In the area of psychopathology, deficits in information processing have been most clearly demonstrated among schizophrenic and minimally brain-damaged individuals. The research in schizophrenia has been based on a cognitive model in which information flows through an input stage, to a processing stage, and finally to a response stage (Neisser, 1967; Sternberg, 1970). Theories that emphasize the input stage tend to consider deficits as a consequence of stimulus contingencies and such perceptual variables as stimulus obscurity and constancy. Buss and Lang (1965) conclude that deficits reported for schizophrenic groups can be most accurately and parsimoniously construed as resulting from interference effects at the input stage. The processing and response stage theories suggest that the relevant aspects of stimulus input are selected for further processing by a hypothetical filter, whose malfunction makes the schizophrenic unable to attend to relevant information and exclude the irrelevant. Issues related to the importance of stimulus complexity and quantity, as compared to simply the rate at which information is processed, are still unresolved.

Children with minimal brain damage, particularly when learning disabilities are present (as they usually are), can also be conceptualized within a cybernetics model. These children may have input problems, particularly from visual and auditory stimuli. These input problems need to be differentiated into peripheral functions (for example, the eye transducing light waves into electrical impulses) and more central input processes (for instance, the occipital cortex receiving, recording, and interpreting light waves). Obviously, central input processes are more akin to perception, and often these input processes are of an intrasensory nature, with various senses involved simultaneously. Learning disabilities also occur because of the child's inability to integrate stimuli correctly. Integration implies forming the correct Gestalt, including proper sequencing of the data. For example, difficulties at this level are illustrated by children who can recite the months of the year, but only by starting with January. If asked what comes after April, they have to start with January. Or when they recount a story they know well, they eventually include the major parts of the story, but in a scrambled sequence.

The next phase of information processing requires both short- and long-term memory, which can also involve any of the senses (such as visual memory or auditory memory). Short-term memory in this context is that memory which can be retained as long as one remains focused. Therefore, children can learn spelling lists while they are attending to them but have no recollection of the words after other activities have interceded. In addition to these problems in input, integration, and memory, these children may also have output problems. These problems may be verbal or motoric. Verbal responses may be divided into spontaneous language (which affords the individual a fraction of a second of time to organize his or her thoughts and select appropriate words) and demand language (which requires the simultaneous organization of one's thoughts and selection of appropriate means of expression). Motor aspects of the output stage can also be divided into fine-motor and gross-motor output. Conceptualizing minimal brain damage in this manner makes it possible to understand the different types of learning disabilities, thereby indicating where in the flow of information processing a malfunction exists.

Personal Views and Recommendations

It is inordinately difficult to describe concretely the procedures to follow in assessing information-processing deficits. Much like other forms of psychiatric diagnostic assessment, the goal is to sensitize the examiner to selected patient behaviors that will prompt further, more detailed examination. While psychological testing has at times been useful in such an examination, its limitation is imposed by the lack of any direct convergence or isomorphic relationship between specific psychological tests and specific clinic behaviors. Although tests cover a range of functions, there is no direct correspondence between scores on given tests and the patient characteristics in which one might be interested. While the examiner may wish to obtain test data—that is, sample patient behaviors obtained under well-defined conditions—the basic step in assessing any deficit is in being alert to behaviors that signal the presence of maladaptive functioning. Information processing requires that information be received (input), integrated, and responded to (output). Each of these processes can be decomposed into contributing elements, such as perception, memory, speech, and motor responses. The examiner's task is to notice the deficiency in one or more of these processes, to be aware of the base rates for that behavior, and then to establish a differential diagnosis by successive approximation. While psychological test data and various neurological examinations may be useful in confirming or refuting the judgment of an information-processing deficit, the most incisive data will be obtained from a careful patient history and behavioral observations.

Application to Particular Variables

Generally speaking, deficits in information processing are not related to demographic or personality characteristics. They appear among various age groups, seem independent of educational level, and are not restricted by socioeconomic status. There are, however, some interesting correlaries that suggest possible links between such deficits and various characteristics.

Sex, for example, while not specifically related to variations in information processing, has not been investigated adequately in research with schizophrenic populations, most of which have been adult males. Similarly, in the area of minimal brain damage, particularly with regard to learning disabilities, approximately four times as many male children as female children are thus classified. Whether this represents a truly sex-linked characteristic or whether it reflects cultural biases in classifying behavior is not at all clear.

Ethnic and racial variables also are potentially confounding in this area. Numerous studies have dealt with the cognitive development of black children from economically disadvantaged backgrounds. Their findings are confounded by (1) the considerable variability in usage of the term *cognitive*; (2) the use of very different tasks to measure cognitive functioning; and (3) the failure, in many instances, to control for subject variability with respect to intelligence, motivation, and the examiner's race. In spite of these limitations, some researchers have suggested that black ghetto children are cognitively impulsive, probably because of various types of deficiencies in language development.

According to Luria (1961) and Vygotsky (1962), language exercises a regulatory effect on cognitive and overt behavior. Speech (initially external speech and eventually inner speech) is considered an effective mediator in the control of behavior and also to provide cues that guide thinking. The maladaptive (impulsive) behavior of black ghetto children has been attributed to (1) their development of a different language (Baratz, 1969); (2) their failure to develop a systematized language (Bernstein, 1966); and (3) deficits in the use of language for transmitting information and self-monitoring (Bereiter and Engelmann, 1968). Because of the often speculative nature of these interpretations, one should exercise considerable caution in assessing the relationship between cognitive functioning and these racial/socioeconomic variables.

References

Baratz, J. "A Bi-Dialectal Task for Determining Language Proficiency in Economically Disadvantaged Negro Children." *Child Development,* 1969, *40,* 889-901.

Bereiter, C., and Engelmann, S. *Teaching Disadvantaged Children in the Preschool.* Englewood Cliffs, N.J.: Prentice-Hall, 1968.

Berlyne, D. E. "Attention as a Problem in Behavior Theory." In D. I. Mostofsky (Ed.), *Attention: Contemporary Theory and Analysis.* New York: Appleton-Century-Crofts, 1970.

Bernstein, B. "Elaborated and Restricted Codes: Their Social Origins and Some Consequences." In A. G. Smith (Ed.), *Communication and Culture.* New York: Holt, Rinehart and Winston, 1966.

Bleuler, E. *Dementia Praecox or the Group of Schizophrenias* [1911]. New York: International Universities Press, 1950.

Broadbent, D. E. *Perception and Communication.* Elmsford, New York: Pergamon Press, 1958.

Buss, A. H., and Lang, P. J. "Psychological Deficit in Schizophrenia. I: Affect, Reinforcement, and Concept Attainment." *Journal of Abnormal Psychology,* 1965, *70,* 2-34.

Dykman, R. A., and Ackerman, P. T. "The MBD Problem: Attention, Intention, and Information Processing." In R. P. Anderson and C. G. Halcomb (Eds.), *Learning Disabilities/Minimal Brain Dysfunction Syndrome.* Springfield, Ill.: Thomas, 1976.

Dykman, R. A., and others. "Specific Learning Disabilities: An Attentional Deficit Syndrome." In H. R. Myklebust (Ed.), *Progress in Learning Disabilities.* Vol. 2. New York: Grune & Stratton, 1971.

Klein, G. S. "The Personal World Through Perception." In R. R. Blake and G. V. Ramsey (Eds.), *Perception: An Approach to Personality.* New York: Ronald Press, 1951.

Laufer, M. W., and Denhoff, E. "Hyperkinetic Behavior Syndrome in Children." *Journal of Pediatrics,* 1957, *50,* 463-473.

Luria, A. R. *The Role of Speech in the Regulation of Normal and Abnormal Behavior.* New York: Liveright, 1961.

Neale, J. M., and Cromwell, R. L. "Attention and Schizophrenia." In B. A. Maher (Ed.), *Progress in Experimental Personality Research.* Vol. 5. New York: Academic Press, 1970.

Neisser, U. *Cognitive Psychology.* New York: Appleton-Century-Crofts, 1967.

Sternberg, S. "Memory Planning: Processes Revealed by Reaction Time Experiments." In J. S. Antrobus (Ed.), *Cognition and Affect.* Boston: Little, Brown, 1970.

Vygotsky, L. *Thought and Language.* New York: Wiley, 1962.

41

Stephanie Z. Dudek

Primary Process Ideation

The concept of primary process remains one of Freud's most original and important contributions. Psychoanalysis is based on the theory of instinctual drives as prime motivators of behavior. Primary process is posited as the mechanism by which unconscious instinctual energy surfaces in the form of images or ideas. It appears when the ego's control over unconscious material is diminished. Its purpose is to serve the pleasure principle—the immediate discharge of tension and the maintenance of a constant state. Instinctual energy (id) is defined as mobile, diffuse, and undifferentiated. The formal structure of primary process is characterized by the kind of mobile (id) energy it processes and the kinds of mechanisms (condensation, symbolism, displacement) which it uses to transform and discharge the energy. It is called ideation rather than thinking by virtue of its closeness to drive, from which it is derived and which it represents in idea or image form. Freud originally reserved the term *thinking* for secondary process (reality oriented) thinking. At present, ideation and thinking tend to be used synonymously. The contents of primary process ideation may be referred to as ideational drive representatives or drive derivatives.

Primary and secondary process served as key concepts in Freud's initial formulation of the development of thought. His primary model of cognition, based on his primary model of action (Rapaport, 1951) postulated that when drive gratification is frustrated (hunger, for example) due to the absence of gratifying object (mother), the drive will manifest itself as a hallucinatory image (mother) in its attempt to establish an identity of perception with the original object. Ideation or fantasy affords the drive impulse some degree of discharge. Until the ego is mature enough to use reality-oriented secondary process thinking aimed at problem solving, primary process will continue to offer immediate discharge of tension by means of wish-fulfilling ideation. The characteristics of the secondary process are its stable and neutralized (socialized) cathexis. Ideas are permanently bound to objects and, therefore, do not shift from one object to another as happens with mobile energy. For example, mother cannot be used simultaneously with breast, or fountain, or apple, and so on. The idea of mother is firmly bound to a specific human being.

The dimension most important to an understanding of the primary process is its formal characteristic as a system for discharging mobile instinctual energy. It makes use of genetically early forms of thought (condensation, symbolism, and displacement) to transform and discharge free, unbound, instinctual energy into ideas that will represent the drive. For a hungry child, a primary process ideational representation of the hunger drive might be breast, apple, or mother. Such a hunger drive will organize the memories or associations that constitute the thought according to principles of wish fulfillment (drive organization of memory) rather than according to reality-oriented logic (conceptual organization). Early drive representations are vague, indistinct, and not attached to stable objects. Their energy cathexis is thus mobile, transferable (thus displacement and symbolism), and fusible (thus condensation). However, instinctual drive is constantly under strain because developmental factors (ego), functioning in the service of the reality principle, maintain control (censorship) over unneutralized (unsocialized) drive by various means (the most prominent of which is repression). The primary process manifests itself when ego control is weakened—for instance, in sleep; in wit; in slips of the tongue; in psychoses; in conditions of diminished consciousness, which allow regression to genetically earlier modes of ideation to occur. Although disguised, the emerging ideation reflects the nature of the repressed drives which are struggling for discharge. Repression does not prevent drive from existing in the unconscious, from organizing itself further, and from seeking to express itself through images or ideas that will reflect its true nature (drive derivatives). Thus, primary process substitutes ideation for action. Ideas and images become the signals and safety valves for drive tension. The quality of the ideation is recognizable (and thus can be "quantified") in loose drive-dominated association, disregard of contradiction, absurdity, indirect representation or representation by the opposite, substitution, allusion, symbolization, neologisms, timelessness, magical thinking, and autistic elaboration. Most of these are variations of, and may be subsumed under, the mechanisms of displacement and condensation (Gill, 1967).

Disregard for reality is characteristic of mobile energy; since they have no permanent object representations, ideas move from appropriate to inappropriate objects and result in irrational thinking. For example, mother may be equated with apple, breast, fountain, tree or any other less rational but personal association. However, a more careful analysis of the ideational form and content reveals that primary process is a special system for processing instinctual drive. The ideas expressed in distorted form are emotionally meaningful to the person using the system. The meaning can be decoded to reveal the person's needs, expectations, fears, or preoccupations. Holt (Holt and Havel, 1960; Holt,

1977) developed a system for scoring and interpreting primary process contents along a continuum from more to less regressed. It comprises both qualitative and quantitative dimensions and identifies drive content and the formal characteristics of thought. It has proved useful in the analysis of creative process and production, dreams, mythology, psychopathological states, effects of subliminal stimulation, and changes in ideas occurring in sensory isolation.

Background and Current Status

Freud first used the concepts of primary and secondary process in 1895 in "Project for a Scientific Psychology." However, this essay did not appear in print during his lifetime. The first published reference to the terms appeared in 1900 in *The Interpretation of Dreams,* and these concepts were integral to his topographic model of psychic functioning. According to this view, the primary process characterizes the unconscious system and gives expression in ideational form to repressed, unconscious drives. The memory traces of the unconscious system (Ucs) are nonverbal. Secondary process is exclusively the expression of the conscious (Cs) and preconscious (Pcs) systems.

Between the years 1900 and 1923, Freud's wide clinical experience led him to conclude that he could not use accessibility to consciousness as a criterion for differentiating primary from secondary process, or as a means of conceptualizing conflict and defense. It was evident that some forms of defense (a function of the ego) are unconscious and some other components (for instance, need for punishment) are inaccessible or accessible to consciousness only through analytic work. Thus, a revision of topographic theory was necessary and resulted in a formulation of the id, ego, and superego systems. The aim of the ego is to gratify the needs of both the id and the superego in a way that will observe to some extent both pleasure and reality principles. The topographical formulation was enlarged to include both aggressive and libidinal energy. Degree of relatedness to reality became the criterion by which to distinguish primary from secondary process along a single continuum. This theory was called structural. (Its main characteristics are summarized in a later section.)

In 1936 Waelder contributed the notion that all psychic activity is multidetermined; ego, id, and superego make their individual contributions, and there is participation from both conscious and unconscious layers of the personality.

The major changes in the concept of primary and secondary process were contributed in 1939 by Hartmann. He pointed out that, although the ego develops through conflict, there is also a conflict-free sphere of the ego. It consists of functions exclusive to the ego (such as perception, thinking, object comprehension, language, recall phenomena, motor development, and the maturation of learning processes). The rudiments of ego development are, therefore, present from the beginning and offer the ego considerable autonomy in its development.

Hartmann, Kris, and Loewenstein (1946) further pointed out that the functions of the ego and the id are not present at birth but differentiate out of an undifferentiated matrix of inborn endowment. This view is consistent with and supported by Piaget's theory of cognitive development. It is obvious that innate apparatuses and reflexes cannot be a part of the id because the id is fluid and unstructured energy. The primary process cannot, therefore, be considered as present at birth. It comes into being through a process of gradual development. The development of innate sensory schemata enables the infant to order his impressions and thus to adapt to the environment (Wolff, 1960). The infant's universe at this point (the first twelve months) is only a totality of pictures emerging at the moment of action and returns to nothingness the moment when action is finished (Piaget, 1937). Until the infant has reached a stage of permanent object representation (which occurs between 12 and 18 months), nothing like primary process ideation can possibly exist (Holt, 1967). Therefore, the origin of ideation, as outlined by Freud in his first model of cognition, is inaccurate. Only when the child achieves object permanence can perception and the "magically" reproduced object lead to the development of new meaning and thus to a system of ideation (Holt, 1967). In this sense, the primary process has initially an adaptive, rather than a maladaptive, function. Faulty synthesis can be expected to arise out of a premature attempt to find order (as the adult understands it), and it will manifest itself in faulty logic. Nevertheless, it is the child's only way to find order and meaning at early developmental stages.

The adaptive function of the primary process was underscored by Kris (1952). He postulated that the ego's organizing function can include control of its own regression, thereby using it in its own service. This formulation is helpful in explaining a variety of phenomena occurring during creative activity, particularly as it relates to the inspirational phase of creativity. Regression in the service of the ego involves rapid shifts of cathexis from conscious to preconscious levels in order that the contents recovered during the process of temporary regression may be used as the raw material of artistic creativity during the conscious stage of elaboration.

Holt's (1967) definition of the primary process summarizes to an important extent its current status. He sees it as a system for making sense out of what can only be a "blooming, buzzing confusion" to the infant. Holt describes primary process as a "special system of processing information in the service of synthetic necessity. It must therefore presuppose the operation of stable structures, and it must be the product of considerable development" (p. 383). Genetic, adaptive, economic, and dynamic components are part of a full explanation of its functioning. The stress on structure means that all structures— ego, id, and superego—can be characterized by primary process, as pointed out by Waelder (1936) in his principle of multiple functioning. This is a radical departure from Freud's (1895) first topographic model, although the germ of the structural idea was already present in *The Interpretation of Dreams* (Freud, 1900). It is evident that primary process undergoes developmental changes and is active throughout life. It may be ordered along a continuum from primary to secondary process, thus reflecting different degrees of mobility of cathexis and different degrees of ego control. Degree of reality contact, and not accessibility to consciousness, becomes the criterion differentiating primary process from secondary process. Thus, access to primary process ideation under ego control, adequate to the demands of the situation, becomes highly desirable and adaptive.

As previously mentioned, the development of a system for identifying, scoring, and analyzing primary process has opened up the concept to research in a number of significant areas—notably, in creative production and schizophrenic pathology. (For further elaboration see Harrow and others, 1976, and Chapter Thirty-Nine in this volume.) Quantitative problems, however, are subject to the difficulties that beset all psychological concepts (including IQ) by virtue of the lack of tight, well-systematized theories. Behavior, whether an overt act or an ideational representation, is remote from the psychological processes that gave rise to it. The same behavior may have different motivations, and vice versa. The techniques for identifying, let alone measuring, hierarchical organizations regulating discharge and transformation of energy by means of structures operating with small units of energy have not yet been developed. While the theory of cathexis offers the possibility of quasi-quantitative measurement (Rapaport, 1951), the difficulties involved in dealing with complex hierarchical levels (which differ not only in degree but in quality of cathexis, in the kinds of structures to which they give rise or of which they are the product, and in the kinds of functions ascribed to them) make interpretation hazardous if not impossible. For example, when the same variable acts both as defense against and as a means of discharge for cathectic energy, it cannot be quantified in the same way as a variable with a single function, although its quantitative identification follows the same ordinal scaling rules. Holt's complex system of identifying and scoring primary process is an admirable attempt to deal with these problems and provides a valuable research instrument, a first step along a long road. It succeeds in describing and highlighting qualitatively the complexity of interrelationships of drive, defense, reality distortion, and creative adaptation, but the use of addition, weighting, proportion of quantities, and the like, is premature. In the wish to go beyond identification and suggestive inference, the system opens up the proverbial "can of worms."

Critical Discussion

General Areas of Concern

There have been many attacks on psychoanalytic theory, some of which have threatened its foundations. Primary process is an intricate part of this theory. Stripped of the concepts of instinctual drive and the unconscious as catalysts, primary process loses its complex, explanatory quality in a system of hierarchical psychic functioning. It becomes simply an expression of a genetically early mode of dealing with the complexity and frustration of the infant's world. As such, primary process is one of the "givens," the way in which the nervous system organizes reality before more mature patterns develop in hierarchical progression (much in the way Hughlings Jackson describes it). Within the context of psychoanalytic theory, the accurate definition of the primary process can extend, clarify, or undermine the main tenets of Freud's systematizing. Problems that have arisen and have been variously resolved include (1) genesis, development, structure, and functions of the primary process; (2) evidence for a structural theory and the consequences of this formulation; and (3) adaptive functions in early and later life.

The genesis, development, structure, and functions of primary process have undergone considerable redefinition since 1900. Once the inaccuracy of Freud's first model of cognition (mounting drive tension—absence of drive object—hallucinatory image of it) became evident, as a result of Piaget's research into the development of sensorimotor intelligence, the concepts about genesis of the primary process and its development and persistence over time had to be reformulated. Holt (1967) has provided a highly original and convincing alternative theory.

Although primary process as ideation emerges at approximately 18 months, its origins are much earlier. Dreaming is a parallel activity which may contribute heavily to the development of primary process. Long before ideation develops, the infant is experiencing a dream state. Rapid eye movements (REM activity) have been observed in infants at 15 days of age and younger. At that time REM consists predominantly of chained sequences of motor activity and sensorimotor schemata. With time, the motor activity decreases, and Holt believes that sooner or later it will be accompanied by phenomenal experience (hallucinatory image). He quotes Roffwarg, Dement, and Fisher (1964, p. 68) as saying "It is likely that what goes on in the infant's mind during the REM period of sleep is fairly closely related to what goes on in his mind when awake. . . . It is possible that, as perception and memory functions develop in the growing infant, dreaming develops in a parallel fashion." At early stages the motor activity during the REM period is probably the infant's way of exercising his sensorimotor schemata in the absence of real objects. Unlike the waking state, where the infant is stimulus bound, the dream state would present images consistent with the enactment of his motor components, but without their external presence. Thus, the dream becomes a way to imagine; it is likely to become more purely perceptual and less motor long before the same is true for waking-state ideational processes (which remain tied to action). Holt states: "The innate capacity to dream may therefore be an important influence in the development of secondary as well as primary process" (p. 382). Exactly when primary process ideation emerges is not at all clear. It is clear to Holt that both systems, primary as well as secondary, develop as an innate function of the central nervous system's dealing with the same experiences and by the growth of the same structures that produce successive versions of the secondary process. The primary process is superseded by the secondary because it is more effective in achieving gratification. Primary process changes its function (becomes maladaptive) if it persists or is given preference when the more reality-oriented secondary process is available.

The consolidation of the primary process is achieved by means of the child's exposure to his or her subculture (the world of myths, legends, fairy tales) and, of course, by the persistence of the dream. A sufficiently consolidated structure is self-sustaining as well as sustained by the structure into which it is inevitably integrated.

The evidence for a structural theory of primary process has been succinctly presented by Holt (1967). His formulation depends on a model of psychic functioning where reality, rather than consciousness, is the criterion for distinguishing between primary and secondary process. In his 1967 article, Holt summarizes a number of reasons why a structural model is necessary to explain primary process: (1) The purposive functioning of the primary process—which uses recognizable mechanisms of displacement, condensation, and symbolism—implies a system of reversible operations of thought. (2) The use of a structural network of drive-organized memories again implies an organization and therefore a structural arrangement. (3) The nonarbitrary functioning of condensation and displacement (predictable modes) points in the same direction. (4) The particular way in which new images are constructed by condensation indicates that there is some kind of arrangement (structure) to bring them together. (5) The stable transformation of original, threatening material by primary process indicates that it can be used and relied on as stable defense (which is a structural concept). (6) The recurrence of identical contents again involves structural constants. (7) The existence of neurotic symptoms, which are highly stable (and often intractable), suggests structuralized forms of primary process. (8) Symbolization, a kind of archaic language that is socially shared, may be seen as a structuralized displacement substitute and also suggests a structural constant. (9) Freud's own conception of the ego and id as shading into each other suggests that some parts of the id are more structured than others, and thus a hierarchical continuum may be posited.

The consequences of a structural model of primary process thinking—as opposed to the topographic, which it replaced in 1923—are enormous. Freed of the topographic (conscious versus unconscious place) model, any product of mental activity can be seen as multiply determined; that is, as the outcome of the interaction among tendencies of id, ego, and superego. Secondary process thinking, when characterized by highly mobile cathexis (as in creative activity), need not be considered as unrealistic or maladaptive as long as the ego maintains sufficient control over it. In fact, the inability to regress to primary process may be seen as maladaptive in certain circumstances. The structural theory also calls attention to the more complex nature of the therapeutic task. According to topographic theory, the analyst's task is to make the unconscious conscious in order to effect cure. In the structural model the focus is directed toward the nature and function of defenses—which are often unconscious and which must be analyzed first, in order to permit the previously warded-off contents to emerge and thus to be integrated into the ego functions.

The concept of regression has also undergone some modification. It has come to include (1) instinctual regression, (2) the shift to predominance of one psychic system over another, (3) the modes of ego and superego functioning at the time of regression, and (4) the extent that these also were regressed. Regression is no longer seen as global; it affects particular functions to different degrees and in different ways.

The persistence of primary process, as a structural concept, is both inevitable and desirable over a lifetime. The shifting back and forth from more to less conscious levels describes the normal functioning of the central nervous system. Primary process therefore has adaptive functions. It can be eradicated only at the price of enormous rigidity. Access to primary process contents assures the personality of a contact with instinctual drives, which might otherwise find no representation. It is difficult to imagine that drives which enter consciousness via the primary process do not have some modifying effect on defenses and controls. The primary process offers sufficient discharge, via ideation, to repressed drives so that equilibrium within the personality is maintained. It prevents functioning that is too highly organized by defenses and, as such, too rigid and too far removed from instinctual integration. It provides a route toward greater self-discharge and possibly greater self-awareness. It offers possibilities to the ego for creative transformation of reappropriated drive material through various forms of sublimative activity. Finally, as an inevitable component of normal reality-oriented thinking, it demonstrates the complexity and multidimensionality of consciousness.

While it has been possible to hypothesize about the structural origins, development, and functioning of the primary process, how a process becomes a structure remains a mystery. Does it, as Piaget suggests for cognitive structures, evolve into a mature structure (schema) partly on the basis of innate apparatuses and partly as a function of experiences? Are many or few structures to be posited in the development of the primary process system? If the assumption is that there are few, do they evolve from simple to complex in a hierarchical fashion, so that "structuring" in a mature organ proceeds, as Hebb (1949) suggested for learning, by a recombining of already established "phase sequences"—in this case simple "structures"? At this point, there is not even a hint of the true state of affairs.

A number of other theoretical questions remain with reference to the fucntioning of primary process. These will be dealt with under the following concerns: (1) the principle of multiple functioning, (2) regression in the service of the ego, (3) the concepts of assimilation and accommodation, and (4) the problem of external object representation (primary process presences).

The principle of multiple functioning (which allows for an interplay of ego, id, and superego contributions to the products of mental activity) is not without its theoretical problems. It certainly mirrors clinical reality better than the id-ego dichotomy postulated by the topographical model. However, the concept of regression, essential to the emergence of primary process, becomes fuzzy in these interactions. In what sense is regression, defined as primitivization of function, occurring? Theory suggests that mental contents can be placed along a continuum from extreme primary to extreme secondary process; this would indicate the degree of ego control or drive presence. Can less than full ego control be equated with ego regression? When ego, id, and superego have combined, by virtue of some degree of lowered defensiveness, to produce mental products that are reality oriented and morally sound and serve the pleasure principle at the same time, can this be labeled regression? Would it not be more appropriate to consider this a sign of integration? In the topographic model, presence of primary process indicated that instinctual drive has escaped ego control and is thus a problem to be remedied. In the structural model, there is, rather, a process of bargaining. At times, id wins out by virtue of its strength; at other times, ego dominates for the same reason; and at other times, ego or superego allows primary process considerable leeway by design.

Regression in the service of the ego is an interesting and useful concept for the understanding of the creative process. Primary process in artistic creativity follows regressive patterns and principles that differ markedly from those posited by Waelder's (1936) multiple functioning. The emergence of primary process in the artist is seldom coordinated with secondary process thinking (ego or superego). It tends to manifest itself in crude and primitive form by using blatantly libidinal and aggressive content. The thought contents are generally at the primary process end of the continuum. The mental functioning is usually characterized by rapid shifts from primary to secondary process, but shifting may also be slow (Kris, 1952). The alternation continues throughout the creative period in the service of the work in progress. The outstanding feature of this regression is that it is under the control of the ego. It can be begun and terminated at will. The primary process contents are the raw material to be transformed by the ego into art products over short or long periods of time. The principle underlying jokes, humor, wit, slips of the tongue, and parapraxes is the same except that the emergence of primary process is sudden and of short duration; although not willed by the ego or superego, it functions in their service.

The concepts of assimilation and accommodation have been used by some researchers synonymously with primary and secondary process. While these may overlap in some aspects of their functioning, the theoretical assumptions underlying each set of concepts are so different that comparisons are inappropriate. Assimilation is a concept developed by Piaget to describe the growth of cognitive structures. It is an invariant mode of processing experience (generally information) in terms of already existing schema. Assimilation is internally motived, although it needs the catalyst of external experience to exercise its function with the purpose of alimenting (nourishing) and thus consolidating existing schemas. When the material being assimilated does not fit the schema, accommodation enters in to change the schema in such a way that the new material can be accommodated. This is the manner in which schema evolve, grow, and become more complex. The purpose is to better apprehend reality. Piaget's concepts do not leave room for drive energy (which is peremptory, purposive, pleasure oriented, irrational, and diffuse). The concepts of repression and defense cannot easily be fitted into Piaget's notion of development of schema. Acquiring new schema may be described as a period of trial and error during which accommodation is attempting to modify assimilative efforts so that an improved schema, one more adapted to reality, may emerge. Assimilation and accommodation work together in response to the organism's need to know its environment cognitively and to overcome obstacles which stand in the way of knowing. The entropy principle is not only foreign but antithetical to Piaget's schematizing. Cognitive life is a constant growth, search, and creative synthesis. The concept of equilibration refers to stability (not to inertia). The distortion of reality, which may result when assimilation tries to fit new data into an old schema, is neither purposeful nor desired as it is in primary process. When new data do not fit an old schema, accommodation automatically enters in an attempt to modify the schema. There can be no accommodation without prior assimilation, and no new schema without their joint collaboration. The efforts required may demand many trials, but eventually a modified (new) schema is the result.

The process is never ending, as long as new experience is available. Secondary process, which has been equated with accommodation, does not work hand in hand with primary process and has no such transforming influence on its contents. The best it can do is control, negate, or repress it. Primary process confronts new situations by using variations of the same old mechanisms—displacement, condensation, symbolization. The goal is pleasure (entropy), not change or new knowledge. Assimilation uses conceptual organization of memory; when it distorts, it is by virtue of new information which indicates that the old schema is outdated. The concepts have so little in common that further comparison seems unnecessary. Although accommodation fits the concept of secondary process better, its relationship to assimilation is so unlike that of secondary to primary process that it is clear these are two universes of discourse that defy comparison.

Schafer (1968) has made a significant contribution to the understanding of the problem of external object representation (identification), as a function of *primary process presences*. When the secondary process has been firmly established, the persistence of primary process as a preferred mode of dealing with drive can only lead to maladaptive behavior. The outcome is a general inability to make adequate contact with reality. This is true in many areas. It is particularly debilitating with respect to externalization of object relationships. In childhood, under normal circumstances drive is intimately tied to the object. In fact, drive is recognized by the object that subserves it. For example, aggression may be intimately but indiscriminately tied to male authority and recognized only in this context. With development and the help of secondary process, the object achieves stability, differentiation, wholeness, and human quality. In time, substitute objects within reality come to be identified with gratification of drive needs, and relationships acquire the quality of mutuality, interaction, and breadth. However, where primary process activity predominates, object representations remain fluid, fragmentary, and partial. They never acquire truly human proportions. The objects are, in fact, activities. The drives—sex, aggression, orality, and so on—will take any object for gratification, using it manipulatively. There is no concept of relationship. Primary process ideation involves a magic fusing of self with object where no independence is needed (since thought is equated with action). A primitive narcissism is perpetuated, and what infantile ties are established are in the nature of fixated introjections which cannot be externalized. An example of a fixated introjection may be an internal image of the mother as a devouring creature. As a result, all females are seen in terms of this internalized image and therefore cannot be perceived in their true nature. Schafer (1968) calls such infantile introjects "primary process presences," and he believes that they may be either introjects or situated in an external space. Their presence, however, interferes with true object representation. By a process of distortion, disguise, and displacement, the internal object or primary process presence is projected upon the external object repetitively. Thus, the external object assumes the form of the subject's wishes or fears and loses its identity. With typical primary process fluidity, subject and object (internal image and person in real world) tend to fuse and substitute for each other as the infantile past obscures the present. Instead of a relationship, an undifferentiated gratifying unity is sought in a make-believe reality. The pattern is generally unconscious, and the primary process presences cannot be integrated by the ego. The result is a typical repetition compulsion (that is, perceiving all new persons in the same fashion regardless of how they may differ). Under such circumstances, identification with external objects is impossible, and the ego remains weak. According to Schafer (1968), primary process presences constitute the strongest forces opposing changes in the personality.

Comparative Philosophies and Theories

The topographic theory and the structural theory that replaced it (Freud, 1923) still offer two basic but significantly differing views of the primary process. Freud used the term *topographic* to designate, in a metaphorical sense, the location of the different systems of the mind (conscious, unconscious, preconscious). He assumed originally that the different systems were possibly separated in space (cerebral topography). He later discarded the idea, substituting for it an economic formulation (modes of discharge). There is still considerable disagreement among psychoanalytic theorists as to whether the topographic *point of view* should be retained along with the structural, although there is no question that the structural point of view has been accepted. Gill (1963) has pointed out that for Freud the topographic was the structural point of view and that Freud used the term to signify *systems*. For Gill the topographic point of view appears unnecessary. He believes that "the relationship of contents to consciousness is rather a phenomenon that is explicable in terms of the more basic hypotheses concerning genetic history, adaptive utility, the economics of energy, structural configurations, and dynamic forces" (p. 159). Thus, the topographic relationship can be subsumed under the five points of view without reducing the importance of the description of mental contents in terms of relationship to consciousness. No other theoretical models (for example, Noy, 1969) offer sufficient logical coherence to be included for discussion in this section.

A schematic comparison of the two theories is presented in Table 1. They have already been summarized in greater detail in preceding sections. Only aspects of each theory that have relevance for primary process are presented. It is evident that, as the relation of the content to consciousness changed in importance and became a descriptive term, the definition of primary process also underwent important changes.

Table 1. Primary Process as Interpreted by Topographic Theory and Structural Theory

Topographic Theory	*Structural Theory*
Developed by Freud in 1895 in "Project for a Scientific Psychology."	
First formulated in 1900 in *The Interpretation of Dreams*.	First formulated in 1923 in *The Ego and the Id*.
Mental apparatus divided into the conscious, preconscious, and unconscious systems.	Mental apparatus divided into the ego, id, and superego systems.
Primary process functioning entirely in service of id.	Primary process functioning in service of id, ego, and superego. Principle of multiple functioning (Waelder, 1936).
Emerges in very early infancy (Freud, 1900).	Can emerge only after object constancy has been established (Holt, 1967).
Primary process superseded by secondary.	Primary process active throughout life.
Primary-secondary process a dichotomy.	Primary-secondary process a continuum.
Criterion of primary process: evidence of unconscious.	Criterion of primary process: degree of reality orientation.
Systemic regression with emergence of unconscious.	Regression possible in all systems; defined as primitivization of function.
Emergence signifies that ego is exercising diminished control or is weak.	Discharge regulated by ego. Emergence can be function of weak or strong ego (for example, regression in service of ego).

(continued on next page)

Table 1 (Continued)

Topographic Theory	Structural Theory
Regression seen as global.	Regression neither global nor uniform.
Connotations of pathology.	Not necessarily pathological or maladaptive.
Defenses operate according to primary process.	Defenses organized along a hierarchical continuum (Gill, 1963).
Id seen as exclusively a motivational concept.	Id is structured (contains inhibiting structures) (Gill, 1963).

Elaboration on Critical Points

For the practicing clinician, the critical questions with respect to primary process are intimately tied to its assessment. They may be formulated as follows: (1) How well can primary process be assessed by existing techniques? (2) To what extent have assessment techniques opened the way to fruitful research? (3) How adequate is the research data in clarifying the concept of the primary process and its usefulness in clinical areas and in elucidating its adaptive and maladaptive functions? Perhaps the best way of responding to these questions is to briefly describe the assessment instruments and the research stemming from their use.

There are two techniques for systematically assessing primary process. Holt (1977; Holt and Havel, 1960) has presented a highly systematized technique within a psychoanalytic framework (to be discussed later). Martindale (1973, 1975), within the context of a behavioral approach different from that of psychoanalysis, constructed an instrument with a specific goal in mind: to analyze literary style and change of style over time. Basing his system on the theories of Berlyne (1971) and Kris (1952), he posited that novelty and disruption of expectation (which are the hallmarks of poetry) are predicated on regression. He therefore developed a 5,000-word regressive imagery dictionary for analyzing the contents of literature. His technique is to apply his regressive word dictionary to an analysis of contents of published literature by means of a computer which was programmed to scan for words labeled as regressive. In Martindale's system, primary process is composed of categories that may be grouped into subdivisions of drives, sensations, defensive symbolization, regressive cognition, and Icarian imagery. His research has indicated that poetic change over time (for example, romantic versus classical) follows an extremely lawful process (Martindale, 1975). For example, the regressive imagery dictionary contains a measure labeled incongruous juxtapositions, which can be used to measure the novelty of thematic drive content in literature or in clinical test situations (Martindale, 1960). He has experimented with simulation of literary change in the following fashion. By inducing a need for novelty in his subjects, he has forced them to be more regressive in their thinking. As a result, they were able to produce more original responses in their writing. He found, as he had predicted, that the speeded-up process of regression led to stylistic disintegration in more creative subjects but not in less creative ones.

Holt attempted to operationalize all the nuances of primary process thinking in ways that would make quantification possible. He used the Rorschach test as a method for eliciting primary process, but he did not tie primary process in any way to Rorschach's perceptanalytic concepts. His measures are directed at (1) formal deviations of thought, as evidenced in condensation, displacement, symbolization, and other derivative forms of deviant thinking; and (2) libidinal and aggressive content in its various forms of expression. He attempted to measure more primitive versus more neutralized or socialized expressions of drive by using two levels (levels 1 and 2). In order to arrive at an index of adaptive regression or regression in the service of the ego, he developed a method for evaluating the need for defense of primary process (Defense Demand) by virtue of its crudity and the effectiveness with which this demand is met (Defense Effectiveness). The formula for the adaptive regression index (REGO) is

$$\frac{DD \times DE}{PPR}$$

All this presupposes that primary process can be added, divided, multiplied, and percentaged. The complexity of Holt's system and the amount of time it takes to score and analyze the data have prevented it from being more widely used. It has, nevertheless, been extensively applied in a large number of research areas—for example, creativity, pathological thinking, developmental studies with young children, tolerance for unusual experiences, effects of psychotherapy, hypnotic regression, sensory isolation, effects of drugs, and cultural differences. Pine (1960) and Eagle (1964) both adopted Holt's system for use with the TAT and other drive content. Dudek (1975) modified Holt's system for use with the Torrance Tests of Creative Thinking (TTCT).

Space limitations make it impossible to present a comprehensive review of this research, but a brief résumé of sixteen sets of findings will be offered:

1. Developmental studies with young children (ages 3 and up) indicate that formal deviations of thought decrease with age while content categories increase and controls and defenses become more effective (Dudek and Verreault, in press; Matalon, 1975; Rivard and Dudek, 1977; Safrin, 1974).

2. Some researchers (Rabie, 1969) have found primary process (obtained by the TAT) to be minimally correlated with ego functions, as reflected in IQ in first-grade children, and not at all when achievement measures were used, while others (Wulach, 1977) have found good correlations with Piaget's measures of preoperational thinking in children ages 4 to 8. Matalon (1975), working with 10-year-old children, found no positive relationships between primary process and IQ, scholastic achievement, perceptual-motor measures, and Piaget's tests of operational and causal thinking. She did find, however, that primary process scores were related to high levels of anxiety, tension, and poor control of aggression.

3. A positive relationship between creativity in artists and primary process ideation (particularly level 1) has repeatedly been found (Dudek, 1968, 1975; Gagnon, 1977; Holt, 1970; Huard, 1972; Myden, 1959; Pine, 1959; Pine and Holt, 1960), thus offering support for the concept of regression in the service of the ego in creativity.

4. In young children, the findings are not clear. Neither overall presence of primary process nor regression in the service of the ego (REGO) scores were found correlated with measures of creativity by Dudek (1975) and Rogolsky (1968), whereas Dudek and Verreault (in press), by adapting the Holt system to the Torrance Tests of Creative Thinking (both verbal and figural forms), were able to demonstrate regression in the service of the ego (REGO) in 10- to 12-year-old children. Wulach (1977), using Rorschach measures and standard Holt scoring, found a negative correlation between REGO and measures of creativity.

5. Although amount of primary process content projected does not differ, when Rorschachs of young art students (mean age 22) are compared with those of renowned mature artists (mean age 40), the latter give a greater amount of libidinal content and have higher Defense Demand and higher Defense Effectiveness scores (Chamberland-Bouhadana, 1977).

6. Successful ("good") artists, as opposed to unsuccessful ("bad") artists, show significantly more level 1 primary process (Dudek, 1968).

7. Successful artists, when compared with a matched group of professionals productive in other areas, do not show greater incidence of primary process content, but they show more libidinal primary process and manifest lower defenses and controls, thus indicating greater access to their own energies (Dudek, Chamberland-Bouhadana, and Gagnon, 1978).

8. Schizophrenics have been shown to project more crude and primitive primary process than neurotic and normal controls (Harrow and others, 1976; Lavoie and others, 1976).

9. Early schizophrenics have been found to give more primary process than chronic schizophrenics (Dudek, 1969, 1970). This was also true of early versus chronic schizophrenics in a maximum security penal institution (Kokis, 1973).

10. Zimet and Fine (1965) found that *process* schizophrenics projected more level 1 primary process than *reactive* schizophrenics. However, Harrow and associates (1976) did not find significant differences between *process* and *reactive* schizophrenics in overall expression of primitive drive content.

11. Harrow and associates (1976) found that patients (whether schizophrenic or not) high on sociopathic or rule-breaking behavior tended to give more primitive drive-dominated thinking.

12. Lavoie and associates (1976) found adaptive regression (REGO) and effectiveness of defense to be positively related to hypnotizability in schizophrenics.

13. Allison (1967), Feirstein (1967), and Maupin (1965) found capacity to regress constructively to be related to tolerance for unusual experiences (religious conversion phenomena, contradictory modes of perception, and Zen meditation, respectively).

14. Experiments in the area of perceptual isolation show that a positive relationship exists between well-controlled primary process and ability to terminate successfully an isolation experience of one week's duration (Wright and Zubek, 1969). Goldberger (1961) did not find such a relationship in an eight-hour isolation experience. He was able to show, however, that interference with reality contact via an isolation chamber results in a decrease in efficiency of secondary process functioning and that persons who projected more primary process to the Rorschach prior to the experiment were better able to withstand the isolation experience (gave less poorly controlled primary process responses during isolation).

15. Primary process ideation in young children does not appear to be a stable characteristic. A longitudinal study (Dudek and Loveless, in press) found considerable variability in the same children from year to year when primary process scores were applied to Torrance Tests of Creative Thinking obtained from the same children over grades 3 through 6. The same was true for fifth- and sixth-grade children when the Rorschach test was used.

16. A cross-sectional study of 500 fifth- and sixth-grade children showed grade 6 children manifesting more effective adaptive regression than grade 5 children (using Dudek's adaptation of Holt's system applied to the Torrance Tests of Creative Thinking). There was also a significantly greater production of primary process and a greater REGO in upper-class as opposed to middle- and lower-class children (Verreault, 1978).

Personal Views and Recommendations

This cursory survey of research using primary process as a tool of evaluation has provided evidence for its usefulness in many types of behavioral and process studies. Some researchers have focused only on content categories; others have used content, effectiveness of defenses and controls, and adaptive regression scores. Theoretically, it should make a difference whether drive expression is well or poorly defended, but this often has not been the case. It is in this area that more research is needed. The inconsistencies probably reflect the inadequacy of primitive quantitative measures when one is dealing with complex, hierarchically organized mental products. How much primary process is enough or too much? Can scores be treated additively, as they have been? What does "undefended or poorly defended primary process" mean? Is defense effectiveness a relevant concept in evaluating all forms of experience (for example, creative activity and tolerance of sensory isolation)? Is defense effectiveness really an index of ego strength? To what extent do situational factors dictate the use of controls and defense as opposed to their abandonment? This type of qualitative analysis has not been attempted; until it has been, the relevance of adaptive regression cannot be meaningfully understood. There is no way as yet to infer when and to what extent the presence of primary process in a test protocol should be interpreted as potential, when it is an index of active contribution (whether negative or positive), and when it should be dismissed as having little influence on the subject's behavior.

Many of the psychoanalytic tenets about primary process, however, have been verified by research data. Thus, there is evidence for its development from crude to more socialized with age, its persistence over a lifetime, and its adaptive as well as maladaptive functions. Where there is evidence of a defective superego, the presence of primary process may suggest acting out (Harrow and others, 1976). It definitely appears to be an index of psychic vitality (in both the negative and positive meanings of the term). Its presence can be seen as indicating a tolerance of unusual experiences, and its absence can be seen as inconsistent with mental health (it is possibly a sign of mental rigidity). It can be experimentally manipulated, and it can be expected to emerge under certain conditions. For all this, its nature and complex functioning are not clear.

Tools for the identification of primary process appear to be adequate, although far from quantitatively perfected; they have opened the way to exploration of many valuable and provocative areas of research. However, with reference to the meaning and function of primary process as identified in Rorschach and other thematic test protocols, inferences are far from definitive. Although Holt's method "works," what it is revealing about the psychic apparatus is still unclear. This is not surprising in view of the fact that there are still divergent psychoanalytic opinions about the meaning and function of the primary process on both a psychodynamic and behavioral level. Some theorists, like Gill (1963), believe (in the spirit of the later Freud) that the id is the most primitive level of an id-ego continuum but one on which "there is already some advance toward secondary process organization, some reality principle, and some structure" (p. 145). Gill is opposed to a force-counterforce dichotomy (repressed id versus repressing ego). A dichotomy automatically defines the primary process along a continuum. Holt's (1967) position is similar. Others, like Noy (1969), stand in strong opposition to Freud's formulations. Noy prefers to see the ego as using the primary process "for all functions aimed at preserving self-continuity and identity and assimilating any new experience and lines of action into the self-schema" (p. 162). His position appears to be based on a fusion, in what seems to be an incompatible format, of Freudian, Piagetian, and information theory conceptualizations. Primary process, for all its development (as is implicit in the notion of a structural model), remains an index of conflict and thus a reflection of the irruption of ego-alien drive representations which are more likely to perturb than to maintain the self-schema. Schafer (1968) has extended the sphere of influence of primary process beyond what can be inferred from Holt's assessment techniques by calling attention to the daydream and to defects in external object representation as a function of *primary process presences*.

Regression in the service of the ego in the artist, which has unquestionably been regarded as a highly adaptive use of the primary process and as a "model" of sublimation in its most desirable form, can be reformulated to serve as an index of a defensive mode of dealing with a frequently undesirable invasion of archaic contents which threaten personality integrity. The binding of this energy within a work of art by repeated attempts at transformation (or working through) may be seen as absorbing large quantities of energy, in a narcissistic way, which might otherwise be directed into intimate interpersonal, libidinal relationships. Examined in the light of criteria of mental health (work, love, and knowledge), the artist's socially valuable and desirable contribution may all too frequently be achieved at very great personal cost, even if it becomes for him or her the only kind of repetition compulsion that achieves a certain degree of personal equilibrium. The fact that artists learn to use regression in the service of the ego and continue to exercise this type of function for ego mastery over a lifetime does not alter the personally costly mode of adaptation.

Holt's method of assessing adaptive regression, which gives an indication of the relative strength of the ego, sheds little light on the personality resources that this ego has at its disposal to direct and control. That is, it tells us little about the presence or absence in the person of talent, imagination, intelligence, resourcefulness, emotional warmth, adaptive sensitivity and receptivity to others, or the quality and intensity of libidinal and aggressive drive outside of the conflictual areas revealed by primary process drive representations. Holt has not chosen to integrate his system into Rorschach's perceptanalytic diagnostic technique. The latter offers this type of information, and its integration into Holt's system would be valuable, albeit a formidable task. Holt's technique of assessing primary process may be regarded as descriptive and suggestive rather than diagnostic. The same applies to existing modifications of Holt's system.

Martindale's approach has a much different focus, and his system has to be evaluated by different criteria. He is not interested in psychodynamic formulations, and his analysis is largely independent of them. The study of literary form and its change over time as a function of the vicissitudes of human imaginal resources focuses on regression as both a catalyst and an index of stylistic change. Regression is seen as a return to more primitive, instinctual modes of imaginative expression, which must, by its nature, depart from the crystallized, conventional styles of expression. It may therefore help to release more original forms of perception. In Martindale's formulation, regression is not dependent on the framework of psychoanalytic theory.

To summarize the section on the nature of ideational drive discharge, the primary process continues to be seen as a mechanism to process and discharge mobile, peremptory instinctual energy in ideational form whatever the circumstances and whichever system it may serve (ego, id, or superego). Its emergence indicates the existence of conflict, frustration, and regression; otherwise, the secondary route would have been taken. Furthermore, the energy discharged is primarily unconscious, even when it is in the service of the ego. If it were conscious and integrated into ego functioning, distortion and disguise would not be necessary for its emergence. The ego's willingness to regress and thus to allow the emergence of drive representations via the primary process does not change the quality of the energy released, nor does the transformation by the ego of the contents into socially acceptable products (such as art) refute the origins of the energy thus transformed. That is, primary process contents (however crude or refined, high or low on the continuum) remain derivatives and representatives of repressed, ego-alien drive; and this is true whether they are willingly released by the (strong) ego or escaped by overwhelming it temporarily. However, there is one consideration. When the ego consciously uses such mechanisms of the primary process as symbolization, displacement, and condensation (for example, in writing poetry), can one assume that it is always repressed drive which is being released? Clearly, the id makes use of the same mechanisms for an entirely different purpose; that is, to counter the defenses of the ego, without regard to reality or mental health. The criterion by which secondary process is differentiated from primary process is by the adequacy of reality contact, whatever the mechanisms used by the ego to achieve its purposes. However, not all unrealistic thinking can be identified as drive dominated; and, as Schafer has pointed out, *unrealistic* is not the logical opposite of *wishful.* Therefore, adequacy of reality contact may not be a sufficient criterion by which to identify primary versus secondary process thought. Perhaps what is relevant is not so much identification of the primary versus the secondary aspects of thinking as evaluation of quality of the effected compromise, which is the successful integration of wish and reality. How to evaluate the extent to which this compromise is adaptive and "healthy" for the individual concerned becomes the crucial problem from both the theoretical and the therapeutic points of view. Not all reality-oriented, socially acceptable thinking is either healthy or desirable. The balance of stresses and strains in the individual cannot be evaluated by looking at the quality of the thinking alone.

The primary process is both a mode of discharge for mobile energy and a defensive system opposing overt energy discharge. It functions both in the service of repression and against it. To the extent that drive discharge is effected by outwitting the censor, it opposes repression and defensive barriers; but to the extent that ideation is the discharge route substituting for action, it is on their side. Thus, both pleasure and reality principles are served by the primary process, each in its own way.

The notion of primary process ideation as a regressive mode for effecting immediate discharge of cathexis in substitute form is, therefore, ambiguous. It really functions to maintain the organism in a passive state, a metaphorically "hallucinatory state" where both action and affect discharge are circumvented. The drive of which the ideation is representative remains repressed, peremptory, and it "proliferates in the dark, as it were" (Freud, 1915, p. 149). The means by which it can rejoin the ego system to obtain gratification and/or integration in a nonideational form are various (for example, through a change in superego or ego strength or a change in reality demands). Whether emergence of primary process ideation contributes to effect the desired changes in any way is speculative.

The adaptive nature of primary process ideation has already been discussed. However, there is an additional component as suggested by the first model of cognition. By using ideation (a passive state), primary process teaches the young organism to delay and to exercise its delaying capacities. As such, it prepares the way for secondary process thinking, of which delay and detour are the main characteristics. This function need not necessarily be very different in normal adults. Under conditions of drive and frustration, some discharge via ideation (for instance, in daydreaming) may lead to healthy lowering of tension before reality-oriented activity, with its large aspect of delay and renunciation, must begin. Moreover, the release of ideational drive representations via primary process ideation (imagery) may sensitize and orient the ego's problem-solving activity into more creative and more individually appropriate solutions.

Finally, the primary process mode of functioning can be (but is not necessarily limited to) ideation. It can affect all areas of the personality, either selectively or as a whole. When massive regression occurs (for example, in psychoses), all areas may be affected at the same time. Thus, in the area of *perception*, primary process results in diffuse, physiognomic, and animistic formal characteristics. *Affect* becomes diffuse and unmodulated and may be discharged in affect storms. *Motility* shows rapid spilling over into action and participation, and often there is grossness of action. The *self* experiences an elimination of boundaries and of inner coherence, so that what is thought and what is real are confused. *Defense* shows weakness, and consciousness is overwhelmed by the emergence of affects and fantasies from the unconscious. The *ego ideal* assumes a megalomanic, unattainable, infantile quality; and the *superego* functions with an archaic severity. The *ego* as a whole demonstrates passivity as opposed to activity. Discharge occurs independent of the ego, and the ego is unable to modify the damming up of impulses by countercathexes. These transformations may occur individually or together. Their emergence is a result of regression, which releases the primary process mode of functioning. The maladaptive effects of the primary process are thus all too evident. As an unwilled uncontrolled emergence of energy, it can be devastating to normal functioning and adjustment.

Application to Particular Variables

The review of the literature has demonstrated the wide applicability of Holt's primary process assessment instrument in research. It can be applied to all age and intelligence groups from whom a verbal or figural document can be obtained. Differences in sex, education, and socioeconomic status may have some culturally understandable effects on primary process ideation, but these do not appear to warrant serious conclusions or inferences at present. The use of primary process as a diagnostic and vocational counseling tool is premature. The presence of primary process has been known to carry both positive and negative influences, but it is not always clear when and to what extent these operate. Absence of primary process in test protocols does not necessary imply that personal and cognitive resources are poorly used. Other knowledge about the sample population is essential to facilitate meaningful interpretation; and, in view of inadequate norms for different populations, interpretation is hazardous. It is difficult to know whether the methodology or the instrument is at fault when ambiguous or negative results are obtained in research. In short, the instrument is wide open for experimental research. It has yielded considerable knowledge about the nature of primary process and about situations where it might be expected to appear. What is still unknown depends as much on conceptual confusion residing within psychoanalytic theory as on the weakness of the assessment tool as developed by Holt.

While primary process measures have been useful in research in schizophrenia, their incidence and significance in psychosomatic and organic disorders have been little explored.

References

Allison, J. "Adaptive Regression and Intense Religious Experiences." *Journal of Nervous and Mental Disease,* 1967, *145,* 452-463.

Arlow, J. A., and Brenner, C. *Psychoanalytic Concepts and the Structural Theory.* New York: International Universities Press, 1973.

Berlyne, D. E. *Aesthetics and Psychobiology.* New York: Appleton-Century-Crofts, 1971.

Chamberland-Bouhadana, G. "Les Modalités de Pensée chez les Artistes Expérimentés et les Artistes Débutants." Unpublished master's thesis, University of Montreal, 1977.

Dudek, S. Z. "Regression and Creativity." *Journal of Nervous and Mental Disease,* 1968, *147,* 535-546.

Dudek, S. Z. "Intelligence, Psychopathology and the Primary Thinking Disorder in Early Schizophrenia." *Journal of Nervous and Mental Disease,* 1969, *148,* 515-527.

Dudek, S. Z. "Effects of Different Types of Psychotherapy on the Personality as a Whole." *Journal of Nervous and Mental Disease,* 1970, *150,* 329-345.

Dudek, S. Z. "Regression in the Service of the Ego in Young Children." *Journal of Personality Assessment,* 1975, *39,* 369-376.

Dudek, S. Z., Chamberland-Bouhadana, G., and Gagnon, P. E. "Regression in the Service of the Ego in Artists, Art Students and Other Professionals." Paper presented at annual convention of Canadian Psychological Association, Ottawa, June 1978.

Dudek, S. Z., and Loveless, R. "Primary Process Thinking as a Creativity Index on Torrance Tests." *Journal of Personality Assessment,* in press.

Dudek, S. Z., and Verreault, R. "Sex and Socio-economic Influences on Adaptive Regression in Young Children." *Journal of Personality Assessment,* in press.

Eagle, C. J. "An Investigation of Individual Consistencies in the Manifestations of Primary Process." Unpublished doctoral dissertation, New York University, 1964.

Feirstein, A. "Personality Correlates of Tolerance for Unrealistic Experiences." *Journal of Consulting Psychology,* 1967, *31,* 387-395.

Freud, S. "Project for a Scientific Psychology" [1895]. In *The Origins of Psychoanalysis: Letters to Wilhelm Fliess, Drafts and Notes: 1887-1902.* New York: Basic Books, 1954.

Freud, S. *The Interpretation of Dreams* [1900]. In *Standard Edition of the Complete Psychological Works of Sigmund Freud.* Vols. 4 and 5. London: Hogarth Press, 1953.

Freud, S. "Formulations of the Two Principles of Mental Functioning" [1911]. In D. Rapaport (Ed.), *Organization and Pathology of Thought.* New York: Columbia University Press, 1951.

Freud, S. *Repression* [1915]. In *Standard Edition.* Vol. 14. London: Hogarth Press, 1957.

Freud, S. *The Ego and the Id* [1923]. In *Standard Edition.* Vol. 19. London: Hogarth Press, 1961.

Gagnon, P. E. "Sublimation d'Agressivité chez les Artistes Peintres." Unpublished master's thesis, University of Montreal, 1977.

Gill, M. M. "Topography and Systems in Psychoanalytic Theory." *Psychological Issues,* 1963, *3* (2) monograph 10.

Gill, M. M. "The Primary Process." In R. R. Holt (Ed.), *Motives and Thought.* New York: International Universities Press, 1967.

Goldberger, L. "Reactions to Perceptual Isolation and Rorschach Manifestations of the Primary Process." *Journal of Projective Techniques,* 1961, *25,* 287-302.

Harrow, M., and others. "Primitive Drive Dominated Thinking: Relationship to Acute Schizophrenia and Sociopathy." *Journal of Personality Assessment,* 1976, *40,* 31-41.

Hartmann, H. *Ego Psychology and the Problem of Adaptation* [1939]. New York: International Universities Press, 1958.

Hartmann, H., Kris, E., and Loewenstein, R. "Comments on the Formation of Psychic Structure." *Psychoanalytic Study of the Child,* 1946, *2,* 11-38.

Hebb, D. O. *The Organization of Behavior.* New York: Wiley, 1949.

Holt, R. R. "The Development of the Primary Process." In R. R. Holt (Ed.), *Motives and Thought.* New York: International Universities Press, 1967.

Holt, R. R. "Artistic Creativity and Rorschach Measures of Adaptive Regression." In B. Klopfer and others (Eds.), *Developments in the Rorschach Technique.* Vol. 3. New York: Harcourt Brace Jovanovitch, 1970.

Holt, R. R. "A Method for Assessing Primary Process Manifestations and Their Control in Rorschach Responses." In M. A. Rickers-Ovsiankina (Ed.), *Rorschach Psychology.* (2nd ed.) New York: Krieger, 1977.

Holt, R. R., and Havel, J. "A Method for Assessing Primary and Secondary Process in the Rorschach." In M. A. Rickers-Ovsiankina (Ed.), *Rorschach Psychology.* New York: Wiley, 1960.

Huard, M. "Les Processus Primaires et Secondaires chez les Musiciens de Jazz Professionnels." Unpublished doctoral dissertation, University of Montreal, 1972.

Kokis, S. "La Pensée des Schizophrènes Récents et Chroniques d'une Institution à Sécurité Maximale à Travers le Test de Rorschach." Unpublished doctoral dissertation, University of Montreal, 1973.

Kris, E. *Psychoanalytic Explorations in Art.* New York: International Universities Press, 1952.

Lavoie, G., and others. "Hypnotic Susceptibility as a Function of Adaptive Regression in Chronic Schizophrenic Patients." *International Journal of Clinical and Experimental Hypnosis,* 1976, *24,* 238-257.

Loveless, R. "Relationship of Primary Process Thinking to Indices of Creativity in Rorschach and Torrance Tests." Unpublished doctoral dissertation, University of Montreal, 1978.

Martindale, C. "The Psychology of Literary Change." Unpublished doctoral dissertation, Harvard University, 1960.

Martindale, C. "An Experimental Simulation of Literary Change." *Journal of Personality and Social Psychology,* 1973, *25,* 319-326.

Martindale, C. *The Romantic Progression: The Psychology of Literary History.* Washington, D.C.: Hemisphere, 1975.

Matalon, E. "Primary Process Thought and Its Relation to Some Areas of Functioning in Ten-Year-Old Children." Unpublished doctoral dissertation, University of Montreal, 1975.

Maupin, E. W. "Individual Differences in Responses to a Zen Meditation Exercise." *Journal of Consulting Psychology,* 1965, *29,* 139-145.

Myden, W. "Interpretation and Evaluation of Certain Personality Characteristics Involved in Creative Production." *Perceptual and Motor Skills,* 1959, *9,* 139-158.

Noy, P. "A Revision of the Psychoanalytic Theory of the Primary Process." *International Journal of Psycho-analysis,* 1969, *50,* 155-178.

Piaget, J. *The Construction of Reality in the Child* [1937]. New York: Basic Books, 1954.

Pine, F. "Thematic Drive Content and Creativity." *Journal of Personality,* 1959, *27,* 136-151.

Pine, F. "A Manual for Rating Drive Content in the Thematic Apperception Test." *Journal of Projective Techniques,* 1960, *24,* 32-45.

Pine, F., and Holt, R. R. "Creativity and Primary Process: A Study of Adaptive Regression." *Journal of Abnormal and Social Psychology,* 1960, *61,* 370-379.

Rabie, V. "A Method for Scoring TAT Drive Content with Children." Unpublished master's thesis, University of Montreal, 1969.

Rapaport, D. "Toward a Theory of Thinking." In D. Rapaport (Ed.), *Organization and Pathology of Thought.* New York: Columbia University Press, 1951.

Rivard, E., and Dudek, S. Z. "Primary Process Thinking in Young Children at Two Developmental Levels." *Journal of Personality Assessment,* 1977, *41,* 120-130.

Roffwarg, H. P., Dement, W. C., and Fisher, C. "Preliminary Observations of the Sleep-

Dream Pattern in Neo-nates, Infants, Children and Adults." In E. Harms (Ed.), *Problems of Sleep and Dreams in Children.* New York: Macmillan, 1964.

Rogolsky, M. M. "Artistic Creativity and Adaptive Regression in Third Grade Children." *Journal of Projective Techniques and Personality Assessment,* 1968, *32,* 53-62.

Safrin, R. "Primary Process Thought in the Rorschachs of Girls at the Oedipal, Latency and Adolescent Stages of Development." Unpublished doctoral dissertation, New York University, 1974.

Schafer, R. "Regression in the Service of the Ego." In G. Lindzey (Ed.), *Assessment of Human Motives.* New York: Holt, Rinehart and Winston, 1958.

Schafer, R. *Aspects of Internalization.* New York: International Universities Press, 1968.

Silverman, L. H., Lapkin, B., and Rosenbaum, I. S. "Manifestations of Primary Process Thinking in Schizophrenics." *Journal of Projective Techniques,* 1962, *26,* 117-127.

Verreault, R. "La Créativité (T.T.C.T.) et la Régression au Service du Moi en Relation avec le Sexe et le Milieu Socio-économique chez les Enfants de 5e et 6e Année." Unpublished doctoral dissertation, University of Montreal, 1978.

Waelder, R. "The Principle of Multiple Function: Observations on Over Determination." *Psychoanalytic Quarterly,* 1936, *5,* 45-62.

Wolff, P. H. *The Developmental Psychologies of Jean Piaget and Psychoanalysis.* New York: International Universities Press, 1960.

Wright, N. A., and Zubek, J. P. "Relationship Between Perceptual Deprivation, Tolerance and Adequacy of Defenses as Measured by the Rorschach." *Journal of Abnormal Psychology,* 1969, *74,* 123-127.

Wulach, J. S. "Piagetian Cognitive Development and Primary Process Thinking in Children." *Journal of Personality Assessment,* 1977, *41,* 230-237.

Zimet, C. N., and Fine, H. J. "Primary and Secondary Process Thinking in Two Types of Schizophrenia." *Journal of Projective Techniques and Personality Assessment,* 1965, *29,* 93-99.

42

Ronald Blackburn

Aggression (Physiological)

Professionals generally agree that "aggression" covers injurious or destructive action, but there is little unanimity about the boundaries of the concept. While aggression may be defined by reference to its antecedents, consequences for the victim, or purposes of the aggressor, each of these realms embraces a different range of phenomena. From the point of view of understanding human violence, there seem to be advantages in distinguishing between classes of injurious behaviors on the basis of functional similarity. As used here, the term *aggression* refers broadly to behavior involving the injury or discomfort of another person, but a distinction is made between angry or hostile aggression (in which injury is the intended outcome) and instrumental or nonhostile aggression (in which injury serves some other purpose). Although clinicians have tended to treat aggression or violence as a unitary category, it is commonly implicit that abnormal or antisocial aggression is hostile aggression. This is a tenuous assumption, since instances of nonhostile aggression are encountered in psychiatric and criminal populations (Bandura, 1973). However, instances of "pure" instrumental aggression may be relatively rare in cases of socially nonsanctioned behavior, and instrumental aggression may be more probable in individuals who have strong tendencies to exhibit angry aggressive behavior. Consequently, attention here is focused primarily on angry or hostile aggression.

Anger is an emotional response to frustration, insult, or attack, and there is now evidence in support of the view that anger makes aggression more probable (Rule and Nesdale, 1976). However, it is widely accepted that whether or not aggressive behavior accompanies anger is largely dependent on learning. The observable response of aggression must, therefore, be distinguished from the inferred mediating state of anger.

Further distinctions are necessary between temporarily aroused states of anger or associated episodes of aggressive behavior, on the one hand, and traits of hostility and aggressiveness, on the other. Hostility in this respect may be regarded as the tendency to experience states of anger, and aggressiveness as the tendency to emit aggressive responses when angry. These have emerged as identifiable personality dimensions in factor analytic studies (Blackburn, 1972). The category of psychopathic personality is also of some relevance in the present context. Although not all individuals diagnosed as psychopathic in clinical practice are aggressive, nonpsychotic individuals who are persistently aggressive are commonly labeled in this way.

This chapter is concerned with the physiological investigation of anger and aggression and with the physiological correlates of hostility and aggressiveness as dispositions. The emphasis is on the psychophysiology of intact human subjects, although some reference is necessary to neuropsychological studies involving surgical intervention in humans and animals. For the clinician, the ultimate interest lies in the extent to which such work may facilitate the evaluation and rehabilitation of abnormal or antisocial individuals. However, the identification of aggression as abnormal or antisocial depends to a large extent on processes of social evaluation, and the difference between abnormal and socially sanctioned (or ignored) aggression is therefore somewhat arbitrary. Consequently, investigations of clinical and nonclinical populations will be considered.

Background and Current Status

The first reported investigation appears to be that of Hill and Watterson (1942), who described an analysis of the electroencephalograms (EEGs) of aggressive personalities. However, current notions of the physiological substrate of aggression can be traced to (1) the classic work of Walter Cannon, who demonstrated the mobilizing function of the sympathetic-adrenal system in preparing the organism for fight or flight; and (2) neurophysiological studies in the 1920s, which clearly implicated the hypothalamus in animal rage and in the integration of autonomic activity.

Cannon believed that emotions are differentiated primarily along a single dimension of intensity of physiological activation. While this view has its modern counterparts, a number of studies have sought to establish that anger is distinguished from other emotions by an identifiable pattern of sympathetic and endocrine discharge. This hypothesis received support from Ax (1953), who found differences between anger and fear. Specifically, although both fear and anger increase sympathetic activity, anger increases diastolic blood pressure, spontaneous skin conductance activity, and muscle tension. He suggested that fear is associated primarily with an increase in the secretion of adrenaline from the adrenal medulla, while anger reflects a mixed pattern of adrenaline and noradrenaline release. Funkenstein, King, and Drolette (1957) modified this hypothesis, on the basis of cardiovascular responses of subjects displaying "anger-out" (verbalized anger) or "anger-in" (verbalized depression) responses to stress. They proposed that, as a result of differential hypothalamic discharge, anger reflects predominantly nonadrenaline increase, whereas fear reflects predominantly adrenaline effects. Although data from several studies have challenged the Funkenstein hypothesis, it has remained a major influence on research in this area.

Other significant developments have centered around the physiology of central mechanisms of aggression in animals, and numerous studies support some degree of localization in the limbic system (Goldstein, 1974; Mark and Ervin, 1970; Moyer, 1971). Electrical stimulation studies have shown that integrated attacking behavior can be elicited from several areas, although there are a number of inconsistent findings, which may reflect variations in electrode placement. Many of the aggressive behavior patterns shown by animals are probably species specific and of little relevance to human aggression. However, affective or defensive aggression is universal among vertebrates, and it appears to be controlled by limbic circuits, including the medial hypothalamus, the amygdala, and the central gray.

Some neurological studies involve stimulation of and recording from limbic areas in human epileptic patients showing abnormal aggression (Mark and Ervin, 1970), and the data suggest that the neural system integrating animal affective aggression also subserves angry aggression in humans. It has been claimed that surgical lesions in the posterior hypothalamus, the amygdala, the thalamus, and the cingulate gyrus reduce the frequency and intensity of abnormal rage reactions in these patients, but this work has been criticized on methodological and ethical grounds (Valenstein, 1973).

Current theories of aggression variously accord physiological processes an initiating, a mediating, or a nonspecific role. While the limbic system may integrate human aggressive reactions, the extent to which this system is controlled and selectively activated by higher cortical functions is undoubtedly considerable. According to some learning theorists (for example, Bandura, 1973), social experience is the primary determinant of the form and intensity of aggressive behavior, as well as the selection of targets and the context in which aggression occurs, and physiological activity accompanying aggression is little different from that associated with a variety of motivated activities. Berkowitz (1969), however, argues that there is an unlearned pattern for anger arousal and that this pattern mediates the relation between frustration and aggression. He also suggests that there may be innate connections between anger and aggression, although these become modified during experience. A more biological approach is advocated by Moyer (1971) and by Mark and Ervin (1970), who believe that internal bodily changes may influence responsiveness to provoking events and may also, under some circumstances, initiate aggressive behavior sequences.

Clearly, the social learning approach, Berkowitz's reactive drive concept, and the biological model assign different degrees of significance to the evaluation of the physiological correlates of aggression. However, these differences are amenable to resolution by empirical means.

Critical Discussion

General Areas of Concern

Psychophysiological investigations of aggression have generally been directed toward three questions: (1) Are there unique physiological response patterns associated with anger instigation or the performance of an aggressive response? (2) Are hostility and aggressiveness (as personality characteristics) associated with particular variables that might predispose to the development or facilitation of aggressive response tendencies? (3) Is abnormal or antisocial aggression determined by specific abnormalities in the nervous system, which might be amenable to pharmacological or surgical intervention? The research generated by these three issues characteristically varies according to whether subjects are drawn from clinical or nonclinical populations; whether the design is correlational or employs experimental manipulation of relevant antecedents and consequences; how aggression, whether viewed as response or trait, is defined; and which physiological variables are measured. To date, the most frequently used measures have been those derived from electrocortical or cardiovascular recordings or from biochemical assays of the blood and urine.

The EEG, the earliest physiological measure examined in relation to aggression, has also been the most widely employed by clinicians. Although automatic frequency and amplitude analysis has been available for some time, clinicians have generally relied on visual analysis of the waveform, as recorded from scalp electrodes. Most attention has been paid to the presence of abnormalities seen in multilead records taken during rest, sleep, or hyperventilation, and these consist mainly of focal or diffuse slow waves in the theta band (4-7 Hz), unusual bursts of activity, and 14-16 Hz spike activity (see Hill, 1963).

A commonly reported finding is that aggressive personalities tend to show a high incidence of EEG abnormalities. For example, in their study of personality disorder in armed forces personnel, Hill and Watterson (1942) found that 65 percent of the aggressive psychopaths showed EEG abnormalities, compared with 32 percent of the inadequate psychopaths, 26 percent of the neurotics, and 15 percent of the nonpatient controls. More recently Williams (1969) made a retrospective comparison of the EEGs of habitually aggressive criminals and offenders who had committed only an isolated act of aggression. Abnormality was found in 65 percent of the former but only 24 percent of the latter, and three quarters of all abnormalities consisted of bilateral slow-wave activity in the theta band and/or focal abnormality in the temporal lobe.

One difficulty with these studies is that the notion of EEG abnormality is ill defined, and it combines several disparate phenomena. Some of these, such as 14-16 Hz spikes, may be of no pathological significance. Moreover, a number of investigators have found no difference between aggressive and nonaggressive subjects. In an early review of these studies, Ellingson (1954) drew attention to a number of methodological shortcomings—notably, criteria of subject selection, criteria of EEG abnormality, lack of controls, and absence of statistical evaluation. Nevertheless, he concluded that rates of 50 percent abnormality had been shown with some consistency in psychopaths and that aggressiveness was the single characteristic most clearly correlated with abnormality. Evaluating more recent data, however, Gale (1975) has been rather skeptical. He argues that few, if any, of the studies in this area are free from the defects pointed to by Ellingson. Given the number of failures of replication, Gale concludes that the evidence favoring an association between EEG abnormality and psychopathy is suspect and that the evidence for an association between abnormality and aggressiveness is, at best, suggestive.

A further problem is that no unequivocal relationship has been established between EEG abnormalities and organic brain dysfunction. The most frequent kind of abnormality is the appearance of slow waves in the theta band, particularly over the temporal lobes. Since this phenomenon is relatively common among children, it has been suggested that in adults it may indicate a "maturational lag." However, no relationship has been found between slow-wave activity and developmental retardation; this hypothesis, therefore, represents no more than a weak inference.

An alternative suggestion has been that temporal lobe abnormalities in the EEG represent limbic dysfunction. This hypothesis gains some support from the work of Mark and Ervin (1970), who have used depth electrode recording in epileptic patients exhibiting behavior disorder. They identified a dyscontrol syndrome, characterized by a history of assaultive behavior, aggression triggered by small amounts of alcohol, impulsive sexual behavior, and serious traffic accidents. In some patients showing this syndrome, abnormal rage reactions have been preceded by epileptiform discharges in depth records, and amygdaloid stimulation has led to violent and destructive episodes. Mark and Ervin believe that a relatively large proportion of individuals showing the dyscontrol syndrome will be found to have either structural brain disorder or functional abnormalities of an epileptic kind. While their data suggest that there may be a causal relationship between brain pathology and aggression (at least in some individuals), one must be cautious in assuming that this finding has wide generality. The majority of patients with temporal lobe epilepsy do not show unusual aggressiveness, and in those who do, rage reactions are most likely to appear during seizure-free periods (Goldstein, 1974). Also, a correlation between brain pathology and abnormal aggression does not necessarily imply causation; that is, aggressive persons may be more likely to engage in activities resulting in head injury.

However suggestive the above data may be, it seems unlikely that limbic pathology provides more than a partial account of EEG abnormality. Dysfunction of deep structures in the brain is not invariably detected in surface EEG recordings, and the extent to which patients with abnormal EEGs suffer from organic disturbance is unknown. One further possible explanation for EEG abnormalities is that they do not, in fact, represent discrete abnormalities but, rather, reflect quantitative departures from normality. Reliance on qualitative visual analysis of the EEG trace seems to have led to an undue emphasis on the possibility of underlying organic pathology, but quantitative analysis indicates that the slow-wave activity varies both within and between individuals as a function of the level of activation. Quantitative analysis also permits a more reliable determination of differences between individuals and between stimulus conditions.

In one of the few studies employing this methodology with aggressive personalities, Blackburn (1975) found no reliable differences between aggressive and unaggressive offenders in amount of theta. Both an inventory measure of aggressiveness and a frequency measure of previous aggression were, in fact, related to higher EEG arousal, as indexed by dominant frequency, rather than to low arousal, as might be expected if high theta activity were characteristic of aggressive personalities. This is consistent with the neurological studies of Sano and associates (1970), which suggest high arousal in aggressive patients. However, in a further analysis Blackburn (1979) found that highly aggressive offenders who are also socially withdrawn and anxious do display high levels of theta activity and also other signs of low arousal, both at rest and during monotonous stimulation. It appears, therefore, that there is no direct relationship between aggressiveness and the presence of theta activity but that high theta levels may be characteristic of aggressive personalities only when other deviant traits are present. Aggressive individuals who are less anxious seem to be characterized by relatively little theta and high arousal. At present, the psychological significance of this finding remains unclear, since the precise behavioral correlates of theta activity have not been established (Schacter, 1977).

Surprisingly little attention has yet been paid to the sympathetic correlates of antisocial aggression. However, several laboratory studies of normal subjects have attempted to determine whether manipulations designed to provoke a state of anger have particular autonomic effects, and also whether aggressive behavior leads to tension reduction, as predicted from the notion of catharsis. In a series of experiments, Hokanson and his colleagues (Hokanson, 1970) recorded cardiovascular activity while subjects were provoked by insult or shock and then permitted to respond aggressively or nonaggressively.

Initial data indicated that insult produced significant elevations of heart rate and systolic blood pressure. Rapid return of these variables to the baseline was found to accompany direct aggression, but not fantasy-, displaced-, or no-aggression conditions. However, a systolic blood pressure response to provocation has not been a universal finding. Some investigators have demonstrated an effect on diastolic but not systolic pressure. A probable reason for these discrepancies lies in the effectiveness with which anger is provoked by the different manipulations employed. Gentry (1970), for example, found that frustration produced a diastolic response but did not influence aggressive responding and that insult facilitated aggression but did not affect blood pressure systematically. A recent study by Frodi (1976) supports rather strongly the proposal that diastolic, rather than systolic, blood pressure is sensitive to anger. She selected provoking conditions which a pretest had established as anger arousing. These produced an increase in diastolic pressure, cardiac rate, and electrodermal level, but they had no significant effect on systolic pressure. Moreover, verbalization of angry thoughts following provocation increased diastolic pressure and the degree of aggression, but it did not affect other autonomic variables.

Some investigators, however, have questioned the notion of a specific physiological pattern in anger and have argued that cognitions about the source of arousal are major determinants of experienced anger and aggression. Zillmann (see, for example, Zillmann and Bryant, 1974) has shown that increased arousal from nonaggressive sources, such as exercise, may intensify aggression when the arousal is attributed to anger. However, the extent to which misattribution of a source of arousal occurs outside the laboratory is an open question.

While Hokanson's early studies provided some limited support for the catharsis hypothesis, his later work has indicated that decreases in arousal accompanying direct aggression may be more a function of the subject's learned mode of coping with a noxious stimulus than an intrinsic characteristic of anger expression. He has hypothesized that tension reduction will accompany any response which, through negative reinforcement, serves to terminate, reduce, or avoid noxious stimulation from others. In a series of experiments, he demonstrated that males reduce tension (as evidenced by recovery of the vasoconstrictive response to shock) most rapidly by making a counteraggressive response but that females reduce tension most rapidly by making nonaggressive responses. However, as predicted by the hypothesis, this pattern was shown to be reversible by manipulation of the response contingencies. Thus, males—who, according to the model, have learned that aggression is the appropriate response to provocation—can learn to experience tension reduction from making nonaggressive responses when these are reinforced, while the converse holds for females. Scarpetti (1974) has extended this model to individual differences and has also demonstrated similar effects on the recovery of the electrodermal response to shock. However, the applicability of the model to angry aggression depends on the adequacy of shock stimulation as a paradigm of anger induction. In these experiments it was not, in fact, established that subjects experienced anger.

Following the earlier studies of Ax (1953) and Funkenstein, King, and Drolette (1957), several studies have examined the hypothesis that levels of adrenaline and noradrenaline are differentially related to fear and anger. Some findings fail to support the hypothesis. Frankenhaeuser (1975) has reviewed studies indicating that adrenaline is elevated by both pleasant and unpleasant states and by a variety of arousing conditions, including unpredictability, uncontrollability, and positive coping. She suggests that the data indicate a relatively nonspecific role of catecholamine secretion in emotional states. Other studies, however, have found a positive correlation between aggressive personality traits and noradrenaline output under arousing conditions; and a differential relationship of catecholamine secretion to personality is also suggested in recent work by Hinton and his colleagues (Hinton and Woodman, 1977; Woodman, Hinton, and O'Neill, in press). In studies of anticipatory stress responses in patients at a maximum security hospital, they isolated a group of offenders who were hyporeactive on electromyographic and cardiovascular responses. These subjects showed very high noradrenaline/adrenaline ratios and low adrenaline levels in both plasma and urine. This pattern was stable over a two-year interval and was not observed in nonoffender patients or normal controls. Offenders showing this pattern had more convictions for assaultive crimes against strangers, with more of them resulting in fatality, than offenders showing smaller catecholamine ratios. It is not clear, however, that these subjects are more persistently aggressive; and, as the investigators note, the low adrenaline levels of this group may be the most significant feature of their anticipatory stress response. It is possible that these are individuals who characteristically deal with stress with coping mechanisms of denial and avoidance, since their personality test scores resemble those of the overcontrolled offender (Megargee, 1971). These results need to be reconciled with those of Lidberg and associates (1976), who found that a small group of aggressive psychopathic criminals displayed significantly lower noradrenaline levels and higher adrenaline secretion than nonpsychopaths under novel but nonstressful conditions and showed a smaller increase in both amines when anticipating stress.

A possible hormonal influence on aggression is the level of androgens. Moyer (1971) proposes that testosterone level may increase or decrease aggressive responding by sensitizing central neural aggression systems. A few studies suggest that androgenizing hormones increase aggression in males, and there have been some clinical reports of aggressive girls who had been exposed to virilizing hormones in utero or early childhood. Attempts have been made in recent studies to determine whether more aggressive individuals are discriminated from unaggressive males by the level of testosterone and its rate of production. Persky, Smith, and Basu (1971) found that both level and production rate of testosterone were significantly related to an inventory scale of aggressiveness in young males but not in older subjects (although several subsequent studies have failed to replicate this finding in either student or criminal samples). Ehrenkrantz, Bliss, and Sheard (1974) found that highly aggressive prisoners had significantly higher levels of plasma testosterone than submissive, unaggressive criminals; however, the aggressive offenders did not differ significantly from offenders who were socially dominant but unaggressive. In view of the largely negative findings in this area, it seems that testosterone secretion may not be a very significant factor in determining individual differences in aggressiveness.

Comparative Philosophies and Theories

The major theoretical issue is whether there is a unique physiological pattern associated with anger arousal and aggressive behavior. Both the biological and reactive drive models seem to predict some degree of autonomic and endocrine differentiation between anger and other aroused states resulting from selective discharge of hypothalamic and other limbic areas in response to a provoking stimulus, as is also postulated by the Funkenstein research. Relevant individual differences might be expected in predispositions to produce these patterns either more intensely or at a lower threshold. In contrast, social learning theory proposes that various aversive stimuli elicit a nonspecific state of emotional arousal, which facilitates whatever response (aggressive or otherwise) is prepotent (Bandura, 1973). Expectations and cognitive labeling of the aroused state determine the nature of the emotion and the response. In these terms, individual differences in arousability might be of relevance in predisposing to aggression, but only if the individual is also exposed to reinforcement for aggression.

Lazarus (1968) emphasizes that cognitive appraisal is the first event in any emotional response. He believes that aversive events are appraised discriminatively and that different appraisals lead to different emotional states. While this model appears to overlap with the reactive drive model, it suggests that individual differences in hostility and aggression may be related to factors affecting cognitive appraisal. Such factors, whether situational or intrapersonal, would be expected to influence the nature of the physiological responses.

Elaboration on Critical Points

The available data on the physiological correlates of anger and aggression do not permit firm statements regarding the preceding models. Although anger manipulations may result in generalized sympathetic activation, the evidence for a differential effect on diastolic blood pressure suggests that there may be a specific pattern for anger. Some data, however, contradict this view, and the evidence on the role played by noradrenaline does not provide strong support for the Funkenstein hypothesis. Similarly, no consistent indications have yet emerged of any physiological pattern associated with hostility or aggressiveness. However, the number of studies to date is small, and it would clearly be premature to discount the possibility of significant predisposing factors.

Personal Views and Recommendations

There is currently a need for research developments in this area along several lines. First, since it is unlikely that any single physiological variable is uniquely associated with anger or aggression, investigators need to examine multivariate patterns rather than single channels of activity. Second, there is a need for more research employing mixed designs, in which both individual differences in hostility and aggression and relevant aggression-inducing conditions are varied. Third, where aggressiveness as a trait is the independent variable, account should be taken of its possible interaction with other traits that might facilitate or inhibit anger experience and aggressive responding. Finally, clinical studies in this area need to take account of cognitive variables that interact with physiological arousal. As Lazarus (1968) has pointed out, emotions are complex responses, with cognitive, physiological, and motor components, and each of these has its own adaptive functions. The potential utility of physiological assessment in this respect is not as a substitute for other forms of assessment but as a necessary adjunct to them.

Application to Particular Variables

Discussion of technical issues in psychophysiological measurement is beyond the scope of this chapter, and the reader is referred to appropriate texts by Venables and Martin (1967) and Greenfield and Sternbach (1972). However, physiological concomitants of aggression are likely to be influenced by a number of individual and demographic variables, which an investigator must take into account.

Developmental variations in physiological responding are considerable, particularly in EEG patterns (Shagass, 1972). Aggression is typically most pronounced in young men, and it may be relevant that both sympathetic reactivity and hormone production decline with age.

Sex appears to be a particularly significant variable affecting the degree of aggression. It is clearly established that males are more aggressive than females, and hormonal differences may be important in this respect. For example, androgenization has been observed to be an antecedent of aggressiveness in some delinquent girls. Stage of the menstrual cycle has also been claimed to be a factor in female violence (Moyer, 1971). However, Hokanson's work (Hokanson, 1970) indicates that sex differences in aggressive responding are associated with physiological activity, which is susceptible to learning. Similarly Frodi (1976) observed sex differences in aggression and physiological responding and concluded that these differences were related to different coping strategies.

Both physical and psychiatric condition must also be taken into account. While no firm data seem to have been collected, disorders affecting the nervous system may influence aggression. Moyer (1971), for example, notes that hypoglycemia is associated with increased irritability and aggression, and the possible association between organic cerebral pathology and aggressive behavior has been discussed above. Among functional psychiatric disorders, there are clear associations between aggression and psychopathic personality, and there have now been a number of studies of the psychophysiology of psychopathy (Hare and Schalling, 1978). However, current thinking in this area associates psychopathy with low levels of autonomic reactivity, which have been hypothesized as resulting in impaired social learning. This model may not be applicable to aggressiveness (Blackburn, 1975, 1979).

Socioeconomic factors may be relevant to the physiological correlates of aggression. There is some evidence for class differences in aggressive behavior arising from variations in socialization practices, and Fine and Sweeney (1967) found socioeconomic correlates of catecholamine secretion which are accounted for in this way.

References

Ax, A. F. "The Physiological Differentiation of Fear and Anger in Humans." *Psychosomatic Medicine,* 1953, *15,* 433-442.

Bandura, A. *Aggression: a Social Learning Analysis.* Englewood Cliffs, N.J.: Prentice-Hall, 1973.

Berkowitz, L. "The Frustration-Aggression Hypothesis Revisited." In L. Berkowitz (Ed.), *Roots of Aggression.* New York: Atherton, 1969.

Blackburn, R. "Dimensions of Hostility and Aggression in Abnormal Offenders." *Journal of Consulting and Clinical Psychology,* 1972, *38,* 20-26.

Blackburn, R. "Aggression and the EEG: a Quantitative Analysis." *Journal of Abnormal Psychology,* 1975, *84,* 358-365.

Blackburn, R. "Cortical and Autonomic Arousal in Primary and Secondary Psychopaths." *Psychophysiology,* 1979, *16,* 143-150.

Ehrenkrantz, J., Bliss, E., and Sheard, M. "Plasma Testosterone: Correlation with Aggressive Behavior and Social Dominance in Man." *Psychosomatic Medicine,* 1974, *36,* 469-475.

Ellingson, R. J. "Incidence of EEG Abnormality Among Patients with Mental Disorders of Apparently Nonorganic Origin: A Critical Review." *American Journal of Psychiatry,* 1954, *111,* 263-275.

Fine, B. J., and Sweeney, D. R. "Socio-economic Background, Aggression and Catecholamine Secretion." *Psychological Reports,* 1967, *20,* 11-18.

Frankenhaeuser, M. "Sympathetic-Adrenomedullary Activity, Behavior and the Psychosocial Environment." In P. H. Venables and M. J. Christie (Eds.), *Research in Psychophysiology.* New York: Wiley, 1975.

Frodi, A. "Experiential and Physiological Processes Mediating Sex Differences in Behavioral Aggression." *Göteborg Psychological Reports,* 1976, *6* (6).

Funkenstein, D., King, S. H., and Drolette, M. *Mastery of Stress.* Cambridge, Mass.: Harvard University Press, 1957.

Gale, A. "Psychopathy and the EEG: a Critical Review." Paper presented at NATO Advanced Study Institute on Psychopathic Behaviour, Les Arcs, France, 1975.

Gentry, W. D. "Effects of Frustration, Attack and Prior Aggression Training on Overt Aggression and Vascular Processes." *Journal of Personality and Social Psychology,* 1970, *16,* 718-725.

Goldstein, M. "Brain Research and Violent Behavior." *Archives of Neurology,* 1974, *30,* 1-35.

Greenfield, N. S., and Sternbach, R. A. (Eds.). *Handbook of Psychophysiology.* New York: Holt, Rinehart and Winston, 1972.

Hare, R. D., and Schalling, D. (Eds.). *Psychopathic Behavior: Approaches to Research.* New York: Wiley, 1978.

Hill, D. "The EEG in Psychiatry." In D. Hill and G. Parr (Eds.), *Electroencephalography.* London: Macdonald, 1963.

Hill, D., and Watterson, D. "Electroencephalographic Studies of the Psychopathic Personality." *Journal of Neurology and Psychiatry,* 1942, *5,* 47-64.

Hinton, J. W., and Woodman, D. D. "Psychophysiological and Biochemical Characteristics of Different Types of Aggressive Offender in a Maximum Security Hospital." Paper presented at annual conference of British Psychological Society, Exeter, 1977.

Hokanson, J. E. "Psychophysiological Evaluation of the Catharsis Hypothesis." In E. I. Megargee and J. E. Hokanson (Eds.), *The Dynamics of Aggression.* New York: Harper & Row, 1970.

Lazarus, R. S. "Emotions and Adaptation: Conceptual and Empirical Relations." In W. J. Arnold (Ed.), *Nebraska Symposium on Motivation.* Lincoln: University of Nebraska Press, 1968.

Lidberg, L., and others. *Excretion of Adrenaline and Noradrenaline as Related to Real Life Stress and Psychopathy.* Report No. 50. Stockholm: Laboratory for Clinical Stress Research, 1976.

Mark, V. H., and Ervin, F. R. *Violence and the Brain.* New York: Harper & Row, 1970.

Megargee, E. I. "The Role of Inhibition in the Assessment and Understanding of Violence." In J. L. Singer (Ed.), *The Control of Aggression and Violence.* New York: Academic Press, 1971.

Moyer, K. E. *The Physiology of Hostility.* Chicago: Markham, 1971.

Persky, H., Smith, K. D., and Basu, G. "Relation of Psychologic Measures of Aggression and Hostility to Testosterone Production in Man." *Psychosomatic Medicine,* 1971, *33,* 265-277.

Rule, B. G., and Nesdale, A. R. "Emotional Arousal and Aggressive Behavior." *Psychological Bulletin,* 1976, *83,* 851-863.

Sano, K., and others. "Results of Stimulation and Destruction of the Posterior Hypothalamus in Man." *Journal of Neurosurgery,* 1970, *33,* 689-707.

Scarpetti, W. L. "Autonomic Concomitants of Aggressive Behavior in Repressors and Sensitizers: a Social Learning Approach." *Journal of Personality and Social Psychology,* 1974, *30,* 772-781.

Schacter, D. L. "EEG Theta Waves and Psychological Phenomena: A Review and Analysis." *Biological Psychology,* 1977, *5,* 47-82.

Shagass, C. "Electrical Activity of the Brain." In N. S. Greenfield and R. A. Sternbach (Eds.), *Handbook of Psychophysiology.* New York: Holt, Rinehart and Winston, 1972.

Valenstein, E. *Brain Control.* New York: Wiley, 1973.

Venables, P. H., and Martin, I. (Eds.). *Manual of Psycho-Physiological Methods.* Amsterdam: North-Holland, 1967.

Williams, D. "Neural Factors Related to Habitual Aggression." *Brain*, 1969, *92*, 503-520.

Woodman, D. D., Hinton, J. W., and O'Neill, M. T. "Plasma Catecholamines and Aggression in Maximum Security Patients." *Biological Psychology*, in press.

Zillmann, D., and Bryant, J. "The Effect of Residual Excitation on the Emotional Response to Provocation and Delayed Aggressive Behavior." *Journal of Personality and Social Psychology*, 1974, *30*, 782-791.

43

George Edmunds

Aggression (Psychological)

The term *aggression* refers generally to interpersonal conflict in which the delivery of suffering is a prominent feature. In the interests of clarity, aggression, which is a motor response, should be distinguished from the constructs of hostility and anger. Hostility is not equivalent to aggression; rather, it is an attitude of dislike or resentment toward other people. Some aggressive acts, however, may be directed by hostile motives, and in these "hostile aggressive" behaviors, the goal is the pain of the victim (Feshbach, 1970). Anger is an emotional state often considered to be a drive for aggression (Berkowitz, 1962). Under certain conditions, emotional arousal is assumed to heighten the probability of aggressive behavior.

There is substantial agreement among experimental psychologists that aggression is a response involving the delivery of noxious stimuli to another organism (Buss, 1971; Kaufmann, 1970). Further, it is acknowledged that such stimuli can be administered in a number of different ways. One meaningful way of classifying aggressive acts requires the assessment, among other things, of the "organ system" employed (physical versus verbal) and the interpersonal contact between the aggressor and victim (direct versus indirect) (Buss, 1961).

At least two further descriptive elements are necessary for classifying aggressive behaviors. First, the basic *motivational* distinction is between hostile aggression, where the goal is the suffering of the victim, and instrumental aggression, which is directed toward the acquisition of extrinsic rewards (such as money, material goods, and status) (Feshbach, 1970). Second, a distinction should be made between reactive and initiatory aggression (Edmunds, 1978). That is, the aggressor may be responding to attack or other noxious events provided by the victim (reactive aggression), or the aggressor himself may make the first move in the aggressive sequence (initiatory aggression).

The reactive-initiatory and hostile-instrumental distinctions are conceptually independent, so that they define four broad classes of aggressive behavior: (1) initiatory instrumental (for example, attacking and robbing innocent persons), (2) reactive instrumental (for example, defense of one's own property against an attacker), (3) reactive hostile (behavior aimed at hurting an attacker), and (4) initiatory hostile (aggression directed toward hurting an innocent victim). Thus, with all four classes of aggression, there is an attempt to hurt the victim, but in the instrumental types, the prime object is to reach an extrinsic goal, and the injury inflicted subserves that purpose. Hostile aggression, by contrast, is designed to hurt the victim with no extrinsic rewards involved.

Background and Current Status

The concept of aggression has its roots in the psychoanalytic tradition. In his initial theorizing, Freud considered aggression the product of frustration of the sexual or ego instincts and, in principle, eradicable. In his later writings, Freud viewed behavior in terms of conflicting life (Eros) and death (Thanatos) instincts, striving, respectively, toward the continuation and cessation of life (Strachey, 1959). A crucial feature of the Thanatos drive is that it requires discharge in one form or another, either against the self or against the external world or in aggressive-erotic activities.

Freud received meager support for his death instinct formulation, and most subsequent drive theorists have adopted the earlier idea of aggression as the product of frustration (Durbin and Bowlby, 1939) or have contended that aggression is an instinct in its own right, not merely the deflection outward of self-directed destructive impulses (Hartmann, Kris, and Loewenstein, 1949).

With the publication in 1939 of the monograph *Frustration and Aggression* by Dollard and his associates, the emphasis began to change from the view that aggression is a drive or an internal impulse to the notion that it is a motor response. According to these investigators, aggression is "an act whose goal response is injury to another organism" (Dollard and others, 1939, p. 11). This definition was later criticized by Buss (1961) on the grounds that the term *goal response* appears to be equivalent to "intent," a concept inconsistent with a behavioral approach by virtue of its teleological implications and the "privacy" of its occurrence. In Buss's view, aggression should be defined as "a response that delivers noxious stimuli to another organism" (p. 3). In turn, Buss' formulation was rejected by Kaufmann (1970) because it made no reference to inner states (which could loosely be called "intentions") and therefore seemed to assess not the behavior of the respondent but, rather, its effects on the victim. In Kaufmann's opinion, an act is classifiable as aggressive if it is directed against a living target and if the attacker has "an expectation or subjective probability greater than zero of reaching the object and of imparting a noxious stimulus to it, or both" (pp. 10-11). Buss (1971) later revised his earlier position and acknowledged that the definition of aggression must involve, in some form, the concept of intent. With this modification, his definition is substantially similar to the position maintained by Kaufmann.

It is now widely accepted that aggressive responses involve the delivery of noxious stimuli and that, in order to be classified as aggressive, pain administration must be intentional behavior. However, aggressive acts serve a wide variety of purposes (self-defense, helping a third party, acquiring commodities, and so on); the infliction of suffering on a victim is merely one of the goals attainable by aggressive means. Viewed in this light, the problem of avoiding the subjectivity apparently inherent in the notion of intent is perhaps obviated to a great extent. The task is not the conceptual one of deciding whether "intent" is to form part of the definition of aggression, but the empirical one of determining what motives underlie given aggressive acts.

Critical Discussion

General Areas of Concern

In psychiatric settings the assessment of aggression has two broad functions: diagnostic (focusing on the role of aggression as a contributory factor in mental illness; the notions of "paranoid" or "projected" aggression exemplify this viewpoint) and predictive (focusing on the prediction of aggressive occurrences, the investigation of experimental hypotheses, and the evaluation of treatment programs). The two types of functions arise from different conceptualizations of aggression, and they demand different measurement strategies. The diagnostic function has primarily been served by techniques aimed at gauging the strength of underlying aggressive drives and their inner- and outer-directed manifestations (Caine, Foulds, and Hope, 1967). Attempts to predict overt aggression in psychiatric patients have consisted mainly of the empirical and intuitive selection of MMPI items (Fisher, 1956; see Buss, 1961, for a review of these strategies). Instruments appropriate for one sort of problem are not necessarily suitable for the other. Thus, data concerning projected or self-directed aggression may be inadequate for detecting assaultive propensities. Likewise, an index of overt aggression may be of scant value for establishing the significance of aggression in personality organization.

The contemporary emphasis is on behavioral aspects of aggression. For this reason, the remainder of this chapter will be devoted principally to prediction issues.

Criminal Violence. Most of the currently available clinical assessment techniques have been developed in psychiatric settings, and there is little evidence that these instruments are capable of predicting (or postdicting) criminally violent behavior (Megargee, 1970; Megargee and Mendelsohn, 1962). A major obstacle to the use of psychiatric instruments with prison samples is that such devices (for instance, the MMPI) typically sample mildly aggressive behavior (such as slapping, swearing, and punching). In contrast, criminal assaultiveness usually takes more serious forms (not infrequently involving the use of weapons). In order to predict violent offending, the content of assessment techniques would need to sample these extreme forms of conduct.

Situational Determinants of Aggression. The main situational determinant of aggression is an aversive stimulus supplied by the victim. In the absence of an event of this kind, there is a lowered probability of aggression (Patterson and Cobb, 1971). The terms *reactive* and *initiatory* were previously introduced to refer, respectively, to aggression in the presence and absence of noxious victim behavior. The propensities to engage in the two forms of activity appear to be unrelated. One of the weaknesses of existing assessment procedures is that they fail to take sufficient account of these different circumstances. Measures of aggression tend to be unidimensional devices (Siegal, 1956), or they relate to such categories as the direction of aggression (Caine, Foulds, and Hope, 1967). These instruments are unlikely to reveal the probability of aggression in specific situations.

Motive and Response Specificity. The points raised in the preceding section are also germane to the matters of motive and response specificity. With regard to motive, it is common practice to distinguish between hostile and instrumentally aggressive behaviors (Feshbach, 1970); the dispositional attributes they represent seem to be largely uncorrelated (Edmunds, 1978). Thus, subjects who would behave aggressively for one form of reward may be unwilling to commit aggression under the other set of incentives. The same is true with respect to classes of aggressive response. Individuals endowed with particular aggressive skills will be inclined to bring these skills into operation on the occasion of aggressive displays and to eschew alternative strategies. Therefore, a highly aggressive person, accustomed to using a certain tactic, could obtain a low score on an aggression inventory simply because the questions asked do not sample his or her preferred mode of responding—for example, when item content concerning mildly aggressive behavior is tested against a criterion of criminal violence. In such cases, extremely assaultive subjects could achieve low scores because they habitually act in an intensely, not mildly, aggressive fashion.

Comparative Philosophies and Theories

The theoretical literature on aggression has been dominated by four major themes: (1) aggression as an instinctive drive (Lorenz, 1966; Storr, 1968); (2) the role of frustration (Berkowitz, 1962); (3) the effects of attack on aggression (Geen, 1968); and (4) the social learning of aggression (Bandura, 1973).

The first three positions assume that an aggressive drive, either self-generated or situation produced, mediates aggressive behavior. Parenthetically, the instinctivist position, in fact, conceives of aggression as a drive rather than as a motor response influenced by drives. This general approach has also been highly influential in assessment, ultimately providing the rationale for the use of projective techniques, as measures of fantasy or "need" aggression, and self-report instruments, in which individuals are asked to indicate their emotional and behavioral reactions to aversive events (Murray, 1943; Zaks and Walters, 1959).

Social learning theory places heavy emphasis on cognitive variables and, while recognizing the role of emotional arousal, assumes that aggressive behaviors are under the control of anticipated consequences. Rather than developing omnibus test batteries, psychologists of this persuasion have concentrated on molecular units of analysis (Patterson and Cobb, 1971), and one school of thought explicitly rejects the value of general personality traits for predicting aggression and other behaviors (Mischel, 1968).

It should be possible, in principle at least, to construct self-report instruments that provide the sensitivity of measurement demanded by social learning theory. But such devices would need to sample individual differences in types of response, across a variety of situations and under an assortment of incentives. The available techniques do not meet these requirements.

Elaboration on Critical Points

Herein, the basic thrust is that assessment techniques must be highly specific to gain applied value. The crucial question confronting any prospective user or constructor of aggression measures concerns the objectives of his or her inquiry. The factors to be considered here are (1) the type of assessment (diagnostic or predictive), (2) the clinical population of interest (psychiatric or criminal), (3) the situational context (reactive or initiatory), (4) the motivation for the aggressive act (hostile or instrumental), and (5) the type of aggressive response.

Prediction programs need to recognize the possibility that aggressive proclivities are specific to immediate environmental influences. That is to say, a "trait" governing the occurrence of a certain type of aggression under one set of circumstances may be irrelevant to or even counterindicative of other types of aggression in the same circumstances or of the same form of aggression in other circumstances.

The question of specificity also arises in evaluating validational evidence. A test that correlates with an empirical criterion may appear to be valid, but if the criterion itself is unsound, so are the data. For example, a significant correlation between a test and a global rating of aggression in psychiatric patients is no guarantee that the instrument will predict specific types of aggression in similar samples or, indeed, aggression of any kind when applied to other samples. The converse is equally true: an instrument invalidated against one criterion or for one population may be quite useful in other settings.

Personal Views and Recommendations

At the outset of a test development program, the objectives and scope of the assessment technique should be accorded careful attention. Consideration should be given to the population of interest and to the type of aggression one proposes to assess. The actual decisions made will depend on the goals of the individual researcher.

The general conceptual approach advocated is an interactionist one. This interactionist position allows for specificity of individuals, motives, situations, and responses. It is the interactions among these variables that determines behavior. In prediction, the practical task is that of establishing the conditions influencing the probability that an individual will perform a certain response. Although the goal of empirical assessment is not necessarily that of predicting particular aggressive acts, it is debatable (in the absence of information regarding the functional equivalence of different responses) whether classes of aggression can be accurately predicted without stipulating the nature of the aggressive responses. In actuality, this may require an assessment of capabilities rather than dispositions (Wallace, 1967).

It seems desirable to have available devices, consisting of subscales, assessing different types of motives and situational determinants of behavior (initiatory instrumental, reactive hostile, and so on), incorporating different forms of aggressive responding, and adapted for use with different populations. Such instruments would probably meet most assessment requirements.

For certain practical purposes, it may be possible to analyze fairly gross behavioral criteria into their constituent elements. Criminal violence, for instance, seems to be predominantly initiatory and instrumental and to involve intense forms of assault. Predictive techniques will be maximally effective if they are sensitive to these facts, and a rational analysis of criteria along such lines may also be fruitful in validation studies.

When assessment is to be used as a guide for making decisions about individual persons, there may be more pragmatic utility, at present, in attempting to isolate stimuli associated with aggressive displays, rather than aspiring to achieve a classification in terms of gross behavioral dimensions. The frequency of aggression is a function of personality variables and the prevalence of relevant situational factors. Therefore, individuals who are not moved to aggressiveness by most environmental stimuli could engage in aggression with high regularity because of extensive exposure to the particular stimuli that do evoke aggression. Football-spectator offending, a source of much contemporary concern in the United Kingdom, appears to be a case in point. For some supporters, the presence of certain stimuli at football matches (such as supporters wearing rival colors or praising opposing teams) could elicit aggressive acts that are reinforced by social approval from members of the aggressor's peer group. Aggression perpetrated by parents against children also occurs in fairly strictly defined sets of conditions. These examples illustrate that normally unaggressive persons can become aggressive in circumstances that do not uniformly elicit aggression across individuals, and so the importance of contextual features is brought into sharp relief.

In other types of aggression, situational parameters may be less prominent but equally potent. Thus, diagnosis for a particular client would entail detecting the range of events that give rise to aggression, and prognosis would involve estimating the incidence of these stimuli in different sorts of environments. A research effort embodying some of the essential elements of this approach has been described by Patterson and Cobb (1971), who have identified social stimuli controlling the exhibition of noxious social responses by problem boys. In planning their own intervention strategies, these authors include provision for altering the behavior of the deviant child and of the controlling agent.

Finally, it should be noted that, in reporting on their aggressive behavior, subjects may disclose information that is potentially harmful to themselves; therefore, confidentiality in the use of the information is essential. Individuals labeled aggressive on the basis of such data may receive untoward treatment from others, with deleterious consequences. The imputation of aggressive characteristics could become a self-fulfilling prophecy by this means.

Application to Particular Variables

It is well documented that males are more physically aggressive than females (Buss, 1961, 1963). There is some evidence that other types of aggression (for instance, verbal) are more characteristic of females (Sears, Maccoby, and Levin, 1957). The effect of education on aggression is a largely unexplored area, but insofar as highly educated individuals would be less inclined to seek rewards by aggressive means, a negative relationship between aggression and educational achievement might be expected. This observation applies also to vocation and aggression. With regard to social class, it is well established that physical aggression is more prevalent among lower-class subjects (Berkowitz, 1962). Any ethnic or racial differences in aggression may be a function of sociocultural factors, such as class, education, and age (Johnson, 1974); in the absence of adequate control over these variables, it is difficult to assess the impact of data (such as crime statistics) pertaining to this matter.

References

Bandura, A. *Aggression: A Social Learning Analysis.* Englewood Cliffs, N.J.: Prentice-Hall, 1973.

Berkowitz, L. *Aggression: A Social-Psychological Analysis.* New York: McGraw-Hill, 1962.

Bowers, K. S. "Situationism in Psychology: An Analysis and a Critique." *Psychological Review,* 1973, *80,* 307-336.

Buss, A. H. *The Psychology of Aggression.* New York: Wiley, 1961.

Buss, A. H. "Physical Aggression in Relation to Different Frustrations." *Journal of Abnormal Psychology,* 1963, *67,* 1-7.

Buss, A. H. "Aggression Pays." In J. L. Singer (Ed.), *The Control of Aggression and Violence: Cognitive and Physiological Factors.* New York: Academic Press, 1971.

Caine, T. M., Foulds, G. A., and Hope, K. *Manual of the Hostility and Direction of Hostility Questionnaire (HDHQ).* London: University of London Press, 1967.

Dollard, J., and others. *Frustration and Aggression.* New Haven, Conn.: Yale University Press, 1939.

Duff, F. L. "Item Subtlety in Personality Inventory Scales." *Journal of Consulting Psychology,* 1965, *29,* 565-570.

Durbin, E. F. M., and Bowlby, L. *Personal Aggressiveness and War.* New York: Columbia University Press, 1939.

Edmunds, G. "Judgements of Different Types of Aggressive Behavior." *British Journal of Social and Clinical Psychology,* 1978, *17,* 121-125.

Endler, N. S., and Hunt, J. McV. "S-R Inventories of Hostility and Comparisons of the Proportions of Variance from Persons, Responses, and Situations for Hostility and Anxiousness." *Journal of Personality and Social Psychology,* 1968, *9,* 309-315.

Feshbach, S. "Aggression." In P. H. Mussen (Ed.), *Carmichael's Manual of Child Psychology.* Vol. 2. (3rd ed.) New York: Wiley, 1970.

Fisher, M. G. "The Prediction of Assaultiveness in Hospitalized Mental Patients." Unpublished doctor's dissertation, Pennsylvania State University, 1956.

Frank, L. K. "Projective Methods for the Study of Personality." *Journal of Psychology,* 1939, *9,* 389-413.

Geen, R. G. "Effects of Frustration, Attack, and Prior Training in Aggressiveness upon Aggressive Behavior." *Journal of Personality and Social Psychology,* 1968, *9,* 316-321.

Hartmann, H., Kris, E., and Loewenstein, R. M. "Notes on the Theory of Aggression." *Psychoanalytic Study of the Child,* 1949, *3,* 9-36.

Hathaway, S. R., and McKinley, J. C. *Minnesota Multiphasic Personality Inventory.* New York: Psychological Corporation, 1951.

Johnson, E. H. *Crime Correction and Society.* London: Dorsey International, 1974.

Kaufmann, H. *Aggression and Altruism.* New York: Holt, Rinehart and Winston, 1970.

Lorenz, K. *On Aggression.* London: Methuen, 1966.

Maddi, S. R. *Personality Theories.* Homewood, Ill.: Dorsey Press, 1976.

Megargee, E. I. "The Prediction of Violence with Psychological Tests." In C. D. Spielberger (Ed.), *Current Topics in Clinical and Community Psychology.* Vol. 2. New York: Academic Press, 1970.

Megargee, E. I., Cook, P. E., and Mendelsohn, G. A. "Development and Evaluation of an MMPI Scale of Assaultiveness in Overcontrolled Individuals." *Journal of Abnormal Psychology,* 1967, *72,* 519-528.

Megargee, E. I., and Mendelsohn, G. A. "A Cross Validation of Twelve MMPI Indices of Hostility and Control." *Journal of Abnormal and Social Psychology,* 1962, *65,* 431-438.

Mischel, W. *Personality and Assessment.* New York: Wiley, 1968.

Murray, H. A. *Thematic Apperception Test Manual.* Cambridge, Mass.: Harvard University Press, 1943.

Norman, W. T. "Relative Importance of Test Item Content." *Journal of Consulting Psychology,* 1963, *27,* 166-174.

Patterson, G. R., and Cobb, J. A. "A Dyadic Analysis of Aggressive Behaviors." In J. P. Hill (Ed.), *Minnesota Symposia on Child Psychology.* Vol. 5. Minneapolis: University of Minnesota Press, 1971.

Sears, R. R., Maccoby, E. E., and Levin, H. *Patterns of Child Rearing.* New York: Harper & Row, 1957.

Siegal, S. M. "The Relationship of Hostility to Authoritarianism." *Journal of Abnormal and Social Psychology,* 1956, *52,* 368-372.

Storr, A. *Human Aggression.* London: Allen Lane, 1968.

Strachey, J. (Ed.). *Collected Papers of Sigmund Freud.* New York: Basic Books, 1959.

Wallace, J. "What Units Shall We Employ? Allport's Question Revisited." *Journal of Consulting Psychology,* 1967, *31,* 56-64.

Zaks, M. S., and Walters, R. H. "First Steps in the Construction of a Scale for the Measurement of Aggression." *Journal of Psychology,* 1959, *47,* 199-208.

44

Robert P. Marinelli

Anxiety

A major problem in the assessment of anxiety results from the ambiguity surrounding the definition of anxiety. This ambiguity occurs because the term *anxiety* is used indiscriminately to refer to a state, a trait, and a process (Spielberger, 1975).

State anxiety (anxiety as an emotional state) is described by Spielberger (1975, p. 137) as "subjective, consciously perceived feelings of tension, apprehension, and nervousness accompanied by or associated with activation of the autonomic nervous system." Anxiety states (A states) are viewed as transient, with fluctuations in intensity over time occurring as a function of the stress perceived by the individual. The occurrence of the anxiety state and its intensity are evaluated through self-report or changes in physiological arousal or motoric behavior.

Trait anxiety (A trait) refers to relatively stable individual differences in proneness to view a wide range of situations as threatening and to respond to these situations with elevations in state anxiety (Spielberger, 1966, 1975). Persons high in trait anxiety are considered "anxiety prone." The assessment of anxiety as a trait focuses on self-reports using personality tests, and/or a complex clinical process of interview and observation.

Process anxiety is "a complex sequence of cognitive, affective, and behavioral events that is evoked by some form of stress" (Spielberger, 1975, p. 137). State anxiety is the core of this complex affective, behavioral, and cognitive process. The process definition appears consistent with definitions of anxiety proposed by modern behavior therapists (Borkovec, Weerts, and Bernstein, 1977).

Background and Current Status

In his psychohistorical review of anxiety, McReynolds (1975) notes that man has always experienced anxiety. However, the *concept* of anxiety did not evolve until the classical Greek period, particularly the Hellenistic period (about 350 B.C.), with its significant cultural change and rising level of self-awareness. McReynolds' thesis is that the study and elaboration of anxiety as a concept occurred during historical periods that encouraged growth in self-awareness and individuality (for instance, in the Hellenistic period and in the Renaissance).

Most social scientists probably believe that anxiety as a *technical term* was admitted to the psychologist's jargon by Freud as a translation of his *Angst* (Freud, 1926, 1936). McReynolds (1975), however, points out that in 1747 the unknown author of *An Enquiry into the Origin of the Human Appetites and Affections* proposed that a state of uncertainty leads to a state of anxiety—thus providing a usage of the word *anxiety* that accords with current usage. Later conceptions of anxiety—by Battie (1758), Kierkegaard (1844), and others (see McReynolds, 1975)—attempted to more clearly define the concept in a global sense but paid little attention to the unique, identifying features of anxiety.

Freud (1926, 1936) led anxiety into the twentieth century by giving it a central position in his theory of personality. Freud's focus was on anxiety as a global motivational force rather than on the experience of anxiety. In building his theory, Freud depended primarily on hypothetico-deductive reasoning based on clinical observation. Learning-oriented theorists (Hull, 1921, 1943, 1952; Mowrer, 1939, 1950) made the first significant movements in using experimental methods for the theoretical study of anxiety. Important postulates in their conceptions are that (1) anxiety is, to a large extent, learned behavior; (2) it motivates trial-and-error behavior; and (3) its reduction reinforces the learning of new habits. These points are considered the touchstone of the drive conceptions of anxiety proposed by Dollard and Miller (1950) and Spence (1956, 1960).

Anxiety is a central explanatory concept in a wide range of psychological theories of personality, psychotherapy, and abnormality. This range of theories includes those that are existential (May, 1950; Tillich, 1952), psychodynamic (Freud, 1926, 1936), and behavioral (Hull, 1943; Mowrer, 1939; Watson and Rayner, 1920; Wolpe, 1958). (See Fischer, 1970, for a review of the position that anxiety plays in theories of behavior and personality.) This concept has been widely applicable to such a wide range of viewpoints because of the nonspecificity and lack of precision in the use of the term. Borkovec, Weerts, and Bernstein (1977, p. 368) point out that anxiety has developed the "multiple personality" of a "transient emotional/physiological *behavior* ("He is anxious today"), a dispositional *trait* ("She is an anxious person"), and a cause or explanation of behavior ("He overeats because of anxiety"; "Her seductiveness is a defense against anxiety").

Existential and psychodynamic theorists emphasize anxiety as a motivational force in the *explanation* of behavior and as a dispositional *trait*. They view human anxiety as a tension or threat, signaling some incongruency or conflict in the person. This tension acts as a motivator, resulting in either positive or negative growth (Corey, 1977; Costello, 1976). Although both theories recognize anxiety as a transient emotional/physiological *behavior*, their focus is on the phenomenological aspects of anxiety, the expressed feelings of distress and uneasiness, rather than on the overt behavioral or physiological indicators. They regard the transient behavioral side of anxiety as simply a sign or signal of a more complex motivational process. In that context, there is no need for extensive study of the transient behavior or its antecedents and consequences (Mischel, 1968).

Existentially oriented therapists do not emphasize the development of methods to assess anxiety. Their procedures focus on what the client says about his or her personal anxiety (in a trait sense) and how this anxiety relates to their theoretical model of psychotherapy (Bugental, 1965; May, 1969).

Psychoanalytically oriented therapists may use written assessment procedures, in addition to the interview, to measure the anxiety trait. Depending on the accessibility of the trait to the individual's level of conscious awareness, objective (paper-and-pencil checklists, scales, inventories, questionnaires) or projective devices are used. An analysis of the responses to these devices provides an indication of the nature and level of anxiety. The type and level of anxiety are considered in the therapeutic process—particularly the anxiety that arises in an attempt to repress basic conflicts. Unconscious defense mechanisms are developed to control this neurotic anxiety (Freud, 1936).

Contemporary theorists and psychotherapists who are social learning or behaviorally oriented do not support the trait description of anxiety. They tend to support a state description; that is, consistent with their focus on behavior, they view anxiety as a transient, emotional behavioral response. Assessment of anxiety would focus on (1) the specific stimulus conditions giving rise to the anxiety response; (2) the identification and quantification of the response; and (3) the consequences from the behaviors, particularly those that are reinforcing. Their assessment procedures, then, would be designed to evaluate the person's motoric, cognitive, and physiological response channels (Borkovec, Weerts, and Bernstein, 1977; Krasner and Ullmann, 1973).

In addition to the study of anxiety as it relates to theories of personality and abnormality, anxiety has also been studied as an entity in its own right. Cattell and Scheier (1961), through their factor analytic studies, provided empirical evidence of two distinct anxiety factors: state and trait anxiety. Spielberger (1966, 1972) and others have organized a number of symposia and have written extensively about the nature and measurement of anxiety and the application of their findings to specific problem areas. (Professionals interested in reviewing other important book-length studies of anxiety should read Appley and Trumbull, 1967; Branch, 1968; Fischer, 1970; Lazarus, 1966; Levitt, 1967; Marks, 1969; and Rourke, 1969.)

Critical Discussion

General Areas of Concern

Ideally, conceptualization of a construct that relates to human behavior should precede assessment of that construct. When that construct is relevant to the state of the human condition, assessment should directly relate to treatment. Although there is general recognition of the importance of anxiety, the definition of anxiety is usually amorphous and differential, dependent on the theory or the theorist. Korchin (1976, p. 49) has written: "No person—bartender, mother, nor clinician-as-layman—is without 'theories' about human behavior." Much the same can be said about social scientists and anxiety. Theories of anxiety abound. Unfortunately, there is little agreement on what constitutes anxiety and less agreement on an integrative theory that attempts to unify differing conceptualizations. There has been little effort to overcome the problem of technical development in anxiety measurement "without sufficient interaction with conceptualization" (Fiske, 1971, p. 10). Although Cattell and Scheier (1961) report over 120 specific procedures to measure anxiety, these procedures usually relate to the researchers' unique operational definitions of anxiety, rather than reflecting some unified concept.

Differences in theoretical orientation to anxiety are probably no more marked than the differences between those individuals who view anxiety as a trait and those who view it as a state. Clinicians who support trait conceptualizations (Cattell and Scheier, 1961; Spence, 1960) view anxiety as a dimension along which individuals differ in a stable manner across situations. This viewpoint typically assigns dispositions to individuals (This person is anxious). This trait of anxiety is considered a personality construct that is usually part of an integrated model to explain behavior or personality. Anxiety as a cross-situational variable is considered a major determinant of behavior in these models (for instance, in Spence's drive theory or in psychoanalytic theory).

Goldfried and Lineham (1977), Hersen (1976), and Mischel (1968, 1969, 1971) have been critical of the trait approach. Generally, these critics contend that there is insufficient evidence to support consistency across situations, particularly as it relates to personality and social behavior. When it comes to measurement of these constructs, concern is that the indirect measurement procedures suffer from low validity, experimenter bias, and an unclear relationship between assessment and treatment (Hersen, 1976). Looking specifically at anxiety, Borkovec, Weerts, and Bernstein (1977) criticize the trait approach because it "does little to provide specific information about a person's behavior" and "assumes that because anxiety is primarily a shorthand *description* of complex behavior, its reification and use as an explanation of maladaptive, irrational, or unusual behavior is inappropriate" (p. 370). They believe that anxiety measurement should focus on "clear specification of stimulus conditions and on objectively quantified responses to these stimuli rather than on the use of psychological tests designed to measure the presence of or changes in a generalized construct" (p. 370).

Comparative Philosophies and Theories

Endler and his associates (Endler, 1973, 1975; Endler and Hunt, 1966) have been critical of the proponents of the person (trait) versus situation (state) issue. Basing his argument in part on a review by Bowers (1972), in which person-by-situation interactions accounted for more variance than either persons or situations, Endler has proposed a person-situation interaction model of anxiety. Endler (1975, p. 147) suggests that the appropriate question should be: "*How* do individual differences and situations *interact* in determining behavior?" He contends that "adequate assessment of a trait such as anxiousness must consider both the responses that characterize the trait and the appropriate evocative situations" (p. 51). Based on the preceding premise, Endler, Hunt, and Rosenstein (1962) devised the S-R Inventory of Anxiousness. The measure assumes that trait anxiety is multidimensional and is made up of three components: Interpersonal, physical danger, and ambiguous anxiety. Later research (Endler and Hunt, 1969) found that in an anxiety-provoking situation the interaction of persons and situations contributed to more of the total anxiety variance than either situations or individual differences did.

Spielberger (1975) has presented two models that integrate state and trait conceptions of anxiety: the trait-state model and the anxiety-as-process model. His trait-state anxiety theory attempts to clarify the characteristics of *A* state and *A* trait and to specify the dimensions of stressful situations that evoke *A* state in persons who differ in *A* trait. According to this theory, either external or internal stimuli that are perceived to be threatening by an individual, as well as the person's level of *A* trait, will evoke an unpleasant *A*-state reaction. The intensity and duration of the *A*-state reaction will be proportional to the individual's cognitive appraisal of the threat, the persistence of the evoking stimuli, and the individual's previous experience in similar situations. The *A*-state reaction may initiate a coping behavior system or defense mechanisms to avoid or minimize the threat and thereby reduce the *A* state.

Spielberger's anxiety-as-process model has state anxiety as a primary component. In the process model, an external or internal stimulus that is interpreted cognitively as threatening to the individual is immediately followed by an increased level of A state. Since A state is experienced as unpleasant, the individual will engage in cognitive and behavioral operations to minimize this discomfort. He will reappraise the stimulus conditions that initiated the process in order to develop future coping mechanisms or to develop means of avoiding the anxiety-arousing situation. If the anxiety is unavoidable, intrapsychic attempts (such as the development of defense mechanisms) may be undertaken.

Elaboration on Critical Points

Probably the most critical question for the assessment specialist in relation to the assessment of anxiety is: Considering the myriad definitions and models of anxiety, which should I choose, how do I go about choosing it/them, and how do I assess anxiety as described by the model that I choose?

Trait anxiety may be assessed by means of trait anxiety inventories or inferred from the frequency and/or intensity of anxiety states over a period of time. The latter method of determining anxiety proneness (trait anxiety) has not been effectively researched and clearly defined. Therefore, the most popular standard methods of assessing trait anxiety are paper-and-pencil inventories. The oldest and probably most widely used measure of trait anxiety is the Manifest Anxiety Scale (MAS) (Taylor, 1951, 1953). The fifty items used in the MAS were taken from the Minnesota Multiphasic Personality Inventory (MMPI) on the basis of their ability to detect clinical anxiety as judged by expert clinicians. The MAS has been used extensively in research on the Spence-Taylor drive theory (Spence, 1956, 1960). A children's form of the Manifest Anxiety Scale (CMAS), developed by Castaneda, McCandless, and Palermo (1956), has been used extensively as a measure of trait anxiety in children (see Gaudry and Spielberger, 1971; Phillips, Martin, and Meyers, 1972).

The MMPI has been used in the development of a number of other trait anxiety scales, two of the most popular being Welsh's A Factor (Dahlstrom and Welsh, 1960) and the Anxiety Index (Welsh, 1952), which were developed on premises similar to those used for the MAS.

Cattell and Scheier (1961) used factor analytic techniques to isolate items from a number of trait measures. These items, which are published as the IPAT Anxiety Scale, relate to the evaluation of anxiety in individuals by clinicians. (For a more detailed discussion of the IPAT Anxiety Scale, see Scheier and Cattell, 1960; Cattell and Warburton, 1968.)

The S-R Inventory of Anxiousness (Endler, Hunt, and Rosenstein, 1962), a multidimensional measure of trait anxiety, assesses anxiety proneness as it relates to interpersonal, physical danger, and ambiguous situations. The S-R Inventory has been criticized for its excessive length (154 responses) and limited applicability (primarily to a college population) (Levitt, 1967). Endler and Okada (1975) have recently developed the S-R Inventory of General Trait Anxiousness (S-R GTA). The S-R GTA, in addition to the three dimensions discussed above, measures anxiety in innocuous daily routines. It overcomes the problem of length (36 items) and applicability mentioned above. Endler (1975) has provided evidence that it is more effective than the S-R Inventory in maximizing the effects of individual differences and minimizing the effects of situations, thus making it a better trait measure.

A number of instruments based on the trait anxiety model have been developed to measure anxiety in testing situations. Most notable among these measures are the Test Anxiety Questionnaire (TAQ) (Mandler and Sarason, 1952), the Test Anxiety Scale (TAS) (Mandler and Cohen, 1958), and the Test Anxiety Scale for Children (TASC) (Sarason and others, 1960). The TAQ is used in measuring test anxiety in adults; the TAS is a high school and college version; and the TASC is a children's version. Although these instruments purport to measure anxiety resulting from a specific set of anxiety-producing situations—namely, tests—they should not be confused as state anxiety measures, since their conceptual underpinnings are clearly based on a trait notion. Gaudry and Spielberger (1971); Phillips, Martin, and Myers (1972); I. G. Sarason (1972, 1975); and S. B. Sarason (1972) provide thorough and thoughtful presentations of test anxiety, particularly as it affects children.

Zuckerman (1960) developed the Affect Adjective Check List (AACL) to measure both trait and state anxiety. The AACL was later expanded by Zuckerman and Lubin (1965) to include scales measuring hostility and depression and was renamed the Multiple Affect Adjective Check List (MAACL). Trait anxiety is measured by the General form of the test; it asks the respondent to check the adjectives that "describe how you generally feel." State anxiety is measured by the Today form; it asks the respondent to check the adjectives that "describe how you feel now—today." The AACL and the MAACL are simple to use and score. Considerable research indicates that they are useful, reliable, and valid measures of state anxiety (Zuckerman and Lubin, 1968). However, the General form does not appear to be impressive as a trait measure (Spielberger, 1972; Spielberger, Gorsuch, and Lushene, 1970).

The State-Trait Anxiety Inventory (STAI), developed by Spielberger and his associates (Spielberger, Gorusch, and Lushene, 1970), also provides separate scales to measure state and trait anxiety. Each of twenty items in the scales asks respondents to check one of four statements describing how they generally feel (trait scale) and how they feel at a particular moment (state scale). A possible limitation of the STAI is that it seems to be a unidimensional scale, restricted to the measurement of interpersonal trait anxiety (Endler, 1975). Considerable evidence (Levitt, 1967; Spielberger, 1972) indicates, however, that the STAI is a useful clinical and research tool.

State anxiety has received only recent professional attention. Whereas trait anxiety was the focal concern of theoreticians and clinicians for over fifty years, during the 1960s state anxiety became a primary concern—largely because of the rising popularity of behavior therapy and its attention to anxiety as a behavioral response. Since behavioralists view anxiety as a transitory, multidimensional response complex occurring in response to external and internal stimuli and involving three major response components (cognitive, motoric, and physiological), attention in assessment focuses on three channels for measuring the response components: self-report, overt motoric behavior, and physiological arousal (Borkovec, Weerts, and Bernstein, 1977; Lick and Katkin, 1976). In addition, attention (via the interview or observation) is given the stimulus conditions evoking the anxiety response, characteristics of the response itself, and consequences of the behavior. (For thorough discussions of the behavioral assessment of anxiety, see Borkovec, Weerts, and Bernstein, 1977; Lick and Katkin, 1976.)

Although attempts should be made to use all three channels in anxiety assessment, clearly the most popular vehicle for evaluating state anxiety is the self-report method—partly because self-report is the only means available to many clinicians and partly because the subjective reporting or labeling of anxiety states is central to their definition (Bellack and Hersen, 1977; Spielberger, 1972). Although self-report is subject to purposeful distortion and a client's ability to discriminate verbally, two types of self-report measures of state anxiety are frequently used: standardized fear or anxiety questionnaires and specific fear or anxiety rating scales. The theorists who distinguish between fear and anxiety point out that fear has a definite referent (for example, fear of snakes), whereas state anxiety is nonspecific, and that fear is correlated with avoidance behaviors, whereas state anxiety has no motor element (Bellack and Hersen, 1977). For our purpose, however, fear responses will be considered anxiety states.

The Fear Survey Schedule (FSS), which was originally developed by Akutagawa (1956) and modified repeatedly, is the most widely used self-report measure of fear. Bellack and Hersen (1977), Hersen (1973), and Tasto (1977) provide thorough reviews of the self-report of fears in general and the FSS in particular. Dickson (1975), in a review of behavioral assessment, concludes that "the FSS is the most sophisticated assessment instrument in the conventional test format that has been yet developed within the behavioral model" (pp. 360-361). Various factor analytic studies of the FSS (using college students as subjects) generally provide evidence of four clusters: (1) fears related to small animals; (2) fears associated with death, physical pain, and surgery; (3) fears about aggression; and (4) fears of interpersonal events (Braun and Reynolds, 1969; Geer, 1965; Rubin and others, 1968; Rubin and others, 1969). The FSS has been used primarily as a pretreatment screening device and as an evaluation of therapeutic effectiveness to determine general classes of objects or events to which the respondent verbalizes fear, particularly stimuli in addition to his presenting fears. Its primary deficit (and that of most questionnaires) is that anxiety or fear is not assessed in specific situations.

In addition to surveys of feared objects or events, a number of scales assess fear or anxiety related to a general theme. Most of these scales employ items requiring the respondent to consider the three anxiety response components (cognitive, motoric, and physiological). Examples are the Acrophobic Questionnaire (Baker, Cohen, and Saunders, 1973), Snake and Spider Questionnaires (Lang, Melamed, and Hart, 1970), Paul's (1966) Personal Report of Confidence as a Speaker, Suinn's (1969) Test Anxiety Behavior Scale, and Watson and Friend's (1969) Social Avoidance of Distress and Fear of Negative Evaluation scales. A review of specific fear measures (Klorman and others, 1974) suggests that these measures generally have adequate reliability and discriminant validity to support their use as screening and outcome measures.

The level of reported anxiety immediately prior to, during, and after exposure to a feared object is important in assessing the level of fear and evaluating the effectiveness of therapeutic interventions. Various measures of this cognitive distress include the Fear Thermometer (FT) (Walk, 1956); Anxiety Differential (AD) (Husek and Alexander, 1963); Autonomic Perception Questionnaire (APQ) (Mandler and Kremen, 1958; Mandler, Mandler, and Uviller, 1958); State-Trait Anxiety Inventory, A-State Scale (STAI) (Spielberger, Gorsuch, and Lushene, 1970); and Affect Adjective Check List, Today form (AACL-T) (Zuckerman, 1960; Zuckerman and Lubin, 1965, 1968). These measures can be divided into two types: (1) relatively unobtrusive and brief scales, which ask respondents to evaluate their level of anxiety by marking a scale item; and (2) more obtrusive and longer scales, usually requiring respondents to rate concepts or check adjectives and describe their current state of anxiety. The Fear Thermometer, the only example of the former type, asks respondents to place a mark somewhere on a 1-to-10 scale to indicate their level of anxiety in a given situation.

Direct observation of the client's motoric responding to anxiety-producing stimuli is another means of assessing state anxiety and serves as the cornerstone of the behavioral assessment process. This type of behavioral measure is generally a standardized analog of fear-producing situations in which subjects are required to perform certain tasks. Level of anxiety is assessed by observers who evaluate the subject's behaviors (usually avoidance behaviors) in relation to the feared tasks. These observational measures include timed behavior checklists (TBCs), behavior avoidance tests (BATs), and role-playing tests (RPTs).

In timed behavior checklists (TBCLs), subjects are asked to carry out a feared behavior and observers rate the occurrence of visible indicators of anxiety over a specified time period on a behavior checklist. TBCLs have been used in the assessment of public-speaking anxiety (Paul, 1966), anxiety in heterosexual interactions (Arkowitz and others, 1975; Borkovec and others, 1974; Glasgow and Arkowitz, 1975; Twentyman and McFall, 1975), fear of snakes (Bernstein and Nietzel, 1974), and fear of insects (Fazio, 1969).

Behavior avoidance tests (BATs) require subjects to progressively approach, increase contact with, or in other ways perform feared behaviors. Distance from the feared object and/or time spent in performing the feared behavior are used as indices of fear. BATs have been used in the assessment of snake phobia (Lang and Lazovik, 1965), claustrophobia (Miller and Bernstein, 1972), obsessive-compulsive behavior (Rachman, Hodgson, and Marks, 1971), acrophobia (Ritter, 1969), and fear of rats (Rutner and Pear, 1972).

In role-playing tests (RPTs), subjects role-play responses to social situations presented on audiotape or videotape or *in vivo*. These responses are evaluated on a number of dimensions, including eye contact, resistance in responding, loudness of voice, speech disruptions, and speech duration. RPTs have been used in the assessment of social anxiety in situations requiring assertive behavior (Eisler and others, 1975; McFall and Marston, 1970; McFall and Twentyman, 1973) and heterosexual competency (Arkowitz and others, 1975). (For a review of the advantages and disadvantages of behavioral measures, see Borkovec, Weerts, and Bernstein, 1977; Lick and Katkin, 1976.)

In addition to contrived laboratory approaches, observation of clients in their natural environment can be an effective means of gathering behavioral data regarding client anxiety. Although this approach may be time consuming, it has the advantage of broadening the range of fear-eliciting situations and individualizing the anxiety assessment process. In spite of apparent advantages, it has rarely been reported in the literature. An exception is Becker and Costello's (1975) use of it with snake-phobic subjects. Methodological problems of assessment in naturalistic settings undoubtedly contribute to its rare occurrence in the literature (Kent and Foster, 1977).

Physiological arousal is almost always considered an important component in state anxiety assessment. The physiological assessment of anxiety usually includes cardiovascular responses and electrodermal responses. (Since an appropriate discussion of these approaches would be complex and lengthy, the reader is referred to thorough reviews by Borkovec, Weerts, and Bernstein, 1977; Lang, 1977; and Lick and Katkin, 1976.) Reviews typically indicate that heart rate is the most consistently used means of assessing the physiological anxiety component, primarily because the simple instrumentation and minimal technical understanding required make it more accessible to the clinician. As instruments become more available (due to increased simplicity and reduced cost), physiological assessment of anxiety may become more commonplace for the clinician. Even now, the simple method of counting pulse beats as a measure of heart rate is available and has been used in behavior therapy (Borkovec, 1973; Paul, 1966). Research by Bell and Schwartz (1975) supports its use; that is, they found a high correlation between subjects' self-monitoring of pulse rate and heart rate measured by sophisticated electronic equipment.

Assessment specialists should recognize that there may be low correlation among self-report, direct observation, and physiological assessment procedures. It is generally assumed that each of these channels is measuring different aspects of anxiety, or "separate-but-interesting anxiety responses" (Borkovec, Weerts, and Bernstein, 1977, p. 403). For the client, it appears safe to say that the most important response channel requiring attention and modification is the one that contributes most to his or her problem.

Personal Views and Recommendations

Too frequently, clinicians select instruments that assess constructs or behaviors (such as anxiety) but fail to consider the nature of the construct or behavior being assessed or the correlation between the definition of the construct or behavior as defined by the makers of the instrument and their theoretical orientation. After considering their views and approaches, clinicians may find that their theoretical stances allow only a state or trait definition. Although "technical eclecticism" (Lazarus, 1971; Woody, 1971) can be worthwhile for practitioners, clinicians must determine for themselves the degree to which they are willing to be atheoretical (in the sense that they are willing to modify their personal theoretical stance).

Theoretical points of view necessarily influence clinicians' views of problems. This is particularly true of anxiety, where anxiety states can be viewed as symptoms of deeper problems or behaviors (in and of themselves) that need to be assessed and treated. In situations where the anxiety (or fear) responses seem to be related to specific objects or events and the client's behavior appears directed toward avoiding the fear-producing stimuli, the assessment modalities developed by behaviorally oriented therapists seem most effective. Behavioral treatment modalities for the treatment of anxiety presented by Meichenbaum (1977), Rimm and Masters (1974), and Wolpe (1973) are recommended in these situations. A significant aspect of the behavioral view of anxiety assessment and treatment is the strong correlation between assessment and treatment, as well as the strong research base on which these procedures rest.

In situations where the problems of anxiety presented are more diffuse (apparently unrelated to specific objects or events and/or directed toward avoiding fear- or anxiety-producing stimuli), more global and less behavioral assessment and treatment modalities (such as existential or psychoanalytic approaches) may be employed. Before these methods are used, however, attempts should be made to specify the stimulus and maintenance conditions. Behaviorally oriented theorists and clinicians probably would argue that, if the stimulus and maintenance conditions have not been specified, the clinician has not looked long and hard enough.

Behavioral approaches are recommended more confidently because they have more of a research base, a better relationship between assessment and treatment, and more clearly defined assessment and treatment procedures than the other approaches. Although comparative studies of the effectiveness of different anxiety assessment and treatment methods as they relate to divergent theoretical orientations would appear to settle this issue, these studies have not been convincingly done. Considering the wide differences in definitions of anxiety and other complex methodological problems with such research, the issue is not likely to be settled in the immediate future.

Application to Particular Variables

Little research has been done relating age to anxiety. Generally, older persons are found to be more anxious, as evaluated by trait anxiety measures. This increase in anxiety is generally thought to be related to deteriorating mental and physical health as age increases (Gaitz and Scott, 1972; Kalimo, Bice, and Novosel, 1970; Kata, 1975).

Questionnaire and self-report data indicate a sex difference in anxiety, with females consistently scoring higher than males in general anxiety (Castaneda, McCandless, and Palermo, 1956; Kalimo, Bice, and Novosel, 1970; Kata, 1975; Phillips, 1962), test anxiety (Lunneborg, 1964; Sarason and others, 1960), and school anxiety (Phillips, 1966). Phillips and his associates (1969) found that sex differences in relation to anxiety are more pronounced in lower-class and minority groups. (For a more complete review of sex differences as they relate to anxiety, particularly in learning situations, see Phillips, Martin, and Myers, 1972.)

Anxiety assessment and education relate on two dimensions: (1) the relationship between level of education and level of anxiety and (2) the relationship between anxiety and performance in educational environments. In his analysis of anxiety in Scandinavian countries, Kata (1975) found that better-educated people were, in general, less anxious; comparable American data were not located. Concerning the effect of anxiety in school settings, general conclusions are that high anxiety is associated with relatively low performance at both the school and university level" (Gaudry and Spielberger, 1971, p. 41). More specifically, "reading is more strongly associated with anxiety in the earlier grades than is arithmetic; arithmetic (mathematics) becomes increasingly associated with anxiety toward the end of the elementary grades" (Gaudry and Spielberger, 1971, p. 41). Another aspect of anxiety in education is test anxiety and its reduction. Experimental studies "strongly suggest that many highly test-anxious persons are not deficient in intellective wherewithal; rather, the problem seems to be that they exaggerate and personalize inordinately the threat of evaluation that may inhere in a given situation" (Sarason, 1972, p. 382). (Persons interested in the role of anxiety in education should also read Phillips, Martin, and Myers, 1972; Sarason, 1975; Sarason and others, 1960.)

It appears that lower-class children are more anxious as a group than middle-class children (Dunn, 1968; Hawkes and Koff, 1969). In his study of Scandinavians, Kata (1975) found that the level of anxiety consistently decreased with an increase in family and individual income. Housing conditions and ownership of property were not found to be related to trait anxiety. Phillips (1966) and Tseng and Thompson (1969) found that lower-class minority children had higher levels of anxiety than other lower-class children. (For more insight into the role of social class and ethnic-racial differences in anxiety, see Phillips, Martin, and Myers, 1972.)

In Scandinavian countries, Kata (1975) found that the higher the prestige of occupations, the lower the level of anxiety of the persons employed in them. Because Kata acknowledges the confounding of education level with this finding and because comparable American findings were not located, his results must be applied with caution.

Physical trauma, poor health, or the threat of physical trauma or poor health can be expected to result in increased anxiety. In general, studies have supported this notion (Bradburn, 1969; Janis, 1958; Kata, 1975; Kegeles, 1963; Levine, 1962; Robbins, 1962). The relationship between physical well-being and anxiety must be viewed with caution. Since many anxiety measures include items related to physical functioning and health, the relationship may be significantly affected by method variance.

The relationship between intellectual functioning and anxiety has been a primary concern of anxiety-as-drive theorists (Spence, 1960) and educational psychologists. Results of these studies generally indicate that as trait anxiety increases, intelligence (as measured by test scores) decreases (Phillips, Martin, and Myers, 1972). However, because the interaction of intelligence, anxiety, and performance is extremely complex, the only safe conclusion is that intellectual ability must be taken into account in this type of research (Gaudry and Spielberger, 1971).

The *Diagnostic and Statistical Manual of Mental Disorders (DSM-II)* assigns anxiety its most significant role in the neuroses: "Anxiety is the chief characteristic of the neuroses. It may be felt directly, or it may be controlled unconsciously and automatically by conversion, displacement, and various other psychological mechanisms. Generally, these mechanisms produce symptoms experienced as subjective distress from which the patient desires relief" (American Psychiatric Association, 1968, p. 39). This classification scheme supports a trait definition of anxiety and is heavily influenced by psychoanalytic theory. The above view also suggests that anxiety may operate indirectly and be controlled (as in hysterical neurosis, conversion and dissociative types, and depressive neurosis); or it may operate directly and be overwhelming (as in phobic neurosis, obsessive-compulsive neurosis, anxiety neurosis, hypochondriacal neurosis, and neurasthenia). Behaviorally oriented theorists and clinicians, most notably Ullmann and Krasner (1969, 1973), are opposed to the trait use of anxiety and the psychoanalytic formulation of abnormal behavior. They have presented a thoughtful reformulation based on socio-psychological principles. In their reformulation of the neuroses, Ullmann and Krasner (1973) reject concepts such as unconscious motivation and conscious malingering. They emphasize that abnormal behaviors are acquired through learning processes and can be modified or unlearned and alternative behaviors acquired through techniques based on the same principles (techniques such as desensitization, role taking, assertion training, and implosion). Rather than being concerned with anxiety as a construct, Ullmann and Krasner (1973) and Bandura (1969) have recommended that the focus be on stimulus conditions and the responses to these stimuli. Although Ullmann and Krasner have recommended abandonment of the term *anxiety,* the approach of social learning theorists to the assessment and treatment of the neuroses emphasizes what would generally be considered a state view of anxiety.

References

Akutagawa, D. A. "A Study in Construct Validity of the Psycho-analytic Concept of Latent Anxiety and a Test of Projection Distance Hypotheses." Unpublished doctoral dissertation, University of Pittsburgh, 1956.

American Psychiatric Association. *Diagnostic and Statistical Manual of Mental Disorders.* (2nd ed.) Washington, D.C.: American Psychiatric Association, 1968.

Appley, M. A., and Trumbull, R. (Eds.). *Psychological Stress.* New York: Appleton-Century-Crofts, 1967.

Arkowitz, H., and others. "The Behavioral Assessment of Social Competence in Males." *Behavior Therapy,* 1975, *6,* 3-13.

Baker, B. L., Cohen, D. C., and Saunders, J. T. "Self-Directed Desensitization for Acrophobia." *Behavior Research and Therapy,* 1973, *11,* 79-89.

Bandura, A. *Principles of Behavior Modification.* New York: Holt, Rinehart and Winston, 1969.

Battie, W. *A Treatise on Madness* [1758]. New York: Brunner/Mazel, 1969.

Becker, H. G., and Costello, C. G. "Effects of Graduated Exposure with Feedback of Exposure Times on Snake Phobias." *Journal of Consulting and Clinical Psychology,* 1975, *43,* 478-484.

Bell, I. R., and Schwartz, G. E. "Voluntary Control and Reactivity of Human Heart Rate." *Psychophysiology,* 1975, *12,* 339-348.

Bellack, A. S., and Hersen, M. "Self-Report Inventories in Behavioral Assessment." In J. D. Cone and R. P. Hawkins (Eds.), *Behavioral Assessment: New Directions in Clinical Psychology.* New York: Brunner/Mazel, 1977.

Bernstein, D. A., and Nietzel, M. T. "Behavioral Avoidance Tests: The Effects of Demand

Characteristics and Repeated Measures on Two Types of Subjects." *Behavior Therapy,* 1974, *5,* 183-192.

Borkovec, T. D. "The Effects of Instructional Suggestion and Physiological Cues on Analogue Fear." *Behavior Therapy,* 1973, *4,* 185-192.

Borkovec, T. D., and others. "Identification and Measurement of a Clinically Relevant Target Behavior for Analogue Outcome Research." *Behavior Therapy,* 1974, *5,* 503-513.

Borkovec, T. D., Weerts, T. C., and Bernstein, D. A. "Assessment of Anxiety." In A. R. Ciminero, K. S. Calhoun, and H. E. Adams (Eds.), *Handbook of Behavioral Assessment.* New York: Wiley, 1977.

Bowers, K. S. "Situationism in Psychology: On Making Reality Disappear." Research Report No. 37. Ontario, Canada: Department of Psychology, University of Waterloo, 1972.

Bradburn, N. M. *The Structure of Psychological Well-Being.* Chicago: Aldine, 1969.

Branch, C. H. *Aspects of Anxiety.* Philadelphia: Lippincott, 1968.

Braun, P. R., and Reynolds, D. N. "A Factor Analysis of a 100 Item Fear Survey Inventory." *Behavior Research and Therapy,* 1969, *7,* 399-402.

Bugental, J. F. T. *The Search for Authenticity: An Existential-Analytic Approach to Psychotherapy.* New York: Holt, Rinehart and Winston, 1965.

Castenada, A., McCandless, B. R., and Palermo, D. S. "The Children's Form of the Manifest Anxiety Scale." *Child Development,* 1956, *27,* 317-326.

Cattell, R. B., and Scheier, I. H. *The Meaning and Measurement of Neuroticism and Anxiety.* New York: Ronald Press, 1961.

Cattell, R. B., and Warburton, F. W. *Objective Personality and Motivation Tests.* Champaign: University of Illinois Press, 1968.

Corey, G. *Theory and Practice of Counseling and Psychotherapy.* Monterey, Calif.: Brooks/Cole, 1977.

Costello, C. G. *Anxiety and Depression.* Montreal: McGill-Queens University Press, 1976.

Dahlstrom, W. G., and Welsh, G. S. *An MMPI Handbook: A Guide to Use in Clinical Practice and Research.* Minneapolis: University of Minnesota Press, 1960.

Dickson, C. R. "Role of Assessment in Behavior Therapy." In P. McReynolds (Ed.), *Advances in Psychological Assessment III.* San Francisco: Jossey-Bass, 1975.

Dollard, J., and Miller, N. E. *Personality and Psychotherapy.* New York: McGraw-Hill, 1950.

Dunn, J. A. "The Approach-Avoidance Model for the Analysis of School Anxiety." *Journal of Educational Psychology,* 1968, *59,* 388-394.

Eisler, R., and others. "Situational Determinants of Assertive Behaviors." *Journal of Consulting and Clinical Psychology,* 1975, *43,* 330-340.

Endler, N. S. "The Person Versus the Situation—A Pseudo Issue? A Response to Others." *Journal of Personality,* 1973, *41,* 287-303.

Endler, N. S. "The Person-Situation Interaction Model for Anxiety." In C. D. Spielberger and I. G. Sarason (Eds.), *Stress and Anxiety.* Vol. 1. Washington, D.C.: Hemisphere, 1975.

Endler, N. S., and Hunt, J. McV. "Sources of Behavioral Variance as Measured by the S-R Inventory of Anxiousness." *Psychological Bulletin,* 1966, *65,* 336-346.

Endler, N. S., and Hunt, J. McV. "Generalizability of Contributions from Sources of Variance in the S-R Inventories of Anxiousness." *Journal of Personality,* 1969, *37,* 1-24.

Endler, N. S., Hunt, J. McV., and Rosenstein, A. J. "An S-R Inventory of Anxiousness." *Psychological Monographs,* 1962, *76* (whole No. 536).

Endler, N. S., and Okada, M. "A Multidimensional Measure of Trait Anxiety: The S-R Inventory of General Trait Anxiousness." *Journal of Consulting and Clinical Psychology,* 1975, *43,* 319-329.

Fazio, A. F. "Verbal and Overt Behavioral Assessment of a Specific Fear." *Journal of Consulting and Clinical Psychology,* 1969, *33,* 705-709.

Fischer, W. F. *Theories of Anxiety.* New York: Harper & Row, 1970.

Fiske, D. W. *Measuring the Concepts of Personality.* Chicago: Aldine, 1971.

Freud, S. *Inhibitions, Symptoms, and Anxiety* [1926]. London: Hogarth Press, 1936.

Freud, S. *The Problem of Anxiety.* New York: Psychoanalytic Quarterly Press, 1936.

Gaitz, C. M., and Scott, J. "Age and the Measurement of Mental Health." *Journal of Health and Social Behavior,* 1972, *13,* 55-67.

Gaudry, E., and Spielberger, C. D. *Anxiety and Educational Achievement.* New York: Wiley, 1971.

Geer, J. H. "The Development of a Scale to Measure Fear." *Behavior Research and Therapy,* 1965, *3,* 45-53.

Glasgow, R. E., and Arkowitz, H. "The Behavioral Assessment of Male and Female Social Competence in Dyadic Heterosexual Interactions." *Behavior Therapy,* 1975, *6,* 488-498.

Goldfried, M. R., and Lineham, M. M. "Basic Issues in Behavioral Assessment." In A. R. Ciminero, K. S. Calhoun, and H. E. Adams (Eds.), *Handbook of Behavioral Assessment.* New York: Wiley, 1977.

Hawkes, T., and Koff, R. "Social Class Differences in Anxiety of Elementary School Children." Paper presented at American Education Research Association conference, 1969.

Hersen, M. "Self-Assessment of Fear." *Behavior Therapy,* 1973, *4,* 241-257.

Hersen, M. "Historical Perspectives in Behavioral Assessment." In M. Hersen and A. S. Bellack (Eds.), *Behavioral Assessment: A Practical Handbook.* Elmsford, N.Y.: Pergamon Press, 1976.

Hull, C. L. "Quantitative Aspects of the Evolution of Concepts: An Experimental Study." *Psychological Monographs,* 1921, *28* (whole No. 23).

Hull, C. L. *Principles of Behavior.* New York: Appleton-Century-Crofts, 1943.

Hull, C. L. *A Behavior System.* New Haven, Conn.: Yale University Press, 1952.

Husek, T. R., and Alexander, S. "The Effectiveness of the Anxiety Differential in Examination Stress Situations." *Educational and Psychological Measurement,* 1963, *23,* 309-318.

Janis, I. L. *Psychological Stress.* New York: Wiley, 1958.

Kalimo, E., Bice, T. W., and Novosel, M. "Cross-Cultural Analyses of Selected Emotional Questions from the Cornell Medical Index." *British Journal of Preventive and Social Medicine,* 1970, *24,* 229-240.

Kata, K. "On Anxiety in the Scandinavian Countries." In I. G. Sarason and C. D. Spielberger (Eds.), *Stress and Anxiety.* Vol. 2. Washington, D.C.: Hemisphere, 1975.

Kegeles, S. S. "Some Motives for Seeking Preventative Dental Care." *Journal of the American Dental Association,* 1963, *7,* 90-98.

Kent, R. N., and Foster, S. L. "Direct Observational Procedures: Methodological Issues in Naturalistic Settings." In A. R. Ciminero, K. S. Calhoun, and H. E. Adams (Eds.), *Handbook of Behavioral Assessment.* New York: Wiley, 1977.

Kierkegaard, S. A. *The Concept of Dread* [1844]. (W. Lorie, Trans.) Princeton, N.J.: Princeton University Press, 1944.

Klorman, R., and others. "Psychometric Description of Some Specific-Fear Questionnaires." *Behavior Therapy,* 1974, *5,* 401-409.

Korchin, S. J. *Modern Clinical Psychology: Principles of Intervention in the Clinic and Community.* New York: Basic Books, 1976.

Krasner, L., and Ullmann, L. P. *Behavior Influences and Personality.* New York: Holt, Rinehart and Winston, 1973.

Lang, P. J. "Physiological Assessment of Anxiety and Fear." In J. D. Cone and R. P. Hawkins (Eds.), *Behavioral Assessment: New Directions in Clinical Psychology.* New York: Brunner/Mazel, 1977.

Lang, P. J., and Lazovik, A. D. "Experimental Desensitization of a Phobia." *Journal of Abnormal and Social Psychology,* 1965, *70,* 395-402.

Lang, P. J., Melamed, B. G., and Hart, J. A. "A Psychophysiological Analysis of Fear Modification Using an Automated Desensitization Procedure." *Journal of Abnormal Psychology,* 1970, *76,* 220-234.

Lazarus, A. A. *Behavior Therapy and Beyond.* New York: McGraw-Hill, 1971.

Lazarus, R. S. *Psychological Stress and the Coping Process.* New York: McGraw-Hill, 1966.

Levine, G. N. "Anxiety About Illness: Psychological and Social Bases." *Journal of Health and Human Behavior,* 1962, *3,* 30-34.

Levitt, E. E. *The Psychology of Anxiety.* Indianapolis: Bobbs-Merrill, 1967.

Lick, J. R., and Katkin, E. S. "Assessment of Anxiety and Fear." In M. Hersen and A. S. Bellack (Eds.), *Behavioral Assessment: A Practical Handbook.* Elmsford, N.Y.: Pergamon Press, 1976.

Lunneborg, P. "Relations Among Social Desirability, Achievement and Anxiety Measures in Children." *Child Development,* 1964, *35,* 169-182.

McFall, R. M., and Marston, A. R. "An Experimental Investigation of Behavioral Rehearsal in Assertive Training." *Journal of Abnormal Psychology,* 1970, *76,* 295-303.

McFall, R. M., and Twentyman, C. T. "Four Experiments on the Relative Contributions of Rehearsal, Modeling and Coaching to Assertion Training." *Journal of Abnormal Psychology,* 1973, *81,* 199-218.

McReynolds, P. "Changing Conceptions of Anxiety: A Historical Review and a Proposed Integration." In I. G. Sarason and C. D. Spielberger (Eds.), *Stress and Anxiety.* Vol. 2. Washington, D.C.: Hemisphere, 1975.

Mandler, G., and Cohen, J. "Test Anxiety Questionnaires." *Journal of Consulting Psychology,* 1958, *22,* 228-229.

Mandler, G., and Kremen, I. "Autonomic Feedback: A Correlational Study." *Journal of Personality,* 1958, *26,* 388-399.

Mandler, G., Mandler, J. M., and Uviller, E. T. "Autonomic Feedback: The Perception of Autonomic Activity." *Journal of Abnormal and Social Psychology,* 1958, *56,* 367-373.

Mandler, G., and Sarason, S. B. "A Study of Anxiety and Learning." *Journal of Abnormal and Social Psychology,* 1952, *47,* 166-173.

Marks, I. M. *Fears and Phobias.* New York: Academic Press, 1969.

May, R. *The Meaning of Anxiety.* New York: Ronald Press, 1950.

May, R. *Love and Will.* New York: Norton, 1969.

Meichenbaum, D. *Cognitive-Behavior Modification.* New York: Plenum, 1977.

Miller, B. V., and Bernstein, D. A. "Instructional Demand in a Behavioral Avoidance Test for Claustrophic Fears." *Journal of Abnormal Psychology,* 1972, *80,* 206-210.

Mischel, W. *Personality and Assessment.* New York: Wiley, 1968.

Mischel, W. "Continuity and Change in Personality." *American Psychologist,* 1969, *24,* 1012-1018.

Mischel, W. *Introduction to Personality*. New York: Holt, Rinehart and Winston, 1971.

Mowrer, O. H. "A Stimulus-Response Analysis of Anxiety and Its Role as a Reinforcing Agent." *Psychological Review*, 1939, *46*, 553-565.

Mowrer, O. H. *Learning Theory and Personality Dimensions*. New York: Ronald Press, 1950.

Paul, G. L. *Insight vs. Desensitization in Psychotherapy: An Experiment in Anxiety Reduction*. Stanford, Calif.: Stanford University Press, 1966.

Phillips, B. N. "Sex, Social Class, and Anxiety as Sources of Variation in School Achievement." *Journal of Educational Psychology*, 1962, *53*, 316-322.

Phillips, B. N. "Conflict Theory and Sex Differences on the CMAS." *American Educational Research Journal*, 1966, *3*, 19-25.

Phillips, B. N., Martin, R. P., and Meyers, J. "Interventions in Relation to Anxiety in School." In C. D. Spielberger (Ed.), *Anxiety: Current Trends in Theory and Research*. Vol. 2. New York: Academic Press, 1972.

Phillips, B. N., and others. "School Stress, Anxiety and Adaptive-Maladaptive Behavior." Unpublished manuscript, 1969.

Rachman, S., Hodgson, R., and Marks, I. M. "Treatment of Chronic Obsessive Compulsive Neurosis." *Behavior Research and Therapy*, 1971, *9*, 237-247.

Rimm, D. C., and Masters, J. C. *Behavior Therapy: Techniques and Empirical Findings*. New York: Academic Press, 1974.

Ritter, B. "The Use of Contact Desensitization, Demonstration-Plus Participation and Demonstration-Alone in the Treatment of Acrophobia." *Behavior Research and Therapy*, 1969, *7*, 157-164.

Robbins, P. R. "Some Explorations into the Nature of Anxieties Relating to Illness." *Genetic Psychology Monographs*, 1962, *66*, 91-141.

Rourke, B. P. (Ed.). *Explorations in the Psychology of Stress and Anxiety*. Don Mills, Ontario: Longmans, 1969.

Rubin, B. M., and others. "Factor Analysis of a Fear Survey Schedule." *Behavior Research and Therapy*, 1968, *6*, 65-75.

Rubin, S. E., and others. "Factor Analysis of the 122 Item Fear Survey Schedule." *Behavior Research and Therapy*, 1969, *7*, 381-386.

Rutner, I. T., and Pear, J. J. "An Observational Methodology for Investigating Phobic Behavior: Preliminary Report." *Behavior Therapy*, 1972, *3*, 437-440.

Sarason, I. G. "Experimental Approaches to Test Anxiety: Attention and the Uses of Information." In C. D. Spielberger (Ed.), *Anxiety: Current Trends in Theory and Research*. Vol. 2. New York: Academic Press, 1972.

Sarason, I. G. "Test Anxiety, Attention, and the General Problem of Anxiety." In C. D. Spielberger and I. G. Sarason (Eds.), *Stress and Anxiety*. Vol. 1. Washington, D.C.: Hemisphere, 1975.

Sarason, S. B. "Anxiety, Intervention and the Culture of the School." In C. D. Spielberger (Ed.), *Anxiety: Current Trends in Theory and Research*. New York: Academic Press, 1972.

Sarason, S. B., and others. *Anxiety in Elementary School Children*. New York: Wiley, 1960.

Scheier, I. H., and Cattell, R. B. *Handbook and Test Kit for the IPAT 8 Parallel Form Anxiety Battery*. Champaign, Ill.: Institute for Personality and Ability Testing, 1960.

Spence, K. W. *Behavior Theory and Conditioning*. New Haven, Conn.: Yale University Press, 1956.

Spence, K. W. *Behavior Theory and Learning: Selected Papers.* Englewood Cliffs, N.J.: Prentice-Hall, 1960.

Spielberger, C. D. "Theory and Research on Anxiety." In C. D. Spielberger (Ed.), *Anxiety and Behavior.* New York: Academic Press, 1966.

Spielberger, C. D. (Ed.). *Anxiety: Current Trends in Theory and Research.* New York: Academic Press, 1972.

Spielberger, C. D. "Anxiety: State-Trait-Process." In C. D. Spielberger and I. G. Sarason (Eds.), *Stress and Anxiety.* Vol. 1. Washington, D.C.: Hemisphere, 1975.

Spielberger, C. D., Gorsuch, R. L., and Lushene, R. E. *State-Trait Anxiety Inventory: Test Manual for Form X.* Palo Alto, Calif.: Consulting Psychologists Press, 1970.

Suinn, R. M. "The STABS, a Measure of Test Anxiety for Behavior Therapy: Normative Data." *Behavior Research and Therapy,* 1969, *7,* 335-339.

Tasto, D. L. "Self-Report Schedules and Inventories." In A. R. Ciminero, K. S. Calhoun, and H. E. Adams (Eds.), *Handbook of Behavioral Assessment.* New York: Wiley, 1977.

Taylor, J. A. "The Relationship of Anxiety to the Conditioned Eyelid Response." *Journal of Experimental Psychology,* 1951, *41,* 81-92.

Taylor, J. A. "A Personality Scale of Manifest Anxiety." *Journal of Abnormal and Social Psychology,* 1953, *48,* 285-290.

Tillich, P. *The Courage to Be.* New Haven, Conn.: Yale University Press, 1952.

Tseng, M. S., and Thompson, D. L. "Need Achievement, Fear of Failure, Perception of Occupational Prestige, and Occupational Aspirations of Adolescents of Differing Socio-economic Groups." Paper presented at American Education Research Association conference, 1969.

Twentyman, C. T., and McFall, R. M. "Behavioral Training of Social Skills in Shy Males." *Journal of Consulting and Clinical Psychology,* 1975, *43,* 384-395.

Ullmann, L. P., and Krasner, L. *A Psychological Approach to Abnormal Behavior.* Englewood Cliffs, N.J.: Prentice-Hall, 1969.

Ullmann, L. P., and Krasner, L. *A Psychological Approach to Abnormal Behavior.* (2nd ed.) Englewood Cliffs, N.J.: Prentice-Hall, 1973.

Walk, R. D. "Self-Ratings of Fear in a Fear-Invoking Situation." *Journal of Abnormal and Social Psychology,* 1956, *52,* 171-178.

Watson, D., and Friend, R. "Measurement of Social-Evaluative Anxiety." *Journal of Consulting and Clinical Psychology,* 1969, *33,* 448-457.

Watson, J. B., and Rayner, R. "Conditioned Emotional Reactions." *Journal of Experimental Psychology,* 1920, *3,* 1-14.

Welsh, G. S. "An Anxiety Index and an Internalization Ratio for the MMPI." *Journal of Consulting Psychology,* 1952, *16,* 65-72.

Wolpe, J. *Psychotherapy by Reciprocal Inhibition.* Stanford, Calif.: Stanford University Press, 1958.

Wolpe, J. *The Practise of Behavior Therapy.* Elmsford, N.Y.: Pergamon Press, 1973.

Woody, R. H. *Psychobehavioral Counseling and Therapy.* New York: Appleton-Century-Crofts, 1971.

Zuckerman, M. "The Development of an Affect Adjective Check List for the Measurement of Anxiety." *Journal of Consulting Psychology,* 1960, *24,* 457-462.

Zuckerman, M., and Lubin, B. *Manual for the Multiple Affect Adjective Check List.* San Diego: Educational and Industrial Testing Service, 1965.

Zuckerman, M., and Lubin, B. *Bibliography for the Multiple Affect Adjective Check List.* San Diego: Educational and Industrial Testing Service, 1968.